29.50 ✓

ST HELENS C

D0353087

WITHDRAWN FROM
ST HELENS COLLEGE LIBRARY

LEGE LIBRARY
WA10 1PZ
e shown below.

009
OM
LIBRARY

THE LAW OF CONTRACT

AUSTRALIA
The Law Book Company
Sydney

CANADA
The Carswell Company
Toronto, Ontario

INDIA
N.M. Tripathi Private Ltd.
Bombay

Eastern Law House (Private) Ltd.
Calcutta

M.P.P. House
Bangalore

Universal Book Traders
Delhi

ISRAEL
Steimatzky's Agency Ltd.
Tel Aviv

PAKISTAN
Pakistan Law House
Karachi

THE LAW OF CONTRACT

by

G. H. TREITEL, Q.C., D.C.L., F.B.A.
Honorary Bencher of Gray's Inn
Fellow of All Souls College, Oxford
Vinerian Professor of English Law

EIGHTH EDITION

LONDON
SWEET & MAXWELL/STEVENS & SONS
1991

First edition 1962
Second edition 1966
Third edition 1970
Fourth edition 1975
Fifth edition 1979
Sixth edition 1983
Seventh edition 1987
Eighth edition 1991

Published in 1991 by
Sweet & Maxwell Limited of
South Quay Plaza, 183 Marsh Way, London E14 9FT
Computerset by Promenade Graphics Limited, Cheltenham
Printed and bound in Great Britain by
Richard Clay (The Chaucer Press) Limited, Bungay, Suffolk

ST. HELENS COLLEGE
346.022 TRE
80111
JULY 1995
LIBRARY

A CIP catalogue record
for this book is available
from the British Library

ISBN 0–421–437200
ISBN 0–421–437308

All rights reserved.
No part of this publication may be
reproduced or transmitted, in any form
or by any means, electronic, mechanical, photocopying,
recording or otherwise, or stored in any retrieval
system of any nature, without the written permission
of the copyright holder and the publisher, application
for which shall be made to the publisher.

©
G. H. Treitel
1991

PREFACE

In the four years since the last edition of this book, there have again been many significant developments in the law of contract. This edition takes account of some 350 new cases and also of a number of statutory changes. These developments have called for much rewriting, so that few pages have escaped entirely without change and about a quarter of the text is new. No more can be done here than to give a brief indication of the principal changes.

The most recent (and, it is to be hoped, the last) group of cases on abandonment of arbitrations by delay has led to a reformulation in Chapter 2 of the objective test of agreement. The discussion of the performance of existing duties as consideration has been rewritten in the light of *Williams* v. *Roffey Bros.*, a decision which has widespread repercussions not only in Chapter 3 but throughout the book. A number of recent cases have provided food for fresh thought on the implication of terms. Other cases, such as *Smith* v. *George S. Bush*, provide new material for the law relating to exemption clauses, particularly under the Unfair Contract Terms Act 1977, while possible developments restricting the effectiveness of standard terms other than exemption clauses are considered in the light of the *Interfoto* case. Parts of the account of mistake have been rewritten in the light of the *Associated Japanese Bank* and *Harlingdon* cases. In the discussion of misrepresentation, the account of the circumstances giving rise to a duty of care has been rewritten in the light of *Caparo* v. *Dickman*, and the effects of non-disclosure are reconsidered in the light of the *Banque Keyser Ullmann* case. Judicial developments in the law relating to the effects of illegal contracts are considered in Chapter 11. The new discussion of gambling with stolen money, in Chapter 12 is based on the decision of the Court of Appeal in *Lipkin Gorman* v. *Karpnale*, which has now been reversed by the House of Lords; a brief note on the decision of the House of Lords (which came too late for discussion in the text) follows this Preface. In Chapter 15, developments in the law of torts (stretching from the *D. & F. Estates* case to *Murphy* v. *Brentwood*) have led to a revision of the discussion of the relationship between liability in negligence to third parties and the doctrine of privity of contract, and of exemption clauses and third parties. Many important new decisions are discussed in the areas of rescission for breach: for example, *The Simona*, *The Dominique*, *Miles* v. *Wakefield*, *Wiluszynski* v. *Tower Hamlets and The Kachenjunga*. Changes in the discussion of frustration take account of *Shepherd* v. *Jerrom* and *The Super Servant Two*. Many new cases on remedies are considered in Chapter 21: for example, *Dean* v. *Ainley* (on the basis for assessing damages); *Vesta* v. *Butcher* (which has led to a rewriting of the section on contributory negligence); and *Rover* v. *Cannon Film Sales* (on the right to claim agreed prepayments, restitution of money and *quantum meruit*).

There have also been significant legislative developments. The provisions of the Law of Property (Miscellaneous Provisions) Act 1989 relating to formal requirements for contracts for the sale of land have their most obvious effect in Chapter 5 (where the account of part performance has been deleted), but also have repercussions in many other parts of the book. The Act has also considerably complicated the discussion of the requirements for the execution of deeds, which now vary according to whether the person executing the deed is an individual, a company incorporated under the Companies Acts, or some other kind of corporation. By contrast, the clean break which the Act makes with the rule in *Bain* v. *Fothergill* (Chapter 21) is to be welcomed. One wishes that the break with the *ultra vires* doctrine (Chapter 13) made by the Companies Act 1989 had been equally clean; further effects of this Act are considered elsewhere, especially in Chapters 14 and 17. The text also takes account of several provisions of the Courts and Legal Services Act 1990: for example, of those as to contingency fees, as to permitting barristers to contract for their services, and as to the dismissal of arbitration claims for want of prosecution.

The number of these new developments, and the complexity of some of them, have led inevitably to an increase in the size of the book, though some of this is the result of a change in typesetting.

It may be unusual for an author to thank his sources, but after many years of working on the law of contract it seems appropriate for me to do so. That work would not have held its continuing fascination, had it not been for the rich, intellectual diet which the English Courts (and indirectly the Bar) have continued to produce in this branch of the law. My debt to them in this respect is far more important than any doubts which I may occasionally have expressed as to their conclusions.

The main work on this edition was completed in August 1990; developments between then and the end of March 1991 (and occasionally somewhat later) have been more briefly incorporated in proof. I am grateful to the publishers for making this possible and for their help in many other respects. I am also grateful to a number of colleagues (in particular to Professor D. D. Prentice) and correspondents for help and advice in various respects; to Robert Spicer for compiling the Index; and to Hilary Williams of the British Museum's Department of Prints and Drawings for help with the cover illustration.

G.H.T.

All Souls College
Oxford
May 6, 1991.

Gambling with stolen money

In *Lipkin Gorman* v. *Karpnale Ltd* the House of Lords has reversed the decision of the Court of Appeal (discussed on pp. 477–480 of this book).

It has held that, where stolen money had been used by a gambler for the purpose of gaming at a casino, the victim of the theft could recover from the casino the amount by which the gambling transactions between the thief and the casino resulted in a balance in the casino's favour. The basis of the decision of the House of Lords was that, although the casino had received the money in good faith, it had not done so for value, since its claim to retain the money could be supported only by reference to contracts which were void under section 18 of the Gaming Act 1845. It made no difference that the thief had used the stolen money to acquire chips, which remained the property of the casino and were merely "a convenient mechanism for gambling with money." The transaction relating to the chips was either part of a single wagering transaction, or itself a contract by way of gaming, or one under which the casino had not given valuable consideration in the sense in which that expression is used in the context of a restitutionary claim (see p. 927 of the text). The decision of the House of Lords has not, indeed, affected the rule (stated on p. 464 of the text) that if the loser of a bet pays the amount lost to the winner, he cannot recover that amount back from the winner; but such a payment was said to be a gift from the loser to the winner, and not valuable consideration for the receipt of payments made by the loser to the winner under void contract. The victim's right to restitution in *Lipkin Gorman's* case was, however, held to have been limited by the defence of change of position. This defence accounted for the fact that the casino was not liable to the full extent of all the stolen money used by the thief for the purpose of the gaming. It was entitled to set off against the total sum so used amounts which it had credited the thief as winnings, and so was liable to the victim of the theft only to the extent to which the relevant gambling transaction had resulted in a balance in its favour.

CONTENTS

TABLE OF CASES

TABLE OF STATUTES

Chapter One

INTRODUCTION[1]

A contract is an agreement giving rise to obligations which are enforced or recognised by law. The factor which distinguishes contractual from other legal obligations is that they are based on the agreement of the contracting parties. This proposition remains generally true, in spite of the fact that it is subject to a number of important qualifications.

The first such qualification is that the law is often concerned with the objective appearance, rather than with the actual fact, of agreement. "If, whatever a man's real intention may be, he so conducts himself that a reasonable man would believe that he was assenting to the terms proposed by the other party, and that other party upon that belief enters into a contract with him, the man thus conducting himself would be equally bound as if he had intended to agree to the other party's terms."[2] This objective principle is based on the needs of commercial convenience. Considerable uncertainty would result if A, after inducing B reasonably to believe that he (A) had agreed to certain terms, could then escape liability merely by showing that he had no "real intention" to enter into that agreement. The principle is an important one; but it would be wrong to say that the law of contract has no concern at all with actual agreement. This would put too much emphasis on the exceptional situation; for in most cases, the appearance corresponds with the fact of agreement. And the principle is not purely objective: A is not bound merely because "a reasonable man would believe that he was assenting to the terms proposed by the other party." In particular, there will be no contract if (in spite of the objective appearance of agreement) B *actually knows* that A in fact has *no* intention to contract with him, or to contract on the terms alleged.[3] A subjective element thus qualifies the objective principle; and this follows from the purpose of that principle, which is to protect B from the prejudice which he might suffer as a result of relying on a false appearance of agreement. There is clearly no need in this way to protect a party who knows that the objective appearance does not correspond with reality.[4] It also follows from the purpose of the objective principle that it will not apply where A's apparent assent is based on a mistake induced by B's negligence.[5] More generally, it may be said that the objective principle applies only where serious inconvenience would be caused by allowing a party to rely on his "real intention." In the interests of convenience the law may sometimes hold that there is a con-

---

[1] See Hughes Parry, *The Sanctity of Contracts in English Law*.

[2] *Smith* v. *Hughes* (1871) L.R. 6 Q.B. 597, 607; *post*, p. 271 *Cambridge Notation Ltd.* v. *B.B.C.* [1990] 3 All E.R. 523, 542. Howarth, 100 L.Q.R. 265; Vorster, 103 L.Q.R. 27d; Howarth, *ibid.* p. 547; Goddard, 7 Legal Studies 263; de Moor, 106 L.Q.R. 632.

[3] *e.g. post*, pp. 8–9, 272.

[4] For the further question whether the objective principle protects the "other party" where he has *no view* on the question whether the objective appearance corresponded with reality, see *post*, p. 9.

[5] *e.g. post*, pp. 273, 286, *cf. Norwich Union Fire Insurance Society Ltd.* v. *Wm. H. Price* [1934] A.C. 455, 463.

tract although there was not even the objective appearance of an agreement.[6] It does not follow that the law is not concerned with any sort of agreement at all: to allege that this was the position "would introduce into the law of contract a novel heresy."[7]

The idea that contractual obligations are based on agreement must, secondly, be qualified because contracting parties are normally expected to observe certain standards of behaviour. These are the result of terms implied by law.[8] For example, a person who sells goods or enters into a contract of employment is bound by many such implied terms. The parties may be able to vary or exclude some such terms by contrary agreement; but unless they do so they are bound by many duties to which they have not expressly agreed and of which they may have never thought. Agreement is clearly not the *sole* factor which determines the legal effects of a contract once it is shown to exist. But it remains an important factor. For example, the intention of the parties determines whether a statement made at the time of contracting has contractual force or is a mere representation[9]; and it determines whether a term which is not expressly stated in the contract should be implied in fact, *i.e.* because the parties must have intended to incorporate it.[10] It has been suggested that in such cases the courts only *say* that the intention of the parties is the determining factor, but really apply rules based on various considerations of policy unconnected with that intention.[11] But a bare assertion that the relevant judgments do not mean what they say should not be accepted unless it is supported by argument. Such an argument can, perhaps, be based on the history of the doctrine of frustration, under which contracting parties may be discharged from liability by supervening impossibility.[12] The doctrine was at one time justified by saying that the parties had impliedly agreed to be discharged in such circumstances; but many lawyers now prefer to say that the parties are discharged by operation of law, whether they would have agreed to discharge or not. This may be true; but the intention of the parties cannot for that reason be wholly disregarded. Before holding that parties are discharged, the court must find out what they contracted about: they may have deliberately run the risk of supervening impossibility. The court must decide whether the parties contracted about a certainty or about a possibility; and it does so by ascertaining, as best it can, their intentions in the matter.

The idea that contractual obligations are based on agreement must, thirdly, be qualified in relation to the scope of the principle of freedom of contract.[13] In the nineteenth century, judges took the view that persons of full capacity should in general be allowed to make what contracts they liked: the law only interfered on fairly specific grounds such as misrepresentation, undue influence or illegality.[14] It did not interfere merely because one party was economically more powerful than the other and so able to drive a hard bargain. This attitude became particularly important

---

[6] *Post*, p. 41.
[7] *The Hannah Blumenthal* [1983] 1 A.C. 854, 916–917.
[8] *Post*, pp. 189 *et seq.*
[9] *Post*, p. 316.
[10] *Post*, p. 185.
[11] Atiyah, *An Introduction to the Law of Contract* (4th ed.), pp. 23–25, 191. (The point was more emphatically put in the 1st ed. at pp. 13, 103).
[12] *Post*, Chap. 20.
[13] For an historical account, see Atiyah, *The Rise and Fall of Freedom of Contract*.
[14] *Post*, Chaps. 4, 10, 11.

when the courts recognised the validity of standard form contracts[15] by which one party excluded or limited his common law liabilities. In the present century this practice of contracting on standard terms has become very common; and it is arguable that a customer who contracts on such standard terms has them imposed on him, and does not really "agree" to them at all. This argument is particularly strong where the supplier has a monopoly, or where all suppliers in a particular field use the same standard terms. The customer may then only be able to accept those terms or do without the goods or services in question; and in many cases he cannot in practice do without. On the other hand, exact equality of bargaining power is probably rare; and there can clearly be much dispute as to the precise degree of pressure which makes the difference between consent reluctantly given and a state of mind which cannot properly be described as consent at all. The amount of pressure which can be brought to bear on the customer does not depend solely on the respective wealth and power of the parties, but also on current market conditions. In a buyer's market, an insistent private customer may be able to induce a normally powerful supplier to modify his standard terms, rather than lose a sale. On the other hand, in a seller's market a customer may be ready to agree to any terms which the seller puts forward, or be willing to take his chance of the contents of any document put forward by the seller. A person may also agree to contract on a set of terms although he does not know in detail what they provide. This is often the position where two businessmen contract on terms settled by a trade association; or where a person takes employment on terms negotiated between his employers and a trade union.[16] In such cases the parties would not deny that they *had* agreed to the terms whatever they might be.

Important inroads on the principle of freedom of contract have been made by legislation passed to redress some real or supposed imbalance of bargaining power. The contents of many service contracts are now regulated in some detail by legislation[17]; and under the Rent Act[18] a system of regulated or controlled rents and security of tenure exists, under which many important aspects of the relationship of landlord and tenant are controlled by legislation. Under other statutes, terms are compulsorily implied into contracts and cannot be excluded by contrary agreement[19]; while the validity of exemption clauses is subject to severe legislative restrictions, especially in contracts between a commercial supplier of goods or services and a consumer.[20] In all these cases the main relationship between the parties is still based on agreement, but many of the obligations arising out of it are imposed or regulated by law.

But there are other cases in which the law plays so large, and the agreement of parties so small, a part that it becomes doubtful whether the relationship can still be called contractual. The agreement of the parties may create a status, such as marriage, the main legal incidents of which are

---

15 *Post*, Chap. 7.

16 *Post*, p. 194.

17 See, *e.g.* Employment Protection (Consolidation) Act 1978, s.49.

18 Previous legislation on this topic is now consolidated in the Rent Act 1977. It is, in general, impossible to "contract out" of the provisions of the Act: see, *e.g.* s.44(2). *Cf.* Leasehold Reform Act 1967, s.23; *Johnson* v. *Moreton* [1980] A.C. 37. Housing Act 1988 Pt. I indicates some return to freedom of contract.

19 Sex Discrimination Act 1975, s.8, amending Equal Pay Act 1970, s.1.

20 *Post*, pp. 229–235.

fixed by law and cannot be varied by the parties at all. Sometimes, the terms on which a person is employed (especially in the public service) are governed in part by legislation; and in one such case it was said that a claim under the "statutory scheme of employment"[21] could not "be dealt with as though it were an ordinary master and servant claim in which the rights of the parties were regulated solely by contract."[22] Similarly, a member of the armed forces is not in any contractual relationship with the Crown, even if he enlists voluntarily.[23] But there are borderline cases in which the mere fact that many of the terms of a relationship are settled by law does not prevent it from being contractual. For example, it has been said that a consultant appointed to a post at a hospital under the National Health Service, works under "an ordinary contract between master and servant," although it is one with a "strong statutory flavour,"[24] as it is governed by regulations made under statutory powers and having the force of law.

In the cases so far considered the parties are free to decide whether or not to enter into the relationship (though the law may fix some or all of its incidents); but there are other cases in which the law to some extent restricts even this freedom. For example, at common law a common innkeeper may be liable criminally[25] or in tort[26] for refusing, without sufficient excuse, to accommodate a guest. By statute injunctions may be granted, and damages awarded, against persons who withhold supplies from retailers on the ground of price-cutting,[27] and against persons whose refusal to make certain contracts amounts to unlawful discrimination on grounds of race or sex[28]; and it is unlawful to refuse a person employment "because he is, or is not, a member of a trade union."[29] Even at common law, a withholding of supplies may, in exceptional circumstances, be restrained by injunction[30]; and it is possible that a refusal to enter into a contract might similarly be restrained where it gave effect to a policy of discrimination even though it was not unlawful by statute; *e.g.* where a person was excluded from an association (and so deprived of the opportunity to do work available only to its members) on religious or political grounds that had no bearing on his competence to do the type of work in question.[31] In

---

21 *Barber* v. *Manchester Regional Hospital Board* [1958] 1 W.L.R. 181, 196.

22 *Barber's* case, *ubi supra*; for the effect of this distinction on remedies, see *post*, pp. 910–911.

23 See *Grant* v. *S. of S. for India* (1877) 2 C.P.D. 445; *Mitchell* v. *R.* (1890) [1896] 1 Q.B. 121n.; *Leaman* v. *R.* [1920] 3 K.B. 663; *Kynaston* v. *Att.-Gen.* (1933) 49 T.L.R. 300; dicta in *Owners of S.S. Raphael* v. *Brandy* [1911] A.C. 413, 415 perhaps suggest the contrary: *cf.* Mitchell, *Contracts of Public Authorities*, p. 41. And see *post*, p. 155.

24 *Barber's* case, *ubi supra*; *cf. R.* v. *E. Berkshire Health Authority, ex p. Walsh* [1985] Q.B. 152; *R.* v. *Derbyshire C.C., ex p. Noble* [1990] I.C.R. 808; *Associated British Ports* v. *T. & G.W.U.* [1989] 1 W.L.R. 939; *Roy* v. *Kensington, etc., Family Practitioner Committee*, *The Times*, March 27, 1990.

25 See *R.* v. *Ivens* (1835) 7 C. & P. 213.

26 *Constantine* v. *Imperial Hotels Ltd.* [1944] K.B. 693.

27 Resale Prices Act 1976, ss.12, 25. *Cf.* also Employment Act 1982, ss.12–14.

28 See Sex Discrimination Act 1975, Pts. II and III and ss.65, 66 and 71 (as amended by Employment Act 1989, ss.1–9); Race Relations Act 1976, Pts. II and III and ss.56, 57 and 62. Injunctions are not available under these Acts in the employment field: *post*, p. 910. See also Courts and Legal Services Act 1990, s.64.

29 Employment Act 1990, s.1(1)(*a*); *cf. ibid.* s.2(1)(*a*); under s.3(5) and Sched. 1 para. 5 the remedy (in the last resort) is by way of compensation.

30 *Acrow (Automation) Ltd.* v. *Rex Chainbelt Inc.* [1971] 1 W.L.R. 1676.

31 A suggestion based on *Nagle* v. *Feilden* [1966] 2 Q.B. 633 (where the refusal was based on sex discrimination before that was made unlawful by statute); *post*, p. 425.

all these cases a relationship which results from some degree of legal compulsion is nevertheless regarded as contractual, because the parties still have considerable freedom to regulate its incidents. But there are other cases in which a relationship created by legal compulsion is clearly not contractual. A person whose property is compulsorily acquired against his will does not make a contract with the acquiring authority even though he receives compensation[32]; a patient to whom medicines are supplied under the National Health Service is not considered to make a contract to buy them, even if he pays a prescription charge[33]; and a person who posts a letter or parcel does not make a contract with the Post Office.[34] The borderline between the two classes of cases is by no means clearly defined: it is, for example, doubtful whether a consumer of gas, electricity or water makes a contract with the bodies which are statutorily obliged to supply these things[35]; or whether there is a contract between a patient and his doctor or dentist under the National Health Service, or between a client and his lawyer under the Legal Aid Scheme.[36]

In spite of the above qualifications, it remains broadly true that the law of contract is concerned with the circumstances in which agreements are legally binding. Thus it deals mainly with the two questions of agreement and legal effects or enforceability. The rules relating to offer and acceptance,[37] for instance, deal with the process of reaching agreement. Those relating to consideration and contractual intention[38] concern the requirements which must normally be satisfied before an agreement will be legally enforced; while the rules relating to misrepresentation and illegality[39] deal with the effect of special circumstances on account of which the law may refuse to enforce agreements which would otherwise be binding. The rules relating to capacity[40] are based partly on the view that certain classes of persons cannot form the requisite contractual intention, and partly on the

---

[32] See *Sovmots Investments Ltd.* v. *S. of S. for the Environment* [1977] Q.B. 411, 443, affirmed but without reference to this point [1979] A.C. 144. If a price is agreed after notice to treat, there is said to be a "statutory contract": *Munton* v. *G.L.C.* [1976] 1 W.L.R. 649; *cf. Harding* v. *Metropolitan Ry.* (1872) L.R. 7 Ch.App. 154, 158. Even where this is not the case, the transaction may be regarded as a contract for the purpose of a particular statute: *Ridge Nominees* v. *I.R.C.* [1962] Ch. 376. The exercise by a "secure tenant" of his right under Part V of the Housing Act 1985 to buy the house or flat which is the subject-matter of his tenancy similarly does not give rise to a contract. Landlord and Tenant Act 1987 Pt. I (Tenants' Right of First Refusal) uses contractual concepts while Pt. III (Compulsory Acquisition by Tenants of their Landlord's Interest) uses those of compulsory purchase.

[33] See *Pfizer Corp.* v. *Ministry of Health* [1965] A.C. 512; *Appleby* v. *Sleep* [1968] 1 W.L.R. 948; *Re Medicaments Reference* [1970] 1 W.L.R. 1339.

[34] *Whitfield* v. *Lord Le Despencer* (1778) Cowp. 754, 764. For exclusion and limitation of liability in tort, see Post Office Act 1969, ss.29, 30 (as amended by British Telecommunications Act 1981, s.70); *American Express Co.* v. *British Airways Board* [1983] 1 W.L.R. 701.

[35] Gas Act 1986, s.10(1) seems to assume that there is no contract with domestic consumers; contrast *ibid.* s.10(7) (non-domestic users receiving supplies under "written contract."). A similar distinction is drawn by Electricity Act 1989, ss.16, 22; *cf.* Water Act 1989, ss.45, 46 (where it is less clear whether the "agreement" in the latter case has contractual force).

[36] *Cf.* Legal Aid Act 1988, s.9(7), 24 and Sched. 3 Pt. 1 para. 2(1); s.16(10) refers to a contract between the legally assisted person and *the Board* (not to one between that person and the legal adviser). For the power of barristers to make contracts for the provision of services as such, and for the power of the General Council of the Bar to prohibit or restrict such contracts, see Courts and Legal Services Act 1990, s.61.

[37] *Post*, Chap. 2.

[38] *Post*, Chaps. 3, 4.

[39] *Post*, Chaps. 9, 11; see also Chaps. 10, 12.

[40] *Post*, Chap. 13.

view that it is undesirable to enforce agreements with such classes of persons. The rules relating to mistake are based partly on the view that there is no agreement when the parties are at cross-purposes on a fundamantal point,[41] and partly on the view that an agreement has no legal effect if both parties were under a fundamental mistake as to the subject-matter.[42] The rules relating to the contents of a contract, performance, breach and frustration[43] are again partly based on the agreement between the parties, and partly on rules of law which determine the precise legal effect of the agreement.

The bulk of the law of contract is concerned with the questions of agreement and legal enforceability; but a number of others will also be discussed in the following chapters. Thus the rules relating to plurality, privity, assignment and agency[44] determine who is bound by, and entitled to the benefit of, an agreement. The rules relating to remedies[45] assume the existence of an enforceable agreement, and deal with the methods of, and limits on, enforcement. These are in principle determined by law. Thus the agreement of the parties is irrelevant to the question whether a contract is to be enforced specifically, or only by an award of damages. But the agreement between the parties may be relevant in determining the precise amount of damages which will be awarded for a breach of contract.

Remedies for breach of contract are discussed in Chapter 21; but one point relating to them may be made at this stage. Such remedies might attempt to do one of two things. First, they might attempt to put the injured party into the position in which he would have been if the contract *had never been made*. This would require the party in breach to restore anything that he had received under the contract, and also to compensate the injured party for any loss that he had suffered by acting in reliance on the contract. Such remedies are said to protect the injured party's *restitution* and *reliance* interests.[46] But remedies for breach of contract go beyond the pursuit of these objectives. Their distinguishing feature is that they seek to put the injured party into the position in which he would have been if the contract *had been performed*.[47] Thus, if a seller agrees to sell goods for less than they are worth, and then fails to deliver them, he is liable to compensate the buyer for having to pay more for substitute goods than the price fixed by the original contract. Conversely, if goods have been sold for more than they are worth the seller can sue for the agreed price[48]: it is quite immaterial that the value of the goods with which he has parted was lower than that price. What the law does in these cases is to protect the injured party's *expectation* interest.[49] Sometimes it does so directly, by actually ordering the party in breach to perform his part of the contract.[50] Sometimes it does so indirectly by ordering him to pay the injured party damages for *loss of his bargain*.

The result of awarding damages on this basis is to compensate the

[41] *Post*, Chap. 8, s.2.
[42] *Post*, Chap. 8, s.1.
[43] *Post*, Chaps. 6, 18, 19, 20.
[44] *Post*, Chaps. 14 to 17.
[45] *Post*, Chap. 21.
[46] *Post*, pp. 831–832.
[47] *Post*, pp. 830–831.
[48] Assuming that the conditions stated on pp. 896–902, *post* are satisfied.
[49] *Post*, p. 830–831.
[50] *Post*, pp. 902–924.

injured party, not because he is worse off than he was before the contract was made, but because the other party has failed to make him better off. The law of contract takes this position in response to the needs of commercial certainty. It is probably going too far to say that business could not be carried on at all if the law did not protect the injured party's expectation interest. Some industries (such as the credit betting industry) are carried on without this, or indeed any other legally recognised, sanction.[51] But in relation to other spheres of commercial activity, such as share and commodity markets and the insurance industry (to take a few random examples)[52] the protection of expectations is of crucial importance. In these cases, that protection promotes stability and furthers one of the central purposes of the law of contract in providing the legal framework required for commercial relations.

---

[51] *Post*, pp. 461–463.

[52] Another may be the sale of houses, where the fact that agreements "subject to contract" have no binding force has been strongly criticised: see *post*, p. 52.

CHAPTER TWO

AGREEMENT[1]

THE first requisite of a contract is that the parties should have reached agreement. Generally speaking, an agreement is made when one party accepts an offer made by the other. Further requirements are that the agreement must be certain and final; and special problems arise from conditional agreements.

SECTION 1. OFFER

1. Offer Defined

(1) The objective test

An offer is an expression of willingness to contract on certain terms, made with the intention that it shall become binding as soon as it is accepted by the person to whom it is addressed.[2] Under the objective test of agreement,[3] an apparent intention to be bound may suffice, *i.e.* the alleged offeror (A) may be bound if his conduct[4] is such as to induce a reasonable person to believe that he intends to be bound, even though in fact he has no such such intention. For example, if A offers to sell a book to B for £10 and B accepts the offer, A cannot escape liability merely by showing that his actual intention was to offer the book to B for £20, or that he intended the offer to relate to a book different from that specified in the offer.[5]

Whether A is actually bound by an acceptance of his apparent offer depends on the state of mind of the alleged offeree (B); to this extent, the test is not purely objective.[6] With regard to B's state of mind, there are three possibilities. First, B actually believes that A has the requisite intention: here the objective test is satisfied so that B can hold A to his apparent offer even though A did not, subjectively, have the requisite intention.[7] The general view is that there is no further requirement that A must also be aware of B's state of mind.[8] Secondly, B knows that, in spite of the objective appearance, A does not have the requisite intention: here A is not

---

[1] Winfield, 55 L.Q.R. 499; Kahn, 72 S.A.L.J. 246; Nussbaum, 36 Col.L.Rev. 920.

[2] *e.g. Storer* v. *Manchester C.C.* [1974] 1 W.L.R. 1403; contrast *Anrdé & Cie* v. *Cook Industries Inc.* [1987] 2 Lloyd's Rep. 463.

[3] *Ante*, p. 1.

[4] For offers made by conduct, see *infra*, at nn. 13 *et seq.*; *The Aramis* [1989] 1 Lloyd's Rep. 213 (where the objective test was not satisfied).

[5] *Cf. Centrovincial Estates plc* v. *Merchant Investors Assurance Co. Ltd.* [1983] Com.L.R. 158; cited with approval in *Whittaker* v. *Campbell* [1984] Q.B. 318, 327 and in *The Antclizo* [1987] 2 Lloyd's Rep. 130, 146, affirmed [1988] 1 W.L.R. 603.

[6] *The Hannah Blumenthal* [1983] 1 A.C. 854, 924.

[7] *The Splendid Sun* [1981] 1 Q.B. 694, as explained in *The Hannah Blumenthal, supra*; *Challoner* v. *Bower* (1984) 269 E.G. 725; *The Multibank Holsatia* [1988] 2 Lloyd's Rep. 486, 493 ("subjective understanding").

[8] The suggestion that A must be aware of B's state of mind was made by Lord Diplock in *The Hannah Blumenthal* [1983] 1 A.C. 854, 916 but Lord Brightman's contrary view, expressed *ibid.* p. 924 has been generally preferred: see *The Multibank Holsatia, supra*, p. 492.

bound; the objective test does not apply in favour of B as he knows the truth about A's actual intention.[9] Thirdly, B has simply not addressed his mind to the question of A's intention, so that B neither believes that A has the requisite intention nor knows that A does not have this intention: this situation has given rise to a conflict of judicial opinion. One view is that A is not bound: in other words, the objective test is only satisfied if A's conduct is such as to induce a reasonable person to believe that A had the requisite intention *and* if B actually held that belief.[10] The opposing view is that (in our third situation) A is bound: in other words, the objective test is satisfied if A's words or conduct would induce a reasonable person to believe that A had the requisite intention, so long as B does not actually know that A does *not* have any such intention.[11] This latter view no doubt facilitates proof of agreement, but it is hard to see why B should be protected in the situation to which it refers. Where B has no positive belief in A's (apparent) intention to be bound, he cannot be prejudiced by acting in reliance on it; and the purpose of the objective test is simply to protect B from the risk of suffering such prejudice.[12] The test embodies a principle of convenience; it is not based on any inherent superiority of objective over subjective criteria. It is therefore submitted that the objective test should not apply to our third situation since in it there is, by reason of B's state of mind, no risk of his suffering any prejudice as a result of the objective appearance of A's intention. For this purpose, it should make no difference whether B's state of mind amounts to knowledge of, or merely to indifference to, the truth.

(2) Conduct as an offer

An offer may be addressed either to an individual, or to a group of persons, or to the world at large; and it may be made expressly or by conduct. At common law, a person who had contracted to sell goods and tendered different goods (or a different quantity) might be considered to make an offer by conduct to sell the goods which he had tendered.[13] It seems that an offer to sell can still be made in this way, though by statute the dispatch of goods without any prior request from the recipient may amount to a gift to him, rather than to an offer to sell.[14]

---

[9] *Ante*, p. 1, and see the authorities cited in n. 11, *infra*.

[10] *The Hannah Blumenthal*, *supra*, as interpreted in *The Leonidas D* [1985] 1 W.L.R. 925; Beatson 102 L.Q.R. 19; Atiyah, *ibid*. 363; *The Agrabele* [1987] 2 Lloyd's Rep. 223, esp. at p. 235; *cf. Cie. Française d'Importation, etc., S.A.* v. *Deutsche Continental Handelsgesellschaft* [1985] 2 Lloyd's Rep. 592, 597; *Amherst* v. *James Walker Goldsmith and Silversmith Ltd*. [1983] Ch. 305.

[11] *The Golden Bear* [1987] 1 Lloyd's Rep. 330, 341 (doubted on another point at p. 31, *post*); this view was approved in *The Antclizo* [1987] 2 Lloyd's Rep. 130, 143 but doubted *ibid*. p. 147 (affirmed [1988] 1 W.L.R. 603 without reference to the point); and *semble* in *Floating Dock Ltd*. v. *Hong Kong and Shanghai Bank Ltd*. [1986] 1 Lloyd's Rep. 65, 77; *The Multibank Holsatia* [1988] 2 Lloyd's Rep. 486, 492 ("at least did not conflict with [B's] subjective understanding"); *The Maritime Winner* [1989] 2 Lloyd's Rep. 506, 515 (using similar language). A dictum in *The Amazonia* [1990] 1 Lloyd's Rep. 238, 242 goes even further in suggesting that there may be a contract even though "*neither* [party] intended to make a contract."

[12] *Ante*, p. 1.

[13] *Hart* v. *Mills* (1846) 15 L.J.Ex. 200; *post*, p. 17; *cf. Steven* v. *Bromley & Son* [1919] 2 K.B. 722; *The Saronikos* [1982] 2 Lloyd's Rep. 277.

[14] Unsolicited Goods and Services Act 1971, ss.1, 6; *quaere* whether this would apply where a seller tendered a quantity grossly in excess of that ordered.

A number of cases raise the further question whether the "conduct" from which an offer may be inferred can take the form of inactivity. The issue in these cases was whether an agreement to submit a dispute to arbitration could be said to have been "abandoned" by long delay, where, over a long period of time, neither party had taken any steps in the arbitration proceedings. In cases of this kind, arbitrators now have a statutory power to dismiss the claim for want of prosecution,[15] so that the question of abandonment by subsequent agreement is no longer likely to arise in this context. But such a question might still arise in the context of the alleged abandonment of some other type of right or remedy,[16] to which no similar legislative provision extends. The arbitration cases indicate that, on the objective test, inactivity may amount to an offer of abandonment when combined with other circumstances (such as the destruction of relevant files),[17] even though those circumstances would not, of themselves, constitute sufficient evidence from which an offer could be inferred. But mere inactivity by one party is unlikely, when standing alone, to have this effect, for it is equivocal and explicable on other grounds, such as inertia or forgetfulness. Consequently, it will not normally suffice to induce a reasonable person in the position of the other party to believe that an offer is being made[18]; and the mere fact that the other party nevertheless had this belief cannot suffice to turn the former party's inactivity into such an offer.[19]

2. Offer Distinguished from Invitation to Treat

When parties negotiate with a view to making a contract, many preliminary communications may pass between them before a definite offer is made. One party may simply respond to a request for information (*e.g.* by stating the price at which he might be prepared to sell a house[20]), or he may make a similar request (*e.g.* where he asks a prospective supplier whether he can supply goods suitable for his purpose).[21] That party is then said to make an "invitation to treat": he does not himself make an offer but, invites the other party to do so. The question whether a statement is an offer or an

---

[15] Arbitration Act 1950, s.13A, as inserted by Courts and Legal Services Act 1990, s.102.

[16] *Cf. Amherst Ltd.* v. *James Walker Goldsmith & Silversmith Ltd.* [1983] Ch. 305; *Collin* v. *Duke of Westminister* [1985] Q.B. 581; *M.S.C. Mediterranean Shipping Co. S.A.* v. *B.R.E. Metro Ltd.* [1985] 2 Lloyd's Rep. 239; *Fenton Ins. Ltd.* v. *Gothaer Versicherungsbank VVaG* [1991] 1 Lloyd's Rep. 172, 180.

[17] *The Splendid Sun* [1981] Q.B. 694, as explained in *The Hannah Blumenthal* [1983] 1 A.C. 854 (though this explanation was doubted in *Cie. Française d'Importation, etc., S.A.* v. *Deutsche Conti Handelsgesellschaft* [1985] 2 Lloyd's Rep. 592, 599); *Tracomin S.A.* v. *Anton C. Nielsen* [1984] 2 Lloyd's Rep. 195 (as to which see *post*, p. 34 n. 34); *The Multibamk Holsatia* [1988] 2 Lloyd's Rep. 486; for the question whether such an offer can be *accepted* by inactivity, see *post*, p. 34.

[18] *The Leonidas D* [1985] 1 W.L.R. 925; *Cie Française d'Importation, etc., S.A.* v. *Deutsche Conti Handelsgesellschaft* [1985] 2 Lloyd's Rep. 592; *The Antclizo* [1988] 1 W.L.R. 603; *The Agrabele* [1987] 2 Lloyd's Rep. 223); *The Maritime Winner* [1989] 2 Lloyd's Rep. 506; *contra*, *The Golden Bear* [1987] 1 Lloyd's Rep. 330 (*sed quaere*: the decision was in part based on the decision at first instance in *The Agrabele* [1985] 2 Lloyd's Rep. 496, but this was reversed on appeal: [1987] 2 Lloyd's Rep. 223); *The Ermoupolis* [1990] 1 Lloyd's Rep. 161, 166 see also *post*, p. 34).

[19] *The Antclizo* [1988] 1 W.L.R. 603; Davenport, 104 L.Q.R. 493.

[20] *e.g. Harvey* v. *Facey* [1893] A.C. 552; *Gibson* v. *Manchester C.C.* [1979] 1 W.L.R. 294; *cf. The Barranduna* [1985] 2 Lloyd's Rep. 419 (quotation of freight rates by carrier not an offer).

[21] *Interfoto Picture Library Ltd.* v. *Stiletto Visual Programmes Ltd.* [1989] Q.B. 433, 436.

invitation to treat depends primarily on the intention with which it was made. It follows from the nature of an offer as described above[22] that a statement is not an offer if it in terms negatives the maker's intention to be bound on acceptance: for example, if it expressly provides that he is *not* to be bound merely by the other party's notification of assent, but only when he himself has signed the document in which the statement is contained.[23] Apart from this type of case, the wording is not conclusive: a statement may be an invitation to treat, although it contains the word "offer."[24] Conversely, a statement may *be* an offer although it is expressed to be an "acceptance,"[25] or although it requests the person to whom it is addressed to *make* an "offer."[26]

The distinction between an offer and an invitation to treat is often hard to draw as it depends on the elusive criterion of intention. But there are certain stereotyped situations in which the distinction is determined, at least prima facie, by rules of law. It may be possible to displace these rules by evidence of contrary intention, but in the absence of such evidence they will determine the distinction between offer and invitation to treat, and they will do so without reference to the intention (actual or even objectively ascertained) of the maker of the statement. This is true, for example, in cases of auction sales and shop displays. These and other illustrations of the distinction will be discussed in the following paragraphs.

(1) Auction sales

At an auction sale, the general rule is that the offer is made by the bidder and accepted by the auctioneer when he signifies his acceptance in the customary manner, *e.g.* by fall of the hammer.[27] Before acceptance the bidder may withdraw his bid and the auctioneer may withdraw the goods. It seems, moreover, that the offer made by each bidder lapses[28] as soon as a higher bid is made. Thus if a higher bid is made and withdrawn the auctioneer can no longer accept the next highest.

When property is put up for auction subject to a reserve price, there is no contract if the auctioneer by mistake purports to accept a bid lower than the reserve price.[29] Where the auction is without reserve, there is no contract *of sale* between the highest bidder and the *owner* of the property if the auctioneer refuses to accept the highest bid. But it has been held that the *auctioneer* is in such a case liable on a separate contract between him and the highest bidder that the sale will be without reserve.[30] Although a mere advertisement of an auction is not an offer to hold it,[31] the actual request

---

[22] *Supra*, at n. 2.

[23] *Financings Ltd.* v. *Stimson* [1962] 1 W.L.R. 1184.

[24] *Spencer* v. *Harding* (1870) L.R. 5 C.P. 561; *Clifton* v. *Palumbo* [1944] 2 All E.R. 497.

[25] *Bigg* v. *Boyd Gibbins Ltd.* [1971] 1 W.L.R. 913.

[26] *Harvela Investments Ltd.* v. *Royal Trust Co. of Canada* (*C.I.*) *Ltd.* [1986] A.C. 207.

[27] Sale of Goods Act 1979, s.57(2); *Payne* v. *Cave* (1789) 3 T.R. 148; *British Car Auctions Ltd.* v. *Wright* [1972] 1 W.L.R. 1519.

[28] *Post*, p. 43.

[29] *McManus* v. *Fortescue* [1907] 2 K.B. 1; on a sale of land, it must be expressly stated whether the sale is with reserve or not: Sale of Land by Auction Act 1867, s.5.

[30] *Warlow* v. *Harrison* (1859) 1 E. & E. 309; *cf. Johnston* v. *Boyes* [1899] 2 Ch. 73, 77. *Contra*, *Fenwick* v. *Macdonald, Fraser & Co. Ltd.* (1904) 6 F. (Ct. of Sess.) 850; Slade, 68 L.Q.R. 238; Gower, 68 L.Q.R. 457; Slade, 69 L.Q.R. 21. Under the American Uniform Commercial Code (hereinafter referred to as U.C.C.) the goods may not be withdrawn once they have been put up, if the auction is without reserve: s.2–328(3).

[31] *Harris* v. *Nickerson* (1873) L.R. 8 Q.B. 286.

for bids seems to be an offer by the auctioneer that he will on the owner's behalf accept the highest bid; and this offer is accepted by the bidding.[32]

(2) Display of goods for sale

The general rule is that a display of price-marked goods in a shop window is not an offer to sell goods but is an invitation to a customer to make an offer to buy.[33] The same is true of an indication of the price at which petrol is to be sold at a filling station[34]: the offer is made by the customer and may be accepted by the seller's conduct in putting petrol into the tank.[35] The position may be different where the station operates on the self-service principle.[36] Similarly, the display of goods on the shelves of a self-service shop is merely an invitation to treat; the customer makes an offer to buy when he carries the goods to the cashdesk, where the shopkeeper may accept or reject it.[37] The general rule is well established, but the reasons given for it are not entirely convincing.

One reason is that "a shop is a place for bargaining, not for compulsory sales."[38] But the modern English shop, in which goods are generally bought on the shopkeeper's terms, is scarcely a place for bargaining; and even if the display of goods were an offer, any resulting sale would not be compulsory: the shopkeeper need not display goods which he does not want to sell. Another argument is that if the display were regarded as an offer, the shopkeeper might be exposed to many actions for damages if more customers purported to accept than his stock could satisfy.[39] But the offer could be construed as one which automatically expired when the shopkeeper's stock was exhausted: this would probably be in keeping with the common expectation of both shopkeeper and customer. It has also been said that, if a display in a self-service shop were an offer, the undesirable result would follow that the customer would be bound to buy as soon as he picked up the goods to examine them.[40] But if the display were an offer, it could be argued that there was no acceptance until the customer did some less equivocal act, such as presenting the goods at the cashdesk.[41]

---

[32] The question whether there is any consideration for the auctioneer's undertaking is discussed *post*, p. 141.

[33] *Timothy* v. *Simpson* (1834) 6 C. & P. 499; *Fisher* v. *Bell* [1961] 1 Q.B. 394; (the actual decision has been reversed: Restriction of Offensive Weapons Act 1961, s.1); dicta in *Wiles* v. *Maddison* [1943] 1 All E.R. 315, 317, may perhaps suggest the contrary.

[34] *Esso Petroleum* v. *Commissioners of Customs & Excise* [1976] 1 W.L.R. 1, 5, 6, 11; *Richardson* v. *Worrall* [1985] S.T.C. 693, 717.

[35] *Re Charge Card Services* [1989] Ch. 497, 512; for acceptance by conduct, see *post*, p. 17.

[36] *Cf. post*, p. 14 at n. 53.

[37] *Pharmaceutical Society of Great Britain* v. *Boots Cash Chemists Ltd.* [1952] 2 Q.B. 795; [1953] 1 Q.B. 401; Unger, 16 M.L.R. 369; D.C.W., 10 N.I.L.Q. 117; Montrose, 10 N.I.L.Q. 178; and *cf. Lacis* v. *Cashmarts Ltd.* [1969] 2 Q.B. 400; *Davies* v. *Leighton* [1978] Crim.L.R. 575.

[38] Winfield, 55 L.Q.R. 518.

[39] *Esso Petroleum* case *supra*, n. 34 at p. 11.

[40] *Boots case* [1952] 2 Q.B. 795, 802.

[41] See *Lasky* v. *Economic Grocery Stores*, 65 N.E. 2d 305 (1946). In *Gillespie* v. *Great Atlantic & Pacific Stores*, 187 S.E. 2d. 441 (1972) and *Sheeskin* v. *Giant Food Inc.*, 318 A 2d. 874 (1974) acceptance was said to take place before the customer presented the goods at the cashdesk, but subject to his power to cancel before that point. *Cf. R.* v. *Morris* [1984] A.C. 320 where taking goods off the shelf of a self-service store *and changing the price-labels* was held to be an "appropriation" within Theft Act 1968, s.3(1); but it does not follow that at this stage there would for the purpose of the law of contract be an acceptance even if the shelf-display amounted to an offer: see, *ibid.* p. 334.

Finally, it may be asked whether the general rule does not sometimes cause injustice. Customers may be induced by a window display to believe that they will be able to buy goods at exceptionally low prices and to wait outside the shop for many hours in reliance on that belief. Is it right to allow the shopkeeper to go back on such a statement at the very moment when the customer demands the goods?[42] Perhaps in exceptional cases window or shelf displays can be offers. The special terms of a display, or the circumstances in which it is made, may be evidence of intention to be bound ousting the prima facie rule that the display is not an offer. But even if this is the case, the customer may still lose his bargain, since an offer can be withdrawn at any time before acceptance.[43]

(3) Advertisements and other displays

Advertisements of rewards for the return of lost or stolen property, or for information leading to the arrest or conviction of the perpetrator of a crime,[44] are invariably treated as offers: they are clearly made with the intention to be bound as no further bargaining is expected to result from them. The same is true of other advertisements of unilateral contracts.[45] Thus in *Carlill* v. *Carbolic Smoke Ball Co.*,[46] an advertisement promising to pay £100 to any user of a carbolic smoke ball who caught influenza was held to be an offer. The intention to be bound[47] was made particularly clear in this case by the statement that the advertisers had deposited £1,000 in their bank "shewing our sincerity."

Advertisements of bilateral contracts are not often held to be offers since such advertisements do often lead to further bargaining, and since the advertiser may legitimately wish, before becoming bound, to assure himself that the other party is able to perform his part of any contract which may result. Thus a newspaper advertisement that goods are for sale is not an offer,[48] an advertisement that an auction sale will be held is not an offer to a person who comes to bid[49]; an advertisement that a scholarship examination will be held is not an offer to a candidate[50]; and the circulation of a price-list by a wine merchant is only an invitation to treat.[51] The same is probably true of a menu displayed, or handed to a customer, in a restaurant.[52] On the other hand, a notice at the entrance to an automatic car park

---

[42] In some of the United States it is an offence to "offer" goods without intending to sell: see 69 Y.L.J. 830; *cf.* also Uniform Deceptive Trade Practices Act, s.2(2) under which this practice can be restrained: see 53 Cornell L.Q. 749. In English law such conduct might conceivably amount to deceit (*cf. post*, p. 307), or to an offence under Pt. III of the Consumer Protection Act 1987, or be the subject of an order under Pt. II of the Fair Trading Act 1973; but these are remote possibilities.

[43] *Post*, p. 40.

[44] *e.g. Gibbons* v. *Proctor* (1891) 64 L.T. 594; *Willaims* v. *Carwardine* (1833) 5 C. & P. 566, 4 B. & Ad. 621, *post*, pp. 35–36.

[45] See *post*, p. 36, for the meaning of "unilateral contracts."

[46] [1893] 1 Q.B. 256.

[47] Contrast *Lambert* v. *Lewis* [1982] A.C. 225, 262, *per* Stephenson L.J. (affirmed without reference to this point [1982] A.C. 271).

[48] *Partridge* v. *Crittenden* [1968] 1 W.L.R. 1204; contrast *Lefkowitz* v. *Great Minneapolis Surplus Stores* 86 N.W. 2d 689 (1957).

[49] *Harris* v. *Nickerson* (1873) L.R. 8 Q.B. 286.

[50] *Rooke* v. *Dawson* [1895] 1 Ch. 480.

[51] *Grainger & Sons* v. *Gough* [1896] A.C. 325; *quaere* whether a price-list sent on request to a single customer could be an offer.

[52] *Cf. Guildford* v. *Lockyer* [1975] Crim.L.R. 236.

may be an offer which can be accepted by driving in[53]; and a display of deck chairs for *hire* has been held to be an offer.[54] No useful purpose is served by attempting to reconcile all the cases on this subject, since the question is one of intention in each case.[55]

(4) Timetables and passenger tickets

There is a remarkable diversity of views on the question just when a contract is made between a carrier and an intending passenger. It has been said that railway companies made offers by issuing advertisements stating the times at and conditions under which trains would run[56]; and that a company which ran buses by so doing made offers to intending passengers.[57] Such offers could be accepted by an indication on the part of the passenger that he wished to travel, *e.g.* by applying for a ticket or getting on the bus. Another view is that the carrier makes the offer at a later stage, by issuing the ticket; and that this offer is accepted by the passenger's retention of the ticket without objection,[58] or (even later) by claiming the accommodation offered in the ticket.[59] On this view the passenger only makes an invitation to treat when he asks for the ticket to be issued to him; and the offer contained in the ticket may be made to, and accepted by, the passenger even though the fare is paid by a third party (*e.g.* the passenger's employer[60]). Where the booking is made in advance, through a travel agent, yet a third view has been expressed: that the contract is concluded when the carrier indicates, even before issuing the ticket, that he "accepts" the booking.[61] The authorities yield no single rule: one can only say that the exact time of contracting depends in each case on the wording of the relevant document and on the circumstances in which it was issued.

(5) Tenders

A statement that goods are to be sold by tender is not normally an offer, so that the person making the statement is not bound to sell to the person making the highest tender.[62] Similarly a statement inviting tenders for the

---

[53] *Thornton* v. *Shoe Lane Parking Ltd.* [1971] 2 Q.B. 163, 169.

[54] *Chapelton* v. *Barry U.D.C.* [1940] 1 K.B. 532.

[55] Contrast *Harvey* v. *Facey* [1893] A.C. 552 with *Philp & Co.* v. *Knoblauch*, 1907 S.C. 994.

[56] *Denton* v. *G.N. Ry* (1856) 5 E. & B. 860; *Thompson* v. *L. M. & S. Ry.* [1930] 1 K.B. 41, 47; perhaps because such companies could not refuse to carry?

[57] *Wilkie* v. *L.P.T.B.* [1947] 1 All E.R. 258, 259.

[58] *Thornton* v. *Shoe Lane Parking Ltd.* [1971] 2 Q.B. 163, 169; *Cockerton* v. *Naviera Aznar S.A.* [1960] 2 Lloyd's Rep. 450. Such acceptance would be by conduct rather than by silence: *cf. post*, p. 33.

[59] *MacRobertson-Miller Airline Service* v. *Commissioner of State Taxation* (1975) 8 A.L.R. 131; the principle resembles that stated in *Heskell* v. *Continental Express Ltd.* [1950] 1 All E.R. 1033, 1037 in relation to carriage of goods by sea.

[60] *Hobbs* v. *L. & S.W. Ry.* (1875) L.R. 10 Q.B. 111, 119, as explained in the *MacRobertson-Miller* case *supra* at p. 147; consideration for the promises of both parties would be provided on the principle of *Gore* v. *Van der Lann* [1967] 2 Q.B. 31, *post*, p. 144.

[61] *The Eagle* [1977] 2 Lloyd's Rep. 70; *The Dragon* [1979] 1 Lloyd's Rep. 257 (affirmed [1980] 2 Lloyd's Rep. 415) *Oceanic Sun Line Special Shipping Co.* v. *Fay* (1988) 165 C.L.R. 97; *The Mikhail Lermontov* [1990] 1 Lloyd's Rep. 579, 594; Hetherington [1990] L.M.C.L.Q. 164; *cf. The Anwar al Sabar* [1980] 2 Lloyd's Rep. 261, 263 (carriage of goods by sea).

[62] *Spencer* v. *Harding* (1870) L.R. 5 C.P. 561.

supply of goods or for the execution of works is not normally an offer.[63] The offer comes from the person who submits the tender and there is no contract until the person asking for the tenders accepts[64] one of them. The preparation of a tender may involve very considerable expense; but the tenderer incurs this at his own risk. The position is different where the person who invites the tenders states in the invitation that he binds himself to accept the highest offer to buy[65] (or, as the case may be, the lowest offer to sell or to provide the specified services).[66] In such cases, the invitation for tenders may be regarded *either* as itself an offer *or* as an invitation to submit offers coupled with an undertaking to accept the highest (or, as the case may be, the lowest) offer; and the contract is concluded as soon as the highest offer to buy (or lowest offer to sell, etc.) is communicated.[67] There is also an intermediate possibility. This is illustrated by a case[68] in which an invitation to submit tenders was sent by a local authority to seven selected parties; the invitation stated that tenders submitted after a specified deadline would not be considered. It was held that the authority was contractually bound to consider (though not to accept) a tender submitted before the deadline.

(6) Sales of shares

A company which, in commercial language,[69] makes an "offer to the public," asking them to subscribe for shares in it, does not in law offer to sell the shares. It invites members of the public to apply for them, reserving the right to decide how many (if any) to allot to each applicant.[70] But where a company resolves to make a "rights" issue of shares to its existing shareholders, entitling each shareholder to buy a number of new shares in proportion to the shares he already holds, the letter informing the shareholder of his rights is regarded as an offer.[71] This letter will set out the precise rights of each shareholder, thus showing an intention on the part of the company to be bound, if the shareholder takes up his rights.

3. Where and When an Offer Takes Effect

In one sense an offer cannot take effect until it is received, for until the offeree knows about it he can take no action in reliance on it. But for the purpose of determining whether a contract can be sued on in a particular court it has been held that an offer sent through the post was made *where* it

---

63 *Ibid.* at p. 564; *cf.* Local Government Act 1988, s.4(2).
64 *Post*, p. 20.
65 *Spencer* v. *Harding*, *supra*, at p. 563.
66 See *William Lacey (Hounslow) Ltd.* v. *Davis* [1957] 1 W.L.R. 932, 939.
67 *Harvela Investments Ltd.* v. *Royal Trust of Canada (C.I.) Ltd.* [1986] A.C. 207, 224–225.
68 *Blackpool and Fylde Aero Club Ltd.* v. *Blackpool B.C.* [1990] 1 W.L.R. 1195. No decision was reached on the quantum of damages: as to this, see *post*, p. 845.
69 And in the terminology of Companies Act 1985, ss.59, 80(1) and 744; Financial Services Act 1986, s.158(4).
70 *e.g. Hebb's Case* (1867) L.R. 4 Eq. 9; *Harris' Case* (1872) L.R. 7 Ch.App. 587; *Wall's Case* (1872) 42 L.J.Ch. 372; *cf. Wallace's Case* [1900] 2 Ch. 671; *Rust* v. *Abbey Life Ins. Co.* [1979] 2 Lloyd's Rep. 335.
71 *Jackson* v. *Turquand* (1869) L.R. 4 H.L. 305.

was posted.[72] The question *when* such an offer was made may also arise for the purpose of determining whether the offer has expired by lapse of time[73] before it was accepted. In *Adams* v. *Lindsell*[74] the defendants offered to sell wool to the plaintiffs by a letter which was misdirected. The letter reached the plaintiffs two days late; but they immediately posted an acceptance which was held binding because the delay arose "entirely from the mistake of the defendants." From this emphasis on the defendants' fault, it seems that the decision might have gone the other way if the delay had been due to some other factor, *e.g.* to an accident in the post. In such a case the time for acceptance probably runs from the moment at which the letter would, but for such accident, have reached the offeree's address. Even where the delay is due to the offeror's fault, the offer may have lapsed before its receipt by the offeree. Obviously, the offer could not be accepted if it reached the offeree only after the date expressly specified in it as the last date for acceptance. The position is probably the same where it is clear to the offeree that there has been such a long delay in the transmission of the offer as to make it obvious to the offeree that the offer was "stale" when it reached him.

SECTION 2. ACCEPTANCE

1. Acceptance Defined

An acceptance is a final and unqualified expression of assent to the terms of an offer. The objective test of agreement applies to an acceptance no less than to an offer.[75] On this test, a mere acknowledgment of an offer would not be an acceptance; nor is there an acceptance where a person who has received an offer to sell goods merely replies that it is his "intention to place an order."[76] Where the offer makes alternative proposals, the reply must make it clear to which of them the assent is directed. In one case an offer to build a freight terminal was made by a tender quoting in the alternative a fixed price and a price varying with the cost of labour and materials. The offeree purported to accept "your tender" and it was held that there was no contract as there was no way of telling which price term had been accepted.[77]

(1) Continuing negotiations

When parties carry on lengthy negotiations, it may be hard to say exactly when an offer has been made and accepted. As negotiations progress, each party may make concessions or new demands and the parties may in the end disagree as to whether they had ever agreed at all. The court must then look at the whole correspondence and decide whether, on its true construction, the parties had agreed to the same terms. If so, there is a contract

---

[72] *Taylor* v. *Jones* (1871) 1 C.P.D. 87.
[73] *Post*, p. 43.
[74] (1818) 1 B. & Ald. 681.
[75] *Ante*, p. 8 *Cf.* in criminal law, *DPP* v. *Holmes*, 152 J.P.N. 738.
[76] *O.T.M. Ltd.* v. *Hydranautics* [1981] 2 Lloyd's Rep. 211, 214.
[77] *Peter Lind & Co. Ltd.* v. *Mersey Docks & Harbour Board* [1972] 2 Lloyd's Rep. 234.

even though both parties, or one of them, had reservations not expressed in the correspondence.[78]

Businessmen do not, any more than the courts, find it easy to say precisely when they reached agreement, and sometimes continue negotiations after they appear to have agreed to the same terms. In such a case, the court will look at the entire course of negotiations to decide whether an apparently unqualified acceptance did in fact conclude the agreement.[79] If it did, the fact that the parties continued negotiations after this point does not affect the existence of the contract between them,[80] unless the continued correspondence can be construed as an agreement to rescind the contract.

(2) Acceptance by conduct

An offer may be accepted by conduct, *e.g.* by supplying or despatching goods in response to an offer to buy.[81] Similarly, an offer to supply goods (made by sending them to the offeree) can be accepted by using them.[82] Conduct will, however, only have this effect if the offeree did the act with the intention (ascertained in accordance with the objective principle[83]) of accepting the offer. Thus an offer by one company to insure a car is not accepted by taking the car out on the road, if there is evidence that the driver intended to insure with another company.[84]

Where it is alleged that an offer has been made, or accepted, by conduct it is often hard to say exactly what terms have been agreed. The difficulty may be so great as to lead to the conclusion that no agreement was reached at all.[85] But the court has considerable power to resolve uncertainties. If the offer is silent as to the rate of payment the court may imply a term that a reasonable amount should be paid.[86] Or the court may import into the contract the terms of another contract between the parties, or of a draft

---

[78] *Kennedy* v. *Lee* (1817) 3 Mer. 441; *cf. Cie de Commerce, etc.*, v. *Parkinson Stove Co.* [1953] 2 Lloyd's Rep. 487; B.S.E., 17 M.L.R. 476; *Port Sudan Cotton Co.* v. *Govindaswamy Chettiar & Sons* [1977] 2 Lloyd's Rep. 5; *Thoresen Car Ferries Ltd.* v. *Weymouth Portland B.C.* [1977] 2 Lloyd's Rep. 614; *O.T.M. Ltd.* v. *Hydranautics* [1981] 2 Lloyd's Rep. 211, 215.

[79] *Hussey* v. *Horne-Payne* (1878) 4 App.Cas. 311; *Bristol, Cardiff & Swansea Aerated Bread Co.* v. *Maggs* (1890) 44 Ch.D. 616; *British Guiana Credit Corporation* v. *Da Silva* [1965] 1 W.L.R. 248; *Container Transport International Inc.* v. *Oceanus Mutual, etc., Association* [1984] 1 Lloyd's Rep. 476; *The Astyanax* [1985] 2 Lloyd's Rep. 109, 112; *The Intra Transporter* [1986] 2 Lloyd's Rep. 132. *Pagnan S.p.A.* v. *Granaria B.V.* [1986] 1 Lloyd's Rep. 547; *Pagnan S.p.A.* v. *Feed Products Ltd.* [1987] 2 Lloyd's Rep. 601, 619.

[80] *Perry* v. *Suffields Ltd.* [1916] 2 Ch. 187; *Davies* v. *Sweet* [1962] 2 Q.B. 300; *Cranleigh Precision Engineering Ltd.* v. *Bryant* [1965] 1 W.L.R. 1293 *The Good Helmsman* [1981] 1 Lloyd's Rep. 377, 409, 416.

[81] *Harvey* v. *Johnston* (1848) 6 C.B. 295, 305; *cf. Steven* v. *Bromley & Son* [1919] 2 K.B. 722, 728; *The Saronikos* [1986] 2 Lloyd's Rep. 277; *Interfoto Picture Library Ltd.* v. *Stiletto Visual Programmes Ltd.* [1989] Q.B. 433, 436; *Re Charge Card Services* [1989] Ch. 497, 512; and see *post*, p. 23.

[82] *Weatherby* v. *Banham* (1832) 5 C. & P. 228; or even by using part of the goods: *cf. Hart* v. *Mills* (1846) 15 L.J.Ex. 200. It is assumed that the goods are not "unsolicited" within Unsolicited Goods and Services Act 1971, ss.1, 6 (*ante*, p. 9).

[83] *Ante*, p. 8.

[84] *Taylor* v. *Allon* [1966] 1 Q.B. 304. The objective principle (*ante*, p. 8) clearly could not apply as the conduct alleged to constitute the acceptance had not come to the notice of the offeror.

[85] *Capital Finance Co. Ltd.* v. *Bray* [1964] 1 W.L.R. 323.

[86] Sale of Goods Act 1979, s.8(2); Supply of Goods and Services Act 1982, s.15(1); *cf. Steven* v. *Bromley & Son*, *supra*; *post*, p. 51.

agreement between them,[87] or even of a contract between one of them and a third party.[88]

(3) Acceptance must be unqualified

A communication may fail to take effect as an acceptance because it attempts to vary the terms of the offer. Thus an offer to sell 1,200 tons of iron is not accepted by a reply asking for 800 tons[89]; an offer to pay a *fixed* price for building work is not accepted by a promise to do the work for a *variable* price[90]; an offer to *supply* goods is not accepted by an "order" for their "supply and installation."[91] Nor, generally, is an offer accepted by a reply which varies one of its other terms (*e.g.* that specifying the time of performance)[92] or by a reply which is intended to introduce an entirely new term.[93] Such replies are not acceptances but counter-offers[94] which the original offeror can accept or reject.

The requirement that the acceptance must be unqualified does not, however, mean that there must be precise *verbal* correspondence between offer and acceptance. An acceptance could be effective even though it departed from the wording of the offer by making express some term which the law would in any case imply. And a reply which adds some new provision by way of indulgence to the offeror (*e.g.* one allowing him to postpone payment) may be an acceptance. Conversely, an acceptance may be effective although the acceptor asks for extra time to pay, so long as he makes it clear that he is prepared to perform in accordance with the terms of the offer even if his request is refused.[95] It is also possible for a communication which introduces a new term to amount at the same time to a firm acceptance and also to a further offer relating to the same subject-matter but emanating from the offeree. In such a case, there will be a contract on the terms of the original offer, but none on the terms of the new offer unless that is, in turn, accepted.[96]

After parties have reached agreement, the offer and acceptance may be set out in formal documents. The purpose of such documents may be merely to record the agreed terms[97]; and where one of the documents per-

[87] *e.g. Brogden* v. *Metropolitan Ry.* (1877) 2 App.Cas. 666; contrast *D. & M Trailers (Halifax) Ltd.* v. *Stirling* [1978] R.T.R. 468.
[88] *e.g. Pyrene Co. Ltd.* v. *Scindia Navigation Co. Ltd.* [1954] 2 Q.B. 402, *post*, p. 558.
[89] *Tinn* v. *Hoffmann & Co.* (1873) 29 L.T. 271; *cf. Holland* v. *Eyre* (1825) 2 Sim. & St. 194; *Jordan* v. *Norton* (1838) 4 M. & W. 155; *Harrison* v. *Battye* [1975] 1 W.L.R. 58.
[90] *North West Leicestershire D.C.* v. *East Midlands Housing Association* [1981] 1 W.L.R. 1396.
[91] *Butler Machine Tool Co. Ltd.* v. *Ex-Cell-O Corp. (England) Ltd.* [1979] 1 W.L.R. 401.
[92] *Ibid.*; *North West Leicestershire D.C.* v. *East Midlands Housing Association* [1981] 1 W.L.R. 1396; *cf. Brinkibon Ltd.* v. *Stahag Stahl und Stahlwarenhandelsgesellschaft mbH* [1983] 2 A.C. 34.
[93] *Jackson* v. *Turquand* (1869) L.R. 4 H.L. 305. *Northland Aircraft Ltd.* v. *Dennis Ferranti Meters Ltd.* (1970) 114 S.J. 845. Statements which are *not* intended to add new terms do not vitiate the acceptance: *Clive* v. *Beaumont* (1847) 1 De G. & Sm. 397; *Simpson* v. *Hughes* (1897) 66 L.J.Ch. 334. *Butler Machine Tool Co. Ltd.* v. *Ex-Cell-O Corporation (England) Ltd.* [1979] 1 W.L.R. 401.
[94] *Jones* v. *Daniel* [1894] 2 Ch. 332; *Von Hartzfeld-Wildenburg* v. *Alexander* [1912] 1 Ch. 284; *Love & Stewart Ltd.* v. *S. Instone & Co. Ltd.* (1917) 33 T.L.R. 457. For a statutory exception, see ULFIS (*post*, p. 28 art. 7(2)); and *cf.* Vienna Convention (*post*, p. 29) art. 19(2).
[95] *Cf. Global Tankers Inc.* v. *Amercoat Europa N.V.* [1975] 1 Lloyd's Rep. 666, 671.
[96] *The Master Stelios* [1983] 1 Lloyd's Rep. 356.
[97] *e.g. O.T.M. Ltd.* v. *Hydranautics* [1981] 2 Lloyd's Rep. 211, 215; *cf. post*, p. 53.

forms this function accurately while the other fails to do so, the discrepancy between them will not prevent the formation of a contract. In such a case, the court can rectify[98] the document which fails to record the agreed terms, and a contract will be concluded on those terms.[99]

(4) The battle of forms

The growing use of printed contract forms by one or both parties has given rise to problems with regard to the rule that the acceptance must correspond to the offer. Two situations call for discussion.

First, A may make an offer to B by asking for a supply of goods or services. B may reply that he is willing to supply the goods or services on his "usual conditions." Prima facie, B's statement is a counter-offer which A is free to accept or reject, and he may accept it by accepting the goods or services. If he does so, it seems clear that there is a contract between A and B, though the question whether B's "usual conditions" form part of it may depend on a number of further factors which will be discussed in Chapter 7.[1]

Secondly, *each* party may purport to contract with reference to his own set of standard terms and these terms may conflict. In *B.R.S.* v. *Arthur V. Crutchley Ltd.*[2] the plaintiffs delivered a consignment of whisky to the defendants for storage. Their driver handed the defendants a delivery note purporting to incorporate the plaintiffs' "conditions of carriage." The note was stamped by the defendants: "Received under [the defendants'] conditions." It was held that this amounted to a counter-offer which the plaintiffs accepted by handing over the goods, and the contract therefore incorporated the defendants' and not the plaintiffs' conditions.

This case gave some support to the so-called "last shot" doctrine: *i.e.* to the view that, where conflicting communications are exchanged, each is a counter-offer so that if a contract results at all (*e.g.* from an acceptance by conduct) it must be on the terms of the final document in the series leading to the conclusion of the contract.[3] But this view requires some modification in the light of *Butler Machine Tool Co. Ltd.* v. *Ex-Cell-O Corporation (England) Ltd.*[4] In that case sellers offered to supply a machine for a specified sum. The offer was expressed to be subject to certain terms and conditions, including a "price escalation clause," by which the amount actually payable by the buyers was to depend on "prices ruling upon date of delivery." In reply, the buyers placed an order for the machine on their own terms and conditions, which differed from those of the sellers in containing no price-escalation clause and also in various other respects.[5] It also contained a tear-off slip to be signed by the sellers and returned to the buyers, stating that the sellers accepted the order "on the terms and conditions stated therein." The sellers did so sign the slip and returned it with a letter saying that they were "entering" the order "in accordance with"

---

[98] *Post*, p. 285.
[99] *Domb* v. *Isoz* [1980] Ch. 548.
[1] *Post*, pp. 197–202.
[2] [1967] 2 All E.R. 285, 287; [1968] 1 W.L.R. 811, 817; *cf. O.T.M. Ltd.* v. *Hydranautics* [1981] 2 Lloyd's Rep. 211; *Muirhead* v. *Industrial Tank Specialities Ltd.* [1986] Q.B. 507, 530; *Sauter Automation* v. *Goodman (Mechanical Services)* (1984) 34 Build.L.R. 81.
[3] As in *Zambia Steel & Building Supplies Ltd.* v. *James Clark & Eaton Ltd.* [1986] 2 Lloyd's Rep. 225.
[4] [1979] 1 W.L.R. 401, esp. at. p. 405; Adams, 95 L.Q.R. 481; Rawlings, 42 M.L.R. 715.
[5] *Ante*, p. 18 at nn. 91 and 92.

their offer. This communication from the sellers was held to be an acceptance of the buyers' counter-offer[6] so that the resulting contract was on the buyers' terms, and the sellers were not entitled to the benefit of the price escalation clause. The sellers' reply to the buyers' order did not prevail (though it was the "last shot" in the series) because the reference in it to the original offer was not made for the purpose of reiterating all the terms of that offer, but only for the purpose of identifying the subject-matter. It would, however, have been possible for the sellers to turn their final communication into a counter-offer by explicitly referring in it not only to the subject-matter of the original offer but also to all its other terms. In that case no contract would have been concluded, since the buyers had made it clear before the machine was delivered that they did not agree to the "price escalation" clause.[7]

Thus it is possible by careful draftsmanship to avoid losing the battle of forms, but not (if the other party is equally careful) to win it. In the *Butler Machine Tool* case, for example, sellers' conditions included one by which their terms were to "prevail over any terms and conditions in Buyer's order"; but this failed (in consequence of the terms of the buyers' counter-offer) to produce the effect desired by the sellers.[8] The most that the draftsman can be certain of achieving is the stalemate situation in which there is no contract at all. Such a conclusion will often be inconvenient,[9] though where the goods are nevertheless delivered it will presumably lead to a liability on the part of the buyers to pay a reasonable price.[10]

(5) Acceptance of tenders

The submission of a tender normally amounts to an offer,[11] and the effect of an "acceptance" of the tender depends on the interpretation of the documents. Where a tender is submitted, for example, for the construction of a building, acceptance will normally create a binding contract unless it is expressly stipulated that there is to be no contract until certain formal documents have been executed.[12] But where a tender is made for an indefinite amount, *e.g.* for the supply of "such quantities (not exceeding 1,000 tons) as you may order" the person to whom the tender is submitted does not incur any liability merely by "accepting" it. He only becomes liable when he places an order for the goods[13]; and he is not bound to place any order at all (unless he has expressly or by necessary implication[14] indicated in his invitation for tenders that he would do so).[15] Once an order has been

---

[6] *Per* Lawton and Buckley L.JJ.; Lord Denning M.R. also uses this analysis, but prefers the alternative approach of considering "the documents . . . as a whole": see p. 405 and *cf. post*, p. 47.

[7] At p. 406, *per* Lawton L.J.

[8] *Cf. Matter of Doughboy Industries Inc.* 233 N.Y.S. 2d. 488, (1962): "The buyer and seller accomplished a legal equivalent to the irresistible force colliding with the immoveable object."

[9] It seems to have been rejected for this reason in *Johnson Matthey Bankers Ltd.* v. *State Trading Corp. of India* [1984] 1 Lloyd's Rep. 427.

[10] *Cf. Peter Lind & Co. Ltd.* v. *Mersey Docks & Harbour Board* [1972] 2 Lloyd's Rep. 234, *ante*, p. 16; McKendrick, 8 O.J.L.S. 197.

[11] *Ante*, p. 14.

[12] *Post*, p. 53.

[13] *Percival* v. *London County Council Asylum, etc. Committee* (1918) 87 L.J.K.B. 677.

[14] *e.g. Sylvan Crest Sand & Gravel Co.* v. *U.S.*, 150 F. 2d. 642 (1945).

[15] *Cf. Harvela Investments Ltd.* v. *Royal Trust Co. of Canada (C.O.) Ltd.*) [1986] A.C. 207.

placed, the party who has submitted the tender is bound to fulfil it.[16] Whether he can withdraw before an order has been placed, or avoid liability with regard to future orders, depends on the interpretation of the tender. If it merely means "I will supply such quantities as you may order" he can withdraw before a definite order is placed.[17] But he will not be entitled to withdraw if the tender means "I hereby bind myself to execute any orders which you may place," and if there is some consideration for this undertaking.[18]

(6) Acceptance by tender

There are exceptional cases in which an invitation for tenders may amount to an offer, *e.g.* where the person issuing the invitation binds himself to accept the highest or the lowest tender.[19] The acceptance then takes the form of the submission of a tender; but difficulties can arise where several tenders are made and one (or more) of them takes the form of a so-called "referential bid." In *Harvela Investments Ltd.* v. *Royal Trust Co. of Canada (C.I.) Ltd.*[20] an invitation for the submission of "offers" for the purchase of shares was addressed to two persons; it stated that the prospective sellers bound themselves to accept the "highest offer." One of the persons to whom the invitations was addressed made a bid of a fixed sum while the other submitted a "referential bid" undertaking to pay either a fixed sum or a specified amount in excess of the bid made by the other, whichever was the higher amount. It was held that the submission of the fixed bid concluded the contract and that the "referential bid" was ineffective. The House of Lords stressed that the bids were, by the terms of the invitation, to be confidential, so that neither bidder would know the amount bid by the other. In these circumstances the object of the invitation, which was to ascertain the highest amount which each of the persons to whom it was addressed was willing to pay, would have been defeated by allowing it to be accepted by a "referential bid."

2. Communication of Acceptance

(1) General rule

The general rule is that an acceptance has no effect until it is communicated to the offeror.[21] One reason for this rule is the difficulty of proving an uncommunicated decision to accept "for the Devil himself knows not the intent of a man."[22] But this is not the sole reason for the rule, which

---

[16] *Great Northern Ry.* v. *Witham* (1873) L.R. 9 C.P. 16; *cf.* similar rule applied to "declarations" under an "open cover" insurance in *Citadel Insurance Co.* v. *Atlantic Union Insurance Co.* [1982] 2 Lloyd's Rep. 543.

[17] *Great Northern Ry.* v. *Witham, supra*, at p. 19

[18] *Percival* v. *London County Council Asylum etc. Committee* (1918) 87 L.J.K.B. 677; *cf. Miller* v. *F. A. Sadd & Son Ltd.* [1981] 3 All E.R. 265. For an exception to the requirement of consideration in the law of insurance, see the *Citadel* case (*supra* n. 16 at. p. 546; *post*, p. 141).

[19] *Ante*, p. 15.

[20] [1986] A.C. 207.

[21] *M'Iver* v. *Richardson* (1813) 1 M. & S. 557; *Mozley* v. *Tinkler* (1835) C.M. & R. 692; *Ex p. Stark* [1897] 1 Ch. 575; *Holwell Securities Ltd.* v. *Hughes* [1974] 1 W.L.R. 155, 157; *The Leonidas D* [1985] 1 W.L.R. 925, 937.

[22] *Anon.* (1478) Y.B. 17 Edw. IV Pasch. f.1–pl. 2, cited in Fifoot, *History & Sources of the Common Law*, p. 253.

applies even where the fact of acceptance could be proved with perfect certainty, *e.g.* where a person writes his acceptance on a piece of paper which he simply keeps[23]; where a company resolves to accept an application for shares, records the resolution, but does not communicate it to the applicant[24]; where a person decides to accept an offer to sell goods to him and instructs his bank to pay the seller, but neither he nor the bank gives notice of this fact to the seller[25]; or where a person communicates the acceptance only to his own agent.[26] The main reason for the rule is that it could cause hardship to an offeror if he were bound without knowing that his offer had been accepted. It follows that there can be a contract if the offeror knows of the acceptance although it was not brought to his notice *by the offeree*.[27] However, there will be no contract if the communication is made by a third party without the authority of the offeree in circumstances indicating that the offeree's decision to accept was not yet regarded by him as irrevocable.[28]

For an acceptance to be "communicated" it must normally be brought to the notice of the offeror. Thus if an oral acceptance is "drowned by an aircraft flying overhead" or is spoken into a telephone after the line has gone dead, or is so indistinct that the offeror does not hear it, there is no contract.[29] The requirement of "communication" may, however, sometimes be satisfied even though the acceptance has not actually come to the notice of the offeror: *e.g.* where a written notice of acceptance is left at his address.[30]

(2) Exceptional cases

In a number of cases, an acceptance is, or may be, effective although it is not communicated to the offeror.

(a) COMMUNICATION TO OFFEROR'S AGENT. The effect of giving an acceptance to the agent of the offeror depends on the nature of the agent's authority.[31] If the agent has authority to *receive* the acceptance, it takes effect as soon as it is communicated to him, *e.g.* if acceptance of an offer made by a company is communicated to its managing director. But if the agent is only authorised to *transmit* the acceptance to the offeror, it may not take effect until the offeror receives it, *e.g.* if a written acceptance is given to a messenger.

(b) CONDUCT OF OFFEROR. An offeror may be precluded from denying that he received the acceptance if "it is his own fault that he did not get it," *e.g.* "if the listener on the telephone does not catch the words of acceptance, but nevertheless does not . . . ask for them to be repeated"[32]; or if

---

23 *Kennedy* v. *Thomassen* [1929] 1 Ch. 426; *Brogden* v. *Metropolitan Ry.* (1877) 2 App.Cas. 666, 692.
24 *Best's Case* (1865) 2 D.J. & S. 650; *cf. Gunn's Case* (1867) L.R. 3 Ch.App. 40.
25 *Brinkibon* v. *Stahag Stahl und Stahlwarenhandelsgesellschaft mbH* [1983] 2 A.C. 34.
26 *Hebb's Case* (1867) L.R. 4 Eq. 9; *Kennedy* v. *Thomassen* [1929] 1 Ch. 426.
27 *Bloxham's Case* (1864) 33 Beav. 529; (1864) 4 D.J. & S. 447; *Levita's Case* (1867) L.R. 3 Ch.App. 36.
28 This seems to be the best explanation of *Powell* v. *Lee* (1908) 99 L.T. 284.
29 *Entores Ltd.* v. *Miles Far East Corp.* [1955] 2 Q.B. 327, 332.
30 *Cf. post*, p. 41.
31 *Henthorn* v. *Fraser* [1892] 2 Ch. 27, 33.
32 *Entores* case [1955] 2 Q.B. 327, 333.

the acceptance is sent during business hours by telex but is simply not read by anyone in the offeror's office when it is there transcribed on his machine.[33]

(c) TERMS OF OFFER. An offer may expressly or impliedly waive the requirement that acceptance must be communicated. Thus where an offer to sell goods is made by sending them to the offeree, it may be accepted by simply using them without communicating this fact to the offeror.[34] Similarly, it seems that, where an offer to buy goods is made by asking the seller to supply them, it may be accepted by simply despatching the goods to the buyer.[35] And a tenant can accept an offer of a new tenancy by simply staying on the premises.[36]

Communication of acceptance is scarcely ever required in the case of an offer of a unilateral contract.[37] Thus in *Carlill* v. *Carbolic Smoke Ball Co.*,[38] the court rejected the argument that the plaintiff should have notified the defendants of her acceptance of their offer. Similarly, where a reward is offered for the return of lost property the finder need not notify the owner in advance of his acceptance: he can accept by finding and returning the thing; and once he has found it the owner probably cannot withdraw.[39]

(d) ACCEPTANCE BY POST. There are many possible solutions to the problem: when does a posted acceptance take effect? Such an acceptance could take effect when it is actually communicated to the offeror, when it arrives at his address, when it should, in the ordinary course of post, have reached him, or when it is posted. As the following discussion will show, each of these solutions is open to objections on the grounds of convenience or justice. This is particularly true where the acceptance is lost or delayed in the post.[40]

(i) *The posting rule.* What is usually[41] called the general rule is that a postal acceptance takes effect when the letter of acceptance is posted.[42] For this purpose a letter is posted when it is in the control of the Post Office,[43] or of one of its employees authorised to receive letters: handing a letter to a postman authorised to *deliver* letters is not posting.[44] An acceptance by telegram similarly takes effect when the telegram is communicated to a person authorised to receive it for transmission to the addressee[45]; and

---

33 *Cf. The Brimnes* [1975] Q.B. 929.
34 *Weatherby* v. *Banham* (1832) 5 C. & P. 228; and see *ante*, p. 9, n. 13.
35 *Cf.* U.C.C., s.2–206(1)(*b*); *Port Huron Machinery Co.* v. *Wohlers*, 221 N.W. 843 (1928).
36 *Roberts* v. *Hayward* (1828) 3 C. & P. 432; but not if the tenant disclaims the intention to accept: *Glossop* v. *Ashley* [1921] 2 K.B. 451.
37 For the meaning of "unilateral contract," see *post*, p. 36.
38 [1893] 1 Q.B. 256; *ante*, p. 13.
39 *Post*, p. 37–40.
40 See, for example *infra*, after n. 51.
41 But see *post*, p. 26.
42 *Henthorn* v. *Fraser* [1892] 2 Ch. 27, 33; *Adams* v. *Lindsell* (1818) 1 B. & Ald. 681; *Potter & Sanders* (1846) 6 Hare 1; *Harris' Case* (1872) L.R. 7 Ch.App. 587. *cf.*, in criminal law, *Treacy* v. *D.P.P.* [1971] A.C. 537 (blackmail); contrast *R.* v. *Baxter* [1972] 1 Q.B. 1 (attempt to obtain by deception).
43 *Brinkibon Ltd.* v. *Stahag Stahl und Stahlwarenhandelsgesellschaft mbH* [1983] 2 A.C. 34, 41.
44 *Re London & Northern Bank* [1900] 1 Ch. 220.
45 *Bruner* v. *Moore* [1904] 1 Ch. 305; *cf. Stevenson, Jacques & Co.* v. *McLean* (1880) 5 Q.B.D. 346; *Cowan* v. *O'Connor* (1888) 20 Q.B.D. 640 (place of acceptance).

it seems that this rule would apply to telemessages, which have replaced inland telegrams.

(ii) *Reasons for the rule.* Various reasons for the rule have been suggested. One is that the offeror must be considered as making the offer all the time that his offer is in the post, and that therefore the agreement between the parties is complete as soon as the acceptance is posted.[46] But this does not explain why posting has any significance at all: any other proof of intention to accept would equally well show that the parties were in agreement. Another suggested reason for the rule is that, if it did not exist "no contract could ever be completed by the post. For if the [offerors] were not bound by their offer when accepted by the [offerees] till the answer was received, then the [offerees] ought not to be bound till after they had received the notification that the [offerors] had received their answer and assented to it. And so it might go on *ad infinitum*."[47] But it would be perfectly possible to hold that the acceptance took effect when it came to the notice of the offeror, whether the offeree knew of this or not. Such a rule would not result in an infinity of letters. Yet another suggested reason for the rule is that the Post Office is the common agent of both parties, and that communication to this agent immediately completes the contract.[48] But the contents of a sealed letter cannot realistically be said to have been communicated to the Post Office, which in any case is at most an agent to *transmit* the acceptance, and not to *receive* it.[49] A mere delivery of the acceptance to such an agent does not of itself complete a contract.[50] Finally, it has been suggested that the rule minimises difficulties of proof: it is said to be easier to prove that a letter has been posted than that it has been received. But this depends in each case on the efficiency with which the parties keep records of incoming and outgoing letters.[51]

The rule is in truth an arbitrary one, little better or worse than its competitors. When a contract is made by post, one of the parties may be prejudiced if a posted acceptance is lost or delayed; for the offeree may believe that there is a contract and the offeror that there is none, and each may act in reliance on his belief. The posting rule favours the offeree, and is sometimes justified on the ground that an offeror who chooses to start negotiations by post takes the risk of delay and accidents in the post; or on the ground that the offeror can protect himself by expressly stipulating that he is not to be bound until actual receipt of the acceptance.[52] Neither justification is wholly satisfactory, for the negotiations may have been started by the offeree[53]; and the offer may be made on a form provided by the offeree,[54] in which case he, and not the offeror, will for practical purposes be in control of its terms. The rule does, however, serve a possibly useful

---

[46] *Henthorn* v. *Fraser* [1892] 2 Ch. 27, 31.

[47] *Adams* v. *Lindsell* (1818) 1 B. & Ald. 681, 683. This case is usually considered to be one of the early leading authorities in support of the "general rule"; but in fact the court does not mention the *posting* of the *acceptance* at all.

[48] *Household, etc., Insurance Co. Ltd.* v. *Grant* (1879) 4 Ex.D. 216, 220.

[49] *Henthorn* v. *Fraser* [1892] 2 Ch. 27, 33.

[50] *Ante*, p. 22.

[51] See Winfield, 55 L.Q.R. 509.

[52] *Household, etc., Insurance Co. Ltd.* v. *Grant* (1879) 4 Ex.D. 216, 223.

[53] It is often hard to tell which party is offeror and which is offeree, especially if the final offer was a counter-offer (*ante* p. 18).

[54] See *post*, p. 30.

function in limiting the offeror's power to withdraw his offer at will[55]: it makes a posted acceptance binding although that acceptance only reaches the offeror after a previously posted withdrawal reaches the offeree.[56]

(iii) *Must be reasonable to use post.* The posting rule only applies when it is reasonable to use the post as a means of communicating acceptance. Generally an offer made in a letter sent by post may be so accepted; but it may be reasonable to accept by post even though the offer was not sent in this way. In *Henthorn* v. *Fraser*[57] the mere fact that the parties lived at a distance justified acceptance by post of an oral offer. It would not normally be reasonable to reply by letter to an offer made by telex[58] or by telephone. Nor would it be reasonable to accept by post if the acceptor knew that the postal service was disrupted.[59]

(iv) *Terms of the offer.* The posting rule can be excluded by the terms of the offer. This may be so even though the offer does not expressly provide when the acceptance is to take effect. In *Holwell Securities Ltd.* v. *Hughes*[60] an offer to sell a house was made in the form of an option expressed "to be exercisable by notice in writing to the Intending Vendor . . . " Such a notice was posted but did not arrive. It was held that there was no contract of sale as the terms of the offer, on their true construction, required the acceptance to be actually communicated.

(v) *Instantaneous communications.* The posting rule does not apply to acceptances made by some instantaneous mode of communication, *e.g.* by telephone or by telex.[61] The reason why the rule does not apply in such cases is that the acceptor will often know at once that his attempt to communicate was unsuccessful,[62] so that it is up to him to make a proper communication. But a person who accepts by letter which goes astray may not know of the loss or delay until it is too late to make another communication. If this is the reason for the distinction between postal and instantaneous communications, it helps to solve the problem whether an acceptance by telemessage dictated over the telephone takes effect when the message is dictated by the sender or when it is communicated to the addressee. It is submitted that it takes effect when dictated, for, if it later goes astray, the acceptor may have no means of knowing this in time to make another communication.[63] Fax messages seem to occupy an intermediate position. The sender will know at once if his message has not been received at all, and where this is the position the message should not amount to an effective acceptance. But if the message is received in such a form that it is wholly or partly illegible, the sender is unlikely to know this

---

[55] *Post*, p. 40. In countries in which the acceptance is only effective when communicated a similar result is often reached by legally limiting the offeror's power to withdraw his offer.

[56] *Post*, pp. 40.

[57] [1892] 2 Ch. 27.

[58] *Cf. Quenerduaine* v. *Cole* (1883) 32 W.R. 185 (telegram).

[59] *Bal* v. *Van Staden* [1902] T.S. 128.

[60] [1974] 1 W.L.R. 155; *cf. New Hart Builders Ltd.* v. *Brindley* [1975] Ch. 342.

[61] *Entores Ltd.* v. *Miles Far East Corp.* [1955] 2 Q.B. 327; *Brinkibon Ltd.* v. *Stahag Stahl und Stahlwarenhandelsgesellschaft mbH* [1983] 2 A.C. 34; *cf. The Pendrecht* [1980] 2 Lloyd's Rep. 55, 66; *Gill & Duffus Landauer Ltd.* v. *London Export Corp. GmbH* [1982] 2 Lloyd's Rep. 627. Such acceptances are therefore governed by the general rule stated at p. 21, *ante*, subject to exceptions (a) to (c) stated at p. 21–23, *ante*. *Cf.* (in tort) *Diamond* v. *Bank of London and Montreal* [1979] Q.B. 333.

[62] See the *Entores* case, *supra*, p. 333 and the *Brinkibon* case, *supra*, p. 43.

[63] *Contra*, Winfield, 55 L.Q.R. 499, 515.

at once, and it is suggested an acceptance sent by fax might well be effective in such circumstances.

(vi) *Applications of the posting rule*. Discussions of this subject sometimes start by stating the "general rule" that an acceptance takes effect when posted, and then proceed to deduce various "consequences" from this rule. In fact few, if any, judges or writers have been prepared to follow all these deductions to their logical conclusions; and it would be more accurate to admit that there is no single or universal rule which determines the effect of a posted acceptance.[64] The effect of such an acceptance has to be considered *as against* various competing factors, such as withdrawal of the offer, loss or delay of the acceptance, subsequent revocation of the acceptance, previous rejection of the offer and so forth. Obviously, a rule laid down in a case concerning the effect of a posted acceptance as against a withdrawal of the offer is no real guide to the solution of a problem concerning the effect of such an acceptance as against a subsequent revocation of the acceptance. The English cases in fact only support three "consequences" of the posting rule. The first (and probably the most important[65]) is that a posted acceptance prevails over a previously posted withdrawal of the offer which had not yet reached the offeree when the acceptance was posted.[66] A second, and more controversial,[67] application of the rule is that an acceptance takes effect on posting even though it never reaches the offeror because it is lost through an accident in the post,[68] and the same rule probably applies where the acceptance is merely delayed through such an accident.[69] Thirdly, the contract is taken to have been made at the *time* of posting so as to take priority over another contract affecting the subject-matter made after the original acceptance had been posted but before it had reached the offeror.[70] Whether a posted acceptance should take effect against *other* competing factors is a question of policy and convenience.[71] The posting rule will not apply where it would lead to "manifest inconvenience and absurdity."[72] Its scope is determined by practical considerations rather than by "deductions" from a "general" rule.

(vii) *Misdirected acceptance*. A letter of acceptance may be lost or delayed because it bears a wrong, or an incomplete, address. Normally, such misdirection will be due to the carelessness of the offeree. Although there is no authority precisely in point,[73] it is submitted that the posting

---

[64] See Evans, 15 I.C.L.Q. 553.

[65] *Ante*, p. 25 at n. 55.

[66] *Harris' Case* (1872) L.R. 7 Ch.App. 587; *Byrne & Co.* v. *Leon van Tienhoven* (1880) 5 C.P.D. 344; *Henthorn* v. *Fraser* [1892] 2 Ch. 27; *Re London & Northern Bank* [1990] 1 Ch. 200; for the contrary view, see *Rhode Island Tool Co.* v. *U.S.*, 130 Ct.Cl. 698, 128 F.Supp. 417 (1955).

[67] *Ante*, p. 24.

[68] *Household, etc., Insurance* v. *Grant* (1879) 4 Ex.D. 216, overruling *British and American Telegraph Co.* v. *Colson* (1871) L.R. 6 Ex. 108.

[69] See *Dunlop* v. *Higgins* (1848) 1 H.L.C. 381, which would probably be followed in England though it is expressly restricted (at p. 402) to the Scots law.

[70] *Potter* v. *Sanders* (1846) 6 Hare 1. This application of the rule can perhaps be explained as a reward for the superior diligence of the first acceptor.

[71] *Brinkibon Ltd.* v. *Stahag Stahl und Stahlwarenhandelsgesellschaft mbH* [1983] 2 A.C. 34, 41; *Gill & Duffus Landauer Ltd.* v. *London Export Corp. GmbH* [1982] 2 Lloyd's Rep. 627, 631.

[72] *Holwell Securities Ltd.* v. *Hughes* [1974] 1 W.L.R. 157, 161.

[73] See, by way of analogy, *Getreide-Import Gesellschaft* v. *Contimar, etc.*, [1953] 1 W.L.R. 207, 793.

rule should not apply to such cases. Even if an offeror can be said to take the risk of accidents in the post, it would be unreasonable to impose on him the further risk of the offeree's carelessness.

It does not follow that a misdirected acceptance should necessarily take effect when received. For such a rule may actually favour the careless acceptor, *e.g.* when an offer is made to sell "at the market price prevailing when this offer is accepted," and the market falls after the misdirected acceptance has been posted. Moreover, the misdirection may be due to the fault of the offeror himself, *e.g.* if he makes the offer in a letter on which his own address is incompletely or illegibly written, or if he uses an out-of-date letter-head.[74] The better rule, therefore, seems to be that a misdirected acceptance takes effect (if at all) at the time which is least favourable to the party responsible for the misdirection.

(viii) *Garbled telegram or telemessage of acceptance.* The effect of such communications has not been determined; but a somewhat similar problem arose in *Henkel* v. *Pape.*[75] The defendant wrote to the plaintiffs that he could "fix an order" for 50 rifles at 34s. each, but the plaintiffs replied that they could not sell for less than 35s. Thereupon the defendant telegraphed "send *three* rifles"; this telegram reached the plaintiffs in the form "send *the* rifles." The plaintiffs sent the defendant 50 rifles, but it was held that the defendant was not bound to accept more than three. As the telegram was either an offer or a counter-offer, the case provides no authority on the effect of a garbled telegram of *acceptance.* But suppose that a seller makes an offer of 50 rifles; that the buyer sends a telemessage asking him to "send the rifles"; and that the message reaches the seller in the form "send three rifles." It is submitted that the seller would be bound by the buyer's version of the message, and could not treat the garbled version as a counter-offer, so long as it was reasonable for the buyer to accept by telemessage. If an offeror takes the risk of such accidents in the post as loss or delay, he should similarly take the risk of errors in the transmission of a telemessage; for in each case the offeree will have no means of knowing that something has gone wrong until it is too late to make another, proper, communication.[76]

(ix) *Revocation of posted acceptance.* An offeree may, after posting an acceptance, attempt to revoke it by a later communication which reaches the offeror before, or at the same time as, the acceptance. There is no English authority on the effectiveness of such a revocation. One view is that the revocation has no effect, since, once a contract has been concluded, it cannot be dissolved by the unilateral act of one party.[77] But this argument has

---

[74] *Cf. Townsend's Case* (1871) L.R. 13 Eq. 148, where the offeror gave his address as "36 Westland Row," omitting "Dublin." The actual reasoning of the case is obsolete since *Household, etc., Insurance* v. *Grant* (1879) 4 Ex.D. 216. Fault of one party may not be the effective cause of the misdirection if the resulting error is obvious to the other party.

[75] (1870) L.R. 6 Ex. 7.

[76] *Cf. ante*, p. 25.

[77] This view is sometimes said to be supported by *Wenckheim* v. *Arndt* (N.Z.) 1 J.R. 73 (1873), where the defendant by letter accepted an offer of marriage; *her mother* sent a telegram purporting to cancel it. The actual decision was that the mother had no authority to act on behalf of her daughter in this way. The view stated in the text is supported by *Morrison* v. *Thoelke*, 155 So. 2d 889 (1963) and by *A to Z Bazaars* (*Pty.*) *Ltd.* v. *Minister of Agriculture* 1974 (4) S.A. 392(C) (discussed by Turpin, [1975] C.L.J. 25) but contradicted by

little to commend it if (as has been suggested above) it is undesirable to resolve what are really issues of policy by making "logical" deductions from some "general" rule as to the effect of posted acceptances. As a matter of policy, the issue is whether the offeror would be unjustly prejudiced by allowing the offeree to rely on the subsequent revocation. On the one hand, it can be argued that the offeror cannot be prejudiced by such revocation as he had no right to have his offer accepted and as he cannot have relied on its having been accepted before he knew of the acceptance. Against this, it can be argued that, once the acceptance has been posted, the offeror can no longer withdraw his offer,[78] and that reciprocity demands that the offeree should likewise be held to his acceptance. For if the offeree could revoke the acceptance he would be able, without risk to himself, to speculate at the expense of the offeror. He could post his acceptance early in the morning of a working day and could, if the market moved against him, revoke his acceptance the same afternoon, while the offeror had no similar freedom of action. It has been suggested[79] that the offeror should take this risk just as much as he takes the risk of loss or delay; but here again it is submitted that while the offeror may take the risks of accidents in the post, he should not have to take risks due entirely to the conduct of the offeree.

So far, it has been assumed that it is in the offeror's interest to uphold the contract. But to hold the acceptance binding as soon as it was posted, in spite of an overtaking communication purporting to revoke it, might cause hardship to the *offeror*. This is particularly true where he has acted in reliance on the revocation. Suppose that A offers to sell B a car. B posts an acceptance of the offer and then telexes: "ignore my letter I do not want the car." A then sells the car to C. Could B change his mind yet again, and claim damages from A? There are several ways of avoiding such an unjust result. The first is to say that there had once been a contract but that it was later rescinded by mutual consent: B's telex was an offer to release A, which A accepted by conduct; communication of such acceptance could be deemed to have been waived. The second is to regard B's telex as a repudiation amounting to a breach of contract; and to say that, by "accepting" the breach, A has put an end to the contract. This analysis is preferable from A's point of view if the sale to C is for a lower price than that to B, for it would enable A to claim the difference from B as damages.[80]

(x) *International sales.* Certain contracts for the international sale of goods are (if the parties so choose) governed by the Uniform Law on the International Sale of Goods (or ULIS).[81] The formation of such contracts is governed by the Uniform Law on the Formation of Contracts for the International Sale of Goods (or ULFIS).[82] Under ULFIS an acceptance does not take effect on posting, but only when it is "communicated"[83] to

Dick v. *U.S.*, 82 F.Supp. 326 (1949). It is also sometimes said to be contradicted by *Dunmore* v. *Alexander* (1830) 9 Shaw 190, but there the first letter was probably an offer; only the dissenting judge regarded it as an acceptance. See generally Hudson, 82. L.Q.R. 169.

78 *Ante*, p. 25.

79 Hudson, 82 L.Q.R. 169, who also argues that the offeror can protect himself by stipulating that he is not to be bound till the acceptance reaches him, or that the offeree is to be bound as soon as he posts the acceptance.

80 *Post*, pp. 756 *et seq.*

81 Uniform Laws on International Sales Act 1967, Sched. 1.

82 Uniform laws on International Sales Act 1967, Sched. 2.

83 ULFIS, Art. 6(1).

the offeror, *i.e.* delivered at his address.[84] Thus there is no contract if the acceptance is lost in the post; though if it is merely delayed there will be a contract unless the offeror promptly repudiates.[85] But a withdrawal of an offer is only effective if it is "communicated" to the offeree before he has "despatched" his acceptance[86]: thus one very important effect of the English posting rule (namely, that a posted acceptance prevails over a previously posted but as yet uncommunicated withdrawal) is preserved. Under ULFIS, effect is given to a revocation of an acceptance which is communicated before or at the same time as the acceptance.[87]

ULIS is eventually intended to be replaced by a more recent United Nations Convention on Contracts for the International Sale of Goods, generally known as the Vienna Convention, which has not yet been ratified by the United Kingdom. Under the Vienna Convention,[88] an offer takes effect when it "reaches" the offeree[89] and an acceptance when it "reaches" the offeror,[90] *i.e.* (in both cases) when it is communicated to the addressee or delivered to his address.[91] Thus there is no contract if the acceptance is lost in the post; but if the acceptance is delayed in transmission, it is effective, unless the offeror informs the offeree promptly on its receipt that he regards the offer as having lapsed.[92] Once an offer has become effective, it cannot be revoked after the offeree has dispatched his acceptance[93]: this again preserves the English position that a posted acceptance prevails over a previously posted withdrawal (referred to in the Convention as a revocation). An acceptance may be withdrawn by a communication which reaches the offeror before (or at the same time as) the acceptance would have become effective[94] if there had been no such withdrawal.

3. Prescribed Method of Acceptance

(1) Compulsory method

Where an offer states that it can only be accepted in a certain way, the offeror is not, in general, bound unless acceptance is made in that way. Thus if the offeror asks for the acceptance to be sent to a particular place an acceptance sent elsewhere will not bind him[95]; nor, if he asks for an acceptance in writing, will he be bound by one that is oral.[96] The rule is particularly strict where the offer is contained in an option.[97] The offeror will, however, be bound if he acquiesces in the different mode of acceptance and so waives the stipulated mode. Alternatively, a contract may be concluded if the purported acceptance (which is ineffective as such for fail-

---

[84] *Ibid.* Art. 12(1).
[85] *Ibid.* Art. 9(2).
[86] *Ibid.* Art. 5(4). Despatch is not defined.
[87] *Ibid.* Art. 10.
[88] See Honnold, *Uniform Law for International Sales*; Bianca and Bonnell, *Commentary on the International Sales Law*; Feltham [1981] J.B.L. 346; Nicholas, 105 L.Q.R. 201.
[89] Art. 15(1).
[90] Art. 18(2).
[91] Art. 24.
[92] Art. 21(2).
[93] Art. 16(1); "dispatch" is not defined.
[94] Art. 22.
[95] *Frank* v. *Knight* (1937) O.Q.P.D. 113; *cf. Eliason* v. *Henshaw* (1819) 4 Wheat. 225.
[96] *Financings Ltd.* v. *Stimson* [1962] 1 W.L.R. 1184.
[97] *Holwell Securities Ltd.* v. *Hughes* [1974] 1 W.L.R. 157.

ure to comply with the stipulated method) can be regarded as a counter-offer and if that counter-offer is then accepted by the counter-offeree.[98] Since such acceptance may be effected by conduct,[99] the contract may be concluded without any further communication between the parties after the orginal, ineffective, acceptance.

Where the offeror prescribes a method of acceptance, he usually does so with some particular object in view, *e.g.* to secure a speedy acceptance, or one which will prevent disputes from arising as to the terms of the agreement. An acceptance which accomplishes that object just as well as, or better than, the stipulated method may, by way of exception to the general rule, bind the offeror.[1] For the purpose of this exception, it must first be determined what object the offeror had in view. If he says "reply by letter sent by return of post" this may simply mean "reply quickly": the words may "fix the time for acceptance and not the manner of accepting."[2] If so, a reply by telex would suffice. But such a reply would not suffice if the offer meant "reply quickly and by letter, I do not like telexes as they are often obscure."

The rules on this subject are based on two assumptions: that the offer is drawn up by the offeror and that stipulations as to the mode of acceptance are put into it for his benefit. In modern conditions, these assumptions are often untrue, for it is increasingly common for an offer to be made on a form provided or drafted by the offeree: *e.g.* where a customer submits a proposal to enter into a hire-purchase agreement; or where an offer is made on a form of tender provided by the offeree. Stipulations as to the mode of acceptance in such documents are usually intended for the protection and benefit of the *offeree*. If the offeree accepts in some other way, this will often be evidence that he has waived the stipulation; and it is submitted that the acceptance ought to be treated as effective unless it can be shown that failure to use the stipulated mode has prejudiced the offeror.[3]

(2) Alternative method: silence

An offer may specify, not that it *must*, but that it *may*, be accepted in a particular way. In cases of this kind, particular difficulty arises from provisions to the effect that the offeree may accept by silence.

(a) Offeree generally not bound. In general, an offeree who simply does nothing on receipt of an offer which states that it may be accepted by silence is not bound. In *Felthouse* v. *Bindley*[4] the plaintiff offered to buy his nephew's horse by a letter in which he said: "If I hear no more about him, I shall consider the horse mine." Later, the horse was, by mistake, included in an auction sale of the nephew's property. The plaintiff sued the auction-

---

[98] *Wettern Electricity Ltd.* v. *Welsh Development Agency* [1983] Q.B. 796.

[99] As in the *Wettern Electricity* case, *supra*; provided, however, that such conduct is accompanied by the requisite contractual intention: see *Harvela Investments Ltd.* v. *Royal Trust Co. of Canada (C.I.) Ltd.* [1986] A.C. 207; and *post*, p. 155.

[1] *Manchester Diocesan Council for Education* v. *Commercial and General Investments Ltd.* [1970] 1 W.L.R. 242.

[2] *Tinn* v. *Hoffmann & Co.* (1873) 29 L.T. 271, 278; *Manchester Diocesan Council for Education* v. *Commercial & General Investments Ltd.*, *supra*.

[3] See *Robophone Facilities* v. *Blank* [1966] 1 W.L.R. 1423 and *cf.* the *Manchester Diocesan* case, *supra*, n. 1. From this point of view, these cases are, it is submitted, to be preferred to *Financings Ltd.* v. *Stimson* [1962] 1 W.L.R. 1184.

[4] (1862) 11 C.B.(N.S.) 869; affirmed (1863) New Rep. 401; Miller, 35 M.L.R. 489. *Cf. Financial Techniques (Planning Services)* v. *Hughes* [1981] I.R.L.R. 32, 35.

eer for damages for the conversion of the horse. It was held that, at the time of the auction, there was no contract for the sale of the horse to the plaintiff because "The uncle had no right to impose upon the nephew the sale of his horse . . . unless he chose to comply with the condition of writing to repudiate the offer . . . "[5] Where an offeree does not wish to accept the offer, it is generally undesirable to put upon him the trouble and expense of rejecting it. But in *Felthouse* v. *Bindley* this was not the position. Before the auction, the nephew had told the auctioneer that he "intended to reserve" the horse for his uncle; and later correspondence showed that, at the time of the auction, the nephew did in fact wish to sell the horse to the uncle. In spite of this it was held that there was no contract because the nephew "had not communicated his intention to the uncle."[6] But the need to communicate an acceptance can be waived; and it seems clear that the uncle's letter did waive it. In view of these facts, the actual decision is hard to support, but this is no criticism of the general rule laid down in the case.

The question whether silence can amount to an acceptance binding the offeree has also arisen in the cases already discussed, in which the issue was whether an agreement to abandon an earlier agreement to submit a claim to arbitration could be inferred from inactivity, in the form of long delay in prosecuting the claim. Such a delay is now in certain circumstances a statutory ground for dismissing the claim for want of prosecution[7] but similar questions of agreement to abandon *other* types of claim or remedy could still be governed by the common law principles developed in the arbitration cases. In these cases, it had been held that, even if one party's inactivity could be regarded as an offer to abandon the arbitration,[8] the mere silence or inactivity of the other did not normally amount to an acceptance. For one thing, such inactivity was often equivocal, being explicable on other grounds (such as forgetfulness).[9] For another, acceptance could not, as a matter of law, be inferred from silence alone[10] "save in the most exceptional circumstances."[11]

(b) OFFEREE EXCEPTIONALLY BOUND? As the above reference to "exceptional circumstances" suggests, there may be exceptions to the general rule that an offeree is not bound by silence. If the offer has been solicited by the offeree, the argument that he should not be put to the trouble of rejecting it loses much of its force,[12] especially if the offer is made on a form provided by the offeree[13] and that form stipulates that silence may amount to

---

[5] At p. 875.

[6] At p. 876.

[7] Arbitration Act 1950, s.13A, as inserted by Courts and Legal Services Act 1990, s.102.

[8] *Ante*, p. 10.

[9] For acceptance by silence *and conduct*, see *post*, p. 33.

[10] *The Leonidas D* [1985] 1 W.L.R. 925, 927.

[11] *The Leonidas D*, *supra* at p. 927. Such "exceptional circumstances" may be illustrated by *The Splendid Sun* [1981] Q.B. 694 (where acceptance may have been by conduct: *post*, p. 34, though it has been said that this case is hard to reconcile with *The Leonidas D*, *supra*: see *The Antclizo* [1987] 2 Lloyd's Rep. 130, 149 (affirmed [1988] 1 W.L.R. 603). *Cf. Cie Française d'Importation etc.* v. *Deutsche Continental Handelsgesellschaft* [1985] 2 Lloyd's Rep. 592, 598; *The Agrabele* [1987] 2 Lloyd's Rep. 223, 224, 235. *The Golden Bear* [1987] 1 Lloyd's Rep. 330 is hard to reconcile with these cases and was apparently doubted in *The Antclizo*, *supra*: see [1987] 2 Lloyd's Rep. 130, 147.

[12] *Cf. Rust* v. *Abbey Life Ins. Co.* [1979] 2 Lloyd's Rep. 335.

[13] *Cf. ante*, p. 30.

acceptance.[14] Again, if there is a course of dealing between the parties the offeror may be led to suppose that silence amounts to acceptance: *e.g.* where a shopkeeper's offers to buy goods from a wholesaler have always been accepted as a matter of course by the despatch of the goods in question.[15] In such a case it may not be unreasonable to impose on the offeree an obligation to reject, especially if the offeror, in reliance on his belief that the goods would be delivered in the usual way, had forborne from seeking an alternative supply. There may also be "an express undertaking or implied obligation to speak"[16] arising out of the course of negotiations between the parties, and failure to perform such an obligation could be held to amount to an acceptance by silence.

Even where silence of the offeree does not amount to an acceptance, it is arguable that he might be liable on a different basis. In *Spiro* v. *Lintern* it was said that "If A sees B acting in the mistaken belief that A is under some binding obligation to him and in a manner consistent only with such an obligation, which would be to B's disadvantage if A were thereafter to deny the obligation, A is under a duty to B to disclose the non-existence of the supposed obligation."[17] Although this statement was made with reference to wholly different circumstances,[18] it could also be applied to certain cases in which an offeror had, to the offeree's knowledge, acted in reliance on the belief that his offer had been accepted by silence. The liability of the offeree would then be based on a kind of estoppel.[19] But the application of this doctrine to cases of alleged acceptance by silence gives rise to the difficulty that such an estoppel can only arise out of a "clear and unequivocal"[20] representation. For this purpose, mere inactivity is not generally sufficient,[21] so that silence in response to an offer will not of itself normally give rise to an estoppel.

It is finally possible for the offeree to be bound by silence if the offeror, to the offeree's knowledge, actually performs in accordance with his offer and so confers a benefit on the offeree; though the better solution in this type of case may be to make the offeree restore the benefit rather than to hold him to an obligation to perform his part of a contract to which he had never agreed.

(c) OFFEROR BOUND? There is some authority for saying that the offeror cannot, any more than the offeree, be bound where the offeree simply remains silent in response to the offer,[22] and the case is not one of the

---

[14] As in *Alexander Hamilton Institute* v. *Jones*, 234 Ill. App. (1924).
[15] As in *Cole-McIntyre-Norfleet Co.* v. *Holloway*, 141 Tenn. 679; 214 S.W. 87 (1919).
[16] *The Agrabele* [1985] 2 Lloyd's Rep. 496, 509, *per* Evans J., whose statement of the relevant legal principles was approved on appeal, though the actual decision was reversed on the facts: [1987] 2 Lloyd's Rep. 223, 225. The case concerned an alleged "abandonment" by delay of an agreement to submit a claim to arbitration; this situation would now be governed by Arbitration Act 1950, s.13A as inserted by Courts and Legal Services Act 1990, s.102 (*ante*, p. 31).
[17] [1973] 1 W.L.R. 1002, 1011.
[18] See *post*, p. 619.
[19] *Post*, pp. 109, 361. The case would not be one of estoppel by convention (*post*, p. 111; for such estoppel is based on an *agreed* assumption of fact, while in cases of the present kind the question is whether there was any agreement.
[20] *Post*, pp. 103, 361.
[21] *Post*, pp. 104–105.
[22] *Fairline Shipping Corp.* v. *Adamson* [1975] Q.B. 180, 189.

exceptional ones discussed above[23] in which an offer can be accepted by silence. But it is submitted that the general rule laid down in *Felthouse* v. *Bindley*[24] does not invariably lead to such a conclusion. For the object of this rule is to protect *the offeree* from having to incur the trouble and expense of rejecting the offer so as to avoid being bound. No such argument can be advanced for similarly protecting the offeror. He may indeed be left in doubt on the question whether his offer has been accepted; but this is not a matter about which he can legitimately complain where he has drawn up his offer in terms which permit (and even encourage) acceptance by silence.[25] Thus it is submitted that the uncle in *Felthouse* v. *Bindley* might have been bound if the nephew had resolved to accept the offer and had, in reliance on its terms, forborne from attempting to dispose of the horse elsewhere. This possibility has, indeed, been judicially doubted,[26] but in the case in which the doubt was raised it was not an express term of the offer that silence would be regarded as acceptance. Where the offeror has included such an express term in his offer, it is submitted that silence in response to the offer by the offeree should be capable of binding the offeror.

It is settled that a creditor can accept his debtor's offer to give additional security for a debt by simply forbearing to sue for the debt.[27] If such forbearance can be regarded as silence, this rule supports the view that acceptance by silence can bind the offeror. Another possible explanation of the rule is that a creditor who forbears accepts by conduct[28] rather than by silence.

(d) SILENCE AND CONDUCT. In *Roberts* v. *Hayward*[29] a tenant accepted his landlord's offer of a new tenancy at an increased rent by simply staying on the premises. It was held that he had accepted the landlord's offer by silence; but it seems better to say that he accepted by conduct and that the landlord waived notice of acceptance.[30] Similarly an offer made *to* a landowner to occupy land under a licence containing specified terms may be accepted by permitting the licensee to occupy the land.[31] An offeree is not, for the present purpose, "silent"merely because his acceptance is not expressed in words. The possibility of acceptance by conduct is, yet again, illustrated by the arbitration cases already mentioned, in which an agreement to abandon the proceedings was alleged to have arisen from delay in prosecuting them. As already noted, legislation has now resolved the practical problems which used to arise from delay in the pursuit of arbitration claims,[32] but the reasoning of the arbitration cases could still apply where it was alleged that some other type of claim or remedy had been abandoned by tacit agreement. According to those cases, an offer of abandonment can

---

[23] At nn. 12–16.
[24] *Ante*, p. 30.
[25] This argument would, however, not apply where the terms of the offer had been drawn up by the *offeree*: *cf. ante*, p. 30.
[26] *Fairline Shipping Corp.* v. *Adamson* [1975] Q.B. 180, 189.
[27] *Post*, p. 84.
[28] *Ante*, p. 17.
[29] (1828) 3 C. & P. 432.
[30] *Cf. ante*, p. 23.
[31] *Wettern Electric Ltd.* v. *Welsh Development Agency* [1983] Q.B. 796.
[32] Arbitration Act 1950, s.13A, as inserted by Courts and Legal Services Act 1990, s.102; *ante*, p. 31.

be accepted by reacting to it, not merely by inactivity,[33] but also by some further conduct: *e.g.* by closing or disposing of relevant files.[34] Where, however, an acceptance is alleged to have taken the form of a forbearance (such as a forbearance to sue), it is obviously very hard to distinguish between "inactivity" or silence on the one hand, and "conduct" on the other.

In *Rust* v. *Abbey Life Ins. Co.*[35] the plaintiff applied and paid for a "property bond" which was allocated to her on the terms of the defendants' usual policy of insurance. After having retained this document for some seven months, she claimed the return of her payment, alleging that no contract had been concluded. The claim was rejected on the ground that her application was an offer which had been accepted by issue of the policy.[36] But it was further held that, even if the policy constituted a counter-offer, this counter-offer had been accepted by "the conduct of the plaintiff in doing and saying nothing for seven months. . . ."[37] Thus mere inaction was said to be sufficient to constitute acceptance; and it seems to have amounted to no more than silence in spite of having been described as "conduct." The conclusion that it amounted to acceptance can, however, be justified in the circumstances. The negotiations had been started by the plaintiff[38] (the counter-offeree), and in view of this fact it was reasonable for the defendants to infer from her long silence that she had accepted the terms of the policy sent to her. The case thus falls within one of the suggested exceptions[39] to the general rule that an offeree is not bound by silence.

4. Acceptance in Ignorance of Offer

(1) Generally ineffective

The general view is that acceptance in ignorance of an offer should have no effect. To create a contract parties must *reach* agreement: it is not enough that their wishes happen to coincide. The act or promise constituting the acceptance must be "given in exchange for the offer."[40] The same considerations apply where a person once knew of the offer but had at the time of the alleged acceptance forgotten it.[41] Thus it has been held in other jurisdictions that a person who gives information for which a reward has been offered cannot claim the reward unless at the time of giving it he knew of

---

[33] *Ante*, p. 31; *cf. Collin* v. *Duke of Westminster* [1985] Q.B. 581.

[34] See *The Splendid Sun* [1981] Q.B. 694, 712, 713 ("closed their files"); *cf. ibid.* 706 ("did so act"); *The Multibank Holsatia* [1988] 2 Lloyd's Rep. 486, 493 (where the offeree had destroyed relevant files, so that the case was not one of mere inaction). *Tracomin S.A.* v. *Anton C. Nielsen A/S* [1984] 2 Lloyd's Rep. 195 can be supported on the same ground even though it was based on the decision at first instance in *The Leonidas D* which was reversed on appeal: [1985] 1 W.L.R. 925, *ante*, pp. 10. There seems to have been no "conduct" amounting to acceptance in *The Golden Bear* [1987] 1 Lloyd's Rep. 300.

[35] [1979] 2 Lloyd's Rep. 355.

[36] *Cf. ante*, p. 13.

[37] [1979] 2 Lloyd's Rep. 335, 340, affirming [1978] 2 Lloyd's Rep. 386, 393.

[38] *Cf. ante*, p. 30.

[39] *Ante*, pp. 31–32.

[40] *R.* v. *Clarke* (1927) 40 C.L.R. 227, 233; *Tracomin S.A.* v. *Anton C. Nielsen* [1984] 2 Lloyd's Rep. 195, 203.

[41] *R.* v. *Clarke*, *supra*, at p. 241.

the offer of reward.[42] The English case of *Gibbons* v. *Proctor*[43] is sometimes thought to support the contrary view, but can be explained on the ground that the plaintiff did know of the offer of reward by the time the information was given on his behalf to the person named in the advertisement.[44]

In the reward cases just considered, it is hard to see what prejudice the offeror would suffer if he had to pay the reward to someone who had complied with the terms of the offer without being aware of it. The reasons for holding that there is no contract in such a case seem to be largely doctrinal; but more practical difficulties can arise where the acts alleged to amount to an acceptance can not only confer rights on the actor, but also deprive him of rights[45] or impose duties on him. This last possibility may be illustrated by reference to *Upton R.D.C.* v. *Powell*[46] where the defendant, whose house was on fire, telephoned the Upton police and asked for "the fire brigade." He was entitled to the service of the Pershore fire brigade free of charge as he lived in its district; but the police called the Upton fire brigade, in the belief that the defendant lived in its district. The Upton fire brigade for a time shared this belief and thought "that they were rendering gratuitous services in their own area." It was held that the defendant was contractually bound to pay for these services. But even if the defendant's telephone call was an offer, it is hard to see how the fire brigade's services, given with no thought of reward, could be an acceptance. It would have been better to give the plaintiffs a quasi-contractual remedy than to hold that there was a contract. The case was only concerned with the rights of the fire brigade, but the fire brigade could also have owed more extensive duties as contractors than as volunteers. It may well be hard to subject a person who reasonably thinks that he is a volunteer to the more stringent duties of a contractor.[47]

(2) Cross-offers

The requirement that the offeree must know of the offer at the time of the alleged acceptance also accounts for the rule that there is no contract if two persons make identical cross-offers, neither party knowing of the other's offer when he makes his own, *e.g.* if A writes to B offering to sell B his car for £5,000 and B simultaneously writes to A offering to buy the car for £5,000. If no further communication took place in such a case, there might be considerable confusion in the minds of both parties as to whether there was indeed a contract between them; and the view that "cross offers are not an acceptance of each other"[48] can be supported on the ground that it tends to promote certainty.

---

[42] *Bloom* v. *American Swiss Watch Co.* (1915) A.D. 100; the American authorities are divided: see Corbin, *Contracts*, s.59.

[43] (1891) 64 L.T. 594, *sub nom. Gibson* v. *Proctor*, 55 J.P. 616. See Hudson, 84 L.Q.R. 513.

[44] "The information ultimately reached Penn at a time when the plaintiff knew that the reward had been offered": 55 J.P. 616.

[45] *e.g. Tracomin S.A.* v. *Anton C. Nielsen* [1984] 2 Lloyd's Rep. 195, 203.

[46] [1942] 1 All E.R. 220.

[47] *Cf. B.S.C.* v. *Cleveland Bridge & Engineering Co. Ltd.* [1984] 1 All E.R. 504, 510. *Quaere* what the position should be where one party thinks that he is giving or getting a gratuitous service while the other thinks that he is contracting.

[48] *Tinn* v. *Hoffmann & Co.* (1873) 29 L.T. 271, 278.

(3) Motive for acceptance

A person who knows of the offer may do the act required for acceptance with some motive other than that of accepting the offer. In *Williams* v. *Carwardine*[49] the defendant offered a reward of £20 to anyone who gave information leading to the conviction of the murderers of Walter Carwardine. The plaintiff knew of the offer, and, thinking that she had not long to live, signed a "voluntary statement to ease my conscience, and in hopes of forgiveness hereafter." This statement resulted in the conviction of the murderers. It was held that the plaintiff had brought herself within the term of the offer and was entitled to the reward. Patteson J. said: "We cannot go into the plaintiff's motives."[50] Similarly, in *Carlill* v. *Carbolic Smoke Ball Co.*[51] the plaintiff recovered the £100, although her predominant motive in using the smoke ball was (presumably) to avoid catching influenza. But in the Australian case of *R.* v. *Clarke*[52] a reward had been offered for information leading to the arrest and conviction of the murderers of two police officers. Clarke, who knew of the offer and was himself suspected of the crime, gave such information. He admitted that he had done so to clear himself of the charge, and with no thought of claiming the reward. His claim for the reward failed as he had not given the information "in exchange for the offer."[53] It seems that an act which is *wholly* motivated by factors other than the existence of the offer cannot amount to an acceptance, but if the existence of the offer plays some part, however small, in inducing a person to do the required act, there is a valid acceptance of the offer.

5. Acceptance in Unilateral Contracts

(1) Classification

A unilateral contract may arise when one party promises to pay the other a sum of money[54] if the other will do (or forbear from doing) something without making any promise to that effect: for example, when one person promises to pay another £100 if he will walk from London to York,[55] or find and return the promisor's lost dog, or give up smoking for a year.[56] In these cases the contract is described as unilateral as the promisee has clearly made no counter-promise to perform the required act or forbearance; it is contrasted with a bilateral contract, in which each party undertakes an obligation and in which acceptance, as a general rule, takes place on communication by the offeree of his counter-promise. The distinction

---

[49] (1833) 5 C. & P. 566; 4 B. & Ad. 621; it must be assumed that the plaintiff knew of the offer: *Carlill* v. *Carbolic Smoke Ball Co. Ltd.* [1892] 2 Q.B. at p. 489, n. 2.

[50] 4 B. & Ad. at p. 623.

[51] [1893] 1 Q.B. 256.

[52] (1927) 40 C.L.R. 227; contrast *Simonds* v. *U.S.*, 308 F. 2d 160 (1962).

[53] At p. 233.

[54] Or to do some other act, or to forbear from doing something. In the text we shall deal only with promises to pay money, by far the most common case.

[55] An old example: *Rogers* v. *Snow* (1573) Dalison 94; *cf. Great Northern Ry.* v. *Witham* (1873) L.R. 9 C.P. 16, 19. Its modern version is the "sponsored walk."

[56] *Cf. Hamer* v. *Sidway*, 124 N.Y. 538 (1881).

between the two types of contract sometimes gives rise to difficulty,[57] because a contract may be in its inception unilateral, but become bilateral in the course of its performance.[58] For example, A may promise to pay B £1000 for some service (such as painting A's house) which B does not promise to render. Here B would not be liable if he did nothing; but once he began the work he might be held to have impliedly promised to complete it, so that at this stage the contract would become bilateral[59] and both parties would be bound by it.

(2) General rules as to acceptance

Once a promise is classified as an offer of a unilateral contract, a number of rules apply to the acceptance of such an offer. First, the offer can be accepted by fully performing the required act or forbearance.[60] Secondly, there is no need to give advance notice of acceptance to the offeror.[61] And thirdly, the offer can, like all other offers, be withdrawn before it has been accepted. But there is much dispute as to the exact stage at which the offer is "accepted" so as to deprive the offeror of the power of withdrawal. It is probable that the offer can be accepted *only* by some performance and not by a counter-promise to walk to York, or to look for the lost dog, or to give up smoking; for such a counter-promise would not be what the offeror had bargained for. Thus the offeror could still withdraw after such a counter-promise had been made. It is less clear whether he can still withdraw after the offeree has *partly* performed the required act or forbearance, *e.g.* if he has walked half-way to York or refrained from smoking for six months. The first problem (which will be discussed here) is whether the offeree has at this stage accepted the offer; the second (to be discussed in Chapter 3[62]) is whether he has provided consideration for the offeror's promise.

(3) Acceptance by part performance

(a) IN GENERAL. According to one view, there is no contract until the required act or forbearance has been completed, and this is said to give effect to the intention of the parties, each of whom intends, until then, to reserve a *locus poenitentiae*.[63] But in most cases[64] it is unlikely that the

---

[57] See generally Llewellyn, 48 Yale L.J. 1, 799. *Cf.* The American Law Institute's Restatement of the Law of Contracts (hereinafter called Restatement, *Contracts*) § 12; the Restatement of the Law Second, Contracts (hereinafter called Restatement 2d., *Contracts*), § 45 substitutes the term "option contract," without any very obvious increase in clarity.

[58] *Cf. The Eurymedon* [1975] A.C. 154, 167–8 ("a bargain initially unilateral but capable of becoming mutual").

[59] See *The Unique Mariner* [1979] 2 Lloyd's Rep. 37, 51–52; contrast *B.S.C.* v. *Cleveland Bridge & Engineering Co. Ltd.* [1984] 1 All E.R. 504, 510–511 where such an implied promise was negatived by the fact that the terms of a bilateral contract were still under negotiation and were never agreed. It is not clear whether the situation discussed in *Offord* v. *Davies* (1862) 12 C.B.N.S. 748, 753 falls into the category of a unilateral or into that of a bilateral contract.

[60] See *Daulia Ltd.* v. *Four Millbank Nominees Ltd.* [1978] Ch. 231, 238; *cf. Harvela Investments Ltd.* v. *Royal Trust of Canada (C.I.) Ltd.* [1986] A.C. 207, 224.

[61] *Carlill* v. *Carbolic Smoke Ball Co.* [1893] 1 Q.B. 256.

[62] *Post*, p. 138.

[63] Wormser in *Selected Readings on the Law of Contracts*, p. 307; but for the same writer's later views see 3 Jl.Leg.Educ. 146.

[64] For a possible exception, see *post*, p. 39.

offeree intends to expose himself to the risk of withdrawal when he has partly performed and is willing and able[65] to complete performance for the sake of securing the promised benefit.[66] The general view is that it would cause hardship to the offeree to allow the offeror to withdraw in such a case; and most writers try to find some reason for saying that part performance prevents the offeror from withdrawing the offer. One possibility is to say that the offeror makes two offers: (1) the principal offer and (2) a collateral one to keep the principal offer open once performance has begun; this latter offer is accepted by beginning to perform.[67] But this analysis is artificial: it is more realistic to say that the principal offer itself is accepted by beginning to perform.[68] It has been objected that this cannot simply be asserted but must be explained.[69] The explanation may be that acceptance is simply the unqualified expression of assent to the terms of the offer by words or conduct. Whether such assent can be inferred from part performance is entirely a question of fact. The sight of a man walking northwards from London may or may not suggest that he does so in response to an offer to pay him £100 if he reaches York, but, if his conduct does clearly suggest this, there is no theoretical difficulty in saying that he has accepted the offer. Factual difficulties might, of course, arise in distinguishing between commencement of performance and mere preparation to perform. Thus it is probable that an offer of a reward for the return of lost property could still be withdrawn after someone had spent time looking for the property without success, but not after he had actually found it and was in the process of returning it to the owner.

English authority on the point is scanty, but a case which supports the above view is *Errington* v. *Errington*.[70] A father bought a house for £750, of which he borrowed £500 on mortgage from a building society. He allowed his son and daughter-in-law to live in the house and told them that if they paid the mortgage instalments, the house would be theirs when the mortgage was paid off. The couple started to live in the house and paid some of the mortgage instalments; but they did not bind themselves to go on making the payments. It was held that this arrangement amounted to a contract which could not, after the father's death, be revoked by his personal representatives. Denning L.J. said: "The father's promise was a unilateral contract—a promise of the house in return for their act of paying the instalments. It could not be revoked by him once the couple entered on performance of the act, but it would cease to bind him if they left it incomplete and unperformed, which they have not done."[71]

---

[65] It is assumed that performance remains within his power. If not, the offeror can withdraw: see *Morrison SS. Co.* v. *The Crown* (1924) 20 Ll.L.R. 283.

[66] Lord Diplock in the *Harvela* case [1986] A.C. 207, 224 can be read as depriving the offeror of the power to withdraw as soon as his offer is *communicated* (*i.e.* before any performance); but in that case the offeree had completely performed the required act by making the requested bid.

[67] McGoveney, *Selected Readings*, p. 300.

[68] Pollock, *Principles of Contract* (13th ed.), p. 19; Ballantine, *Selected Readings*, p. 312.

[69] McGoveney, *ubi supra*.

[70] [1952] 1 K.B. 290. The reasoning of this case was doubted, but not on this point, in *National Provincial Bank Ltd.* v. *Ainsworth* [1965] A.C. 1175, 1239–1240, 1251–1252 and in *Ashburn Anstalt* v. *Arnold* [1989] Ch. 1, 17: see *post*, p. 538, n. 41. For another possible illustration, see *Beaton* v. *McDivitt* (1988) 13 N.S.W.L.R. 162, 175.

[71] [1952] 1 K.B. 290, 295.

(b) CONTINUING GUARANTEES. The view that part performance of a uni lateral contract can amount to an acceptance is further supported by the law relating to continuing guarantees. These may be divisible, where each advance constitutes a separate transaction; or indivisible *e.g.* where, on A's admission to an association, B guarantees all liabilities that A may incur as a member of the association.[72] If the guarantee is divisible, it can be revoked at any time with regard to future advances[73]; but an indivisible guarantee cannot be revoked after the creditor has begun to act on it by giving credit to the principal debtor.[74] This rule applies even though the contract of guarantee is unilateral in the sense that the creditor has not made any promise to the guarantor (in return for the guarantee) to give credit to the debtor.

(c) BANKERS' IRREVOCABLE CREDITS. This subject is explained in Chapter 3[75]; here it need only be said that the essence of the system is that a bank, on the instruction of its customer (usually a buyer of goods) notifies a third person (usually the seller) that it has opened an irrevocable credit in his favour. This amounts to a promise to pay him a stipulated sum if he will present certain specified documents to the bank. The general view is that the bank cannot revoke the promise once it has been notified to the seller; and, as the seller makes no promise *to the bank*, this result is sometimes explained in terms of the unilateral contract between these parties. In most cases there will be some act of part performance by the seller, *e.g.* in shipping the goods so as to procure the required documents. But the bank's promise is regarded as binding as soon as it is notified to the seller, *i.e.* before he has done any act in response to it. The binding force of such irrevocable credits is not, therefore, easily explicable in terms of acceptance of an offer.

(d) ESTATE AGENTS' CONTRACTS. Where an estate agent is engaged to negotiate the sale of a house, it is arguable that the client's promise to pay a commission on sale gives rise to a unilateral contract, for in one case of this kind it was said that "No obligation is imposed on the agent to do anything."[76] It is settled that the client can, without liability, revoke his instructions before a claim to commission has accrued, in spite of the fact that the agent has made considerable efforts to find a purchaser.[77] Hence this line of cases could be said to support the view that the offeror (the client) can withdraw after part performance by the offeree (the agent) of the unilateral contract. But the better explanation is that this is one of the exceptional cases in which, on the true construction of the offer, a *locus poenitentiae* is reserved to the client even after part performance. This view is supported by the fact that the right to revoke instructions exists even where the contract is bilateral because the agent has, expressly or by implication, made some promise, *e.g.* one to use his best endeavours to effect a

---

72 As in *Lloyd's* v. *Harper* (1880) 16 Ch.D. 290.
73 As in *Offord* v. *Davies* (1862) 12 C.B.N.S. 748.
74 *Lloyd's* v. *Harper*, *supra*.
75 *Post*, p. 138.
76 *Luxor (Eastbourne) Ltd.* v. *Cooper* [1941] A.C. 108, 124. In fact the agent often does undertake to do something; *infra*, nn. 78, 79. See generally Murdoch, (1975) 91 L.Q.R. 357.
77 *Post*, p. 644.

sale[78] or one to bear advertising expenses.[79] Such promises have been found to exist where the agent has been appointed "sole agent," but in practice they are commonly made by other agents as well. A "sole agent" is entitled to damages if the client sells through another agent,[80] but not if he simply revokes his instructions or sells "privately," without the help of any agent at all.[81] These rules apply irrespective of the unilateral or bilateral nature of the contract; so that the estate agency cases shed little, if any, light on the question of acceptance in unilateral contracts.

(e) EXTENT OF RECOVERY. Where a unilateral contract takes the shape of a promise to pay a sum of money, it is generally assumed that the promisee must either get nothing or the full sum. Perhaps some compromise is possible. Suppose the promisee has walked half-way to York before the offer is withdrawn. It is arguable that he should desist and recover his expenses, or a reasonable sum.[82] This might be fairer to both parties than the "all or nothing" solutions which are usually canvassed.[83]

SECTION 3. TERMINATION OF OFFER

1. Withdrawal

(1) Communication to offeree generally required

As a general rule, an offer can be withdrawn at any time before it is accepted.[84] It is not withdrawn merely by acting inconsistently with it, *e.g.* by disposing of the subject-matter.[85] Notice of the withdrawal must be given and must actually reach the offeree: mere posting will not suffice. In *Byrne & Co.* v. *Leon van Tienhoven*[86] the defendants in Cardiff on October 1 posted an offer to sell tinplates to the plaintiffs in New York. This offer reached the plaintiffs on October 11, and they immediately accepted it by a telegram which they confirmed by a letter of October 15. Meanwhile, the defendants had on October 8 posted a letter withdrawing their offer, but that letter of withdrawal did not reach the plaintiffs until October 20. It was held that there was a contract since the withdrawal had not been communicated when the offer was accepted. Thus there was a

---

78 *Christopher* v. *Essig* [1958] W.N. 461; *John McCann & Co.* v. *Pow* [1974] 1 W.L.R. 1643, 1647; *Wood* v. *Lucy* (*Lady Duff-Gordon*), 118 N.E. 214 (1917) (where such a promise was implied). It is an open question whether such a promise is sufficiently certain to have legal effect, *post*, pp. 48, 153.

79 *Cf. Bentall, Horsley & Baldry* v. *Vicary* [1931] 1 K.B. 253.

80 *Hampton & Sons Ltd.* v. *George* [1939] 3 All E.R. 627; *Christopher* v. *Essig* [1958] W.N. 461, *post*, p. 646.

81 *Post*, p. 646.

82 Unless the plaintiff has a "substantial or legitimate interest" in going on, this may be the law under the principles laid down in *White & Carter* (*Councils*) *Ltd.* v. *McGregor* [1962] A.C. 413, *post*, pp. 898–902.

83 Fuller & Perdue, 46 Y.L.J. at p. 411.

84 *Routledge* v. *Grant* (1828) 4 Bing 653; *Offord* v. *Davies* (1862) 12 C.B.N.S. 748; *Tuck* v. *Baker* [1990] 2 E.G.L.R. 195; Dunmore v. *Alexander* (1830) 8 Shaw 190. For statutory exceptions, see Companies Act 1985, s. 82(7); ULFIS (*ante*, p. 28) Art. 5(2); and see Vienna Convention (*ante*, p. 29) Art. 16(2).

85 *Adams* v. *Lindsell* (1818) 1 B. & Ald. 681; *Stevenson, Jacques & Co.* v. *McLean* (1880) 5 Q.B.D. 346; contrary dicta in *Dickinson* v. *Dodds* (1876) 2 Ch.D. 463, 472 would no longer be followed.

86 (1880) 5 C.P.D. 344. Under Consumer Credit Act 1974, s.69(1)(ii) and (7) posting is, exceptionally, sufficient.

contract in spite of the fact that the parties were demonstrably not in agreement, for when the plaintiffs first knew of the defendants' offer, the defendants had already ceased to intend to deal with the plaintiffs. The rule is based on convenience; for no one could rely on a postal offer if it could be withdrawn by a letter already posted but not yet received.

(2) Exceptions

The general rule that the withdrawal must be "brought to the mind of"[87] the offeree is subject to a number of exceptions. First, the requirement cannot be taken quite literally where an offer is made to a company whose mail is received, opened and sorted in different offices and then distributed to be dealt with in various departments. Is a letter withdrawing such an offer communicated when it is received, or when it is opened, or when it is actually read by the responsible officer?[88] In the interests of certainty it would probably be held that communication took place when the letter was "opened in the ordinary course of business or would have been so opened if the ordinary course was followed."[89] Secondly (as the concluding words of the passage just quoted suggest) the general rule may be displaced by the conduct of the offeree. A withdrawal which was delivered to the offeree's last known address would be effective if he had moved without notifying the offeror. Similarly, a withdrawal which had reached the offeree would be effective even though he had simply failed to read it after it had reached him: this would be the position where a withdrawal by telex or fax reached the offeror's office during business hours even though it was not actually read by the offeree or by any of his staff till the next day.[90] Of course the withdrawal would not be effective in such a case, if it had been sent to the offeree at a time when he and all responsible members of his staff were, to the offeror's knowledge, away on holiday or on other business.[91] A third exception to the requirement that a withdrawal must be actually communicated relates to offers made to the public, *e.g.* of rewards for information leading to the arrest of the perpetrator of a crime. As it is impossible for the offeror to ensure that the notice of withdrawal comes to the attention of everyone who knew of the offer, it seems to be enough for him to take reasonable steps to bring the withdrawal to the attention of such persons, even though it does not in fact come to the attention of them all.[92]

(3) Communication need not come from offeror

Although withdrawal must be communicated to the offeree, it need not be communicated by the offeror. It is sufficient if the offeree knows from any reliable source that the offeror no longer intends to contract with him. Thus in *Dickinson* v. *Dodds*[93] it was held that an offer to sell land could not

---

[87] *Henthorn* v. *Fraser* [1892] 2 Ch. 27, 32.

[88] *Cf. Curtice* v. *London, etc., Bank* [1908] 1 K.B. 291, 300–301 (notice to countermand a cheque).

[89] *Eaglehill Ltd.* v. *J. Needham (Builders) Ltd.* [1973] A.C. 992, 1011, discussing notice of dishonour of a cheque; contrast *The Pendrecht* [1980] 2 Lloyd's Rep. 56, 66 (telex notice of arbitration).

[90] *Cf. The Brimnes* [1975] Q.B. 929 (notice withdrawing ship from charterparty).

[91] *Cf. Brinkibon Ltd.* v. *Stahag Stahl und Stahlwarenhandelsgesellschaft mbH* [1983] 2 A.C. 34, 42 (communication of acceptance).

[92] *Shuey* v. *U.S.*, 92 U.S. 73 (1875).

[93] (1876) 2 Ch.D. 463; *cf. Cartwright* v. *Hoogstoel* (1911) 105 L.T. 628.

be accepted after the offeror had, to the offeree's knowledge decided to sell the land to a third party. The decision is based on the fact that there is in such a case no agreement between the parties. But this would be equally true if the offeree had not heard of the withdrawal at all before he accepted the offer: yet in that case there is a contract.[94] The rule that communication of withdrawal need not come from the offeror can be a regrettable source of uncertainty. It puts on the offeree the possibly difficult task of deciding whether his source of information is reliable, and it may also make it hard for him to tell exactly when the offer was withdrawn. In *Dickinson* v. *Dodds*, for example, it is not clear whether this occurred when the plaintiff realised that the defendant had (a) sold the land to the third party, or (b) begun to negotiate with the third party, or (c) simply decided not to sell to the plaintiff. Certainty would be promoted if the rule were that the withdrawal must be communicated by the offeror, as well as to the offeree.

2. Rejection

An offer is terminated by rejection.[95] An attempt to accept an offer on new terms, not contained in the offer, may be a rejection of the offer accompanied by a counter-offer.[96] An offeree who makes such an attempt cannot later accept the original offer. In *Hyde* v. *Wrench*[97] the defendant offered to sell a farm to the plaintiff for £1,000. The plaintiff replied by making an offer to buy for £950 and when that was rejected he purported to accept the original offer to sell for £1,000. It was held that there was no contract as the plaintiff had, by making a counter-offer of £950, rejected the original offer.

A communication from the offeree *may* be construed as a counter-offer (and hence as a rejection) even though it takes the form of a question as to the offeror's willingness to vary the terms of the offer.[98] But such a communication is not *necessarily* a counter-offer: it may be a mere inquiry or request for information made without any intention of rejecting the terms of the offer. Whether the communication is a counter-offer or a request for information depends on the intention, objectively ascertained,[99] with which it was made. In *Stevenson, Jacques & Co.* v. *McLean*[1] an offer was made to sell iron to the plaintiffs who asked by telegram whether they might take delivery over a period of four months. It was held that this telegram was not a counter-offer but only a request for information as it was "meant . . . only as an inquiry" and as the offeror "ought to have regarded it" in that sense.[2] Similarly, if an offer is made for the sale of a house at a specified price, an inquiry whether the intending vendor is prepared to reduce the price will not amount to a rejection if the inquiry is "merely exploratory."[3]

It seems that a rejection has no effect unless it is actually communicated to the offeror. There is no ground of convenience for holding that it should take effect when posted. The offeree will obviously not act in reliance on it

---

[94] *Byrne & Co.* v. *Leon van Tienhoven* (1880) 5 C.P.D. 344, *ante*, p. 40.
[95] *Tinn* v. *Hoffmann & Co.* (1873) 29 L.T. 271, 278.
[96] *Ante*, p. 18.
[97] (1840) 3 Beav. 334.
[98] See the treatment in *Tinn* v. *Hoffman* (1873) 29 L.T. 271, 278 of the plaintiff's letter of November 27.
[99] *Ante*, p. 8.
[1] (1880) 5 Q.B.D. 346.
[2] At pp. 349–350; in fact the offeror did not so regard it but sold the iron to a third party.
[3] *Gibson* v. *Manchester C.C.* [1979] 1 W.L.R. 294, 302.

as he derives no rights or liabilities from it; and the offeror will not know that he is free from the offer until the rejection is actually communicated to him. Hence if a letter of rejection is overtaken by an acceptance sent by telex there should be a contract, provided that the offeree has made his final intention clear to the offeror. But once the rejection had reached the offeror he should not be bound by an acceptance posted after the rejection and also reaching the offeror after the rejection. To hold the offeror bound,[4] merely because the acceptance was *posted* before the rejection had reached him, could expose him to serious hardship, particularly when he had acted on the rejection, *e.g.* by disposing elsewhere of the subject-matter. If the offeree has posted a rejection and then wishes, after all, to accept the offer, he should ensure that his subsequently posted acceptance actually comes to the notice of the offeror before the latter receives the rejection.

3. Lapse of Time

An offer which is expressly stated to last for a fixed time cannot be accepted after that time; and an offer which stipulates for acceptance "by return" (of post) must normally[5] be accepted either by a return postal communication or by some other no less expeditious method. An offer which contains no express provision limiting its duration determines after lapse of a reasonable time.[6] What is a reasonable time depends on such circumstances as the nature of the subject-matter and the means used to communicate the offer. Thus an offer to sell a perishable thing, or one whose price is liable to sudden fluctuations, would determine after a short time. The same is true of an offer made by telegram or telemessage.[7]

The period that would normally constitute a reasonable time for acceptance may be extended if the conduct of the offeree within that period indicates an intention to accept and this is known to the offeror. Such conduct would often of itself amount to acceptance, but this possibility may be ruled out by the terms of the offer, which may require the acceptance to be by written notice sent to a specified address.[8] In such a case the offeree's conduct, though it could not *amount* to an acceptance, could nevertheless prolong the time for giving a proper notice of acceptance. For the offeree's conduct to have this effect, it must be known to the offeror; for if this were not the case the offeror might reasonably suppose that the offer had not been accepted within the normal period of lapse, and act in reliance on that belief: *e.g.* by disposing elsewhere of the subject-matter.

4. Occurrence of Condition

An offer which expressly provides that it is to determine on the occurrence of some condition cannot be accepted after that condition has occurred; and such a provision may also be implied. Thus where a person examines goods and subsequently makes an offer to buy or hire-purchase them, it

---

[4] Under the "posting rule," *ante*, p. 23.

[5] *Ante*, p. 29.

[6] *Ramsgate Victoria Hotel Co. Ltd.* v. *Montefiore* (1866) L.R. 1 Ex. 109; *Cemco Leasing S.p.A.* v. *Rediffusion Ltd.* [1987] F.T.L.R. 201.

[7] *Quenerduaine* v. *Cole* (1883) 32 W.R. 185.

[8] As in *Manchester Diocesan Council for Education* v. *Commercial and General Investments Ltd.* [1970] 1 W.L.R. 241.

may be an implied term of the offer that the goods should remain in substantially the same state in which they were when the offer was made. Such an offer cannot be accepted after the goods have been seriously damaged.[9] Similarly, an offer to insure the life of a person cannot be accepted after he has suffered serious injuries by falling over a cliff.[10] On the same principle, it is submitted that the offer which is made by bidding at an auction by implication provides that it is to lapse as soon as higher bid is made.[11]

5. Death

One possible view is that the death of either party terminates the offer, as the parties can no longer reach agreement.[12] But there may be a contract in spite of a demonstrable lack of agreement if to hold the contrary would cause serious inconvenience.[13] In accordance with this principle, it is submitted that the death of either party should not of itself determine the offer except in the case of such "personal" contracts as are determined by the death of either party.[14]

(1) Death of an offeror

The effect of the death of the offeror has been considered in a number of cases concerning continuing guarantees. In general a continuing guarantee, *e.g.* of a bank overdraft, is divisible[15]: it is a continuing offer by the guarantor, accepted from time to time as the banker makes loans to his customer. Each loan is a separate acceptance, turning the offer *pro tanto* into a binding contract. It seems that such a guarantee is not terminated merely by the death of the guarantor.[16] But it is terminated if the bank knows that the guarantor is dead and that his personal representatives have no power under his will to continue the guarantee[17]; or if for some other reason it is inequitable for the bank to charge the guarantor's estate.[18] If the guarantee expressly provides that it can only be terminated by notice given by the guarantor *or his personal representatives*, the death of the guarantor, even if known to the bank, will not terminate the guarantee: express notice must be given.[19]

(2) Death of offeree

Two cases have some bearing on the effect of the death of the offeree. In *Reynolds* v. *Atherton*[20] an offer to sell shares was made in 1911 "to the

---

[9] *Financings Ltd.* v. *Stimson* [1962] 1 W.L.R. 1184.
[10] *Canning* v. *Farquhar* (1885) 16 Q.B.D. 722 (the offer here came in the form of a counter-offer from the insurance company: see p. 733); *Looker* v. *Law Union & Rock Ins. Co. Ltd.* [1928] 1 K.B. 554. Contrast p. 255, n. 54, *post*.
[11] *Ante*, p. 11.
[12] *Dickinson* v. *Dodds* (1876) 2 Ch.D. 463, 475.
[13] *Ante*, p. 41.
[14] *e.g.* contracts of employment or agency: *post*, p. 651. In such a case any *contract* would be determined by death even if the *offer* were not so determined; but the legal effects of saying that there was never any contract might differ from those of saying that there had been a contract which was determined.
[15] *Ante*, p. 39.
[16] *Bradbury* v. *Morgan* (1862) 1 H. & C. 249; *Harris* v. *Fawcett* (1873) L.R. 8 Ch.App. 866, 869; *Coulthart* v. *Clementson* (1879) 5 Q.B.D. 42, 46.
[17] *Coulthart* v. *Clementson* (1879) 5 Q.B.D. 42.
[18] *Harris* v. *Fawcett* (1873) L.R. 8 Ch.App. 866.
[19] *Re Silvester* [1895] 1 Ch. 573.
[20] (1921) 125 L.T. 690; affirmed, (1922) 127 L.T. 189.

directors of" a company. An attempt to accept the offer was made in 1919 by the survivors of the persons who were directors in 1911 and by the personal representatives of those who had since died. The purported acceptance was held to be ineffective; and Warrington L.J. said obiter that an offer "made to a living person who ceases to be a living person before the offer is accepted . . . is no longer an offer at all." The actual ground for the decision, however, was that the offer had, on its true construction, been made to the directors of the company for the time being, and not to those who happened to hold office in 1911. In *Kennedy* v. *Thomassen*[21] an offer to buy annuities was accepted by the solicitors of the annuitant after she had, without the solicitors' knowledge, died. This acceptance was held to be ineffective on the grounds that the solicitors' authority was terminated by their client's death and that the acceptance was made under a mistake.[22] Neither case supports the view that an offer can never be accepted after the offeree's death. It is submitted that, where an offer related to a contract which was not "personal,"[23] it might, on its true construction, be held to have been made to the offeree or to his executors, and that such an offer could be accepted after the death of the original offeree.

6. Supervening Incapacity

(1) Mental patients

If an offeror became a mental patient he would not be bound by an acceptance made after this fact had become known to the offeree, or after the patient's property had been made subject to the control of the court. But the other party would be bound; and an offer made to a person who later became a mental patient could be accepted so as to bind the other party. These rules can readily be deduced from the law as to contracts with mental patients.[24]

(2) Corporations

(a) COMPANIES INCORPORATED UNDER THE COMPANIES ACT 1985. Such a company may lose its capacity to do an act by altering its memorandum of association.[25] If the company nevertheless entered into transactions after depriving itself of the capacity to do so, those transactions were formerly *ultra vires* and void.[26] Now the general rule[27] is that acts done by the company can no longer be called into question on the ground that the company lacked capacity to do them by reason of anything in its memorandum[28]; and that, in favour of a person dealing with the company is good faith, the power of the board of directors to bind the company, or to authorise others to do so, is deemed to be free of any limitation under

---

21 [1929] 1 Ch. 426.
22 *Cf. post*, p. 249.
23 *Supra*, at n. 14.
24 *Post*, pp. 501–503 *et seq*.
25 *Post*, p. 504.
26 *Post*, p. 504.
27 See generally *post*, pp. 504–507.
28 Companies Act 1985, s.35(1) (as substituted by Companies Act 1989, s.108.

the company's constitution.[29] But a member of the company may bring proceedings to restrain the doing of acts beyond the company's capacity, or beyond the powers of the directors, except where such acts are done in fulfilment of legal obligations arising from previous acts of the company.[30] The effect of these provisions must be considered on offers made *to* and *by* the company.

(i) *Company as offeree.* A company may receive an offer to enter into a contract and then alter its memorandum and so deprive itself of the capacity to enter into that contract. If it nevertheless accepts the offer, the acceptance is effective in favour of a person who deals with the company in good faith; but before the company has accepted the offer, it can be restrained from doing so in proceedings brought by one of its members.

(ii) *Company as offeror.* A company may make an offer to enter into a contract and then alter its memorandum and so deprive itself of the capacity to enter into that contract. An acceptance of that offer is nevertheless effective in favour of a person dealing with the company in good faith; but it is not entirely clear whether in this situation a member of the company could take proceedings to prevent the conclusion of the contract. Such proceedings only lie to restrain "the doing of an act"[31] by the company and since the relevant act on the company's part (*i.e.* the making of the offer) would already have been done when the company still had capacity to do it, there seems to be nothing for the member to restrain, unless holding the offer open could be described as a continuing act.

Of course, the company itself could normally withdraw the offer and would be likely to do so in pursuance of the policy which had led it to change its memorandum. But this possibility would not be open to the company where it had bound itself not to withdraw the offer, *i.e.* where it had granted a legally enforceable option[32]; and in such a case it is clear that a member could not take proceedings to prevent the conclusion of the contract since such proceedings cannot be taken "in respect of an act to be done in fulfilment of a legal obligation arising from a previous act of the company[33]: *i.e.* in the case put, from the grant of the option.

(b) OTHER CORPORATIONS. Companies may also be incorporated by Royal Charter or by special legislation. Charter corporations have the legal capacity of a natural person so that an alteration of the charter would not affect the validity of an offer or acceptance made by the corporation.[34] The legal capacity of corporations incorporated by special statute is governed by the statute, and acts not within that capacity are *ultra vires* and void. An alteration of the statute could therefore prevent the company from accepting an offer made to it, and from being bound by the acceptance of an offer made by it, where the offer was made before the alteration came into effect. In practice, the problem is likely to be dealt with in the statute which changes the capacity of the corporation.

---

[29] *Ibid.* s.35A(1).

[30] *Ibid.* ss.35(2), 35A(4).

[31] *Ibid.*

[32] For legally enforceable options, see *post*, p. 140, n. 98; Mowbray, 71 L.Q.R. 242; Lücke, 3 Adelaide L. Rev. 200.

[33] Companies Act 1985, ss.35(2), 35A(3) (as substituted by Companies Act 1989, s.108).

[34] *Post*, pp. 503–504; but a corporation could bring proceedings to restrain the conclusion of the contract: *ibid.*

SECTION 4. SPECIAL CASES

In some situations already discussed, the analysis of agreement into offer and acceptance gives rise to considerable difficulty,[35] and in others, to be discussed in this section, such analysis is impossible or highly artificial.[36] For this reason, it has been suggested that the analysis is "out of date"[37] and that "you should look at the correspondence as a whole and at the conduct of the parties and see therefrom whether the parties have come to an agreement."[38] The objection to this view, however, is that it provides too little guidance for the courts (or for the legal advisers of the parties) in determining whether agreement has been reached. For this reason, the situations to be discussed below are best regarded as exceptions[39] to a general requirement offer and acceptance. This approach is supported by cases in which it has been held that there is no contract precisely because there was no offer and acceptance[40]; and by those in which the terms of a contract have been held to depend on the analysis of the negotiation into offer, counter-offer and acceptance.[41]

1. Multipartite Agreements

In *The Satanita*[42] the plaintiff and the defendant entered their yachts for a regatta. Each signed a letter, addressed to the secretary of the club which organised the regatta, undertaking to obey certain rules during the race. It was held that there was a contract between all the competitors on the terms of the undertaking, though it is not clear whether the contract was made when the competitors entered their yachts or when they actually began to race. In either event, it is difficult to analyse the transaction into offer and acceptance. If the contract was made when the yachts were entered, one would have to say that the entry of the first competitor was an offer and that the entry of the next was an acceptance of that offer and (simultaneously) an offer to yet later competitors; but this view is artificial and unworkable even in theory unless each competitor knew of the existence of previous ones. It would also lead to the conclusion that entries which were put in the post together were cross-offers and thus not binding on each other.[43] If the contract was made when the race began, then it seems that

---

[35] See *ante*, pp. 10, 16–17, 19–20.

[36] *Gibson* v. *Manchester C.C.* [1978] 1 W.L.R. 520, 523, reversed [1979] 1 W.L.R. 294; *cf. The Eurymedon* [1975] A.C. 154, 167; Pollock, *Principles of Contract* (13th ed.), p. 5.

[37] *Butler Machine Tool Co. Ltd.* v. *Ex-Cell-O Corp. (England) Ltd.* [1979] 1 W.L.R. 401, 404; *cf. Port Sudan Cotton Co.* v. *Govindaswamy Chettiar & Sons* [1977] 2 Lloyd's Rep. 5, 10; *Interfoto Picture Library Ltd.* v. *Stiletto Visual Programmes Ltd.* [1989] Ch. 433, 443.

[38] *Gibson* v. *Manchester C.C.* [1978] 1 W.L.R. 520, 523, reversed [1979] 1 W.L.R. 294.

[39] *Gibson* v. *Manchester C.C.* [1979] 1 W.L.R. 294, 297; *The Good Helmsman* [1981] 1 Lloyd's Rep. 377, 409.

[40] *The Kapetan Markos NL (No. 2)* [1987] 2 Lloyd's Rep. 323, 331 ("What was the mechanism for offer and acceptance?"); *cf. The Good Helmsman* [1981] 1 Lloyd's Rep. 377, 409; *The Aramis* [1989] 1 Lloyd's Rep. 213, Treitel [1989] L.M.C.L.Q. 162. The "offer and acceptance" analysis was also regarded as decisive in many of the arbitration cases discussed at pp. 10, 31, *ante*, though it was viewed with scepticism in *The Multibank Holsatia* [1988] 2 Lloyd's Rep. 486, 491 and in *The Maritime Winner* [1989] 2 Lloyd's Rep. 506, 515.

[41] *e.g.* The "battle of forms" cases discussed at pp. 19–20, *ante*.

[42] [1895] P. 248; affirmed sub nom. Clarke v. *Dunraven* [1897] A.C. 59; Phillips, 92 L.Q.R. 499.

[43] *Ante*, p. 35.

each competitor simultaneously agreed to terms proposed by the officers of the club, and not that each proposed an identical set of terms amounting at the same time to an offer to the others and to an acceptance of the offers at that instant made by them. Even if the second view of the facts could be taken, the "offers" and "acceptances" would all occur at the same moment. Thus they would be cross-offers and would not create a contract. The competitors, no doubt, reached agreement, but they did not do so by a process which can be analysed into offer and acceptance.

2. Reference to Third Party

Where two negotiating parties reach deadlock, they may ask a third party to break it. If both simultaneously assent to a solution proposed by him, there is a contract, but it is again impossible to say which party has made the offer and which the acceptance.[44] The same is true where the parties negotiate through a single broker who eventually obtains their consent to the same terms.[45]

3. Sale of Land

There is some difficulty in analysing into offer and acceptance a transaction such as the sale of land where parties agree "subject to contract" so that they are not bound until formal contracts are exchanged.[46] Strictly an "offer" subject to contract does not satisfy the definition of offer[47] since the person making it has no intention to be bound immediately on acceptance. However, the *agreement* is made by the usual process: the only reason why parties are not bound until they exchange formal contracts is that the terms of their agreement expressly negative for the time being the intention to enter into legal relations. Alternatively, a party can be regarded as making the offer when he submits a signed contract for exchange[48]; and this would be accepted when the exchange took place.

SECTION 5. CERTAINTY

An agreement is not a binding contract if it lacks certainty, either because it is too vague or because it is obviously incomplete.[49]

1. Vagueness

An agreement may be so vague that no definite meaning can be given to it without adding new terms. Thus in *G. Scammell & Nephew Ltd.* v. *Ouston*[50] the House of Lords held that an agreement to buy goods "on hire-purchase" was too vague to be enforced, since there were many kinds of hire-purchase agreements in widely different terms, so that it was impossible to say on which terms the parties intended to contract. Similarly, agreements "subject to war clause,"[51] "subject to strike and lockout

---

[44] Pollock, *Principles of Contract* (13th ed.), p. 5.
[45] *Pagnan* S.p.A. v. *Feed Products Ltd.* [1987] 2 Lloyds's Rep. 601, 616.
[46] *Post*, p. 52.
[47] *Ante*, p. 8.
[48] See *Christie Owen & Davies* v. *Rapacioli* [1974] Q.B. 781.
[49] Fridman, 76 L.Q.R. 521; Lücke, 6 Adelaide L.Rev. 1.
[50] [1941] A.C. 251.
[51] *Bishop & Baxter Ltd.* v. *Anglo-Eastern Trading Co.* [1944] K.B. 12.

clause,"[52] and "subject to *force majeure* conditions"[53] have been held too vague, there being no evidence in any of the cases of a customary or usual form of such clauses or conditions.[54] Similar reasoning has sometimes been applied where agreements were made subject to the "satisfaction" of one party. The problems arising from such provisions are discussed later in this Chapter.[55]

But the courts do not expect commercial documents to be drafted with strict precision, and will, particularly if the parties have acted on an agreement,[56] do their best to avoid striking it down on the ground that it is too vague.[57]

(1) Custom

Apparent vagueness can be resolved by custom. Thus a contract to load coal at Grimsby "on the terms of the usual colliery guarantee" was upheld on proof of the terms usually contained in such guarantees at Grimsby.[58] The courts often enforce commercial contracts expressed in abbreviations whose meaning is certain and notorious.

(2) Reasonableness and trade usage

Vague phrases can be interpreted in the light of what is reasonable. This was done in *Hillas & Co. Ltd.* v. *Arcos Ltd.*,[59] where the House of Lords upheld an agreement for the sale of timber "of fair specification," made between persons well acquainted with the timber trade: the standard of reasonableness was applied to make the vague phrase certain. An undertaking to grant a lease of a shop "in prime position" has similarly been held not to be too uncertain to be enforced since the phrase was commonly used by persons dealing with shop property, so that its meaning could be determined by expert evidence.[60]

(3) Duty to resolve uncertainty

An agreement containing a vague phrase may be binding because one party is under a duty to resolve the uncertainty. In one case an agreement to sell goods provided for delivery "free on board . . . good Danish port."

---

[52] *Love & Stewart Ltd.* v. *S. Instone & Co.* (1917) 33 T.L.R. 475.

[53] *British Electrical, etc. Industries Ltd.* v. *Patley Pressings Ltd.* [1953] 1 W.L.R. 280.

[54] For further illustrations, see *post*, p. 408.

[55] *Post*, p. 60.

[56] *Brown* v. *Gould* [1972] Ch. 53, 57–58; *Tito* v. *Waddell* (*No. 2*) [1977] Ch. 106, 314; *The Tropwind* [1982] 1 Lloyd's Rep. 232; *Sudbrook Trading Estate Ltd.* v. *Eggleton* [1983] 1 A.C. 444.

[57] See *Rahcassi Shipping Co.* v. *Blue Star Line* [1969] 1 Q.B. 173; *Nea Agrex S.A.* v. *Baltic Shipping Co. Ltd.* [1976] Q.B. 933; *Grace Shipping Inc.* v. *C.F. Sharpe & Co.* (*Malaysia*) *Pte.* [1987] 1 Lloyd's Rep. 207; *Ashburn Anstalt* v. *Arnold* [1989] Ch. 1; *Deutsche Schachtbau-und-Tiefbohrgesellschaft mbH* v. *Ras Al Khaimah National Oil Co.* [1990] 1 A.C. 295, 306, reversed on other grounds *ibid.* pp. 329 *et seq.*; *Anangel Atlas Compania Naviera S.A.* v. *Ishikawajima Harima Heavy Industries Co. Ltd. (No. 2)* [1990] 2 Lloyd's Rep. 526, 546.

[58] *Shamrock SS. Co.* v. *Storey & Co.* (1899) 81 L.T. 413; *cf. Hart* v. *Hart* (1881) 18 Ch.D. 670; *Malcolm* v. *Chancellor, Masters and Scholars of the University of Oxford*, *The Times*, December 19, 1990.

[59] (1932) 147 L.T. 503 (and see *post*, p. 56); *Sweet & Maxwell Ltd.* v. *Universal News Services Ltd.* [1964] 2 Q.B. 699; *cf. Greater London Council* v. *Connolly* [1970] 2 Q.B. 100; *Finchbourne Ltd.* v. *Rodrigues* [1976] 3 All E.R. 581.

[60] *Ashburn Anstalt* v. *Arnold* [1989] Ch. 1, 27.

It was held that the agreement was not too vague: it amounted to a good contract under which the buyer was bound to select the port of shipment.[61]

(4) Meaningless phrases

The court will make considerable efforts to give meaning to an apparently meaningless phrase[62]; but, even where these efforts fail, such phrases do not necessarily vitiate the agreement. In *Nicolene Ltd.* v. *Simmonds*[63] steel bars were bought on terms which were certain except for a clause that the sale was subject to "the usual conditions of acceptance;" but there were no such usual conditions. It was held that the phrase was meaningless, but that this did not vitiate the whole contract: the words were severable and could be ignored. The same possibility exists where a clause is self-contradictory. Thus where an arbitration clause provided for arbitration of "any dispute" in London and of "any other dispute" in Moscow the court disregarded the clause and determined the dispute itself.[64] Such cases show that the question whether a meaningless clause vitiates the contract, or can be ignored, depends on the importance which the parties may be considered to have attached to it. If it is simply verbiage, not intended to add anything to an otherwise complete agreement, or if it relates to a matter of relatively minor importance, it can be ignored. But if the parties intend it to govern some vital aspect of their relationship, its vagueness will vitiate the entire agreement.

2. Incompleteness

(1) Agreement in principle only[65]

Parties may reach agreement on essential matters of principle, but leave important points unsettled, so that their agreement is incomplete. There is, for example, no contract if an agreement for a lease fails to specify the date on which the term is to commence.[66] Similarly, an agreement for the sale of land by instalments is not a binding contract if it provides for conveyance of "a proportionate part" as each instalment of the price is paid but fails to specify which part was to be conveyed on each payment.[67]

On the other hand, the agreement does not have to be worked out in meticulous detail. Under the Sale of Goods Act 1979, an agreement for the sale of goods may be binding as soon as the parties have agreed to buy and sell, the remaining details being determined by the standard of reasonable-

[61] *David T. Boyd & Co.* v. *Louis Louca* [1973] 1 Lloyd's Rep. 209; *cf. Siew Soon Wah* v. *Yong Tong Hong* [1973] A.C. 831; *Pagnan S.p.A.* v. *Feed Products Ltd.* [1987] 2 Lloyd's Rep. 601.

[62] *The Tropwind* [1982] 1 Lloyd's Rep. 232.

[63] [1953] 1 Q.B. 543; discussed in *Heisler* v. *Anglo-Dal Ltd.* [1954] 1 W.L.R. 1273; *cf. Slater* v. *Raw*, *The Times*, October 15, 1977; *The Scaptrade* [1981] 2 Lloyd's Rep. 425, 432, (affirmed without reference to this point [1983] 2 A.C. 694), and see *post*, p. 53.

[64] *E. R. J. Lovelock* v. *Exportles* [1968] 1 Lloyd's Rep. 163.

[65] Lücke, 3 Adelaide L.Rev. 46.

[66] *Harvey* v. *Pratt* [1965] 1 W.L.R. 1025; and see *Re Day's Will Trusts* [1962] 1 W.L.R. 1419.

[67] *Bushwall Properties Ltd.* v. *Vortex Properties Ltd.* [1976] 1 W.L.R. 591; Emery, [1976] C.L.J. 215.

ness or by law. Even agreement as to the price is not essential in such a case. Section 8(2) of the Act provides that, if no price is determined by the contract, a reasonable price must be paid. Under section 15(1) of the Supply of Goods and Services Act 1982, a reasonable sum must similarly be paid where a contract for the supply of services fails to fix the remuneration to be paid for them.[68] These statutory provisions assume that the agreement amounts to a contract in spite of its failure to fix the price or remuneration. The very fact that the parties have not reached agreement on this vital point may indicate that there is *no* contract, *e.g.* because the price or remuneration is to be fixed by further agreement.[69] In such a case, the statutory provisions for payment of a reasonable sum do not apply. There may, however, be a claim for payment of such a sum at common law: for example, where work is done in the belief that there was a contract or in the expectation that the negotiations between the parties would result in the conclusion of a contract.[70] Such liability arises in restitution, in spite of the fact that there was *no* contract. It follows that the party doing the work, though he is entitled to a reasonable sum, is not liable in damages, *e.g.* for failing to do the work within a reasonable time.[71] If the claim were made under a contract by virtue of section 15(1) of the 1982 Act, the party doing the work would be both entitled and liable.

Even an agreement for the sale of land dealing only with the barest essentials may be regarded as complete if that was the clear intention of the parties. Thus in *Perry* v. *Suffields Ltd.*[72] an offer to sell a public-house with vacant possession for £7,000 was accepted without qualification. It was held that there was a binding contract, in spite of the fact that many important points such as the date of completion[73] and the question of paying a deposit, were left open.[74] In another case[75] a buyer and seller of corn feed pellets had reached agreement on the "cardinal terms of the deal: product, price, quantity, period of shipment, range of loading ports and governing contract terms."[76] The agreement was held to have contractual force even though the parties had not yet reached agreement on a number of other important points, such as the loading port,[77] the rate of loading and certain payments (other than the price) which might in certain events become payable under the contract. And a publisher's oral commitment to publish a book has been held to amount to a binding contract even though no details were specified in the agreement and nothing more precise was said about the author's remuneration than that he was to be paid a royalty to be agreed, or, in default of agreement, a fair one.[78] In all these cases,

---

68 *Cf.*, at common law, *Way* v. *Latilla* [1937] 3 All E.R. 759; *The Tropwind* [1982] 1 Lloyd's Rep. 232; and see, as to agents' commissions, *post*, p. 643.

69 *e.g. May & Butcher* v. *R.* [1934] 2 K.B. 17n; *Courtney & Fairbairn Ltd.* v. *Tolaini Bros. (Hotels) Ltd.* [1975] 1 W.L.R. 297; Dugdale and Lowe [1976] J.B.L. 312; *Chamberlain* v. *Boodle & King* [1982] 1 W.L.R. 1443 n.

70 *Post*, p. 934.

71 *B.S.C.* v. *Cleveland Bridge & Engineering Co. Ltd.* [1984] 1 All E.R. 504.

72 [1916] 2 Ch. 187; *Elias* v. *George Sahely & Co. (Barbados) Ltd.* [1982] 3 All E.R. 801.

73 *Cf. Storer* v. *Manchester C.C.* [1974] 1 W.L.R. 1403.

74 For the resolution of such points, see *post*, p. 53.

75 *Pagnan S.p.A.* v. *Feed Products Ltd.* [1987] 2 Lloyd's Rep. 601.

76 *Ibid.* p. 611.

77 *Cf. ante*, p. 50 at n. 61.

78 *Malcolm* v. *Chancellor, Masters and Scholars of the University of Oxford, The Times*, December 19, 1990.

the courts took the view that the parties intended to be bound at once in spite of the fact that further significant terms were to be agreed later; and that even their failure to reach such agreement would not invalidate the contract unless without such agreement the contract was unworkable or too uncertain[79] to be enforced.

(2) Further agreement expressly required

An agreement may be incomplete because it expressly requires further agreement to be reached on points as yet left open.

(a) AGREEMENTS "SUBJECT TO CONTRACT." Agreements for the sale of land by private treaty are usually[80] made "subject to contract." Such an agreement is incomplete until the details of a formal contract have been settled and approved by the parties.[81] Even when a formal contract has been approved, it is usually not binding until there has been an exchange of the contractual documents.[82] In such a case there is no uncertainty as to the terms of the agreement, but neither party intends to be legally bound until the "exchange of contracts" takes place.[83] This state of the law, which enables either party with impunity to go back on a concluded agreement, has been described as "a social and moral blot on the law"[84]; and there are indications that the courts are prepared to mitigate the former strictness of the requirement of "exchange of contracts." Thus it has been held that the exchange may be effected by telephone or telex[85]; that certain technical slips in the process may be disregarded[86]; that exchange is not necessary where the parties use the same solicitor[87]; and (in Australia) that where the two parts do not match precisely there may nevertheless be a contract, the discrepancy being remedied by rectification.[88] The parties may also create a binding contract by a subsequent agreement to remove the effect of the words "subject to contract," thus indicating their intention henceforth to

---

[79] See *ante*, p. 49.

[80] Not always: *Storer* v. *Manchester C.C.* [1974] 1 W.L.R. 1403; *Tweddell* v. *Henderson* [1975] 1 W.L.R. 1496, 1501–1502; *Elias* v. *George Sahely & Co. (Barbados) Ltd.*, *supra*.

[81] *Winn* v. *Bull* (1877) 7 Ch.D. 29. *Cf. The Nissos Samos* [1985] 1 Lloyd's Rep. 378, 385; *The Intra Transporter* [1985] 2 Lloyd's Rep. 159, 163, affd. [1986] 2 Lloyd's Rep. 132; *The Junior K* [1988] 2 Lloyd's Rep. 583; (sale of ship and charterparty intended to be "subject to details" not binding before details settled); Debattista [1985] L.M.C.L.Q. 241; *Ronald Preston & Partners* v. *Markheath Securities* [1988] 2 E.G.L.R. 23 (agreement to pay fee to estate agent "subject to contract" not legally binding).

[82] *Eccles* v. *Bryant & Pollock* [1948] Ch. 93; *Santa Fé Land Co. Ltd.* v. *Forestal Land Co. Ltd.* (1910) 26 T.L.R. 534; *cf. Coope* v. *Ridout* [1921] 1 Ch. 291; *Chillingworth* v. *Esche* [1924] 1 Ch. 97; *Raingold* v. *Bromley* [1931] 2 Ch. 307; *D'Silva* v. *Lister House Development Ltd.* [1971] Ch. 17.

[83] *Post*, p. 150.

[84] *Cohen* v. *Nessdale* [1981] 3 All E.R. 118, 128 (affirmed [1982] 2 All E.R. 97); *cf.* Law Commission Papers Nos. 65 and 91.

[85] *Domb* v. *Isoz* [1980] Ch. 548.

[86] *Harrison* v. *Battye* [1975] 1 W.L.R. 58.

[87] *Smith* v. *Mansi* [1963] 1 W.L.R. 26; exchange is also unnecessary in the case of a deed, which takes effect as soon as it has been duly executed (*post* pp. 144–146: *Vincent* v. *Premo Enterprises Ltd.* [1969] 2 Q.B. 609; *D'Silva* v. *Lister House Development Ltd.* [1971] Ch. 17.

[88] *Sindel* v. *Georgiou* (1984) 1454 C.L.R. 661; for rectification see *post*, p. 285.

be legally bound.[89] Subsequent conduct may also give rise to liability on other grounds: where one party to the agreement encourages the other to believe that he will not withdraw, and the other acts to his detriment in reliance on that belief, the former may be liable on the basis of "proprietary estoppel."[90] In "a very strong and exceptional context"[91] the court may even infer that the parties intended to be legally bound when executing the original document, even though it is expressed to be "subject to contract." This was held to be the position where a document containing these words laid down an elaborate time-table and imposed a duty on the purchaser to approve the draft contract (subject only to reasonable amendments) and required him then to exchange contracts.[92] It seems that, in these circumstances, the words "subject to contract" merely meant that the parties had not yet settled all the details of the transaction and did not negative the intention to be bound.

Agreements for the sale of land by auction or by tender are not normally made "subject to contract." The intention of the parties in such cases is to enter into a binding contract as soon as an offer to buy has been accepted. In one case[93] of a sale by tender, the words "subject to contract" were, by a clerical error, typed on one of the contractual documents. In these highly exceptional circumstances,[94] the words were held to be meaningless, so that there was a binding contract.

(b) EXECUTION OF FORMAL DOCUMENT REQUIRED. The effect of a stipulation that an agreement is to be embodied in a formal written document depends on its purpose.[95] One possibility is that the agreement is regarded by the parties as incomplete, or as not intended to be legally binding,[96] until the terms of the formal document are agreed and the document is duly executed in accordance with the terms of the preliminary agreement (*e.g.* by signature).[97] An alternative possibility is that such a document is intended only as a solemn record of an already complete and binding agreement[98]; for example, a contract of insurance is generally regarded as complete as soon as the insurer initials a slip setting out the main terms of

---

[89] *Law* v. *Jones* [1974] Ch. 112, as explained in *Daulia* v. *Four Millbank Nominees* [1978] Ch. 231, 250; *Cohen* v. *Nessdale* [1981] 3 All E.R. 118, 127; [1982] 2 All E.R. 97, 104; see also *Tiverton Estates Ltd.* v. *Wearwell* [1975] Ch. 146; the subsequent agreement would now have to satisfy formal requirements more stringent than those in force at the time of the decisions cited in this note: see *post*, p. 163.

[90] See the discussion at p. 128, *post* of *Att.-Gen. of Hong Kong* v. *Humphreys Estate* (*Queen's Gardens*) [1987] A.C. 114.

[91] *Alpenstow Ltd.* v. *Regalian Properties Ltd.* [1985] 1 W.L.R. 721, 730; Harpum [1986] C.L.J. 356.

[92] *Alpenstow Ltd.* v. *Regalian Properties Ltd.*, *supra.*

[93] *Michael Richard Properties Ltd.* v. *St. Saviour's Parish* [1975] 3 All E.R. 416; Emery [1976] C.L.J. 28.

[94] See *Munton* v. *G.L.C.* [1976] 1 W.L.R. 649.

[95] *Von Hatzfeldt-Wildenburg* v. *Alexander* [1912] 1 Ch. 284, 288–289.

[96] *B.S.C.* v. *Cleveland Bridge & Engineering Co. Ltd.* [1984] 1 All E.R. 504.

[97] *Okura & Co. Ltd.* v. *Navara Shipping Corp. S.A.* [1982] 2 Lloyd's Rep. 537; *cf. R.* v. *Sevenoaks D.C.*, *ex p. Terry* [1985] 3 All E.R. 226; *The Nissos Samos* [1985] 1 Lloyd's Rep. 378, 385; *The Intra Transporter* [1985] 2 Lloyd's Rep. 159, 163; affd. [1986] 2 Lloyd's Rep. 132.

[98] *Rossiter* v. *Miller* (1878) 3 App.Cas. 1124; *cf. Fowle* v. *Freeman* (1804) 9 Ves. 351; *Filby* v. *Hounsell* [1896] 2 Ch. 737; *Branca* v. *Cobarro* [1947] K.B. 854; *E. R. Ives Investments Ltd.* v. *High* [1967] 2 Q.B. 379; *Elias* v. *George Sahely & Co.* (*Barbados*) *Ltd.* [1982] 3 All E.R. 801; *The Blankenstein* [1985] 1 W.L.R. 435; *The Anemone* [1987] 1 Lloyd's Rep. 547; *Malcolm* v. *Chancellor, Masters and Scholars of the University of Oxford*, *The Times*, December 19, 1990; *The Great Marine (No. 2)* [1990] 2 Lloyd's Rep. 250.

the contract, even though the execution of a formal policy is contemplated.[99] The question whether an agreement which expressly requires the execution of a formal document is incomplete depends on the purpose of the requirement in each case; and there is no point multiplying examples.

(c) TERMS LEFT OPEN. The parties to an agreement may be reluctant to commit themselves to a rigid long-term arrangement, particularly when prices and other factors affecting performance are likely to fluctuate. They therefore attempt sometimes to introduce an element of flexibility into the agreement; a number of devices which have been used for this purpose are considered in the following discussion.

(i) *Terms "to be agreed."* One possibility is to provide that certain matters (such as prices, quantities or delivery dates) are to be agreed later, or from time to time. The question whether the resulting agreement is a binding contract then depends primarily on the intention of the parties; and inferences as to this intention may be drawn both from the importance of the matter left over for further agreement, and from the extent to which the parties have acted on the agreement.

Sometimes such agreements have no contractual force. In *May & Butcher* v. *R.*[1] an agreement for the sale of tentage provided that the price, dates of payment and manner of delivery should be agreed from time to time. The House of Lords held that the agreement was incomplete as it left vital matters still to be settled. Had the agreement simply been silent on these points, they could perhaps have been settled in accordance with the provisions of the Sale of Goods Act 1979[2]; or by the standard of reasonableness; but the parties showed that this was not their intention by providing that such points were to be settled by further agreement between them. It has similarly been held that a lease at "a rent to be agreed" was not a binding contract,[3] and that the same was true of an option to purchase land "at a price to be agreed."[4]

In the above cases, the most natural inference to be drawn from the fact that the parties left such an important matter as the price to be settled by further agreement was that they did not intend to be bound until they had agreed on the price. But where it can be inferred that they intended to be bound immediately, in spite of the provision requiring further agreement, a binding contract can be created at once[5]; for the courts are "reluctant to

[99] *Ionides* v. *Pacific Insurance Co.* (1871) L.R. 6 Q.B. 674, 684; *Cory* v. *Patton* (1872) L.R. 7 Q.B. 304; *General Reinsurance Corp. v. Forsakringsaktiebolaget Fennia Patria* [1983] Q.B. 856; *Hadenfayre Ltd.* v. *British National Insurance Soc. Ltd.* [1984] 2 Lloyd's Rep. 393; *The Zephyr* [1984] 1 Lloyd's Rep. 56, 69–70 (reversed in part on other grounds [1985] 2 Lloyd's Rep. 529); under Marine Insurance Act 1906, s.22, the contract is complete, though evidence of it may not be admissible: *post*, p. 165. Under an "open cover" arrangement, it is not the initialing of the slip but the declaration of the insured that creates the obligation of the insurer: *Citadel Insurance Co.* v. *Atlantic Union Insurance Co.* [1985] 2 Lloyd's Rep. 543.

[1] [1934] 2 K.B. 17n.; *cf. British Homophone Ltd.* v. *Kunz* (1935) 152 L.T. 589; *The Shamah* [1981] 1 Lloyd's Rep. 40, 83; *The Good Helmsman* [1981] Lloyd's Rep. 377, 409. *Pancommerce S.A.* v. *Veecheema B.V.* [1983] 2 Lloyd's Rep. 304, 307; *The Gudermes* [1985] 2 Lloyd's Rep. 623.

[2] *Ante*, p. 51.

[3] *King's Motors (Oxford) Ltd.* v. *Lax* [1970] 1 W.L.R. 426; *cf. King* v. *King* (1981) 41 P. & C.R. 311 (rent review clause).

[4] See *Brown* v. *Gould* [1972] Ch. 52 (where, however, the option was binding as it specified *criteria* for determining the price: *post*, p. 56).

[5] *Pagnan S.p.A.* v. *Freed Products Ltd.* [1987] 2 Lloyds's Rep. 601.

hold void for uncertainty any provision that was intended to have legal effect."[6] This judicial attitude is illustrated by *Foley* v. *Classique Coaches Ltd.*[7] The plaintiff owned a petrol-filling station and adjoining land. He sold the land to the defendants on condition that they should enter into an agreement to buy petrol for the purpose of their motor-coach business exclusively from him. This agreement was duly executed, but the defendants broke it, and argued that it was incomplete because it provided that the petrol should be bought "at a price agreed by the parties from time to time." The Court of Appeal rejected this argument and held that, in default of agreement, a reasonable price must be paid.[8] *May & Butcher* v. *R.* was distinguished on a number of grounds: the agreement in *Foley's* cse was contained in a stamped document; it was believed by both parties to be binding and had been acted upon for a number of years; it contained an arbitration clause in a somewhat unusual form which was construed to apply "to any failure to agree as to the price"[9]; and it formed part of a larger bargain under which the defendants had acquired the land at a price which was no doubt fixed on the assumption that they would be bound to buy all their petrol from the plaintiff.[10] While none of these factors in itself is conclusive,[11] their cumulative effect seems to be sufficient to distinguish the two cases.[12]

Thus an agreement is not incomplete *merely* because it calls for some further agreement between the parties.[13] Of course the parties may later fail to agree on the matters left outstanding. But this failure only vitiates the contract if it makes the agreement "unworkable or void for uncertainty."[14] Often, the failure will not have this effect, for it may be possible to resolve the uncertainty in one of the ways already discussed, *e.g.* by applying the standard of reasonableness.[15] There can be no doubt as to the commercial convenience of this approach. Businessmen often intend to make agreements binding in principle without being able or willing at the

---

[6] *Brown* v. *Gould* [1972] Ch. 53, 57–58; *cf. Smith* v. *Morgan* [1971] 1 W.L.R. 803, 807; *Snelling* v. *John G. Snelling Ltd.* [1973] 1 Q.B. 87, 93; *Queensland Electricity Generating Board* v. *New Hope Colliery Pty. Ltd.* [1989] 1 Lloyd's Rep. 205, 210.

[7] [1934] 2 K.B. 1.

[8] *Cf. British Bank for Foreign Trade* v. *Novinex* [1949] 1 K.B. 623; *Sykes (Wessex) Ltd.* v. *Fine Fare Ltd.* [1967] 1 Lloyds's Rep. 53; *Beer* v. *Bowden* [1981] 1 W.L.R. 522; *Thomas Bates & Sons Ltd.* v. *Wyndham's (Lingerie) Ltd.* [1981] 1 W.L.R. 505, 518–519; *The Tropwind* [1982] 1 Lloyd's Rep. 232, 236; *Voest Alpine Intertrading GmbH* v. *Chevron International Oil Co. Ltd.* [1987] 2 Lloyd's Rep. 547; *Malcolm* v. *Chancellor, Masters and Scholars of the University of Oxford, The Times*, December 19, 1990.

[9] [1934] 2 K.B. 10; the clause covered disputes as to "the *subject matter or* construction of this agreement," while the arbitration clause in *May & Butcher* v. *R.* covered "disputes with reference to or arising out of this agreement." For the distinction between the two forms of clause, see *Heyman* v. *Darwins* [1942] A.C. 356, 385, 392; *cf.* also *Vosper Thorneycroft Ltd.* v. *Ministry of Defence* [1976] 1 Lloyd's Rep. 58; *Queensland Electricity Generating Board* v. *New Hope Collieries Pty. Ltd.* [1989] 1 Lloyds's Rep. 205.

[10] Scrutton L.J. said at p. 7 that he was glad to decide in favour of the plaintiff "because I do not regard the appellants' [defendants'] contention as an honest one."

[11] R.S.T.C., 49 L.Q.R. 316.

[12] *Foley's* case was approved by the House of Lords in *G. Scammell & Nephew Ltd.* v. *Ouston* [1941] A.C. 251.

[13] *Cf. Wilson Smithett & Cape (Sugar) Ltd.* v. *Bangladesh Sugar & Food Industries Ltd.* [1986] 1 Lloyd's Rep. 378, 386.

[14] *Pagnan S.p.A.* v. *Feed Products Ltd.* [1987] 2 Lloyd's Rep. 601, 619.

[15] *Ante*, p. 49; or by imposing on one party the duty to resolve the uncertainty: p. 50 at n. 61; *Pagnan S.p.A.* v. *Feed Products Ltd., supra.*

time precisely to settle all the details. For example, contracts of insurance may be made "at a premium to be arranged" when immediate cover is required but there is no time to go into all the details at once: such agreements are perfectly valid and a reasonable premium must be paid.[16] All this is not to say that the courts will hold parties bound when they have not yet reached substantial agreement[17]; but once they have reached such agreement it is not necessarily fatal that some points (even important ones) remain to be settled by further negotiation.

(ii) *Options and rights of pre-emption.* We have seen that an option to purchase land "at a price to be agreed" is not a binding contract; but such an option must be distinguished from a "right of pre-emption" by which a landowner agrees to give the purchaser the right to buy "at a figure to be agreed" should the landowner wish to sell.[18] An *option* is an offer which becomes a contract of sale when the purchaser accepts it by exercising the option; and it cannot have this effect where it fails to specify the price. A *right of pre-emption* is not itself an offer but an undertaking to make an offer in certain specified future circumstances. An agreement conferring such a right is therefore not void for uncertainty merely because it fails to specify the price. It obliges the land-owner to offer the land to the purchaser at the price at which he is in fact prepared to sell; and if the purchaser accepts that offer there is no uncertainty as to price.[19] This is so even though the parties have described the right as an "option" when its true legal nature is that of a right of pre-emption.[20]

(iii) *Criteria or machinery specified in the agreement.* An agreement may fail to specify matters such as price or quality but lay down criteria for determining those matters. For example, in *Hillas & Co. Ltd.* v. *Arcos Ltd.*[21] an option to buy timber was held binding even though it did not specify the price, since it provided for the calculation of the price by reference to the official price list. Similarly, an option to renew a lease "at a rent to be fixed having regard to the market value of the premises" has been held binding as it provided a criterion (though not a very precise one) for resolving the uncertainty.[22] Even a provision that hire under a charterparty was in certain specified events to be "equitably decreased by an amount to be mutually agreed" has been held to sufficiently certain to be enforced: it was said that "equitably" meant "fairly and reasonably"[23] and that a "purely objective standard has been prescribed."[24]

Alternatively, the agreement may provide *machinery* for resolving matters originally left open. Perhaps the most striking illustration of this

---

[16] *Glicksten & Son Ltd.* v. *State Assurance Co.* (1922) 10 Ll.L.R. 604; *cf.* Marine Insurance Act 1906, s.31(2); contrast *American Airline Inc.* v. *Hope* [1973] 1 Lloyd's Rep. 233, affd. [1974] 2 Lloyd's Rep. 301 ("at an additional premium *and geographical area* to be agreed").

[17] See *Shakleford's Case* (1866) L.R. 1 Ch.App. 567; *Bertel* v. *Neveux* (1878) 39 L.T. 257; *Loftus* v. *Roberts* (1902) 18 T.L.R. 532; *The Intra Transporter* [1986] 2 Lloyd's Rep. 132; *Pagnan S.p.A.* v. *Granaria B.V.* [1986] 2 Lloyd's Rep. 547.

[18] *Pritchard* v. *Briggs* [1980] Ch. 339.

[19] *Smith* v. *Morgan* [1971] 1 W.L.R. 803; *cf. Snelling* v. *John G. Snelling* [1973] 1 Q.B. 87, 93; *Miller* v. *Lakefield Estates Ltd.* [1988] 1 E.G.L.R. 212 (where some doubts were expressed about *Smith* v. *Morgan*).

[20] See *Fraser* v. *Thames Television Ltd.* [1984] Q.B. 44.

[21] (1932) 147 L.T. 503; *cf. Miller* v. *F. A. Sadd & Son Ltd.* [1981] 3 All E.R. 265.

[22] *Brown* v. *Gould* [1972] Ch. 53.

[23] *Didymi Corp.* v. *Atlantic Lines & Navigation Co. Inc.* [1988] 2 Lloyd's Rep. 108, 116, 118.

[24] *Ibid.* p. 117.

possibility is provided by cases in which such matters are to be resolved by the decision of one party: for example a term, by which interest rates are expressed to be variable on notification by the creditor, is perfectly valid.[25] Agreements are *a fortiori* not incomplete merely because they provide that outstanding points shall be determined by arbitration[26] or by the valuation of a third party. The Sale of Goods Act 1979 provides that if the third party "cannot or does not make the valuation, the agreement is avoided"[27]; but an agreement is not necessarily ineffective merely because the agreed machinery fails to work. Thus in *Sudbrook Trading Estate Ltd.* v. *Eggleton*[28] a lease gave the tenant the option to purchase the premises "at such price as may be agreed upon by two Valuers, one to be nominated by" each party. The landlord having refused to appoint a valuer, the House of Lords held that the option did not fail for uncertainty. It amounted, on its true construction, to an agreement to sell at a reasonable price to be determined by the valuers; and the stipulation that each party should nominate one of the valuers was merely "subsidiary and inessential."[29] So long as the agreed machinery is of this character,[30] the court can, on its failure to operate, substitute other machinery: for example, it can itself fix the price with the aid of expert evidence. This is so not only where the agreed machinery fails because of one party's refusal to operate it,[31] but also where it fails for some other reason, such as the refusal of a designated valuer to make the valuation.[32]

(d) CONTRACT TO MAKE A CONTRACT. In some cases of incomplete agreements it is said that there is a "contract to make a contract." This expression may refer to a number of different situations. One possibility is that the parties may agree to execute a formal document incorporating terms on which they have previously agreed. Such a "contract to make a contract" is perfectly binding.[33] For example, in *Morton* v. *Morton*[34] an agreement "to enter into a separation deed containing the following clauses" (of which a summary was then given) was held to be a binding contract. The grant of an option to purchase can similarly be described as a contract by which one party binds himself to enter into a further contract if the other so elects; and neither of these contracts is void for uncertainty.[35] But a further possibility is that the parties have simply agreed to negotiate. In spite of dicta to the contrary,[36] it has been held that a mere agreement to negotiate is not a contract "because it is too uncertain to have any binding

---

[25] *Lombard Tricity Finance Ltd.* b. *Paton* [1989] 1 All E.R. 918.

[26] *Arcos Ltd.* v. *Aronson* (1930) 36 Ll.L.R. 108; *cf. Thomas Bates & Son Ltd.* v. *Wyndham's (Lingerie) Ltd.* [1981] 1 W.L.R. 505, where a lease was rectified (*post*, p. 286) to include such a clause; *Queensland Electricity Generating Board* v. *New Hope Collieries Pty. Ltd.* [1989] 1 Lloyd's Rep. 205.

[27] Sale of Goods Act 1979, s.9(1); *cf. Pym* v. *Campbell* (1856) 6 E. & B. 370.

[28] [1982] 1 A.C. 444; Robertshaw, 46 M.L.R. 493.

[29] *Re Malpas* [1985] Ch. 42, 50; *Tito* v. *Waddell* (*No.* 2) [1977] Ch. 106, 314; *Didymi Corp.* v. *Atlantic Lines & Navigation Co. Inc.* [1988] 2 Lloyd's Rep. 108, 115.

[30] *i.e.* not if it is "essential."

[31] As in the *Sudbrook* case, *supra*.

[32] As in *Re Malpas*, *supra*.

[33] Subject to statutory exceptions: see Consumer Credit Act 1974, s.59.

[34] [1942] 1 All E.R. 273.

[35] See *The Messiniaki Bergen* [1983] 1 Lloyd's Rep. 424, 426.

[36] *Chillingworth* v. *Esche* [1924] 1 Ch. 97, 113; *Hillas & Co. Ltd.* v. *Arcos Ltd.* (1932) 147 L.T. 503, 515. See F.P., 48 L.Q.R. 141; F.W. McC., *Ibid.* 310; Williams, 6 M.L.R. 81.

force."[37] It therefore does not impose any obligation to negotiate, or to use best endeavours to reach agreement,[38] or to accept proposals that "with hindsight appear to be reasonable."[39] The position is different once the parties have reached agreement on all essential points and so established a contract. The court may then imply a term that they are to negotiate in good faith so as to settle outstanding details which are to be incorporated in the formal document setting out the full terms of the contract between them.[40]

SECTION 6. CONDITIONAL AGREEMENTS

An agreement is conditional if its operation depends on an event which is not certain to occur. Discussions of this topic are made difficult by the fact that in the law of contract the word "condition" bears many senses: it is "a chameleon-like word which which takes on its meanings from its surroundings."[41] At this stage, we are concerned with only one of these meanings; but to clear the ground it is necessary to draw a number of preliminary distinctions.

The word "condition" may refer either to an *event*, or to a *term* of a contract (as in the phrase "conditions of sale"[42]). Where "condition" refers to an event, that event may be either an occurrence which neither party undertakes to bring about, or the performance by one party of his undertaking. The first possibility is illustrated by a contract by which A is to work for B, and B is to pay A £50, "if it rains tomorrow." Here the obligations of both parties are contingent on the happening of the specified event which may be described as a *contingent* condition. The second possibility is illustrated by the ordinary case in which A agrees to work for B at a weekly wage payable at the end of the week. Here the contract is immediately binding on both parties, but B is not liable to pay until A has performed his promise to work. Such performance is a condition of B's liability,[43] and, as A has promised to render it, the condition may be described as *promissory*.[44] In this Chapter our sole concern is with contingent conditions; promissory conditions will be discussed in Chapter 18.[45]

Contingent conditions may be precedent or subsequent. The condition is precedent if it provides that the contract is not to be binding until the specified event occurs. It is subsequent if it provides that a previously binding

---

37 *Courtney & Fairbairn Ltd.* v. *Tolaini Bros. (Hotels) Ltd.* [1975] 1 W.L.R. 297, 301; *cf. Von Hatzfeldt-Wildenburg* v. *Alexander* [1912] 1 Ch. 284, 249; *Malozzi* v. *Carapelli S.p.A.* [1976] 1 Lloyd's Rep. 407; *The Scaptrade* [1981] 2 Lloyd's Rep. 425, 432 (affirmed without reference to this point [1983] 2 A.C. 694); *Nile Co. for the Export of Agricultural Crops* v. *H. & J. M. Bennett (Commodities) Ltd.* [1986] 1 Lloyd's Rep. 555, 587; *The Jing Hong Hai* [1989] 2 Lloyd's Rep. 523, 526.

38 *The Scaptrade*, (*supra*, n. 37) [1981] 2 Lloyd's Rep. at p. 432; *The Junior K.* [1988] 2 Lloyd's Rep. 583. Contrast, in the United States, *Hoffman* v. *Red Owl Stores Inc.*, 133 N.W. 2d. 267 (1965).

39 *Pagnan S.p.A.* v. *Granaria BV* [1985] 1 Lloyd's Rep. 256, 270; affd. [1986] 2 Lloyd's Rep. 547.

40 *Donwin Productions Ltd.* v. *E.M.I. Films Ltd.*, *The Times*, March 9, 1984.

41 *The Varenna* [1984] Q.B. 599, 618.

42 *Property and Bloodstock Ltd.* v. *Emerton* [1968] Ch. 94, 118; *cf.* also *post*, p. 000.

43 *Post*, p. 662.

44 For the distinction between *promissory* and *contingent* condition see Chalmers, *Sale of Goods* (18th ed.) Appendix 2, Note A.

45 *Post*, pp. 662–667; 689–703.

contract is to determine on the occurrence of the event: *e.g.* where A contracts to pay an allowance to B until B marries.[46]

An agreement which is subject to a contingent condition precedent is not fully binding until the specified event occurs; nor does either party undertake that it will occur. But an agreement subject to such a condition may impose some degree of obligation on the parties or on one of them. Whether it has this effect, and if so what degree of obligation is imposed, depends on the true construction of the condition.[47]

One possibility is that, before the event occurs, each party is free to withdraw from the agreement. In *Pym* v. *Campbell*[48] an agreement for the sale of a patent was executed, but the parties at the same time agreed that it should not "be the agreement" unless a third party approved of the invention. He did not approve, and it was held that the buyer was not liable for refusing to perform. The written agreement was "not an agreement at all."[49] If this is taken literally, either party could have withdrawn even before the third party had given his opinion.

A second possibility is that, before the event occurs, the main agreement is not binding; but that, so long as the event can still occur, one (or both) of the parties cannot withdraw. Thus in *Smith* v. *Butler*[50] A bought land from B on condition that a loan to B (secured by a mortgage on the premises) would be transferred to A.[51] It was held that A could not withdraw before the time fixed for completion: he was bound to wait until then to see whether B could arrange the transfer.

A third possibility is that, before the events, the main agreement is not binding; but that in the meantime neither party must do anything to prevent the occurrence of the event. Thus in *Mackay* v. *Dick*[52] an excavating machine was sold on condition that it could excavate at a specified rate on the buyer's property; but the buyer refused to provide facilities for a proper trial. It was held that the buyer was in breach. Similarly, the seller would have been liable in damages, had he refused to subject the machine to a proper test. The same principle is, again, illustrated by a case[53] in which a professional footballer was transferred for a fee, part of which was to be paid only after he had scored 20 goals. Before he had done so, the new club dropped him from their first team, and they were held to be in breach as they had not given the player a reasonable opportunity to score the 20 goals.

---

[46] *Cf. Brown* v. *Knowsley B.C.* [1986] I.R.L.R. 102 (appointment to "last only as long as sufficient funds were provided" from specified sources), and (*semble*) *Gyllenhammar & Partners International* v. *Sour Brodogradevna Industria* [1989] 2 Lloyd's Rep. 403 (contract to "become null and void" if certain consents were not obtained).

[47] For special difficulties where the condition is implied, see *Bentworth Finance Ltd.* v. *Lubert* [1968] 1 Q.B. 680; Carnegie 31 M.L.R. 78.

[48] (1856) 6 E. & B. 370.

[49] *Ibid.* p. 374.

[50] [1900] 1 Q.B. 694, *cf. Felixstowe Dock & Ry. Co.* v. *British Transport Docks Bd.* [1976] 2 Lloyd's Rep. 656; *Alan Estates Ltd.* v. *W. G. Stores Ltd.* [1982] Ch. 511, 520.

[51] On agreements "subject to finance," see Coote, 40 Conv. (N.S.) 37; Furmston, 3 O.J.L.S. 438, discussing *Meehan* v. *Jones* (1982) 149 C.L.R. 571.

[52] (1881) 6 App.Cas. 251. The condition is described as subsequent in *Colley* v. *Overseas Exporters* [1921] 3 K.B. 302, 308. *Cf.* also *Shipping Corp. of India* v. *Naviera Letasa* [1976] 1 Lloyd's Rep. 132 and *C.I.A. Barca de Panama S.A.* v. *George Wimpey & Co. Ltd.* [1980] 1 Lloyd's Rep. 598.

[53] *Bournemouth & Boscombe Athletic F.C.* v. *Manchester United F.C.*, *The Times*, May 22, 1980. *Cf.* also *post*, p. 645.

The duty not to prevent the occurrence of the condition has been explained as resting on an implied term and this explanation limits the scope of the duty in a number of ways. For example, the implied term may be only to the effect that a party will not *deliberately* prevent the occurrence of the condition[54]; or (even more narrowly) that he will not *wrongfully* do so.[55] The latter type of implication may allow a party to engage in certain kinds of prevention but not in others: for example, it may allow a company which has promised an employee the opportunity of earning a bonus to deprive him of that opportunity by going out of business, but not by simply dismissing him, before the bonus has become due.[56] The implied term can also be excluded by an express contrary provision and, in particular, by a provision making the operation of a contract depend on the "satisfaction" of one of the parties with the subject-matter or other aspects relating to the other's performance. Thus it has been held that there was no contract where a house was bought "subject to satisfactory mortgage"[57] and where a boat was bought "subject to satisfactory survey."[58] The buyer in such cases is not bound if he expresses his dissatisfaction, in spite of the fact that such expression is a deliberate act on his part which prevents the occurrence of the condition. The same is true where goods are bought on approval and the buyer does not approve them.[59] But in some cases in the present group the courts do place restrictions on the freedom of action of the party on whose satisfaction the operation of the contract depends. Thus where a ship was sold "subject to satisfactory completion of two trial voyages" it was said that such a stipulation was to be construed as "subject to bona fides"[60]; and it has also been held that the party on whose satisfaction the operation of the contract depends must at least provide facilities for, or not impede, the inspection referred to in the agreement.[61] Of course if the result of the inspection is unsatisfactory, the principal obligation of the contract will not take effect.[62]

A fourth possibility is that, before the event occurs, the main agreement is not binding but that one of the parties undertakes to use reasonable efforts to bring the event about (without absolutely undertaking that his efforts will succeed). This construction was applied, for instance, where land was sold subject to the condition that the purchaser should obtain

[54] See *Blake & Co.* v. *Sohn* [1969] 1 W.L.R. 1412.

[55] See *Thompson* v. *ASDA-MFI Group plc* [1988] Ch. 241.

[56] Example based on *Thompson* v. *ASDA-MFI Group plc*, *supra* and on *post*, p. 645; but effect may be given to *express* term permitting an employer to act in this way: see *Micklefield* v. *S.A.C. Technology Ltd.* [1990] 1 W.L.R. 1002.

[57] *Lee-Parker* v. *Izett* (*No.* 2) [1975] 1 W.L.R. 775; distinguished in *Janmohammed* v. *Hassam*, *The Times*, June 10, 1976.

[58] *Astra Trust Ltd.* v. *Adams & Williams* [1969] 1 Lloyd's Rep. 81 doubted in *The Merak* [1976] 2 Lloyd's Rep. 250, 254 and in *Ee* v. *Kahar* (1979) 40 P. & C.R. 223 (as to which see *infra*, n. 61); *cf. Wishart* v. *National Association of Citizens Advice Bureaux*, *The Times*, June 30, 1990.

[59] *Cf.* Sale of Goods Act 1979, s.18, rule 4.

[60] *The John S. Darbyshire* [1977] 2 Lloyd's Rep. 457, 464; *cf. BV Oliehandel Jongkind* v. *Coastal International Ltd.* [1983] 2 Lloyd's Rep. 463; *The Nissos Samos* [1985] 1 Lloyd's Rep. 378, 385; contrast *The Junior K* [1988 2 Lloyd's Rep. 583, 589 (where the words were held to negative contractual intention). See also *El Awadi* v. *Bank of Credit & Commerce International S.A.* [1990] 1 Q.B. 606, 619.

[61] *The Merak* [1976] 2 Lloyd's Rep. 250; *cf. Ee* v. *Kahar* (1979) 40 P. & C.R. 223 (where the sale was simply "subject to survey"—omitting the word "satisfactory"—thus falling, it is submitted, within the principle of *Mackay* v. *Dick*, *supra* n. 52).

[62] As in *The John S. Darbyshire* [1977] 2 Lloyd's Rep. 457.

planning permission to use the land as a transport depot: he was bound to make reasonable efforts to obtain the permission, but he was free from liability when those efforts failed.[63] Similarly, where goods are sold "subject to export (or import) licence," the party whose duty it is to obtain the licence[64] does not prima facie promise absolutely that a licence will be obtained,[65] but only undertakes to make reasonable efforts to that end.[66] The principal obligations to buy and sell will not take effect if no licence is obtained[67]; but if the party who should have made reasonable efforts has failed to do so he will be liable in damages,[68] unless he can show that any such efforts, which he could have made would (if made) have necessarily have been unsuccessful.[69] The same principles have been applied where an agreement was made "subject to the approval of the court"; and where an agreement was made to assign a lease which could only be assigned with the consent of the landlord. In such cases the requisite approval or consent must be sought; but the main agreement does not become binding until the approval or consent is given,[70] and if it is refused the principal obligation will not take effect.[71]

It will be seen that in cases falling within the second, third and fourth categories discussed above, a distinction must be drawn between two types of obligation: the principal obligation of each party (*e.g.* to buy and sell) and a subsidiary obligation, *i.e.* one not to withdraw, not to prevent occurrence of the condition, or to make reasonable efforts to bring it about. One possible view is that the party who fails to perform the subsidiary obligation is to be treated as if the condition had occurred; and that he is then liable on the principal obligation. Thus in *Mackay* v. *Dick*[72] the buyer was held liable *for the price*; but there was no discussion as to the remedy. In principle it seems wrong to hold him so liable, for such a result ignores the

---

63 *Hargreaves Transport Ltd.* v. *Lynch* [1969] 1 W.L.R. 215 (condition not satisfied); *Richard West & Partners (Inverness) Ltd.* v. *Dick* [1969] 2 Ch. 424 (similar condition satisfied); contrast *Tesco Stores Ltd.* v. *Gibson* (1970) 214 E.G. 835 (no obligation on purchaser to apply for planning permission).

64 As to which party has this duty, see *H. O. Brandt & Co.* v. *H. N. Morris & Co.* [1917] 2 K.B. 784; *A. V. Pound & Co.* v. *M. W. Hardy & Co.* [1956] A.C. 588.

65 The prima facie rule may be excluded by express words which do, on their true construction, impose an absolute duty; *e.g. Peter Cassidy Seed Co. Ltd.* v. *Osuustukkukauppa* [1957] 1 W.L.R. 273; *C. Czarnikow Ltd.* v. *Centrala Handlu Zagranicznego "Rolimpex"* [1979] A.C. 351, 371; *Congimex Companhia Geral, etc., S.A.R.L.* v. *Tradax Export S.A.* [1983] 1 Lloyd's Rep. 250; *Pagnan S.p.A.* v. *Tradax Ocean Transport S.A.* [1987] 3 All E.R. 565; Yates and Carter, 1 J.C.L. 57.

66 *Re Anglo-Russian Merchant Traders and John Batt & Co. (London) Ltd.* [1917] 2 K.B. 679; *Coloniale Import-Export* v. *Loumidis & Sons* [1978] 2 Lloyd's Rep. 560; *Overseas Buyers Ltd.* v. *Granadex S.A.* [1980] 2 Lloyd's Rep. 605. Where the contract is expressly subject to the approval of a public authority, there may not even be a duty to make reasonable efforts to secure that approval: see *Gyllenhammar Partners International* v. *Sour Brodegradevna Industria* [1989] 2 Lloyd's Rep. 403.

67 *Charles H. Windschuegl Ltd.* v. *Alexander Pickering & Co. Ltd.* (1950) 84 Ll.L.Rep 89, 92–93; *Brauer & Co. (Great Britain) Ltd.* v. *James Clark (Brush Materials) Ltd.* [1952] 2 All E.R. 497, 501; *cf.* the cases on sales of goods "to arrive" discussed in Benjamin's *Sale of Goods* (3rd ed.), §§ 1942–1947.

68 *e.g. Malik* v. *C.E.T.A.* [1974] 1 Lloyd's Rep. 279; *Agroexport* v. *Cie Européenne de Céréales* [1974] 1 Lloyd's Rep. 499.

69 See Benjamin's *Sale of Goods* (3rd ed.), § 1569; *Overseas Buyers Ltd.* v. *Granadex S.A.*, *supra*, at p. 612.

70 *Smallman* v. *Smallman* [1972] Fam. 25.

71 *Shires* v. *Brock* (1977) 247 E.G. 127.

72 (1881) 6 App.Cas. 251, *ante*, p. 59.

possibility that the machine might have failed to come up to the standard required by the contract, even if proper facilities for trial had been provided. It is submitted that the correct result in cases of this kind is to award *damages* for breach of the subsidiary obligation: in assessing such damages, the court can take into account the possibility that the condition might not have occurred, even if there had been no such breach.[73] To hold the party in breach liable for the full performance promised by him, on the fiction that the condition had occurred, seems to introduce into this branch of the law a punitive element that is inappropriate to a contractual action.[74] The most recent authority rightly holds that this doctrine of "fictional fulfilment" of a condition does not form part of English law.[75]

Where a condition is inserted entirely for the benefit of one party, that party may waive the condition. He can then sue[76] and be sued[77] on the contract as if the condition had occurred. Obviously this rule does not apply to cases falling within the first of the categories discussed above, in which there is no contract at all before the condition occurs.

---

[73] *Bournemouth & Boscombe Athletic F.C.* v. *Manchester United F.C.*, *The Times*, May 22, 1980; *cf. The Blankenstein* [1985] 1 W.L.R. 435 (*post*, p. 749); *Alpha Trading Ltd.* v. *Dunshaw-Patten Ltd.* [1981] Q.B. 290 (*post* p. 646); *George Moundreas & Co. S.A.* v. *Navimpex Centrala Navala* [1985] 2 Lloyd's Rep. 515.

[74] *Cf. post*, p. 829.

[75] *Thompson* v. *ASDA-MFI Group plc* [1988] Ch. 241, 266 (where the condition was said at p. 251 to be subsequent).

[76] *Wood Preservation Ltd.* v. *Prior* [1969] 1 W.L.R. 1077; contrast *Heron Garages Properties Ltd.* v. *Moss* [1974] 1 W.L.R. 148.

[77] *McKillop* v. *McMullan* [1979] N.I. 85.

CHAPTER THREE

CONSIDERATION[1]

SECTION 1. INTRODUCTION

1. General

IN English law, a promise is not, as a general rule, binding as a contract unless it is either made in a deed[2] or supported by some "consideration." The purpose of the requirement of consideration is to put some legal limits on the enforceability of agreements even where they are intended to be legally binding[3] and are not vitiated by some factor such as mistake, misrepresentation, duress or illegality.[4] The existence of such limits is not a peculiarity of English law: for example, in some civil law countries certain promises which in England are not binding for "want of consideration" cannot be enforced unless they are made in some special form, *e.g.* by a notarised writing.[5] The view was, indeed, at one time put forward that consideration was only evidence of the intention of the parties to be bound, and that (at any rate in the case of certain commercial contracts), such evidence could equally well be furnished by writing.[6] But the view that agreements (other than those contained in deeds), were binding without consideration merely because they were in writing was rejected in England over 200 years ago,[7] though it has from time to time been revived as a proposal for law reform.[8] The present position therefore is that English law limits the enforceability of agreements (not in deeds) by reference to a complex and multifarious body of rules known as "the doctrine of consideration."

The basic feature of that doctrine is the idea of reciprocity: "something of value in the eye of the law"[9] must be given for a promise in order to make it enforceable as a contract. An informal gratuitous promise therefore does not amount to a contract.[10] A person or body to whom a promise of a gift is made from purely charitable or sentimental motives gives nothing for the promise; and the claims of such a promisee are obviously less compelling than those of a person who has given (or promised) some return for the promise.[11] The invalidity of informal gratuitous promises of this kind can also be supported on the ground that their enforcement could

---

[1] Shatwell, 1 Sydney L.R. 289; Sutton, *Consideration Reconsidered*.

[2] *Post*, p. 144.

[3] *Post*, Chap. 4.

[4] *Post*, Chaps. 8–11.

[5] See generally von Mehren, 72 Harv.L.Rev. 1009.

[6] *Pillans* v. *Van Mierop* (1765) 3 Burr. 1663.

[7] *Rann* v. *Hughes* (1778) 7 T.R. 350 n.; 4 Bro. P.C. 27. In the United States, writing is in many jurisdictions, at least for some purposes, regarded as a substitute for consideration: see Fuller & Eisenberg, *Basic Contract Law* (4th ed.), pp. 17–18.

[8] *Post* p. 147.

[9] *Thomas* v. *Thomas* (1842) 2 Q.B. 851, 859.

[10] *Re Hudson* (1885) 54 L.J. Ch. 811; *Re Cory* (1912) 29 T.L.R. 18; *Williams* v. *Roffey Bros. & Nicholls (Contractors Ltd.)* [1991] 1 Q.B. 1, 19.

[11] *Cf.* Eisenberg, 47 U. of Chi.L.Rev. 1.

prejudice third parties such as creditors of the promisor.[12] Such promises, too, may be rashly made[13]; and the requirements of executing a deed or giving value provide at least some protection against this danger.

The doctrine of consideration has, however, also struck at many promises which were not "gratuitous" in any ordinary or commercial sense. These applications of the doctrine were brought within its scope by stressing that consideration had to be not merely "something of value," but "something of value *in the eye of the law*."[14] The law in certain cases refused to recognise the "value" of acts or promises which might well be regarded as valuable by a layman. This refusal was based on many disparate policies; so that "promises without consideration" included many different kinds of transactions which, at first sight, had little in common.[15] It is this fact which is the cause of the very great complexity of the doctrine; and which has also led to its occasional unwarranted extensions and hence to demands for reform of the law.[16]

2. Definitions

(1) Benefit and detriment

The traditional definition of consideration concentrates on the requirement that "something of value" must be given and accordingly states that consideration is either some detriment to the promisee (in that he may give value) or some benefit to the promisor (in that he may receive value).[17] Usually, this detriment and benefit are merely the same thing looked at from different points of view. Thus payment by a buyer is consideration for the seller's promise to deliver and can be described as a detriment to the buyer or as a benefit to the seller; and conversely delivery by a seller is consideration for the buyer's promise to pay and can be described either as a detriment to the seller or as a benefit to the buyer. It should be emphasised that these statements relate to the consideration *for the promise of each party* looked at separately. For example, the seller suffers a "detriment" when he delivers the goods and this enables him to enforce the buyer's promise to pay the price. It is quite irrelevant that the seller has made a good bargain and so gets a benefit from the performance of the contract. What the law is concerned with is the consideration *for a promise*—not the consideration *for a contract*.

(a) EITHER SUFFICIENT. Under the traditional definition it is sufficient if there is either a detriment to the promisee or a benefit to the promisor. Thus detriment to the promisee suffices even though the promisor does not

---

[12] *Eastwood* v. *Kenyon* (1840) 11 A. & E. 438, 451.

[13] *Beaton* v. *McDivitt* (1988) 13 N.S.W.L.R. 162, 170.

[14] *Supra*, at n. 9; *post*, p. 65.

[15] *Cf.* Corbin, *Contracts*, Vol. I, p. 489: "The doctrine of consideration is many doctrines."

[16] See *post* p. 146.

[17] *Currie* v. *Misa* (1875) L.R. 10 Ex. 153, 162. See also *Barber* v. *Fox* (1682) 2 Wms. Saund. 134, n. (e); *Cooke* v. *Oxley* (1790) 3 T.R. 653, 654; *Jones* v. *Ashburnham* (1804) 4 East 455; *Bainbridge* v. *Firmstone* (1838) 8 A. & E. 743, 744; *Thomas* v. *Thomas* (1842) 2 Q.B. 851, 859; *Bolton* v. *Madden* (1873) L.R. 9 Q.B. 55, 56; *Gore* v. *Van der Lann* [1967] 2 Q.B. 31, 42; *Argy Trading Development Co. Ltd.* v. *Lapid Developments Ltd.* [1977] 1 W.L.R. 444, 455; *Midland Bank & Trust Co. Ltd.* v. *Green* [1981] A.C. 513, 531; *R.* v. *Braithwaite* [1983] 1 W.L.R. 385, 391; *Johnsey Estates Ltd.* v. *Lewis Manley (Engineering) Ltd.* [1987] 2 E.G.L.R. 69, 70.

benefit[18]: for example where A guarantees B's bank overdraft and the promisee bank suffers detriment by advancing money to B. The view of Sir William Holdsworth, indeed, was that "Detriment to the promisee is of the essence of the doctrine, and benefit to the promisor is, when it exists, merely an accident."[19] But in a number of cases[20] promises have been held enforceable in spite of the fact that there was no apparent detriment to the promisee; and these cases support the view that benefit to the promisor is sufficient to satisfy the requirement of consideration.

(b) BENEFIT AND DETRIMENT MAY BE FACTUAL OR LEGAL. The traditional definition of consideration lacks precision because the key notions of "benefit" and "detriment" are used in at least two senses. They may mean, first, any act[21] which is of some value, or, secondly, only such acts the performance of which is not already legally due from the promisee. In the first sense, there is consideration if a benefit or detriment is *in fact* obtained or suffered. When the words are used in the second sense this factual benefit or detriment is disregarded, and a notion of what may be called legal benefit or detriment is substituted.[22] Under this notion, the promisee may provide consideration by doing anything that he was not legally bound to do, whether or not it actually occasions a detriment to him or confers a benefit on the promisor; while conversely he may provide no consideration by only doing what he was legally bound to do, however much this may in fact occasion a detriment to him or confer a benefit on the promisor. The English courts have not consistently adopted either of these senses of the words "benefit" and "detriment." In some of the situations to be discussed in this Chapter, factual benefit is stressed[23] even though legal detriment may also have been present; while in others the absence of a legal detriment or benefit has in the past been regarded as decisive.[24] The most recent authority[25] regards factual benefit to the promisor as sufficient in one such situation, even in the absence of a legal benefit to him or of a legal detriment to the promisee. It is possible, though not yet certain, that this approach may spread to at least some[26] of the situations in which the courts have in the past insisted on legal benefit or detriment.

(2) Other definitions

The traditional definition of consideration in terms of benefit and detriment is often regarded as unsatisfactory. One cause of dissatisfaction is that it is wrong to talk of benefit and detriment when both parties expect to, and actually may, benefit from the contract. But this kind of argument falls, with respect, into the error of treating the subject-matter of the defi-

---

[18] *O'Sullivan* v. *Management Agency & Music Ltd.* [1985] Q.B. 428, 459.

[19] *History of English Law*, Vol. 8, p. 11.

[20] *e.g. post*, pp. 78, 89, 119.

[21] Or forbearance, or promise to do or to forebear. For the sake of simplicity references in the text are confined to the doing of an act.

[22] Corbin § 172 rightly points out that use of this terminology does not explain *why* legal benefit or detriment is necessary; but the present point is simply that the terms are sometimes used in this sense.

[23] *e.g.* in *Bolton* v. *Madden* (1873) L.R. 9 Q.B. 55, *post*, p. 78.

[24] *e.g.* in some of the existing duty cases discussed on pp. 88–89, *post.*

[25] *Williams* v. *Roffey Bros. & Nicholls (Contractors) Ltd.* [1991] 1 Q.B. 1, *post*, p. 89.

[26] *e.g.* to the variation cases discussed *post*, pp. 96–98; but probably not to the forbearance to sue cases discussed *post*, pp. 82–84.

nition as the consideration *for a contract*,[27] when the definition is actually concerned with the consideration *for a promise*.[28] Another cause of dissatisfaction is the artificial reasoning that is sometimes necessary to accommodate the cases within the traditional definition. Sir Frederick Pollock has, accordingly, described consideration simply as "the price for which the promise is bought."[29] This statement has been approved in the House of Lords[30]; but if it is to be regarded as a definition of consideration it is defective in being so vague as to give no help in determining whether consideration exists on a given set of facts. A view which leads to even more uncertainty is that consideration "*means* a reason for the enforcement of promises"[31]—that reason being simply "the justice of the case."[32] But "the justice of the case" is in almost all the decided cases highly debatable, so that the suggested definition provides no basis for formulating a coherent legal doctrine. A modification of the suggested definition, describing consideration as "a reason for the recognition of an obligation"[33] is open to the same objection. Of course the traditional definition does not provide complete (or even a very high degree of) certainty. But it does state the doctrine in a way which gives some basis for predicting the course of future decisions; and it has more support in the authorities than any other definition. For these reasons it will be used in this Chapter.

(3) Mutual promises

So far we have discussed performance by one party as consideration for the promise of the other: for example, payment by a buyer as the consideration for the seller's promise to deliver, or delivery by a seller as consideration for the buyer's promise to pay. It is, however, also well settled that mutual promises can be consideration for each other. Hence if a seller promises to deliver goods in six months' time and the buyer to pay for them on delivery, there is an immediately binding contract from which neither party can withdraw, though, of course, performance cannot be claimed till the appointed time. Implied, no less than express, promises can constitute consideration for each other.[34]

Some difficulty has been felt in explaining the rule that mutual promises can be consideration for each other. At first sight, it might seem that the mere giving of a promise was not a detriment, nor its receipt a benefit, so as to make the counter-promise binding. It will not do to say that the person making the promise suffers a detriment because he is legally bound to perform it; for if this assumption is made about one of the promises, it must

---

[27] There are traces of this approach in: *Williams* v. *Roffey Bros. & Nicholls (Contractors) Ltd.* [1991] 1 Q.B. 1, 23: "If both parties benefit from an agreement it is not necessary that each also suffered a detriment."

[28] *Ante*, p. 64.

[29] *Principles of Contract*, (13th ed.), p. 133.

[30] *Dunlop Pneumatic Tyre Co. Ltd.* v. *Selfridge Ltd.* [1915] A.C. 847, 855.

[31] Atiyah, *Consideration in Contracts: A Fundamental Restatement*, Canberra, 1971, p. 60. For an earlier, similar statement, see Llewellyn, 40 Yale L.J. at p. 741 (1931)—"any sufficient justification for court enforcement"; but no attempt is made to suggest that this actually is the law. For criticism of Atiyah's views, see Treitel, 50 A.L.J. 439.

[32] Atiyah (*supra*, n. 31), pp. 52, 58.

[33] Atiyah, *Essays in Contract*, 179, 183.

[34] *Thoresen Car Ferries Ltd.* v. *Weymouth Portland B.C.* [1977] 2 Lloyd's Rep. 614, 619; *The Aramis* [1989] 1 Lloyd's Rep. 213, 225 (where the claim failed for want of contractual intention).

also be made of the other, so that the "explanation" assumes the very point in issue. Probably the reason for the rule is simpler. A person who makes a commercial promise expects to have to perform it (and is in fact under considerable pressure to do so). Correspondingly, one who receives such a promise expects it to be kept. These expectations, based on commercial morality, can without abuse of language be called a detriment and a benefit; and they satisfy the requirement of consideration in the case of mutual promises.

As a general rule a promise is only regarded as consideration for a counter-promise if its performance would also have been so regarded.[35] It follows that a mere promise to accept a gift cannot be consideration for the promise to make it. Similary, we shall see that a debtor who actually pays part of a debt does not thereby provide consideration for the creditor's promise to release the balance[36] and the position is exactly the same if the debtor *promises* part payment in return for the creditor's counter-promise to accept the part payment in full settlement.

(4) Invented consideration

Normally, a party enters into a contract with a view to obtaining the consideration provided by the other: for example, the buyer wants the goods and the seller the price. In the United States it has been said that this is essential, and that "Nothing is consideration that is not regarded as such by both parties."[37] But English courts do not insist on this requirement and often regard an act or forbearance as the consideration for a promise even though it may not have been the object of the promisor to secure it.[38] They may also regard the possibility of some prejudice to the promisee as a detriment without regard to the question whether it has in fact been suffered.[39] These practices may be called "inventing consideration,"[40] and the temptation to adopt one or the other of them is particularly strong when the act or forbearance which was actually bargained for cannot be regarded as consideration for some reason which is thought to be technical and without merit. In such cases the practice of inventing consideration may help to make the operation of the doctrine of consideration more acceptable; but

---

[35] *Thorp* v. *Thorp* (1702) 12 Mod. 445, 449.

[36] *Post*, p. 115.

[37] *Philpot* v. *Gruninger*, 14 Wall, 570, 577 (1872); Restatement, *Contracts* § 75(1); Restatement 2d, *Contracts* § 71(1) and (2); Williston, *Contracts* (rev. ed.), Vol. 1, at p. 320; Corbin, *Contracts*, § 172, is more sceptical. Restatement 2d, *Contracts* § 72 also supports the converse proposition, namely that anything is consideration if it is bargained for, even if there is no element of benefit or detriment; but this is subject to important exceptions, especially where what is bargained for is the performance of an existing duty or the settlement of an invalid claim: §§ 73, 74: as to these topics, see *post*, pp. 82–84, 85–93.

[38] See for example, *post*, pp. 83, 92, 142, 260; *cf* Pollway Ltd. v. *Abdullah* [1974] 1 W.L.R. 493, discussed by Zuckerman, 38 M.L.R. 384; Thornely [1975] C.L.J. 26; *The Alev* [1989] 2 Lloyd's Rep. 138, 147.

[39] *e.g. infra*, n. 42.

[40] Atiyah, *Essays in Contract*, 183 accuses me of having "invented the concept of invented consideration"; but all that I can claim to have invented is a phrase for describing what the courts sometimes actually do. The phrase does not imply approval of the practice: see *infra* after n. 41. Nor does the phrase necessarily imply inconsistency between decisions, as Atiyah suggests *ibid.*: courts could *consistently* hold that an act or forbearance was consideration although it was not the promisor's object to secure it. In fact, the decisions on the point are not perfectly consistent with each other: see *infra* at notes 42 and 43; but that is hardly unusual in a common law system.

the practice may also be criticised[41] on the ground that it gives the courts a wide discretion to hold promises binding (or not) as they please. Thus the argument that the promisee *might* have suffered prejudice by acting in reliance on a promise is in some cases made a basis of decision,[42] while in others precisely the same argument is rejected.[43] The courts have not been very consistent in the exercise of this discretion and its existence is a source of considerable uncertainty in this branch of the law.

(5) Motive and consideration

In *Thomas* v. *Thomas*[44] a testator shortly before his death expressed a desire that his widow should during her life have the house in which he lived, or £100. After his death, his executors "in consideration of such desire" promised to convey the house to the widow during her life or for so long as she should continue a widow, "provided nevertheless and it is hereby further agreed" that she should pay £1 per annum towards the ground rent, and keep the house in repair. In an action by the widow for breach of this agreement, the consideration for the executors' promise was stated to be the widow's promise to pay and repair. An objection that the declaration omitted to state part of the consideration, namely the testator's desire, was rejected. Patteson J. said: "Motive is not the same thing with consideration. Consideration means something which is of value in the eye of the law, moving from the plaintiff."[45] This remark should not be misunderstood: a common motive for making a promise is the desire to obtain the consideration; and an act or forbearance on the part of the promisee may fail to constitute consideration precisely because it was not the promisor's motive to secure it: for example, where A promises to give B £1,000 and B thereupon buys a fur coat. What Patteson J. meant was that a motive for promising does not amount to consideration unless two further conditions are satisfied, *viz.*: (i) that the thing secured in exchange for the promise is "of some value in the eye of the law"[46]; and (ii) that it moves from the plaintiff.[47] Consideration and motive are not opposites; the former concept is a subdivision of the latter. The consideration for a promise is (unless it is nominal or invented)[48] always a motive for promising; but a motive for making a promise is not necessarily consideration for it in law. Thus the testator's desire in *Thomas* v. *Thomas* was a motive for the executors' promise, but not part of the consideration for it. The widow's promise to pay and repair was another motive for the executors' promise and did constitute the consideration.

---

[41] Holmes, *The Common Law*, p. 292. In the United States there is less need to invent consideration because of the existence of a broad doctrine of promissory estoppel: see Restatement, *Contracts*, and Restatement 2d, *Contracts*, § 90.

[42] *Shadwell* v. *Shadwell* (1860) 9 C.B.(N.S.) 159, 174: the consideration was said by Erle C.J. to consist of the possibility that the promisor "*may* have made a most material change in his position . . ."

[43] In *Offord* v. *Davies* (1862) 12 C.B.(N.S.) 748: the argument of counsel (at p. 750) that "the plaintiff *might* have altered his position in consequence of the guarantee" was rejected, Erle C.J. being again a member of the court.

[44] (1842) 2 Q.B. 851.

[45] At p. 859.

[46] *Post*, pp. 79–93.

[47] *Post*, pp. 77–79.

[48] *Ante*, p. 67, *post*, p. 71. In *Thomas* v. *Thomas* the consideration may not have been adequate, but it was not nominal: *cf. post*, p. 72.

(6) Consideration and condition

Thomas v. *Thomas* also illustrates the difference between consideration and condition[49]: the plaintiff's remaining a widow was not part of the consideration but a condition of her entitlement to enforce the executors' promise. On the other hand, in *Re Soames*[50] A promised £3,000 to B if B would set up a school, in the running of which A was to have an active part. It was held that, by establishing the school, B had provided consideration for A's promise. It seems that the distinction between consideration and condition depends, in such cases, on whether "a reasonable man would or would not understand that performance of the condition was requested as the price or exchange for the promise."[51] In *Thomas* v. *Thomas* the executors had not requested the plaintiff to remain a widow; while in *Re Soames* a request that B should establish the school could be inferred from A's expressed intention to participate in its management. The distinction is further illustrated by *Carlill* v. *Carbolic Smoke Ball Co.*[52] where the plaintiff provided consideration for the defendants' promise by using the smokeball; but her catching influenza was only a condition of her entitlement to enforce that promise.

(7) Limited effects of promises without consideration

A promise that is not supported by consideration may nevertheless give rise to certain legal effects. In particular, the law may place restrictions on the revocability of a promise where the promisee has acted on it in a way that the promisor could have anticipated but had not requested[53]; and it may give a remedy against a promisor who would be unjustly enriched if he were allowed freely to revoke his promise after such action in reliance on it by the promisee.[54] These limited legal effects of promises without consideration will be discussed later in this Chapter[55]: here it is only necessary to emphasise that they do not give such promises the full consequences of binding contracts. Thus the restrictions on their revocability may be only temporary[56] and breach of the promise may not entitle the injured party to the full loss of bargain damages normally awarded for breach of contract,[57] or may not entitle him to them as of right.[58] Only a promise supported by consideration (or one or made in a deed) has these full contractual effects. "Contract" does not exhaust the category of promises or agreements having *some* legal effects[59]; it refers, more narrowly, to those promises or

[49] *i.e.* a *contingent* condition: see *ante*, p. 58.
[50] (1897) 13 T.L.R. 439.
[51] Williston, *Contracts*, rev. ed., § 112. For example, A's promise to convey Blackacre to B if B will build a house on it could be enforced by B once he had built the house. See *Raffaele* v. *Raffaele* [1962] W.A.R. 29; Allan, 79 L.Q.R. 239; *cf. Errington* v. *Errington* [1952] 1 K.B. 290 (*ante*, p. 38); *The Castle Alpha* [1989] 2 Lloyd's Rep. 383, 387; contrast *Dickinson* v. *Abel* [1969] 1 W.L.R. 295, where A's promise to pay £10,000 to B if A bought Blackacre from its owners was held to be "nothing but a conditional promise made without consideration" as B had not done (or been asked to do) anything to bring about the sale.
[52] [1893] 1 Q.B. 256; *ante*, p. 13.
[53] *Post*, pp. 101–111, 120–124, 125–126.
[54] *Post*, p. 125.
[55] For references, see *supra*, nn. 53 and 54.
[56] *Post*, pp. 106–107, 121–123, 131–132.
[57] *Ante*, p. 6, *post*, Chap. 21; *cf.* Restatement 2d, *Contracts* § 90 ("the remedy . . . may be limited as justice requires").
[58] *Post*, p. 132.
[59] *Cf.* Duncanson, 39 M.L.R. 268.

agreements leading to the full measure of enforceability to be discussed later in this book.[60] Moreover, while promises without consideration may have some legal effects, the promisee can still gain a number of important practical advantages by showing that he provided consideration. If the promise was supported by consideration, the promisee will not need to show action in reliance on the promise, or unjust enrichment of the promisor; the promise will not be revocable but enforceable according to its terms; and the promisee will be entitled to full loss of bargain damages as of right. The limited effects of promises without consideration may have mitigated some of the rigours of the strict doctrine; but they have not eliminated consideration as an essential requirement of a binding contract.[61]

SECTION 2. ADEQUACY

1. Consideration need not be Adequate

Under the doctrine of consideration, a promise has no contractual force unless *some* value has been given for it. But the courts do not, in general, ask whether adequate value has been given,[62] or whether the agreement is harsh or one-sided.[63] The reason for this is not that the courts *cannot* value the promise of each party: they have to do just this when assessing damages.[64] It is rather that they *should* not interfere with the bargain actually made by the parties. The fact that a person pays "too much" or "too little" for a thing may be evidence of fraud or mistake, or it may induce the court to imply a warranty or to hold that a contract has been frustrated. But it does not of itself affect the validity of the contract. This state of the law sometimes causes dissatisfaction, for example, when it is alleged that "excessive" profits have been made out of government contracts[65] or when, in times of scarcity, it is said that "excessive" prices are charged for goods or services or accommodation. Such problems are, however, more appropriately dealt with by special legislation or by administrative measures than by the ordinary process of civil litigation. The courts are not well equipped to develop a system of price-control, and their refusal, as a general rule, to concern themselves with the adequacy of consideration is a reflection of this fact. At the same time, the general rule is subject to a number of exceptions, to be discussed later in this book.[66] These indicate that the courts are by no means insensitive to the problem of unequal bargains; but in none of them is a promise held invalid *merely* because adequate value for it has not been given. Some additional factor is required to bring a case within one of the exceptions: for example, the existence of a

---

[60] *Post*, Chap. 21.

[61] *Post*, p. 108.

[62] *Haigh* v. *Brooks* (1840) 10 A. & E. 309, 320; *Westlake* v. *Adams* (1858) 5 C.B.(N.S.) 248, 265; *Wild* v. *Tucker* [1914] 3 K.B. 36, 39; *cf. Langdale* v. *Danby* [1982] 1 W.L.R. 1123; *C.C.C. Films (London) Ltd.* v. *Impact Quadrant Films Ltd.* [1985] Q.B. 16, 27; *Brady* v. *Brady* [1989] A.C. 755, 775; *Normid Housing Association Ltd.* v. *R. John Ralphs* [1989] 1 Lloyd's Rep. 265, 272; *cf.* Barton, 103 L.Q.R. 118.

[63] *Gaumont-British Pictures Corp.* v. *Alexander* [1936] 2 All E.R. 1686; *Midland Bank & Trust Co. Ltd.* v. *Green* [1981] A.C. 513, 532.

[64] *Post*, p. 830.

[65] See [1964] *Public Law* 391; *cf* the report into allegations of overcharging by Bristol Siddeley Engines Ltd. (H.C. Paper 129, Session 1967–1968); see Turpin, 31 M.L.R. 241; Turpin, *Government Contrasts*, pp. 196 *et seq.*

[66] *Post*, pp. 370–371, 409, 909; Waddams, 39 M.L.R. 393, Tiplady, 46 M.L.R. 601.

relationship in which one party is able to take an unfair advantage of the other. The general rule remains that "no bargain will be upset which is the result of the ordinary interplay of forces."[67]

2. Nominal Consideration

(1) Sufficiency of nominal consideration

The rule that consideration need not be adequate makes it possible to evade the doctrine of consideration, *i.e.* to make a gratuitous promise binding by means of a nominal consideration, *e.g.* £1 for the promise of valuable property, or a peppercorn for a substantial sum of money. Such cases are merely extreme applications of the rule that the courts will not judge the adequacy of consideration.[68] If, however, it appears on the face of the agreement that the consideration must as a matter of arithmetic be worth less than the performance of the counter-promise, there would seem to be no contract: for example, where A promised to pay B £100 in return for £1 to be simultaneously paid by B. It is assumed in the example that both sums are simply to be paid in legal tender. An agreement to exchange a specific coin or coins of a particular description for a sum of money greater than their face value (*e.g.* 20 shilling pieces bearing the date 1900 for £100) would be a good contract. The same would be true of an agreement to pay a sum in one currency in exchange for one payable in another, and of an agreement to pay a larger sum tomorrow in exchange for a smaller sum paid today.

Where an agreement is legally binding on the ground that it is supported by nominal consideration, the doctrine of consideration does not serve its main purpose, of distinguishing between gratuitous and onerous promises. But the law has no settled policy against enforcing all gratuitous promises. It only refuses to enforce *informal* gratuitous promises; and the deliberate use of a nominal consideration can be regarded as a form to make a gratuitous promise binding. In some cases it may, indeed, be undesirable to give promises (or transfers) supported by nominal consideration the same legal effect as promises supported by substantial consideration; but these cases are best dealt with by special rules.[69] Such rules are particularly necessary where the promise operates to the prejudice of third parties. For example, the danger that promoters of companies might use the device of nominal consideration to the prejudice of shareholders is avoided by imposing fiduciary duties on the promoters.[70]

---

[67] *Lloyds Bank Ltd.* v. *Bundy* [1975] Q.B. 326, 336, *per* Lord Denning M.R.

[68] Atiyah, *Essays in Contract* p. 194 argues that there is no logical connection between the two rules, relying on the fact that in many of the United States the courts recognise the principle that consideration need not be adequate, while rejecting the device of nominal consideration. The answer to this argument lies in Holmes' aphorism (The *Common Law* p. 1) that "the life of the law has not been logic: it has been experience": American courts which reject the device of nominal consideration do so on policy grounds which have nothing to do with logic.

[69] Thus a nominal consideration was disregarded in *Milroy* v. *Lord* (1862) 4 D.F. & J. 264, discussed *post*, p. 589 and for the purposes of the Law of Property Act 1925, " 'valuable consideration' . . . does not include a nominal consideration in money"; s.205(1)(xxi).

[70] *Post*, p. 358. For other ways of protecting third parties from being prejudiced by contracts made for inadequate consideration see Insolvency Act 1986, ss.238, 339, 423; Trustee Act 1925, s.13; Law of Property Act 1925, s.172; Inheritance (Provisions for Family and Dependants) Act 1975, ss.10(2)(*b*), 10(5)(*b*), 11(2)(*c*); *cf.* Companies Act 1985, ss.103, 320.

(2) Nominal and inadequate consideration

It is not normally necessary to distinguish between "nominal" and "inadequate" consideration, since both equally suffice to make a promise binding. The need to draw the distinction may, however, arise in some of the exceptional cases[71] in which the law treats promises or transfers supported only by nominal consideration differently from those supported by substantial or "valuable" consideration (even though it may be inadequate).

One view is that a nominal consideration is one that is of only token value,[72] while an inadequate consideration is one that has substantial value even though it is manifestly less than that of the performance promised or rendered in return. A second view is that " 'Nominal consideration' and a 'nominal sum' appear . . . , as terms of art, to refer to a sum or consideration which can be mentioned as consideration but is not necessarily paid."[73] This view was expressed by Lord Wilberforce in *Midland Bank & Trust Co. Ltd.* v. *Green*,[74] where a husband sold a farm, said to be worth £40,000, to his wife for £500. It was held that the wife was, for the purposes of the Land Charges Act 1925, s.13(2) a "purchaser for money or money's worth" so that the sale to her prevailed over an unregistered option to purchase the land, which had been granted to one of the couple's sons.[75] It was not necessary to decide whether the consideration for the sale was nominal but Lord Wilberforce said that he would have had "great difficulty" in so holding; and that "To equate 'nominal' with 'inadequate' or even 'grossly inadequate' consideration would embark the law on inquiries which I cannot think were ever intended by Parliament"[76]: *i.e.* inquiries into the adequacy of the price. On the facts of the case the £500 was in fact paid and was more than a mere token, so that the consideration was not nominal on either of the two views stated above. But if the stated consideration had been only £1, or a peppercorn, it is submitted that it would have been nominal even if it had been paid, or delivered, in accordance with the intention of the parties. So to hold would not lead to enquiries as to the adequacy of consideration; for the distinction between a consideration that is a mere token and one that is inadequate (or even grossly inadequate) is, it is submitted, clear as a matter of common sense. It certainly gives rise to no more difficulty than the concept of a consideration which is "mentioned as a consideration but not necessarily paid." On this test, the question whether consideration was nominal would presumably turn on the intention of the parties; and, in the present context, this would be an even more than usually elusive criterion, since no guidance could be obtained from the terms of the contract, those terms being, in cases of this kind, often deliberately drafted so as to conceal the true nature of the transaction.

---

[71] *Supra* at nn. 69 and 70.

[72] This seems to be the sense in which 10s. was described as "nominal" consideration (for the assignment of a debt) in *Turner* v. *Forwood* [1951] 1 All E.R. 746.

[73] *Midland Bank & Trust Co. Ltd.* v. *Green* [1981] A.C. 513, 532.

[74] *Supra.*

[75] For later successful proceedings by the son against his parents in conspiracy see [1982] Ch. 529.

[76] [1981] A.C. 513, 532. In other legislative contexts such an inquiry may be intended: *e.g.* by use of the phrase "full and valuable consideration" in Inheritance (Provision for Family and Dependants) Act 1975, s.1(3).

3. Attitude of Equity

Equity recognised the general rule that the validity of a contract could not be challenged merely on the ground of inadequacy of consideration.[77] But it sometimes refused specific performance of a contract, or set it aside, or even reopened it (*i.e.* varied its terms) on the ground that adequate value had not been given to a party who was thought to need special protection.[78]

Equity also refuses to aid a "volunteer"—*i.e.* a person who has given no substantial consideration but can nonetheless enforce a promise at law because it was made in a deed or supported by nominal consideration.[79] It was evidently thought that even such formal gratuitous promises did not deserve the same degree of enforcement as those for which substantial value had been given.

SECTION 3. PAST CONSIDERATION

1. The General Rule

The consideration for a promise must be given in return for the promise. If A makes a present of a car to B and a year later B promises to pay A £500 there is no consideration for B's promise as A did not give B the car in return for it. This reasoning very often applies where there is an interval of time between an act and the promise said to have been given in return for it. The alleged consideration is then said to be "past consideration" and therefore bad.[80] Thus if a thing is guaranteed *after* it has been sold there is no consideration for the guarantee.[81] Similarly, a promise to pay a sum of money may be made to an employee after his retirement or to an agent after the termination of the agency. If the sole consideration for the promise is the service previously rendered by the employee or agent under the terminated contract, it will be a past consideration so that the promise will not be contractually binding.[82] It will only be so binding if some consideration, other than the past service, has been provided by the promisee. Such other consideration may consist in his giving up rights which are outstanding (or are in good faith believed to be outstanding) under the original contract,[83] or in his promising or accomplishing some other act or forbearance not due from him under the original contract: for example, in his validly promising not to compete with the promisor.[84]

---

[77] See, *e.g. Cheale* v. *Kenward* (1858) 3 D. & J. 27; *Townend* v. *Toker* (1866) L.R. 1 Ch.App. 446.

[78] *Tennent* v. *Tennents* (1870) L.R. 2 Sc. & Div. 6, 9, *post* pp. 370–371, 909.

[79] *Jefferys* v. *Jefferys* (1841) Cr. & Ph. 138; *post*, p. 916.

[80] *Dent* v. *Bennett* (1839) 4 My. & Cr. 269; *Eastwood* v. *Kenyon* (1840) 11 A. & E. 438.

[81] *Thorner* v. *Field* (1612) 1 Bulst. 120; *Roscorla* v. *Thomas* (1842) 3 Q.B. 234. In the latter case, an oral warranty had in fact been given at the time of sale (see 11 L.J.Q.B. 214 and 6 Jur. 929) but was presumably regarded as "void" for want of written evidence: see *post*, p. 170.

[82] *Cf. Simpson* v. *John Reynolds* [1975] 1 W.L.R. 617; *Murray* v. *Goodhews* [1978] 1 W.L.R. 489, where payments made in such circumstances were for tax purposes held to be voluntary.

[83] *e.g. Bell* v. *Lever Bros. Ltd.* [1932] A.C. 161 (where the value of the rights given up in return for the payment was uncertain in amount since it included not only future salary but also possible future commission).

[84] *Cf. Wyatt* v. *Kreglinger and Fernau* [1933] 1 K.B. 793, where the ex-employee's claim would have succeeded if the restraint undertaken by him had not been invalid (*post*, p. 410).

In determining whether consideration is past, the court is not, it is submitted, bound to apply a strictly chronological test. If the consideration and the promise are substantially one transaction, the exact order in which these events occur is not decisive.[85] Thus guarantees are often given by manufacturers to persons who buy their products from retailers. The buyer may have to send a card to the manufacturer to claim the benefit of the guarantee, and he generally does so after he has bought the goods. It seems that the consideration for the guarantee is not past, for the sale and the giving of the guarantee are substantially one transaction. This is certainly the understanding of the buyer, who thinks that he is buying guaranteed goods.

The question whether consideration is past is one of fact: the wording of the agreement is not decisive. Thus in *Re McArdle*[86] a promise made "in consideration of your carrying out" certain work was held to be gratuitous as the work had already been done. Conversely, a promise made "in consideration of your having today advanced . . . £750" has been held binding on proof that the advance was made at the same time as the promise.[87]

2. Past Acts or Promises requested by Promisor

Even an act done before a promise was made can be consideration for it if three conditions are satisfied: the act must have been done at the request of the promisor; it must have been understood that payment would be made; and the payment, if it had been promised in advance, must have been legally recoverable.[88] In such a case the promisee is, quite apart from the subsequent promise, entitled to a *quantum meruit* for his services. The promise can be regarded either as fixing the amount of that *quantum meruit*[89] or as being given in consideration of the promisee's releasing his *quantum meruit* claim.

On the other hand, a past service which was not done at the request of the promisor, or one for which payment was not expected, or one for which payment, though expected, is not recoverable, cannot support a subsequent promise to pay for it.[90]

The consideration for a promise by A can consist not only of a past *act* done by B at A's request, but also of an earlier *promise* made by B at A's request. Thus in *Pao On* v. *Lau Yiu Long*[91] the plaintiffs had promised the defendants that for one year they would not sell certain shares in a company of which the defendants were the principal shareholders. This promise had been made at the request of the defendants, who were anxious to prevent the value of their own holding from being depressed by a sudden sale of the plaintiffs' shares. Later, the defendants gave the plaintiffs a

---

85 *Thornton* v. *Jenkyns* (1840) 1 Man. & G. 166; *Tanner* v. *Moore* (1846) 9 Q.B. 1; *National Westminster Bank* v. *Cullinane, The Times,* October 27, 1982.

86 [1951] Ch. 669.

87 *Goldshede* v. *Swan* (1847) 1 Ex. 154. The burden of providing that the consideration was not past is on the person seeking to enforce the promise: *Savage* v. *Uwechia* [1961] 1 W.L.R. 455.

88 *Re Casey's Patents* [1892] 1 Ch. 104, 115–116; *cf. Lampleigh* v. *Brathwait* (1615) Hob. 105.

89 *Kennedy* v. *Broun* (1863) 13 C.B.(N.S.) 677, 740; *Rondel* v. *Worsley* [1969] 1 A.C. 191, 236, 278, 287.

90 *Kennedy* v. *Broun, supra*; *Rondel* v. *Worsley, supra.*: promise to pay barrister for past professional services not binding since he could not sue for his fees; see now Courts and Legal Services Act 1990, s.61.

91 [1980] A.C. 614.

guarantee in which they promised to indemnify the plaintiffs against any loss which they might suffer if, during the year, the shares fell in value.[92] The Privy Council rejected the argument that the consideration for the guarantee was past.[93] It consisted in the plaintiffs' promise not to sell the shares; for although that promise had been made before the guarantee was given, it had been made at the defendants' request and on the understanding that the plaintiffs were to be compensated for it by some form of protection against the risk of a fall in the value of those shares.

3. Antecedent Debt

In a number of cases it has been held that the mere existence of an antecedent debt does not constitute "value" for a transfer by the debtor as it amounts only to past consideration.[94] These cases are not directly concerned with the enforceability of promises between promisor and promisee: indeed, in one of them such enforceability at common law could hardly have been disputed since the transfer was made in a deed.[95] The cases may, however, be relevant by analogy to the enforceability of promises; and, in principle, it seems that, where the only possible consideration for a promise is an antecedent debt owed by the promisor to the promisee, that consideration is past, so that the promise is not contractually binding.[96] In practice, however, the creditor (*i.e.* the promisee) will often provide consideration for such a promise by forbearing, on the strength of it, to sue for the debt.[97]

4. Moral Obligation

In the eighteenth and early nineteenth centuries, an attempt was made (originally by Lord Mansfield) to define consideration so as to include certain pre-existing "moral" obligations. In accordance with this theory it was held that an executor was personally liable on a promise to pay a legacy if he had sufficient assets of the deceased in his hands to pay his debts and legacies[98]; that a promise by a discharged bankrupt to pay a debt contracted before the discharge was binding[99]; and that a promise to pay a statute-barred debt[1] or one contracted during minority[2] was binding. In some of these cases, the consideration for the promise was said to be the "moral" obligation of the defendant to pay the debt.

---

92 This guaranteee replaced an earlier agreement which was less favourable to the plaintiffs.

93 For the further argument that the consideration was no more than the promise to perform an existing contractual duty, see *post*, p. 93.

94 *Roger* v. *Comptoir d'Escompte de Paris* (1869) L.R. 2 C.P. 393; *Re Barker's Estate* (1875) 44 L.J. Ch. 487; *Wigan* v. *English & Scottish Law Life Assurance Society* [1909] 1 Ch. 291.

95 *Wigan's* case, *supra*.

96 *e.g. Hopkinson* v. *Logan* (1839) 5 M. & W. 241.

97 *Post*, p. 84.

98 *Atkins* v. *Hill* (1775) 1 Cowp. 284; *Hawkes* v. *Saunders* (1782) 1 Cowp. 289, an alternative ground for the decision given by Buller J. was that the defendant's equitable (as opposed to "moral") obligation to pay the legacy was consideration for the promise.

99 *Trueman* v. *Fenton* (1772) 2 Cowp. 544.

1 *Hyeling* v. *Hastings* (1699) 1 Ld. Raym. 389.

2 *Post*, p. 492; *cf. Lee* v. *Muggeridge* (1813) 5 Taunt. 36 (promise by a woman after her husband's death to pay debt incurred during marriage); for attempts to restrict or define the doctrine, see *Littlefield* v. *Shee* (1831) 2 B. & Ad. 811; *Meyer* v. *Haworth* (1838) 8 A. & E. 467.

In this context, the term "moral obligation" was used in a narrow sense. It was restricted to cases in which the defendant's obligation was not legally enforceable (or, at any rate, not enforceable in the particular court in which the action on the promise was brought[3]) because it suffered from some specific legal defect. It did not follow that any "moral" obligation was consideration. Thus in *Eastwood* v. *Kenyon*[4] the guardian of a young girl had raised a loan to pay for her maintenance and education, and to improve her estate. She subsequently came of age and married; and her husband promised the guardian to pay the amount of the loan. In dismissing the guardian's action on this promise, the court rejected the argument that the husband's promise was binding merely because he was under a moral obligation to perform it. Lord Denman C.J. said that argument would "annihilate the necessity for any consideration at all, inasmuch as the mere fact of giving a promise creates a moral obligation to perform it."[5] The moral obligation to *perform* a promise cannot be the consideration for it even in the most general sense: it cannot be the reason for *making* the promise. The case also shows that the mere existence of an antecedent moral obligation (in the ordinary sense of the phrase) to reimburse the guardian did not amount to consideration for the husband's promise. From this point of view, the case provides the classic illustration of the requirement that the consideration for a promise must not be past.

Many of the cases in which promises were held binding under the old "moral obligation" theory would now go the other way. For example, an executor who has assets of the deceased in his hands is no longer personally liable on a promise to pay legacies[6]; a promise by a discharged bankrupt to pay in full debts incurred before his discharge is only binding if supported by fresh consideration[7]; and the same is true of a promise to pay a debt after it has become statute-barred.[8]

On the other hand, a promise by an adult to pay a debt (or to perform some other obligation) contracted during minority is enforceable[9]; and *Eastwood* v. *Kenyon*[10] did not purport to overrule the "moral obligation" theory in its original narrow sense, that a promise to perform an earlier obligation which suffered from some specific legal defect might be binding. In this sense the theory was restated by Lord Denman himself only two years after his decision in *Eastwood* v. *Kenyon*[11] and applied 23 years later in a case[12] that was mentioned with approval by Scrutton L.J. in 1918.[13] In this narrow sense, the "moral obligation" theory may still survive, though its scope has been restricted and the label has become unfashionable.

---

[3] As in *Hawkes* v. *Saunders, supra*, n. 98.
[4] (1840) 11 A. & E. 438.
[5] *Ibid.* at p. 450; *cf. Monkman* v. *Stephenson* (1840) 11 A. & E. 411, 416.
[6] Williams, Mortimer and Sunnucks, *Executors and Administrators and Probate*, (6th ed.), p. 700.
[7] *Jakeman* v. *Cook* (1878) 4 Ex.D. 26; *Re Bonacina* [1912] 2 Ch. 394; *Wild* v. *Tucker* [1914] 3 K.B. 36.
[8] Limitation Act 1980, s.29(7); *cf.* as to time bars imposed by contract, *The Ion* [1980] 2 Lloyd's Rep. 245, 249.
[9] *Post*, p. 492.
[10] (1840) 11 A. & E. 438.
[11] *Roscorla* v. *Thomas* (1842) 3 Q.B. 234, 237.
[12] *Flight* v. *Reed* (1863) 1 H. & C. 703.
[13] *J. Evans & Co.* v. *Heathcote* [1918] 1 K.B. 418, 437.

5. Statutory Exceptions

There are two exceptions to the rule that past consideration is no consideration.

First, an "antecedent debt or liability," though normally a past consideration,[14] is good consideration for a bill of exchange.[15]

Secondly, the Limitation Act 1980[16] provides that, where a debtor in a writing signed by him[17] "acknowledges" a debt, it shall be deemed to have accrued on and not before the date of the acknowledgment. An "acknowledgment" need not take the form of a promise[18]; but if it does take this form the promise can extend the period of limitation even though the only consideration for it was the antecedent debt, and thus past. Further acknowledgments made within such an extended period or periods have the same effect.[19] But once the debt has become statute-barred the right to sue for it cannot be revived by any subsequent acknowledgment[20]: to this extent, the old "moral obligation" theory as applied to statute-barred debts[21] has been reversed.

SECTION 4. CONSIDERATION MUST MOVE FROM THE PROMISEE

1. Promisee must provide Consideration

The rule that consideration must "move from the promisee"[22] means that a person to whom a promise was made can only enforce it if he himself provided the consideration for it. He cannot sue if the consideration for the promise moved from a third party. Thus if a man says to his son-in-law "I will pay you £1,000 if your father does the same," and the father does so, the son-in-law cannot enforce the promise. But the promisee need not provide the whole consideration for the promise: thus he can enforce a promise, the consideration for which was provided partly by himself and partly by his agent or partner or by some other co-promisee.[23]

2. Consideration need not move to Promisor

While consideration must move from the promisee, it need not move to the promisor.[24] It follows that the requirement of consideration may be

---

[14] *Ante*, p. 75.

[15] Bills of Exchange Act 1882, s.27(1)(*b*). Such consideration is not *necessarily* past: it might consist of forbearance of the creditor to sue for the debt or in his treating the bill as conditional payment: see *Currie* v. *Misa* (1875) L.R. 10 Ex. 153 and *cf. post.* pp. 84, 655.

[16] s.27(5).

[17] *Ibid.* s.30(1).

[18] An admission of liability suffices: *Surrendra Overseas Ltd..* v. *Government of Sri Lanka* [1977] 1 W.L.R. 481; *cf. Re Overmark Smith Warden Ltd.* [1982] 1 W.L.R. 1195.

[19] Limitation Act 1980, s.29(7).

[20] *Ibid.*

[21] *Ante*, p. 75.

[22] *Barber* v. *Fox* (1682) 2 Wms.Saund. 134, n. (*e*); *Thomas* v. *Thomas* (1842) 2 Q.B. 851, 859; *Tweddle* v. *Atkinson* (1861) 1 B. & S. 393, 398, 399; *Pollway Ltd.* v. *Abdullah* [1974] 1 W.L.R. 493, 497; *cf. Dickinson* v. *Abel* [1969] 1 W.L.R. 295; a dictum to the contrary in *McEvoy* v. *Belfast Banking Co.* [1935] A.C. 24, 43, has been convincingly criticised by S.J.B. in 51 L.Q.R. 419, *post*, p. 522.

[23] *Jones* v. *Robinson* (1847) 1 Ex. 454; *Fleming* v. *Bank of New Zealand* [1900] A.C. 577. For the position where the *whole* consideration is provided by a co-promisee, see *post*, p. 522.

[24] *Re Wyvern Developments Ltd.* [1974] 1 W.L.R. 1097.

satisfied where the promisee suffers some detriment at the promisor's request, but confers no corresponding benefit on the promisor. Thus the promisee may provide consideration by giving up a job[25] or the tenancy of a flat,[26] even though no direct benefit results to the promisor from these acts. Consideration may also move from the promisee without moving to the promisor where the promisee at the promisor's request confers a benefit on a third party, *e.g.* by entering into a contract with the third party.[27] This possibility is illustrated by the case in which goods are bought and paid for by the use of a cheque card or credit card. The issuer of the card makes a promise to the supplier of the goods that the cheque will be honoured or that the supplier will be paid; and the supplier provides consideration for this promise by supplying the goods to the customer.[28] In the case of the credit card transaction, there is also consideration in the shape of the discount allowed by the supplier of the goods to the issuer of the card: this is both a detriment to the supplier and a benefit to the issuer.[29]

3. Benefit to Promisor sufficient

The rule that consideration must move from the promisee at first sight strongly supports the view that the essence of consideration is detriment to the promisee. But the promisee may confer a benefit on the promisor or on a third party without in fact[30] suffering any detriment himself. Thus in *Bolton* v. *Madden*[31] the plaintiff and defendant were entitled, as subscribers to a charity, to vote on the disposition of its funds. The plaintiff promised to vote at one meeting for a person whom the defendant wished to benefit, and the defendant promised in return to vote at the next meeting for a person whom the plaintiff wished to benefit. In an action on the defendant's promise, it was argued that there was no consideration for it as the plaintiff "incurred neither trouble nor prejudice."[32] But the court held the agreement binding on the ground that consideration had moved from the plaintiff when he had at the defendant's request conferred a benefit on a third party. It could be argued that the plaintiff had suffered a legal detriment[33] by voting in accordance with his promise as he was not previously bound to do so. But this was not the basis of the decision.

The view that consideration can move from the promisee though he in fact suffers no detriment is, supported by two further rules to be discussed later in this Chapter. The first is that performance of an existing contractual duty (or a promise to perform such a duty) can constitute consideration if it benefits the promisor[34]: this benefit "moves" from the promisee

[25] *Jones* v. *Padavatton* [1969] 1 W.L.R. 628.
[26] *Tanner* v. *Tanner* [1975] 1 W.L.R. 1346; contrast *Horrocks* v. *Forray* [1976] 1 W.L.R. 230; *Coombes* v. *Smith* [1986] 1 W.L.R. 808.
[27] See *International Petroleum Refining Supply Ltd.* v. *Caleb Brett & Son Ltd.* [1980] 1 Lloyd's Rep. 569, 594 (where the promisor benefited indirectly since promisor and third party were associated companies).
[28] See *R.* v. *Lambie* [1982] A.C. 449; *Re Charge Card Services Ltd.* [1987] Ch. 150, affirmed [1989] Ch. 497.
[29] *Customs & Excise Commissioners* v. *Diner's Club Ltd.* [1989] 1 W.L.R. 1196. 1207.
[30] *Ante*
[31] (1873) L.R. 9 Q.B. 55.
[32] At p. 57.
[33] *Ante*, p. 65.
[34] *Post*, pp. 89, 93.

in that it is conferred by him, even though it may cause him no detriment[35] in the sense that he was already bound to do the acts in question. The second is that a composition agreement between a debtor and his creditors is binding[36] because it benefits the creditors; and this benefit can be said to "move" from the debtor in that his co-operation is essential to the making and performance of the composition agreement. It could be said that the debtor suffers a legal detriment by signing the agreement when he is not bound to do so. But the rule is not based on this invented consideration.[37] It is based on benefit to the promisors.[38]

SECTION 5. CONSIDERATION MUST BE OF SOME VALUE

1. Must be of Economic Value

An act, forbearance or promise will only amount to consideration if the law recognises that it has some economic value. It may have such value even though the value cannot be precisely quantified. But "natural affection of itself is not a sufficient consideration,"[39] and the same is true of other merely sentimental motives for promising. This is the reason why in *Thomas* v. *Thomas*[40] the desire of the testator that his widow should live in his house was not part of the consideration for the executors' promise that she might do so. Similar reasoning may also explain the decision in *White* v. *Bluett*[41] that a son had not provided consideration (for his father's promise not to sue him on a promissory note) by promising not to bore his father with complaints.

2. Illusory Consideration

A promise may appear to be made for some consideration which is really illusory and which must therefore be disregarded.

One such situation would arise when the consideration is impossible to perform and this is known to both parties. For example, a promise by A to pay B £100 in return for B's promise to let A have all the wine in B's cellar would probably be regarded as a gratuitous promise if, at the time when the promise was made, both A and B knew[42] that there was no wine in the cellar. The position would be different if B's promise was to deliver the *future* contents of the cellar. In that case, A would be buying the chance of

---

35 *Williams* v. *Roffey Bros. & Nicholls (Contractors) Ltd.* [1991] 1 Q.B. 1, 16.

36 *Post*, p. 119, the application of this rule in *West Yorks Darracq Agency Ltd.* v. *Coleridge* [1911] 2 K.B. 326 is hard to support, since there the creditors got nothing and so received no benefit. The consideration was said at p. 329 to be benefit to the debtor, but he was the person *to* whom the promise was made, and benefit to the promisee is obviously no consideration. If it were, there would be consideration for every gratuitous promise.

37 See *ante*, p. 67. The creditors do not bargain for the debtor's signature but for a dividened. If the debtor's signature were the consideration it could equally well be so regarded in a composition with a single creditor, but this would be contrary to *Foakes* v. *Beer* (1884) 9 App.Cas. 605, *post*, p. 115.

38 *Post* p. 119.

39 *Bret* v. *J.S.* (1600) Cro.Eliz. 756.

40 (1842) 2 Q.B. 851; *ante*, p. 68.

41 (1853) 23 L.J.Ex. 36. Pollock C.B. said at p. 37 that the son had "no right" to bore his father with complaints; but the son certainly had no legal duty not to do this and it is arguable that his forbearance did amount to consideration. Perhaps the decision can be explained on the ground that the father, in spite of his promise, retained the note.

42 There could be a good contract if the parties were in doubt on this point: see *Smith* v. *Harrison* (1857) 26 L.J. Ch. 412, *post*, p. 258.

the cellar's containing wine[43]; and the value of that chance would be illusory only if the question whether any wine was to be put into the cellar had been left entirely to B's discretion.[44]

A second situation in which consideration would be illusory is where the promisee would have accomplished the act or forbearance anyway, even if the promise had not been made. This would be the position if A promises to pay B, who happens to be fond of port, £5 if B will drink the glass of port that he had just poured for himself; or if C promises D, who has religious objections to smoking, £5 if he will not smoke for a week. Since "it is no consideration to refrain from a course of conduct which it was never intended to pursue,"[45] such promises would not be legally binding. But where the promise provided *an* inducement for the act or forbearance, the requirement of consideration is satisfied even though there were also other inducements operating on the mind of the promisee.[46] It seems that the burden of proving that the requested act or forbearance would have been accomplished, even if the promise had not been made, is on the promisor.[47]

Consideration would again be illusory where it was alleged to consist of a promise the terms of which left performance entirely to the discretion of the promisor.[48] A person does not provide consideration by promising to do something "if I feel like it," or "unless I change my mind"; and the same principle may apply in analogous cases. Thus a promise may be illusory if it is accompanied by a clause effectively[49] excluding all liability of the promisor for breach.[50] And a promise to buy "so much coal as I may decide to order" would be an illusory consideration for the seller's counter-promise to deliver, which could therefore not be enforced.[51] On the other hand, the buyer would provide consideration by promising to buy from the seller "*all* the coal I require"; for in such a case, even if the buyer does not promise to have any requirements, he does at least give a definite undertaking not to deal with anybody else.[52] Similarly, a promise which is subject to cancellation by A may nevertheless constitute consideration for a counter-promise from B where A's power to cancel is limited by the

---

[43] *Cf. Brady* v. *Brady* [1989] A.C. 755, 774 ("at the date of the promise").

[44] *Infra* at n. 48.

[45] *Arrale* v. *Costain Civil Engineering Ltd.* [1976] 1 Lloyd's Rep. 98, 106; *Colchester B.C.* v. *Smith* [1991] 2 All E.R. 29, 57; *cf. Beaton* v. *McDivitt* (1988) 13 N.S.W.L.R. 162.

[46] *Brikom Investments Ltd.* v. *Carr* [1979] Q.B. 467, 490.

[47] *Cf.* the analogous rule in cases of "proprietary estoppel" (*post*, p. 130): *Greasley* v. *Cook* [1980] 1 W.L.R. 1306; and misrepresentation (*post*, p. 307: *Smith* v. *Chadwick* (1884) 9 App.Cas. 187, 196.

[48] For another problem arising out of such promises, see *post*, p. 153.

[49] See *post*, Chap. 7. If the clause were ineffective, this fact would give reality to an otherwise illusory promise.

[50] *Firestone Tyre & Rubber Co. Ltd.* v. *Vokins* [1951] 1 Lloyd's Rep. 32; *cf.* the discussion of *The Cap Palos* [1921] P. 458, in the *Suisse Atlantique Case* [1967] 1 A.C. 361, 432.

[51] See *Wickham & Burton Coal Co.* v. *Farmer's Lumber Co.* 189, 179 N.W. 417 (1923); for an exception, see *Citadel Insurance Co.* v. *Atlantic Union Insurance Co.* [1982] 2 Lloyd's Rep. 543; *post*, p. 140.

[52] The validity of "requirement" contracts is assumed in such cases as *Metropolitan Electric Supply Co.* v. *Ginder* [1901] 2 Ch. 799 and *Dominion Coal Co. Ltd.* v. *Dominion Steel & Iron Co. Ltd.* [1909] A.C. 293. Similarly, a contract by a manufacturer to sell his entire output to a particular buyer is binding even though he does not bind himself to have any output: see, for example, *Donnell* v. *Bennett* (1883) 22 Ch.D. 835 and *cf.* Howward, 2 U. of Tas.L.R. 446; Adams, 94 L.Q.R. 73. For the possible illegality of such promises, see *post*, pp. 416–420.

express terms of the promise, *e.g.*, where it can only be exercised within a specified time. Such a limitation on the power to cancel may also be implied, so that (for example) A could not cancel after B had begun to perform his counter-promise. A's promise would then constitute consideration, so that B would be liable if he failed to complete the performance. Finally, the objection that a promise amounts only to illusory consideration on the grounds here discussed can be removed if the promise is performed: such actual performance can constitute consideration even though the person who has rendered it was not legally obliged to do so.[53]

3. Trivial Acts

Since consideration need not be adequate, acts or omissions of very small value can be consideration. Thus it has been said that there was consideration for a promise to give a man £50 "if you will come to my house"[54]; that the act of executing a deed could be consideration for a promise to pay money although the deed was void[55]; that to give up a piece of paper without reference to its contents was consideration[56]; and even that to show a person a document was consideration.[57] In *Chappell & Co. Ltd.* v. *Nestlé Co. Ltd.*,[58] chocolate manufacturers sold gramophone records for 1s. 6d. plus three wrappers of their 6d. bars of chocolate. It was held that the delivery of the wrappers formed part of the consideration, though the wrappers were of little value and were in fact thrown away. If the delivery of the wrappers formed part of the consideration it could, presumably, have formed the whole of the consideration, so that a promise to deliver records for wrappers alone would have been binding.

4. Gift of Onerous Property

A promise to give away onerous property is binding if the donee promises in return to discharge obligations attached to it. Thus a promise to give away a leasehold house is binding if the donee promises to perform the donor's covenants under the lease, *e.g.* to repair and to pay rent[59]; a promise to give away a freehold house is binding if the donee promises to pay outstanding mortgage instalments or other charges[60]; and a promise to give away partly paid-up shares in a company is binding if the donee promises to pay further calls which may be made on the shares.[61] Of course if the prop-

---

[53] *Cambridge Notation Ltd.* v. *B.B.C.* [1990] 3 All E.R. 523, 538.
[54] *Gilbert* v. *Ruddeard* (1608) 3 Dy. 272b (n); *cf. Denton* v. *G.N. Ry.* (1856) 5 E. & B. 860.
[55] *Westlake* v. *Adams* (1858) 5 C.B.(N.S.) 248; perhaps there was also an element of compromise in this case: *cf. post*, p. 82.
[56] *Haigh* v. *Brooks* (1839) 10 A. & E. 309, 334; contrast *Foster* v. *Dawber* (1861) 6 Ex. 839.
[57] *Sturlyn* v. *Albany* (1587) Cro.Eliz. 67; *March* v. *Culpepper* (1628) Cro.Car. 70. Contrast *Re Charge Card Services Ltd.* [1987] Ch. 150, 164, affirmed [1989] Ch. 497 (production of charge card and signature of voucher not the consideration for a supply of goods, evidently because such "consideration" would be blatantly "invented": *ante*, p. 67).
[58] [1960] A.C. 87; *cf. Lipkin Gorman* v. *Karpnale Ltd.* [1989] 1 W.L.R. 1340 (*post*, p. 478): consideration for a cheque said at pp. 1350, 1364 to be gaming chips, of little intrinsic value, and services supplied, or to be supplied, by the casino; contrast *ibid.* pp. 1382, 1383.
[59] *Price* v. *Jenkins* (1877) 5 Ch.D. 619; *Johnsey Estates Ltd.* v. *Lewis Manley (Engineering) Ltd.* [1987] 2 E.G.L.R. 69. In so far as *Thomas* v. *Thomas* (1842) 2 Q.B. 851, *ante*, p. 68, takes a contray view, it seems to be inconsistent with *Price* v. *Jenkins* (where the "case which is not reported" mentioned at p. 620 closely resembles *Thomas* v. *Thomas*).
[60] *Merritt* v. *Merritt* [1970] 1 W.L.R. 1121.
[61] *Cheale* v. *Kenward* (1858) 3 D. & J. 27.

erty is worth more than the obligations attached to it, there will be an element of gift in such transactions; and safeguards are provided by law to ensure that certain categories of third parties, such as creditors of the promisor, are not prejudiced by this aspect of the transaction.[62]

5. Compromise and Forbearance to Sue

A promise not to enforce a valid claim[63] is clearly good consideration for a promise given in return.[64] If, for example, A is injured by the admitted negligence of B, they can validly compromise the claim, A's promise not to sue B constituting the consideration for B's promise to pay the agreed compensation. Similarly, a creditor to whom a sum of money has become due may promise to give the debtor extra time to pay in return for the debtor's promise to pay higher interest or to give additional security. In such a case there is good consideration for the debtor's promise: he benefits by getting extra time to pay, while the creditor suffers a detriment in that he is, for a time, kept out of his money.[65] There is such benefit to the debtor and detriment to the creditor even if the creditor only promises to forbear for a limited time; and if no time is specified, the court will infer that he undertook to forbear for a reasonable time.[66] The principles just stated apply, not only to a promise not to enforce a claim, but also to a promise to abandon a good defence[67]; and to a promise to abandon a particular remedy, *e.g.* to one to abandon arbitration proceedings.[68]

Two further possibilities call for discussion: the creditor's claim may be *invalid or doubtful*; and he may not promise to forbear but simply *forbear in fact* from enforcing his claim against the debtor.

(1) Invalid and doubtful claims

It used to be thought that a promise by A not to enforce a claim which was invalid was no consideration for a promise given by B in return: if B was not liable, he did not benefit from A's promise not to sue him and A lost nothing by giving up a worthless right.[69] This reasoning still applies where the sole[70] consideration provided by A is his forbearance to enforce a claim which is clearly invalid and which he either knows to be invalid or does not believe to be valid. Thus a promise by a bookmaker not to sue his client for the amount of lost bets[71] is no consideration for a promise made in return by the client.[72]

---

[62] Insolvency Act 1986, ss.238, 339; *ante*, p. 71, n. 70.
[63] For promises to abandon defences and remedies, see *infra* at nn. 67 and 68.
[64] *e.g. Greene* v. *Church Commissioners for England* [1974] Ch. 467; *cf. Centrovincial Estates plc* v. *Merchant Investors Assurance Co. Ltd., The Times*, March 8, 1983 (as to which see *ante*, p. 8, n. 5); *The Attika Hope* [1988] 1 Lloyd's Rep. 439, 442 (forbearance to sue third party).
[65] *Crowther* v. *Farrer* (1850) 15 Q.B. 677.
[66] *Payne* v. *Wilson* (1827) 7 B. & C. 423; *Oldershaw* v. *King* (1857) 2 H. & N. 517.
[67] See *Banque de l'Indochine* v. *J. H. Rayner* (*Mincing Lane*) *Ltd.* [1983] Q.B. 711.
[68] *The Leonidas D* [1985] 1 W.L.R. 925, 933, where there was no such abandonment: see *ante* p. 10.
[69] *Jones* v. *Ashburnham* (1804) 4 East 455.
[70] The position is different where there is also other consideration: *The Siboen and the Sibotre* [1976] 1 Lloyd's Rep. 293, 334.
[71] For the invalidity of the bookmaker's claim, see *post*, p. 462.
[72] *Hyams* v. *Coombes* (1912) 28 T.L.R. 413; *Burrell & Sons* v. *Leven* (1926) 42 T.L.R. 407; *Poteliakhoff* v. *Teakle* [1938] 2 K.B. 816; *cf. Edwards* v. *Baugh* (1843) 11 M. & W. 641; *Goodson* v. *Baker* (1908) 98 L.T. 415, *contra*, seems wrong.

But a promise to abandon a claim which is doubtful in law is good consideration: it involves at any rate the possibility of benefit to one party or detriment to the other, for the claim may turn out to have been well founded. Thus in *Haigh* v. *Brooks*[73] the defendant promised to pay the plaintiffs sums of money if they would give up a guarantee which he had previously given them. The defendant's promise was held binding although the validity of the guarantee was in doubt. "There was in the guarantee an ambiguity that might be explained, . . . so as to make it a valid contract, and therefore this was a sufficient consideration for the promise declared upon."[74]

It has, further, been held that a promise to abandon a claim which is *clearly* bad in law but which is believed by the promisee to be valid is good consideration.[75] One possible reason for this rule is that otherwise "in no case of a doubtful claim could a compromise be enforced."[76] But this argument hardly applies where the claim is not "doubtful" but *clearly* bad. Another possible reason for the rule is that the party forbearing suffers detriment because "he gives up what he believes to be a right of action"[77]; but, in general, consideration must be something of value, not something believed to be of value. In fact the party forbearing would be worse off, if he did not forbear, for he would lose his action and the costs. A further suggestion is that the party forbearing suffers detriment in that it becomes more difficult to get up his case, the longer he waits[78]; this is a possible detriment (even though his action is bound to fail) as the failure may be more expensive than it would have been, had he sued promptly. The party forbearing might also suffer detriment if as a result of the agreement he loses the right to sue a third party who is liable on the original cause of action.[79] The party to whom the forbearance is given also benefits: "instead of being annoyed with an action, he escapes from the vexations incident to it."[80] There is some difficulty in relying on this benefit as the consideration, since it may also exist where the claim is *known* to be bad, in which case the compromise is not binding.[81] Perhaps this last rule is based on public policy rather than on want of consideration. As Tindal C.J. said in *Wade* v. *Simeon*[82] "It is almost *contra bonos mores* and certainly contrary to the principles of natural justice that a man should institute proceedings against another when he is conscious that he has no good cause of action." If compromises of such claims were upheld, improper pressure might be brought to bear on persons who "owed" void debts.

The rule that a promise to abandon a claim which is clearly bad but believed to be valid is good consideration is subject to a number of safeguards. There must be a "reasonable claim,"[83] (*i.e.* one made on reason-

---

[73] (1839) 10 A. & E. 309.
[74] At p. 334.
[75] *Cook* v. *Wright* (1861) 1 B. & S. 559; *Callisher* v. *Bischoffsheim* (1870) L.R. 5 Q.B. 449; *Holsworthy U.D.C.* v. *Holsworthy R.D.C.* [1907] 2 Ch. 62; *cf. Horton* v. *Horton* [1961] 1 Q.B. 215.
[76] *Callisher* v. *Bischoffsheim, supra*, at p. 451.
[77] *Ibid.* at p. 452.
[78] *Cook* v. *Wright, supra*, at p. 569.
[79] *Ibid.* at pp. 569–570.
[80] *Callisher* v. *Bischoffsheim, supra*, at p. 452.
[81] *Supra* at n. 72.
[82] (1846) 2 C.B. 548, 564; *cf. Edwards* v. *Baugh* (1843) 11 M. & W. 641, 646.
[83] *Cook* v. *Wright, supra*, at p. 569.

able grounds) and the party forbearing must honestly believe that his claim had at any rate a fair chance of success.[84] He must not conceal from the other party any facts which, if known to the latter, would enable him to resist the claim.[85] And he must show that he seriously intended to enforce the claim.[86]

The cases on this question all concern claims the validity of which was doubtful in law. It seems that the same rules apply where the claim was doubtful because of a dispute about the facts. A settlement based on a simple *mistake* of fact made by both parties might be void for mistake.[87] But it will not be void where both parties knowingly take the risk that the actual facts may turn out to be different from the facts as they were supposed to be. This element of risk is always present when parties negotiate a settlement on disputed facts.

(2) Actual forbearance

A person may forbear from enforcing a claim without expressly promising to do so. The question then arises whether this actual forbearance is consideration for some promise or act of the other party, for example for a promise by him to give security, or for giving the security. Sometimes actual forbearance may be evidence of an implied promise to forbear.[88] Thus the acceptance of a cheque in payment of a debt may be evidence of a promise not to sue the debtor so long as the cheque is not dishonoured, or at least for a reasonable time.[89]

But even where no such promise to forbear can be implied, an actual forbearance may constitute consideration. In *Alliance Bank* v. *Broom*[90] the defendant owed £22,000 to his bank, who pressed him to give some security. He promised to do so, but the bank made no counterpromise not to sue him. It was held that there was consideration for the defendant's promise as the bank had given, and the defendant received "some degree of forbearance."[91] On the other hand, in *Miles* v. *New Zealand Alford Estate Co.*[92] a company had bought land and was dissatisfied with the purchase. The vendor later promised to make certain payments to the company, and it was alleged that the consideration for this promise was the company's forbearance to take proceedings to rescind the contract. A majority of the Court of Appeal held that there was no consideration for the vendor's promise as no proceedings to rescind were ever intended; and Cotton L.J. added that "it must be shown that there was something which would bind the company not to institute proceedings."[93] Bowen L.J. dissented from his proposition,[94] relying on *Alliance Bank* v. *Broom*; but it may be possible to reconcile the cases by reference to the types of claim forborne. A bank to which £22,000 is owed is virtually certain to take steps to enforce

---

[84] *Callisher* v. *Bishchoffsheim*, *supra*, at p. 452.
[85] *Miles* v. *New Zealand Alford Estate Co.* (1886) 32 Ch.D. 267, 284.
[86] *Cook* v. *Wright*, *supra*, at p. 569; *The Proodos C.* [1980] 2 Lloyd's Rep. 390, 392.
[87] *Post*, Chap. 8; Andrews [1989] L.M.C.L.Q. 431.
[88] *Re Wyvern Developments Ltd.* [1974] 1 W.L.R. 1097.
[89] *Baker* v. *Walker* (1845) 14 M. & W. 465; *Elkington* v. *Cooke-Hill* (1914) 30 T.L.R. 670.
[90] (1864) 2 Dr. & Sm. 289; *cf.* also *Brikom Investments Ltd.* v. *Carr* [1979] Q.B. 467, 490.
[91] At p. 292.
[92] (1886) 32 Ch.D. 267; *cf. Hunter* v. *Bradford Property Trust Ltd.*, 1970 S.L.T. 173.
[93] At p. 285.
[94] At p. 291; his view was approved by Lord Macnaghten in *Fullerton* v. *Provincial Bank of Ireland* [1903] A.C. 309, 314.

its claim, but a dissatisfied purchaser of land is much less certain to take proceedings for rescission. It may, therefore, be reasonable to say that mere forbearance will amount to consideration in relation to the former type of claim, but that a promise to forbear is necessary where it is problematical whether the claim will ever be enforced at all. A promise to forbear is also, of course, necessary where that is what the debtor bargains for.

Where the consideration consists of a *promise* to forbear which specifies no time the creditor must forbear for a reasonable time.[95] There is no such requirement where the consideration consists of *actual forbearance*: here it is enough that the debtor had "a certain amount of forbearance."[96]

A forbearance only amounts to consideration for a promise or performance that is induced by it. In *Wigan* v. *English & Scottish Law Life Assurance Society*[97] a debtor executed a mortgage of an insurance policy in favour of his creditor. It was held that the creditor, who knew nothing of the mortgage, had not provided consideration for it merely by having forborne to sue for his antecedent debt. But Parker J. added[98] that if the creditor had been told of the mortgage and if, "on the strength of" it, he had actually forborne to sue for the debt, he would have provided consideration. The difficult question is to determine when the creditor forbears "on the strength of" the debtor's act or promise. He clearly does so where the debtor *expressly* requested the forbearance[99] but in *Alliance Bank* v. *Broom*[1] the bank's forbearance was held to constitute consideration even though the defendant had not expressly requested it. The case has been explained on the ground that the debtor had impliedly requested forbearance.[2] But where the forbearance is not requested expressly or by implication, it is no consideration. In *Combe* v. *Combe*[3] a husband during divorce proceedings promised to pay his wife an annual allowance. In an action to enforce this promise, the wife argued, *inter alia*, that she had given consideration for it by forbearing to apply to the court for a maintenance order. But her argument was rejected as she had not forborne at the husband's request.[4]

6. Performance of Existing Duty[5]

Much difficulty arises in determining whether a person who does, or promises to do, what he was already legally bound to do thereby provides consideration for a promise made to him. As he was already legally bound to do the act, he suffers no legal detriment.[6] But he may suffer a factual detriment[7] if he actually does the act: this may be more troublesome to him than to pay damages. The promisor may also get a factual benefit, as

---

[95] *Ante* p. 82.
[96] *Alliance Bank* v. *Broom* (1864) 2 Dr. & Sm. 289, 292.
[97] [1909] 1 Ch. 291: *cf. ante*, p. 75.
[98] At p. 298.
[99] *Crears* v. *Hunter* (1887) 19 Q.B.D. 341, 344.
[1] (1864) 2 Dr. & Sm. 289.
[2] *Fullerton* v. *Provincial Bank of Ireland* [1903] A.C. 309, 313.
[3] [1951] 2 K.B. 215.
[4] *Quaere* whether such a request should not have been implied.
[5] Davis, 6 C.L.J. 202; Reynolds and Treitel, 7 Malaya Law Rev. 1, Aivazian, Trebilcock & Penny, 22 *Osgoode Hall L.J.* 173.
[6] *Ante*, p. 65.
[7] *Ante*, p. 65.

damages might not fully compensate him for the loss which he would suffer if the duty were broken. Denning L.J. has therefore said that the performance of an existing duty, or the promise to perform it, was of itself good consideration.[8] This radical view has not been accepted; but the requirement of consideration in this group of cases has been mitigated by recognising that it can be satisfied where the promisee has conferrred a factual (as opposed to a legal) benefit on the promisor.[9]

(1) Duty imposed by law

In certain cases a person cannot enforce a promise made to him in return for performing, or promising to perform, a duty imposed by law (as opposed to one imposed by contract). Thus a public officer cannot enforce a promise to pay him money for doing his duty as such,[10] and generally a person does not provide consideration for forbearing to engage in a course of conduct that is criminal.[11] To allow enforcement of such promises would encourage extortion; and it is this ground of public policy, rather than want of consideration, that accounts for most of the authorities that establish the present rule. The position was different where no such grounds of public policy existed: for example, promises to pay rewards for information that might lead to the arrest of a felon were often enforced[12] though, till 1968, a person who had such information was bound to communicate it to the police, and indeed committed an offence[13] if he failed to do so. Public policy was not offended by the enforcement of such promises, as they might induce people to look for the information and so promote the interests of justice. These cases show that an act may constitute consideration even though there is a public duty to do it.

The contrary view is, indeed, supported by *Collins* v. *Godefroy*[14] where an attorney had been subpoenaed to give evidence and had been promised a guinea a day for attendance. This was held to be "a promise without consideration" as he was already bound to attend. But the reasoning is hard to reconcile with the reward cases just mentioned; and the actual decision has long ceased to represent the practice in such cases.[15] A subpoena must be

---

[8] *Ward* v. *Byham* [1956] 1 W.L.R. 496, 498; *Williams* v. *Williams* [1957] 1 W.L.R. 148, 151.

[9] *Post*, pp. 89, 93.

[10] *Wathen* v. *Sandys* (1811) 2 Camp. 640; *Morris* v. *Burdett* (1808) 1 Camp. 218; *Bilke* v. *Havelock* (1813) 3 Camp. 374; *Morgan* v. *Palmer* (1825) 2 B. & C. 729, 736.

[11] *Brown* v. *Brine* (1975) L.R. 1 Ex.D. 5 (forbearance to commit criminal libel).

[12] *England* v. *Davidson* (1840) 11 A. & E. 856; *Neville* v. *Kelly* (1862) 12 C.B.(N.S) 740; *Bent* v. *Wakefield and Barnsley Union Bank* (1878) 4 C.P.D. 1. Contrast *Maryland Casualty Co.* v. *Matthews*, 209 F.Supp. 822 (1962) where a similar claim *by a detective* failed on grounds of public policy.

[13] *i.e.* misprision of felony: *Sykes* v. *D.P.P.* [1962] A.C. 528. This offence was abolished by Criminal Law Act 1967, s.1. The offence of concealing an arrestable offence created by s.5(1) of that Act is narrower in scope than the former offence of misprision of felony; it is only committed if the person withholding the information accepts or agrees to accept some consideration (other than making good the loss) for not disclosing it. *Cf. post*, p. 393. For the definition of "arrestable offence," see now Police & Criminal Evidence Act 1984, s.24.

[14] (1831) 1 B. & Ad. 950; *cf. Willis* v. *Peckham* (1820) 1 Br. & B. 515; *Thoresen Car Ferries Ltd.* v. *Weymouth Portland B.C.* [1977] 2 Lloyd's Rep. 614, 619.

[15] *Re Working Men's Mutual Society* (1882) 21 Ch.D. 831; *Chamberlain* v. *Stoneham* (1889) 24 Q.B.D. 113.

accompanied by a tender of "conduct money"[16]; this includes the reasonable expenses of attending the trial, and, in certain cases, compensation for loss of time. It seems that all witnesses who attend in a professional capacity, whether they are strictly expert witnesses or not, are entitled to compensation for loss of time; and expert witnesses can validly contract for payment.[17]

In *Ward* v. *Byham*[18] the father of an illegitimate child promised to pay its mother £1 per week "providing you can prove that (the child) is well looked after and happy, and also that she is allowed to decide for herself whether or not she wishes to come and live with you." The mother began to look after the child, and it was held that she could enforce the father's promise although she was under a statutory duty to maintain the child. One basis of the decision is that the mother had provided consideration by showing that she had made the child happy, etc.: in this way she can be said to have conferred a factual benefit on the father, even though she may not have suffered any detriment.[19] But if a son's promise not to bore his father is not good consideration,[20] it is hard to see why a mother's promise to make her child happy should stand on a different footing. There is, with respect, force in Denning L.J.'s view, that the mother provided consideration by merely performing her legal duty to support the child.

There is, moreover, no doubt that a person can provide consideration by doing, or promising, *more* than he is by law obliged to do. Thus in *Glasbrook Bros. Ltd.* v. *Glamorgan C.C.*[21] mine-owners who feared violence from strikers asked, and promised to pay, for a greater degree of police protection than the police reasonably thought necessary. It was held that the police authority had provided consideration for this promise by giving the extra protection, and that accordingly the promise was enforceable. The position in cases of this kind is now regulated by statute. Section 15(1) of the Police Act 1964 provides that payment can be claimed for "special police services" rendered at the "request" of the person requiring them. Such a request can be implied from conduct, *e.g.* where a person organises an event which cannot safely take place without such special services. On this reasoning, a football club has been held liable to a police authority for the cost of policing matches played on its ground.[22] Such liability arises irrespective of contract.

The cases so far discussed under this heading raise the problem whether payment can be recovered (or retained) for a service which *has been* rendered in the performance of a public duty. But further problems can arise where a statute imposes two duties: one on a public authority to render specified services and one on the recipient to pay for them. In such a case the recipient does not provide consideration for the authority's promise to render the services merely by promising to pay for them; but his promise to *make use of* the services (being something that he is not bound by the stat-

[16] Supreme Court Act 1981, s.36(4). A subpoenaed witness (other than an expert witness) is not entitled to more than this and if he threatens to withhold or alter his evidence unless he is paid more he may be guilty of blackmail: *R.* v. *Clear* [1968] 1 Q.B. 670; *semble* the same result could be reached under Theft Act 1968, s.21.

[17] See Taylor, *Evidence*, (12th ed), pp. 801 *et seq.*

[18] [1956] 1 W.L.R. 496.

[19] *Williams* v. *Roffey Bros. & Nicholls (Contractors) Ltd.* [1991] 1 Q.B. 1, 13.

[20] *White* v. *Bluett* (1853) 23 L.J. Ex. 36; *ante*, p. 79.

[21] [1925] A.C. 270.

[22] *Harris* v. *Sheffield United F.C. Ltd.* [1988] Q.B. 77.

ute to do) can amount to consideration for the authority's promise to render them.[23]

(2) Duty imposed by contract with promisor

When A was bound by contract with B to do, or to forbear from doing, something, the law at one time took the view that A's performance of that duty (or his promise to perfom it) was no consideration for a new promise by B. Recent authority qualifies that view but the extent of the qualification is uncertain, so that any statement of the present position can only be tentative. The cases fall into three groups.

(a) CASES IN WHICH THERE WAS NO CONSIDERATION. The view that there was no consideration for B's new promise was first established in cases in which seamen who had bound themselves to serve for a voyage were promised higher wages by the masters of their ships if they performed their duty by working the ships home. It was held that these promises were not binding. Originally this conclusion was based on the ground of public policy that the enforcement of such promises might lead to extortion.[24] But in one of the reports of *Stilk* v. *Myrick*[25] the result was also supported on the ground that the men provided no consideration by only doing what they were already bound to do; and this is the explanation of such cases which is now commonly accepted.[26] On the same principle, a promise to pay extra freight for the carriage of goods to the agreed destination cannot be enforced by the carrier[27]; and a debtor's promise to pay in stated instalments a debt that is already due is no consideration for the creditor's promise not to take bankruptcy proceedings in respect of the debt.[28] The view that the new promises in such cases should not be enforced seems to be based on two related lines of reasoning.

The first rests on the need to protect the promisor from extortion, in the shape of the promisee's refusal to perform unless he is promised extra pay. But this argument is much reduced in importance now that such a refusal may constitute duress.[29] Where the refusal *does* amount to duress, a promise induced by it can be avoided (and money paid in pursuance of it be recovered back) on that ground.[30] This is true even where the promise *is* supported by consideration: for example, because the promisee has undertaken, not merely to perform his duties under the original contract, but

---

[23] *Thoresen Car Ferries* v. *Weymouth Portland B.C.* [1977] 2 Lloyd's Rep. 614, 619.

[24] *Harris* v. *Watson* (1791) Peake 102; *cf. Scotson* v. *Pegg* (1861) 6 H. & N. 295, 299.

[25] That in (1809) 2 Camp. 317; the other report, in 6 Esp. 129, does not mention consideration at all and makes the decision turn on public policy. Both grounds are stated in *Harris* v. *Carter* (1854) 3 E. & B. 559.

[26] *Harrison* v. *Dodd* (1914) 111 L.T. 47; *Swain* v. *West (Butchers) Ltd.* [1936] 3 All E.R. 261; *The Atlantic Baron* [1979] Q.B. 705, 712; *Pao On* v. *Lau Yiu Long* [1980] A.C. 614, 633; *Sybron Corp.* v. *Rochem Ltd.* [1984] Ch. 112, 129; *The Alev* [1989] 1 Lloyd's Rep. 138, 147.

[27] *The Proodos C.* [1980] 2 Lloyd's Rep. 390; *cf. Atlas Express Ltd.* v. *Kafco (Importers and Distributors) Ltd.* [1989] Q.B. 833.

[28] *Vanbergen* v. *St. Edmund's Properties Ltd.* [1933] 2 K.B. 223.

[29] *Post*, pp. 363–365.

[30] As in *The Universe Sentinel* [1983] 1 A.C. 366; *B. & S. Contracts & Designs* v. *Victor Green Publications* [1984] I.C.R. 419 *post*, p. 364; *Atlas Express Ltd.* v. *Kafco (Importers and Distributors) Ltd.* [1989] Q.B. 833; and in *T. A. Sundell & Sons Pty. Ltd.* v. *Emm Yannoulatos (Overseas) Pty. Ltd.* [1956] 56 S.R. (N.S.W.) 323. The position would have been the same in *The Atlantic Baron* [1975] Q.B. 705 if the victim of the duress had not affirmed the contract.

also to render some additional performance.[31] If, on the other hand, the promisee's refusal to perform the original contract does *not* amount to duress, it has been held that the promise cannot be impugned merely on the ground that the refusal amounted to an abuse by the promisee of a dominant bargaining position.[32] To allow a promise to be invalidated on this ground alone would introduce an intermediate category of promises unfairly obtained; and this would (in the words of Lord Scarman) "be unhelpful because it would render the law undcertain."[33]

The second reason for the view that the new promise should not be enforced was that the promisee suffered no legal detriment[34] in performing what was already due from him, nor did the promisor receive any legal benefit in receiving what was already due to him. But this reasoning takes no account of the fact that the promisee may in fact suffer a detriment: for example, the wages that a seaman could earn elsewhere may exceed those that he would earn under the original contract together with the damages that he would have to pay for breaking it. Conversely, the promisor may in fact benefit from the actual performance of what was legally due to him: in *Stilk* v. *Myrick* the master got his ship home and this may well have been worth more to him than any damages that he could have recovered from the crew.

(b) FACTUAL BENEFIT TO PROMISOR. The foregoing discussion shows that a new promise by B in consideration of A's performing his duty to B under an earlier contract between them is not necessarily obtained by duress; and that A's performance of the duty may in fact benefit B. Where both these conditions are satisfied, it has been held that A can enforce B's new promise.

In *Williams* v. *Roffey Bros. & Nicholls (Contractors) Ltd.*[35] B had engaged A as carpentry sub-contractor, for the purpose of performing a contract between B and X to refurbish a number of flats. The amount payable by B to A under the subcontract was £20,000 but B later promised to make extra payments to A, who undertook no additional obligation in return.[36] B made this new promise because B's own surveyor recognised that the originally agreed sum of £20,000 was too low, and because B feared that A (who was in financial difficulties) would not be able to complete his work on time, and so expose B to penalties for delay under his contract with X. It was held that B's promise to make the extra payments to A was supported by consideration in the shape of the "practical benefits"[37] obtained by B from A's performance of his duties under the original

---

[31] *e.g. The Atlantic Baron* [1979] Q.B. 705; *post*, p. 91 at n. 46; *The Alev* [1989] 1 Lloyd's Rep. 138.

[32] *Pao On* v. *Lau Yiu Long* [1980] A.C. 614, 632.

[33] *Ibid.*, p. 634. This statement was made in a case involving three parties, but it is of general application: *Williams* v. *Roffey Bros. & Nicholls (Contractors) Ltd.* [1991] 1 Q.B. 1, 15.

[34] *Ante*, p. 65.

[35] [1991] 1 Q.B. 1; Adams and Brownsword, 53 M.L.R. 536.

[36] The payments under the original contract were found to be due in unspecified instalments while those under the new promise were due as each flat was completed, but no attempt was made to argue that this change in the times when payment was due *might* have been to A's disadvantage and therefore provided consideration. There is perhaps a hint to this effect in Russell L.J.'s judgment at p. 19.

[37] *Ibid.* p. 11; *cf. ibid.* pp. 19, 23; followed in *Anangel Atlas Compania Naviera S.A.* v. *Ishikawajima-Harima Heavy Industries Co. Ltd. (No. 2)* [1990] 2 Lloyd's Rep. 526, where "promisor" and "promisee" appear to have been transposed in a passage at p. 545.

contract between them.[38] Since no allegation of duress on A's part had been made by B, the new promise by B to pay extra could not be avoided on this ground. There had been no threat by A to break his original contract; indeed, the initiative for the agreement containing the promise of extra pay seems to have come from B.

The consideration for B's promise in the *Williams* case appears to have been the factual benefit obtained by B from A's actual performance of his earlier contract with B. This element of factual benefit has been regarded as consideration where a person performs or (promises to perfom) a contractual duty owed to a third party[39]; and the *Williams* case is to be welcomed in bringing the two-party cases in line with those involving three parties.[40] But it is by no means clear how the case is, from this point of view, to be reconciled with *Stilk* v. *Myrick* and with the line of more recent decisions which have followed that case. As has been suggested above, the master in *Stilk* v. *Myrick* also obtained a factual benefit (in getting his ship home); and such a factual benefit will very often be obtained by B where he secures actual performance from A (as opposed to having to sue him for non-performance of the original contract).

In the *Williams* case, *Stilk* v. *Myrick* was not overruled; indeed Purchas L.J. described it as a "pillar stone of the law of contract."[41] But he added that the case might be differently decided today[42]; while Glidewell L.J. said that the present decision did not "contravene" but did "refine and limit"[43] the principle of the earlier case; and Russell L.J. said that the "rigid approach" to consideration in *Stilk* v. *Myrick* was "no longer necessary or desirable."[44] The conclusion which may tentatively be drawn from these statements is that the factual benefit to B in securing A's performance of the earlier contract will normally suffice to constitute consideration. The insistence in the earlier cases on the stricter requirement of legal benefit or detriment is no longer justified by the need to guard against extortion, now that this risk is more satisfactorily dealt with by the expanding concept of duress.

(c) OTHER CONSIDERATION. The promisee may provide other consideration for the new promise by doing, or promising to do, more than he was bound by the original contract to do. Thus a seaman is entitled to extra wages if, during the voyage, he is promoted and so undertakes additional

---

[38] In fact, B did not secure the whole of this benefit, but this was because his wrongful failure to make the extra payments justified A's refusal to continue with the work: see *post*, p. 689.

[39] *Post*, p. 92.

[40] In *Stilk* v. *Myrick ante*, p. 88 the distinction was ignored: no one even asked whether the original contract was with the promisor (the master) or with a third party (the shipowner). It is clear from the report in Espinasse that the action was brought against the master. *Cf.* also *Turner* v. *Owen* (1862) 3 F. & F. 176; *B. & S. Contracts & Designs* v. *Victor Green Publications Ltd.* [1984] I.C.R. 419.

[41] [1991] 1 Q.B. 1, 20.

[42] *Ibid.* p. 21. But he was not prepared to accept *Watkins* v. *Carrig* 21 A 2d. 591 (1941), where a contractor who had agreed to do excavating work unexpectedly struck hard rock and was held entitled to enforce a promise to pay nine times the originally agreed sum. That case was said not to represent English law in *The Atlantic Baron* [1979] Q.B. 705, 714, *cf.* also *Finland SS Co. Ltd.* v. *Felixstowe Dock Ry. Co.* [1980] 2 Lloyd's Rep. 390.

[43] [1991] 1 Q.B. 1, 16.

[44] *Ibid.* p. 18.

duties.[45] The same principle was applied where shipbuilders claimed an increase in the agreed price for a supertanker on the ground that the currency in which that price was to be paid had been devalued. The contract required the builders to give a performance guarantee, and it was held that they provided consideration for the prospective owners' promise to pay the price increase by making a corresponding increase in their performance guarantee.[46]

The promisee similarly provides other consideration where, before the new promise is made, circumstances arise which justify his refusal to perform the original contract. Thus the crew of a ship may be justified in refusing to complete a voyage because so many of their fellows have deserted that completion will involve hazards of a kind not originally contemplated. If they are induced to go on by a promise of extra pay, they do something which they were not bound to do, and can recover the extra pay.[47] The same principle applies where the contract is determined by notice or by mutual consent. Thus a promise to pay an employee higher wages after he has lawfully determined his contract by notice is binding. Or the parties might agree to rescind the contract and substitute a new one, at a higher rate of pay[48]; but this would in practice be hard to distinguish from a simple promise to pay higher wages for continuing to work under the original contract.[49] If the original contract is void, voidable or unenforceable, performance of the work specified would, it seems, be consideration for a promise of extra pay; and if the original contract was in fact good but was believed to be defective the new promise might still be binding on the analogy of the rule that forbearance to litigate an invalid claim may amount to consideration.[50] A final possibility is that the contract may provide, expressly or by implication, for revision of pay scales from time to time; and in such a case an agreement to pay higher (or to accept lower) wages would clearly be binding.[51]

(3) Duty imposed by contract with a third party

Two problems arise under this heading. The first is whether, if A is under a contractual duty to B, the *performance* of this duty can constitute consideration for a promise made to A by C. The second is whether A's *promise* to perform his contractual duty to B can constitute consideration for a counter-promise made to A by C.

(a) PERFORMANCE OF THE DUTY. It is now generally accepted that actual performance of a contractual duty owed to a third party can constitute con-

45 *Hanson* v. *Royden* (1867) L.R. 3 C.P. 47; *semble*, such extra pay is recoverable notwithstanding failure to comply with the formal requirements now contained in Merchant Shipping Act 1970, s.1; *cf. post*, p. 161, n. 4.

46 *The Atlantic Baron* [1979] Q.B. 705; Coote [1980] C.L.J. 40; Adams, 42 M.L.R. 557.

47 *Hartley* v. *Ponsonby* (1857) 7 E. & B. 872; *O'Neil* v. *Armstrong, Mitchell & Co.* [1895] 2 Q.B. 418; *Palace Shipping Co.* v. *Caine* [1907] A.C. 386; *Liston* v. *S.S. Carpathian (Owners)* [1915] 2 K.B. 42.

48 See *Schwartzreich* v. *Bauman-Basch Inc.* 131 N.E. 887 (1921); Dekoven, 35 U. of Chi.L. Rev. 173.

49 *Cf. post* pp. 96, 173.

50 *Ante*, p. 82; *cf. Anangel Atlas Compania Naviera S.A.* v. *Ishikawajima Harima Heavy Industries Co. Ltd. (No. 2)* [1990] 2 Lloyd's Rep. 526.

51 *e.g. Pepper & Hope* v. *Daish* [1980] I.R.L.R. 13; *cf. Lombard Tricity Finance Ltd.* v. *Paton* [1989] 1 All E.R. 98 (credit agreement providing for increases in interest rates to be made by lender).

sideration.[52] Two mid-nineteenth century cases which support this view are not wholly conclusive, since in each of them the promisee did, or may have done, *more* than he was bound under the earlier contract to do, and so provided additional consideration.[53] But it is harder to find any such additional consideration in *Shadwell* v. *Shadwell*.[54] An uncle wrote to his nephew: "I am glad to hear of your intended marriage with Ellen Nicholl; and as I promised to assist you at starting, I am happy to tell you that I will pay you £150 yearly during my life. . . . " A majority of the Court of Common Pleas held that the nephew had provided consideration for the uncle's promise by marrying Ellen Nicholl. It was said that there was a detriment to the nephew in that he "may have made a most material change in his position, and induced the object of his affection to do the same, and may have incurred pecuniary liabilities resulting in embarrassments"[55]; and that there was a benefit to the uncle in that the marriage was "an object of interest to a near relative."[56] The majority does not refer to the fact that the nephew was already bound contractually[57] to marry Ellen Nicholl. It could perhaps be argued that he forbore from trying to persuade her to postpone the wedding or to put an end to the engagement[58]; but this forbearance can scarcely be regarded as consideration in the absence of any suggestion that he contemplated the possibility.[59] The argument that the uncle benefited fares little better, for that benefit, as described by the court, was a purely sentimental one. It is, moreover, very doubtful whether, on the true construction of the uncle's letter, the nephew's marriage to Ellen Nicholl was intended to be the consideration for the uncle's promise, or only a condition.[60] Byles J., who dissented, treated it as a condition and also thought that the uncle's promise was not made with any contractual intent. His view was subsequently approved,[61] so that the correctness of the actual decision in *Shadwell* v. *Shadwell* is very much in doubt. But for what the decision is worth, it does support the view that the performance of a contractual duty owed to a third party can be good consideration for a promise. More recent authority on the point also supports that view. In *The*

[52] For the contrary view, see *McDevitt* v. *Stokes* 192 S.W. (1917). In *Pfizer Corp.* v. *Ministry of Health* [1965] A.C. 512 Lord Reid said that there was no contract where a chemist supplied drugs to a patient under the National Health Service in return for a prescription charge, because the chemist is "bound by his contract with the appropriate authority to supply the drug . . . " (at p. 536). But it seems from the context that Lord Reid was considering whether the relationship was consensual (*ante*, p. 5) and was not thinking of the problem of consideration.

[53] *Scotson* v. *Pegg* (1861) 6 H. & N. 295; *Chichester* v. *Cobb* (1866) 14 L.T. 433. The question in these cases was whether A provided consideration for C's promise by performing a contractual duty owed by A to B. There is no doubt that C's promise to perform a duty owed by B to A (or the performance of such a promise) can constitute consideration for a promise (express or implied) by A to C: see, *e.g.* *Brandt* v. *Liverpool, etc. S.N. Co.* [1924] 1 K.B. 575; *The Aramis* [1989] 1 Lloyd's Rep. 213, 225 (where C's claim failed for want of contractual intention: *post*, p. 155).

[54] (1860) 9 C.B.(N.S.) 159.

[55] *Ibid.* p. 174.

[56] *Ibid.*

[57] Now there would be no such contractual obligation: Law Reform (Miscellaneous Provisions) Act 1970, s.1.

[58] *Cf. De Cicco* v. *Schweitzer* 117 N.E. 807 (1917).

[59] *Ante*, p. 80.

[60] *Ante*, p. 69.

[61] *Jones* v. *Padavatton* [1969] 1 W.L.R. 328, 333.

Eurymedon[62] A (a firm of stevedores) had unloaded goods from B's ship. Some of these belonged to C who, for present purposes,[63] may be taken to have promised A not to sue him for damaging the goods. It was held that A had provided consideration for this promise by unloading the goods even if he was already bound by a contract with B to unload them.

(b) PROMISE TO PERFORM THE DUTY. It was at one time thought that a mere promise to perform a contractual duty owed to a third party could not constitute consideration. Thus in *Jones* v. *Waite*[64] it was said that a promise by A to C that A will pay a debt owed by A to B is no consideration for a promise made by C to A. This view seems to be based on the idea that A suffers no (legal) detriment by promising to pay a debt that he was already bound to pay; nor did it appear that C gained any benefit as a result of the promise. It is, however, possible for C to gain such a benefit: for example, where C promises A some benefit in return for A's promise not to carry out his intention of breaking a contract with the B company in which C has an interest. This was the position in *Pao On* v. *Lau Yiu Long*[65] where the plaintiffs, having entered into a contract with a company, refused to perform it unless the defendants, who were shareholders in the company, guaranteed them against loss which might be incurred as a result of the performance of one of the terms of that contract. The guarantee was given in consideration of the plaintiffs' promise to perform their contractual obligations to the company; and was held binding[66] on the ground that "A promise to perform, or the performance of, a pre-existing contractual obligation to a third party can be valid consideration."[67] This view seems, with respect, to be preferable to that expressed in *Jones* v. *Waite*; for the guarantee was certainly not gratuitous in a commercial sense.

It will, of course, be open to the promisor to avoid liability if he can show that the promisee's refusal to perform the contract with the third party amounted to duress[68] not merely with regard to the third party, but also with regard to the promisor himself.

SECTION 6. RESCISSION AND VARIATION

A contract may be rescinded or varied by subsequent agreement. The object of rescission is to release the parties from the contract, while that of variation is to alter some term of the contract. Such subsequent agreements give rise to problems of consideration, which will be discussed here, and to problems of form, to be discussed in Chapter 5. One aspect of the consider-

---

62 [1975] A.C. 154; followed in *The New York Star* [1981] 1 W.L.R. 138.

63 For a discussion of this point, see *post*, pp. 554–555.

64 (1839) 5 Bing. N.C. 341, 351, affirmed on another ground (1842) 9 Cl. & F. 107; contrast *Morton* v. *Burn* (1837) 7 A. & E. 19 (promise to pay assignee).

65 [1980] A.C. 614.

66 For rejection of the argument that the consideration was past, see *ante*, pp. 74–75.

67 [1980] A.C. 614, 632. *Cf. Scotson* v.*Pegg* (1861) 6 H. & N. 295, 301. In *The Eurymedon, supra*, at p. 168, a promise to perform a contractual duty owed to a third party is said to be consideration because it is a *benefit* to the promisee. This is puzzling at first sight, since consideration must be a detriment to the promisee or a benefit to the promisor. The reference, however, is to a case in which A's promise to C is said to be the consideration for C's counter-promise to A, and it is the validity of C's counter-promise which is in issue. In relation to the counter-promise, C is the promisor, and the benefit that he gets from A's promise satisfies the orthodox test of consideration. *Cf. ante*, p. 64.

68 See *ante*, p. 88.

ation problem has already been dealt with in discussing cases such as *Stilk* v. *Myrick*.[69] In those cases, the question was whether the performance by A of his obligations under the old contract could be consideration for a new promise from B. Our present problem is whether there is consideration for a promise by B to accept in discharge of A's obligations some performance *other* than that originally undertaken by A, or to grant A a total release from the contract. Even if there is no such consideration B's subsequent promise may, nevertheless, have some limited legal effect.

1. Rescission

An agreement to rescind a contract will generate its own consideration whenever each party has outstanding rights under the contract against the other. This is most obviously true where the contract is wholly executory and neither party is in breach.[70] Thus a contract for the sale of goods to be delivered and paid for on a future day can be rescinded by mutual consent at any time before the day fixed for performance. It is also clear that a contract can be rescinded by agreement after both parties have broken it.[71] And a partly executed contract can be rescinded by agreement so long as there are outstanding obligations on both sides: thus a lease for seven years can be rescinded by mutual consent after it has run for three years. In all these cases there is consideration for the rescission in that each party gives up his rights against the other under the original contract. It is, of course, essential, that *each* party should promise to give up his rights. If only one party does so, the other making no counterpromise, the former party's promise will be "entirely unilateral and unsupported by any consideration."[72]

An agreement to rescind a contract may also fail to generate its own consideration (and so lack contractual force) where only one party has outstanding rights under the contract. This will often be the position where the contract has been wholly executed by that party. Suppose that goods are sold and delivered but not paid for, and the parties then agree to "rescind" the contract. If the agreement means that the buyer is to return the goods and to be released from his liability to pay the price, there is good consideration for the promise of each party. But if it simply means that the buyer is not to pay the price, it is a gratuitous promise by the seller.[73] Conversely, goods may be sold, delivered and paid for, but turn out to be defective. Here an agreement to "rescind" would be a gratuitous promise if it simply released the seller from his liability under the original contract for the defects. Similarly, A may agree to sell goods to B for cash on delivery on a future day. If, when that day came, B tendered the price but A failed to deliver the goods, A would be liable in damages; and a rescission of the contract at this stage would be gratuitous if it merely released A from that

---

[69] *Ante*, p. 88.

[70] *Foste* v. *Dawber* (1851) Ex. 839, 850; *cf. The Trado* [1982] 1 Lloyd's Rep. 157.

[71] *e.g. Morris* v. *Baron & Co.* [1918] A.C. 1.

[72] *Collin* v. *Duke of Westminster* [1985] Q.B. 581, 598.

[73] *Commissioner of Stamp Duties* v. *Bone* [1977] A.C. 511, 519. ("A debt can only be truly released and extinguished by agreement for valuable consideration or under seal.") This rule seems with respect, to have been overlooked in a dictum in *Brikom Investments Ltd.* v. *Carr* [1979] Q.B. 467, 488 accordingly to which "waiver" of instalments of rent could extinguish the tenant's liability to pay. The landlord's actual promise in that case was supported by consideration: *ante*, p. 84; *post*, p. 97.

liability. This is what is meant by the statement that rescission after breach requires separate consideration.[74]

That statement must, however, be qualified where the contract is a continuing one, such as one to deliver goods by instalments. An agreement to "rescind" such a contract after one defective instalment had been delivered and paid for would not be a gratuitous release of the seller from his liability for the defects, for he would be giving up his rights to have future instalments accepted and paid for. It is only where the defect is of such a kind as to give the buyer the right as a matter of law to treat the contract as repudiated[75] that the seller may be said to give up nothing in return for the buyer's promise not to sue for the defect. Even in such a case, however, this result would not necessarily follow; for so long as the seller in good faith believed that the contract remained binding he would provide consideration by forbearing to enforce it.[76]

Where the rescinding agreement does not generate its own consideration, it must be supported by separate consideration: there must, in technical language, be not only accord but also satisfaction. Thus a buyer of goods may agree to release a seller who has become liable in damages for non-delivery, if the seller will pay him £50. The agreement to release the seller is the accord; payment of the £50 is the satisfaction.[77] On payment of the £50, the seller is released from his liability in damages.

It was formerly said that an executory accord, *i.e.* one which had not yet been followed by satisfaction, had no effect: that it neither released the party in breach nor gave the other party any new right of action.[78] But it is settled that an executory accord can be enforced by the party to whom the satisfaction was offered,[79] and it may release the party by whom it was offered. In *Elton Cop Dyeing Co.* v. *Broadbent & Son Ltd.*,[80] a buyer of machinery claimed damages for breach of warranty. A compromise was reached by which the buyer agreed to withdraw his action and the seller to repair the machinery, bearing half the cost. The buyer then sued on the original contract, but was defeated by plea of accord and satisfaction. He had, on the true construction of the compromise, taken the seller's *promise* to repair in discharge of his original cause of action. The rule that the party in breach cannot rely on an executory accord only applies when the accord, on its true construction, means that he is only to be discharged when he has given satisfaction.

There is one long-established exception to the rule that accord without satisfaction does not discharge a contract after breach. If the holder of a bill of exchange or promissory note at or after its maturity absolutely, unconditionally and in writing renounces his rights against any person liable on the bill or note, the latter is discharged.[81] The exception provides a comparatively simple way of evading the general rule: the creditor can take a bill or note in satisfaction of the debt and then renounce it.

[74] *Atlantic Shipping & Trading Ltd.* v. *Louis Dreyfus & Co.* [1922] 2 A.C. 250, 262.
[75] *Post*, pp. 659 *et seq*.
[76] *Ante*, p. 82.
[77] *British-Russian Gazette Ltd.* v. *Associated Newspapers Ltd.* [1933] 2 K.B. 616, 643.
[78] *Bayley* v. *Homan* (1837) 3 Bing.N.C. 915; *cf. Morris* v. *Baron & Co.* [1918] A.C. 1, 36.
[79] *Henderson* v. *Stobart* (1850) 5 Ex. 99.
[80] (1919) 89 L.J.K.B. 186; *cf. Cartwright* v. *Cooke* (1832) 3 B. & Ad. 701; *Crowther* v. *Farrer* (1850) 15 Q.B. 677.
[81] Bills of Exchange Act 1882, s.62.

2. Variation

Four situations call for discussion.

First, a variation of a contract may amount to a rescission of the old contract followed by the making of a new one relating to the same subject-matter. The question whether there is consideration for the rescission then depends on the principles just discussed.[82] If there is consideration for the rescission there is also consideration for the new contract. "The same consideration which existed for the old agreement is imported into the new agreement, which is substituted for it."[83] The distinction between a variation by way of a rescission followed by the making of a new contract, and a simple variation appears to be one of degree.[84] The courts may be more ready to regard a renegotiation as falling into the former category where the original contract is wholly executory.

Secondly, the parties may agree to vary their contract in a way that can benefit either party. Such a variation generates its own consideration.[85] This would be the position if a lease were varied by altering the date on which notice of termination could be given[86]; or if a contract of sale were varied by altering the currency in which payment was to be made.[87] In the latter case, it would make no difference that the new currency was later devalued in relation to the old, for at the time of the variation it could not be certain how the two currencies would move in relation to each other: hence either party *might* benefit from the variation. If a variation is, taken as a whole, capable of benefiting either party, the requirement of consideration will be satisfied even though a particular term of the variation is for the sole benefit of one.[88] A variation does not, however, generate its own consideration if, though capable of benefiting either party, it is in fact made wholly for the benefit of one. For example, a variation as to the place at which a debt is to be paid may benefit either party and thus provide consideration for a promise by the creditor to accept part payment in full settlement. But it will not have this effect if it is introduced solely for the benefit of the debtor.[89] Similarly, an agreement to reduce the quantity of goods to be delivered and paid for under a contract for the sale of goods may benefit either party; but if it is made purely for the seller's convenience it will not be consideration for the buyer's promise to accept the smaller quantity; nor conversely.[90]

Thirdly, the parties may agree to vary the contract in a way that can confer a legal benefit[91] on only one party. In some situations, it is settled that such a variation does not generate its own consideration: thus a promise by

---

[82] *Ante*, pp. 94–95.
[83] *Stead* v. *Dawber* (1839) 10 A. & E. 57, 66.
[84] *Post*, p. 173; *cf. ante*, p. 91.
[85] *E.g.*, *Anangel Atlas Compania Naviera S.A.* v. *Ishikawajima-Harima Heavy Industries Co. Ltd (No. 2)* [1990] 2 Lloyd's Rep. 526.
[86] *Fenner* v. *Blake* [1900] 1 Q.B. 427.
[87] *W. J. Alan & Co. Ltd.* v. *El Nasr Export & Import Co.* [1972] 2 Q.B. 189; *Woodhouse A.C. Israel Cocoa Ltd. S.A.* v. *Nigerian Produce Marketing Co.* [1972] A.C. 741, 757.
[88] *Ficom S.A.* v. *Sociedad Cadex Ltda.* [1980] 2 Lloyd's Rep. 118, 132.
[89] *Vanbergen* v. *St. Edmund's Properties Ltd.* [1933] 2 K.B. 233; *cf. Continental Grain Export Corp.* v. *S.T.M. Grain Ltd.* [1979] 2 Lloyd's Rep. 460, 476.
[90] *Ibid.*
[91] *Ante*, p. 65.

a creditor to accept part payment of a debt in full settlement is not binding unless it is supported by some separate consideration.[92] Such separate consideration could be provided by some further variation which may benefit the creditor: for example, by a debtor's promise to make the part payment *before* the day when the debt becomes due.[93] In other situations, it is arguable[94] that the variation may be supported by consideration if, though capable of conferring a legal benefit on only one party, it can also confer a factual benefit[95] on the other, *e.g.* where it secures eventual delivery of goods to a buyer when strict insistence on the original contract would have led to nothing but litigation.

Fourthly, there is the apparently paradoxical possibility that the parties may agree to vary a contract even before that contract has been concluded. This may be the position where parties negotiate on the basis of formal documents and one of them represents that the proposed contract will be on terms less favourable to himself than those set out in the documents. If the documents are nevertheless executed without alteration, the representation may then be enforceable as a collateral contract. The consideration for the promise contained in the representation is provided by the representee when he executes the documents (and so enters into the principal contract) at the request of the representor and in reliance on the representation. In *Brikom Investments Ltd.* v. *Carr*[96] the plaintiffs, who owned blocks of flats, negotiated with their tenants for the sale of long leases of the flats on terms requiring the tenants to contribute to the cost of (*inter alia*) roof maintenance. At the time of the negotiations, the roof was in need of repairs, and the plaintiffs promised to execute these "at our own cost." It was held that one of the tenants had provided consideration for this promise by executing the agreement for the lease, and the lease itself; and that the promise was accordingly binding as a collateral contract. It followed that the plaintiffs could not enforce the term in the lease under which the tenant would (but for the collateral contract) have been liable to contribute to the cost of the roof repairs.[97] Greater difficulty would have arisen if the tenant had already executed the documents before the landlord's promise had been made,[98] for in that case the execution of the documents would have been past consideration.[99] The tenants could, however, have succeeded, even in such a case, on an alternative ground. The plaintiffs had been guilty of unreasonable delay in executing the repairs, and the tenants would, by forbearing to take proceedings in respect of that

---

[92] *Post*, p. 115.

[93] *Post*, pp. 117–118.

[94] On the analogy of the reasoning of *Williams* v. *Roffey Bros. & Nicholls (Contractors) Ltd.* [1991] 1 Q.B. 1, *ante*, p. 89.

[95] *Ante*, p. 65.

[96] [1979] Q.B. 467.

[97] This was agreed by all members of the Court of Appeal. For other grounds for the decision, see *post*, pp. 119, 122–123.

[98] From the grounds of appeal as stated on pp. 472–473 of the report, it seems that reliance was placed on pre-contract representations; *cf.* the statement at p. 490 that the landlord's promise was made "at the time when the leases were granted." According to Lord Denning M.R. at p. 480 "some of the tenants" had already signed agreements for leases when the representations were made; but that does not seem to have been the position with regard to any of the cases before the court.

[99] *Ante*, p. 73.

breach,[1] have provided consideration for the plaintiff's promise to bear the cost of the repairs.

A variation which is not supported by consideration has no contractual effect. But it may have limited effect as a waiver, or in equity.[2]

3. Waiver[3]

(1) At common law

Where a party promises to relinquish some or all of his rights under a contract, he is sometimes said to have "waived" those rights. Unfortunately, however, "the word 'waiver' . . . covers a variety of situations different in their legal nature. . . . "[4] Of the many senses in which it is used, three are relevant to the present discussion.[5]

(a) To MEAN RESCISSION. Sometimes waiver means total rescission of the contract: "The waiver spoken of in the case is an entire abandonment and dissolution of the contract."[6] This usage assumes that the rescission is supported by consideration.[7] It has been judicially criticised so far as it refers to a purported release without consideration. "To say that a claim is to be waived is incorrect. If a right has accrued, it must be released or discharged by deed or upon consideration."[8]

(b) To MEAN VARIATION. Waiver is occasionally used to refer to a variation which is contractually binding because it is supported by consideration.[9] It is also used to refer to a variation which, though supported by consideration, is for some other reason not binding contractually. This usage occurs in the context of the rule that a contract which is required to be in, or evidenced in, writing can be rescinded but not varied orally.[10] Here waiver is sometimes used to refer to a variation as opposed to a rescission. For example, in one case a written contract for the sale of iron called for delivery in June; later the delivery date was orally extended at the request of the buyer. In spite of the extension, the buyer failed to take delivery, and the seller recovered damages for breach of the original contract: "There was no fresh agreement . . . which can be regarded as having been substituted for the original written contract. There was nothing more than a waiver by the defendants of a delivery by the plaintiff in June."[11]

---

[1] See [1979] Q.B. 467, 490; *cf. ante*, p. 84. Delay in *executing* the repairs was a breach irrespective of the question of who was to *pay* for them.

[2] *Post*, pp. 98–111, 120–124.

[3] Ewart, *Waiver Distributed*; Cheshire and Fifoot, 63 L.Q.R. 283; Stoljar, 35 Can.Bar.Rev. 485; Dugdale and Yates, 39 M.L.R. 681.

[4] *The Laconia* [1977] A.C. 850, 871 *cf. Kammins Ballrooms Co. Ltd.* v. *Zenith Investments (Torquay) Ltd.* [1971] A.C. 850, 882–883; *The Athos* [1983] 1 Lloyd's Rep. 127, 134; *The Kachenjunga* [1990] 1 Lloyd's Rep. 391, 397.

[5] For further senses, see *post* pp. 709–714.

[6] *Price* v. *Dyer* (1810) 17 Ves. 356, 364.

[7] *Ante*, p. 94.

[8] *Atlantic Shipping & Trading Co. Ltd.* v. *Louis Dreyfus & Co.* [1922] 2 A.C. 250, 262; *cf. The Ion* [1980] 2 Lloyd's Rep. 245, 249.

[9] *Semble*, this is the sense in which the word is used by Roskill and Cumming-Bruce L.JJ. in *Brikom Investments Ltd.* v. *Carr* [1979] Q.B. 467, 488, 491; for the consideration for the "waiver," see *ante* p. 97; *cf. Shamsher Jute Mills Ltd.* v. *Sethia (London) Ltd.* [1987] 2 Lloyd's Rep. 388, 392.

[10] *Post*, p. 172.

[11] *Hickman* v. *Haynes* (1875) L.R. 10 C.P. 598, 604.

(c) TO MEAN FORBEARANCE. A variation may not be contractually binding for want of consideration or of contractual intention, or because it fails to comply with a legal requirement that it must be in, or evidenced in, writing.[12] It may nevertheless have certain limited legal effects, which are sometimes said to arise because one party has "waived" his rights. To distinguish such arrangements from contractually binding variations, they will here be referred to as "forbearances."[13] Their effects are as follows:

(i) The party requesting the forbearance cannot refuse to accept the varied performance. Thus, if a seller at the request of the buyer delivers late, the buyer cannot refuse to accept on the ground that delivery was not made at the time specified in the original contract.[14]

(ii) If the varied performance is actually made and accepted, neither party can claim damages on the ground that performance was not in accordance with the original contract. Thus, in the above example the seller who delivers late, or the buyer who takes delivery late, is not liable in damages. But if the contract is not performed at all, the damages are assessed on the footing that the breach took place at the end of the extended period.[15]

(iii) The cases that give rise to the greatest difficulty are those in which the party *granting* the forbearance refuses to perform, or to accept performance, in accordance with it.

Suppose, for example, that a buyer agrees, at the seller's request, to accept late delivery. The buyer cannot then claim damages for the seller's failure to deliver within the contract period[16]; but a further set of problems can arise if, after expiry of that period but within the extended period, the seller tenders delivery, and the buyer refuses to accept it. One possible view is that the seller cannot derive rights from a forbearance which is not binding as a contract, and that therefore he is not entitled to damages for the buyer's refusal to take delivery within the extended, but outside the original, contract period. A claim for such damages was accordingly rejected in *Plevins* v. *Downing*,[17] where the agreement to extend the delivery dates had no contractual force since it was oral[18] and probably unsupported by consideration, having been made at the request, and for the sole benefit, of the seller.[19]

But in many cases the party for whose benefit the forbearance was granted was allowed to enforce the contract in accordance with the new terms. In *Hartley* v. *Hymans*[20] a buyer of cotton agreed to allow the seller to make late delivery. It was held that he was liable in damages for peremptorily refusing to take delivery after the period originally specified in the contract had expired. Similarly, a party may acquiesce in a method of pay-

---

[12] *Post*, pp. 172–173.

[13] *Cf. The Kachenjunga* [1990] 1 Lloyd's Rep. 391, 397.

[14] *Hickman* v. *Haynes, supra*; *Levey & Co.* v. *Goldberg* [1922] 1 K.B. 688; *cf. British and Beningtons Ltd.* v. *N.W. Cachar Tea Co.* [1923] A.C. 48.

[15] *Ogle* v. *Vane* (1868) L.R. 3 Q.B. 272.

[16] *Cf. The Kachenjunga* [1989] 1 Lloyd's Rep. 354, 358, affirmed [1990] 1 Lloyd's Rep. 391.

[17] (1876) 1 C.P.D. 220.

[18] For this reason alone, the variation could not then have been enforced as a contract: *post*, p. 172.

[19] *Ante*, p. 96.

[20] [1920] 3 K.B. 475; *cf. Tyers* v. *Rosedale & Ferryhill Iron Co.* (1875) L.R. 10 Ex. 195; *Besseller Waechter Glover & Co.* v. *South Derwent Coal Ltd.* [1938] 1 K.B. 408; and see *Leather Cloth Co.* v. *Hieronimus* (1875) L.R. 10 Q.B. 104 (variation of route of shipment).

ment other than that specified in the contract so as to indicate that the new method is to become the "accepted method."[21] He cannot then refuse to perform his part simply because the other party has not performed his obligation to pay strictly in accordance with the terms originally agreed[22]; nor can he peremptorily require performance strictly in accordance with those terms.[23] In these cases it is sometimes said that there is no variation of the contract, but only a variation of the mode of performance; or that there is no variation, but only a waiver[24] in the sense of forbearance.

Such a forbearance differs from a variation which is supported by consideration in that it does not irrevocably alter the rights of the parties under the original contract. The party granting the forbearance *can generally retract it*, provided that he gives reasonable notice of his intention to do so to the party for whose benefit it was granted.[25] Thus, in *Charles Rickards Ltd.* v. *Oppenhaim*[26] a contract for the sale of a car provided for delivery on March 20. The car was not delivered on that day but the buyer continued to press for delivery and finally told the seller on June 29 that he must have the car by July 25 at the latest. It was held that the buyer could not have refused peremptorily to accept the car merely because the original delivery date had gone by, as he had continued to press for delivery; but that he could refuse on the seller's failure to comply with a notice to deliver within a reasonable time. Here the notice did give the seller a reasonable time to deliver, so that the buyer was justified in refusing to take the car after July 25. *A fortiori*, the buyer could have refused to take delivery if the original delivery date had been extended only for a fixed time and if delivery had not been made by the end of that time.[27]

A forbearance may, however, become irrevocable as a result of subsequent events: for example if a buyer indicates that he is willing to accept goods of a different quality from those contracted for, and the seller, in reliance on that assurance, so conducts himself as to put it out of his power to supply goods of the contract quality within the contract period.[28]

The distinction between a forbearance and a variation is sometimes said to depend on the intention of the parties[29]: a statement is a forbearance if the party making it intends to reserve a power to retract; but a variation if he intends permanently to abandon his rights under the contract. The courts were, however, anxious to avoid the unjust effects of the rules as to

---

[21] *The Scaptrade* [1981] 2 Lloyd's Rep. 425, 431 (where this requirement was not satisfied), affirmed without reference to this point [1983] 2 A.C. 694.

[22] *Panoutsos* v. *Raymond Hadley Corp. of N.Y.* [1917] 2 K.B. 473; *Tankexpress A/S* v. *Cie. Financière Belge des Petroles, S.A.* [1949] A.C. 76; *Plasticmoda Soc.* v. *Davidsons (Manchester) Ltd.* [1952] 1 Lloyd's Rep. 527.

[23] *Mitas* v. *Hymans* [1951] 2 T.L.R. 1215.

[24] *e.g.* in *Plevins* v. *Downing* (1876) 1 C.P.D. 220, 225; *Besseller Waechter Glover & Co.* v. *South Derwent Coal Co. Ltd.* [1938] 1 K.B. 408, 416; *The Kachenjunga* [1989] 1 Lloyd's Rep. 354, 358; [1990] 1 Lloyd's Rep. 391, 397–398.

[25] *Banning* v. *Wright* [1972] 1 W.L.R. 972, 981. *Ficom S.A.* v. *Sociedad Cadex Ltda.* [1980] 2 Lloyd's Rep. 118, 131; *Bremer Handelsgesellschaft mbH* v. *Raiffeisen Hauptgenossenschaft E.G.* [1982] 1 Lloyd's Rep. 599.

[26] [1950] 1 K.B. 616; *cf. Cape Asbestos Co. Ltd.* v. *Lloyds Bank Ltd.* [1921] W.N. 274, 276; *Bird* v. *Hildage* [1948] 1 K.B. 91; *State Trading Corp. of India* v. *Cie. Française d'Importation et de Distribution* [1983] 2 Lloyd's Rep. 679, 681.

[27] *Cf. Nichimen Corp.* v. *Gatoil Overseas Inc.* [1987] 2 Lloyd's Rep. 46, where similar fixed term extensions were granted by a seller.

[28] *Toepfer* v. *Warinco A.G.* [1978] 2 Lloyd's Rep. 569, 576.

[29] *Stead* v. *Dawber* (1839) 10 A. & E. 57, 64.

variations that were not contractually binding because they were oral or gratuitous. Hence they often interpreted a subsequent agreement as a forbearance, so as to give it at least some legal effects.

(2) In equity[30]

The common law rules as to waiver in the sense of forbearance are defective in two ways. First, they rest on the tenuous distinction between forbearance and variation, which can be deduced from the judgments, but does not provide any very solid basis for distinguishing between the actual decisions. It is hard to see, for instance, why the buyer in *Plevins* v. *Downing*[31] was allowed to reject late delivery, while the buyer in *Hartley* v. *Hymans*[32] was not allowed to do so. Secondly, the common law rules produced the paradoxical result that, the more a party purported to bind himself by a subsequent agreement, the less he was likely to be bound. An attempt permanently to renounce a right would be a variation, and ineffective for want of writing or consideration. But an attempt to suspend a right would be effective, to a limited extent, as a forbearance.

(a) HUGHES V. METROPOLITAN RY. Equity devised a more satisfactory approach to the problem by concentrating, not on the intention of the party granting the forbearance, but on the conduct of that party and on its effect on the position of the other party. The leading case is *Hughes* v. *Metropolitan Ry.*,[33] where a landlord gave his tenant notice requiring him to do repairs within six months. During the six months he began to negotiate with the tenant for the purchase of his lease. When the negotiations broke down, he immediately claimed to forfeit the lease on the ground that the tenant had not done the repairs. The claim was rejected, Lord Cairns saying that if one party leads the other "to suppose that the strict rights arising under the contract will not be enforced, or will be kept in suspense or held in abeyance, the person who otherwise might have enforced those rights will not be allowed to enforce them where it would be inequitable having regard to the dealings which have thus taken place between the parties."[34]; The landlord had by his conduct led the tenant to suppose that during the negotiations he would not enforce his right to forfeit. Hence he could not forfeit immediately the negotiations broke down: he had to give the tenant a reasonable time from that date to do the repairs. This equitable rule can now be applied to arrangements which might formerly have been regarded as variations ineffective at common law for want of consideration.[35] For reasons to be discussed later in this Chapter[36] the doctrine

[30] Denning, 15 M.L.R. 1; Wilson, 67 L.Q.R. 330; Sheridan, 15 M.L.R. 325; Gordon [1963] C.L.J. 222; Wilson [1965] C.L.J. 93; Thompson [1983] C.L.J. 257.

[31] (1876) 1 C.P.D. 220; *ante*, p. 99.

[32] [1920] 3 K.B. 475; *ante*, p. 99.

[33] (1877) 2 App.Cas. 439.

[34] At p. 448.

[35] *e.g. Charles Rickards Ltd.* v. *Oppenhaim* [1950] K.B. 616 (where both common law and equitable principles were applied). The principle in *Hughes* v. *Metropolitan Ry.* was said in *Brikom Investments Ltd.* v. *Carr* [1979] Q.B. 467, 489 to be "an illustration of *contractual* variation of strict contractual rights." This description was apt on the facts of that case, where the promise not to enforce such rights was supported by consideration: *ante*, p. 97. But the principle stated in *Hughes* v. *Metropolitan Ry.* applies even in the absence of such consideration: *cf. post*, p. 122.

[36] *Post*, p. 109.

is often (if somewhat misleadingly) referred to as "equitable" or "promissory" estoppel.

(b) Relationships within the doctrine. The rights which the equitable doctrine prevents a promisor or representor from enforcing normally arise out of a contract between him and the other party. But the doctrine can also apply where the relationship giving rise to rights and correlative duties is non-contractual: *e.g.* to prevent the enforcement of a liability imposed by statute on a company director for signing a bill of exchange in which the company's name is not correctly given[37]; or to prevent a man from ejecting a woman, with whom he had been cohabiting, from the family home.[38] On the other hand, it has been said that the doctrine "has no application as between landowner and a trespasser."[39] Hence the mere fact that a landowner has for some time failed or neglected to enforce his rights against a trespasser does not prevent him from subsequently doing so without notice.

It has, indeed, been suggested that the doctrine can even apply where, before the making of the promise or representation, there is no legal relationship of any kind giving rise to rights and duties between the parties[40]; or where there is only a putative contract between them: *e.g.* where the promisee is induced to believe that a contract into which he had undoubtedly entered was between him and the promisor, when in fact it was between the promisee and another person.[41] But it is submitted that these suggestions mistake the nature of the doctrine, which is to restrict the enforcement by the promisor of previously existing rights against the promisee. Such rights can only arise out of a legal relationship existing between these parties before the making of the promise or representation. To apply the doctrine where there was no such relationship would contravene the rule (to be discussed below) that the doctrine creates no new rights.[42]

(c) When applicable. The operation of the doctrine is subject to the following requirements:

(i) *Promise or representation.* There must be a promise (or an assurance or representation in the nature of a promise)[43] which is intended to affect the legal relationship between the parties[44] and which indicates that the promisor will not insist on his strict legal rights,[45] arising out of that relationship, against the promisee. Here, as elsewhere, the law applies an objective test. It is enough if the promise induces the promisee reasonably

---

[37] *Durham Fancy Goods Ltd.* v. *Michael Jackson (Fancy Goods) Ltd.* [1968] 2 Q.B. 839.

[38] *Maharaj* v. *Chand* [1986] A.C. 898.

[39] *Morris* v. *Tarrant* [1971] 2 Q.B. 143, 160.

[40] See *Evenden* v. *Guilford City F.C.* [1975] Q.B. 917, 924, 926 (actual decision overruled in *Secretary of State for Employment* v. *Globe Elastic Thread Co. Ltd.* [1980] A.C. 506); *cf.*, in Australia, *Waltons Stones (Interstate) Ltd.* v. *Maher* (1988) 164 C.L.R. 387.

[41] *The Henrik Sif* [1982] 1 Lloyd's Rep. 456, 466; the acutal decision can perhaps be explained as one of liability for actionable non-disclosure: *post*, p. 359.

[42] *Post*, p. 107. Some doubt as to the correctness of *The Henrik Sif*, *supra*, is expressed by Webster J. (who decided the case) in *Shearson Lehman Hutton Inc.* v. *MacLaine Watson & Co. Ltd.* [1989] 2 Lloyd's Rep. 570, 596, 604.

[43] *James* v. *Heim Galleries* (1980) 256 E.G. 819, 821; *Collin* v. *Duke of Westminster* [1985] Q.B. 581, 595.

[44] *Spence* v. *Shell* (1980) 256 E.G. 55, 63.

[45] Or that he will not rely on an available defence: *cf. post*, pp. 108–109, 361.

to believe that the other party will not insist on his strict legal rights.[46] A mere threat to do something is not sufficient, nor, probably, is a representation or promise by a person that he *will* enforce a legal right: thus the doctrine does not apply where A tells B that he will exercise his right to cancel a contract between them unless by a specified date B has paid sums due under the contract to A.[47]

To bring the equitable doctrine into operation, the promise or representation must be "clear" or "unequivocal," or "precise and unambiguous." This requirement seems to have originated in the law relating to estoppel by representation[48]; and it is now frequently stated in relation to "waiver"[49] and "promissory estoppel."[50] It does not mean that the promise or representation must be express[51]; it may equally well be implied. For example, in *Hughes* v. *Metropolitan Ry.*[52] itself the landlord made no express promise that he would not enforce his right to forfeit the lease; but an implication of such a promise fairly arose from the course of the negotiations between the parties. There is some support for the view that the promise must have the same degree of certainty as would be needed to give it contractual effect if it were supported by consideration.[53] Thus if the statement could not take effect as a contract because it was too vague,[54] or if it was insufficiently precise to amount to an offer,[55] it will not bring the equitable doctrine into operation.[56]

The requirement that the promise or representation must be "clear" or "unequivocal" is essential to prevent a party from losing his legal rights merely because he has granted some indulgence by failing throughout to

---

[46] *Bremer Handelsgesellschaft mbH* v. *Vanden Avenue-Izegem P.V.B.A.* [1978] 2 Lloyd's Rep. 109, 126; *Bremer Handelsgesellschaft mbH* v. *Mackprang Jr.* [1979] 1 Lloyd's Rep. 221 (both these cases concerned "waiver"; *cf. infra*, n. 49).

[47] *Drexel Burnham Lambert International NV* v. *El Nasr* [1986] 1 Lloyd's Rep. 356.

[48] *Low* v. *Bouverie* [1981] 3 Ch. 82, 106; *Woodhouse A.C. Israel Cocoa Ltd. S.A.* v. *Nigerian Produce Marketing Co. Ltd.* [1972] A.C. 741; *The Shakleford* [1978] 2 Lloyd's Rep. 155, 159.

[49] *Finagrain S.A. Geneva* v. *P. Kruse Hamburg* [1976] 2 Lloyd's Rep. 508, 534; *The Laconia* [1977] A.C. 850, 871; *Bremer Handelsgesellschaft mbH* v. *Vanden Avenne-Izegem P.V.B.A.* [1978] 2 Lloyd's Rep. 109, 126; *The Mihalios Xilas* [1979] 1 W.L.R. 1018, 1024; *Avimex S.A.* v. *Dewulf & Cie.* [1979] 2 Lloyd's Rep. 57, 67; *Bremer Handelsgesellschaft GmbH* v. *Westzucker GmbH* [1981] 1 Lloyd's Rep. 207, 212; *Prosper Homes* v. *Hambro's Bank Executor & Trustee Co.* (1979) 39 P. & C.R. 395; *Bremer Handelsgesellschaft mbH* v. *Finagrain Cie. Commerciale Agricole & Financière S.A.* [1981] 2 Lloyd's Rep. 259, 266; *The Rio Sun* [1981] 2 Lloyd's Rep. 489 and [1982] 1 Lloyd's Rep. 404; *The Athos* [1983] 1 Lloyd's Rep. 127, 134–135; *Bremer Handelsgesellschaft mbH* v. *Deutsche Conti-Handelsgesellschaft mbH* [1983] 1 Lloyd's Rep. 689; for the analogy between waiver and the equitable doctrine here under discussion, see *ante*, p. 101; *post*, p. 110.

[50] *B.P. Exploration Co. (Libya) Ltd.* v. *Hunt (No. 2)* [1979] 1 W.L.R. 783, 812 (affd. without reference to this point [1983] 2 A.C. 352); *Spence* v. *Shell* (1980) 256 E.G. 55, 63; *James* v. *Heim Galleries* (1980) 256 E.G. 819, 821; *The Post Chaser* [1981] 2 Lloyd's Rep. 695, 700; *The Scaptrade* [1983] Q.B. 529, 534–535 ("equitable estoppel") (affd. without reference to this point [1983] A.C. 694); *Goldworthy* v. *Brickell* [1987] Ch. 378, 410.

[51] *Spence* v. *Shell* (1980) 256 E.G. 55, 63.

[52] (1877) 2 App.Cas. 439; *cf. The Post Chaser* [1981] 2 Lloyd's Rep. 695, 700.

[53] *The Winson* [1980] 2 Lloyd's Rep. 213, 222; reversed on other grounds [1982] A.C. 939; *Drexel Burnham Lambert International NV* v. *El Nasr* [1986] 1 Lloyd's Rep. 357; *The Antclizo* [1987] 2 Lloyd's Rep. 130, 142 (affd. [1988] 1 W.L.R. 603, where the law was criticised on other grounds; legislative Reform followed in Courts and Legal Services Act 1990, s.102, *ante*, p. 10); *cf. ante*, p. 48 for the requirement of certainty.

[54] *Ante*, pp. 48–49.

[55] *Ante*, p. 8.

[56] *The Winson* [1980] 2 Lloyd's Rep. 213, 223; reversed on other grounds [1982] A.C. 939.

insist on strict performance of a contract[57]; or because he has offered some concession in the course of negotiations for the settlement of a dispute arising out of the contract. Thus the requirement was not satisfied where one of the parties to such negotiations throughout insisted on strict compliance with the terms of the contract.[58] Nor was it satisfied where he accepted less than that to which he was entitled but did so subject to an express reservation of his rights.[59] Failure, in the course of negotiations of this kind, to object to a defect or deficiency in performance is likewise insufficient if the injured party did not know and could not reasonably have known of it[60] or if full performance remained possible and continued to be demanded by that party.[61] On the other hand, failure to object to a known defect or deficiency within a reasonable time of its discovery[62] may be regarded as an unequivocal indication of the injured party's intention not to insist on his strict legal rights.[63] The position seems to be the same where the defect or deficiency, though not actually known to the injured party, was obvious or could have been discovered by him, if he had taken reasonable steps.[64] But where more than one matter is in dispute between the parties, "emphatic reliance upon some important disputed point does not by itself . . . imply any unequivocal representation that compliance with other parts of the bargain is thereby waived."[65]

Although a promise or representation may be made by conduct, mere inactivity will not suffice for the present purpose since "it is difficult to imagine how silence and inaction can be anything but equivocal."[66] Unless

---

[57] *The Scaptrade* [1981] 2 Lloyd's Rep. 425, 431, [1983] Q.B. 529, 535 affd. [1983] 2 A.C. 694; *cf. Cape Asbestos Co. Ltd.* v. *Lloyds Bank Ltd.* [1921] W.N. 274, 276; *Bunge S.A.* v. *Compagnie Européenne des Céréales* [1982] Lloyd's Rep. 306; *Bremer Handelsgesellschaft mbH* v. *Raiffeisen Hauptgenossenschaft E.G.* [1982] 2 Lloyd's Rep. 599; *Bremer Handelsgesellschaft mbH* v. *Bunge Corp.* [1983] 1 Lloyd's Rep. 476.

[58] *V. Berg & Son Ltd.* v. *Vanden Avenne-Izegem P.V.B.A.* [1977] 1 Lloyd's Rep. 500; *cf. Edm. J. M. Mertens & Co. P.V.B.A.* v. *Veevoeder Import Export Vimex B.V.* [1979] 2 Lloyd's Rep. 372.

[59] *Finagrain S.A. Geneva* v. *P. Kruse Hamburg* [1976] 2 Lloyd's Rep. 508; *cf. Cook Industries Inc.* v. *Meunerie Liègeois S.A.* [1981] 1 Lloyd's Rep. 359, 368; *Bremer Handelsgesellschaft mbH* v. *Deutsche Conti Handelsgesellschaft mbH* [1983] 2 Lloyd's Rep. 45; *Peter Cremer* v. *Granaria B.V.* [1981] 2 Lloyd's Rep. 583; *cf. The Winson* [1980] 2 Lloyd's Rep. 213 (as to which see n. 56, supra).

[60] *Avimex S.A.* v. *Dewulf & Cie.* [1979] 2 Lloyd's Rep. 57.

[61] *The Mihalios Xilas* [1979] W.L.R. 1018; *Bremer Handelsgesellschaft mbH* v. *C. Mackprang Jr.* [1981] 1 Lloyd's Rep. 292, 299; *Bremer Handelsgesellschaft mbH* v. *Westzucker GmbH* [1981] 1 Lloyd's Rep. 207, 212–213; *Peter Cremer* v. *Granaria B.V.* [1981] 2 Lloyd's Rep. 583; *The Post Chaser* [1981] 2 Lloyd's Rep. 695, 700.

[62] See *The Laconia* [1977] A.C. 850 (where retention of an under-payment accepted without authority by the payee's bank was held not to amount to a waiver). Contrast *The Superhulls Cover Case* [1990] 2 Lloyd's Rep. 431 (where the deficiency was not known).

[63] *e.g. Bremer Handelsgesellschaft mbH* v. *Vanden Avenne-Izegem P.V.B.A.* [1978] 2 Lloyd's Rep. 109.

[64] See *Bremer Handelsgesellschaft mbH* v. *C. Mackprang Jr.* [1979] 1 Lloyd's Rep. 221, where there was a division of opinion on the point in the Court of Appeal. Contrast, for a different type of waiver, pp. 712–714, *post.*

[65] *The Athos* [1983] 1 Lloyd's Rep. 127, 135.

[66] *The Leonidas D* [1985] 1 W.L.R. 925, 937; *cf. Cook Industries* v. *Tradax Export S.A.* [1983] 1 Lloyd's Rep. 327, 332 (affirmed [1985] 2 Lloyd's Rep. 454); *The August P. Leonhardt* [1985] 2 Lloyd's Rep. 28, 33; *MSC Mediterranean Shipping Co. SA* v. *B.R.E. Metro Ltd.* [1985] 2 Lloyd's Rep. 239; *Cie. Française d'Importation, etc.,* v. *Deutsche Continental Handelsgesellschaft* [1985] 2 Lloyd's Rep. 592. 598; *The Antclizo* [1986] 1 Lloyd's Rep. 181, 187 (affd. [1988] 1 W.L.R. 603); *The Superhulls Cover Case* [1990] 2 Lloyd's Rep. 431, 452; and see *ante*, p. 103, n. 55).

the law took this view, mere failure to assert a contractual right could lead to its loss; and the courts have on a number of occasions rejected this clearly undesirable conclusion. Thus it has been held that there is "no ground for saying that mere delay, however lengthy, destroys the contractual right"[67]; and that the mere failure to prosecute a claim regarded by both parties as hopeless did not amount to a promise to abandon it.[68] The only circumstances in which "silence and inaction" can have this effect are the exceptional ones (discussed elsewhere in this book[69]) in which the law imposes a duty to disclose facts or to clarify a legal relationship and the party under the duty fails to perform it.

(ii) *Reliance.* The requirement of reliance means that the promise or representation must in some way have influenced the conduct of the party to whom it was made. Although the promise need not form the sole inducement,[70] it must (it is submitted) be *some* inducement. Hence the requirement would not be satisfied if it could be shown that the other party's conduct was not influenced by the promise at all,[71] so that he was not in any way prejudiced by it.[72] But if this is a matter of "mere speculation,"[73] or if the promise or representation "was one of the factors . . . relied upon,"[74] it would form a sufficient inducement. In other words, where the conduct intended by the promisor has followed after the making of the promise, it will be up to the promisor to establish that the conduct was not induced by the promise.[75]

There is sometimes said to be a further requirement, namely that the promisee must have suffered some "detriment" in reliance on the promise.[76] This may mean that the promisee must have done something which he was not previously bound to do and as a result have suffered loss, *e.g.* by incurring expenditure in reliance on the promise. The alleged requirement of "detriment" in this sense is based on the analogy of estoppel.[77] But that analogy is (as we shall see)[78] inexact; and the equitable doctrine can clearly operate even though there is no "detriment" in this sense.[79] It is enough if the promisee has altered his position in reliance on the promise so that it

---

[67] *Amherst* v. *James Walker Goldsmith & Silversmith Ltd.* [1983] Ch. 305, 315; *cf.*, in another context, *The Nai Genova* [1984] 1 Lloyd's Rep. 353, 365.

[68] *Collin* v. *Duke of Westminster* [1985] Q.B. 581.

[69] *Post*, pp. 352–359, *ante*, p. 32; see for example, *The Lutetian* [1982] 2 Lloyd's Rep. 140, 158; *P. S. Chellaram & Co. Ltd.* v. *China Ocean Shipping Co.* [1989] 1 Lloyd's Rep. 43.

[70] *Cf. post*, pp. 305–306.

[71] See *Fontana N.V.* v. *Mautner* (1979) 254 E.G. 199; *Raiffeisen Hauptgenossenschaft* v. *Louis Dreyfus & Co.* [1981] 1 Lloyd's Rep. 345, 352; *Cook Industries Ltd.* v. *Meunerie Liègeois S.A.* [1981] 1 Lloyd's Rep. 359, 368; *The Scaptrade* [1983] Q.B. 529, 536, affirmed without reference to this point [1983] 2 A.C. 694; *Bremer Handelsgesellschaft mbH* v. *Bunge Corp.* [1983] 1 Lloyd's Rep. 476; *Bremer Handelsgesellschaft mbH* v. *Deutsche-Conti Handelsgesellschaft mbH* [1983] 1 Lloyd's Rep. 689.

[72] *Ets. Soules & Cie.* v. *International Trade Development Co. Ltd.* [1980] 1 Lloyd's Rep. 129; *The Multibank Holsatia* [1988] 2 Lloyd's Rep. 486, 493.

[73] *Brikom Investments Ltd.* v. *Carr* [1979] Q.B. 467, 482.

[74] *Ibid.* at p. 490 (*per* Cumming-Bruce L.J., whose decision was based on the different ground discussed *ante*, p. 97).

[75] *Cf.* the similar rule in cases of "proprietary estoppel" stated *post*, p. 130.

[76] *e.g. Fontana N.V.* v. *Mautner* (1979) 254 E.G. 199; *Meng Long Development Pte Ltd.* v. *Jip Hong Trading Co. Pte Ltd.* [1985] A.C. 511, 524. *cf.* Wilson, 67 L.Q.R. 344.

[77] For the requirement of detriment in cases of estoppel, see *post*, p. 361; *Carr* v. *L. & N.W. Ry.* (1875) L.R. 10 C.P. 310, 317.

[78] *Post*, pp. 109–110.

[79] *W. J. Alan & Co. Ltd.* v. *El Nasr Export & Import Co.* [1972] 2 Q.B. 189, 213.

would be inequitable to allow the promisor to act inconsistently with it.[80] Thus the requirement can be satisfied if the promisee has forborne from taking steps to safeguard his legal position (as in *Hughes* v. *Metropolitan Ry.*[81] itself); or if he has performed or made efforts to perform the original obligation as altered by the promise (for example, where a seller who has been promised extra time for delivery continues to make efforts to perform after the originally agreed delivery date has gone by).

(iii) *Inequitable.* It must be "inequitable" for the promisor to go back on the promise. This requirement cannot be defined with anything approaching precision, but the basic idea is that the promisee must have acted in reliance on the promise in one of the ways just described, so that he cannot be restored to the position in which he was before he took such action.[82] If the promisee can be restored to that position, it will not be inequitable for the promisor to go back on the promise. In one case[83] the promisor re-asserted his strict legal rights only two days after the promise had been made. It was held that this was not "inequitable," since the promisee had not, in this short period, suffered any prejudice: he could be, and was, restored to exactly the same position as that in which he had been before the promise was made. Sometimes, moreover, extraneous circumstances will justify the promisor in going back on the promise without notice. In *Williams* v. *Stern*[84] the plaintiff gave the defendant a bill of sale of furniture as security for a loan; the bill entitled the defendant to seize the furniture if the plaintiff defaulted in paying instalments due under it. When the fourteenth instalment became due, the plaintiff asked for extra time, and the defendant said that he "would not look to a week." Three days later he seized the furniture because he had heard that the plaintiff's landlord intended to distrain it for arrears of rent. It was held that the defendant's seizure was justified. There was no consideration for his promise to give time, nor did *Hughes* v. *Metropolitan Ry.*[85] apply. Brett L.J. said: "Has there been any misconduct on the part of the defendant? I think not: it appears that a distress by the plaintiff's landlord was threatened; and under those circumstances I do not blame the defendant for changing his mind."[86] His conduct was not "inequitable."

(d) EFFECT GENERALLY SUSPENSORY. The equitable doctrine, like the common law doctrine of waiver,[87] does not extinguish, but only suspends, rights. In *Hughes* v. *Metropolitan Ry.* the landlord was not forever prevented from enforcing the covenant: he could have enforced it on giving reasonable notice requiring the tenant to do the repairs. This aspect of the matter was stressed in *Tool Metal Manufacturing Co. Ltd.* v. *Tungsten*

---

[80] *James* v. *Heim Galleries* (1980) 256 E.G. 819, 825; *The Post Chaser* [1981] 2 Lloyd's Rep. 695, 701; *The Superhulls Cover Case* [1990] 2 Lloyd's Rep. 431, 454.

[81] (1877) 2 App.Cas. 439; *ante* p. 101.

[82] *Maharaj* v. *Chand* [1986] A.C. 898.

[83] *The Post Chaser* [1981] 2 Lloyd's Rep. 693; *cf. Bremer Handelsgesellschaft mbH* v. *Bunge Corp.* [1983] 1 Lloyd's Rep. 476, 484; *Bremer Handelsgesellschaft mbH* v. *Deutsche-Conti Handelsgesellschaft mbH* [1983] 1 Lloyd's Rep. 689; *The Trado* [1982] 1 Lloyd's Rep. 157, 160.

[84] (1879) 5 Q.B.D. 409.

[85] (1877) 2 App.Cas. 439; *ante*, p. 101.

[86] At p. 413.

[87] *i.e.* in the sense of forbearance, *ante*, p. 100.

Electric Co. Ltd.,[88] where a licence for the use of a patent provided that the licensees should pay "compensation" if they manufactured more than a stated number of articles incorporating the patent. In 1942 the owners of the patent agreed to suspend the obligation to pay "compensation" until a new agreement was made. They later gave notice to end the suspension. It was held that they were once again entitled to the payments after the expiry of a reasonable time from the giving of notice.

Subsequent events may, however, in exceptional circumstances, give the doctrine an extinctive effect. They can, most obviously, lead to this result where they make it impossible for the promisee to perform his original obligation. In *Birmingham & District Land Co.* v. *L. & N.W. Ry.*[89] a building lease bound the tenant to build by 1885. The lessor agreed to suspend this obligation; but in 1886, while the suspension was still in force, the land was compulsorily acquired by a railway company, so that performance of the tenant's obligation became impossible. The tenant recovered statutory compensation from the railway company on the footing that the building lease was still binding; but clearly his obligation to build was utterly extinguished. Even where performance of the original obligation has not become literally impossible, the doctrine may sometimes have an extinctive effect. For example, in *Ogilvy* v. *Hope-Davies*[90] a vendor of land indicated on August 15 that he would not insist on the contractual completion date of August 30. It was held that no question of reinstating the contractual completion date could arise "because the time was far too short."[91] The doctrine has an extinctive effect in such cases because subsequent events, or the passage of time, though not making performance of the original obligation impossible, have made it highly inequitable to require such performance even after reasonable notice.[92]

(e) CREATES NO NEW RIGHTS. The equitable doctrine prevents the enforcement of existing rights, but it does not create entirely new rights or extend the scope of existing ones. It would not, for example, enable employees in a case like *Stilk* v. *Myrick*[93] to recover the extra pay that they had been promised. The point was settled in *Combe* v. *Combe*,[94] where a husband during divorce proceedings promised to pay £100 per annum to his wife who, in reliance on this promise, forbore from applying to the court for maintenance. It was held that the equitable doctrine did not enable her to enforce the husband's promise since it did not "create new causes of action where none existed before."[95] The scope of the equitable doctrine is limited in this way because "it would be wrong to extend the doctrine of promissory estoppel, whatever its precise limits at the present day, to the extent of abolishing in this back-handed way the doctrine of

---

[88] [1955] 1 W.L.R. 761; *cf. Banning* v. *Wright* [1972] 1 W.L.R. 972, 981, *The Post Chaser* [1981] 2 Lloyd's Rep. 695, 701; *The Kachenjunga* [1990] 1 Lloyd's Rep 391, 399.

[89] (1888) 40 Ch.D. 268. *Cf. Durham Fancy Goods Ltd.* v. *Michael Jackson (Fancy Goods) Ltd.* [1968] 2 Q.B. 839.

[90] [1976] 1 All E.R. 683; *The Ion* [1980] 2 Lloyd's Rep. 245; *Voest Alpine Intertrading GmbH* v. *Chevron International Oil Co.* [1987] 2 Lloyd's Rep. 547, 560.

[91] *Ogilvy* v. *Hope-Davies* [1976] 1 All E.R. 683, 696.

[92] See *Maharaj* v. *Chand* [1986] A.C. 898; *cf. W. J. Alan & Co. Ltd.* v. *El Nasr Export & Import Co.* [1972] Q.B. 189 (where the actual decision was that there was a variation supported by consideration: *ante*, p. 96.)

[93] (1809) 2 Camp. 317; 6 Esp. 129; *ante*, p. 88.

[94] [1951] 2 K.B. 215.

[95] [1951] 2 K.B. at p. 219.

consideration."[96] The view that the equitable doctrine does not create new causes of action seems to have been doubted[97] or ignored[98] by dicta in later cases; but the promises in these cases created new rights on the perfectly orthodox ground that they were, in fact, supported by consideration.[99] *Combe* v. *Combe* therefore still stands as the leading English[1] authority for the proposition that the doctrine creates no new rights[2] and this proposition has been reaffirmed in a number of later cases.[3]

The essentially defensive nature of the equitable doctrine is sometimes expressed by saying that it operates as a shield and not as a sword.[4] In other words, its normal effect is merely to protect the promisee from being sued on the original obligation. But the statement is apt to mislead, for the equitable doctrine can assist a plaintiff no less than a defendant. For example, a creditor may threaten to seize property on which a debt is secured, after having indicated that he would not insist on punctual payment. In such a case the debtor will, if the requirements of the equitable doctrine[5] are satisfied, be able to restrain the creditor's threatened seizure by injunction.[6] Similarly, a seller may tender goods after the originally agreed delivery date, in reliance on the buyer's promise to accept late delivery. If the buyer without justification refuses to accept the delivery, the seller will be entitled to damages.[7]

The equitable doctrine can also assist the promisee as plaintiff in that it may prevent the promisor from relying on a defence which would, but for the promise, have been available to him: *e.g.* the defence that a claim

---

[96] *Brikom Investments Ltd.* v. *Carr* [1979] Q.B. 467, 486; *cf. Combe* v. *Combe* [1951] 2 K.B. 215, 219–220; *Tool Metal Manufacturing Co. Ltd.* v. *Tungsten Electric Co. Ltd.* [1955] 1 W.L.R. 761, 764; *Beesly* v. *Hallwood Estates Ltd.* [1960] 1 W.L.R. 549, 561; *Drexel Burnham Lambert International N.V.* v. *El Nasr* [1986] 1 Lloyd's Rep. 357, 365 contrast *Vaughan* v. *Vaughan* [1953] Q.B. 762, 768; Denning, 15 M.L.R. 1.

[97] *Re Wyvern Developments Ltd.* [1974] 1 W.L.R. 1097, 1104–1105; Atiyah, 38 M.L.R. 65 and see Allan, 79 L.Q.R. 238. The point was left open in *The Henrik Sif* [1982] 1 Lloyd's Rep. 456, 466–468 (as to which see *ante*, p. 102).

[98] *Evenden* v. *Guildford City F.C.* [1975] Q.B. 917, 924, 926; Napier, [1976] C.L.J. 38; and see next note.

[99] *e.g. Secretary of State for Employment* v. *Globe Elastic Thread Co. Ltd.* [1980] A.C. 506, overruling *Evenden's* case, *supra.* Lord Wilberforce remarked at p. 518 that "To convert this [contract] into an estoppel is to turn the doctrine of promissory estoppel . . . upside down."

[1] In the United States a similar doctrine can give rise to a cause of action: see *Restatement, Contracts*, § 90 and *Restatements*, 2d, *Contracts* § 90. In English law, the need to use the doctrine to give rise to a cause of action is less acute than in the United States because of the wider powers of English courts to "invent" consideration: see *ante*, p. 67. The American position has also been taken in Australia: see *Waltons Stores (Interstate) Ltd.* v. *Maher* (1988) 164 C.L.R. 387; Duthie, 104 L.Q.R. 362; Sutton, 1 J.C.L. 205.

[2] *Cf. post*, p. 361 for the similar rule in cases of estoppel by representation of fact. Contrast the position in cases of proprietary estoppel: *post*, p. 131. For the position in cases of estoppel by convention, see *post*, pp. 113–114.

[3] *Argy Trading Development Co. Ltd.* v. *Lapid Developments Ltd.* [1977] 1 W.L.R. 444, 457; *Aquaflite Ltd.* v. *Jaymar International Freight Consultants Ltd.* [1980] 1 Lloyd's Rep. 36; *The Proodos C.* [1980] 2 Lloyd's Rep. 390, 394; *James* v. *Heim Galleries* (1980) 256 E.G. 819, 821; *Brikom Investments Ltd.* v. *Seaford* [1981] 1 W.L.R. 863; *cf. Taylors Fashions Ltd.* v. *Liverpool Victoria Trustees Co. Ltd.* [1982] Q.B. 133 n. at p. 152.

[4] *Combe* v. *Combe* [1951] 2 K.B. 215, 224.

[5] *i.e.* those discussed at pp. 102–106, *ante*.

[6] Such a claim would have succeeded in *Williams* v. *Stern* (1879) 5 Q.B.D. 409 (*ante*, p. 106), if the creditor's conduct had been "inequitable."

[7] *Cf. Hartley* v. *Hymans* [1920] 3 K.B. 475, applying the corresponding doctrine of common law forbearance (*ante*, p. 99). And see Jackson, 81 L.Q.R. 223.

which the promisee has made against him is time-barred,[8] or that the claim has been satisfied.[9] In such cases, the doctrine will, once again, enable the promisee to win an action that, but for the doctrine, he would have lost. But the promisee's cause of action will have arisen independently of the promise which brought the equitable doctrine into operation: the effect of the doctrine is merely to prevent the promisor from relying on some circumstance that would, if the promise had not been made, *have destroyed the promisee's original cause of action*. This situation must be distinguished from that in which the promisor's "defence" is that (apart from the promise) the promisee's alleged *cause of action never existed at all*. It is submitted that the equitable doctrine should not prevent the promisor from relying on a "defence" of this kind. If the doctrine were allowed to operate in this way, it would give the promisee a new cause of action based on the promise, even though the promise was not supported by consideration; and such a result would be inconsistent with the essentially defensive nature of the doctrine.[10]

(f) ANALOGY WITH ESTOPPEL. The equitable doctrine has certain features in common with the doctrine of estoppel by representation.[11] Each is based on a representation followed by reliance on the part of the representee, and each is defensive in nature in that neither is capable in itself of giving rise to new rights. On the other hand, there are many significant differences between the two doctrines. The most important of these is that the equitable doctrine is brought into operation by a representation of *intention*, or a *promise*. For this reason, and because the doctrine was developed in equity, it is often referred to as "promissory" or "equitable" estoppel.[12] True estoppel by representation, on the other hand, cannot be based on a representation of intention, but only on one of *existing fact*. This rule was laid down in *Jorden* v. *Money*,[13] where it was held that a representation by

---

[8] See *The Ion* [1980] 2 Lloyd's Rep. 245; *P. S. Chellaram & Co. Ltd.* v. *China Ocean Shipping Co.* [1989] 1 Lloyd's Rep. 413; *cf. Commonwealth of Australia* v. *Verwayen* (1990) 64 A.L.J.R. 540; Spence, 107 L.Q.R. 221.

[9] *Cf. post*, p. 362.

[10] *Cf.* the criticism (*ante*, p. 102) of *The Henrik Sif* [1982] 1 Lloyd's Rep. 456.

[11] *Post*, p. 361.

[12] *e.g. Woodhouse A.C. Israel Cocoa Ltd.* v. *Nigerian Produce Marketing Co. Ltd.* [1972] A.C. 741, 758; *Ogilvy* v. *Hope-Davies* [1976] 1 All E.R. 683, 689; *Ets. Soules & Cie* v. *International Trade Development Co. Ltd.* [1980] 1 Lloyd's Rep. 129, 133; *The Ion* [1980] 2 Lloyd's Rep. 245, 250; *Peter Cremer* v. *Granaria B.V.* [1981] 2 Lloyd's Rep. 583, 587; *The Post Chaser* [1981] 2 Lloyd's Rep. 695, 700; *The Kachenjunga* [1990] 1 Lloyd's Rep. 391, 398. Contrast *Brikom Investments Ltd.* v. *Carr* [1979] Q.B. 467, 485, 489, where Roskill L.J. prefers to refer simply to the principle of *Hughes* v. *Metropolitan Ry.* (1877) 2 App.-Cas. 439. *Amherst* v. *James Walker Goldsmiths & Silversmiths Ltd.* [1983] Ch.305, 316 somewhat puzzlingly seems to distinguish between "promissory" and "equitable" estoppel. Terminological difficulty is compounded by the occasional use of the phrase "equitable estoppel" to refer to true estoppel by representation: see *infra*, n. 14.

[13] (1854) 5 H.L.C. 185; criticised by Jackson, 81 L.Q.R. 84. Atiyah (*ante*, p. 66 n. 31, pp. 53–57), argues that *Jorden* v. *Money* does not support the proposition for which it is usually cited, but that there was a contract in the case, which was unenforceable for want of written evidence. But no such contract was alleged by the plaintiff: as Lord Cranworth said at p. 215, "it is put entirely on the ground of misrepresentation." The orthodox view is also unequivocally supported by Lord Selborne (who was counsel in *Jorden* v. *Money*) in his speech in *Maddison* v. *Alderson* (1883) 8 App.Cas. 467, 473. For recent statements of the rule that there must be a representation of fact see *Argy Trading Development Co. Ltd.* v.

a creditor that he *would not* enforce a bond did not give rise to an estoppel. This difference between estoppel by representation and the equitable doctrine cannot be satisfactorily explained by arguing that the requirement of a representation of existing fact did not exist in equity but only at common law.[14] *Jorden* v. *Money* was an appeal from the Court of Appeal in Chancery and was, no less than *Hughes* v. *Metropolitan Ry.*,[15] decided on equitable principles. And the rule that an estoppel can only be based on a representation of existing fact is stated in many equity cases.[16] There are, moreover, other significant differences between the two doctrines. The equitable doctrine may operate even though there is no such "detriment" as is required to bring the doctrine of estoppel into play.[17] And the effect of the equitable doctrine is only to suspend rights,[18] while estoppel, where it operates, has a permanent effect.

(g) ANALOGY WITH WAIVER. It is submitted that the characteristics just mentioned indicate that the equitable doctrine is not truly analogous with estoppel by representation. As Denning J. has pointed out, the authorities which support it "although they are said to be cases of estoppel, are not really such."[19] The doctrine has closer affinities with the common law rules of waiver in the sense of forbearance: both are based on promises, or representations of intention; and both are suspensive (rather than extinctive) in effect. The main difference between them is that the equitable doctrine discards the oversubtle and unfortunate common law distinction between a variation and a forbearance.[20]

There is now much judicial support for these submissions. Thus Lord Pearson has said that "promissory estoppel" was "far removed from the familiar estoppel by representation of fact and seems . . . to be more like waiver of contractual rights."[21] In many later cases "waiver" and "promissory estoppel" (or the rule in *Hughes* v. *Metropolitan Ry.*)[22] are treated as substantially similar doctrines.[23] The two expressions have been des-

---

Lapid Development Ltd. [1977] 1 W.L.R. 444, 450; *Spence* v. *Shell* (1980) 256 E.G. 55, 63; *T.C.B. Ltd.* v. *Gray* [1986] Ch. 621, 634, affd. [1988] 1 All E.R. 108; so-called "estoppel by convention" (*post*, p. 111) is similarly based on an assumption of *fact*, including one of private right (*cf. post*, p. 113, n. 36).

[14] Estoppel by representation of fact (*post*, p. 361) was recognised at common law at least as long ago as *Freeman* v. *Cooke* (1848) 2 Ex. 654; but sometimes this form of estoppel is (confusingly referred to as "equitable estoppel": *e.g.* in *Lombard North Central plc* v. *Stobart* [1990] Tr.L.R. 105, 107. In that case, an estoppel arose from a finance company's statement that no more than £1,003 was due under a conditional sale, when the actual sum due was nearly five times as much. This statement was clearly a representation of *fact* rather than a *promise*.

[15] (1877) 2 App.Cas. 439; *ante*, p. 101.

[16] *Pigott* v. *Stratton* (1859) 1 D.F. & J. 33, 51; *Citizens' Bank of Louisiana* v. *First National Bank of New Orleans* (1873) L.R. 6 H.L. 352, 360; *Maddison* v. *Alderson* (1883) 8 App.-Cas. 467, 473; *Chadwick* v. *Manning* [1896] A.C. 231, 238.

[17] *Ante*, p. 105.

[18] *Ante*, p. 106.

[19] *Central London Property Trust Ltd.* v. *High Tree House Ltd.* [1947] K.B. 130, 134; *post*, p. 120.

[20] *Ante*, p. 99.

[21] *Woodhouse A.C. Israel Cocoa Ltd.* v. *Nigerian Produce Marketing Co. Ltd.* [1972] A.C. 741, 762.

[22] (1877) 2 App.Cas. 439; *ante*, p. 101.

[23] *Ogilvy* v. *Hope-Davies* [1976] 1 All E.R. 683, 688–689; *Finagrain S.A. Geneva* v. *P. Kruse Hamburg* [1976] 2 Lloyd's Rep. 508, 534; *Bremer Handelsgesellschaft mbH* v. *C. Mackprang Jr.* [1979] 1 Lloyd's Rep. 221, 226; *Brikom Investments Ltd.* v. *Carr* [1979] Q.B. 467,

cribed as "two ways of saying exactly the same thing"[24]; and the courts often use them interchangeably when discussing situations in which it is alleged that one party has indicated that he will not enforce his strict legal rights against the other. This usage indicates that the equitable doctrine more closely resembles waiver (in the sense of forbearance) than true estoppel by representation of fact.

(h) DISTINGUISHED FROM PROMISES SUPPORTED BY CONSIDERATION. Under the equitable doctrine, certain limited effects are given to a promise without consideration. But it is nevertheless in the interests of the promisee to show, if he can, that he did provide consideration so that the promise amounted to a contractually binding variation. Such proof will free him from the many rules that restrict the scope of the equitable doctrine: he need not then show that he has "relied" on the promise, or that it would be "inequitable" for the other party to go back on it; the variation will permanently affect the rights of the promisor and not merely suspend them (unless it is expressed so as to have only a temporary effect); and a contractual variation can not only reduce or extinguish existing rights but also create new ones. Where parties agree to modify an existing contract, the equitable doctrine (and its common law counterpart of waiver) may have reduced, but they have by no means eliminated, the practical importance of the doctrine of consideration.

(i) DISTINGUISHED FROM ESTOPPEL BY CONVENTION. Estoppel by convention may arise where both[25] parties to a transaction have acted on an agreed assumption as to the existence of a state of facts, or as to the true construction of a document.[26] The parties are then precluded from denying the truth of that assumption, if it would be unjust to allow them (or one of them) to go back on it.[27] Such an estoppel differs from estoppel by representation and from promissory estoppel in that it does not depend on any "clear and unequivocal" representation or promise[28]: it can arise where the assumption was based on a mistake spontaneously made by the party relying on it, and acquiesced in by the other party.

488, 489, 490; *Bremer Handelsgesellschaft mbH* v. *Westzucker GmbH* [1981] 1 Lloyd's Rep. 207, 212–213; *Bremer Handelsgesellschaft mbH* v. *Mackprang Jr.* [1981] 1 Lloyd's Rep. 292, 298; *Bremer Handelsgesellschaft mbH* v. *Bunge Corp.* [1983] 1 Lloyd's Rep. 476, 484; *B.I.C.C. Ltd.* v. *Burndy Corp.* [1985] Ch. 232, 253. In *W. J. Alan & Co. Ltd.* v. *El Nasr Export Co.* [1972] 2 Q.B. 189, 212 waiver is described as an instance of the principle of *Hughes* v. *Metropolitan Ry.* (*supra*), which, however, is said to be of "wider" scope; *cf. The Ion* [1980] 2 Lloyd's Rep. 245, 249–250. In *Brikom Investments Ltd.* v. *Carr* [1979] Q.B. 467, 485, 489 the principle of *Hughes* v. *Metropolitan Ry.* (*supra*) is, unusually, regarded as distinct from "promissory estoppel" but rather as an illustration of "waiver," thus suggesting a difference between the two concepts—perhaps in the *Brikom* case the waiver amounted to a contractual variation supported by consideration: *cf. post*, p. 122.

[24] *Prosper Homes* v. *Hambro's Bank Executor & Trustee Co.* (1979) 39 P. & C.R. 395, 401.

[25] There can be no such estoppel where one party is not yet in existence: see *Rover International Ltd.* v. *Cannon Film Sales Ltd.* [1987] B.C.L.C. 540, revsd. in part on other grounds [1989] 1 W.L.R. 912 (company not yet formed: see *post*, p. 637).

[26] Spencer Bower and Turner, *Estoppel by Representation*, (3rd ed. 1977) p. 157; Dawson, 9 Legal Studies 16; for qualification of this formulation, see *The Vistafjord* [1988] 2 Lloyd's Rep. 343, 351; and see *Shearson Lehman Hutton Inc.* v. *Maclaine Watson & Co. Ltd.* [1989] 2 Lloyd's Rep. 570, 596.

[27] *The Vistafjord* [1988] 2 Lloyd's Rep. 343.

[28] *Troop* v. *Gibson* (1986) 277 E.G. 1134.

(i) *Requirements.* Estoppel by convention was discussed in *Amalgamated Investment & Property Co. Ltd.* v. *Texas Commerce International Bank Ltd.*,[29] where A had negotiated with the X Bank for a loan to B (one of A's subsidiaries) for the purpose of acquiring and developing a property in the Bahamas. It was agreed that the loan was to be secured by a mortgage on that property and also by a guarantee from A. In the guarantee, A promised the X Bank, in consideration of the Bank's giving credit to B, to "pay you . . . all moneys . . . due . . . *to you*" from B. This was an inappropriate form of words since the loan to B was not made directly by the X Bank but by one of its subsidiaries, the Y Bank, with money provided by the X Bank: hence, if the guarantee were read literally, it would not apply to the loan since no money was due from B to the X Bank. The Court of Appeal, however, took the view that this literal interpretation would defeat the intention of the parties, and held that, on its true construction, the guarantee applied to the loan made by the Y Bank.[30] But even if the guarantee did not, on its true construction, produce this result, A was estopped from denying that the guarantee covered the loan by the Y Bank, as both A and the X Bank had assumed, when they negotiated the loan, that the guarantee did cover it; and as the X Bank continued subsequently to act on that assumption in granting various indulgences to A in respect of the loan to B and of another loan made directly by the X Bank to A. It made no difference that the assumption was not induced by any representation made by A but originated in the X Bank's own mistake: the estoppel was not one by representation but by convention.[31] The same principle was applied in *The Vistafjord*[32] where an agreement for the charter of a cruise ship had been negotiated by agents on behalf of the owners. Both the agents and the owners throughout believed that commission on this transaction would be payable under an earlier agreement but, on its true construction, this agreement gave no such rights to the agents. It was held that estoppel by convention precluded the owners from relying on the true construction of the earlier agreement, so that the agents were justified in retaining the amount of the commission out of sums received by them from the charterers.

To give rise to an estoppel by convention, the mistaken assumption of the party claiming the benefit of the estoppel must, however, have been acquiesced in by the party alleged to be estopped; and both parties must have conducted themselves on the basis of such a shared assumption: the estoppel "requires communications to pass across the line between the parties. It is not enough that each of two parties acts on an assumption not communicated with each other."[33] Such communication may be effected by the conduct of one party, known to the other.[34] But no estoppel by convention arose where each party spontaneously made a different mistake and there was no subsequent conduct by the party alleged to be estopped

---

[29] [1982] Q.B. 84.

[30] *Cf.* on the issue of construction, *T.C.B. Ltd.* v. *Gray* [1988] 1 All E.R. 108; *Bank of Scotland* v. *Wright* [1990] BCC 663.

[31] *Cf. The Leila* [1985] 2 Lloyd's Rep. 172; and see *infra*, n. 35.

[32] [1988] 2 Lloyd's Rep. 343.

[33] *The Captain Gregos (No. 2)* [1990] 2 Lloyd's Rep. 395, 405, following *The August P. Leonhardt* [1985] 2 Lloyd's Rep. 28, 35.

[34] As in *The Vistafjord* [1988] 2 Lloyd's Rep. 343, 351 ("very clear conduct crossing the line . . . of which the other party was full cognisant").

from which any acquiescence in the other party's mistaken assumption could be inferred.[35]

(ii) *Effect of estoppel by convention.* The effect of this form of estoppel is to preclude a party from denying an agreed assumption of fact or as to the meaning of a document.[36] One such assumption may be that a particular promise has been made[37]: thus it is possible to describe the result in the *Amalgamated Investment & Property* case by saying that A was estopped from denying that it had promised the X Bank to repay any sum left unpaid by B to the Y Bank. But, although estoppel by convention may thus take effect in relation to a promise, it is quite different in nature from promissory estoppel. In cases of promissory estoppel, the promisor or representor is not estopped from denying that the promise or representation *has been made*: on the contrary, this must be proved to establish that kind of estoppel. The doctrine of promissory estoppel is concerned with the *legal effects* of a promise that has been shown to exist. Estoppel by convention, on the other hand, may operate so as to prevent a party from denying that a promise *has been made* or from disputing its terms: it does not specify the *legal effects* of the assumed promise. Hence it has been said that the effect of estoppel by convention is not to give rise to an enforceable contract without consideration: "Estoppel by convention is not dependent on contract but on a common assumption."[38] In the *Amalgamated Investment & Property* case, once A was estopped from denying the *existence* of the promise described above, no question arose as to its legal *validity*. There could be no doubt that that promise was supported by consideration[39]: this was provided by the X Bank in making funds available to the Y Bank to enable it to make a loan to B, and in inducing the Y Bank to make that loan.[40] Where the assumed promise is one that would, if actually made, have been unsupported by consideration, both types of estoppel can, however, operate in the same case: estoppel by convention to establish the existence of the promise, and promissory estoppel to determine its legal effect.[41]

(iii) *Whether estoppel by convention can create new rights.* We have seen that promissory estoppel cannot "create new causes of action where none

---

[35] *The August P. Leonhardt* [1985] 2 Lloyd's Rep. 28, reversing [1984] 1 Lloyd's Rep. 332, which had been followed in *The Leila*, *supra*, n. 31. The present status of *The Leila* therefore remains in some doubt but the two cases can be reconciled on the ground that in *The Leila* there was, while in *The August P. Leonhardt* there was not, conduct by the party alleged to be estopped from which acquiescence in the other party's mistaken belief could be inferred.

[36] *Amalgamated Investment & Property* case [1982] 2 Q.B. 84, 126, 130; at p. 122 the estoppel is said to apply to an assumption of "fact or law"; *cf. The Vistafjord* [1988] 2 Lloyd's Rep. 343, 351; *Shearson Lehman Hutton Inc.* v. *Maclaine Watson & Co. Ltd.* [1989] 2 Lloyd's Rep 570, 596; *semble*, the reference to law is intended to meet the objection that the construction of a document is often said to be a matter of "law." Such an assumption of "law" could be described as one of private rights: *cf. post*, p. 299. For the difference between the requirements of estoppel by convention and relief for mistake in equity, see *post*, p. 279.

[37] Such an assumption is one of fact (and not as to the future).

[38] *The Vistafjord* [1988] 2 Lloyd's Rep. 343, 351. For this reason the citation in *Williams* v. *Roffey Bros. & Nicholls (Contractors) Ltd.* [1991] 1 Q.B. 1, 17–18 of the *Amalgamated Investment & Property* case seems, with respect, to be of doubtful relevance. In the *Williams* case there was no doubt that the promise had been made; and the actual decision was that it was supported by consideration and thus legally effective: *ante*, p. 89.

[39] This was also true in *The Vistafjord* [1988] 2 Lloyd's Rep. 343, *ante*, p. 112.

[40] It is enough that consideration moved from the promisee (the X Bank): *ante*, p. 77.

[41] *e.g.* (apparently) *Troop* v. *Gibson* (1986) 277 E.G. 1134.

existed before"[42]; and we shall see that the same principle applies to estoppel by representation.[43] Estoppel by convention resembles estoppel by representation in that it prevents a party from denying *facts*, and one would therefore expect estoppel by convention to operate only where its effect was defensive in substance. The question whether estoppel by convention is so limited was discussed in the *Amalgamated Investment & Property* case where, however, it was not necessary to decide the point. The action was brought because the X Bank had sought to apply money due from it to A under another transaction in discharge of A's alleged liability under A's guarantee of B's debt. Hence the effect of the estoppel was to provide the X Bank with a defence to A's claim for a declaration that it was not entitled to apply the money in that way. Eveleigh L.J. said: "I do not think that the bank could have succeeded in a claim on the guarantee itself."[44] Brandon L.J. seems to have taken the view that the bank could have sued on the guarantee, but to have based that view on the ground that the loan agreement between A and the X Bank imposed an obligation on A to give the guarantee: hence it was that agreement, and not the estoppel per se, which would have given rise to the X Bank's cause of action, if it had sued on the guarantee.[45] Lord Denning M.R. expressed the principle of estoppel by convention in such a way as to enable it to give rise to a cause of action[46]; but he was alone in stating the principle so broadly.[47] In *The Vistafjord*[48] the estoppel similarly operated defensively. This factor was not stressed in the judgments, but there is no suggestion in them that in this respect estoppel by convention differs from estoppel by representation, which does not, of itself, give rise to a cause of action.[49] It is indeed, possible for estoppel by convention (as it is for promissory estoppel[50]) to deprive the defendant of a *defence* and so to enable the plaintiff to win an action which otherwise he would have lost[51]; but even in such cases the estoppel does not create the cause of action, for the *facts giving rise to it* exist independently of the estoppel. No other authority squarely supports the view that estoppel by convention can, of itself, create a new cause of action; and the present position seems to be that it cannot, any more than promissory estoppel, produce this effect.

(iv) *Invalidity of assumed term.* A party is not liable on the basis of estoppel by convention where the terms which he is prevented by such an estoppel from denying would, if actually incorporated in the contract, have been

---

42 *Combe* v. *Combe* [1951] 2 K.B. 215, 219; *ante*, p. 107.
43 *Post*, p. 361.
44 [1982] Q.B. 84, 126.
45 *Ibid.* p. 132.
46 *Ibid.* p. 122. A similar view may be hinted at in *Williams* v. *Roffey Bros. & Nicholls (Contractors) Ltd.* [1991] 1 Q.B. 1, 17–18; but see *ante*, p. 113, n. 38.
47 *Keen* v. *Holland* [1984] 1 W.L.R. 251, 261–262.
48 [1988] 2 Lloyd's Rep. 343; *ante*, p. 112. In *Shearson Lehman Hutton Inc.* v. *Maclaine Watson & Co. Ltd.* [1989] 2 Lloyd's Rep. 570 the estoppel would likewise (if supported on the facts) have operated defensively.
49 *Post*, p. 361.
50 *Ante*, pp. 108–109.
51 This was the effect of the estoppel in *The Amazonia* [1990] 1 Lloyd's Rep. 238, where it operated to prevent a party from relying on facts giving rise to a mistake nullifying consent (*post*, p. 249) and where the effect of allowing him to rely on those facts would have been to bar the other party's claim by lapse of time. *Cf. Colchester B.C.* v. *Smith* [1991] 2 All E.R. 29.

invalid[52]; nor does such an estoppel prevent a party from relying on the true legal effect (as opposed to the meaning[53]) of an admitted contract merely because the parties have entered into it under a mistaken view as to that effect.[54]

4. Part Payment of a Debt

(1) General rule

The general rule of common law is that a creditor is not bound by an undertaking to accept part payment in full settlement of a debt. An accrued debt can only be discharged by accord and satisfaction.[55] A promise by the debtor to pay part of the debt provides no consideration for the accord, as it is merely a promise to perform part of an existing duty owed to the creditor. And the actual part payment is no satisfaction under the rule in *Pinnel*'s case that "Payment of a lesser sum on the day in satisfaction of a greater sum cannot be any satisfaction for the whole."[56] This rule was finally approved by the House of Lords in *Foakes* v. *Beer*.[57] Mrs. Beer had obtained a judgment against Dr. Foakes for £2,090 19s. Sixteen months later Dr. Foakes asked for time to pay. Thereupon the parties entered into a written agreement[58] under which Mrs. Beer undertook not to take "any proceedings whatsoever" on the judgment, in consideration of an immediate payment by Dr. Foakes of £500 and on condition[59] of his paying specified instalments "until the whole of the said sum of £2,090 19s. shall have been paid and satisfied." Some five years later, when Dr. Foakes had paid £2,090 19s., Mrs. Beer claimed £360[60] for interest on the judgment debt. The House of Lords upheld her claim, and the actual decision does not appear to be unjust; for it seems that Mrs. Beer only intended to give Dr. Foakes time to pay, and not to forgive interest.[61]

The rule in *Pinnel*'s case may sometimes have served the useful purpose of protecting a creditor against a debtor who had too ruthlessly exploited the tactical advantage of being a potential defendant in litigation.[62] For example, in *D. & C. Builders Ltd.* v. *Rees*[63] the plaintiffs had done building work for the defendant and had presented an account of which some £482 was outstanding. Six months after payment had first been demanded,

---

[52] See *Keen* v. *Holland* [1984] 1 W.L.R. 251; contrast *The Amazonia* [1990] 1 Lloyd's Rep. 238 (illegality under foreign law).

[53] *Ante*, p. 113.

[54] *Keen* v. *Holland, supra*, n. 52.

[55] *Ante*, p. 95.

[56] (1602) 5 Co.Rep. 117a; *Cumber* v. *Wane* (1721) 1 Stra. 426; *McManus* v. *Bark* (1870) L.R. 5 Ex. 65; *Underwood* v. *Underwood* [1894] P. 204; *Tilney Engineering* v. *Admos Knitting Machinery* [1987] 2 C.L. 21; *Re Broderick* (1986) 6 N.I.J.B. 36.

[57] (1884) 9 App.Cas. 605; Dixon, *Jesting Pilate*, 159–165.

[58] Drawn up by Dr. Foakes solicitor: (1884) 9 App.Cas. at p. 625.

[59] Dr. Foakes made no promise to pay the instalments.

[60] *Beer* v. *Foakes* (1883) 11 Q.B.D. 221, 222.

[61] Lords Fitzgerald and Watson thought that the agreement did not, on its true construction, cover interest. Lords Selborne and Blackburn sympathised with this view but felt unable to adopt it as the operative part of the document was too "clear" to be controlled by the recitals.

[62] As Dr. Foakes appears to have done. Kelly, 27 M.L.R. 540, argues that there is consideration in giving up this advantage, as there is in the compromise of a disputed claim. This may be so, but a compromise is only binding if there is a *bona fide* dispute as to liability (*ante* p. 83) and there was no such dispute in *Foakes* v. *Beer*.

[63] [1966] 2 Q.B. 617; Chorley, 29 M.L.R. 165; Cornish, 29 M.L.R. 428.

the defendant's wife (acting on his behalf) offered the plaintiffs £300 in full settlement. They accepted this offer as they were in desperate straits financially; and there was some evidence that the defendant's wife knew this.[64] It was held that the plaintiffs could sue for the balance; and a majority[65] of the Court of Appeal based their decision on the rule in *Pinnel*'s case.

On the other hand, it is arguable that the function of protecting the creditor in such a situation is now better performed by the expanding concept of duress[66] and that the rule in *Pinnel*'s case no longer serves any useful purpose. The rule is, moreover, open to the objection that it applies to any agreement to accept part payment of a debt, even though it is a perfectly fair and reasonable transaction,[67] and in *Foakes* v. *Beer* Lord Blackburn criticised the rule on the ground that part payment was often more beneficial to the creditor than strict insistence on his full legal rights.[68] A factual benefit[69] of a similar kind has been accepted as sufficient consideration for a promise to make a payment for the performance of an existing contractual duty owed by the promisee to the promisor[70]; and the law would be more consistent, as well as more satisfactory in its practical operation, if it adopted the same approach to cases of part payment of a debt. Agreements of the kind here under discussion would then be binding unless they had been made under duress. But the rule in *Foakes* v. *Beer* is open to challenge only in the House of Lords. In the meantime, its operation is mitigated by limitations on its scope at common law and by evasions of it in equity.

(2) Common law limitations

(a) DISPUTED CLAIMS. The rule does not apply where the creditor's claim (or its amount) is disputed in good faith.[71] In such cases, the value of the claim is doubtful and the debtor accordingly provides consideration by paying something, even though it is less than the amount claimed. It makes no difference that the amount paid is small in relation to the amount claimed, or that the creditor has a good chance of succeeding on the claim; for the law will not generally investigate the adequacy of consideration.[72]

(b) UNLIQUIDATED CLAIMS. Even where the claim is undisputed, the rule only applies if the claim is also a "liquidated" one, *i.e.* a claim for a fixed sum of money, such as one for money lent or for the agreed price of goods or services. It does not apply to "unliquidated" claims[73] such as claims for damages or for a reasonable remuneration (where none is fixed by the contract). In such cases, the claim is of uncertain value; and even if the over-

---

[64] [1966] 2 Q.B. at p. 622.
[65] Lord Denning M.R. based his decision on a different ground: *post*, p. 124.
[66] *Cf. ante*, p. 88 and *post*, pp. 363–365. A debtor who by any deception dishonestly induces the creditor to accept part payment of a debt in full settlement may also be guilty of an offence under Theft Act 1978, s.2: see Treitel in *Essays in Memory of Sir Rupert Cross*, pp. 90–92.
[67] *e.g.* on the facts of *Central London Property Trust Ltd.* v. *High Trees House Ltd.* [1947] K.B. 130; *post*, p. 120.
[68] (1884) 9 App.Cas. 605, 617–620.
[69] *Ante*, p. 65.
[70] *Williams* v. *Roffey Bros. & Nicholls (Contractors) Ltd.* [1991] 1 Q.B. 1, *ante*, p. 89.
[71] *Cooper* v. *Parker* (1885) 15 C.B. 822; *Re Warren* (1884) 53 L.J. Ch. 1016.
[72] *Ante*, p. 70. But the fact that the sum received is much smaller than that claimed may be evidence that the recipient has not accepted it in full settlement: *Rustenburg Platinum Mines Ltd.* v. *Pan Am* [1979] 1 Lloyd's Rep. 19.
[73] *Wilkinson* v. *Byers* (1834) 1 A. & E. 106; *Ibberson* v. *Neck* (1886) 2 T.L.R. 427.

whelming probability is that it is worth more than the sum paid, the possibility that it may be worth less suffices to satisfy the requirement of consideration.

A claim that was originally unliquidated may subsequently become liquidated by act of the parties. For example, in *D. & C. Builders* v. *Rees*[74] it does not seem that the contract fixed the price of the work to be done by the plaintiffs. When they presented their account they had only an unliquidated claim (for a reasonable remuneration); and if at this stage they had accepted £300 in full settlement they would not have been protected by the rule in *Foakes* v. *Beer*. That rule only became applicable because the defendant had, by retaining the account without protest, impliedly agreed that it correctly stated the sum due, and so turned the plaintiffs' claim into a liquidated one.[75]

A creditor may have two claims against the same debtor, one of them liquidated and the other unliquidated; or a single claim which is partly liquidated and partly unliquidated. A promise by the creditor to release the *whole* claim will not be binding if the debtor pays no more than the liquidated amount and if his liability to pay this amount is undisputed. For example, in *Arrale* v. *Costain Civil Engineering Ltd.*[76] an employee was injured at work. Legislation in force at the place of work gave him a right against the employers to a fixed lump sum of £490 and it was assumed that he also had a common law right to sue the employers in tort for unliquidated damages.[77] It was held that any promise[78] which he might have made not to pursue the common law claim was not made binding by payment of the £490. The employers had not provided any consideration for such a promise since, in making that payment, they merely did what they were already bound to do.[79]

(c) VARIATIONS IN DEBTOR'S PERFORMANCE. Consideration for a creditor's promise to accept part payment in full settlement can be provided by the debtor's doing any act that he was not previously bound by the contract to do.[80] For example, payment of a smaller sum at the creditor's request before the due day is good consideration for a promise to forego the balance, for it is a benefit to the creditor to receive (and a corresponding detriment to the debtor to make) such early payment.[81] The same applies, *mutatis mutandis*, where payment of a smaller sum is made at the creditor's request at a place different from that originally fixed for payment,[82] or in a different currency.[83] Again, payment of a smaller sum accompanied at the

---

[74] [1966] 2 Q.B. 617.

[75] *Cf. Amantilla* v. *Telefusion* (1987) 9 Con. L.R. 139, where a builder's *quantum meruit* claim which had not been disputed was treated as "liquidated claim" for the purpose of Limitation Act 1980, s.29(5)(*a*).

[76] [1976] 1 Lloyd's Rep. 98; *cf. Rustenburg Platinum Mines Ltd.* v. *Pan Am* [1979] 1 Lloyd's Rep 19, 24.

[77] *Cf. post*, p. 189.

[78] Lord Denning M.R. and Stephenson L.J. took the view that no such promise had been made.

[79] *Per* Stephenson and Geoffrey Lane L.JJ. Lord Denning M.R. based his decision on a different ground: *post*, p. 124.

[80] *e.g. Re William Porter & Co.* [1937] 2 All E.R. 261: *Ledingham* v. *Bermejo Estancia Co. Ltd.* [1947] 2 All E.R. 748.

[81] *Pinnel's* case, *ante*, p. 115.

[82] *Ibid.*

[83] *Cf. ante*, p. 96.

creditor's request by the delivery of a chattel is good consideration for a promise to forego the balance: "The gift of a horse, hawk or robe, etc., in satisfaction is good. For it shall be intended that a horse, hawk or robe, etc., might be more beneficial than the money. . . ."[84]

(d) FORBEARANCE TO ENFORCE CROSS-CLAIMS. The debtor may have a cross-claim against the creditor; and forbearance to enforce such a claim can constitute consideration for the creditor's promise to accept part payment in full settlement. For example, where a landlord promises to accept part payment of rent in full settlement, the tenant may provide consideration for this promise by forbearing to sue the landlord for breach of the latter's obligation to keep the premises in repair.[85]

(e) PAYMENT BY THIRD PARTY. Part payment by a third party, if accepted by the creditor in full settlement of the debtor's liability,[86] is a good defence to a later action by the creditor against the debtor for the balance.[87]

It is generally agreed that this rule does not depend on any contract between debtor and creditor, so that it can apply even though no promise was made to the debtor and no consideration moved from him. The rule has therefore been explained on other grounds. One such ground is that it would be a fraud on the third party to allow the creditor to sue the debtor for the balance of the debt.[88] The difficulty with this reasoning is that the mere breach of a promise does not usually amount to fraud at common law; it only has this effect if the promisor had no intention of performing the promise when he made it.[89] A second reason for the rule is that the court will not help the creditor to break his contract with the third party by allowing him to recover the balance of the debt from the debtor. On the contrary, it has been held that where A (the creditor) contracts with B (the third party) not to sue C (the debtor), and A nevertheless does sue C, B can intervene so as to obtain a stay of the action.[90] A third explanation is suggested by *Hirachand Punamchand* v. *Temple*,[91] where the defendant was indebted to the plaintiff on a promissory note. The plaintiff accepted a smaller sum from the defendant's father in full settlement. It was held that he could not later sue the defendant for the balance of the debt, because the promissory note was extinct: the position was the same as if the note had been cancelled.[92] This reasoning again does not depend on any contract between the plaintiff and the defendant, for the cancellation of a promissory note can release a person liable on it irrespective of contract and without consideration.[93]

---

84 *Pinnel's* case, *supra*. Many cases formerly supported the view that part payment by a negotiable instrument, made at the request of the creditor and accepted by him in full settlement, discharged the debt. But these cases were overruled in *D. & C. Builders Ltd.* v. *Rees* [1966] 2 Q.B. 617.
85 *Brikom Investments Ltd.* v. *Carr* [1979] Q.B. 467; as explained *ante*, p. 97.
86 See *post*, p. 657 for this requirement.
87 *Welby* v. *Drake* (1825) 1 C. & P. 557; *Cook* v. *Lister* (1863) 13 C.B.(N.S.) 543, 595.
88 See the authorities cited in n. 87, *supra*.
89 *Post*, p. 297.
90 *Snelling* v. *John G. Snelling Ltd.* [1973] 1 Q.B. 87, distinguishing *Gore* v. *Van der Lann* [1967] 2 Q.B. 31, where no promise was made not to sue C.
91 [1911] 2 K.B. 330.
92 At p. 336.
93 *Ante*, p. 95.

(f) COMPOSITION AGREEMENTS. A debtor who cannot pay all his creditors in full may be able to induce them to agree with himself and each other to accept a dividend in full settlement of their claims.[94] A creditor who has accepted a dividend under such an agreement cannot sue the debtor for the balance of his original demand.[95] If the debtor fails to pay the agreed dividend, the original debt revives.[96]

One reason why such composition agreements are binding is again said to be that a creditor who sued for the balance of his debt would commit a fraud on the others.[97] On this view it is unnecessary to look for any consideration moving from the debtor. Another possible reason for the rule is that the debtor may be prejudiced by forbearing to have himself adjudicated bankrupt. But it is hard to see how this can be consideration if the debtor's whole object in agreeing to the composition was to avoid bankruptcy.[98] And if such a forbearance were consideration for a composition with several creditors, why is it not consideration for a composition with one? The same objection applies to the theory that the debtor can provide consideration by the act of executing the composition agreement. The debtor may, however, provide consideration by procuring a third party to act as surety for his promise to pay the dividend.[99] A final justification for the rule, stated in some of the relevant judgments, is that there is consideration for the creditors' promise to forgo the balance since each creditor benefits from the arrangement: he is certain to get some payment, while in the scramble for priority which would take place if there were no composition agreement he might get nothing at all.[1]

(g) COLLATERAL CONTRACT. An agreement to accept part payment of a debt in full settlement may take effect as a collateral contract if the requirements of contractual intention and consideration are satisfied. This was the position in *Brikom Investments Ltd.* v. *Carr*[2] where a tenant's liability to contribute to the maintenance costs of a block of flats was held to have been reduced by a collateral contract under which the landlord undertook

---

94 Provision for publicity and substantial agreement among creditors is made by the Deeds of Arrangement Act 1914 (repealed in part by Insolvency Act 1985 s.235 and Sched. 10 Pt. III and amended by Insolvency Act 1986, s.439(2)). *Oral* agreements are not caught by the 1914 Act; *Hughes & Falconer* v. *Newton* [1939] 2 All E.R. 869. "Voluntary arrangements" under Insolvency Act 1986 Pts. I and VIII do not derive their force from contract, but from statute: under ss.5(2) and 260(2), they may bind a creditor who did not attend the meeting summoned under the statutory procedure so long as he had notice of, and was entitled to vote at, the meeting.

95 *Good* v. *Cheesman* (1831) 2 B. & Ad. 328; *Boyd* v. *Hind* (1857) 1 H. & N. 938; the bare *agreement* to pay a dividend may operate as satisfaction, if the parties so intend: *Bradley* v. *Gregory* (1810) 2 Camp. 383.

96 *Evans* v. *Powis* (1847) 1 Ex. 601.

97 *Wood* v. *Roberts* (1818) 2 Stark. 417; *Cook* v. *Lister* (1863) 13 C.B.(N.S.) 543, 595.

98 *Cf. ante*, p. 80. The position might be different if the debtor really did intend to go into bankruptcy and the creditors dissuaded him by promising to accept part payment in full settlement.

99 As in *Bradley* v. *Gregory* (1810) 2 Camp. 383.

1 *Good* v. *Cheesman* (1831) 2 B. & Ad. 328, 334; *Garrard* v. *Woolner* (1832) 8 Bing. 258, 265; *West Yorks Darracq Agency Ltd.* v. *Coleridge* [1911] 2 K.B. 326 is an unwarranted extension of the principle since the creditor got nothing: *ante*, p. 79, n. 36. Even in such cases, the debtor may get the benefit of the agreement if, when he is sued by one creditor, the others can intervene to stay the action under *Snelling* v. *John G. Snelling Ltd.* [1973] 1 Q.B. 87, *ante*, p. 118.

2 [1979] Q.B. 467.

to execute certain roof repairs at his own expense.[3] The landlord's claim for contribution in this case was probably unliquidated; but the principle seems to be equally applicable where a creditor enters into a collateral contract to accept part payment in full settlement of a liquidated claim.

(3) Equitable evasion

The common law limitations leave in existence the general and often inconvenient rule that a creditor is not bound by a promise to accept part payment of a debt in full satisfaction. Two attempts have been made to evade this rule in equity.

(a) EQUITABLE RELEASE. A number of early cases may support the view that in equity a creditor could release a debt by simply saying that he had done so, or was doing so.[4] Other cases, on the contrary, hold that a release was not good in equity unless it was also good at law.[5] A possible distinction between the two lines of cases is that in the first the creditor says "I hereby release the debt," while in the second he says "I promise not to sue the debtor."[6] The former statement could be regarded as a completed gift of the debt by the creditor to the debtor[7] and the latter as a mere promise or covenant not to sue[8] (which would not be binding without consideration). But the distinction is tenuous, and it is doubtful whether the doctrine of equitable release, if it was ever established, has survived *Jorden* v. *Money*.[9]

(b) EQUITABLE FORBEARANCE. Under the rule in *Hughes* v. *Metropolitan Ry.*[10] a promise by a contracting party not to enforce his legal rights has (even where it is not supported by consideration) at least a limited effect in equity. Before 1947, this rule had not been applied to a creditor's promise to accept part payment of a debt in full settlement. Such an extension of the rule seemed to be barred by *Foakes* v. *Beer.*[11] The possibility of making the extension was, however, suggested in *Central London Property Trust Ltd.* v. *High Trees House Ltd.*[12] The plaintiffs had in 1937 let a block of flats to the defendants for 99 years at a rent of £2,500 per annum. In 1940 the plaintiffs agreed to reduce the rent to £1,250 per annum as many of the flats were unlet because of war-time conditions. After the end of the war, the plaintiffs demanded the full rent for the last two quarters of 1945 and Denning J. upheld their claim on the ground that, as a matter of construc-

---

[3] For the consideration supporting this promise, see *ante* p. 97, for other grounds for the decision, see *post*, pp. 122–123.

[4] *Wekett* v. *Raby* (1724) 2 Bro.P.C. 386; *Richards* v. *Syms* (1740) 2 Eq.Ca.Abr. 617; *Eden* v. *Smyth* (1800) 5 Ves. 341; *Flower* v. *Marten* (1837) 2 My. & Cr. 459.

[5] *Cross* v. *Sprigg* (1849) 6 Hare 552 (reversed on other grounds: 2 Mac. & G. 113); *Major* v. *Major* (1852) 1 Drew. 165; *Luxmore* v. *Clifton* (1867) 17 L.T. 460.

[6] See *Reeves* v. *Bryner* (1801) 6 Ves. 516, distinguishing *Eden* v. *Smyth, supra.*

[7] *Cf. Gray* v. *Barton*, N.Y. 68 (1873). If a creditor can make a gift of a debt to a third party by assignment (*post*, pp. 588 *et seq.*) why should he not be able to make such a gift to the debtor?

[8] *Cf.* the distinction between a release and a covenant not to sue which is drawn (for another purpose) in the law relating to joint debtors: *post*, p. 517.

[9] *Ante*, p. 109.

[10] (1877) 2 App.Cas. 439; *ante*, p. 101.

[11] (1884) 9 App.Cas. 605; *ante*, p. 115.

[12] [1947] K.B. 130; Denning, 15 M.L.R. 1; Wilson, 67 L.Q.R. 330; Sheridan, 15 M.L.R. 325; Bennion, 16 M.L.R. 441; Guest, 30 A.L.J. 187; Turner, 1 N.Z.U.L.R. 185; Campbell, *ibid.* 232.

tion, the 1940 agreement was only intended to apply while the war-time conditions lasted. But he also said that the plaintiffs would have been precluded by the equitable doctrine of *Huges* v. *Metropolitan Ry.*[13] from suing for the full rent for the period which *was* covered by the 1940 agreement. He added: "The logical consequence no doubt is that a promise to accept a smaller sum, if acted upon, is binding notwithstanding the absence of consideration."[14] The requirements and effects of the equitable doctrine have already been discussed.[15] Three points give rise to particular difficulty in its application to cases of part payment of a debt.

(i) *Effect generally suspensory.* The first difficulty is to reconcile the remarks of Denning J. in the *High Trees* case with *Foakes* v. *Beer.*[16] If the plaintiff in *Foakes* v. *Beer* could go back on her promise not to ask for interest, why could not the plaintiffs in the *High Trees* case go back on their promise not to ask for the full rent in, say, 1941, when war-time difficulties of letting still prevailed? One possibility is to say that *Foakes* v. *Beer* was decided on purely common law principles, without reference to equity[17]; and is therefore "no longer valid"[18]; but this is unsatisfactory, as the rule that part payment of a debt was no discharge was clearly recognised in equity.[19] Another possibility, and one which does less violence to the authorities, is to say that the creditor's right to the balance of his debt is not extinguished but only suspended.[20] This is generally the sole consequence of the rule in *Hughes* v. *Metropolitan Ry.*[21] and may often give effect to the intention of the parties.[22] Of course where the intention is to extinguish, and not merely to suspend, the creditor's right to the balance, the suggestion that he is permanently bound by his promise not to sue for the balance[23] may seem to be an attractive one.[24] But such an extension of the principle of *Hughes* v. *Metropolitan Ry.* would require the overruling of *Foakes* v. *Beer.* It is, no doubt, with such difficulties in mind that Lord Hailsham L.C. has said that the *High Trees* principle "may need to be reviewed and reduced to a coherent body of doctrine by the courts."[25]

For the present the better view is that the principle only suspends rights; but the meaning of this statement is not entirely clear where the promisee is under a continuing obligation to make periodical payments, *e.g.* of rent

---

[13] *Ante* p. 101.
[14] [1947] K.B. 130, 134; *cf. Combe* v. *Combe* [1951] 2 K.B. 215, 220.
[15] *Ante*, pp. 101–111.
[16] (1884) 9 App.Cas. 605, *ante*, p. 115.
[17] *High Trees* case, *supra.* at p. 133.
[18] *Arrale* v. *Costain Civil Engineering Ltd.* [1976] 1 Lloyd's Rep. 98, 102.
[19] *Bidder* v. *Bridges* (1887) 37 Ch.D. 406; *Re Warren* (1884) 53 L.J.Ch. 1016.
[20] *Ajayi* v. *R. T. Briscoe (Nig.) Ltd.* [1964] 1 W.L.R. 1326, 1330; Unger, 28 M.L.R. 231; *cf. Re Venning* [1947] W.N. 196. Gordon [1963] C.L.J. 222 objects to giving the creditor's promise even this limited effect, arguing that the equitable principle is limited to relief against forfeiture. But though *Hughes* v. *Metropolitan Ry.* was a case of this kind, the equitable principle had developed since 1877 and is no longer restricted to such cases: see Wilson [1965] C.L.J. 93.
[21] *Ante* p. 106.
[22] *e.g.* in *Ajayi* v. *R. T. Briscoe (Nig.) Ltd., supra*: see *post*, p. 122, n. 30.
[23] Originally made by Lord Denning in the *High Trees* case at p. 134 and repeated by him in *D. & C. Builders Ltd.* v. *Rees* [1966] 2 Q.B. 617, 624. *cf. W. J. Alan & Co. Ltd.* v. *El Nasr Export & Import Co.* [1972] 2 Q.B. 189, 213; and *ibid.* 218, 220; but in that case there was consideration: *ante*, p. 96.
[24] Provided that there was no duress: *cf. ante*, p. 88; *post*, p. 124.
[25] *Woodhouse A.C. Israel Cocoa Ltd.* v. *Nigerian Produce Marketing Co. Ltd.* [1972] A.C. 741, 758.

under a lease,[26] or of royalties under a licence to use a patent,[27] or of instalments under a hire-purchase agreement.[28] In such cases the statement may mean one of two things: first, that the promisor can only claim the full amount of payments which fall due after the expiry of a reasonable notice of the retraction of the promise[29]; or, secondly, that he is then entitled, not only to future payments in full, but also to the unpaid balance of *past* ones. Of course the second of these views might sometimes be at variance with the intention of the parties at the time of the promise.[30] On the other hand it is hard to see why a debtor whose liability accrues from time to time should, for the present purpose of the present rule, be in a more favourable position than one whose liability is to pay a single lump sum; nor is it clear which of the two views should apply where a debtor who owed a lump sum promised to pay it off in instalments and the creditor first made, and then gave reasonable notice revoking, a promise to accept reduced instalments. In such a case, it is at least arguable that the intention of the creditor is only to give extra time for payment. Hence the total debt remains due, and the only effect of the promise is to extend the period over which it is to be repaid.[31]

There may, however, be exceptional cases where the creditor's right is wholly extinguished. We have seen that a forbearance cannot be retracted where subsequent events, or the passage of time, make it highly inequitable[32] to require performance of the original obligation, even after reasonable notice. This principle could be applied to cases of the present kind, so that the creditor's right to the balance might be extinguished if, in reliance on his promise, the debtor had undertaken new commitments in relation to the subject-matter: *e.g.* if the tenant in the *High Trees* case had used the rebate to modernise the flats.[33]

The creditor's right was also held to have been wholly extinguished in *Brikom Investments Ltd.* v. *Carr.*[34] In that case, long leases of flats provided that the tenants should pay (*inter alia*) contributions in respect of certain expenses incurred by the landlords on repairs. During negotiations leading to the execution of the leases, the landlords had promised to put

---

26 As in the *High Trees* case.

27 As in the *Tool Metal* case [1955] 1 W.L.R. 761; *ante*, p. 106.

28 As in *Ajayi* v. *R. T. Briscoe (Nig.) Ltd.* [1964] 1 W.L.R. 1326; *cf. Meng Long Development Pte. Ltd.* v. *Jip Hong Trading Pte. Ltd.* [1985] A.C. 511, 524.

29 *Banning* v. *Wright* [1972] 1 W.L.R. 972, 981; *cf. W. J. Alan & Co. Ltd.* v. *El Nasr Export & Import Co.* [1972] 2 Q.B. 189, 213. This view is apparently regarded as correct in the *Tool Metal* case, *supra*; but the case is not conclusive as the liability of the licensee to make the payments *during* the suspension period was not directly considered by the House of Lords.

30 This would be so in cases like the *High Trees* and *Tool Metal* cases—but not in a case like *Ajayi* v. *R. T. Briscoe (Nig.) Ltd.*, *supra*, n. 28 as the promise there "was not intended to be irrevocable": *Meng Long Development Pte. Ltd.* v. *Jip Hong Trading Pte. Ltd.* [1985] A.C. 511, 524. *J. T. Sydenham & Co. Ltd.* v. *Enichem Elastometers Ltd.* [1989] 1 E.G.L.R. 257, 260 (discussed by Cartwright, [1990] C.L.J. 13) purports to give the "estoppel" an extinctive effect; but the amount of rent due in that case was in dispute, so that the actual decision is explicable on the ground stated at p. 116, *ante*.

31 *Hardwick* v. *Johnson* [1978] 1 W.L.R. 683 (where the creditor was said at p. 699 to have agreed to "postpone" the debtor's obligation to pay instalments).

32 *Ante*, p. 107 at n. 92.

33 *Cf.* Mitchell, 2 Univ. of Western Australia Annual Law Review 245, 251; and see the defence of "change of position" in an action for the recovery back of money paid: Jones, 73 L.Q.R. 48; Goff & Jones, *The Law of Restitution*, (3rd ed.), pp. 691–699.

34 [1979] Q.B. 467.

the roof into repair "at our own cost." This was held to amount to a collateral contract[35] with one of the original tenants, precluding the landlords from enforcing against her the provision in the lease requiring her to contribute to the cost of the roof repairs. It was further held that claims for contributions to the cost of those repairs could not be made against assignees and sub-assignees of original tenants, even though there were no collateral contracts with these persons. Lord Denning M.R. based this conclusion on the *High Trees* principle which, in his view, was available not only between the original parties, but also in favour of, and against, their assigns.[36] The extinctive effect of the principle can perhaps be supported in these circumstances on the ground that the original tenants, the assignees and the sub-assignees had all, in reliance on the landlord's promise, undertaken fresh commitments by entering into long leases of the flats. Roskill and Cumming-Bruce L.JJ., on the other hand, treated the case, not as one of "promissory estoppel,"[37] but as one of "waiver."[38] It seems that the latter expression here refers to a variation supported by consideration[39]; for the consideration provided by the tenants[40] could equally support the landlords' promise whether that promise was regarded as a collateral contract[41] or as a variation of the principal contract itself. On this interpretation of the case, there is no difficulty in accounting for the extinctive effect of the landlords' promise. It amounted to a variation supported by consideration, so that the liability of the original tenants to contribute to the cost of the repairs in question was extinguished; and once it had been so extinguished it was not revived on assignment of the leases.

(ii) *Reliance.* One difficulty which has been felt about the *High Trees* case is that a tenant who is bound to pay £2,500 per annum for 99 years suffers no "detriment," in the sense in which that word is used in the law of estoppel,[42] by paying half that rent for part of the period. Ingenious attempts have been made to find some "detriment" in the case[43]; but Lord Denning himself has said extra-judicially that there was none.[44] Nor is the requirement mentioned in the *High Trees* case itself, or in any later statements of the principle. And if such "detriment" is not necessary for the purpose of the rule in *Hughes* v. *Metropolitan Ry.*[45] it is hard to see why it should be necessary for the purpose of its offshoot, the *High Trees* rule. All that is necessary is that the tenant should have acted in reliance on the promise in such a way that it would be inequitable for the landlord to act

---

35 *Ante*, p. 97.
36 [1979] Q.B. 467, 484–485.
37 *Ibid.* pp. 485, 490.
38 *Ibid.* p. 488, 490.
39 *Cf. ante*, p. 98.
40 *Ante*, p. 97. Roskill L.J. at p. 489 refers to *Hughes* v. *Metropolitan Ry.* (1877) 2 App.Cas. 439 (*ante* p. 101) as stating a principle of "contractual variation of strict contractual rights." It is respectfully submitted that this phrase should be interpreted to refer simply to *variations of contracts*, rather than to *contractually binding variations*; for the *Hughes* principle clearly applies to variations which are not contractually binding (but revocable on reasonable notice) because they are not supported by consideration.
41 *Ante*, p. 97.
42 *Cf. ante*, p. 105.
43 *e.g.* Wilson, 67 L.Q.R. 330, 344.
44 15 M.L.R. 1, 6–8.
45 See *ante*, p. 105.

inconsistently with it. This requirement was satisfied on the facts of the *High Trees* case, no less than on those of *Hughes* v. *Metropolitan Ry.*

(iii) *Inequitable.* When the debtor makes the part payment in reliance on the creditor's promise, it becomes prima facie "inequitable" for the creditor peremptorily to go back on his promise. But other circumstances may indicate that it would not be "inequitable" for the creditor to reassert his claim for the full amount.[46] It has been suggested that one such circumstance may be the conduct of the debtor in obtaining the promise. Thus in *D. & C. Builders Ltd.* v. *Rees*[47] Lord Denning M.R. held that the *High Trees* principle did not apply because the builders' promise to accept £300 in full settlement of their claim for £482 had been obtained by taking undue advantage of their desperate financial position. The difficulty with this reasoning is that most debtors who offer part payment in full settlement try to exert some form of "pressure" against their creditors. The law now recognises that it is possible for such pressure to amount to duress[48]; and where it has this effect the promise should clearly not bring the *High Trees* principle into operation. Where, on the other hand, there is no duress, the operation of the *High Trees* principle should not be excluded merely because it could be said that the creditor's promise had, in some sense, been "improperly obtained." Such an intermediate category between promises obtained by duress and those not so obtained should, here as elsewhere,[49] be rejected as "unhelpful because it would make the law uncertain."[50]

SECTION 7. PROPRIETARY ESTOPPEL

Proprietary estoppel is said to arise in certain situations in which a person has done acts in reliance on the belief that he has, or will acquire, rights in or over another's land. Usually, but not invariably, these acts consist of erecting buildings on, or making other improvements to, the land in question. Where the requirements of proprietary estoppel are satisfied, the landowner is precluded from denying the existence of the rights in question, and may indeed be compelled to grant them. Because the estoppel precludes him from denying the existence of rights in property, it has come to be known as "proprietary estoppel."[51] It is distinct[52] from promissory estoppel, both in the conditions which must be satisfied before it comes into operation and in its effects. But under both doctrines some legal effects are given to promises which are not contractually binding for want of consideration; and it is this aspect[53] of proprietary estoppel which calls for discussion in the present Chapter.

---

46 *Cf. ante*, p. 106.

47 [1966] 2 Q.B. 617, Winder, 82 L.Q.R. 165; *ante*, p. 115. *Cf. Arrale* v. *Costain Civil Engineering Ltd.* [1976] 1 Lloyd's Rep. 98, 102.

48 *Ante*, p. 88, *post*, pp. 363–365.

49 *Ante*, p. 89.

50 *Pao On* v. *Lau Yiu Long* [1980] A.C. 614, 634.

51 *Jones* v. *Jones* [1977] 1 W.L.R. 438, 442; *Pascoe* v. *Turner* [1979] 1 W.L.R. 431, 436; *Re Sharpe* [1980] 1 W.L.R. 219, 233; *Greasley* v. *Cooke* [1980] 1 W.L.R. 1306, 1311.

52 *Fontana N.V.* v. *Mautner* (1980) 254 E.G. 199, 207; and see *post*, p. 134.

53 For wider discussions, see Davies, 8 Sydney L.Rev. 200 and 7 Adelaide L.Rev. 200; Moriarty, 100 L.Q.R. 376.

1. Nature and Scope of the Doctrine

Proprietary estoppel operates in a variety of cases so disparate that it has been described as "an amalgam of doubtful utility."[54] The cases can be divided broadly into two categories.

In the first, one person acts under a mistake as to the existence or as to the extent of his rights in or over another's land. Even though the mistake was in no way induced by the landowner, he might be prevented from taking advantage of it, particularly if he "stood by" knowing of the mistake, or actively encouraged the mistaken party to act in reliance on his mistaken belief.[55] These cases of so-called "acquiescence"[56] do not raise any questions as to the enforceability of promises and therefore do not call for further discussion in this Chapter.[57]

In the second group of cases, there is not merely "acquiescence" by the landowner, but "encouragement."[58] The other party acts in reliance on the landowner's promise, or on conduct or a representation from which a promise can be implied,[59] that the promisee has a legally enforceable[60] interest in the land or that one will be created in his favour. The question then arises, to what extent such a promise can be enforced, even though it may not be supported by consideration, or fail to satisfy the other requirements (such as certainty) of a binding contract.

(1) Bases of liability

(a) EXPENDITURE ON ANOTHER'S LAND IN RELIANCE ON A PROMISE. In *Dillwyn* v. *Llewelyn*[61] a father executed a memorandum "presenting" a named estate to his son "for the purpose of furnishing himself with a dwelling house." The son spent £14,000 in building a house on the land; and it was held (after the father's death) that he was entitled to have the fee simple of the estate conveyed to him. Many subsequent cases similarly give some degree of legal enforceability to a promise by a landowner in reliance on which the promisee has spent money on making improvements to the promisor's land: for example, where A built a bungalow on B's land in reliance on B's promise that A could stay there for the rest of his life[62]; where A spent money on extending or improving B's house in reliance on a similar promise by B[63]; and where, in reliance on such a promise, A actually did

---

[54] *Amalgamated Investment & Property Co. Ltd.* v. *Texas Commerce International Bank Ltd.* [1982] Q.B. 84, 103.

[55] *Wilmott* v. *Barber* (1880) 15 Ch.D. 96; *cf. Taylors Fashions Ltd.* v. *Liverpool Victoria Trustee Co. Ltd.* [1982] Q.B. 133 n.

[56] *Wilmott* v. *Barber* (1880) 15 Ch.D. 96, 105.

[57] Nor do they call for discussion in Chapter 8, as the mistake is not one that prevents the formation of a contract, or is alleged to do so.

[58] *Ramsden* v. *Dyson* (1866) L.R. 1 H.L. 129, 170. Contrast *Att.-Gen. of Hong Kong* v. *Humphreys Estate (Queen's Gardens)* [1987] A.C. 114, where there was no encouragement.

[59] See *Lloyd's Bank Plc* v. *Rossett* [1991] 1 A.C. 107 (where this requirement was not satisfied).

[60] See *Coombes* v. *Smith* [1986] 1 W.L.R. 808 (where there was no belief in the existence of a *legally enforceable* right); *cf. Brinnand* v. *Ewens* (1987) 19 H.L.R. 415.

[61] (1862) 4 D.F. & G. 517; Allan, 79 L.Q.R. 238.

[62] *Inwards* v. *Baker* [1965] 2 Q.B. 507.

[63] *Hussey* v. *Palmer* [1972] 1 W.L.R. 1286; *Pascoe* v. *Turner* [1979] 1 W.L.R. 431; *semble* spending money on mere maintenance would not suffice: *Griffiths* v. *Williams* [1978] E.G. Digest of Cases 919.

the work of improvement him- or herself.[64] Cases of this kind can be explained on the basis of unjust enrichment: in all of them, the landowner would benefit unjustly if he were allowed to disregard his promise and to take back the land after having induced the promisee to make improvements to it. But this explanation will not account for cases in which the doctrine has been applied even though the promisee's expenditure on another's land did not result in any benefit to the landowner at all.[65] It follows that, although unjust enrichment of the promisor may be the most obvious basis of proprietary estoppel, it cannot provide complete explanation of the doctrine.

(b) OTHER ACTS DONE IN RELIANCE ON THE PROMISE. The operation of proprietary estoppel is not confined to cases in which the promisee has incurred expenditure on, or done work to, the promisor's land. It can also apply where the promisee has conferred some other benefit on the promisor[66]; and even where no work has been done on the promisor's land and he has not received any other benefit. This indeed appears from one of the illustrations given by Lord Westbury in *Dillwyn* v. *Llewelyn*: if "A gives a house to B, but makes no formal conveyance, and the house is afterwards included, with the knowledge of A, in the marriage settlement of B, A would be bound to complete the title of the parties claiming under the settlement."[67] Similarly, the doctrine operated in the absence of any expenditure on the promisor's land in *Crabb* v. *Arun D.C.*[68] In that case A (a local authority) by its conduct represented to B that B had a right of way from his land over adjoining land owned by A. In reliance on that representation, B sold part of his own land, so that the only access from the remainder to the nearest public highway was by means of the right of way across A's land. It was held that B had a right to cross A's land for the purpose of access to his retained land. Detrimental reliance by the promisee can therefore give rise to a proprietary estoppel even though no benefit is conferred on the promisor.[69]

(c) ALTERNATIVE EXPLANATION: CONTRACT. In *Dillwyn* v. *Llewelyn* Lord Westbury, while referring to the parties to the transaction as "donor" and

---

[64] *Eves* v. *Eves* [1975] 1 W.L.R. 1338; *Jones* v. *Jones* [1977] 1 W.L.R. 438.

[65] *Canadian Pacific Railway* v. *The King* [1931] A.C. 414; *Armstrong* v. *Sheppard & Short* [1959] 2 Q.B. 384.

[66] *e.g. Tanner* v. *Tanner* [1975] 1 W.L.R. 1346 (services rendered to promisor in managing his property); *Greasley* v. *Cooke* [1980] 1 W.L.R. 1306 (personal and nursing services); *cf. Plimmer* v. *Mayor of Wellington* (1884) 9 App.Cas. 699 and *E. R. Ives Investments Ltd.* v. *High* [1967] 2 Q.B. 379 (where the landowner benefited from improvements to his land but also—and more significantly—in other ways); *Grant* v. *Edwards* [1986] Ch. 638, 657; *Maharaj* v. *Chand* [1986] A.C. 898 (where, because of local legislation, proprietary estoppel was not argued); *Re Basham* [1986] 1 W.L.R. 1498; contrast *Howard* v. *Jones* (1988) 19 Fam. L. 231 (contribution to running cost of *another* property insufficient).

[67] (1862) 4 D.F. & G. 517, 521.

[68] [1976] Ch. 179. The case was described in *Amalgamated Investment & Property Co. Ltd.* v. *Texas Commerce International Bank Ltd.* [1982] Q.B. 84, 121 as one of "estoppel by convention"; but this would require a dealing between A and B on the basis of common assumption (*ante*, p. 112), while in *Crabb's* case the dealing was between B and a purchaser from him. In *Waltons Stores (Interstate) Ltd.* v. *Maher* (1988) 62 A.L.J.R. 110, 115 *Crabb's* case was described as one of "promissory estoppel" (see *ante*, p. 109); but the requirements of that doctrine (in particular, the requirement of a pre-existing legal relationship: *ante*, p. 102) were not satisfied in *Crabb's* case, and the effect of the estoppel differed from promissory estoppel in giving rise to a new right: *cf. ante*, p. 107.

[69] *Cf. Hammersmith & Fulham B.C.* v. *Top Shop Centres Ltd.* [1990] Ch. 237.

"donee" also said that the son's expenditure "supplied a valuable consideration originally wanting"[70] and in discussing a hypothetical example similar to the facts of the case before him he concluded "that the donee acquires a right from the subsequent transaction to call upon the donor to perform that contract and to complete the imperfect donation."[71] These passages may suggest that he regarded the memorandum as a kind of unilateral contract by which the father promised to convey the land if the son built a house on it. The terms of the memorandum make it improbable that a modern court would so regard it; it is more likely that these terms would now be regarded as negativing contractual intention.[72] However, in a number of later cases the rights of a person who had expended money on the property of another have been explained as being based on contract[73]; and often such an explanation was sufficiently plausible to make reliance on a doctrine of proprietary estoppel unnecessary. A unilateral contract to transfer an interest in land has been held to arise out of a promise to make the transfer if the promisee would pay instalments due under a mortgage on the house[74]; it can equally arise out of a promise to make the transfer if the promisee will make improvements to the land, or indeed do any other act.[75] But there are, it is submitted, obstacles to treating all cases of proprietary estoppel as depending on contract.[76] One, already mentioned, is that the promises in cases of this kind are often made in a family context, without contractual intention. A second is that the terms of the alleged contract are often too vague to satisfy the requirement of certainty.[77] This difficulty accounts for the view of the Court of Appeal that there was no contract in *Crabb* v. *Arun D.C.*[78]: there may have been an implied promise to grant the plaintiff some right of way across the defendants' land, but no financial or other terms were specified in that promise, so that it would not (even if supported by consideration) have been sufficiently certain to give rise to a contract. Moreover, many arrangements which can give rise to proprietary estoppel are made without any attempt to comply with the stringent formal requirements now imposed on the making of contracts for the disposition of interests in land.[79] Failure to comply with these require-

---

70 (1862) 4 D.F. & G. 517, 521.

71 *Ibid.* p. 521.

72 *Cf. post*, p. 152.

73 *e.g. Plimmer* v. *Mayor of Wellington* (1884) 9 App.Cas. 699 as explained in *Canadian Pacific Railway* v. *The King* [1931] A.C. 414, 428; *Eves* v. *Eves* [1975] 1 W.L.R. 1338; *Tanner* v. *Tanner* [1975] 1 W.L.R. 1346; *cf. Re Sharpe* [1980] 1 W.L.R. 219, 224; and see *E. R. Ives Investments Ltd.* v. *High* [1967] 2 Q.B. 379 (where there was a contract between the defendant and the plaintiff's predecessor in title).

74 *Errington* v. *Errington* [1952] 1 Q.B. 290; see *ante*, p. 38, n. 70 for authorities doubting this case on other points.

75 *e.g. Tanner* v. *Tanner* [1975] 1 W.L.R. 1346; merely to maintain the house in repair could be sufficient for the present purpose, even if it did not suffice to raise a proprietary estoppel: *ante*, p. 125 n. 63.

76 *Cf. Beaton* v. *McDivitt* (1988) 13 N.S.W. L.R. 162, 170–171.

77 *Ante*, p. 48.

78 [1976] Ch. 179; Atiyah, 92 L.Q.R. 174, criticises the view that there was no contract but the argument is based on the fallacy that, merely because a promise has *some* legal effects, it must necessarily have *all* the effects of a contract: *cf. ante*, p. 69, and *post*, p. 136; Millett, 92 L.Q.R. 342; Duncanson, 39 M.L.R. 268.

79 Law of Property (Miscellaneous Provisions) Act 1989, s.2(1)–(3). Previously, Law of Property Act 1925, s.40 (replacing part of Statute of Frauds 1677, s.4 and now repealed) had required either a note or memorandum in writing as evidence of the contract, or "part per-

ments will not prevent such arrangements from giving rise to a proprietary estoppel,[80] but it will prevent them from taking effect as contracts. The possibility of explaining proprietary estoppel on the basis of contract is therefore in practice likely to be restricted to cases where the arrangement does *not* purport to dispose of an interest in land, *e.g.* where it amounts to no more than a promise to grant a licence to occupy the land.[81]

(2) Conditions of liability

(a) KINDS OF PROMISES CAPABLE OF GIVING RISE TO A PROPRIETARY ESTOPPEL. A promise may give rise to a proprietary estoppel even though it is not express but is implied: for example, from the fact that the parties acted on the common assumption that one of them was to have the right to reside on the other's property.[82] The promise must be of such a kind that it is reasonable for the promisee to rely on it; and it must induce him to believe that a legal right has been, or will be, created in his favour. It follows that a promise will not give rise to proprietary estoppel if it expressly disclaims legal effect: for example, in one case[83] it was held that no proprietary estoppel arose out of an agreement for the transfer of a number of flats "subject to contract," it being well known that the effect of these words was to negative the intention to be legally bound.[84] The promisee may have formed "the confident and not unreasonable hope"[85] that the promise would not be withdrawn; but no *belief* to this effect had been encouraged[86] by the promisor or relied on by the promisee. It seems that a proprietary estoppel could arise out of such an agreement if one of the parties *did* encourage such a belief in the other and the other acted to his detriment in reliance on that belief.[87]

The rights which the promisee believes to have been created must, as a general rule, be rights in or over the property of the promisor. Thus a representation by a planning authority to the effect that a landowner does not need permission to carry out development on his *own* land is not capable of giving rise to a proprietary estoppel.[88] The promisor may, however, make

formance" of the contract: The latter requirement was often satisfied by the conduct of the promisee giving rise to proprietary estoppel. *Cf.* the reference to "part performance" in *Dillwyn* v. *Llewelyn* (1862) 4 D.F. & G. 517, 521.

[80] *Post*, p. 164.

[81] The earlier legislation referred to in n. 79, *supra*, did not apply to a licence to occupy land: *Wright* v. *Stavert* (1860) 2 E. & E. 721; *cf. Taylor* v. *Waters* (1816) 7 Taunt. 374 (licence to use opera box). The position seems to be the same under Law of Property (Micellaneous Provisions) Act 1989, s.2(6).

[82] *e.g. Re Sharpe* [1980] 1 W.L.R. 219.

[83] *Att.-Gen. of Hong Kong* v. *Humphreys Estates* (*Queen's Gardens*) [1987] 1 A.C. 114; the case was said in *Walton Stores (Interstate) Ltd.* v. *Maher* (1988) 62 A.L.J.R. 110, 116 to be "not a case of proprietary estoppel" but (apparently) one of *promissory* estoppel. But most of the authorities relied on in the *Humphreys Estates* case were cases of proprietary estoppel; the leading cases on promissory estoppel were not cited; and if the requirements of encouragement and reliance had been satisfied the estoppel would have created a new right, which in English law is not the effect of promissory estoppel: *ante*, p. 107.

[84] *Ante*, p. 52; *post*, p. 150.

[85] [1987] 1 A.C. 114, 124.

[86] *Cf. ante*, p. 125; *Brinnand* v. *Ewens* (1987) 19 H.L.R. 415; and (in a different context) *Kelly* v. *Liverpool Maritime Terminals* [1988] I.R.L.R. 310, where authorities on proprietary estoppel are cited in a case unconnected with property.

[87] This is assumed in *Att.-Gen. of Hong Kong* v. *Humphreys Estate* (*Queen's Gardens*) *supra* n. 79, where the Privy Council at p. 124 stress that there had been *no* such encouragement.

[88] *Western Fish Products Ltd.* v. *Penwith D.C.* [1981] 2 All E.R. 204 (decided in 1978).

two promises, the first of which relates to the promisor's land while the second relates to that of the promisee; and the two promises may be so closely linked as to form in substance a single transaction. If the doctrine of proprietary estoppel applies to that transaction as a whole, it can provide the promisee with a remedy in respect of the second promise even though that promise, standing alone, could not have given rise to proprietary estoppel because it related only to the promisee's land. In one case,[89] for example, A promised B (1) to sell blackacre to B to enable B to build on it, and (2) to buy whiteacre from B so that B could pay for the building operations on blackacre. B carried out the building work envisaged in the first of A's promises and it was held that the doctrine of proprietary estoppel provided B with a remedy in respect of the second promise (which had no contractual force), even though that promise related only to B's land. But it was recognised that the doctrine could not have applied to the second promise if it had stood alone and not formed part of a transaction also relating to A's land.[90] It could not, for example, have applied if A had simply made a non-contractual promise to B to buy whiteacre from B, knowing that B intended to use the proceeds of the sale to buy shares from C, and if B had then entered into a contract to that effect with C. Normally, the doctrine applies to promises to *grant* rights in land *to* the promisee; it only applies to promises to *acquire* such rights *from* him where they are inextricably linked with promises of the former kind.

(b) SUBJECT-MATTER OF THE PROMISE. In the cases to which the doctrine has so far been applied, the subject-matter of the promise has always been (or at least included[91]) land. The question whether a promise can give rise to a proprietary estoppel where its subject-matter is property of some other kind remains an open one.[92] Even if the doctrine is extended to such promises, its scope will remain narrower than that of so-called promissory estoppel[93]: it is essential that the promisee should be induced to believe that he will *acquire an interest* in the property which is the subject-matter of the promise. It is not enough that the promise should in some other way relate to property: for example, the doctrine of proprietary estoppel would not apply on the facts of *Central London Property Trust* v. *High Trees House Ltd.*[94]

(c) DETRIMENTAL RELIANCE. The promisee must have relied on the promise or representation to his detriment.[95] The requirement has been

[89] *Salvation Army Trustee Co.* v. *West Yorks Metropolitan C.C.* (1981) 41 P. & C.R. 179.

[90] *Ibid.* p. 191. The case was approved but distinguished in *Att.-Gen. of Hong Kong* v. *Humphreys Estate (Queen's Gardens)* [1987] A.C. 114, 126–127.

[91] See *Re Basham* [1986] 1 W.L.R. 1498.

[92] *Western Fish Products Ltd.* v. *Penwith D.C.* [1981] 2 All E.R. at p. 217; *cf.* the reference *ibid.* at p. 218, and in *Crabb* v. *Arun D.C.* [1976] Ch. 179, 187, to the decision of the Court of Appeal in *Moorgate Mercantile Co.* v. *Twitchings* [1976] Q.B. 225; that decision was reversed by the House of Lords: [1977] A.C. 890.

[93] See *ante*, pp. 101–111, 120–124.

[94] [1947] K.B. 130; *ante*, p. 120.

[95] This was the view of the majority of the Court of Appeal in *Greasley* v. *Cooke* [1980] 1 W.L.R. 1306; the requirement is assumed to exist in *Taylors Fashions Ltd.* v. *Liverpool Victoria Trustees Co. Ltd.* [1982] Q.B. 133 n and stated in *Grant* v. *Edwards* [1986] Ch. 638, 657; *cf. Lloyds Bank Plc* v. *Rosset* [1990] 1 All E.R. 1111, 1116. The fact that there was no such reliance was one reason why the claim based on proprietary estoppel failed in *Western Fish Products Ltd.* v. *Penwith D.C.*, *supra*: see [1981] 2 All E.R. at p. 217, in *Coombes* v. *Smith* [1986] 1 W.L.R. 808, in *Att.-Gen. of Hong Kong* v. *Humphreys Estate*

doubted[96] but in the absence of any such reliance it is hard to see why failure to perform a merely gratuitous promise should be regarded as giving rise to any legal liability. The existence of the requirement is also supported by the rules as to the revocability of the promise, to be discussed below.[97]

Where a promise has been made which is capable of inducing detrimental reliance, and which is in fact followed by such reliance, the question may arise whether the promise actually did induce the reliance. The burden on this issue is on the promisor: that is, it is up to the promisor, in order to escape liability, to show that the promisee would have done the acts in question anyway, even if the promise had not been made.[98] The position appears to be different where a proprietary estoppel arises because both parties have acted under a mistake as to their rights in the land.[99] Here it seems to be up to the party relying on the proprietary estoppel to show that his conduct in relation to the property was in fact induced by his belief that he had an interest in it.[1]

(d) WHETHER RELIANCE MUST RELATE TO SPECIFIC PROPERTY. The authorities are divided on the question whether, to give rise to a proprietary estoppel, the reliance must relate to identifiable property. According to one case, the promisee's conduct must relate to "some specific asset" in which an interest is claimed; so that proprietary estoppel did not arise merely because B rendered services to A in the expectation of receiving some indeterminate benefit under A's will.[2] But in another case reliance on a similar expectation (induced by A's promise) was held sufficient even though it did not relate to any "particular property."[2a] The latter case can perhaps be explained on the ground that the promise did to some extent identify the property.[3] It is submitted that the view that the promise must relate to identified or identifiable property is to be preferred; for without some such limitation on the scope of proprietary estoppel the doctrine could extend to any gift promise on which the promisee had relied to his detriment. Such a very broad doctrine would be fundamentally inconsistent with the doctrine of consideration[4] and, indeed, with the rule that the doctrine of promissory estoppel gives rise to no rights.[5]

2. Effects of the Doctrine

(1) Revocability

A promise which is capable of giving rise to a proprietary estoppel may be revocable by its express terms. Thus if the landowner promises to allow the

(*Queen's Gardens*) [1987]. A.C. 114, and in *Mecca Leisure* v. *The London Residuary Body* [1988] C.L.Y. 1375; different conditions of liability apply to a *donatio mortis causa*: see *Sen* v. *Hedley* [1991] N.L.J. R. 384.

[96] By Lord Denning M.R. in *Greasley* v. *Cooke, supra* at p. 1311. The argument may be influenced by the analogy of promissory estoppel (see *ante*, p. 105); but the two doctrines are distinct: *post*, p. 134.

[97] *Post*, pp. 130–131.

[98] *Greasley* v. *Cooke, supra*; *cf. Grant* v. *Edwards* [1986] Ch. 638; *Re Basham* [1986] 1 W.L.R. 1498; *Hammersmith & Fulham B.C.* v. *Top Shop Centres Ltd.* [1990] Ch. 237.

[99] *Ante*, p. 125.

[1] *Taylors Fashions Ltd.* v. *Liverpool Victoria Trustees Co. Ltd.* [1982] Q.B. 133 note; *cf. Coombes* v. *Smith* [1986] 1 W.L.R. 808.

[2] *Layton* v. *Martin* [1986] 2 F.L.R. 227.

[2a] *Re Basham* [1986] 1 W.L.R. 1498, 1508.

[3] By referring to the promisor's cottage.

[4] See, *e.g. ante*, p. 63.

[5] *Ante*, p. 107.

promisee to stay on the land "until I decide to sell," then the promisee cannot, merely by spending money on improvements to the land, acquire any right to stay there for a longer period.[6] Even where the promise is not expressed to be revocable, it can be revoked before the promisee has acted on it. Thus in *Dillwyn* v. *Llewelyn*[7] it seems that the father could have revoked his promise before the son had started to build on the land[8] and in *Crabb* v. *Arun D.C.*[9] the promise to grant a right of way could have been revoked before the promisee had, by selling off part of his land, made it impossible for himself to obtain access to the retained land except by means of the promised right of way. In this respect proprietary estoppel resembles so-called promissory estoppel (under which promises are similarly revocable[10]) and differs from contractually binding promises which are not revocable unless they expressly or impliedly so provide. The cases on proprietary estoppel assume that once the promisee has acted on the representation, he cannot be restored to his original position. Where he has spent money on improvements to land, this will generally be the case. Where a restoration of the status quo is physically possible, it seems that a promise giving rise to a proprietary estoppel could be revoked even after the promisee had acted on it, provided that the promisor in fact restored the promisee to the position in which he was before he had acted in reliance on the promise.

In the situations just discussed, revocation of the promise may prevent a proprietary estoppel from arising. It is also possible for the requirements of proprietary estoppel to be satisfied, but for the promise to be none the less revocable, because the court considers it appropriate in this way to limit the effects to be given to the promise.[11]

(2) Operation of proprietary estoppel

Granted that the conditions required to give rise to a proprietary estoppel have been satisfied, the effect of the doctrine is said to be to confer an "equity" on the promisee. Two further questions then arise: namely, what is the extent of that "equity," and what are the remedies for its enforcement.[12] In practice these questions tend to merge into each other; but an attempt to deal with them in turn will be made in the following discussion.

(a) EXTENT OF THE EQUITY. At one extreme, the promisee may be entitled to conveyance of the fee simple in the property which is the subject-matter of the promise, as in *Dillwyn* v. *Llewelyn*.[13] On the other hand, in *Inwards* v. *Baker*,[14] where a son had also built a house for himself at his father's suggestion on the latter's land, the result of the estoppel was only to entitle the son to occupy the house for life. Similar results were reached in a number of later cases in which the promisee made improvements to the

---

[6] *E. & L. Berg Homes* v. *Gray* (1979) 253 E.G. 473.

[7] (1862) D.F. & G. 517; *ante*, p. 125.

[8] *Cf. Pascoe* v. *Turner* [1979] 1 W.L.R. 431, 435 (where before the promisee's action in reliance on the promise she was said to be only a licensee at will).

[9] [1976] Ch. 179; *ante*, p. 126.

[10] *Ante*, p. 106.

[11] See *post*, p. 132, at n. 18.

[12] *Crabb* v. *Arun D.C.* [1976] Ch. 179, 193, *per* Scarman L.J.

[13] (1862) D.F. & G. 517; or, in the exceptional circumstances discussed on p. 129 *ante*, at n. 89, to an order requiring the promisor to *acquire* the promisee's land.

[14] [1965] 2 Q.B. 507; Maudsley, 81 L.Q.R. 183.

promisor's property (or otherwise acted to his detriment) in reliance on a promise, or common understanding, that the promisee would be entitled to reside there for as long as he or she wished to do so[15]; or for some shorter period: *e.g.* until her children had left school.[16] *Dillwyn* v. *Llewelyn* can be reconciled with these cases by reference to the terms of the respective promises: in the former case, the promise was expressed as an outright gift of the property, while in the latter cases it amounted to no more than an assurance that the promisee would be entitled to reside in the property for the specified period. Another way of giving effect to a promise of the latter kind is by the grant of a long, non-assignable lease at a nominal rent, on terms that ensured that the right of occupation was personal to the promisee.[17] In other cases, not concerned with rights of personal occupation but with the right to keep and use structures on promisor's land, the promisee has been held entitled only to a revocable licence.[18]

Where the promise is one to allow the promisee access to his own land over that of the promisor, the effect of the proprietary estoppel will be to entitle the promisee to an easement or licence on terms.[19] Such terms, if not agreed between the parties, may be imposed by the court: they can specify the extent of the permitted user as well as any payment that the promisee may be required to make for the exercise of the right.[20] However, an order for such payment was held not to be appropriate in one case, because the promisor had already obtained other benefits under the agreement.[21] It may also be inappropriate for other reasons, as the following discussion of the promisee's remedy will show.

(b) REMEDY. In deciding what remedy to grant to the promisee, the court may take into account not only the terms of the promise and the extent of the promisee's reliance on it, but also the conduct of the promisor after the occurrence of the facts giving rise to the proprietary estoppel. Thus in *Crabb* v. *Arun D.C.*[22] the defendants acted without warning in blocking the plaintiff's access to his land. In view of this "high-handedness"[23] and the resulting loss to the plaintiff, he was not required to make the payment that would otherwise have been a condition of the exercise of the right of way. Similarly, in *Pascoe* v. *Turner*[24] a proprietary estoppel arose when a man told a woman with whom he had formerly cohabited that the house in which they had lived was hers, and she later spent some £230 of her limited resources on repairs and improvements to it. The Court of Appeal relied on the man's "ruthlessness"[25] in seeking to evict the promisee as a ground for ordering him to convey the fee simple to her. The submission that she

---

[15] *Jones* v. *Jones* [1977] 1 W.L.R. 438; *Re Sharpe* [1980] 1 W.L.R. 219; *Greasley* v. *Cooke* [1980] 1 W.L.R. 1306.

[16] *Tanner* v. *Tanner* [1975] 1 W.L.R. 1346 (where there was a contract: *cf. ante*, p. 127).

[17] *Griffiths* v. *Williams* [1978] E.G. Digest of Cases 919; *cf. Jones* v. *Jones* [1977] 1 W.L.R. 438.

[18] *Canadian Pacific Railway* v. *The King* [1931] A.C. 414; *Armstrong* v. *Sheppard & Short* [1959] Q.B. 384.

[19] *E. R. Ives Investments Ltd.* v. *High* [1967] 2 Q.B. 379; *Crabb* v. *Arun D.C.* [1976] Ch. 179.

[20] *Crabb* v. *Arun D.C.*, [1976] Ch. 179, 199.

[21] *E. R. Ives Investments Ltd.* v. *High* [1967] 2 Q.B. 379.

[22] [1976] Ch. 179.

[23] [1976] Ch. at p. 199; *cf. ibid.* at p. 189.

[24] [1979] 1 W.L.R. 431; Sufrin, 42 M.L.R. 574.

[25] At p. 439.

should have no more than an irrevocable licence to occupy the house was rejected since this would not protect her against a bona fide purchaser from the promisor. The result seems, with respect, unduly punitive; and intermediate possibilities (such as granting the promisee a long lease[26]) were not put before the court.

Pascoe v. *Turner* illustrates a situation in which the grant of an irrevocable licence to remain on the property may constitute an unsatisfactory remedy because it will not adequately secure the promisee's possession. It may also be unsatisfactory on account of its inflexibility: thus in *Inwards* v. *Baker*[27] the promisee would have had no remedy, had he wanted to move elsewhere; nor would his dependants have had any remedy, had he died shortly after completing the house. In such cases a remedy by way of compensation in money would be more satisfactory for the promisee; and it would also have the advantage for the promisor that he would not be impeded in dealing with the property for an indefinite time.[28] Such a remedy was granted in *Dodsworth* v. *Dodsworth*[29] where the promisees spent £700 on improvements to the promisor's bungalow in reliance on an implied promise (not intended to give rise to legal relations) that the promisee and his wife could live there as if it were their home. The Court of Appeal held that to give the promisees a right of occupation for an indefinite time would confer on them a greater interest than had been contemplated by the parties; and that the most appropriate remedy was to repay them their outlay on improvements. Where there is evidence that the improved property has increased in value by reason of market fluctuations, it is submitted that the amount recoverable by the promisee should be increased correspondingly; conversely it should be reduced where the market value of the property has declined.

In *Dodsworth* v. *Dodsworth*[30] the court awarded compensation even though, when the action was brought, the promisee was still in possession of the improved property. More commonly this form of remedy is granted where the promisee is no longer in possession, having either left voluntarily[31] or been lawfully ejected as a result of legal proceedings.[32] Where the promisee has been wrongly ordered to give up possession, compensation in money is similarly available,[33] though in such a case the court may alternatively order the promisee to be put back into possession of the premises.[34] The compensation has been assessed in a variety of ways: at the cost of improvements made with the promisee's money[35] at a proportionate interest in the property[36]; or at the reasonable value of the right of occupation,

---

26 As in *Griffiths* v. *Williams* [1978] E.G. Digest of Cases 919.

27 [1965] 2 Q.B. 507.

28 *Cf.* criticisms of the present law by Browne-Wilkinson J. in *Re Sharpe* [1980] 1 W.L.R. 219, 226.

29 [1973] E.G. Digest of Cases 233; to the extent that the reasoning is based on the provisions of Settled Land Act 1925, s.1, it is criticised in *Griffiths* v. *Williams* [1978] E.G. Digest of Cases 919.

30 [1973] E.G. Digest of Cases 233.

31 As in *Hussey* v. *Palmer* [1972] 1 W.L.R. 1286 and *Eves* v. *Eves* [1975] 1 W.L.R. 1338.

32 As in *Plimmer* v. *Mayor of Wellington* (1884) 9 App.Cas. 699.

33 *Tanner* v. *Tanner* [1975] 1 W.L.R. 1346 (where there was a contract).

34 *Ibid.*

35 *Hussey* v. *Palmer* [1972] 1 W.L.R. 1286.

36 *Eves* v. *Eves* [1975] 1 W.L.R. 1338.

based (presumably) on the cost to the promisee of equivalent alternative accommodation.[37]

(3) Proprietary and promissory estoppels contrasted[38]

Proprietary and promissory estoppels have a number of points in common. Both can arise from promises[39]; consideration is not, while action in reliance is, a necessary condition for their operation[40]; and both are, within limits, revocable.[41] But there are also many important points of difference between the two doctrines.

The scope of proprietary is in two respects narrower than that of promissory estoppel. First, proprietary estoppel is restricted to situations in which one party acts under the belief that he has or will be granted an interest in or over the property (generally the land) of another. A promissory estoppel may, on the other hand, arise (if other necessary conditions are satisfied[42]) out of *any* promise that strict legal rights will not be enforced: there is no need for those rights to relate to land or other property.

Secondly proprietary estoppel requires the promisee to have acted to his detriment,[43] while promissory estoppel may operate even though the promisee merely performs a pre-existing duty and so suffers no detriment in the sense of doing something that he was not previously bound to do.[44] This difference between the two doctrines follows from the fact that promissory estoppel is (unlike proprietary estoppel) only concerned with the variation of rights arising out of a pre-existing legal relationship between promisor and promisee.

On the other hand, the scope of proprietary is in two respects wider than that of promissory estoppel. First, promissory estoppel only arises out of a representation or promise that is "clear" or "precise and unambiguous."[45] Proprietary estoppel, on the other hand, can arise where there is no actual promise: for example, where one party makes improvements to another's land under a mistake[46] and the other either knows of the mistake[47] or seeks to take unconscionable advantage of it.[48]

Secondly (and most importantly), while promissory estoppel is essentially defensive in nature,[49] proprietary estoppel can give rise to a cause of action.[50] The promisee is not only entitled to raise the estoppel as a defence to an action of trespass or to a claim for possession: he may sue to

---

[37] *Tanner* v. *Tanner* [1975] 1 W.L.R. 1346.
[38] Evans [1988] Conv. 346.
[39] *Ante*, pp. 102, 120, 125. For use of the expressions "promissory estoppel" see *ante*, p. 109.
[40] *Ante*, pp. 105, 121, 129.
[41] *Ante*, pp. 106, 121, 130.
[42] *Ante*, pp. 101–107, 120–124.
[43] *Ante*, p. 129.
[44] *Ante*, p. 105.
[45] *Ante*, p. 103.
[46] *Ante*, pp. 131–132.
[47] *Wilmott* v. *Barber* (1880) 15 Ch.D. 96, 105 (the claim in that case failed as the party against whom it was made did not know of the extent of his own rights or of the other party's mistake).
[48] *Taylors Fashions Ltd.* v. *Liverpool Victoria Trustees Co. Ltd.* [1982] Q.B. 133 n.
[49] *Ante*, p. 107.
[50] *Crabb* v. *Arun D.C.* [1976] Ch. 179, 187; *Taylors Fashions Ltd.* v. *Liverpool Victoria Trustees Co. Ltd.* [1982] Q.B. 133 n. at p. 148.

have the land conveyed to him,[51] or for compensation[52] or for such other remedy as is regarded by the court as appropriate.[53] Although the authorities support this second distinction between the two kinds of estoppel, they do not make any attempt to explain or justify it. It is submitted that the explanation is in part historical and terminological. Proprietary estoppel was originally explained in terms of *acquiescence*[54] or *encouragement*.[55] Hence no conflict with the requirement that *promises* must be supported by consideration was perceived; or where it was perceived the facts were said to give rise to a contract.[56] Promissory estoppel, on the other hand, dealt principally with the renegotiation of contracts; it obviously depended on giving binding effect to promises, and did so in the context of releases and variations, in which the common law requirement of consideration had long been established.[57] The rule that promissory estoppel gives rise to no cause of action was evolved to prevent what would otherwise be an obvious conflict between the doctrines of promissory estoppel and consideration. In cases of proprietary estoppel there was no such conflict where liability was based on "acquiescence"; and where it was based on "encouragement" the conflict, though sometimes real enough, was at least less obvious. There are, moreover, two aspects of proprietary estoppel which help to justify the distinction. These are that the acts done by the promisee are not ones which he was under any previous legal obligation to perform; and that generally their effect would be unjustly to enrich the promisor if he were allowed to go back on his promise.[58] In these respects, the facts on which proprietary estoppel is based provide more compelling grounds for relief[59] than those commonly found in cases of promissory estoppel.

While the two doctrines are in these respects distinct it can also be argued that they have a common basis, namely that it would be unconscionable for the promisor to go back on his promise after the promisee has acted on it to his detriment; and that the precise labels to be attached to them are "immaterial."[60] It is perhaps for these reasons that the distinction between the two kinds of estoppel was described as "not . . . helpful" by Scarman L.J. in *Crabb* v. *Arun D.C.*[61] That decision was, in a later case, said to illustrate "the virtual equation of promissory estoppel and proprietary estoppel,"[62] perhaps

---

[51] *e.g. Dillwyn* v. *Llewelyn* (1862) 4 D.F. & G. 517.

[52] *e.g. Eves* v. *Eves* [1975] 1 W.L.R. 1338.

[53] See *ante*, pp. 132–133.

[54] *Wilmott* v. *Barber* (1880) 15 Ch.D. 96, 105.

[55] *Ramsden* v. *Dyson* (1866) L.R. 1 H.L. 129, 170.

[56] *Dillwyn* v. *Llewelyn* (1862) 4 D.F. & G. 517, 522; *ante*, pp. 126–127.

[57] *Ante*, pp. 93–98.

[58] See the reference to the landowner's "profit" in *Ramsden* v. *Dyson* (1866) L.R. 1 H.L. 129, 141 and *cf. ante*, p. 126.

[59] See Fuller and Eisenberg, *Basic Contract Law* (3rd ed.) 70: "Unjust enrichment presents a more urgent case for judicial intervention than losses through reliance which do not benefit the defendant." *Cf.* Fuller and Perdue, 46 Yale L.J. 52, 56 (1936).

[60] *Taylors Fashions Ltd.* v. *Liverpool Victoria Trustee Co. Ltd.* [1982] Q.B. 133 note, at p. 153, where, however, a distinction is also drawn between "promissory estoppel" and the principle in *Ramsden* v. *Dyson* (1866) L.R. 1 H.L. 129 (*i.e.* proprietary estoppel).

[61] [1976] Ch. 179, 193.

[62] *Taylors Fashions Ltd.* v. *Liverpool Victoria Trustees Co. Ltd.* [1982] Q.B. 133 n. at p. 153. The use of "promissory estoppel" to describe a typical *proprietary* estoppel situation in *Griffiths* v. *Williams* [1978] E.G. Digest of Cases 919, 921 may well be a misprint.; *cf.* also *ante*, p. 126, n. 68.

because it extended the operation of proprietary estoppel beyond the situations originally within its scope, namely those in which the promisor would be unjustly enriched by the work done by the promisee on his land unless some legal effect were given to the promise. Nevertheless it is submitted that the doctrines are distinct in the respects stated above.[63] Attempts to unite them by posing "simply" the question whether it would be "unconscionable"[64] for the promisor to go back on his promise are, it is submitted, unhelpful[65] as they provide no basis on which a legal doctrine capable of yielding predictable results can be developed.

(4) Proprietary estoppel and contract contrasted

We have seen that some cases which have been said to support the doctrine of proprietary estoppel can be explained on the alternative basis that there was a contract between the parties.[66] But in other cases no such equation is possible; for proprietary estoppel can operate even though the conditions required for the creation of a contract are not satisfied. The need to discuss the doctrine in this Chapter arises precisely because a promise can give rise to a proprietary estoppel even though it is not supported by consideration; and it can also give rise to such an estoppel even though it cannot take effect as a contract because it is not sufficiently certain or because it fails to comply with formal requirements. Moreover, the effect of a proprietary estoppel differs from that of a contract. Sometimes, indeed, the result of a proprietary estoppel is to give effect to the promise in the terms in which it was made[67]; but such a result does not follow as of right. We have seen that the promisee's rights may depend not only on the terms of the promise and on the extent to which he has acted on it, but also on the subsequent conduct of the promisor. Thus in *Crabb* v. *Arun D.C.* the promisee would have had to make some payment for the right of way but for the "high-handedness"[68] of the promisor; and in *Pascoe* v. *Turner* the promisee would not have been entitled to the fee simple of the house (but only to an irrevocable licence for life) if the promisor had not shown a "ruthless"[69] determination to evict her. The rights arising under a binding contract are fixed once for all at its formation and not subject to such variation in the light of the court's approval or disapproval of the subsequent conduct of one of the parties. For this reason, and because proprietary estoppel may be revocable,[70] it will generally be more advantageous to a party to show the existence of a binding contract, if he can, than to rely on a proprietary estoppel.

---

[63] At nn. 42 to 53

[64] *Taylors Fashions Ltd.* v. *Liverpool Victoria Trustees Co. Ltd.* [1982] Q.B. 133 n. at p. 155; *cf. Habib Bank Ltd.* v. *Habib Bank A.G. Zürich* [1981] 1 W.L.R. 1265, 1285; *Amalgamated Investment & Property Co. Ltd.* v. *Texas Commerce International Bank Ltd.* [1982] Q.B. 84, 104, 122.

[65] *Cf. Haslemere Estates Ltd.* v. *Baker* [1982] 1 W.L.R. 1009, 1119 where Megarry V.-C., rejecting the argument that proprietary estoppel arises "whenever justice and good conscience requires it," said "I do not think that the subject is as wide and indefinite as that."

[66] *Ante*, p. 126.

[67] *e.g. Dillwyn* v. *Llewelyn* (1862) 4 D.F. & G. 517.

[68] [1976] Ch. 179, 199.

[69] [1979] 1 W.L.R. 431, 438.

[70] *Ante*, p. 130.

SECTION 8. SPECIAL CASES

1. Defective Promises[71]

Mutual promises are generally consideration for each other,[72] but difficulty is sometimes felt in treating a promise as consideration for another if the first promise suffered from some defect by reason of which it was not legally binding. The law on this topic is based rather on expediency than on any supposedly logical deductions which might be drawn from the doctrine of consideration. The question whether a defective promise can constitute consideration for a counter-promise depends on the policy of the rule of law making the former promise defective.

One group of cases concerns contracts made between persons, one of whom lacks contractual capacity.[73] A minor can enforce a promise made to him under such a contract, even though the only consideration for that promise is his own promise, which does not bind him by reason of his minority.[74] The same rule applies to contracts with mental patients.[75] A contrasting group of cases concerns promises which are illegal (*e.g.* for restraint of trade). The party who makes such a illegal promise cannot enforce the counter-promise (*e.g.* to pay a sum of money) if the illegal promise constitutes the sole consideration for the counter-promise.[76] Indeed, where the promise of one party is illegal, the counter-promise cannot be enforced, even though there is also some other consideration for it, if the illegal promise was the main consideration for it.[77]

Where a defective *promise* did not amount to consideration its *performance* was nevertheless sometimes held to provide consideration for the counter-promise.[78] A similar principle accounts for the rule that a victim of misrepresentation, duress or undue influence can sue but not be sued: by suing, he affirms the contract, makes his own promise binding on himself, and so supplies consideration for the other party's promise. But where the promise of one party is illegal, even its performance does not entitle that party to enforce the counter-promise,[79] for the law must not give him any incentive to perform the illegal promise.

Where one of the promises is defective by statute, the terms of the statute may solve the problem whether the person giving the defective promise can sue.[80] Thus a party who gives a promise which is defective under section 4 of the Statute of Frauds 1677, or under section 34 of the Matrimonial Causes Act 1973, may be entitled to sue although he (or she) is not

---

[71] Treitel, 77 L.Q.R. 83.
[72] *Ante*, pp. 66.
[73] See Chap. 13 *post*.
[74] *Holt* v. *Ward Clarencieux* (1732) 2 Stra. 937; *post*, p. 492.
[75] *Post*, p. 501.
[76] *e.g. Wyatt* v. *Kreglinger & Fernau* [1933] 1 K.B. 793.
[77] See *Goodinson* v. *Goodinson* [1954] 2 Q.B. 118; the actual decision is obsolete in view of Matrimonial Causes Act 1973, s.34, *post*, p. 395.
[78] *Fishmongers' Co.* v. *Robertson* (1843) 5 Man. & G. 131; (unsealed promise made by a corporation). Before the Corporate Bodies Contracts Act 1960, (*post*, p. 510) such a promise generally did not bind the corporation; and, while executory, it was no consideration for a counter-promise: *Kidderminster Corp.* v. *Hardwick* (1873) L.R. 9 Ex. 13.; *cf. Lipkin Gorman* v. *Karpnale Ltd.* [1989] 1 W.L.R. 1340, 1370.
[79] *e.g. Wyatt* v. *Kreglinger & Fernall* [1933] 1 K.B. 793.
[80] See *Laythoarp* v. *Bryant* (1836) 2 Bing.N.C. 735.

bound.[81] Where a statute invalidates a promise but does not provide for the effect of its invalidity on the other party's promise, it seems that the invalid promise is not good consideration[82]; but, unless the promise is illegal, the party giving it can sue if he actually performs his promise.[83]

2. Unilateral Contracts[84]

There is no difficulty in seeing the consideration for a promise giving rise to a unilateral contract when the required act or forbearance (such as walking to York or not smoking for a year) has been completed.[85] In such cases the promisee clearly suffers a detriment. The promisor may also obtain a benefit: *e.g.* where he promises a reward for the return of lost property and it is actually returned to him. But it has been suggested that if the promisee has begun, but not yet completed, the required act or forbearance the promisor can still withdraw. At this stage, there is said to be no consideration for the promise, since the promisee is not bound to complete performance.[86] But it may be detriment to walk part of the way to York, or to forbear from smoking for part of the year. Difficult questions of fact may, indeed, arise in determining whether performance has actually begun. This is particularly true where the stipulated performance was a forbearance; but if an actual forbearance to sue can constitute good consideration,[87] it must in principle be possible to tell when a forbearance has begun. Thus commencement of performance (whether of an act or of a forbearance) may provide consideration for the promise and so deprive the promisor of the power to withdraw it.

The further suggestion has been made that a unilateral contract may be made as soon as the offer is received by the offeree[88]; and this could be interpreted to mean that the contract was binding even before the offeree had acted on it in any way. But at this stage the offeree has clearly not provided any consideration, and in the case in which the suggestion was made no problem of consideration arose as the offeree had in fact completed the required act[89] before any attempt to withdraw the offer was made. Except in the case of bankers' irrevocable credits (to be discussed below), the better view is that an offer of a unilateral contract is not binding on receipt, but only when the offeree has begun to render the required performance.

3. Bankers' Irrevocable Credits

When goods are sold to a foreign buyer, the contract often provides for payment by irrevocable credit.[90] The buyer instructs his bank to open an

---

[81] *Post*, pp. 168, 395. For more elaborate provisions of this kind, see Financial Services Act 1986 ss.5, 56, 131 and 132.

[82] *Clayton* v. *Jennings* (1760) 2 W.Bl. 706.

[83] This, it is submitted, is the best justification for *Rajbenback* v. *Mamon* [1955] 1 Q.B. 283; see 77 L.Q.R. 95. For another view, see Unger 19 M.L.R. 99.

[84] *Ante*, pp. 36 *et seq*.

[85] *Ante*, p. 37. For controversy whether the act must be "requested" by the promisor in cases of unilateral contracts, see A.L.G., 67 L.Q.R. 456; Smith, 69 L.Q.R. 99; A.L.G., 69 L.Q.R. 106.

[86] Wormser, in *Selected Readings on the Law of Contracts*, at p. 307; but for the same writer's later views, see 3 Jl.Leg.Educ. 146.

[87] *Ante*, p. 84.

[88] *Harvela Investments Ltd.* v. *Royal Trust Co. of Canada (C.I.) Ltd.* [1986] 1 A.C. 207, 224 ("when the invitation was received").

[89] By submitting the requested bid: *cf. ante*, p. 15.

[90] See generally *Guaranty Trust Co. of N.Y.* v. *Hannay* [1918] 2 K.B. 623, 659.

irrevocable credit in favour of the seller; and the bank then notifies the seller that such a credit has been opened in his favour, and that he will be paid when he tenders specified shipping documents to the bank. It is generally thought that the bank is bound by this arrangement and is not entitled to withdraw simply because the shipping documents have not yet been tendered.[91] But it is very doubtful whether there is any consideration, moving from the seller, for the bank's promise to him.[92]

One possible solution is to say that the bank makes an offer of a unilateral contract, for which the seller provides consideration by performing his contract with the buyer.[93] As in the case of other unilateral contracts, steps taken in the performance would be enough, *e.g.* beginning to manufacture the goods. If the seller already had the goods when he received notification of the credit one could find consideration in his forbearing to make other attempts to dispose of them. Another possibility is that, because the seller is not bound to deliver the goods to the buyer until he receives notification of the credit, his becoming so bound on such notification is the consideration for the bank's promise.[94] But as the seller's becoming bound in this way does not result from any act (or even forbearance) by him at this stage, it is hard to see how it can amount to consideration for the promise by the bank. Yet another suggestion is that the seller might provide consideration by forbearing to sue the buyer for the price. But the bank would not, on this view, be bound before the seller had acted, or forborne, in some such way. The widely held commercial view is that the bank is bound as soon as the seller is notified of the credit. If (as seems probable) this view also represents the law, it is best regarded as exception to the doctrine of consideration.[95]

4. Firm Offers

A "firm" offer is one containing a promise not to revoke it for a specified period of time. Such a promise is not binding unless the offeree has provided some consideration for it. Thus in *Dickinson* v. *Dodds*[96] it was held

---

[91] See *Hamzeh Malas & Sons* v. *British Imex Industries Ltd.* [1958] 2 Q.B. 127, 129 (where in fact there was consideration of the most orthodox kind, the seller having paid the bank a confirmation commission: see *British Imex Industries Ltd.* v. *Midland Bank Ltd.* [1958] 1 Q.B. 542, 544); *W. J. Alan & Co. Ltd.* v. *El Nasr Export & Import Co.* [1972] 2 Q.B. 189, 208; *cf. ibid.* p. 218; *Offshore International S.A.* v. *Banco Central S.A.* [1977] 1 W.L.R. 399, 401; *Trendtex Trading Corp.* v. *Central Bank of Nigeria* [1977] Q.B. 529, 551; *The American Accord* [1983] 1 A.C. 168, 183.

[92] Davis, *The Law Relating to Commercial Credits* (3rd ed.), Chap. 7; Gutteridge & Megrah, *The Law of Bankers' Commercial Credits* (7th ed.), pp. 26 *et seq.*; Ellinger, *Documentary Letters of Credit*, pp. 39 *et seq.*

[93] *Cf. Guaranty Trust Co. of N.Y.* v. *Hannay* [1918] 2 K.B. 623, 659; *Urquhart Lindsay & Co.* v. *Eastern Bank* [1922] 1 K.B. 318, 321; *ante*, p. 39.

[94] The suggestion is sometimes said to be supported by dictum in *Dexters Ltd.* v. *Schenker & Co.* (1923) 14 Ll.L. Rep. 586, 588; but the judgment does not purport to go beyond *Urquhart Lindsay & Co.* v. *Eastern Bank, supra*, n. 93. The seller does not *promise* the bank to perform his contract with the buyer, so that cases such as *Pao On* v. *Lau Yiu Long* [1980] A.C. 614 (*ante*, p. 93) do not help with the problem of consideration for the bank's promise to him.

[95] *Cf.* in the United States, U.C.C. ss.5–105.

[96] (1876) 2 Ch.D. 463; *cf. Cooke* v. *Oxley* (1790) 3 T.R. 653; *Routledge* v. *Grant* (1828) 4 Bing. 653; *Head* v. *Diggon* (1828) 3 M. & Ry. 97.

that an offer to sell land "to be left over until Friday"[97]; could be withdrawn on Thursday. Consideration for the promise is most obviously provided if the offeree pays (or promises to pay) a sum of money for it and so buys an option.[98] It may also be provided by some other promise: for example, in the case of an offer to sell a house, the offeree may provide consideration for the offeror's promise to hold the offer open, by promising to apply for a mortgage on the house; and, in the case of an offer to buy shares, the offeree may provide consideration for the offeror's promise not to revoke the offer for a specified time, by promising not to dispose of those shares elsewhere during that time. The performance of the offeree's promises in such cases could likewise provide consideration for the offeror's promise to keep the offer open. It seems that the promise can also become binding as a unilateral contract. Thus a seller may promise to keep an offer open for a fixed period if the buyer can raise the necessary money; and if the buyer makes efforts to that end (without actually promising to do so) it is arguable that he has by part performance accepted the seller's offer of a unilateral contract to keep the principal offer open. On the other hand the equitable doctrine of *Hughes* v. *Metropolitan Ry.*[99] will not avail the offeree since it does not create new causes of action where none existed before.[1] Nor does it seem likely that an offeree who suffers loss as a result of the withdrawal of the offer will be able to claim damages in tort[2] for misrepresentation.[3]

The general rule can lead to inconvenience, so much so that there are some situations in which it has been said that "the market would disdain"[4] to take the point that there was no consideration for a promise to keep an offer open. In the case of certain international sales, the rule has been expressly abolished by legislation.[5] It is also subject to a common law exception in the law of insurance where an underwriter who initials a slip under an "open cover" arrangement is regarded as making a "standing offer" which the insured can accept from time to time by making "declarations" under it. The underwriter's commitment is regarded as binding even though there is no consideration for his implied promise not to revoke

[97] *Quaere* whether this meant that the offer would not be withdrawn before Friday, or only that it should lapse on Friday and not before. The latter interpretation was given to a stipulation that an offer should be "open all Monday" in *Stevenson, Jacques & Co.* v. *McLean* (1880) 6 Q.B.D. 346.

[98] An option supported by consideration is a contract even if it is not (as was held in *Re Button's Lease* [1964] Ch. 263) a contract *of purchase. cf. ante*, p. 46, n. 32; *Greene* v. *Church Commissioners for England* [1974] Ch. 467, disapproving a dictum in *Beesly* v. *Hallwood Estates Ltd.* [1960] 1 W.L.R. 549, 555 (actual decision affirmed [1961] Ch. 549) the dictum was also doubted in *Spiro* v. *Glencrown Properties* [1991] 1 All E.R. 600, 606; *United Scientific Holdings Ltd.* v. *Burnley B.C.* [1978] A.C. 904, 945.

[99] (1877) 2 App.Cas. 439; *ante*, p. 101.

[1] *Ante*, p. 107.

[2] *Cf. Holman Construction Ltd.* v. *Delta Timber Co. Ltd.* [1972] N.Z.L.R. 1081; and see *Blackpool and Fylde Aero Club Ltd.* v. *Blackpool B.C.* [1990] 1 W.L.R. 1195, 1202.

[3] *i.e.* under *Hedley Byrne & Co. Ltd.* v. *Heller & Partners Ltd.* [1964] A.C. 465; *post*, p. 308.

[4] *Jaglom* v. *Excess Insurance Co. Ltd.* [1972] 2 Q.B. 250, 258. For the view that the statement in *Jaglom's* case was not an offer, but an acceptance (and binding as such) see *General Reinsurance Corp.* v. *Forsakringsaktiebolaget Fennia Patria* [1983] Q.B. 856, 863–864.

[5] ULFIS Art. 5(2) (*ante*, p. 28); *cf.* Vienna Convention (*ante*, p. 29) Art. 16(2); U.C.C. s.2–205, limiting the period of irrevocability to three months on the theory that unlimited irrevocability could unreasonably prejudice the offeror.

the "standing offer."[6] But even with these mitigations, the rule can still cause hardship to an offeree who has acted in reliance on the assurance that the offer will be kept open for a stated time. A builder may submit a tender in reliance on offers from suppliers of materials expressed to remain "firm" for a fixed period.[7] If those offers are withdrawn within that period and after his tender has been accepted, he may be gravely prejudiced. Further legislation limiting the right to withdraw such firm offers seems to be desirable.[8]

5. Auction Sales Without Reserve[9]

Where goods are put up for auction without reserve, there is no contract *of sale* if the auctioneer refuses to knock the goods down to the highest bidder; but the auctioneer is liable to the highest bidder on a separate promise that the sale will be without reserve.[10] It has been said that there is no consideration for this promise as the highest bidder is not bound by his unaccepted bid.[11] But it seems that the bidder suffers a detriment by bidding on the strength of the promise, for he runs the risk of being bound by a contract of sale[12]; and the auctioneer benefits as the bidding is driven up. Hence there is consideration for the separate promise, and it makes no difference to the auctioneer's liability *on this promise* that he would not be liable if he did not put the goods up for sale at all (since an advertisement of an auction is not an offer to hold it)[13] or that there was no contract of sale because of his refusal to accept the highest bid.[14]

6. Novation of Partnership Debts

When the composition of a partnership changes, it is usual to arrange that the debts owed by the existing partners should be transferred by novation[15] to the new partners. Two situations may be considered.

(1) A and B are in partnership; A retires and C is admitted as a new partner; it is agreed between A, B and C, and the creditors of the old firm of A and B, that A shall cease to be liable for the firm's debts, and that C shall undertake such liability. The result is that the creditors can sue C and can no longer sue A. They provide consideration for C's promise to pay by abandoning their claim against A; and A provides consideration for their promise to release him by procuring a substitute debtor, C.

(2) A and B are in partnership; A retires; it is agreed between A, B and the creditors of the firm that A shall cease to be liable and that B shall be solely liable. It seems that the creditors cannot sue A, but it is hard to see

---

[6] *Citadel Insurance Co.* v. *Atlantic Union Insurance Co.* [1982] 2 Lloyd's Rep. 543, 546.

[7] For conflicting American authorities, see *James Baird Co.* v. *Gimbel Bros.* 64 F. 2d. 344 (1933); *Drennan* v. *Star Paving Co.* 51 Cal. 2d. 409, 333 P. 2d. 757 (1958). For a review of Canadian authorities, see *Northern Construction Co.* v. *Gloge Heating & Plumbing* [1986] 2 W.W.R. 649, holding a subcontractor bound by his offer.

[8] *Post*, p. 147.

[9] See also *ante*, p. 11.

[10] *Warlow* v. *Harrison* (1859) 1 E. & E. 309; approved in *Harris* v. *Nickerson* (1873) L.R. 8 Q.B. 286, 288; *Johnston* v. *Boyes* [1899] 2 Ch. 73, 77.

[11] For controversy on this point, see Slade, 68 L.Q.R. 238; Gower, *ibid.* 457; Slade, 69 L.Q.R. 21.

[12] An "invented" consideration: see *ante*, p. 67.

[13] *Harris* v. *Nickerson* (1873) L.R. 8 Q.B. 286; *ante*, p. 11.

[14] *Ibid.*

[15] *Post*, p. 577, *cf.* Partnership Act 1890, s.17(3).

what consideration moves from him. In one case it was said that there was consideration in that a remedy against a single debtor might be easier to enforce than one against several, all of whom are solvent[16]; thus the creditors benefit by the release of A. This is a possible, if invented[17] consideration.

7. Gratuitous Bailments

A gratuitous bailment may be for the benefit of the bailee or for the benefit of the bailor.

The first possibility is illustrated by *Bainbridge* v. *Firmstone*[18] where the defendant asked for, and received, permission from the plaintiff to weigh two boilers belonging to the plaintiff. In performing this operation, the defendant damaged the boilers; and he was held liable for breach of his promise to return them in good condition. The court rejected the argument that, as the defendant was not paid to weigh, or look after, the boilers, there was no consideration for his promise. Patteson J. said: "I suppose the defendant thought he had some benefit; at any rate there is a detriment to the plaintiff from his parting with the possession for even so short a time."[19] It is more doubtful whether there would be any consideration moving from the defendant for any promise by the plaintiff to allow the defendant to have possession of the boilers. A mere promise by the defendant to return the boilers might not suffice as it would only be a promise to perform a duty imposed by law on all bailees; but a promise to look after the boilers or to improve them in some way would probably be regarded as consideration moving from the defendant.[20]

Different problems arise where the bailment is for the benefit of the bailor, for example where A undertakes the safekeeping of B's chattel without reward. In such a case parting with the possession is hardly a detriment to B. A's duty to look after the thing[21] does not arise out of contract but is imposed by the general law. It follows that A's *only* duty is that imposed by the law. Thus A is under no obligation before he actually receives the thing; and if he promised to do anything which went beyond the duty imposed by law (for example, to keep the property in repair) he would only be bound by this promise if B had provided some consideration for it apart from the delivery of the chattel.[22] To constitute such consideration, it is not necessary to show that A profited from the transaction; thus it is enough if B reimburses (or promises to reimburse) any expenses that A has incurred for the purpose of performing his promise.[23] This follows from the rule that the law generally does not enquire into the adequacy of consideration.[24]

---

16 *Lyth* v. *Ault* (1852) 7 Ex. 669; *Thompson* v. *Percival* (1834) 5 B. & Ad. 925 is based on reasoning which is obsolete after *D. & C. Builders Ltd.* v. *Rees* [1967] 2 Q.B. 617.

17 *Ante*, p. 67.

18 (1838) 8 A. & E. 743.

19 At p. 744.

20 *Cf. Verrall* v. *Farnes* [1966] 1 W.L.R. 1254, a case relating to land; followed in *Mitton* v. *Farrow* (1980) 255 E.G. 449.

21 See *Coggs* v. *Bernard* (1703) 2 Ld.Raym. 909; *Mitchell* v. *London Borough of Ealing* [1979] Q.B. 1; *Port Swettenham Authority* v. *T. W. Wu. & Co.* [1979] A.C. 580, 590.

22 *Cf. Charnock* v. *Liverpool Corporation* [1968] 1 W.L.R. 1498; *post*, p. 525.

23 *C.C.C. Films (London) Ltd.* v. *Impact Quadrant Films Ltd.* [1985] Q.B. 16, 27.

24 *Ante*, p. 70.

8. Gratuitous Services

A promise to render services without reward is not supported by consideration and is therefore not binding contractually. For example, where A gratuitously promises to insure B's property but fails to do so, he is not liable to B for breach of contract if the property is lost or damaged.[25] Occasionally it may be possible to find consideration in an indirect benefit which a person who promises to render gratuitous services obtains from the arrangement: *e.g.* in the form of favourable publicity.[26]

Even where the promise is not supported by consideration, the promisor may be liable in tort for negligence if he actually renders the gratuitous services but fails to exercise due care in rendering them and so causes loss. A banker who gives a negligent credit reference may be liable on this ground even though he makes no charge to the person to whom the information is given.[27] Similarly, where A gratuitously promised to insure B's property and did so negligently, so that the policy did not cover the loss that occurred, A was held liable to B in tort.[28] In one case, a person was even held liable in tort for negligently giving free advice to a friend in connection with the purchase of a second-hand car which turned out to be seriously defective.[29]

The most important distinction between the two groups of cases discussed above is that between non-feasance and misfeasance in the performance of a promise to render gratuitous services. For this purpose, non-feasance means complete failure to pursue a *promised course of action*, while misfeasance means carelessness in the pursuit of that course of action, leading to failure to achieve a *promised result*. The first group of cases shows that non-feasance gives rise (in the absence of consideration) to no liability in contract, while the second shows that misfeasance can give rise to liability in tort. There is no liability in tort for simple non-feasance; for to impose such liability would amount to holding "that the law of England recognises the enforceability of a gratuitous promise. On the face of it, this would be inconsistent with fundamental principle."[30] In cases of pure non-feasance, the promisee will therefore only have a remedy if he can show that he provided consideration for the promise. If he can show

---

25 *Argy Trading & Development Co. Ltd.* v. *Lapid Developments Ltd.* [1977] 1 W.L.R. 444; *cf.* the New York case of *Thorn* v. *Deas* 4 Johns. 84 (1809); modern American authorities are divided: Corbin, *Contracts*, s.205, n. 54.

26 *Cf. De la Bere* v. *Pearson* [1908] 1 K.B. 280, 287.

27 See *Hedley Byrne & Co. Ltd.* v. *Heller & Partners Ltd.* [1964] A.C. 465; *cf. post*, p. 308.

28 *Wilkinson* v. *Coverdale* (1793) 1 Esp. 75.

29 *Chaudhry* v. *Prabhakar* [1989] 1 W.L.R. 29 where the defendant conceded that he owed a duty of care to the plaintiff and two members of the Court of Appeal seem to have regarded this concession as correct; Brown [1989] L.M.C.L.Q. 148.

30 *The Zephyr* [1985] 2 Lloyd's Rep. 529, 538, disapproving the contrary view expressed at first instance [1984] 1 Lloyd's Rep. 58, 85 and there based on authorities which were all cases of misfeasance. *The Zephyr* itself was also such a case: [1984] 1 Lloyd's Rep. at pp. 79, 86 ("he was making the position steadily worse"). *A fortiori*, there is no liability in tort for pure omission where *no* promise has been made: see *Reid* v. *Rush & Tompkins Group plc* [1990] 1 W.L.R. 212 and *Van Oppen* v. *Clerk to the Bedfort Charity Trustees* [1990] 1 W.L.R. 235, though in the latter case it was said at p. 260 that a voluntary assumption of responsibility by one party followed by reliance on it by the other might in exceptional cases give rise to such liability. The nature of the exception is not clear; in the last two cases it was held that there was *no* duty on respectively an employer and a school to advise an employee or the parents of a pupil to insure against forseeable risks of injury.

this he may also be in a better position with regard to damages, even in cases of misfeasance.[31]

In *Gore* v. *Van der Lann*[32] a corporation issued a free travel pass to the plaintiff who "in consideration of my being granted a free pass" undertook that the use of the pass by her should be subject to certain conditions. One of these was that neither the corporation nor its servants were to be liable to her for loss or injury suffered while she was boarding, alighting from, or being carried in, the corporation's vehicles. The plaintiff was injured while boarding a corporation bus; and it was held the issue and acceptance of the free pass amounted to a contract.[33] Willmer L.J. said that "Each party gave good consideration by accepting a detriment in return for the advantages gained."[34] The parties were, as a result of the issue of the pass, brought into a relationship of passenger and carrier which gave rise to duties quite independently of contract; and it was the promise not to enforce these obligations which constituted the consideration moving from the plaintiff. It does not follow that a promise not to sue for defective performance can in all cases amount to consideration for a promise to render a gratuitous service. Thus if A promised to carry B's goods to London free of charge and B promised not to sue A for negligently damaging them on the way, A would not be under any contractual liability for failing to pick up the goods. But he might be liable if he did pick them up and then unloaded them short of the agreed destination.

SECTION 9. PROMISES IN DEEDS

Consideration is not necessary for the validity of a promise in a deed. The binding force of such a promise does not depend on contract at all. Thus it can take effect although the person in whose favour it was made did not know of it.[35] To take effect as a deed, an instrument must make it clear on its face that it is intended to be a deed and must be validly executed as such.[36] At common law, execution of an instrument as a deed had in all cases to be under seal, but the requirement of sealing has been abolished in the case of an instrument executed as a deed by an individual.[37] To be validly executed as a deed, such an instrument must be signed[38] by the individual making it.[39] The instrument must also be witnessed (by one attesting witness if it is signed by the maker, and by two if it is signed at his direction[40]) and delivered.[41] There is also no longer any requirement of sealing for the execution of a deed by a company incorporated under the Companies Acts: a document signed by a director and secretary, or by two directors, of such a company and expressed to be executed by the company

[31] *Cf. post*, pp. 322–325.
[32] [1967] 2 Q.B. 31; Harris, 30 M.L.R. 584; Odgers, 86 L.Q.R. 69; and see *post*, p. 156, on the issue of contractual intention.
[33] This contract was void, so far as it purported to exclude liability for personal injury, by virtue of s.151 of the Road Traffic Act 1960, now Public Passenger Vehicles Act 1981, s.29; *post*, p. 228.
[34] [1967] 2 Q.B. 31, 42.
[35] *Hall* v. *Palmer* (1844) 3 Hare 532; *Macedo* v. *Stroud* [1922] 2 A.C. 330.
[36] Law of Property (Miscellaneous Provisions) Act 1989, s.1(2).
[37] *Ibid*, s.1(1)(*b*).
[38] Making one's mark suffices: *ibid.* s.1(4).
[39] *Ibid.* s.1(3)(*a*).
[40] *Ibid.*
[41] *Ibid.* s.1(3)(*b*).

has the same effect as if executed under the common seal of the company[42]; and (even if the company has no common seal[43]) a document executed by the company which makes it clear on its face that it is intended to be a deed has effect upon delivery as a deed.[44] Execution by corporations other than companies incorporated under the Companies Acts remains subject to the common law requirement of sealing and delivery.

The common law requirement of sealing has been laxly interpreted. There need be no actual seal: it is enough if the document indicates where the seal is meant to be, and is signed with the intention of executing it as a deed.[45]

Delivery does not mean transfer of possession, but conduct indicating that the person who has executed the deed intends to be bound by it.[46] Delivery can be effected by giving the deed to the beneficiary, or to a third person to hold for him, but it is perfectly possible for the grantor to "deliver" the deed and yet keep possession of it.[47] A deed sealed by a corporation is deemed, in favour of a purchaser, to have been duly executed if certain statutory requirements are satisfied.[48] In such a case there is no separate requirement of "delivery." In the case of a document executed by a company incorporated under the Companies Acts, the rules just stated apply even if the document is *not* sealed: in favour of a purchaser, a document is deemed to have been duly executed if it purports to be signed by a director and the secretary or by two directors; and where the document makes it clear on its face that it is intended to be a deed, it is deemed to have been delivered upon its being executed.[49]

A document may be executed as a deed and delivered with the intention that it is to take effect only on the occurrence of some condition. The document is then said to be delivered as an escrow. It will become effective as a deed only if the condition occurs; though it may then relate back to the date of the original delivery. For example, if the document is a lease, rent under it is payable from that date, unless the document specifies some other date.[50] Even before the occurrence of the condition, the document has some legal effect; it cannot be revoked by the grantor so long as it remains possible for the condition to occur.[51] The document will, however, cease to have this effect if the condition fails to occur within the time specified for its occurrence by the document.[52] Where no such time is specified,

---

[42] Companies Act 1985, s.36A(4) (as inserted by Companies Act 1989, s.130(1)).
[43] See *ibid.* s.36A(3).
[44] *Ibid.* s.36A(5).
[45] *First National Securities Ltd.* v. *Jones* [1978] Ch. 109; Hoath, 43 M.L.R. 415. Contrast *TCB Ltd.* v. *Gray* [1987] Ch. 48; *Rushingdale S.A.* v. *Byblos Bank S.A.L.* 1985 P.C.C. 342.
[46] *Xenos* v. *Wickham* (1866) L.R. 2 H.L. 296; *cf. Beesly* v. *Hallwood Estates Ltd.* [1960] 1 W.L.R. 549, 562; *affirmed* [1961] Ch. 105; *Vincent* v. *Premo Enterprises (Voucher Sales) Ltd.* [1969] 2 Q.B. 609; Yale [1970] C.L.J. 52.
[47] *Doe* v. *Knight* (1826) 5 B. & C. 671.
[48] Law of Property Act 1925, s.74(1); *D'Silva* v. *Lister House Developments Ltd.* [1971] Ch. 17.
[49] Companies Act 1985, s.36A(6), as inserted by Companies Act 1989, s.130(1).
[50] *Alan Estates Ltd.* v. *W. G. Stores Ltd.* [1982] Ch. 511.
[51] *Ibid.* pp. 520–521 and 527 rejecting a dictum in *Terrapin International Investments* v. *I.R.C.* [1976] 1 W.L.R. 665, 669 that before the condition is fulfilled the escrow has "no effect whatsoever"; *cf. ante*, p. 59.
[52] *Glessing* v. *Green* [1975] 1 W.L.R. 863.

a term is likely to be implied that the condition must be fulfilled within a reasonable time.[53]

It is sometimes difficult to distinguish between a deed which has not been delivered at all and one which has been delivered as an escrow.[54] The distinction depends on the intention of the grantor. If he reserves an overriding power to recall the deed at his discretion, it is not delivered as an escrow but is simply an undelivered deed.[55]

SECTION 10. PROPOSALS FOR REFORM

The doctrine of consideration has attracted much criticism on general and on particular grounds. It has been said that the doctrine is an historical accident; that foreign systems do without it; and that it can easily be evaded, *e.g.* by the device of nominal consideration.[56] But these criticisms fail to come to grips with the fundamental question: whether it is desirable to enforce informal gratuitous promises. So long as the rights and interests of third parties are adequately protected,[57] the enforcement of such promises may do no harm. On the other hand English law does recognise, in the deed, a perfectly safe and relatively simple means of making gratuitous promises binding. Many such promises are in fact made by deed for tax purposes; and for this reason the legal enforceability of promises to give money to charitable institutions presents no serious problem in England.[58] Moreover, the small amount of extra effort, which the execution of a deed requires the promisor to make, may be a useful safeguard against rash promises.[59] The availability of the deed does not solve the problem of action in reliance on an *informal* gratuitous promise; but where there is such action the court may be able to invent consideration, or to give at least some effect to the promise under the doctrine of waiver or in equity.[60]

The requirement of consideration may also cause inconvenience where a promise is reasonably regarded by the parties as having been made for value, but is for some reason treated by the law as gratuitous.[61] This is particularly true in the existing duty cases, and in the cases on part payment of a debt. In those cases the doctrine of consideration may indeed at one time have performed a useful function in protecting a promisor against undue pressure or other undesirable conduct on the part of the promisee.[62] But this function is now more satisfactorily provided by the expanding notion of duress[63]; and recent authority recognises this point, by holding that the requirement of consideration can be satisfied by the performance of an

---

[53] *Alan Estates Ltd.* v. *W. G. Stores Ltd.* [1982] Ch. 511, 520.

[54] See *Vincent* v. *Premo Enterprises (Voucher Sales) Ltd.* [1969] 2 Q.B. 609; *Kingston* v. *Ambrian Investments Ltd.* [1975] 1 W.L.R. 161.

[55] *Windsor Refrigerator Co. Ltd.* v. *Branch Nominees Ltd.* [1961] Ch. 88, 102; actual decision reversed on other grounds [1961] Ch. 375.

[56] *Ante*, p. 71.

[57] *Cf. ante*, p. 71, *Eastwood* v. *Kenyon* (1840) 11 A. & E. 438, 450 and *Horrocks* v. *Forray* [1976] 1 W.L.R. 230 (where a finding that there was no consideration helped to protect the creditors of the alleged promisor).

[58] There appear to be only two reported cases in which such claims failed for want of consideration; *Re Hudson* (1885) 54 L.J.Ch. 811 and *Re Cory* (1912) 29 T.L.R. 18.

[59] *Cf. post*, p. 161.

[60] *Ante*, pp. 67, 98–110, 120–124.

[61] *e.g. ante*, pp. 86–87, 88–89, 115–116.

[62] See *ante*, pp. 86, 88–89, 115–116.

[63] *Ante*, p. 88; *post*, p. 363.

existing duty, even if it causes no legal detriment to the promisee, so long as it results in a factual benefit to the promisor.[64] On the other hand, the function of the doctrine in providing protection against the different risk of being bound by rashly made gratuitous promises remains an important one and must be taken into account in formulating proposals for reform. The following such proposals were made in 1937 by the Law Revision Committee[65]:

(1) That a promise in writing should be binding, though not supported by consideration. But it is doubtful whether the mere use of writing would provide a sufficient safeguard against rash gratuitous promises.[66] The recently attenuated formalities for the execution of deeds[67] seem to serve this purpose, without putting serious obstacles in the way of the creation of legally binding formal gratuitous promises.

(2) That past consideration should be good consideration. But the first proposal accepts that the law should not, in general, enforce informal gratuitous promises. Promises supported only by a past consideration fall into this category, and it is hard to see why they should be treated differently from other promises of this kind.

(3) That performance of an existing duty should always be good consideration for a promise. This is a desirable reform, and recent cases have moved towards it by holding that such a promise is binding (unless procured by duress) if the performance of it results in a factual benefit to the promisor.[68]

(4) That the rule that consideration must move from the promisee should be abolished. This proposal raises the same issues as that to modify the doctrine of privity and will be discussed in Chapter 15.[69]

(5) That a promise to keep an offer open should be binding. The present law can cause hardship to offerees[70]; and some reform is clearly desirable. At the same time, simple reversal of the present law could cause hardship to offerors: *e.g.* where an offer is made by a customer on a form provided by a supplier and expressed to be irrevocable; or where the period of irrevocability is not specified so that the offeror is left subject to an indefinite obligation without acquiring any corresponding right. The Law Commission has accordingly sought to balance the interests of both parties by proposing[71] that a firm offer is to be binding if it is made *in the course of a business* and is expressed to be irrevocable for a *definite period* (which is not to exceed six years).

(6) That, in a unilateral contract, the promisor should not be entitled to revoke once the promisee has started to perform: this, it is suggested, is already the law.[72]

(7) That a creditor's promise to accept part payment of a debt in full settlement should bind him. This is a desirable reform: the creditor is ade-

---

64 *Pao On* v. *Lau Yiu Long* [1980] A.C. 614, *ante*, p. 93; *Williams* v. *Roffey Bros. & Nicholls (Contractors) Ltd.* [1991] 1 Q.B. 1, *ante*, p. 89.

65 6th Interim Report, Cmnd. 5449; Hamson, 54 L.Q.R. 233; Hays, 41 Col.L.Rev. 849; Chloros, 17 I.C.L.Q. 137.

66 *Cf. post*, p. 161.

67 *Ante*, p. 144.

68 *Ante*, pp. 89–90.

69 *Post*, pp. 574–575.

70 *Ante*, p. 141.

71 Working Paper No. 60 (1975).

72 *Ante*, pp. 37–39, 138.

quately protected by the law of duress against improper pressure by an unscrupulous debtor.[73]

(8) That a promise which the promisor knows, or reasonably should know, will be relied upon by the promisee and is acted upon by him to his detriment should be binding.[74] Such promises already have a limited effect.[75] Whether and to what extent they should be made fully binding as contracts is really part of the larger question—whether informal gratuitous promises should be made binding. The fact of reliance by the promisee no doubt strengthens the case for giving the promisee *some* remedy. The present law (largely developed since 1937) represents a compromise between two views: that gratuitous promises on which the promisee has relied should either be fully binding or not be binding at all. The compromise could be carried further[76] by providing that the promisee, while not necessarily entitled in full to the promised performance,[77] should at least be compensated to the extent to which he has been prejudiced as a result of his reliance on the promise.[78]

---

[73] *Ante*, p. 116.

[74] *Cf.* Restatements, *Contracts*, § 90. Restatement 2d, *Contracts*, § 90 imposes somewhat less stringent conditions and concludes: "The remedy . . . may be limited as justice requires."

[75] *Ante*, pp. 98–109, 120–124.

[76] *e.g.* by allowing "promissory estoppel" (*ante*, p. 109) to give rise to a cause of action or by extending the categories of cases covered by proprietary estoppel (*ante*, p. 124).

[77] The qualification would not preclude such enforcement at the discretion of the court, as at present in cases of proprietary estoppel: *ante*, p. 132.

[78] *Cf.* p. 40, *ante*, and *supra*, n. 74.

CHAPTER FOUR

CONTRACTUAL INTENTION

AN agreement, though supported by consideration, is not binding as a contract[1] if it was made without any intention of creating legal relations.

SECTION 1. ILLUSTRATIONS

1. Mere Puffs

A statement inducing a contract may be so vague, or so clearly one of opinion, that the law refuses to give it any contractual effect.[2] Even a statement that is perfectly precise may nevertheless not be binding if the court considers that it was not seriously meant. Thus in *Weeks* v. *Tybald*[3] the defendant "affirmed and published that he would give £100 to him that should marry his daughter with his consent." The court held that "It is not reasonable that the defendant should be bound by such general words spoken to excite suitors." Similarly, in *Lambert* v. *Lewis*[4] a manufacturer stated in promotional literature that his product was "foolproof" and that it "required no maintenance." These statements did not give rise to a contract between the manufacturer and a dealer (who had bought the product from an intermediary) as they were "not intended to be, nor were they, acted on as being express warranties."[5]

2. Other Statements Inducing a Contract

A statement inducing a person to enter into a contract may be *either* "mere representation" *or* a term of the contract. The distinction between these categories turns on the intention with which the statement was made.[6] In most cases on this subject the question is merely as to the *contents* of a contract which is admitted to exist. But sometimes the test of intention determines the very existence of the contract itself. This happens when a statement inducing a principal contract can for some reason not take effect as one of its terms, but only as collateral contract.[7] Thus in *Heilbut, Symons & Co.* v. *Buckleton*[8] the plaintiff said to the defendants' manager that he understood the defendants to be "bringing out a rubber company."

---

1 For enforcement on other grounds, see *John Fox* v. *Bannister King & Rigbeys* [1988] Q.B. 925, 928 (agreement between solicitors enforced in exercise of court's jurisdiction to enforce "honourable conduct" on the part of solicitors).

2 *Post*, p. 296.

3 (1605) Noy 11; *cf. Dalrymple* v. *Dalrymple* (1811) 2 Hag.Con. 54, 105.

4 [1982] A.C. 225; affirmed, so far as the manufacturer's liability was concerned, but on other grounds, *ibid*. p. 271.

5 [1982] A.C. 225, 262; contrast *Carlill* v. *Carbolic Smoke Ball Co. Ltd.* [1893] 1 Q.B. 256, *ante*, p. 13.

6 *Post*, pp. 315 *et seq*.

7 *Post*, pp. 164, 183–185, 319–320, 525.

8 [1913] A.C. 30. A decision described as "catastrophic" by Atiyah in *The Rise and Fall of Freedom of Contract* at p. 772, but followed by the House of Lords in *I.B.A.* v. *E.M.I. Electronics Ltd.* (1980) 14 Build. L.R. 1 (*post*, p. 525).

The manager replied that they were, on the strength of which statement the plaintiff applied for, and was allotted, shares in the company. It turned out not to be a rubber company and the plaintiff claimed damages, alleging that the defendants had warranted that it was a rubber company. The claim failed as nothing said by the defendants' manager was intended to have contractual effect. "Not only the terms of such contracts, but the existence of an *animus contrahendi* on the part of all the parties to them must be clearly shewn."[9]

3. Intention Expressly Negatived

The intention to be legally bound may be negatived by an express provision in the agreement. It is a question of construction whether a particular provision has this effect.

(1) Honour clauses

In *Rose & Frank Co.* v. *J. R. Crompton & Bros. Ltd.*[10] an agency agreement provided: "This arrangement is not entered into, nor is this memorandum written, as a formal or legal agreement, and shall not be subject to legal jurisdiction in the Law Courts . . . but is only a definite expression and record of the purpose and intention of the . . . parties concerned, to which they each honourably pledge themselves. . . . " It was held that the agreement was not a legally binding contract as it was not intended to have this effect. On the other hand, contractual intention was not negatived where an arbitration clause in a reinsurance contract provided that "this treaty shall be interpreted as an honourable engagement rather than as a legal obligation . . . " The contract as a whole was clearly intended to be binding and the purpose of the words quoted was merely to free the arbitrator "to some extent from strict legal rules"[11] in interpreting the agreement.

(2) Agreement subject to contract

Agreements for the sale of land are commonly made "subject to contract." These words normally negative contractual intention, so that the parties are not bound until formal contracts are exchanged.[12]

(3) "Ex gratia" compromise

In *Edwards* v. *Skyways Ltd.*[13] employers promised a dismissed employee an "ex gratia payment." It was held that the words "ex gratia" did not negative contractual intention but only meant that the employers did not admit any pre-existing liability to make the payment.

---

9 At p. 47; *Unit Construction Co. Ltd.* v. *Liverpool Corp.* (1972) 221 E.G. 459; *The Kapetan Markos NL* (*No. 2*) [1987] 2 Lloyd's Rep. 323, 332. For possible effects of the Misrepresentation Act 1967, s.2 on such statements, see *post*, p. 314.

10 [1925] A.C. 445; [1923] 2 K.B. 261; *cf.* similar provisions in football pool coupons: *Jones* v. *Vernon's Pools* [1938] 2 All E.R. 464; *Appleson* v. *Littlewoods* [1939] 1 All E.R. 464; *Guest* v. *Empire Pools* (1964) 108 S.J. 98.

11 *Home Insurance Co.* v. *Administratia Asigurarilor* [1983] 2 Lloyd's Rep. 674, 677; *cf. Overseas Union Ins. Ltd.* v. *International Ins. Ltd.* [1988] 2 Lloyd's Rep. 65; *Home & Overseas Ins. Co. Ltd.* v. *Mentor Ins.* (*U.K.*) *Ltd.* [1989] 1 Lloyd's Rep. 473.

12 *Ante*, p. 52. *Rose & Frank Co.* v. *J.R. Crompton & Bros. Ltd.* [1923] 2 K.B. 261, 294.

13 [1964] 1 W.L.R. 349. It was admitted that there was consideration moving from the plaintiff.

4. Social and Domestic Arrangements

Many social arrangements do not amount to contracts because they are not intended to be legally binding. "The ordinary example is where two parties agree to take a walk together, or where there is an offer and an acceptance of hospitality."[14] Similarly it has been held that the winner of a competition held by a golf club could not sue for his prize where "no one concerned with that competition ever intended that there should be any legal results flowing from the conditions posted and the acceptance by the competitor of those conditions"[15]; that the rules of a competition organised by a "jalopy club" for charitable purposes did not have contractual force[16]; that "car pool" and similar arrangements between friends or neighbours did not amount to contracts even though one party contributed to the running costs of the other's vehicle[17]; and that the provision of free residential accommodation for close friends did not amount to a contract as it was an act of bounty, done without any intention to enter into legal relations.[18]

Many domestic arrangements are not intended to be legally binding. In *Balfour* v. *Balfour*[19] a husband who worked abroad promised to pay an allowance of £30 per month to his wife, who had to stay in England on medical grounds. The wife's attempt to enforce this promise by action failed for two reasons: she had not provided any consideration, and the parties did not intend the arrangement to be legally binding. On the second ground alone, most domestic arrangements between husband and wife are not contracts. Atkin L.J. said: "Those agreements, or many of them, do not result in contracts at all . . . even though there may be what as between other parties would constitute consideration for the agreement. . . . They are not contracts . . . because the parties did not intend that they should be attended by legal consequences. . . . "[20] It has been said that the facts of *Balfour* v. *Balfour* "stretched that doctrine to its limits"[21]; but the doctrine itself has not been judicially questioned and the cases provide many other instances of its application.[22] It does not of course prevent a husband from making a binding contract with his wife: he can be her tenant[23]; and binding separation agreements are often made when husband and wife agree to

---

14 *Balfour* v. *Balfour* [1919] 2 K.B. 571, 578; *Rose & Frank Co.* v. *J.R. Crompton & Bros. Ltd.* [1923] 2 K.B. 261, 293; *Wyatt* v. *Kreglinger & Fernau* [1933] 1 K.B. 793, 806.

15 *Lens* v. *Devonshire Club* (1914) *The Times*, December 4; referred to in *Wyatt's* case, *supra*, from which the quotation in the text is taken.

16 *White* v. *Blackmore* [1972] 2 Q.B. 651.

17 *Coward* v. *M.I.B.* [1963] 1 Q.B. 259; overruled, but not on the issue of contractual intention, in *Albert* v. *M.I.B.* [1972] A.C. 301; *Buckpitt* v. *Oates* [1968] 1 All E.R. 1145, criticised on this point by Karsten, 32 M.L.R. 88. The actual decisions are obsolete by reason of Road Traffic Act 1988, ss.145, 149; *cf.* also s.150. But an issue of contractual intention might still arise if one party to such an arrangement simply failed to turn up at the agreed time.

18 *Heslop* v. *Burns* [1974] 1 W.L.R. 1241.

19 [1919] 2 K.B. 571; Hedley, 5 O.J.L.S. 391.

20 At p. 578: it would clearly be undesirable to enforce such agreements in accordance with their original terms, however much the position of the parties had changed.

21 *Pettit* v. *Pettit* [1970] A.C. 806, 816; *cf. Gould* v. *Gould* [1970] 1 Q.B. 275 where there was a division of opinion, the majority holding that there was no contractual intention where a husband on leaving his wife promised to pay her £15 per week so long as he could manage it. And see generally Ingman [1970] J.B.L. 109.

22 *e.g. Gage* v. *King* [1961] 1 Q.B. 188; *Spellman* v. *Spellman* [1961] 1 W.L.R. 921; *cf. Lloyd's Bank plc.* v. *Rosset* [1991] 1 A.C. 107.

23 *Pearce* v. *Merriman* [1904] 1 K.B. 80; contrast *Morris* v. *Tarrant* [1971] 2 Q.B. 143.

live apart.[24] Similarly, where a man before marriage promised his future wife to leave her a house if she married him, she was able to enforce the promise although it was made informally and in affectionate terms.[25]

Such issues of contractual intention can also arise between parents and children. An informal promise by a parent to pay a child an allowance during study is not normally a contract, though it may become one, if, for example, it is part of a bargain made to induce the child to give up some occupation so as to enter on some particular course of study.[26] Similarly, where a mother bought a house as a residence for her son and daughter-in-law on the terms that they should pay her £7 per week to pay off the purchase price, this was held to amount to a contractual licence which the mother could not revoke so long as either of the young couple kept up the payments.[27] On the other hand, there is normally no contract where a mother agrees to nurse her child who has fallen ill or been injured, even though performance of the agreement makes it necessary for her to give up her job.[28]

The principle of *Balfour* v. *Balfour* can also apply where persons other than husband and wife share a common household. While that household is a going concern, many arrangements will be made about its day-to-day management, and it is unlikely that these will be intended to be legally binding. But this may not be true of the financial terms which form the basis on which the household was established. In one case a young couple were induced to sell their house, and move in with their elderly relations, by the latters' promise to leave them a share of the proposed joint home. The argument that this promise was not intended to be legally binding was rejected as the young couple would not have taken the important step of selling their own house on the faith of a merely social arrangement.[29] Similar reasoning was used in a later case[30] in which a man promised a woman that the house in which they had lived together (without being married) should be available for her and the couple's children. It was held that the promise had contractual force because, in reliance[31] on it, the woman had moved out of her rent-controlled flat. In another case of this kind,[32] the

---

[24] *e.g. Merrit* v. *Merrit* [1970] 1 W.L.R. 1121; *Re Windle* [1975] 1 W.L.R. 1628; *Tanner* v. *Tanner* [1975] 1 W.L.R. 1346 (where the parties were not married) as explained in *Horrocks* v. *Forray* [1976] 1 W.L.R. 230; *cf. post.*, p. 388.

[25] *Synge* v. *Synge* [1894] 1 Q.B. 466, *cf. Jennings* v. *Brown* (1842) 9 M. & W. 496 (promise to discarded mistress).

[26] See *Jones* v. *Padavatton* [1969] 1 W.L.R. 328, 333; *cf. Shadwell* v. *Shadwell* (1860) 9 C.B. N.S. 159; *ante*, p. 92.

[27] *Hardwick* v. *Johnson* [1978] 1 W.L.R. 683 *per* Roskill and Browne L.JJ.; Lord Denning M.R. thought that there was no contract but reached the same conclusion on other grounds; *cf. Collier* v. *Holinshead* (1984) 272 E.G. 941.

[28] If there is very clear evidence of contractual intention there may be a binding contract, as in *Haggar* v. *de Placido* [1972] 1 W.L.R. 716. But in practice such "contracts" were only made as a device to enable the value of the mother's services to be recovered from a tortfeasor who had injured the child, and for this purpose they are now unnecessary: *Donnelly* v. *Joyce* [1974] Q.B. 454.

[29] *Parker* v. *Clark* [1960] 1 W.L.R. 286; *cf. Schaefer* v. *Schuhman* [1972] 1 W.L.R. 1286; Lee, 88 L.Q.R. 320; *Tanner* v. *Tanner* [1975] 1 W.L.R. 1346.

[30] *Tanner* v. *Tanner* [1975] 1 W.L.R. 1346.

[31] Contrast *Horrocks* v. *Forray* [1976] 1 W.L.R. 320 and *Coombes* v. *Smith* [1986] 1 W.L.R. 808, where there was no such reliance and hence no contract.

[32] *Eves* v. *Eves* [1975] 1 W.L.R. 1338, 1345, *per* Browne L.J. and Brightman J. For the effects of failure to comply with formal requirements where the contract is one for the disposition of an interest in Land, see *post*, p. 164.

fact that the promisee had helped to improve the property was relied on to support the conclusion that an express or implied promise, giving her an interest in the property, had contractual force. New formal requirements for contracts for the disposition of interests in land[33] make it unlikely[34] that such an arrangement could now take effect as such a contract, but the same result could be reached by holding that the promise had taken effect as a constructive trust.[35]

In view of the informality of many house-sharing arrangements, it may be hard in a particular case to say just what obligation is created. In *Hussey* v. *Palmer*[36] a lady spent £600 on having a room added to her son-in-law's house, on the understanding that she could live there for the rest of her life. When she left voluntarily, about a year later, it was held that there was no contract *of loan* in respect of the £600[37] but there was probably a contract to allow her to live in the room for the rest of her life.

An agreement between persons who share a common household may have nothing to do with the management of the household. Thus in *Simpkins* v. *Pays*[38] three ladies who lived in the same house took part in a fashion competition run by a newspaper, agreeing to pool their entries and to share the prize which any entry might win. The court rejected the contention that the agreement to share was not intended to be legally binding.

5. Agreements Giving Wide Discretion to One Party

Contractual intention may be negatived where the terms of a promise leave its performance entirely to the discretion of the promisor.[39] In *Taylor* v. *Brewer*[40] the plaintiff agreed to do work for a committee who resolved that he should receive "such remuneration . . . as should be deemed right." The plaintiff's claim for a reasonable remuneration for work done failed: the promise to pay was "merely an engagement of honour."[41] This case is now more often distinguished than followed,[42] but it would still be applied if the wording made it clear that the promise was not intended to be legally binding.[43]

An agreement may give one party a discretion to rescind. That party will

---

33 Law of Property (Miscellaneous Provisions) Act 1989, s.2, *post*, p. 163.

34 s.2(1) of the 1989 Act (*supra*) requires the contract to be made in writing by incorporating all its "expressly agreed" terms in a document; and if the promise in *Eves* v. *Eves*, *supra*, n. 32, was indeed implied it could be argued that there were no "expressly agreed" terms.

35 *Eves* v. *Eves* [1975] 1 W.L.R. 1338, 1342, *per* Lord Denning M.R.: *cf. Grant* v. *Edwards* [1986] Ch. 638; contrast *Burns* v. *Burns* [1984] Ch. 317; Lowe and Smith, 47 M.L.R. 341; Dewar, *ibid.* p. 735. The formal requirements imposed by the 1989 Act (*supra*, n. 33) do not apply to "the creation or operation of . . . constructive trusts": s.2(5).

36 [1972] 1 W.L.R. 1286.

37 But she recovered the £600 on equitable grounds. *Cf. Re Sharpe* [1980] 1 W.L.R. 219, where there was both a loan and an equitable right in the lender.

38 [1955] 1 W.L.R. 975.

39 *Cf. ante*, p. 80 for the question whether such a promise can constitute consideration for a counter-promise.

40 (1813) 1 M. & S. 290; *cf. Shallcross* v. *Wright* (1850) 12 Beav. 558; *Roberts* v. *Smith* (1859) 28 L.J.Ex. 164.

41 1 M. & S. at p. 291.

42 *Post*, p. 643; *cf. Re Brand's Estate* [1936] 3 All E.R. 374.

43 *Cf. Re Richmond Gate Property Co. Ltd.* [1965] 1 W.L.R. 335; *post*, p. 648.

not be bound if his promise means "I will only perform if I do not change my mind." But the power to rescind may only be inserted as a safeguard in certain eventualities which are not exhaustively stated: for example, a contract for the sale of land may entitle the vendor to rescind if the purchaser persists in some requisition or objection which the vendor is "unable *or unwilling* to satisfy." In such a case there is a contract and the court will control the exercise of the power to rescind by insisting that the vendor must not rescind "arbitrarily, or capriciously, or unreasonably. Much less can he act in bad faith."[44]

6. Letters of Intent or of Comfort[45]

An issue of contractual intention may arise where parties in the course of negotiations exchange "letters of intent" or where one party gives to the other a "letter of comfort." The terms of such documents may negative contractual intention.[46] This was, for example, held to be the case where a company had issued a "letter of comfort" to a lender in respect of a loan to one of its subsidiaries.[47] The letter stated that "it is our policy that [the subsidiary] is at all times in a position to meet its liabilities in respect of the loan." This was interpreted to be no more than a statement of the company's present policy: it was not an undertaking that the policy would not be changed, since neither party had intended the statement to take effect as a contractual promise. On the other hand, where the language of such a document does not in terms negative contractual intention, it is open to the courts to hold the parties bound by the document; and they will, in particular, be inclined to do so where the parties have acted on the document for a long period of time or have expended considerable sums of money in reliance on it.[48] The fact that the parties envisage that the letter is to be superseded by a later, more formal, contractual document does not, of itself, prevent it from taking effect as a contract.[49]

7. Collective Agreements

Agreements as to rates of wages and conditions of work are commonly reached after collective bargaining between trade unions and employers or associations of employers. The general common law view was that such

[44] *Selkirk* v. *Romar Investments Ltd.* [1963] 1 W.L.R. 1415, 1422. *cf.* also the authorities on agreements subject to the "satisfaction" of one party, discussed *ante*, p. 60. For the possible effect of Unfair Contract Terms Act 1977, s.3(2)(*b*)(i), see *post*, p. 232.

[45] Lake, *Letters of Intent*.

[46] *Snelling* v. *John G. Snelling Ltd.* [1973] Q.B. 87; *cf. Montreal Gas Co.* v. *Vesey* [1900] A.C. 595; *B.S.C.* v. *Cleveland Bridge & Engineering Ltd.* [1984] 1 All E.R. 504.

[47] *Kleinwort Benson Ltd.* v. *Malaysian Mining Corp.* [1989] 1 W.L.R. 379; Reynolds, 104 L.Q.R. 353; Davenport [1988] L.M.C.L.Q. 290; Prentice, 105 L.Q.R. 346; Ayres and Moore, [1989] L.M.C.L.Q. 281; Tyree, 2 J.C.L. 279.

[48] *Cf. Turriff Construction Ltd.* v. *Regalia Knitting Mills* (1971) 22 E.G. 169 (letter of intent held to be a collateral contract for preliminary work); *Wilson Smithett & Cape (Sugar) Ltd.* v. *Bangladesh Sugar and Food Industries Ltd.* [1986] 1 Lloyd's Rep. 378 (letter of intent held to be an acceptance); *Chemco Leasing S.p.A.* v. *Rediffusion* [1987] 1 F.T.L.R. 201 (letter of intent held to be an offer but to have lapsed before acceptance).

[49] *Ante*, p. 53.

collective agreements were prima facie not intended to be legally binding[50] as between the trade unions and the employers.[51]; The Trade Union and Labour Relations Act 1974 goes further in providing that a collective agreement is "*conclusively* presumed not to have been intended by the parties to be a legally enforceable contract" unless it is in writing and expressly provides the contrary (in which case the agreement is conclusively presumed to have been intended by the parties to be a legally enforceable contract).[52] To displace the presumption that a collective agreement is not intended to be a legally binding contract, the agreement must provide that it was intended to be *legally* binding. The presumption is not displaced by a statement that the parties shall be "bound" by the agreement, for this may mean that they are bound in honour only.[53]

8. Other Cases

The cases in which there is no intention to create legal relations cannot be exhaustively classified. Contractual intention may, for example, be negatived by evidence that "the agreement was a goodwill agreement . . . made without any intention of creating legal relations"[54]; and by many other factors. Thus in one case it was said that an arrangement which was believed simply to give effect to pre-existing rights was not a contract because the parties had no intention to enter into a *new* contract.[55] In another case a statement was made on behalf of the Government that a certain neutral ship would be allowed to leave a British port if specified conditions were met. It was held that the statement did not have contractual force as it was "merely an expression of intention to act in a particular way in a certain event."[56] And in *President of the Methodist Conference* v. *Parfitt*[57] it was held that the appointment of a person as a Minister of the Methodist Church did not give rise to a contract as the relationship was not one "in which the parties intended to create legal relations between themselves so

---

50 Kahn-Freund in (Ed.) Flanders and Clegg, *The System of Industrial Relations in Great Britain*, Chap. 2; and in (Ed.) Ginsberg, *Law and Opinion in England in the 20th Century*, p. 215; Grunfeld, *Modern Trade Union Law*, pp. 219–220; Wedderburn, *The Worker and the Law*, (3rd ed.), pp. 318–322; Report of the Royal Commission on the Trade Unions and Employers' Associations (Cmnd. 3623, 1968) §§ 470–471 *Ford Motor Co. Ltd.* v. *A.E.F.*. [1969] 1 W.L.R. 339; Selwyn, 32 M.L.R. 377; Hepple [1970] C.L.J. 122; Lewis, 42 M.L.R. 613.

51 For the position between employer and employee where the terms of a collective agreement are incorporated in individual contracts of employment, see *post*, p. 194.

52 s.18(1) and (2) *The Universe Sentinel* [1983] A.C. 366, 380. *The Rosso* [1982] 2 Lloyd's Rep. 120; *cf. Cheall* v. *APEX* [1983] 1 A.C. 180, 189 (inter-union agreement); provisions making collective agreements legally binding seem to be very rare: see *Commission of the European Communities* v. *United Kingdom* [1984] I.C.R. 192, 195.

53 *N.C.B.* v. *N.U.M.* [1986] I.C.R. 736.

54 *Orion Ins. Co. plc.* v. *Sphere Drake Ins. plc.* [1990] 1 Lloyd's Rep. 465, 505.

55 *Beesly* v. *Hallwood Estates Ltd.* [1960] 1 W.L.R. 549, 558, affirmed on other grounds [1961] Ch. 105; *cf. Harvela Investments Ltd.* v. *Royal Trust Co. of Canada (C.I.) Ltd.* [1986] A.C. 207. See also *The Aramis* [1989] 1 Lloyd's Rep. 213, Treitel [1989] L.M.C.L.Q. 162; contrast *The Amazonia* [1990] 1 Lloyd's Rep. 238, 241–242 (where the parties did intend to make a new contract, containing additional terms); and *The Eurymedon* [1975] A.C. 514 and *Pyrene* v. *Scindia Navigation Co. Ltd.* [1954] 2 Q.B. 402 (in these two cases, belief that one party was acting under another contract with a third party did not negative contractual intention).

56 *Rederiaktiebolaget Amphitrite* v. *R.* [1921] 2 K.B. 500, 503.

57 [1984] Q.B. 368.

as to make the agreement . . . enforceable in the courts."[58] Even the intention of only one of the parties may lead to the same result: thus the question whether a contract of employment exists between the Crown and one of its civil servants has been said to depend on proof of the necessary contractual intention on the part of the Crown.[59]

Contractual intention may be negatived by the vagueness of a statement or promise. Thus, in one case a promise by a husband to allow his deserted wife to stay in the matrimonial home was held not to have contractual force because it did not state for how long or on what terms she could stay there: this showed that it was "not intended by him, or understood by her, to have any contractual basis or effect."[60] So, too, the use of deliberately vague language was held to negative contractual intention where a property developer reached an "understanding" with a firm of solicitors to employ them in connection with a proposed development, but neither side entered into a definite commitment.[61]

The fact that a statement was made in jest or anger may also negative contractual intention. Thus in *Licenses Insurance Corporation* v. *Lawson*[62] the defendant was a director of the plaintiff company and of another company. The plaintiff company held shares in the other company and resolved, in the defendant's absence, to sell them. At a later meeting this resolution was rescinded after a heated discussion during which the defendant said that he would make good any loss which the plaintiff company might suffer if it kept the shares. It was held that the defendant was not liable on this undertaking. Nobody at the meeting regarded it as a contract; it was not recorded as such in the minute book; and the defendant's fellow-directors at most thought that he was bound in honour.

There are conflicting decisions on the question whether the issue and acceptance of a free travel pass amounts to a contract. In *Wilkie* v. *L.P.T.B.*[63] it was held that such a pass issued by a transport undertaking to one of its own employees did not amount to a contract. But the contrary conclusion was reached in *Gore* v. *Van der Lann*[64] where the pass was issued to an old age pensioner. This conclusion was based on the ground that an application for the pass had been made on a form couched in contractual language; and *Wilkie's* case was distinguished on the ground that the pass there was issued to the employee "as a matter of course . . . as one of the privileges attaching to his employment."[65] But as the pass in *Gore's* case was issued expressly on the "understanding" that it only consti-

---

[58] *Ibid.* p. 378; approved in *Davies* v. *Presbyterian Church of Wales* [1986] 1 W.L.R. 323 (no contract of employment between pastor and Presbyterian Church); Woolman, 102 L.Q.R. 356. *Santokh Singh* v. *Guru Nanak Gurdwara* [1990] I.C.R. 309 (no contract of employment between Sikh minister of religion and his Temple).

[59] See *R.* v. *Civil Service Appeal Board, ex p. Bruce* [1988] I.C.R. 649, affirmed on other grounds [1989] I.C.R. 171; *McLaren* v. *Home Office* [1990] I.C.R. 824; under Employment Act 1988, s.30(1), the relationship may, for certain purposes "be deemed to constitute a contract."

[60] *Vaughan* v. *Vaughan* [1953] 1 Q.B. 762, 765; *cf. Booker* v. *Palmer* [1942] 2 All E.R. 674; *Horrocks* v. *Forray* [1976] 1 W.L.R. 230; *Jones* v. *Padavatton* [1969] 1 W.L.R. 328; and see *Gould* v. *Gould* [1970] 1 Q.B. 275; *Layton* v. *Morris, The Times*, December 11, 1985.

[61] *J. H. Milner & Son* v. *Percy Bilton Ltd.* [1966] 1 W.L.R. 1582.

[62] (1896) 12 T.L.R. 501.

[63] [1947] 1 All E.R. 258.

[64] [1967] 2 Q.B. 31; *ante*, p. 144.

[65] [1967] 2 Q.B. 31, 41.

tuted a licence subject to conditions the distinction seems, with respect, to be a tenuous one.

9. Proof of Contractual Intention

The question of contractual intention is, in the last resort, one of fact[66]; but in the case of an ordinary commercial relationship the courts do not require proof that the parties actually intended to be bound.[67] On the contrary, the onus of proving that there was no such intention "is on the party who asserts that no legal effect was intended, and the onus is a heavy one."[68] In deciding whether the onus has been discharged, the courts will be influenced by the importance of the agreement to the parties, and by the fact that one of them has acted in reliance on it.[69] They will also normally apply an objective test[70]: for example, where an agreement for the sale of a house is *not* "subject to contract,"[71] both parties are likely to be bound even though one of them subjectively believed that he would not be bound till the usual exchange of contracts had taken place.[72] Of course the objective test is here (as elsewhere)[73] subject to the limitation that it does not apply in favour of a party who knows the truth: thus in the example just given the party who did not intend to be bound would not be bound if this state of mind was actually known to the other party.[74] The incidence of the burden of proof and the objective test may explain two controversial decisions, in each of which there was a difference of opinion on the issue of contractual intention.

The first is *Esso Petroleum Ltd.* v. *Commissioners of Customs and Excise.*[75] Esso supplied garages with tokens called "World Cup coins," instructing them to give away one coin with every four gallons of petrol sold. The scheme was advertised by Esso and also on posters displayed by the garages. By a majority of four to one, the House of Lords held that there was no "sale" of the coins; but the majority was equally divided on the question whether there was any contract at all with regard to the coins.

---

[66] See *Zakhem International Construction Ltd.* v. *Nippon Kohan KK* [1987] 2 Lloyd's Rep. 596.

[67] Certain hire-purchase agreements must contain the following notice: "This is a Hire-Purchase Agreement regulated by the Consumer Credit Act 1974. Sign it only if you want to be legally bound by its terms." (Consumer Credit (Agreements) Regulations 1983 S.I. No. 1553).

[68] *Edwards* v. *Skyways Ltd.* [1964] 1 W.L.R. 349, 355; *cf. The Polyduke* [1978] 1 Lloyd's Rep. 211; *Financial Techniques (Planning Services) Ltd.* v. *Hughes* [1981] I.R.L.R. 32. *The Zephyr* [1985] 2 Lloyd's Rep. 529, 537 (disapproving [1984] 1 Lloyd's Rep. 58, 63–64); *Yani Haryanto* v. *E.D. & F. Man (Sugar) Ltd.* [1986] 2 Lloyd's Rep. 44. If the agreement is intended to give rise to legal relations, its precise legal *effects* are similarly not determined by the subjective intentions of the parties or one of them: see *Street* v. *Mountfort* [1985] A.C. 809 where an agreement was held as a matter of law to take effect as a lease even though the lessor clearly intended it to take effect only as a licence. *Cf. A.G. Securities* v. *Vaughan* [1990] 1 A.C. 417; contrast *Ogwr B.C.* v. *Dykes* [1989] 1 W.L.R. 295.

[69] *Ante*, p. 152; *Kingswood Estate Co. Ltd.* v. *Anderson* [1963] 2 Q.B. 169; *cf. South West Water Authority* v. *Palmer*, (1982) 263 E.G. 438.

[70] *Ante*, pp. 1, 8.

[71] *Ante*, p. 52.

[72] *Tweddell* v. *Henderson* [1975] 1 W.L.R. 1496; *Storer* v. *Manchester C.C.* [1974] 1 W.L.R. 1403, 1408.

[73] *Ante*, pp. 8–9.

[74] *Pateman* v. *Pay* (1974) 232 E.G. 457.

[75] [1976] 1 W.L.R. 1; Atiyah, 39 M.L.R. 335.

Those who thought that there was a contract[76] relied on the incidence of the burden of proof, and on the argument that "Esso envisaged a bargain of some sort between the garage proprietor and the motorist."[77] But this argument relates rather to the intention of Esso than to that of the alleged contracting parties. With regard to *their* intention, it is submitted that the more realistic view is that of Lords Dilhorne and Russell, who relied on the language of the advertisements (in which the coins were said to be "going free"), and on the minimal value of the coins, as negativing contractual intention.

The second case is *J. Evans & Son (Portsmouth) Ltd.* v. *Andrea Merzario Ltd.*[78] The representative of a firm of forwarding agents told a customer, with whom the firm had long dealt, that henceforth his goods would be packed in containers and assured him that these would be carried *under* deck. About a year later, such a container was carried *on* deck and lost. At first instance,[79] Kerr J. held that the promise was not intended to be legally binding since it was made in the course of a courtesy call, not related to any particular transaction, and indefinite with regard to its future duration. The Court of Appeal, however, held[80] that the promise did have contractual force, relying principally on the importance attached by the customer to the carriage of his goods under deck, and on the fact that he would not have agreed to the new mode of carriage but for the promise. The case is no doubt a borderline one, but it is submitted that Kerr J.'s view accords more closely with the objective test of contractual intention. In most cases, that test prevents the *promisor* from relying on his subjective intention not to enter into a contractual undertaking. But it should equally prevent the *promisee's* subjective intention or belief from being decisive and require that party's belief to be one which would have been apparent to a reasonable person in the position of the promisor. The Court of Appeal appears with respect to have attached too much weight to the customer's subjective state of mind, and too little weight to the circumstances in which the promise was made.

SECTION 2. INTENTION AND CONSIDERATION

In the United States, the view has been put forward by Williston[81] that "the common law does not require any positive intention to create a legal obligation as an element of contract." No one disputes that an agreement is not a contract if the parties expressly provide that it is not to be legally binding. But it is said that an agreement containing no such provision will generally be a contract although no positive intention to create a legal obligation existed in the minds of the parties. This theory can be interpreted in two ways.

The first interpretation simply emphasises the rule as to burden of proof

---

[76] Lords Simon and Wilberforce. Lord Fraser, who dissented on the main issue, took the same view.

[77] [1976] 1 W.L.R. at p. 6.

[78] [1976] 1 W.L.R. 1078; Adams, 40 M.L.R. 227; *cf. El Awadi* v. *Bank of Credit and Commerce International* [1990] 1 Q.B. 606, 617.

[79] [1975] 1 Lloyd's Rep. 162.

[80] 1 W.L.R. 1078.

[81] Williston, *Contracts*, Section 21; Tuck, 21 Can.B.Rev. 123; Shatwell, 1 Sydney L.R. at p. 293; Unger, 19 M.L.R. 96. Hedley, 5 O.J.L.S. 391.

and the objective test, stated above.[82] Thus Williston says: "If, under the circumstances, a reasonable person would understand[83] the words used as importing that the speaker promised to do something if given a requested exchange therefor, it is immaterial what intention the offeror may have had." This statement is no doubt true in the case of an ordinary commercial contract; but it is harder to apply where words are spoken in jest or in anger.[84] Williston admits that there is no contract in such cases; and this admission can perhaps be explained on the ground that a person to whom a promise is made in *obvious* jest or anger would know that it was not intended to be binding, so that the objective test would not be satisfied. Another difficulty is that Williston's test is, if taken quite literally, wide enough to cover ordinary social and domestic arrangements. Williston sees no reason why these "should not create a contract, if the requisites for the formation of a contract exist." No doubt it is possible that in exceptional circumstances and by use of clear words acceptance of an invitation to a party could create a contract. But would it do so *merely* because "the speaker promised to do something if given a requested exchange therefor?" Would acceptance of an invitation to a bottle-party normally create a contract? And can Williston's view be reconciled with the "car pool" cases[85] mentioned above?

The second, and more extreme, version of the theory is that there is no requirement of contractual intention at all. A promise is binding if it is supported by consideration; nothing else is necessary. Social and domestic arrangements are not contracts, even if they involve reciprocal promises or performances, because the promise of one party is not given as the price for the other's: there is no bargain. "The family circle differs from the market place in that it is not the setting for bargaining but for an exchange of gifts or gratuitous services."[86] This is said to be the true basis of *Balfour* v. *Balfour*.[87] But this view merely makes the requirement of intention part of the definition of consideration: one cannot tell whether mutual promises constitute a bargain or an "exchange of gifts" without regard to the intention of the parties. Nor can one on this view explain why mere puffs or statements made in jest or anger do not give rise to contractual obligations; why a defendant who concedes that there was consideration has any case left to argue on the issue of intention[88] or why there was no contract in *Heilbut, Symons & Co.* v. *Buckleton*.[89] It is, finally, inconsistent with cases such as *President of the Methodist Conference* v. *Parfitt*[90] where there was an agreement and consideration,[91] and the conclusion that the appointment did not amount to a contract was based solely on the ground that the

---

[82] *Ante*, p. 157.
[83] See *Edwards* v. *Skyways Ltd.* [1964] 1 W.L.R. 349, 356 for the difficulties which may arise in determining this question, especially where one of the parties is a corporation.
[84] See *ante*, p. 156.
[85] *Ante*, p. 151.
[86] Unger, *loc. cit.*; *cf.* Hepple [1970] C.L.J. 122.
[87] [1919] 2 K.B. 571.
[88] As in *Edwards* v. *Skyways Ltd.* [1964] 1 W.L.R. 349. *cf. Re Beaumont* [1980] Ch. 444, 453, recognising that consideration may be provided "under a contract *or otherwise*."
[89] [1913] A.C. 30; *ante*, p. 149.
[90] [1984] Q.B. 368, *ante*, p. 155.
[91] [1984] Q.B. 368, 378.

parties did not intend that it should give rise to legal relations between them.[92]

It is submitted that neither version of the theory is satisfactory. Many of the decisions discussed in this Chapter are expressly based on the absence of an intention to create legal relations, and cannot be satisfactorily explained in any other way. They show that such intention is recognised by English law as a separate requirement for the formation of contracts.

[92] *Ibid*; *cf.* also *R.* v. *Civil Service Appeal Tribunal, ex p. Bruce* [1988] I.C.R. 649, 659, 665; affd. on other grounds [1989] I.C.R. 171.

CHAPTER FIVE

FORM

SECTION 1. GENERAL RULE

A LEGAL system is said to require that a contract shall be made in a certain form if it lays down the manner in which the conclusion of the contract is to be marked or recorded. In modern legal systems, such formal requirements generally consist of writing, sometimes with additional requirements, *e.g.* those of a deed or (in some countries) of authentication by a notary. It has even been said that consideration is a form,[1] but more usually "form" refers to requirements which have nothing to do with the contents of an agreement. In this sense consideration is not generally a form, though the giving of peppercorn to make a gratuitous promise binding might be so regarded.[2]

Form may be *sufficient* to make a promise binding, as we have seen in discussing the effect of a gratuitous promise made in a deed.[3] But in this Chapter we shall discuss cases in which form is a *necessary* requirement which must be satisfied (granted that there is agreement, consideration and contractual intention) before the contract is fully effective. Such a requirement may serve one of several purposes. First, it promotes certainty, as it is usually relatively easy to tell whether the required form has been used. A requirement of writing also simplifies the problem of ascertaining the contents of the agreement. Secondly, form has a cautionary effect: a person may hesitate longer before executing a deed than he would before making an oral promise. Thirdly, form has a protective function: it is used to protect the weaker party to a contractual relationship by ensuring that he is provided with a written record of the terms of the contract. For example, an employee must be informed in writing of the terms of his employment,[4] and a tenant must (in certain cases) be given a rent-book containing certain particulars of his tenancy.[5] Both the second and the third purposes of form are illustrated by the elaborate formal requirements that protect a hirer under certain hire-purchase agreements. He must be given a document to be signed by him inside a "signature box;" this must contain a notice warning him that he is signing a hire-purchase agreement. A similar box must contain a notice telling him of his statutory right of cancellation.[6] It is

---

[1] Holmes, *The Common Law*, p. 273: "Consideration is a form as much as a seal." See also Fuller, 41 Col.L.Rev. 799.

[2] See *The Alev* [1989] 1 Lloyd's Rep. 138, 147.

[3] *Ante*, p. 144.

[4] Employment Protection (Consolidation) Act 1978, s.1; the actual contract need not be in writing. Administrative machinery for securing compliance with s.1 is provided by s.11.

[5] Landlord and Tenant Act 1985, s.4; the actual lease is not required by this Act to be in writing. Failure to comply with s.4 is an offence under s.7 of the Act; but does not make the contract invalid: *Shaw* v. *Groom* [1970] 2 Q.B. 504. *Cf.* Estate Agents Act 1979, s.18 for information which estate agents must give to their clients.

[6] Consumer Credit (Agreements) Regulations (1983 S.I. No. 1553 Sched. 5), made under Consumer Credit Act 1974, s.60. They apply where the price is under £15,000: Consumer Credit (Increase of Monetary Limits) Order (1983 S.I. No. 1878).

scarcely fanciful to suggest that these boxes fulfil in a modern context some of the functions formerly performed by use of the seal.[7] Form may finally serve what has been called a "channelling" purpose[8]: that is, the use of a certain form may help to distinguish one type of transaction from another.

Form has, on the other hand, the disadvantage that it is time-consuming and clumsy and that it is a source of technical pitfalls. Even the relatively simple requirement of writing is open to these objections and has therefore been regarded as inconvenient from a commercial point of view. Thus the general rule is that contracts can be made quite informally.[9]

SECTION 2. STATUTORY EXCEPTIONS

The general rule is subject to many exceptions. These now all depend on statutes which deal with specific types of contracts. Some such contracts must be made by deed, some must be in writing, and others must be evidenced by a note or memorandum in writing. No attempt can be made in this book to give a complete list of these exceptions. A few illustrations must suffice.

1. Contracts which must be made by Deed

A lease for more than three years must be made by deed.[10] If it is not so made, it is "void for the purpose of creating a legal estate."[11] But it operates in equity as an agreement for a lease,[12] which can be specifically enforced if it complies with the formal requirements (to be discussed below)[13] for contracts for the disposition of interests in land. Thus between the parties to the lease lack of a deed is not fatal. But, unless the tenant happens to have registered the lease as a land-charge, he can be turned out by a third party to whom the landlord has sold the land.[14]

2. Contracts which must be in Writing

(1) Illustrations of such contracts

Under nineteenth century legislation, contracts which must be in writing include bills of exchange, promissory notes[15] and bills of sale.[16] Two more recent statutes impose the requirement of writing on regulated consumer credit agreements and on most contracts for the sale or other disposition of interests in land.

Under the Consumer Credit Act 1974, regulated consumer credit agreements (including hire-purchase agreements), and certain other agreements[17] are "not properly executed"[18] unless certain formalities are

---

[7] See *ante*, p. 144.
[8] See Von Mehren, 72 H.L.R. 1009, 1017.
[9] *Beckham* v. *Drake* (1841) 9 M.& W. 79, 92.
[10] Law of Property Act 1925, ss.52, 54(2).
[11] *Ibid*. s.52.
[12] *Walsh* v. *Lonsdale* (1882) 21 Ch.D. 9.
[13] *Post*, pp. 163–165.
[14] Law of Property Act 1925, s.199(1)(i); Land Charges Act 1925, ss.10(1) Class (iv); 13(2).
[15] Bills of Exchange Act 1882, ss.3(1), 17(2).
[16] Bills of Sale Act 1878 (Amendment) Act 1882.
[17] Such as consumer hire agreements (s.15) and security instruments (s.105).
[18] s.61(1).

complied with. A regulated consumer credit agreement is one by which a creditor provides an individual debtor with credit[19] not exceeding £15,000.[20] Both parties must sign a document in the form prescribed by government regulations.[21] This must legibly set out all the express terms of the contract[22] and contain a notice of the debtor's statutory right to cancel during the "cooling off" period (where this applies),[23] as well as certain other information.[24] A copy must also be given to the debtor.[25]

Under section 2 of the Law of Property (Miscellaneous Provisions) Act 1989, most contracts for the sale or disposition of an interest in land[26] must be "made in writing."[27] All the terms expressly[28] agreed by the parties must be incorporated in the document (or documents, where contracts are exchanged).[29] The terms may be incorporated either by being set out in the document, or by reference.[30] The document must also be signed by or on behalf of each party.[31] The requirement of writing does not apply to short leases for less than three years, to sales at public auctions or to transactions in certain forms of investment securities (*e.g.* unit trust investing in land).[32]

(2) Effect of non-compliance

The effect of failing to comply with a statutory requirement of writing is far from uniform.

A bill of sale is void unless it is in writing in the statutory form.[33] But if the sort of promise which is normally contained in a bill of exchange or promissory note is made orally, it can result in a perfectly valid contract. The contract will simply not have the legal and commercial characteristics of a bill or note.[34]

In the case of regulated consumer credit agreements, the 1974 Act provides an intermediate solution. An agreement which is not properly executed can be enforced *against the debtor* on an order of the court only.[35] No such order can be made if the agreement has not been signed by the debtor,[36] or if (in the case of a cancellable agreement) the debtor has not been given a copy or notice of his right to cancel.[37] In the case of other formal defects, the court has a wide discretion. It can take into account the prejudice caused to the debtor and the degree of culpability of the credi-

---

[19] As defined by s.9.
[20] s.8; Consumer Credit (Increase of Monetary Limits) Order (1983 S.I. No. 1878); certain agreements are exempt under s.16.
[21] s.61(1)(*a*); for exceptions, see s.74. *Cf. ante*, pp. 161–162.
[22] s.61(1)(*b*) and (*c*).
[23] s.64(5); *cf.* Insurance Companies Act 1982, s.76.
[24] Consumer Credit Act 1974, s.55(1).
[25] ss.62, 63.
[26] As defined in Law of Property (Miscellaneous Provisions) Act 1989, s.2(6).
[27] *Ibid.* s.2(1).
[28] This word makes it unnecessary to set out *implied* terms in the document.
[29] Law of Property (Miscellaneous Provisions) Act 1989, s.2(1).
[30] *Ibid.* s.2(2).
[31] *Ibid.* s.2(3).
[32] *Ibid.* s.2(5).
[33] *Supra*, n. 16.
[34] *Post*, p. 595.
[35] s.65(1). The defective agreement is thus unenforceable only and not void: *Reg.* v. *Modupe*, *The Times*, February 27, 1991.
[36] s.127(3).
[37] s.127(4).

tor[38]; order enforcement conditionally or subject to variations[39]; reduce the amount payable by the debtor[40]; or enforce the agreement as if it did not include a term omitted from the document signed by the debtor.[41] This flexible approach goes far to meet the objection that formal requirements can give rise to unmeritorious defences based on technical slips.[42]

Section 2 of the Law of Property (Miscellaneous Provisions) Act 1989 requires a contract for the sale or other disposition of an interest in land to be "made in writing." The effect of these words is that the contract does not come into existence if the parties fail to comply with the statutory formal requirements. This could cause hardship where one party has partly performed such a contract, or otherwise acted in reliance on it, *e.g.* by making improvements to the land in question. But such hardship can be avoided by other judicially developed doctrines, such as proprietary estoppel or constructive trust.[43] Under these doctrines, the court can make an order for the transfer of the land to the party who has acted in reliance on the contract.[44] But the remedy is limited in various ways[45] and does not necessarily lead to enforcement of the contract as such.[46] In this respect the position of the party who has acted in reliance on the defective contract is now less favourable than it was before the 1989 Act.[47] Further remedies are available where the document fails to comply with the statutory requirement because it does not incorporate *all* the express terms on which the parties had orally agreed. If that failure was due to a mistake in recording those terms, it may be possible to rectify the document, *i.e.* to bring it into line with what was actually agreed.[48] If the failure is due to some other cause, it is sometimes possible to treat the omitted term as a collateral contract, separate from the contract contained in the document. This can only be done if the omitted term is not so "interwoven with the substance of the transaction"[49] as to form an essential term of it; for to treat an essential term as collateral would conflict with the statutory requirement that the document must incorporate all the expressly agreed terms. It seems that the parties must intend the term to take effect as a separate contract, and

---

[38] s.127(1)(i).

[39] s.127(1)(ii).

[40] s.127(2).

[41] s.127(5).

[42] *Cf.* Mobile Homes Act 1983, s.1, under which the court can order the site-owner to comply with the formal requirements imposed by the Act.

[43] *Ante*, pp. 124–136, 153 n. 35. The concluding words of s.2(5) of Law of Property (Miscellaneous Provisions) Act 1989 are intended to preserve these rules: see Law Com. No. 164 paras. 4.3, 5.4 and 5.5.

[44] *Ante*, p. 131.

[45] *Ibid.*; *cf.* also *ante*, p. 130.

[46] *Ante*, p. 136.

[47] Under Law of Property Act 1925, s.40 (re-enacting part of s.4 of the Statute of Frauds 1677 and now repealed with effect from September 27, 1989) failure to comply with the statutory requirement of written evidence only made the contract unenforceable; and "part performance" enabled the party so performing to enforce the contract.

[48] For the conditions in which rectification is available, see *post*, pp. 285–290; the possibility of rectification is recognised by Law of Property (Miscellaneous Provisions) Act 1989, s.2(4), which provides that the contract is deemed to come into being at such time as may be specified in the court order rectifying the document. See also Law Com. No. 164, para. 5.6.

[49] *Preece* v. *Lewis* (1963) 186 E.G. 113, decided under Law of Property Act 1925, s.40 (*supra*, n. 47) but, *semble*, equally applicable under Law of Property (Miscellaneous Provisions) Act 1989, s.2(1); see also Law Com. No. 164, paras. 5.7, 5.8.

not merely as part of the main contract. Where this requirements is satisfied, two consequences follow. First, a document which omits the term can nevertheless satisfy the statutory requirement of incorporating *all* the terms of the main contract. Secondly, the collateral contract is binding, even if oral, so long as it is not itself one which is required to be in writing,[50] and so long as evidence of it is admissible under the parol evidence rule.[51]

3. Contracts which must be Evidenced in Writing

(1) In general

Some statutes do not require contracts to be made in writing, but only to be evidenced by a written document. A contract of marine insurance, for example, is "inadmissible in evidence" unless it is embodied in a marine policy signed by the insurer and containing particulars specified by statute.[52] This is not a requirement of the making or validity of such a contract: it is enough if the policy is executed *after* the making of the contract. Other statutory provisions are less exacting; they are satisfied if there is merely a "note or memorandum" in writing. The Statute of Frauds 1677 applied this requirement to six classes of contracts. Its object was to prevent fraudulent claims based on perjured evidence; but it worked badly and it was, whenever possible, whittled down by judicial construction. This process is illustrated by the interpretation of its provisions relating to contracts of guarantee, the only type of contract to which the formal requirements imposed by the Statute still apply.[53]

(2) Contracts of guarantee

(a) DEFINITION. Section 4 of the Statute of Frauds provides: "No action shall be brought . . . whereby to charge the defendant upon any special promise to answer for the debt, default or miscarriage of another person" unless there is written evidence of the promise. This provision applies whether the liability guaranteed is contractual or tortious.[54] But it does not apply in the following cases.

(i) *Promise to debtor.* The Statute only applies where a third person promises the creditor to pay the debt. It does not apply where the third party's promise is made to the debtor.[55]

(ii) *Indemnity.* The Statute applies to a guarantee, but not to an indemnity. A guarantee is a promise to pay another's debt if he fails to pay. An indemnity is a promise to indemnify the creditor against loss arising out of the principal contract.[56] In the case of a guarantee the liability of the principal debtor is primary and that of the guarantor only secondary; thus if for

---

[50] *Angell* v. *Duke* (1875) L.R. 10 Q.B. 174 (and see next note); *Record* v. *Bell*, *The Times*, December 21, 1990.

[51] *Post*, pp. 183–185; in *Angell* v. *Duke*, *supra*, where the evidence of the collateral contract was later rejected under the parol evidence rule: (1875) 32 L.T. 320.

[52] Marine Insurance Act 1906, ss.22, 23 and 24.

[53] For the repeal of other relevant provisions contained (or formerly contained) in the Statute, see Law Reform (Enforcement of Contracts) Act 1954; Law of Property (Miscellaneous Provisions) Act 1989, ss.2(8) and 4, Sched. 2.

[54] *Kirkham* v. *Marter* (1819) 2 B. & Ald. 613.

[55] *Eastwood* v. *Kenyon* (1840) 11 A. & E. 438.

[56] *Birkmyr* v. *Darnell* (1704) 1 Salk. 27; *Argo Caribbean Group* v. *Lewis* [1976] 2 Lloyd's Rep. 289; *cf. post*, p. 356.

some reason the principal debtor is not liable, the guarantor is not liable either. A promise to indemnify creates primary liability which arises even though the promisee has no enforceable rights under the principal contract.[57]

It follows from the nature of a guarantee that there can be no guarantee if there never was a principal debtor: *e.g.* if A promises to pay B for doing work for C, which C has not ordered so that C is not liable to pay B for it.[58] Nor is a contract a guarantee if there once was a principal debtor, but if the whole object of the contract is that his liability should cease and that of the new promisor be substituted for it. Thus a promise by a father to pay his son's creditor, if the creditor will release the son, is an indemnity.[59] But a promise may be an indemnity in spite of the fact that there is a principal debtor whose liability continues. This is the position if the person making the promise undertakes not merely to pay if the principal debtor fails to do so, but "to put the [creditor] in funds in any event."[60]

It can hardly be said that there is less danger of perjury in the case of an indemnity than in the case of a guarantee. The distinction between them has accordingly been criticised for having "raised many hair-splitting distinctions of exactly that kind which bring the law into hatred, ridicule and contempt by the public."[61] It can only be explained historically as a device for restricting the scope of the Statute of Frauds.

(iii) *Part of larger transaction.* The Statute of Frauds only applies to a guarantee which stands alone and not to one which is part of a larger transaction. It did not, for example, apply where the defendant introduced clients to a firm of stockbrokers on the terms that he was to receive half the commissions earned, and to pay half the losses incurred, by the stockbrokers on transactions with such clients.[62] The promise to pay losses was enforceable, though oral, as it formed part of a larger transaction in which the defendant was interested otherwise than as guarantor. Similarly the guarantee given by a *del credere* agent is not within the statute. Such an agent guarantees the solvency of the third party between whom and his principal he makes a contract: that is, he promises the principal to pay if the third party does not. The main object of a *del credere* agency is to enable the principal to sell and the agent to earn his commission. "Though it may terminate in a liability to pay the debt of another, that is not the immediate object for which the consideration is given."[63] On the wording of the Statute, it is hard to justify the special treatment of these cases. Perhaps it could be said that such promises are more likely to be made than purely disinterested guarantees: hence there is less danger of perjury.

(iv) *Protection of property.* A guarantee is not within the Statute of Frauds if it is given to protect some proprietary interest of the guarantor. Thus A may buy goods from B which are held by C as security for a debt owed by B to C. If A induces C to deliver the goods to him by promising to

---

[57] *Yeoman Credit Ltd.* v. *Latter* [1961] 1 W.L.R. 828; in Consumer Credit Act 1974, s.189(1), "security" includes both guarantee and indemnity.

[58] *Lakeman* v. *Mountstephen* (1874) L.R. 7 H.L. 17.

[59] *Goodman* v. *Chase* (1818) 1 B. & Ald. 297.

[60] *Guild & Co.* v. *Conrad* [1894] 2 Q.B. 885, 892; *cf. Thomas* v. *Cook* (1828) 8 B. & C. 728; *Wildes* v. *Dudlow* (1874) L.R. 19 Eq. 198; *Re Hoyle* [1893] 1 Ch. 84.

[61] *Yeoman Credit Ltd.* v. *Latter* [1961] 1 W.L.R. 828, 835.

[62] *Sutton & Co.* v. *Grey* [1894] 1 Q.B. 285.

[63] *Couturier* v. *Hastie* (1852) 8 Ex. 40, 56. The actual decision was reversed on another point: (1856) 5 H.L.C. 673, *post*, p. 258.

pay B's debt in case B does not pay it, A's promise is not within the Statute of Frauds.[64] The main object of A's promise is said to be to protect his own property and not to guarantee B's debt. This rule may again be justified on the ground that such promises are more likely to be made than purely disinterested guarantees. But if this is so, it is hard to see why the rule is restricted to cases in which the interest is strictly proprietary. The rule has, for example, been held not to apply where the guarantee was given to protect the assets of a company in which the guarantor was a substantial shareholder or debenture holder.[65] It was said that to enforce an oral guarantee in such a case would amount to repealing the Statute.[66] But this is also true where the interest protected is a strictly proprietary one.

So many subtle distinctions have been drawn to whittle away the application of the Statute to contracts of guarantee that it seems a pity that this part of the Statute has not been repealed. The object of retaining it was to protect guarantors, but it is doubtful whether it has this effect. It has been said that the standard form of a bank guarantee strips the guarantor "of virtually all those rights which the law would otherwise confer upon him—at any rate where they might conflict with the banker's interest."[67] Even if the requirement of written evidence did protect the guarantor, it would not do so very effectively, for it can fairly easily be evaded by making the contract one of indemnity.

(b) TYPE OF EVIDENCE REQUIRED. Contracts within the Statute of Frauds must be evidenced by a signed note or memorandum in writing. The exact nature of the evidence required was not specified by the Statute, but the following rules have been laid down by Parliament and by the courts. Many of the relevant cases concern contracts to which the Statute no longer applies; but the principles to be derived from them still apply, where appropriate, to contracts of guarantee.

(i) *Parties.* The memorandum must identify the parties by naming or describing them,[68] and state the capacity in which they contract.[69] It may sufficiently describe the parties without actually naming them. For example, a party can even be sufficiently described by a pronoun.[70]

(ii) *Consideration.* It has been provided by statute that the memorandum of guarantee need not state the consideration for the guarantee.[71]

(iii) *Terms.* The memorandum must contain the material[72] terms of the contract. If the memorandum states only some of the material terms, the

---

[64] *Fitzgerald* v. *Dressler* (1859) 7 C.B.(N.S.) 374.

[65] *Harburg India Rubber Comb Co.* v. *Martin* [1902] 1 K.B. 778; *Davys* v. *Buswell* [1913] 2 K.B. 47; *The Anemone* [1987] 1 Lloyd's Rep. 547.

[66] *Harburg* case, *supra*, at p. 787.

[67] Holden, *Security for Bankers' Advances*, (7th ed.), p. 198. In relation to regulated agreements, statutory protection is provided by Consumer Credit Act 1974, Pt. VIII and s.127. The Unfair Contract Terms Act 1977, will not generally help the guarantor; *post*, p. 246, n. 59.

[68] *Williams* v. *Jordan* (1877) 6 Ch.D. 517 ("Sir" not sufficient); *Re Lindrea* (1913) 109 L.T. 623 (Christian name sufficient).

[69] *Vandenbergh* v. *Spooner* (1866) L.R. 1 Ex. 316; *Newell* v. *Radford* (1867) L.R. 3 C.P. 52; *Dewar* v. *Mintoft* [1912] 2 K.B. 373.

[70] *Carr* v. *Lynch* [1900] 1 Ch. 613.

[71] Mercantile Law Amendment Act 1856, s.3.

[72] *Hawkins* v. *Price* [1947] Ch. 645; *cf. Beckett* v. *Nurse* [1948] 1 K.B. 535; *Tweddell* v. *Henderson* [1975] 1 W.L.R. 1496; *Marshall* v. *Berridge* (1881) 19 Ch.D. 233; *Edwards* v. *Jones* (1921) 124 L.T. 740.

parties will be "distinctly at issue as to what the contract was, and the very object of the Statute of Frauds was to prevent parol evidence being gone into to elucidate that which the parties failed to make distinct by reducing it into writing."[73] There is some authority for the view that if a term has been omitted from the memorandum the plaintiff may waive the term if it is solely for his benefit and not of major importance, and enforce the contract without the term.[74] Conversely, if the omitted term is for the benefit of the defendant, the plaintiff may be able to enforce the contract on agreeing to perform it.[75]

(iv) *Signature.* The memorandum must be signed by the party to be charged or by his agent lawfully authorised[76] to sign for him.

The requirement that the memorandum must be "signed" is liberally interpreted. A party need not sign his full name: initials will do.[77] The signature may be printed,[78] and may be in any part of the document, not necessarily at the bottom.[79] It may be put on the document before the contract was made so long as it is "recognised" at the time of contracting. Thus a form printed before the contract is made and bearing one party's name is "signed" by that party if he at the time of contracting submits it to the other party for signature: he thereby "recognises" his own "signature."[80] These rules are lax, but a document is not signed by a party merely because his name occurs somewhere within it: the signature must authenticate the whole document. Thus if a memorandum is headed "Articles of Agreement between A & B" and concludes "As witness our hands . . . " the parties must actually subscribe: the mention of their names at the beginning is clearly not intended as a signature.[81] A party is not considered to have signed a document merely because he adds his signature to it as witness to the signature of the other party.[82]

The writing need only be signed by "the party to be charged." Thus the contract can be enforced against a party who has signed by one who has not.[83]

(v) *Memorandum need not be prepared as such.* The memorandum need not be prepared for the purpose of satisfying the statutory requirements of written evidence. A writing which comes into existence before an action is brought[84] on the contract will suffice so long as it acknowledges or recog-

---

[73] *Caddick* v. *Skidmore* (1857) 2 D. & J. 52, 56.

[74] *North* v. *Loomes* [1919] 1 Ch. 378; *Beckett* v. *Nurse* [1948] 1 K.B. 535; *Turner* v. *Hatton* [1952] 1 T.L.R. 1148. The point was not argued in *Tweddell* v. *Henderson* [1975] 1 W.L.R. 1496.

[75] *Martin* v. *Pycroft* (1852) 2 D.M. & G. 785; *Scott* v. *Bradley* [1971] Ch. 850 (refusing to follow *Burgess* v. *Cox* [1951] Ch. 383 on this point).

[76] The cases on this point concern the authority of auctioneers and are obsolete now that no formal requirements apply either to sales of goods (Law Reform (Enforcement of Contracts) Act 1954) or to sales of land by public auction (Law of Property (Miscellaneous Provisions) Act 1989, s.2(5)(*b*)).

[77] *Chichester* v. *Cobb* (1866) 14 L.T. 433; *Hill* v. *Hill* [1947] Ch. 231, 240.

[78] *Schneider* v. *Norris* (1814) 2 M. & S. 286; *cf. Godwin* v. *Francis* (1870) L.R. 5 C.P. 295 (telegram).

[79] *Ogilvie* v. *Foljambe* (1817) 3 Mer. 53; *Durrell* v. *Evans* (1862) 1 H. & C. 174; *Evans* v. *Hoare* [1892] 1 Q.B. 593.

[80] *Schneider* v. *Norris*, *supra*; *Evans* v. *Hoare*, *supra*; *Cohen* v. *Roche* [1927] 1 K.B. 169; *Leeman* v. *Stocks* [1951] Ch. 941.

[81] *Hubert* v. *Treherne* (1842) 3 Man. & G. 743.

[82] *Gosbell* v. *Archer* (1835) 1 A. & E. 500.

[83] *Laythoarp* v. *Bryant* (1836) 2 Bing.N.C. 735; as to specific performance, see *post*, pp. 909–910.

[84] See *Lucas* v. *Dixon* (1889) 22 Q.B.D. 357; *Farr, Smith & Co.* v. *Messers* [1928] 1 K.B. 397.

nises the existence of the contract.[85] Thus an offer signed by one party and orally accepted by the other,[86] a recital or disposition in a will,[87] a letter written by one of the parties to his own agent[88] and pleadings in a previous action between different parties[89] have been held sufficient. A letter repudiating liability is a sufficient memorandum if it admits the terms of the contract but denies the construction put upon them by the other party; but not if it denies that a contract was ever made on the terms alleged.[90]

(vi) *Joinder of documents.* Where no single document fully records the transaction it may be possible to produce a sufficient memorandum by joining together two or more documents.

Joinder is, in the first place, possible where one document expressly or impliedly *refers* to another transaction. If that transaction is also recorded in a document, and that document was in existence when the first was signed[91] the two documents can be joined.[92]

Joinder may be effected via an intermediate document. Thus in one case[93] three telexes were involved: the first was addressed by the creditor to the guarantor and set out the terms of the guarantee; the second was addressed by the debtor to the guarantor and referred to the terms of the guarantee; and the third was addressed by the guarantor to the creditor's agent and referred to the second (and thus indirectly to the first) telex. It was held that the telexes constituted a sufficient memorandum since the third referred to the second, which in turn referred to the first. Even where there is no express reference in one document to the other, they can be joined if, on placing them side by side, it becomes obvious without the aid of oral evidence that they are connected.[94] It seems that the original and the photocopy of a document (one signed by one party and the other by the other) could be joined on this ground.[95] But if the document signed by the defendant contains no reference to another document or transaction, and if the connection between the two documents can only be established by oral evidence, joinder is not permitted.[96]

---

85 *Tweddell* v. *Henderson* [1975] 1 W.L.R. 1496.

86 *Reuss* v. *Picksley* (1866) L.R. 1 Ex. 342; *Lever* v. *Koffler* [1901] 1 Ch. 543; *Parker* v. *Clark* [1960] 1 W.L.R. 286.

87 *Re Hoyle* [1893] 1 Ch. 84; *Schaefer* v. *Schuhmann* [1972] A.C. 572; contrast *Maddison* v. *Alderson* (1883) 8 App.Cas. 467, where there was probably no contract at all.

88 *Gibson* v. *Holland* (1865) L.R. 1 C.P. 1.

89 *Grindell* v. *Bass* [1920] 2 Ch. 487. The position is probably different where reliance is placed on pleadings in an earlier action between the *same* parties; *Hardy* v. *Elphick* [1974] Ch. 65.

90 See *Buxton* v. *Rust* (1872) L.R. 7 Ex. 279; *Thirkell* v. *Cambi* [1919] 2 K.B. 591; *cf. Dobell* v. *Hutchison* (1835) 3 A. & E. 355.

91 For recognition of, and an exception to, this requirement, see *Re Danish Bacon Co. Ltd.* v. *Staff Pension Fund* [1971] 1 W.L.R. 248, a case arising under Law of Property Act 1925, s.53(1)(*c*).

92 *Long* v. *Millar* (1879) 4 C.P.D. 450; *cf. Reading Trust Ltd.* v. *Spero* [1930] 1 K.B. 492; *Holiday Credit Ltd.* v. *Erol* [1977] 1 W.L.R. 704; *Elias* v. *George Sahely & Co. (Barbados) Ltd.* [1983] 1 A.C. 646, where joinder is said at p. 655 to be possible even though the second document has no contractual force.

93 *The Anemone* [1987] 1 Lloyd's Rep. 547.

94 *Sheers* v. *Thimbleby* (1879) 13 T.L.R. 451; *cf. Burgess* v. *Cox* [1951] Ch. 383 (disapproved on another point in *Scott* v. *Bradley* [1971] Ch. 850).

95 *Stokes* v. *Whicher* [1920] 1 Ch. 411, 419 (top and carbon copies).

96 *Timmins* v. *Moreland Street Property Co.* [1958] Ch. 110; *cf. Boydell* v. *Drummond* (1809) 11 East 192; Contrast *Stokes* v. *Whicher* [1920] 1 Ch. 411; *Pearce* v. *Gardner* [1899] 1 Q.B. 688.

(c) EFFECT OF NON-COMPLIANCE. Failure to comply with the requirements just described does not make the contract void[97] but only enforceable.[98] The contract can be made orally, but it can only be enforced by action if a note or memorandum of it exists, signed by the party against whom enforcement is sought. As the contract is not void, money paid or property transferred under it cannot be recovered back merely because the contract is not evidenced in writing.[99] For example, a guarantor could not recover back from the creditor money which he had paid or property which he had deposited under a guarantee of which there was no sufficient note or memorandum. Similarly, a security given for the guarantor's performance would not be void merely because the guarantee was unenforceable: thus an action could be brought on a cheque given to the creditor in payment of sums due from the debtor.[1]

The Statute of Frauds could cause hardship to a party who had wholly or partly performed a contract which was unenforceable for want of written evidence. To meet this hardship, Equity developed the doctrine of part performance, under which the party who had rendered such performance could enforce the contract in spite of the lack of a proper note or memorandum. This doctrine was applied almost exclusively to contracts for the sale or other disposition of interests in land. It can no longer apply to such contracts since they must now be *made in* writing.[2] The result of failure to comply with this (more stringent) requirement is that no contract comes into existence; and there can be no part performance of a non-existent contract. There is, therefore, no longer any need to discuss the doctrine of part performance as it was applied to such contracts.[3] The doctrine of part performance was in the past restricted to contracts which were specifically enforceable in Equity, or perhaps (more narrowly) to contracts for the disposition of interests in land.[4] Contracts of guarantee would hardly ever (if at all) fall within even the broader of these two formulations. The normal remedy against a guarantor would be a common law action for the amount which he had promised to pay, and not a claim for specific performance.[5] Accordingly, the doctrine of part performance has not in the past been applied to contracts of guarantee.[6] The possibility of its being so applied in the future cannot be categorically ruled out,[7] since it is conceivable that a contract of guarantee might, in exceptional circumstances, be specifically enforceable[8]; if so, acts done by the creditor in reliance on the guarantee

---

[97] For the now rejected view that the contract was void, see dicta in *Carrington* v. *Roots* (1837) 2 M. & W. 248, 255, 257.

[98] *Leroux* v. *Brown* (1852) 12 C.B. 801; *Elias* v. *George Sahely & Co. (Barbados) Ltd.* [1983] 1 A.C. 646, 650.

[99] *Thomas* v. *Brown* (1876) 1 Q.B.D. 714; *cf. post*, pp. 890–891.

[1] *Low* v. *Fry* (1935) 152 L.T. 585.

[2] Law of Property (Miscellaneous Provisions) Act 1989, s.2(1)). For other devices by which such hardship may now be avoided, see *ante*, p. 164.

[3] For such discussion, see pp. 144–146 of the previous edition of this book.

[4] See *Britain* v. *Rossiter* (1879) 11 Q.B.D. 123; *McManus* v. *Cooke* (1887) 35 Ch.D. 681.

[5] The common law remedy would normally be "adequate" and so exclude specific performance: *post*, p. 907. A debtor's promise to give security may be specifically enforceable because damages for breach of it may be hard to quantify (*post*, p. 904); but no such difficulty arises in quantifying the liability of the guarantor.

[6] *Cf. Maddison* v. *Alderson* (1883) 8 App.Cas. 467, 490.

[7] The point was left open in *The Anemone* [1987] 1 Lloyd's Rep. 546, 557.

[8] *e.g.* if the debt guaranteed is one to pay an annuity to a person other than the promisee, as in *Beswick* v. *Beswick* [1968] A.C. 58; *cf. post*, pp. 905, 907, 918.

might be regarded as sufficient part performance. But the possibility seems to be a remote one, and the safest conclusion is that it is highly unlikely that the doctrine will be applied to contracts of guarantee.

SECTION 3. FORMAL REQUIREMENTS FOR RESCISSION AND VARIATION

So far in this Chapter we have been concerned with formal requirements for the making, proof or enforceability of a contract. It is finally necessary to consider the impact of form where a contract which complies with such a requirement, or which is (though it is not required to be) made by deed or in writing, is rescinded or varied by subsequent agreement of the parties.[9] Our present concern is with formal requirements only. The requirement of consideration for rescission and variation is discussed in Chapter 3.[10]

1. Rescission

The general principle is that formal requirements which apply to the making of a contract do not apply to its rescission by mutual consent. For example, a contract of guarantee can be rescinded orally[11]; and the same appears to be true of a contract for the disposition of an interest in land.[12] Somewhat greater difficulty arises where the rescinding agreement is itself a contract which is subject to formal requirements. Suppose, for example, that A in writing guarantees X's debt to B and that the guarantee is later rescinded by an oral agreement by which A guarantees Y's debt to B. The oral agreement is a valid contract[13] so that the guarantee of X's debt is rescinded, but B cannot enforce[14] the guarantee of Y's debt since that guarantee is not evidenced in writing. The position is less certain where the original contract is one which must be made in writing and where the rescinding agreement is also such a contract: for example, where both agreements were contracts for the disposition of an interest in land and the first did, but the second did not, comply with the formalities required for the making such contracts.[15] The second agreement is not itself a valid contract to make the new disposition; and one possible view is that that agreement, not having been properly "made,"[16] is totally ineffective and so cannot operate even to rescind the first. An alternative (and, it is submitted, a preferable) view is that the second agreement is merely ineffective as a contract for the disposition of an interest in land. On this view, it can nevertheless amount to an agreement, supported by good consideration,[17]

---

[9] Our sole concern here is with this type of rescission. Formal requirements are sometimes imposed where a contract is "rescinded" without the consent of a party because of his failure in performance: *post*, p. 681 n. 15.

[10] *Ante*, pp. 93–98.

[11] *Cf. Morris* v. *Baron & Co.* [1918] A.C. 1.

[12] Law of Property (Miscellaneous Provisions) Act 1989, s.2(1) (*ante*, p. 163) provides that such a contract shall be "*made* in writing" and says nothing about how it can be *unmade*.

[13] *Ante*, p. 170.

[14] See *Morris* v. *Baron & Co.*, *supra*; *Goman* v. *Salisbury* (1648) 1 Vern. 240.

[15] *Supra*, n. 12.

[16] Law of Property (Miscellaneous Provisions) Act 1989, s.2(1).

[17] *Ante*, p. 94.

to rescind the first contract.[18] Hence the first contract is rescinded but the second is not binding.

At common law, a deed could only be rescinded by deed,[19] but this rule did not apply in equity, which now prevails.[20]

2. Variation

Difficult problems used frequently to arise out of oral variations of contracts which had to be evidenced in writing. Many of the cases concern contracts which can now be made orally,[21] or which must now be made in writing[22]; but the rules laid down in them continue to apply to contracts which still have to be in, or evidenced in, writing.[23]

An oral variation of a contract which had to be evidenced in writing could be regarded as a rescission of the old contract, followed by the making of a new one affecting the same subject-matter. If so, the old contract was effectively rescinded, but the new one could not be enforced for want of writing.[24] Alternatively, it could be said that the parties had simply tried to vary a term, or to add one to the original contract. If so, the original contract remained in force, but the variation, being oral, had no effect. In this sense, a contract which had to be evidenced in writing could not be varied orally. For example, a written guarantee may provide that the guarantor was only to be liable if the creditor gave notice of the debtor's default within one week of its occurrence. If the guarantor then says orally that he will not insist on this requirement, that oral variation does not have contractual force.[25] It seems that the position would be the same in the case of an oral variation of a contract which must be made in writing: for example, where a written contract for the sale of land required the vendor to make good title, and the purchaser later said orally that he would not insist on good title being made to part of the land.[26] This oral statement would not have contractual force; it therefore would not, in an action by the vendor for the price, prevent the purchaser from raising the defence that good title to the whole had not been made.[27]

In the above examples, the result would have been the same if the sub-

---

[18] The mere rescission of a contract for the disposition of an interest in land does not itself appear to amount to a "disposition": see the definition of "disposition" in Law of Property Act 1925, s.205(i)(ii), incorporated into Law of Property (Miscellaneous Provisions) Act 1989 by s.2(6) of the latter Act.

[19] *West* v. *Blakeway* (1841) 2 Man. & G. 729; *Spence* v. *Healey* (1853) 8 Ex. 668. The rule applied whether or not the contract was by law required to be made by deed.

[20] *Berry* v. *Berry* [1929] 2 K.B. 316, 319.

[21] *i.e.* since the Law Reform (Enforcement of Contracts) Act 1954: *ante*, p. 165.

[22] Law of Property (Miscellaneous Provisions) Act 1989, s.2(1).

[23] *Ante*, pp. 162–167.

[24] *Morris* v. *Baron & Co.* [1918] A.C. 1. *Robinson* v. *Page* (1826) 3 Russ. 114; *Tyers* v. *Rosedale & Ferryhill Iron Co. Ltd.* (1875) L.R. 10 Ex. 195.

[25] Example based on *Goss* v. *Nugent* (1835) 5 B. & Ad. 58, where the contract was one for the disposition of an interest in land which then only required to be evidenced (not made) in writing.

[26] These were the facts of *Goss* v. *Nugent*, *supra*.

[27] On the facts of the example given in the text, it seems that the vendor could not rely on "waiver" or "promissory estoppel" since those doctrines do not create causes of action (*ante*, p. 107); and since, on the bare facts stated, there is in any case no reliance by the vendor on the subsequent agreement nor are there circumstances making it "inequitable" for the purchaser to reassert his rights (see *ante*, pp. 106, 124).

sequent oral agreement had been regarded as a rescission: the guarantor or purchaser would not have been *liable* on the original contract because it was rescinded, nor under the new agreement because it was oral. But the distinction between (on the one hand) a rescission followed by a new agreement and (on the other) a variation would have been crucial if it had been the guarantor or the purchaser who been suing to assert *rights* under the original contract.[28] Had the oral agreement been a rescission, he would have failed. Had it been a variation, he could have sued on the original agreement: this would have remained in force,[29] and the subsequent oral agreement would not have been effective to vary it, though it might have had some effect as a waiver (in the sense of forbearance), or in equity.[30]

Whether a subsequent agreement is a rescission or a variation depends on the extent to which it departs from the original agreement. It is a rescission if it alters the original agreement in some essential way; but if it does not go "to the very root of the original contract"[31] it is only a variation. The distinction is one of degree. In *Morris* v. *Baron & Co.*[32] a dispute arising out of a contract for the sale of goods (which then had to be evidenced in writing) was orally compromised: it was agreed that the buyer should have extra time to pay and that he should have an option whether he would take the goods not yet delivered. This compromise was held to be a rescission as it dealt with an essential matter, the quantity of goods to be delivered. On the other hand, alterations in the place and time of delivery have been held to be variations only, so that the original agreements could still be enforced.[33]

The foregoing discussion concerns contracts which are subject to some formal requirement imposed by law. If, however, a contract which is not subject to any such legal requirement merely happens to have been executed in writing or by deed, it can be varied informally. At common law, indeed, a deed could not be varied except by another deed; but this rule did not apply in equity which now prevails. Accordingly it was held in *Berry* v. *Berry*[34] that a separation agreement which had been made by deed (though there was no legal requirement that it should be so made) could be varied by a subsequent agreement that was not made by deed. Later cases apply this rule where the original contract *was* by law required to be made by deed.[35] These decisions are hard to reconcile with the reasoning of cases which hold that a contract required to be evidenced in writing cannot be

---

[28] *e.g.* if in *Goss* v. *Nugent*, *supra* n. 25, the *purchaser* had been suing to enforce the original contract; or if a guarantee had contained a promise by the creditor to advance at least £1m, to the debtor and the guarantor were claiming damages for loss suffered by himself (*e.g.* as shareholder of a debtor company) for breach of his undertaking.

[29] *Robinson* v. *Page* (1826) 3 Russ. 114; *Tyers* v. *Rosedale & Ferryhill Iron Co. Ltd.* (1875) L.R. 10 Ex. 195.

[30] *Ante*, pp. 101 *et seq.*

[31] *British and Beningtons Ltd.* v. *N.W. Cachar Tea Co.* [1923] A.C. 48, 68.

[32] [1918] A.C. 1.

[33] *e.g.* the *British and Beningtons* case, *supra*; *Hickman* v. *Haynes* (1875) L.R. 10 C.P. 598; *The Arawa* [1980] 2 Lloyd's Rep. 135; *cf. United Dominions Corp. (Jamaica) Ltd.* v. *Shoucair* [1969] 1 A.C. 340 (temporary variation in rate of interest held not to amount to rescission of a mortgage).

[34] [1929] 2 K.B. 316.

[35] *Plymouth Corporation* v. *Harvey* [1971] 1 W.L.R. 549 (lease for seven years), and possibly *Mitas* v. *Hyams* [1951] 2 T.L.R. 1215 (where the length of the lease is not stated).

varied orally.[36] They are best explained on the ground that, though the variations were not contractually binding, they nevertheless had a limited effect under the rules of waiver in the sense of forbearance,[37] or in equity.[38]

[36] *e.g. Goss* v. *Nugent* (1833) 5 B. & Ad. 58; *Morris* v. *Baron & Co.* [1918] A.C. 1, *supra.*
[37] *Ante*, p. 99.
[38] *Ante*, pp. 101 *et seq.*

CHAPTER SIX

THE CONTENTS OF A CONTRACT

THE contents of a contract depend primarily on the words used by the parties in entering into the contract: these make up its express terms. A contract may, in addition, contain terms which are not expressly stated, but which are implied, either because the parties so intended, or by operation of law, or by custom or usage.

SECTION 1. EXPRESS TERMS

Where a contract is made orally, the ascertainment of its terms raises in the first place the pure question of fact: what did the parties say? Once this has been determined, a further question can arise as to the meaning of the words used. In answering this question, the court applies the objective test of agreement. Under that test, a party cannot enforce the contract in the sense which he gave to the words, if that sense differs from the one which the other party reasonably gave to them.[1]

Further difficulties in ascertaining the express terms of a contract can arise where a contract is, or appears to be, reduced to writing.

1. Joinder of Documents

(1) Incorporation by express reference

The terms of a contract may be contained in more than one document. One of these may expressly refer to another,[2] *e.g.* where a contract is made subject to standard terms settled by a trade association. Those terms are then incorporated by reference into the contract; if there are several editions of the standard terms, the contract is prima facie taken to refer to the most recent edition.[3] It may also incorporate amendments validly made by the association.[4]

The parties may purport to incorporate one document in another by express reference, not realising that the terms of the two documents conflict. In *Adamastos Shipping Co.* v. *Anglo-Saxon Petroleum Co.*[5] clause 1 of a charterparty provided: "This bill of lading shall have effect subject to the Carriage of Goods by Sea Act of the United States 1936, which shall be deemed to be incorporated herein. . . . " The object of this clause was to reduce the shipowner's duty to provide a seaworthy ship from the absolute duty existing at common law to that of due diligence imposed by the Act.[6] But section 5 of the Act stated that its provisions "shall not be applicable to

[1] *Eyre* v. *Measday* [1986] 1 All E.R. 488; *Thake* v. *Maurice* [1986] Q.B. 644; Grubb [1986] C.L.J. 197; *post*, p. 740.

[2] *Cf.* Law of Property (Miscellaneous Provisions) Act 1989, s.2(2).

[3] *Smith* v. *South Wales Switchgear Ltd.* [1978] 1 W.L.R. 165.

[4] *Shearson Lehman Hutton Inc.* v. *Maclaine Watson & Co.* [1989] 2 Lloyd's Rep. 570, 589.

[5] [1959] A.C. 133; applied in *The Oceanic Amity* [1984] 2 All E.R. 140.

[6] *Cf.* Carriage of Goods by Sea Act 1971, s.3 and Sched., Art. III.(1)(a).

charterparties. . . . " Two difficulties arose out of this contract. First, the parties had described their contract as "this bill of lading" when it was a charterparty; but, as this was a simple mistake, it was held that the phrase could be taken to mean "this charterparty." Secondly, the parties had apparently provided that the charterparty was to take effect subject to an Act which expressly provided that it did *not* apply to charterparties. The House of Lords could have held the whole contract meaningless or rejected clause 1 of the charterparty, or rejected section 5 of the United States Act. The House chose the last course, and so gave effect to the intention of the parties that there should be a contract under which the shipowner was only bound to use due diligence to provide a seaworthy ship. The case is a good illustration of the anxiety of the courts to make sense, if possible, of loosely and sometimes carelessly drafted commercial documents.

(2) No express reference

A contract may be contained in several documents even though one does not expressly refer to the other. Suppose, for example, that a series of dealings takes place under a "master contract," a formal document being executed each time an individual contract is made. All these contracts may be subject to the master contract, even though they do not refer to it.[7] Similarly, a policy of insurance can be read together with the rules of the mutual insurance society which had issued it,[8] although the policy does not expressly refer to the rules,[9] and a contract to purchase securities may be held to incorporate the terms of a prospectus on the faith of which they were bought.[10] Such incorporation without express reference appears to depend on the intention of the parties, determined in accordance with the objective test of agreement.

2. The Parol Evidence Rule

(1) Statement of the rule

The parol evidence rule states that evidence cannot be admitted (or that, even if admitted, it cannot be used) to add to, vary or contradict a written instrument.[11] In relation to contracts, the rule means that, where a contract has been reduced to writing, neither party can rely on evidence of terms alleged to have been agreed, which is extrinsic to the contractual document, *i.e.* not contained in it. Although the rule is generally stated as applying to *parol* evidence, it applies just as much to other forms of extrinsic evidence. Of course if a contractual document incorporates another document by reference, evidence of the second document is admissible,

---

[7] *Panorama Developments (Guildford) Ltd.* v. *Fidelis Furnishing Fabrics Ltd.* [1971] 2 Q.B. 711.

[8] *Edwards* v. *Aberayron Insurance Society Ltd.* (1876) 1 Q.B.D. 563.

[9] For difficulties relating to joinder where contracts have to be evidenced in writing, see *ante*, pp. 169–170.

[10] *Jacobs* v. *Batavia & General Plantations Trust Ltd.* [1924] 1 Ch. 287; affirmed [1924] 2 Ch. 329; another possible explanation of the case is that there was a collateral contract: *post*, p. 183.

[11] *Jacobs* v. *Batavia & General Plantations Trust Ltd.* [1924] 1 Ch. 287, 295. For a recent statement of the rule, see *Rabin* v. *Gerson Berger Association Ltd.* [1986] 1 W.L.R. 526, 531, 537.

but the rule prevents a party from relying on evidence that is extrinsic to both documents.[12]

There are obvious grounds of convenience for the application of the parol evidence rule to contracts: certainty is promoted by holding that parties who have reduced a contract to writing should be bound by the writing and by the writing alone.[13] On the other hand, the parol evidence rule will in practice be invoked where a dispute arises after the time of contracting as to what was actually said at that time; and in such cases one of the parties could feel aggrieved if evidence on the point were excluded merely because the disputed term was not set out in the contractual document. Evidence extrinsic to the document is therefore admitted in a number of situations (to be discussed below) which fall outside the scope of the rule.

(2) Cases in which extrinsic evidence is admissible

(a) WRITTEN AGREEMENT NOT THE WHOLE AGREEMENT. When a contract is reduced to writing, there is a presumption that the writing was intended to include all the terms of the contract; but this presumption is rebuttable.[14] If the written document was not intended to set out all the terms on which the parties had actually agreed extrinsic evidence of it is admissible. In *Allen* v. *Pink*[15] the buyer of a horse received a note as follows: "Bought of G. Pink, a horse for the sum of £7 2s. 6d. G. Pink." Evidence of an oral warranty that the horse would go quietly in harness was admitted as the note was "meant merely as a memorandum of the transaction, or as an informal receipt for the money, not as containing the terms of the contract itself." This case should be contrasted with *Hutton* v. *Watling*[16] where a document was headed "To sale of a business," set out a number of terms, contained a receipt for the price of the goodwill, and was signed over a 6d. stamp. In an action by the purchaser to enforce one of the clauses of the written document, the vendor argued that the document was only a memorandum of a provisional agreement for the sale of goodwill, which had already been fully performed. Evidence to this effect was held inadmissible as the document was not intended to be a mere memorandum but a "true record of the contract."[17] It seems that a document which is simply intended to form a record of a previously concluded contract will prima facie be a mere memorandum[18]; while a document the execution of which marks the actual conclusion of a contract is more likely to be taken to contain all the terms of the contract.

It has been argued that the right of a party to rely on extrinsic evidence

---

[12] *Jacobs* v. *Batavia & General Plantations Trust Ltd., supra.*

[13] *Rabin* v. *Gerson Berger Association Ltd.* [1986] 1 W.L.R. 526, 534, 537.

[14] *Gillespie Bros. & Co.* v. *Cheney, Eggar & Co.* [1896] 2 Q.B. 59, 62.

[15] (1838) 4 M. & W. 140; *cf. Harris* v. *Rickett* (1859) 4 H. & N. 1; *Malpas* v. *L. & S. W. Ry. Co.* (1866) L.R. 1 C.P. 336; *Roe* v. *R. A. Naylor Ltd.* (1918) 87 L.J.K.B. 958; *J. Evans & Son (Portsmouth) Ltd.* v. *Andrea Merzario* [1976] 1 W.L.R. 1078, 1083; *Yani Haryanto* v. *E. D. & F. Man (Sugar) Ltd.* [1986] 2 Lloyd's Rep. 44, 46–47; *Anangel Atlas Compania Naviera S.A.* v. *Ishikawajima-Harima Heavy Industries Co. Ltd. (No. 2)* [1990] 2 Lloyd's Rep. 526, 545; *Guardian Ocean Cargoes Ltd.* v. *Banco do Brasil, The Times*, February 27, 1991.

[16] [1948] Ch. 398.

[17] [1948] Ch. 398, at p. 404.

[18] This view would account for the special position of bills of lading: as to this see *Leduc* v. *Ward* (1888) 20 Q.B.D. 475; *S.S. Ardennes (Cargo-Owners)* v. *S.S. Ardennes (Owners)* [1951] 1 K.B. 55.

in the present group of cases turns the parol evidence rule (as applied to contracts) into "no more than a circular statement."[19] For if the rule only applies where the written document is intended to contain *all* the terms of the contract, evidence of other terms would be useless even if admitted (since *ex hypothesi* they would not form part of the contract); while the rule never prevents a party from relying on evidence of terms which *were* intended to be part of the contract. Accordingly, on this view, no injustice is caused by the operation of the rule.[20] There is much force in this view in cases in which, at the time of contracting, both parties actually shared a common intention. But in most cases in which the rule is invoked this is not the position: the dispute arises precisely because the parties had different intentions, and one alleges, while the other denies, that terms not set out in the document were intended to form part of the contract. In such cases, the court will attach importance to the appearance of the document: if it *looks* like a complete contract to one of the parties taking a reasonable view of it, it will prevent the other party from relying on extrinsic evidence to show that the contract also contained other terms.[21] This result has been described as being simply an application of the objective test of agreement[22]; but, even if it can be so regarded, it is such a common and frequently recurring application of this test as to amount to an independent rule. In cases of the present kind, moreover, the law goes beyond the normal objective test. That test normally requires the party relying on it to prove that he reasonably believed that the other party was contracting on the terms alleged.[23] Where a document *looks* like a complete contract, the party relying on it does not have to prove that he had such a belief: he can rely on a presumption to that effect which it is up to the other party to rebut.[24] As laymen are known to attach greater importance than the law does to writing in a contractual context, it will be hard for the party relying on extrinsic evidence to rebut the presumption that the written document was an exclusive record of the terms agreed. Moreover, the objective test normally prevents a party from relying on his "private but uncommunicated intention as to what was to be agreed."[25] The presumption that applies in the case of an apparently complete contractual document goes beyond this: it prevents a party from relying on evidence of intention that was not "private and uncommunicated" at all, but simply not recorded in the document. For these reasons, it is submitted that the admissibility of extrinsic evidence, where it is proved that the document was not in fact intended to contain all the terms of the contract, does not turn the rule into a merely "circular statement." Whether it also supports the conclusion that the rule is not one that "could lead to evidence being unjustly excluded"[26] is perhaps more doubtful. The primary purpose of the rule, like that of the objective test of agreement, is to promote certainty, sometimes even at the expense of justice. Where the parties have brought into being an apparently complete

---

[19] Law Commission Report on *The Parol Evidence Rule* (Law Com. No. 154), para. 2.7; Marston [1986] C.L.J. 192; *Wild* v. *Civil Aviation Authority* (unrep.) (1987) C.A.T. No. 85/N3/4250, *per* Ralph Gibson L.J.

[20] Law Com. No. 154, *ubi supra*; and see also para. 1.7.

[21] Wedderburn [1959] C.L.J. 58, 62, Cross on *Evidence* (7th ed.), p. 703.

[22] Law Com. No. 154, *supra*, para. 2.14, 2.17.

[23] *Ante*, pp. 1, 8.

[24] *Ante*, p. 177 at n. 14.

[25] Law Com. No. 154, *supra*, para. 2.14.

[26] *Ibid*. para. 2.7.

contractual document, the rejection of evidence of extrinsic terms that were actually agreed may cause injustice to the party relying on those terms, while the reception of such evidence may cause injustice to the other party, if he reasonably believed that the document formed an exclusive record of the contract.[27] The question is which, on balance, is the greater injustice. Where the evidence is rejected because the party relying on it cannot overcome the presumption arising from the fact that the document *looks* like a complete contract, the greater injustice would appear to lie in the exclusion of the evidence; for the presumption seems to be based on the nature and form of the document, rather than on the actual belief of the party relying on it, that it formed an exclusive record of the contract.[28]

(b) VALIDITY. The rule only prevents a party from relying on extrinsic evidence as to the contents of the contract, and not as to its validity. Such evidence can therefore be used to show that the contract was not binding for want of consideration or of contractual intention,[29] or to establish some invalidating cause such as incapacity, misrepresentation, mistake[30] or *non est factum*.[31] Evidence has similarly been held admissible to show that provisions in an agreement purporting to be a licence to occupy a room (as opposed to a lease of it) were a "mere sham"[32] in that they had failed to state the parties' true intention and had been inserted simply in an attempt to evade the Rent Act.

(c) IMPLIED TERMS. The rule only prevents a party from relying on extrinsic evidence as to the express terms of the contract. Where the contract is silent on a matter on which a term is normally implied by law, parol evidence may be given to support, or to rebut, the usual implication. Thus a buyer of coal can show that he made known to the seller the particular purpose for which he required the coal, so as to raise the implication that he relied on the seller's skill and judgment.[33] Conversely, a person who takes out a policy of marine insurance can show that the insurer knew the ship to be unseaworthy, and so negative the usual implied warranty of seaworthiness.[34]

(d) ORAL WARRANTIES. Where parties enter into a written contract of sale, the rule would prima facie prevent the buyer from relying on evidence of oral undertakings as to the quality of the subject-matter; but this appli-

---

[27] For the rejection of evidence in such circumstances, see *Hutton* v. *Watling* [1948] Ch. 398, 404; and *cf. Rabin* v. *Gerson Berger Association Ltd.* [1986] 1 W.L.R. 526 where the rule was applied to a declaration of trust but said at p. 536 to apply to contracts.

[28] The Law Commission had, before publishing the Report referred to in n. 19, *supra*, provisionally recommended the abolition of the rule: Law Commission Working Paper No. 76 (1976); *cf.* Administration of Justice Act 1982, s.21 (making extrinsic evidence admissible in certain cases for interpretation of wills).

[29] *Clever* v. *Kirkman* (1876) 33 L.T. 672; *Zahem International Construction Ltd.* v. *Nippon Kohan K.K.* [1987] 2 Lloyd's Rep. 596; *Kleinwort Benson Ltd.* v. *Malaysian Mining Corp.* [1989] 1 W.L.R. 379, 392; *Orion Inc. Co. plc* v. *Sphere Drake Ins. plc* [1990] 1 Lloyd's Rep. 465, 498.

[30] *Campbell Discount Co.* v. *Gall* [1961] 1 Q.B. 431 reversed on other points, by Consumer Credit Act 1974, s.56 and by *Branwhite* v. *Worcester Works Finance Ltd.* [1969] 1 A.C. 552; *post*, pp. 610, 933.

[31] *Roe* v. *R. A. Naylor Ltd.* (1918) 87 L.J.K.B. 958, 964; *post*, p. 291.

[32] *A.G. Securities* v. *Vaughan* [1990] 1 A.C. 417, 469, 475; *Mikeover* v. *Brady* [1989] 3 All E.R. 618, 625.

[33] *Gillespie Bros. & Co.* v. *Cheney, Eggar & Co.* [1896] 2 Q.B. 59.

[34] *Burges* v. *Wickham* (1863) 3 B. & S. 669; Blackburn J. dissented on this point.

cation of the rule is subject to two qualifications. First, an exclusion clause contained in a written contract can be overridden by an express oral warranty given at the time of sale.[35] Secondly, an oral statement of fact may operate as a misrepresentation in spite of its purported incorporation into the contract as a warranty[36]; and where this is the case, the oral statement can be used as evidence, not of the contents of the contract, but of an invalidating cause.

(e) OPERATION OF THE CONTRACT. Extrinsic evidence can be used to show that the contract does not yet operate, or that it has ceased to operate. Thus in *Pym* v. *Campbell*[37] a written agreement for the sale of a patent was drawn up, and evidence was admitted of an oral stipulation that the agreement should not *become operative* until a third party approved of the invention. It seems from the reasoning of the court that evidence of an oral stipulation that the agreement should *cease to bind* if the third party disapproved of the invention would not have been admissible. On the other hand, evidence is admissible to show that a written contract has been varied or rescinded.[38] It is not easy to deduce from the purpose of the parol evidence rule why evidence should be admissible in the first and third, but not in the second of these cases.

(f) EVIDENCE AS TO PARTIES. Extrinsic evidence can be used to show in what capacities the parties contracted. Thus in *Newell* v. *Radford*[39] the written record of a contract read "Mr. Newell, 32 sacks of culasses at 39s. 280lbs., to await orders. John Williams." Evidence was admitted that Newell was a baker and Williams' principal a flour dealer, so as to show which party was buyer and which seller.

Where a person contracts ostensibly as principal evidence is admissible to prove that he really acted as another's agent so as to entitle the latter to sue[40] unless such evidence contradicts the express description of the agent in the contract.[41] As the ostensible contracting party is in such cases personally liable even if he acted as agent, the evidence would not normally relieve him from liability. But in *Wake* v. *Harrop*[42] an agent signed a charterparty on behalf of the charterer, but so as to make himself personally liable. He did so after an oral agreement with the shipowner that he should not be personally liable. It was held that the agent could rely on the oral agreement, if not at law, at any rate by way of equitable defence.

(g) DEFENCE TO SPECIFIC PERFORMANCE. Failure to perform an oral promise may be available as a defence when the party who made it claims

---

[35] *Post,* p. 223.

[36] Misrepresentation Act 1967, s.1(*a*); *post,* p. 336.

[37] (1856) 6 E. & B. 370. According to this report a new trial was sought on the ground of misdirection; but the other reports (25 L.J.Q.B. 277; 2 Jur.(N.S.) 641 and 4 W.R. 528) are probably more accurate in stating that it was sought on the ground of improper reception of evidence.

[38] *Morris* v. *Baron & Co.* [1918] A.C. 1; *Goss* v. *Nugent* (1833) 5 B. & Ad. 58, 65. It does not, of course, follow from the admissibility of evidence of a variation that the variation can be enforced: as to this, see *ante*, pp. 172–174.

[39] (1867) L.R. 3 C.P. 52.

[40] *Humfrey* v. *Dale* (1857) 7 E. & B. 266; *affirmed* (1858) E.B. & E. 1004.

[41] *Post,* p. 631.

[42] (1861) 6 H. & N. 768; *affirmed* 1 H. & C. 202.

specific performance of the written agreement.[43] Alternatively, in such a case, the court may have a discretion to order specific performance on the terms that the plaintiff performs the oral undertaking.[44] The authorities which support these propositions concerned contracts for the disposition of interests in land, and in such cases the contract now generally has to be made in writing by incorporating *all* its express terms in a contractual document.[45] Failure to incorporate the oral promise would therefore prevent the contract from coming into existence,[46] and would lead to the dismissal of a claim (whether for specific performance or for damages) on that ground, unless the promise could be said to take effect only as a collateral contract.[47] But the reasoning of the older authorities would still apply where specific performance was sought of a contract which was in fact in writing, even though there was no legal requirement to this effect.[48]

(h) AID TO CONSTRUCTION. Where the words of the contract are "clear," extrinsic evidence cannot be used to explain their meaning,[49] unless they have a special meaning by custom.[50] Extrinsic evidence can, on the other hand, be used to explain words or phrases which are ambiguous,[51] or which, if taken literally, make no sense,[52] as well as technical terms. There are, however, restrictions on the use of certain types of extrinsic evidence as an aid to construction. First, evidence of *prior negotiations* is generally inadmissible, being unhelpful since "It is only the final document which records a consensus."[53] If that document contains ambiguous expressions, evidence of precontract communications is however admissible to show that the parties had attached an agreed meaning to these expressions.[54] Secondly, evidence of the *conduct* of the parties *after* the making of the contract will not be admitted on the issue of construction. For if such evidence were admitted the undesirable result might follow "that a contract meant one thing the day it was signed but, by reason of subsequent events,

---

43 *Martin* v. *Pycroft* (1852) 2 D.M. & G. 785, 795; *cf. Scott* v. *Bradley* [1971] Ch. 850.

44 See *London & Birmingham Ry.* v. *Winter* (1840) Cr. & Ph. 57.

45 Law of Property (Miscellaneous Provisions) Act 1989, s.2(1), *ante*, p. 163. Before this section came into force, the contract only had to be evidenced in writing, and failure to comply with this requirement did not prevent enforcement if there had been "part performance" by the claimant: *ante*, p. 170.

46 *Ante*, p. 164.

47 *Ibid.*; *post*, p. 183.

48 *e.g.* if it was a lease for less than three years (*ante*, p. 163) or a contract for the sale of "unique" goods (*post*, pp. 905–907).

49 *Bank of New Zealand* v. *Simpson*, [1900] A.C. at p. 189; *Edward Lloyd Ltd.* v. *Sturgeon Falls Pulp Co.* (1901) 85 L.T. 162; *Lovell & Christmas Ltd.* v. *Wall* (1911) 104 L.T. 85.

50 *Post,* p. 183.

51 *Robertson* v. *Jackson* (1845) 2 C.B. 412; *Bank of New Zealand* v. *Simpson* [1900] A.C. 182; *cf. Scarfe* v. *Adams* [1981] 1 All E.R. 843; *Pao On* v. *Lau Yiu Long* [1980] A.C. 614, 631; *Forsikringsaktieselskapet Vesta* v. *Butcher* [1989] A.C. 582, 909–910; *Shearson Lehman Hutton Inc.* v. *Maclaine Watson & Co. Ltd.* [1989] 2 Lloyd's Rep. 570, 591; *Anangel Atlas Compania Naviera S.A.* v. *Ishikawajima-Harima Heavy Industries (No. 2)* [1990] 2 Lloyd's Rep. 526, 554.

52 *The Sounion* [1987] 1 Lloyd's Rep. 230 ("grates and stoves" on ships which no longer carried such implements).

53 *Prenn* v. *Simmonds* [1971] 1 W.L.R. 1381, 1384; *Arrale* v. *Costain Civil Engineering Ltd.* [1976] 1 Lloyd's Rep. 49; *The Ionio* [1985] 2 Lloyd's Rep. 271, 274; *cf. Rabin* v. *Gerson Berger Association Ltd.* [1986] 1 W.L.R. 526.

54 *The Karen Oltman* [1976] 2 Lloyd's Rep. 708; *cf. The Pacific Colocotronis* [1981] 2 Lloyd's Rep. 40.

meant something different a month or a year later."[55] Such evidence may be admissible to show what the terms of the original contract were,[56] or that the written terms were a "mere sham,"[57] or that the contract had been varied, or to raise an estoppel[58]; but it cannot be used to elucidate the original meaning of the contract. Thirdly, it has been said that evidence of the "parties' intentions"[59] will not be admitted on the issue of construction. What seems to be meant is that the purposes of the parties[60] will not be considered. So far as their intentions relate (for example) to the identity of the subject-matter, evidence of them is no doubt admissible.[61]

(i) To PROVE CUSTOM. Evidence of custom is admissible "to annex incidents to written contracts[62] in matters with respect to which they are silent."[63] It is generally said that the evidence can be used to add to, but not to contradict, the written contract. Thus the evidence cannot be used where the custom, if actually written into the contract, would make it "insensible or inconsistent."[64] For example, in *Palgrave, Brown & Son Ltd.* v. *S.S. Turid (Owners)*[65] a charterparty provided that the expenses of discharging the cargo should be borne by the charterer "as customary." A custom that these expenses should be borne by the shipowner was held to be inconsistent with the charterparty. This is a clear case; but others present more difficulty. In *Brown* v. *Byrne*[66] a bill of lading provided for payment of freight at a specified rate. The consignee claimed that he was entitled to make a customary deduction of three months' interest. One possible view was that the contract provided for payment of one sum and the custom for payment of another, so that the custom contradicted the contract. But the court held that the custom merely added to the contract, because the customary discount was calculated on the rate of freight laid down in the contract. On the other hand, in *Krall* v. *Burnett*[67] a bill of lading provided for "freight payable in London." Evidence of a custom that

---

[55] *James Miller & Partners* v. *Whitworth Street Estates (Manchester) Ltd.* [1970] A.C. 583, 603, 606; *Wickman Ltd.* v. *Schuler A.G.* [1974] A.C. 325; *cf. Houlder Bros. & Co. Ltd.* v. *Commissioners of Public Works* [1908] A.C. 276, 285; *The Good Helmsman* [1981] 1 Lloyd's Rep. 377, 416; *Macedonia Maritime Co.* v. *Austin Pickersgill Ltd., The Times*, January 26, 1989. For an exception, see *Wilson* v. *Maynard Shipbuilding Consultants A.B.* [1978] Q.B. 665, 675–676.

[56] *Ferguson* v. *Dawson & Partners (Contractors) Ltd.* [1976] 1 W.L.R. 1213; *Mears* v. *Safecar Securities Ltd.* [1983] Q.B. 54, 77.

[57] *A.G. Securities* v. *Vaughan* [1990] 1 A.C. 417, 469, 475; *Mikeover* v. *Brady* [1989] 3 All E.R. 618, 625; *ante*, p. 179.

[58] *James Miller & Partners Ltd.* v. *Whitworth Street Estates (Manchester) Ltd.* [1970] A.C. 583, 611, 615; *cf. Amalgamated Investment & Property Co. Ltd.* v. *Texas Commerce International Bank Ltd.* [1982] Q.B. 84, 119.

[59] *Prenn* v. *Simmonds, supra*, n. 53, at p. 1385; *Pritchard* v. *Briggs* [1980] Ch. 338; *The Good Helmsman* [1981] 1 Lloyd's Rep. 377, 416; *The Scaptrade* [1981] 2 Lloyd's Rep. 425, 432, affirmed without reference to this point [1983] 2 A.C. 694; *Rabin* v. *Gerson Berger Association Ltd.* [1986] 1 W.L.R. 526, 533; *Transpetrol Ltd.* v. *Transol Olieprodukten Nederland BV* [1989] 1 Lloyd's Rep. 309, 310.

[60] *Prenn* v. *Simmonds, supra,* at p. 1385.

[61] *Post,* p. 183.

[62] Including those made by deed: *Wigglesworth* v. *Dallison* (1779) 1 Doug. 201.

[63] *Hutton* v. *Warren* (1836) 1 M. & W. 466, 475.

[64] *Humfrey* v. *Dale* 7 E. & B. 266, 275; affirmed (1858) E.B. & E. 1004.

[65] [1922] 1 A.C. 397; *cf. Mowbray Robinson & Co.* v. *Rosser* (1922) 91 L.J.K.B. 524.

[66] (1854) 3 E. & B. 703.

[67] (1877) 25 W.R. 305.

this meant "freight payable *in advance*[68] in London" was rejected as inconsistent with the contract. The distinction between customs which add to and customs which contradict the written contract is in these borderline cases largely one of emphasis.

Custom can also be used as an aid to construction.[69] For this purpose, evidence of custom is admissible even though it contradicts the ordinary meaning of the words used in the contract. Thus in *Smith* v. *Wilson*[70] evidence was admitted of a local custom to show that "1,000 rabbits" meant "1,200 rabbits."

(j) TO IDENTIFY THE SUBJECT-MATTER. Extrinsic evidence is admissible to identify the subject-matter of a contract: for example, to show that "your wool" meant not only wool produced by the plaintiff but also wool produced on a neighbouring farm[71]; and to define the exact area of land conveyed where the conveyance fails to make this clear.[72] Similarly, such evidence is admissible to define the extent of a party's obligations under a contract: *e.g.* to show that a contract to pump oil out of a stranded tanker only obliged the party rendering the service to take away so much oil as to avert the risk of pollution.[73] Where a lease contains a covenant to repair, evidence can be given as to the character of the premises in order to determine the extent of the obligation imposed by the covenant.[74] On the same principle, evidence is admissible to show whether a guarantee relates to one debt only or is a continuing one,[75] and to which of a number of transactions a guarantee relates.[76]

(k) RECTIFICATION. A document may be meant to record a previous oral agreement, but fail accurately to do so. Such a document can sometimes be rectified, *i.e.* brought into line with the previous oral agreement.[77] When this is done evidence of the previous oral agreement must inevitably be admitted. This does not mean that a party can claim rectification merely by alleging that terms which were in fact agreed were not incorporated in the document. The remedy of rectification is based on a *mistake* in the recording of a previous oral agreement.[78] In most of the cases in which the parol evidence rule is invoked the parties make no such mistake: they know perfectly well that the extrinsic term is not incorporated in the document, so that rectification is not available.

(l) COLLATERAL AGREEMENTS.[79] Even where extrinsic evidence cannot be used to vary, add to or contradict the terms of a written agreement, it may

---

[68] And thus payable even though the ship failed to reach its destination: *post*, p. 816.
[69] *e.g. Norden Steam Co.* v. *Dempsey* (1876) 1 C.P.D. 654; *cf. Robertson* v. *Jackson* (1845) 2 C.B. 412.
[70] (1832) 3 B. & Ad. 728.
[71] *Macdonald* v. *Longbottom* (1859) 1 E. & E. 977.
[72] *Scarfe* v. *Adams* [1981] 1 All E.R. 843.
[73] *The Pacific Colocotronis* [1981] 2 Lloyd's Rep. 40; *cf. Essex C.C.* v. *Ellam* [1989] 2 All E.R. 494 (evidence admissible as to legal nature of payments made under covenant).
[74] *Burges* v. *Wickham* (1863) 3 B. & S. 669, 698.
[75] *Heffield* v. *Meadows* (1869) L.R. 4 C.P. 595.
[76] *Perrylease Ltd.* v. *Imecar Ltd.* [1988] 1 W.L.R. 463.
[77] *Post*, pp. 285 *et seq.*
[78] *Post*, p. 285; *cf. Rabin* v. *Gerson Berger Association Ltd.* [1986] 1 W.L.R. 526, 534.
[79] See also *ante*, p. 164 and *post*, pp. 319–320.

be possible to show that the parties made two related contracts, one written and the other oral. In *Mann* v. *Nunn*[80] the plaintiff orally agreed to take a lease of the defendant's premises if the defendant would first do certain repairs. A written agreement was later executed, but did not refer to the defendant's promise to do the repairs. The plaintiff was nonetheless able to enforce this promise. "The parol agreement neither alters nor adds to the written one, but is an independent agreement."[81]

Thus evidence is admissible if it proves an "independent agreement"; but it is often hard to say whether the evidence has this effect or whether it varies, or adds to, the terms of the main contract. The test seems to be whether the evidence relates to a term which would go to the essence of the whole transaction: if so, it cannot be regarded as evidence of a collateral contract and will be inadmissible.[82]

In *Mann* v. *Nunn* the lease contained no provisions as to putting the premises in repair, so that the landlord's promise merely *added* to it. According to two later cases, evidence of a collateral contract is inadmissible if it *varies* or *contradicts* a term actually set out in the main written contract. In the first,[83] a lease of a furnished house specified the furniture to be included. Evidence of a collateral agreement, made before the lease, to put in more furniture, was held inadmissible. In the second,[84] rent under a lease was payable quarterly in advance. Evidence of a collateral agreement allowing the tenant (in effect) to pay the rent in arrear was similarly held inadmissible.

On the other hand, in *City & Westminster Properties* (1934) *Ltd.* v. *Mudd*[85] a lease contained a covenant to use the premises for business purposes only. The tenant had been induced to sign it by an oral assurance that the lessors would not object to his continuing to reside on the premises (as he had done in the past). In spite of the fact that this assurance contradicted the lease, evidence of it was held admissible to prove a collateral contract. The case is hard to distinguish from the earlier authorities[86]; and it may be argued that evidence of a collateral contract should not, any more than evidence of custom,[87] be allowed to contradict the main written contract. But evidence of custom is meant to elucidate the meaning of the written document itself, and it could hardly do this by introducing contra-

---

[80] (1874) 30 L.T. 526; *cf. Walker Property Investments* (*Brighton*) *Ltd.* v. *Walker* (1947) 177 L.T. 204.

[81] *Mann* v. *Nunn, supra,* at p. 527. For other requirements of collateral contracts, see *post,* pp. 319–320.

[82] *e.g. Mitchill* v. *Lath* 160 N.E. 646 (1928) *cf.* (in the context of formal requirements) *Preece* v. *Lewis* (1963) 186 E.G. 113. Failure to incorporate in the contractual document a term which is a *collateral* contract does not make the main contract ineffective under Law of Property (Miscellaneous Provisions) Act 1989, s.2(1): see *ante*, p. 164.

[83] *Angell* v. *Duke* (1875) 32 L.T. 320; for previous proceedings in this case, see (1875) L.R. 10 Q.B. 174; *ante,* p. 165.

[84] *Henderson* v. *Arthur* [1907] 1 K.B. 10.

[85] [1959] Ch. 129; *cf. Couchman* v. *Hill* [1947] K.B. 554, where one reason for the decision was that the oral warranty was a collateral contract; and *Brikom Investments Ltd.* v. *Carr* [1979] Q.B. 467 (*ante,* p. 97), where no point as to admissibility of evidence seems to have been taken.

[86] The fact that the tenant actually *refused* to sign the lease until he was given the oral assurance may distinguish *Mudd's* case from *Angell* v. *Duke* and *Henderson* v. *Arthur, supra.*

[87] *Ante*, p. 182.

dictory terms. Evidence of a collateral agreement is not meant to determine the content or meaning of a written document, but to give effect to an independent agreement. There is no compelling reason why this agreement should not contradict the written document.

It can be argued that the collateral contract device largely destroys the parol evidence rule, especially if *Mudd*'s case is right. But some limitations on this device are imposed by the requirements that a statement only operates as a collateral contract if intended to be legally binding and is supported by separate consideration.[88] Such consideration will often be provided by the promisee's act of entering into the main contract.[89] But this act could not be consideration for the collateral promise if that promise was made *after* the conclusion of the main contract; for in that case the act would be no more than past consideration[90] for the collateral contract.

(m) CONSIDERATION. In *Turner* v. *Forwood*[91] a person assigned a debt due to him from a company to one of its directors by a deed stated to have been made for a nominal consideration. It was held that evidence was admissible to show that there was a substantial consideration for the assignment.[92] This evidence did not really contradict the deed as the nominal consideration was only mentioned as a matter of form.[93] Where an agreement states a substantial consideration, evidence of *additional* consideration is also admissible, so long as it does not contradict that stated in the written agreement.[94]

SECTION 2. IMPLIED TERMS[95]

Implied terms may be divided into three groups. The first consists of terms implied in fact, that is, terms which were not expressly set out in the contract, but which the parties must have intended to include. The second consists of terms implied in law, that is, terms imported by operation of law, although the parties may not have intended to include them. The third consists of terms implied by custom.

1. Terms Implied in Fact

The principle on which a court acts in implying terms in fact has been stated by MacKinnon L.J. as follows: "Prima facie that which in any contract is left to be implied and need not be expressed is something so obvious that it goes without saying; so that, if while the parties were making their bargain, an officious bystander were to suggest some express provision for it in the agreement, they would testily suppress him with a

---

[88] *Ante*, p. 149; *post*, p. 320.
[89] *e.g.* in *City of Westminster Properties (1934) Ltd.* v. *Mudd* [1959] Ch. 129.
[90] *Ante*, p. 73.
[91] [1951] 1 All E.R. 746.
[92] *Cf. ante*, p. 71.
[93] *i.e.* to avoid the implication of a use: *Cross on Evidence*, (7th ed.), p. 701.
[94] *Pao On* v. *Lau Yiu Long* [1980] A.C. 614, 631.
[95] Lücke, 5 Adelaide L.Rev. 31.

common 'Oh, of course!' "[96] For example, in one case[97] a vendor of land undertook that, if he later *sold* certain adjoining land, he would give the purchaser the "first refusal" of it. A term was implied to prevent the vendor from defeating the purchaser's expectation by disposing of the land to a third party by way of *gift*.

The implication of a term in fact is also often said to be subject to a test of "business efficacy." Thus such a term has been described by Lord Wright as one "of which it can be predicated that 'it goes without saying,' some term not expressed but necessary to give the transaction such business efficacy as the parties must have intended."[98] The relationship between this "business efficacy" test and MacKinnon L.J.'s "officious bystander" test is, however, not entirely clear. One view is that *both* tests must be satisfied: in other words, that the party seeking to establish the term must show "that the implication was necessary, that the contract would have made no sense without it, *and* that the term was omitted . . . because it was so obvious that there was no need to make it explicit."[99] But if it can be established, as a matter of fact, that both parties regarded the term as obvious and would have accepted it, had it been put to them at the time of contracting, that should suffice to support the implication of the term in fact; for the purpose of such an implication is simply "to give effect to the intention of the parties."[1] A second view is that it is sufficient to satisfy *either* test, so that "a term will be implied only where it is necessary in a business sense to give efficacy to a contract *or* where the term is one which the parties must obviously have intended."[2] This view in turn gives rise to difficulty where it is clear that one party (at least) would *not* have agreed to the term, even though a reasonable person would have regarded it as necessary to give business efficacy to the contract. In such a case, there seems to be no room for an implication in fact; for the implication would clearly not "give effect to the intention of the parties."[3] It is submitted that, in the present context, "business efficacy" is merely a practical test for determining the intention of the parties: in most cases, it can be assumed that they would have agreed to a term which is necessary to make their agreement work. This seems to be the meaning of Lord Wright's

---

[96] *Shirlaw* v. *Southern Foundries (1926) Ltd.* [1939] 2 K.B. 206, 227 (affirmed [1940] A.C. 701); *cf. Comptoir Commercial Anversois* v. *Power, Son & Co.* [1920] 1 K.B. 868, 899–900; MacKinnon L.J.'s test is viewed with some scepticism in *The Manifest Lipkowy* [1989] 2 Lloyd's Rep. 138, 142, but (*semble*) approved *ibid.* at p. 143. In *The Bonde* [1991] 1 Lloyd's Rep. 136, 145 the officious bystander is, unusually, regarded as answering, rather than as posing, the question assumed to have been put.

[97] *Gardner* v. *Coutts & Co.* [1968] 1 W.L.R. 173; *cf. Vosper Thorneycroft* v. *Minister of Defence* [1976] 1 Lloyd's Rep. 58; *Essoldo* v. *Ladbroke Group, The Times*, December 26, 1976; *Bournemouth & Boscombe Athletic F.C.* v. *Manchester United F.C., The Times*, May 22, 1980; *Fraser* v. *Thames Television Ltd.* [1984] Q.B. 44, 57; *The Dadomar General T.J. Park* [1986] 2 Lloyd's Rep. 68.

[98] *Luxor (Eastbourne) Ltd.* v. *Cooper* [1941] A.C. 108, 137; *cf. Comptoir Commercial Anversois* v. *Power, Son & Co.* [1920] 1 K.B. 868, 899–900; *Barclays Bank plc* v. *Taylor* [1989] 1 W.L.R. 1066, 1074; Burrows, 3 N.Z.U.L.R. 121.

[99] *Stubbs* v. *Trower Still and King* [1987] I.R.L.R. 321, 324 (emphasis added).

[1] *Luxor (Eastbourne) Ltd.* v. *Cooper* [1941] A.C. 108, 137.

[2] *The Manifest Lipkowy* [1989] 2 Lloyd's Rep. 138, 143 (emphasis added) and 144; *cf. The C Joyce* [1986] 2 All E.R. 177, 182; *Barrett* v. *Lounava (1982) Ltd.* [1990] 1 Q.B. 348, 355: *The Choko Star* [1990] 1 Lloyd's Rep. 516, 524, 526.

[3] *Luxor (Eastbourne) Ltd.* v. *Cooper*, *supra* at n. 1.

statement (quoted above) in which the two tests are stated in apposition and evidently regarded as meaning much the same thing.[4] It follows that, as a general rule, satisfaction of either test is sufficient; but that satisfaction of the "business efficacy" test will not itself support an implication in fact where the "officious bystander" test is actually negatived by evidence.

The "business efficacy" test also serves to emphasise the fact that the courts will not imply a term merely because it would be reasonable to do so[5]; "they will not . . . improve the contract which the parties have made for themselves, however desirable the improvement might be."[6] The standard of reasonableness may, indeed, be used in interpreting *express* terms that are imprecise or ambiguous[7]; but the test for implying a new term in fact is to ask whether the parties would have agreed to it—not whether it would have been reasonable for them to have done so. It follows that a term cannot be implied in fact if it actually conflicts with the express terms of the contract[8]; and the courts are also reluctant to imply a term "where the parties have entered into a carefully drafted written contract containing detailed terms agreed between them."[9] Although the contrary is sometimes suggested,[10] the test of implication under the officious bystander test is subjective: what would the parties have agreed?—not what would a reasonable person in their position have agreed? This view is supported by the fact that attempts to imply terms in fact commonly fail for one of two further reasons.

First, one of the parties may simply not know of the matter to be implied or of the facts on which the implication is to be based.[11] For example, in *Spring* v. *N.A.S.D.S.*[12] a trade union argued that it was an implied term of its contract with one of its members that the union should be able to comply with the Bridlington agreement which regulated the transfer of members from one union to another. The argument was rejected on the ground that, if the member had been asked whether he had agreed to allow the union to comply with the Bridlington agreement, his reply would more probably have been a puzzled "What's that?" than a testy "Oh, of

---

[4] *Cf. K. C. Sethia (1944) Ltd.* v. *Partabmull Rameshwar* [1950] 1 All E.R. 51, 59 (affirmed [1951] 2 Lloyd's Rep. 89): "unless, considering the matter from the point of view of business efficacy, it is clear that both parties intended a given term to operate"; *The Good Luck* [1989] 2 Lloyd's Rep. 238, 268 (revsd. on other grounds, *The Times*, May 17, 1991): "what would the parties, if asked, have said, *also known* as the business efficacy test" (emphasis added); *The Bonde* [1991] 1 Lloyd's Rep. 136, 145.

[5] *Reigate* v. *Union Manufacturing Co. (Ramsbottom) Ltd.* [1918] 1 K.B. 592, 605; *Bandar Property Holdings Ltd.* v. *J. S. Darwen (Successors) Ltd.* [1968] 2 All E.R. 305; *Lupton* v. *Potts* [1969] 1 W.L.R. 1749; *Liverpool City Council* v. *Irwin* [1977] A.C. 239; *Duke of Westminster* v. *Guild* [1985] Q.B. 688, 698; *The Mammoth Pine* [1986] 3 All E.R. 767, 770.

[6] *Trollope & Colls Ltd.* v. *N.W. Metropolitan Hospital Board* [1973] 1 W.L.R. 601, 609.

[7] *Paula Lee Ltd.* v. *Robert Zehil & Co. Ltd.* [1983] 2 All E.R. 390; *cf. ante*, p. 49.

[8] *Duke of Westminster* v. *Guild* [1985] Q.B. 688, 700. *Cf. Johnston* v. *Bloomsbury Health Authority* [1991] I.R.L.R. 118, *per* Legatt L.J. and Browne-Wilkinson V.C.

[9] *Shell U.K. Ltd.* v. *Lostock Garages Ltd.* [1976] 1 W.L.R. 1187, 1200; *Duke of Westminster* v. *Guild* [1985] Q.B. 688; contrast *Associated Japanese Bank (Internatinal)* v. *Crédit du Nord SA* [1989] 1 W.L.R. 255; *The Maira (No. 3)* [1988] 2 Lloyd's Rep. 126, revsd. on other grounds [1990] 1 A.C. 637.

[10] *e.g. The Dadomar General T.J. Park* [1986] 2 Lloyd's Rep. 68, 70 ("reasonable men faced with the suggested term . . . "); *cf. Fal Bunkering of Sharjah* v. *Grecale Inc. of Panama* [1990] 1 Lloyd's Rep. 369, 372–373 (where both tests would have led to the same result).

[11] *McCutcheon* v. *David MacBrayne Ltd.* [1964] 1 W.L.R. 125, 128, 134.

[12] [1956] 1 W.L.R. 585.

course."[13] Again, in *K. C. Sethia* (1944) *Ltd.* v. *Partabmull Rameshwar*[14] sellers of Indian jute to Italian buyers could not perform their contract because they failed to obtain a quota for shipment to Italy. They argued that the contract was impliedly "subject to quota," but one reason why the argument was rejected was that the buyers did not know that the sellers had no quota for Italy.

Secondly, it may not be clear that both parties would in fact have agreed to the alleged term.[15] Where their interests are opposed, an implication that may be regarded as obvious by one party may well be rejected by the other. For example, in *Luxor* (*Eastbourne*) *Ltd.* v. *Cooper*[16] the defendant had employed an estate agent to sell two cinemas and promised to pay him a commission "on completion of sale." Before the agent had effected a sale, the defendant sold the cinemas himself. It was held that no term could be implied to the effect that the defendant should not (except for good cause) refuse to sell to a person introduced by the agent, since it was not clear that both parties would have agreed to such a term. Similarly, in *Shell U.K. Ltd.* v. *Lostock Garages Ltd.*[17] a written contract provided that Shell should supply petrol and oil to the defendant garage company which undertook, (*inter alia*) to buy such goods solely from Shell.[18] During a price war, Shell reduced the price of petrol to neighbouring garages, so that the defendant could only trade at a loss. A majority of the Court of Appeal refused to imply a term that Shell should not "abnormally discriminate" against the defendant. One ground for rejecting the implication was that Shell would not have agreed to it[19]; another was that the alleged implication was too vague.[20]

The requirement that both parties must have agreed to the implication also explains another group of cases in which the courts have refused to imply a term in agency agreements that the principal will not, by going out of business, deprive the agent of a chance of earning his commission.[21] On the other hand, where a seller's agent had negotiated a sale of particular goods, a term was implied that the seller would not, by breaking that contract of sale, deprive the agent of his right to commission.[22] This implied term only made the seller liable to the agent if he broke one particular con-

---

[13] [1956] 1 W.L.R. 585 at p. 599; *cf. Spence* v. *Cosmos Air Holidays Ltd.*, *The Times*, December 6, 1989.

[14] [1950] 1 All E.R. 51 (affirmed [1951] 2 Lloyd's Rep. 89).

[15] *Attica Sea Carriers Corp.* v. *Ferrostaal Poseidon Bulk Reederei GmbH* [1976] 1 Lloyd's Rep. 250; *Frobisher* (*Second Investments*) *Ltd.* v. *Kiloran Trust Co. Ltd.* [1980] 1 W.L.R. 425; *Tadd* v. *Eastwood* [1985] I.C.R. 132.

[16] [1941] A.C. 108; *cf. Lonrho* v. *Shell Petroleum Co.* [1981] Com.L.R. 74 (affirmed without reference to the point [1981] 2 All E.R. 456).

[17] [1976] 1 W.L.R. 1187; Russell, 40 M.L.R. 582.

[18] See *post,* p. 417 as to such agreements.

[19] *Cf. The Good Luck* [1989] 2 Lloyd's Rep. 238, 273 (revsd. on other grounds, *The Times*, May 17, 1991).

[20] *Cf. Watford B.C.* v. *Watford R.D.C.* (1986) 86 L.G.R. 524, 529.

[21] *Rhodes* v. *Forwood* (1876) 1 App.Cas. 256; *cf. Hamlyn & Co.* v. *Wood* [1891] 2 Q.B. 488; *Lazarus* v. *Cairn Line Ltd.* (1912) 106 L.T. 378. Contrast cases in which the principal has expressly promised to stay in business: *Reigate's Case* [1918] 1 K.B. 592; *cf. Ogdens Ltd.* v. *Nelson* [1905] A.C. 109.

[22] *Alpha Trading Ltd.* v. *Dunshaw-Patten* [1981] Q.B. 290; *post*, p. 646. Contrast *The Manifest Lipkowy* [1989] 2 Lloyd's Rep. 138 where it was held that no such term could be implied in an arrangement between a seller and the *buyer's* agent that the commission was to be deducted from the proceeds of sale.

tract of sale. It did not otherwise restrict his freedom to go out of business, and it was therefore less likely that he would have refused to agree to it if it had been put to him at the time when the agency agreement was made.

Even where both parties accept that *some* term should be implied, an implication in fact may still fail because they disagree as to the exact formulation of that term.[23]

2. Terms Implied in Law

Many of the obligations arising out of a contract are, at any rate presumptively, determined by rules of law; and some such obligations are said to be the result of implied terms. For example, in a contract of employment the employee impliedly undertakes that he is reasonably skilled,[24] that he will faithfully serve his employer[25] and not act against the employer's interests,[26] and that he will indemnify his employer against all liabilities incurred by the employer as a result of his wrongful acts.[27] The employer, on the other hand, impliedly undertakes that he will not require the employee to do any unlawful act[28] and that he will provide safe premises.[29] Similarly, a surgeon carrying out an operation impliedly undertakes to exercise due care and skill, but he does not impliedly guarantee that the operation will achieve the desired result.[30–31]

Many terms that are implied in law have been put into statutory form. For example, a number of important terms implied into contracts for the sale of goods are stated in sections 12 to 15 of the Sale of Goods Act 1979, and similar terms are implied by statute into hire-purchase agreements,[32] other contracts for the supply of goods[33] and contracts for the supply of services.[34] The power to exclude these terms is now severely restricted by statute.[35]

This is not the place for a detailed analysis of the terms implied by law into particular types of contracts. But points of general interest arise out of the distinction between terms implied in fact, terms implied in law, and legal duties independent of implied terms.

---

23 *Abbott* v. *Sullivan* [1952] 1 K.B. 189; *Trollope & Colls Ltd.* v. *N.W. Metropolitan Hospital Bd.* [1973] 1 W.L.R. 601, 609, 610.

24 *Harmer* v. *Cornelius* (1858) 5 C.B.(N.S.) 236.

25 *Hivac Ltd.* v. *Park Royal Scientific Instruments Ltd.* [1946] Ch. 169; *cf. Secretary of State* v. *ASLEF (No. 2)* [1972] 2 Q.B. 455; *Faccenda Chicken Ltd.* v. *Fowler* [1987] Ch. 117.

26 *Wessex Dairies Ltd.* v. *Smith* [1935] 2 K.B. 80; *Sanders* v. *Parry* [1967] 1 W.L.R. 753.

27 *Lister* v. *Romford Ice & Cold Storage Co. Ltd.* [1957] A.C. 555; *post*, pp. 191–192.

28 *Gregory* v. *Ford* [1951] 1 All E.R. 121.

29 *Matthews* v. *Kuwait Bechtel Corp.* [1959] 2 Q.B. 57; Webber, (1959) 22 M.L.R. 521; Jolowicz [1959] C.L.J. 163. *Cf. Johnstone* v. *Bloomsbury Health Authority* [1991] I.R.L.R. 118 (implied undertaking not to injure employee's health). See also Employers' Liability (Defective Equipment) Act 1969.

30–31 *Eyre* v. *Measday* [1986] 1 All E.R. 488; *Thake* v. *Maurice* [1986] Q.B. 644 *post*, p. 740. In determining whether he has *expressly* given such a guarantee, the court will apply the objective test: *ante*, p. 176.

32 Supply of Goods (Supplied Terms) Act 1973, ss.8–11, as substituted by Consumer Credit Act 1974, s.112 and Sched. 4 para. 35.

33 Supply of Goods and Services Act 1982, ss.2–5, 7–10.

34 Supply of Goods and Services Act 1982, ss.13–14.

35 *Post*, pp. 229–230, 232–233.

(1) Terms implied in law distinguished from terms implied in fact

The implication of a term in fact is based on the inference that the parties intended to incorporate the term into their contracts[36]; but no such inference is necessary for the implication of a term in law.[37] This point can be illustrated in a number of ways.

(a) COMPLEXITY. Some statutory implied terms, such as the implied condition as to fitness for a particular purpose set out in section 14(3) of the Sale of Goods Act 1979, are extremely complex. If an officious bystander tried to read, and explain, this subsection to a chemist and an intending buyer of a hot-water bottle, he might be testily suppressed, but scarcely with a common "of course." And the question whether any, and if so what, term is to be implied at common law often turns on distinctions which are so subtle that they can scarcely be based on the intention of both parties.[38]

(b) CITATION OF AUTHORITIES. The question whether any, and if so what, term should be implied in law is often decided exclusively by the citation of earlier cases.[39] This is done to determine the content of a rule of law and not to ascertain the intention of the parties.

(c) NEGATIVING THE IMPLICATION. A term implied in law can sometimes be excluded by a definite contrary agreement, but it is not necessarily excluded by circumstances which would prevent the implication of a term in fact. In *Sterling Engineering Co. Ltd.* v. *Patchett*[40] it was held to be an implied term in a contract of service between an inventor and his employers that the inventor was trustee of his inventions and of the resulting patents for the employers. It was further held that this implied term could not be excluded by a mere "understanding" to the contrary, though obviously the term could not have been implied *in fact* if such an "understanding" had been proved.

(2) Implied terms as legal duties

Terms implied by law are, in truth, simply duties prima facie arising out of certain types of contracts, or, as it has been put, "legal incidents of those . . . kinds of contractual relationship."[41] It has indeed been said of such terms that "the test of implication is necessity" rather than "the imposition of a term."[42] In this respect terms implied in law might therefore seem to resemble terms implied in fact, since one test for the implication of the latter kind of terms is that the implication must be necessary to give

---

[36] This is true though the implication of even such terms may be a question of "law" in the sense that it is an inference based on primary facts: see *O'Brien* v. *Associated Fire Alarms* [1968] 1 W.L.R. 1916.

[37] For recent recognition of the distinction between the two processes, see *The Dadomar General T.J. Park* [1986] 2 Lloyd's Rep. 68, 70; *The Choko Star* [1990] 1 Lloyd's Rep. 516, 526.

[38] See, *e.g.* the contrast between *Young & Marten Ltd.* v. *McManus Childs Ltd.* [1969] 1 A.C. 454 and *Gloucestershire C.C.* v. *Richardson* [1969] 1 A.C. 480.

[39] *e.g. Yeoman Credit Ltd.* v. *Apps* [1962] 2 Q.B. 508.

[40] [1955] A.C. 534.

[41] *Mears* v. *Safecar Securities Ltd.* [1983] Q.B. 54, 78; *Johnstone* v. *Bloomsbury Health Authority* [1991] 1 I.R.L.R. 118, *per* Stuart-Smith L.J.

[42] *Tai Hing Cotton Mill Ltd.* v. *Liu Chong Hing Bank Ltd.* [1986] A.C. 80, 104–105; *Reid* v. *Rush & Tompkins Group plc* [1990] 1 W.L.R. 212, 220; *Barrett* v. *Lounava (1982) Ltd.* [1990] 1 Q.B. 348, 358–359.

business efficacy to the contract.[43] But in the context of terms implied in fact the reason for this requirement is that it provides evidence of common intention: the parties are assumed to have agreed to a term, without which their contract would not work. In the context of terms implied in law the courts do not look for any such evidence of common intention; and the view that the implication of such terms is based on "necessity" may, with respect, be doubted as a general requirement. "Necessity" cannot, for example, justify the complex implied term of fitness of goods for a particular purpose, set out in section 14(3) of the Sale of Goods Act 1979: it is perfectly possible to imagine a workable contract of sale which did not contain such a term. In other contracts, moreover, terms have been implied in law in spite of the fact that the implication was *not* necessary to give business efficacy to the contract.[44] There is, in such cases, often no practical distinction between the implication of a term in law and the imposition of a duty. One recent decision refers to a term implied in law indiscriminately as an "implied term" and as an "implied obligation"[45] and describes that obligation (to repair the outside of premises subject to a tenancy) as one which must be "imposed on"[46] the landlord. There are many other cases in which the same process can with equal plausibility be described as either the implication of a term in law or as the imposition of a legal duty. Where a term is implied in law, the two operations are, as a practical matter, indistinguishable. It is, for example, commonly said that a landlord *impliedly covenants* that his tenant shall have quiet possession, and that the tenant is under an *obligation* not to commit waste.[47] One could just as well say that the landlord was under an obligation to let the tenant have quiet possession, and that the tenant impliedly covenanted not to commit waste. Again, it is said that a party who enters into an arrangement which can only take effect if a given state of circumstances continues impliedly promises not to put an end to it.[48] But in a case in which this rule was applied, Lord Atkin said: "Personally I should not so much base the law on an implied term, as on a positive rule of the law of contract that conduct of either promisor or promisee which can be said to amount to himself 'of his motion' bringing about the impossibility of performance is in itself a breach."[49]

This point would not be worth stressing if the true nature of the inquiry before the court were not sometimes obscured by the use of the expressions "implied term" and "legal duty" to convey the same idea, and by the failure to distinguish between terms implied in fact and terms implied in law. In *Lister* v. *Romford Ice and Cold Storage Co. Ltd.*[50] a lorry driver injured a third party by negligent driving in the course of his employment. The third party recovered damages from the employers, who obtained judgment for an indemnity from the driver on the ground that he had broken the implied term in the contract of employment to drive with

---

[43] *Ante*, p. 186.
[44] See *Liverpool City Council* v. *Irwin* [1977] A.C. 239, 255, *post* pp. 192–193.
[45] *Barrett* v. *Lounava (1982) Ltd.* [1990] 1 Q.B. 348, 359.
[46] *Ibid.* p. 358.
[47] See Megarry and Wade, *Law of Real Property* (5th ed.), pp. 693, 702.
[48] *Stirling* v. *Maitland* (1864) 5 B. & S. 840.
[49] *Southern Foundries (1926) Ltd.* v. *Shirlaw* [1940] A.C. 701, 717; *cf. The Dadomar General T.J. Park* [1986] 2 Lloyd's Rep. 68, 70.
[50] [1957] A.C. 555.

proper care.[51] The driver in turn argued that the contract also contained an implied promise by the employers. This was formulated in various ways: as a promise to indemnify the driver against liability to third parties if the employers were insured, or if they were required by law to be insured, or if they ought as reasonable and prudent persons to have been insured. The House of Lords, by a majority, held that no such term could be implied. Some of the reasons given by the majority are reasons against the implication of a term *in fact*. The implication was not "precise and obvious"[52]; it was not necessary to give business efficacy to the contract[53]; and it was not clear that both parties would have agreed to it.[54] But many terms implied *in law* would fail to pass these tests. Whether such terms should be implied is not a question of intention, but one of policy. In fact the House of Lords in *Lister's* case was to a large extent concerned with considerations of policy. The argument that seems to have weighed most heavily with the majority was that it would be undesirable to allow a driver to recover an indemnity from his employer as he might then drive less carefully. Considerations of this kind always influence the implications of terms in law; but they have nothing to do with the intention of the parties, and hence with the implication of terms in fact.

The distinction between the two types of implication is clearly drawn in the later case of *Reid* v. *Rush & Tompkins Group plc*,[55] where an employee was injured, while working abroad, as a result of the fault of a third party who could not be traced. He argued that his contract of employment contained an implied term obliging his employers to warn him to insure against such risks; but the argument was rejected on two separate grounds. First, no such term *could* be implied in fact since it would not have been agreed by the parties. And secondly, no such term *should* be implied in law by the court as the exact scope of such an implication raised issues of policy which could only be resolved by the legislature.

But there may be cases in which, though no term can be implied in fact, it may be desirable to attach certain "legal incidents"[56] to a contract, or, in other words, to impose a legal duty. This point has sometimes been overlooked,[57] so that it was occasionally held that no terms *should* be implied in law merely because none *could* be implied in fact. But the distinction between the two operations is clearly illustrated in *Liverpool City Council*

---

[51] Employers' insurers have agreed not to make such claims against employees, so that the decision has little practical effect. See 272 L.T. 67 for a summary of the report of an Interdepartmental Committee set up in 1957. Semble, the validity of the alleged term would not be affected by Unfair Contract Terms Act 1977, s.4 (*post*, p. 233). since that section does not seem to apply to *implied* promises to indemnify or to cases where the liability to indemnify arises from the negligence of the promisor himself. For an unsuccessful attempt by a third party to claim the indemnity, see *Morris* v. *Ford Motor Co. Ltd.* [1973] Q.B. 792.

[52] [1957] A.C. 555, 574.

[53] At p. 583.

[54] At p. 578.

[55] [1990] 1 W.L.R. 212.

[56] *Ante*, p. 190 at n. 41.

[57] *e.g.* in *Abbott* v. *Sullivan* [1952] 1 K.B. 189 where, it is submitted, a term might well have been implied in law (though on the principle stated at *ante*, p. 189 none could be implied in fact). *The Aramis* [1989] 1 Lloyd's Rep. 213 is open to criticism on similar grounds: see Treitel, [1989] L.M.C.L.Q. 162. *Cf. John* v. *Rees* [1970] Ch. 345 where a term was implied in law.

v. *Irwin.*[58] The House of Lords there held that it was an implied term of a lease of a maisonette in a Council block that the landlord should take reasonable care to keep the common parts of the block in a reasonable state of repair. The term was clearly not implied in fact: the "officious bystander" test was not satisfied[59]; nor was the implication necessary to give business efficacy to the contract.[60] The implication arose because the nature of the relationship made it desirable to place some obligation on the landlord as to the maintenance of the common parts of the premises. It amounted to the imposition of a legal duty, in spite of the fact that no term could be implied in fact.

In deciding whether to imply a term in law, the courts are guided by general policy considerations affecting the type of contract in question; and to this extent considerations of reasonableness and fairness may enter into the implication of such terms.[61] When it is said that the courts will not imply a term into a contract merely because it is reasonable to do so[62] the reference is to a different type of operation: that of implying a term into an individual contract simply because the contract would be fairer with than without the term.[63] The courts do not regard it as their proper function to rewrite contracts in this way.[64]

(3) Doubtful cases

Sometimes it is not clear whether a particular term is implied in fact or in law. In *The Moorcock*[65] the defendants owned a wharf and made a contract to allow the plaintiffs to unload their ship at the wharf. The ship was damaged by settling at low water on a ridge of hard ground. It was held that the defendants were liable for this damage as they were in breach of an implied term that they would take reasonable care to see that the berth was safe. The case is generally regarded as the leading authority on terms implied in fact, but some passages in the judgment also refer to terms implied in law. Lord Esher M.R. said that it must be implied that the defendants had "undertaken to see that the bottom of the river is reasonably fit, or at all events that they have taken reasonable care to find out that the bottom of the river is reasonably fit for the purpose. . . ."[66] Had these alternatives been put to the parties, they might well have disagreed. This suggests that the term was not implied in fact but in law. Again, in a famous passage, Bowen L.J. said: "An implied warranty, or, as it is called, *a covenant in law* . . . is in all cases founded on the presumed intention of the parties *and upon reason*. . . . In business transactions such as this, what the law desires to effect by the implication is to give such business efficacy to the transaction as must have been intended at all events by both

[58] [1977] A.C. 239; MacIntyre [1977] C.L.J. 15; *Duke of Westminster* v. *Guild* [1985] Q.B. 688, 697–698; *Sim* v. *Rotherham M.B.C.* [1987] Ch. 216, 245.

[59] At pp. 258, 266. This was also the position in *Barrett* v. *Lounava (1982) Ltd.* [1990] 1 Q.B. 348 (where a term was nevertheless implied in law).

[60] [1977] A.C. at p. 255.

[61] *Cf. Re Charge Card Services Ltd.* [1989] Ch. 497, 513 ("What is the fair term to imply"); contrast *The Choko Star* [1990] 1 Lloyd's Rep. 516, 526 (reasonableness not sufficient).

[62] *Ante,* p. 187.

[63] [1977] A.C. 239, 258.

[64] *Ante,* p. 187.

[65] (1889) 14 P.D. 64.

[66] At p. 67.

parties who are businessmen."[67] The two italicised phrases show that Bowen L.J. was not exclusively concerned with the actual intention of the parties, on which terms implied in fact are based; and it does not seem that the "officious bystander" test[68] was satisfied. The most that could have been implied in fact was that the wharf-owner was to be under *some* obligation in relation to the safety of the berth; but the intention of the parties was not decisive in defining the precise extent of that obligation. *The Moorcock* therefore seems to illustrate the process of implication in law rather than that of implication in fact. It differs from the category of terms implied in law discussed above, in that the implication relates to a particular transaction rather than to a group of contracts; it resembles that category, however, in that the implication is based on objective criteria of reasonableness.

3. Custom or Usage

We have seen that evidence of custom is admissible to add to, but not to contradict, a *written* contract.[69] Further, *any* contract (whether written or not) may be deemed to incorporate any relevant custom of the market, trade or locality in which it is made, unless the custom is inconsistent with the express (or necessarily implied) terms, or with the nature, of the contract. In cases of such inconsistency the custom is said to be "unreasonable," and only binds a party if he knew of it. A custom which is "reasonable" binds both parties, whether they knew of it or not.[70] It is sometimes said that the incorporation of custom into a contract is based on the presumed intention of the parties,[71] but this is a somewhat unrealistic view. For the question whether a custom binds depends on whether it is "reasonable," and this question often gives rise to complex issues of law and fact on which the parties are unlikely to have a common (or any) view.[72]

The terms of collective agreements between trade unions and employers may be incorporated in the employment contracts of individual employees by express reference,[73] or by being acted on over a period of time.[74] Between employer and union, such agreements normally have no contractual force because they are not intended to be legally binding.[75] But when their terms are incorporated in individual contracts of employment, those terms can, if so intended,[76] become legally binding between employer and employee.[77] It has, moreover, been suggested that the terms of collective

---

67 At p. 68 (italics supplied).

68 *Ante*, p. 185.

69 *Ante*, p. 182.

70 *Reynolds* v. *Smith* (1893) 9 T.L.R. 494 for other illustrations, see *post*, p. 614.

71 *e.g.* in *Produce Brokers Co. Ltd.* v. *Olympia Oil & Cake Co. Ltd.* [1916] 1 A.C. 314, 324.

72 *Cf. The Maira* (*No.* 3) [1990] 1 A.C. 637, 681.

73 *Hooker* v. *Lange, Bell & Co.* [1937] 4 L.J.N.C.C.R. 199; *Camden Exhibition & Display Ltd.* v. *Lynott* [1966] 1 Q.B. 555. Special requirements exist for the incorporation of "no strikes" clauses in collective agreements into employment contracts: Trade Union and Labour Relations Act 1974, s.18(4).

74 *N.C.B.* v. *Galley* [1958] 1 W.L.R. 16.

75 *Ante*, p. 154.

76 See *N.C.B.* v. *N.U.M.* [1986] I.C.R. 736 where this intention was said to have been negatived. *Cf. Hulland* v. *Saunders* [1945] K.B. 78 (parties contracting out of collective agreement).

77 *Robertson* v. *British Gas Corp.* [1983] I.C.R. 351; *Marley* v. *Forward Trust Group*, [1986] I.C.R. 891; *Alexander* v. *Standard Telephone and Cables Ltd.* [1990] I.C.R. 291, 303.

agreements may be incorporated in contracts of employment as "crystallised custom."[78] The "custom" may be incorporated even in contracts with employees who are not members of the union which has negotiated the agreement,[79] so long as there is some evidence of intention to incorporate it.[80] Moreover, once the terms of the collective agreement have been incorporated in the contract of employment, the employee can enforce rights (*e.g.* to a minimum wage) under that contract, even after the collective agreement itself has, as between the union and the employer, been brought to an end.[81]

Terms may, again, be implied by trade usage. For example, where the owner of a crane hired it out to a contractor who was also engaged in the same business, it was held that the hirer was bound by the owner's usual terms though these were not actually communicated at the time of contracting.[82] They were, however, based on a model supplied by a trade association; and references in the judgment to the fact that they were reasonable and prevalent in the trade[83] suggest that they were incorporated on a principle similar to that which applies to customary terms.

[78] Kahn-Freund in (ed.) Flanders & Clegg, *The System of Industrial Relations in Great Britain*, Chap. 2, p. 58, and in (ed.) Kahn-Freund, *Labour Relations and the Law*, pp. 26–27; Wedderburn, *The Worker and the Law* (2nd ed.), pp. 188–197.

[79] Gayler & Purvis, *Industrial Law* (2nd ed.), p. 353.

[80] *Young* v. *Canadian Northern Ry.* [1931] A.C. 83.

[81] *Gibbons* v. *Associated British Ports Authority* [1985] I.R.L.R. 376.

[82] *British Crane Hire Corp. Ltd.* v. *Ipswich Plant Hire Ltd.* [1975] Q.B. 303; *The Ulyanovsk* [1990] 1 Lloyd's Rep. 425, 431. And see generally Hoggett, (1970) 33 M.L.R. 518.

[83] [1975] Q.B. 303, 311, 313; contrast *Salsi* v. *Jetspeed* [1977] 2 Lloyd's Rep. 57 (where there was no evidence of usage).

CHAPTER SEVEN

STANDARD FORM CONTRACTS[1]

THE terms of many contracts are set out in printed standard forms which are used for all contracts of the same kind, and are only varied so far as the circumstances of each contract require. Such terms are often settled by a trade association for use by its members for contracting with each other or with members of the outside public. Standard contract forms are even provided by legislation[2] or under statutory authority.[3]

One object of these standard forms is to save time. The work of insurers, carriers and bankers, for example, would become impossibly complicated if all the terms of every contract they made had to be newly settled for each transaction.[4] Standard form contracts are also a device for allocating contractual risks: they can be used to determine in advance who is to bear the expense of insuring against those risks[5]; and they also facilitate the quotation of differential rates: *e.g.* where a carrier's form provides for goods to be carried either at his or at the customer's risk, and the charge is adjusted accordingly. Between businessmen bargaining at arm's length such uses of standard forms can be perfectly legitimate[6]; and this may also be true where one party to the transaction is a private consumer but is nevertheless likely to have insured against the risk quite apart from the contract.[7] But a less defensible object of standard form contracts has been to exploit and abuse the superior bargaining power of commercial suppliers of goods or services when contracting with private consumers. In particular, the supplier could use the form to exclude or limit his liability, while the consumer generally could not insist on varying the terms submitted to him; indeed he might not be aware of them or understand their effect only in part, if at all. Even between businessmen, the use of unusual or very broadly drafted exemption clauses could lead to similar hardship.

To some extent, the courts were able to redress the balance in favour of parties prejudicially affected by exemption clauses in standard form con-

---

[1] Prausnitz, *The Standardisation of Commercial Contracts*; Coote, *Exception Clauses;* Yates and Hawkins, *Standard Business Contracts*; Lawson, *Exclusion Clauses* (3rd ed.).

[2] *e.g.* Companies' Articles of Association: see Companies Table A–F Regulations (1985 S.I. No. 805) as amended by Companies Table A–F (Amendment) Regulations (S.I. 1985 No. 1052).

[3] *e.g.* the Statutory Form of Conditions of Sale made by the Lord Chancellor under s.46 of the Law of Property Act 1925.

[4] *Cf.* also Schmitthoff, 17 I.C.L.Q. 551.

[5] See *The Maratha Envoy* [1978] A.C. 1, 8; *Photo Production Ltd.* v. *Securicor Transport Ltd.* [1980] A.C. 827, 843, 851; *cf. A Schroeder Music Publishing Co. Ltd.* v. *Macaulay* [1974] 1 W.L.R. 308, 316.

[6] See *Marston Excelsior Ltd.* v. *Arbuckle Smith & Co. Ltd.* [1971] 1 Lloyd's Rep. 70, 95; *Photo Production* case *supra*, at p. 851; *Ailsa Craig Fishing Co. Ltd.* v. *Malvern Fishing Co. Ltd.* [1983] 1 W.L.R. 964, 966. In some cases liability is even limited by statute: *e.g.* Merchant Shipping Act 1979, ss.17, 18 and Sched. 4; see also s.35; Carriage of Goods by Sea Act 1971, Sched. Art. IV. 5 (as amended by Merchant Shipping Act 1981, ss.2, 3).

[7] *e.g.* in the car-park cases, such as *Hollins* v. *J. Davy Ltd.* [1963] 1 Q.B. 844. Contrast *Mendelssohn* v. *Normand Ltd.* [1970] 1 Q.B. 177 (where luggage stolen from a parked car did not belong to the owner of the car).

tracts. But legislative intervention has become increasingly common, the most important changes being contained in the Unfair Contract Terms Act 1977.[8] Under this Act, many exemption clauses are either wholly ineffective or subject to a requirement of reasonableness. In a significant number of cases, however, standard form contracts and exemption clauses are not affected by the Act[9] and remain subject to the rules of common law. These therefore still require discussion, though many of the cases from which they are derived would, on their particular facts, now be differently decided under the 1977 (or some other) Act.

The legislative and judicial restrictions on the efficacy of provisions in standard form contracts are largely concerned with exemption clauses. In other cases (to be discussed at the end of this Chapter)[10] legal intervention has been less marked so that there are still situations in which it can be argued that unfair use may be made of standard form contracts.

SECTION 1. EXEMPTION CLAUSES

A party who wishes to rely on a clause excluding or limiting liability[11] must show that the clause has been incorporated in the contract, and also that, on its true construction, it covers the breach which has occurred and the resulting loss or damage. Even if he can show these things, he may still find that the clause is invalid or inoperative.

1. Incorporation in the Contract

An exemption clause can be incorporated in the contract by signature, by notice, or by course of dealing.

(1) Signature

A person who signs a contractual document is bound by its terms even though he has not read them. In *L'Estrange* v. *F. Graucob Ltd.*[12] the proprietress of a café bought an automatic cigarette vending machine. She signed, but did not read, a sales agreement which contained an exemption clause "in regrettably small print."[13] It was held that she was bound by the clause, so that she could not rely on defects in the machine, either as a defence to a claim for part of the price, or as entitling her to damages. It would have made no difference had she been a foreigner who could not read English.[14]

---

[8] *Post*, pp. 226–244.
[9] *Post*, pp. 241–244.
[10] *Post*, pp. 245–248.
[11] For the distinction between these and certain other kinds of clauses, see *post*, pp. 219–220.
[12] [1934] 2 K.B. 394; *Levison* v. *Patent Steam Cleaning Co. Ltd.* [1978] Q.B. 69; *The Polyduke* [1978] 1 Lloyd's Rep. 211; *Singer (U.K.) Ltd.* v. *Tees & Hartlepool Port Authority* [1988] 2 Lloyd's Rep. 164, 166; for criticism, see *McCutcheon* v. *David MacBrayne Ltd.* [1964] 1 W.L.R. 125, 133; *cf.* Spencer [1973] C.L.J. 104; Samek, 52 Can.Bar Rev. 351.
[13] [1934] 2 K.B. 394, 405.
[14] *The Luna* [1920] P. 22. The signer might be able to rely on the doctrine of *non est factum* (*post*, p. 291), but if this applied there would be no contract at all.

(2) Notice[15]

If the exemption clause is set out, or referred to,[16] in a document which is simply handed by one party to the other, or displayed where the contract is made, it will only be incorporated in the contract if reasonable notice of its existence is given to the party adversely affected by it. Whether such notice has been given depends on the following factors.

(a) NATURE OF THE DOCUMENT. An exemption clause is not incorporated in the contract if the document in which it is set out (or referred to) is not intended to have contractual force. In *Chapelton* v. *Barry U.D.C.*[17] the plaintiff hired a deck chair from the defendants for three hours. He paid 2d., and was given a ticket which he did not read. It was held that the defendants were not protected by an exemption clause printed on the ticket as it was a mere voucher or receipt. It did not purport to set out the conditions on which the plaintiff had hired the chair, but only to show for how long he had hired it, and that he had paid the fee.

On the other hand, a document is contractual if the party to whom it was handed knows it was intended to have this effect, or if it was delivered to him in such circumstances as to give him reasonable notice of the fact that it contained conditions.[18] The mere fact that the document is called a "receipt" will not prevent it from having contractual effect.[19] A document is also contractual if it is obvious to a reasonable person that it must have been intended to have this effect. This will be the case if the document is of a kind that generally contains contractual terms.[20] Whether a document falls into this class depends on current commercial practice, which may vary from time to time. In 1877 it was said that railway cloakroom tickets were not contractual as there was no general practice that they contained conditions.[21] But by 1951 such tickets were said to be contractual documents because most people knew that they commonly contained conditions.[22]

(b) DEGREE OF NOTICE. The party relying on the exemption clause need not show that he actually brought it to the notice of the other party, but only that he took reasonable steps to do so. The test is whether the former party took such steps[23]—not whether the latter should, in the exercise of reasonable caution, have discovered or read the clause.[24] Where the clause is printed on a ticket, it is not enough to show that the party to whom it was

---

[15] Clarke [1976] C.L.J. 451.

[16] For the sufficiency of incorporation by reference, see *Circle Freight International Ltd.* v. *Mideast Gulf Exports* [1988] 2 Lloyd's Rep. 427; *cf. ante*, p. 175.

[17] [1940] 1 K.B. 532; *cf. Henson* v. *London & North Eastern Ry.* [1946] 1 All E.R. 653; *The Eagle* [1977] 2 Lloyd's Rep. 70; Clarke [1978] C.L.J. 22.

[18] *Harling* v. *Eddy* [1951] 2 K.B. 739, 746; *Parker* v. *South Eastern Ry.* (1877) 2 C.P.D. 416; *The Polyduke* [1978] 1 Lloyd's Rep. 211.

[19] *Watkins* v. *Rymill* (1883) 10 Q.B.D. 178.

[20] *Nunan* v. *Southern Ry.* [1923] 2 K.B. 703, 707; *Thompson* v. *London, Midland & Scottish Ry.* [1930] 1 K.B. 41, 46.

[21] *Parker* v. *South Eastern Ry.*, *supra*, n. 18, at p. 424.

[22] *Alexander* v. *Railway Executive* [1951] 2 K.B. 882, 886.

[23] *Parker* v. *S.E. Ry.* (1877) 2 C.P.D. 416, 424; *cf. Burnett* v. *Westminster Bank Ltd.* [1966] 1 Q.B. 742.

[24] *Parker* v. *S.E. Ry.* (1877) 2 C.P.D. 416; *cf. Birch* v. *Thomas* [1972] 1 W.L.R. 294, a case that would now fall within Road Traffic Act 1988, s.149; *cf.* also *ibid.* s.150.

handed knew that there was writing on the ticket,[25] for the writing might not have been intended to have contractual effect.

The question whether adequate notice has been given turns principally on two factors: the steps taken to give notice and the nature of the exempting conditions.

(i) *Steps taken to give notice.* Where the notice is contained in a contractual document it is normally sufficient for the exempting condition to be prominently set out or referred to on the face of the document. In *Thompson* v. *L.M. & S. Ry.*[26] the plaintiff asked her niece to buy a railway excursion ticket for her. The ticket (which cost 2s. 7d.) had on its face the words "see back" and on the back a statement that it was issued subject to the conditions set out in the company's time-tables, which could be bought for 6d. These conditions included an exemption clause. The plaintiff could not read the words on the ticket as she was illiterate; and the jury found that the defendants had not taken reasonable steps to bring the conditions to the plaintiff's notice. But the Court of Appeal held that there was no evidence to support this finding as the notice was clear and as the ticket was a common form contractual document. Hence the exemption clause was held to be incorporated in the contract. The case is an extreme one since the time-table cost nearly a fifth of the fare paid by the plaintiff and was evidently a volume of some size, the exemption clause being set out on its 552nd page.[27] The likelihood of its being bought (let alone read) by an excursion passenger was, to say the least, remote; and it seems probable that the steps taken to incorporate the clause would not now be regarded as sufficient.[28] The principle that such a clause can be incorporated by reference[29] nevertheless seems to be a sound one. Many common contractual documents would become impossibly bulky if it were to be rejected.

On the other hand, the clause is unlikely to be incorporated if there are no words on the face of the document drawing attention to it,[30] or if the words are made illegible by a date stamp,[31] or if the exemption clause is buried in a mass of advertisements.[32] It is not necessary, *as a matter of law,* to print words such as "see back" or "see inside" on the face of the document.[33]

In *Thompson's* case, the illiteracy of the plaintiff was treated as immaterial; but the position may be different where the person relying on the clause knows or should know of the other party's disability. In an earlier case[34] some reliance was placed on the fact that the other party was a steerage passenger and so belonged to a class of persons who could not be expected to read clauses in small print. Extra steps may have to be taken to bring the notice home to a person suffering from a *known* disability: for

---

[25] This was the majority view in *Parker* v. *S.E. Ry., supra.* Bramwell L.J. dissented on this point.

[26] [1930] 1 K.B. 41; *cf. Hood* v. *Anchor Line* [1918] A.C. 837.

[27] [1930] 1 K.B. 41, 46.

[28] *Cf. The Mikhail Lermontov* [1990] 1 Lloyd's Rep. 579, 594.

[29] *Cf. Smith* v. *South Wales Switchgear Ltd.* [1978] 1 W.L.R. 165 (indemnity clause).

[30] *Henderson* v. *Stevenson* (1875) L.R. 2 Sc. & Div. 470 (where dicta that the ticket was not a contractual document are not *ratio: Harris* v. *G.W. Ry.* (1876) 1 Q.B.D. 515, 532); *Richardson, Spence & Co.* v. *Rowntree* [1894] A.C. 217.

[31] *Sugar* v. *London, Midland & Scottish Ry.* [1941] 1 All E.R. 172.

[32] *Stephen* v. *International Sleeping Car Co. Ltd.* (1903) 19 T.L.R. 620.

[33] *Burke* v. *South Eastern Ry.* (1879) 5 C.P.D. 1.

[34] *Richardson, Spence & Co.* v. *Rowntree* [1894] A.C. 217.

example translating it to a party who is known not to understand the language in which it is expressed, if such a step is reasonably practicable.[35] A person trying to incorporate the terms of a document should, however, beware of translating only part of it; for by doing this he may suggest that the rest is of no importance and so be unable to rely on it.[36]

(ii) *Nature of the clause.* The more unusual or unexpected a particular term is, the higher will be the degree of notice required to incorporate it. If the clause is of such a nature that the party adversely affected would not normally expect it, then the other party will not be able to incorporate it by simply handing over or displaying a document containing the clause. He must go further and "make it conspicuous"[37] or take other special steps to draw attention to it. For example, a person who drives his car into a car-park might expect to find in his contract a clause excluding the proprietor's liability for loss of or damage to the car. But in *Thornton* v. *Shoe Lane Parking Ltd.*[38] the car-park ticket referred to a condition purporting to exclude liability for *personal injury*.[39] It was held that adequate notice of this condition had not been given, even though the steps taken by the proprietor might have been sufficient to incorporate the more usual clauses excluding or limiting liability for property damage. As Denning L.J. had said in an earlier case: "Some clauses I have seen would need to be printed in red ink on the face of the document with a red hand pointing to it before the notice could be held to be sufficient."[40]

(c) TIME OF NOTICE. An exemption clause is only incorporated in the contract if the steps required to give notice of it are taken before or at the time of contracting. In *Olley* v. *Marlborough Court*[41] the plaintiff booked a room in the defendant's hotel. She later saw a notice in her bedroom exempting the defendants from liability for articles lost or stolen unless handed to the management for safe custody. It was held that the contract was made at the reception desk when the defendants agreed to accept the plaintiff as a guest. The notice in the bedroom could not have been seen by the plaintiff until later and was therefore not incorporated in the contract.

(3) Course of dealing

Parties may for some time have dealt with each other on terms that exempted one of them from liability and that were usually incorporated by signature or notice. On the occasion in question, however, the usual document may by some oversight not have been handed over or signed at the time of contracting; and the question then arises whether the usual exemp-

---

[35] *Geier* v. *Kujawa, Weston & Warne Bros. Transport* [1970] 1 Lloyd's Rep. 364; the notice in that case would now be invalid under Road Traffic Act 1988, s.149.

[36] *H. Glynn (Covent Garden) Ltd.* v. *Wittleder* [1959] 2 Lloyd's Rep. 409.

[37] *Crooks* v. *Allen* (1870) 5 Q.B.D. 38, 40.

[38] [1971] 2 Q.B. 163; *cf. The Eagle* [1977] 2 Lloyd's Rep. 70; *Interfoto Picture Library Ltd.* v. *Stiletto Visual Programmes Ltd.* [1989] Q.B. 433, discussed at p. 246, *post*; *Shearson Lehman Hutton Inc.* v. *Maclain Watson & Co. Ltd.* [1989] 2 Lloyd's Rep. 570, 612; Chandler and Holland, 104 L.Q.R. 359; McLean, [1988] C.L.J. 172; Macdonald [1988] J.B.L. 375 and 8 Legal Studies 48; Swanton, 1 J.C.L. 223.

[39] Where the injury is caused *by negligence* such a provision is now ineffective: *post*, p. 228.

[40] *J. Spurling Ltd.* v. *Bradshaw* [1956] 1 W.L.R. 461, 466.

[41] [1949] 1 K.B. 532; *cf. The Eagle* [1977] 2 Lloyd's Rep. 70; *The Dragon* [1979] 1 Lloyd's Rep. 257, affirmed without reference to this point [1981] 1 W.L.R. 120; *Oceanic Sun Line Special Shipping Co.* v. *Fay* (1988) 165 C.L.R. 197.

tion clause is nevertheless incorporated in that particular transaction. A negative answer to this question was suggested by Lord Devlin in *McCutcheon* v. *David MacBrayne Ltd.* where he said: "Previous dealings are relevant only if they prove knowledge of the terms, *actual and not constructive, and consent to them.*"[42] But this view is inconsistent with at least one earlier case[43] and it has been rejected by the House of Lords. The present position is that if there has been a long consistent course of dealing on terms incorporating an exemption clause, then those terms may apply to a particular transaction even though in relation to it the usual steps to incorporate the clause have not been taken.[44] Of course the terms will not apply if the transaction in question was not part of a *consistent* course of dealings[45]; if the transactions were spread over a long period of time and their number was so small that they could not be said to give rise to a course of dealing[46]; if the steps necessary to incorporate the clause had never been taken at any stage of the dealings between the parties[47]; or if the terms of each transaction in the series had been separately negotiated and expressly agreed between the parties.[48]

The fact that there has been a long course of dealing may also be relevant to the degree of notice required when the party claiming the benefit of a clause seeks to alter it to his own advantage. As the other party is reasonably entitled to assume that the course of dealing is continuing on the accustomed terms, it seems that special steps would have to be taken to draw his attention to any such alteration.[49]

The course of dealing referred to in the present discussion is one between the parties to the contract.[50] A term may also be implied into a contract because of a general course of dealing amounting to a trade cus-

---

[42] [1964] 1 W.L.R. 125, 134 (italics supplied).

[43] *J. Spurling Ltd.* v. *Bradshaw* [1956] 1 W.L.R. 461.

[44] *Hardwick Game Farm* v. *Suffolk Agricultural, etc., Association* [1969] 2 A.C. 31, 90, 104, 105, 113, 130; and see *Britain & Overseas Trading (Bristles)* v. *Brookes Wharf and Bull Wharf* [1967] 2 Lloyd's Rep. 51; *S.I.A.T. di dal Ferro* v. *Tradax Overseas S.A.* [1978] 2 Lloyd's Rep. 470, affirmed [1980] 1 Lloyd's Rep. 53; *George Mitchell (Chesterhall) Ltd.* v. *Finney Lock Seeds Ltd.* [1983] Q.B. 284, 295, affirmed without reference to this point [1983] 2 A.C. 803; *Circle Freight International Ltd.* v. *Mideast & Gulf Exports Ltd.* [1988] 2 Lloyd's Rep. 427.

[45] *McCutcheon* v. *David MacBrayne Ltd.*, *supra*, n. 42, can be explained on the ground that the parties contracted sometimes on one set of terms and sometimes on another. *Cf.* also *Burnett* v. *Westminster Bank Ltd.* [1966] 1 Q.B. 742, and *Mendelssohn* v. *Normand Ltd.* [1970] 1 Q.B. 177.

[46] On this question, contrast *Hollier* v. *Rambler Motors (A.M.C.) Ltd.* [1972] 2 Q.B. 71 (three or four transactions in five years not sufficient) and *Metaalhandel J.A. Magnum BV* v. *Ardfields Transport Ltd.* [1988] 1 Lloyd's Rep. 197, 203 ("isolated affairs") with *The Havprins* [1983] 2 Lloyd's Rep. 356, 362 (three transactions in five years sufficient, though incorporation was "not by course of dealing alone," and with the *Hardwick Game Farm* case, *supra*, n. 44, (three or four contracts a month for three years held to be sufficient).

[47] *Smith* v. *Taylor* [1966] 2 Lloyd's Rep. 231.

[48] *Johnson Matthey Bankers Ltd.* v. *State Trading Corp. of India* [1984] 1 Lloyd's Rep. 427, 433.

[49] See *Pancommerce Co. S.A.* v. *Veecheema B.V.* [1983] 2 Lloyd's Rep. 304, 305 ("in bold type"); and contrast *Burnett* v. *Westminster Bank Ltd.* [1966] 1 Q.B. 742 with *Re Bond Worth Ltd.* [1980] Ch. 228. In the last two cases the actual issue was as to the variation of a continuing contract: sufficient notice had been given in the first, but not in the second case.

[50] Or between one of them and a group of companies to which the other belongs, as in the *S.I.A.T.* case, *supra*, n. 44, and in *The Raphael* [1982] 2 Lloyd's Rep. 42.

tom or usage.[51] Such an implication can arise even though the parties to the particular contract in question have not previously dealt with each other. It seems that exemption clauses, no less than other types of terms, can be incorporated in this way.

2. Construction

Under this heading we shall first discuss in general terms the principle that exemption clauses are construed *contra proferentem*; we shall then consider two special applications of that principle to cases in which a party relies on an exemption clause to protect him from liability for negligence or for certain particularly serious breaches.

(1) Contra proferentem rule

Exemption clauses are strictly construed against parties who rely on them. A provision that a seller gives "no *warranty*, express or implied" does not protect him from liability for breach of condition[52]; nor does a clause protecting him from liability for breach of *implied* conditions and warranties cover breach of an *express* term of the contract[53]; nor does a provision in a hire-purchase agreement that "no warranty, condition or description or representation *is* given" exclude liability for breach of a collateral undertaking *previously* given.[54]

If the words are ambiguous they are construed in the way least favourable to the party relying on them.[55] In *Houghton* v. *Trafalgar Insurance*[56] a five-seater car was involved in an accident while carrying six people. The driver's insurance policy exempted the insurers from liability for damage caused "whilst the car is carrying any *load* in excess of that for which it was constructed." The insurers were held liable as the clause did not extend to cases where the car was carrying too many *passengers*. Similarly, in *Beck & Co.* v. *Szymanowski*[57] a contract for the sale of cotton provided that "The *goods delivered* shall be deemed to be in all respects in accordance with the contract," unless the buyer gave notice of a complaint within 14 days of the arrival of the goods. This clause did not prevent the buyers from claiming damages for *short delivery*: "The damages are claimed not in respect of goods delivered but in respect of goods which were not delivered."[58]

Although the *contra proferentem* rule applies to all exemption clauses, the courts do not apply it with the same rigour to clauses which merely limit liability as they do to those which purport totally to exclude it[59]; for while it

---

[51] *British Crane Hire Corp. Ltd.* v. *Ipswich Plant Hire Ltd.* [1975] Q.B. 303; *ante*, p. 195. The dispute concerned an indemnity clause, but the principle seems equally applicable to exemption clauses: *cf. Smith* v. *South Wales Switchgear Ltd.* [1978] 1 W.L.R. 165; *Victoria Fur Traders* v. *Roadline U.K. Ltd.* [1981] 1 Lloyd's Rep. 571.

[52] *Wallis, Son & Wells* v. *Pratt & Haynes* [1911] A.C. 394; *Harling* v. *Eddy* [1951] 2 K.B. 739; for the distinction between conditions and warranties, see *post*, pp. 689 *et seq.*; for statutory restrictions on exemption clauses in contracts for the sale of goods, see *post*, pp. 229–230; 232–233.

[53] *Andrews Bros. (Bournemouth) Ltd.* v. *Singer & Co. Ltd.* [1934] 1 K.B. 17.

[54] *Webster* v. *Higgins* [1948] 2 All E.R. 127; *cf. J. Evans & Son (Portsmouth) Ltd.* v. *Andrea Merzario Ltd.* [1976] 1 W.L.R. 1078, 1084.

[55] *Cf. Morris* v. *C. W. Martin & Sons Ltd.* [1966] 1 Q.B. 716; *post*, p. 560.

[56] [1954] 1 Q.B. 247.

[57] [1924] A.C. 43.

[58] At p. 50.

[59] *Ailsa Craig Fishing Co. Ltd.* v. *Malvern Fishing Co.* [1983] W.L.R. 964; Palmer, 45 M.L.R. 327; *George Mitchell (Chesterhall) Ltd.* v. *Finney Lock Seeds Ltd.* [1983] 2 A.C. 803, 814.

is thought "inherently improbable" that the injured party will agree to a total exclusion of the other party's liability "there is no such high degree of improbability that he would agree to a limitation of . . . liability."[60]

(2) Negligence

By statute, clauses purporting to exempt a party from liability for negligence are now often ineffective[61]; and the negligence of the party in breach may also support the conclusion that the statutory requirement of reasonableness has not been satisfied.[62] But even where it remains possible to exclude liability for negligence, "clear words" must be used for this purpose, since the courts regard it as "inherently improbable that one party to a contract should intend to absolve the other party from the consequence of his own negligence."[63] The requirement is most obviously satisfied where the exemption clause expressly refers to negligence: *i.e.* uses the word "negligence"[64] or some synonym for it.[65] It may be satisfied, even though there is no such express reference to negligence, if the words are nevertheless wide enough to cover negligence: *e.g.* if the clause exempts a party from "all liability whatsoever."[66] But the effectiveness of such general words for the purpose of excluding liability for negligence depends on a further distinction: namely that between cases in which, but for the clause, the party relying on it may be liable irrespective of negligence, and those in which his only possible liability is for negligence.[67]

(a) PARTY LIABLE IRRESPECTIVE OF NEGLIGENCE. If there is a realistic possibility (as opposed to a merely fanciful one[68]) that a party can be made liable irrespective of negligence, an exemption clause in general terms will not normally be construed so as to cover liability for negligence.[69] For example, a common carrier of goods is strictly liable if they are lost or damaged. A clause exempting him from liability "for loss or damage"[70] would be construed to refer to his strict liability only. The position is the same where it is doubtful in law whether the party relying on the clause is liable irrespective of negligence: here again a clause which does not refer to negligence will not prima facie be construed to exempt him from liability

---

[60] *Ailsa Craig* case, *supra*, at p. 970.

[61] Unfair Contract Terms Act 1977, s.2; *post*, pp. 228–229, 231.

[62] *George Mitchell (Chesterhall) Ltd.* v. *Finney Lock Seeds Ltd.* [1983] 2 A.C. 803; *post*, p. 209.

[63] *Gillespie Bros. Ltd.* v. *Roy Bowles Transport Ltd.* [1973] Q.B. 400, 419; *cf. Sonat Offshore S.A.* v. *Amerada Hess Development Ltd.* [1988] 1 Lloyd's Rep. 145, 157.

[64] *e.g. Spriggs* v. *Sotheby Parke Bernet & Co.* [1986] 1 Lloyd's Rep. 487.

[65] *Canada SS. Lines Ltd.* v. *The King* [1952] A.C. 192, 208.

[66] *Canada SS. Lines Ltd.* v. *The King, supra*, at p. 208; such general words do not amount to an *express* reference to negligence: see *Smith* v. *South Wales Switchgear Ltd.* [1978] W.L.R. 165, 173 and *Smith* v. *U.M.B. Chrysler (Scotland)* 1978 S.C.(H.L.) 1, 12, disapproving dicta in *Gillespie* v. *Roy Bowles Transport Ltd.* [1973] Q.B. 400, 420, 421; *The Raphael* [1982] 2 Lloyd's Rep. 42.

[67] *Canada SS. Lines Ltd.* v. *The King* [1952] A.C. 192, 208.

[68] See *Hair & Skin Trading Co. Ltd.* v. *Norman Airfreight Carriers Ltd.* [1974] 1 Lloyd's Rep. 442; *Gallagher* v. *B.R.S.* [1974] 2 Lloyd's Rep. 440, 448; *Smith* v. *South Wales Switchgear Ltd.* [1978] 1 W.L.R. 165, 178; *The Raphael, supra*, n. 66.

[69] *Canada SS. Lines Ltd.* v. *The King* [1952] A.C. 192, esp. at p. 208; *White* v. *J. Warwick & Co. Ltd.* [1953] 1 W.L.R. 1285; Gower, 17 M.L.R. 155.

[70] See *Rutter* v. *Palmer* [1922] 2 K.B. 87; *cf. Dorset CC* v. *Southern Felt Roofing Co.* (1990) 9 Tr.L.R. 96.

for negligence.[71] But in all the cases just described it is not absolutely necessary, to refer expressly to negligence; for the rule is one of construction only and "should not be applied rigidly or mechanically so as to defeat [the] intentions [of the parties]."[72] Thus in one case[73] a charterparty provided that the shipowners were to be liable *only* for negligent stowage, want of personal diligence in making the ship seaworthy, and personal default. It was held that by accepting liability *only* for these three causes the shipowners had excluded liability for negligence of the crew resulting in the stranding of the ship. In another case[74] a clause excluded liability for loss or damage "however caused which can be covered by insurance." This was similarly held to cover negligence even though the party relying on the clause could have been liable (as a common carrier) irrespective of negligence.

The fact that the clause only *limits* (and does not wholly *exclude*) liability is relevant to the issue of construction. Thus a seller is strictly liable for defects in goods; so that prima facie general words might not exclude liability for defects due to his negligence. But where a seller of seeds undertook to replace defective seeds or to refund the price paid for them, it was held that a clause which clearly excluded "all [further] liability" did, as a matter of construction, apply where he was negligent in supplying seeds which were defective; and one reason given for this conclusion was that the rules limiting the scope of exemption clauses in cases of negligent breach "cannot be applied in their full rigour to limitation clauses."[75] The question in all the above cases is whether the intention of one party to exclude liability for negligence has been made sufficiently clear to the other. An express reference to negligence is the safest, but not the only, way of achieving this result.

(b) PARTY ONLY LIABLE FOR NEGLIGENCE. Where a contracting party is only liable for negligence, the rule of construction discussed above obviously does not apply. It follows that in such cases an exemption clause in general terms (*i.e.* one not specifically referring to negligence) *can* cover negligence.[76] For example, in *Rutter* v. *Palmer*[77] a customer left a car with a garage for sale on the terms that "customers' cars are driven by our staff at customers' sole risk." It was held that the garage proprietor was protected by this clause from liability caused by the negligence of one of his staff, as this was the obvious meaning of the clause.

It used, moreover, to be thought that, in cases of the present kind, a clause in general terms necessarily *did* cover negligence, since "it would

---

[71] *The Emmanuel C* [1983] 1 Lloyd's Rep. 310; *The Oceanic Amity* [1984] 2 All E.R. 140, 151.

[72] *The Golden Leader* [1980] 2 Lloyd's Rep. 573, 574.

[73] *The Golden Leader, supra.*

[74] *Joseph Travers & Sons Ltd.* v. *Cooper* [1915] K.B. 73; and see *A. E. Farr Ltd.* v. *Admiralty* [1953] 1 W.L.R. 965.

[75] *George Mitchell (Chesterhall) Ltd.* v. *Finney Lock Seeds Ltd.* [1983] 2 A.C. 803, 814; but the fact that the seller was negligent was relevant for the purpose of the statutory reasonableness test: *post*, p. 237.

[76] *e.g. J. Archdale Ltd.* v. *Comservices Ltd.* [1954] 1 W.L.R. 459; *White* v. *Blackmore* [1972] 2 Q.B. 651; *Scottish Special Housing Association* v. *Wimpey Construction U.K. Ltd.* [1986] 1 W.L.R. 995.

[77] [1922] 2 K.B. 87; *cf. Levison* v. *Patent Steam Carpet Cleaning Co. Ltd.* [1978] Q.B. 69, 83–84; *The Raphael* [1982] 2 Lloyd's Rep. 42.

otherwise lack subject-matter"[78]: it would have no effect if it did not exclude the only liability which the defendant could incur. But this reasoning no longer prevails. Even where the defendant's only liability is for negligence, the clause must make it clear that liability is to be excluded. It may do so by general words not containing any express reference to negligence.[79] But in *Hollier* v. *Rambler Motors (A.M.C.) Ltd.*[80] a customer's car had been left with the defendants for repair and was damaged in a fire caused by their negligence. It was held that they could not rely on a provision[81] that they were "not responsible for damage caused by fire to customer's cars on the premises." This was so even though they were only liable for fire if it was due to their negligence: the provision only operated as a warning to the customer that the garage proprietors were not liable for loss caused by a fire which was *not* due to their negligence. Obviously, however, a clause cannot be construed merely as such a warning if it expressly exempts a party from liability for negligence.[82]

Even where a defendant is only liable for negligence and clearly intends to exclude that liability, general words may fail to protect him. In *Re Polemis*[83] a clause in a charterparty provided that liability for fire should be *mutually* excepted, *i.e.* that neither shipowner nor charterer should be liable for fire. The shipowner was a common carrier and therefore liable without negligence. Thus the clause would not exempt him from liability for negligence, but only from strict liability. In view of this, it was held that the clause did not exempt the charterer from liability for negligence either, although he was only liable for negligence.

3. Seriousness of breach

Before the courts had statutory powers to control exemption clauses, they were reluctant to allow a party to rely on such a clause where he had committed a breach that was particularly serious. Effect was given to this policy by two techniques. One was to construe the exemption clause narrowly, so that it would not apply where such a serious breach had occurred, unless the intention that it should apply in spite of the gravity of the breach was made very clear. Another was to say that, as a matter of substantive law, it was impossible by any clause (however widely drafted) to exclude liability for certain breaches which were "fundamental."[84] This substantive doctrine of fundamental breach was developed by the courts as a device for protecting consumers. But it was not restricted to consumer cases; and, when applied to commercial transactions negotiated at arm's length, it was

---

78 *Alderslade* v. *Hendon Laundry* [1945] K.B. 189, 192; *cf. Gibaud* v. *Great Eastern Ry.* [1921] 2 K.B. 426; *The Ballyalton* [1961] 1 W.L.R. 929.

79 *Alderslade* v. *Hendon Laundry Ltd.* [1945] K.B. 189, as explained in *Hollier* v. *Rambler Motors (A.M.C.) Ltd.* [1972] 2 Q.B. 71; *Hair & Skin Trading Co. Ltd.* v. *Norman Airfreight Carriers Ltd.* [1974] 1 Lloyd's Rep. 442. For similar construction of indemnity clauses, see *Gillespie Bros. & Co. Ltd.* v. *Roy Bowles Transport Ltd.* [1973] Q.B. 400, *Arthur White (Contractors) Ltd.* v. *Tarmac Civil Engineering Ltd.* [1967] 1 W.L.R. 1506 and *Thompson* v. *T. Lohan (Plant Hire) Ltd.* [1987] 1 W.L.R. 649; and *cf. The Super Servant Two* [1990] 1 Lloyd's Rep. 1, 8 (similar construction of cancellation clause).

80 [1972] 2 Q.B. 71; *cf. Olley* v. *Marlborough Court* [1949] 1 K.B. 532.

81 Which was actually not incorporated in the contract: *ante*, p. 201 at n. 46.

82 *Spriggs* v. *Sotheby Parke Bernet & Co.* [1986] 1 Lloyd's Rep. 487.

83 [1921] 3 K.B. 560.

84 *e.g. Karsales (Harrow) Ltd.* v. *Wallis* [1956] 1 W.L.R. 936; and see Grunfeld, 24 M.L.R. 62; Guest, 77 L.Q.R. 98; Montrose [1964] C.L.J. 60, 254.

liable to upset perfectly fair bargains for the reasonable allocation of contractual risks. When, in the *Suisse Atlantique* case[85] in 1966, an attempt was made to apply the doctrine in such a context, the House of Lords rejected the view that the doctrine was one of substantive law and held that it was one of construction only, so that liability for even a fundamental breach could be excluded so long as the words of the clause were sufficiently clear. In the following years the lower courts were reluctant to accept this position, no doubt because they feared that it would weaken the doctrine of fundamental breach as a consumer-protecting device. But the substantive doctrine was no longer needed for this purpose once the effectiveness of exemption clauses came to be restricted by the Unfair Contract Terms Act 1977[86]; and, where these restrictions did not apply, it was desirable, in the interests of commercial certainty, to allow the parties to allocate risks between themselves by clearly drafted exemption clauses.[87] In the *Photo Production*[88] case in 1980 the House of Lords therefore reasserted the view that the doctrine of fundamental breach was a rule of construction only. That view was again affirmed by the House of Lords in the *George Mitchell* case in 1983, where Lord Bridge said that the *Photo Production* case had given "the final quietus to the doctrine that a 'fundamental breach' of contract deprived the party in breach of the benefit of clauses in the contract excluding or limiting his liability."[89]

In the course of the development just described, the House of Lords overruled a small number of cases that were consistent only with the substantive doctrine[90]; but it did not cast doubt on many other decisions in which the seriousness of the breach had been a ground for holding that an exemption clause afforded no protection. A difficult question is therefore left unresolved as to the status of these decisions. One possible view is that they are all obsolete, as the question whether a clause applies to a particular breach simply depends in each case on whether the words of the clause are sufficiently clear to cover that breach. On this view, nothing more need or can be said about "fundamental breach" than that all exemption clauses are to be construed *contra proferentem*,[91] and that, the more serious the breach is, the less likely it is that the clause will apply. A second possible view is that the earlier cases are to be reinterpreted rather than rejected or ignored. In support of this view, it can be said that some of the earlier judgments explicitly proceeded on the basis that the rule was one of construction,[92] while others, though based on the substantive doctrine, have been explained as illustrations of the rule of construction,[93] or as retaining their

---

[85] [1967] 1 A.C. 361 discussed at p. 216, *post*.

[86] *Photo Production Ltd.* v. *Securicor Transport Ltd.* [1980] A.C. 827, 843.

[87] *Ibid.*

[88] *Supra*; discussed *post* at p. 216.

[89] *George Mitchell (Chesterhall) Ltd.* v. *Finney Lock Seeds* [1983] 2 A.C. 803, 813; *cf. The Antares* [1987] 1 Lloyd's Rep. 424, 428.

[90] *i.e. Charterhouse Credit Co. Ltd.* v. *Tolly* [1963] 2 Q.B. 683 ("though the result might have been reached on construction of the contract": *Photo Production* case, *supra*, at p. 845); *Harbutt's "Plasticine" Ltd.* v. *Wayne Tank Co. Ltd.* [1970] 1 Q.B. 477; *Wathes (Western) Ltd.* v. *Austins (Menswear) Ltd.* [1976] 1 Lloyd's Rep. 14.

[91] *Ante*, p. 202.

[92] *Gibaud* v. *G.E. Ry.* [1921] 2 K.B. 426: see the *Suisse Atlantique* case [1967] 1 A.C. 361, 412; and see the judgment of Pearson L.J. in *U.G.S. Finance Ltd.* v. *National Mortgage Bank of Greece* [1964] 1 Lloyd's Rep. 446, 453.

[93] *e.g. Levison* v. *Patent Steam Cleaning Co.* [1978] Q.B. 69: see the *Photo Production* case [1980] A.C. 827, 845, 846; and *cf.* the *Charterhouse* case, *supra*, n. 90.

validity on other special grounds.[94] For these reasons, it is submitted that the second view is to be preferred. The cases concerning serious breaches resemble those (discussed above) concerning negligent breaches: they can be regarded as illustrations of the *contra proferentem* rule, but they amount to particular or special applications of that rule and therefore still provide guidance on the scope and effects of the rule of construction which applies where the breach is of a certain degree of seriousness. They can be said to give rise to a presumption or prima facie rule that general words will not exclude liability for certain very serious breaches; but that presumption or rule can be displaced if the words of the clause are sufficiently clear. At the same time, it should be emphasised that the practical importance of the cases on this topic is likely to be confined to situations in which the validity of the exemption clause is not affected by the Unfair Contract Terms Act 1977. The outcome of a case will obviously not depend on whether the clause covers the breach if, on the assumption that it does, it would be simply ineffective under the Act[95]; and if under the Act the clause is subject to the requirement of reasonableness,[96] the outcome is more likely to depend on the question whether that requirement was satisfied than on the construction of the clause.[97]

In the following discussion, we shall first describe the breaches to which the rule of construction applies, bearing in mind that the occurrence of such a breach does not *necessarily* lead to the conclusion that the clause will not cover it: there is only a presumption that it will not be construed to have this effect, and this presumption can be overcome if the words of the clause are sufficiently clear. It will then be necessary to consider the exact effects (or present operation) of the rule of construction.

(a) SCOPE OF THE RULE. For the purpose of the rule of construction described above, a breach may be a serious one either because of the nature of the term broken, or because of the consequences of the breach, or because of the manner in which the breach was committed.

(i) *Nature of the term broken.* The legal consequences of a breach often depend on the nature of the term broken. The leading distinction is between three categories of terms known respectively as conditions, warranties and intermediate terms. This distinction is discussed in Chapter 18[98]; here it is only necessary to say that breach of condition of itself gives the injured party the right to rescind the contract while breach of warranty or of an intermediate term does not have this effect. But the law recognises yet a further category, the so-called "fundamental term," which is "narrower than a condition of the contract"[99] and it is this category of fundamental term that is significant for the present purpose. Such a term is one

---

[94] *i.e.* the deviation cases: see *post* pp. 210–213, 222.

[95] *i.e.* in the situations described at pp. 228–231 *post*.

[96] *i.e.* in the situations described at pp. 231–235 *post*.

[97] *e.g.* in *George Mitchell (Chesterhall) Ltd.* v. *Finney Lock Seeds Ltd.* [1983] 2 A.C. 803, *post*, pp. 209, 237–238.

[98] *Post*, pp. 689–704.

[99] *Smeaton Hanscomb & Co. Ltd.* v. *Sassoon I. Setty & Co. (No. 1)* [1953] 1 W.L.R. 1468, 1470; *R. W. Green Ltd.* v. *Cade Bros. Farms* [1978] 1 Lloyd's Rep. 602. A passage in *Photo Production Ltd.* v. *Securicor Transport Ltd.* [1980] A.C. 827, 849–850, can be interpreted as treating the two concepts as identical (*cf. post*, p. 211, n. 33) but only for the purpose of the rule that breaches of both give rise to a right to rescind: see *post*, p. 704. It is respectfully submitted that Devlin J. was correct in treating them as distinct for the *present* purpose, *i.e.* the scope of an exemption clause.

that specifies the essential purpose of the contract, so that breach of the term turns the performance rendered into one which is not merely defective, but essentially different from that promised: for example, where a person who had contracted to sell peas instead delivered beans[1]; or where a seller of mahogany logs instead delivered pine logs.[2] In a number of cases exemption clauses have been held not to cover breaches of this kind. It has, for example, been held that a seller of "foreign refined rape oil" could not rely on an exemption clause where what he delivered was not "foreign refined rape oil"[3]; that a seller of a new car would be in breach of a fundamental term if he delivered a second-hand car[4]; and that a shipowner who had contracted to provide cruise accommodation was not protected by an exemption clause when he substituted an inferior ship and a much less attractive itinerary.[5]

The same rule can apply where what is supplied is not literally a different thing from what was bargained for, but is so seriously defective as to be different in substance.[6] In *Pinnock Bros.* v. *Lewis & Peat Ltd.*[7] copra cake was sold "not warranted free from defect" but was so adulterated by castor beans as to poison the cattle to which it was fed. It was held that "where a substance quite different from that contracted for has been delivered, that clause has no application, as such a difference of substance cannot be said to constitute a 'defect.' " In other similar cases, the actual decisions were based on the view that the supplier could not as a matter of substantive law exclude liability for defects of this very serious kind.[8] This reasoning used to be particularly common where seriously defective or unroadworthy cars were supplied under contracts of sale or hire-purchase[9]; but these cases must now be explained on the ground that the exemption clauses in them did not, as a matter of construction, apply to the breaches that had occurred. On the other hand, a party does not lose the protection of an exemption clause merely because his performance suffers from a defect that entitles (or would, but for the clause, have entitled) the other party to reject the defective performance. Thus a seller of "mahogany logs equal to sample" would not be in breach of a fundamental term (but only in breach of condition[10]) if he delivered mahogany logs that were not equal to sample.[11] Similarly, the supplier of a motor vehicle which corresponds with the contractual description does not commit a breach of a fundamental term

---

1 See *Chanter* v. *Hopkins* (1838) 4 M. & W. 399, 404; for a modern application, *cf. The Bow Cedar* [1980] 2 Lloyd's Rep. 601.

2 *Smeaton Hanscomb & Co. Ltd.* v. *Sassoon I. Setty & Co. (No. 1)* [1953] 1 W.L.R. 1468, 1470.

3 *Nichol* v. *Godts* (1854) 10 Ex. 191; *cf. Wieler* v. *Schilizzi* (1856) 17 C.B. 619.

4 *Andrews Bros. (Bournemouth) Ltd.* v. *Singer & Co.* [1934] 1 K.B. 17, as explained in *Karsales (Harrow) Ltd.* v. *Wallis* [1956] 1 W.L.R. 17.

5 *Anglo-Continental Holidays Ltd.* v. *Typaldos Lines* [1976] 2 Lloyd's Rep. 61.

6 *Cf. Topfell Ltd.* v. *Galley Properties Ltd.* [1979] 1 W.L.R. 446, 450 (vendor of a house not protected where he failed to give vacant possession); and see *post*, pp. 673–674.

7 [1923] 1 K.B. 690.

8 *e.g. Karsales (Harrow) Ltd.* v. *Wallis, supra.*

9 For statutory restrictions on exemption clauses in these cases, see *post*, pp. 229–230, 232–233. Before 1964, similar restrictions were subject to low financial limits, making them in practice ineffective.

10 *Ante*, p. 207; *post*, p. 694; Sale of Goods Act 1979, s.15(2)(*a*).

11 *Smeaton Hanscomb & Co. Ltd.* v. *Sassoon I. Setty & Co. (No. 1)* [1953] 1 W.L.R. 1468, 1470.

merely because he breaks some implied undertaking as to the fitness of the vehicle for the purpose for which it was supplied.[12]

In these cases of defective performance, it is often hard to tell whether the performance rendered is so essentially different from that promised as to amount to a breach of a fundamental term. This depends on the answer to a preliminary question of construction: what is the essence of the bargain that the parties have made?[13] The "peas and beans" example may be contrasted with a case put by Lord Devlin: "If an anxious hostess is late in the preparation of a meal, she can perfectly well say: 'Send me peas or if you haven't got peas send beans, but for heaven's sake send something.' That would be a contract for peas, beans or anything else *ejusdem generis* and is a perfectly sensible contract to make."[14] In such a case, the supplier would not have been in breach at all if he had sent beans; but more difficulty arises where the supplier is undoubtedly in breach and the question is whether that breach makes the article supplied as different from that contracted for as peas are from beans. This question gave rise to much difference of judicial opinion in *George Mitchell (Chesterhall) Ltd.* v. *Finney Lock Seeds Ltd.*[15] where the defendants agreed to sell to the plaintiffs 30 lbs of "a cabbage seed"[16] which was later invoiced to them as "Finney's Late Dutch Special," a variety of winter white cabbage. It was "common ground . . . that the seed agreed to be sold was seed for a winter white cabbage"[17] and "conceded that what was supplied was not the winter white cabbage which to everybody's knowledge was what the plaintiffs had ordered and the defendants had agreed to sell."[18] As a result of the breach, the plaintiffs' crop failed; it was fit for neither human nor animal consumption. The defendants were no doubt in breach and the question whether the performance rendered was essentially or fundamentally different from that promised depended on how their essential or fundamental obligation under the contract was to be described. Was it an obligation to deliver "cabbage seed" or one to deliver "vegetable seed" or simply one to deliver "seed"? Parker J.[19] and a majority of the Court of Appeal held that the essential obligation was one to deliver vegetable seed and that a clause limiting the sellers' liability did not cover their breach of that obligation. Oliver L.J. said: "what was delivered to the plaintiffs simply was not fulfilment of the contract, even a defective fulfilment, any more than delivery of a motor bicycle would be a fulfilment of a contract for the sale of a car."[20] But the House of Lords held that the clause did as a matter of construction cover the breach (though it did not in the end protect the defendants as it failed to satisfy the statutory requirement of reasonableness[21]). Lord

---

[12] *Astley Industrial Trust Ltd.* v. *Grimley* [1963] 1 W.L.R. 584.
[13] See Melville, 19 M.L.R. 26; Unger [1957] J.B.L. 30.
[14] [1966] C.L.J. at p. 212.
[15] [1981] 1 Lloyd's Rep. 476 (Parker J.); [1983] Q.B. 284 (C.A.); [1983] 2 A.C. 803 (H.L.).
[16] [1981] 1 Lloyd's Rep. 476, 477.
[17] *Ibid.*
[18] *Ibid.* At first instance counsel for the defendant further conceded that he would not be able to rely on the clause limiting the defendant's liability "if what had been delivered had been beetroot seed or carrot seed" and "that to get within any distance of success he must establish that what was delivered was cabbage seed": [1981] 1 Lloyd's Rep. 476, 479. This concession was withdrawn on appeal: [1983] Q.B. 284, 303.
[19] [1981] 1 Lloyd's Rep. 476, 480.
[20] [1983] Q.B. 284, 305.
[21] *Post*, p. 236.

Bridge said: "In my opinion this is not a 'peas and beans' case at all"[22]: in other words, he seems to have regarded the defendants' essential obligation as one simply to deliver "seed." Such a narrow view of a party's essential obligation obviously extends the scope of exemption clauses for it increases the range of cases in which a breach can be described as giving rise to defective performance, as opposed to a failure, to perform an essential obligation.

(ii) *Deviation and analogous rules.* In a contract for the carriage of goods by sea, the term as to the route is regarded as fundamental, so that benefit of an exemption clause is normally lost by a shipowner who has without justification[23] deviated, *i.e.* departed from the agreed or usual route.[24] The same is true where a warehouseman has stored the goods in a place other than that agreed[25]; and where a bailee such as a cleaner or carrier has parted with the possession of goods entrusted to him in the course of unauthorised subcontracting.[26] On the other hand, such a person will not lose the protection of an exemption clause merely because he has broken some other term: for example the shipowner may be protected although he has broken his undertaking to supply a seaworthy ship[27]; and the warehouseman may be protected although he is in breach of his obligation to exercise reasonable care in looking after the goods.[28] The reason for the distinction is sometimes said to be that the terms as to the route and as to the place where the goods are to be stored are fundamental, while the other terms mentioned are not. The special importance of the term as to route has been explained on the ground that the owner of the goods may lose his insurance cover if the ship departs from the agreed route[29]: it is therefore thought necessary to give him a remedy against the carrier (in spite of the exemption clause) as if the latter were an insurer. In fact the goods-owner may not suffer the hardship on which the rule is based, since his insurance policy may provide that he is to be "held covered" in case of deviation at a premium to be arranged.[30] The special rule as to the effects

---

[22] [1983] 2 A.C. 803, 813.

[23] See *Kish* v. *Taylor* [1912] A.C. 604, 617; Carriage of Goods by Sea Act 1971, Sched., Art. IV 4: deviation may be justified for the purpose of saving life or property at sea.

[24] *Joseph Thorley Ltd.* v. *Orchis S.S. Co. Ltd.* [1907] 1 K.B. 660; *James Morrison & Co. Ltd.* v. *Shaw Savill & Albion Co. Ltd.* [1916] 2 K.B. 783; *Stag Line Ltd.* v. *Foscolo, Mango & Co. Ltd.* [1932] A.C. 328. For the application of the same principle to carriage on deck, see *J. Evans & Sons (Portsmouth) Ltd.* v. *Andrea Merzario* [1976] 1 W.L.R. 1078, and *The Chanda* [1989] 2 Lloyd's Rep. 494; but contrast (in cases of a *statutory* limitation of liability), *The Antares (No. 2)* [1987] 1 Lloyd's Rep. 424, where dicta at p. 430 suggest that on deck carriage is no longer regarded as a special case. *Cf. L. & N.W. Ry.* v. *Neilson* [1922] 2 A.C. 263 (carriage by land).

[25] *Woolf* v. *Collis Removal Services* [1948] 1 K.B. 11, 15; *cf. United Fresh Meat Co. Ltd.* v. *Charterhouse Cold Storage Ltd.* [1974] 2 Lloyd's Rep. 286.

[26] *Davies* v. *Collins* [1945] 1 All E.R. 247; *Garnham, Harris & Elton Ltd.* v. *Alfred W. Ellis (Transport) Ltd.* [1967] 1 W.L.R. 940.

[27] *The Europa* [1908] P. 84; *Kish* v. *Taylor* [1912] A.C. 604.

[28] *J. Spurling Ltd.* v. *Bradshaw* [1956] 1 W.L.R. 461; *Kenyon Son & Craven Ltd.* v. *Baxter Hoare & Co. Ltd.* [1971] 1 W.L.R. 519; *cf. Mayfair Photographic Supplies Ltd.* v. *Baxter Hoare & Co. Ltd.* [1972] 1 Lloyd's Rep. 410.

[29] See *Hain S.S. Co.* v. *Tate & Lyle Ltd.* (1936) 41 Com.Cas. 350, 354.

[30] See *State Trading Corp. of India* v. *S. M. Golodetz Ltd.* [1989] 2 Lloyd's Rep. 277, 289. But such clauses may fail to provide satisfactory protection: for example, in *Vincentelli* v. *Rowlett* (1911) 16 Com.Cas. 310 the insurer "arranged" the premium at an amount equal to the loss. *Quaere*, whether such conduct is consistent with Marine Insurance Act 1906, s.31(2) under which such a premium must be reasonable.

of deviation has accordingly been criticised.[31] It can be explained either as an application of the rule of construction normally applied to breach of a fundamental term,[32] or as a rule which, on account of its historical and commercial background, must be treated as *sui generis.*[33]

Once a term has been identified as fundamental, the next question to arise in this group of cases is whether that term has been broken. For this purpose it is first necessary to construe that term to see what obligation it imposes. Thus a warehouseman commits a breach of a fundamental term if he stores the goods elsewhere than at the agreed place. But the court cannot apply the rule that, prima facie, exemption clauses are not to be construed so as to cover such a breach until it has first determined exactly where the goods were to be stored. In *Gibaud* v. *G.E. Ry*[34] a contract to store a bicycle in a railway station cloakroom was interpreted as one to store in the cloakroom or in any convenient place nearby. Accordingly, an exemption clause was held to apply when the bicycle was stolen, even though it had been stored in the station hall and not in the cloakroom.

A similar principle applies in the deviation cases. In determining the content of the carrier's obligation as to route, the court will have regard not only to the agreed or usual route (if any)[35] but also to any liberty to deviate given by the contract of carriage. But because of the actual or assumed importance of the term specifying the route, such liberties are restrictively construed. In *Glyn* v. *Margetson*[36] a contract for the carriage of oranges from Malaga to Liverpool gave the carrier a wide liberty to deviate. It was held that this provision did not apply where the ship first went east from Malaga, retraced her course, and then made for Liverpool. The general words of the clause were to be limited with reference to "the main object and intent"[37] of the contract—in this case a voyage from Malaga to Liverpool. The clause only justified the carrier in calling at ports *on the route* between those places. Such a restrictive interpretation can to some extent be overcome by permitting the carrier to call at any port "although in a contrary direction to or out of or beyond the route." In *Connolly Shaw Ltd.* v. *A/S Det Nordenfjeldske D/S*[38] a deviation clause containing these words was included in a contract for the carriage of lemons from Palermo to London. It was held that the clause justified deviation to Hull, involving a delay of three days on a voyage of 22 days. But it would not have justified a deviation to Vladivostock, though that was literally within its terms. It only gave the carrier such liberties as could be used "without frustrating the contract."[39]

Clauses permitting a change of route in circumstances beyond the control of the parties are more generously construed. In *G. H. Renton & Co.*

---

[31] *Farr* v. *Hain S.S. Co.* 121 F 2d. 940, 944 (1941). This case arose from the same facts as *Hain S.S. Co.* v. *Tate & Lyle Ltd., supra*; *cf.* Livermore, 2 J.C.L. 241.

[32] *The Antares* [1987] 1 Lloyd's Rep. 424, 430; *State Trading Corp. of India* v. *S. M. Golodetz Ltd.* [1989] 2 Lloyd's Rep. 277, 289.

[33] *Photo Production Ltd.* v. *Securicor Transport Ltd.* [1980] A.C. 827, 845, *per* Lord Wilberforce; *cf. ibid.* at p. 850, where Lord Diplock treats deviation as a breach of "condition": as to this see *ante*, p. 207, n. 99.

[34] [1921] 2 K.B. 426; contrast *Davies* v. *Collins* [1945] 1 All E.R. 247; *post*, p. 658.

[35] See *Frenkel* v. *MacAndrew & Co. Ltd.* [1929] A.C. 545.

[36] [1893] A.C. 351.

[37] *Ibid.* 355.

[38] (1934) 49 Ll.L.R. 183.

[39] *Ibid.* p. 190.

v. *Palmyra Trading Corporation of Panama*[40] timber was shipped from Canada for carriage to London or Hull: if strikes prevented discharge at these ports, "the Master may discharge the cargo at . . . any other convenient port." Strikes at London and Hull made discharge at those ports impossible, and the master discharged the cargo at Hamburg. It was held that the carriers were entitled to rely on the clause; for it only applied in a specified emergency and did not enable them to alter the contractual destination at will.

Assuming that the carrier's departure from the agreed or usual route cannot be justified by a deviation clause or otherwise,[41] he normally loses the protection of other exemption clauses in the contract. This rule is quite different in nature from that which applies in the supply of goods and similar cases previously discussed.[42] In those cases, the term is regarded as fundamental because the effect of its breach is that the injured party receives a performance essentially different from that promised. In the deviation cases, on the other hand, the courts are not concerned with the *effect* of the breach: *any* departure from the agreed route "however for practical purposes irrelevant"[43] normally deprives the shipowner of the benefit of the exemption clause. Yet it can hardly be said that a voyage actually accomplished after a minor deviation is essentially different from the voyage bargained for. It is, moreover, irrelevant that the deviation did not cause, or increase the risk of, loss. Thus in *Joseph Thorley Ltd.* v. *Orchis SS. Co. Ltd.*[44] a cargo of beans was damaged through being mixed with poisonous earth. The carrier lost the benefit of his exemption clause because he had deviated, though the deviation had not caused the loss.[45] And in *James Morrison & Co.* v. *Shaw, Savill & Albion Co. Ltd.*[46] a ship was sunk by enemy action while deviating. The shipowner lost the benefit of his exemption clause even though the ship *might* just as probably have been sunk on her proper route. He would only have been protected had he been able to show that the loss *must* have occurred anyway, *i.e.* even if the ship had not deviated.

The deviation cases do, however, have one thing in common with the supply of goods cases: the *manner* in which the breach is committed is irrelevant. In the supply of goods cases, this point is assumed without argument; and in the deviation cases, so long as the carrier's act is voluntary,[47] it makes no difference that the deviation was quite innocent. In *L. & N.W. Ry.* v. *Neilson*[48] the label came off a vanload of theatrical properties and its contents were despatched to various wrong destinations by a stationmaster. In spite of the fact that he had acted under an honest mistake, the railway company lost the protection of its exemption clause. From this point of

---

40 [1957] A.C. 149; and see *post*, p. 218.
41 See *ante*, p. 210 n. 23.
42 *Ante*, pp. 207–210.
43 *Suisse Atlantique* case [1967] 1 A.C. 361, 423.
44 [1907] 1 K.B. 660.
45 *Aliter* if loss is due to inherent vice or the nature of the goods themselves: *Internationale Guano etc.* v. *Robert MacAndrew & Co.* [1909] 2 K.B. 360.
46 [1916] 2 K.B. 783.
47 See *Rio Tinto Co. Ltd.* v. *Seed Shipping Co. Ltd.* (1926) 24 Ll.L.Rep. 321, 326, where there was in fact no departure from the route.
48 [1922] 2 A.C. 263. The deviation was no doubt "deliberate" (p. 274) in the sense that the defendants' servant knew where he was sending the goods: but it was not "deliberate" in the sense that he knew he was sending them to a wrong destination. *Cf. infra*, p. 213.

view, the supply of goods, deviation and analogous cases may be contrasted with the next group to be discussed.

(iii) *Manner of breach.* The courts are generally reluctant to construe exemption clauses so as to apply to acts amounting to a *deliberate* disregard of the main purpose of the contract. They assume that "the parties never contemplated that such a breach should be excused or limited."[49] In accordance with this assumption, it has been held that a tug-owner could not rely on a clause which protected him from liability for "omission" and "default," where he had deliberately abandoned the tow[50]; and that a carrier of goods by sea could not rely on a clause, which protected him from liability after the goods were "discharged," where he had delivered the goods to a person who, as the carrier knew, had no authority to receive them.[51]

The former substantive doctrine of fundamental breach was often invoked in cases in which a bailee of goods had delivered them to the wrong person. It was held that exemption clauses did not apply where the misdelivery was deliberate[52] or reckless,[53] but could apply where it was merely negligent.[54] Thus the manner of breach was the crucial point, for the term broken and the effect of the breach were always the same: because of delivery to the wrong person, the goods were lost to the owner. These cases gave rise to much difficulty. For one thing, a "deliberate" breach was hard to define[55]; for another it was puzzlingly held that a deliberate misdelivery by an employee did not deprive the employer of the protection of an exemption clause where the employee had acted with the intention of defrauding his employer.[56] The need for "reconciling" the cases has largely disappeared now that each must be explained as turning on the construction of the clause. The fact that the breach was deliberate would be a ground[57] for holding that the clause was not intended to cover the breach; but it would no longer be a decisive ground. Thus an exemption clause may apply to a breach in spite of the fact that it is deliberate if it is of only trivial importance: "for example, a deliberate delay of one day in unloading."[58] This may be so even where a deliberate but trivial breach gives rise to unexpectedly serious consequences.[59]

---

49 *Suisse Atlantique* case [1967] 1 A.C. 361, 435; *cf. ibid.* pp. 394, 397.

50 *The Cap Palos* [1921] P. 458.

51 *Sze Hai Tong Bank Ltd.* v. *Rambler Cycle Co. Ltd.* [1959] A.C. 576; so far as *contra*, *Chartered Bank of India* v. *British India Steam Navigation Co. Ltd.* [1990] A.C. 369 would no longer be followed: see Guest, 77 L.Q.R. 98, 116–118; Wedderburn [1990] C.L.J. 11.

52 *Alexander* v. *Railway Executive* [1951] 2 K.B. 882.

53 *J. Spurling Ltd.* v. *Bradshaw* [1956] 1 W.L.R. 461, 466; *cf. United Fresh Meat Co. Ltd.* v. *Charterhouse Cold Storage Ltd.* [1974] 2 Lloyd's Rep. 286, 291.

54 *Hollins* v. *J. Davy Ltd.* [1963] 1 Q.B. 844; Guest, (1963) 26 M.L.R. 301; *cf. Gallagher* v. *B.R.S.* [1974] 2 Lloyd's Rep. 446; *The New York Star* [1981] 1 W.L.R. 138; *P. S. Chellaram & Co. Ltd.* v. *China Ocean Shipping Co.* [1989] 1 Lloyd's Rep. 413.

55 Probably it meant delivery "to someone known to have no right" to the goods: *Hollins* v. *J. Davy Ltd.* (*supra*) at p. 856.

56 *John Carter* (*Fine Worsteds*) *Ltd.* v. *Hanson Haulage* (*Leeds*) *Ltd.* [1965] 2 Q.B. 495—a case now to be "treated with caution": *W. & J. Lane* v. *Spratt* [1970] 1 All E.R. 162, 172. *cf.* also *Levison* v. *Patent Steam Carpet Cleaning Co. Ltd.* [1978] Q.B. 82 (where, on such facts, there is said to be a fundamental breach).

57 *e.g. The Cap Palos* [1921] P. 458; *Sze Hai Tong Bank Ltd.* v. *Rambler Cycle Co. Ltd.* [1959] A.C. 576; *supra* at n. 52.

58 *Suisse Atlantique* case [1967] 1 A.C. 361, 435.

59 *e.g. Photo Production Ltd.* v. *Securicor Transport Ltd.* [1980] A.C. 827, 840 (fire started deliberately but without the intention of burning down the factory).

(iv) *Consequences of breach.* Even though a breach is not deliberate, or one of a fundamental term, it may still, by reason of its practical consequences be sufficiently serious to attract the operation of the rule of construction. Failure to perform at the agreed time is always a breach of the same term; but an exemption clause may be construed so as to cover only slight delays and not those that are so prolonged as to cause serious prejudice to the injured party.[60] Again, goods supplied under a contract of sale or hire-purchase may not be fit for the particular purpose for which the customer has acquired them. The supplier is not, merely because he has failed to perform the implied condition as to fitness,[61] in breach of a fundamental term[62] but in a number of cases it has been held that he was not protected by an exemption clause because the defect was so serious as to make the thing practically useless for the customer's purposes.[63] The same result was reached where the proprietor of a parking garage had undertaken to keep a car which had been parked there locked, but left it unlocked, so that the customer's luggage was stolen.[64] In all these cases, the crucial factor was not the nature of the term broken, but the consequence of the breach: for this reason, it was the *breach*, rather than the *term broken*, that was described as fundamental.[65]

The rule of construction most clearly applies where the breach is such that the defective performance becomes "totally different from what the contract contemplates."[66] But the examples given in the preceding paragraph show that the rule can apply even where the breach does not make the performance *totally* different from that promised: it is sometimes enough if the breach causes *serious* prejudice to the injured party. Thus the rule was applied against suppliers of motor vehicles that were seriously defective,[67] even though they could still be described as the motor vehicles that were, under the contracts, to be supplied.[68] It has further been suggested that the rule of construction applies whenever the breach "entitles the injured party to treat it as repudiatory and rescind a contract."[69] This may merely refer to the general principle that an injured party wishing to rescind a contract on account of the other party's breach must show that the breach was a "serious" one.[70] But there are many exceptions to this principle: for example: a party may be entitled to rescind for breach of con-

---

[60] See, *e.g. Bontex Knitting Works Ltd.* v. *St. John's Garage* [1943] 2 All E.R. 690; [1944] 1 All E.R. 381; *Suisse Atlantique* case [1967] 1 A.C. 361; *cf. Brandt* v. *Liverpool, etc., S.N. Co. Ltd.* [1924] 1 K.B. 575, 597, 601.

[61] *Ante*, p. 189, *post*, p. 229.

[62] *Ante*. p. 207.

[63] *Yeoman Credit Ltd.* v. *Apps* [1962] 2 Q.B. 508; *Farnsworth Finance Facilities Ltd.* v. *Attryde* [1970] 1 W.L.R. 1053.

[64] *Mendelssohn* v. *Normand Ltd.* [1970] 1 Q.B. 177; Treitel, 32 M.L.R. 685.

[65] For the distinction between breach of a fundamental term and fundamental breach, see *Suisse Atlantique* case [1967] 1 A.C. 361, 393, 421; *United Fresh Meat Co. Ltd.* v. *Charterhouse Cold Storage Ltd.* [1947] 2 Lloyd's Rep. 286; *cf.* (in the context of stipulations as to time) *United Scientific Holdings Ltd.* v. *Burnley B.C.* [1978] A.C. 904, 945.

[66] *Suisse Atlantique* case [1967] 1 A.C. at p. 393.

[67] *Yeoman Credit Ltd.* v. *Apps* [1962] 2 Q.B. 508; *Farnsworth Finance Facilities Ltd.* v. *Attryde* [1970] 1 W.L.R. 1053.

[68] Thus in *Yeoman Credit Ltd.* v. *Apps, supra*, it was held that there was a fundamental breach but *no* "total failure of consideration": *cf. post*, p. 930.

[69] *Suisse Atlantique* case, *supra*, n. 66 at p. 397.

[70] *Post*, p. 670. Lord Diplock in the *Photo Production* case [1980] A.C. 827, 849 and in *The Afovos* [1983] 1 W.L.R. 12, 195, 202 uses "fundamental breach" to refer to this type of breach.

dition even though the breach does not cause him serious prejudice, or indeed any prejudice at all.[71] It is clear that the rule of construction with which we are here concerned would not apply merely because there had been a breach of condition.

It is impossible to define with precision the degree of seriousness of the prejudice (resulting from the breach) that is required to bring the rule of construction into operation. One can only say that the court's reluctance to construe a clause so as to apply to a particular breach will, in general, be directly proportioned to the gravity of that breach. The point may be illustrated by reference to *Kenyon Son & Craven Ltd.* v. *Baxter Hoare & Co. Ltd.*[72] where nuts stored in a warehouse were seriously damaged by rats as a result of the warehouseman's "gross and culpable" failure to take care to prevent such damage. It was held that the warehouseman was protected by an exemption clause which, on its true construction, covered the events which had occurred; but Donaldson J. said that the warehouseman would not have been protected if he had stored the nuts in the open or in an area which was prohibited by the contract.[73]

(b) NATURE OF THE RULE. At this stage, it is necessary to discuss the nature of the rule of construction, to illustrate its operation, and to consider a possible limitation on its scope.

(i) *In General.* Where a breach falls within the scope of the rule of construction, the effect of the rule is that an exemption clause will only cover the breach if it is "most clearly and unambiguously expressed,"[74] so that general words which can fairly be said to apply only to less serious breaches will be construed so as not to cover the serious breach which has occurred.[75] It would, indeed, be wrong "to create ambiguities by strained construction."[76] But general words which at first sight appear to cover even the most serious breach may not be construed in this sense, if to give them this effect "would lead to an absurdity, or because it would defeat the main object of the contract or perhaps for some other reason."[77] For example, a bailee who had undertaken to deliver goods to one person could not rely on such general words if he deliberately delivered the goods to another person, or threw them into the sea.[78] In such cases it is said that the exemption clause "cannot be taken to refer" to the "total breach."[79] According to another formulation of the rule, there is a "strong, though rebuttable, presumption that in inserting a clause of exclusion or limitation . . . the parties are not contemplating breaches of fundamental terms."[80]

(ii) *Illustrations of breach covered.* An important element in the formulation of the rule just quoted is that the presumption is rebuttable; and it will

---

[71] *Post*, pp. 689, 694.
[72] [1971] 1 W.L.R. 519; Legh-Jones and Pickering, 86 L.Q.R. 513.
[73] [1971] 1 W.L.R. 519 at p. 532.
[74] *Ailsa Craig Fishing Co. Ltd.* v. *Malvern Fishing Co. Ltd.* [1983] 1 W.L.R. 964, 966.
[75] *e.g. Levison* v. *Patent Steam Cleaning Co.* [1978] Q.B. 69, now said to be explicable on construction in *Photo Production Ltd.* v. *Securicor Transport Ltd.* [1980] A.C. 827, 845–846.
[76] *Ailsa Craig* case, *supra*, at p. 966; *Photo Production Ltd.* v. *Securicor Transport Ltd.* [1980] A.C. 827, 851; *George Mitchell (Chesterhall) Ltd.* v. *Finney Lock Seeds Ltd.* [1983] 2 A.C. 803, 814; *Singer (U.K.) Ltd.* v. *Tees & Hartlepool Port Authority* [1988] 2 Lloyd's Rep. 164, 169.
[77] *Suisse Atlantique* case [1967] 1 A.C. 361, 398.
[78] *Sze Hai Tong Bank Ltd.* v. *Rambler Cycle Co. Ltd.* [1959] A.C. 576, 587.
[79] *Suisse Atlantique* case, *supra* at p. 432.
[80] *Ibid.* p. 427.

be rebutted if the court is satisfied that the clause was intended to cover the breach which has occurred. In a number of cases, the House of Lords has therefore given effect to clauses excluding or restricting liability in spite of the seriousness of the breach. In the *Suisse Atlantique*[81] case, the liability of charterers for long delays was limited to $1000 per day by a demurrage clause even though it was accepted[82] that those delays amounted to a "fundamental breach."[83] In the *Photo Production*[84] case a security firm which had been engaged to safeguard a factory was protected by an exemption clause which was "clearly and fairly susceptible of one meaning only,"[85] even though the firm's breach resulted in the factory's total destruction by fire. In the *Ailsa Craig*[86] case, a security firm was likewise protected by a clause limiting its liability to £1,000, even though the firm had committed a "total" breach of its undertaking to provide a continuous security service for fishing boats, leading to a loss valued at £55,000. As the potential loss which might be caused by the breach was very great in proportion to the sums that could be charged for the service, and as the loss suffered was likely to have been covered by insurance, it was not inherently improbable that the owners of the boats should have agreed to the limitation of liability.

The current approach to the construction of exemption clauses is illustrated by *George Mitchell (Chesterhall) Ltd.* v. *Finney Lock Seeds Ltd.*[87] Farmers had ordered seed from a firm of seed merchants for a winter white cabbage and were, because of the merchants' negligence, supplied with seed that was admittedly not winter white cabbage seed[88] and that was found to be "in no commercial sense vegetable seed at all."[89] As a result, the farmers' crop failed totally, causing them a loss valued at over £60,000; and the actual decision was that the seed merchants were not protected by a clause in the contract limiting their liability to the return of the price (some £200) since the statutory requirement of reasonableness was not satisfied.[90] But before reaching this conclusion the House of Lords held that the clause did, as a matter of construction, cover the (no doubt extremely serious) breach which had occurred. The clause provided that, "in the event of seeds agreed to be sold by us not complying with the express terms of the contract of sale . . . or any seeds proving defective in varietal purity," the merchants would "replace the defective seeds" or repay the price; that this was to be "the limit of our obligation"; and that, except to the extent just stated, the merchants excluded "all liability for any loss or damage" and for any consequential loss or damage "arising from the use of any seeds . . . supplied by us . . . or any failure in the performance of or any defect in any seeds supplied by us." Lord Bridge said that the clause, read as a whole "unambiguously" limited the merchants' liability and that it was "only possible to read an ambiguity into it by the

[81] [1967] 1 A.C. 371; Drake, 30 M.L.R. 531; Fridman, 7 Alberta L.Rev. 281; Treitel, 29 M.L.R. 546.
[82] [1967] 1 A.C. 371, 419, 430.
[83] *Ibid.* p. 396.
[84] [1980] A.C. 827; *post*, p. 221.
[85] [1980] A.C. 827, 851; *Swiss Bank Corp.* v. *Brink's-Mat Ltd.* [1986] 2 Lloyd's Rep. 79, 92.
[86] [1983] 1 W.L.R. 964; Palmer, 45 M.L.R. 322.
[87] [1983] 2 A.C. 803; Clarke [1983] C.L.J. 32; Adams, 46 M.L.R. 147.
[88] [1981] 1 Lloyd's Rep. 476, 477.
[89] *Ibid.* p. 478.
[90] *Post*, p. 238.

process of strained construction"[91] which had been deprecated in the *Ailsa Craig* and *Photo Production* cases.[92] The adoption of such a "strained construction" by the lower courts in the *George Mitchell* case had come "dangerously near to reintroducing by the back door the doctrine of 'fundamental breach' which this House in the *Photo Production* case had so forcibly evicted from the front."[93]

(iii) *Illustrations of breaches not covered.* It is clear from the four House of Lords cases just considered that clear words in an exemption or limitation clause can cover even a very serious breach; but one feature of the *George Mitchell* case perhaps deserves some emphasis. It will be recalled that Lord Bridge described the case as "not a 'peas and beans' case at all. The relevant condition applies to 'seeds,' "[94] and seeds had indeed been supplied. If the articles supplied had been plastic pellets designed for roof insulation but resembling seeds in appearance, no "strained construction" would have been necessary to hold that the clause did not apply: the things supplied would simply not have been "seeds." In theory the merchants could have drafted a clause to cover even such a breach but in practice they would find it difficult to persuade a court that a clause "unambiguously" had such a very wide ambit. This kind of difficulty may be illustrated by contrasting the *George Mitchell* case with the more recent decision of the House of Lords in *The T.F.L. Prosperity*.[95] In that case, a clause in a charterparty exempting the shipowner from liability for "damage" was held not to cover the economic loss suffered by the charterer by reason of the fact that the ship was not of the dimensions specified in the contract. The effect of construing the clause so as to cover this kind of loss would, in the words of Lord Roskill, have been that "the charter virtually ceases to be a contract . . . and becomes no more than a statement of intent by the owners in return for which the charterers are obliged to pay large sums of hire, though if the owners fail to carry out their promises as to description or delivery, [the charterers] are entitled to nothing in lieu,"[96] and he rejected that construction on the ground that it did not accord with "the true common intention of the parties."[97] Such an approach to the construction of exemption or limitation clauses is, moreover, not confined to extreme cases of this kind. In *The Chanda* delicate machinery was damaged while being carried on the defendant's ship. The damage occurred because the machinery had, in breach of the contract of carriage, been stowed on deck, over the ship's forward hatch. It was held that the defendant was not entitled to rely on a limitation of liability clause in the contract of carriage because this clause could "hardly have been intended to protect the shipowner who, as a result of the breach, exposed the cargo to such palpable risk of damage."[98] The result was based, not on any substantive rule of law, but on "contractual intention."[99]

---

[91] [1983] 2 A.C. 803, 814. All the other members of the House of Lords agreed with Lord Bridge's speech.
[92] See *ante*, p. 215 at n. 76.
[93] [1983] 2 A.C. 803, 813.
[94] *Ibid.* and see *ante*, p. 210.
[95] [1984] 1 W.L.R. 48.
[96] *Ibid.* pp. 58–59.
[97] *Ibid.* p. 59. *Cf.*, in a different context, *Bishop* v. *Bonham* [1988] 1 W.L.R. 742.
[98] [1989] 2 Lloyd's Rep. 494, 505; Davenport, 105 L.Q.R. 521.
[99] [1989] 2 Lloyd's Rep. 494, 505.

(iv) *Total breach.* In discussing the scope of the rule of construction, we distinguished between breaches that caused *serious* prejudice and those that made performance *totally* different from that bargained for.[1] Clear words can, no doubt, exclude liability for serious breaches, but it is less certain whether the same is true where the words purport to cover breaches that are indeed total. Two suggestions in the *Suisse Atlantique* case bear on the point.

The first suggestion was made by Lord Wilberforce, when he said that the court could refuse to apply an exemption clause literally if to give effect to the clause would be to "deprive one party's stipulation of all contractual force."[2] The clause might then turn the party's promise into one to perform only if he felt like it; and a promise of this kind might not amount to a contract at all on the ground that it was illusory.[3] Such a situation should be contrasted with that in the *Ailsa Craig* case[4] where the clause was expressed to cover "failure in the provision of services." It was held to apply even on the assumption that the failure was "total"[5]; but the clause only *limited* the defendants' liability, and therefore did not make their promise illusory. If an exemption clause would, on its literal meaning, make a promise illusory, the court might reject that meaning; but such a decision could be explained on the ground that the court was rejecting the literal meaning of the clause so as to give effect to the construction of the contract as a whole.

The second suggestion is based on Lord Reid's statement in the *Suisse Atlantique* case, that an exemption clause might "apply to at least *some cases* of fundamental breach without being so widely drawn that it can be cut down by applying the ordinary principles of construction."[6] The italicised words suggest that there might be *other* cases in which this would not be true: for example, if a shipowner to whom goods had been entrusted for carriage deliberately threw them into the sea,[7] if the defendants in the *Photo Production* case had deliberately burnt down the plaintiffs' factory[8] or if the defendants in the *George Mitchell* case had supplied plastic pellets instead of seeds. In such cases the court might refuse to give effect to the clause (even if it was literally wide enough to cover the breach) because to do so would "lead to an absurdity."[9]

(c) CLAUSES TO WHICH THE RULE APPLIES. The principles of strict construction which operate in cases of serious breach apply to clauses that limit, as well as to those that wholly exclude, liability; but they do not apply to limitation clauses "in their full rigour."[10] In the *George Mitchell* case Lord Bridge relied on the fact that the clause only limited liability in support of

[1] *Ante*, p. 214.
[2] *Suisse Atlantique* case [1967] 1 A.C. 361, 432.
[3] *Ante*, pp. 79, 153, *cf. Firestone Tyre & Rubber Co. Ltd.* v. *Vokins & Co. Ltd.* [1951] 1 Lloyd's Rep. 32, 39: "It is illusory to say—'we promise to do a thing but we are not liable if we do not do it.' "
[4] [1983] 1 W.L.R. 964.
[5] *Ibid.* p. 971.
[6] [1967] A.C. 361, 399.
[7] *Cf. ante*, p. 213.
[8] This was not the position: see [1980] A.C. 827, 840 where Lord Wilberforce says that, though the fire was started deliberately by one of the defendants' employees, "it was not established that he intended to burn down the factory."
[9] *Suisse Atlantique* case [1967] 1 A.C. 361, 398.
[10] [1983] 2 A.C. 803, 814; *cf. ante*, p. 202.

the conclusion that the clause applied to a negligent breach even though it did not refer to negligence[11]; and the distinction between the two types of clauses is also relevant in considering whether a clause applies to a particularly serious breach. In the *Ailsa Craig*[12] case the House of Lords emphasised that the clause did not wholly exclude liability; and this was also true of the clause in the *Suisse Atlantique*[13] case. The clause in the *Photo Production*[14] case was, indeed, one of total exclusion, but it only excluded liability to the extent that the defendants were not personally at fault.

Exclusion and limitation clauses must be distinguished from clauses that fix damages in advance.[15] The distinction can be illustrated by reference to the *Suisse Atlantique*[16] case where a further ground for the decision was that the purpose of the demurrage clause was not to limit damages but rather to fix in advance the damages payable in the event of certain breaches.[17] Under a limitation clause the owners would have recovered such loss as they could prove, with an upper limit of $1,000 per day. Under the demurrage clause they were entitled to $1,000 per day even if they could not prove any loss at all, or only a smaller loss. In the circumstances, the clause operated to limit the liability of the charterers; but it differed from a limitation clause in that it was capable of benefiting either party. Therefore there was less need to apply strict rules of construction to it.[18]

This is true of arbitration clauses.[19] Although such clauses may be said to exclude a remedy (in restricting a party's right to sue on the contract in a court of law),[20] their main purpose is not to deprive a party of rights to compensation, but to set up machinery for determining these rights. The same is also true of a clause which merely prevents a party from asserting his rights by some specified procedure: *e.g.* by way of set-off (as opposed to cross-action).[21]

Clauses which assume that there has been a breach and exclude or limit liability must be distinguished from those which define a contracting party's duty.[22] For example, a building contract may provide for completion by a fixed date and contain an "exception" for delays caused by strikes. This may only be another way of saying that the builder will complete by the agreed date, if strikes permit: he is under no higher duty.[23] The clause in *G. H. Renton & Co.* v. *Palmyra Trading Corporation*[24] permitting discharge at ports other than London or Hull was of the same nature. In these cases, failure to complete on the day named, or to get to the specified

---

[11] *Ibid.*; *cf. ante*, p. 204.
[12] [1983] 1 W.L.R. 964.
[13] [1967] 1 A.C. 361.
[14] [1980] A.C. 827.
[15] *Post*, pp. 883 *et seq.*
[16] [1967] 1 A.C. 361.
[17] [1967] 1 A.C. 361, 395. 421, 435–436.
[18] *Semble* the rule does not apply to qualifications of provisions increasing a party's normal liability: *Adams* v. *Richardson & Starling Ltd.* [1969] 1 W.L.R. 1465.
[19] *Woolf* v. *Collis Removal Service* [1948] 1 K.B. 11. *Cf.* Unfair Contract Terms Act 1977, s.13(2).
[20] *Post*, p. 395.
[21] *The Fedora* [1986] 2 Lloyd's Rep. 441.
[22] See *The London Lion* [1980] 2 Lloyd's Rep. 456, 468; *The Saudi Prince* [1988] 1 Lloyd's Rep. 1.
[23] *Semble*, the position is the same under Unfair Contract Terms Act 1977, s.3(2)(*b*)(i). See further, *post*, p. 227.
[24] [1957] A.C. 149; *ante*, pp. 211–212.

ports, is *not a breach at all.*[25] On the other hand, a clause which provided that a builder was not to be liable for loss or damage due to his defective workmanship would be an exemption clause, for it would be absurd to suppose that a building contract should impose no duty at all with respect to the standard of workmanship.[26] This is all the more obvious where the clause only limits, and does not wholly exclude, liability. The rule of strict construction applies to exemption clauses, but it has been said that it does not apply to clauses which merely define the duties of a contracting party.[27] In borderline cases the distinction between the two types of clauses will not be easy to draw; but one important test is whether the events in which a clause operates are beyond the control of the party relying on it. If they are, the clause is likely to be regarded as a provision defining the contractual duty rather than as an exemption clause.[28]

(d) EFFECTS OF AFFIRMATION OR RESCISSION. A serious breach of the kind discussed above normally gives the injured party two remedies: he can claim damages, and he can rescind (or terminate) the contract.[29] An exemption clause may affect one or both of these remedies. If it only excludes or restricts the extent to which the party in breach is to be liable in *damages,* it will not affect the injured party's remedy by way of *rescission* at all. This is true even though the clause is, as a matter of construction, held to apply to the serious breach that has occurred. Thus in the *Suisse Atlantique*[30] case the clause covered the serious breach which had occurred, and so limited the shipowners' damages; but it did not deprive them of their right to rescind the contract by sailing their ship away. Conversely, a contract may contain a non-rejection or non-cancellation clause which excludes the right to rescind but makes no reference to damages. Such a clause may take away the right to rescind even for a very serious breach, but it would not prevent the injured party from claiming damages.

The right to rescind may be lost by affirmation; and it was held to have been so lost in the *Suisse Atlantique* case when the shipowners, with knowledge of the existence of that right, took no steps to rescind the charterparty.[31] The case therefore supports the view[32] that affirmation after a serious breach does not affect the operation of an exemption clause which only excludes or restricts *the right to damages* for that breach[33]: that right continues, after affirmation, to depend on the construction of the clause.

The position was at one time thought to be different if the injured party did not affirm the contract but rescinded it on account of the serious breach. It was argued that, by rescinding, the injured party could bring the whole contract to an end; and that in this way he could unilaterally get rid

[25] *The Angelia*, [1973] 1 W.L.R. 210, 230, disapproved, but on another point, in *The Nema* [1982] A.C. 724; *post*, p. 795.
[26] *Cf.*, in another context, *The Union Amsterdam* [1982] 2 Lloyd's Rep. 832, 836.
[27] *The Angelia, supra,* at p. 231; *Kenyon Son & Craven Ltd.* v. *Baxter Hoare & Co.* [1971] 1 W.L.R. 519, 522.
[28] *The Angelia, supra,* at p. 231; contrast *Blackburn* v. *Liverpool, etc., S.N. Co.* [1902] 1 K.B. 290 ("exception" expressly including negligence).
[29] *Post*, pp. 743 *et seq*.
[30] [1967] 1 A.C. 361; *ante*, p. 216.
[31] [1967] 1 A.C. at pp. 395, 398, 409, 410, 437.
[32] This view is also supported by *Chandris* v. *Isbrandtsen-Moller Inc.* [1951] 2 K.B. 240; reversed on another ground [1951] 1 K.B. at p. 256. For the apparently contrary decision in *Charterhouse Credit Ltd.* v. *Tolly* [1963] 2 Q.B. 683, see *ante*, p. 206, n. 90.
[33] *Cf.* Unfair Contract Terms Act 1977, s.9(2); *post*, p. 238.

of an exemption clause even though the clause, on its true construction, excluded or restricted the right to damages for the breach.[34] But this line of argument amounted to a reintroduction of the substantive doctrine after the *Suisse Atlantique* case; and it was rejected in *Photo Production Ltd.* v. *Securicor Transport Ltd.*[35] The defendants in that case agreed to provide a "night patrol service" for the plaintiffs' factory for a weekly charge of £8 15s. One of their employees started a small fire which got out of control so that the factory, worth £650,000, was destroyed. The contract contained a clause which, on its true construction, applied to this breach, in spite of the seriousness of its effects.[36] In holding that the defendants were protected by the clause, the House of Lords rejected the argument that the plaintiffs could get rid of the clause by rescinding the contract on account of the breach. Such action on their part could only absolve them from their obligation of further performance *after* they had elected to rescind.[37] It could not operate retrospectively so as to deprive the party in breach of the benefit of the clause with respect to loss suffered *before* that election had been made.

Where a party exercises his right to rescind for breach, he may, however, be prima facie entitled to damages not only in respect of past loss but also in respect of prospective loss, *i.e.* loss which he will suffer after rescission, as a result of the other party's wrongful repudiation.[38] Suppose, for example, that in the *Suisse Atlantique* case the shipowners had justifiably rescinded when only half the period of the charter had expired, and that they had found alternative employment for the ship. They would then, but for any exemption clauses, have been entitled to damages in respect of (i) detention of the ship before rescission and (ii) loss suffered thereafter if the alternative employment of the ship was less profitable than that under the original contract. The demurrage clause limited the damages for the past loss recoverable under the first head, but it did not even purport to affect the damages for prospective loss recoverable by reason of wrongful repudiation under the second head. When Lord Reid said that the shipowners would have been entitled to damages over and above the agreed demurrage if, instead of affirming the charterparty, they had justifiably terminated it,[39] he was (it is submitted) referring to this prospective loss. It should be emphasised that the demurrage clause did not cover this type of loss but only damages for detention under the first head. If an exemption clause on its true construction did cover prospective loss under the second head, it is submitted that the injured party could not, by simply rescinding the contract on account of the breach, get rid of the clause so as to recover full damages in respect of loss of this kind. To allow him to do so would not, indeed, infringe the principle that rescission for breach has no retrospective effect; but it would be inconsistent with the rejection of the substantive doctrine of fundamental breach. This submission is supported by a

---

[34] *e.g. Harbutt's "Plasticine" Ltd.* v. *Wayne Tank Co. Ltd.* [1970] 1 Q.B. 447, overruled in *Photo Production Ltd.* v. *Securicor Transport Ltd.* [1980] A.C. 827.

[35] [1980] A.C. 827. Guest, 96 L.Q.R. 324; Sealy [1980] C.L.J. 252; Palmer and Yates [1981] C.L.J. 108; Nicol and Rawlings, 43 M.L.R. 567.

[36] *Ante*, p. 216.

[37] [1980] A.C. 827, 844–845, 849–850.

[38] *Post*, p. 748.

[39] [1967] 1 A.C. 361, 398, *cf. ibid.* pp. 419 and 437. It does not seem that Lord Wilberforce intends to cast doubt on this dictum when in the *Photo Production* case at p. 842 he criticised a different passage of Lord Reid's speech.

dictum of Lord Diplock in the *Photo Production* case that liability for such loss can be "excluded or modified by express words."[40] Clauses which regulate "the manner in which liability . . . is to be established,"[41] *e.g.* by providing that a claim must be made within one year, similarly continue to govern the future relations of the parties even after rescission for serious breach.[42] Arbitration clauses likewise survive such rescission.[43]

To the general rule that termination does not retrospectively deprive a party of the benefit of exemption clauses, there is or may be an exception. In the deviation cases, it is commonly held that the carrier is deprived of the benefit of exemption clauses in respect of loss which has occurred before the owner of the goods elected to terminate the contract.[44] One possible explanation for this state of the law is that it follows, as a matter of construction, from the special considerations which affect deviation. If the cargo-owner loses the benefit of his insurance cover as soon as the ship deviates,[45] it might well be his intention that the shipowner should be fully liable from that point, and not from some later point at which the cargo-owner learns of the deviation and elects to terminate the contract. On this view, the deviation cases would be "assimilated into the general law of contract,"[46] so that a shipowner would not be retrospectively deprived of the protection of an exemption clause *merely* because the ship had deviated: he would only be so deprived where the clause was, on its true construction, intended to have such retrospective effect. An alternative possibility is simply to regard the deviation cases as exceptional or *sui generis.*[47] Whichever may be the true explanation, the authority of the deviation cases was expressly recognised in the *Photo Production* case.[48]

(e) BURDEN OF PROOF. An exemption clause may, as a matter of construction, be held not to cover certain serious breaches, and it may be alleged that the loss which has been suffered is due to such a breach. The question then arises whether it is up to the plaintiff to show that the breach which has occurred was of this kind or whether it is up to the defendant to show that the loss was not due to a breach of this kind (but to one that is covered by the clause).

This question has arisen in a number of cases in which goods were lost by a bailee to whom they had been entrusted for storage, carriage or cleaning. On the one hand, it can be argued that the bailee should not have the burden of proving that the loss was not due to the serious breach alleged, as it is notoriously difficult to prove a negative. On the other hand there is the argument that the result in these cases generally depends on the *manner* of the breach; that the bailee will generally be in a better position than the bailor to know how the goods were lost; and that the bailor should not have the burden of proving facts peculiarly accessible to the other party. After some conflict in the authorities, the latter argument has prevailed, so that

---

40 [1980] A.C. 827, at p. 849.
41 *The New York Star* [1981] 1 W.L.R. 138, 145.
42 *Ibid.*
43 *Heyman* v. *Darwins Ltd.* [1942] A.C. 356.
44 See the authorities cited at pp. 210–213, *ante.*
45 *Ante*, p. 210.
46 *The Antares* (*No. 2*) [1987] 1 Lloyd's Rep. 424, 428; *State Trading Corporation of India* v. *S. M. Golodetz Ltd.* [1989] 2 Lloyd's Rep. 277, 289; *cf. ibid.* at p. 287.
47 *Photo Production* case, [1980] A.C. 827, 845; *cf. ibid.* p. 850.
48 *Ibid.*; *ante*, p. 211.

the burden is on the bailee to show that the breach was not so serious as to fall outside the scope of the exemption clause.[49]

The above cases all concern breaches by bailees of their duty with regard to the safekeeping of the goods. They do not necessarily apply where the breach consists of delay in performance and is alleged to be serious because of its *consequences*.[50] In such cases it is probably the plaintiff who has the burden of proving that the delay is so serious as not to be covered by the clause. This is consistent with the principle of the bailment cases; for the consequences of the breach on the plaintiff's position would be a matter peculiarly within *his* (rather than the defendant's) knowledge.

3. Other Common Law Limitations

Even if an exemption clause on its true construction covers the breach that has occurred, its effectiveness is subject to a number of further common law limitations. These are much reduced in importance by the statutory limitations to be discussed later in this Chapter[51]; but they retain their practical importance in cases to which the statutory limitations do not apply.[52]

(1) Misrepresentation

In *Curtis* v. *Chemical Cleaning & Dyeing Co. Ltd.*,[53] the plaintiff took a dress to the defendants to be cleaned. She signed a receipt after being told that it exempted the defendants from liability for certain specified kinds of damage, when it actually exempted them for liability "for any damage, however arising." It was held that the defendants could not rely on the clause as they had induced the plaintiff to sign the receipt by misrepresenting its contents. Denning L.J. said[54] that mere failure to draw attention to the existence or extent of the exemption clause might in some circumstances amount to misrepresentation.

(2) Overriding undertaking

An exemption clause in a document with reference to which the parties contract can be overridden by an express inconsistent undertaking given at or before the time of contracting. Thus a buyer of goods by auction can recover damages for breach of an oral undertaking given at the time of sale although the printed conditions of sale exempt the seller from all liability for defects.[55] To bring this rule into operation, there must be an "express

---

[49] *Levison* v. *Patent Steam Cleaning Co. Ltd.* [1978] Q.B. 68, following *Woolmer* v. *Delmer Price Ltd.* [1955] 1 Q.B. 291, and distinguishing *Hunt & Winterbotham (West of England) Ltd.* v. *B.R.S. (Parcels) Ltd.* [1962] 1 Q.B. 617. See also *J. Spurling Ltd.* v. *Bradshaw* [1956] 1 W.L.R. 461, 466, 470; and *cf. United Fresh Meat Co. Ltd.* v. *Charterhouse Cold Storage Ltd.* [1974] 2 Lloyd's Rep. 286 (deterioration of goods in a warehouse); Handford, 38 M.L.R. 577; Males [1978] C.L.J. 24.

[50] *e.g.* in cases like the *Suisse Atlantique* case, [1967] 1 A.C. 361; *ante*, p. 216.

[51] *Post*, pp. 226–245.

[52] *Post*, pp. 241–244. Theoretically, the common law limitations could be used to impugn a clause which satisfied the statutory reasonableness test (*post*, pp. 231–235); but in practice it is unlikely that the statutory test could be satisfied where one of the common law limitations applied.

[53] [1951] 1 K.B. 805; *cf. Horry* v. *Tate & Lyle Refineries Ltd.* [1982] 2 Lloyd's Rep. 416, 422.

[54] At p. 809.

[55] *Couchman* v. *Hill* [1947] K.B. 554; *Harling* v. *Eddy* [1951] 2 K.B 739; these cases can also be explained on another ground: *ante*, p. 184; *cf. Brikom Investments Ltd.* v. *Carr* [1979] Q.B. 467, 480.

specific oral promise"[56] which is inconsistent with the exemption clause: a party is not prevented from relying on a clause merely because no reference was made to it at the time of contracting, so that (in this sense) it can be said to be inconsistent with the terms expressly agreed. Where a series of contracts is made under a master agreement, an obligation imposed by that agreement may similarly override an exemption clause contained in a written document evidencing the terms of the particular contract in question.[57]

(3) Excluding liability for fraud

The power to exclude liability for misrepresentation *inducing* a contract has been limited by section 3 of the Misrepresentation Act 1967[58]; but that section does not affect contractual provisions purporting to exclude liability for fraud in the *performance* of a contract. It seems unlikely that such a provision would now be regarded as effective. In *Tullis* v. *Jacson*[59] the parties to a building contract agreed to submit disputes to the arbitration of an architect, whose award was to be final, and not to be set aside for "any pretence, suggestion, charge or insinuation of fraud." An attempt to challenge the award on the ground that it was not made in good faith failed because of this provision. But this decision has been judicially criticised[60] and is in any event limited in two ways. Such a clause would not protect a party from liability for his *own* fraud[61] and an exemption clause cannot *by general words* exclude liability for fraud.[62]

(4) Excluding liability for breach of fiduciary duty

The promoter of a company is under a fiduciary duty to the company not to make a profit out of the promotion without disclosing it to the company.[63] He cannot contract out of this duty.[64] It is submitted that any attempt by a person who is under a fiduciary duty to exempt himself from liability for a deliberate breach of that duty would be similarly ineffective.

(5) Excluding "natural justice"

Members of an association may agree to submit certain disputes to a domestic tribunal, such as the disciplinary committee of a trade union. Such a tribunal is prima facie bound by certain rules of "natural justice." It must

---

[56] *George Mitchell (Chesterhall) Ltd.* v. *Finney Lock Seeds Ltd.* [1983] Q.B. 284, 309, affirmed without reference to this point [1983] 2 A.C. 803.

[57] *Gallagher* v. *B.R.S. Ltd.* [1974] 2 Lloyd's Rep. 440; *J. Evans & Son (Portsmouth) Ltd.* v. *Andrea Merzario* [1976] 1 W.L.R. 1078; *cf. Mendelssohn* v. *Normand Ltd.* [1970] 1 Q.B. 177.

[58] *Post*, p. 345.

[59] [1892] 3 Ch. 441. In so far as this case decides that the architect's decision was final on a point of law, it will not be followed: *Re Davstone Estates Ltd.'s Leases* [1969] 2 Ch. 378.

[60] *Czarnikow* v. *Roth, Schmidt & Co.* [1922] 2 K.B. 478, 488.

[61] *S. Pearson & Son Ltd.* v. *Dublin Corporation* [1907] A.C. 351, 353, 362; *cf. Garden Neptune Shipping Ltd.* v. *Occidental Worldwide Investment Corp.* [1990] 1 Lloyd's Rep. 330, 335.

[62] *S. Pearson & Son Ltd.* v. *Dublin Corporation, supra*; *Walker* v. *Boyle* [1982] 1 W.L.R. 495. *Cf. Schneider* v. *Heath* (1813) 3 Camp. 506 and *Re Englefield Holdings* [1962] 1 W.L.R. 1119.

[63] See Gower, *Modern Company Law* (4th ed.), pp. 326 *et seq.*

[64] *Gluckstein* v. *Barnes* [1900] A.C. 240. This rule is quite independent of the statutory provisions set out, *post*, p. 358.

give each party a fair hearing and a chance to rebut the case that is made against him; and its members must not have any pecuniary interest in the dispute or any other interest which is likely to bias them.[65] In a number of cases[66] Lord Denning M.R. has said that a provision in the rules of an association would be void if it purported to oust the rules of "natural justice." Such rules "are more like by-laws than a contract"[67] and can, like by-laws,[68] be held invalid for unreasonableness. An attempt to oust the rules of "natural justice" would be unreasonable and thus ineffective.[69]

(6) Unreasonableness

It is sometimes said that exemption clauses may be held invalid on the ground that they are "unreasonable in themselves or irrelevant to the main purpose of the contract"[70] or "so unreasonable that no-one could contemplate that they exist."[71] Unreasonableness of the latter kind can certainly be relevant to the process of incorporation of a clause in a contract, in the sense that the degree of notice required for this purpose increases in proportion to the unusualness of the clause.[72] Some dicta go further and suggest that even a properly incorporated clause can be invalid on the ground of unreasonableness.[73] But no decision squarely supports this view, which is also rejected in other dicta.[74] Now that many exemption clauses are subject to a requirement of reasonableness under the Unfair Contract Terms Act 1977,[75] it seems unlikely that the courts will impose a similar requirement at common law.[76] Such a development would be open to the objections that it would apply a reasonableness test precisely in those cases which Parliament had decided to exclude from the scope of that test in the

---

[65] See de Smith, *Judicial Review of Administrative Action* (4th ed.), Chaps. 4 and 5, for a full account of these rules.

[66] *Lee* v. *Showmen's Guild* [1952] 2 Q.B. 329; *Bonsor* v. *Musicians' Union* [1954] Ch. 479 (dissenting): the majority decision was reversed by the House of Lords [1956] A.C. 104, without reference to this point. *Cf. Edwards* v. *SOGAT* [1971] Ch. 354, 382; *Enderby Town F.C. Ltd.* v. *The F.A. Ltd.* [1971] Ch. 591, 606; *Breen* v. *A.E.U.* [1971] 2 Q.B. 175, 190; and see *London Export Corp.* v. *Jubilee Coffee Roasting Co.* [1958] 1 W.L.R. 661.

[67] *Bonsor's* case (*supra*) [1954] Ch. at p. 485.

[68] *Kruse* v. *Johnson* [1898] 2 Q.B. 291.

[69] For the contrary view, see *Maclean* v. *The Workers' Union* [1929] Ch. 602, 603; Citrine, *Trade Union Law* (3rd ed.), p. 278; *cf. Russell* v. *Duke of Norfolk* [1949] 1 All E.R. 109, where a majority of the Court of Appeal held that an undertaking to observe the rules of natural justice could not be implied into a contract the terms of which gave the domestic tribunal an absolute discretion. See also *Fontaine* v. *Chesterton* (1968) S.J. 690, discussed in *John* v. *Rees* [1970] Ch. 345, 398–400.

[70] *Watkins* v. *Rymill* (1883) 10 Q.B.D. 178, 189.

[71] *Thompson* v. *London, Midland & Scottish Ry.* [1930] 1 K.B. 41, 56.

[72] *Ante*, p. 200; *cf.* (in relation to terms other than exemption clauses) *post*, pp. 246–247.

[73] See Lord Denning M.R. in *Thornton* v. *Shoe Lane Parking Ltd.* [1971] 2 Q.B. 163, 170; *Gillespie Bros. & Co. Ltd.* v. *Roy Bowles Transport Ltd.* [1973] Q.B. 400, 416; *Levison* v. *Patent Steam Carpet Cleaning Co. Ltd.* [1978] Q.B. 68, 69; *Re Brocklehurst (dec'd)* [1978] Ch. 14, 31 (dissenting); *Standard Chartered Bank Ltd.* v. *Walker* [1982] 1 W.L.R. 1410, 1416.

[74] *Van Toll* v. *South Eastern Ry.* (1862) 12 C.B.N.S. 75, 85; *Grand Trunk Ry. of Canada* v. *Robinson* [1915] A.C. 740, 747; *Ludditt* v. *Ginger Coote Airways Ltd.* [1947] A.C. 233, 242.

[75] *Post*, pp. 231–235.

[76] *Clark* v. *West Ham Corp.* [1909] 2 K.B. 858 is best explained as turning on the construction of the relevant statute.

1977 Act[77]; and that, if such a requirement existed at common law, many of the provisions of the Act[78] would scarely have been necessary.

(7) Third parties

The question whether exemption clauses can protect or prejudice third parties is discussed in Chapter 15.

4. The Unfair Contract Terms Act[79]

The most important limitations on the efficacy of exemption clauses are now statutory. Many (but not all) of these are contained in the Unfair Contract Terms Act 1977. The Act follows earlier legislation in using two techniques of control: some exemption clauses[80] are simply made ineffective, while others are subjected to a requirement of reasonableness. Other legislation using these same techniques will be incorporated in the following discussion of the 1977 Act. Legislation using different techniques will be separately considered.

(1) Preliminary definitions

The operation of the Act depends on a number of preliminary definitions.

(a) "BUSINESS LIABILITY" and "DEALING AS CONSUMER." The Act defines "business liability" as "liability for breach of obligations or duties arising (a) from things done or to be done by a person in the course of a business (whether his own business or another's); or (b) from the occupation of premises used for business purposes of the occupier."[81] Such a person will in the following discussion be called B.

A person "deals as consumer" if he does not make (or hold himself out as making) the contract in the course of a business *and* the other party does make the contract in the course of a business.[82] For this purpose, a contract is only made "in the course of" a business if it forms part of the *regular* course of dealing of that business.[83] In the case of contracts for the supply of goods it is also necessary that the goods are of a type ordinarily supplied for private use or consumption.[84] A buyer by auction or competitive tender is not to be regarded as dealing as consumer.[85] In the following discussion a person who deals as consumer will be called C.

---

[77] The argument would not apply to contractual terms *other than* exemption clauses, discussed at pp. 246–247, *post*, in relation to which there is no statutory reasonableness test similar to that existing under the 1977 Act.

[78] *i.e.* those imposing the requirement of reasonableness: *post*, pp. 231–235.

[79] Thompson, *Unfair Contract Terms Act 1977*; Coote, (1978) 41 M.L.R. 312; Sealy [1978] C.L.J. 15; Reynolds, [1978] 1 L.M. C.L.Q. 201; Adams and Brownsword, 104 L.Q.R. 94.

[80] The Act also deals with certain notices not having contractual effect, *e.g.* in ss.2 and 11(3). Such notices were formerly used to exclude or restrict tort liability and are beyond the scope of this book.

[81] s.1(3). "Business" includes a profession and activities of government departments or local or public authorities: s.14. Liability to persons gaining access to premises for recreational or educational purposes is excepted, in certain circumstances, by Occupiers' Liability Act 1984, s.2

[82] s.12(1)(*a*) and (*b*).

[83] *R. & B. Customs Brokers Ltd.* v. *United Dominions Trust Ltd.* [1988] 1 W.L.R. 321 (company held to have dealt as consumer in buying a car for use of one of its directors, having only made two or three such purchases in the past); Price, 52 M.L.R. 245; Jones and Harland, 2 J.C.L. 266.

[84] s.12(1)(*c*).

[85] s.12(2).

Generally, contracts will be made between B and C, or between B1 and B2. It is, however, impossible to have a contract between two persons each of whom deals as consumer, since it is part of the definition of dealing as consumer that one party does, while the other does not, make the contract in the course of a business. If, for example, a car were sold "privately" (neither buyer nor seller acting in the course of a business) there would be no dealing as consumer. However, a person can deal as consumer in disposing of goods, no less than in acquiring goods or services: for example, if the "private" (non-business) owner of a car transferred it to a car dealer in part-exchange for a new car, he would deal as consumer in relation to the first as well as to the second vehicle.

(b) EXCLUDING OR RESTRICTING LIABILITY. The Act limits the effectiveness of clauses that "exclude or restrict" liability. To the same extent it also prevents a party from doing certain analogous things: for example, from imposing a short time limit within which claims must be brought, or from excluding a particular remedy (such as rejection) without affecting another (such as damages).[86] Other provisions which do not in terms exclude or restrict liability may nevertheless have this effect in substance. For example, provision in a contract between X and Y that Y will indemnify X for any liability which X may incur to Y is in substance a clause excluding X's liability to Y and will be treated as such for the purposes of the Act.[87] The same may be true of a clause requiring an employee to work such long hours as to suffer an injury to his health for which the employer would (but for the clause) be liable.[88] On the other hand, a valid agreed damages clause[89] is probably not subject to the Act, for such a clause may extend as well as restrict liability. An agreement in writing to submit present or future differences to arbitration is not to be treated as excluding or restricting liability.[90]

In two cases, the Act prevents a party from excluding or restricting *duties* (as opposed to *liabilities*): namely where a provision purports to exclude (i) the duty of care giving rise to liability in negligence[91] or (ii) the duties arising out of terms implied by law in contracts for the supply of goods.[92] Apart from these cases, the Act does not strike at provisions that specify the duties of the parties. Thus a provision purporting to exclude or restrict a seller's duty as to the fitness of goods for a particular purpose would only be effective to the extent permitted by the Act[93]; but the effectiveness of a clause qualifying a provision as to the time of delivery (*e.g.* by making it "subject to strikes" or "subject to availability") would be governed by the rules of common law.[94]

At common law a distinction is sometimes drawn between clauses which exclude or restrict liability and those which prevent it from arising[95]; and in some cases this distinction is no doubt relevant for the purposes of the Act.

[86] s.13(1).
[87] *Phillips Products Ltd.* v. *Hyland* [1987] 1 W.L.R. 659, *post*, p. 234.
[88] *Johnstone* v. *Bloomsbury Health Authority* [1991] I.R.L.R. 118.
[89] *Ante*, p. 219; *post*, p. 883.
[90] s.13(2).
[91] See the reference to ss.2 and 5 in s.13(1).
[92] See the reference to ss.6 and 7 in s.13(1); *cf.* s.30.
[93] See s.6(1) and (2).
[94] s.3(2)(*b*)(ii) would not apply to such a clause: see *post*, p. 232.
[95] *Cf. ante*, p. 219.

For example, if a seller of goods expressly warned the buyer *not* to use goods for a specified purpose, any implied term of fitness for that particular purpose would be negatived, and the warning would not be subject to the Act.[96] But to give such effect to all provisions which might at common law prevent liability from arising would, it has been said, "emasculate"[97] the Act. In *Smith* v. *Eric S. Bush*[98] the House of Lords has therefore held that a clause purporting to exclude responsibility for negligence on the part of the valuer of a house was subject to the test of reasonableness under the Act. The decision was based on section 13(1) of the Act, by which a term purporting to exclude the duty of care giving rise to liability in negligence is to be treated as a term excluding or restricting liability. In order to determine whether such a duty existed, the court must disregard the term purporting to exclude it, and ask itself whether, but for the existence of the term, there would have been such a duty; if so, the effectiveness of term is then subject to the restrictions imposed by the Act. It seems likely that the courts will also "look behind" certain other clauses which are similarly being used in an obvious attempt to evade the Act.[99]

(2) Ineffective terms

In the following cases, attempts to exclude or restrict liability are wholly ineffective under the 1977 Act and other legislation.

(a) NEGLIGENCE LIABILITY: DEATH OR PERSONAL INJURY. By section 2(1) of the 1977 Act, B[1] cannot by any contract term or notice exclude or restrict his[2] liability for death or personal injury[3] resulting from negligence[4] to any person (whether C or not). Provisions excluding *strict* liability for death or personal injury are not affected by section 2(1). Under other enactments, any provision in a contract for the carriage of passengers by rail[5] or by road in a public service vehicle[6] is void if it purports to negative or limit the liability of the carrier in respect of the death or personal injury of the passenger. These enactments do not expressly refer to negligence, but since

---

[96] *Wormell* v. *R.H.M. Agriculture (East) Ltd.* [1987] 1 W.L.R. 1091; *cf. Harlingdon & Leinster Enterprises Ltd.* v. *Christopher Hull Fine Art Ltd.* [1990] 1 All E.R. 737, 753, and the examples given at p. 219, *ante*.

[97] *Smith* v. *Eric S. Bush* [1990] 1 A.C. 831, 848.

[98] *Supra*, n. 97; *cf. Davies* v. *Parry* [1988] 1 E.G.L.R. 147.

[99] *Cf. post*, p. 346. *Smith* v. *Eric S. Bush*, *supra*, only deals with clauses purporting to exclude the duty of care giving rise to liability in negligence. It seems that the "but for" test there formulated would not apply to sale of goods cases such as *Wormell* v. *R.H.M. Agriculture (East) Ltd.*, *supra*, n. 96: in order to determine for what "particular purpose" goods had been bought, a warning such as the one given in that case would, it is submitted, have to be taken into account.

[1] See s.1(3); *ante*, p. 226.

[2] s.2 does not prevent a contracting party from excluding or restricting the liability of a *third* party: *The Chevalier Roze* [1983] 2 Lloyd's Rep. 438, 442. For the effect of the section on indemnity clauses, see *post*, p. 234.

[3] As defined by s.14.

[4] As defined by s.1(1). "Negligence" is there stated to include "breach . . . of any obligation, arising from the . . . terms . . . of a contract, to take reasonable care . . . ;" for the purpose of this definition the court must apply the "but for" test (*supra*, n. 99), *i.e.* it must disregard a clause the effect of which is (or would be, if the clause were valid) to exclude liability for such a breach: *Phillips Products Ltd.* v. *Hyland* [1987] 1 W.L.R. 659.

[5] Transport Act 1962, s.43(7).

[6] Public Passenger Vehicles Act 1981, s.29. *Cf.* also Financial Services Act 1986, s.84 (dealing with purely financial loss).

the carrier is not liable in the absence of negligence[7] their scope is restricted to negligence liability.

Section 2(1) does not apply where death or personal injury results from a breach of contract or duty which can be, and is, committed without negligence: for example, where a seller supplies defective goods to a buyer, where a producer incurs "product liability" in respect of defective products, or where a person who does work for the provision of a dwelling fits defective components.[8] Clauses purporting to exclude liability for such breaches may, however, be ineffective under other provisions of the Act,[9] or under other legislation.[10]

(b) "GUARANTEES" OF CONSUMER GOODS. Section 5 deals with provisions in "guarantees" of goods of a type ordinarily supplied for private use or consumption. It does not apply between the parties to the contract for the supply of the goods[11]: their relations are regulated by sections 6 and 7. It is aimed at the relations between manufacturer and customer under so-called manufacturers' guarantees.[12]

The section defines a "guarantee" as a written promise or assurance that defects will be made good.[13] It provides that B[14] cannot by means of such a guarantee exclude or restrict liability for loss or damage that arises from defects in the goods while in "consumer use" and results from the negligence of a person concerned in the manufacture or distribution of the goods.[15] Goods are in "consumer use" when a person is using them or has them in his possession otherwise than *exclusively* for the purpose of a business. Thus generally section 5 will apply only between B and C. But it may also apply in certain other circumstances: for example, where a car is bought in the course of a business (so that the buyer does not deal as consumer) and used partly for business and partly for private purposes.

(c) SALE OF GOODS AND HIRE-PURCHASE. Section 6(1) provides that liability for breach of the undertakings as to title implied by statute[16] into contracts for the sale or hire-purchase of goods cannot be excluded or restricted by reference to any contract term. Section 6(2) lays down the same rule, but only "as against a person dealing as consumer," in relation to the statutorily implied terms as to correspondence of the goods with description or sample, and as to their quality or fitness for a particular purpose.[17]

As a general principle the only types of terms made completely ineffec-

---

[7] *Readhead* v. *Midland Ry.* (1869) L.R. 4 Q.B. 376; *Barkway* v. *S. Wales Transport Co. Ltd.* [1950] 1 All E.R. 392, 403–404.

[8] For strict liability in such cases, see *post*, p. 738.

[9] *e.g.* ss.6, 7.

[10] Defective Premises Act 1972, s.1(1) ("proper materials") and s.6(3). Consumer Protection Act, 1987, ss.5 and 7(1); *post*, p. 230.

[11] s.5(3).

[12] See *ante*, p. 74 and *post*, p. 523.

[13] s.5(2)(*b*); making good is defined so as to include payment of compensation.

[14] See s.1(3).

[15] s.5(1). Consumer Protection Act 1987, s.7 (*post*, p. 231) could also apply to such a guarantee.

[16] By Sale of Goods Act 1979, s.12 and Supply of Goods (Implied Terms) Act 1973, s.8 as substituted by Consumer Credit Act 1974, s.192 and Sched. 4, para. 35.

[17] By Sale of Goods Act 1979, ss.13–15 and Supply of Goods (Implied Terms) Act 1973, ss.9–11 as substituted by Consumer Credit Act 1974, s.192 and Sched. 4, para. 35; *Hughes* v. *Hall and Hall* [1981] R.T.R. 430.

tive by the Act are those purporting to exclude or restrict "business liability."[18] Section 6(4), however, provides that the liabilities referred to "in this section" are not only "business liabilities . . . but include those arising under any contract of sale of goods or hire-purchase agreement." It follows that a private (non-business) seller cannot exclude or restrict liability for breach of the implied undertakings as to title. At first sight, s.6(4) suggests that an attempt by a private seller to exclude or restrict liability for breach of the implied undertakings as to correspondence with description, etc., (referred to in section 6(2)) is equally ineffective. But section 6(2) only applies "as against a person dealing as consumer," and a person can only so deal if "the other party does make the contract in the course of a business."[19] Since a private seller does not contract "in the course of a business," it seems that a person who buys from such a seller does not "deal as consumer" and is not protected by section 6(2); he is only protected by the requirement of reasonableness.[20] In some cases, indeed, the statutorily implied condition only arises at all where the supplier acts in the course of a business. This is true of the implied conditions as to merchantable quality and fitness for a particular purpose.[21] Here the private supplier is never subject to the statutorily implied term at all, and so the issue of the validity of a clause excluding liability for breach of it cannot arise.[22]

(d) OTHER CONTRACTS FOR THE SUPPLY OF GOODS. Section 7 deals with contracts for the supply of goods other than contracts of sale and hire-purchase: for example, contracts of exchange, pledge or hire. By statute, such contracts contain implied terms as to title, correspondence with description or sample, quality and fitness for a particular purpose.[23] As against C, B[24] cannot, in such contracts, exclude or restrict liability in respect of the failure of the goods to correspond with their description or with a sample, or in respect of their quality or fitness for a particular purpose.[25] So far as liability for breach of the implied terms as to title is concerned, a distinction must be drawn. Such liability cannot be excluded by B[26] where the contract is one by which he transfers or agrees to transfer the property in the goods to another (not necessarily C): this rule would, for example, apply to a contract of exchange. But where the contract is not one by which property is transferred or to be transferred (*e.g.* where it is one of pledge or hire) attempts by B[27] to exclude or restrict such liability are subject only to the test of reasonableness.[28]

(e) PRODUCT LIABILITY. Under Part I of the Consumer Protection Act 1987, producers, and certain other persons engaged in the distribution, of products which are defective, in the sense of being unsafe, are liable if the defect causes death or personal injury or certain kinds of damage to prop-

---

[18] See s.1(3) of the 1977 Act.
[19] s.12(1)(*b*).
[20] s.6(3), *post*, p. 232.
[21] Sale of Goods Act 1979, s.14(2) and (3); Supply of Goods (Implied Terms) Act 1973, s.10(2) and (3) as substituted by Consumer Credit Act 1974, s.192 and Sched. 4, para. 35.
[22] See further *post*, pp. 232–233.
[23] Supply of Goods and Services Act 1982, ss.2–5, 7–10.
[24] Unfair Contract Terms Act 1977, s.1(3).
[25] *Ibid.* s.7(2).
[26] ss.1(3) and 7(3A), as inserted by Supply of Goods and Services Act 1982, s.17(2).
[27] Unfair Contract Terms Act 1977, s.1(3).
[28] *Ibid.* s.7(4), as amended by Supply of Goods and Services Act 1982, s.17(3).

erty. Section 7 of the 1987 Act provides that such "product liability" (which arises without proof of negligence and irrespective of contract) cannot be limited or excluded by any contract term, notice or other provision.

(f) DANGEROUS GOODS. Under Part II of the Consumer Protection Act 1987, it is an offence to supply goods which do not comply with a general safety requirement laid down by the Act and in safety regulations made under the Act. Failure to perform an obligation imposed by such a regulation gives a civil remedy to any person who may be affected by a contravention of the obligation; and the resulting liability cannot be excluded by any contract term, notice or other provision.[29]

(3) Terms subject to the requirement of reasonableness

In the following cases, exemption clauses are, under the 1977 Act, subject to the requirement of reasonableness. Where the requirement applies, the burden of showing that it is satisfied lies on the party so claiming.[30]

(a) NEGLIGENCE LIABILITY: HARM OTHER THAN DEATH OR PERSONAL INJURY. By section 2(2) the requirement applies to a contract term or notice by which B[31] seeks to exclude or restrict his[32] liability for negligence[33] giving rise to loss or damage other than death or personal injury. The subsection does not apply to provisions excluding or restricting *strict* liability[34]; on the other hand it is not confined to cases where the other party deals as consumer. In both these respects, it resembles section 2(1).

(b) CONSUMER CONTRACTS AND STANDARD FORM CONTRACTS. Section 3 applies to two situations: to any contract between B and C; and to a contract in which a party (not necessarily C) deals with B on the latter's "written standard terms of business."[35] In such cases B cannot "by reference to any contract term," except insofar as it satisfies the requirement of reasonableness, do any of the following three things:

(i) Under section 3(2)(*a*) B cannot exclude or restrict any liability in respect of his own breach. This provision refers to "any liability": not merely to liability for negligence. It thus includes strict liability[36] for breach of contract.

(ii) Under section 3(2)(*b*)(i) B cannot "claim to be entitled . . . to render a contractual performance substantially different from that which was reasonably expected of him." This would, for example, subject to the requirement of reasonableness provisions in a tour operator's contract purporting to entitle him to change the advertised route, accommodations or means of transport.[37] B cannot rely on the provision even though he is not actually obliged to render the performance expected: the criterion is the

---

29 Consumer Protection Act 1987, ss.10, 41(1) and (4).

30 Unfair Contract Terms Act 1977, s.11(5).

31 s.1(3).

32 See *ante*, p. 228, n. 4. For the effect of the section on indemnity clauses, see *post*, p. 234.

33 As defined by s.1(1).

34 See *ante*, p. 229. A contract term or notice purporting to exclude certain types of property damage is ineffective irrespective of reasonableness: Consumer Protection Act 1987, ss.5, 7(1), *ante*, p. 230.

35 s.3(1). The section does not apply to specially negotiated contracts: *The Flammar Pride* [1990] 1 Lloyd's Rep. 434, 438.

36 *Post*, p. 737.

37 *e.g.* it would apply to a situation such as that which arose in *Anglo-Continental Holidays Ltd.* v. *Typaldos Lines (London) Ltd.* [1967] 2 Lloyd's Rep. 61.

reasonable expectation of the other party, not the obligation of B under the contract.

(iii) Under section 3(2)(*b*)(ii) B cannot "claim to be entitled . . . in respect of the whole or any part of his contractual obligation to render no performance at all." This would apply where an agreement is on its true construction held to impose a contractual obligation but gives or purports to give B a wide discretion whether to perform at all or to the full extent promised. The criterion is not (as it is under section 3(2)(*b*)(i)) what the other party reasonably expects: it is the obligation undertaken by B. If the "contract term" gave B a totally free discretion whether to perform or not, there might be no "contractual obligation" on B at all; and in such a case the requirement of reasonableness need not be satisfied. Section 3(2)(*b*)(ii) would also not apply to a clause defining B's duty[38] in such a way that in the circumstances which have occurred no duty arose; *e.g.* where B promised to perform "subject to strikes" and strikes have prevented performance.

In a number of other situations, the scope of section 3(2)(*b*)(ii) is harder to determine. A contract may provide that B is entitled to cancel in certain events: *e.g.* on the other party's failure to perform (whether or not it amounts to a breach) or on some other event, such as the other party's death.[39] Or it may provide that B is only bound to perform when the other party's performance has been rendered in full, or when some prescribed part of the performance has been rendered.[40] For example, a building contract may provide that nothing is to be paid till the work is completed, or that instalments of the price are to be paid as specific parts of the work are done. Such provisions might at first sight appear to be literally within section 3(2)(*b*)(ii); but it does not seem to have been the purpose of that enactment to alter the law as to cancellation clauses of the kind mentioned above, or as to the effect of the other party's breach on the obligations of B. It is submitted that the scope of the enactment must be narrowed by a restrictive interpretation of the opening words of section 3(2), according to which B cannot do the three things specified in the subsection "by reference to any contract term." These words should be taken to mean "by reference *only* to such a term"—not by reference to it combined with other circumstances justifying B's refusal, such as a failure by the other party to perform his part.

(c) SUPPLY OF GOODS. By section 6(3), the requirement of reasonableness applies to a term in a contract for the sale or hire-purchase of goods purporting to exclude or restrict liability for breach of the statutorily implied terms[41] as to correspondence of the goods with description or sample, or as to their quality or fitness for a particular purpose, where the buyer or hire-purchaser deals otherwise than as consumer.[42] A similar rule is laid down by section 7(3) with regard to terms in other contracts for the supply of goods (such as contracts of hire or exchange) purporting to exclude liability for breach of similar terms implied by law in such contracts.[43] Section 7 only applies to terms purporting to exclude or restrict "business liability"[44]

---

38 *Ante*, p. 227; s.3 is *not* referred to in s.13(1).
39 *Post*, p. 680.
40 *Post*, pp. 683–689.
41 *Ante*, p. 229, n. 16.
42 See *ante*, p. 229 for the position where he deals as consumer.
43 *Ante*, p. 230 at n. 23.
44 s.1(3).

so that section 7(3) is restricted to the case where the supplier acts in the course of a business and the acquirer does not deal as consumer. Section 6 is however not restricted to the case where the supplier acts in the course of a business.[45] A term by which a private seller seeks to exclude or restrict liability for breach of the statutorily implied terms (even against a buyer who acts in the course of a business) is therefore under section 6(3) subject to the requirement of reasonableness. However, the statutorily implied terms as to merchantable quality and fitness for a particular purpose only arise where the supplier acts in the course of a business.[46] A private supplier is under no liability in respect of such matters unless he gives an express undertaking. There is nothing in the Act to prevent him from restricting his liability for breach of such an *express* undertaking, *e.g.* by limiting his liability to a specified sum. In this respect he is in a better position than a business supplier, whose right so to limit his liability for breach of an express term may be subject to the requirement of reasonableness under section 3, *e.g.* if he deals on his "written standard terms of business."

We have seen that B cannot exclude or restrict his liability for breach of the implied terms as to title in contracts of sale and hire-purchase, and in certain other contracts under which he transfers or agrees to transfer the property in goods[47] (such as contracts of exchange). In contracts for the transfer or supply of goods which fall outside this group, section 7(4)[48] applies the requirement of reasonableness to terms by which B seeks to exclude or restrict such liability: this would, for example, be the position in contracts of pledge,[49] or hire. As section 7 only applies to "business liability,"[50] a private supplier's right to exclude or restrict liability in respect of defects of title in contracts of this kind is in no way affected by the Act. This is also true where a private supplier enters into a contract (other than one of sale or hire-purchase) by which he transfers or agrees to transfer the property in goods: for example, where the contract is one of exchange.[51] Where, on the other hand, the contract is one of sale or hire-purchase, a term by which even a private supplier seeks to exclude or restrict liability for breach of the implied undertakings as to title is simply ineffective,[52] without regard to its reasonableness.

(d) INDEMNITY CLAUSES. A contract may provide that if one party incurs a liability under it, whether to the other party or to a third party, then the other party shall indemnify the first against such liability. For example, a contract for the hire of a vehicle with a driver may contain a clause by which the hirer promises to indemnify the owner for any injury, loss or damage caused by the negligence of the driver.

Section 4 of the Act applies the requirement of reasonableness to a con-

---

[45] s.6(4).

[46] Sale of Goods Act 1979 s.14(2) and (3); Supply of Goods (Implied Terms) Act 1973, s.10(2) and (3), as substituted by Consumer Credit Act 1974, s.192 and Sched. 4, para. 35.

[47] *Ante*, pp. 229, 230.

[48] As amended by Supply of Goods and Services Act 1982, s.17(3).

[49] See Supply of Goods and Services Act 1982, s.1(2)(*e*).

[50] Unfair Contract Terms Act 1977, s.1(3).

[51] The restriction on the effectiveness of terms excluding liability for breach of the implied terms as to title in such contracts is imposed by Unfair Contract Terms Act 1977, s.7(3A) (*ante*, p. 230, n. 26) which, like the rest of s.7 only applies to "business liability": s.1(3).

[52] s.6(1); *ante*, p. 229.

tract term by which C undertakes to indemnify another person in respect of a business liability[53] incurred by the other for negligence or breach of contract. The operation of the section, and its relationship to other provisions of the Act, can best be explained by distinguishing between two situations, based on the example just given.

(i) *Injury, loss or damage caused to a third party.* Where the driver negligently injures, or causes loss or damage to, a third party, section 4 subjects the indemnity clause to the requirement of reasonableness, but only if the hirer dealt as consumer. The clause is therefore not subject to the requirement of reasonableness, under section 4, if the contract of hire was between B1 and B2. Nor is the clause treated as an exemption clause for the purposes of the Act, since it does not "exclude or restrict" the liability of the owner to the third party: it simply determines by whom (as between owner and hirer) that liability is to be borne.[54] It follows that section 2 does not apply and that the clause is neither ineffective (in case of personal injury)[55] nor subject to the requirement of reasonableness (in case of other loss or damage).[56] Section 4 likewise does not apply to an indemnity clause in a contract between two parties neither of whom acts in the course of a business, since neither party to such a contract "deals as consumer."[57] Here again the clause is not subject to section 2, both because it is not an exemption clause and because section 2 is restricted to "business liability."[58] The clause is likewise not an exemption clause for the purpose of other restrictions (already discussed)[59] imposed by the Act on the operation of exemption clauses.

(ii) *Injury, loss or damage caused to indemnifier.* Where (in our example) the driver negligently injures, or causes loss or damage to, the hirer himself, section 4 again subjects the indemnity clause to the requirement of reasonableness if the hirer dealt as consumer. In addition, the clause is regarded as an exemption clause for the purposes of the Act since there is no difference of substance between the owner's saying to the hirer "I am not liable to you" and his saying "you must indemnity me against any damages which I may have to pay to you."[60] The clause is therefore subject not only to section 4 but also to other provisions of the Act, for example to section 2. This point is significant for two reasons. First, in cases of personal injury the clause is not merely subject to the requirement of reasonableness, as it would be if section 4 alone applied: the clause is simply ineffective under section 2(1). Secondly, in cases of other loss or damage the requirement of reasonableness must be satisfied, not only in contracts between B and C, as would be the case if section 4 alone applied: it must be satisfied also in contracts between B1 and B2, since section 2 applies even in favour of a person who does not deal as consumer. An indemnity clause in the present type of case will likewise be treated as an exemption clause

[53] s.1(3).
[54] *Thompson* v. *T. Lohan (Plant Hire) Ltd.* [1987] 1 W.L.R. 649; Sealy [1988] C.L.J. 6; Adams and Brownsword [1988] J.B.L. 146.
[55] Unfair Contract Terms Act 1977, s.2(1), *ante*, p. 228.
[56] *Ibid.* s.2(2), *ante*, p. 231.
[57] *Ante*, p. 227.
[58] Unfair Contract Terms Act 1977, s.1(3).
[59] *e.g.* those imposed by ss.6 and 7, *ante*, pp. 229–230, 232–233.
[60] *Phillips Products Ltd.* v. *Hyland* [1987] 1 W.L.R. 659.

for the purpose of other restrictions (already discussed)[61] imposed by the Act on the operation of exemption clauses.

(e) MISREPRESENTATION. The 1977 Act[62] amends section 3 of the Misrepresentation Act 1967, which had originally applied a requirement of reasonableness to terms excluding or restricting liability for misrepresentation. Such terms are now subject to the requirement of reasonableness as newly defined by the 1977 Act. The requirement applies to all contracts, and is not restricted to "business liabilities" or to contracts in which one party "deals as consumer." It is further discussed in Chapter 9.[63]

(4) Partly effective terms

Under the 1977 Act, a term may be partly effective and partly ineffective. There are two types of situations in which this may be the position.

First, a clause may be drafted so as to exclude or restrict both a liability which cannot be excluded or restricted at all, and one which can be excluded by a provision which satisfies the requirement of reasonableness or by one which is effective subject only to common law restrictions. A clause may, for example, purport to limit the liability of a seller of goods for *any* breach to the return of the contract price. Such a provision is wholly ineffective to protect him from liability for breach of the implied undertaking as to title.[64] But this does not make the clause entirely void.[65] Thus the seller could rely on it to limit his liability for some other breach: for example, for breach of the statutorily implied terms as to quality if the buyer was not dealing as consumer and the clause satisfied the requirement of reasonableness.[66] He could similarly rely on it to limit liability for late delivery (or simple non-delivery) subject only to common law restrictions.[67] These conclusions follow from the fact that the Act nowhere invalidates contractual provisions as such: it simply says that specified liabilities cannot be excluded or restricted "by reference" to them.

Secondly, the Act provides that terms subject to the requirement of reasonableness are ineffective "except in so far as,"[68] or effective "only in so far as,"[69] they satisfy the requirement of reasonableness. In most cases, the term will either satisfy the requirement (and so be effective) or fail to satisfy it (and so be ineffective). But the words "in so far as" make it possible for the court to hold one part of a term valid and another invalid. Thus where a clause in a contract for the sale of goods imposed a short time limit on all claims and also limited the seller's liability to the amount of the con-

[61] See n. 59, *supra*.
[62] s.8.
[63] *Post*, p. 345.
[64] s.6(1).
[65] *Cf. George Mitchell (Chesterhall) Ltd.* v. *Finney Lock Seeds Ltd.* [1983], Q.B. 284, 303, 309 decided under an earlier and now superseded statutory requirement of reasonableness and affirmed without reference to this point in [1983] 2 A.C. 803.
[66] s.6(3).
[67] Such breaches are not covered by s.6. If the buyer was not dealing as consumer and the seller was not dealing on his written standard terms of business, the Act would not apply to such a case: see *post*, p. 241.
[68] ss.2(2), 3(2), 4(1), and 7(4).
[69] ss.6(3) and 7(3).

tract price, it was held that the first part of the clause was reasonable, and the second unreasonable.[70]

In the situation just described, what appears to be a single clause is treated as severable and the court, having severed the clause, then determines separately the reasonableness of each of its parts. It seems unlikely, however, that where a clause (or a severable part of one) was unreasonable, the court would actually modify it so as to make it reasonable: *e.g.* by allowing a limitation of liability where the contract had provided for total exclusion,[71] or by striking out an unreasonably low limitation in the contract and substituting a higher one that the court regarded as reasonable. To do this would, it is submitted, be inconsistent with the wording of section 11(1) of the 1977 Act, under which the requirement of reasonableness "is that the term shall have been a fair and reasonable one to be included." This means that the reasonableness test has to be applied to the term actually in the contract (or to each such term, if the contract contains more than one) and not to some other term which in the court's view might reasonably have been included.

(5) Rules relating to reasonableness

A judicially administered requirement of reasonableness is open to the objection that it is a source of uncertainty.[72] To meet this objection, the Act lays down a rule as to the time for determining reasonableness and it also provides guidelines for this purpose. In addition, the Act lays down two rules as to the effects of breach on the requirement; their object is to prevent undue restrictions on its scope.

(a) TIME FOR DETERMINING REASONABLENESS. The question whether the requirement is satisfied is determined by reference to the time at which the contract was made.[73] If the term was a fair and reasonable one to be included having regard to the circumstances that were or should have been known to or in the contemplation of the parties *at that time,* its effectiveness will not be impaired by subsequent events.

(b) GUIDELINES. The Act lays down two guidelines for determining the reasonableness of provisions limiting a person's liability to a specific sum of money: regard is to be had to (a) the resources which that person could expect to be available to him for the purpose of meeting the liability, and (b) how far it was open to him to cover himself by insurance.[74] Under the second of these guidelines, a clause limiting the liability of a manufacturer for defects would not be reasonable if he could have insured against the liability without materially raising the price of his product.[75] On the other hand, a clause limiting the liability of a person engaged in the storage or

[70] *R. W. Green Ltd.* v. *Cade Bros. Farms* [1978] 1 Lloyd's Rep. 602, decided under an earlier and now superseded statutory requirement of reasonableness.

[71] *George Mitchell (Chesterhall) Ltd.* v. *Finney Lock Seeds Ltd.* [1983] 2 A.C. 803, 816.

[72] Treitel, *Doctrine and Discretion in the Law of Contract*, pp. 13–19. For the American experience under UCC ss.2–302, see Leff, 115 U. of Pa L.Rev. 485; Ellinghaus, 78 Y.L.J. 757.

[73] s.11(1). In the case of a non-contractual notice (*ante*, pp. 226, 231) the relevant time is the time when the liability arose or but for the notice would have arisen: s.11(3).

[74] s.11(4). The subsection is in terms applicable only to terms which *limit* (as opposed to those which wholly *exclude*) liability: *The Flammar Pride* [1990] 1 Lloyd's Rep. 434, 438.

[75] *George Mitchell (Chesterhall) Ltd.* v. *Finney Lock Seeds Ltd.* [1983] A.C. 803, 817, decided under earlier and now superseded legislation not containing this guideline.

carriage of goods would be reasonable if he had little knowledge of the nature or value the goods, and if the goods could be more cheaply insured by their owner than by the bailee.[76] In applying the second guideline, the court considers the *availability* of insurance to the defendant, rather than his *actual* insurance position.[77]

Where a provision in a contract for the supply of goods is subject to the requirement of reasonableness under sections 6 or 7 of the Act,[78] five further guidelines are provided.[79] These include the strength of the bargaining positions of the parties relative to each other, whether the customer "received an inducement to agree to the term" (*e.g.* in the form of a lower price), whether he could have bought elsewhere without being subjected to a similar term, and the customer's knowledge or means of knowledge of the existence and extent of the terms.[80] Under these guidelines, the fact that the contract was in a standard form settled after negotiations between trade associations to which both parties belonged is relevant to the issue of reasonableness; for it helps to show that its terms were "not imposed by the strong upon the weak."[81]

These guidelines no doubt help to reduce the uncertainty to which the requirement of reasonableness gives rise; but the restrictions on their scope are hard to understand. Thus it is not easy to see why the strength of the bargaining positions of the parties is relevant only in contracts for the supply of goods; nor why the five guidelines[82] which can apply where a seller delivers goods of the wrong *quality*[83] do not also apply where he delivers goods of the wrong *quantity*.[84] It seems that the courts can remedy this defect by applying the guidelines to cases which do not fall literally within them: for example, the guidelines stated in relation to contracts for the supply of goods can be applied by analogy to other types of contracts.[85]

Even in relation to the situations covered by them, the statutory guidelines are by no means exhaustive; indeed it has been said that it is "impossible to draw up an exhaustive list of factors to be taken into account when a judge is faced with this very difficult question."[86] In *Smith* v. *Eric S. Bush*[87] the House of Lords held that a term purporting to exclude the liability for

---

[76] *Singer (U.K.) Ltd.* v. *Tees & Hartlepool Port Authority* [1988] 2 Lloyd's Rep. 164.

[77] *Ibid.* at p. 169; *The Flammar Pride* [1990] 1 Lloyd's Rep. 434, 439.

[78] *Ante*, pp. 232–233.

[79] s.11(2) and Sched. 2.

[80] The question whether a provision *is* a term of the contract is, however, a separate question, as is recognised by the concluding words of s.11(2).

[81] *R. W. Green Ltd.* v. *Cade Bros. Farms Ltd.* [1978] 1 Lloyd's Rep. 602, 607; *supra*, n. 70; *The Zinnia* [1984] 2 Lloyd's Rep. 211; contrast *George Mitchell (Chesterhall) Ltd.* v. *Finney Lock Seeds Ltd.* where the conditions were not negotiated by the National Farmers Union but simply introduced by seed merchants without objection from farmers: see [1983] 2 A.C. 803, 817.

[82] *Supra*, n. 79.

[83] The requirement of reasonableness applies to terms purporting to exclude or restrict B's liability in such cases if the buyer does not deal as consumer: s.6(3).

[84] The requirement of reasonableness applies to terms purporting to exclude or restrict B's liability in such cases if the contract is made on his "written standard terms of business": s.3.

[85] *Singer (U.K.) Ltd.* v. *Tees & Hartlepool Port Authority* [1988] 2 Lloyd's Rep. 164, 169; *The Flammar Pride* [1990] 1 Lloyd's Rep. 434, 439.

[86] *Smith* v. *Eric S. Bush* [1990] 1 A.C. 831, 858.

[87] [1990] 1 A.C. 831; Kaye, 52 M.L.R. 841; for other factors relevant to the issue of reasonableness, see *George Mitchell (Chesterhall) Ltd.* v. *Finney Lock Seeds Ltd.* [1983] 2 A.C. 803, decided under an earlier (now superseded) statutory reasonableness test.

negligence of surveyors to buyers of dwelling houses did not satisfy the reasonableness test. The principal factors leading to this conclusion were that there was no equality of bargaining power, that the houses were of modest value so that it was not reasonable to expect the plaintiffs to seek alternative sources of information, *e.g.* by commissioning their own structural survey, and that the surveyors could easily have insured against the risk without unduly increasing their charges.[88] On the other hand, the House of Lords indicated that a disclaimer might be reasonable if the task undertaken had been of one of great difficulty and complexity, or if the value of the subject-matter had been very high, so that insurance against professional liability would have been very expensive or impossible to obtain.[89] Another factor relevant to the issue of reasonableness is the availability, to the party seeking to rely on the term, of an opportunity to discover the defect in respect of which he is seeking to exclude liability. Thus where the seller of a car was a company which had been brought into the transaction purely to provide finance, it was said that the test of reasonableness would have been satisfied (if the buyer had not dealt as consumer)[90] because the company had never seen the car.[91]

(c) NATURE OF DECISION ON REASONABLENESS. A decision on the issue of reasonableness is not merely an exercise of judicial discretion[92]; for it involves the application of statutory and judge-made guidelines. Nevertheless in the *George Mitchell* case Lord Bridge described such a decision as one on which there "will sometimes be room for a legitimate difference of judicial opinion"; and as one with which an appellate court should not interfere "unless satisfied that it proceeded on some erroneous principle or was plainly and obviously wrong."[93] The purpose of these remarks is clearly to discourage appeals on the issue of reasonableness.

(d) EFFECTS OF RESCISSION OR AFFIRMATION. Section 9(1) of the Act provides that effect may be given to a term which satisfies the requirement of reasonableness even though the contract has been terminated[94]; while section 9(2) provides that the requirement of reasonableness is not excluded by affirmation of the contract.[95]

(e) EFFECT OF SERIOUSNESS OF BREACH. Earlier in this Chapter, we saw that the question whether exemption clauses covered certain particularly serious breaches was one of construction.[96] If the clause does not cover such a breach, no issue of reasonableness will arise; but even if the clause does cover the breach it may still fail to satisfy the requirement of reasonableness, as in the *George Mitchell* case.[97] Hence reasonableness under the Act and the rules of construction applicable at common law remain separ-

---

[88] *Smith* v. *Eric S. Bush* [1990] 1 A.C. 831, 851–854, 858–859.
[89] *Ibid.* p. 859.
[90] *Ante*, p. 226.
[91] *R. & B. Customs Brokers Ltd.* v. *United Dominions Trust Ltd.* [1988] 1 W.L.R. 321, 332; *ante*, p. 226.
[92] *George Mitchell (Chesterhall) Ltd.* v. *Finney Lock Seeds Ltd.* [1983] 2 A.C. 803, 816. *Cf. Comemsco Ltd.* v. *Contrapol* (unrep.) referred to by Kerr L.J. in [1983] Q.B. 284, 315.
[93] [1983] 2 A.C. 803, 810; *Phillips Products Ltd.* v. *Hyland* [1987] 1 W.L.R. 659, 669.
[94] *Cf.* the common law position, *ante*, p. 220.
[95] *Ibid.*
[96] *Ante*, pp. 205–223.
[97] [1983] 2 A.C. 803: see *ante* p. 236 at n. 75.

ate requirements of the effectiveness of exemption clauses[98]; though as a practical matter the importance of the rules of construction will be reduced where the clause is subject to the statutory requirement of reasonableness. The two sets of rules also differ from each other in that reasonableness is determined by reference to the time of contracting,[99] while the question whether a clause covers a particular breach may depend on the manner in which the breach has been committed, or on its consequences,[1] and these circumstances can obviously be known only at or after the time of breach.

(6) Restrictions on evasions

The Act invalidates two possible devices for evading its provisions.

(a) SECONDARY CONTRACT. The first such device is that the term restricting or excluding liability may be contained, not in the principal contract itself, but in another (secondary) contract. To meet this possibility, section 10 provides that "A person is not bound by any contract term prejudicing or taking away rights of his which arise under, or in connection with the performance of, another contract,[2] so far as those rights extend to the enforcement of another's liability which this Part of this Act[3] prevents[4] that other from excluding or restricting." Unfortunately, section 10 uses different terminology from that employed elsewhere in the Act,[5] and this fact gives rise to a number of difficulties of interpretation.

Section 10 refers to a contract term "prejudicing or taking away rights," not to one "excluding or restricting liability." The statutory explanation of the latter phrase[6] therefore does not apply to section 10. In particular, it is by no means clear whether the section would cover a secondary contract excluding a particular *remedy,* or one imposing onerous conditions (such as short time limits) on the enforcement of a liability; or whether it would apply to a subsequent agreement to submit disputes under the original contract to arbitration.[7]

The exact scope of section 10 is also in doubt in relation to consumer contracts and contracts on written standard terms. Section 3(2) applies the requirement of reasonableness to terms in such contracts which (a) exclude or restrict liability for breach, or (b) purport to entitle a party to render a performance substantially different from that reasonably expected of him, or to render no performance at all. Clearly, a secondary contract seeking to achieve result (a) is within section 10 and thus ineffective. But is the same true of a secondary contract seeking to achieve result (b)? The concluding words of section 10 give rise to a difficulty because the rights affected by

---

[98] See the *George Mitchell* case, *supra*, and *R. W. Green Ltd.* v. *Cade Bros. Farms Ltd.* [1978] 1 Lloyd's Rep. 602.

[99] *Ante*, p. 236.

[1] *Ante*, pp. 213–215.

[2] s.10 does not apply where a contract between A and B takes away A's right to sue a third party, C, *in tort*, since A's right against C does not arise "under . . . another contract:" *The Chevalier Roze* [1983] 2 Lloyd's Rep. 438, 422.

[3] *i.e.* Pt. I, which extends to England and Wales.

[4] *i.e.* (*semble*) by making it totally ineffective or by subjecting it to the requirement of reasonableness.

[5] Perhaps because s.10 was introduced at a late stage in the Parliamentary proceedings on the Act.

[6] s.13(1) *ante*, pp. 227–228.

[7] See s.13(2) which, unlike s.10, uses the standard terminology of the Act—"excluding or restricting liability."

the secondary contract must "extend to the enforcement of another's *liability* which . . . this Act prevents the other from excluding or restricting." Section 3(2) appears to contrast terms *excluding or restricting liability* with terms purporting to *entitle a party to render a performance substantially different,* etc. It is at least doubtful whether section 10 is apt to cover a secondary agreement having the latter effect.

Section 10 must also be considered in relation to a perfectly genuine renegotiation of a contract. Suppose a contract contains a provision limiting the liability of a party and that the provision is subject to, and satisfies, the requirement of reasonableness. Subsequently, the parties agree on a lower limit of liability which would also (had it been originally incorporated in the contract) have satisfied the requirement of reasonableness. If the subsequent agreement is within section 10, it seems to be totally ineffective, and incapable of validation by being shown to be reasonable. But this—surely undesirable—result can be avoided by arguing that the subsequent agreement is a variation of the original contract, so that the new terms do not prejudice rights "which arise under . . . *another* contract." The new limit of the defaulting party's liability becomes a term of the main contract and is, as such, subject to the same requirement of reasonableness as the original term limiting that liability.

Section 10 may also, if taken literally, apply in the following situation. Suppose that a person suffers loss as a result of a breach of contract and that under the Act a term in that contract excluding or restricting liability for the breach would be ineffective or subject to the requirement of reasonableness. The contract may in fact not contain any such term. Nevertheless an agreement made after the breach, by which the party in breach pays a sum of money to the injured party in satisfaction of his claim, appears to fall within the words of section 10. Yet it can hardly be supposed that the section was intended to strike at genuine out-of-court settlements. One can only hope that the courts will be prepared to cut down its wide language so as to restrict it to its intended scope.[7a] As the marginal note indicates, this is limited to "evasions" of the principal provisions of the Act.

(b) CHOICE OF LAW CLAUSES. A second possible way of evading the Act is to provide that a contract which would otherwise be subject to its provisions shall be governed by the law of a foreign country (which imposes no such restriction on the effectiveness of contract terms). By section 27(2), the Act applies, even though the contract contains such a clause, where the clause was imposed wholly or mainly to evade the Act; and also where one of the parties dealt as consumer, was habitually resident in the United Kingdom, and the essential steps necessary to the making of the contract were taken there. Further restrictions on the efficacy of choice of law clauses are contained in the EEC Convention on the Law Applicable to Contractual Obligations (also known as the Rome Convention), which has the force of law in the United Kingdom.[8] Article 5 of the Convention[9] provides that, where specified conditions are satisfied,[10] such a clause in a con-

---

[7a] See *Tudor Grange Holdings Ltd.* v. *Citibank NA*, *The Times*, April 30, 1991.
[8] Contracts (Applicable Law) Act 1990, s.2.
[9] *Ibid.* Sched. 1.
[10] See Art. 5(2); these conditions relate mainly to the place where the steps leading to the conclusion of the contract are taken.

tract for the supply of goods or services[11] to a consumer is not to have the effect of depriving the consumer of mandatory rules[12] of law of the country of his habitual residence.

(7) Situations not covered by the Act

These fall into two categories: those which are not within the scope of the provisions of the Act, and those which would be within the scope of its provisions if they were not specifically excepted. In all such cases the rules of common law stated earlier in this Chapter continue to apply.

(a) CASES NOT WITHIN THE SCOPE OF THE ACT. Contract terms excluding or restricting the liability of a person not acting in the course of a business are generally unaffected by the Act. The Act only limits such a person's right to exclude or restrict certain liabilities arising out of contracts for the sale and hire-purchase of goods[13] and for misrepresentation.[14] Even terms excluding or restricting business liability may be outside the scope of the Act: this is the position where a contract between B1 and B2, not made on written standard terms of business,[15] excludes or restricts a liability other than one for breach of the implied terms in contracts for the supply of goods dealt with in sections 6 and 7 of the Act.[16] For example, a clause by which B1 excluded or limited liability to B2 for delay in delivering goods, or for short delivery or for an express undertaking as to quality going beyond those implied by law, would be completely outside the scope of the Act.

(b) CASES SPECIFICALLY EXCEPTED. Some or all of the provisions of the Act do not apply in the following cases.

(i) *The principal group* of contracts excepted[17] from some of the provisions of the Act is listed in Schedule 1.

Paragraph 1 of the Schedule lists a number of contracts to which sections 2, 3 and 4 do not apply. In the excepted cases, contract terms[18] excluding or restricting liability for negligence, terms in consumer contracts and provisions in written standard terms of business and indemnity clauses are not subject to the provisions of those sections.[19] The contracts within paragraph 1 of the Schedule are contracts of insurance and any contract "so far as it relates" to the creation, transfer or termination of an interest in land or in any patent, trade mark, copyright or other intellectual property; the formation, dissolution or constitution of a company or the rights or obli-

---

[11] *i.e.* "rules of . . . law . . . which cannot be derogated from by contract:" Art. 3(3).

[12] With certain exceptions specified in Art. 5(4) (contracts of carriage and contracts of service where the services are to be performed exclusively in a country other than that of the consumer's habitual residence).

[13] ss.6(1) and 6(4) *ante*, pp. 229–230, 233.

[14] s.8 *post*, pp. 345–348.

[15] See s.3(1).

[16] *Ante*, pp. 229–230, 232–233; it is assumed that there is no "product liability" (*ante*, p. 230).

[17] By s.1(2).

[18] s.2 also deals with certain notices not having contractual effect, but the wording of s.1(2) ("in relation to contracts") indicates that the exclusions in Sched. 1 only apply to contract terms.

[19] *Ante*, pp. 228–229, 231–232, 233–235.

gations of its members; and the creation or transfer of securities or any right or interest in securities. Contracts of insurance are *wholly* excepted, but a contract falling within the other categories is only excepted "*so far as* it relates" to the matter specified. Where a contract relates to such matters and also to others, the Act is excluded with regard to the former: *e.g.* it does not apply to a contract of employment so far as that contract confers a share option.[20] In the case of a contract for the transfer of an interest in land, it is uncertain whether the whole contract is excepted from sections 2, 3 and 4, or whether only those parts of it which "relate to" *the transfer* are so excepted.

Paragraph 2 of the Schedule lists three contracts: contracts of marine salvage or towage, charterparties of ships or hovercraft, and contracts for the carriage of goods by ship or hovercraft.[21] These contracts are subject to section 2(1), which provides that B[22] cannot by any contract term exclude or restrict his liability for death or personal injury resulting from negligence. But they are excepted from the remainder of section 2, as well as from sections 3 and 4, except in favour of C. Since some contracts within this group may involve the hire of a chattel[23] they are also excepted from section 7 which limits the extent to which liability for breach of certain implied terms in such contracts can be excluded or restricted.[24]

Paragraph 3 of the Schedule deals with the case where goods are carried by ship or hovercraft under a contract which either specifies that means of carriage only for part of the journey[25] or makes no provision for the means of carriage. Such contracts may not be contracts *for* the carriage of goods by ship or hovercraft, but are nevertheless excepted from the operation of sections 2(2), 3 and 4 in the same way as such contracts.

By paragraph 4 of the Schedule, sections 2(1) and (2) do not apply to contracts of employment "except in favour of the employee." The liability of the employee for negligence can therefore be restricted or excluded; but the employer cannot exclude or restrict such liability as against the employee. Since section 2 only applies to "business liabilities" the need for paragraph 4 may not at first sight be apparent. But "business liability" includes liability for breach of a duty arising from things done in the course of *another* person's business[26] so that liability incurred by an employee (whether to his employer or to a third party) can be a "business liability." Moreover, "business" includes profession[27] so that an employee who in the course of his employment exercises a profession could incur a "business liability" which, but for paragraph 4, would attract the operation of section 2(1) and (2).

Paragraph 5 of the Schedule excepts from section 2(1) the validity of a

---

[20] *Micklefield* v. *S.A.C. Technology Ltd.* [1990] 1 W.L.R. 1002.

[21] See, for example *The European Enterprise* [1989] 2 Lloyd's Rep. 185. Certain contracts for the carriage of goods by sea also come within the exception provisions of s.29, *post*, p. 243.

[22] s.1(3).

[23] *e.g.* a demise charterparty.

[24] *Ante*, pp. 232–233.

[25] This situation commonly arises where the goods are carried in a container from one inland destination to another in an overseas country.

[26] s.1(3).

[27] s.14.

discharge and indemnity given on or in connection with an award of compensation for pneumoconiosis.[28]

(ii) *Contracts for the international supply of goods.* In such contracts,[29] none of the limits "imposed by this Act" on contract terms which exclude or restrict liability apply.[30] However, it seems that the limits contained in section 3 of the Misrepresentation Act 1967 do apply: they were not "imposed by this [*i.e.* the 1977] Act" even though the 1977 Act amends section 3 of the Misrepresentation Act.[31]

Under the Unfair Contract Terms Act, the requirement of reasonableness sometimes applies to terms which do not "exclude or restrict" liability; for example, it applies to terms entitling a party to render a performance substantially different from that reasonably expected of him, or to render no performance at all,[32] and to indemnity clauses.[33] Where such terms or clauses are contained in a contract for the international supply of goods, the requirement of reasonableness does not apply.[34]

(iii) *Contractual provisions authorised or required under legislation or international agreements.* An increasingly common technique for controlling exemption clauses (and other contract terms) is found in international conventions, for example those regulating the international carriage of goods and passengers. Many such conventions have been given the force of law by statute.[35] These conventions often lay down a limitation of liability and then provide that any attempt at further reduction in the contract is void. This position is preserved by the 1977 Act.[36]

(iv) *Choice of law clauses.* The Act is intended to deal with contracts having some substantial connection with some part of the United Kingdom. A contract may be governed by English law though its connection with England is tenuous (or even non-existent); this can happen if it contains an express term that it is to be governed by English law. Section 27(1)[37] accordingly provides that sections 2 to 7[38] do not apply where a contract is governed by the law of a part of the United Kingdom only by choice of the parties and would apart from that choice have been governed by the law of some country outside the United Kingdom. The point is of considerable commercial importance as contracts having no substantial

---

[28] This matter is governed by an agreement originally made between the N.C.B. and the N.U.M.: H.L., Deb., Vol. 384, col. 518.

[29] As defined by s.26(3) and (4). Generally such contracts will be between persons acting in the course of a business, but this is not an essential part of the definition.

[30] s.26(1).

[31] s.8, *ante*, p. 235.

[32] See s.3(2)(*b*). *ante*, pp. 231–232.

[33] See s.4, *ante*, pp. 233–235.

[34] s.26(2).

[35] *e.g.* Carriage by Air Act 1961, Sched. 1, Arts. 22, 23(1) and 32; Carriage of Goods by Road Act 1965, Sched. Arts. 23, 41; Carriage of Goods by Sea Act 1971, Sched. Arts. III. 8 and IV. 5; Carriage by Railway Act 1972, Sched. Arts. 6(2), 7 and 10; Carriage of Passengers by Road Act 1974, Sched. Arts. 13, 16 and 23(1) (not yet fully in force); Merchant Shipping Act 1979, ss.14 and 16, and Sched. 3 Part I, Arts. 7, 8, 18 and Part III (not yet fully in force: for transitional provisions, see Unfair Contract Terms Act 1977, s.28); International Transport Conventions Act 1983, s.1

[36] s.29. Certain contracts for the carriage of goods by sea are within both this exception and the somewhat more restricted exception of Sched. 1, para. 2(*c*)

[37] As amended by Contracts (Applicable Law) Act 1990, s.5 and Sched. 4.

[38] *Ante*, pp. 228–235.

connection with England are quite commonly made subject to English law by choice of the parties.

5. Other Legislation

Other legislation illustrates two further techniques for dealing with exemption clauses.

(1) Supervised bargaining

This technique requires the bargain to be made under the supervision of the court or some administrative body. For example, the Landlord and Tenant Act 1985 provides that in certain leases covenants by the landlord to repair are implied.[39] These can be excluded but only by a court order made with the consent of both parties.[40] The court's supervision ensures that no unfair advantage is taken of the tenant.

(2) Administrative control: Fair Trading Act 1973

The legislative techniques so far discussed simply deprive an exemption clause of legal validity. This might be a wholly ineffective means of controlling such clauses, particularly in cases between consumers on the one hand and commercial suppliers of goods and services on the other. If a contract contained an invalid exemption clause the consumer might believe that he was bound by it and so not pursue his claim. Even if he did make a claim, the supplier might settle it so as to avoid a judicial declaration of invalidity, and then continue to use the clause. To remedy this situation, the intervention of a public authority was required; and provision for this method of control is made by the Fair Trading Act 1973.

The Act provides for the appointment of a Director General of Fair Trading,[41] one of whose duties is to keep under review the carrying on of commercial activities which relate to goods and services supplied to consumers.[42] It also sets up a Consumer Protection Advisory Committee[43] to which the Director or a Minister can refer the question whether a "consumer trade practice . . . adversely affects the economic interests of consumers."[44] A "consumer trade practice" is defined to include "the terms and conditions . . . on or subject to which goods or services are or are sought to be supplied" and "the manner in which those terms or conditions are communicated."[45] It can thus refer both to the substance of exemption clauses and to the manner of their incorporation in the contract. If the practice has the effect of making terms and conditions of consumer transactions to be "so adverse to [consumers] as to be inequitable,"[46] it may be prohibited by delegated legislation with criminal sanctions[47]: in other words, continued use of an exemption clause may become a criminal

[39] s.11; *cf.* Housing Act 1988, s.16.
[40] Landlord and Tenant Act 1985, s.12.
[41] s.1.
[42] s.2(1)(*a*).
[43] s.3.
[44] s.14(1).
[45] s.13(*a*) and (*b*).
[46] s.17(2)(*d*).
[47] s.23.

offence. As a result of Orders[48] made under the Act it is now an offence for a person who sells goods in the course of a business to a consumer to apply (or to purport to apply) to the transaction an exemption clause which would be void under the statutory provisions discussed earlier in this Chapter.[49] However, under section 26 of the Act the mere fact that such an offence has been committed does not make "a contract . . . void or unenforceable": the point of the section seems to be that the *whole contract* is not invalid, so that the supplier can enforce other provisions in it. For example, if the goods were not seriously defective he could sue for the price in spite of the fact that the contract contained a punishable exemption clause.

Where a course of conduct is "detrimental to the interests of consumers" and "unfair" to them, the Director General must try to obtain an assurance that it will be discontinued.[50] If such an assurance is not given, he can obtain an order from the Restrictive Practices Court to restrain the course of conduct.[51] For this purpose "unfair" is defined to include breaches of both the criminal and civil law,[52] and so it presumably includes the use of practices (including exemption clauses) made criminal under the Act.

The Director is, moreover, under a duty to encourage trade associations to prepare "codes of practice for guidance in safeguarding and promoting the interests of consumers."[53] These codes have in some instances led to the adoption of standard contracts considerably more favourable to consumers than those previously in use.[54] It may be that the requirement of reasonableness under the Unfair Contract Terms Act 1977[55] will prove to be of greater practical importance in negotiations between the Director and businessmen or trade associations than in private litigation initiated by consumers.

SECTION 2. OTHER CASES

The problem caused by standard form contracts is by no means confined to exemption clauses. It is equally acute where a contract purports to confer rights on one of the parties, or to deprive the other of some protection which the law normally gives him.

1. Illustrations

The first such situation is illustrated by cases concerning the question: at what point of time is an estate agent entitled to his commission? This question is discussed in Chapter 17.[56] Here it need only be noted that the courts

---

[48] Consumer Transactions (Restrictions on Statements) Order 1976 (S.I. 1976 No. 1813) as amended by Consumer Transactions (Restrictions on Statements) (Amendment) Order 1978 (S.I. 1978 No. 127). For a successful prosecution, see *Hughes* v. *Hall & Hall* [1981] R.T.R. 430. The *contra proferentem rule* (*ante*, p. 202) can here operate *in favour* of the proponent of the clause: see *Cavendish Woodhouse* v. *Mancy* (1984) 82 L.G.R. 376 where no offence was committed by a seller of furniture "as seen," since these words did not exclude liability but only confirmed that the customer had seen the goods.

[49] *Ante*, pp. 228–230 (completely ineffective terms).

[50] s.34(1).

[51] ss.35, 37.

[52] s.34(2) and (3).

[53] s.123(3).

[54] Borrie, L.S. Gaz. January 26, 1977, at p. 71.

[55] *Ante*, pp. 231–235.

[56] *Post*, pp. 643–645.

have tried, by various more or less strained constructions, to uphold the principle that no commission is payable if no sale takes place (unless the sale falls through because of the client's default). But in the end the courts were unable to maintain this principle in the teeth of clearly worded contracts entitling the agent to his commission whether a sale resulted from his efforts or not[57]; and legislation regulating the activities of estate agents has done nothing to resolve this problem.[58]

The second such situation is illustrated by bank guarantees which commonly "strip a guarantor of virtually all those rights which the law would otherwise confer upon him—at any rate where they might conflict with the banker's interests."[59] A somewhat similar situation arises in contracts of insurance. Statements by the assured, some of which may be quite unimportant, are often expressly made the basis of the contract, with the result that the insurer can repudiate liability for some quite trivial misstatement.[60]

2. The Common Law Position

The courts have to a limited extent been able to protect the weaker contracting party in some such situations. They have, for example, held that the rules which govern the incorporation and construction of exemption clauses[61] also apply to certain terms[62] which purport to confer rights on the party relying on the standard terms. This reasoning also forms one basis of *Interfoto Picture Library Ltd.* v. *Stiletto Visual Programmes Ltd.*[63] In that case, the defendants (an advertising agency) had hired photographic tranparencies from the plaintiffs under a contract allegedly incorporating the terms of the plaintiffs' delivery note, which had been sent with the goods. One of these terms purported to make the defendants liable for a "holding charge" of £5 per day (an unusually high rate)[64] for each transparency retained for more that 14 days. In holding that the defendants were not liable to pay this charge, both members of the Court of Appeal regarded it as crucial that the plaintiffs had failed to take reasonable steps to bring the term to the attention of the defendants. But while Dillon L.J. drew from this failure the orthodox conclusion that the term had not been incorporated in the contract,[65] it is less clear exactly why Bingham L.J. regarded the failure as vital. It seems that he so regarded it (even on the assumption, that the terms of the delivery note *had* been incorporated into the contract),[66] because, on account of the failure, it would not be "fair to hold

---

[57] Note, however, the view of Lord Denning M.R. in *Jaques* v. *Lloyd D. George & Partners Ltd.* [1968] 1 W.L.R. 625, stated *post*, p. 645, n. 56.

[58] Estate Agents Act 1979, s.18 merely requires the agent to inform the client of the circumstances in which commission will become due. Regulations under s.19 may, however, limit the amount of *precontract* deposits that may be sought by estate agents.

[59] Holden, *Security for Bankers' Advances* (7th ed.), p. 198. The Unfair Contract Terms Act 1977 will not generally help the guarantor since it is *his* liability and not that of the bank which is in issue.

[60] *Post*, p. 355. The Unfair Contract Terms Act 1977 does not alter this position: *ante*, p. 241.

[61] *Ante*, pp. 197–202.

[62] *e.g.* indemnity clauses: *ante*, p. 199, n. 29 and some clauses conferring rights to be paid: *Sonat Offshore S.A.* v. *Amerada Hess Development Ltd.* [1988] 1 Lloyd's Rep. 191.

[63] [1989] Q.B. 433.

[64] *Ibid.* p. 436: a reasonable rate would have been £3.50 per transparency per week.

[65] *Ante*, p. 200.

[66] [1989] Q.B. at p. 445: "I do not think that the defendants could successfully contend that [the conditions] were not incorporated in the contract."

[the defendants] bound by the condition in question."[67] He went on to suggest that "this may yield a result not very different from the civil law principle of good faith, at any rate so far as the formation of the contract is concerned."[68] The reference here to "formation" seems to indicate that Bingham L.J. was, after all, concerned with the incorporation of the clause and perhaps intended to make the point that "this unreasonable and extortionate clause"[69] was not incorporated *merely* because the formal requirements of offer and acceptance had been satisfied[70]: there must, in addition, be "fair" notice, and the degree of notice required increases with the unusualness or unreasonableness of the clause.[71] But once the requisite degree of notice has been given, the English common law does not, as a general rule, control the *substance* of the clause; it does not impose any general requirement that contracts must be reasonable or that contractual rights must be exercised reasonably.[72] The rejection by the courts of the substantive doctrine of fundamental breach[73] can be said to support this general common law rule.

There may, indeed, be highly exceptional cases in which the common law is prepared to recognise exceptions to its general rule. Thus it has been suggested that a term in a contract for the deposit of goods at a railway station would be void for unreasonableness if it provided that £1,000 was to be forfeited if the goods were not collected within 48 hours.[74] The far-fetched nature of the example suggests that this common law exception to the general rule is not likely to have much practical importance. The invalidity of penalty clauses[75] could be regarded as another common law exception to the general rule; but this exception is limited in scope as a clause is only penal if it requires a payment[76] to be made *on breach*: not if it specifies some other event on which the payment is to be made.[77]

3. Legislative Control

While the courts have found it hard to protect the weaker party against the harsh operation of terms other than exemption clauses, a number of specific points have been dealt with by legislation. Under the Unfair Contracts Terms Act 1977, certain indemnity clauses are subject to the requirements of reasonableness.[78] An elaborate system of legislative control exists in relation to regulated consumer credit agreements. To a considerable extent, the contents of such agreements are prescribed by the Consumer Credit Act 1974 and by delegated legislation[79]: the debtor is given a cool-

---

67 *Ibid.*
68 *Ibid.*
69 *Ibid.*
70 *Cf. ante*, p. 47.
71 See *ante*, p. 200.
72 See, for example *Margaronis Navigation Agency Ltd.* v. *Henry W. Peabody of London Ltd.* [1965] 1 Q.B. 300; *Innisfail Laundry* v. *Dawe* (1963) 107 S.J. 437; for exceptions, see *ante*, pp. 60, 154, and *post*, p. 893; and *cf. Paula Lee Ltd.* v. *Robert Zehil & Co. Ltd.* [1983] 2 All E.R. 390.
73 *Ante*, p. 206.
74 *Parker* v. *South Eastern Ry.* (1876) 2 C.P.D. 416, 428.
75 *Post*, pp. 883 *et seq.*
76 Or some other performance: *post*, p. 887.
77 *Post*, pp. 880–890; in the example in *Parker's* case, *supra*, at n. 74, it seems that failure to collect the goods is not a breach, so that the clause is not a penalty.
78 *Ante*, pp. 233–235.
79 *Ante*, pp. 162–163.

ing-off period[80]; the creditor's power to terminate on the death of the debtor is restricted[81] and he can only terminate for default after giving a notice calling on the debtor to make good the default[82]; the debtor has the right to make early payment and thereby to earn certain rebates[83]; and in the case of a regulated hire-purchase agreement he can terminate in certain circumstances on making prescribed payments.[84] Any term in such an agreement is void to the extent of its inconsistency with any such legislative provision for the protection of the debtor.[85] Contracts for the provision of financial services are similarly subject to detailed legislative control.[86] The need for such legislation is based on the assumption that, at common law, the principle of freedom of contract applies[87] to contractual provisions of the kind discussed in this Section.

---

80 s.67.
81 s.86.
82 s.87.
83 ss.94, 95.
84 ss.99, 100.
85 s.173.
86 Financial Services Act 1986, especially s.48 and rules made thereunder; see also Sched. 8 and s.130.
87 *Cf. post*, pp. 355–356, 371–373.

CHAPTER EIGHT

MISTAKE[1]

IN *Bell* v. *Lever Bros. Ltd.*,[2] Lord Atkin said: "If mistake operates at all, it operates so as to negative or in some cases to nullify consent." Mistake *negatives* consent where it prevents the parties from reaching agreement, *e.g.* because they intend to contract about different things. It *nullifies* consent where the parties reach an agreement which is based on a fundamental mistaken assumption, *e.g.* if a contract is made to paint a portrait of someone who, unknown to either party, has just died. At law, the effect of mistake is to make a contract void[3]; but this rule is confined within very narrow limits. It is thought to be in the interests of commercial convenience that, in general, apparent contracts should be enforced. In equity, mistake has a wider scope, but its effect is less drastic. Certain special rules apply to documents mistakenly signed.

SECTION 1. MISTAKE NULLIFYING CONSENT

1. Fundamental Mistake at Common Law

Consent may be nullified if both parties make a *fundamental* mistake of fact.[4] In such cases, the extreme injustice of holding one of the parties to the contract outweighs the general principle that apparent contracts should be enforced. The following types of mistake can be "fundamental" for this purpose.

(1) Mistake as to the existence of the subject-matter

Consent is nullified where both parties are mistaken as to the existence of the subject-matter. Thus it has been held that a separation deed between a man and a woman, who mistakenly thought that they were married to each other, was void, because it purported to deal with a marriage which did not exist[5]; and that a contract to buy an annuity was void where, at the time of the contract, the annuitant had died, so that the annuity no longer existed.[6]

---

[1] Champness, *Mistakes in the Law of Contract*; Palmer, *Mistake and Unjust Enrichment*; Stoljar, *Mistake and Misrepresentation*; Lawson, 52 L.Q.R. 79; Tylor, 11 M.L.R. 257; Wade, 7 C.L.J. 361; Grunfeld, 13 M.L.R. 50; 15 M.L.R. 297; Slade, 70 L.Q.R. 385; Atiyah, 73 L.Q.R. 340; Atiyah and Bennion, 24 M.L.R. 421; Shatwell, 33 Can. Bar Rev. 164; Bamford, 72 S.A.L.J. 166, 282; Stoljar, 28 M.L.R. 265; Sutton, 7 N.Z.U.L.R. 40 (discussing possible reforms); Cartwright, 103 L.Q.R. 594; other articles dealing specifically with mistakes as to identity are cited *post*, p. 262.

[2] [1932] A.C. 161, 217.

[3] *Associated Japanese Bank (International) Ltd.* v. *Crédit du Nord S.A.* [1989] 1 W.L.R. 255, 268.

[4] Not of law: *cf. Gee* v. *News Group Newspapers*, *The Times*, June 8, 1990; unless the mistake is as to *foreign* law, which is treated as a matter of fact in English courts: *The Amazonia* [1990] 1 Lloyd's Rp. 236.

[5] *Galloway* v. *Galloway* (1914) 30 T.L.R. 531.

[6] *Strickland* v. *Turner* (1852) 7 Ex. 208.

Contracts for the sale of non-existent goods illustrate the same point, but give rise to further difficulties, which are discussed below.[7]

(2) Mistake as to the identity of the subject-matter

Such a mistake usually arises where one party intends to deal with one thing and the other with a different thing. Here consent is negatived,[8] and not nullified. Consent could, however, be nullified if both parties thought that they were dealing with one thing when they were in fact dealing with another.[9] Mistake as to a fundamental quality (discussed below[10]) may sometimes be regarded as affecting the identity of the subject-matter.

(3) Mistake as to the possibility of performing the contract

Consent may be nullified if both parties believe that the contract is capable of being performed when this is not the case.

(a) PHYSICAL IMPOSSIBILITY. In *Sheikh Bros. Ltd.* v. *Ochsner*[11] a contract was made for the exploitation of sisal, growing on land belonging to A. The contract provided that B was to cut and process the sisal and to deliver an average of 50 tons of sisal fibre per month to A. It was held that the contract was void because the land was not capable of producing 50 tons of fibre per month.

(b) LEGAL IMPOSSIBILITY. A contract may be void if it provides for something to be done which cannot, as a matter of law, be done. For example, a person cannot acquire property which he already owns, and Lords Atkin and Wright have said that, if he purports to do so in the mistaken belief that the property belongs to the other contracting party, the contract is void.[12] On the other hand, a contract is not void merely because it purports to dispose of property which belongs to a third party,[13] for in such a case the vendor might be able to acquire the property and then make a proper transfer.

One special case of legal impossibility is illegality. A contract involving the commission of a crime is often illegal.[14] The contract may be illegal even though both parties believe it to be lawful, so that in a sense they were under a mistake as to the legal possibility of performing it. Persons may, moreover, agree to do what is the *actus reus* of crime, but may not commit a crime if they do the act because they lack *mens rea*. Such an agreement might not be illegal, but would probably be void for legal impossibility.

---

[7] *Post*, pp. 258–260 *et seq.*
[8] *Post*, pp. 266–267.
[9] *Cf. Diamond* v. *British Columbia Thoroughbred Breeders' Society* (1966) 52 D.L.R. (2d) 146, where two horses at an auction were confused by the auctioneer *and* by the bidders; but the court held that the difference was one of quality only: *sed quaere*.
[10] *Post*, pp. 251–257 *et seq.*
[11] [1957] A.C. 136; the case cannot be dismissed as turning on the Indian Contract Act, as the Privy Council expressly applied the principles laid down in *Bell* v. *Lever Bros. Ltd.* [1932] A.C. 161.
[12] *Bell* v. *Lever Bros. Ltd.* [1932] A.C. 161, 218; *Norwich Union Fire Insurance Society Ltd.* v. *Price* [1934] A.C. 455, 463. The proposition supported by these dicta remains valid even though, to the extent that they are based on *Cooper* v. *Phibbs* (1867) L.R. 2 H.L. 149, they may involve a misinterpretation of that case: see Matthews, 105 L.Q.R. 599.
[13] *Bell* v. *Lever Bros. Ltd., ubi supra; Clare* v. *Lamb* (1875) L.R. 10 C.P. 334.
[14] *Post*, pp. 378 *et seq.*

(c) COMMERCIAL IMPOSSIBILITY. In *Griffith* v. *Brymer*[15] a contract was made for the hire of a room for the purpose of viewing Edward VII's coronation procession. The contract was held void[16] because, when it was made, the procession had (unknown to the parties) already been cancelled. Performance may have been physically and legally possible, but its commercial object was defeated. It could also be said that the parties had made a mistake about a quality of the subject-matter. On this view, the present status of the decision depends on the discussion that follows.

(4) Mistake as to quality

Where the subject-matter of the contract lacks some quality which it is believed to have, the first question is whether the quality forms part of the contractual description of the thing. If it does and "the article does not answer the description of that which is sold,"[17] the contract is valid and the party who gave the description is in breach.[18]

If there is no contractual misdescription, mistake as to quality generally does not nullify consent. This is so whether the mistake prejudices the buyer (so that he pays "too much") or the seller (so that he charges "too little"). In *Scott* v. *Littledale*[19] a contract for the sale of tea was held valid at law in spite of a mistake as to its quality and hence as to its value. The same rule applies where the mistake affects, not the value of the subject-matter, but its utility to the buyer. In *Harrison & Jones* v. *Bunten & Lancaster*[20] a contract was made for the sale of " 'Sree' brand Calcutta kapok." It was held that the contract was valid even though both parties believed such kapok to be pure, when in fact it was impure, and therefore of no use to the buyer.[21]

These cases illustrate the general rule, but it does not follow from them that a mistake as to quality can *never* make a contract void at law. In *Kennedy* v. *Panama, etc., Royal Mail Co.*,[22] the plaintiff applied for shares in a company on the faith of an untrue statement that the company had secured a contract to carry mail for the New Zealand Government. The shares were allotted to him, and the actual decision was that the resulting contract between him and the company was valid.[23] But in reaching this conclusion Blackburn J. referred to the Roman doctrine of *error in substantia*, by which mistakes as to quality may make a contract void if they relate to the "substance" of the subject-matter, *e.g.* to the metal of which a thing is

---

[15] (1903) 19 T.L.R. 434; *cf. post*, p. 784.

[16] So that the hirer recovered back the money he had paid for the room. This appears to be the only reported "Coronation Case" in which the hirer of a room or seat was held entitled to recover back his money. *Cf. post*, p. 809.

[17] *Gompertz* v. *Bartlett* (1853) 2 E. & B. 849, 853; *cf. Gurney* v. *Womersley* (1854) 4 E. & B. 133. Contrast *Harlingdon and Leinster Enterprises Ltd.* v. *Christopher Hull Fine Art Ltd.* [1990] 1 All E.R. 737, where a false attribution, made in good faith, was held not to form part of the contractual description on the sale of a painting by one art dealer to another.

[18] *Gompertz* v. *Bartlett, supra.*

[19] (1858) 8 E. & B. 815; *cf. Hall* v. *Conder* (1857) 2 C.B.(N.S.) 22; *Pope & Pearson* v. *Buenos Ayres New Gas Co.* (1892) 8 T.L.R. 758

[20] [1953] 1 Q.B. 646.

[21] It is not clear whether *both* parties thought that the kapok was pure, but this was assumed: see [1953] 1 Q.B. 646, 657.

[22] (1867) L.R. 2 Q.B. 580. Contrast *Emmerson's Case* (1866) L.R. 1 Cl. 433 (where special statutory provisions affected the result).

[23] There being then no remedy for innocent misrepresentation at common law: *post*, pp. 295, 326, 329.

made.[24] He added: "And . . . the principle of our law is the same as that of the civil law; and the difficulty in every case is to determine whether the mistake or misapprehension is as to the substance of the whole consideration, going, as it were, to the root of the matter, or only to some point, even though a material point, an error as to which does not affect the substance of the whole consideration."[25] This principle did not help the plaintiff as he got the very shares he bargained for and as his mistake did not affect the substance of the whole transaction. But it can be inferred from Blackburn J.'s approval of the Roman texts that, in his view, mistake as to quality could in some cases make a contract void in English law.

Whether this view is correct now depends on the decision of the House of Lords in *Bell* v. *Lever Bros. Ltd.*[26] Bell and Snelling had agreed with Lever Bros. to serve for five years as chairman and vice-chairman of a company controlled by Lever Bros. Before the end of this period Lever Bros. wished to terminate these service contracts, and the parties entered into compensation agreements under which Bell and Snelling received between them £50,000 for loss of office. Lever Bros. then discovered that Bell and Snelling had broken their service contracts in a way that would have justified their summary dismissal without compensation.[27] It was found that Bell and Snelling had forgotten about these breaches of the service contracts when the compensation agreements were made, so that they were not guilty of fraudulent concealment.[28] The remaining issue was whether the compensation agreements were void for mistake, so that Lever Bros. could recover back the £50,000 which they had paid under those agreements.[29] They had made the compensation agreements in the belief that the service contracts were valid when in fact they were voidable. They had paid £50,000 to get rid of Bell and Snelling, when they might have got rid of them for nothing. Wright J. and a unanimous Court of Appeal held that the compensation agreements were void as Lever Bros. had made them under a fundamental mistake. But the House of Lords, by a narrow majority, reversed this decision. The mistake related only to a quality of the service contracts, and was not fundamental. Lord Atkin said: "The contract released is the identical contract in both cases,[30] and the party paying for release gets exactly what he bargained for."[31] Lord Thankerton stressed that mistake even as to a fundamental quality was of no effect unless it related to some assumption which *both* parties regarded as essential. In his view there was nothing to show that Bell and Snelling regarded the validity of the service contracts as vital: only Lever Bros. did so.[32]

It might be thought that, if a mistake as to a quality which is worth £50,000 is not fundamental, no mistake as to quality can ever have this

---

[24] Lawson, 52 L.Q.R. 79; De Zulueta, *The Roman Law of Sale*, p. 26. The Romans did not call such an error one of "quality" but an English lawyer could so describe it.

[25] *Kennedy* v. *Panama, etc., Royal Mail Co., supra.* at p. 588.

[26] [1932] A.C. 161.

[27] *Post*, p. 648; the harshness of this rule may account for the eventual decision in the case.

[28] Nor were they under any duty to disclose their breaches of duty: *cf. post*, p. 359.

[29] *Post*, p. 933.

[30] *i.e.* whether the service contracts were valid or voidable. *Cf. Robert A. Munro & Co. Ltd* v. *Meyer* [1930] 2 K.B. 312.

[31] *Bell* v. *Lever Bros. Ltd., supra*, at p. 223. It was particularly important for Lever Bros. to get rid of Bell and Snelling by May 1, 1929, but this fact is not stressed in the speeches of Lords Atkin and Thankerton.

[32] At p. 235.

effect; and indeed one view of *Bell* v. *Lever Bros. Ltd.* is that it was simply a "quite exceptional case."[33] But once one accepts the principle that a mere mistake as to value is not fundamental, the size of that difference cannot be decisive. The speeches in *Bell* v. *Lever Bros.* clearly recognise that some mistakes as to quality may be fundamental. Lord Atkin said that mistake as to quality "will not affect assent unless it is the mistake of both parties, and is as to the existence of some quality which makes the thing without the quality essentially different from the thing as it was believed to be."[34] Lord Thankerton said that a mistake as to subject-matter must relate to "something which both must necessarily have accepted in their minds as an essential and integral element of the subject-matter."[35]

These are stringent requirements, which make the common law doctrine of mistake "markedly narrower in scope than the civilian doctrine"[36] referred to by Blackburn J. in the dictum cited above.[37] It follows that generally a mistake as to quality will not make a contract void. According to Lord Atkin, it would not have this effect if a man bought a horse mistakenly believed to be sound[38]; if he bought a dwelling-house mistakenly believed to be inhabitable; if he bought a garage on a road which was about to be starved of all traffic by the construction of a by-pass; and (most difficult of all): "A buys a picture from B; both A and B believe it to be the work of an old master and a high price is paid. It turns out to be a modern copy. A has no remedy in the absence of representation or warranty"[39] *i.e.* the contract is valid. The same view is taken in *Leaf* v. *International Galleries*,[40] where it was said that a contract for the sale of a picture would not be void if the parties mistakenly believed that it was by Constable. Similarly it was held in *Solle* v. *Butcher*[41] that a lease was not void because the parties mistakenly believed the premises to be free from rent control; in *Magee* v. *Pennine Insurance Co. Ltd.*[42] it was said that a compromise of a claim under an insurance policy was not void because the parties mistakenly believed that the policy was valid when in fact it was voidable[43]; in *F. E. Rose (London) Ltd.* v. *W. H. Pim Jnr. & Co. Ltd.*[44] it was said that a contract for the sale of horse-beans would not be void because the parties believed that they were dealing with a type of horse-beans more valuable than those contracted for; and in *Oscar Chess Ltd.* v. *Williams* it was said

[33] *Associated Japanese Bank (International) Ltd.* v. *Crédit du Nord S.A.* [1989] 1 W.L.R. 255, 267.
[34] At p. 218.
[35] At p. 235.
[36] *Associated Japanese Bank (International) Ltd.* v. *Crédit du Nord S.A.* [1989] 1 W.L.R. 255, 268.
[37] *Supra*, at n. 25.
[38] *Cf. Naughton* v. *O'Callaghan* [1990] 3 All E.R. 191 (horse sold by auction with wrong pedigree said at p. 197 to be "a different animal altogether," but it was not suggested that the contract was void).
[39] At p. 224. Contrast *Smith* v. *Zimbalist*, 2 Cal.App. 2d 234; 38 P. 2d 170 (1934) (violins mistakenly believed to be by Stradivarius and Guarnerius: held buyer not liable for the price on grounds of mistake *and* breach of warranty).
[40] [1950] 2 K.B. 86, 89; *post*, pp. 256–257. *Cf. Harlingdon and Leinster Enterprise Ltd.* v. *Christopher Hull Fine Art Ltd.* [1990] 1 All E.R. 737, where the buyer's claim (which failed) was based solely on breach; no attempt was made to base it on mistake as to the authenticity of the picture.
[41] [1950] 1 K.B. 671.
[42] [1969] 2 Q.B. 507; 85 L.Q.R. 454; Harris, 32 M.L.R. 688.
[43] Relief was given in the last two cases on equitable grounds; *post*, pp. 281, 283.
[44] [1953] 2 Q.B. 450, 459.

that a contract for the sale of a car would not be void because the parties made a mistake as to its age, so that the buyer paid more than he would have done, had he known the truth.[45]

But according to other dicta and decisions a mistake as to quality can sometimes make a contract void. Thus it has been said that a contract for the sale of land believed to be freehold could be avoided if it turned out to be leasehold.[46] In *Bell* v. *Lever Bros. Ltd.* Greer L.J. said in the Court of Appeal that a contract for the sale of a horse, believed to be a racehorse, would be void if it turned out to be a carthorse[47]: it may be significant that Lord Atkin, in his example of the *unsound* horse,[48] did not contradict this suggestion. Similarly, in *Scott* v. *Coulson*[49] a policy on the life of one Death was sold for £460 on the assumption that Death was alive. The price paid was therefore fixed in relation to the surrender value of the policy. In fact Death was dead, so that the policy had matured and was worth £777. The vendor successfully claimed to have the contract set aside and Vaughan Williams L.J. said[50] that it was void at law. Again, in the *Associated Japanese Bank*[51] case one Bennett purported to sell and lease back machinery, with a view to raising money on the security of the machinery; payments to be made by him under the lease were guaranteed by the defendant. In fact no such machinery existed, so that the lease was voidable for fraud; and it was said that the guarantee was void for mistake. And in *Nicholson & Venn* v. *Smith-Marriott*[52] the defendants put up for auction table napkins "with the crest of Charles I and the authentic property of that monarch." On the faith of this description the lot was bought for £787 10s., but the napkins were Georgian and worth £105 only. The buyer recovered damages for breach of contract but Hallett J. also said that the contract might have been treated by the buyer[53] as void for mistake. The transaction could be regarded in two ways. The parties may have intended to buy and sell antique table linen: in this case a mistake as to its exact age, provenance or value would not be fundamental. Alternatively, the parties may have intended to buy and sell a Carolean relic; in this case their mistake would be fundamental and make the contract void.

The cases and examples concerning mistakes as to quality cannot be perfectly reconciled; but there is a principle which runs through them. A thing has many qualities. A car may be black, old, fast and so forth. For any particular purpose one or more of these qualities may be uppermost in the

---

45 [1957] 1 W.L.R. 370, 373. *cf. Wood* v. *Boynton*, 64 Wis. 265; 25 N.W. 42 (1885) (sale of uncut stone believed to be a topaz for $1: in fact it was a diamond worth $700: held, contract valid). Contrast Restatement, *Contracts*, § 503, Ill. 3, but see Restatement 2d, *Contracts* § 154 Ill. 3.

46 *Durham* v. *Legard* (1865) 34 Beav. 611, possibly expressing a purely equitable view.

47 [1931] 1 K.B. 557, 597. *Cf. Sherwood* v. *Walker*, 66 Mich. 568; 33 N.W. 919 (1887) (sale of cow, believed to be barren, for no more than $80; in fact she was a breeder worth at least $750: held, contract invalid).

48 [1932] A.C. 224; *supra*, n. 39.

49 [1903] 2 Ch. 249.

50 At p. 252.

51 *Associated Japanese Bank (International) Ltd.* v. *Crédit du Nord S.A.* [1989] 1 W.L.R. 255; Treitel 104 L.Q.R. 501; Cartwright [1988] L.M.C.L.Q. 300; Marston [1989] C.L.J. 175.

52 (1947) 177 L.T. 189.

53 It may be objected that Hallett J. held the contract *valid* by giving the buyer damages. But where one party negligently causes the other to make a mistake, the former cannot rely on the mistake to escape liability: *McRae* v. *Commonwealth Disposals Commission* (1951) 84 C.L.R. 377, 408; *post*, p. 261.

minds of the persons dealing with the thing. Some particular quality may be so important to them that they actually use it to *identify* the thing. If the thing lacks that quality, it is suggested that the parties have made a fundamental mistake, even though they have not mistaken one thing for another, or made a mistake as to the existence of the thing.[54] The matter may be tested by imagining that one can ask the parties, immediately after they made the contract, what its subject-matter was. If, in spite of the mistake, they would give the right answer the contract is valid at law. Thus in *Bell* v. *Lever Bros. Ltd.*, the parties would have said, quite rightly. "We are contracting about a service agreement." In *Nicholson & Venn* v. *Smith-Marriott* they might have said, rightly, "We are contracting about antique table linen," in which case the contract would be valid; or they might have said, wrongly, "We are contracting about a Carolean relic," in which case the contract would be void.

Most of the cases and illustrations given above can be explained in this way; but three of them give rise to particular difficulty.

The first is *Scott* v. *Coulson*, where the subject-matter of the contract would no doubt have been described as "an insurance policy" so that the contract ought to have been valid at law. The view that the contract was void is also very hard to reconcile with *Bell* v. *Lever Bros. Ltd.* If the difference between a valid and a voidable contract is not fundamental, why is there a fundamental difference between a contingent and an accrued debt?[55]

A second source of difficulty is that the contract of guarantee in the *Associated Japanese Bank* case was held to be *void*. The subject-matter of that contract was not the machinery, but the lease, and this contract was not void but only voidable for fraud. Yet the compensation agreements in *Bell* v. *Lever Bros. Ltd.* were held *valid* even though their subject-matter, too, consisted of the earlier service contracts which were also voidable and not void. One possible way of distinguishing the cases is to explain *Bell* v. *Lever Bros. Ltd.* on the ground that the House of Lords there wished to mitigate the hardship which resulted to the employees from their being subject to summary dismissal for comparatively trivial breaches of duty.[56] Another is that the *Associated Japanese Bank* case is to be explained on the ground that the guarantee there was part of a composite transaction intended to raise money on the security of the alleged machinery, so that "the analogy of the classic *res extincta* cases . . . [was] fairly close."[57] Hence the crucial fact was that guarantor and lessor both mistakenly

---

[54] Contrast p. 44, *ante*. The rule that deterioration of the subject-matter after offer may preclude acceptance is distinct from the principles discussed in this Chapter. It operates even though the parties at the time of the formation of the alleged contract were perfectly well aware of the true facts; and it may operate even though the change is not "fundamental" in our present sense: for example, the sale of a life-insurance policy would probably not be void for mistake merely because at the time of sale the person insured had (unknown to the parties to the sale) suffered serious injury. For another view, see Atiyah, 2 Ottawa L.Rev. 337, 339.

[55] In *Bell* v. *Lever Bros. Ltd.* [1932] A.C. at p. 236 Lord Thankerton regards the contract in *Scott* v. *Coulson* as one for the sale of a non-existent subject-matter. But it is hard to see in what sense a policy of insurance ceases to exist when it matures.

[56] *Ante*, p. 252, n. 27.

[57] *Associated Japanese Bank (International) Ltd.* v. *Crédit du Nord S.A.* [1989] 1 W.L.R. 255, 269.

believed that *the machinery* existed: this was more important than their state of mind as to the legal effect of the fraud on *the lease*.

The third source of difficulty is Lord Atkin's example of a modern copy bought for a high price in the belief that it is an old master, supported by dicta in *Leaf* v. *International Galleries*.[58] The assumption behind these statements seems to be that the parties would identify the subject-matter simply as "a picture"; but on the bare facts of Lord Atkin's example this seems to be a questionable assumption. Suppose that A has just paid B £5 million for what both believe to be a painting by Rembrandt. If A were asked "what have you just bought?" he would almost certainly reply "a Rembrandt"—not "a picture." With the greatest respect, this type of case stands on a different level from Lord Atkin's other examples.[59] Nor are the dicta in *Leaf* v. *International Galleries* conclusive, for the plaintiff did not claim that the contract was void. He only claimed to rescind it for misrepresentation.[60] It is submitted on the bare facts given in Lord Atkin's example the contract should be held void. Of course in practice the facts of cases of this kind are likely to be more complex. On the one hand, it may be a term of the contract that the picture is authentic, in which case the seller is liable for breach of contract[61] so that no question of mistake will arise. On the other hand, a picture may be sold speculatively, in which case the contract will be valid and the seller will not be in breach, even though the buyer's belief in the authenticity of the picture turns out to be incorrect. Between these extremes lies the large group of cases in which both parties may believe the picture to be authentic but in which there can be no certainty on the point; scholarly or expert opinion as to the authenticity of a picture may vary from time to time.[62] In cases within this group, it has been held that the seller does not impliedly undertake that the picture is genuine (at least where the sale was by one dealer to another, and the

---

[58] [1950] 2 K.B. 86. *Cf.* also *Hindle* v. *Brown* (1907) 98 L.T. 44, where only misrepresentation was discussed.

[59] *Ante*, p. 253. The answer to the question "what have you just bought?" would in those cases be: "a horse," "a house," and "a garage."

[60] Nor did he claim damages for breach of warranty, though Denning and Jenkins L.J. thought that this remedy was open to him. The receipt described the picture as "One original oil painting Salisbury Cathedral by J. Constable, £85": [1950] 1 All E.R. at p. 694. *Cf.* also 66 T.L.R. (Pt. 1) 1031, 1032. The only report which says that there was a representation that the picture was by "*John* Constable" is that in the *Law Reports*, where the statement is that of the reporter and not of any member of the court. In the usage of art auctioneers "John Constable" would mean that the picture was considered to be the work of the famous painter, but "J. Constable" would not; and the seller may have been adopting this usage. The All E.R. and T.L.R. reports seem to be preferable, for it is hard to imagine that a dealer would have been prepared to give a contractual undertaking that the picture was "by John Constable" when the price was as little as £85. *Cf. Harlingdon and Leinster Enterprises Ltd.* v. *Christopher Hull Fine Art Ltd.* [1990] 1 All E.R. 737, 746, stating that, at least between art dealers, the principle of *caveat emptor* applied. In *Peco Arts Inc.* v. *Hazlitt Gallery Ltd., supra*, the buyer claimed no more than the return of the price plus interest; it seems that any claim for damages for breach of contract or for misrepresentation would have been statute-barred.

[61] As in *Peco Arts Inc.* v. *Hazlitt Gallery Ltd.* [1983] 1 W.L.R. 1315 (where it was a term of the contract that the subject-matter of the sale was a drawing by J.A.D. Ingres, but it turned out to be a copy. The seller admitted liability to return the price as money paid under "a common mistake of fact"; the only issue was whether the claim was statute-barred.

[62] See *Firestone & Parson Inc.* v. *Union League of Philadelphia* 672 F. Supp. 819 (1987), affirmed 833 F. 2d. 304; *cf. Luxmoore-May* v. *Messenger May Baverstock* [1990] 1 W.L.R. 1009, 1028.

seller indicates that he is not an expert on the work of the artist in question)[63]; and it is submitted that the element of uncertainty would make it equally inappropriate to regard such a case as one in which the contract was void for mistake.

The suggested test for determining whether a mistake is fundamental, presupposes that both parties would give the same answer to the question "what are you contracting about?" If they would give different answers, the mistake, whatever else its effect may be, will not *nullify* consent. A seller may intend to sell antique table linen and the buyer to buy a Carolean relic. If the parties are thus at cross-purposes consent may be *negatived*. The question whether the buyer could rely on the mistake as making the contract void at law would then depend on factors discussed later in this Chapter.[64]

(5) Mistake as to quantity

Mistake as to quantity has generally been dealt with in equity; but it seems that it can also invalidate a contract at law. In *Cox* v. *Prentice*[65] a silver bar was sold under a mistake as to its weight. The buyer (who was the party prejudiced by the mistake) obtained a verdict for damages for the difference in value between the weight of the bar as it was, and as it was believed to be. The court added that the plaintiff could have recovered back the price he paid for the bar, which suggests that he had the option of treating the contract as void or valid.[66] Similarly, Lord Atkin in *Bell* v. *Lever Bros Ltd.* said: "I agree that an agreement to take an assignment of a lease for five years is not the same thing as to take an assignment of a lease for three years, still less a term for a few months,"[67] though it is not clear from the context whether Lord Atkin thought that such a mistake could make a contract void. And in *Barrow, Lane & Ballard Ltd.* v. *Phillips & Co. Ltd.*[68] a contract for the sale of an "indivisible parcel" of 700 bags of nuts was held to be void because, unknown to the parties, only 591 bags were in existence.

2. Cases in which a Fundamental Mistake Does Not Nullify Consent

In two situations, a contract may not be void, even though the parties have made a fundamental mistake of fact.

(1) Construction of the contract

When a contract is made on the basis of a fundamental assumption which turns out to be false, there are in theory four possible solutions: that neither party shall be bound, or that one shall be bound, or that the other shall be bound, or that both shall be bound.

In the cases of fundamental mistake so far discussed, the first solution has been applied, so that neither party could sue the other, and money paid under the contract could be recovered back. In such cases the contract may

---

[63] *Harlingdon and Leinster Enterprises Ltd.* v. *Christopher Hull Fine Art Ltd.* [1990] 1 All E.R. 737.
[64] *Post*, pp. 261 *et seq.*
[65] (1815) 3 M. & S. 344; *cf. Devaux* v. *Connolly* (1849) 8 C.B. 640, 659.
[66] As to this option, see *post*, p. 261.
[67] [1932] A.C. at p. 223.
[68] [1929] 1 K.B. 574.

properly be called void.[69] But where the parties intend to adopt one of the other solutions the contract is, generally speaking, perfectly valid. Thus, contracts of marine insurance may contain a "lost or not lost" clause: the effect of this is that both parties are bound although the thing insured had (unknown to them) perished at the time of the contract.[70] That is, the insurer has to pay on the policy if the loss is covered by it; and the person insured has to pay the premium even though the loss is caused by an excepted peril, *i.e.* by one not covered by the policy. Similarly, a sale of "my title, *if any*" to certain land could bind both parties even though the seller had no title (unless he knew this fact).[71] And in *Clark* v. *Lindsay*[72] a contract for the hire of a room overlooking the route of one of Edward VII's coronation processions provided that, if the procession were postponed, the hirer should have the use of the room on any later day on which the procession did take place. It was held that the contract was not void even though it was made after the originally planned procession had (unknown to the parties) been cancelled.

In these cases the express terms of the contract deal with the possibility that certain assumed facts may not exist; but in others more difficult questions of construction may have to be answered. Two cases concerning mining leases illustrate the point. In one the tenant promised to dig at least 1,000 tons of clay and to pay a royalty of 2s. 6d. per ton, but there was not so much clay in the land. It was held that the tenant was not liable in respect of the deficiency: he had not warranted that enough clay could be extracted from the land.[73] In the other the tenant of a coal mine agreed to raise a minimum quantity of coal and to pay a minimum rent *in any event*. He was held liable to pay this rent, though there was not so much coal in the mine, because the parties had appreciated the risk and had thrown it on the tenant.[74]

A similar question of construction arose in *Couturier* v. *Hastie*,[75] where a contract was made for the sale of "a cargo of about 1,180 quarters of Salonika Indian corn of fair average quality when shipped, per the '*Kezia Page*' . . . free on board, and including freight and insurance, to a safe port in the United Kingdom, payment at two months from this date upon handing over shipping documents." Before the contract was made, the cargo had, unknown to the parties, become overheated and been sold at Tunis to prevent further deterioration. The seller argued that the buyer was nevertheless liable for the price: what he had bought was an interest in a maritime adventure, or such rights as the seller had under the shipping documents, against which payment was to be made.[76] But the House of Lords rejected this argument and held that the buyer was not liable. Lord Cranworth L.C. said: "The whole question turns upon the construction of the contract . . . Looking to the contract . . . alone it appears to me clearly

---

[69] *Norwich Union Fire Insurance Society Ltd.* v. *Price* [1934] A.C. 455, 463; *Barclays Bank Ltd.* v. *W. J. Sims & Cooke (Southern) Ltd.* [1980] Q.B. 677, 695 ("void for mistake").

[70] *Cf.* Marine Insurance Act 1906, Sched. 1, r. 1.

[71] See *Smith* v. *Harrison* (1857) 26 L.J.Ch. 412.

[72] (1903) 88 L.T. 198.

[73] *Clifford* v. *Watts* (1870) L.R. 5 C.P. 577.

[74] *Bute* v. *Thompson* (1844) 13 M. & W. 487.

[75] (1856) 5 H.L.C. 673; Atiyah, 73 L.Q.R. 487.

[76] This would normally have satisfied the buyer, as he could have claimed the insurance money. But the policy in question was "warranted free from average unless generally" and so did not cover the loss which had actually occurred, as it was not a total loss.

that what the parties contemplated . . . was that there was an existing something to be sold and bought."[77] The contract was for the sale of existing goods—not for the sale of the goods *or* the documents representing them. A similar issue may arise in relation to an accessory contract. The actual decision in the *Associated Japanese Bank* case[78] was that the guarantor was not liable since the guarantee, on its true construction, contained an undertaking (express or implied) that the machinery was in existence.

These cases should be contrasted with *McRae* v. *Commonwealth Disposals Commission*,[79] where the defendants purported to sell to the plaintiffs the wreck of an oil tanker, said to be lying on the Jourmand Reef, and to contain oil. The plaintiffs sent out an expedition to salvage the tanker but found that there was not and never had been any such tanker. The High Court of Australia held that the defendants had impliedly undertaken that there was a tanker there; and that, being in breach of this undertaking, they were liable in damages.[80]

Thus there may be a good contract about a non-existent subject-matter if on the true construction of the contract the risk of non-existence is thrown on one party. In *Couturier* v. *Hastie* the risk was not thrown on the buyer: he was not liable for the price. It is more doubtful whether the risk was thrown on the seller, *i.e.* whether the buyer could have claimed damages for non-delivery. In *McRae's* case the court thought that prima facie the seller in *Couturier* v. *Hastie*, had promised that the goods were in existence[81]: on this view, the contract in that case was not void and the seller could have been held liable on it. But in *Barrow, Lane & Ballard Ltd.* v. *Phillips & Co. Ltd.*,[82] Wright J. said "Where a contract relates to specific goods which do not exist, the case is not to be treated as one in which the seller warrants the existence of those specific goods, but as one in which there has been failure of consideration and mistake." The English courts would probably adopt this approach. Prima facie a seller would not be held to undertake that the goods existed, any more than the buyer would bind himself to pay for them in any event. Thus, neither party is bound and the contract can properly be called void. This explains why the contract in *Couturier* v. *Hastie* has for long been regarded as void[83] for mistake, although the words "void" and "mistake" do not occur in any of the judgments. Similarly, in the *Associated Japanese Bank*[84] case Steyn J., having rejected the claim on the issue of construction, considered the alternative argument based on mistake and held that the claim also failed on this further and *separate* ground. Mistake and construction are thus not necessarily mutually exclusive processes. Construction only displaces mistake (as a ground of invalidity) where it is clear from the words of the contract or from the surrounding circumstances that one party or the other promised to undertake responsibility in any event.

In *McRae's* case the tanker never existed; in *Couturier* v. *Hastie* the

---

[77] *Couturier* v. *Hastie, supra*, at p. 681.
[78] *Associated Japanese Bank (International) Ltd.* v. *Crédit du Nord S.A.* [1989] 1 W.L.R. 255, *ante*, p. 254.
[79] (1951) 84 C.L.R. 377.
[80] For the assessment of damages, see *post*, p. 831.
[81] At p. 407.
[82] [1929] 1 K.B. 574, 582; *ante*, p. 257.
[83] Sale of Goods Act 1979, s.6, originally enacted in 1893, and discussed below.
[84] [1989] 1 W.L.R. 255, *ante*, p. 254.

goods originally existed but had, before the contract was made, "perished" as a commercial entity. This distinction, unimportant in principle, gives rise to difficulty because section 6 of the Sale of Goods Act 1979 provides that "Where there is a contract for the sale of specific goods, and the goods without the knowledge of the seller have perished at the time when the contract is made, the contract is void." At first sight this section prevents the buyer from recovering damages even though the seller has expressly guaranteed that the goods exist, and the seller from recovering the price or damages even though the buyer has expressly promised to pay whether or not the goods exist. The problem may be of more theoretical than practical interest, for it does not seem that contracts on such terms are at all common. In practice the more important question is whether section 6 would apply if the sale was one of alternatives (*e.g.* of the goods *or* the shipping documents representing them[85]) or if it was simply a sale of the documents. Probably section 6 would not apply as such transactions would, in the events which had happened, be sales of things in action and not of goods at all.[86]

If the parties are conscious of a doubt as to the existence of the goods, and one of them expressly undertakes to bear the risk that they may not exist, there seems to be no strong reason against upholding the contract. But in view of section 6 some ingenuity is required to reach this result. One possible argument is that section 6 is only a rule of construction which can be ousted by proof of contrary intention.[87] But many other sections of the Act expressly provide that they are subject to contrary agreement and there is no such provision in section 6.[88] Another possibility is to say that the main contract is void but that the seller can be held liable on a collateral contract that the goods do exist. But if nothing had been done under the main contract it would be hard to find any consideration for the seller's promise under the collateral contract. It is just possible that such consideration could be found in the act of purporting to enter into the main contract, especially if it involved the execution of a document.[89] There is even more difficulty in seeing how the buyer's promise to pay can be expressed

[85] But for this possibility, *Couturier* v. *Hastie* would scarcely have reached the House of Lords. The writer is not aware of any English case in which the court was called upon to consider a simple sale of goods "lost or not lost" at the time of the contract unless the buyer was entitled under the contract to documents giving him rights against the carrier or insurer in respect of the loss of the goods in certain events.

[86] See the definition of "goods" given in s.61(1) of the Sale of Goods Act 1979. The normal contract for the sale of goods on c.i.f. terms is not regarded as a sale of documents but as a sale of goods to be performed by the delivery of documents: *Arnhold Karberg & Co.* v. *Blythe, Green Jourdain & Co.* [1916] 1 K.B. 495, 510, 514; *Hindley & Co. Ltd.* v. *East Indian Produce Co. Ltd.* [1973] 2 Lloyd's Rep. 515, 517; *Congimex Companhia Geral, etc., S.A.R.L.* v. *Tradax Export S.A.* [1983] 1 Lloyd's Rep. 250, 253 ("sale of documents representing goods"—and not merely things in action); Benjamin's *Sale of Goods*, 3rd ed. § 1617. *Couturier* v. *Hastie* provides an early illustration of a c.i.f. contract.

[87] Atiyah, 73 L.Q.R. 340; *Sale of Goods*, (8th ed.), p. 77.

[88] s.55(1) provides that "Where any right, duty or liability would arise under a contract of sale of goods by implication of law, it may (subject to the Unfair Contract Terms Act 1977) be negatived or varied by express agreement . . . ." But this does not affect the position, since the effect of s.6 is that *no* "right, duty or liability would arise" and that there is *no* contract of sale. Atiyah (*ubi supra*) argues that under s.6 liability might arise to restore the price; but this would hardly be a liability which "would arise under a contract of sale."

[89] *Cf. ante*, p. 81. Such a consideration would be blatantly invented (*ante*, p. 67).

as a collateral contract, for it seems to be merely a reiteration of his principal obligation under the main contract. It is finally possible that a seller who warrants that goods exist may be liable in damages for negligent misrepresentation[90]; but the damages on such a claim would be differently assessed from those for breach of contract,[91] and the claim would fail if the seller was wholly innocent.[92]

(2) Conduct of the parties

A party may be liable, even where he did not expressly or impliedly take the risk of the mistake, if he was at fault in inducing the mistake in the mind of the other party. This was a further ground for the decision in *McRae's* case,[93] where it was said that a party could not rely on a mistake consisting "of a belief which is . . . entertained without any reasonable ground, and . . . deliberately induced by him in the mind of the other party."[94] In such a situation one party may be able to rely on the mistake while the other cannot. Thus in *Nicholson & Venn* v. *Smith-Marriott*[95] the plaintiff could have relied on mistake to recover back his money while the defendant could not have relied on it to resist the plaintiff's claim for damages.

SECTION 2. MISTAKE NEGATIVING CONSENT

Mistake negatives consent where the parties are so much at cross-purposes that they do not reach agreement. This may happen where one party is mistaken about the identity of the other, where one party intends to deal with one thing and the other with a different one, or where one party intends to deal on one set of terms and the other on a different set of terms. A mistake as to the other party or as to the subject-matter of the contract has no effect unless it is fundamental, and it is this requirement which links the present group of cases with those in which consent is nullified.

The mere existence of a mistake which negatives consent does not make a contract void. The mistake must also induce the contract, and be operative. In many cases, the last requirement will not be satisfied, so that there will often be a contract in spite of the fact that consent was negatived.

---

90 At common law, if there was a "special relationship" (*post*, p. 309); and possibly under s.2(1) of the Misrepresentation Act 1967 (*post*, p. 312). But that subsection only applies "Where a person has entered into a contract . . . " and it is not clear whether these words cover the case where the "contract" is wholly void.

91 *Post*, p. 322. *Cf.* the damages recovered in *McRae's* case (*post*, p. 832).

92 *Post*, p. 329.

93 (1951) 84 C.L.R. 377.

94 (1951) 84 C.L.R. 377, 408. In *Associated Japanese Bank (International) Ltd.* v. *Crédit du Nord S.A.* [1989] 1 W.L.R. 255, 268 Steyn J. carries the principle further by ommitting the second requirement (*i.e.* that of inducement) stated in the passage quoted in the text above from *McRae's* case. That principle should be distinguished from "estoppel by convention" as applied in cases such as *Amalgamated Investment & Property Co. Ltd.* v. *Texas Commerce International Bank Ltd.* [1982] Q.B. 84; *ante*, p. 112. The mistake in that case related to the existence of a promise which, if made, was undoubtedly a valid contract, and not to facts on which the validity of that contract depended.

95 (1947) 177 L.T. 189.

1. Types of Mistake

(1) Mistake as to the person[96]

(a) REQUIREMENT OF FUNDAMENTAL MISTAKE. A mistake is fundamental, so that consent is negatived, if one party is mistaken as to the *identity* of the other. In *Cundy* v. *Lindsay*[97] the plaintiffs received an order for handkerchiefs from a dishonest person called Blenkarn, who gave his address as 37, Wood Street, Cheapside. He signed his name to make it look like Blenkiron & Co., a respectable firm known by reputation to the plaintiffs and carrying on business at 123, Wood Street. The plaintiffs sent the goods to "Blenkiron & Co., 37, Wood Street," where Blenkarn took possession of them. He did not pay for the goods and he later sold them to the defendants. It was held that there was no contract between the plaintiffs and Blenkarn, as the plaintiffs did not intend to deal with him but with someone else. Thus no property in the handkerchiefs passed to Blenkarn,[98] so that he could pass none to the defendants, who were accordingly liable for conversion.

But a mistake by one party as to an *attribute* of the other will not as a general rule put the parties so seriously at cross-purposes as to negative consent. In *King's Norton Metal Co. Ltd.* v. *Edridge, Merrett & Co. Ltd.*[99] the plaintiffs received an order for wire from "Hallam & Co." which was described on the letter-head as a substantial firm having a large factory in Sheffield and depôts in various other places. In fact "Hallam & Co." consisted solely of an impecunious rogue called Wallis. The plaintiffs sent the goods to "Hallam & Co." on credit. Wallis took possession of them, failed to pay, and sold them to the defendants. It was held that the plaintiffs had contracted with "the writer of the letters."[1] Thus property in the goods passed to Wallis, so that he could pass it to the defendants, who were accordingly not liable for conversion. As Wallis and "Hallam & Co." were one and the same person, the plaintiffs had not made any mistake as to the identity, but only one as to the credit-worthiness, of the other contracting party, whom they identified as the writer of the letter. The essential point is that "Hallam & Co." *was* Wallis, just as much a "Currer Bell" *was* Charlotte Brontë.

In both the above cases, the dispute was between one of the contracting parties and a third party who later acquired the subject-matter. The effect of holding the contract void was to prejudice the third party even though he might have acted in the most perfect good faith. The Law Reform Committee has criticised this result and has recommended "that contracts which are at present void because the owner of the goods was deceived or mistaken as to the identity of the persons with whom he dealt should in future be treated as voidable so far as third parties are concerned."[2] This recommendation has not been implemented by legislation, but in many cases the courts have protected the third party by confining the category of mistakes as to identity within narrow limits. This in turn can cause hardship to the

---

[96] Goodhart, 57 L.Q.R. 228; Williams, 23 Can.Bar Rev. 271, 380; Wilson, 17 M.L.R. 515; Unger, 18 M.L.R. 259; Smith & Thomas, 20 M.L.R. 38.
[97] (1878) 3 App.Cas. 459; *cf. Baillie's Case* [1898] 1 Ch. 110.
[98] *Cf. post*, p. 311.
[99] (1897) 14 T.L.R. 98.
[1] At p. 99.
[2] 12th Report (1966) Cmnd. 2958, para. 15.

mistaken party who may (as in *Cundy* v. *Lindsay*) be an equally innocent dupe of the other party to the alleged contract. The mistaken party is not likely to suffer such hardship where the dispute is between the contracting parties themselves; for if the mistake is induced by the other party's misrepresentation, the mistaken party will be entitled to rescind for that misrepresentation.[3] He will only[4] need to rely on mistake as such where the mistake arises without any misrepresentation.[5]

Where a contract is in writing, the parties to that contract are prima facie[6] the persons described as such in the writing. In *Hector* v. *Lyons*[7] a father conducted negotiations for the purchase of a house, and, when these were successfully concluded, instructed his solicitors to draw up the contract in the name of his son (who was a minor) as purchaser. Contracts were duly exchanged naming the son as purchaser and it was held that the father could not enforce the contract against the vendor, even though the vendor believed that she was dealing with the father. It was said that the identity of vendor and purchaser was established by the terms of the written contract. These certainly showed that the father was *not* a party to the contract; but it is less clear whether there was a contract between the vendor and the son. It is arguable that the vendor had made a mistake as to the identity of the other party: she believed that the other party was the father when actually it was the son. But it does not follow that there was no contract between the vendor and the son since that mistake, even if fundamental, would not have been operative (unless it was known[8] to the son). Hence it seems that the vendor could have been held liable in damages to the son.[9]

(b) MISTAKE INTER PRAESENTES. The difficulty of deciding whether the mistake is one of attribute or of identity is particularly acute where the parties who are alleged to have contracted have come physically face to face. In *Phillips* v. *Brooks Ltd.*,[10] a rogue called North entered the plaintiff's shop and asked to see pearls and rings. He selected (*inter alia*) a ring worth £450, produced a chequebook, claimed to be Sir George Bullough (a wealthy man known by name to the plaintiff) and gave Sir George's address. The plaintiff checked this address in a directory, and then allowed North to take away the ring in exchange for a cheque, which was dishonoured. North later pledged the ring with the defendant. The plaintiff claimed that there was never any contract between him and North, so that the latter had no title to the ring which he could pass to the defendant. But Horridge J. held that the plaintiff had "contracted to sell and deliver [the ring] to the person who came into his shop . . . who obtained the sale and delivery by means of the false pretence that he was Sir George Bul-

---

[3] *Post*, pp. 31 *et seq*.

[4] Contrary authorities such as dicta in *Gordon* v. *Street* [1899] 2 Q.B. 641 and the decision in *Sowler* v. *Potter* [1940] 1 K.B. 271 are no longer law: see *Gallie* v. *Lee* [1969] 2 Ch. 17, 33, 41, 45, affd. without reference to this point [1971] A.C. 1004; *Lewis* v. *Averay* [1972] 1 Q.B. 198, 206.

[5] *e.g.* in *Craven-Ellis Ltd.* v. *Canons Ltd.* [1936] 2 K.B. 403, *post*, p. 266.

[6] Subject to the possible application of the principles of agency (*post*, pp. 631–634).

[7] (1989) 58 P. & C.R. 156.

[8] *Post*, pp. 271–272; the other conditions there discussed, in which a mistake negativing consent may be operative, were plainly not satisifed.

[9] *Post*, p. 488. As the son was a minor, the remedy of specific performance was not available to him, nor was he liable on the contract: *ibid.*

[10] [1919] 2 K.B. 243; *cf. Dennant* v. *Skinner* [1948] 2 K.B. 164.

lough."[11] "His intention was to sell to the person present and identified by sight and hearing."[12] The plaintiff's mistake, therefore, was not one of identity. An alternative ground for the decision, suggested by Lord Haldane, is that the sale was concluded before any mention was made of Sir George Bullough, and that the mistake only induced the plaintiff to let North take the ring away on credit.[13] But this explanation was rejected in a later judicial discussion of the case[14]; and it is only doubtfully consistent with the reported facts. North made an offer to buy when he selected the ring[15]; and it is not clear whether he said that he was Sir George Bullough before or after the offer was accepted.[16]

The same result was reached in the more recent case of *Lewis* v. *Averay*,[17] where the plaintiff had advertised his car for sale and was visited by a rogue who falsely claimed to be a well-known actor called Richard Greene. By this pretence the rogue induced the plaintiff to sell the car to him on credit and to let him take it away in exchange for a cheque, which was dishonoured. The plaintiff claimed the car from the defendant, who had bought it in good faith from the rogue; but the claim failed as the contract between the plaintiff and the rogue was not void for mistake. The presumption that the plaintiff intended to contract with the person physically before him had not been overcome[18]: his mistake was not one of identity[19] but as to the credit-worthiness of the other party.[20]

It does not follow from *Phillips* v. *Brooks* or *Lewis* v. *Averay* that there can be no fundamental mistake as to the person merely because the parties alleged to have contracted were in each other's presence. There may, in the first place, be such a mistake where A induces B to deal with him by pretending to act as agent for C, while in fact intending to contract on his own behalf.[21] In such a case it could be said that there was no mistake as to the identity of A, but rather one as to the capacity in which he purported to contract.[22] Secondly, a mistake about a person who was present could also be one of identity where he had adopted a physical disguise: for example, where A induced B to deal with him by disguising himself as C, and C was personally known to B, so that B thought that A was C. And there are, thirdly, further exceptional circumstances in which a mistake about a person present at the time of the alleged contract can be one as to his identity.

---

[11] [1919] 2 K.B. at p. 246.
[12] *Ibid.* at p. 247.
[13] *Lake* v. *Simmons* [1927] A.C. 487, 501.
[14] *Lewis* v. *Averay* [1972] 1 Q.B. 198, 206.
[15] *Ante*, p. 12.
[16] Three of the reports of the case (88 L.J.K.B. 952, 35 T.L.R. 470 and 24 Com.Cas. 263) suggest that North said he was Sir George Bullough as soon as he entered the shop; while two ([1919] 2 K.B. 243, 121 L.T. 249) suggest that he said this a little later.
[17] [1972] 1 Q.B. 198; A.L.G. 88 L.Q.R. 161; Turpin [1972] C.L.J. 19; *cf.* (in criminal law) *Whittaker* v. *Campbell* [1984] Q.B. 319.
[18] [1972] 1 Q.B. 198 at pp. 208, 209.
[19] Lord Denning M.R. said at p. 207 that there *was* a mistake of identity but that it did not make the contract void. With respect, this approach cannot be reconciled with *Cundy* v. *Lindsay* (1878) 3 App.Cas. 459, *ante*, p. 262.
[20] [1972] 1 Q.B. at p. 209.
[21] *Hardman* v. *Booth* (1863) 1 H. & C. 803; *cf. Higgons* v. *Burton* (1857) 26 L.J.Ex. 342. Contrast *Midland Bank plc* v. *Brown Shipley & Co. Ltd.* [1990] N.L.J.R. 1753 (identity of person acting as mere messenger not fundamental).
[22] *cf. Ingram* v. *Little* [1961] 1 Q.B. 31, 50, 66.

This possibility is illustrated by *Ingram* v. *Little*,[23] where the plaintiffs had, again, advertised their car for sale and been visited by a rogue who falsely claimed to be "P. G. M. Hutchinson of Stanstead House, Stanstead Road, Caterham." They agreed to sell the car to him on credit, but only after one of them had checked in a telephone directory that there was a person of that name living at that address. The rogue sold the car to the defendants from whom the plaintiffs claimed it when the rogue's cheque was dishonoured. A majority of the Court of Appeal upheld the claim on the ground that the plaintiffs had intended to deal with the Hutchinson of Stanstead House and not with the person before them *as such*. The case was doubted in *Lewis* v. *Averay*,[24] though it can perhaps be supported on its very special facts: *i.e.* on the ground that the plaintiffs had refused to clinch the deal until they had consulted the telephone directory.[25]

(c) DISTINCTION BETWEEN IDENTITY AND ATTRIBUTE. The above discussion shows that it may be difficult to say precisely what mistake has been made: *i.e.* whether B thought that A was C, as opposed to merely thinking that A was not A or making a mistake about A's credit-worthiness. In other cases, it may be clear what mistake has been made, but disputed whether it should be described as one of identity or attribute. This difficulty is illustrated by *Lake* v. *Simmons*.[26] A woman called Esmé Ellison told the plaintiff that she was married to one Van der Borgh (with whom she was in fact living as his mistress); and that he wanted to give her a necklace which he wished to see on approval. The plaintiff let her have possession of the necklace and entered it in his book as being out on approval to Van der Borgh. Esmé Ellison absconded with the necklace, and the actual decision was that the plaintiff had not "entrusted" the necklace to her as a "customer" within the terms of an insurance policy.[27] Lord Haldane also said that there was no contract, since there was no *consensus*. The plaintiff "thought that he was dealing with a different person, the wife of Van der Borgh. . . . He never intended to contract with the woman in question."[28] "Nothing short of a belief in her *identity as a wife* who was transacting for her husband as the real customer would have induced the [plaintiff] to act as he did."[29]

These remarks can be interpreted in two ways. One possible view is that Esmé Ellison's "identity as a wife" was important in inducing a mistake as to the *capacity* in which she dealt: the plaintiff intended to deal with her as agent for Van der Borgh, while she intended to contract (if at all) on her own behalf.[30] A second possibility is that the plaintiff's mistake was one as to her *identity*: he identified her as the wife of Van der Borgh and not by the more usual process of sight and hearing. This possibility raises the question how the distinction between identity and attributes should in this context be drawn.

It is submitted that the test formulated for the purpose of defining funda-

[23] [1961] 1 Q.B. 31.
[24] [1972] 1 Q.B. 198 at pp. 206, 208 (Megaw L.J.).
[25] *Ibid.* at p. 208 (Phillimore L.J.).
[26] [1927] A.C. 487.
[27] As to this point, contrast *John Rigby (Haulage) Ltd.* v. *Reliance Marine Insurance Co.* [1956] 2 Q.B. 468.
[28] *Lake* v. *Simmons* [1927] A.C. at p. 500.
[29] *Ibid.* at p. 502.
[30] As in *Hardman* v. *Booth* (1863) 1 H. & C. 803; *ante*, p. 264 at n. 21.

mental mistakes as to the subject-matter[31] should also (with appropriate modifications) be applied in the present context. A person may be identified by reference to any one of his attributes. If a mistake is made as to that attribute, there can be said to be a mistake as to identity. This is the basis of the second possible explanation of Lord Haldane's remarks in *Lake* v. *Simmons*. It is also supported by a dictum of Greene L.J. in *Craven-Ellis* v. *Canons Ltd.*,[32] where a director's service agreement was held "void *ab initio*" as neither he nor those who appointed him had the necessary qualification shares. One reason for this conclusion was that the agreement was made "under a mistake as to the present existence of an essential fact recognised by the law as the foundation of the contract."[33] Other hypothetical cases can be imagined which would come within the same principle. A college may hold a private dance and intend to sell tickets only to past or present members. In such a case the identifying attribute of an applicant for tickets might be his or her membership of the college.

The principle, then, is that a mistake as to *the* attribute by which a person is identified is in law regarded as a mistake of identity. In applying this principle, the law indeed makes certain prima facie assumptions about the way in which a person is identified: prima facie, a person physically present is identified by sight and hearing, and an unknown correspondent as "the writer of this letter." The situations discussed above show that these assumptions can be rebutted by showing that the mistaken party identified the other party in some other, unusual way. But one attribute on which the mistaken party cannot in law rely for this purpose is that of the other party's credit-worthiness. In deciding whether the other party is credit-worthy, the mistaken party takes a business risk. It would be impracticable to allow an error of judgment on such a point to negative consent.

(d) WHETHER ONE PERSON MUST BE MISTAKEN FOR ANOTHER. In most cases of mistaken identity, one person is mistaken for another *existing* person; but the process of identification (described above) suggests that this is not a necessary requirement. If, in *Ingram* v. *Little*,[34] it had been shown that Mr. P. G. M. Hutchinson had died six months before the transaction, this would have made no difference to the process by which the plaintiffs identified the rogue; and it ought not to have affected the decision. If B thinks that A is C, there can be a mistake as to identity so long as C is or was a distinct entity from A (as opposed to a mere alias) and is so regarded by B.

(e) UNDISCLOSED PRINCIPALS. A person who knows that another is unwilling to contract with him may employ an agent to make the contract without disclosing the existence of his principal. In some such cases the undisclosed principal is not allowed to intervene and take the benefit of the contract. But the contract is not void since the agent can always (fraud apart) enforce it. These cases are discussed in Chapter 17.[35]

(2) Mistake as to the subject-matter

Consent is negatived if one party intends to deal with one thing, and the other with a different one. This principle may have been applied in *Raffles*

[31] *Ante*, pp. 254–255.
[32] [1936] 2 K.B. 403.
[33] *Ibid.* at p. 413.
[34] [1961] 1 Q.B. 31.
[35] *Post*, pp. 632–633.

v. *Wichelhaus*,[36] where the plaintiff sold to the defendant "125 bales of Surat cotton . . . to arrive *ex Peerless* from Bombay," and tendered cotton from a ship called *Peerless* which had sailed from Bombay in December. The defendant refused to accept the goods, alleging that he had intended to buy the cotton shipped on another *Peerless* which had sailed from Bombay in October: thus it was argued that there was no agreement between the parties. Judgment was given for the defendant, but as no reasons were stated it is hard to tell whether the ground of decision was that there was *no* contract,[37] or that there *was a* contract to deliver cotton from the October *Peerless* which could not be performed by delivering cotton from the December *Peerless*.[38]

Consent was clearly negatived in *Falck* v. *Williams*.[39] The defendants and the plaintiffs were negotiating about two charterparties: one to carry shale from Sydney to Barcelona, and one to carry copra from Fiji to Barcelona. The plaintiffs' agent sent a coded telegram intending to confirm the copra charter, but the telegram was ambiguous and was understood by the defendants to refer to the shale charter. It was held that there was no contract. Similarly, consent is negatived if a buyer at an auction thinks that the lot for which he is bidding consists of hemp when it consists of hemp and tow.[40]

On the other hand, consent is not generally negatived by a mere mistake as to quality: thus it was held in *Smith* v. *Hughes*[41] that if a person buys oats, thinking that they are old, from a seller who knows that they are new, there is a good contract. Similarly, a contract for the sale of goods is not void merely because the seller, under a mistake as to the quality of the goods, charges a lower price than he would have done, had he known the truth.[42] In such cases, the parties are at cross-purposes, but not to such an extent that they are not in agreement at all. A mistake as to quality can only negative consent if it is a mistake as to a fundamental quality by which the thing is identified.[43]

(3) Mistake as to the terms of the contract

Consent is negatived if the parties intend to contract on different terms, *e.g.* if A sells goods to B for so many "pounds" intended by A to mean sterling and by B to mean a different currency[44]; or if A intends to sell rab-

---

[36] (1864) 2 H. & C. 906.

[37] *Smith* v. *Hughes* (1871) L.R. 6 Q.B. 597, 609. There was no allegation that the seller intended to deal with the cargo of the December rather than the October *Peerless*. The case was decided on a demurrer so that the facts were never proved.

[38] *Van Praagh* v. *Everidge* [1902] 2 Ch. 266, 269. On this view the buyer could have got damages for the seller's failure to deliver cotton from the October *Peerless*.

[39] [1900] A.C. 176.

[40] *Scriven Bros. & Co.* v. *Hindley & Co.* [1913] 3 K.B. 564.

[41] (1871) L.R. 6 Q.B. 597.

[42] *Dip Kaur* v. *Chief Constable of Hampshire* [1981] 1 W.L.R. 578; but the invalidity of the contract is not decisive for the purpose of criminal liability: *R.* v. *Morris* [1984] A.C. 320; *Dobson* v. *GAFLAC* [1990] Q.B. 274.

[43] As defined *ante*, pp. 254–255.

[44] See *Woodhouse A. C.Israel Cocoa Ltd.* v. *Nigerian Produce Marketing Co.* [1972] A.C. 741, 768; *cf. Felthouse* v. *Bindley* (1862) 11 C.B.(N.S.) 869 ("30" intended to mean pounds by buyer but guineas by seller); *Smidt* v. *Tiden* (1874) L.R. 9 Q.B. 446.

bit skins at a fixed price per piece when B intends to buy at the same price per pound, there being about three pieces to the pound.[45]

Mistakes as to the person and mistakes as to the subject-matter only negative consent if they are fundamental. There seems to be no such requirement where the mistake is as to the terms of the contract. A sale of oats is not void merely because they are believed by one party to be old but known by the other to be new. The mistake is as to the subject-matter and is not fundamental.[46] But according to *Smith* v. *Hughes*[47] a sale of oats believed by one party to be *warranted* to be old and not intended by the other party to be so warranted may be void for mistake. The mistake is as to a term of the contract and negatives consent although the term relates to a quality of the subject-matter which is not fundamental. This distinction seems to be generally accepted, but the reason for it is not easy to see. If a quality is not fundamental, a mistake as to its existence does not destroy consent. Why should consent be destroyed by mistake as to a warranty of that same quality? Is it really true, in the latter case, that the parties have not agreed at all? An alternative explanation for this aspect of *Smith* v. *Hughes* will be put forward later in this Chapter.[48]

2. Mistake must Induce the Contract

A mistake will only negative consent if it induced the mistaken party to enter into the contract. If that party takes the risk that the facts are not as he supposed them to be,[49] or if he is simply indifferent as to the matter to which the mistake relates, the validity of the contract will not be affected. For example, in *Mackie* v. *European Assurance Soc.*[50] the plaintiff took out an insurance policy through an agent, believing that the agent was acting for one company when in fact he was acting for another. It was held that the policy with the latter company was not void for mistake. The plaintiff's intention "was not to remain uninsured for one hour and in what office it was was a secondary consideration, provided it would meet its engagements and was able to do so."[51]

This case should be contrasted with *Boulton* v. *Jones*.[52] The plaintiff had just bought the shop of one Brocklehurst when the defendant sent his servant to the shop with an order, addressed to Brocklehurst, for a quantity of pipe hose. The plaintiff supplied the goods, no doubt thinking that the defendant did not care from whom he obtained them. The defendant was apparently satisfied with the goods and used them. He had clearly made a fundamental mistake, in that he thought he was dealing with Brocklehurst when he dealt with Boulton. Ordinarily, that mistake would have had no effect, since it would not matter to the defendant whether the goods were

---

[45] *Hartog* v. *Colin & Shields* [1939] 3 All E.R. 566.

[46] *Supra*, after n. 41.

[47] (1871) L.R. 6 Q.B. 597; *cf. London Holeproof Hosiery Co. Ltd.* v. *Padmore* (1928) 44 T.L.R. 499; *Sullivan* v. *Constable* (1932) 49 T.L.R. 369.

[48] *Post*, pp. 272–273.

[49] *Wales* v. *Wadham* [1977] 1 W.L.R. 199, 220; (approved on the issue of mistake in *Jenkins* v. *Livesey* [1985] A.C. 424); *cf. ante*, pp. 258, 260.

[50] (1869) 21 L.T. 102; *cf. Fellowes* v. *Gwydyr* (1829) 1 Russ. & My. 83.

[51] (1869) 21 L.T. at p. 105.

[52] (1857) 2 H. & N. 564; L.J.Ex. 117; 6 W.R. 107.

supplied by Boulton or by Brocklehurst. But Brocklehurst owed money to the defendant, who had intended to set off this debt against the price of the goods. He could thus show that it was important for him to contract with Brocklehurst rather than with Boulton. It was therefore held that there was no contract so that the defendant was not liable for the price of the goods. To have held him liable would have been unjust as it would have deprived him of the benefit of his set-off against Brocklehurst. But the result of holding him not liable was almost equally unjust. The defendant got the goods for nothing but retained his right to sue Brocklehurst for the amount which the latter owed him. It seems that on such facts the defendant should be under some quasi-contractual liability,[53] or that he should at least be bound to transfer his claim against Brocklehurst to the plaintiff.[54]

In a number of English cases, reference has been made to the following passage from the French writer Pothier: "Whenever the consideration of the person with whom I am willing to contract enters as an element into the contract which I am willing to make, error in regard to the person destroys my consent and consequently annuls the contract. . . . On the contrary, when the consideration of the person with whom I thought I was contracting does not enter at all into the contract, and I should have been equally willing to make the contract with any person whatever as with him with whom I thought I was contracting, the contract ought to stand." This passage has sometimes been interpreted to mean that mistake will make a contract void if it relates to a personal attribute of the other party but for the existence of which the mistaken party would not have contracted.[55] If it means this, it does not represent English law,[56] for a mistake must be fundamental, and a mistake as to the person is only fundamental if one person is mistaken for another or if the mistake relates to *the* attribute by which a person is identified.[57] But it seems that the purpose of the passage is not to define when a mistake is fundamental but to distinguish between cases in which it does, and those in which it does not, induce the contract. This is made clear by the examples given by Pothier: a contract by which an artist is commissioned to paint a picture is void if mistakenly made with the wrong artist; but a contract to sell a book is not void simply because the bookseller thinks he is contracting with Peter when in fact he is contracting with Paul. In both cases the mistake is fundamental, one person being mistaken for another. The difference between them is that in the first case the mistake induces the contract, while in the second it does not.

The requirement that the mistake must induce the contract applies not only to mistake as to the person but also to other types of mistake. If in *Raffles* v. *Wichelhaus*[58] both ships *Peerless* had sailed from Bombay on the same day and had arrived at the same time, it might not have mattered to the buyer which cargo he got. In that case he could not have escaped liab-

---

[53] *Cf. post*, p. 936.
[54] Goff and Jones, *The Law of Restitution* (3rd ed.), pp. 395–387.
[55] *e.g.* in *Sowler* v. *Potter* [1940] 1 K.B. 271, 274; see *ante*, p. 263, n. 4 as to this case.
[56] *Lewis* v. *Averay* [1972] 1 Q.B. 198, 206.
[57] *Ante*, pp. 265–266.
[58] (1864) 2 H. & C. 906; *cf. Ind's Case* (1872) L.R. 7 Ch.App. 485 (validity of share transfer not affected by which shares the transferee gets, so long as he gets the quantity contracted for).

ility by saying that he intended to buy the cargo in the one ship while the seller intended to sell the cargo in the other.

3. When Mistake is Operative

(1) Contract generally valid

A mistake which negatives consent does not necessarily make the contract void. On the contrary, the general rule is that a party is bound, in spite of his mistake, if "whatever [his] real intention may be, he so conducts himself that a reasonable man would believe that he was assenting to the terms proposed by the other party, and that other party upon that belief[59] enters into a contract with him. . . . "[60] This "objective principle" is sometimes regarded as a kind of estoppel by representation. But such estoppel only operates in favour of a person who acts on a representation to his detriment[61]; while a person who invokes the objective principle need only show that he has entered into the contract in reliance on the appearance of the agreement created by the other's conduct. He need not show that he has, as a result of entering into that contract, suffered any actual detriment.[62]

The operation of the objective principle is most easily illustrated by the case of a person who by mistake bids for the wrong lot at an auction. Although the parties may not be *ad idem*,[63] (as they intended to deal with different things), the bidder is prevented by the objective principle from relying on the mistake and so from saying that the contract is void.[64] The same principle applies to mistakes as to the person[65] and as to the terms of the contract. Thus a seller who, as a result of some miscalculation, offers goods at a price lower than that which he would have asked but for the mistake cannot, after the offer has been accepted, generally rely on the mistake to make the contract void.[66] Similarly, where a landlord as a result of

---

59 For the submission that the mistaken party must *actually* hold this belief, see *ante*, p. 9.

60 *Smith* v. *Hughes* (1871) L.R. 6 Q.B. 597, 607. This principle contains no requirement of negligence and is in this respect wider in scope than that which prevents a mistake which *nullifies* consent from being operative on account of the conduct of one of the parties: *ante*, p. 261.

61 *Post*, p. 361; such detrimental reliance is also necessary for "estoppel by convention," discussed *ante* at p. 112. Reliance, though not "detriment" is also necessary for "promissory" estoppel: *ante* p. 105.

62 Williston, in *Selected Readings on the Law of Contracts*, p. 119; Atiyah's contrary suggestion in 94 L.Q.R. 193, 202 is inconsistent with the cases discussed in the following paragraph, and with *Centrovincial Estates plc.* v. *Merchant Investors Assurance Co. Ltd.*, [1983] Com.L.R. 158. That decision is described by Atiyah in his *Introduction to the Law of Contract* (4th ed.), p. 477 as "absurd and unjustifiable"; but it has been twice cited with approval in the Court of Appeal: see *Whittaker* v. *Campbell* [1984] Q.B. 318, 327; *The Antclizo* [1987] 2 Lloyd's Rep. 130, 146 (affd. [1988] 1 W.L.R. 603). In further support of his view, Atiyah relies (102 L.Q.R. 363) on *The Hannah Blumenthal* [1983] 1 A.C. 854, *ante*, p. 8. But the principal question in that case was whether A's conduct had induced B reasonably to believe that A was making an offer to B. Conduct amounting to reliance (not necessarily detrimental) by B is *one* way in which such an offer can be accepted (*ante*, pp. 17, 33), but it is not the *only* way: an express acceptance in so many words would be equally effective.

63 *Van Praagh* v. *Everidge* [1903] 1 Ch. 434.

64 *Robinson, Fisher & Harding* v. *Behar* [1927] 1 K.B. 513.

65 *Cornish* v. *Abington* (1859) 4 H. & N. 549; *Re Reed* (1876) 3 Ch.D. 123, so far as *contra*, seems wrong.

66 This would have been the position in *Hartog* v. *Colin & Shields* [1939] 3 All E.R. 566 (*post*, p. 273) if the court had not taken the view that the plaintiff must have known of the defendant's mistake.

a clerical error offers to grant a tenancy at a rent of £1,000 per annum, he cannot, after the offer has been accepted, escape from the transaction merely by showing that his real intention was to make the offer at a rent of £2,000 per annum.[67] The position is the same where a person signs a document under some other mistake about its terms or legal effects: he cannot, in general, say that the contract is void because of his mistake.[68]

(2) Exceptional cases in which mistake is operative

Where the objective principle applies, the contract is valid in spite of the existence of a mistake, so that it is unnecessary to go into the difficult question whether the mistake is fundamental. That question need only be answered in the following three exceptional situations, in which the objective principle does not apply, so that the mistake is *operative*.

(a) AMBIGUITY. There may be such ambiguity in the circumstances that a reasonable person could not draw any relevant inference from them at all. Thus in *Raffles* v. *Wichelhaus*[69] a reasonable person could not have deduced with which cargo the parties intended to deal. Similarly, if parties stipulate for the payment of freight "per charterparty" but there are two charterparties in the case providing for payment of different rates of freight, the reasonable person again cannot put any definite interpretation on the promises.[70] In these cases, therefore, the mistake is operative and makes the contract void.

(b) MISTAKE KNOWN TO OTHER PARTY. The objective principle applies where A so conducts himself as to induce B reasonably to believe that A is contracting with him; but it does not apply where B actually knows that (in spite of the objective appearance) A has no such intention.[71] It follows that the objective principle will not apply, and that the mistake will be operative, if A's mistake is known to B. This is the reason why the contract in *Cundy* v. *Lindsay*[72] was void. Lindsays may have behaved so as to induce a reasonable person to believe that they were dealing with Blenkarn, but the mistake was operative as Blenkarn knew that they had no such intention. The case would have been different if Blenkarn had written to Lindsays in good faith and they had misread his signature for "Blenkiron & Co." In such a case, Lindsays could not have relied on their mistake, had they simply sent the goods to Blenkarn's address, unless it had been clear to Blenkarn from the contractual documents that they did not intend to deal with him but with Blenkiron & Co.[73]

In *Boulton* v. *Jones* the defendant's order was addressed to Brocklehurst, so that Boulton knew it was not meant for him. It is not clear whether he also knew *why* the order was not meant for him, *i.e.* whether he

---

[67] *Centrovincial Estates plc.* v. *Merchant Investors Assurance Co. Ltd.*, *supra* n. 62.
[68] *Blay* v. *Pollard & Morris* [1930] 1 K.B. 628; *cf. L'Estrange* v. *F. Graucob Ltd.* [1934] 2 K.B. 394, a case of ignorance rather than mistake.
[69] (1864) 2 H. & C. 906; *cf. Hickman* v. *Berens* [1895] 2 Ch. 638.
[70] *Smidt* v. *Tiden* (1874) L.R. 9 Q.B. 446.
[71] *Ante*, pp. 1, 8–9.
[72] (1878) 3 App.Cas. 459.
[73] *Cf. The Unique Mariner* [1978] 1 Lloyd's Rep. 438, 451–452.

knew that Brocklehurst owed money to Jones.[74] Probably such knowledge is not essential to make the contract void. A person who accepts an offer knowing that it is addressed to another must take the risk that the mistake may turn out to be material.

The rule that a mistake of one party is operative if known to the other is further illustrated by *Smith* v. *Hughes*.[75] Oats were bought by sample, the buyer thinking that they were old when, in fact, they were new. He refused to accept them, as he had no use for new oats. In an action for the price, the trial judge told the jury to find for the buyer (1) if the word "old" had actually been used in the negotiations, *i.e.* if the oats had been *expressly described* as old; or (2) if "the [seller] believed the [buyer] to believe, or to be under the impression, that he was *contracting for the purchase of old oats*." The jury found for the buyer, but did not say which of these two questions they had answered in his favour. If they thought that the word "old" had been used, their verdict was clearly correct. But they might have based their verdict on their answer to the second question, so that the court had to decide whether this question was correctly formulated.

If the buyer's mistake had been *as to the subject-matter*, it could not in law negative consent at all because it was not fundamental.[76] The seller's knowledge of the buyer's mistake would not alter this. But if the mistake had been *as to the terms of the contract* it could negative consent although it was not fundamental.[77] There would have been such a mistake if the buyer believed that the seller *warranted* the oats to be old, while the seller intended to sell without warranty. Prima facie this mistake would not be operative: the objective principle would apply, the buyer having behaved so as to induce the seller reasonably to believe that the buyer was buying oats of the same quality as those in the sample. The mistake would only be operative if the seller knew of the buyer's mistake—*i.e.* if he knew that the buyer believed he was buying the oats with a warranty that they were old.[78]

Thus if the buyer thought the oats *were old* there was a good contract even if the seller knew of this mistake; but if the buyer thought the oats were *warranted to be old* and the seller knew of this, quite different, mistake the contract was void. The court ordered a new trial because the direction to the jury did not clearly distinguish between the two mistakes which the buyer might have made.

It has been suggested above[79] that it is hard to see why a mistake as to a warranty of quality should negative consent when a mistake as to the existence of the quality itself does not have this effect. The distinction is based on *Smith* v. *Hughes*; and it is submitted that if the buyer did believe the oats to have been warranted old, and the seller knew this, the buyer could have been absolved from liability on an alternative ground. In such a case it could be said that there *was* a contract under which the seller was bound by the warranty that the oats were old, because he had behaved so as to induce the buyer reasonably to believe that he was contracting on those

[74] The only report of the case which suggests that Boulton did know this is in 6 W.R. 107, where counsel for the defendants says at p. 108: "The plaintiff knew that Brocklehurst was indebted to the defendants . . . ."
[75] (1871) L.R. 6 Q.B. 597.
[76] *Ante*, p. 267.
[77] *Ante*, p. 268.
[78] *Cf. Hartog* v. *Colin & Shields* [1939] 3 All E.R. 566 (*post*, p. 273).
[79] *Ante*, p. 268.

terms.[80] Breach of the warranty that the oats were old could justify the buyer's refusal to accept new oats.[81]

(c) MISTAKE NEGLIGENTLY INDUCED. A mistake is operative where one party has negligently led the other to make it. In *Scriven Bros.* v. *Hindley & Co.*[82] the defendant at an auction bid for two lots believing that both were lots of hemp, whereas one was a lot of hemp and tow. Normally, he could not have relied on this mistake,[83] but he was able to do so in this case because the mistake was caused by the misleading nature of the catalogue and by the conduct of one of the seller's servants. This principle is distinct from that which applies in cases of ambiguity.[84] Where a mistake is negligently induced, the circumstances need not be so perfectly ambiguous that each party's view of the contract is equally tenable. If auction particulars are so obscure as to lead a purchaser to make a mistake, the mistake will be operative even though the particulars, properly interpreted, can only bear the meaning intended by the vendor.[85]

(3) Mistake may operate against one party only

If A's mistake is deliberately induced by B, then A can treat the contract as void, but it does not follow that B can do so. It seems probable that in *Cundy* v. *Lindsay* Blenkarn could have been sued for the price of the handkerchiefs.[86] The same may be true even where B does not in any way bring about A's mistake. In *Hartog* v. *Colin & Shields*[87] the defendants intended to offer hare skins for sale at a stated price "per piece," but inadvertently offered to sell at that price "per pound." A pound contained, on average, three pieces. The plaintiff purported to accept this offer. It was held that there was "no contract"[88] as the plaintiff must have known of the defendants' mistake in expressing their offer.[89] But it is possible that the defendants could have held the plaintiff liable on his acceptance if a fall in the market had made them wish to do so.

4. Theoretical Basis

It has been suggested[90] that the cases discussed in this Section do not depend on mistake at all, but on the rule that there is no contract if offer

---

80 This is in fact the argument of counsel for the buyer as reported in 40 L.J.Q.B. at p. 223. But in the *Law Reports*, counsel is reported as saying: "The parties were not *ad idem*" (p. 600).

81 It is true that now refusal to accept is (as a general rule) only justified by a breach of *condition* (*post*, pp. 689 *et seq.*). But the terms "warranty" and "condition" were probably not used in their present sense in 1871: see *post*, p. 691; *cf. Hardwick Game Farm* v. *Suffolk Agricultural, etc. Association* [1969] 2 A.C. 31, 83.

82 [1913] 3 K.B. 564.

83 *Ante*, pp. 270–271.

84 *Ante*, p. 271.

85 *Cf. Swaisland* v. *Dearsley* (1861) Beav. 430, in equity, but *Scriven Bros. & Co.* v. *Hindley & Co.* [1913] 3 K.B. 564 shows that the common law is the same.

86 So in the agency situation discussed at p. 264, *ante*, the agent might have been liable: *cf. Bell* v. *Balls* [1897] 1 Ch. 663, 669.

87 [1939] 3 All E.R. 566.

88 *Ibid.* p. 567.

89 *Cf. Watkin* v. *Watson-Smith, The Times*, July 3, 1986.

90 Slade, 70 L.Q.R. 385; Shatwell, 33 Can.Bar Rev. 164; Atiyah, 2 Ottawa L.Rev. 337, esp. at pp. 344–350 and *Essays in Contract*, pp. 253–260; *cf. Whittaker* v. *Campbell* [1984] Q.B. 319, 327—but in that case the mistake was as to attribute only, and so not fundamental: see *ibid.* p. 329.

and acceptance do not correspond. If, for example, contract notes are exchanged by which A agrees to sell "St. Petersburgh clean hemp ex *Annetta*" but B agrees to buy "Riga Rhine hemp ex *Annetta*"[91] it is as plausible to say that there is no contract because offer and acceptance do not correspond as it is to say that there is no contract because the parties intended to deal with different things.

But there are also difficulties in the way of this "offer and acceptance" theory.[92] It clearly does not mean that there is a good contract merely because the express words of the offer correspond with those of the acceptance. In *Raffles* v. *Wichelhaus*,[93] there was, so far as appears from the report, no lack of verbal correspondence between offer and acceptance, and yet (on one view of the case) there was no contract.

Another version of the same theory is that the full terms of the offer, as intended by the offeror, must correspond with the full terms of the acceptance, as intended by the offeree. But on this view it is hard to see why some discrepancies prevent the formation of a contract, while others do not. Two cases may be contrasted. In the first, A intends to sell oats which are new; B intends to buy oats which are old. In the second, A intends to sell cotton ex *Peerless* (December); B intends to buy cotton ex *Peerless* (October). The contract in the first case is expressed to be for "oats" and in the second for "cotton ex *Peerless*." In both cases offer and acceptance correspond verbally. In neither case would they correspond if each party expressed his full intention. Yet in the first case there is a good contract, while in the second there is none. This version of the "offer and acceptance" theory makes no allowance for the crucial distinction between mistakes which are fundamental and those which are not.

A third version of the theory is that the required correspondence is between offer and acceptance *as construed by the court*. On this view *Raffles* v. *Wichelhaus* can be explained on the ground that offer and acceptance were so ambiguous that the court could not, in the context, determine their meaning at all. But this version of the theory makes it hard to explain the distinction drawn in *Smith* v. *Hughes* between a mistake as to the age of the oats and a mistake as to a warranty as to their age; and, more generally, to say why offer and acceptance should have been held to correspond in some of the cases discussed in this Section, but not in others. It seems that this version of the "offer and acceptance" theory will still raise the same difficulties that have to be resolved under the doctrine of mistake. If the offer and acceptance correspond verbally, the court is unlikely to hold that they do not correspond on their true construction unless the parties are very seriously at cross-purposes; and such a process of construction would not appear to differ substantially from the application of the principle of fundamental mistake.[94]

---

[91] As in *Thornton* v. *Kempster* (1814) 5 Taunt. 786.

[92] *Cf.* Devlin L.J. (dissenting) in *Ingram* v. *Little* [1961] 1 Q.B. 31.

[93] (1864) 2 H. & C. 906; *ante*, pp. 266–267, 271.

[94] Atiyah, *supra*, n. 90 at pp. 350 and 260, suggests that the courts are "in fact using" the construction technique and not the mistake technique, citing *Sullivan* v. *Constable* (1932) 48 T.L.R. 369. On the other hand, it seems that the mistake technique was used in *Dennant* v. *Skinner* [1948] 2 K.B. 164 and in *Lewis* v. *Averay* [1972] 1 Q.B. 198. It is also accepted in the Law Reform Committee's 12th Report (1966) Cmnd. 2958, para. 15. The difficulty of determining which technique was used by the majority in *Ingram* v. *Little* [1961] 1 Q.B. 31 may support the view expressed in the text that there is little (if any) practical difference between them.

SECTION 3. MISTAKE IN EQUITY

The common law of mistake can be a source of hardship in a number of situations. First, a contract may be held valid because of the narrow common law definition of a "fundamental" mistake. The result is that a person may have to pay for something that he does not want[95] or for something that is nearly worthless.[96] Secondly, a contract may be valid at common law, in spite of the existence of a fundamental mistake, because of the objective principle.[97] Here again the mistaken party can suffer hardship through being held to a contract which he did not intend to make[98] though this hardship must be weighed against that which the other party might suffer if the contract were held invalid.[99] In both these situations, the common law emphasises the needs of commercial certainty, at the expense of the demands of justice in individual cases. Thirdly, an innocent third party may suffer hardship where the contract is *void* at common law, as in *Cundy* v. *Lindsay*.[1]

Equity differs from the common law principally in mitigating the first of these hardships: it gives relief for certain types of mistake which the common law disregards. It also provides more flexible remedies. At common law there is no power of apportionment, so that the whole loss resulting from a mistake has to be suffered by one party, even though both are equally innocent. The powers of adjustment available in equity can lead to more satisfactory solutions.[2] Equity, however, only deals to a very limited extent with the hardship that can result from the operation of the objective principle[3]; and it provides no relief from the hardship to third parties that can arise when the contract is void at law.

Equity's more liberal treatment of mistake to some extent sacrifices the requirements of certainty emphasised by the common law. One cannot in this field have certainty and justice at the same time; and the present state of English law presents a somewhat incongruous appearance, with common law striving for certainty while equity tries to promote justice. It may be that the common law has over-stressed the need for certainty. This is suggested by the fact that the American rules on this subject are much closer to those of English equity than to those of the English common law,[4] and do not seem to have caused widespread inconvenience. Nor has such inconvenience resulted from the rule that a contract can be set aside for even a wholly innocent misrepresentation.[5] Yet from the representor's

---

[95] *e.g. Smith* v. *Hughes* (1871) L.R. 6 Q.B. 597 (assuming that the only mistake was as to the age of the oats).
[96] *e.g. Bell* v. *Lever Bros. Ltd.* [1932] A.C. 161.
[97] *Ante*, p. 270.
[98] *Cf. post*, p. 280.
[99] The other party can invoke the objective principle even though he has not suffered any detriment by relying on the appearance of agreement induced by the conduct of the mistaken party: *ante*, p. 270.
[1] (1878) 3 App.Cas. 459; for a proposal for reform, see *ante*, p. 262.
[2] The statutory powers of adjustment available in cases of frustration (*post*, pp. 810–818) do not apply to cases of mistake: *e.g.* the defendant in a case like *Griffith* v. *Brymer* (1903) 19 T.L.R. 434 (*ante*, p. 251) would even now have no statutory claim for his expenses.
[3] *Post*, p. 280; contrast *ante*, p. 270.
[4] See Williston, *Contracts*, rev. ed., § 1544; *cf.* his criticism in § 1570, n. 3 of *Bell* v. *Lever Bros. Ltd.*; Restatement 2d, *Contracts* §§ 152, 153.
[5] *Post*, Chap. 9.

point of view this rule creates almost as much uncertainty as would a broad doctrine of mistake.

At first sight, it may seem odd still to provide a separate discussion of mistake in equity. A more satisfactory approach, it might be thought, would simply be to look at each mistake situation and to ask whether the law (including equity) provided any relief.[6] But this approach would not help towards an understanding of the present law, because equitable remedies for mistake differ in several ways from those available at common law. They are not only more flexible but also discretionary and liable to be barred by the various factors to be discussed below.[7] Even today it is therefore not enough to know that there is *some* remedy for mistake in a given case. It can still make a practical difference whether the remedy is available at common law (because the contract is void) or in equity (even though the contract is not void).

1. Types of Mistake Dealt With in Equity

(1) Mistake of fact

(a) MISTAKE NOT FUNDAMENTAL. Equity may give relief to a person who has made a mistake which is not fundamental in the narrow common law sense: for example to a purchaser who buys under a mistake as to the vendor's title,[8] though at law the contract would be valid unless the title happened to be in the purchaser himself.[9] Similarly, equity can give relief if a vendor intends to sell property subject to a right of way or a mortgage, but the purchaser believes he is buying without incumbrance.[10] Conversely, equitable relief can be given to a vendor who sells property to which he has a greater right than he thinks he has: *e.g.* if he thinks that he has only a half-share in property when he is in fact entitled to the whole.[11] Many other cases in which equitable relief was given for mistakes that were not fundamental in the common law sense are considered later in this Chapter in the discussion of the various forms that such relief can take.[12]

(b) MISTAKE AS TO VALUE. Occasionally, equity has even intervened where a mistake has been made by a vendor which merely affects the value of the thing sold.[13] Similarly, in *Re Garnett*[14] a testator left half his estate to his sister and the other half to be shared equally between his nieces, who lived with the sister. The nieces later released their shares to the sister in consideration of a payment of £10,500. The releases were set aside on the ground that the shares of the nieces were worth over £15,000. However, where a contract price is fixed by the valuation of a third party, equity will not intervene merely because that valuation is too high[15] or too low. The

---

[6] Phang, 9 Legal Studies 291.
[7] *Post*, p. 285.
[8] *Hitchcock* v. *Giddings* (1817) 4 Price 135.
[9] *Ante*, p. 250.
[10] *Manser* v. *Back* (1848) 6 Hare 433; *Torrance* v. *Bolton* (1872) L.R. 8 Ch.App. 118.
[11] *Colyer* v. *Clay* (1843) 7 Beav. 188.
[12] *Post*, pp. 279–290, especially at pp. 281–284.
[13] *Cocking* v. *Pratt* (1749) 1 Ves.Sen. 400; *Evans* v. *Llewellin* (1787) 1 Cox CC. 333; *Walters* v. *Morgan* (1861) 3 D.F. & J. 718; *Bettyes* v. *Maynard* (1882) 46 L.T. 766; *cf. Scott* v. *Coulson* [1903] 2 Ch. 249, *ante*, p. 254.
[14] (1885) 31 Ch.D. 1; *cf. Jones* v. *Rimmer* (1880) 14 Ch.D. 588.
[15] *Campbell* v. *Edwards* [1976] 1 W.L.R. 403.

remedy (if any) of the party prejudiced by the mistake is against the valuer.[16]

(c) NO RELIEF FOR MISTAKE AS TO EXPECTATION. Equity will grant relief for a mistake as to facts existing at the date of the contract; but not for "one which related to the expectation of the parties."[17] The distinction is illustrated by *Amalgamated Investment & Property Co. Ltd.* v. *John Walker & Sons Ltd.*[18] where a contract was made for the sale of a London warehouse which the purchaser (to the vendor's knowledge) intended to redevelop. Before the contract was made, a government official had decided that the warehouse ought to be listed as a building of special architectural or historic interest. But the actual listing only took place after the conclusion of the contract; its effect was to make it harder to obtain permission to redevelop. If such permission were refused the value of the property would be reduced by some £1,500,000 below the contract price of £1,710,000. The Court of Appeal held that equity could not intervene[19] merely because the purchaser mistakenly believed that the property was "suitable for and capable of being developed."[20] No doubt the official's decision, if known, would have affected the negotiations; but that decision did not amount to a listing, and therefore did not affect the quality of the subject-matter at the time of contracting. It only affected the extent of the risk that permission to redevelop might be refused—a risk which would have existed, though to a lesser extent, quite apart from any question of listing.

(2) Mistake of law

At common law, relief is only given for a mistake of "fact" as opposed to one of "law." But the distinction between these two categories is not always easy to draw[21] or to justify[22]; and equity gives relief for certain types of mistake that the common law would, or might, regard as mistakes of law.

(a) PRIVATE RIGHT. A mistake as to private right can avoid a contract, even at law, but only[23] if it results in an attempt by a person to buy his own property.[24] Such a mistake may be based on a pure mistake of fact, *e.g.* if A is wrongly thought to be older than B. More usually, the mistake arises out of the misconstruction of a document, such as a will or settlement.[25] It may also result from a mistake about the law, *e.g.* as to the age at which a person can marry or make a will, or as to the contractual capacity of a person under a disability. In such cases the mistake seems to be a pure mistake of law, though, like many mistakes of law, it may affect private rights.

---

16 If he is negligent: *post*, p. 310.
17 *Amalgamated Investment & Property Co. Ltd.* v. *Walker & Sons Ltd.* [1977] 1 W.L.R. 164, 172.
18 *Supra*; Brownsword, (1977) 40 M.L.R. 467.
19 Whether by rescission or by refusal of specific performance.
20 [1977] 1 W.L.R. at p. 171.
21 *Cf. post*, pp. 298–300 for the similar distinction between representations of "fact" and of "law."
22 *Cf. Avon C.C.* v. *Howlett* [1983] 1 W.L.R. 605, 620 (where Slade L.J. said that the courts should not be "quick to extend" the category of mistakes of "law" in the context of a claim for the recovery of money paid under a mistake).
23 *British Homophone Ltd.* v. *Kunz* (1932) 152. L.T. 589.
24 *Cf. ante*, p. 250.
25 As in *Cooper* v. *Phibbs* (1877) L.R. 2 H.L. 149.

(b) PURE MISTAKE OF LAW. There is some support for the view that equity can relieve against a pure mistake of law of the kind last mentioned, even though it does not result in an attempt by a person to buy his own property. In *Allcard* v. *Walker*[26] a married woman executed a settlement containing a covenant to settle after-acquired property. Under the then existing law a married woman could not bind herself by such a covenant. In later divorce proceedings she agreed to an order varying the settlement, mistakenly believing that the settlement and the covenant were valid. It was held that the order could be set aside. Since orders made by consent may for this purpose have the effect of contracts,[27] the case supports the view that in equity a contract can be set aside for pure mistake of law. Stirling J., apart from affirming this proposition, also said that the mistake was one as to private right: he relied on the analogy of *Cooper* v. *Phibbs*,[28] where equitable relief was granted to a person who had taken a lease of land to which he was already entitled beneficially, though not at law, neither party being at the time of the transaction aware of the true state of the title. But the mistake in that case was one as to the construction of the documents[29] on which the title to the land in question depended. The mistake in *Allcard* v. *Walker* was one as to the general law then governing the contractual capacity of married women and it is now doubtful whether relief can be given in equity for such a pure mistake of law. In *Solle* v. *Butcher*[30] all the members of the Court of Appeal seem to have assumed that such relief was not available; the court was divided only on the question whether the mistake was one of law.

(c) MISTAKE AS TO CONSTRUCTION. Law and equity can give relief where a contract is made under a mistake as to private rights arising out of a misconstruction of documents that specify those rights. Equity can also sometimes give relief where one of the parties has misinterpreted the contract itself. The mere fact that A has misinterpreted the contract does not entitle him to enforce it against B in the sense in which A understood it[31]; and, in general, the court will enforce the contract, properly interpreted, at the suit of either A[32] or B.[33] But the court can, in its discretion, refuse B specific performance on the ground that A has misinterpreted the contract[34];

[26] [1896] 2 Ch. 369; *cf. Stone* v. *Godfrey* (1854) 5 D.M. & G. 76, 90; *Re Saxon Life Assurance Soc.* (1862) 2 J. & H. 408, 412 (affd. 1 D.J. & S. 29). *Cf. Gibson* v. *Mitchell* [1990] 1 W.L.R. 1304, where the court puzzlingly distinguishes at p. 1309 between a mistake of law as to the "effect" and "consequences" of the transaction. The actual decision is based on the Variation of Trusts Act 1958.

[27] *Huddersfield Banking Co. Ltd.* v. *Henry Lister & Son Ltd.* [1895] 2 Ch. 273; *cf. Sport International Bussum BV* v. *Inter-Footwear Ltd.* [1984] 1 W.L.R. 776. But a "consent" order may be merely one to which a party submits without objection in which case it does not amount to a contract: *Siebe Gorman & Co. Ltd.* v. *Pneupac Ltd.* [1982] 1 W.L.R. 185; and in matrimonial proceedings consent orders are not now regarded as contracts: *Thwaite* v. *Thwaite* [1982] Fam. 1; *Jenkins* v. *Livesey* [1985] A.C. 424.

[28] (1867) L.R. 2 H.L. 149; Matthews, 105 L.Q.R. 599.

[29] It made no difference that one of these was a private Act of Parliament: *cf. post*, p. 299 n. 33.

[30] [1950] 1 K.B. 671; *post*, p. 281.

[31] *Midland Great Western Ry. of Ireland* v. *Johnson* (1858) 6 H.L.C. 798.

[32] *Berners* v. *Fleming* [1925] Ch. 264.

[33] *Powell* v. *Smith* (1872) L.R. 14 Eq. 85; *Hart* v. *Hart* (1881) Ch.D. 670.

[34] *Watson* v. *Marston* (1853) 4 D.M. & G. 230.

and if A's mistake is induced (even innocently) by B, A may be entitled to have the contract set aside.[35]

A mistake as to the *contents* of a contract is clearly one of fact.[36] Action in reliance on such a mistake may give rise to an estoppel by convention. The requirements and effects of such an estoppel are discussed in Chapter 3[37]; they differ from the kind of relief with which we are concerned in this Chapter. Such relief is sought by a party who wishes to *impugn* the binding force of a contract, *e.g.* by asking to have it set aside. Estoppel by convention is, on the other hand, invoked by a party who seeks to *rely*[38] on the contract, as understood by him. This accounts for the fact that the requirements of such an estoppel are more stringent than those of relief for mistake. Estoppel by convention requires action in reliance on an agreed but mistaken assumption; usually this takes the form of acts done in the performance of the contract. There is no such requirement where a party merely seeks to set aside, or to resist the enforcement of, a contract on the ground of mistake: he need show no more than that he entered into the contract under the mistake, and that it falls into one of the categories (discussed above) for which equity gives relief.

(3) Mistaken inferences

Many cases involve an inquiry into the physical circumstances from which some inference then has to be drawn. The physical circumstances are called the primary facts of the case and the inference is called a secondary fact. Questions of secondary fact are for some purposes treated as questions of law and for others as questions of fact.[39]

The cases of mistake dealt with at common law involve mistakes as to primary facts. But equity goes further and gives relief against mistakes of secondary fact, or mistaken inferences. In *Solle* v. *Butcher*[40] a flat was extensively altered and then let. Both landlord and tenant mistakenly thought that, as a result of the alterations, the flat had changed its "identity," so that it was no longer subject to the Rent Acts. In the Court of Appeal, the mistake was variously described as one of fact, as to private rights, or of law.[41] It is submitted that it is best described as a mistake of secondary fact. The parties were under no mistake as to the primary facts: they knew what work had been done in the flat. Their mistake was as to the inference to be drawn from those facts and this mistake enabled the court to give equitable relief.

2. Forms of Equitable Relief

Equity may give relief by refusal of specific performance, rescission and rectification. The discretion to refuse specific performance is the most freely available form of relief. As it leaves the contract enforceable at law, the requirements of certainty are not too seriously prejudiced. Rescission and rectification, on the other hand, have repercussions at law and are more closely circumscribed.

---

[35] *Wilding* v. *Sanderson* [1897] 2 Ch. 534; *Faraday* v. *Tamworth Union* (1917) 86 L.J. Ch. 436.
[36] *Post*, p. 299.
[37] *Ante*, p. 111.
[38] Though probably only by way of defence: see *ante*, p. 114.
[39] *Cf. post*, p. 000, *Benmax* v. *Austin Motor Co. Ltd.* [1955] A.C. 370.
[40] [1950] 1 K.B. 671.
[41] At pp. 685, 693, 705 (Jenkins L.J. dissenting).

(1) Refusal of specific performance

(a) ABSOLUTE REFUSAL. Specific performance will clearly be refused where the contract is *void* at law, *e.g.* where a person contracts to buy his own property[42] or where one party, to the knowledge of the other, makes a mistake as to the terms of the contract[43]; or as to its binding force.[44]

Specific performance may also be refused where the contract is *valid* at law because the mistake is not one of fact, or not fundamental,[45] or not operative because of the objective principle.[46] Thus in *Day* v. *Wells*[47] the defendant instructed an auctioneer to sell cottages thinking that he had told the auctioneer to put a reserve price on them. The auctioneer sold without reserve, at a lower price and it was held that the defendant could not be compelled to perform specifically. Similarly, in *Wood* v. *Scarth*[48] a landlord agreed to let a public house, intending to take a premium but failing to say so. He successfully resisted a claim for specific performance, though he was later held liable in damages at law.[49]

Where the contract is valid, refusal of specific performance is a matter for the discretion of the court. In exercising that discretion, the court must weigh the hardship caused by granting specific performance against the uncertainty caused by refusing it. Two cases may be contrasted. In *Malins* v. *Freeman*[50] the defendant at an auction bid for one lot under the mistaken impression that he was bidding for another. Although he was clearly liable at law,[51] it was held that specific performance should not be ordered against him. But in *Tamplin* v. *James*[52] the defendant at an auction bid for an inn and a shop mistakenly believing that the lot included a certain garden. The Court of Appeal ordered specific performance, stressing the uncertainty which would result from allowing the defendant to rely on his own mistake. James L.J. said that a defendant could only rely on a mistake to which the plaintiff had not contributed "where a hardship amounting to injustice would have been inflicted upon him by holding him to his bargain, and it was unreasonable to hold him to it."[53] The two cases may be reconciled by saying that it is a "hardship amounting to injustice" to force a person to take one property when he thinks he has bought another, but not to force a person to take a property which is less extensive than he thought.

Since the object of refusing specific performance is to avoid hardship to the party prejudiced by the mistake, it follows that, where the contract is valid at law, only that party can rely on the mistake. Thus if A thinks that he is buying more than B intends to sell, A can specifically enforce the contract for the smaller quantity intended by B.[54] But where the contract is

---

[42] *Jones* v. *Clifford* (1876) 3 Ch.D. 779.
[43] *Webster* v. *Cecil* (1861) 30 Beav. 62. It seems reasonable to deduce from the report that the plaintiff knew of the defendant's mistake; but this fact is not actually stated.
[44] *Pateman* v. *Pay* (1974) 232 E.G. 457.
[45] *e.g. Jones* v. *Rimmer* (1880) 14 Ch.D. 588.
[46] *Ante*, pp. 270–271.
[47] (1861) 30 Beav. 220.
[48] (1855) 2 K. & J. 33.
[49] (1858) 1 F. & F. 293.
[50] (1837) 2 Keen 25.
[51] *Ante*, p. 270.
[52] (1880) 15 Ch.D. 215; *cf. Calverley* v. *Williams* (1790) 1 Ves.Jun. 209.
[53] *Tamplin* v. *James, supra*, at p. 221; *cf. Stewart* v. *Kennedy* (1890) 15 App.Cas. 75, 105.
[54] *Preston* v. *Luck* (1884) 27 Ch.D. 497.

void at law, neither party can specifically enforce it[55] unless the circumstances are such that, even at law, one party, but not the other, can rely on the mistake.[56]

(b) SPECIFIC PERFORMANCE ON TERMS. Equity can take a middle course between refusing specific performance and granting it in spite of the mistake: it can, where the contract is valid at law, grant specific performance on terms. Thus in *Baskcomb* v. *Beckwith*[57] an estate was sold in lots, on the terms that the purchaser of each lot should covenant not to build a public house on it. The vendor kept one of the lots himself, and proposed to build a public house on it, but the plan of the lots did not make this clear. It was held that the vendor could specifically enforce the contract but only if he covenanted not to build a public house on the land retained by him. Similarly, equity can order specific performance with compensation, *i.e.* abatement or increase of the purchase price, where the value of the property sold is less or greater than supposed because of some misdescription of the property.[58]

(2) Rescission[59]

(a) EQUITABLE JURISDICTION TO RESCIND. Where the mistake is not fundamental in the common law sense, so that the contract is valid at law, equity may nevertheless set the contract aside. In this way, it relieves the party prejudiced by the mistake from hardship; but it will only do so if he in turn does justice to the other party. Thus in *Solle* v. *Butcher*[60] a flat was let for £250 per annum. For reasons already stated,[61] the parties thought that the flat was free from rent control, when in fact it was subject to the Rent Acts and to a standard rent of £140 per annum. Had the landlord realised this, he could, before granting the lease, have increased the rent to about £250 per annum, on account of the work done by him to the flat; but he had no right to make such an increase during the currency of a lease already granted. The tenant claimed a declaration that the standard rent was £140 per annum and repayment of the excess; the landlord claimed rescission of the lease. It was held that the lease could be rescinded, though it was valid at law. As it would have caused considerable hardship to the tenant to turn him out of the flat, the court gave him the option of staying on if he paid the standard rent plus the amount by which the landlord could have increased it, had he been aware of the true position when he granted the lease.

(b) RESTRICTED TO CONTRACTS VALID AT LAW. At first sight, it would seem that the power to impose terms when a contract is set aside only exists where the contract is valid at law[62]; for when the contract is void at law each party is entitled to ignore it completely. There is nothing to "set aside" and consequently no power to impose terms. There are, however, two difficulties in the way of this view.

---

55 *Higginson* v. *Clowes* (1808) 15 Ves. 516 (vendor's claim); *Clowes* v. *Higginson* (1813) 1 V. & B. 524 (purchaser's claim).
56 *Ante*, p. 273.
57 (1869) L.R. 8 Eq. 100.
58 *Post*, p. 673.
59 *Cf. post*, pp. 329 *et seq.*
60 [1950] 1 K.B. 671; *ante*, p. 279.
61 *Ante*, p. 279.
62 *Ingram* v. *Little* [1961] 1 Q.B. 31, 62.

The first arises from *Cooper* v. *Phibbs*.[63] In that case A was the legal owner of land to which B was beneficially entitled in equity. A improved the land and later agreed to grant a lease of it to B, together with other land of which A was both legal and beneficial owner. It was held that the agreement must be set aside for mistake (neither party having been aware of B's entitlement to part of the land); and that B could get back rent which he had paid under the agreement. But B had to compensate A for the improvements, and to pay a reasonable rent for that part of the land in which he had no interest when the agreement was made. Some later dicta have treated *Cooper* v. *Phibbs* as a case of a contract which was void at law[64]; and this view of the case may give rise to the impression that equity can impose terms even where the contract is void at law. But the actual decision in *Cooper* v. *Phibbs* was that the agreement "ought to be set aside,"[65] this form of relief being then necessary because the legal title to the land was not vested in B.[66] It is, moreover, submitted that, in imposing terms on B (which in any event he did not contest)[67] the court gave effect to obligations that were based, not on any purported contract, but on general principles of equity or restitution. The crucial point was not that A and B had purported to enter into a contract under a mistake, but that A had conferred benefits on B, by the retention of which B would be unjustly enriched.[68] *Cooper* v. *Phibbs* does not support the view that equity can impose terms merely because parties have entered into a void contract.

The second difficulty arises from a number of statements by Lord Denning to the effect that the contract in cases such as *Cundy* v. *Lindsay*[69] would now be voidable in equity.[70] The attraction of this view is that it would enable the court in such cases to protect innocent third parties. But he has also said that there was "no contract at all"[71] in *Cundy* v. *Lindsay*; and this view is certainly the more consistent with the decision. Unless *Cundy* v. *Lindsay* is reversed by legislation or by the House of Lords, there can be nothing to rescind in such a case.

(c) SCOPE OF THE JURISDICTION. The precise scope of the equitable jurisdiction to set a valid contract aside on terms is obscure. The mistake must be of more than trivial importance[72] but apart from this it is hard to say when a mistake which is not regarded as fundamental at law will justify rescission. It has been suggested that a mistake as to the age of a car or as

---

[63] (1867) L.R. 2 H.L. 149.
[64] See *ante*, p. 250.
[65] (1867) L.R. 2 H.L. 149, 167, 173.
[66] See Matthews, 105 L.Q.R. 599.
[67] (1867) L.R. 7 H.L. 149, 154.
[68] *Cf. post*, p. 623 in respect of the improvements; and *post*, p. 936 in respect of the rent (showing that even where a contract is void there may be liability at law in respect of benefits obtained under it).
[69] (1878) 3 App.Cas. 459; *ante*, p. 262.
[70] *Solle* v. *Butcher* [1950] 1 K.B. 671, 692; *Lewis* v. *Averay* [1972] 1 Q.B. 198, 207; and see his statement in *Magee* v. *Pennine Insurance Co. Ltd.* [1969] 2 Q.B. 507, 514, that "a common mistake, even on a most fundamental matter, does not make a contract void at law: but makes it voidable in equity." This view would very much increase the scope of the equitable jurisdiction but it appears to be inconsistent with many of the cases discussed in Sections 1 and 2 of this Chapter. *Cf. Associated Japanese Bank (International) Ltd.* v. *Crédit du Nord S.A.* [1989] 1 W.L.R. 255, 266, describing Lord Denning's view as an "individual opinion."
[71] *Gallie* v. *Lee* [1969] 2 Ch. 17, 33 (affd. [1971] A.C. 1004).
[72] *Debenham* v. *Sawbridge* [1901] 2 Ch. 98.

to the authenticity of a painting might suffice.[73] The equitable jurisdiction has been exercised in a number of cases since *Solle* v. *Butcher*: for example, to set aside a lease because the parties mistakenly thought that the premises had been used only for business purposes when in fact they had been used for residential purposes and so were subject to the Rent Acts[74]; and to set aside a lease of premises to be used as offices for 15 years when it was discovered that the lessors had planning permission for such use for only 3 years.[75] Again, in *Grist* v. *Bailey*[76] a house was sold for £850, both parties believing that it was in the occupation of a protected tenant. In fact the protected tenant had died before the sale so that vacant possession of the house could be obtained, making it worth £2,250. It was held that the contract was not void at law, but that it could be set aside in equity on the terms that the vendor should give the purchaser an opportunity of buying for a "proper vacant possession price."[77] The case seems to go very far in protecting the vendor. And in *Magee* v. *Pennine Insurance Co. Ltd.*[78] a claim was made against an insurance company under a policy of motor insurance. The company compromised the claim by agreeing to pay £385. It did so in the belief that the policy was binding when it was "in truth voidable"[79] for innocent misrepresentation. Lord Denning (with whom Fenton Atkinson L.J. agreed[80]) held that the compromise, though valid at law, was voidable in equity, so that the company was not liable to pay the £385. Rather surprisingly, no terms (*e.g.* as to return of premiums) were imposed so that the decision again seems to be unduly favourable to the insurance company. Winn L.J. dissented on the ground that the case was indistinguishable from *Bell* v. *Lever Bros. Ltd.*[81]; and this point, which is not satisfactorily answered by the majority,[82] raises once again the problem of the relationship between that leading case and the equitable jurisdiction to rescind.

One view is that the equitable jurisdiction could have been exercised in *Bell* v. *Lever Bros. Ltd.*, if an attempt had been made to invoke it; but the difficulty with this argument is that some of the relevant equity cases were in fact cited to the House of Lords.[83] Another view is that the equitable jurisdiction is simply inconsistent with *Bell* v. *Lever Bros. Ltd.*, so that a contract which is valid at law cannot be set aside for a mistake which is not

---

[73] *Oscar Chess Ltd.* v. *Williams* [1957] 1 W.L.R. 370, 373; *Leaf* v. *International Galleries* [1950] 2 K.B. 86, 89.

[74] *Peters* v. *Batchelor* (1950) 100 L.J. News 718.

[75] *Laurence* v. *Lexcourt Holdings Ltd.* [1978] 1 W.L.R. 1128.

[76] [1967] Ch. 532.

[77] [1967] Ch. at p. 543.

[78] [1969] 2 Q.B. 507.

[79] *Ibid.* p. 514.

[80] But he also purported to apply "the proposition which was accepted by all their Lordships in *Bell* v. *Lever Bros. Ltd.*" (p. 517) which suggests that his decision may have been based on common law principles.

[81] [1932] A.C. 161.

[82] Lord Denning said that if the plaintiff "had no valid claim on the insurance policy, it is not equitable that he should have a good claim on the agrement to pay £385 . . . " (at p. 515). But equally Bell and Snelling "had no valid claim" on their service contracts, and yet the compensation agreements were not set aside in *Bell* v. *Lever Bros. Ltd.*

[83] *e.g. Harris* v. *Pepperell* (1867) L.R. 5 Eq. 1; *Paget* v. *Marshall* (1884) 28 Ch.D. 255. As to these cases, see *post*, p. 286; *cf. Associated Japanese Bank International Ltd.* v. *Crédit du Nord S.A.* [1989] 1 W.L.R. 255, 256.

fundamental in the narrow common law sense[84]; but, however cogent the arguments in support of this view may be, it has not impressed the courts, who have accepted the existence of the equitable jurisdiction. A third view is that the equitable jurisdiction depends on the conduct of the parties. Thus it was said in *Solle* v. *Butcher* that the party seeking rescission must not himself be at fault[85]; while conversely contracts have been set aside at the suit of one party because the other behaved improperly in inducing the mistake,[86] or because it was unconscientious for him to insist on his legal advantage after becoming aware of the mistake.[87] The difficulty with this view is that there is no definition of "fault" for this purpose so that it does little to clarify the scope of the equitable jurisdiction. A final possibility is that the common law principles laid down in *Bell* v. *Lever Bros. Ltd.* determine the rights of the parties while the equitable jurisdiction simply entitles the court to vary these at its discretion; but this, too, is unsatisfactory because it is almost impossible to determine on what basis the discretion will be exercised. In the present confused state of the authorities one can only conclude that the courts recognise the existence of the equitable jurisdiction; but no clear answer can be given to the question just when a contract which is valid at common law will be rescinded in equity.

So far, we have considered cases in which the contract was valid at law because the mistake was not *fundamental*. It may also be valid at law because the mistake is, under the objective principle, not *operative*[88]: here equity may refuse specific performance against the mistaken party,[89] leaving the other to his remedy at law. But it will not rescind[90] and so deprive the other party of his remedy at law on the contract. Accordingly, equity will, in general, follow the common law rule that a mistake is not operative if the mistaken party, A, has so conducted himself as to induce the other party, B, reasonably to believe that A agreed to the terms proposed by B. In particular, a person cannot have a contract set aside because of a mistake which he made because he failed to act with due diligence.[91]

The equitable jurisdiction to set a contract aside is discretionary and will, it seems, only be exercised if enforcement of the contract would cause hardship to the mistaken party.[92]

---

[84] A.L.G., 66 L.Q.R. 169; Atiyah & Bennion, 24 M.L.R. 421, 439.

[85] [1950] 1 K.B. 693; *cf. Harrison & Jones Ltd.* v. *Bunten & Lancaster Ltd.* [1953] 1 Q.B. 646, 654 (equitable relief refused as neither party was at fault): *Laurence* v. *Lexcourt Holdings Ltd.* [1978] 1 W.L.R. 1128 (relief granted as party prejudiced by mistake was not, while the other party was, at fault); *The Lloydiana* [1983] 2 Lloyd's Rep. 313, 318 (relief refused as mistake entirely due to fault of allegedly mistaken party); *Associated Japanese Bank International Ltd.* v. *Crédit du Nord S.A.* [1989] 1 W.L.R. 255, 270 (equitable relief would have been available, had the contract not been void at law, as claimant was "not at fault in any way").

[86] *e.g. Cocking* v. *Pratt* (1749) 1 Ves.Sen. 400; *Evans* v. *Llewellin* (1787) 1 Cox C.C. 333; *Torrance* v. *Bolton* (1872) L.R. 8 Ch. App. 118; *cf. Beauchamp* v. *Winn* (1873) L.R. 6 H.L. 223, 233.

[87] *e.g. Hitchcock* v. *Giddings* (1817) 4 Price 135; *Bettyes* v. *Maynard* (1882) 46 L.T. 766, but see *Riverlate Properties Ltd.* v. *Paul* [1975] Ch. 133, 140–141.

[88] *Ante*, p. 270.

[89] *Ante*, p. 280.

[90] *Riverlate Properties Ltd.* v. *Paul* [1975] Ch. 133; *post*, p. 286.

[91] *Att.-Gen.* v. *Tomline* (1877) 7 Ch.D. 388; *Soper* v. *Arnold* (1877) 37 Ch.D. 96; 14 App.Cas. 429. For the common law position

[92] *Mills* v. *Fox* (1887) 37 Ch.D. 153.

(d) LOSS OF RIGHT TO RESCIND.[93] In the following cases the right to rescind for mistake is, or may be, barred.

(i) *Lapse of time.* A person who claims rescission must do so with reasonable promptness.[94] It is not clear whether time runs from the making of the contract or from the discovery of the mistake or from the time when the mistake should, with reasonable diligence, have been discovered. The last test probably applies in cases of innocent misrepresentation[95] but in one case of mistake rescission was allowed as long as 20 years after the original transaction.[96]

(ii) *Third party rights.* The contract will not be rescinded to the prejudice of a third party who has, before rescission is claimed, acquired an interest in the subject-matter.[97]

(iii) *Impossibility of restitutio in integrum.* The right to rescind can only be exercised if the claimant can put the other party into substantially the same position as that in which he was before the contract was made. This may be impossible because of some act done by the other party in reliance on the contract, *e.g.* by a lessee's farming land comprised in a lease made under a mistake on the part of the lessor[98] or by a daughter's marrying in reliance on a settlement made under a mistake on the part of her father.[99] Or restitution may be impossible because of the way in which the claimant has dealt with the subject-matter: he may have consumed it, or disposed of it. Restitution need not be precise; a contract can be rescinded if substantial restitution is still possible and if the court can, by making allowances for depreciation etc. do justice between the parties.[1] And, although restitution must in this sense be possible, it will not always be ordered: thus the contract may, as in *Solle* v. *Butcher*,[2] be rescinded on terms which do not restore the pre-contract position.

(iv) *Execution of the contract no bar.* It was formerly the law that certain contracts could not be rescinded for innocent misrepresentation after they had been executed.[3] But this rule did not (and does not) apply to rescission in equity on the ground of mistake.[4]

(3) Rectification

Contracting parties may execute a document purporting to contain the terms previously agreed between them. If, as a result of a mistake, the document fails to contain all those terms, or contains different terms, the court may rectify it so as to bring it into line with the earlier agreement.[5] Having been developed in equity, rectification is a discretionary remedy.[6]

---

[93] *Cf.* the similar but not identical rules in cases of misrepresentation: *post*, pp. 338 *et seq*.
[94] *Cf. Bell* v. *Cundall* (1750) Amb. 101.
[95] *Post*, p. 345.
[96] *Re Garnett* (1885) 31 Ch.D. 1.
[97] *Cf. Bell* v. *Cundall* (1750) Amb. 101.
[98] *Powell* v. *Smith* (1872) L.R. 14 Eq. 85.
[99] *Hart* v. *Hart* (1881) 18 Ch.D. 670.
[1] *Cf. post*, p. 341.
[2] [1950] 1 K.B. 671; *ante*, p. 281.
[3] *Post*, p. 337.
[4] *e.g. Solle* v. *Butcher, supra*. For a discussion of contrary Australian cases, see Allan, 4 Univ. of Western Australia Annual L.Rev. 391.
[5] *Murray* v. *Parker* (1854) 19 Beav. 305; *Crane* v. *Hegeman-Harris Co. Inc.* [1939] 1 All E.R. 662, affd. [1939] 4 All E.R. 68; for a passage omitted from these reports, see [1971] 3 All E.R. 245; *The Rhodian River* [1984] 1 Lloyd's Rep. 373.
[6] *Re Butlin's S.T.* [1976] Ch. 251, 263.

It is available where there has been a mistake, not in the making, but in the recording, of a contract: "Courts of equity do not rectify contracts; they may and do rectify instruments."[7] Rectification can be ordered although the contract is one which must be in, or evidenced in, writing.[8] The availability of the remedy depends on the following rules.

(a) MISTAKE OF BOTH PARTIES OR KNOWN TO ONE

(i) *Mistake of one party generally insufficient.* A contractual document[9] will, in general, only be rectified if it fails to record the intention of *both* parties. Thus if A lets a house to B and both agree that the rent is to be £200 per month, the lease can be rectified if by mistake it states the monthly rent to be only £100. But if all the time A intended to charge £200 while B only intended to pay £100 the lease could not be rectified to conform with A's intention,[10] for this would force on B a contract to which he had never agreed. Rectification could, however, be ordered if B, when he executed the lease, knew of A's mistake,[11] or if B was guilty of fraud.[12] In such cases, the remedy would cause no injustice to B.

Some cases formerly supported the view that, where the intention of only one party was inaccurately recorded, the court could intervene, by forcing the other to choose between having the contract rescinded or having it rectified.[13] But these cases conflicted with the objective principle[14] in that they deprived the other party of a bargain on terms which had every appearance of being offered to him; and they were overruled in *Riverlate Properties Ltd.* v. *Paul.*[15] A landlord had granted a lease of part of a house intending to make the tenant liable for part of the cost of external repairs; but the tenant did not know of this intention, nor did the lease contain any provision to this effect. It was held that the landlord was not entitled to have the lease rectified so as to conform with his intention, or to force the tenant to choose between having it so rectified and having it rescinded.

(ii) *One party indifferent.* In *Van der Linde* v. *Van der Linde*[16] a brother covenanted to pay his sister "an annual sum of £400." These words failed to achieve the brother's object of securing a tax advantage, but would have achieved it if the covenant had been to pay "such annual sum as shall after deduction of income tax amount to £400." The brother's claim for rectifi-

---

[7] *Mackenzie* v. *Coulson* (1869) L.R. 8 Eq. 369, 375; *The Olympic Pride* [1980] 2 Lloyd's Rep. 67, 72.

[8] *Olley* v. *Fisher* (1886) 34 Ch.D. 367; *Johnson* v. *Bragge* [1901] 1 Ch. 28; *U.S.A.* v. *Motor Trucks Ltd.* [1924] A.C. 196; *May* v. *Platt* [1900] 1 Ch. 616, if *contra*, is not law: *Craddock Bros.* v. *Hunt* [1923] 2 Ch. 136; Law Com. No. 164, para. 5, 6. The position was different before the Judicature Act 1873: *Woollam* v. *Hearn* (1802) 7 Ves. 211; *Squire* v. *Campbell* (1836) 1 My. & Cr. 459; but s.24(7) of that Act altered the law. See now s.49 of the Supreme Court Act 1981.

[9] A voluntary settlement can be rectified on account of a mistake of the settlor alone: *Re Butlin's S.T.* [1976] Ch. 251.

[10] *Faraday* v. *Tamworth Union* (1917) 86 L.J.Ch. 436; *W. Higgins Ltd.* v. *Northampton Corp.* [1927] 1 Ch. 128; *cf. Lloyd* v. *Stanbury* [1971] 1 W.L.R. 535; *The Nai Genova* [1984] 1 Lloyd's Rep. 353; *The Ypatia Halcoussi* [1985] 2 Lloyd's Rep. 364, 370.

[11] *Garrard* v. *Frankel* (1862) 30 Beav. 445, 451; *A. Roberts & Co. Ltd.* v. *Leicestershire C.C.* [1961] Ch. 555, discussed by R.E.M., 77 L.Q.R. 313; *The Olympic Pride, supra* n. 7 at p. 72; *Thomas Bates & Son Ltd.* v. *Wyndham's (Lingerie) Ltd.* [1981] 1 W.L.R. 505.

[12] *Blay* v. *Pollard & Morris* [1930] 1 K.B. 628, 633.

[13] *Harris* v. *Pepperell* (1867) L.R. 5 Eq. 1; *Paget* v. *Marshall* (1884) 28 Ch.D. 255.

[14] *Ante*, p. 270.

[15] [1975] Ch. 133.

[16] [1947] Ch. 306.

cation was rejected primarily because there was not sufficient evidence of mistake. It was also said that rectification could not be ordered because the sister had no view as to "the intention of the document."[17] In *Whiteside* v. *Whiteside*[18] the court refused to rectify a similar covenant between husband and wife, partly because there was no evidence of the common intention of the parties, and partly because there was no issue between the parties at all: the husband went on paying the wife as if the covenant had already been rectified. But such an issue can be manufactured by simply refusing to make a single payment. If the document in fact fails to express the intention of the parties, rectification can be ordered even though there is no dispute between them *inter se*, but only one between them and the Revenue authorities.[19]

(iii) *Customary terms.* A document may be rectified if it fails to record terms implied by custom into an agreement even though there is no evidence that the parties actually intended such terms to be incorporated. Thus in *Caraman, Rowley & May* v. *Aperghis*[20] sellers were prevented by war from performing a contract for the sale of sultanas. Similar contracts normally contained a "*force majeure*" clause which would have protected the sellers; but in this case the clause was inadvertently left out. It was held that the contractual document could be rectified by the inclusion of a "*force majeure*" clause, whether or not the buyer knew that such a clause was usual. In such a case the customary term is, by implication, part of the *contract*[21] even though the *document* is not rectified. But it may be convenient to have the document rectified, especially if the contract is a long-term one, or if it affects, or is likely to come into the hands of, a third party.

(b) TYPES OF MISTAKE. Rectification is most frequently ordered where the terms of a document do not correspond with those of the agreement between the parties, *e.g.* where the rent is misstated in a lease, or the area of land to be conveyed is misstated in a conveyance.[22] For this purpose, "the agreement" refers to the terms actually agreed between the parties. Thus where those terms were accurately recorded in a lease it was held that rectification was not available merely because they had not been correctly stated in the earlier written agreement for the lease.[23] The only "mistake" of the parties was as to the effect of that written agreement, and to rectify the lease would have defeated, rather than given effect to, the intention of the parties.

Rectification is also available where a person who intends to sign a document in one capacity does so in another, *e.g.* where the name of a person to whom a bill of exchange is meant to be payable is put in as drawer instead

[17] At p. 312.
[18] [1950] Ch. 65; *cf. Rabin* v. *Gerson Berger Assocation Ltd.* [1986] 1 W.L.R. 526, 534 (where no claim for rectification was made); *Sherdley* v. *Sherdley* [1986] 1 W.L.R. 732, 744, revsd. on other grounds [1988] A.C. 213.
[19] *Re Colebrook's Conveyances* [1973] 1 W.L.R. 1379; *cf. Re Slocock's Will Trust* [1979] 1 All E.R. 359; *Seymour* v. *Seymour, The Times*, February 16, 1989; *Lake* v. *Lake* [1989] S.T.C. 865.
[20] (1923) 40 T.L.R. 124.
[21] *Ante*, p. 194.
[22] *e.g. Murray* v. *Parker* (1854) 19 Beav. 305; *Beale* v. *Kyte* [1907] 1 Ch. 564; *Blacklocks* v. *J. B. Developments (Godalming) Ltd.* [1982] Ch. 183.
[23] *London Regional Transport* v. *Wimpey Group Services* (1987) 53 P. & C.R. 356.

of as payee.[24] The court may also rectify a document executed under a mistake as to its meaning or legal effect[25]; but such a mistake will not be a ground for rectification if the true legal effect of the document was fully explained to the party claiming to have made the mistake.[26] A mere misnomer can sometimes be corrected as a matter of construction, in which case there may be no need to rectify the document.[27]

(c) Prior contract not necessary. The court can rectify a document which was preceded by a *concluded agreement* or a "continuing common intention"[28] even though there was no prior *binding contract*.[29] Thus before executing a policy of insurance an underwriter may initial a slip setting out a summary of the essential terms of the policy. If a policy is later executed and found to be at variance with the slip, it can be rectified although the slip was binding in honour only.[30] Similarly, in *Joscelyne* v. *Nissen*[31] an agreement for the transfer of a business and premises was negotiated between a father and daughter, it being understood that the father should continue to live in the premises and that the daughter should pay his gas and electricity bills. No provision for such payments was made in the formal contract finally executed. Rectification was ordered even though, before execution of the document, the agreement between the parties had no contractual force. It was enough if there was "some outward expression of accord" and if this was "adhered to in intention by the parties to the subsequent written contract."[32] On the other hand, a document cannot be rectified to bring it into line with mere steps in the antecedent negotiations,[33] for these may not have led to a concluded agreement on the particular point, or, if they did, that agreement may not have been maintained till the execution of the document.

(d) Document accurately recording prior agreement. It follows from the principle that equity rectifies instruments and not contracts[34] that a document which accurately records a prior agreement cannot be rectified merely because that agreement was made under some mistake. In *F. E.*

---

[24] *Druiff* v. *Parker* (1868) L.R. 5 Eq. 131.

[25] *Re Colebrook's Conveyances* [1973] 1 W.L.R. 1379; *cf. Jervis* v. *Howle & Talke Colliery Ltd.* [1937] Ch. 67, following *Burroughes* v. *Abbott* [1922] 1 Ch. 86; *Tucker* v. *Bennett* (1887) 38 Ch.D. 1; *Re Butlin's S.T.* [1976] Ch. 251. No claim for rectification was made in *Keen* v. *Holland* [1984] 1 W.L.R. 251 (where a mistake as to legal effect was held not sufficient to give rise to an estoppel by convention: *ante*, p. 114.

[26] *Constantinidi* v. *Ralli* [1953] Ch. 427.

[27] *Nittan U.K. Ltd.* v. *Solent Steel Fabrications Ltd.* [1981] 1 All E.R. 633.

[28] *The Olympic Pride* [1980] 2 Lloyd's Rep. 67, 72; *The Pina* [1991] 1 Lloyd's Rep. 146, 250.

[29] For the now rejected contrary view, see *Mackenzie* v. *Coulson* (1869) L.R. 8 Eq. 369, 375.

[30] *Eagle Star, etc., Insurance Co.* v. *Reiner* (1927) 43 T.L.R. 259; Arnould, *Marine Insurance*, (16th ed.) sect. 49; *cf. Symington & Co.* v. *Union Insurance Society of Canton* (1928) 34 Comm.Cas. 233.

[31] [1970] 2 Q.B. 86; Bromley, 87 L.Q.R. 532; Kavanagh, 34 M.L.R. 102; *cf. Wilson* v. *Wilson* [1969] 1 W.L.R. 1470; *Michael Richards Properties* v. *St. Saviour's Parish* [1975] 3 All E.R. 416, 423; *The Olympic Pride, supra* n. 28, at p. 72.

[32] [1970] 2 Q.B. 86, 99; *Shipley U.D.C.* v. *Bradford Corp.* [1936] Ch.375, 396; *cf. Crane* v. *Hegeman-Harris Co. Inc.* [1939] 1 All E.R. 662, 664–665; criticised in *F. E. Rose (London) Ltd.* v. *W. H. Pim, Jnr., & Co. Ltd.* [1953] 2 Q.B. 450, 461; distinguished in *Ashville Investments Ltd.* v. *Elmer Construction Ltd.* [1989] Q.B. 488, 516, and in *Ethiopian Oilseeds & Pulses Corp.* v. *Rio del Mar Foods Inc.* [1990] 1 Lloyd's Rep. 86; approved in *Joscelyne* v. *Nissen* [1970] 2 Q.B. 86; *Earl* v. *Hector Whaling* [1961] 1 Lloyd's Rep. 459, 470.

[33] *Lovell & Christmas Ltd.* v. *Wall* (1911) 104 L.T. 85, 88.

[34] *Ante*, p. 286.

Rose (London) Ltd. v. *W. H. Pim, Jnr. & Co. Ltd.*[35] the plaintiffs had received an order from a customer for "Moroccan horsebeans described here as feveroles" and asked the defendants (their suppliers) what "feveroles" were. The defendants replied that feveroles were just horsebeans and orally agreed to sell "horsebeans" to the plaintiffs. When this contract was reduced to writing, the goods were again described as "horsebeans." In fact there were three types of Moroccan horsebeans: feves, feveroles and fevettes. The defendants supplied feves, which were less valuable than feveroles. It was held that the written contract could not be rectified by inserting "feveroles" after "horsebeans," as it accurately recorded the previous oral agreement.[36]

(e) CLEAR EVIDENCE. When rectification is claimed, the court has to guard against two dangers. The first is that the remedy may result in imposing on a party terms to which he might not in fact have agreed. The second is that the "certainty and ready enforceability [of written agreements] would be hindered by constant attempts to cloud the issue by reference to precontract negotiations."[37] For these reasons, rectification will only be ordered if there is strong and convincing evidence that the document failed accurately to record the intention of the parties.[38] The court is, in particular, reluctant to rectify a contract solely on the oral evidence of the party claiming rectification[39] but there is no absolute rule preventing rectification on such evidence.[40] The requirement of clear evidence seems to be less strict when rectification is sought of a voluntary deed, or of a voluntary provision in a deed.[41]

(f) EXECUTED CONTRACTS. Although the contrary has been suggested[42] execution of a contract is no bar to rectification. Thus leases and conveyances are often rectified on the ground that they are inconsistent with the contracts which preceded them.[43] Any other view would conflict with the whole concept of rectification, for the formal document which it is sought to rectify often *is* the execution of the prior contract.

(g) RESTITUTIO IN INTEGRUM IMPOSSIBLE. Impossibility of restoring the parties to the position in which they were before the contract is, in general,

---

[35] [1953] 2 Q.B. 450; *cf. The Ypatia Halcoussi* [1985] 2 Lloyd's Rep. 364, 371.

[36] The contract was not void for mistake: *ante*, p. 253. Nor could the buyers rescind for misrepresentation as they had resold the horsebeans: *cf. post*, p. 338, but they might now be able to claim damages under Misrepresentation Act 1967, s.2(1) (*post*, p. 312). They might also (as Denning L.J. suggested) be able to claim damages for breach of a collateral warranty, if the necessary *animus contrahendi* on the part of the seller could be shown (*ante*, p. 149, *post*, p. 319).

[37] *The Olympic Pride* [1980] 2 Lloyd's Rep. 67, 73.

[38] *Fowler* v. *Fowler* (1859) 4 D. & J. 250, 265; *Fredensen* v. *Rothschild* [1941] 1 All E.R. 430, 436; *Joscelyne* v. *Nissen* [1970] 2 Q.B. 86; *Ernest Scragg & Sons Ltd.* v. *Perseverence Banking & Trust Co.* [1973] 2 Lloyd's Rep. 101; *The Olympic Pride, supra*, n. 37, at p. 73; *Blacklocks* v. *J. B. Developments (Godalming) Ltd.* [1982] Ch. 183, 191. On the question whether the evidence must come up to the standard required in criminal cases contrast *Earl* v. *Hector Whaling* [1961] 1 Lloyd's Rep. 459 with *The Pina* [1991] 1 Lloyd's Rep. 246, 250.

[39] *Tucker* v. *Bennett* (1887) 38 Ch.D. 1; *Fredensen* v. *Rothschild, supra.*, *Thomas Bates & Son Ltd.* v. *Wyndham's (Lingerie) Ltd.* [1981] 1 W.L.R. 505, 514, 521.

[40] *Cook* v. *Fearn* (1878) 48 L.J.Ch. 63.

[41] See *Hanley* v. *Pearson* (1879) 13 Ch.D. 545.

[42] *e.g.* in *May* v. *Platt* [1900] 1 Ch. 616, criticised in *Thompson* v. *Hickman* [1907] 1 Ch. 550.

[43] *e.g. Murray* v. *Parker* (1854) 19 Beav. 305; *Cowen* v. *Truefitt Ltd.* [1899] 2 Ch. 309; *Stait* v. *Fenner* [1912] 2 Ch. 504.

no bar to rectification. For example, a marriage settlement can be rectified after the marriage has taken place.[44]

(h) LIMITATIONS ON THE REMEDY. Rectification is not available in the following cases:

(i) *Lapse of time.* A claim for rectification is barred by lapse of time. It is not clear whether time begins to run when the contract was made[45] or when the mistake is discovered[46] or when it should by the exercise of reasonable diligence have been discovered. The last view probably applies in cases of innocent misrepresentation[47]; and there seems to be no good reason for applying a different rule where rectification is claimed.

(ii) *Third party rights.* The right to claim rectification, like the other equitable rights, can be asserted against a purchaser with notice of the mistake,[48] but not against a bona fide purchaser for value without notice.[49]

(iii) *Judgment.* A claim for rectification is barred by a judgment in proceedings in which the issue of rectification could have been (though it was not) raised.[50] But judgment in proceedings in which the question of rectification could *not* have been raised is no bar to a later claim for rectification.[51]

(iv) *Assignment.* It has been suggested that, even where a contracting party can claim rectification, a person to whom he assigns his rights cannot do so.[52] The basis for this suggestion seems to be that in such circumstances rectification might produce an undeserved windfall for the assignee.

(v) *Instruments which cannot be rectified.* The articles of association of a company cannot be rectified once they have been registered, even if they contain a simple clerical error.[53] To allow rectification would cut across the scheme laid down by the Companies Acts for the registration and alteration of such documents.

In *Phillipson* v. *Kerry*[54] it was held that a deed poll cannot be rectified, though, if executed under a mistake, it can be set aside. One possible reason for this rule, given in the judgment, is that a voluntary gift cannot be rectified. But as it is now clear that a voluntary deed *inter partes* can be rectified,[55] there does not seem to be any convincing reason for the rule.

The court cannot rectify a settlement which is binding, not as a contract, but by virtue of a court order.[56] If a mistake is made in drawing up such an order, it is more convenient to ask the court which made it to vary it than to ask another court to rectify it.

---

[44] *Cook* v. *Fearn* (1878) 48 L.J. Ch. 63; *Johnson* v. *Bragge* [1901] 1 Ch. 28.

[45] *Bloomer* v. *Spittle* (1872) L.R. 13 Eq. 427.

[46] *Beale* v. *Kyte* [1907] 1 Ch. 564.

[47] *Post*, p. 345.

[48] *Craddock Bros.* v. *Hunt* [1923] 2 Ch. 136; *Blacklocks* v. *J. B. Developments (Godalming) Ltd.* [1982] Ch. 183.

[49] *Smith* v. *Jones* [1954] 1 W.L.R. 1089; *cf. Garrard.* v. *Frankel* (1862) 30 Beav. 445.

[50] *Caird* v. *Moss* (1886) 33 Ch.D. 22.

[51] *Crane* v. *Hegeman-Harris Co. Inc.* [1939] 4 All E.R. 68 (*ante*, p. 285, n. 5).

[52] *Napier* v. *Williams* [1911] 1 Ch. 361; the actual decision would now be different because of Law of Property Act 1925, s.82. Where the assignment forms part of a conveyance, the assignee can claim rectification by virtue of Law of Property Act 1925, s.63(1): *Boots the Chemist* v. *Street* (1983) 268 E.G. 817.

[53] *Scott* v. *Frank F. Scott (London) Ltd.* [1904] Ch. 794.

[54] (1863) 32 Beav. 628.

[55] *Bonhote* v. *Henderson* [1895] 1 Ch. 742; *Re Butlin's S.T.* [1976] Ch. 251; *Re Slocock's Will Trust* [1979] 1 All E.R. 359.

[56] *Mills* v. *Fox* (1887) 37 Ch.D. 153.

SECTION 4. DOCUMENTS MISTAKENLY SIGNED

1. Development

As a general rule, a person is bound by his signature to a document whether he reads it or understands it, or not. But at the end of the sixteenth century an exception to this rule was established. It was held in *Thoroughgood's Case*[57] that if a person who could not read executed a deed after it had been incorrectly read over to him, he was not bound by it. He could plead *non est factum*: it is not my deed.

In the nineteenth century, it was settled that this doctrine was no longer confined to persons who were unable to read. The reason for this extension of the doctrine was the insistence on the requirement of *consensus ad idem* in contract. A person who signed a document without being aware of its nature was not bound because "the mind of the signer did not accompany the signature."[58] But if too wide a scope were given to this argument, it could lead to results that were inconsistent with the objective principle[59] and with the general common law requirement that a mistake must be fundamental if it is to negative consent.[60]

The objective principle does not operate in favour of a person who *knows* of the mistake of the signer[61]; and if that person has induced the mistake by some misrepresentation about the document which is alleged to contain the contract between him and the signer, then the signer will be entitled to avoid the contract on that ground.[62] Often, however, the document purports to be a contract between the signer and someone other than the fraudulent party. For example, A may induce B to sign a guarantee of A's bank overdraft by representing that it is an insurance proposal. Here the document is an apparent contract, not between A and B, but between B and *the bank*, which may reasonably believe that B has assented to the terms of the document. As the bank is not responsible for the fraud of A, B's only hope is to plead *non est factum*; but success of the plea would deprive the bank of the protection of the objective principle.

Even if the document is an apparent contract only between A and B, the latter may try to invoke the doctrine of *non est factum* because it may provide a better remedy for him than rescission on the ground of A's fraud. This will be the position where B has under the contract parted with property and an innocent third party has later acquired an interest in that property for value.[63] If the doctrine of *non est factum* applies, the contract will be void so that B will be entitled to the return of the property; while if the contract is only voidable for A's fraud the third party will be protected. In cases of mistaken identity, the current trend is to protect such innocent third parties by a strict insistence on the requirement that the mistake must

---

[57] (1584) 2 Co.Rep. 9a; *cf. Hitchman* v. *Avery* (1892) 8 T.L.R. 698; *Lloyds Bank plc.* v. *Waterhouse*, *The Independent*, February 27, 1990, *per* Purchas L.J.

[58] *Foster* v. *Mackinnon* (1869) L.R. 4 C.P. 704, 711; *cf.* (in criminal law). *R.* v. *Davies* [1982] 1 All. E.R. 513, 516.

[59] *Ante*, p. 270.

[60] *Ante*, pp. 262–267, but see p. 268.

[61] *Ante*, p. 271.

[62] *Post*, p. 329; *Lloyds Bank plc.* v. *Waterhouse*, *The Independent*, February 27, 1990, *per* Woolf L.J. and Sir Edward Eveleigh.

[63] As in *Gallie* v. *Lee* [1971] A.C. 1004, *post*, p. 292.

be fundamental[64]; and a similar trend can be seen also in the *non est factum* cases.

2. Present Scope of the Doctrine

For the reasons just stated, the scope of the doctrine of *non est factum* is now restricted in the following ways:

(1) Persons to whom the plea is available

The nineteenth century extension of the doctrine to persons who could read has been called "one of the less happy developments in our law"[65] and it has been suggested that the doctrine should not apply in favour of such persons if they were of full age and capacity.[66] But this very narrow view of the doctrine was rejected by the House of Lords in *Gallie* v. *Lee.* In the words of Lord Reid, the doctrine may apply to "those who are permanently or temporarily unable through no fault of their own to have without explanation any real understanding of the purport of a particular document, whether that be from defective education, illness or innate incapacity,"[67] and to these must be added persons who have been tricked into signing the document.[68] The doctrine may thus apply not only to the blind and illiterate but also to persons who are senile, of very low intelligence or unable to read English. But it will not normally protect literate persons of full capacity.[69]

(2) Serious mistake required

In their desire to restrict the scope of the doctrine, the courts have insisted that *non est factum* can only be pleaded where the mistake of the signer was a serious one. Formerly, they gave effect to this policy by drawing a distinction between the "character"[70] of a document and its "contents."[71] But in *Gallie* v. *Lee*[72] the House of Lords rejected this distinction as unworkable,[73] and put in its place the requirement that the difference between the document as it was and as it was believed to be must be radical or substantial or fundamental.[74] Under this test, the seriousness of the mistake is to be judged by "difference in practical result" rather than by "difference in legal character."[75] The facts of the case were that a widow of 78 wanted to help her nephew Parkin to raise money on the security of her leasehold house, provided that she could continue to live there rent free for the rest of her life. Parkin did not want to raise the loan in his own name, or to

---

[64] *Ante*, pp. 262 *et seq.*
[65] *Gallie* v. *Lee* [1969] 2 Ch. 17, 43 *per* Salmon L.J.
[66] *Ibid.* pp. 36–37.
[67] [1971] A.C. 1004, 1016.
[68] *Ibid.* p. 1025.
[69] *Ibid.* pp. 1016, 1025.
[70] *e.g. Foster* v. *Mackinnon* (1869) L.R. C.P. 704 (bill of exchange endorsed in the belief that it was a guarantee: plea upheld).
[71] *e.g. Howatson* v. *Webb* [1907] 1 Ch. 537; affd. [1908] 1 Ch. 1 (mortgage of land executed in the belief that it was a conveyance: plea rejected).
[72] [1971] A.C. 1004.
[73] *Muskham Finance Ltd.* v. *Howard* [1963] 1 Q.B. 904 is, for example, hard to reconcile with *Howatson* v. *Webb, supra.* See also *Gallie* v. *Lee* [1969] 2 Ch. 17, 31–32, *per* Lord Denning M.R.
[74] [1971] A.C. at pp. 1017, 1019, 1021, 1026, 1034.
[75] *Ibid.* p. 1017.

become owner of the house as he feared that this would enable his wife (from whom he was separated) to enforce her claim for maintenance against him. He therefore arranged that an intermediary called Lee should raise the money on a mortgage of the house; and as a first step in this scheme a document was prepared which was in fact an assignment on sale of the lease to Lee for £3,000. The widow did not read this document as her glasses were broken, but she signed it after being told by Lee that it was a deed of gift to Parkin (who witnessed the document). Lee raised money by mortgaging the house to a building society, but he made no payment either to Parkin or to the widow. It was held that the doctrine of *non est factum* did not apply as the widow's mistake was not sufficiently serious. She believed that the document would enable her nephew to raise money on the security of the house, and the document was in fact designed to achieve this aim, though by a different process from that contemplated by her.[76]

(3) Mistake as to identity

We have seen that consent may be negatived, so as to make a contract void, where A deals with B in the mistaken belief that B is C.[77] But if a person signs a document expressed to be in favour of B, he cannot plead *non est factum* merely because he thought that the party named in the document was C. Thus in *Gallie* v. *Lee*[78] the doctrine was inapplicable even though the plaintiff thought that she was making a gift to Parkin when in fact she was making a conveyance to Lee. The reason for this rule may be that the mistaken party can discover the mistake by reading the document.

(4) Ignorance

The plea of *non est factum* is not open to a person who signs a document in the belief that it is "only a form" without having any precise idea as to its nature.[79] Thus in *Gillman* v. *Gillman*[80] a wife, shortly before her husband left her, signed a document which was in fact a separation deed. She did not know this when she signed it, but neither had she any definite idea as to what it was that she was signing. It was held that she was bound by the deed.

(5) Mistake as to capacity

The rule just stated is subject to an exception where a person signs a document under a mistaken belief as to the capacity in which he signs. Thus in *Lewis* v. *Clay*[81] the defendant was induced to sign two promissory notes by the fraudulent representation that his signature was required as a witness and that the documents were of a private nature. The plea of *non est factum* succeeded even though the defendant could not say precisely what type of document he thought he had signed.

---

[76] *Cf. Mercantile Credit Ltd.* v. *Hamblin* [1965] 2 Q.B. 242; *Avon Finance Co.* v. *Bridger* [1985] 2 All E.R. 281.

[77] *e.g. Cundy* v. *Lindsay* (1873) 3 App.Cas. 459

[78] [1971] A.C. 1004; *cf. Howatson* v. *Webb* [1907] 1 Ch. 535; affd. [1908] 1 Ch. 1. For discussion of the mistaken identity point, see *Gallie* v. *Lee* [1969] 2 Ch. 17, 44.

[79] *Hunter* v. *Walters* (1871) L.R. 7 Ch.App. 75; *cf. National Provincial Bank of England* v. *Jackson* (1886) 33 Ch.D. 1.

[80] (1946) 174 L.T. 272; *cf. Mercantile Credit Co. Ltd.* v. *Hamblin* [1965] 2 Q.B. 242 (but in that case the signer escaped liability on another ground).

[81] (1897) 67 L.J.Q.B. 224.

(6) Carelessness

Carelessness of the signer excludes the doctrine of *non est factum*. This was a second ground for the decision in *Gallie* v. *Lee*[82]: the widow could not rely on the doctrine as she had been careless in signing the document without reading it. For the same reason, a person cannot rely on the doctrine if he signs a document containing blanks which are later filled in otherwise than in accordance with his instructions.[83]

In this context, the standard of care cannot be that of the reasonable person, for such a person will not normally be able to rely on the doctrine of *non est factum* at all.[84] One has to assume that the person relying on the doctrine falls within the class of persons to whom it is available, and then to ask whether that person took such care as one so disadvantaged could have been expected to take. In *Gallie* v. *Lee* itself, this test was not satisfied; for, although the widow would not be expected to follow the intricacies of conveyancing, she could at least be expected to make sure that the person named in the document as transferee was the person intended by her. It does not follow that failure to read the document will exclude the plea of *non est factum* in all cases: the plea might, for example, still be available if reading the document would not have revealed its true character to a person of the signer's limited capabilities.[85]

---

[82] [1971] A.C. 1004; overruling *Carlisle & Cumberland Banking Co.* v. *Bragg* [1911] 1 K.B. 489. See also *Vorley* v. *Cooke* (1857) 1 Giff. 230, 236, *Hunter* v. *Walters* (1871) L.R. 7 Ch.App. 75, 87; *Lewis* v. *Clay* (1897) 67 L.J.Q.B. 224, 226; *Howatson* v. *Webb* [1908] 1 Ch. 1; *Credit Lyonnais* v. *F. T. Barnard & Associates* [1976] 1 Lloyd's Rep. 557. *Avon Finance Co.* v. *Bridger* [1985] 2 All E.R. 281.

[83] *United Dominion's Trust Ltd.* v. *Western* [1976] Q.B. 513; Marston, [1976] C.L.J. 218.

[84] *Ante*, p. 292.

[85] [1971] A.C. 1004, 1023.

CHAPTER NINE

MISREPRESENTATION[1]

A PERSON may be able to claim relief if he was induced to enter into a contract by a misleading statement. As the grounds for, and forms of, relief are numerous and complex, it may be helpful to begin this Chapter with a summary of the more important rules. In the first place the representation must be of a kind which the law recognises as giving rise to liability: this excludes "mere puffs" and certain statements of law or of opinion or as to the future. A number of general conditions of liability must next be satisfied: the representation must be unambiguous and material, and must have been relied upon by the representee. If these requirements are satisfied the representee may be able to claim damages or to rescind the contract or to do both these things.

There is a common law right to damages where the representation is fraudulent; where it is negligent there is a common law and a statutory right to damages and these two rights are by no means identical in scope. Damages can also be claimed where the representation is binding contractually. Where a representation which has no contractual force is wholly innocent, there is no *right* to damages; but the court has in certain circumstances a *discretion* to award damages in lieu of rescission. Even where damages cannot be claimed under any of these rules, the court may still sometimes order the representor to pay the representee a sum of money by way of "indemnity."

The representee can rescind the contract whether the representation is fraudulent, negligent or wholly innocent, though the distinction between these various kinds of representation may to some extent determine the conditions of rescission and its effects. A contract may be rescinded even though the representation has become one of its terms, but the relationship between this rule and the rules governing the right to rescind a contract for breach gives rise to many difficulties. The court may, in its discretion, refuse to allow rescission and award damages instead. The right to rescind may also be lost as a result of a number of supervening factors; and the power to contract out of liability for misrepresentation is severely restricted by statute.

The above rules apply to active misrepresentation. Non-disclosure calls for separate treatment, which will be followed by a discussion of the relationship between estoppel and misrepresentation.

SECTION 1. MEANING OF "REPRESENTATION"

The general rule is that no relief will be given for a misrepresentation as such unless it is a statement of *existing fact*. There may, therefore, be no remedy if the statement falls into one of the following categories.

---

[1] Allen, *Misrepresentation* (1988).

1. Mere Puffs

These are statements which are so vague that they have no effect at law or in equity. To describe land as "fertile and improvable" is mere sales talk which affords no ground for relief.[2] But there is a liability for more precise claims, *e.g.* that use of a carbolic smoke-ball will give immunity from influenza.[3] The distinction is between indiscriminate praise, and specific promises or assertions of verifiable facts.

2. Statements of Fact and of Opinion or Belief

Some statements of opinion are mere puffs. Others, while more specific, yet have no legal effect as they are not positive assertions of fact but only statements of opinion or belief. Thus assertions that an anchorage was safe and that a piece of land had the capacity to support 2,000 sheep have been held to be mere statements of opinion.[4] In each case, the party making the statement had (as the other party knew) no personal knowledge of the facts on which it was based: it was understood that he could only state his belief. If that party has or professes to have some special knowledge or skill as to the matter stated, the statement is likely to be treated as one of fact.[5]

A statement may, in terms, be one of opinion or belief, but by implication involve a statement of fact. Thus it is a misrepresentation of fact for a person to say that he holds an opinion which he does not hold, *e.g.* to say that he thinks a picture is a Rembrandt when he thinks it is a copy.[6] And if the facts on which an opinion is based are particularly within the knowledge of the person stating the opinion, he may be taken to have represented that those facts exist. If the vendor of a house describes it as "let to a most desirable tenant," when the tenant has for long been in arrears with his rent, he misrepresents a fact, "for he impliedly states that he knows facts which justify his opinion."[7] The same principle applies where a person makes a statement of belief quite honestly but fails to check the facts on which it appears to be based, when he could easily have done so.[8]

3. Representations as to the Future

A representation as to the future does not, of itself, give rise to any cause of action[9] unless it is binding as a contract. Thus if A induces B to lend him money by representing that he will not borrow from anybody else, B can-

---

[2] *Dimmock* v. *Hallett* (1866) L.R. 2 Ch.App. 21; *cf. ante*, p. 149.
[3] *Carlill* v. *Carbolic Smoke Ball Co.* [1893] 1 Q.B. 256.
[4] *Anderson* v. *Pacific Fire & Marine Insurance Co.* (1872) L.R. 7 C.P. 65; *Bissett* v. *Wilkinson* [1927] A.C. 177.
[5] *e.g. Esso Petroleum Co. Ltd.* v. *Mardon* [1976] Q.B. 801, *post*, p. 312; *Box* v. *Midland Bank Ltd.* [1979] 2 Lloyd's Rep. 391 (reversed as to costs only [1981] 1 Lloyd's Rep. 434).
[6] *Jendwine* v. *Slade* (1797) 2 Esp. 571, 573; *Brown* v. *Raphael* [1958] Ch. 636, 641; contrast *Harlingdon and Leinster Enterprises Ltd.* v. *Christopher Hull Fine Art Ltd.* [1990] 1 All E.R. 537; *cf.* Marine Insurance Act 1906, s.20(5); *Highlands Ins. Co.* v. *Continental Ins. Co.* [1987] 1 Lloyd's Rep. 109.
[7] *Smith* v. *Land & House Property Corp.* (1884) 28 Ch.D. 7, 15.
[8] *Brown* v. *Raphael* [1958] Ch. 636 contrast *Humming Bird Motors* v. *Hobbs* [1986] R.T.R. 276 (*post*, p. 319), where the seller was not negligent in stating his (mistaken) belief.
[9] It may be a ground for refusing specific performance: *post*, p. 909. It may also, in combination with other circumstances, give rise to a proprietary estoppel: see *ante*, pp. 124–136.

not sue A if he does borrow elsewhere, unless the representation is made part of the contract of loan or amounts to a collateral contract.[10]

A person who promises to do something may simply be making a statement as to his future conduct; if so, he does not misrepresent a fact merely because he fails to do what he said he would do. But he may also be making a statement of his present intention; if so, he does misrepresent a fact if, when he made the statement, he had no such intention. The courts tend to construe such statements in the second of these two ways in order to protect the interests of persons deceived by them.[11] In *Edgington* v. *Fitzmaurice*[12] the directors of a company induced the plaintiff to lend money to the company by representing that the money would be used to improve the company's buildings and to expand its business. In fact the directors intended to use the money to pay off the company's existing debts. They were held liable in deceit. Bowen L.J. said: "There must be a mis-statement of an existing fact; but the state of a man's mind is as much a fact as the state of his digestion. It is true that it is very difficult to prove what the state of a man's mind at a particular time is, but if it can be ascertained it is as much a fact as anything else. A misrepresentation as to the state of a man's mind is, therefore, a mis-statement of fact."[13]

This principle is not restricted to statements of intention. A person may misrepresent a fact if he states an expectation or a *belief* which he does not hold as to some future event. The Marine Insurance Act 1906 expressly provides that a marine policy can be avoided for an untrue representation of expectation or belief.[14] Such a statement may, moreover, like one of opinion,[15] amount to a misrepresentation of fact (though it was honestly made) if it involves an implied assertion that the representor has reasonable grounds for his opinion or belief.[16] For example, a shipowner who says that his ship is "expected ready to load" at a particular port on or about a specified date impliedly represents that he honestly holds that belief, and that he does so on reasonable grounds. If he has no reasonable grounds for holding the belief, he misrepresents a fact.[17]

A person may similarly state his intention of doing something and thereby impliedly assert that he has reasonable grounds for thinking that he has the capacity to do it. There is no logical reason why such an implied assertion should not also be regarded as one of fact. It could further be argued that a person who incurs a debt may impliedly represent that he has

---

[10] *Cf. Ex p. Burrell* (1876) 1 Ch.D. 537, 552. Failure to perform a promise is, similarly, not a false "statement" for the purpose of the Trade Descriptions Act 1968: *Beckett* v. *Cohen* [1972] 1 W.L.R. 1593; *R.* v. *Sunair Holidays Ltd.* [1973] 1 W.L.R. 1105; unless the promise also contains a statement of present intention: see n. 13, *infra*.

[11] *Cf.* Theft Act 1968, s.15(4); Theft Act 1978, s.5(1); *R.* v. *Gilmartin* [1983] Q.B. 953; *R.* v. *Grantham* [1984] Q.B. 675.

[12] (1885) 29 Ch.D. 459.

[13] At p. 482; *cf. British Airways Bd.* v. *Taylor* [1976] 1 W.L.R. 13; *Smith Kline & French Laboratories Ltd.* v. *Long* [1988] 1 W.L.R. 1; *Kleinwort Benson Ltd.* v. *Malaysian Mining Corp.* [1989] 1 W.L.R. 379, 396.

[14] s.20(1) and (3).

[15] *Ante*, p. 296.

[16] Under s.20(5) of the Marine Insurance Act 1906, a representation of expectation or belief is true if made in good faith (as in *The Zephyr* [1985] 2 Lloyd's Rep. 529, 538). This rule does not in practice differ substantially from that stated in the text, as a person who lacks reasonable grounds for his statement will find it hard to prove good faith.

[17] *The Mihalis Angelos* [1971] 1 Q.B. 164, 194, 205.

reasonable grounds for thinking that he will be able to pay it[18]; and that, if he had no such grounds, the creditor should be able to rescind the contract. But the common understanding is that the creditor's only remedy (in the absence of fraud, such as an express misrepresentation as to solvency) is an action to recover the debt; and the whole scheme set up by the law of bankruptcy for the distribution of an insolvent debtor's estate would be seriously disrupted if some creditors could rescind (and so regain title to goods with which they had parted) on the ground that the debtor had, by merely incurring the debt, impliedly asserted that he had reasonable grounds for thinking that he would be able to pay. An implied assertion of this kind will[19] not be a sufficient ground for rescinding a contract.

A statement of intention may also be coupled with an *express* statement of existing fact. Thus a statement by A that he *had* sold flour and *would* pay over the proceeds to B is a misrepresentation of fact if A had made no such sale.[20]

4. Statements of Fact and Law[21]

(1) Effect of the distinction

At common law, there is no civil remedy for a misrepresentation of law, as opposed to one of fact. In equity, too, a money claim cannot be based on a misrepresentation of law[22]; and the same is probably true of claims for damages under the Misrepresentation Act 1967.[23] It is sometimes assumed that a misrepresentation of law is not even a ground for rescission in equity.[24] But this is more doubtful. It has been said that *wilful* misrepresentation of law is ground for equitable relief.[25] And equity gives relief for misrepresentation as to private rights[26] whether or not these are rightly called misrepresentation of fact.

(2) Illustrations of the distinction

(a) POWERS OF COMPANIES. A number of cases deal with the question whether a misrepresentation by a director of a company as to its powers is one of law or one of fact. In one case directors represented that they had power under the private Act incorporating the company to issue new preference shares ranking *pari passu* with an existing issue. This was held to be a representation of law.[27] But in another case directors who had power to borrow with the consent of the shareholders borrowed without such con-

---

[18] See the authorities cited in n. 11, *supra*.

[19] *Amalgamated Metal Trading Ltd.* v. *D.T.I.*, *The Times*, March 21, 1989.

[20] *Babcock* v. *Lawson* (1880) 5 Q.B.D. 284; *cf. Ismail* v. *Polish Ocean Lines Ltd.* [1976] Q.B. 893: statement that goods *were* so packed that they *would* withstand the voyage.

[21] Hudson, 1958 S.L.T. 16.

[22] See *Rashdall* v. *Ford* (1866) L.R. 2 Eq. 750; *Beattie* v. *Ebury* (1872) L.R. 7 Ch.App. 777; *Eaglesfield* v. *Londonderry* (1876) 4 Ch.D. 693.

[23] *André & Cie. S.A.* v. *Ets. Michel Blanc & Fils* [1979] 2 Lloyd's Rep. 427, 432, 434–435.

[24] *e.g.* in *Wauton* v. *Coppard* [1899] 1 Ch. 92 and *Mackenzie* v. *Royal Bank of Canada* [1934] A.C. 468. But in both cases the representation was held to be one of fact.

[25] *West London Commercial Bank* v. *Kitson* (1884) 13 Q.B.D. 360, 362–363; this formulation appears to exclude the possibility of relief for *negligent* misrepresentation of law. For certain purposes in the law of theft, a deliberate or reckless deception as to fact *or law* is sufficient: Theft Act 1968, s.15(4); Theft Act 1978, s.5(1).

[26] *Post*, p. 300. *André & Cie. S.A.* v. *Ets. Michel Blanc & Fils, supra*, n. 23, at pp. 431, 432.

[27] *Beattie* v. *Ebury* (1872) L.R. 7 Ch.App. 777.

sent. It was held that they had impliedly made a representation of fact, *viz.*, that they had obtained the shareholders' consent.[28]

(b) EFFECT OF A DOCUMENT. A representation as to the effect of a document may be one as to its contents or one as to its meaning. In the former case, the representation is clearly one of fact.[29] A representation as to the meaning of a document whose contents are known may be one of law since for many purposes the construction of a document is a question of law; but for the present purpose it is more likely to be treated as a representation of private right, and hence as one of fact.[30]

(c) EFFECT OF A STATUTE. A representation as to the meaning of an Act of Parliament is clearly one of law.[31] The same, it is submitted, is generally true of a representation as to the contents. But in *West London Commercial Bank* v. *Kitson*[32] the directors of a company represented that they had authority to accept bills on behalf of the company. Under the private Acts incorporating it, the company had no power to accept, or to authorise anyone to accept, bills. The representation was held to be one of fact as it related to the contents of a private Act. It is, however, submitted that there is no longer any ground for distinguishing between private and public Acts for this purpose[33]; and that a representation as to the contents of any Act of Parliament would, like a representation as to its effects, be one of law.

(d) APPLICABILITY OF A RULE OF LAW. A statement that a statute or rule of common law applies to a known state of facts may be one of fact or of law according to the circumstances. Thus a statement that the Rent Acts applied to a house which was known to be in the occupation of the Crown was a misrepresentation of law, for it involved the erroneous proposition of law that the Rent Acts bound the Crown.[34] But a statement that the Rent Acts did not apply to a flat because its identity was wrongly thought to have been changed by work done to it was a misrepresentation of fact.[35] The proposition of law involved in this statement—that the Rent Acts did not apply where the identity of the flat had changed—was accurate. The only misrepresentation was one of fact, *viz.*, as to the change of identity.

---

[28] *Cherry* v. *Colonial Bank of Australasia* (1869) L.R. 3 P.C. 24; *cf. Firbank's Executors* v. *Humphreys* (1886) 18 Q.B.D. 54. Now that a company incorporated under the Companies Acts is liable, to a person dealing with it in good faith, on a contract even though it is *ultra vires* (*post*, p. 506), the need for a remedy for misrepresentation is less acute; but the representee may still prefer rescission to enforcement.

[29] *Wauton* v. *Coppard* [1889] 1 Ch. 92.

[30] *Ante*, p. 277; *infra* at n. 36; *Horry* v. *Tate & Lyle Refineries Ltd.* [1982] 2 Lloyd's Rep. 417; *Cornish* v. *Midland Bank plc* [1985] 3 All E.R. 513; in *National Westminster Bank plc* v. *Morgan* [1985] A.C. 686 no claim based on misrepresentation was made.

[31] *Cf. National Pari-Mutuel Association* v. *R.* (1930) 47 T.L.R. 110 (*mistake* of law).

[32] (1884) 13 Q.B.D. 360.

[33] Such a distinction may formerly have been based on the lack of publicity for private Acts; but it cannot be maintained after Interpretation Act 1889, s.9 (now Interpretation Act 1978, s.3). The question whether a representation as to the contents of a subordinate law is one of "law" might similarly depend on the question whether the law has been published under the Statutory Instruments Act 1946; but there seems to be no authority on the point.

[34] *Territorial & Auxiliary Forces Association* v. *Nichols* [1949] 1 K.B. 35; see now Rent Act 1977, s.154. *cf. Harse* v. *Pearl Life Assurance Co.* [1904] 1 K.B. 558, *post*, pp. 438–439.

[35] *Solle* v. *Butcher* [1950] 1 K.B. 671; *ante*, p. 279.

(e) PRIVATE RIGHT. A representation as to private right is for the present purpose treated as one of fact.[36] Thus representations that A's shares are pledged to B, that C has a patent in a certain invention and that D's product embodies E's invention have all been treated as representations of fact.[37]

(f) STATEMENTS OF LAW AND FACTS. A statement may contain a misrepresentation of law and one of fact. If so, it seems that the availability of relief depends on which part of the statement provided the representee's major inducement to enter into the contract.[38]

Sometimes the same statement may be one of law or fact, according to the circumstances. Thus the statement that A is unmarried is one of fact if it amounts to an assertion that A had never gone through a ceremony of marriage. If it amounts to an assertion that a ceremony in which A is known to have taken part was invalid, the following distinction has been drawn by Jessel M.R.: if the person making the statement tells "the whole story and all the facts" and *concludes* that A is still unmarried, the statement is one of law but if he simply says that A is single, he states a fact.[39] But it is hard to see the force of this distinction,[40] unless statements of the latter kind are regarded as analogous to statements as to private rights. In borderline cases of this kind, "representations of fact shade into representations of law"[41]; and the distinction between them is hard to justify on grounds of policy.[42]

(g) REPRESENTATION OF FOREGN LAW. In an English court, foreign law is a matter of fact.[43] A representation of foreign law is therefore regarded as one of fact.[44]

SECTION 2. GENERAL CONDITIONS OF LIABILITY

Where a representation does not have contractual force, it will only give rise to the remedies discussed in Sections 3 and 4 of this Chapter if it is unambiguous and material and if the representee has relied on it.

1. Unambiguous

A statement may be intended by the representor to bear a meaning which is true, but be so obscure that the representee understands it in another sense, in which it is untrue. In such a case the representor is not liable if his interpretation is the correct one[45]; and even if the court holds that the

[36] *Cf. ante*, p. 277 *André & Cie. S.A.* v. *Ets. Michel Blanc & Fils* [1979] 2 Lloyd's Rep. 427, 431, 432.

[37] *Mackenzie* v. *Royal Bank of Canada* [1934] A.C. 468; *Begbie* v. *Phosphate Sewage Co. Ltd.* (1875) L.R. 10 Q.B. 491; *Lyle-Mellor* v. *Lewis* [1956] 1 W.L.R. 29; *cf. Taylors Fashions Ltd.* v. *Liverpool Victoria Trustee Co. Ltd.* [1982] Q.B. 133 (note), 158.

[38] *Cf. Holt* v. *Markham* [1923] 1 K.B. 504.

[39] *Eaglesfield* v. *Londonderry* (1876) 4 Ch.D. 693, 702–703.

[40] The Court of Appeal disagreed with Jessel M.R.'s conclusion that the mistake in *Eaglesfield's* case was one of law; but how much of his reasoning was disapproved is not clear.

[41] *Brikom Investments Ltd.* v. *Seaford* [1981] 1 W.L.R. 863, 869; *cf. Amalgamated Investment & Property Co. Ltd.* v. *Texas Commerce International Bank Ltd.* [1982] Q.B. 84, 122.

[42] For criticism of the distinction see *André & Cie. S.A.* v. *Ets. Michel Blanc & Fils* [1979] 2 Lloyd's Rep. 427, 431.

[43] Dicey and Morris, *The Conflict of Laws*, (11th ed.) Rule 18.

[44] *André & Cie. S.A.* v. *Ets. Michel Blanc & Fils* [1979] 2 Lloyd's Rep. 427, 431, 432.

[45] *McInerny* v. *Lloyds Bank Ltd.* [1974] 1 Lloyd's Rep. 246, 254.

representee's interpretation was the correct one, the representor is not guilty of fraud.[46] This is so in spite of the fact that the representor's interpretation was an unreasonable one, so long as he honestly believed in it.[47] *A fortiori* the representee cannot sue in deceit if the representation is ambiguous and he did not in fact understand it in a different sense from that intended by the representor.[48] But it does not follow from the fact that the representor was not guilty of fraud that the representee has no remedy at all. If he reasonably understood the ambiguous statement in a sense in which the representor did not mean it, and which was untrue, he can rely on it as a defence to specific performance.[49]

A representor is guilty of fraud if he makes an ambiguous statement intending it to bear a meaning which is to his knowledge untrue, and if the statement is reasonably understood in that sense by the representee. In such a case it is no defence for the representor to show that, on its true construction, the statement bore a meaning that was in fact true.[50]

2. Material

A misrepresentation generally has no effect unless it is material.[51] That is, it must be one which would affect the judgment of a reasonable person in deciding whether, or on what terms, to enter into the contract; or one that would induce him to enter into the contract without making such inquiries as he would otherwise make.[52] Thus in a contract of insurance it is material that the subject-matter has been grossly overvalued[53] or that a previous proposal for insuring it has been declined[54]; in a contract for a loan of money it is material that the lender is a notoriously ruthless money-lender[55]; and in an auction sale of a house it is material who owns the house "as it was, to a certain extent, a guarantee as to the character of the sale."[56] A misrepresentation may be material although the representor in good faith thinks that it is not material.[57]

There are two exceptions to the requirement of materiality. First, a person who has successfully perpetrated a fraud cannot be heard to say that the representation which he used to achieve this end was immaterial.[58]

---

[46] *Akerhielm* v. *De Mare* [1959] A.C. 789; *Gross* v. *Lewis Hillman Ltd.* [1970] Ch. 445; and *cf. post*, p. 354.

[47] *Quaere* whether it could make him liable in negligence: do *Hedley Byrne & Co. Ltd.* v. *Heller & Partners Ltd.* [1964] A.C. 465 and s.2(1) of the Misrepresentation Act 1967 apply to bad drafting?

[48] *Smith* v. *Chadwick* (1884) 9 App.Cas. 187.

[49] *New Brunswick & Canada Ry.*, v. *Muggeridge* (1860) 1 Dr. & Sm. 363, 382; and see *post*, p. 354.

[50] *The Siboen and the Sibotre* [1976] 1 Lloyd's Rep. 293, 318.

[51] *McDowell* v. *Fraser* (1779) 1 Dougl. 247, 248, *per* Lord Mansfield.

[52] *Traill* v. *Baring* (1864) 4 D.J. & S. 318, 326; *Dimmock* v. *Hallett* (1866) L.R. 2 Ch.App. 21, 29, 30; Marine Insurance Act 1906, s.20(2): this provision expresses the general law: *Locker & Woolf Ltd.* v. *W. Australian Insurance Co. Ltd.* [1936] 1 K.B. 408, 414; *Industrial Properties Ltd.* v. *A.E.I. Ltd.* [1977] Q.B. 580, 597, 601; *Highland Ins. Co.* v. *Continental Ins. Co.* [1987] 1 Lloyd's Rep. 109; *cf. Walker* v. *Boyle* [1982] 1 W.L.R. 495, 503.

[53] *Ionides* v. *Pender* (1874) L.R. 9 Q.B. 531.

[54] *Locker & Woolf Ltd.* v. *W. Australian Insurance Co. Ltd.*, *supra*.

[55] *Gordon* v. *Street* [1899] 2 Q.B. 641.

[56] *Whurr* v. *Devenish* (1904) 20 T.L.R. 385.

[57] *Lindenau* v. *Desborough* (1828) 8 B. & C. 586; *Joel* v. *Law Union & Crown Insurance Co.* [1908] 2 K.B. 863, 883; *cf.* (in criminal law) *R.* v. *Millward* [1985] Q.B. 519.

[58] *Smith* v. *Kay* (1859) 7 H.L.C. 750; *cf. Gordon* v. *Street*, *supra*. *Quaere* whether this strict rule would be applied to a negligent misrepresentation.

Secondly, every representation is material if the contract so provides. Thus if a policy of insurance provides that statements by the assured in the proposal form shall be the basis of the contract, or are warranted to be true, such statements are material,[59] however unimportant they may be in themselves.

The requirement of materiality has been doubted[60]; but in evaluating these doubts a distinction should, it is submitted, be drawn between two reasons why the misrepresentation would not affect the judgment of a reasonable person. This may be the position either because of the *circumstances in which the representation was made*, or because of its *contents*. The first possibility is illustrated by *Museprime Properties Ltd.* v. *Adhill Properties Ltd.*,[61] where a purchaser by auction of commercial property was allowed to rescind for a representation by the auctioneer that higher rents could still be negotiated, when in fact the rents had been fixed for the next rent review period. The court held that it was sufficient for the purchaser to show that his bid had actually been affected by the representation, even if no reasonable bidder would have allowed it to affect his bid. This conclusion can, with respect, be regarded merely as an application of the rule that the representee may be entitled to relief even though he had the opportunity to discover the truth.[62] The second of the two possibilities mentioned above arises where the matter misrepresented is not "material" because it had little (or only a trivial) effect on the value of the subject-matter. The representation in the *Museprime* case was certainly "material" in this sense. What is an "immaterial" representation (in the same sense) can be illustrated by supposing that the auctioneer in that case had represented the tenant to be 40 years old when actually he was 39 or 41, that this representation had (for some reason) been a factor inducing the representee's successful bid, and that its falsity had caused no, or no substantial, loss to the representee. If the representor has made such a representation in good faith it is hard to see why a representee should be entitled to any relief when, by definition, the representation would not have influenced a reasonable person. Damages would be no more than nominal, and a claim to rescind for such a misrepresentation has been rejected as totally unmeritorious.[63]

3. Reliance

The person to whom the misrepresentation was made must have relied on it. He therefore cannot rescind, or claim damages, for misrepresentation[64] if the representation did not come to his notice,[65] if he knew the truth, if he took a deliberate risk as to the truth of the matter stated, if he would have

---

[59] *Andersen* v. *Fitzgerald* (1853) 4 H.L.C. 484; *London Assurance* v. *Mansel* (1879) 11 Ch.D. 363, 368; and see *post*, p. 355.

[60] Goff and Jones, *The Law of Restitution*, (3rd ed.) p. 168; *Chitty on Contracts*, (26th ed.), Vol. I, § 427.

[61] [1990] 2 E.G.L.R. 196.

[62] *Post*, p. 303.

[63] *Industrial Properties Ltd.* v. *A.E.I. Ltd.* [1977] Q.B. 580; *cf.* Restatement 2d. *Contracts* § 162, Ill. 4.

[64] The position is different where he claims damages for breach of contract: see *post*, pp. 315–316.

[65] *Ex p. Biggs* (1859) 28 L.J.Ch. 50.

entered into the transaction even though he had known the truth,[66] or if he relied on his own information.[67]

(1) Truth known to agent

A person cannot claim relief for misrepresentation if the truth, though not known to him, was known to his agent while acting within the scope of his authority.[68] But the principal may claim such relief if the agent found out the truth while acting for the other party,[69] or in fraud of the principal,[70] or in any way outside the scope of his authority.

(2) Testing accuracy

A person who himself tests the accuracy of the representation can be said to rely on his own judgment, rather than on the representation. Accordingly, he cannot obtain relief for innocent[71] (or probably for negligent[72]) misrepresentation. But this rule does not apply in cases of fraud. In *S. Pearson & Son Ltd.* v. *Dublin Corporation*[73] the plaintiffs undertook to execute works for the corporation on the faith of plans supplied by it. The contract provided that the plaintiffs should satisfy themselves of the accuracy of the plans.[74] It was held that this provision would not protect the corporation if the plans were fraudulent. It is not clear what steps, if any, the plaintiffs took to test the accuracy of the plans. But it is submitted that if, in spite of taking some such steps, they had failed to discover the truth, the corporation should still have been liable on proof of fraud.

(3) Opportunity to find out the truth

A person may be entitled to relief even though he had, but did not take, the opportunity to test the accuracy of the representation.[75] This rule is most frequently applied to cases of fraud,[76] but *Smith* v. *Eric S. Bush*[77] shows that it can also apply where the misrepresentation was negligent. The plaintiffs in that case had bought a house with the aid of a mortgage,

---

[66] *J.E.B. Fasteners Ltd.* v. *Marks Bloom & Co.* [1983] 1 All E.R. 583 (as to which see *post*, p. 306); *The Lucy* [1983] 1 Lloyd's Rep. 188; *cf. Beaumont* v. *Humberts* [1988] 2 E.G.L.R. 171.

[67] *Jennings* v. *Broughton* (1854) 5 D.M. & G. 126; *cf. Cooper* v. *Tamms* [1988] 1 E.G.L.R. 257; *The Morning Watch* [1990] 1 Lloyd's Rep. 547, 556.

[68] *Bawden* v. *London Assurance* [1892] 2 Q.B. 534; *Strover* v. *Harrington* [1988] Ch. 390.

[69] *Newsholme* v. *Road Transport Insurance Co. Ltd.* [1929] 2 K.B. 356.

[70] *Wells* v. *Smith* [1914] 3 K.B. 722.

[71] *Clarke* v. *Mackintosh* (1862) 4 Giff. 134; *Redgrave* v. *Hurd* (1881) 20 Ch.D. 1, 14, discussing *Attwood* v. *Small* (1838) 6 Cl. & F. 232.

[72] *McInerny* v. *Lloyd's Bank Ltd.* [1974] 1 Lloyd's Rep. 246, 254.

[73] [1907] A.C. 351.

[74] For such provisions, see *post*, p. 346.

[75] *Dobell* v. *Stevens* (1825) 3 B. & C. 623; *Reynell* v. *Sprye* (1852) 1 D.M. & G. 660; *Central Ry. of Venezuela* v. *Kisch* (1867) L.R. 2 H.L. 99; *Redgrave* v. *Hurd* (1881) 20 Ch.D. 1; *Smith* v. *Land & House Property Corporation* (1884) 28 Ch.D. 7; *Aaron's Reefs Ltd.* v. *Twiss* [1896] A.C. 273; *cf., The Arta* [1985] 1 Lloyd's Rep. 534; *Rignal Developments Ltd.* v. *Halil* [1988] Ch. 190, 199, *aliter*, if a person reads a document revealing the truth, but simply fails to understand it: *Ex p. Briggs* (1866) L.R. 1 Eq. 483.

[76] *e.g. Gordon* v. *Selico Ltd.* (1986) 278 E.G. 53, 61; *Strover* v. *Harrington* [1988] Ch. 390, 410; *Horsfall* v. *Thomas* (1862) 1 H. & C. 90, so far as *contra*, was doubted in *Smith* v. *Hughes* (1871) L.R. 6 Q.B. 597, 605.

[77] [1990] 1 A.C. 831; Allen, 105 L.Q.R. 511 Horton Rogers [1989] C.L.J. 366.

relying on a valuation which had been negligently conducted by a surveyor engaged by the lender. Their claim in negligence against the surveyor succeeded in spite of the fact that they might have discovered the truth if they had conducted their own independent survey; for it was neither reasonable to expect them to take this step, nor likely that they would do so, since the house in question was one of modest value. But the House of Lords indicated[78] that the position might be different on the purchase of commercial or industrial premises, or even of residential property of high value. The principle appears to be that failure to make use of an opportunity to discover the truth may defeat a claim for negligent misrepresentation where, but only where, it is reasonable to expect the representee to make use of the opportunity.

In *Redgrave* v. *Hurd*,[79] it was held that an opportunity to discover the truth was no bar to relief even where the misrepresentation was innocent. In that case, a person was induced to buy a solicitor's practice and house by an innocent misrepresentation as to the value of the practice. He was allowed to rescind even though he had the opportunity of examining the accounts of the practice and so discovering the truth. It should, however, be noted that, when *Redgrave* v. *Hurd* was decided, all misrepresentations which were not fraudulent were described as "innocent."[80] Now, the law distinguishes between negligent and wholly innocent misrepresentations[81]; and it further distinguishes between cases in which it was, and those in which it was not, reasonable for the representee to make use of an opportunity to discoverthe truth.[82] Where it *was* reasonable to expect the representee to make use of such an opportunity, and he fails to do so, the reasoning of *Smith* v. *Eric S. Bush*[83] indicates that a claim based on negligence will fail; and the position should, *a fortiori*, be the same where the misrepresentation is wholy innocent.[84] To this extent, it is submitted that the rule in *Redgrave* v. *Hurd* no longer applies.[85] Where it is *not* reasonable to expect the representee to make use of the opportunity to discover the truth, and he fails to do so, the actual decision in *Smith* v. *Eric S. Bush* shows that a claim based on negligence will nevertheless succeed; but it is less clear whether the same result should follow where the misrepresentation was wholly innocent, so that both parties were equally innocent. *Redgrave* v. *Hurd* stands as an authority for the proposition that, in the case last put, failure to make use of the opportunity to discovery the truth is no bar to relief. It can be supported on the ground that there is actual, and reasonable, reliance on the misrepresentation in such a case.

---

[78] *Cf.* pp. 854, 872 (dealing with the issue of reasonableness under the Unfair Contract Terms Act 1977); *Kijowski* v. *New Capital Properties* (1990) 15 Con.L.R. 1.

[79] (1881) 20 Ch.D. 1; *Laurence* v. *Lexcourt Holdings Ltd.* [1978] 1 W.L.R. 1128.

[80] Now that damages can be recovered for negligent misrepresentation it is arguable that the carelessness of the representee is a ground for reducing the damages under the Law Reform (Contributory Negligence) Act 1945 (*post*, p. 871); but this Act would not affect a right to *rescind* for misrepresentation.

[81] See *post*, pp. 312, 320.

[82] *Supra* at n. 78.

[83] *Ibid.*

[84] *Cf. McInerny* v. *Lloyds Bank Ltd.* [1974] 1 Lloyd's Rep. 246, 254 and *The Nai Genova* [1984] 1 Lloyd's Rep. 353, 365 (where the plaintiff's carelessness prevented him from relying on an estoppel).

[85] *Cf. Archer* v. *Brown* [1985] Q.B. 401, 416 (doubting *Redgrave* v. *Hurd* on another point).

(4) Representation addressed to another

A person may rely on a representation even though it was not made directly to him: *e.g.* where A makes a misrepresentation to B which later comes to the notice of C and induces C to contract with A. If A intended to bring about this result he is liable to C.[86]

A representation made by A to B may also make A liable to C where it was reasonable for A to anticipate that the representation would be passed on to C and that C would act on it in some other way than by entering into a contract with A.[87] This possibility is illustrated by cases such as *Smith* v. *Eric S. Bush*,[88] where a representation in a report as to the value or condition of a house was made by A to B, was then passed on by B to C, and induced C to buy the house from X. Where the contract induced by the misrepresentation is not made between A and C, difficult questions may arise in determining whether A owed any duty to C: it has, for example, been held that accountants engaged by a company to audit its accounts owed no duty to persons who had lent money to, or bought shares in, the company merely because those persons had dealt with the company in reliance on misleading statements in the accounts.[89] The question wheher such a duty of care is owed by the representor to the representee is discussed later in this Chapter; the point of the present discussion is simply that the requirement of reliance on the representation may be satisfied even though the representation is not addressed directly by the representor to the representee.

Where A by misrepresentation induces B to buy something from him, he will not be liable to C merely because B repeats the misrepresentation when later reselling the subject-matter to C. In one such case it was held that the misrepresentation was "spent"[90] when the contract was made between A and B, so that C could not rely on it against A. He might, however, be able to do so if he could show that A knew that B intended to resell and was likely to repeat the misrepresentation on the occasion of the sale to C.[91]

(5) Other inducements

A person who relies on a misrepresentation can claim relief although he also relied on other inducements. Thus in *Edgington* v. *Fitzmaurice*[92] the plaintiff was induced to lend money to a company by (i) the misrepresen-

[86] *Pilmore* v. *Hood* (1838) 5 Bing.N.C. 97; *cf. Langridge* v. *Levy* (1837) 2 M. & W. 519; *Brikom Investments Ltd.* v. *Carr* [1979] Q.B. 467, 485. Contrast *Peek* v. *Gurney* (1873) L.R. 6. H.L. 377; criticised by Gower, *Modern Company Law*, (4th ed.), p. 374.

[87] But not in the absence of such circumstances: *The Zephyr* [1985] 2 Lloyd's Rep. 529, 539 (and see *post*, p. 540); *Bank Leumi Le Israel B.M.* v. *British National Insurance Co.* [1988] 1 Lloyd's Rep. 71, 77; *cf. Beaumont* v. *Humberts* [1988] 2 E.G.L.R. 171.

[88] [1990] 1 A.C. 831; *Yianni* v. *Edwin Evans & Sons* [1982] Q.B. 438.

[89] *Al Saudi Banque* v. *Clark Pixley* [1990] Ch. 313; *Caparo Industries plc* v. *Dickman* [1990] 2 A.C. 605.

[90] *Gross* v. *Lewis Hillman Ltd.* [1970] Ch. 445, 461.

[91] *Ibid. cf. The Sennar (No. 2)* [1985] 1 W.L.R. 490.

[92] (1885) 29 Ch.D. 459; *The Siboen and the Sibotre* [1976], Lloyd's Rep. 293, 324; *Horry* v. *Tate & Lyle Refineries Ltd.* [1982] 2 Lloyd's Rep. 417, 422; *cf.* (in cases of duress) *Barton* v. *Armstrong* [1976] A.C. 104; and *ante*, p. 105.

tations which have already been discussed,[93] and (ii) his mistaken belief that he would have a charge on the assets of the company. He was able to claim damages for deceit even though he admitted that he would not have lent the money, had he not held this mistaken belief.

But if a person to whom two statements, one true and one untrue, are made relies exclusively on the true one, he has no right to relief. Thus in *Heilbut, Symons & Co.* v. *Buckleton*[94] the plaintiff bought shares in a company after being told (i) that it was a rubber company (which was untrue), and (ii) that the defendants were "bringing it out" (which was true). One reason given by Lord Atkinson for dismissing the plaintiff's claim for damages was that the plaintiff had relied on the second statement to the exclusion of the first.

(6) Distinguished from materiality

The rule that the representee must rely on the representation is distinct from the requirement of materiality. Whether a representation is material depends, in general,[95] on the significance which would be attached to it by a reasonably prudent man of business. Whether the representee has relied on the representation depends on his own actual state of mind. The mere fact that a representation is material gives rise to no "inference of law" that the representation was relied on.[96] For example, in *J.E.B. Fasteners Ltd.* v. *Marks Bloom & Co.*[97] the plaintiffs took over a company after seeing its accounts, which were inaccurate, having been negligently prepared by the defendants (a firm of accountants). A duty of care seems to have arisen because the accounts had been "impliedly confirmed directly to the plaintiff . . . with a particular transaction in contemplation,[98] and the misrepresentation was clearly material but the plaintiffs' claim for damages was dismissed as they had not relied at all on the accounts. Their object in taking over the company was to secure the services of two of its directors and they would have proceeded with the transaction even if the accounts had shown the company's true financial state. The distinction between the two requirements of materiality and reliance is further supported by the fact that the law may insist on the former even where it recognises an exception to the latter.[99]

The distinction is sometimes obscured by the use of the word "material" to mean "material to the representee." Thus in *Smith* v. *Chadwick*[1] the plaintiff bought shares in a company on the faith of a prospectus which contained the untrue statement that one Grieve was a director of the company. The plaintiff's claim for damages was dismissed: the statement was "imma-

---

[93] *Ante*, p. 297.
[94] [1913] A.C. 30; *ante*, p. 149.
[95] *Ante*
[96] *Smith* v. *Land & House Property Corp.* (1884) 28 Ch.D. 7, 16.
[97] [1983] 1 All E.R. 583 1 All E.R. 538, affirming [1981] 3 All E.R. 289. The question whether the defendants owed any duty to the plaintiffs was only discussed at first instance; on this point see *post*, p. 310.
[98] *Al Saudi Banque* v. *Clark Pixley* [1990] Ch. 313, 335.
[99] *e.g.* in the law of non-disclosure (*post*, p. 355) as it affects marine insurance: *Container Transport International* v. *Oceanus Mutual, etc., Insurance* [1984] 1 Lloyd's Rep. 476, 510.
[1] (1884) 9 App.Cas. 187.

terial" as the plaintiff had never heard of Grieve. It is more accurate to say that for this reason the plaintiff did not rely on the statement, which was clearly material in the sense that it could influence a reasonably prudent man of business.

(7) Burden of proof

For the purpose of the present requirement, the representee need only show that the representation was made and that it was capable of inducing the contract. The burden then passes to the representor to show that the representee would have entered into the contract anyway, even if the misrepresentation had not been made.[2]

SECTION 3. DAMAGES FOR MISREPRESENTATION[3]

In this Section, we shall discuss the five grounds on which damages can be recovered for misrepresentation, and consider the relationship between them. We shall also refer, in the context of misrepresentation, to the power of criminal courts to make compensation orders in criminal cases.

1. Fraud

At common law a person who suffers loss as a result of acting in reliance on a fraudulent statement can recover damages in an action of deceit. He can generally do this whether he rescinds the contract or not[4] though he cannot pursue both remedies if this results in his recovering twice over for the same loss.[5]

In *Derry* v. *Peek*[6] the House of Lords decided that a statement is only fraudulent if made (i) with knowledge of its falsity, or (ii) without belief in its truth, or (iii) recklessly, not caring whether it is true or false. Fraud is a serious charge which must be clearly and distinctly proved.[7] A person who negligently makes a false statement will now often be liable in damages, but it may still be important that he is not guilty of fraud at common law. One reason for this is that the damages for fraud may not be the same as damages for negligence.[8] Another is that certain special rules may apply to rescission for fraud.[9]

---

[2] *Smith* v. *Chadwick* (1884) 9 App.Cas. 187, 196.

[3] Greig, 87 L.Q.R. 179.

[4] *Newbigging* v. *Adam* (1886) 34 Ch.D. 582, 592 ("an alternative or cumulative remedy, as the case may be"); *Archer* v. *Brown* [1985] Q.B. 401, 415 ("damages as well as rescission"). Under the rule in *Houldsworth* v. *City of Glasgow Bank* (1880) 5 App.Cas. 317, a person who was induced by fraud to subscribe for shares in a company could not claim damages unless he also rescinded; so that if he lost the right to rescind he had no remedy at all; but this rule has been reversed by Companies Act 1989, s.13.

[5] *Archer* v. *Brown, supra*, at p. 415.

[6] (1889) 14 App.Cas. 337. The actual decision was reversed by the Directors Liability Act 1890; see now Financial Services Act 1986, ss.150, 166.

[7] *Wallingford* v. *Mutual Society* (1880) 5 App.Cas. 685.

[8] *Post*, p. 325.

[9] *Post*, pp. 333–334, 340, 345; *cf.* p. 321.

A statement may be fraudulent although it was made without bad motive and without intention to cause loss. Thus in *Polhill* v. *Walter*[10] an agent purported to accept a bill of exchange on behalf of his principal, knowing that he had no authority to do so but believing that his principal would ratify. He was held liable in deceit. This case should be contrasted with *Angus* v. *Clifford*.[11] The directors of a company which had bought a gold mine issued a prospectus containing extracts from an engineer's report said to have been "prepared for the directors." It had in fact been prepared for the sellers of the mine. The directors knew this, but were held not liable for fraud as they did not at the time of issuing the prospectus appreciate the importance of the words "prepared for the directors." Thus it seems that a person is not guilty of fraud if he knows that his statement is false but does not appreciate its materiality.

Responsibility for a statement may be divided between principal and agent or between several agents of the same principal. If an agent within the scope of his authority makes a statement which he knows to be false, the principal is liable for the fraud of the agent.[12] If the agent who made the statement did not know that it was false, but the principal, or another agent did know this, the principal is in general not liable for fraud.[13] The *mens rea* required for fraud cannot be established by adding together the states of mind of several persons, each of whom is innocent. But if the principal or the second agent stood by, knowing that the representation was being made and that it was false, the principal would be guilty of fraud or liable for the fraud of the second agent.[14] In such a case the principal or second agent has *mens rea*, though he made no representation. The same rule applies where the representation is innocently made by the principal, and the agent stands by knowing that the representation is going to be made and that it is false.

2. Negligence at Common Law

(1) Duty of care

A misrepresentation is negligent if it is made carelessly and in breach of a duty owed by the representor to the representee to take reasonable care that the representation is accurate. It used to be thought that such a duty could only arise out of a pre-existing contract between representor and representee, or where the relationship between them was "fiduciary."[15] But this narrow view was rejected in *Hedley Byrne & Co. Ltd.* v. *Heller &*

---

[10] (1832) 3 B. & Ad. 114; *cf. Foster* v. *Charles* (1830) 6 Bing. 396; *Edgington* v. *Fitzmaurice* (1885) 29 Ch.D. 459, 481; *Watts* v. *Spence* [1976] Ch. 165, 176 (where fraud was not alleged).

[11] [1891] 2 Ch. 449.

[12] *S. Pearson & Son Ltd.* v. *Dublin Corporation* [1907] A.C. 351; *Briess* v. *Woolley* [1954] A.C. 333; *cf. Rignal Developments Ltd.* v. *Halil* [1988] Ch. 190, 198.

[13] *Cornfoot* v. *Fowke* (1840) 6 M. & W. 358; *Gordon Hill Trust Ltd.* v. *Segall* [1941] 2 All E.R. 379; *Armstrong* v. *Strain* [1952] 1 K.B. 232; Devlin, 53 L.Q.R. 344; Gower, 15 M.L.R. 232. For liability in negligence, see *infra*.

[14] *London County Freehold* v. *Berkeley Property Co. Ltd.* [1936] 2 All E.R. 1039; *The Siboen and the Sibotre* [1976] 1 Lloyd's Rep. 293, 321.

[15] *Nocton* v. *Ashburton* [1914] A.C. 932.

Partners Ltd.[16] The plaintiffs in that case suffered loss as a result of having given credit to a firm called Easipower Ltd., in reliance on a reference carelessly given by Easipower's bank, who knew of the purpose for which the reference was required. The actual decision was that the bank was not liable because the reference had been given "without responsibility."[17] But the House of Lords made it clear that, had there been no such disclaimer, the bank would have owed some duty to the plaintiffs.[18]

(2) Relationships giving rise to duty

(a) SPECIAL RELATIONSHIPS. Such a duty can arise at common law if there is a "special relationship" between the parties. In a number of cases it has been said that, for this purpose, three conditions must be satisfied: it must be reasonably foreseeable by the representor that the representee will rely on the statement; there must be sufficient "proximity" between the parties; and it must be just and reasonable for the law to impose the duty.[19] Foreseeable *reliance* by the representor on the representee's statement or advice is the single most important requirement of the special relationship.[20] But while it is a necessary condition of liability, it is not a sufficient one. Thus a purely social relationship will not normally suffice to give rise to a duty, so that no action normally lies at common law where a person suffers loss as a result of acting on careless friendly advice,[21] even if it is given by a professional person.[22] This is one situation[23] in which it would not normally be fair and reasonable to impose legal liability.

On the other hand, there was a "special relationship" between the plaintiffs and the bank in *Hedley Byrne*'s case,[24] and it is clear from dicta in that case, from earlier decisions which were overruled[25] or rehabilitated[26] by it, and from later cases, that a duty of care can arise where there is a professional relationship even though it is not contractual. Thus the duty may

---

[16] [1964] A.C. 465; Stevens, 27 M.L.R. 121; Payne, 6 Univ. of W. Australia L. Rev. 467; Honoré, 8 J.S.P.T.L. 284; Craig, 92 L.Q.R. 213.

[17] *Semble* this provision would now be subject to the test of reasonableness by virtue of Unfair Contract Terms Act 1977, ss.2(1) and 13(1): see *Smith* v. *Eric S. Bush* [1990] 1 A.C. 831, 875–876; *ante*, pp. 227–228.

[18] Contrast *Royal Bank Trust Co. (Trinidad)* v. *John Norbert Pampellone* [1987] 1 Lloyd's Rep. 218 (bank not liable for contents of information where it only undertook to pass on such information as was available to it: its only duty was to transmit such information accurately).

[19] *Smith* v. *Eric S. Bush* [1990] 1 A.C. 831, 865; *Al Saudi Banque* v. *Clark Pixley* [1990] Ch. 313; *Caparo Industries plc.* v. *Dickman* [1990] 2 A.C. 605, 617–618 (where it is also said at p. 632 that "these requirements are, at least in most cases, merely facets of the same thing"); *cf. Yuen Kun Yeu* v. *Att.-Gen of Hong Kong* [1988] A.C. 175; *Davies* v. *Radcliffe*, *The Times*, April 6, 1990.

[20] *Murphy* v. *Brentwood D.C.* [1990] 2 All E.R. 908, 929–930, 934.

[21] [1964] A.C. at p. 482; see *ibid.* p. 531 for possible exceptions. In *Chaudhry* v. *Prabakhar* [1989] 1 W.L.R. 29 (*ante*, p. 143) the existence of a duty was conceded; this concession was approved by two members of the Court, who, however, also recognised (at pp. 36 and 34) that advice given in "family, domestic or social relationships" would not normally be actionable.

[22] *Mutual Life and Citizens' Assurance Co. Ltd.* v. *Evatt* [1971] A.C. 793, 806.

[23] For another, see *infra* at n. 33.

[24] [1964] A.C. at pp. 494, 502, 538, 539.

[25] *Candler* v. *Crane, Christmas & Co.* [1951] 2 K.B. 164.

[26] *Cann* v. *Willson* (1883) 39 Ch.D. 39.

be owed by barristers,[27] solicitors,[28] accountants,[29] surveyors, valuers,[30] analysts, etc. even to persons other than their immediate clients who rely on their statements, where the conditions (stated above) which give rise to a duty of care are satisfied. The relationship between the parties in cases of this kind is more likely to be regarded as sufficiently proximate if the statement was made with a view to the particular transaction which it induced, than where it was not made with a view to this (or to such a) transaction. There was accordingly sufficient proximity between a surveyor and the prospective purchaser of a house, where the surveyor had been commissioned by a building society to report on the value of that house, knowing that his report would be passed on to the purchaser, where it was so passed on, and the house was bought in reliance on it.[31] Similarly, an accountant's report on the financial state of a company can give rise to liability to an intending lender or investor if it was made for the purpose of providing such a person with the information on which his decision whether or not to make the loan or investment is likely to be, and is in fact, based.[32] But the position is different where auditors are appointed by a company to enable the company to perform its statutory obligation to produce audited annual accounts. In such a case there is no sufficient proximity between those auditors and prospective lenders to, or investors, in the company, or even between the auditors and shareholders in the company who, in reliance on the accounts, buy additional shares.[33] The reason why no duty is owed to these persons is that the audited accounts are produced simply for the purpose of satisfying the statutory obligation described above, and not to induce the transactions in question.

---

[27] The immunity of barristers from liability for negligence in the conduct of litigation is not affected by *Hedley Byrne*'s case; see *Rondel* v. *Worsley* [1969] 1 A.C. 191; *Somasundram* v. *Melchior & Co.* [1988] 1 W.L.R. 1394 (extending the rule to a limited extent to solicitors); Courts and Legal Services Act 1990, s.63 but they may be liable for negligence in respect of certain kinds of pre-trial work; see *Saif Ali* v. *Sydney Mitchell & Co.* [1980] A.C. 198; Zander, 42 M.L.R. 319.

[28] *Cf. Ross* v. *Caunters* [1980] Ch. 297 (as to which see *post*, p. 539, n. 45).

[29] See the overruling in *Hedley Byrne*'s case, *supra*, of *Candler* v. *Crane Christmas & Co.*, *supra*.

[30] *Yianni* v. *Edwin Evans & Son* [1982] Q.B. 438; *Smith* v. *Eric S. Bush* [1990] 1 A.C. 831; *ante*, p. 305. For the liability in negligence of architects and valuers issuing certificates on which their clients pay, see *Sutcliffe* v. *Thackrah* [1974] A.C. 727; *Campbell* v. *Edwards* [1976] 1 W.L.R. 403; *Arenson* v. *Arenson* [1977] A.C. 405. For similar liability of auditors, *cf. Burgess* v. *Purchase & Sons Ltd.* [1983] Ch. 216.

[31] *e.g. Yianni* v. *Edwin Evans and Sons* [1982] Q.B. 438; *Davies* v. *Parry* (1988) 20 H.L.R. 452; *Roberts* v. *J. Hampson & Co.* [1990] 1 W.L.R. 94; *Smith* v. *Eric S. Bush* [1990] 1 A.C. 831; (where *Yianni's* case is cited with approval at pp. 852–853, 864, 875); contrast *Beaumont* v. *Humberts* [1988] 2 E.G.L.R. 171.

[32] See note 29, *supra*, *J.E.B. Fasterners Ltd.* v. *Marks Bloom & Co.* [1981] 3 All E.R. 583 (affirmed [1983] 1 All E.R. 583 on other grounds) is now explicable (if at all) only on the ground stated at p. 306, *ante*; *cf. Caparo Industries plc* v. *Dickman* [1990] 2 A.C. 605, 625, 647–648; *Morgan Crucible Co. plc* v. *Hill Samuel Bank Ltd.* [1991] 1 All E.R. 148; contrast *James McNaughton Paper Group* v. *Hicks Anderson & Co.* [1991] 1 All E.R. 134, where the circumstances in which the report was prepared negatived the duty.

[33] *e.g. Al Saudi Banque* v. *Clark Pixley* [1990] Ch. 313; *Caparo Industries plc* v. *Dickman* [1990] 2 A.C. 605; Flemming, 106 L.Q.R. 349; *cf. Huxford* v. *Stoy Hayward & Co.* (1989) 5 B.C.C. 421 (auditors called in by company's bank held to owe no duty to shareholders); *The Morning Watch* [1990] 1 Lloyd's Rep. 547 (no duty owed to buyer of a yacht in respect of certificate issued by Lloyd's); *Al Nakib Investments (Jersey) Ltd.* v. *Longcroft* [1990] 1 W.L.R. 1390.

Two further alleged requirements of the relationships giving rise to a duty of care call for discussion.

(i) *Assumption of responsibility?* The first is that in many such relationships the person making the representation can be said voluntarily to have assumed responsibility; and this factor is sometimes mentioned as an ingredient of liability for negligent misrepresentation at common law.[34] The authorities are, however, divided on the weight to be attached to this point. One view is that the references to assumption of responsibility are merely descriptive of the relationships which give rise to a duty of care; another view is that such voluntary assumption is an essential ingredient of liability in cases of this kind. Some of the decisions can only be reconciled with the second view by a process of *ex post facto* rationalisation[35]; and it is submitted that the weight of recent authority shows that the first view is to be preferred.[36]

(ii) *Professional skill?* The second feature of the relationships (discussed above) which give rise to a duty of care is that the person making the statement does so in the exercise of some professional skill. The absence of this factor was held to negative liability in *Mutual Life and Citizen's Insurance Co. Ltd.* v. *Evatt*,[37] where a company carelessly gave misleading information about an associated company to a prospective investor in the latter company. As a result the investor suffered loss, but the majority of the Privy Council held that the first company was not liable in negligence as it was not and did not purport to be engaged in the business of giving skilled advice on investments.[38] The majority regarded this as an essential ingredient of liability[39]; but the prevailing view is that, so long as other conditions of liability are satisfied, the representator may be liable even though he was not in the business of giving advice[40] and even though the representee did not seek his advice (but only asked for information).[41] Thus in *Anderson & Sons Ltd.* v. *Rhodes (Liverpool) Ltd.*[42] a commission agent made a representation to a seller of potatoes about the solvency of his principal, the buyer. It was held that the agent owed a duty of care to the seller.

(b) COMMERCIAL RELATIONSHIPS. A duty of care may exist at common law even in a purely commercial relationship, such as that of buyer and seller

---

34 *Yuen Kun-yeu* v. *Att.-Gen. of Hong Kong* [1988] A.C. [1988] A.C. 175, 196; *Simaan General Contracting Co.* v. *Pilkington Glass Ltd. (No. 2)* [1988] Q.B. 758, 784; *Chaudhry* v. *Prabakhar* [1989] 1 W.L.R. 29, 34; *Shearson Lehman Hutton Inc.* v. *Maclaine Watson & Co. Ltd.* [1989] 2 Lloyd's Rep. 570, 636.

35 *e.g. Anderson & Son Ltd.* v. *Rhodes (Liverpool) Ltd.* [1967] 2 All E.R. 850; *Esso Petroleum Co. Ltd.* v. *Mardon* [1976] Q.B. 801.

36 *Smith* v. *Eric S. Bush* [1990] 1 A.C. 831, 862, 871 and (*semble*); *Caparo Industries plc* v. *Dickman* [1990] 2 A.C. 605, 623, 628, 637; *The Morning Watch* [1990] 1 Lloyd's Rep. 547; *Reid* v. *Rush and Tompkins Group plc* [1990] 1 W.L.R. 212 leaves the point open.

37 [1971] A.C. 793; A.L.G., 87 L.Q.R. 147; Rickford, 34 M.L.R. 328.

38 [1971] A.C. 793, 809.

39 At pp. 805, 809.

40 The views of the minority in *Evatt's* case were preferred to those of the majority by Ormrod L.J. in *Esso Petroleum Co. Ltd.* v. *Mardon* [1976] Q.B. 801, 827 and by Lord Denning M.R. (dissenting) and Shaw L.J. in *Howard Marine & Dredging Co. Ltd.* v. *A. Ogden & Sons (Excavations) Ltd.* [1978] Q.B. 574, 591, 600. The point was left open in *Caparo Industries plc* v. *Dickman* [1990] 2 A.C. 605, 637.

41 *Box* v. *Midland Bank Ltd.* [1979] 2 Lloyd's Rep. 391 (reversed as to costs only [1981] 1 Lloyd's Rep. 434).

42 [1967] 2 All E.R. 850; Dias [1967] C.L.J. 155; Dean, 31 M.L.R. 322; contrast *Jones* v. *Still* [1965] N.Z.L.R. 1071; McKenzie, 29 M.L.R. 337.

or landlord and tenant. For example, in *Esso Petroleum Co. Ltd.* v. *Mardon*[43] a tenant was induced to take a lease of a petrol station from an oil company by a statement made by an experienced salesman on the company's behalf, as to the potential future turnover of the premises. As the tenant had relied on the salesman's superior knowledge and experience, it was held that the company was under a duty of care at common law. On the other hand there are many commercial relationships in which each party consciously relies on his own skill or judgment[44] or where it is reasonable for the representor to assume that the representee will be advised by4 his own experts.[45] In such cases there would be no duty of care at common law; though, even in the absence of a "special relationship," there can be liability in damages under the Misrepresentation Act.[46]

(3) Effects of negligence on other rules

The main importance of *Hedley Byrne*'s case lies in its recognition of liability in damages for negligent misrepresentation; but it may also have a further, less easily predictable, impact on the law of misrepresentation. Before the decision, there was, for most practical purposes, no separate legal category of negligent misrepresentation. This state of affairs had an important influence on the development of the law relating to the effect of misrepresentation on contract. Many of the rules on this topic provided that one result should follow if the representation was fraudulent, and another if it was innocent.[47] For these purposes, "innocent" simply meant "not fraudulent."[48] It is now necessary to accommodate negligent misrepresentation within this scheme, and to ask whether, for the purpose of any given rule, negligence is to be treated in the same way as fraud, or in the same way as innocence, or in some third way. There is as yet very little guidance as to how questions of this kind are going to be answered. The only thing that is certain is that a negligent misrepresentation is treated like a fraudulent one in that it gives rise to a claim for damages.

3. Misrepresentation Act 1967, section 2(1)

This subsection creates a statutory liability for misrepresentation. It provides: "Where a person has entered into a contract after a misrepresentation has been made to him by another party thereto and as a result thereof he has suffered loss, then, if the person making the misrepresentation would be liable to damages in respect thereof had the misrepresentation been made fraudulently, that person shall be so liable notwithstanding that the misrepresentation was not made fraudulently, unless he proves that he had reasonable ground to believe and did believe up to the time the contract was made that the facts represented were true."

---

43 [1976] Q.B. 801; Gravells 39 M.L.R. 462; *cf.* dicta in *Hedley Byrne*'s case [1964] A.C. 465, 486, 514, 528–529.

44 *Oleificio Zucchi S.A.* v. *Northern Sales Ltd.* [1965] 2 Lloyd's Rep. 496, 519; *cf. Jones* v. *Still* [1965] N.Z.L.R. 1071; *Amalgamated Metal Trading Ltd.* v. *D.T.I., The Times*, March 31, 1989.

45 *McInerny* v. *Lloyds Bank Ltd.* [1974] 1 Lloyd's Rep. 246.

46 S.2(1), *infra*; on the facts of *Esso Petroleum Co. Ltd.* v. *Mardon*, *supra*, n. 43, there would now be liability under this provision, as well as at common law.

47 *Ante*, pp. 298, 301, 303, *post*, pp. 333–334, 340, 345.

48 *Cf. ante*, p. 304; *post*, p. 320.

(1) Scope of the subsection

The statutory liability differs from common law liability for negligent misrepresentation in two ways.

First, it is not necessary under the subsection to ask whether there was a "special relationship," giving rise to a duty of care, between the parties[49]: it is enough if the representation is made by one contracting party to the other. For this reason, it has been said that the subsection imposes an "absolute obligation"[50]; but these words cannot be taken to refer to the *standard* of liability. This is far from "absolute," for under the concluding words of section 2(1), the representor can, in effect, escape liability by proving that his belief in the truth of the facts stated was not formed carelessly.

Secondly, the subsection reverses the burden of proof. At common law, the representee must prove negligence, while under the subsection the representor is liable "unless he proves that he had reasonable ground to believe and did believe up to the time the contract was made that the facts represented were true." The difficulty of discharging this burden is illustrated by a case in which, during negotiations for the hire of barges, the owner's agent mis-stated their deadweight capacity, relying on an erroneous statement in Lloyd's Register. It was held that the burden had not been discharged since reference to documents in the owner's possession would have disclosed the true state of affairs.[51] The burden would, on the other hand, probably be discharged if the representor could show that he was himself the victim of an earlier fraud and that he had innocently repeated a representation previously made to him,[52] or that he had reasonably relied on an expert's report on the point in question.[53] The subsection only requires him to prove that he had reasonable ground for his belief, so that his actual means of knowledge are relevant: accordingly, a layman may succeed in discharging the burden where an expert would fail.

Under the subsection, a contracting party can be held liable for a representation made on his behalf by his agent.[54] But the agent himself is not liable under the subsection,[55] though he will be liable in negligence at common law if the representee can establish that there was a "special relationship" between himself and the agent, and that the agent was in breach of the resulting duty of care. There are two further situations in which the subsection does not apply, though there may be liability in negligence at common law: namely, where (as in *Hedley Byrne*'s[56] case) the representation is made by a stranger to the contract; and where the negotiations between representor and representee do not reach the stage of a concluded contract.

---

[49] *Howard Marine & Dredging Co. Ltd.* v. *A. Ogden & Sons (Excavations) Ltd.* [1978] Q.B. 574, 596; Sills, 96 L.Q.R. 15; Sealy [1978] C.L.J. 229; *Cemp Properties (U.K.)* v. *Dentsply Research & Developments Corp.* [1989] 2 E.G.L.R. 205.

[50] *The Skopas* [1983] 1 W.L.R. 857, 861; *cf.* the *Howard Marine* case, *supra*, at p. 596.

[51] *Howard Marine* case, *supra*; *cf. Walker* v. *Boyle* [1982] 1 W.L.R. 495, 509.

[52] As in *Oscar Chess Ltd.* v. *Williams* [1957] 1 W.L.R. 370; *post*, p. 317; *cf. Humming Bird Motors* v. *Hobbs* [1986] R.T.R. 276 *post*, p. 319.

[53] *Cooper* v. *Tamms* [1988] 1 E.G.L.R. 257.

[54] *Gosling* v. *Anderson* (1972) 223 E.G. 1743; *Howard Marine* case, *supra*.

[55] *The Skopas* [1983] 1 W.L.R. 857; Owen [1984] C.L.J. 27.

[56] *Ante*, p. 308; *Kleinwort Benson Ltd.* v. *Malaysian Mining Corp.* [1989] 1 W.L.R. 379, 386.

(2) The fiction of fraud

Section 2(1) has the effect of imposing liability in damages for careless misrepresentation; but instead of simply providing that the representor shall be liable in damages[57] it says that he shall be so liable if he "would be liable to damages . . . had the misrepresentation been made fraudulently." This fiction of fraud seems to be quite unnecessary; and it could have the mischievous consequence of importing rules which have been developed in the context of fraudulent misrepresentation and which are quite inappropriate where there is no actual fraud. In the Parliamentary debates on the Act, Lord Reid suggested that the effect of the fiction might be to apply to the new cause of action the extended period of limitation which applies where an action is "based upon"[58] fraud. But he added that this result would be "rather unreasonable"[59] and a more recent dictum indicates that the fiction of fraud would not be applied to this situation.[60] Further support for the view that the fiction is not to be literally applied is provided by a case in which the Court of Appeal has held[61] that a principal may be liable under the subsection for his agent's misrepresentation even though there is no such shared responsibility for the statement as is required to make the principal liable in cases of fraud.[62] It is to be hoped that the courts will similarly reject certain other consequences[63] which could be deduced from the fiction of fraud.

(3) Effect of affirmation

The right to *rescind* a contract for misrepresentation can be lost by affirmation[64]; but such affirmation does not deprive the representee of his right to damages under section 2(1). Such damages can therefore in principle be recovered if, after having entered into the contract, the representee discovers the truth and nevertheless performs the contract.[65] Of course the right to damages may be limited in such cases: *e.g.* if the matter to which the misrepresentation relates was so serious that performance with knowledge of the truth amounts to failure on the part of the representee to mitigate his loss.[66]

---

57 *Cf.* Financial Services Act 1986, ss.150, 166.
58 See now Limitation Act 1980, s.32(1).
59 274 H.L. 936.
60 *Garden Neptune Shipping Ltd.* v. *Occidental Worldwide Investment Corp.* [1990] 1 Lloyd's Rep. 330, 335.
61 *Gosling* v. *Anderson* (1972) 223 E.G. 1743.
62 *Ante*, p. 308.
63 *e.g.* the rules as to damages for fraud (*post*, p. 325); the rule that a fraudulent statement need not be material (*ante*, p. 301) and the rule in *S. Pearson Ltd.* v. *Dublin Corp.* [1970] A.C. 351 (*ante*, p. 303), and the rule that a person cannot exclude liability for his own fraud (*ante*, p. 224): see the *Garden Neptune* case, *supra*, n. 60. On the other hand the rule that a representation as to a third person's credit must be in writing to give rise to liability under Statute of Frauds Amendment Act 1828, s.6 only applies to *fraudulent* misrepresentation: *Banbury* v. *Bank of Montreal* [1918] A.C. 626; and in *The Pacific Colocotronis* [1984] Q.B. 713, 718–719 it seems to have been thought that the fiction of fraud applied in this context, for it was "common ground" that the requirement of writing equally applied for the purpose of an action under Misrepresentation Act 1967, s.2(1).
64 *Post*, p. 343.
65 *Production Technology Consultants* v. *Barlett* [1986] 1 E.G.L.R. 82: *cf.* at common law *Arnison* v. *Smith* (1889) 41 Ch.D. 348 (where, however, the plaintiffs did not have full knowledge of their right to rescind and so could not be said to have affirmed).
66 *Post*, p. 866.

4. Contractual Statements

So far, in this Section, we have assumed that the misrepresentation induces the representee to enter into the contract, but that it does not actually form part of the contract or otherwise acquire contractual force. If the misrepresentation does have contractual force, the representee is entitled to recover damages for breach of contract. He may also be entitled to rescind the contract for breach or for misrepresentation. The relation between these various rights will be considered below[67]; here we are concerned only with the right to damages. This differs from the rights to damages previously considered in this Section in two ways: it can arise without fraud or negligence, and it is governed by different rules as to assessment of damages and remoteness.[68] It also differs in a number of ways from the power of the court to award damages in lieu of rescission, which will be considered below.[69] That power is discretionary, while damages for breach of contract can be recovered as of right; a representee cannot rescind for misrepresentation *and* claim damages in lieu of rescission, while (if the misrepresentation has become a term of the contract) he may be able to rescind and claim damages for breach of contract[70]; a party who once had the right to rescind, but has lost it, probably cannot claim damages in lieu of rescission,[71] though he can claim damages for breach of contract; and the two causes of action are, once again, governed by different rules as to assessment of damages and remoteness.

For all these reasons it is still necessary to distinguish between contractual statements and "mere" representations inducing a contract,[72] though the provisions of the Misrepresentation Act as to damages will probably reduce the practical importance of the distinction. A contractual statement may either be a term of the main contract or a collateral contract.

(1) Term of main contract

Where a contract is in writing, a descriptive statement may actually be made in the contractual document. Such a statement will clearly be a contractual term if it is said to be the basis of the contract.[73] Subject to such express provisions, the question whether the statement is a term or a mere representation is one of construction.[74] The same is true where the statement is contained in a written offer, the acceptance of which concludes the contract.[75] Where a descriptive statement is contained in a contractual document it may[76] be a term even though it did not induce the party com-

---

67 *Post*, pp. 322–325, 336–337.
68 *Post*, pp. 322–325.
69 *Post*, pp. 320–322.
70 *Post*, pp. 322.
71 *Post*, p. 322.
72 Atiyah, 1971 Alberta L.Rev. 347, and *Essays in Contract* 275.
73 *e.g. London Assurance* v. *Mansel* (1879) 11 Ch.D. 363
74 *Behn* v. *Burness* (1863) 1 B. & S. 751, 754 (statement in charterparty as to position of ship).
75 *The Larissa* [1983] 2 Lloyd's Rep. 325, 330.
76 Though reliance may be relevant in determining whether the statement was intended as a term: see *Harlingdon & Leinster Enterprises Ltd.* v. *Christopher Hull Fine Art Ltd.* [1990] 1 All E.R. 737.

plaining of its untruth to enter into the contract,[77] and, indeed, even though he was at the time of contracting quite unaware of its existence.[78]

Often a statement inducing a contract will not be set out in the contractual document, but will be made during the negotiations leading up to the contract. The question whether such a statement was a mere representation or a term of the contract used to be treated as one of fact and left to the jury.[79] Now, few cases of this kind are tried by jury, but the orthodox view is that the question remains one of fact: with what intention was the statement made?[80] This intention would, in general, be objectively ascertained.[81] It is impossible to lay down any strict rules for determining when such an intention can be said to exist. But a number of guiding principles can be deduced from the cases.

(a) VERIFICATION. A statement is unlikely to be a term of the contract if the person making it expressly asks the other party to verify its truth. In *Ecay* v. *Godfrey*[82] the seller of a boat said that it was sound but advised the buyer to have it surveyed. This advice negatived any intention to warrant the soundness of the boat. The same principle applies where the circumstances are such that the person to whom the statement was made would normally be expected to verify it. This is the reason traditionally given for the view that statements made by sellers of houses in pre-contract negotiations are rarely regarded as warranties: the buyer is expected to rely on a survey, commissioned by himself or his building society, for information with regard to the state of the premises.[83] It has indeed been held that, if the buyer relies on a survey negligently conducted by a surveyor commissioned by the building society he may have a right of action in tort against that surveyor, in spite of the fact that he might have discovered the truth by commissioning his own survey.[84] But that does not affect the present point, which is that the buyer normally has no cause of action *in contract* against the seller in respect of statements made by the latter about the condition of the property.

On the other hand, a statement is likely to be a term of the contract if it is intended to prevent the other party from finding out the truth, has this effect, and induces him to contract in reliance on it. In *Schawel* v. *Reade*[85] the buyer of a horse was about to examine it when the seller said: "You need not look for anything; the horse is perfectly sound. If there was anything the matter with the horse I should tell you." The buyer, relying on this statement, bought the horse without examination. The actual decision turned on the trial judge's direction to the jury, which was held to be correct; but all the members of the House of Lords also agreed with the jury's

---

[77] *Ibid.* pp. 744, 747, 751.
[78] *Cf. ante*, p. 197: the principle of incorporation by signature can here work *in favour* of the signer.
[79] *e.g. Power* v. *Barham* (1836) 4 A. & E. 473; *Miller* v. *Cannon Hill Estates Ltd.* [1931] 2 K.B. 113.
[80] *Howard Marine & Dredging Co. Ltd.* v. *A. Ogden & Son (Excavations) Ltd.* [1978] Q.B. 574, 595.
[81] *Ante*, pp. 1, 8.
[82] (1947) 80 Ll.L.R. 286; *cf. Mahon* v. *Ainscough* [1952] 1 All E.R. 337; *Eustace* v. *Kempe-Roberts* [1964] C.L.Y. 3280.
[83] See *Longman* v. *Blount* (1896) 12 T.L.R. 520; *Green* v. *Symons* (1897) 13 T.L.R. 301; *cf. Terence Ltd.* v. *Nelson* (1937) 157 L.T. 254.
[84] *Smith* v. *Eric S. Bush* [1990] 1 A.C. 831; *ante*, p. 305.
[85] [1913] 2 I.R. 64.

view that the statement was a warranty. On the other hand, in the earlier case of *Hopkins* v. *Tanqueray*,[86] the buyer of a mare was about to examine her when the seller said: "You have nothing to look for. I assure you that she is perfectly sound." The buyer, relying on this statement, the next day bought the mare, without further examination, at an auction at Tattersalls. It was held that the seller's statement was not a warranty. The case turns on the special fact that sales at Tattersalls were known by both parties to be without warranty unless the contrary was expressly stated in the catalogue.

(b) IMPORTANCE. A statement is likely to be a term of the contract where its importance is such that, if it had not been made, the representee would not have entered into the contract at all. In *Bannerman* v. *White*[87] an intending buyer of hops asked whether sulphur had been used in their cultivation, adding that, if it had been used, he would not even bother to ask the price. The seller assured him that sulphur had not been used and this assurance was held to be a term of the contract. Such a statement can be a term of the contract even though it conflicts with a previous written statement. Thus in *Couchman* v. *Hill*[88] a heifer was put up for auction under printed conditions of sale which provided that no warranty was given. The plaintiff asked whether the heifer was in calf, adding that, if she were, he would not bid. He bought the heifer after being assured that she was not in calf, and it was held that this assurance was a term of the contract.

These cases should be contrasted with *Oscar Chess Ltd.* v. *Williams*,[89] where the defendant sold to the plaintiffs for £280 a car honestly described as a 1948 Morris 10. It was in fact a 1939 model worth £175. The statement that the car was a 1948 model was held not to be a term of the contract. In this case, the plaintiffs might still have bought (though for less money) had they known the truth; but if the plaintiffs in *Bannerman* v. *White* and *Couchman* v. *Hill* had known the truth, they would not have bought at all.

(c) SPECIAL KNOWLEDGE. The question whether a statement is a contractual term or a mere representation may turn on the relative capacities of the parties to ascertain the truth of what was stated.[90] Thus in *Oscar Chess Ltd.* v. *Williams* the seller was a private person to whom the car had been previously sold as a 1948 model, with a forged logbook. The main reason why the seller's statement as to the age of the car was not a term of the contract was that he had no special knowledge as to the age of the car, while the buyers were car dealers, and so in at least as good a position as the seller to know whether the statement was true.[91] The case may be contrasted with *Dick Bentley Productions Ltd.* v. *Harold Smith (Motors) Ltd.*[92] where a dealer sold a Bentley car, representing that it had only done 20,000 miles since a replacement engine was fitted, when in fact it had done

[86] (1854) 15 C.B. 130.
[87] (1861) 10 C.B.(N.S.) 844.
[88] [1947] K.B. 554. Alternatively, the statement was said to be a collateral contract: *post* see also *Otto* v. *Bolton* [1936] 2 K.B. 46.
[89] [1957] 1 W.L.R. 370.
[90] *Cf. Esso Petroleum Co. Ltd.* v. *Mardon* [1976] Q.B. 801, where this test was applied to determine the existence of a collateral contract (*post*, p. 319).
[91] *Cf. Routledge* v. *McKay* [1954] 1 W.L.R. 615; *Hummingbird Motors* v. *Hobbs* [1986] R.T.R. 276 (*post*, p. 319), where the seller was not a dealer, though he occasionally sold cars; and see *Harrison* v. *Knowles & Foster* [1918] 1 K.B. 608; *The Larissa* [1983] 2 Lloyd's Rep. 325, 330.
[92] [1965] 1 W.L.R. 623.

nearly 100,000 miles since then. He was clearly in a better position than the buyer to know whether the representation was true, and it was held to be a warranty. Salmon L.J. based this conclusion on the orthodox test of contractual intention,[93] while Lord Denning M.R. took the different view, that any inducing representation was prima facie a warranty, though the representor could "rebut this inference if he can show that it really was an innocent misrepresentation, in that he was in fact innocent of fault in making it, and that it would not be reasonable for him in the circumstances to be bound by it."[94] But the view that an inducing misrepresentation has contractual force unless the misrepresentor can disprove "fault" is hard to reconcile with the many cases in which representors have escaped liability for breach of contract without having disproved "fault"; and in some of these the representors were clearly careless.[95] Even the fact that the representor was in a better position than the representee to know the truth is not always decisive.[96] In *Gilchester Properties Ltd.* v. *Gomm*[97] a statement by the vendor of a block of flats as to the rent at which the flats were let was held to be a mere representation, though obviously the vendor was in a better position than the purchaser to know the truth. Of course a representor who is guilty of "fault" may be liable in damages at common law or under the Misrepresentation Act[98]; but such liability may differ in extent from liability for breach of contract.[99]

The *Oscar Chess* and *Dick Bentley* cases are sometimes reconciled by saying that the sale in the first was by a private seller and in the second by a dealer. This distinction was, however, disregarded in *Beale* v. *Taylor*[1]; where a car was sold by a private seller to a private buyer. The seller had previously advertised the car as a "Herald convertible, white, 1961, twin carbs." In fact the car was an amalgam of two cars, the back being taken from a 1961 model and the front from an earlier one; but the seller did not know this and it was not suggested that he was negligent in not knowing it. The court treated the statement in the advertisement as part of the contractual description of the car, for breach of which the buyer could recover damages. It does not seem to have been argued that the terms of the advertisement constituted a "mere" representation; and the case is hard to reconcile with *Oscar Chess Ltd.* v. *Williams,* which was not cited to the court.[2]

(d) Opinion. Statements of opinion which are so vague that they cannot be verified are mere puffs and have no effect. But a statement which is one of opinion in the sense that it states a fact which is difficult, but not impossible, to verify may be a term of the contract. In *Jendwine* v. *Slade*[3] Lord Kenyon held that statements that two pictures were respectively by Claude Lorrain and Teniers were not warranties. The authenticity of pictures

---

93 At p. 629.

94 At pp. 627–628. Contrast his dissenting judgment in *Howard Marine & Dredging Co. Ltd.* v. *A. Ogden & Son (Excavations) Ltd.* [1978] Q.B. 574, 591, applying the test of whether the statement was "intended to be binding."

95 *e.g. Redgrave* v. *Hurd* (1881) 20 Ch.D. 1; *ante*, p. 304.

96 See criticisms in *Heilbut, Symons & Co.* v. *Buckleton* [1913] A.C. 30, 50 of *De Lassalle* v. *Guildford* [1901] 2 K.B. 215 on this point.

97 [1948] 1 All E.R. 493.

98 *Ante*, pp. 307–314.

99 *Post*, pp. 322–325; the claim in the *Dick Bentley* case was limited to £400.

1 [1967] 1 W.L.R. 1193; Koh [1968] C.L.J. 11.

2 The seller conducted his own case.

3 (1797) 2 Esp. 571; *cf. Gee* v. *Lucas* (1867) 16 L.T. 357.

painted "some centuries back" could only be a matter of opinion. But later cases show that this is not an inflexible rule. In *Power* v. *Barham*[4] it was held that a statement that certain pictures were by Canaletto could be a warranty, *Jendwine* v. *Slade* being distinguished on the ground that Canaletto was "not a very old painter."[5] Similarly, in *Leaf* v. *International Galleries*[6] the Court of Appeal indicated that a representation made in 1945 that a picture was a Constable could be a warranty; though the position will be different where the seller of a picture makes an attribution but expressly disclaims expert knowledge.[7] Nor will a statement be a warranty as to a quality if the statement is *expressly* one of opinion or belief. Thus where the seller of a car said that, to the best of his knowledge and belief, the odometer reading was correct, it was held that he had not given a warranty of such correctness, and that he was not liable merely because, unknown to him, the odometer had been tampered with before he had acquired the car.[8]

(2) Collateral contract[9]

It may not be possible for a statement made during the negotiations leading up to the contract to take effect as one of its terms. The contract may be in writing, so that extrinsic evidence cannot be used to add to it, or to vary it[10]; or the statement may be oral and the contract one which the law requires to be in, or evidenced in, writing.[11] In such cases[12] the oral statement may nevertheless be enforceable as a "collateral contract". There are then two contracts between the parties: the main (written) contract and the collateral (oral) contract, both relating to the same subject-matter. Thus in *De Lassalle* v. *Guildford*[13] the intending lessee of a house refused to execute the lease unless the landlord first assured him that the drains were in good order. The landlord gave this assurance, which was not incorporated in the lease. He was nonetheless held liable, when the drains were found to be defective, for breach of a collateral contract. The statement made, on behalf of the landlord in *Esso Petroleum Co. Ltd.* v. *Mardon*,[14] was similarly held to amount to a collateral contract.

A statement can, it seems, only take effect as a collateral contract if two conditions are satisfied. First, it must have been intended to have contractual effect, as in the case of a statement forming part of the main contract. Secondly, there must be some indication that the parties intended the statement to take effect as a collateral contract and not simply as a term in the main contract.

---

[4] (1836) 4 A. & E. 473.
[5] *Ibid.* at p. 476. He had died in 1768.
[6] [1950] 2 K.B. 86. *Quaere*, however, whether there was such a warranty; *ante*, p. 256, n. 60.
[7] *Harlingdon and Leinster Enterprises Ltd.* v. *Christopher Hull Fine Art Ltd.* [1990] 1 All E.R. 737.
[8] *Humming Bird Motors* v. *Hobbs* [1986] R.T.R. 276. Liability in negligence was also excluded; and the seller had not misrepresented his knowledge or belief: *cf. ante*, p. 296.
[9] Wedderburn [1959] C.L.J. 58.
[10] *Ante*, pp. 176, *et seq.*, especially at pp. 183–185.
[11] *Angell* v. *Duke* (1875) L.R. 10 Q.B. 174; *Jameson* v. *Kinmell Bay Land Co. Ltd.* (1931) 47 T.L.R. 593; *Hill* v. *Harris* [1965] 2 Q.B. 601; Law Com. No. 164, paras. 5.7–5.8; *ante*, p. 164.
[12] See *J. Evans & Son (Portsmouth) Ltd.* v. *Andrew Merzario Ltd.* [1976] 1 W.L.R. 1078, 1083.
[13] [1901] 2 K.B. 215.
[14] [1976] Q.B. 801; *ante*, p. 312.

These requirements have already been discussed[15] and it will suffice here to recall the statement of principle by Lord Moulton in *Heilbut, Symons & Co.* v. *Buckleton*[16]: "There may be a contract the consideration for which is the making of some other contract. . . . Such collateral contracts, the sole effect of which is to vary or add to the terms of the principal contract, are therefore viewed with suspicion by the law . . . Not only the terms of such contracts but the existence of an *animus contrahendi* on the part of all the parties to them must be clearly shewn."[17]

In one respect a person who relies on a statement as a collateral contract is at first sight in a worse position than one who relies on it as a term of the main contract: since a collateral contract exists apart from the main contract, it must be supported by *separate* consideration. But this requirement would usually be satisfied by entering into the main contract. The only cases in which this analysis could give rise to difficulty are those in which the party relying on the collateral contract was already bound to enter into the main contract[18]; *e.g.* where a lease was executed in performance of an agreement to enter into it.[19] Even in such cases, however, the act of entering into the main contract[20] (*i.e.* the execution of the lease) would constitute consideration for the collateral contract if that act in fact conferred a benefit on the other party.[21]

The question whether evidence of a collateral contract is admissible if it actually *contradicts* the main written contract has been discussed in Chapter 6.[22]

5. Damages in Lieu of Rescission

(1) Misrepresentation Act 1967, section 2(2)

Before the Misrepresentation Act, damages could not be awarded for a wholly innocent misrepresentation (*i.e.* for one that was neither fraudulent nor negligent[23]) if it did not have contractual force.[24] The principal remedy for innocent misrepresentation was rescission, though when the court rescinded a contract it could make some form of monetary adjustment by granting an "indemnity."[25] This position was unsatisfactory since, in cases

---

[15] *Ante*, pp. 164, 183–185.

[16] [1913] A.C. 30, 47; *ante*, p. 150. In *J. Evans & Son (Portsmouth) Ltd.* v. *Andrea Merzario Ltd.* [1967] W.L.R. 1078, 1081 Lord Denning M.R. described "much of what was said in that case as entirely out of date"; *cf.* his dissenting judgment in *Howard Marine & Dredging Co. Ltd.* v. *A. Ogden & Sons (Excavations) Ltd.* [1978] Q.B. 574, 590. But, though damages may be recoverable under Misrepresentation Act 1967, s.2 for statements which do not satisfy Lord Moulton's test, that test remains good law so far as *contractual* liability is concerned: *I.B.A.* v. *E.M.I. (Electronics) Ltd.* (1980) 14 Build.L.R. 1 (*post*, p. 525).

[17] *Cf. Hill* v. *Harris* [1965] 2 Q.B. 601.

[18] See *ante*

[19] See the discussion of *Brikom Investments Ltd.* v. *Carr* [1979] Q.B. 467, *ante*, p. 97.

[20] *Williams* v. *Roffey Bros. & Nicholls (Contractors) Ltd.* [1991] 1 Q.B. 1.

[21] *Ante*, p. 89.

[22] *Ante*, pp. 183–185.

[23] See *ante*, pp. 304, 312.

[24] *Redgrave* v. *Hurd* (1881) 20 Ch.D. 1, where the representor would now almost certainly be liable in damages for negligence at common law, or under Misrepresentation Act 1967, s.2(1): see *Archer* v. *Brown* [1985] Q.B. 401, 416, suggesting that *Redgrave* v. *Hurd* does not (so far as damages are concerned) "represent the law since the Misrepresentation Act." *Cf. ante*, p. 304.

[25] *Post*, pp. 327–329.

of wholly innocent misrepresentation, the entire transaction would have to be set aside (even though the misrepresentation related to a matter of relatively minor importance), if any remedy at all were to be given to the representee. Section 2(2) of the Misrepresentation Act partly cures this defect by giving the court a discretionary power to declare the contract subsisting and to award damages in lieu of rescission. It provides: "Where a person has entered into a contract after a misrepresentation has been made to him otherwise than fraudulently, and he would be entitled, by reason of the misrepresentation, to rescind the contract, then, if it is claimed, in any proceedings arising out of the contract, that the contract ought to be or has been rescinded, the court or arbitrator may declare the contract subsisting and award damages in lieu of rescission, if of opinion that it would be equitable to do so, having regard to the nature of the misrepresentation and the loss that would be caused by it if the contract were upheld, as well as to the loss that rescission would cause to the other party."

(2) Scope of the subsection

(a) DISCRETIONARY. The power to award damages in lieu of rescission is discretionary: neither party has a right that this remedy shall be granted. The concluding words of the subsection specify the factors which the court can consider in deciding whether to exercise the power. It seems that the court can take into account the contents of the representation; and balance the interests of the parties in on the one hand seeking and on the other resisting rescission. Usually the representor will want to resist rescission and two factors are likely to induce the court to exercise its discretion in his favour and to leave the representee to his remedy in damages. These are the relatively minor significance of the representation and the absence of fault on the misrepresentor's part.[26] On the other hand, the "policing function"[27] of the remedy of rescission may also be taken into account: this was the ground on which the court refused to uphold a contract of reinsurance which had been induced by a broker's material misrepresentation.[28]

(b) IN LIEU OF RESCISSION. Damages under the subsection may only be awarded "in lieu of rescission," so that the representee cannot rescind *and* claim such damages. If he rescinds on account of a wholly innocent misrepresentation[29] which has no contractual force,[30] any claim for monetary compensation will continue to be governed by the principles which determine the extent of an indemnity.[31] The misrepresentee can, however, still rescind *and* claim damages for fraud, since fraudulent misrepresentation is expressly excepted from the subsection; and there is nothing in the subsection to prevent him from rescinding *and* claiming damages for negligence at common law or under section 2(1).[32] The suggestion that the victim of an "innocent" misrepresentation can now rescind and claim

---

[26] See *The Lucy* [1983] 1 Lloyd's Rep. 188, 202.
[27] *Highlands Ins. Co.* v. *Continental Ins. Co.* [1987] 1 Lloyd's Rep. 109, 118.
[28] *Ibid.*
[29] *Supra*, at n. 23.
[30] For "incorporated misrepresentations" see *infra* and *post*, pp. 336–337.
[31] *Post*, pp. 327–329.
[32] As in *F. & H. Entertainments* v. *Leisure Enterprises* (1976) 240 E.G. 445.

damages under "section 2"[33] cannot, it is submitted, be interpreted to mean that the representee can rescind *and* claim damages under section 2(2) in spite of the fact that the representor was not negligent and has succeeded in discharging the burden of proof under section 2(1). Such an interpretation would be plainly inconsistent with the words of section 2(2), that the damages which can be awarded under it are "in lieu of rescission."

A further consequence of the rule that damages under the subsection are "in lieu of rescission" is more controversial. Such damages are available where a person "would be entitled, by reason of the misrepresentation, to rescind the contract." It is not clear from these words whether the court can award damages if the representee once had the right to rescind but had lost it[34] before the claim under section 2(2) was made. The fact that the court's power is to award damages "in lieu of rescission," and the description of the factors to which the court is to have regard in determining whether to exercise its discretion, suggest that the court must have some real choice in the matter and therefore support the view that damages in lieu cannot be awarded where the right to rescind has been lost.[35] On the other hand it is hard, as a matter of policy, to see why the factors which bar the right to rescind should limit the discretion to award damages. The intervention of third party rights, for instance, may make it highly inappropriate to rescind the contract, but it does not follow that it should prevent the court from awarding monetary compensation to the representee.

(c) INCORPORATED MISREPRESENTATION. A representation originally made to induce a contract may become a term of the contract by being subsequently incorporated in it; and this does not affect the right to rescind for misrepresentation.[36] In such cases the representee is entitled as of right to *damages* for breach of contract; this right is not subject to the discretion of the court. The question whether his right to "*rescind*" for breach of contract is affected by section 2(2) will be discussed below.[37]

6. Basis of Assessment and Remoteness

Where a representee claims damages, questions may arise as to the basis of assessment and remoteness. These questions are discussed generally in Chapter 21,[38] but some special factors relating to misrepresentation must be considered here.

(1) Basis of assessment

Liability for misrepresentation may arise in tort (where the representation is made fraudulently or negligently) or in contract (where the representation has contractual force). This distinction affects the assessment of damages in the most common case of misrepresentation: namely, where

[33] *Archer* v. *Brown* [1985] Q.B. 401, 415; the suggestion is *obiter* as the case was one of fraud, and "innocent" may have been intended simply to mean "not fraudulent."
[34] *Post*, pp. 337–345.
[35] *Cf. The Lucy* [1983] 1 Lloyd's Rep. 188, 201–202. But the right to damages *under s.2(1)* survives loss of the right to rescind by affirmation: *ante*, p. 314.
[36] *Post*, p. 336.
[37] *Post*, p. 337.
[38] *Post*, pp. 836–864.

the subject-matter of a contract is represented to have some quality which in fact it lacks. The general principle is that in tort the plaintiff is entitled to such damages as will put him into the position in which he would have been if the tort had not been committed; while in contract he is to be put into the position in which he would have been if the contract had been performed.[39] It is thought to follow that in tort the plaintiff is entitled to be put into the position in which he would have been if the representation *had not been made*, while in contract he is entitled to be put into the position in which he would have been if the representation *had been true*.[40] If the representation induces the plaintiff to buy something which, but for the misrepresentation, he would not have bought at all, it follows that the damages in tort are prima facie the amount by which the actual value of the thing bought is less than *the price* paid for it.[41] In contract, on the other hand, the damages are prima facie the amount by which the actual value of the thing bought is less than *the value which it would have had if the representation had been true*.[42]

Some examples may help to make this clear. Suppose, first, that the plaintiff would have made a good bargain if the representation had been true: *e.g.* he has bought something for £100 which would have been worth £150 if the representation had been true but which is actually worth only £90. Here in tort the plaintiff can recover £10 and in contract £60. Suppose next that the plaintiff would have made a bad bargain even if the representation had been true: *e.g.* he has bought something for £100 which would have been worth £50 if the representation had been true but is in fact worth only £10. Here in tort the plaintiff can recover £90 and in contract £40.

There is some conflict in the authorities as to which of these bases of assessment is to be adopted for the purpose of section 2(1) of the Misrepresentation Act 1967. One view is that damages under the subsection are to be assessed on a contractual basis[43]; but the now more generally held view

---

[39] *McGregor on Damages* (15th ed.), 1988, § 11.

[40] *Smith Kline French Laboratories Ltd.* v. *Long* [1989] 1 W.L.R. 1, 6.

[41] This rule is stated in many cases: see, for example, *Davidson* v. *Tulloch* (1860) 3 Macq. 783, 790; *Peek* v. *Derry* (1887) 37 Ch.D. 541, 578 (reversed on liability 14 App.Cas. 337); *Twycross* v. *Grant* (1877) 2 C.P.D. 496, 504; *Cackett* v. *Keswick* [1902] 2 Ch. 456, 468; *McConnel* v. *Wright* [1903] 1 Ch. 546, 554; *Broome* v. *Speake* [1903] 1 Ch. 586, 605, 623 (affirmed [1904] A.C. 342); *Stevens* v. *Hoare* (1904) 20 T.L.R. 407; *Heineman* v. *Cooper* [1987] H.L.R. 262; *Saunders* v. *Edwards* [1987] 1 W.L.R. 1116, 1121; *Strover* v. *Harrington* [1988] Ch. 390, 411; *Westgate* v. *Bracknell D.C.* (1987) 19 H.L.R. 735; *Smith* v. *Eric S. Bush* [1990] 1 A.C. 831, 851; *Hussey* v. *Eels* [1990] 2 Q.B. 227, 241; the assessment in *Roberts* v. *J. Hampson & Co.* [1990] 1 W.L.R. 94 is (if correctly reported) hard to reconcile with the normal basis of assessment. For the position where a lender is induced to advance money on the security of a house in reliance on a negligent surveyor's report: see *Swingcastle Ltd.* v. *Gibson* [1991] 2 All E.R. 353. See *McGregor on Damages* (15th ed.), § 1724; *Spencer Bower and Turner on Actionable Misrepresentation* (3rd ed.), pp. 237–258. Where the value of the thing bought declines after the sale, the time for assessing that value should (for the present purpose) be the time when the truth was or could with reasonable diligence have been discovered, unless the plaintiff acted reasonably in keeping it after that date: see *Naughton* v. *O'Callaghan* [1990] 3 All E.R. 191; *cf. post*, pp. 849–859.

[42] See, for example, Sale of Goods Act 1979, s.53(3); an alternative measure is the cost of making the defect good (*post*, p. 837).

[43] *Davis & Co. (Wines) Ltd.* v. *Afa Minerva (E.M.I.) Ltd.* [1974] 2 Lloyd's Rep. 27, 32.

is that such damages are "the same as in an action of deceit,"[44] *i.e.* that they are to be assessed on a tortious basis. It is submitted that the latter is the correct view since the reference to fraud in section 2(1) indicates that the statutory cause of action is tortious in nature. Accordingly, the tortious basis of assessment applies where the representee has received something which lacked a quality that it was represented to have.

A representation may have contractual force, but the contract may be to the effect, not that the representation is true, but that the representor has taken due care in making it. This was the position in *Esso Petroleum Co. Ltd.* v. *Mardon*[45] where a tenant was induced to take a lease of a petrol station by a statement made on behalf of the landlord that the future annual turnover could be estimated at 200,000 gallons. The estimate had been carelessly made and the actual turnover was much lower. The landlord was held liable both for negligence at common law and for breach of collateral warranty.[46] But even on the latter basis the tenant did not recover damages for loss of his bargain[47] (*i.e.* for loss of the profit that he would have made on a turnover of 200,000 gallons); for the warranty was not that 200,000 gallons would be sold but only that the estimate had been prepared with due care. The damages were in fact assessed on a tort basis, so as to put the tenant into the position in which he would have been if he had not taken the lease. In view of this fact, it is not easy to see why the Court of Appeal placed so much emphasis on its view that the landlord was liable in contract as well as in tort.

In the cases so far discussed, the misrepresentations were made *by* the seller and related to the quality of the subject-matter. They may also be made *to* the seller and relate to his willingness to contract with a particular buyer.[48] In one case,[49] manufacturers of pharmaceuticals were induced to sell tablets to a company by the defendant's representation that the company intended to resell them in Central Africa; in fact they were resold in Holland. If the plaintiffs had known the truth, they would not have sold to the company; but that sale did not affect their capacity to supply other customers. In these circumstances, the proper way of putting the plaintiffs into the position in which they would have been, if the representation had not been made, was to ensure that they should receive the market value of the tablets. As this value was not shown to exceed the contract price, the

---

[44] *F. & H. Entertainments Ltd.* v. *Leisure Enterprises Ltd.* 240 E.G. 455 (the reference is simply to s.2, but it is clear from the context that subs. (1) is meant); *André & Cie. S.A.* v. *Ets. Michel Blanc & Fils* [1977] 2 Lloyd's Rep. 166, 181 (affirmed, without reference to this point [1979] 2 Lloyd's Rep. 427); *Cemp Properties (U.K.)* v. *Dentsply Research & Development Corp.* [1989] 2 E.G.L.R. 205; *Naughton* v. *O'Callaghan* [1990] 3 All E.R. 191, 196; *Royscott Trust Ltd.* v. *Rogerson*, *The Times*, April 3, 1991; *Cf. Box* v. *Midland Bank Ltd.* [1979] 2 Lloyd's Rep. 391 (reversed as to costs only [1981] 1 Lloyd's Rep. 434); *Archer* v. *Brown* [1985] Q.B. 401, 426–427 (denying an item of loss of bargain damages); *Sharneyford Supplies Ltd.* v. *Edge* [1987] Ch. 305, 303, disapproving a contrary dictum in *Watts* v. *Spence* [1975] Ch. 165, 175 (the actual reasoning of these last two cases has been made obsolete by Law of Property (Miscellaneous Provisions) Act 1989, s.3, *post*, p. 883); Taylor, 45 M.L.R. 139; Cartwright [1987] Conv. 423.

[45] [1976] Q.B. 801.

[46] *Ante*, pp. 312, 319.

[47] [1976] Q.B. 801, 820.

[48] *Cf. ante*, pp. 262–266.

[49] *Smith Kline & French Laboratories Ltd.* v. *Long* [1989] 1 W.L.R. 1.

defendant was liable for no more than the contract price, less that part of it which had already been paid by the company.

(2) Remoteness

The fact that the subject-matter lacks a quality that it was represented to have may, apart from affecting its value, also cause the representee to suffer consequential loss. For example, where diseased cows are sold under representations of soundness and infect other animals of the buyer, he may be able to recover for the loss of those animals[50]; and where a business is sold under misrepresentation as to its profitability the buyer may be able to recover damages for losses suffered in the course of running the business.[51] Consequential losses can, however, only be recovered if they are not too remote[52]; and the rules as to remoteness are more favourable to the plaintiff in actions of deceit than they are in actions for breach of contract. Lord Denning M.R. has gone so far as to say that "In contract the damages are limited to what may reasonably be supposed to have been in the contemplation of the parties. In fraud they are not so limited. The defendant is bound to make reparation for all the actual damage directly flowing from the fraudulent inducement. . . . It does not lie in the mouth of the fraudulent person to say that they could not reasonably have been foreseen."[53] This view may be too sweeping in the sense that some totally unforeseeable *kind* of loss may be irrecoverable even in actions of deceit[54]; but the degree of foreseeability required in such actions is certainly lower than in a contractual action.[55]

In an action based on negligent misrepresentation at common law, the loss must be reasonably foreseeable, that being the general rule applied in actions for negligence.[56] This rule may be less favourable to the plaintiff than the rule in deceit but it is probably more favourable than the rule in a contractual action.[57] Where the action is brought under section 2(1) of the Misrepresentation Act, one possible view is that the deceit rule will be applied by virtue of the fiction of fraud.[58] But it is submitted that the severity of the deceit rule can only be justified in cases of actual fraud[59] and that remoteness under section 2(1) should depend, as in actions based on negligence, on the test of foreseeability.

---

[50] *Mullett* v. *Mason* (1866) L.R. 1 C.P. 559 (fraud); *Smith* v. *Green* (1875) 1 C.P.D. 92 (breach of contract).

[51] *Doyle* v. *Olby (Ironmongers) Ltd.* [1969] 2 Q.B. 158; Treitel, 32 M.L.R. 526; *cf. Naughton* v. *O'Callaghan* [1990] 3 All E.R. 191. As to exemplary damages, see *post*, p. 829.

[52] *Post*, pp. 854–866.

[53] [1969] 2 Q.B. 158, 167.

[54] *Cf. Mullen* v. *Mason* (1866) L.R. 1 C.P. 559, 564; *Doyle* v. *Olby (Ironmongers) Ltd.* [1969] 2 Q.B. 158, 169.

[55] Especially after *The Heron II* [1969] 1 A.C. 350, *post*, p. 856. In *Archer* v. *Brown* [1985] Q.B. 401, 417–418 both tests were satisfied.

[56] *The Wagon Mound* [1961] A.C. 388; *cf. Esso Petroleum Co. Ltd.* v. *Mardon* [1976] Q.B. 801, 822.

[57] See *The Heron II* [1969] 1 A.C. 350; *post*, pp. 856–858.

[58] *Ante*, p. 314; *cf. Cooper* v. *Tamms* [1988] 1 E.G.L.R. 257, 263 (where the actual decision was that the defendant was not liable as there had been no reliance on the misrepresentation). *Royscott Trust Ltd.* v. *Rogerson*, *The Times*, April 3, 1991, where there seems to have been a difference of judicial opinion on the point.

[59] *Cf. Shepheard* v. *Broome* [1904] A.C. 342, 345, 346, where the House of Lords protested against being compelled by statute to treat a person who was morally innocent as if he were guilty of fraud.

(3) Misrepresentation Act 1967, section 2(2)

Under this subsection "damages" may be awarded in lieu of rescission even though the misrepresentation is wholly innocent[60] and even though it has no contractual force. There is, therefore, no reason for regarding these damages as being either tortious or contractual. They are really *sui generis*, and the subsection gives no clue as to the basis of assessment or as to the rules as to remoteness that govern an award under it. If the legislative history could be taken into account it would perhaps support the view that the contractual basis was not to be applied[61]; and indeed it seems unreasonable to make a person who has not guaranteed the truth of his representations liable as if he had. On the other hand, a person should not actually profit from even a wholly innocent non-contractual misrepresentation; and accordingly he should be liable for the amount by which the actual value of what he has transferred is less than the price received by him. So far as remoteness is concerned, the very strict deceit rule should obviously not apply against a misrepresentor who is wholly innocent; and it may be doubted whether he should be liable for consequential loss at all. The view that he should not be so liable can perhaps be supported by reference to section 2(3) which provides that damages may be awarded under subsection (2) against a person who is also liable under subsection (1), "but where he is so liable any award under the said subsection (2) shall be taken into account in assessing his liability under the said subsection (1)." It can be inferred from this that damages under subsection (2) are meant to be less than damages under subsection (1). One possible explanation for this may be that remoteness is governed by the deceit rule under subsection (1) and by the negligence rule under subsection (2). But if (as has been submitted above) remoteness under subsection (1) is in fact governed by the negligence rule, an alternative explanation must be found for the inference based on subsection (3); and this may be that consequential loss is not recoverable at all under subsection (2). The result would be that a wholly innocent misrepresentor would *only* be liable for the amount by which the actual value was less than the price; while a negligent misrepresentor could be made liable for this amount under subsection (1) or (2), and, in addition, for foreseeable consequential loss under subsection (1).

7. Limit of the Right to Damages

(1) Cases in which damages cannot be recovered

Although the availability of damages for misrepresentation has been greatly extended by *Hedley Byrne*'s case and the Misrepresentation Act, there is still no *right* to damages for a wholly innocent misrepresentation which has no contractual force. In the case of such a misrepresentation, the court has a discretionary power to award damages in lieu of rescission; but it cannot rescind the contract, or regard it as rescinded *and* award damages. If the representee wishes to rescind for a wholly innocent non-contractual misrepresentation, and if the court does not think it equitable

---

[60] *i.e.* even though it is neither fraudulent nor negligent and even though the representor has discharged the burden of proof under s.2(1).

[61] At one stage an amendment was introduced to apply the contractual basis to actions under s.2(2): Standing Committee G, February 23, 1966. But it was withdrawn without discussion.

to declare the contract subsisting and award damages in lieu of rescission, the old rule that damages cannot be recovered for innocent misrepresentation[62] will continue to apply. In such a case the representee may, however, be entitled to invoke the equitable jurisdiction to award an indemnity.

(2) Indemnity

In rescinding a contract, equity will so far as possible force each party to restore benefits received from the other. In the simplest case, the seller will have to restore the price and the buyer the thing sold. It is sometimes necessary, as part of the process of rescission, to go further and to order one party to "restore" a benefit not received directly by him. Suppose, for example, that a buyer rescinds after having, under the terms of the contract, paid the price to a third party. There is little doubt that in such a case rescission would entitle the buyer to recover the money so paid from the seller.[63]

On the same principle, the buyer can sometimes recover an "indemnity" in respect of certain expenses; while other expenses are regarded as damages and may therefore be irrecoverable in cases of wholly innocent non-contractual misrepresentation. The distinction can be illustrated by reference to *Whittington* v. *Seale-Hayne*.[64] The plaintiff had taken a lease of the defendant's premises for the purpose of breeding poultry; he had done so in reliance on a representation that the premises were in good sanitary condition. In fact the water supply was poisoned so that the plaintiff's manager became ill and most of the birds died. The defendant submitted to rescission and agreed to repay £20 in respect of rent and rates paid, and repairs done, by the plaintiff under the lease. On the other hand, claims for loss of profits and loss of stock were disallowed as they were clearly claims for damages. Further claims for removal expenses[65] and medical expenses were disallowed on the same ground: they were not claims for an indemnity, for such claims could be made only in respect of expenses incurred in discharging obligations *created* by the contract.[66] The important distinction is that between the money spent on rates and repairs on the one hand, and the removal and medical expenses on the other. It is that the lease obliged the tenant to pay rates and to do repairs, but not to move in and employ a manager. The tenant's undertaking to pay rates and to do repairs was really *part of the price* for the lease of the premises. If the lease had provided that the landlord should do these things, he would no doubt have charged a higher rent, which he would clearly have had to restore. He was under a similar liability in respect of part of the price not paid directly to him, or not paid in cash. The tenant's removal and medical expenses could not be regarded in this way. On the facts of the case a claim for damages under section 2(1) of the Misrepresentation Act would now almost certainly succeed[67]; but if the defendant could discharge the burden of proof under that subsection the plaintiff would still be restricted to a claim for an

---

62 *Ante*, p. 320.
63 Any question between seller and third party would not be the concern of the buyer.
64 (1900) 82 L.T. 49; 16 T.L.R. 181; 44 S.J. 229.
65 On this point, *cf. Redgrave* v. *Hurd* (1881) 20 Ch.D. 1.
66 For a possible extension of the right to necessary maintenance costs, see *Lagunas Nitrate Co.* v. *Lagunas Syndicate* [1899] 2 Ch. 392.
67 *Cf. ante*, p. 320, n. 24.

indemnity. He could not rescind *and* get damages under section 2(2) of the Act.

The distinction between indemnity and damages, it is submitted, is that stated in the preceding paragraph, but there is thought to be some conflict of opinion on the point in *Newbigging* v. *Adam*.[68] The plaintiff was induced by the defendants' fraud to enter into a partnership with them and another person. On rescinding the contract of partnership he was clearly entitled to get back the money which he had paid for his share. The Court of Appeal held that he was also entitled to be indemnified against his liability to pay debts incurred by the partnership.[69] The crucial point is that it is a term of a contract of partnership, or a legal incident of it,[70] that each partner is liable for the partnership debts. Hence any partner who pays such debts performs an obligation *under that contract*, though of course the debts also arise under another contract (*i.e.* that with the creditor of the partnership). Accordingly Cotton L.J. said that the plaintiff was entitled to an indemnity "against the obligations which he has *contracted under the contract which is set aside*."[71] Bowen L.J. similarly said that he was entitled to be restored to his original position "so far as regards the rights and obligations *created by the contract into which he has been induced to enter*."[72] Only Fry L.J. appears to state a broader view when he says that the plaintiff is entitled to an indemnity not only against obligations "created by" the contract but also against such "obligations *entered into under the contract* as are within the reasonable expectation of the parties to the contract."[73] What seems to have troubled Fry L.J. is that the *debts of the partnership* were not "created by" the contract of partnership. But the plaintiff's *liability to contribute to the payment of those debts* clearly was "created by" or "contracted under" that contract. In the context of *Newbigging* v. *Adam*, it is submitted that Fry L.J.'s statement does not conflict with the distinction drawn above between indemnity and damages. The point can be illustrated by supposing that the tenant in *Whittington* v. *Seale-Hayne*[74] had employed a builder to do the repairs and a furniture remover to move in his furniture. The debt to the builder would not of course have been "created by" the lease, but the tenant's obligation to repair was so created, thus entitling him to an indemnity against the cost of its performance: this would amount, prima facie, to the sum due to the builder. The debt to the furniture remover would simply have been incurred *in reliance* on the lease: it would obviously not have been "created by" the lease; nor even would it have been "entered into under" the lease within Fry L.J.'s formulation.

The grant of an indemnity amounts only to "working out the proper result of setting aside a contract in consequence of misrepresentation."[75] It is ancillary to rescission. It follows that if the right to rescind is barred, the court cannot grant an indemnity unless the misrepresentor consents to

---

[68] (1886) 34 Ch.D. 582.

[69] In the House of Lords it was held that the question of indemnity did not arise because the debt in question was not enforceable against the firm: *Adam* v. *Newbigging* (1888) 13 App.-Cas. 308.

[70] *Cf.* Partnership Act 1890, s.41.

[71] (1886) 34 Ch. 582, 589 (italics supplied).

[72] *Ibid.* pp. 592–593 (italics supplied).

[73] *Ibid.* p. 596 (italics supplied).

[74] *Ante*, p. 327.

[75] *Newbigging* v. *Adam, supra*, at p. 589.

rescission.[76] Where the right to rescind is barred, the court may[77] have no power to award damages in lieu of rescission; and if this is the position the victim of a wholly innocent misrepresentation might still be left, in such a case, without any remedy.

8. Compensation Orders in Criminal Cases

In this book our main concern is with civil liability. But misrepresentation may involve criminal liability, for example, where a person obtains property, services or a pecuniary advantage by deception,[78] or where, in the course of a trade or business, he applies a false trade description to goods or makes a false statement as to the provision of services or accommodation.[79] The court by or before which such a person is convicted may order the offender to pay compensation "for any . . . loss or damage resulting from that offence . . . ."[80] Such an order may be made even though the conduct constituting the offence does not give rise to any civil liability in damages[81]: for example where a person is convicted under the Theft Act 1968 or 1978 on account of a misrepresentation of law.[82] In the more common case where the criminal conduct also involves civil liability, the making of a compensation order is no bar to later civil proceedings. The damages in those proceedings will be *assessed* on normal principles, without reference to the order; but, to prevent double recovery, the sum so assessed will be reduced by the amount paid under the compensation order.[83]

SECTION 4. RESCISSION FOR MISREPRESENTATION

1. Introduction

It is impossible to understand the authorities on this subject without referring to the difference between the rules of common law and equity before the Judicature Acts 1873–1875.

At common law the general rule was that a contract could be rescinded *for misrepresentation* only on the ground of fraud; but this requirement of fraud was subject to several qualifications. If an innocent misrepresentation became a term of the contract, it might give rise to a right to rescind the contract *for breach*.[84] If it led to a fundamental *mistake* it might make the contract void so that each party could, on returning what he had got under the contract, recover back what he gave. This was sometimes called "rescinding" the contract, though strictly there was no need to rescind

---

[76] As in *Whittington* v. *Seale-Hayne* (1900) 16 T.L.R. 181, where the right to rescind was probably barred by the execution of the lease; see now *post*, p. 338.
[77] *Ante*, p. 326.
[78] Theft Act 1968, ss.15, 16; Theft Act 1978, ss.1, 5.
[79] Trade Descriptions Act 1968, ss.1, 14.
[80] Powers of Criminal Courts Act 1973, s.35, as amended by Criminal Justice Act 1988, s.104; *R.* v. *Oddy* [1974] 1 W.L.R. 1212; *R.* v. *Inwood* (1974) 60 Cr.App.R. 70. *Cf.* Financial Services Act 1986, ss.47, 61.
[81] *R.* v. *Chappell, The Times*, May 26, 1986.
[82] Theft Act 1968, s.15(4); Theft Act 1978 s.5(1).
[83] Powers of Criminal Courts Act 1973, s.38, as substituted by Criminal Justice Act 1988, s.105.
[84] *Post*, pp. 659 *et seq*.

since the contract was void *ab initio*.[85] Rescission was also available at common law in certain cases of *non-disclosure*.[86]

In equity, on the other hand, there was a general rule that a contract could be rescinded for "innocent misrepresentation"[87]; this phrase covered every misrepresentation which was not fraudulent, and so included negligent misrepresentation.[88] Now that the equitable rule prevails, the distinction between rescission at common law and in equity is of small (if any) importance; but the fact that the distinction once existed may account for some of the surviving differences between rescission for fraudulent and for innocent misrepresentation.

2. Various Meanings of "Rescission"

Bowen L.J. once said that "A fallacy may possibly lurk in the use of the word 'rescission' "[89]; and it is a great pity that subsequent lawmakers have not taken this observation to heart. The Misrepresentation Act, in particular, uses the expressions "rescind," "rescinded" and "rescission" without attempting to define them. They have in the past been used in a number of senses, and it is impossible to say that one of these rather than another is the "correct" one: "there is no primary meaning."[90] The following distinctions, in particular, are relevant in this Chapter.

(1) Rescission for misrepresentation and for breach

Where a misrepresentation is not a term of the contract, the process which may be referred to as "rescission for misrepresentation" amounts to setting the contract aside for all purposes,[91] so as to restore, as far as possible, the state of things which existed before the contract. Where, on the other hand, a misrepresentation has become a term of the contract[92] the victim of the misrepresentation may seek "rescission for breach," and this may also result in a restoration of the state of things which existed before the contract.[93] But there is a vital difference between the two processes.[94] Rescission for misrepresentation involves an allegation that there was a defect in the *formation* of the contract; and if this allegation is substantiated it follows that the contract is avoided *ab initio*. Rescission for breach, on the other hand, involves an allegation that there was a defect in the *performance* of the contract; and the existence of such a defect does not lead to the conclusion that the contract should be treated as if it had never existed. It follows that a party who rescinds for breach can also claim damages for breach of the contract[95]; while one who rescinds for misrep-

---

[85] See *Kennedy* v. *Panama, etc., Royal Mail Co. Ltd.* (1867) L.R. 2 Q.B. 580, 587, stating the common law position before the Judicature Acts.

[86] *Post*, p. 360; see, for example, *Ionides* v. *Pender* (1874) L.R. 9 Q.B. 531; the distinctions formerly drawn between various kinds of insurance are no longer of importance now that all policies can be rescinded in equity for innocent misrepresentation and non-disclosure: see *London Assurance* v. *Mansel* (1879) 11 Ch.D. 363, 367.

[87] See *Redgrave* v. *Hurd* (1881) 20 Ch.D. 1.

[88] *Ante*, pp. 304, 312.

[89] *Mersey Steel and Iron Co.* v. *Naylor Benzon & Co.* (1882) 9 Q.B.D. 648, 671.

[90] *Buckland* v. *Farmar & Moody* [1979] 1 W.L.R. 221, 232.

[91] *The Kachenjunga* [1990] 1 Lloyd's Rep. 391, 398 ("wipe it out altogether").

[92] *Post*, p. 336.

[93] *Post*, p. 927.

[94] *Johnson* v. *Agnew* [1980] A.C. 367, 392–393; *cf. Buckland* v. *Farmar & Moody* [1979] 1 W.L.R. 221, 232.

[95] *Post*, p. 748.

resentation has, by treating the contract as if it never existed, prima facie lost the right to claim damages for its breach.[96] If such a conclusion were to cause hardship to the representee the court could exercise its discretion under section 2(2) of the Misrepresentation Act to declare the contract subsisting.[97]

(2) Rescinding and pleading misrepresentation as a defence

A party who "rescinds" a contract (whether for misrepresentation or for breach) may take active steps to this end: *e.g.* by seeking the cancellation of the contract, or a declaration of its invalidity, or the return of money or property with which he has parted under the contract, on restoring what he obtained under it. Alternatively he may simply rely on the misrepresentation (or breach) as a defence to an action on the contract; and this process is not necessarily governed by the same rules as the active process of rescission.[98]

3. Rescission for Misrepresentation

(1) Contract voidable

The general rule is that misrepresentation makes the contract voidable at the option of the representee.[99] In *Redgrave* v. *Hurd*,[1] for instance, the defendant was induced to buy a solicitor's house and practice by an innocent misrepresentation as to the value of the practice. It was held that he could rescind the contract and so get back the deposit he had paid.

Misrepresentation makes a contract voidable and not void[2]; and this has important effects on the rights of third parties. If a person obtains goods under a contract which is void for mistake, property in the goods may not pass to him so that the goods can be recovered by the owner from a third person into whose hands they have come.[3] But if a person obtains goods under a contract which is only voidable for misrepresentation, a voidable title passes to him and the former owner's right to avoid it is lost when an innocent third party for value acquires an interest in the goods.[4]

The position of the third party in such cases should be contrasted with that of a third party to whom a chose in action[5] is assigned. The assignee takes "subject to equities"[6] and one such "equity" is the possibility of rescission for misrepresentation. Thus if A induces B to sell him a gold

[96] *Cf.* the rule that a party cannot rescind in part while affirming some particular term of the contract: *post*, p. 344.

[97] *Ante*, p. 321. See further *post*, p. 337.

[98] *Post*, pp. 333–334.

[99] *Clough* v. *L. & N.W. Ry.* (1871) L.R. 7 Ex. 26, 34; *Urquhart* v. *Macpherson* (1878) 3 App.-Cas. 831, 838; *cf. Whittaker* v. *Campbell* [1984] Q.B. 319 (where, however, the distinctions drawn in the law of contract were said at p. 329 not to be decisive in criminal law).

[1] (1881) 20 Ch.D. 1.

[2] See the authorities cited in n. 4 below; for a contrary dictum, see *Pilgrim* v. *Rice-Smith* [1977] 1 W.L.R. 671, 675; Phillips, 93 L.Q.R. 497.

[3] *e.g. Cundy* v. *Lindsay* (1878) 3 App.Cas. 459; *ante*, p. 262.

[4] *White* v. *Garden* (1851) 10 C.B. 919; *Stevenson* v. *Newnham* (1853) 13 C.B. 285; the third party must give value: *Scholefield* v. *Templer* (1859) 4 D. & J. 429; and see generally *ante*, pp. 262–266.

[5] For the meaning of "chose in action," see *post*, p. 576.

[6] *Post*, p. 592; *cf.* Marine Insurance Act 1906, s.50(2); *William Pickersgill & Sons Ltd.* v. *London & Provincial Marine, etc. Insurance Co. Ltd.* [1912] 3 K.B. 614 (non-disclosure).

watch on credit by some fraud (not giving rise to a fundamental mistake) and pledges the watch to C, C's right to retain the watch is not affected by A's fraud. But if A by fraud induces B to buy a worthless watch, said to be of gold, and assigns the benefit of B's promise to pay for it to C as security for a loan, C's right to sue B is affected by A's fraud.[7]

It looks at first sight strange that the third party's position should depend on whether the fraudulent person was buyer or seller. One reason for treating the two cases differently may be that the law gives greater protection to proprietary than to contractual rights; and this distinction could be justified by saying that the assignee of a chose in action takes a greater business risk than the pledgee of a chattel. But some cases will still cause difficulty. For example, a person may fraudulently induce a company to allot shares to him and then sell them to an innocent third party. It is disputed whether shares are to be regarded as choses in action or as property in possession,[8] and it is therefore not clear whether the third party would take subject to the company's "equity" of rescission, or whether the company's right to rescind would be barred by the third party's acquisition of a proprietary interest.

(2) Mode of rescission

Sometimes a contract is rescinded by bringing legal proceedings, but rescission can also be effected quite informally, by simply giving notice to the other party. Legal proceedings may, however, be necessary to work out the consequences of rescission. This is most obviously true where, as a result of rescission, a sum of money becomes due to the representee and the representor refuses to pay it. It may also be desirable to have a court order stating that a formal transaction (such as a lease or a transfer of shares) has been or ought to be set aside. Even in such a case rescission is the act of the representee and not that of the court, so that the time at which it takes effect is when the representee gives the notice or commences legal proceedings—not the time of the court's order.[9] In other cases no legal proceedings are necessary to give effect to the consequences of rescission: thus where goods have been obtained by fraud rescission can be effected by simply taking them back.[10]

All these modes of rescission involve some degree of notice to the representor; but it has been held that this is not always necessary. In *Car & Universal Finance Co. Ltd.* v. *Caldwell*[11] the owner of a car was induced by fraud to sell it to a rogue who absconded and could not be traced. On discovering the fraud, the owner notified the police and the Automobile Association and asked them for help in recovering the car. It was held that these acts were enough to rescind the contract, so that an innocent third party who later bought the car got no title to it. It would no doubt be hard on the owner to hold that he could only rescind by communicating with the rogue, for this would deprive him of the right to rescind whenever the rogue disappears. But the actual decision is equally hard on the third

---

[7] Good faith on the part of C is assumed in both examples.
[8] See Gower, *Modern Company Law* (4th ed.), pp. 397–401.
[9] *Reese Silver Mining Co.* v. *Smith* (1869) L.R. 4 H.L. 64.
[10] *Re Eastgate* [1905] 1 K.B. 465.
[11] [1965] 1 Q.B. 525.

party[12]; and the Law Reform Committee has recommended that it should be reversed.[13] It only applies where the representor has disappeared or for some other reason cannot be reached.[14]

The general principles determining the mode of rescission apply whether the representation is fraudulent or negligent or innocent. But in *Caldwell's* case the Court of Appeal left open the question whether the rule there laid down applies where the misrepresentation is negligent. The question is perhaps academic since negligent representors are not likely to go into hiding; but it is submitted that the rule can only be justified, if at all, by the strong need to protect victims of fraud and that it should not be applied in cases of negligent or wholly innocent misrepresentation. It is also questionable whether the rule that a contract can be rescinded by simply taking back goods delivered under it should be applied except in cases of fraud.

(3) Misrepresentation as a defence

The operation of misrepresentation as a defence to an action to enforce the contract is illustrated by further reference to *Redgrave* v. *Hurd.*[15] The defendant there successfully relied on the misrepresentations as to the value of the practice by way of defence to the vendor's claim for specific performance.

Since this process of pleading misrepresentation as a defence is a form of "rescission"[16] it is, in general, subject to the requirement that the representee must return what he got under the contract.[17] But this requirement does not always apply where the representor is guilty of actual fraud. For example where a ship was insured after she had, to the knowledge of the assured, been lost, it was held that the insurer could repudiate liability under the policy on the ground of fraud, and also keep the premiums.[18] The result is to leave the insurer with a windfall; but the rule may perhaps be justified by the strong need to discourage fraud.[19] Even this justification

---

[12] Such a third party may, in appropriate circumstances, be protected by s.25 of the Sale of Goods Act 1979. *Newtons of Wembley Ltd.* v. *Williams* [1965] 1 Q.B. 560; but the scope of this protection is limited: see Thornley [1965] C.L.J. 24.

[13] 12th Report (1966) Cmnd. 2958, para. 16; *cf. Macleod* v. *Ker*, 1965 S.C. 253, where the Court of Session decided a very similar case in favour of the third party, saying at p. 257: "By no stretch of imagination could we treat an intimation to the police as of any materiality to found a plea of rescission of contract." *Caldwell's* case was not mentioned.

[14] *Empresa Cubana de Fletes* v. *Lagonisi Shipping Co. Ltd.* [1971] 1 Q.B. 488, 505 (actual decision overruled in *The Laconia* [1977] A.C. 850).

[15] (1881) 20 Ch.D. 1.

[16] *Ante*, p. 331.

[17] *Ante*, p. 331; *post*, p. 338.

[18] See *Tyler* v. *Horne* (1785) and *Chapman* v. *Fraser* (1795), related in *Park on Marine Insurance* (8th ed.), pp. 455, 456; *Feise* v. *Parkinson* (1812) 4 Taunt. 639, 641; *Anderson* v. *Thornton* (1853) 8 Exch. 425, 428; MacGillivray & Parkington *Insurance Law* (8th ed.), §§ 1004, 1026–1028; Colinvaux, *Law of Insurance* (5th ed.), p. 132. *Contra, Fowkes* v. *Manchester, etc., Assurance* (1863) 3 B. & S. 917, 929, where Blackburn J. is reported to have said that in cases of *fraudulent* misrepresentation the premiums could be recovered back. But the corresponding passages in 11 W.R. 622, 623 and 8 L.T. 309, 311 refer to *innocent* misrepresentation; and these reports are to be preferred as they make the statement consistent with the earlier authorities, from which Blackburn J. showed no intention of departing. See also Marine Insurance Act 1906, s.84(1) and (3), restating the common law rule.

[19] If the assured could recover back the premiums, the only risk to which he would be exposed under the civil law would be that of not being able to sue on the policy; and where he had already lost the property this would be no risk at all.

is, however, hard to square with the further rule that, if the insurer takes the initiative by suing for rescission, he does have to return the premiums.[20] This is also the position where he relies on a negligent or wholly innocent misrepresentation as a defence[21]; unless the policy provides for forfeiture of premiums if *any* false statement is made in the proposal form.[22]

A further situation in which a person can plead fraud as a defence without restoring what he has obtained under the contract is illustrated by *Berg* v. *Sadler & Moore*.[23] The plaintiff was a retail tobacconist, and knew that the defendants (who were wholesalers) would not supply him as he had been put on a stop-list[24] for price-cutting. He therefore sent one Reece to the defendants to buy cigarettes, ostensibly in his own name. Reece paid with money supplied by the plaintiff but when the defendants discovered the true facts they refused to deliver the cigarettes or to pay back the price. A claim by the plaintiff for the return of the price failed, so that (as in the insurance cases discussed above) the defendants were left with a windfall. The court justified this result on the ground that the plaintiff had been engaged in an attempt to perpetrate a *criminal* fraud; and the rule seems to be based on the supposed need to deter such fraud, though it is far from clear why adequate deterrence is not provided by the criminal law. The rule would probably not apply where the fraud was not criminal: *e.g.* where a statement was made with knowledge of its falsity but without dishonest intent.[25] The rule should certainly not apply where the misrepresentation was only negligent or where it was innocent.

(4) Application to sale of goods

It has been doubted whether the equitable remedy of rescission for innocent misrepresentation applies at all to a contract for sale of goods.[26] The remedy is not mentioned in the Sale of Goods Act 1979, and in *Re Wait* Atkin L.J. said that "the total sum of legal relations (meaning by the word 'legal' existing in equity as well as in common law) arising out of the contract for the sale of goods may well be regarded as defined by the Code."[27] Section 62(2) of the Act admittedly saves the rules of "common law" so far as they are not inconsistent with the Act, but it has been held in other jurisdictions that "common law" here does not include equity, and that the equitable right to rescind a contract for the sale of goods for innocent misrepresentation has not (if it ever existed) survived the Act.[28] But it is submitted that this view should be rejected for the following reasons.

First: the Act plainly does not deal with every aspect of a contract for the

[20] *Barker* v. *Walters* (1844) 8 Beav. 92, 96; *London Assurance* v. *Mansel* (1879) 11 Ch.D. 363; *cf. The Litsian Pride* [1985] 1 Lloyd's Rep. 437, 515. *Quaere* whether an insurer who only claims a *declaration* that he is entitled to avoid the policy on the ground of fraud (as in *Fire, etc., Insurance* v. *Greene* [1964] 2 Q.B. 687) must return the premiums.

[21] *Feise* v. *Parkinson* (1812) 4 Taunt. 639; *Anderson* v. *Thornton* (1853) 8 Exch. 425.

[22] *Kumar* v. *Life Insurance Corp. of India* [1974] 1 Lloyd's Rep. 147; Hasson, 38 M.L.R. 93.

[23] [1937] 2 K.B. 158; Allen, 54 L.Q.R. 201; Goodhart, *ibid.* 216; Treitel in *Essays in Memory of Sir Rupert Cross*, pp. 107–108.

[24] This practice is now unlawful: *post*, p. 569.

[25] See *Polhill* v. *Walter* (1832) 3 B. & Ad. 114, *ante*, p. 308.

[26] Atiyah, 22 M.L.R. 76; but see his *Sale of Goods* (8th ed.), pp. 520–521.

[27] [1927] 1 Ch. 606, 635.

[28] *Riddiford* v. *Warren* (1901) 20 N.Z.L.R. 572; followed in *Watt* v. *Westhoven* [1933] V.L.R. 458.

sale of goods. It does not, for example, deal with assignment but clearly the benefit of a contract for the sale of goods can be assigned.[29] The Act can only deal exhaustively with the topics to which its enacting sections refer. One of those topics, admittedly, is remedies and Atkin L.J. said that the rules contained in the Act as to (*inter alia*) the "remedies" of the parties appear to be "complete and exclusive statements of the legal relations both at law and in equity."[30] Even this may, with respect, be doubted. Breach of a contract for the sale of goods may be restrained by injunction,[31] and such a contract may be rectified,[32] although these remedies are not mentioned in the Act. In any event, it seems that Atkin L.J. used the term "remedies" in the sense in which it is used in Part VI of the Act, *i.e.* to mean remedies *for breach* of contract[33]; and rescission for misrepresentation is not such a remedy.[34] In an earlier case, Atkin J. himself had said that, if the seller had made a misrepresentation, the buyer "would be entitled to rescind the contract."[35]

Secondly: it is submitted that in section 62(2) "common law" does include equity. The subsection saves the rules of "common law" . . . relating to the law of principal and agent and the effect of fraud, *misrepresentation*, duress or coercion, mistake, *or other invalidating cause*." Misrepresentation is here regarded as an invalidating cause distinct from fraud and mistake. But at common law an innocent misrepresentation did not invalidate a contract for the sale of goods,[36] unless it induced a fundamental mistake. Hence the saving of the rules as to the effect of misrepresentation can only refer to the rules of equity. Moreover, it would be strange if the Act saved the rules of common law, but not those of equity, relating to mistake and agency.

Thirdly: the authorities support the view that a contract for the sale of goods can be rescinded for innocent misrepresentation. In *Leaf* v. *International Galleries*[37] and *Long* v. *Lloyd*[38] the right to rescind such contracts for innocent misrepresentation was held to be barred—in the first case by lapse of time and in the second by acceptance.[39] The decision in each case was that the right to rescind had been lost: not that it never existed. In *Goldsmith* v. *Roger*[40] a contract for the sale of a boat was induced by an innocent[41] misrepresentation of the buyer; and it was held that the seller could "rescind" in the sense of being able to rely on the misrepresentation as a defence.

---

[29] *Re Wait* [1927] 1 Ch. 606, 636.
[30] *Ibid.*
[31] See *post*, pp. 923–924.
[32] *e.g. Caraman, Rowley & May* v. *Aperghis* (1928) 40 T.L.R. 124; the same assumption was made (though the claim for rectification failed) in *F. E. Rose (London) Ltd.* v. *W. H. Pim Jr. & Co. Ltd.* [1953] 2 Q.B. 450, *ante*, pp. 228–229.
[33] See the sub-headings before ss.49 and 51.
[34] Unless Atkin L.J.'s remarks are interpreted in this way the first three sections of the Misrepresentation Act would not apply to contracts for the sale of goods; but obviously no court would reach this conclusion.
[35] *Re Harrison & Micks, Lambert & Co.* [1917] 1 K.B. 755, 761.
[36] *Ante*, p. 329. Negligent misrepresentation was not recognised as a separate category in 1893, when the Sale of Goods Act was originally passed.
[37] [1950] 2 K.B. 86.
[38] [1958] 1 W.L.R. 753.
[39] *Cf. post*, pp. 343–344.
[40] [1962] 2 Lloyd's Rep. 249.
[41] *i.e.* not fraudulent: *cf. ante*, pp. 304, 312, 330.

Fourthly: if a contract for the sale of goods could not be rescinded for innocent misrepresentation the injured party would have no remedy at all for an innocent misrepresentation not incorporated in the contract. Such an unjust result ought not to be reached in the absence of a clear statutory provision to that effect.

4. Incorporated Misrepresentation

(1) Misrepresentation Act 1967, section 1(a)

Before the Misrepresentation Act it was clear that a person could rescind a contract for a misrepresentation which did *not* form part of the contract; but it was doubtful whether this right to rescind survived where the misrepresentation was later incorporated in the contract as one of its terms.[42] Section 1(*a*) of the Act now provides that a person shall be entitled to rescind notwithstanding that the misrepresentation has become a term of the contract if he would otherwise be entitled to rescind without alleging fraud. This right to rescind will therefore normally[43] exist when a statement of fact (as opposed to a promise) is made to induce a contract and later becomes one of its terms. But section 1(*a*) does not take away any remedies for breach of contract; and the relation between these remedies and the statutory right to rescind is obscure.

Apart from the Misrepresentation Act, breach of contract gives rise sometimes to a right to damages only, and sometimes to a right to damages and also to a right to treat the contract as repudiated, or, in other words, to "rescind for breach."[44] Where an incorporated misrepresentation gives rise to a right to damages *and* to a right to rescind for breach, these rights can presumably still be exercised independently of section 1 (and the right to rescind for breach is probably unaffected by section 2(2)).[45] Where the incorporated misrepresentation gives rise (apart from the Act) to a right to damages only, the representee can ignore his right to rescind under the Act and claim damages for breach of contract. But it is not clear whether he can still claim such damages if he does "rescind" under section 1(*a*). If "rescind" here refers to "rescission for misrepresentation" it is arguable that such rescission destroys all outstanding liabilities under the contract, including liability in damages for its breach. This view might cause hardship where a representee has rescinded out of court (*e.g.* by returning defective goods) but the court could probably come to his rescue by declaring the contract subsisting under section 2(2) of the Act. It is true that damages in lieu of rescission under that subsection may be less than damages for breach of contract[46]; but one effect of declaring the contract subsisting might be to revive the right to damages for breach of contract, *i.e.* for the untruth of the incorporated misrepresentation.[47]

---

[42] See *Cie Française de Chemin de Fer Paris-Orléans* v. *Leeston Shipping Co.* (1919) 1 Ll.L.R. 235; *Pennsylvania Shipping Co.* v. *Cie Nationale de Navigation* (1936) 155 L.T. 294.
[43] *I.e.* subject to the principles stated in Section 2 of this Chapter.
[44] *Ante*, p. 330; *post*, pp. 659 *et seq*.
[45] *Infra*, next heading
[46] *Ante*, p. 326.
[47] A possibility which was overlooked in 30 M.L.R. at p. 372.

(2) Misrepresentation Act 1967, section 2(2)

This subsection, which gives the court a discretion to declare the contract subsisting, and award damages in lieu of rescission,[48] may limit the right to rescind for an incorporated misrepresentation. Where the representee does not rescind but simply claims damages for breach of contract, the subsection clearly has no effect, for the court's discretion depends on a claim having been made "that the contract ought to be or has been rescinded." Where the representee does claim "rescission" it is first necessary to ask what would be the effect of the incorporated misrepresentation viewed purely as a breach of contract. If its only effect as a breach would be to give rise to a right of damages, any claim to "rescind" must be a claim to "rescind for misrepresentation" which is subject to the discretion of the court, so that the court could refuse to allow rescission and confine the plaintiff to a claim for damages. If on the other hand, the effect of the incorporated misrepresentation as a breach would be to give rise to a right to damages and also to a right to "rescind for breach," the position is less clear. One view is that a representee who treats the contract as repudiated thereby claims "that the contract ought to be or has been rescinded"; and this view has the attraction that it enables the court to restrict the right to "rescind for breach" which has sometimes been exercised by parties who have not suffered any appreciable loss as a result of the breach.[49] On the other hand there is no hint in the legislative history of the Act that any such reform was intended; and if such a change in the law has been made it would be an extraordinarily partial one, for it would only apply to breaches resulting from representations *of fact* made before the contract (and not to breaches of *promises*). The better view seems to be that "rescinded" in section 2(2) refers only to "rescission for misrepresentation" as the subsection deals with the case of a person "who is entitled, *by reason of the misrepresentation* to rescind the contract"; and that, accordingly, the right to "rescind for breach" is not subject to the discretion of that court.

SECTION 5. LIMITS TO THE RIGHT TO RESCIND

The right to rescind a contract may be barred by a number of factors. Before these are considered, two points must be made with regard to the effects of the Misrepresentation Act 1967.

1. Effects of Misrepresentation Act 1967

First, the Act has abrogated one restriction on the right to rescind. Before the Act, it had been held that certain contracts could not be rescinded for innocent misrepresentation after they had been "executed." This rule applied, in particular, where a contract for the disposition of an interest in land was performed by execution of the conveyance or lease[50]; and where a contract for the sale of shares was performed by transfer of the shares.[51] But most applications[52] of the rule were hard to justify, and its scope was

---

[48] *Ante*, p. 320.
[49] See, for example, *post*, pp. 680, 695.
[50] *Angel* v. *Jay* [1911] 1 K.B. 666 (lease).
[51] *Seddon* v. *North Eastern Salt Co.* [1905] 1 Ch. 326.
[52] *e.g.* in the cases cited in the last two notes. The rule may have served some useful purpose in relation to contracts for the sale of land and to long leases: *cf.* Law Reform Committee 10th Report Cmnd. 1782 (1962) paras. 6 and 7.

uncertain. It was reversed by section 1(*b*) of the Act, which provides that a person who would otherwise be entitled to rescind a contract for misrepresentation without alleging fraud[53] shall be so entitled notwithstanding that the contract has been performed. The buyer of a house can therefore rescind for misrepresentation even after conveyance and even though the misrepresentation was wholly innocent.

Secondly, the right to rescind a contract for misrepresentation is now subject to the discretion of the court under section 2(2) of the Act.[54] In the case just put, of a house-purchaser claiming rescission for wholly innocent misrepresentation, the court might well prefer to declare the contract subsisting and to award damages in lieu of rescission. For if (as would often be the case) the vendor had used the purchase-money to buy another house, rescission might cause him severe hardship. This would be a factor which the court could take into account under section 2(2),[55] so that rescission would probably be allowed only where the buyer had suffered very serious prejudice as a result of the misrepresentation. Section 2(2) may, similarly, operate in cases which are not precisely covered by the bars to rescission but in which the court nevertheless considers that damages would be a more appropriate remedy than rescission. It is, however, still necessary to define the bars to rescission because if one of them has arisen the court has *no* discretion to allow rescission and, on one possible interpretation of section 2(2),[56] cannot award damages either.

2. Bars to Rescission

(1) Restitution impossible

Normally, a party who wishes to rescind a contract for misrepresentation is required to restore to the other any benefits that he has obtained under the contract: for example, a buyer who wants to rescind with a view to getting back the price must give back the goods. If the benefit obtained is a sum of money[57] there is never any difficulty in complying with this requirement: the representee restores an equivalent sum. However, where he has obtained a benefit other than money, he may for some reason be unable to restore it; and this impossibility of restitution will sometimes bar the right to rescind.

(a) CHANGES MADE BY MISREPRESENTEE. Where a contract of sale has been induced by a misrepresentation of the seller, the buyer may lose the right to rescind if he has so changed the subject-matter that he can no longer restore what he obtained under the contract. An obvious illustration is provided by the case of the buyer of an animal who has slaughtered it: he cannot rescind on returning the corpse.[58] Similarly, the purchaser of a business cannot get back his purchase-money after carrying on the business for four

---

[53] The rule that an executed contract could not be rescinded never applied to cases of fraudulent misrepresentation, so that it was not necessary to change the law in such cases.

[54] *Ante*, p. 321. Rescission was said to be a discretionary remedy even before the 1967 Act: see *Spence* v. *Crawford* [1939] 3 All E.R. 271, 288; but this principle would be hard to apply to rescission by some extra-judicial act of the representee (*ante*, pp. 332–333).

[55] *Ante*, p. 321.

[56] *Ante*, pp. 321–322.

[57] Or the release of an obligation to pay money, as in *The Siboen and the Sibotre* [1976] 1 Lloyd's Rep. 293; see esp. p. 337.

[58] *Clarke* v. *Dickson* (1858) E.B. & E. 148, 155.

months and disposing of some of its assets,[59] or after changing a partnership into a limited company[60]; nor can the purchaser of a mine rescind after he has worked it out.[61] On the same principle a person cannot rescind after he has disposed of the subject-matter of the contract unless, perhaps, he has been able to get it back.[62]

(b) DETERIORATION OR DECLINE IN VALUE. In the cases discussed above, deterioration or decline in value barred the right to rescind because it was due to the acts of the representee. Where it is due to other causes, different rules apply. The right to rescind is clearly not barred where the subject-matter deteriorates precisely because it lacks a quality that it was represented to possess. Thus a person who is induced to enter into a partnership by a misrepresentation as to its solvency can still rescind after the bankruptcy of the firm.[63] The position is the same where the deterioration or decline in value is not related to the misrepresentation but is due to some external cause. In *Armstrong* v. *Jackson*[64] a broker purported to buy shares for a client, but in fact sold his own shares to the client. Five years later, when the shares had fallen in value from nearly £3 to 5s., it was held that the client could rescind. He still had the identical shares and was able to return them, together with the dividends he had received. McCardie J. said: "It is only . . . where the plaintiff has sustained loss by the inferiority of the subject-matter or a substantial fall in its value that he will desire to exert his power of rescission. . . . If mere deterioration of the subject-matter negatived the right to rescind, the doctrine of rescission would become a vain thing."[65]

Similarly, a contractual right to reject is not lost simply because the subject-matter deteriorates without the fault of the party claiming to rescind. In *Head* v. *Tattersall*[66] the buyer of a horse was allowed to return it for breach of "warranty"[67] although it had been seriously injured through no fault of his. Bramwell B. added that the right to reject would not be lost if "the injury were caused by reason of a trial necessary to test the warranty."[68] It is submitted that these rules also apply where the buyer is induced to buy by a misrepresentation which has been incorporated in the contract.[69]

(c) CHANGES MADE BY MISREPRESENTOR. In the cases considered, the misrepresentation was that of the seller; and the question was whether the buyer (*i.e.* misrepresent*ee*) could rescind even though he could not restore the subject-matter in its original state. A sale may also be induced by a misrepresentation on the part of the buyer, *e.g.* as to his solvency or as to the value of the subject-matter. The question then arises whether the seller's

---

59 *Sheffield Nickel Co. Ltd.* v. *Unwin* (1877) 2 Q.B.D. 215.
60 *Clarke* v. *Dickson* (1858) E.B. & E. 148; *quaere* whether this is *per se* decisive; *Western Bank of Scotland* v. *Addie* (1867) L.R. 1 Sc. & Div. 145, 159.
61 *Clarke* v. *Dickson, supra*; *Lagunas Nitrate Co.* v. *Lagunas Syndicate* [1899] 2 Ch. 392.
62 This suggestion might cause difficulty where the plaintiff has on a falling market bought the subject-matter back for less than the amount for which he had previously sold it, so that he would actually make a profit out of rescission: see *Marr* v. *Tumulty* 175 N.E. 356 (1931).
63 *Adam* v. *Newbigging* (1886) 34 Ch.D. 582; (1888) 13 App.Cas. 308.
64 [1917] 2 K.B. 822.
65 At p. 829.
66 (1871) L.R. 7 Ex. 7.
67 *i.e.* a "condition" in the modern terminology used at *post*, p. 689.
68 (1871) L.R. Ex. 7, 12.
69 *Cf. Long* v. *Lloyd* [1958] 1 W.L.R. 753, 760.

right to rescind is affected by some dealing with the subject-matter by the buyer (who in such a case is the misrepresent*or*). Obviously, it may be so affected in a practical sense where the buyer actually consumes the property or so alters it that the seller has no interest in getting it back. As a matter of law, however, a buyer who is guilty of fraud cannot rely on his own dealings[70] with the subject-matter as a bar to the seller's right to rescind. In *Spence* v. *Crawford*[71] A was induced by the fraud of B to enter into a contract by which (i) A sold to B shares in a company, and (ii) B undertook to relieve A of his liability under a guarantee of the company's bank overdraft, and to procure the release of securities deposited by A with the bank. A duly transferred the shares, while B relieved A of his liability to the bank and freed the securities by giving his own personal guarantee to the bank. The constitution of the company was later altered and some of the shares in it were sold. It was held that this dealing with the shares did not bar A's right to rescind. The question whether it would have had this effect if B's misrepresentation had been innocent was left open.[72]

(d) Benefit to misrepresentee. The mere fact that the misrepresentee has received a benefit under the contract does not bar his right to rescind, if the misrepresentor has not been put to any expense in conferring that benefit. Thus in *Spence* v. *Crawford* the fact that B had relieved A of his liability to the bank and freed his securities did not bar A's right to rescind. B was not put to any expense *by merely giving* the guarantee the bank, nor was he ever asked to pay anything under it, as the company prospered. We shall see that B did suffer some loss as a result of giving his guarantee, but this did not bar A's claim to rescind as he was able to make allowance for it.[73]

Conversely, a right to rescind is not lost *merely* because the representor has acted on the contract to his prejudice. In *Mackenzie* v. *Royal Bank of Canada*[74] a wife was induced by misrepresentation to deposit share certificates with a bank as security for the overdraft of a company controlled by her husband. She was able to rescind although the bank had, after the deposit, advanced further money to the company. She did not have to "restore" this money as it had not been received by her. It is sometimes said that the object of rescission is to restore the parties to the situation in which they would have been if the contract had never been made,[75] but in the light of *Mackenzie*'s case such statements are not quite accurate. The essence of the requirement of restitution is that the representee should not be unjustly enriched at the representor's expense. That the representor should not be prejudiced is a secondary consideration, which is only taken into account when some benefit has been received by the representee.

(e) Precise restitution impossible. The general rule that a representee had to restore what he had got under the contract was very strictly applied at common law where a person sought to recover his money on rescission *for breach*. The rule was so strict that a person who had agreed to buy an interest in land lost the right to get his money back merely by going into

---

70 Nor on the other party's dealings at his request: *cf. Hulton* v. *Hulton* [1917] 1 K.B. 813 (destruction of letters).
71 [1939] 3 All E.R. 271.
72 At p. 281. The effect of negligence in such a situation is also unclear.
73 *Post*, p. 341.
74 [1934] A.C. 468.
75 *e.g. Gillett* v. *Peppercorne* (1840) 3 Beav. 78, 81.

possession under the contract. The benefit of even such temporary possession was thought to make restitution impossible.[76] The authorities supporting this rule were sometimes cited in cases of rescission *for misrepresentation*[77]; though it is by no means clear whether the strict common law rule ever extended to such cases. The point is no longer of any importance, since a more flexible rule was developed by equity in cases of misrepresentation, and this rule now prevails.

In equity a representee who is able to make substantial, though not precise, restitution can rescind if he returns the subject-matter of the contract in its altered state, accounts for any profits derived from it and makes allowance for deterioration caused by his dealing with it. Thus a person who has gone into possession under a contract to buy, or take a lease of, land can rescind[78] on terms of paying rent for the period of his occupation.[79] Similarly, in *Erlanger* v. *New Sombrero Phosphate Co.*[80] a company bought and worked a phosphate mine, but did not so work it out as to make restitution utterly impossible. It was held that the company could rescind the sale for breach of fiduciary duty by one of its promoters on terms of returning the mine and accounting for the profits of working it. Lord Blackburn said that equity could "take accounts of profits and make allowance for deterioration. And I think the practice has always been for a court of equity to give this relief whenever, by the exercise of its powers, it can do what is practically just, though it cannot restore the parties precisely to the state they were in before the contract."[81]

These powers of adjustment are normally exercised where the misrepresentee is a buyer who claims back his money. They may also be available in the converse case where the misrepresentee is a seller who claims back his property, as in *Spence* v. *Crawford*.[82] The fraudulent buyer in that case had performed his contractual undertaking to relieve the seller of certain obligations to a bank. He was asked by the bank to sell some stock to maintain his liquidity, and the sale resulted in a loss to him of £1,000. The final order made in that case was that the seller should recover back his shares plus the dividends received by the buyer; but that he should repay the purchase price plus interest, and make allowance in respect of part[83] of the £1,000 lost by the buyer on the sale of his stock.

When ordering rescission the court can set off benefits received by one party against those received by the other. In *Hulton* v. *Hulton*,[84] a wife set aside a separation deed on the ground of the husband's fraud. It was held that she need not repay £500 per annum which she had received under the

---

[76] *Hunt* v. *Silk* (1804) 5 East 449; *Blackburn* v. *Smith* (1848) 2 Ex. 783 (both cases of pure breach); *post*, pp. 928–929.

[77] *e.g.* in *Clarke* v. *Dickson* (1858) E.B. & E. 148.

[78] *Redgrave* v. *Hurd* (1881) 20 Ch.D. 1.

[79] *Hulton* v. *Hulton* [1917] 1 K.B. 813, 826. It seems that no such terms were imposed in *Redgrave* v. *Hurd, supra* where the buyer got back the whole of his deposit in spite of having been in possession for a short time.

[80] (1878) 3 App.Cas. 1218; *cf. Gillett* v. *Peppercorne* (1840) 3 Beav. 78; *The Lucy* [1983] 1 Lloyd's Rep. 188, 202.

[81] At pp. 1278–1279; approved in *Guiness plc* v. *Saunders* [1990] 2 A.C. 663, 698, but distinguished as the agreement in the latter case was not voidable but void.

[82] [1939] 3 All E.R. 271; *ante*, p. 340.

[83] This seems to have been a compromise, adopted to avoid the need to take complicated cross-accounts.

[84] [1917] 1 K.B. 813.

deed since the husband had received corresponding advantages, *viz.* freedom from his obligation to maintain the wife, and the destruction of certain letters at his request. But she had to account for a debt owed by her to the husband which had been released by the deed, since no benefit corresponding to this release had been received by the husband.

(f) IMPROVEMENTS IN THE SUBJECT-MATTER. In the cases so far discussed, it has been assumed that the dealings with the subject-matter have decreased its value. They may also improve it; and this possibility gives rise to two problems. The first is whether such dealings bar the right to rescind; the second is what allowance (if any) is to be awarded in respect of the improvements. These may be made either by the misrepresentee or by the misrepresentor.

(i) *Made by the Misrepresentee.* One illustration of this possibility is provided by *Boyd & Forrest* v. *Glasgow & S.W. Ry.*[85] Contractors alleged that they had been induced to enter into a contract to build a railway by misrepresentations as to the strata. After the railway had been built, they claimed to rescind, with a view to recovering a *quantum meruit* (exceeding the contract price) for the cost of the work. The claim failed on a number of grounds, one of which was that the right to rescind was barred since it was no longer possible to restore the railway company to its original position. This is an unusual application of the requirement of restoration, which normally prevents the representee from rescinding unless he can *give back* benefits that he has *received*. In this case, the requirement prevented rescission because the representee could not *take back* benefits that he had *conferred*. Nevertheless the decision appears to be correct. It was not practicable to restore the parties to their pre-contract position, so that "rescission" made very little sense. The more convenient remedy is damages and on such facts this would now generally be available under section 2(1) of the Misrepresentation Act.[86]

A second, and perhaps more common, illustration of this situation is provided by the case of a person who is induced by misrepresentation to buy something which he improves before discovering the truth. In such a case, the improvements probably do not bar the right to rescind; and their cost can often be claimed as damages.[87] Where the representation is wholly innocent and the contract has been rescinded, there will be no such claim[88]; but the representee might be able to set off the cost of the improvements against his liability[89] to make allowance for benefits received by him under the contract.[90]

(ii) *Made by the misrepresentor.* In *Spence* v. *Crawford*[91] the fraudulent buyer was allowed something in respect of his loss on sale of stock. This loss did not produce any directly corresponding increase in the value of what he had bought; and it was incurred in consequence of something that he was *obliged* under the contract to do. It does not follow from the decision that a buyer who obtains property by misrepresentation can, if the seller claims rescission, insist on an allowance for improvements which he

---

[85] 1915 S.C.(H.L.) 20.
[86] *Ante,* p. 312.
[87] *Ante,* pp. 307 *et seq.*
[88] *Ante,* pp. 326 *et seq.*
[89] *Ante,* p. 341.
[90] *Cf. Cooper* v. *Phibbs* (1867) L.R. 2 H.L. 149, *ante,* p. 282.
[91] [1939] 3 All E.R. 271; *ante,* pp. 340, 341.

has made *without* being contractually bound to do so. It can be argued on the one hand that the seller would get a windfall if he did not have to pay anything for the improvements[92]; and on the other that he should not be forced to pay for improvements (which he may not want or be able to afford) as a condition of getting back his property. The better view, probably, is that if the seller claims rescission, he should have to make some allowance (based on increase in value rather than the cost of work to the buyer).[93] If the seller is unwilling or unable to pay the allowance he can generally fall back on his alternative remedy of damages.[94]

(2) Third party rights

The right to rescind a contract may be barred by the intervention of third party rights. For example, a person who has been induced by fraud to sell goods cannot rescind after the goods have been bought by an innocent third party.[95] On the same principle, a person cannot rescind an allotment of shares in a company after the company has gone into liquidation. At that point the rights of third parties intervene in that the assets of the company have to be collected for distribution among the company's creditors.[96] This should be contrasted with the rule in the bankruptcy of an individual that the trustee in bankruptcy takes the property "subject to equities," including the right of rescission. Thus in *Load* v. *Green*[97] the plaintiff was by fraud induced to sell goods to one Bannister, who became bankrupt. It was held that the plaintiff could disaffirm the contract and recover the value of his goods from Bannister's trustee in bankruptcy. It is difficult to find any convincing reason for this distinction between winding up of insolvent companies and individual bankruptcy. It seems to be based on the assumption that third parties place greater reliance on a company's nominal share capital (especially if the company is a new one, or has just raised new capital) than on an individual's appearance of wealth.

(3) Affirmation

A contract cannot be rescinded for misrepresentation if the representee expressly or by conduct affirms it after discovering the truth.[98] Thus a person who is induced by misrepresentation to buy goods cannot rescind if, after discovering the truth, he uses them[99]; a person who is induced by misrepresentation to subscribe for shares in a company cannot rescind if, after discovering the truth, he accepts dividends, votes at meetings or tries to sell the shares[1]; a person who is induced by misrepresentation to take a lease cannot rescind if, after discovering the truth, he stays on and pays rent[2]; *a fortiori* a mining lease cannot be rescinded if, after discovering the truth,

---

92 *e.g.*, *Williams* v. *Logue*, 122 So. 490 (1929).
93 *Cf. Walker* v. *Galt*, 171 F. 2d 613 (1948).
94 *Ante*, pp. 307 *et seq*.
95 *Ante*, pp. 331–332; and see *post*, p. 374.
96 *Re Scottish Petroleum Co.* (1883) 23 Ch.D. 413.
97 (1846) 15 M. & W. 216.
98 *Cf.* the loss of the right to rescind *for breach* on similar grounds: *post*, p. 709.
99 *United Shoe Machinery Co. of Canada* v. *Brunet* [1909] A.C. 330; *cf. Long* v. *Lloyd* [1958] 1 W.L.R. 753.
1 *Western Bank of Scotland* v. *Addie* (1867) L.R. 1 Sc. & Div. 145; *Scholey* v. *Central Ry. of Venezuela* (1870) L.R. 9 Eq. 266n.; *Ex. p. Briggs* (1866) L.R. 1 Eq. 483.
2 *Kennard* v. *Ashman* (1894) 10 T.L.R. 213.

the lessee continues to work the mine.[3] Use of the subject-matter for the sole purpose of testing the accuracy of the representation does not, however, amount to affirmation.[4]

On a principle analogous to affirmation a person cannot set aside one part of a contract while affirming the rest. In *Urquhart* v. *Macpherson*[5] a deed dissolving a partnership contained a clause by which each partner released his claims against the others. One partner sought to set aside the release on the ground of fraud. It was held he could not do so while affirming the rest of the deed. Similarly, an insurance company can rescind a policy for non-disclosure, but it cannot repudiate a particular claim while purporting to recognise that the policy is still in force.[6]

A person can only affirm after he has discovered the truth. To hear rumours that the representation may be untrue is not discovery of the truth for this purpose.[7] But if the representee knows all the facts from which a reasonable person would deduce the truth, he may be taken to know it.[8]

Our present concern is with affirmation as a bar to the right to rescind for misrepresentation; but it must also be compared with certain bars to the right to rescind for breach. In *Leaf* v. *International Galleries*[9] Denning L.J. said: "An innocent misrepresentation is much less potent than a breach of condition; and a claim to rescission for innocent misrepresentation must at any rate be barred when the right to reject for breach of condition is barred." The right to reject for breach of condition is barred by "acceptance," and this takes place when the buyer intimates that he accepts the goods; or, if he has had a reasonable opportunity of examining the goods, when they have been delivered to him and he does an act inconsistent with the ownership of the seller; or when after lapse of a reasonable time he retains the goods without intimating that he had rejected them.[10] A buyer may "accept" before discovering the truth,[11] and a literal reading of Denning L.J.'s dictum would suggest that acceptance will always deprive him of the right to rescind for innocent misrepresentation. But it is submitted that the dictum must be read, according to its context, to refer to cases in which a claim to rescission is resisted on the ground of lapse of time. In other words, it only means that lapse of time amounting to acceptance will also bar the right to rescind for misrepresentation. If the buyer, in ignorance of the true facts, "accepts" in some other way he may nevertheless be able to rescind for misrepresentation; and he may, by virtue of section 1(*a*) of the Misrepresentation Act, be able to do this even where the misrepresentation had been incorporated in the contract.

---

[3] *Vigers* v. *Pike* (1842) 8 Cl. & F. 562.

[4] *Long* v. *Lloyd* [1958] 1 W.L.R. 753 (first trip); *cf. Lindsay Petroleum Co.* v. *Hurd* (1874) L.R. 5 P.C. 221 (sinking exploratory well no bar to rescission).

[5] (1878) 3 App.Cas. 831.

[6] *West* v. *National Motors & Accident Insurance Union Ltd.* [1955] 1 W.L.R. 343. It is not clear why the company adopted this ambivalent attitude: see p. 347 of the report. The result might have been different had fraud been alleged; *ante*, p. 333.

[7] *Central Ry. of Venezuela* v. *Kisch* (1867) L.R. 2 H.L. 99.

[8] *Scholey* v. *Central Ry. of Venezuela* (1870) L.R. 9 Eq. 266n.; *Long* v. *Lloyd* [1958] 1 W.L.R. 753, 760. Contrast, in cases of breach, *post*, pp. 712 *et seq*.

[9] [1950] 2 K.B. 86, 90.

[10] Sale of Goods Act 1979, s.35.
Sale of Goods Act 1979, s.35; *post* p. 715.

[11] *e.g.* where he has a reasonable opportunity of examining the goods but does not discover the truth.

Affirmation may be inferred from failure to rescind. The courts are particularly ready to draw this inference where a person wishes to rescind an allotment of shares in a company. He must not only tell the company that he rescinds, but must also take active steps to remove his name from the company's register. He is not allowed to wait and see whether the company will prosper.[12] But where several persons have been induced by misrepresentation to become shareholders they may agree among themselves and with the company that one of them will take proceedings for rescission and that the others will be bound by the outcome of the proceedings. Such an agreement makes it impossible for the other shareholders to speculate on the success of the company or on the outcome of the proceedings. Hence their right to rescind is preserved.[13]

(4) Lapse of time

In cases of fraud or breach of fiduciary duty, lapse of time does not itself bar rescission. It is simply evidence of affirmation.[14] This view is supported by the rule that time only begins to run from the discovery of the truth[15]; and by the rule that time spent in negotiations to settle the dispute does not bar rescission.[16]

In *Leaf* v. *International Galleries*[17] the plaintiff was induced to buy a picture by the innocent misrepresentation that it was "by J. Constable."[18] Five years later he sought to rescind but it was held that his right to do so was barred by lapse of time. As he claimed rescission immediately on discovering the truth, the lapse of time cannot be regarded as evidence of affirmation. Thus it seems that the right to rescind for *innocent* misrepresentation is barred by lapse of time even though there is no evidence of affirmation. The length of time required for this purpose seems to be such as would enable a reasonably diligent inquirer to discover the truth. This rule probably applies to a negligent misrepresentation in the same way as to a wholly innocent one.

SECTION 6. EXCLUDING LIABILITY FOR MISREPRESENTATION

Contract terms excluding liability for misrepresentation may be ineffective under general rules relating to exemption clauses, discussed elsewhere in this book.[19] In addition, section 3 of the Misrepresentation Act 1967[20] provides: "If a contract contains a term which would exclude or restrict (*a*) any liability to which a party to a contract may be subject by reason of any misrepresentation made by him before the contract was made; or (*b*) any remedy available to another party to the contract by reason of such a misrepresentation, that term shall be of no effect except in so far as it satis-

[12] *First National Reinsurance Co. Ltd.* v. *Greenfield* [1921] 2 K.B. 260.
[13] *Pawle's* Case (1869) L.R. 4 Ch.App. 497.
[14] *Clough* v. *L.N.W. Ry.* (1871) L.R. 7 Ex. 26, 35; *cf.* (in cases of breach) *post*, p. 711.
[15] *Gillet* v. *Peppercorne* (1840) 3 Beav. 78; *Armstrong* v. *Jackson* [1917] 2 K.B. 822; *Lindsay Petroleum Co.* v. *Hurd* (1874) L.R. 5 P.C. 221, 241; *Aaron's Reefs Ltd.* v. *Twiss* [1896] A.C. 273, 287.
[16] *Erlanger* v. *New Sombrero Phosphate Co.* (1878) 3 App.Cas. 1218, 1248.
[17] [1950] 2 K.B. 86.
[18] *Ante*, p. 256, n. 60.
[19] See especially *ante*, p. 223.
[20] As amended by Unfair Contract Terms Act 1977, s.8(1).

fies the requirement of reasonableness as stated in section 11(1) of the Unfair Contract Terms Act 1977; and it is for those claiming that the term satisfies that requirement to show that it does."

1. Scope of the Misrepresentation Act 1967, section 3

(1) Excluding or restricting liabilities or remedies

The section covers not only clauses excluding or limiting a party's liability but also certain analogous terms: for example clauses which impose a short time limit within which claims must be brought, or which exclude a particular remedy (such as rescission) without affecting another (such as damages).[21] On the other hand, they probably do not cover a valid agreed damages clause, since this might in some circumstances extend rather than restrict liability.[22] Some terms which purport to define a duty rather than to exclude or restrict a liability[23] are probably outside the scope of the section: *e.g.* a term which indicates that the representor is in good faith passing on information supplied to him by a third party, or one which indicates that a written document formed an exclusive record of the terms of the contract.[24] The same may be true of certain other terms which do not exclude or restrict liability but prevent it from arising. It seems, for example, that the section would not apply to a term in a contract made through an agent negativing his ostensible authority to make representation as to the subject-matter.[25] But it would be comparatively easy to evade section 3 if the courts were not to some extent prepared to look behind clauses purporting to "prevent liability from arising." It has therefore been held that a statement can take effect as a misrepresentation in spite of the fact that it is made in a document expressly warning the representee to make his own enquiries into its accuracy.[26] Similarly, a clause commonly used by auctioneers provides that all representations in the catalogue are statements of opinion only. If the court, on applying the tests stated earlier in this Chapter,[27] concluded that the representation would, but for the clause, be one of fact, it might well hold that the clause was within section 3.

The section applies to terms excluding or restricting "*any* remedy." This

---

[21] *Cf. ante*, p. 227 for a similar definition in s.13 of the Unfair Contract Terms Act 1977. That definition only applies in terms for the purposes of Pt. I of 1977 Act, which is not considered to include (though it amends) s.3 of the Misrepresentation Act 1967: see s.11(1) of the 1977 Act. An arbitration clause is excluded from the definition in s.13 of the 1977 Act, but may be covered by s.3 of the Misrepresentation Act.

[22] *Cf. ante*, p. 227; *post*, pp. 883–890.

[23] *Ante*, p. 227.

[24] *McGrath* v. *Shaw* (1989) 57 P. & C.R. 452.

[25] See *Overbrooke Estates Ltd.* v. *Glencombe Properties Ltd.* [1974] 1 W.L.R. 1335; Coote, [1975] C.L.J. 17. This case was decided under the original version of s.3, but the amendment made by the Unfair Contract Terms Act 1977, s.8(1) appears not to affect the point. *Cf. Museprime Properties Ltd.* v. *Adhill Properties Ltd.* [1990] 2 E.G.L.R. 196, 200.

[26] *Walker* v. *Boyle* [1982] 1 W.L.R. 495; *cf. Cremdean Properties Ltd.* v. *Nash* (1977) 244 E.G. 547; *South Western General Property Co. Ltd.* v. *Marton* (1982) 263 E.G. 1090. The reasoning of *Smith* v. *Eric S. Bush* [1990] 1 A.C. 831 (*ante*, p. 228) might also be applied by analogy, even though it is not directly applicable to cases falling within section 3 of the 1967 Act since (i) it is based on the definition exemption clauses in s.13(1) of the Unfair Contract Terms At 1977, and this definition does not apply for the purpose of 1967 Act; and (ii) the misrepresentation in that case did not induce any contract between misrepresentor and misrepresentee: *cf. post*, p. 347.

[27] *Ante*, p. 296.

phrase obviously covers the normal remedies of damages and rescission. It probably also covers terms restricting or excluding the right to plead misrepresentation as a defence,[28] for this could be described as a "remedy" in a broad sense. Similarly, a term excluding or restricting the right to retake goods obtained by fraud[29] would be within the section.

(2) "Party to a contract"

This section only applies to provisions excluding or restricting the liability of a "party to a contract," and the subsequent words of the section show that this means *the* contract induced by the misrepresentation. The section therefore would not apply to disclaimers of liability in cases such as *Hedley Byrne & Co. Ltd.* v. *Heller & Partners Ltd.*[30] and in *Smith* v. *Eric S. Bush*[31] since the contracts induced by the misrepresentations in those cases were not made with the representor but with a third person. Such disclaimers of liability for negligence in giving advice in the course of a business would, however, be subject to the test of reasonableness under the Unfair Contract Terms Act 1977.[32] The scope of that test is, however, as will be seen below, in several ways significantly narrower than that of section 3 of the Misrepresentation Act 1967.

(3) "By reason of any misrepresentation made"

The section clearly applies to terms excluding or restricting liability for mere misrepresentations. It equally clearly does not apply to terms which only exclude or restrict liability for breaches of pure promises (as opposed to statements of fact) or for breaches of implied terms not dependent on statements of fact. Terms which exclude or restrict liability only for such breaches may be subject to the test of reasonableness under the Unfair Contract Terms Act 1977. But the scope of the test under that Act is limited[33]: it does not, for example, generally apply to contracts made otherwise than in the course of a business, nor does it apply to certain specified contracts, such as contracts for the sale of houses.[34] The scope of section 3 of the Misrepresentation Act is not so limited; and the difference in the scope of the two Acts gives rise to two problems. In discussing these, we shall assume that the case is one in which the reasonableness test under the 1977 Act does not apply.

(a) INCORPORATED MISREPRESENTATION. Where a misrepresentation is incorporated in the contract, the right to rescind for misrepresentation is preserved by section 1(*a*), and a term purporting to exclude or restrict that right would be within section 3. But a term may purport to exclude or restrict liabilities or remedies available only because the representation has been incorporated in the contract: for example, it may provide that the representee is only to recover out-of-pocket expenses and not to have

---

[28] *Ante*, p. 333.
[29] *Ante*, p. 332.
[30] [1964] A.C. 465; *ante*, p. 308.
[31] [1990] 1 A.C. 831; *ante*, p. 228.
[32] *i.e.*, under s.2(2) (*ante*, p. 231) and possibly under s.3(2) (*ante*, pp. 231–232).
[33] *Ante*, pp. 241–244.
[34] If the sale were a private sale, it would be completely outside the scope of the 1977 Act: *ante*, p. 241. Even if the seller acted in the course of a business, and the buyer dealt as consumer, the reasonableness test would not apply to the contract "so far as it relates to" the transfer of an interest in land: *ante*, p. 241.

damages for loss of his bargain.[35] It seems that such a term would not be within section 3, for the liability which it purported to exclude would not arise by reason of the *making* of the representation, but by reason of its *incorporation* into the contract. This conclusion is, however, subject to the point next to be discussed.

(b) PROVISION APPLICABLE TO MISREPRESENTATION AND BREACH. A single term may exclude liability for misrepresentation *and* for breach of contract. A clause excluding liability "for all defects" would have this effect where some defects were merely represented not to exist and others amounted to breaches of contract. Section 3 provides that where a term would exclude or restrict any liability for misrepresentation "*that term* shall be of no effect except in so far as" the test of reasonableness is satisfied. It seems to follow that the *whole* term may be subject to the reasonableness test and not only the part of it which excludes liability for misrepresentation, unless that part is severable.[36] If this is correct, a term excluding liability for "misrepresentation" in general terms could be ineffective (if unreasonable) to exclude contractual liability for an incorporated misrepresentation.

(4) "Before the contract was made"

Section 3 applies to terms excluding or restricting liability for misrepresentations made before the conclusion of the contract. It does not apply to terms excluding or restricting liability for misrepresentations made in the course of *performing* a contract. However, in general[37] such liability is only likely to be incurred by a person who acts in the course of a business and is negligent: *e.g.* by one who gives negligent professional advice. In such a situation a term excluding or restricting liability is subject to the test of reasonableness under the Unfair Contract Terms Act 1977.[38] If the representation was fraudulent, a clause excluding liability for it is probably void at common law.[39]

2. The Reasonableness Test

Section 3 applies "the test of reasonableness *as stated in section 11(1)* of the Unfair Contract Terms Act 1977" to terms excluding or restricting liability for misrepresentation. Section 11(1) provides that, in order to determine whether the test of reasonableness is satisfied, regard is to be had to the time of contracting: this rule is expressly stated to apply for the purposes of section 3 of the Misrepresentation Act 1967. The 1977 Act also lays down certain guidelines for determining reasonableness; these take effect under section 11(2) and 11(4) of that Act.[40] At first sight, none of these guidelines apply for the purpose of section 3 of the Misrepresentation Act, since section 3 only refers to section 11(1) of the 1977 Act. However, the guidelines

[35] *Cf. ante*, pp. 322–325.
[36] *Cf. ante*, p. 236.
[37] For an exception, see *Chaudhry* v. *Prabhakar* [1989] 1 W.L.R. 29. *Semble*, a disclaimer of liability in such a situation would not be subject to the reasonableness test under either Act.
[38] *i.e.* s.2(2) (*ante*, p. 231) and possibly s.3(2) (*ante*, pp. 231–232).
[39] *Ante*, p. 224; the point might be of some importance if the liability were not a "business liability" within the Unfair Contract Terms Act 1977.
[40] *Ante*, pp. 236–238.

contained in section 11(4) are there said to apply where "the question arises (under this *or any other* Act) whether the term . . . satisfies the test of reasonableness." In view of the italicised words, those guidelines[41] are, it is submitted, applicable for the purpose of section 3 of the Misrepresentation Act. Moreover the statutory guidelines are not exhaustive for this purpose: in this respect their position under section 3 is indistinguishable from that under the 1977 Act.[42]

Under section 3 (as under the Unfair Contract Terms Act 1977)[43] the court will generally hold the term to be either wholly ineffective[44] or fully valid; but it can also, if the clause is severable, uphold it in part, *i.e.* "in so far as" it satisfies the test of reasonableness.[45]

SECTION 7. NON-DISCLOSURE

1. General Rule

(1) No duty of disclosure

As a general rule, a person who is about to enter into a contract is under no duty to disclose material facts known to him but not to the other party. Thus it has been held that a landlord is not liable in deceit if before letting his house he fails to tell the tenant that it is in a ruinous condition[46]; and that a person who applies for the post of governess is not bound to divulge the fact that she is a divorcee.[47] Sometimes the rule may appear to operate harshly; but if a general duty of disclosure did exist it would be very hard to say exactly what must be disclosed in any particular case.

(2) Representation by conduct

A person may make a representation by conduct[48] and, if he fails to correct the impression given by his conduct, he cannot rely on the general rule that there is no duty of disclosure.[49] Active concealment of a defect amounts to misrepresentation[50]; and even conduct falling short of this may suffice. In the words of Blackburn J.: "The defendant, by taking the cow to a public market to be sold . . . thereby furnishes evidence of a representation that, so far as his knowledge goes, the animal is not suffering from any infectious disease. . . . The case might be different where the sale takes place privately."[51]

---

41 *Ante*, p. 236 at n. 74.

42 Ante, p. 237.

43 *Ante*, pp. 231–232.

44 See *Walker* v. *Boyle* [1982] 1 W.L.R. 495; *cf. Howard Marine & Dredging Co. Ltd.* v. *A. Ogden & Sons (Excavations) Ltd.* [1978] Q.B. 574.

45 *Ante*, p. 235.

46 *Keates* v. *Cadogan* (1851) 10 C.B. 591.

47 *Fletcher* v. *Krell* (1872) 42 L.J.Q.B. 55; *cf. The Unique Mariner* [1978] 1 Lloyd's Rep. 438, 449; *Lloyds Bank* v. *Egremont* [1990] 2 FLR 351.

48 *Curtis* v. *Chemical Cleaning & Dyeing Co. Ltd.* [1951] 1 K.B. 805, 808.

49 *Walters* v. *Morgan* (1861) 3 D.F. & J. 718, 723.

50 *Schneider* v. *Heath* (1813) 3 Camp. 506; *cf.* Insurance Companies Act, 1982, s.73 ("dishonest concealment of material facts"); *cf. Sybron Corp.* v. *Rochem Ltd.* [1984] Ch. 112, 130 ("covering up and deliberately concealing"); *Gordon* v. *Selico Ltd.* (1986) 278 E.G. 53.

51 *Bodger* v. *Nicholls* (1873) 28 L.T. 441, 445.

(3) Latent defects

It has been said that a person must disclose latent defects in the subject-matter of the contract which are known to him.[52] Some of the cases which may appear to support this view can be explained on the ground of active misrepresentation[53] by words or by conduct. But it does not seem that English law recognises a general duty to disclose known latent defects. In the dictum quoted above, Blackburn J. did not base liability on any such general duty, but on the defendant's conduct in taking the cow to market. The dictum was cited without comment in *Ward* v. *Hobbs*[54] where pigs were taken to Newbury market and sold there "with all faults." The seller knew that the pigs were diseased but he did not disclose this fact to the buyer. It was held that the buyer had no remedy as there was no general duty to disclose known latent defects and as any representation which might be inferred from the seller's conduct in taking the pigs to market was negatived by the words "with all faults." These words might, on such facts, now only have this effect if they satisfied the statutory test of reasonableness.[55] Moreover, if the thing sold suffers from a latent defect of which the seller knows, and if that defect causes injury to the buyer, or harm to other property belonging to him, then the seller's failure to warn the buyer of the defect may make him liable in negligence; and it has been suggested that *Ward* v. *Hobbs* may require reconsideration in the light of this possibility.[56] But such liability will not extend to cases in which the defect caused no loss to the buyer except in making the thing sold less valuable than he had supposed it to be.[57] Cases of this kind will continue to be governed by the general rule that there is no duty of disclosure.[58]

That general rule has been applied where land sold was subject to a latent physical defect.[59] It is possible that on a sale of land latent defects in title must be disclosed[60]; but even here the better view appears to be that there is no general duty of disclosure.[61] An undisclosed defect of this kind

---

[52] *Horsfall* v. *Thomas* (1862) 1 H. & C. 90, 100.

[53] *e.g. Hill* v. *Gray* (1816) 1 Stark. 434, as explained in *Keates* v. *Cadogan* (1815) 10 C.B. at p. 600.

[54] (1878) 4 App.Cas. 13.

[55] *Ante*, pp. 232–233; *semble* the buyer did not deal as consumer: if he did the term would be ineffective under Unfair Contract Terms Act 1977, s.6(2).

[56] *Hurley* v. *Dyke* [1979] R.T.R. 265, 303. For a similar duty to disclose one's own *breach* where it may lead to danger, see *post*, p. 359.

[57] *Cf. post*, p. 542.

[58] The view that negligent *conduct* can, in exceptional circumstances, give rise to liability in tort for such loss may be supported by *Junior Books Ltd.* v. *Veitchi Co.* [1983] A.C. 520; but the restrictive interpretation placed on this case by later decisions (*post*, pp. 540–545) makes it highly unlikely that such liability will be extended to cases of pure non-disclosure. It has been held that there is no such liability in tort even where (exceptionally) there *is* a duty of disclosure because the contract is *uberrimae fidei* (*post*, p. 357): *Banque Keyser Ullmann S.A.* v. *Skandia (U.K.) Insurance Co. Ltd.* [1990] 1 Q.B. 665, 798–800; [1990] 2 All E.R. 947, 959, 960 (where the decision was affirmed on other grounds). *A fortiori* there should be no liability in tort for mere non-disclosure where there is *no* duty of disclosure; and this is the situation under discussion at this point.

[59] *Shepherd* v. *Croft* [1911] 1 Ch. 521.

[60] *Selkirk* v. *Romar Investments Ltd.* [1963] 1 W.L.R. 1415, 1423; *F. & H. Entertainments Ltd.* v. *Leisure Enterprises Ltd.* (1976) 120 S.J. 331, 240 E.G. 455; *Faruqi* v. *English Real Estates* [1979] 1 W.L.R. 963.

[61] Megarry and Wade, *The Law of Real Property* (5th ed.), p. 622 n. 75. For criticisms, see *Let the buyer be well informed*: recommendations of the Conveyancing Standing Committee of the Law Commission.

is only a ground for relief if it is unusual,[62] or if it leads to a breach of contract[63] or to an operative mistake.[64] It can also, if known to the vendor, prevent him from relying on a term of the contract under which the purchaser is deemed to have made enquiries relating to the matter in question and to have knowledge of it.[65]

The general rule that there is no duty of disclosure also applies where the buyer knows (but the seller does not) of some latent quality which makes the subject-matter of the contract *more* valuable. Thus a contract for the sale of land is binding even though the buyer, but not the seller, knew that it contained valuable minerals.[66]

2. Exceptions

There are many important exceptions to the rule that there is no liability for non-disclosure. In these exceptional cases, a person is, in general, only bound to disclose facts known to him.[67] But a person may be under a duty to disclose facts known to his agent, if the knowledge has been acquired within the scope of the agent's authority and if it was the agent's duty to communicate it to the principal.[68] He may also be under a duty to disclose facts which he ought to have known, if there is a "special relationship" between the parties within *Hedley Byrne & Co. Ltd.* v. *Heller & Partners Ltd.*[69]

Where a duty of disclosure exists, it generally continues until the contract becomes legally binding.[70] But where a contract is regarded as binding as a matter of business the duty to disclose may cease at that point even though the contract is not yet binding in law. Thus in contracts of insurance the duty ceases when the insurer initials a slip saying that he will accept the risk, even where there is no legally binding contract until a policy is executed.[71] Conversely the duty may continue even after the conclusion of the contract. Thus a person who takes a fidelity bond for the honesty of one of his servants is under a continuing duty to disclose to the surety any acts of dishonesty on the part of the servant.[72] Similarly, an insurance policy may provide that the insured is to be held covered in certain events which affect the risk, at a premium to be arranged; and in such cases the duty of

---

[62] *Molyneux* v. *Hawtrey* [1903] 2 K.B. 487; *cf. Carlish* v. *Salt* [1906] 1 Ch. 335; *Celsteel Ltd.* v. *Alton House Holdings Ltd. (No. 2)* [1986] 1 All E.R. 598, 607 (not reported on this point in [1986] 1 W.L.R. 666).

[63] *e.g. Flight* v. *Booth* (1834) 1 Bing. N.C. 370; *Peyman* v. *Lanjani* [1985] Ch. 457, 496.

[64] *Ante*, Chap. 8.

[65] *Rignall Developments Ltd.* v. *Halil* [1988] Ch. 190.

[66] *Smith* v. *Hughes* (1871) L.R. 6 Q.B. 587, 604; *quaere* whether the contract would be specifically enforced: *post*, p. 909. *Cf.* also *Phillips* v. *Homfray* (1871) L.R. 7 Ch.App. 770. For a statutory exception, see Company Securities (Insider Dealing) Act 1985, imposing criminal penalties on "insider dealing," but without affecting the validity of resulting transactions: s.8(3).

[67] *Blackburn, Low & Co.* v. *Vigors* (1887) 12 App.Cas. 531.

[68] *Proudfoot* v. *Montefiore* (1867) L.R. 2 Q.B. 511; *Joel* v. *Law Union and Crown Insurance Co.* [1908] 2 K.B. 863.

[69] [1964] A.C. 465; *ante*, p. 308.

[70] *Container Transport International Inc.* v. *Oceanus Mutual, etc., Association* [1984] 1 Lloyd's Rep. 476, 486.

[71] *Cory* v. *Patton* (1872) L.R. 7 Q.B. 304; *Citadel Insurance Co.* v. *Atlantic Union Insurance Co.* [1982] 2 Lloyd's Rep. 543, 548. Section 2(1) of the Misrepresentation Act (requiring belief in the truth of the "facts represented" up to the time that the contract was made) would not apply to pure non-disclosure: *cf. post*, p. 360.

[72] *Phillips* v. *Foxall* (1872) L.R. 7 Q.B. 666.

disclosure in relation to those events continues throughout the currency of the contract.[73]

The duty of disclosure exists in the following cases.

(1) Representation falsified by later events

A person may have to disclose material facts which come to his notice[74] before the conclusion of a contract if they falsify a representation previously made by him.[75] In *With* v. *O'Flanagan*[76] negotiations for the sale of a medical practice were begun in January, when the practice was said to be worth £2,000. A contract of sale was made on May 1, by which time the practice had become worthless because of the intervening illness of the vendor. The contract was set aside on the ground that the vendor ought to have communicated this change of circumstances to the purchasers. But there would probably be no need to disclose minor variations in the income of the practice.[77] And it is uncertain to what extent a duty of disclosure is imposed on a person who makes a statement as to his financial position which influences a series of transactions extending, perhaps, over many years. Clearly, the representor does not have to disclose every change in that position over such a long period. A time must come when the representation loses its force and the representee begins to rely rather on his own judgment.[78]

There are conflicting decisions on the question whether a duty of disclosure arises where during negotiations a party makes a representation as to his present intention but changes his mind before the conclusion of the contract. In *Traill* v. *Baring*[79] an insurance company made a proposal for reinsurance to a second company, stating that it would retain part of the risk. This was its intention when it made the representation but before the proposal was accepted it disposed of that part of the risk. It was held that the "change of intention"[80] of the first company should have been disclosed to the second company. On the other hand, in *Wales* v. *Wadham*[81] a husband who had left his wife made her an offer of financial provision after she had declared her intention of not remarrying. She accepted the offer after having decided to marry again. If the husband had known this, he would have made a lower offer; but it was held that the wife was not bound to disclose her change of mind. The duty of disclosing changed circumstances was said only to apply where the original representation was one of

---

[73] *The Litsian Pride* [1985] 1 Lloyd's Rep. 437, 512.

[74] Or, which, if there is a "special relationship," should have come to his notice, had he exercised reasonable care.

[75] The rule does not apply where no such previous representation has been made: *English* v. *Dedham Vale Properties Ltd.* [1978] 1 W.L.R. 93, 104.

[76] [1936] Ch. 575; *cf. Traill* v. *Baring* (1864) 4 D.J. & S. 318; *British Equitable Insurance Co.* v. *Great Western Ry.* (1869) 38 L.J.Ch. 132; *Davies* v. *London & Provincial Marine Insurance Co.* (1878) 8 Ch.D. 469; *Zamir* v. *S. of S. for the Home Dept.* [1980] A.C. 730, 750. In view of these authorities, *Turner* v. *Green* [1895] 2 Ch. 205, where this point was not argued, cannot be supported. See also Financial Services Act 1986, ss.147, 164.

[77] For the possible application of the Misrepresentation Act, see *post*, p. 361.

[78] *Cf. Argy Trading Development Co. Ltd.* v. *Lapid Developments Ltd.* [1977] 1 W.L.R. 444, 461–462.

[79] (1864) 4 D.J. & S. 318.

[80] *Ibid.* pp. 326, 330.

[81] [1977] 1 W.L.R. 199.

fact: not where it was one of *intention*.[82] The view that the wife was not bound to disclose her decision to remarry was disapproved by the House of Lords in *Jenkins* v. *Livesey*,[83] but only on the ground that the agreement for financial provision had been embodied in a consent order made in matrimonial proceedings; and that parties seeking such an order were, by statute,[84] under a duty to make full and frank disclosure to the court which made the order. So far as common law liability for fraud and non-disclosure was concerned, *Wales* v. *Wadham* was approved, though unfortunately without any reference to *Traill* v. *Baring*. It may be possible to reconcile the two decisions by saying that in *Traill* v. *Baring* the first company had, before acceptance of its offer, not merely changed its mind but acted accordingly, while the wife in *Wales* v. *Wadham* had not actually remarried when she accepted the husband's offer; or by saying that the wife's statement in the latter case was as to an intention so intrinsically likely to be changed that the husband should not have relied on the statement.[85] Subject to these possible distinctions, it is submitted that the principle in *Traill* v. *Baring* is to be preferred; for, in cases of this kind, what was originally a misrepresentation of intention becomes by the time of contracting one of fact, *viz*. as to the representor's state of mind at that time.[86] And there is no difficulty in specifying exactly what should be disclosed, so that the reason for the general rule against imposing a duty of disclosure does not apply.

(2) Statement literally true, but misleading

A person is guilty of misrepresentation, though all the facts stated by him are true, if his statement is misleading as a whole because it does not refer to other facts affecting the weight of those stated. In *Notts Patent Brick and Tile Co*. v. *Butler*[87] the purchaser of land asked the vendor's solicitor whether the land was subject to restrictive covenants. The solicitor replied that he was not aware of any, but failed to add that this was because he had not troubled to read the relevant documents. The solicitor's reply, though literally true, amounted to a misrepresentation entitling the purchaser to rescind.

Dicta in cases of this kind sometimes suggest a wider common law duty of disclosure, co-extensive with that which exists in contracts *uberrimae fidei*[88]; but, properly construed, they do not have this effect. In *New Brunswick and Canada Ry*. v. *Muggeridge*[89] the defendant successfully resisted a claim for specific performance of a contract to take up shares in a company

---

82 *Ibid*. p. 211.
83 [1985] A.C. 424.
84 Matrimonial Causes Act 1973, ss.23–25.
85 *Cf. ante*, p. 303.
86 *Ante*, p. 297.
87 (1886) 16 Q.B.D. 778; *cf. Tapp* v. *Lee* (1803) 3 B. & P. 367; *R*. v. *Kylsant* [1932] 1 K.B. 442; *Faruqi* v. *English Real Estates* [1979] 1 W.L.R. 963; *The Lucy* [1983] 1 Lloyd's Rep. 188 (where relief was denied as the requirement of reliance was not satisfied: *ante*, p. 303); *Cemp Properties (U.K.) Ltd*. v. *Dentsply Research & Development Corp*. [1989] 2 E.G.L.R. 205.
88 *Post*, pp. 354–357.
89 (1860) 1 Dr. & Sm. 363; approved in *Central Ry. of Venezuela* v. *Kisch* (1867) L.R. 2. H.L. 99.

on the ground that the prospectus which induced him to make the contract did not make it clear that the company's interest in certain land was contingent. Kindersley V.-C. said that persons who issue such a prospectus "are bound to state everything with strict and scrupulous accuracy, and not only to abstain from stating as facts that which is not so, but to omit no one fact within their knowledge which might in any degree affect the nature, or extent or quality of the privileges and advantages, *which the prospectus holds out as an inducement* to take the shares."[90] As the italicised words show, this means that if the prospectus mentions some inducement, no fact must be omitted which is relevant *to that inducement*. It does not mean that the prospectus must state all material facts whatsoever. At common law, "the duty of disclosure is not the same in the case of a prospectus inviting share subscriptions as in the case of a proposal for marine insurance.[91] In an honest prospectus many facts and circumstances may be lawfully omitted" although some subscribers might regard them as material.[92] But the courts look carefully at a prospectus to see whether it is on the whole misleading[93]; and the analogy between a company prospectus and a contract *uberrimae fidei* has become very close now that a general duty of disclosure is imposed by statute on persons who issue a prospectus.[94] Since, however, the only remedy for breach of this duty appears to be by way of damages,[95] the common law rules on the topic are still significant where a claim is made to rescind the contract or allotment induced by the prospectus.

The common law principles just stated apply to contracts to enter into a partnership,[96] in which there is no statutory duty of disclosure.

(3) Custom

In *Jones* v. *Bowden*[97] the plaintiff bought pimento which had been damaged by sea water. It was usual in the trade, when pimento had been so damaged, to declare this, but the seller failed to make such a declaration. He was held liable in deceit as, in view of the custom, his silence amounted to misrepresentation.

(4) Contracts uberrimae fidei

There is a duty to disclose material facts in some types of contracts, in which one party is in a particularly strong position, and the other in a particularly weak one, to know the material facts.

(a) INSURANCE. "It has been for centuries in England the law in connection with insurance of all sorts, marine, fire, life, guarantee and every kind of policy, that, as the underwriter knows nothing and the man who comes to him to ask him to insure knows everything, it is the duty of the

---

[90] At p. 381; *cf. Dimmock* v. *Hallett* (1866) L.R. 2 Ch.App. 21, 28.
[91] *Infra* at n. 98.
[92] *Aaron's Reefs Ltd.* v. *Twiss* [1896] A.C. 273, 287.
[93] See *Oakes* v. *Turquand* (1867) L.R. 2 H.L. 325.
[94] Financial Services Act 1986, s.163; *cf. ibid.* s.146; *post*, p. 358.
[95] See *post*, p. 358, n. 42.
[96] Pollock, *Partnership* (15th ed.), p. 83.
[97] (1813) 4 Taunt. 847.

assured . . . to make a full disclosure to the underwriters, without being asked, of all the material circumstances."[98]

(i) *Material facts to be disclosed.* The assured must disclose all such facts as a reasonable or prudent insurer would take into account in deciding whether, or at what premium, to take the risk.[99] A policy of marine insurance can therefore be avoided if the assured conceals the real value of the cargo[1]; or if he fails to declare that it may be carried on deck (thus increasing the risk),[2] that the ship carrying the cargo had already been stranded,[3] or that she had been engaged in smuggling, so that those operating her faced criminal charges.[4] Similarly a policy of life insurance can be avoided if the assured fails to disclose that a number of other insurance offices had declined proposals to insure his life,[5] or that there was a doubt as to his mental health.[6] And a policy of insurance on jewellery can be avoided if the insurer is not told that jewellery had on several occasions been stolen from the assured.[7] A policy can also be avoided on the ground of non-disclosure of facts material to the risk[8] by the insurer,[9] *e.g.* if he accepts a premium for insuring a voyage which he knows to have been safely accomplished.

(ii) *Facts which need not be disclosed.* The assured need not disclose facts which the insurer himself knows or ought to know, facts which diminish the risk, facts which both parties have equal means of knowing, "general topics of speculation,"[10] and facts the disclosure of which is waived by the insurer.[11]

(iii) *Basis of contract clauses.* The duty of disclosure gives a generous measure of protection to insurers, but they often add that the accuracy and completeness of the answers given by the assured to questions in the proposal form shall be the basis of the contract.[12] The result is that quite unimportant misstatements or failure to disclose some quite trivial matter can vitiate a policy[13]; and this position has repeatedly been criticised. Thus Fletcher Moulton L.J. has said: "I wish I could adequately warn the public against such practices on the part of insurance offices. . . . Few of those who insure have any idea how completely they leave themselves in the hands of the insurers, should the latter wish to dispute the policy when it

---

[98] *Rozanes* v. *Bowen* (1928) 32 Ll.L.R. 98, 102.

[99] *Lambert* v. *Co-operative Insurance Society Ltd.* [1975] 2 Lloyd's Rep. 485; Marine Insurance Act 1906, s.18(2); *Woolcott* v. *Sun Alliance, etc. Insurance Ltd.* [1978] 1 W.L.R. 493, 498; *Woolcott* v. *Excess Insurance Co. Ltd.* [1979] 1 Lloyd's Rep. 231, [1979] 2 Lloyd's Rep. 210; *Container Transport International* v. *Oceanus Mutual, etc., Association* [1984] 2 Lloyd's Rep. 476; for criticism and proposals for reform, see Law Com. 104 paras. 3.17–3.19, 4.43–4.53.

[1] *Ionides* v. *Pender* (1874) L.R. 9 Q.B. 531.

[2] *Hood* v. *West End Motor Car Packing Co.* [1917] 2 K.B. 38.

[3] *Proudfoot* v. *Montefiore* (1867) L.R. 2 Q.B. 511.

[4] *Inversiones Mannia S.A.* v. *Sphere Drake Ins. Co. plc* [1989] 1 Lloyd's Rep. 69.

[5] *London Assurance* v. *Mansel* (1879) 11 Ch.D. 363.

[6] *Lindenau* v. *Desborough* (1828) 8 B. & C. 586.

[7] *Rozanes* v. *Bowen* (1928) 32 Ll.L.R. 98.

[8] See *Banque Keyser Ullmann S.A.* v. *Skandia (U.K.) Insurance Co. Ltd.* [1990] 2 All E.R. 947 (where the facts in question were not so material).

[9] *Carter* v. *Boehm* (1766) 3 Burr. 1905, 1909 ("either party"). No such duty is owed to, or by, an assignee of the policy: *The Good Luck* [1989] 2 Lloyd's Rep. 238 (revsd. on other grounds, *The Times*, May 17, 1991).

[10] *Carter* v. *Boehm, supra,* at p. 1910.

[11] Colinvaux, *Law of Insurance* (5th ed.), p. 96; *Roberts* v. *Plaisted* [1989] 2 Lloyd's Rep. 341.

[12] Hasson, (1971) 34 M.L.R. 29.

[13] *Dawsons Ltd.* v. *Bonnin* [1922] 2 A.C. 413.

falls in."[14] And the Law Commission has recommended that basis of the contract clauses should cease to have this effect.[15] Meanwhile, the courts do their best to protect policyholders by construing the basis of the contract clauses strictly against the insurance companies.[16]

(iv) *Insurance distinguished from suretyship or guarantee.* A contract of insurance must be distinguished from a contract of suretyship or guarantee, since it is disputed whether the latter type of contract is *uberrimae fidei*.[17]

A promise to pay another person's debt if he fails to pay it is normally a contract of guarantee, but it is possible to insure against non-payment of a debt, or against some other breach of contract. In *Seaton* v. *Heath*[18] A guaranteed a loan of £15,000 made by B to X. B then obtained a promise from C "in consideration of a premium of 50s. per cent." to "guarantee" A's solvency. The contract between B and C was held to be one of insurance. But in *Trade Indemnity Co. Ltd.* v. *Workington Harbour Board*[19] A agreed to build a dock for B. C gave B a "guarantee" of £50,000 that A would complete the work, and it was held that this was not a contract of insurance.

The distinction between the two types of contract is that a guarantor is usually provided by the debtor,[20] while an insurer is usually sought out by the creditor. Thus the creditworthiness of the debtor is a matter about which a guarantor is likely to know at least as much as the creditor[21]; while an insurer is likely to know less about it than the creditor, having probably had no previous dealings with the debtor. Hence a higher duty of disclosure is owed to the insurer.[22]

(v) *Basis of duty of disclosure in insurance contracts.* In *William Pickersgill & Sons Ltd.* v. *London, etc., Insurance Co.*[23] Hamilton J. said: "The rule imposing an obligation to disclose upon the intending assured does not rest upon a general principle of common law, but arises out of an implied condition, contained in the contract itself, precedent to the liability of the underwriter to pay." One possible interpretation of this dictum is that, in contracts of insurance, there is a *contractual* duty of disclosure based on an implied term in the contract. This duty, being mutual,[24] would rest on the underwriter no less than on the insured; and failure to perform it would amount to a breach of contract, giving rise to a right, not only to rescind the contract, but also to recover damages for its breach. But the current view is that the "condition . . . precedent" is contingent only and not promissory.[25] That is, the party who fails to make the disclosure required

---

[14] *Joel* v. *Law Union & Crown Insurance Co.* [1908] 2 K.B. 863, 885; *cf. West* v. *National Motor & Accident Insurance Union Ltd.* [1955] 1 W.L.R. 343, 348.

[15] Law Com. 104 para. 7.4; *cf.* Law Reform Committee Fifth Report, Cmnd. 63 (1957). Contracts of insurance are excepted from the relevant provisions of the Unfair Contract Terms Act 1977: *ante*, p. 241.

[16] *Joel's* case, *supra* n. 14.

[17] *Post*, p. 357.

[18] [1899] 1 Q.B. 782; reversed on another ground [1900] A.C. 135.

[19] [1937] A.C. 1.

[20] *The Zuhal K* [1987] 1 Lloyd's Rep. 151, 155.

[21] *e.g.* where the debtor is a company and the guarantor is one of its directors.

[22] *Cf. Re Denton's Estate* [1904] 2 Ch. 178, 188.

[23] [1912] 3 K.B. 614, 621.

[24] *Ante*, p. 355.

[25] See *ante*, p. 58 for the distinction between contingent and promissory conditions.

of him cannot enforce the contract, but is not, merely on account of the non-disclosure, liable in damages for breach of the contract.[26] Nor does the non-disclosure give the other party a right to claim damages in tort for negligence. It has been said that the effect of allowing such a claim would be to undermine the general common law principle that there is no duty of disclosure in the negotiations leading to the conclusion of a contract.[27] That general principle is attenuated in insurance contracts only to the extent that the law provides a remedy by way of rescission for non-disclosure of material facts.

(b) FAMILY ARRANGEMENTS. There is a duty to make full disclosure in certain family arrangements, *e.g.* in agreements between members of a family for settling disputes as to the family property. Thus parties to an agreement for the division of the property of a deceased member of the family must disclose to each other all facts known to them which bear on their rights to the estate, or on its value.[28]

(5) Contracts in which there is a limited duty of disclosure

In some cases there is a duty to disclose certain specified facts, or to disclose unusual facts.

(a) SURETYSHIP OR GUARANTEE. Contracts of suretyship or guarantee are sometimes said to be *uberrimae fidei*[29]; but the better view is that they do not fall into this category.[30] The creditor is only bound to disclose unusual circumstances, which the surety would not commonly expect.[31] But an employer who takes a fidelity bond, by which the honesty of one of his employees is guaranteed, is under a somewhat higher duty: he must disclose to the surety any acts of dishonesty by the employee of which he has notice[32]; even if such acts occur after the execution of the bond.

---

[26] *Banque Keyser Ullmann S.A.* v. *Skandia (U.K.) Insurance Co. Ltd.* [1990] 1 Q.B. 665, 779–781; approved on this point [1990] 2 All E.R. 947, 959, 960, where the case was affirmed on other grounds. *Cf. March Cabaret Club & Casino Ltd.* v. *London Assurance* [1975] 1 Lloyd's Rep. 169, 175; *The Good Luck* [1990] 1 Q.B. 818, 888; Clarke [1989] C.L.J. 363; Davenport [1989] L.M.C.L.Q. 251; revsd. on other grounds, *The Times*, May 17, 1991. In one case of breach of a statutory duty of disclosure, the position is the exact converse of that in the insurance cases: damages are available, but rescission is not: see *post*, p. 358, n. 42.

[27] *Banque Keyser Ullmann S.A.* v. *Skandia (U.K.) Insurance Co. Ltd.* [1990] 1 Q.B. 665, 801–802, as to which see *supra*, n. 26.

[28] *Gordon* v. *Gordon* (1817) 3 Swan. 400; *Greenwood* v. *Greenwood* (1863) 1 D.J. & S. 28. *cf. Tennent* v. *Tennents* (1870) L.R. 2 Sc. & Div. 6. Contrast *Wales* v. *Wadham* [1977] 1 W.L.R. 199, 218, *ante*, p. 000, where the rule did not apply as the parties bargained at arm's length.

[29] *Railton* v. *Matthews* (1844) 10 Cl. & F. 934, 943; *March Cabaret Club & Casino Ltd.* v. *London Assurance* [1975] 1 Lloyd's Rep. 169, 175; *Wales* v. *Wadham* [1977] 1 W.L.R. 199, 214.

[30] *Davies* v. *London & Provincial Marine Insurance Co.* (1878) 8 Ch.D. 469, 475; *L.G.O.C. Ltd.* v. *Holloway* [1912] 2 K.B. 72, 81, 83. The point was left open in *Mackenzie* v. *Royal Bank of Canada* [1934] A.C. 468, 475 and in *Trade Indemnity Co. Ltd.* v. *Workington Harbour & Dock Board* [1937] A.C. 1, 18.

[31] *National Provincial Bank of England Ltd.* v. *Glanusk* [1913] 3 K.B. 335, 338; *Cooper* v. *National Provincial Bank* [1946] K.B. 1, 7.

[32] *L.G.O.C. Ltd.* v. *Holloway, supra*. The giving of such bonds is "insurance business" within Insurance Companies Act 1982, s.95(*a*).

(b) SALE OF LAND. There is in general no duty on a seller of land to disclose latent physical defects, but there may be a duty to disclose *unusual* defects of title which a reasonably prudent purchaser could not be expected to discover.[33]

(c) CERTAIN COMPROMISES. There can be a valid compromise of a claim which is bad in law if it is believed to be valid and is made in good faith. But the compromise is only valid if the person making the claim discloses to the other party all facts known to him which affect the validity of the claim.[34]

(d) EXEMPTION CLAUSES. In some cases failure to disclose or draw attention to the terms of a contractual document may (while not affecting the validity of the contract as a whole) deprive one party of the benefit of an exemption clause.[35]

(6) Fiduciary relationship

A duty of disclosure may arise from the relationship of the parties. There is clearly such a duty where the relationship is one to which the equitable doctrine of undue influence applies.[36] The duty in such cases is indeed not discharged by mere disclosure; more stringent conditions must be satisfied before a person who is under the duty can take the benefit of a transaction with the person to whom the duty is owed.[37] But there are other cases in which a person is under a fiduciary duty which he can discharge merely by making full disclosure. This is the position between principal and agent,[38] partners,[39] and between a company and its promoters.[40] A company promoter owes no such common law duty to persons who subscribe for shares in the company on the faith of a prospectus issued by him,[41] but he does owe them an extensive statutory duty of disclosure.[42]

(7) Statute

Under the Financial Services Act 1986, extensive duties of disclosure are imposed on persons who apply for an official listing of securities on the Stock Exchange, and on those who issue a prospectus inviting subscriptions for unlisted securities.[43]

Parties to matrimonial proceedings who seek a consent order from the Family Division for the settlement of their financial and proprietary

---

[33] *Ante*, p. 351.
[34] *Ante*, pp. 83–84.
[35] *Ante*, p. 223.
[36] *Post*, pp. 366–369.
[37] *Post*, pp. 369–370.
[38] *e.g. Armstrong* v. *Jackson* [1917] 2 K.B. 822; *ante*, p. 339.
[39] Pollock, *Law of Partnership* (15th ed.), p. 8.
[40] Gower, *Modern Company Law* (4th ed.), pp. 326 *et seq.*; *Erlanger* v. *New Sombrero Phosphate Co.* (1879) 3 App.Cas. 1218.
[41] *Heyman* v. *European Central Ry.* (1868) L.R. 7 Eq. 154.
[42] *Infra*. Breach of this duty gives rise to a right to damages against those responsible for the prospectus, but not to a right to rescind an allotment of shares: *Re South of England Natural Gas Co.* [1911] 1 Ch. 573. This position seems to be unaffected by the Financial Services Act 1986, ss. 150, 166: see *Palmer's Company Law*, (24th ed.), § 23–170.
[43] ss. 146, 163; *cf.* also ss.144(2)(a) and 162(1):

arrangements must make full and frank disclosure of relevant circumstances to the court that is asked to make the order.[44]

(8) Duty to clarify legal relationship

A duty of disclosure may arise where A sees B acting in reliance on a view of a legal relationship between them which is to A's knowledge false.[45] In the authorities which support the existence of such a duty, the effect of its breach has simply been to give rise to an estoppel[46]; but it is conceivable that such a breach might also invalidate a contract.

(9) Duty of disclosure in performance of contract

So far, we have considered exceptional cases in which a duty of disclosure may exist in the negotiations leading to the conclusion of a contract. It is also possible for a duty of disclosure to arise in the course of the *performance* of an already existing contract. For example, an employee may be bound to disclose breaches of duty of fellow-employees who have defrauded the employer[47]; though he is not bound to disclose his own breaches of duty,[48] let alone his intention to commit breaches of duty in the future.[49] A contracting party may also be under a duty to disclose his own breaches of the contract on the ground that they may lead to danger of physical injury to persons or to property.[50] A professional man may be under certain duties of disclosure towards the person who has engaged his services; but again these duties arise out of the contract (or relationship giving rise to liability in tort)[51] between them: their performance is not a prerequisite for its creation. Sometimes, failure to perform a duty of disclosure imposed by one contract may vitiate a second contract between the same parties: thus in one case it was held that an employee's failure to perform his duty under his contract of employment to disclose frauds being perpetrated by his subordinates on his employers entitled the employers to rescind an arrangement with the employee under which he had obtained considerable benefits on "early retirement."[52] Similarly, it has been suggested that, where a bank lends money on a mortgage to one of its customers, it is under a duty "to proffer to her some adequate explanation of the nature and effect of the document which she had come to sign."[53]

---

[44] *Jenkins* v. *Livesey* [1985] A.C. 424.

[45] *Bell* v. *Marsh* [1903] 1 Ch. 528, 541; *Spiro* v. *Lintern* [1973] 1 W.L.R. 1002, 1010–1011, quoted *ante*, p. 32; *The Henrik Sif* [1982] 1 Lloyd's Rep. 456; *The Lutetian* [1982] 2 Lloyd's Rep. 140, 158. Contrast *The Tatra* [1990] 2 Lloyd's Rep. 51 (where A had no such knowledge).

[46] *Post*, p. 361. *Cf.* also the cases of "estoppel by convention" discussed at p. 111, *ante*. In those cases, the mistake is shared by both parties, so that it is inappropriate to talk of a duty of disclosure: *cf. ante*, p. 351 at n. 67.

[47] *Sybron Corp.* v. *Rochem Ltd.* [1984] Ch. 112, 126–127, 129; Kerr L.J. treated the case as one of "covering up and deliberately concealing": *ibid.* at p. 130.

[48] *Bell* v. *Lever Bros.* [1932] A.C. 161.

[49] *Horcal* v. *Gatland* [1984] I.R.L.R. 288.

[50] *The Zinnia* [1984] 2 Lloyd's Rep. 211, 218.

[51] See the discussion of the extent of a surgeon's duty of disclosure before carrying out an operation: *Sidaway* v. *Bethlehem Royal Hospital* [1985] A.C. 871; and the duty of a doctor carrying out a vasectomy to warn the patient that sterility might not be permanent: *Thake* v. *Maurice* [1986] Q.B. 644.

[52] *Sybron Corp.* v. *Rochem Ltd.* [1984] Ch. 112; Honeyball [1983] C.L.J. 218.

[53] *Cornish* v. *Midland Bank plc* [1985] 3 All E.R. 513, 523, where the bank was in fact guilty of active misrepresentation.

3. Effects of Non-disclosure

(1) In general

Cases of liability for non-disclosure can be divided into two kinds. First, there are cases in which no misrepresentation has been made in so many words, but one can be inferred from conduct or from the surrounding circumstances, *e.g.* where a representation is falsified by later events, or where a statement is literally true but misleading, or where disclosure is required by custom.[54] Secondly, there are cases of what may be called "pure" non-disclosure, in which no such inference can be drawn, but the law nevertheless gives a remedy for non-disclosure, *e.g.* in contracts of insurance, or by statute.[55]

In the first of the above groups of cases, non-disclosure can give rise to the same remedies as active misrepresentation, that is, to a right to rescind and to a common law right to damages for deceit, or for negligence. The position is more complex in the second group of cases, *i.e.* in those of "pure" non-disclosure. We have seen that failure to perform the duty of disclosure in contracts *uberrimae fidei* gives rise to a right to rescind, but not to one to damages either for breach of contract or for negligence at common law.[56] Conversely, breach of the statutory duty of disclosure imposed on persons issuing a company prospectus has been held to give rise to a right to damages, but not to one to rescind.[57] On the other hand, it seems that failure to perform a duty of disclosure in the performance of a contract[58] can give rise to a right to damages and to one to rescind, in accordance with the rules relating to the effects of breach, to be discussed later in this book.[59] General statements about the effects of cases of "pure" non-disclosure are best avoided: the effects depend on the purpose of the rule of law by which the duty of disclosure is imposed.

(2) Effects of Misrepresentation Act 1967

The Misrepresentation Act repeatedly uses the expression "misrepresentation made." This refers primarily to active misrepresentation and not to the category of "pure" non-disclosure,[60] as described above. The Act therefore does not impose liability for such non-disclosure where none existed before.[61] Nor does it affect any liability for, or defence based on, such non-disclosure which did exist before the Act. It follows that liability in negligence for "pure" non-disclosure could only be imposed (if at all) at common law and not under section 2(1); that the court has no discretion in cases of such non-disclosure to award damages in lieu of rescission under section 2(2); and that a term whose sole effect was to exclude or restrict liability for such non-disclosure is not affected by section 3.

On the other hand, the distinction between cases of "pure" non-

---

54 *Ante*, pp. 352–354.
55 *Ante*, pp. 354, 358.
56 *Ante*, p. 357.
57 *Ante*, p. 358, n. 42.
58 *Ante*, p. 359.
59 *Post*, pp. 659 *et seq.*; 747 *et seq.*
60 The Act has not altered the common law meaning of "misrepresentation": *André & Cie. S.A.* v. *Ets. Michel Blanc & Fils* [1979] 2 Lloyd's Rep. 427, 435.
61 *Banque Keyser Ullmann S.A.* v. *Skandia (U.K.) Ins. Co. Ltd.* [1990] 1 Q.B. 665, 789–790, affirmed [1990] 2 All E.R. 947.

disclosure, and those in which a misrepresentation, though not made in so many words, can be inferred from conduct, probably applies for the purposes of the Act. It is submitted that the Act would apply to cases of the latter kind,[62] *e.g.* where a representation had been made by conduct,[63] and where a representation had been made which was literally true but misleading because it was obscure or only told part of the truth.[64] It seems probable that the Act would also apply where the representation was true when it was made but was falsified by later events.[65] Section 2(1) in particular might be thought to apply to such a case as it requires the representor to show that he believed "up to the time the contract was made that the facts represented were true." It could be argued that there was no "misrepresentation made" if the facts originally stated were then true; but the answer to this may be that the representation can be treated as a continuing one and that it would become a *mis*representation when the falsifying event occurred.

SECTION 8. MISREPRESENTATION AND ESTOPPEL

Under the doctrine of estoppel by representation[66]; a person who makes precise and unambiguous[67] representation[68] of fact[69] may be prevented from denying the truth of the statement if the person to whom it was made was intended to act on it, and did act on it to his detriment.[70] It is generally said that the doctrine does not give rise to a cause of action[71] but only to a defence. Thus if A agrees to let a house to B, representing that the drains are sound when they are not, B cannot rely on the doctrine of estoppel to found a claim for damages against A.[72] But the doctrine could provide B with a defence: for example, if A, immediately after the execution of the lease, brought an action for breach of covenant to repair.[73] Such a defence could be pleaded even though B had affirmed (and not rescinded) the lease.

In addition to providing a defence to the representee, estoppel may

---

[62] See Hudson, 85 L.Q.R. 524.

[63] *Ante*, p. 349.

[64] *Ante*, p. 353.

[65] *Ante*, p. 352.

[66] In this Chapter our only concern is with this kind of estoppel. Estoppel by negligence is beyond the scope of this book. For the distinction, see Cross on *Evidence* (7th ed.), pp. 96–98; *Moorgate Mercantile Co.* v. *Twitchings* [1977] A.C. 890. For promissory estoppel, estoppel by convention and proprietary estoppel, see *ante*, pp. 101–115, 120–136.

[67] See *Low* v. *Bouverie* [1891] 3 Ch. 82 and *Woodhouse A.C. Israel Cocoa Ltd.* v. *Nigerian Produce Marketing Co.* [1972] A.C. 741, where this requirement was not satisfied; *cf. The Junior K* [1988] 2 Lloyd's Rep. 583, 589. But it has been said that "reasonable clarity is sufficient": *The Shakleford* [1978] 2 Lloyd's Rep. 155, 159.

[68] Non-disclosure or inaction will not normally suffice: *Laurie & Morewood* v. *Dudin & Sons* [1926] 1 K.B. 223; *Moorgate Mercantile Co.* v. *Twitchings, supra*, n. 66; *The Nai Genova* [1984] 1 Lloyd's Rep. 353, 363; *Tai Hing Cotton Mill Ltd.* v. *Liu Chong Hing Bank* [1986] A.C. 80, 110, 392; *The Leonidas D* [1985] 1 W.L.R. 925; *The Tatra* [1990] 2 Lloyd's Rep. 51 and see *ante*

[69] As distinct from one of law: see *Territorial & Auxiliary Forces Association* v. *Nichols* [1949] 1 K.B. 35; *The Argo Hellas* [1984] 1 Lloyd's Rep. 296, 304; and from a representation as to the future (or a promise): see *ante*, pp. 00, 000–000.

[70] *e.g. Lombard North Central plc* v. *Stobart* [1990] Tr.L.R. 105.

[71] *Low* v. *Bouverie, supra*, n. 67; *The Anemone* [1987] 1 Lloyd's Rep. 546, 557.

[72] Of course, there might be a claim for damages under one of the five heads discussed at pp. 10, 33–34, *ante*.

[73] *Cf. Oades* v. *Spafford* [1949] 1 K.B. 74.

remove one that would otherwise be available to the representor. Thus it may help a plaintiff no less than a defendant.[74] In *Burrowes* v. *Lock*[75] a beneficiary under a trust fund proposed to assign his share for value to the plaintiff, who, before advancing any money, asked the trustee whether the beneficiary had previously encumbered his share. The trustee replied that there was no encumbrance, having forgotten that 10 years earlier the beneficiary had in fact encumbered his share. It was held that the trustee was estopped from denying the truth of his statement. Thus he was liable to pay the assigned share to the plaintiff, free from the earlier encumbrance. The assignee here had an independent cause of action against the trustee based on the assignment. And the trustee was, by his representation, deprived of the defence that he was already bound to pay part of the fund to the previous encumbrancer. Similarly, a warehouseman may make a contractual promise to deliver goods out of his warehouse; and if the promise is coupled with an untrue statement about the goods (*e.g.* that they are in good condition, or in the warehouse, when they are not), he may be estopped from denying the truth of the statement.[76] The cause of action is based on the contractual promise, and the effect of the estoppel is simply to remove a defence.[77] And a person who has entered into a voidable contract may indicate that he is not going to exercise his power to avoid it. The effect of such a representation will be that he is bound by the contract without any power of avoidance[78]; and this result may be explained on the ground of either affirmation or estoppel. If the second explanation is adopted, it is again not the estoppel but the contract which constitutes the cause of action: the effect of the estoppel is simply to remove the power of avoidance.

---

[74] Jackson, 81 L.Q.R. 223; *cf. ante*, p. 108.
[75] (1805) 10 Ves. 470, as explained in *Low* v. *Bouverie, supra*; see Sheridan, *Fraud in Equity*, pp. 31–36.
[76] See *Coventry Shepherd & Co.* v. *G.E. Ry.* (1883) 11 Q.B.D. 76; *cf. Alicia Hosiery Ltd.* v. *Brown Shipley & Co. Ltd.* [1970] 1 Q.B. 195, 206; *Griswold* v. *Haven*, 25 N.Y. 595 (1862).
[77] *e.g. European Asian Bank* v. *Punjab & Sind Bank* [1983] 2 All E.R. 508; *The Uhenbels* [1986] 2 Lloyd's Rep. 294, 300.
[78] *Janred Properties Ltd.* v. *Ente Nazionale Italiano per il Turismo* [1989] 2 All E.R. 444.

CHAPTER TEN

DURESS AND UNDUE INFLUENCE[1]

THE consent of a contracting party may have been obtained by some form of pressure which the law regards as improper. The victim of such pressure may be entitled to relief under the common law of duress, and under the equitable rules of undue influence. He is also protected by certain special statutory provisions.

SECTION 1. DURESS AT COMMON LAW

A contract is voidable[2] at common law if it was made under duress. At one time the common law concept of duress was a very narrow one. It was restricted to actual or threatened physical violence to, or unlawful constraint of, the person of the contracting party.[3] In *Latter* v. *Bradell*[4] a housemaid was ordered by her mistress to submit to a medical examination, on a suspicion of pregnancy which turned out to be unfounded. She cried and protested but submitted. Her claim for damages for assault failed: it was held that her consent to the examination had not been vitiated by duress as no physical violence was threatened or inflicted.

The original common law[5] view that only unlawful violence to the person (actual or threatened) could constitute duress was open to the objection that it failed to give due weight to the coercive effect of other illegitimate conduct or threats. It was therefore rejected in *The Siboen and the Sibotre*,[6] where Kerr J. said that a plea of "compulsion or coercion" would also be available in other circumstances: *e.g.* where a person had been forced to enter into a contract under an imminent threat of having his house burnt down, or a valuable picture slashed.[7] His views have been accepted in later cases, so that the question now to be asked is whether there has been "coercion of the will, which vitiates consent."[8] In *The Universe Sentinel*,[9] for example, trade union officials threatened to induce

---

[1] Winder, 3 M.L.R. 97; 4 Conv.(N.S.) 274.

[2] In *Barton* v. *Armstrong* [1976] A.C. 104 certain deeds were declared "void" for duress; *cf.* Lanham, 29 M.L.R. 615. But the general view is that a contract procured by duress is only voidable: *Pao On* v. *Lau Yiu Long* [1980] A.C. 614, 634; *The Universe Sentinel* [1983] 1 A.C. 366, 383, 400 and *Deputy* v. *Stapleford* 19 Cal. 302 (1861) (contract procured by flogging, etc., held "voidable"). A marriage is voidable for duress: Matrimonial Causes Act 1973, s.12(*c*).

[3] *Cumming* v. *Ince* (1847) 11 Q.B. 112, 120; the violence threatened had to be unlawful: *Biffin* v. *Bignell* (1862) 7 H. & N. 877; *Smith* v. *Monteith* (1844) 13 M. & W. 427.

[4] (1880) 50 L.J.C.P. 166; (1881) 50 L.J.Q.B. 448.

[5] Admiralty took a broader view in cases concerning salvage agreements: see *The Port Caledonia* [1903] P. 184.

[6] [1976] 1 Lloyd's Rep. 293. Beatson, 92 L.Q.R. 496; Beatson, "The Use and Abuse of Unjust Enrichment:" Essays in the Law of Restitution, Chap. 5.

[7] At p. 335.

[8] *Pau On* v. *Lau Yiu Long* [1980] A.C. 614, 636; *cf. The Atlantic Baron* [1979] Q.B. 705; *The Proodos C* [1980] 2 Lloyd's Rep. 390, 393; Coote [1980] C.L.J. 40; Atiyah, 98 L.Q.R. 197; *The Evia Luck* (*No. 2*) [1990] 1 Lloyd's Rep. 319.

[9] [1983] 1 A.C. 366; Napier, [1983] C.L.J. 43; Jones, *ibid*. 47.

the crew of a ship to break their contracts of employment and so to prevent the ship from leaving port. In view of the "catastrophic"[10] financial consequences which the shipowners would suffer if these threats were carried out, it was conceded that they constituted "economic duress,"[11] vitiating the shipowners' consent to an agreement to make certain payments to the union. To be capable of giving rise to such duress, the threat must be illegitimate either because what is threatened is a legal wrong[12] (as in the examples so far given) or because the threat itself is wrongful (as in the case of the blackmailer's threat to disclose his victim's conduct to third parties[13]) or because it is contrary to public policy.[14] Whether the threat actually gives rise to duress must then be considered by reference to its coercive effect in each case: no particular type of threat is regarded either as *ipso facto* having such an effect, or as being incapable, as a matter of law, of producing it.

Even under this more flexible test, mere "commercial pressure"[15] will not suffice; nor will a threat amount to duress *merely* because what is threatened is a legal wrong. The point can be illustrated by reference to cases in which a party is induced to enter into a contract by a threat to break an earlier contract. Such a threat *may* amount to duress. Thus cases such as *D. & C. Builders* v. *Rees*[16] have been explained[17] on the ground that the creditor's promise to accept part payment in full settlement had been obtained by duress. Similarly, in *B & S Contracts and Designs Ltd.* v. *Victor Green Publications Ltd.*[18] a contractor who had undertaken to erect stands for an exhibition at Olympia told his client, less than a week before the exhibition was due to open, that the contract would be cancelled unless the client paid an additional sum to meet claims which were being made against the contractor by his workforce. The consequence of not having the stands erected in time would have been disastrous for the client in that it would have gravely damaged his reputation and might have exposed him to heavy claims for damages from exhibitors to whom space on the stands had been let. In these circumstances it was held that the payment had been made under duress and that the client was entitled to recover it back.

It does not follow from such cases that *any* threat to break a contract will amount to duress.[19] In *Pao On* v. *Lau Yiu Long*[20] the plaintiffs threatened

---

[10] [1983] 1 A.C. 366, 383.

[11] *Ibid.*

[12] Hence a threat merely to exercise one's rights under a contract is not illegitimate: *The Olib*, *Financial Times*, February 8, 1991.

[13] [1983] 1 A.C. 401.

[14] *The Evia Luck (No. 2)* [1990] 1 Lloyd's Rep. 319, 329; *cf. The Evia Luck* [1986] 2 Lloyd's Rep. 165, 178.

[15] *The Siboen and the Sibotre* [1976] 1 Lloyd's Rep. 293, 336.

[16] [1966] 2 Q.B. 617; *ante*, p. 115. *Cf. The Atlantic Baron* [1979] Q.B. 705, *ante*, p. 91; *Nixon* v. *Furphy* (1925) 25 S.R. (N.S.W.) 151; *T. A. Sundell & Sons Pty. Ltd.* v. *Emm Yannoulatos (Overseas) Pty. Ltd.* (1956) 56 S.R. (N.S.W.) 323; contrast *Smith* v. *Charlick* (1923–4) 34 C.L.R. 38 (payment to avoid threat not to enter into *future* contracts); *Williams* v. *Roffey Bros. & Nicholls (Contractors) Ltd.* [1991] 1 Q.B. 1 (where no threat was made and duress was not pleaded).

[17] In *The Siboen and The Sibotre, supra*, at p. 335.

[18] [1984] I.C.R. 419; Palmer and Catchpole, 48 M.L.R. 102; *cf. The Alev* [1989] 1 Lloyd's Rep. 138; *Atlas Express Ltd.* v. *Kafco (Importers & Distributors) Ltd.* [1989] Q.B. 833; Chandler, [1989] L.M.C.L.Q. 270; Flemming, [1989] C.L.J. 362; Phang, 53 M.L.R. 107.

[19] *The Siboen and The Sibotre, supra*, at p. 335; *cf. post*, pp. 550–551.

[20] [1980] A.C. 614; *Cf. Alec Lobb (Garages) Ltd.* v. *Total Oil (Great Britain) Ltd.* [1983] 1 W.L.R. 87.

to break a contract with a company unless the defendants, who were shareholders in the company, gave them a guarantee against loss resulting from the performance of that contract. The defendants, thinking that the risk of such loss was small, gave the guarantee to avoid the adverse publicity which the company might suffer if the contract was not performed. In these circumstances, it was held that there was no "coercion of the will," so that the guarantee was not vitiated by duress. In deciding whether the threat actually coerced the person to whom it was addressed, the court will also consider what alternative courses of action (other than submission to the threat) were reasonably available to that person: for example there will be no economic duress if it would have been reasonable for him to have resisted the threatened wrong by taking legal proceedings.[21]

The view that unlawful violence to the person was necessary to constitute duress had led in a number of nineteenth century cases to the conclusion that a contract could not be invalidated by "duress of goods." This meant than an agreement to pay money for the release of goods unlawfully detained, or to prevent their unlawful seizure, was valid.[22] But it had also been held that money which had actually been paid for such a purpose could be recovered back.[23] Parke B. in several cases stated this strange distinction with apparent complacency.[24] Its effect was not wholly clear. It could hardly have meant that a person who was successfully sued for money which he had agreed to pay for the release of his goods could then recover back what he had been compelled to pay in the first action. It seems to have meant that money which was simply paid for the release of the goods could be recovered back; while money to be paid under an agreement for their release could be sued for and could not (if paid) be recovered back. But if it meant this it was inconsistent with at least one case[25] in which money paid under such an agreement was recovered back; and if this was right it would have been very strange if the agreement to pay the money had been enforceable.[26] Recent authority supports the view that the "duress of goods" cases now depend on the modern, flexible, test of duress, so that the question in each case is whether there had in fact been "coercion of the will"[27]; and that this test governs both the validity of the contract and the right to recover back money paid under it.[28]

The rule that money extorted by duress can be recovered back also applies where an unlawful charge is levied by unlawful threats, for

---

[21] *e.g. Hennessy* v. *Craigmyle & Co.* [1986] I.C.R. 461.

[22] *Skeate* v. *Beale* (1841) 11 A. & E. 983; and see *infra*, n. 24. It is assumed that the seizure is not *known* to be unlawful, for, in that case, there would be no consideration for the promise to pay: *ante*, p. 83, and see *Atlee* v. *Backhouse* (1836) 3 M. & W. 633, 650.

[23] *Astley* v. *Reynolds* (1731) 2 Str. 915; *Valpy* v. *Manley* (1845) 1 C.B. 594; *Green* v. *Duckett* (1883) 11 Q.B.D. 275; *Maskell* v. *Horner* [1915] 3 K.B. 106; *T. D. Keegan Ltd.* v. *Palmer* [1961] 2 Lloyd's Rep. 449, 457.

[24] *Atlee* v. *Backhouse* (1836) 3 M. & W. 633, 650; *Oates* v. *Hudson* (1851) 6 Ex. 346; *Parker* v. *Bristol & Exeter Ry.* (1851) 6 Ex. 702, 705.

[25] *Tamvaco* v. *Simpson* (1866) L.R. 1 C.P. 363, where the only question discussed by the Exchequer Chamber was whether the detention was lawful.

[26] *Cf.* Beatson [1974] C.L.J. 97 (suggesting that the cases of valid agreements should be explained as compromises or on similar grounds).

[27] *Pao On* v. *Lau Yiu Long* [1980] A.C. 614, 636.

[28] *The Universe Sentinel* [1983] 1 A.C. 366; *cf. The Atlantic Baron* [1979] Q.B. 705, (where the claim there failed on the ground of affirmation); *Lloyds Bank Ltd.* v. *Bundy* [1975] Q.B. 326, 337; *The Alev* [1989] 1 Lloyd's Rep. 138.

example, if a carrier refuses to carry goods unless he is paid more than he is legally entitled to charge.[29] But it does not apply where the demand for the money is not backed by any threat[30]; or where it is backed only by a threat to take legal proceedings[31]: if such a payment could be recovered back, no compromise would be secure.

As in the case of misrepresentation, it is not necessary to show that duress was the sole cause inducing the contract.[32] It is enough if it was *an* inducement; and once the fact of duress is established the burden is on the party exerting the duress to show that it did not in fact induce the contract.[33]

SECTION 2. UNDUE INFLUENCE IN EQUITY

1. Actual Pressure

Equity gives relief on the ground of undue influence where an agreement has been obtained by certain kinds of improper pressure which were thought not to amount to duress at common law because no element of violence to the person was involved.[34] For example, a promise to pay money can be set aside if obtained by a threat to prosecute the promisor,[35] or his close relative, or his spouse, for a criminal offence.[36] The party who claims relief on the ground of actual undue influence must show that such influence existed and had been exercised,[37] that the transaction resulted from that influence, and that the transaction was manifestly to his disadvantage.[38]

2. Special Relationships

In a number of situations (to be described below) the relationship between the parties is such as to give rise to a presumption of undue influence[39]; and in these situations there is no need to show that undue influence existed and had been exercised. There was formerly some support for the view that, in such cases, the transaction could be set aside on grounds of public policy, even though it was not disadvantageous to the party claiming

---

[29] *Parker* v. *Bristol & Exeter Ry.*, *supra*, n. 24; Great Western Ry. v. *Sutton* (1869) L.R. 4 H.L. 226; Winfield, 60 L.Q.R. 341.

[30] *Twyford* v. *Manchester Corpn.* [1946] Ch. 236; discussed by Marsh, 62 L.Q.R. 333.

[31] *Brown* v. *M'Kinally* (1795) 1 Esp. 279; *William Whiteley Ltd.* v. *R.* (1910) 101 L.T. 741.

[32] *Ante*, pp. 305–306.

[33] *Barton* v. *Armstrong* [1976] A.C. 104.

[34] *Turnbull & Co.* v. *Duvall* [1902] A.C. 429; *Chaplin & Co.* v. *Brammal* [1908] 1 K.B. 233; *Avon Finance Co.* v. *Bridger* [1985] 2 All E.R. 281, 285.

[35] Such a threat was formerly thought to be incapable of giving rise to duress at common law: *Flower* v. *Sadler* (1882) 10 Q.B.D. 572.

[36] *Williams* v. *Bayley* (1866) L.R. 1 H.L. 200; *Kaufman* v. *Gerson* [1904] 1 K.B. 591; *Société des Hôtels Réunis (S.A.)* v. *Hawker* (1913) 29 T.L.R. 578; *Mutual Finance Ltd.* v. *Wetton* [1937] 2 K.B. 389.

[37] *Howes* v. *Bishop* [1909] 2 K.B. 390; *Bank of Montreal* v. *Stuart* [1911] A.C. 120, 127.

[38] *Bank of Credit & Commerce International S.A.* v. *Aboody* [1990] 1 Q.B. 923; Cretney, 105 L.Q.R. 169; Dixon, [1989] C.L.J. 359.

[39] *Allcard* v. *Skinner* (1887) 36 Ch.D. 145.

relief.[40] But the House of Lords has rejected this view and has held that the basis of relief was "not a vague 'public policy' but specifically the victimisation of one party by the other."[41] It follows that the presumption of undue influence is not, of itself, a ground for relief. It absolves the claimant from having to show that the alleged influence actually existed and had been exercised but it does not absolve him from the need to establish that the transaction which he seeks to set aside is manifestly to his disadvantage.[42]

Relief can be given on the ground of undue influence even though the person to whom the gift or promise was made obtained no personal benefit from it. Thus the rule applies where the head of a religious order uses a gift wholly for the purposes of the order and where a trustee extracts a promise from one beneficiary solely for the benefit of the other.[43]

(1) Relationships in which the presumption applies

The question whether the presumption applies to a given relationship is in many cases settled by authority. Thus it applies between parent and child,[44] guardian and ward,[45] religious adviser and disciple,[46] doctor and patient,[47] solicitor and client[48] and trustee and *cestui que trust*.[49] It applies to some, but not all, transactions between fiancé and fiancée: thus it has been applied to a settlement made before marriage by which the wife agreed, in return for a small immediate payment, to give up large sums which were to accrue to her as a widow; but it would not apply to the gift of an extravagant engagement ring.[50] The rule does not apply between hus-

---

[40] *Ibid.* p. 171; *Lloyds Bank Ltd.* v. *Bundy* [1975] Q.B. 326, 342; *cf. Hylton* v. *Hylton* (1745) 2 Ves.Sen. 547, 549 ("public utility").

[41] *National Westminster Bank plc* v. *Morgan* [1985] A.C. 686, 706; Cope, 60 A.L.J. 87; *cf. Alec Lobb (Garages) Ltd.* v. *Total Oil (Great Britain) Ltd.* [1985] 1 W.L.R. 173; *Hart* v. *O'Connor* [1985] A.C. 1000, 1024; *Cornish* v. *Midland Bank plc* [1985] 3 All E.R. 513; *Petrou* v. *Woodstead Finance Ltd.* [1986] F.L.R. 158; *Midland Bank plc* v. *Shephard* [1988] 3 All E.R. 17, 21.

[42] See the authorities cited in n. 41, *supra.* Dicta in *National Westminster Bank plc* v. *Morgan, supra*, at p. 704 and in *Cornish* v. *Midland Bank plc, supra*, at pp. 518, 520 suggest that the presumption can only arise if the transaction is wrongful; but this would, with respect, leave no scope for the operation of any presumption. The relationship in these cases was *not* one of those to which the presumption applies; and the dicta perhaps use the phrase "presumption of undue influence" to refer to *all* the circumstances which must exist to give rise to a claim for relief. For the continued existence of the presumption, see *Goldsworthy* v. *Brickell* [1987] Ch. 378; Tiplady, 45 M.L.R. 579; and for the survival of the distinction between *actual* and *presumed* undue influence, see *Coldunell Ltd.* v. *Gallon* [1986] 1 All E.R. 429, 434. For qualification of the requirement that the party seeking relief must show that the transaction was disadvantageous to him, see *infra* at n. 48 and *post*, p. 370 at n. 77.

[43] *Allcard* v. *Skinner, supra*; *Ellis* v. *Barker* (1871) L.R. 7 Ch.App. 104; *cf. Bullock* v. *Lloyds Bank* [1955] Ch. 317.

[44] *Bullock* v. *Lloyds Bank, supra*; *Cocking* v. *Pratt* (1749) 1 Ves.Sen. 400; *Powell* v. *Powell* [1900] 1 Ch. 243.

[45] *Hylton* v. *Hylton,* (1754) 2 Ves.Sen. 547; *Hatch* v. *Hatch* (1804) 9 Ves. 292; the *de facto* relation of guardian and ward suffices: *Archer* v. *Hudson* (1846) 15 L.J.Ch. 211.

[46] *Allcard* v. *Skinner, supra*; *Nottidge* v. *Prince* (1860) 2 Giff. 246; *cf. Tufton* v. *Sperni* [1952] 2 T.L.R. 516; *Roche* v. *Sherrington* [1982] 1 W.L.R. 599, 606.

[47] *Dent* v. *Bennett* (1839) 4 My. & Cr. 269; *Radcliffe* v. *Price* (1902) 18 T.L.R. 466; *cf. Re. C.M.G.* [1970] Ch. 574 (authorities in charge of mental hospital and patient residing there).

[48] *Wright* v. *Carter*[1903] 1 Ch. 27; *cf. Wintle* v. *Nye* [1959] 1 W.L.R. 284.

[49] *Ellis* v. *Barker* (1871) L.R. 7 Ch.App. 104; *Thomson* v. *Eastwood* (1877) 2 App.Cas. 215.

[50] *Zamet* v. *Hyman* [1961] 1 W.L.R. 1442; qualifying *Re Lloyds Bank Ltd.* [1931] 1 Ch. 289.

band and wife,[51] or between employer and employee.[52] Nor does it apply to all relationships which are fiduciary in the sense that they give rise to a duty of disclosure: thus it does not apply between agent and principal.[53] The rule may apply even after the relationship has ceased if the influence continues, for example, between solicitor and ex-client[54]; and between parent and child for a "short" time[55] after the child has come of age, but not once the child is "emancipated" from parental control.[56] Even the marriage of a child does not necessarily have this effect.[57]

The presumption is not confined to these relationships; nor is it restricted to relationships in which one party can be said to have acquired "domination" over the other.[58] It applies whenever the relationship between the parties is such that one of them is by reason of the confidence reposed in him by the other able to take unfair advantage of the other. In *Tate* v. *Williamson*,[59] the defendant became financial adviser to an extravagant Oxford undergraduate who sold him his estate for half its value and then drank himself to death at the age of 24. His executors successfully claimed that the sale of the estate should be set aside. Lord Chelmsford said: "The jurisdiction exercised by courts of equity over the dealings of persons standing in certain fiduciary relations has always been regarded as one of the most salutary description. . . . The courts have always been careful not to fetter this jurisdiction by defining the exact limits of its exercise."[60] A modern illustration of the principle is provided by *O'Sullivan* v. *Management Agency & Music Ltd.*[61] where the relationship between the plaintiff (then a young and unknown composer and performer of music) and his manager was held to be one giving rise to a presumption of undue influence; and transactions which turned out to be unfair to the plaintiff when he later became a celebrity were accordingly set aside.

A number of cases have raised the question whether the presumption can apply between banker and customer where the bank is asked to lend money on the security of the customer's home. In *Lloyds Bank Ltd.* v. *Bundy*[62] a father gave his bank a guarantee of his son's business debts and mortgaged his house to the bank as security for the guarantee. It was held that the presumption applied since, for the purpose of the transaction, the father had placed himself entirely in the hands of the bank manager, and

---

[51] *Howes* v. *Bishop* [1909] 2 K.B. 390; *Bank of Montreal* v. *Stuart* [1911] A.C. 120; *Mackenzie* v. *Royal Bank of Canada* [1934] A.C. 468; *Gillman* v. *Gillman* (1946) 174 L.T. 272. *National Westminster Bank plc* v. *Morgan* [1985] A.C. 686, 703; *Kings North Trust Ltd.* v. *Bell* [1986] 1 W.L.R. 119, 127; *Coldunell Ltd.* v. *Gallon* [1986] 1 All E.R. 429, 437; Andrews, [1986] C.L.J. 195; *Midland Bank plc* v. *Shephard* [1988] 3 All E.R. 17.

[52] *Matthew* v. *Bobbins* (1980) 256 E.G. 603.

[53] *Re Coomber* [1911] 1 Ch. 723; but if the duty of disclosure is broken, the injured party need not show that the transaction is to his manifest disadvantage: *Bank of Credit & Commerce International S.A.* v. *Aboody* [1990] 1 Q.B. 923, 962.

[54] *McMaster* v. *Byrne* [1952] 1 All E.R. 1362; *cf. Allison* v. *Clayhills* (1907) 97 L.T. 709, 711.

[55] See *Re Pauling's Settlement Trusts* [1964] Ch. 303, 337.

[56] *Bainbrigge* v. *Browne* (1881) 18 Ch.D. 188.

[57] *Lancashire Loans Ltd.* v. *Black* [1934] 1 K.B. 380.

[58] *Goldsworthy* v. *Brickell* [1987] Ch. 378, 404.

[59] (1866) L.R. 2 Ch.App. 55. For similar relationships between the aged and their advisors or companions, see *Inche Noriah* v. *Shaik Allie bin Omar* [1929] A.C. 127; *Re Craig* [1971] Ch. 95; contrast *Hunter* v. *Atkins* (1834) 3 My. & K. 113; *Re Brocklehurst* [1978] 1 Ch. 14.

[60] At p. 60; *cf. Tufton* v. *Sperni* [1952] 2 T.L.R. 516; *National Westminster Bank plc* v. *Morgan* [1985] A.C. 686, 708–709; *Goldsworthy* v. *Brickell* [1987] Ch. 378.

[61] [1985] Q.B. 428; *cf.* also *Horry* v. *Tate & Lyle Refineries Ltd.* [1982] 2 Lloyd's Rep. 417.

[62] [1975] Q.B. 326, especially at p. 342. Carr, 38 M.L.R. 463; Sealy [1975] C.L.J. 17.

had been given no opportunity to seek independent advice. But this was an exceptional case which turned on its "very special facts"[63]: normally the presumption does not apply between banker and customer. In *National Westminster Bank plc* v. *Morgan*[64] a wife joined her husband in mortgaging the family home to their bank, after being assured by the bank manager that the mortgage covered no more than the amount of the original advance. This assurance was honestly given but it was mistaken: the mortgage extended to all further liabilities of the husband to the bank. No such further liabilities were in fact incurred; and, after the husband's death, it was held that the mortgage could not be set aside on the ground of undue influence since the bank manager had not acquired a sufficient degree of influence[65] over the wife, nor was the transaction unfair to her. If she had suffered loss as a result of the bank manager's misstatement, her remedy would have been to claim damages for negligence or for misrepresentation[66]—not to have the mortgage set aside.

Where the necessary relationship is alleged to exist, the burden of proving that it does exist is on the party seeking to set the transaction aside.[67] Once this burden has been discharged, it is up to the party benefiting from the transaction to rebut the presumption of undue influence[68] in one of the ways to be discussed below.

The presumption does not apply, even though one of the special relationships exists, if it cannot possibly have influenced the particular transaction. Thus it has been suggested that the presumption would not apply if a solicitor bought a horse from a client who had retained him to conduct an action for slander.[69]

(2) Rebutting the presumption

The presumption of undue influence is rebutted if the party benefiting from the transaction shows that it was "the free exercise of independent will."[70] The most usual way of doing this is to show that the other party had independent advice before entering into the transaction.[71] But the mere fact that independent advice was given will not necessarily save the transaction. The advice must be competent and based on knowledge of all the relevant facts.[72] It has been suggested that the independent adviser must also

---

[63] *National Westminster Bank plc* v. *Morgan* [1985] A.C. 686, 698; also approving at p. 709 the *ratio* of the majority in *Lloyds Bank Ltd.* v. *Bundy* on the presumption of undue influence. *Cf. Cornish* v. *Midland Bank plc* [1985] 3 All E.R. 513, 518.

[64] [1985] A.C. 686; Andrews [1985] C.L.J. 192; Tiplady, 48 M.L.R. 579; *Bank of Baroda* v. *Panessar* [1987] Ch. 335; *cf. Lloyd's Bank* v. *Egremont* [1990] 2 FLR 351.

[65] At p. 708. A relationship of trust (as opposed to domination) may suffice: *Goldsworthy* v. *Brickell* [1987] Ch. 378, 404.

[66] As in *Cornish* v. *Midland Bank plc, supra*; no such claim was made in *National Westminster Bank plc* v. *Morgan*: see [1985] A.C. 686, 698.

[67] *Lloyds Bank Ltd.* v. *Bundy* [1975] Q.B. at p. 342; *cf. Re Craig* [1971] Ch. 95; *Coldunell Ltd.* v. *Gallon* [1986] Q.B. 1184. For the statement in *National Westminster Bank plc* v. *Morgan* [1985] A.C. 686, 707 ("The wrongfulness of the transaction must . . . be shown") *cf. ante* p. 367, n. 42; there was *no* presumption of undue influence in that case.

[68] *Allcard* v. *Skinner* (1887) 36 Ch.D. 145; *Re Craig, supra*.

[69] *Allison* v. *Clayhills* (1907) 97 L.T. 709, 711.

[70] *Inche Noriah* v. *Shaik Allie bin Omar* [1929] A.C. 127, 136.

[71] *Allcard* v. *Skinner* (1887) 36 Ch.D. 145, 190; *Bullock* v. *Lloyds Bank* [1955] Ch. 317 *Horry* v. *Tate & Lyle Refineries Ltd.* [1982] 2 Lloyd's Rep. 417, 421.

[72] *Inche Noriah* v. *Shaik Allie bin Omar* [1929] A.C. 127.

approve the transaction, and that his advice must be followed.[73] This may be necessary where the influence is particularly strong, or where a very large gift is made; but it is not necessary in every case.[74] There is indeed no invariable rule that independent advice is necessary to save the transaction[75]; but the beneficiary would lack elementary prudence if he did not ensure that independent advice was given.

Particularly stringent rules apply where a solicitor buys from his client.[76] The solicitor must show that the client was fully informed of all the relevant facts; (generally) that the client was separately advised; and that the transaction was a fair one: thus it can be set aside simply on the ground of undervalue.[77] A solicitor must make full disclosure even where the presumption of undue influence has been rebutted.[78]

3. Unconscionable Bargains

Equity can give relief against unconscionable bargains in certain cases in which one party is in a position to exploit a particular weakness of the other. The burden of justifying such a transaction is on the former party.[79]

(1) Catching bargains[80]

Equity can set aside or modify an agreement with an "expectant heir" made in anticipation of his expectations. The transaction need not amount to a sale of or charge on the expectation.[81] Thus equity can relieve against a *post-obit* bond, by which a debtor promises his creditor a certain sum if the debtor survives a named person and becomes entitled to a share in his estate.[82] Nor is the equitable jurisdiction confined to "heirs": relief can be given to a young man whose sole expectation of wealth is from his father, who is still alive.[83]

A person who sold a reversionary interest at one time only had to prove that the sale was at an undervalue to obtain relief. The law was changed by the Sales of Reversions Act 1867, now re-enacted in section 174 of the Law of Property Act 1925. This provides that no sale of a "reversionary interest" (which includes a mere expectancy) shall be opened or set aside merely on the ground of undervalue; but the section expressly preserves the jurisdiction of the court to set aside or modify unconscionable bargains. Undervalue remains "a material element in cases in which it is not the sole equitable ground for relief,"[84] and may still form the sole ground for relief if it is "so gross as to amount of itself to evidence of fraud."[85] Fraud is not

[73] *Powell* v. *Powell* [1900] 1 Ch. 243, 246; *Wright* v. *Carter* [1903] 1 Ch. 27.
[74] *Re Coomber* [1911] 1 Ch. 723, 730.
[75] *Inche Noriah* v. *Shaik Allie bin Omar* [1929] A.C. 127, 135; *Re Brocklehurst* [1978] Ch. 14.
[76] *Cf.* also the provisions of the Solicitors Act 1974, ss.56, 57, for regulating the remuneration of solicitors.
[77] *Wright* v. *Carter* [1903] 1 Ch. 27; the same rule applies where a trustee buys from his *cestui que trust*: *Thomson* v. *Eastwood* (1877) 2 App.Cas. 215. It follows that in these cases the party claiming relief need not show that the transaction was to his manifest disadvantage: *cf. Bank of Credit & Commerce International S.A.* v. *Aboody* [1990] 1 Q.B. 923, 962.
[78] *Moody* v. *Cox & Hatt* [1917] 2 Ch. 71.
[79] *Aylesford* v. *Morris* (1873) L.R. 8 Ch.App. 484.
[80] Dawson, 45 Mich.L.Rev. 267–279.
[81] *Aylesford* v. *Morris* (1873) L.R. 8 Ch.App. 484.
[82] See *Chesterfield* v. *Janssen* (1750) 2 Ves.Sen. 125.
[83] *Nevill* v. *Snelling* (1880) 15 Ch.D. 679.
[84] *O'Rorke* v. *Bolingbroke* (1877) 2 App.Cas. 814, 833.
[85] *Fry* v. *Lane* (1888) 40 Ch.D. 312, 321.

here used in its common law sense[86] but means "an unconscientious use of the power arising out of" the relative positions of the parties.[87]

(2) Dealing with poor and ignorant persons

In *Evans* v. *Llewellin*[88] a poor man became entitled to a share of an estate worth £1,700. He sold it for 200 guineas cash, and was later able to set the transaction aside as it was "improvidently obtained." It seems that equity may give such relief when unfair advantage is taken of a person who is poor, ignorant or weak-minded, or is for some other reason in need of special protection.[89] Specific performance may be refused on similar grounds.[90] The equitable rule is based on unconscientious conduct by the stronger party: relief will not be granted merely because the transaction is unfair.[91] *A fortiori,* mere inadequacy of consideration is not a ground for relief where the parties have bargained on equal terms.[92]

(3) Inequality of bargaining power[93]

A number of judicial statements give some support to the view that one party to a contract may be entitled to relief if the other has taken unfair advantage of the fact that there is a marked inequality of bargaining power between them.

The first group of such statements is concerned with the special problem of the validity of covenants in restraint of trade.[94] This depends on whether the covenant is "reasonable,"[95] and the adequacy of consideration is taken into account in determining the issue of reasonableness.[96] The fairness of the bargain (which to some extent depends on the relative bargaining positions of the parties) is therefore obviously relevant to the validity of the restraint; but the fact that it is taken into account for this purpose scarcely supports a general principle of relief against harsh bargains on the ground of inequality of bargaining power.

Such a principle was, however, stated (as an alternative ground of decision) by Lord Denning M.R. in *Lloyds Bank Ltd.*v. *Bundy*.[97] He referred to a number of rules (discussed earlier[98] in this Chapter) under

---

86 *Ante*, p. 307.
87 *Aylesford* v. *Morris* (1873) L.R. 8 Ch.App. 484, 491.
88 (1787) 1 Cox C.C. 333; mentioned with approval in *Fry* v. *Lane, supra*; *Longmate* v. *Ledger* (1860) 2 Giff. 157; *Clark* v. *Malpas* (1862) 4 D.F. & J. 401; *Baker* v. *Monk* (1864) 4 D.J. & S. 338; *Lloyds Bank Ltd.* v. *Bundy* [1975] Q.B. 326, 337; *Watkin* v. *Watson-Smith, The Times*, July 3, 1986.
89 *e.g. Creswell* v. *Potter* (1968) [1978] 1 W.L.R 255n. (wife in course of divorce proceedings transferring her share in the matrimonial home to husband without getting independent advice and for inadequate consideration); *cf. Backhouse* v. *Backhouse* [1978] 1 W.L.R. 243.
90 *e.g. Falcke* v. *Gray* (1859) 4 Drew. 651: *post*, p. 909.
91 *Alec Lobb (Garages) Ltd.* v. *Total Oil (Great Britain) Ltd.* [1985] 1 W.L.R. 173; *Hart* v. *O'Connor* [1985] A.C. 1000.
92 See *Collier* v. *Brown* (1788) 1 Cox C.C. 428; *Coles* v. *Trecothick* (1804) 9 Ves. 234, 246; *Western* v. *Russell* (1814) 3 V. & B. 187.
93 Clark, *Inequality of Bargaining Power*, Thal, 8 O.J.L.S. 17.
94 *A. Schroeder Music Publishing Co.* v. *Macaulay* [1974] 1 W.L.R. 1308, 1315; *cf. Clifford Davis Management* v. *W.E.A. Records* [1975] 1 W.L.R. 61; *Shell U.K. Ltd.* v. *Lostock Garages Ltd.* [1976] 1 W.L.R. 1187, 1197; Wooldridge, [1977] J.B.L. 312.
95 *Post*, pp. 406–410.
96 *Post*, pp. 409–410.
97 [1975] Q.B. 326; *ante*, p. 368.
98 *Ante*, pp. 366–371.

which the law gave relief against harsh or unfair contracts; and he derived from them the following generalisation: "The English law gives relief to one who, without independent advice, enters into a contract upon terms which are very unfair or transfers property for a consideration which is grossly inadequate, when his bargaining power is grievously impaired by reason of his own needs or desires, or by his own ignorance or infirmity, coupled with undue influence or pressures brought to bear on him by or for the benefit of the other."[99] The other members of the Court of Appeal based their decision solely on the equitable doctrine of undue influence.[1] Thus, while expressing "some sympathy"[2] for Lord Denning's principle, they did not find it necessary to express a concluded opinion on it. It follows that the principle does not form the ground for the decision.[3]

In a number of later cases, Lord Denning nevertheless repeated his view that the law recognised a principle of "inequality of bargaining power."[4] The scope of the alleged principle seems to be very wide: it can apparently apply to such disparate transactions or terms as the contract in *Lloyds Bank Ltd.* v. *Bundy*,[5] the renegotiation of a contract,[6] the settlement of a tort claim,[7] and the inclusion of an exemption clause in a cleaning contract made in standard form.[8] No clear limit to the principle is stated except that a bargain will not be upset if it is "the result of the ordinary interplay of forces."[9] Reference by Lord Denning to "the American policy of inadequate bargaining power"[10] are from his point of view scarcely reassuring; for the lengths to which American courts have gone in implementing this policy would hardly be acceptable in England without express statutory authority. It is, for example, hard to imagine an English court holding that a consumer could keep goods after paying only part of the price simply because the seller's profit on the full contract price would be excessive.[11] The regulation of these and similar matters is in England, by general consent, left to the legislature.[12]

For these reasons, Lord Denning's principle lacks judicial[13] support in England. On the contrary, in *Pao On* v. *Lau Yiu Long*[14] the Privy Council, having held that the contract was not voidable for duress,[15] also rejected

---

[99] [1975] Q.B. 326, 339. *Cf.* the rules against "collateral advantages" in mortgages: Megarry and Wade, *Law of Real Property*, (4th ed.), pp. 940–943. And see Beatson, 1 O.J.L.S. 426.

[1] *Ante*, p. 368; *cf. Horry* v. *Tate & Lyle Refineries Ltd.* [1982] 2 Lloyd's Rep. 417, 422.

[2] [1975] Q.B. 326, 347 (Sir Eric Sachs, with whom Cairns L.J. agreed); *cf. Backhouse* v. *Backhouse* [1978] 1 W.L.R. 243, 251.

[3] *National Westminster Bank Ltd.* v. *Morgan* [1985] A.C. 686, 708–709.

[4] *Arrale* v. *Costain Civil Engineering Ltd.* [1976] 1 Lloyd's Rep. 98, 102; *Levison* v. *Patent Steam Carpet Cleaning Co. Ltd.* [1978] Q.B. 69, 78.

[5] [1975] Q.B. 326.

[6] *D. & C. Builders* v. *Rees* [1966] 2 Q.B. 617.

[7] *Arrale* v. *Costain Civil Engineering Ltd.* [1976] 1 Lloyd's Rep. 98.

[8] *Levison* v. *Patent Steam Carpet Cleaning Co. Ltd.* [1978] Q.B. 69.

[9] *Lloyds Bank Ltd* v. *Bundy* [1975] Q.B. 326, 336.

[10] *Ibid.* p. 333 (in argument).

[11] *Jones* v. *Star Credit Corp.* 298 N.Y.S. 2d 264 (1969).

[12] See *Lloyds Bank Ltd.* v. *Bundy* [1975] Q.B. at p. 336; *cf. post*, pp. 373, 425–426.

[13] Inequality of bargaining power may also be relevant to the exercise of *statutorily* conferred discretions: see, for example Unfair Contract Terms Act 1977, Sched. 2 para. (*a*) (*ante*, p. 237); Consumer Credit Act 1974, s.138(3)(*b*) and (4)(*b*) (*post.* p. 375); Matrimonial Causes Act 1973, s.23, as interpreted in *Edgar* v. *Edgar* [1980] 1 W.L.R. 1410. But such discretions cannot provide any basis for a general *common law* principle.

[14] [1980] A.C. 614.

[15] *Ante*, pp. 364–365.

the argument that agreements were invalid if they were procured by "an unfair use of a dominant bargaining position."[16] To treat this as a ground of invalidity distinct from duress would, in Lord Scarman's words, "be unhelpful because it would render the law uncertain."[17] In *National Westminster Bank plc* v. *Morgan* Lord Scarman again expressed similar views when questioning "whether there is any need in the modern law to erect a general principle of relief against inequality of bargaining power."[18] Parliament having dealt with a number of specific instances in which superior bargaining power might be abused,[19] he doubted "whether the courts should asume the burden of formulating further restrictions"[20]; and the need for them to do so has also been reduced by the widening of the scope of duress.[21] Decisions of the lower courts have similarly rejected the argument that inequality of bargaining power is, of itself, a ground of invalidity[22]; and this is true even in the restraint of trade cases, in which the courts have traditionally taken the "fairness" of the bargain into account.[23]

4. Bars to Relief

Relief for undue influence is barred on grounds similar to those which limit the right to rescind for misrepresentation.

(a) IMPOSSIBILITY OF RESTITUTION. As in cases of misrepresentation, the party seeking rescission must restore benefits that he has obtained under the contract, but he is not required to make *precise* restitution: the principle of allowing rescission for misrepresentation so long as equity can achieve a result that is "practically just"[24] applies also where rescission is sought on the ground of undue influence. The point is illustrated by *O'Sullivan* v. *Management Agency & Music Ltd.*[25] where the plaintiff sought to set aside for undue influence a number of management, sole agency, recording and publishing agreements and transfers of copyrights. On the one hand the defendants argued that rescission should not be allowed as they could no longer be restored to their pre-contract position in view of the work which they had done to promote the plaintiff's success; on the other hand the plaintiff argued that rescission for undue influence was (unlike rescission for misrepresentation) not subject to any requirement of restitution at all. The court rejected both arguments, holding that, even though precise restitution was not possible, rescission could be ordered so long as the court could do substantial justice. This could be done by upholding the plaintiff's claim for rescission while allowing the defendants a reasonable remuneration for their work on behalf of the plaintiff. In this respect the case resembles those in which contracts have been rescinded for

[16] [1980] A.C. 614, 634.
[17] *Ibid.*
[18] [1985] A.C. 686, 708.
[19] See, for example, *ante*, pp. 226–244 for legislative restrictions on exemption clauses.
[20] [1985] A.C. 686, 708; *cf. Lloyds Bank Ltd.* v. *Bundy* [1975] Q.B. 326, 336.
[21] *Ante*, p. 363.
[22] *Burmah Oil Co.* v. *Bank of England, The Times*, July 4, 1981; *Horry* v. *Tate & Lyle Refineries Ltd.* [1982] 2 Lloyd's Rep. 417, 422; *Alec Lobb (Garages) Ltd.* v. *Total Oil (Great Britain) Ltd.* [1985] 1 W.L.R. 173.
[23] The *Alec Lobb* case, *supra*, concerned restraint of trade.
[24] *Erlanger* v. *New Sombrero Phosphate Co.* (1878) 3 App.Cas. 1218, 1279; *ante*, p. 341.
[25] [1985] Q.B. 428; *ante*, p. 368.

misrepresentation, subject to similar allowances in respect of improvements made to the subject-matter by the misrepresentor.[26]

(b) AFFIRMATION. A claim to relief on the ground of undue influence is barred by affirmation[27] of the transaction after the influence (or the relationship giving rise to a presumption of influence) has ceased. It has been held that affirmation is effective though made without independent advice and in ignorance of the right to have the transaction set aside.[28] It is submitted that the law on this point should be brought into line with the rule in cases of misrepresentation and breach, that affirmation requires knowledge by the injured party of the right to rescind.[29]

(c) DELAY. The victim of undue influence must "seek relief within a reasonable time after the removal of the influence under which the gift was made."[30] If with knowledge or means of knowledge of his rights he fails to seek relief he is assumed to have ratified the transaction.

(d) THIRD PARTY RIGHTS. The right to set the transaction aside cannot be exercised against a third party who in good faith acquires an interest for value in the subject-matter. Thus in *Bainbrigge* v. *Browne*[31] children who were not yet emancipated[32] charged their property as security for their father's debts. They could not set this transaction aside against the father's creditors who did not know that they were not emancipated and gave value (presumably) by forbearing to sue the father. Similarly, in *Coldunell Ltd.* v. *Gallon*[33] a son had by undue influence induced his parents (aged 86 and 91) to mortgage their house to enable his father to borrow £20,000 for the purpose of providing financial help to the son in his business. The lender was unaware of the son's influence over the parents and had done his best to warn them to seek independent advice. It was held that the parents were not entitled to have the transaction set aside against the lender.[34] And in *O'Sullivan* v. *Management Agency & Music Ltd.*[35] relief was not available against a company which had acquired some of the plaintiff's copyrights and tapes in good faith and for value.

A transaction can, however, be set aside against a third party who does not give value, and against one "with notice of the equity . . . or with notice of the circumstances from which the court infers the equity."[36] Thus if an unemancipated child guarantees his parent's debt he can set the guarantee aside against a creditor who knows of the nature of the relationship, or deliberately shuts his eyes to it.[37] The position is the same where the relationship between debtor and guarantor, though not one to which the presumption of undue influence applies, is such that the debtor in fact had a dominating influence over the guarantor, and the creditor knew this fact

[26] See *ante*, pp. 342–343.
[27] *Cf.* (in cases of duress) *The Atlantic Baron* [1979] Q.B. 705.
[28] *Mitchell* v. *Homfray* (1882) 8 Q.B.D. 587.
[29] *Ante*, p. 344 *post*, pp. 712–714.
[30] *Allcard* v. *Skinner* (1887) 36 Ch.D. 145, 187.
[31] (1881) 18 Ch.D. 188.
[32] *Ante*, p. 368.
[33] [1986] 1 All E.R. 1184; *cf. Midland Bank plc* v. *Perry* [1988] 1 FLR 161.
[34] The house had been sold and the parents accommodated elsewhere, so that there was no longer any issue as to possession.
[35] [1985] Q.B. 428, 459–460.
[36] *Bainbrigge* v. *Browne* (1881) 18 Ch.D. at p. 197.
[37] *Maitland* v. *Irving* (1846) 15 Sim. 437; *Lancashire Loans Ltd.* v. *Black* [1934] 1 K.B. 380.

or should have been aware of it. This was, for example, held to be the position where a wife guaranteed the debts of her husband, who had acquired a dominating influence over her[38]; and where an elderly couple, who were under the influence of their adult son, guaranteed his debt to a moneylender, and secured the guarantee by a mortgage on the house in which they were living in retirement.[39] In both cases the transactions were set aside as the creditor either knew of the circumstances giving rise to the undue influence of the debtors over the guarantors, or was taken to know of it because he had left all the arrangements for obtaining the security to the debtor and so constituted him his agent for this purpose.[40]

SECTION 3. MONEYLENDING AND CONSUMER PROTECTION

1. Extortionate Credit Bargains

The rate of interest which could be charged by moneylenders was at one time regulated by statute. After the Usury Laws Repeal Act 1854, the lender was free to charge such interest as he could get, and for nearly 50 years the activities of moneylenders were subject only to the equitable rules as to unconscionable bargains.[41] Statutory powers to control moneylending contracts were, however, given to the courts by the Moneylenders Acts 1900 and 1927, and are now contained in the Consumer Credit Act 1974. Under that Act, the court has power to "reopen" any "extortionate credit bargain."[42] The Act provides that a credit bargain is extortionate if the payments to be made under it are "grossly exorbitant" *or* if it "otherwise grossly contravenes the ordinary principles of fair dealing."[43] These are stringent requirements: a bargain is not "extortionate" merely because it is harsh or even unconscionable.[44] Factors to be taken into account in determining whether a credit bargain is extortionate include the prevailing level of interest rates; matters affecting the debtor (such as his age and business capacity, and the degree to which he was under financial pressure when he made the bargain); and the degree of risk accepted by the creditor.[45] Under these provisions, it has been held that payments were not "grossly exorbitant" where interest at an annual rate of 48 per cent. was charged on a loan which was made with very little security, and on the very day on which the borrower applied for it, so as to enable him to complete

---

[38] *Turnbull & Co.* v. *Duvall* [1902] A.C. 429; *Chaplin & Co. Ltd.* v. *Brammall* [1908] 1 K.B. 233, as explained in *Howes* v. *Bishop* [1909] 2 K.B. 390, 397, and in *Coldunell Ltd.* v. *Gallon* [1986] Q.B. 1184, 1197.

[39] *Avon Finance Co.* v. *Bridger* [1985] 2 All E.R. 281.

[40] As in *Turnbull & Co.* v. *Duvall, supra, Chaplin & Co. Ltd.* v. *Brammall, supra*, *Avon Finance Co.* v. *Bridger*, *supra* and *Barclays Bank plc* v. *Kennedy* (1989) 21 H.L.R. 132; *cf. Kings North Trust Ltd.* v. *Bell* [1986] 1 W.L.R. 119 (a case of fraud). There was no such agency in *Coldunell Ltd.* v. *Gallon* [1986] Q.B. 1184, *Perry* v. *Midland Bank* [1987] FLR 237, *Midland Bank Plc* v. *Shephard* [1988] 3 All E.R. 17, *Bank of Boroda* v. *Shaw* [1988] 3 All E.R. 24; or in *Lloyds Bank* v. *Egremont* [1990] 2 FLR 351; and see Oldham [1989] C.L.J. 184.

[41] See *Nevill* v. *Snelling* (1880) 15 Ch.D. 679.

[42] Consumer Credit Act 1974, s.137(1); *cf.* Insolvency Act 1986 ss.244, 343.

[43] Consumer Credit Act 1974, s.138(1); if the debtor or any surety alleges that a credit bargain is extortionate, the burden is on the creditor to prove the contrary: *ibid.* s.171(7).

[44] *Davies* v. *Directloans Ltd.* [1986] 1 W.L.R. 823.

[45] Consumer Credit Act 1974, s.138(2)–(4); *Davies* v. *Directloans Ltd.*, *supra.*

the purchase of a house already heavily encumbered with other charges[46]; and that a bargain did not "grossly contravene the principles of fair dealing" where (in accordance with the principles already discussed[47]) the lender's conduct was not tainted by the exercise of undue influence over the borrower by a third person.[48]

In "reopening" the transaction, the court has a wide discretion "to do justice between the parties."[49] It can alter the terms of the bargain in order to relieve the debtor "from payment of any sum in excess of that fairly due and reasonable"; order repayment of excessive sums paid; and grant various other forms of relief to the debtor or to a surety.[50]

2. Consumer Trade Practices

Under the Fair Trading Act 1973, action may be taken by delegated legislation against certain "consumer trade practices."[51] Two groups of such practices are particularly relevant at this point: those which have the effect of "subjecting consumers to undue pressure to enter into relevant consumer transactions,"[52] and those which cause the terms of such transactions to be so adverse to consumers as to be inequitable.[53] The remedies[54] under the Act are by way of criminal prosecution and proceedings by the Director General of Fair Trading before the Restrictive Practices Court.[55] The mere fact that a prohibited form of "pressure" had induced the contract would not therefore invalidate the contract[56]; though if it had caused loss to the consumer he could get compensation in criminal proceedings in which the other party had been convicted.[57]

A similar policy against a form of economic duress appears to underlie the statutory provisions giving consumers a "cooling-off" period in certain cases. For example a person who is induced to sign a regulated consumer credit agreement[58] at home is entitled to cancel it within such a period.[59]

---

[46] *Ketley* v. *Scott* [1981] I.C.R. 241; *cf. Petrou* v. *Woodstead Finance Ltd.* [1986] F.L.R. 158 (42.5 per cent. not extortionate on short term loan).

[47] *Supra*, at n. 40.

[48] *Coldunell Ltd.* v. *Gallon* [1986] Q.B. 1184.

[49] Consumer Credit Act 1974, s.137(1).

[50] *Ibid.* s.139(2).

[51] *Ante*, p. 244.

[52] Fair Trading Act 1973, s.17(2)(*c*).

[53] *Ibid.* s.17(2)(*d*).

[54] Where satisfactory assurances that the practice will be discontinued are not obtained: see s.34.

[55] *Ante*, pp. 244–245.

[56] Fair Trading Act 1973, s.26; *ante*, p. 245.

[57] Powers of Criminal Court Act 1973, s.35

[58] *Ante*, p. 163.

[59] Consumer Credit Act 1974, ss.67–68; *cf.* Insurance Companies Act 1982, s.76; Financial Services Act 1986, s.56.

CHAPTER ELEVEN

ILLEGALITY[1]

THE law may refuse to give full effect to a contract on the ground of illegality, *i.e.* because the contract involves the commission of a legal wrong or is in some other way contrary to public policy.

SECTION 1. THE PROBLEM OF CLASSIFICATION

English writers commonly divide the cases in which contracts are affected by illegality into a number of classes.[2] One object of this classification is to make it possible to generalise about the *effects* of illegality; but it is doubtful whether any of the suggested classifications achieve this object to any considerable extent. Another object of classification is purely expository, and this does no harm so long as it is not actually misleading.

One classification is based on the nature of the objectionable conduct. Thus Sir Frederick Pollock divided the cases into those where the contract was contrary to (1) positive law, (2) morals or good manners, and (3) public policy; but he admitted that this classification was "only approximate."[3] The main difficulty with it is that the second category is hard to define and that it may overlap with the third. For this reason the second category is not used in the present Chapter. It can also be argued that public policy is the ground for invalidating *all* contracts affected by illegality, so that the third category includes the other two. But if all illegal contracts fell into a single category, there would be no point in attempting to classify them, even for purposes of exposition.

A second classification is based on the source of the rule infringed. Thus it is sometimes said that a contract is more likely to be invalid for violation of a statute than for violation of a rule of common law. The distinction is appropriate where a statute expressly prohibits or invalidates a contract.[4] But it is not decisive where the statute contains no such express prohibition and the illegality consists only in the method of making or performing the contract.[5] In *St. John Shipping Corp.* v. *Joseph Rank Ltd.*[6] a shipowner committed a statutory offence by overloading his ship while performing a number of contracts for the carriage of goods. Devlin J. held that he was nonetheless entitled to freight, because the object of the statute was to prevent overloading and not to prohibit contracts. This object was to be achieved by imposing a fine, and not by subjecting the shipowner to the additional financial loss which would result from invalidating the contracts

---

[1] Furmston (1966) U. of Tor.L.J. 267.

[2] The fashion seems to have been started by Sir Frederick Pollock (*infra*, n. 3). It has not spread to the United States. Williston, *Contracts* (rev. ed.), s.1628, says: "There seems to be no importance to these distinctions."

[3] *Principles of the Law of Contract*, (13th ed.), Chap. 8, p. 261.

[4] *e.g.* Fair Trading Act 1973, Part XI (pyramid selling). *Cf. post*, pp. 432, 455.

[5] See *Shaw* v. *Groom* [1970] 2 Q.B. 540; *London & Harrogate Securities Ltd.* v. *Pitts* [1976] 1 W.L.R. 1063.

[6] [1957] 1 Q.B. 267.

of carriage. It is submitted that this approach should not be confined to cases in which the offence is statutory.[7] It would have been just as appropriate, and would probably have led to the same result, had the shipowner been convicted of manslaughter committed in the course of the voyage.

Classification may proceed, thirdly, by the legal consequences of the contracts concerned. Thus Sir John Salmond distinguished between "illegal" and "nugatory" contracts[8]; and the same classification has been adopted by later writers who distinguish between "illegal" and "void" contracts. This classification cannot, of course, lead to any deductions about the legal effects of the contracts in question as it assumes that those consequences are already known. Unfortunately, those who use the classification cannot always agree on this vital point. Thus some regard an agreement by a married person to marry as "illegal,"[9] while others regard it as "void."[10] Moreover, the classification tries to do the impossible. The nature of the illegality which may affect a contract varies almost infinitely in seriousness.[11] To classify these contracts by their effects into only two groups is likely to result in a misleading degree of oversimplification.

In Section 2 of this Chapter, 22 types of illegal contracts are listed; for purposes of exposition they are divided into two groups, namely contracts involving the commission of a legal wrong and contracts contrary to public policy. The second group includes one particularly important type of contracts, those in restraint of trade. Because of the complexity of the law relating to such contracts, they will be discussed under an independent heading. The exact effects of illegality should ideally be discussed separately in relation to each type of contract, but such treatment would be inordinately long. An attempt will therefore be made in Section 3 of this Chapter to provide a general discussion of the effects of illegality. This approach can be justified on the ground that many of the relevant rules apply to all types of illegal contracts; but it is also often true that the effects vary with the type of illegality. Where this is the case, the general propositions in Section 3 will be qualified accordingly.

SECTION 2. TYPES OF ILLEGALITY

1. Contracts Involving the Commission of a Legal Wrong

(1) Contracts amounting to a legal wrong

A contract is illegal[12] if the mere making of it is a legal wrong. Thus a contract to "rig the market" by offering inflated prices for shares in a particular company is illegal as it is a criminal conspiracy.[13] A contract to finance

---

[7] *Wetherell* v. *Jones* (1832) 3 B. & Ad. 221, 225–226; *Coral Leisure Group* v. *Barnett* [1981] I.C.R. 503, 509. For a similar approach in case of a civil wrong, see *The Ypatianna* [1988] Q.B. 345, 369–370.

[8] Salmond and Winfield, *Law of Contracts*, Chap. 7; Salmond and Williams, *Law of Contracts*, Chap. 14.

[9] Salmond and Winfield, *supra*; Salmond and Williams, *supra*. An agreement to marry is no longer a contract, but may have other legal consequences: *post*, p. 387.

[10] Cheshire, Fifoot and Furmston, *The Law of Contract* (11th ed.), p. 380.

[11] Corbin, *Contracts*, s.1373.

[12] Except to the extent that a statute provides the contrary: *e.g.* Sex Discrimination Act 1975, s.77; (as amended by Sex Discrimination Act 1986, s.6); Race Relations Act 1976, s.72.

[13] *Scott* v. *Brown* [1892] 2 Q.B. 724; *cf. Harry Parker Ltd.* v. *Mason* [1940] 2 K.B. 590.

another person's litigation in return for a share in the proceeds used to amount to the crime and tort of champerty; and accordingly the contract was illegal.[14] Although criminal and tortious liability for champerty have been abolished[15] a champertous agreement remains, as a general rule, illegal.[16] By statute, however, an agreement may validly be made in writing, by which a client promises to pay a "conditional fee" to a person providing him with advocacy or litigation services. The condition may be that the litigation for which that person is engaged ends in the client's favour, and the fee may include a percentage (at a rate not exceeding that specified by order made by the Lord Chancellor) of the amount recovered.[17] A contract to stifle a prosecution for treason is illegal as it amounts to compounding. It is also an offence for a person who knows that an arrestable offence has been committed, and that he has information which may help to secure the conviction of the offender, to accept or agree to accept any consideration (other than the making good of the loss or injury caused by the offence) for not disclosing the information.[18] The mere making of some contracts is expressly made criminal by statute: it is, for example, an offence to sell a flick-knife[19], to agree to indemnify a surety in criminal proceedings against liability to forfeit a recognisance,[20] and to deal for payment in human organs.[21] Such contracts are no doubt illegal. And where the making or variation of a contract is prohibited by a court order, disobedience of the order amounts to contempt of court; and the prohibited contract, or variation, is illegal.[22]

(2) Contracts to commit a crime

A contract for the deliberate commission of a crime is obviously illegal.[23] Such a contract would also amount to conspiracy. But many statutory crimes can be committed without criminal intent[24]; and there are cases in which only one of the parties to a contract has any criminal intent. The exact effects of illegality on such contracts, where one or both parties act in good faith, will be considered later in this Chapter.[25]

---

[14] *Re Thomas* [1894] 1 Q.B. 747.
[15] Criminal Law Act 1967, ss.13(1), 14(1).
[16] *Ibid.* s.14(2); *Trendtex Trading Corp.* v. *Crédit Suisse* [1982] A.C. 679.
[17] Courts and Legal Services Act 1990, s.58, reversing the common law position as stated in *Wallersteiner* v. *Moir (No.* 2) [1975] Q.B. 373. Conditional fee agreement with surveyors are valid at common law: *Pickering* v. *Sogex Services* (1982) 262 E.G. 700; *Picton Jones & Co.* v. *Arcadia Developments* [1989] 1 E.G.L.R. 43.
[18] Criminal Law Act 1967, s.5(1); "arrestable offence" is defined in Police and Criminal Evidence Act 1984, s.24(1), which applies by virtue of s.119 and Sched. 6, para. 17 for the purposes of the 1967 Act.
[19] Restriction of Offensive Weapons Act 1959, s.1(1)(*a*).
[20] Bail Act 1976, s.9.
[21] Human Organ Transplants Act 1989, s.1.
[22] *Clarke* v. *Chadburn* [1985] 1 W.L.R. 78.
[23] *e.g. Bostel Bros. Ltd.* v. *Hurlock* [1949] 1 K.B. 74 (evasion of building licensing regulations); *Bigos* v. *Bousted* [1951] 1 All E.R. 92 (evasion of exchange control legislation); *cf. Ashton* v. *Turner* [1981] Q.B. 137 (agreements, probably not contractual, to commit burglary); *Pitts* v. *Hunt* [1990] 3 All E.R. 344. Ignorance of the law makes no difference: see *Belvoir Finance Co. Ltd.* v. *Stapleton* [1971] 1 Q.B. 210.
[24] In such a case there is no criminal liability for conspiracy: Criminal Law Act 1977, s.1(2).
[25] *Post*, pp. 430–435.

(3) Contracts to commit a civil wrong

A contract is illegal where its object is the *deliberate* commission of a civil wrong. Thus contracts to assault[26] or defraud[27] a third party are illegal: and the same is true of a contract by an insolvent debtor to pay one of his creditors in fraud of the others.[28] Similarly a contract may be illegal if its object is to procure one party to break a contract known by both to be binding on him.[29]

Where a contract involves the *unintentional* commission of a civil wrong two types of cases call for discussion.

(a) ONE PARTY INNOCENT. One party may know that the performance of the contract will involve the commission of a civil wrong, while the other is innocent. In *Clay* v. *Yates*[30] the plaintiff agreed with the defendant to print a book with a dedication. He refused to print the dedication on discovering that it was libellous, but claimed the cost of printing the book. The defendant did not plead illegality but argued that the obligation to print the book with the dedication was "entire,"[31] and that the plaintiff could not recover anything as he had only performed in part. In rejecting this argument, Pollock C.B. said that there was an implied undertaking to pay "for so much of the work *as is lawful*"[32]; while Martin B. said that the defendant was liable "to pay the plaintiff for that part *which he has performed*."[33] The further question arises whether the plaintiff could have recovered the cost of printing the dedication, if he had printed it without knowing the facts which made it libellous. Pollock C.B.'s test would seem to deny recovery in such a case, while Martin B.'s test would allow it; and it is submitted that the latter is the preferable view.[34]

(b) BOTH PARTIES INNOCENT. If neither party knows that performance of the contract involves the commission of a civil wrong the contract is not illegal. A contract for the sale of goods belonging to a third party may make buyer and seller liable to that third party in tort[35] even though they believed that the goods belonged to the seller; but such a contract has never been held illegal.[36]

(4) Use of subject-matter for unlawful purpose

A contract which is in itself lawful may be illegal if its subject-matter is to be used for an unlawful purpose. In *Langton* v. *Hughes*[37] the plaintiff sold Spanish juice, isinglass and ginger to a brewer knowing that the latter

---

[26] *Allen* v. *Rescous* (1676) 2 Lev. 174.
[27] *Begbie* v. *Phosphate Sewage Co. Ltd.* (1875) L.R. 10 Q.B. 491; *cf. Customs & Excise Commissioners* v. *Oliver* [1980] 1 All E.R. 355 (sale of goods stolen, or known to have been stolen, by seller).
[28] *Cockshott* v. *Bennett* (1788) 2 T.R. 763; *Mallalieu* v. *Hodgson* (1851) 16 Q.B. 689.
[29] For a full discussion, see Lauterpacht, 52 L.Q.R. 494.
[30] (1856) 1 H. & N. 73.
[31] *Post*, p. 683.
[32] *Clay* v. *Yates*, *supra*, at p. 79.
[33] At p. 80.
[34] *Cf.* Williams, 8 C.L.J. at p. 54; Martin B.'s view may be reconciled with *Frank W. Clifford Ltd.* v. *Garth* [1956] 1 W.L.R. 570; *post*, p. 448, on the ground that the builder in that case took a conscious risk of illegality.
[35] *Post*, p. 931.
[36] Sale of Goods Act 1979, s.12 assumes that the contract is valid.
[37] (1813) 1 M. & S. 593; *cf. Gas Light & Coke Co.* v. *Turner* (1839) 6 Bing.N.C. 324.

intended to put them into his beer. The contract was held to be illegal because an Act of 1802 made it an offence to use anything except malt and hops to flavour beer. Later cases suggest that this rule only applies if the seller to some extent "participates" in the illegal purpose[38]; but it seems that such participation would readily be inferred if he knew of that purpose and made its achievement possible by delivering the goods.

(5) Unlawful method of performance

A contract which is lawful in itself may be performed in a way which involves one or both parties in criminal liability. It used to be thought that the contract was illegal[39] if its performance involved breach of a statute passed for the protection of the public; but that if the statute was passed only for the protection of the revenue the contract was not illegal.[40] But the distinction between these two types of statutes is by no means decisive.[41] Even where the object of the statute is to protect the public (or a section of it) a contract involving a breach of it is not invariably illegal. Thus a contract to grant (or to transfer) a lease is not illegal merely because the landlord has committed a statutory offence by receiving or demanding an illegal premium. The tenant can accordingly enforce the contract, though without having to pay the premium.[42] Similarly, a tenancy is not illegal merely because the landlord has committed a statutory offence by failing to give his tenant a rent-book. Here the illegality relates to a merely collateral matter, so that the contract can be enforced even by the offender: *i.e.* the landlord can sue for the rent.[43] On the other hand, a contract may be illegal although it only violates a statute passed for the protection of the revenue.[44] The test for determining whether an otherwise lawful contract is illegal because its performance involved the breach of a statute is that laid down in *St. John Shipping Corp.* v. *Joseph Rank Ltd.*[45]: did the statute only intend to penalise *conduct* or also to prohibit *contracts*? Some statutes expressly solve this problem: a contract for the supply of goods is not, for example to be void or unenforceable merely because, in performing it, the seller has committed an offence under the Trade Descriptions Act 1968.[46]

---

[38] *Hodgson* v. *Temple* (1813) 5 Taunt. 181; *Pellecat* v. *Angell* (1835) 2 Cr.M. & R. 311; *cf. Foster* v. *Driscol* [1929] 1 K.B. 470; for similar reasoning in a case involving unlawful method of performance, see *Ashmore, Benson Pease & Co. Ltd.* v. *A. V. Dawson Ltd.* [1973] 1 W.L.R. 828; *post*, p. 430.

[39] *Little* v. *Poole* (1829) 9 B. & C. 192; *Fergusson* v. *Norman* (1838) 5 Bing.N.C. 76; *Cundell* v. *Dawson* (1847) 4 C.B. 376; *Victorian Daylesford Syndicate* v. *Dott* [1905] 2 Ch. 624; *Brightman & Co.* v. *Tate* [1919] 1 K.B. 463; *Anderson Ltd.* v. *Daniel* [1924] 1 K.B. 138 (actual decision reversed by Fertilisers and Feeding Stuffs Act 1926, s.1(2)).

[40] *Johnson* v. *Hudson* (1805) 11 East 180; *Brown* v. *Duncan* (1829) 10 B. & C. 93; *Smith* v. *Mawhood* (1845) 14 M. & W. 452; *Learoyd* v. *Bracken* [1894] 1 Q.B. 114; *cf. Wetherell* v. *Jones* (1832) 3 B. & Ad. 221.

[41] *Cope* v. *Rowlands* (1836) 2 M. & W. 149, 157.

[42] *Ailion* v. *Spiekermann* [1976] Ch. 158.

[43] *Shaw* v. *Groom* [1970] 2 Q.B. 504; *cf. London & Harrogate Securities Ltd.* v. *Pitts* [1976] 1 W.L.R. 1063; *Yango Pastoral Co. Ltd.* v. *First National Chicago Australia Ltd.* (1978) 139 C.L.R. 410.

[44] Thus a contract whose object is to evade or to delay the payment of income tax is now illegal: *Napier* v. *National Business Agency Ltd.* [1951] 2 All E.R. 264; *cf. Miller* v. *Karlinski* (1945) 62 T.L.R. 85; *post*, p. 398.

[45] [1957] 1 Q.B. 267; *ante*, p. 377. *Credit Lyonnais* v. *P. T. Barnard & Associates* [1976] 1 Lloyd's Rep. 557; *cf. Curragh Investments Ltd.* v. *Cook* [1974] 1 W.L.R. 1559; and see *post*, p. 433.

[46] s.35; *cf.* Fair Trading Act 1973, s.26; and see *post*, pp. 432–433.

A statute may subject contracts to a licensing or similar requirement, so that they can only be lawfully performed with the consent of some public body. Such a statute may expressly prohibit (and so render illegal) a contract made in breach of its provisions[47]; and even where the statute does not expressly prohibit the contract, it may do so by implication. Such an implication is most likely to arise where *both* parties are prohibited from making or performing the contract; but the position may be the same even where the statutory prohibition is directed at only one of the parties. At common law, this was the position where an insurer committed a statutory offence by engaging in certain types of insurance business without government authorisation[48]; by statute, such contracts are no longer illegal, but only unenforceable against the other party.[49]

A licensing or similar requirement may apply merely to the performance of a particular contract (as opposed to the carrying on of a business): *e.g.* where a licence is required for the erection of a building or for the export or import of goods. Such a contract is not illegal if it is expressly or by implication made subject to the relevant consent.[50] It will only be illegal if it is performed without such licence or consent[51] or if the parties intend to perform it even though no licence or consent is obtained.[52] A party may, however, guarantee that the licence will be obtained; if so, the undertaking can be enforced against him as a collateral contract, even though the main contract is illegal.[53] He may also be liable in damages for failing to perform an express or implied promise to make reasonable efforts to obtain the licence.[54]

(6) Contracts to indemnify against liability for unlawful acts

(a) CRIMINAL LIABILITY. A contract to indemnify a person against criminal liability is illegal if the crime is one which can only be, or in fact is, committed with guilty intent.[55] But the position is less clear where the crime is one of strict liability. In *Cointat* v. *Myham & Sons*[56] the defendants sold to a butcher the carcass of a pig, which was unfit for food. The butcher innocently exposed it for sale and was consequently convicted and fined £20. It was held that he could recover this sum from the defendants; but the legality of their implied promise to indemnify him was not discussed. This case has been criticised on the ground that "punishment inflicted by a criminal court is personal to the offender" and is fixed "having regard to

---

[47] *Cf. Re Mahmoud and Ispahani* [1921] 2 K.B. 716, *post*, p. 432.
[48] *Bedford Ins. Co. Ltd.* v. *Instituto de Resseguros do Brazil* [1985] 1 Q.B. 966; *Phoenix General Ins. Co. of Greece* v. *Halvanon Ins. Co. Ltd.* [1988] Q.B. 216, where the statute was not contravened and where *Stewart* v. *Oriental Fire & Marine Ins. Co. Ltd.* [1986] 1 Q.B. 988 was disapproved; *Re Cavalier Ins. Co. Ltd.* [1989] 2 Lloyd's Rep. 430.
[49] Financial Services Act 1986, s.132; *post*, p. 433.
[50] *Michael Richards Properties Ltd.* v. *St. Saviour's Parish* [1975] 3 All E.R. 416;
[51] *e.g. J. Dennis & Co. Ltd.* v. *Munn* [1949] 2 K.B. 327. For an exception, see *S.A. Ancien Maison Marcel Bauche* v. *Woodhouse Drake & Carey (Sugar) Ltd.* [1982] 2 Lloyd's Rep. 516.
[52] *e.g. Bigos* v. *Bousted* [1951] 1 All E.R. 92.
[53] *Peter Cassidy Seed Co. Ltd.* v. *Osuustukkuk-Auppa* [1957] 1 W.L.R. 273, as explained in *Walton (Grain and Shipping) Ltd.* v. *British Trading Co.* [1959] 1 Lloyd's Rep. 223, 236; *cf. post*, p. 434. Both cases concerned foreign licensing requirements.
[54] *Ante*, p. 61, *post*, p. 741.
[55] *Colburn* v. *Patmore* (1834) 1 C.M. & R. 73; *Fitzgerald* v. *Leonard* (1893) L.R. 33 Ir. 675.
[56] [1913] 2 K.B. 220; reversed on another ground [1914] W.N. 46.

the personal responsibility of the offender in respect of the offence."[57] One object of imposing strict criminal liability is to make a person take care not to commit the offence; and this object might be defeated by allowing him to recover the fine from a third party. Nonetheless it seems that the courts will allow a person to recover an indemnity against criminal liability if they are satisfied that he is wholly innocent. For example, in *Osman* v. *J. Ralph Moss Ltd.*[58] the plaintiff had been convicted of driving while uninsured. He was morally innocent, having been told by his insurance agent that he was properly insured, and it was held that his fine could be included in the damages recoverable from the agent for breach of contract.

(b) CIVIL LIABILITY. A contract to indemnify a person against civil liability may be illegal if the wrong is intentionally and knowingly committed: for example, a contract to indemnify a person against liability for deceit is illegal.[59] Similarly, a person who publishes what he knows to be a libel cannot recover an indemnity from the person who instigated the publication,[60] for the tendency of such an agreement might be to increase the circulation of the libel. On the other hand, a contract to keep a communication confidential, and to indemnify the maker against any liability resulting from its disclosure, has been held valid even where the communication contained a malicious libel[61]—apparently because the tendency of such an agreement is to restrict the circulation of the libel.

A contract to indemnify a person against civil liability is perfectly valid if the liability was incurred innocently or negligently.[62] Indeed, in many such cases a promise to indemnify, far from being illegal, is actually implied in law. The general principle is that where A at B's request does an act which is not "manifestly tortious," B must indemnify A for any liability incurred by A if the act turns out to be injurious to C.[63] The cases provide many illustrations of the validity of such express or implied promises to indemnify. Thus the innocent publisher of a libel can recover an indemnity from the person who instigated the publication.[64] An agent can recover an indemnity from his principal if he is made liable in conversion for selling a third person's property on the principal's instructions.[65] An employer can insure himself against civil liability for the tort of his employee; and he may also be entitled to an indemnity against such liability from the employee under the contract of employment.[66] And where A holds property which is claimed by B and C, a promise by one of them to indemnify A against liab-

[57] *Askey* v. *Golden Wine Co.* (1948) 64 T.L.R. 379, 380; *cf. Simon* v. *Pawsons & Leafs Ltd.* (1932) 38 Com.Cas. 151, 158; *Crage* v. *Fry* (1903) 67 J.P. 240; *R. Leslie Ltd.* v. *Reliable Advertising, etc. Agency Ltd.* [1915] 1 K.B. 652.

[58] [1970] 1 Lloyd's Rep. 313.

[59] *Brown Jenkinson & Co. Ltd.* v. *Percy Dalton (London) Ltd.* [1957] 2 Q.B. 621.

[60] *W. H. Smith & Sons* v. *Clinton* (1909) 99 L.T. 840.

[61] *Weld-Blundell* v. *Stephens* [1919] 1 K.B. 520; *Bradstreets British Ltd.* v. *Mitchell and Carpanayoti & Co. Ltd.* [1933] Ch. 190; contrast *Howard* v. *Odham's Press Ltd.* [1938] 1 K.B. 1. And see *Distillers Co. Ltd.* v. *Times Newspapers Ltd.* [1975] Q.B. 613.

[62] *Betts* v. *Gibbins* (1834) 2 A. & E. 57; *cf. Yeung* v. *Hong Kong & Shanghai Banking Corp.* [1981] A.C. 787.

[63] *The Nogar Marin* [1988] 1 Lloyd's Rep. 412, 417.

[64] *Daily Mirror Newspapers Ltd.* v. *Exclusive News Agency* (1937) 81 S.J. 924; Defamation Act 1952, s.11.

[65] *Adamson* v. *Jarvis* (1827) 4 Bing. 66; *Betts* v. *Gibbins*, *supra* n. 62.

[66] *Lister* v. *Romford Ice & Cold Storage Co. Ltd.* [1957] A.C. 555; *ante*, p. 191.

ility to the other if he delivers the property to the promisor is perfectly valid.[67]

(c) CIVIL LIABILITY ARISING OUT OF CRIMINAL ACTS. Where an act amounts both to a crime and to a civil wrong, a promise to indemnify the wrongdoer against civil liability incurred as a result of the act is often illegal. For example, in *Gray* v. *Barr*[68] a husband shot and killed his wife's lover in circumstances amounting in the view of the Court of Appeal to manslaughter (though in the criminal proceedings he had been acquitted). It was held that the husband could not recover under an insurance policy (even if it covered the occurrence) the damages which he had had to pay to the lover's estate. The decision was based on the public interest in deterring armed violence; but it does not follow that promises to indemnify against civil liability are necessarily invalid merely because the act giving rise to that liability also amounts to a crime. There are, in particular, two types of cases in which they may be upheld.

First, a promise to indemnify a person against civil liability can be enforced, even though the act giving rise to that liability is criminal, if the crime is one of strict liability or is in fact committed without *mens rea*. Thus in *Gray* v. *Barr* the possibility was left open that a person who committed manslaughter in circumstances amounting to little more than an error of judgment might be able to recover an indemnity from his insurance company.[69] The view that such an indemnity is recoverable is supported by a dictum in a later case, according to which the test "is not the label which the law applies to the crime which has been committed, but the nature of the crime itself."[70] Similarly, if the butcher in *Cointat* v. *Myham & Son*[71] had had to pay damages for breach of contract to a customer who was poisoned by the pork, he should have been able to claim an indemnity against this loss from the defendant.

A second possible exception exists in the law of motor insurance. In *Tinline* v. *White Cross Insurance*[72] a motorist, who was insured against liability for "accidental personal injury" to third parties, killed a pedestrian by driving with criminal negligence, and was convicted of manslaughter. He successfully sued the insurers for the damages which he had had to pay to

---

67 *e.g. Betts* v. *Gibbins* (1834) 2 A. & E. 57.

68 [1971] 2 Q.B. 554; criticised (on another point) in *D.P.P.* v. *Newbury* [1977] A.C. 500. Flemming, 34 M.L.R. 177; *cf. Haseldine* v. *Hosken* [1933] 1 K.B. 822; *R.* v. *National Insurance Commissioner, ex p. Connor* [1981] 1 Q.B. 758.

69 [1971] 1 Q.B. 544, 581; *cf. Gregory* v. *Ford* [1951] 1 All E.R. 121 (employment contract). It has been held that a person convicted of manslaughter cannot at common law take under his victim's will irrespective of his degree of moral culpability: *Re Giles* [1972] Ch. 544; *Re Royse* [1985] Ch. 22; Price 48 M.L.R. 723; but in *Re H* [1990] 1 FLR 441 the court refused to apply this rule where the person so convicted had, by reason of his diminished responsibility, "no responsibility at all" for the offence. Moreover, the court has power under Forfeiture Act 1982, s.2 to modify the rule: see *Re K* [1986] Ch. 180; Cretney, 10 O.J.L.S. 289.

70 *R.* v. *National Insurance Commissioner, ex p. Connor* [1981] Q.B. 758, 765 (where a claim for widow's benefit under the Social Security Act 1975 was rejected as the claimant had been convicted of manslaughter by *deliberately* stabbing her husband to death). *Semble*, that on such facts the result would not be affected by Forfeiture Act, 1982, s.4. though by Social Security Act 1986, s.76, Social Security Commissioners now have the same discretion as the High Court to modify the "forfeiture" rule (*supra*, n. 69).

71 [1913] 2 K.B. 220.

72 [1921] 3 K.B. 327; followed in *James* v. *British General Insurance Co. Ltd.* [1927] 2 K.B. 311; doubted in *Haseldine* v. *Hosken* [1933] 1 K.B. 822 but approved in *Marles* v. *Philip Trant & Sons Ltd.* [1954] 1 Q.B. 29, 40, and in *Gray* v. *Barr* [1971] 1 Q.B. 544, 568, 581.

the deceased. The motorist only has this right where the crime is committed negligently—not where it is committed deliberately.[73] But even in the latter case the position of the innocent victim of the motorist's crime is protected by giving him rights in certain circumstances against the insurer[74] or against the Motor Insurers' Bureau.[75] The existence of such rights is obviously necessary to maintain the effectiveness of the scheme of compulsory motor insurance.

(7) Promises to pay money on the commission of an unlawful act

A contract may be illegal if it provides for the payment of money to a person in the event of his doing an unlawful act, *e.g.* if A promises B £5 if B breaks the speed limit. Such a promise is not easy to distinguish from one to make a driver (or the cost of one) available to a motorist if he should be disqualified for a driving offence. A recommendation that such contracts[76] should be declared by statute to be unenforceable and void[77] has been accepted in principle, but legislation has not been introduced, as the insurance industry has agreed to discontinue the practice of issuing policies of this kind.[78]

A life insurance policy was never wholly illegal merely because it provided that the sum insured was to be paid even if the assured committed suicide (which was formerly a crime). It could clearly be enforced if he died in some other way. In *Beresford* v. *Royal Exchange Assurance*[79] it was, however, held that such a policy could not be enforced by the personal representatives of the assured if he did commit suicide; to allow a man, or his estate, to benefit from his own crime was said to be against public policy.[80] But if the assured assigned the policy and then committed suicide, the assignees were entitled to the policy moneys since it was they, and not the assured, who benefited from the crime.[81] It is hard to see the force of this distinction where, as in *Beresford's* case, the assured was bankrupt, so that the only people who could benefit were his creditors.

(8) Effect of changes in the law

In relation to contracts which involve the commission of a legal wrong it is necessary to consider the effect of changes in the law, both on contracts in existence at the time of the change and on contracts made after the change.

---

[73] *Gardner* v. *Moore* [1984] A.C. 548, 560.

[74] *Post*, p. 571.

[75] *Post*, p. 571; *Hardy* v. *M.I.B.* [1964] 2 Q.B. 743; *Gardner* v. *Moore* [1984] A.C. 548, 560–561.

[76] See *D.T.I.* v. *St. Christopher's Motorist Association* [1974] 1 W.L.R. 99.

[77] Road Traffic Law Report, HMSO 1988 (The North Report) paras. 16.32–16.35.

[78] The Road User and the Law 1989, Cm. 576.

[79] [1938] A.C. 586; Goodhart, 52 L.Q.R. 575.

[80] This principle applies even though the contract is not illegal: it has been applied to prevent recovery on a policy of life insurance where the assured was executed for felony though the policy did not in terms refer to this contingency: *Amicable Soc.* v. *Bolland* (1830) 4 Bligh (N.S.) 194, criticised by Devlin, *The Enforcement of Morals* at p. 53 and Furmston (1966) U. of Tor.L.J. at p. 274. *Cf. Davitt* v. *Titcumb* [1989] 3 All E.R. 417: murderer not allowed to benefit indirectly from policy on joint lives of victim and himself; *Geismar* v. *Sun Alliance* [1978] Q.B. 383: insurer not liable to pay for loss of goods smuggled into this country; liability for loss of *other* goods covered by the policies seems not to have been disputed; contrast *Euro-Diam Ltd.* v. *Bathurst* [1990] Q.B. 1, *post*, p. 434.

[81] *White* v. *British Empire, etc. Assurance Co.* (1868) L.R. 7 Eq. 394.

First, the law may change so that previously lawful conduct becomes a legal wrong. The effect of such a change may be to frustrate existing contracts[82] and to make future contracts illegal. Whether it actually has this effect will depend on principles stated in *St. John Shipping Corp.* v. *Joseph Rank Ltd.*[83]

A second kind of change is one by which conduct previously amounting to a legal wrong ceases to be so; and prima facie the effect of such a change in the law is that future contracts involving such conduct will be valid. This would clearly be the case where the conduct in question had been criminal under some regulatory statute (for example, one requiring certain work to be licensed) which was then repealed. But there are exceptions to this general rule. First, a statute abrogating a rule of law under which certain conduct was unlawful may expressly preserve a rule under which a contract involving such conduct was previously illegal: this is the position (in general[84]) with regard to champertous agreements.[85] Secondly, it is possible that, even after an act has ceased to be a legal wrong, a contract involving its commission would still be contrary to public policy. Thus a contract to do a homosexual act which was formerly, but is no longer,[86] criminal would probably be regarded as illegal where it promoted sexual immorality,[87] so that it fell, within one of the established heads of contracts which were against public policy.[88] But where this is not the case it is submitted that contracts should not generally be regarded as contrary to public policy merely because they involve conduct which was formerly criminal. Thus it is submitted that a contract to render services in connection with a lawful abortion is valid even though it would have been a contract to commit a crime before the Abortion Act 1967. Similarly it is submitted that the reasoning of *Beresford's* case is obsolete now that suicide is no longer a crime.[89]

The effect of this second kind of change in the law on contracts already in existence when the law was changed is more problematical. Changes in the law made after action brought are generally disregarded[90] but there seems to be no authority on the effect of changes in the law between the making of the contract and the commencement of the action. One possible view is that the validity of the contract must be determined, once for all, when it is made. But it is submitted that, so long as the act in question is lawful *when it is done,* no useful purpose is served by holding the contract invalid. The statute may itself solve the problem by specifying whether and if so to what extent the change in the law has retrospective effect.

2. Contracts Contrary to Public Policy: in General[91]

A contract which does not involve the commission of a legal wrong may be illegal because its tendency is to bring about a state of affairs of which the law disapproves on grounds of public policy. A contract is only illegal for

---

82 *Post*, p. 786.
83 [1957] 1 Q.B. 267, *ante*, p. 377.
84 For an exception, see Courts and Legal Services Act 1990, s.58, *ante*, p. 379.
85 *Ante*, p. 379.
86 Sexual Offences Act 1967.
87 *Cf.*, in criminal law, *R.* v. *Ford* [1977] 1 W.L.R. 1083.
88 *Post*, p. 390.
89 Suicide Act 1961; *cf. Gray* v. *Barr* [1971] 2 Q.B. 544, 582.
90 *Hitchcock* v. *Way* (1837) 6 A. & E. 943.
91 Lloyd, *Public Policy*; Winfield, 42 H.L.R. 76.

this reason if its harmful tendency is clear, that is, if injury to the public is its probable and not merely its possible consequence.[92]

Such contracts are often called "illegal."[93] It is sometimes said that they are only "void" or "unenforceable"[94]; but these statements only emphasise that no specific legal wrong is involved. So long as this point is borne in mind, no harm is done by using the traditional terminology in which these contracts are "illegal."[95]

(1) Agreements by married persons to marry

An agreement to marry was formerly regarded as a contract, the breach of which gave rise to an action for damages. It was, however, thought to be against public policy to allow such actions to be brought on a promise by a married person to marry. Such a promise might be one to commit bigamy, but even where this was not the case the promise was illegal. Thus in *Spiers* v. *Hunt*[96] a promise by a man to marry the plaintiff after his wife's death was held to be illegal as it had a tendency to break up the marriage, to encourage sexual immorality and even to lead to crime. These arguments are far from convincing and in *Fender* v. *St. John Mildmay*[97] the House of Lords held that they did not apply where the promise was made by a married man after he had obtained a decree nisi of divorce. But the promise was against public policy where, when it was made, a divorce (which later took place) was merely contemplated,[98] and also where the promisor believed that he was entitled to have his marriage annulled because of his wife's impotence.[99]

Actions for breach of promise of marriage were abolished by section 1 of the Law Reform (Miscellaneous Provisions) Act 1970,[1] so that the cases just discussed are, strictly speaking, obsolete. However, section 2 of the Act provides that "where an agreement to marry is terminated" the formerly engaged couple is to be treated for the purpose of certain rights[2] in, and disputes about, property as if they had been married. Difficult problems with regard to rights in property can obviously arise when an ex-fiancée makes a claim under section 2 against a man who, when he promised to marry her, was already married to someone else. Perhaps such difficulties can be overcome by holding that the "agreement" in section 2 must not be contrary to public policy in the sense of the old law. But the analogy between an "agreement" within the section and a valid contract under the old law is far from perfect; and, so long as the property interests of the wife (or former wife) are protected an ex-fiancée may sometimes be allowed to take the benefit of section 2 even though she could not before the Act have claimed damages. This might, for example, be the position

---

[92] *Fender* v. *St. John Mildmay* [1938] A.C. 1, 13; *cf. Multiservice Bookbinding Ltd.* v. *Marden* [1979] Ch. 84, 104.

[93] *e.g. Hermann* v. *Charlesworth* [1905] 2 K.B. 123, 136; *McEllistrim's Case* [1919] A.C. 548, 571; *cf.* Criminal Law Act 1967, s.14(2) ("contrary to public policy or otherwise illegal").

[94] *e.g. Bennett* v. *Bennett* [1952] 1 K.B. 249, 260; *Pao On* v. *Lau Yiu Long* [1980] A.C. 614, 634–635. *O'Sullivan* v. *Management Agency & Music Ltd.* [1985] Q.B. 428, 447, 448, 469.

[95] *Cf. Mogul S.S. Co. Ltd.* v. *McGregor Gow & Co.* [1892] A.C. 25, 46.

[96] [1908] 1 K.B. 720; *Wilson* v. *Carnley* [1908] 1 K.B. 729.

[97] [1938] A.C. 1.

[98] *Skipp* v. *Kelly* (1926) 42 T.L.R. 258.

[99] See *Siveyer* v. *Allison* [1935] 2 K.B. 403.

[1] Cretney, 33 M.L.R. 534.

[2] Not all: *Mossop* v. *Mossop* [1989] Fam. 77.

where the agreement to marry was made after the original marriage had broken up, but before a decree nisi had been obtained.

Under the old law, a promisee who did not know that the promisor was married could take advantage of the general rule allowing innocent parties in certain cases to sue on illegal contracts[3] and so recover damages for breach of promise of marriage.[4] Clearly, this cause of action has been abolished by the 1970 Act. But it was also held before the Act that a woman who innocently went through a ceremony of marriage with a man who, unknown to her, was married, could, after his death, recover damages from his estate for breach of an implied warranty that he was single.[5] The 1970 Act makes special provision for this situation by giving the innocent party certain rights against the other party's estate.[6] It does not in terms abolish the action for breach of the implied warranty, and it is arguable that such an action could still be brought by an innocent promisee.[7] But the implied warranty is based on the assumption that, if the promisor had been single, the promise would have been actionable. In destroying this assumption, the Act has removed the substratum of the implied warranty; and it is submitted that no action could now be brought on it.[8]

(2) Agreements between spouses for future separation

It was at one time thought that all separation agreements between spouses were inconsistent with the duties arising out of marriage and therefore invalid. This rule still applies if the agreement is made while the spouses are living together or before marriage. In *Brodie* v. *Brodie*[9] a man felt obliged to marry a woman who shortly afterwards gave birth to a child of which he was the reputed father. An agreement made before the marriage that the parties should not live together was held invalid. The result of the rule is that the husband cannot, while he is living with his wife or before marriage, make a binding promise to provide for his wife in the event of a separation.[10] But an agreement regulating the rights of spouses who are already separated is valid[11] as it does not encourage any breach of marital duty; at most, it creates favourable conditions for the continuance of a breach which has already taken place. And where spouses who are separated become reconciled, they can validly provide for future separation: the law recognises that, unless they could do this, reconciliation would be less likely.[12]

(3) Agreements in contemplation of divorce

At common law, an arrangement or agreement between parties to divorce proceedings (about such matters as the wife's maintenance) was invalid if it

---

[3] *Post*, pp. 431–435.
[4] *Wild* v. *Harris* (1849) 7 C.B. 999; *Millward* v. *Littlewood* (1850) 5 Ex. 775.
[5] *Shaw* v. *Shaw* [1954] 2 Q.B. 429.
[6] s.6.
[7] *Cf. post*, p. 434.
[8] For a dispute on this point, see Thomson, (1971) 87 L.Q.R. 159; L.C.B.G., *ibid.* 314.
[9] [1917] P. 271; *cf. Scott* v. *Scott* [1959] P. 103n. (*tamquam sororem* agreement before marriage invalid).
[10] The rule does not apply where the marriage is a polygamous one contracted abroad, under which the husband can divorce the wife at will: see *Shahnaz* v. *Rizwan* [1965] 1 Q.B. 390.
[11] *Wilson* v. *Wilson* (1848) 1 H.L.C. 538; *Hart* v. *Hart* (1881) 18 Ch.D. 670.
[12] *Harrison* v. *Harrison* [1910] 1 K.B. 35; *Macmahon* v. *Macmahon* [1913] 1 I.R. 428.

was made with a corrupt intention, for example, if it amounted to a bribe to institute, or carry on, the proceedings,[13] or to a conspiracy to deceive the court. But it was valid if it was an honest attempt to minimise the difficulties which had arisen between the parties.[14] The law on this topic was formerly influenced by the rule that collusion was a bar to divorce; but the abolition of this rule "completely alters the public policy on this point,"[15] so that an agreement is no longer invalid merely because it is collusive. Indeed, the court now has a statutory power to express its view as to the "reasonableness" of arrangements or agreements in contemplation of divorce.[16] In exercising this jurisdiction the court will be primarily concerned with the fairness of the agreement[17]; but it will also be influenced by the old distinction between honest compromises and bargains which are corrupt for reasons other than their collusive nature.[18]

(4) Agreements inconsistent with parental responsibility

At common law a father had the custody of his legitimate child and a contract by which he purported to assign that custody to any person was contrary to public policy as it was "repugnant entirely to his parental duty."[19] By statute, both parents have "parental responsibility"[20] for their child if they were married to each other at the time of the child's birth; if they were not, the mother has parental responsibility.[21] In the latter case, the parents may enter into a "parental responsibility agreement" providing for the father to have parental responsibility for the child[22]; but freedom of contract in making such an agreement, and in bringing it to an end, is severely restricted so as to protect the interests of the child.[23] The effect of such an agreement seems to be that parental responsibility is vested in both parents: the mother does not lose such responsibility since "a person who has parental responsibility for a child may not surrender or transfer such responsibility to another."[24] This statutory provision resembles the common law principle stated above and seems to be based on similar grounds of public policy. The person with parental responsibility may "arrange for some or all of it to be met by one or more persons acting on his behalf."[25] In such a case the responsibility is not transferred but vicariously performed.[26]

---

[13] *Hope* v. *Hope* (1857) 8 D.M. & G. 731; *Churchward* v. *Churchward* [1895] P. 7.
[14] *Scott* v. *Scott* [1913] P. 52.
[15] *Sutton* v. *Sutton* [1984] Ch. 184, 194.
[16] Matrimonial Causes Act 1973, s.7; *cf.* Domestic Proceedings and Magistrates' Courts Act 1978, s.6 (as substituted by Matrimonial and Family Proceedings Act 1984, s.10).
[17] *Dean* v. *Dean* [1978] Fam. 161.
[18] *Mulhouse* v. *Mulhouse* [1966] P. 39; *Nash* v. *Nash* [1965] P. 266; *Gosling* v. *Gosling* [1968] P. 1; *semble* these criteria will continue to apply despite the abolition of collusion as a bar to divorce.
[19] *Vansittart* v. *Vansittart* (1858) D. & J. 249, 259; *Walrond* v. *Walrond* (1858) Johns 18; *cf.* *Cole* v. *Gower* (1805) 6 East 110. *Cf.* also Adoption Act 1976, ss.57, 57A and 58, as amended by Children Act 1989, ss.88(1) and 108(7) (prohibition of advertisements and regulation of payments in connection with adoption).
[20] As defined by Children Act 1989, s.3.
[21] *Ibid.* s.2(1); and see s.2(4), abolishing the former common law rule.
[22] *Ibid.* s.4(1)(*b*).
[23] *Ibid.* ss.4(1) and (3), 1(1).
[24] *Ibid.* s.2(9).
[25] *Ibid.*
[26] *Cf. post*, p. 658.

(5) Agreements in restraint of marriage

Some contracts are invalid on the ground that they unjustifiably restrict a person's freedom to marry. This is true, for example, of a promise by a widow to pay £100 if she remarries,[27] and of a promise not to marry anyone except a specified person (not amounting to a promise to marry that person).[28] It may be that such promises are valid if they are limited in duration or otherwise reasonable: *e.g.* if a limited restraint is imposed for the sake of a person's health or (conceivably) of his moral well-being.[29] It is also possible that a promise not to marry anyone except a member of a fairly large group (for example, some religious denomination) might be valid.

So far we have considered actual promises not to marry, or to pay a sum of money on marriage. It seems that a contract is not invalid merely because it may in some other way deter one of the parties from marrying. Thus a promise to pay an allowance, or to permit a person to occupy a house, until the promisee's marriage, is valid.[30] Such promises may tend to discourage marriage, but they do not actually impose a contractual liability on a person as a result of marriage.[31]

(6) Marriage brokage contracts[32]

A marriage brokage contract is one by which a person promises in return for a money consideration to procure the marriage of another. Until the eighteenth century such contracts were valid at common law, thus making it possible for servants of young heiresses to obtain payment for assisting their charges to elope with fortune-hunters.[33] Equity therefore prevented the enforcement of these contracts "that marriages may be on a proper foundation . . . and to prevent that influence which servants more especially would gain over young ladies."[34] The principle is not restricted to contracts to procure a marriage between one of the contracting parties and a *particular* third person. Thus a contract by which a marriage bureau simply undertakes to make efforts to find a spouse for a client has been held invalid, because it involved "the introduction of the consideration of a money payment into that which should be free from any such taint."[35] The harmful tendencies of such contracts are by no means self-evident.

(7) Contracts promoting sexual immorality

A contract may be illegal if its object is sexually immoral. The common law originally applied this principle to all cases in which a contract could be said to promote such an object. But a distinction is now drawn between con-

---

[27] *Baker* v. *White* (1690) 2 Vern. 215; *cf. Hartley* v. *Rice* (1808) 10 East 22.

[28] *Lowe* v. *Peers* (1768) 2 Burr. 2225.

[29] *Cf. Denny* v. *Denny* [1919] 1 K.B. 583; *post*, p. 400.

[30] *Gibson* v. *Dickie* (1815) 3 M. & S. 463; the same point was assumed in *Thomas* v. *Thomas* (1842) 2 Q.B. 851.

[31] Contrast the position in the restraint of trade cases, *post*, p. 411. It is probably thought that stipulations which deter persons from trading are more likely to prejudice the public than those which deter them from marrying.

[32] Powell, 6 C.L.P. 254.

[33] *e.g. Goldsmith* v. *Bruning* (1700) 1 Eq.Ca.Abr. 89, pl. 4.

[34] *Cole* v. *Gibson* (1750) 1 Ves.Sen. 503, 506.

[35] *Hermann* v. *Charlesworth* [1905] 2 K.B. 123, 130; *post*, p. 446.

tracts with purely meretricious purposes and those which are intended to regulate stable extra-marital relationships.

(a) MERETRICIOUS PURPOSES. A promise by a man to pay a woman money if she will become his mistress is illegal.[36] A promise to pay money to a woman with whom the promisor had illicitly cohabited in the past is not contrary to public policy since it does not *promote* immorality. It is simply void because the consideration for it is past,[37] but it will be valid if made in a deed.[38] The validity of a promise in a deed made *during* cohabitation depends on its purpose. If it is simply a gift, or voluntary bond, it is as valid as one given after cohabitation.[39] But if its object is to secure the continuance of cohabitation, it is illegal.[40] A bond given after cohabitation would also be invalid if it were merely given to secure the performance of a promise of payment made before cohabitation. A promise to pay must be distinguished from a completed gift. In *Ayerst* v. *Jenkins*[41] a man settled property on a woman with whom he was cohabiting. A claim by his personal representatives to have the settlement set aside failed. "The voluntary gift of part of his own property by one *particeps criminis* to another is in itself neither fraudulent nor prohibited by law."[42]

A contract is also illegal if it indirectly promotes sexual immorality. Thus in *Pearce* v. *Brooks*[43] a contract to hire out a brougham to a prostitute for the purposes of her profession was held to be illegal. The same would be true of a contract of employment by which the employee undertook to procure prostitutes for the employer's clients.[44] On the other hand, a contract to let a room to a prostitute who practises her profession elsewhere is valid "because persons of that description must have a place to lay their heads."[45] In the somewhat questionable case of *Lloyd* v. *Johnson*[46] a contract to wash a prostitute's linen was held valid even though the linen included a quantity of gentlemen's nightcaps.

In the cases on this subject "immorality" always means extra-marital sexual intercourse. A contract might promote some other form of activity that could be described as immoral and sexual. For example, a contract might be made to publish an indecent book whose publication did not amount to a crime. Such a contract might formerly have been regarded as

---

36 *Franco* v. *Bolton* (1797) 3 Ves. 368; *Benyon* v. *Nettlefold* (1850) 3 Mac. & G. 94.

37 *Beaumont* v. *Reeve* (1846) 8 Q.B. 483; *Binnington* v. *Wallis* (1821) 4 B. & Ald. 650 suggests that such a promise is binding if made by a man who was a seducer, but this is based on the wide view of the "moral obligation" theory of consideration, which no longer prevails: *ante*, p. 75 and see *Jennings* v. *Brown* (1842) 9 M. & W. 496, 501.

38 *Annadale* v. *Harris* (1727) 2 P.Wms. 432; *affirmed* 1 Bro.P.C. 250; *Turner* v. *Vaughan* (1767) 2 Wils.K.B. 339; *Knye* v. *Moore* (1822) 1 S. & S. 61. It is stressed in some of the old cases that the promisor was the seducer and that the payment was promised as "praemium pudicitiae." Thus it was doubtful whether the rule applied in favour of a common prostitute: *Bainham* v. *Manning* (1691) 2 Vern. 242; *Whaley* v. *Norton* (1687) 1 Vern. 483; *contra*, *Hill* v. *Spencer* (1767) Amb. 641, 836.

39 *Gray* v. *Mathias* (1800) 5 Ves. 286; *Hall* v. *Palmer* (1844) 3 Hare 532.

40 *The Lady Cox's Case* (1734) 3 P.Wms. 339; *Walker* v. *Perkins* (1764) 3 Burr. 1568.

41 (1873) L.R. 16 Eq. 275.

42 At p. 283.

43 (1866) L.R. 1 Ex. 213; *cf. Upfill* v. *Wright* [1911] 1 K.B. 506; a case viewed with some scepticism in *Heglibiston Establishment* v. *Heyman* (1977) 36 P. & C.R. 351.

44 See *Coral Leisure Group* v. *Barnett* [1981] I.C.R. 503, 508 (where no such undertaking had, on the facts, been established).

45 *Appleton* v. *Campbell* (1826) 2 C. & P. 347; *cf. Bowry* v. *Bennett* (1808) 1 Camp. 348.

46 (1798) 1 B. & P. 340.

invalid on account of its "grossly immoral" tendency.[47] "But at the present day the difficulty is to identify what sexual conduct is to be treated as grossly immoral"[48]; so that it is less likely that such a contract would now be struck down on this ground.

(b) STABLE RELATIONSHIPS. The traditional common law approach to immoral contracts is progressively being abandoned in cases concerning the arrangements between persons who live together in a common household as husband and wife without being married. It has for example been held that a licence under which such a couple occupied furnished accommodation was not contrary to public policy.[49] The law also recognises that legal effects can flow from agreements between such persons with respect to the house in which they live. Where the house is owned by one of them, the agreement can confer legally enforceable rights on the other, such as a contractual licence to remain there,[50] or a share in the value of the house in respect of the contribution made by the other to its acquisition, maintenance or improvement.[51] By statute a spouse who is a victim of domestic violence can exclude the other from the matrimonial home; and this remedy is expressly stated to apply "to a man and a woman who are living in the same household as it applies to the parties to a marriage."[52] The opening of a bank account by one party to such a relationship with funds intended to belong to both jointly has been held (on proof of the appropriate intention) to amount to a declaration of trust in favour of the other.[53] It seems, although the point has not yet been decided in England, that an express contract between such persons to "pool" their earnings and acquisitions would not be regarded as contrary to public policy.[54] And "when an illegitimate child has been born, there is certainly nothing contrary to public policy in the parents coming to an agreement which they intend to be binding in law, for the maintenance of the child and mother."[55]

These illustrations[56] suggest that the old common law rule governing immoral contracts will in future be confined to meretricious relationships. Domestic arrangements between parties to the present group of stable relationships will often not be contracts because they were not made with that intention.[57] But they should not, if the requirement of contractual intention is satisfied, be struck down on grounds of public policy.[58]

---

[47] *Cf. Glyn* v. *Weston Feature Film Co.* [1916] 1 Ch. 261 (refusal to protect copyright in immoral book) approved in *Att.-Gen.* v. *Guardian Newspapers* (*No.* 2) [1990] A.C. 109, 262, 276 (refusal to protect copyright in book written in breach of fiduciary duty).

[48] *Stephens* v. *Avery* [1988] Ch. 449, 453 (protection of confidential information concerning lesbian relationship).

[49] *Somma* v. *Hazlehurst* [1979] 1 W.L.R. 1014 (disapproved on another point in *Street* v. *Mountford* [1985] A.C. 809); *cf.* also *Watson* v. *Lucas* [1980] 1 W.L.R. 1493.

[50] *Tanner* v. *Tanner* [1975] 1 W.L.R. 1346; *Chandler* v. *Kerley* [1978] 1 W.L.R. 693.

[51] *Eves* v. *Eves* [1975] 1 W.L.R. 1338.

[52] Domestic Violence and Matrimonial Proceedings Act 1976, s.2(1); *Davis* v. *Johnson* [1978] A.C. 264.

[53] *Paul* v. *Constance* [1977] 1 W.L.R. 527.

[54] *Marvin* v. *Marvin* 557 P. 2d 106 (1976); and see *The Times*, August 14, 1981. *Cf. Latham* v. *Latham* 547 P. 2d 144 (1975).

[55] *Horrocks* v. *Forray* [1976] 1 W.L.R. 230, 239.

[56] *Cf.* also *post*, p. 613; *Heglibiston Establishment* v. *Heyman* (1977) 36 P. & C.R. 351.

[57] *Ante*, p. 151.

[58] Devlin, 39 M.L.R. 1, 12; Dwyer, 93 L.Q.R. 386.

(8) Contracts interfering with the course of justice

A contract may be illegal because the mere making of it amounts to a conspiracy to pervert the course of justice: *e.g.* where a person promises another money for giving false evidence on his behalf in criminal proceedings[59] or where two men agree to bribe a prosecution witness to withdraw a charge of rape.[60] A contract may also (even though it does not amount to a criminal conspiracy) be illegal if its object is to interfere with the course of public justice. Before the distinction between felonies and misdemeanours was abolished, a contract to stifle a prosecution for a misdemeanour was not itself an offence but such contracts were often held illegal. Thus contracts to stifle prosecutions for perjury, riot, assault on a police officer, interfering with a public road, and obtaining by false pretences were held illegal.[61] But this rule was not applied where the misdemeanour was of a "private" nature. Thus in *McGregor* v. *McGregor*[62] it was held that a husband and wife who had taken out cross-summonses for assault against each other could validly compromise them in a separation agreement. It has similarly been held that a prosecution for trade-mark offences could be compromised by agreement between the owner and the offender[63]; and it has been said that the same principle applies to criminal libel.[64]

The old cases must now be read in the light of the abolition of the distinction between felonies and misdemeanours and of the creation of the new offence of concealing an arrestable offence.[65] That offence is not committed by a person who withholds information which may lead to the conviction of the offender in consideration only of the making good of the loss or injury caused by the offence[66]; and it is doubtful whether an agreement to this effect should now be held illegal.[67] One view is that the agreement may still be illegal, even though it does not itself amount to an offence, for this was precisely the position under the old law where an agreement was made to stifle a prosecution for a misdemeanour. A second view is that, where the only consideration is the making good of the loss, no public interest is harmed by upholding the agreement; and this view can be supported by reference to the old cases concerning misdemeanours of a "private" nature. A third view is that the legality of an agreement to stifle a prosecution (not amounting to a conspiracy to pervert the course of justice or to the offence of concealing an arrestable offence) should depend on the

---

59 *R.* v. *Andrews* [1973] Q.B. 422.

60 *R.* v. *Panayiotou* [1973] 3 All E.R. 112.

61 *Collins* v. *Blantern* (1767) 2 Wils.K.B. 341; *Keir* v. *Leeman* (1846) 9 Q.B. 371; *Windhill Local Board of Health* v. *Vint* (1890) 45 Ch.D. 351; *Clubb* v. *Huston* (1865) 18 C.B.(N.S.) 414 (embezzlement); *cf. Howard* v. *Odham's Press Ltd.* [1938] 1 K.B. 42 (contract not to disclose confession of fraud); and *cf. post*, p. 403, n. 58. Contracts to stifle a prosecution for a felony were sometimes held illegal on this ground (*e.g. Rawlings* v. *Coal Consumers' Association* (1874) 43 L.J.M.C. 111; *Whitmore* v. *Farley* (1881) 45 L.T. 99), but were also illegal as they formerly amounted to compounding. For threats to prosecute, see *ante*, p. 366.

62 (1888) 21 Q.B.D. 424.

63 *Fisher & Co.* v. *Apollinaris Co.* (1875) L.R. 10 Ch.App. 297.

64 *Ibid.*, p. 303.

65 Criminal Law Act 1967, ss.1, 5(1), *ante*, p. 379.

66 Criminal Law Act 1967, s.5(1).

67 Hudson, 43 M.L.R. 532.

question whether it was in the public interest that the prosecution should be brought; and it is submitted that this is the best view.[68]

The principle of public policy is not confined to contracts to stifle a prosecution: thus a contract to indemnify a surety in criminal proceedings is illegal.[69] Nor is the principle restricted to contracts affecting criminal proceedings. Thus agreements to obstruct bankruptcy proceedings[70] and corrupt agreements relating to matrimonial proceedings[71] are illegal. It has also been said that a contract by which a witness promised one party to a civil dispute not to give evidence for the other would be contrary to public policy.[72] An ordinary civil claim can, of course, be validly compromised, even though the facts giving rise to the claim also amount to a crime. But in such a case an agreement to abandon "any legal proceedings" may be illegal, as this phrase is wide enough to refer to possible civil *and* criminal proceedings.[73]

(9) Contracts purporting to oust the jurisdiction of the courts

A contract is contrary to public policy if it purports to deprive the courts of a jurisdiction which they would otherwise have. Thus in *Anctil* v. *Manufacturers' Life Insurance Co.*[74] it was held that a clause in an insurance policy providing that it should in certain events become "incontestable" did not prevent the court from deciding whether the assured had any insurable interest.[75] Such agreements are contrary to public policy because they would, if valid, make it possible to evade or contravene many peremptory rules of law.

(a) ILLUSTRATIONS. The rule restricting the parties' power by contract to oust the jurisdiction of the courts is further illustrated by the following cases:

(i) *Agreements for maintenance.* A husband may, as part of a separation agreement or in the course of matrimonial proceedings, promise to pay his wife an allowance in return for the wife's promise not to apply to the court for maintenance. In *Hyman* v. *Hyman*[76] the House of Lords held that such an agreement did not prevent the wife from applying to the court for maintenance. The contract was illegal, since "The wife's right to future main-

---

68 It might be relevant that the offence was a "serious arrestable offence" as defined by Police and Criminal Evidence Act 1984, s.116 (though the Act does not use the definition for this purpose).

69 *Herman* v. *Jeuchner* (1885) 15 Q.B.D. 561. It is now an offence to make such an agreement: Bail Act 1976, s.9.

70 *Elliott* v. *Richardson* (1870) L.R. 5 C.P. 744; *cf. Murray* v. *Reeves* (1828) 8 B. & C. 421; *Hall* v. *Dyson* (1852) 17 Q.B. 785; *Kearley* v. *Thomson* (1890) 24 Q.B.D. 742; *Coppock* v. *Bower* (1838) 4 M. & W. 361 (agreement to abandon election petition on ground of bribery illegal); *Norman* v. *Cole* (1800) 3 Esp. 253 (money paid for help in procuring a pardon).

71 *Ante*, p. 389.

72 *Harmony Shipping Co. S.A.* v. *Saudi Europe Line Ltd.* [1979] 1 W.L.R. 1380, 1386.

73 *Lound* v. *Grimwade* (1888) 39 Ch.D. 605.

74 [1899] A.C. 604.

75 But such clauses are effective to prevent the insurer from contesting certain matters of fact, *e.g.* that statements in the proposal form were true: see Colinvaux, *Laws of Insurance* (5th ed.), p. 369.

76 [1929] A.C. 601. The principle laid down in this case has survived the abolition of collusion as a bar to divorce: see *cf. Dean* v. *Dean* [1978] Fam. 161, 167.

tenance is a matter of public concern which she cannot barter away."[77] But this rule had one unfortunate result: if the husband failed to pay the promised allowance, the wife could not sue him for it, since a promise cannot be enforced if the sole or main consideration for it is illegal.[78] By statute, the wife can, if such an agreement is in writing, sue the husband for the promised allowance, in spite of the fact that her own promise not to apply to the court is void.[79]

(ii) *Arbitration clauses*. There was never any doubt about the validity of such clauses if they simply provided that the parties were to resort to arbitration before going to court. In *Scott* v. *Avery*[80] a clause of this kind was upheld as it did not purport to oust the jurisdiction of the court, but simply to lay down at what stage the cause of action upon which that jurisdiction might be exercised arose. At common law a party who disregarded such a clause and went to court without first resorting to arbitration was only liable in damages[81]; but by statute the court as a general rule[82] may (and in certain cases must)[83] stay the action.[84] Thus it can, in effect, ensure that arbitration clauses are observed.

On the other hand, an arbitration clause might be invalid at common law on one of two grounds. First, such a clause was invalid to the extent that it purported to deprive the parties of the right to go to court to sue on a completed cause of action, or to exclude the power granted to the courts by statute to control the decisions of arbitrators on points of law.[85] This rule was justified by the argument that, if such a clause were valid, an arbitrator who decided a dispute on principles at variance with the general law would be subject to no control at all[86]; and this would be particularly undesirable

[77] [1929] A.C. at. p. 629. But such an agreement is not contrary to public policy if it only ousts the jurisdiction of a foreign court: *Addison* v. *Brown* [1954] 1 W.L.R. 779; nor if it is sanctioned by order of the court: *L.* v. *L.* [1962] P. 101; *Minton* v. *Minton* [1979] A.C. 593. The court can, however, later increase periodical payments due to the wife under such an agreement: *Wright* v. *Wright* [1970] 1 W.L.R. 1219; *Jessel* v. *Jessel* [1979] 1 W.L.R. 1148. The court can also take the wife's promise into account when exercising its discretion whether to make an award in her favour: *Edgar* v. *Edgar* [1980] 1 W.L.R. 1410.

[78] *Bennett* v. *Bennett* [1952] 1 K.B. 249; *aliter* if only a subsidiary part of the consideration was illegal: *Goodinson* v. *Goodinson* [1954] 2 Q.B. 118; *cf. Sutton* v. *Sutton* [1984] Ch. 184 (where *each* party promised not to invoke the jurisdiction of the court); and see *post*, p. 446.

[79] Matrimonial Causes Act 1973, s.34. For a dispute on this point, see Dew, 56 Law Soc. Gaz. 365; J. H. H., 101 S.J. 73; 78 *Law Notes* 177; Treitel, 77 L.Q.R. 93–95. In *Sutton* v. *Sutton*, *supra*, the agreement was oral, so that s.34 did not apply.

[80] (1855) 5 H.L.C. 811; *cf. Atlantic Shipping & Trading Co. Ltd.* v. *Louis Dreyfus & Co.* [1922] 2 A.C. 250; *Persson* v. *London County Buses* [1974] 1 W.L.R. 569.

[81] *Doleman & Sons* v. *Ossett Corporation* [1912] 3 K.B. 257, 267.

[82] For an exception in cases of certain arbitration agreements in contracts with consumers, see Consumer Arbitration Act 1988.

[83] Arbitration Act 1975 s.1(1), applying to certain arbitration agreements with an international element: see *Associated Bulk Carriers Ltd.* v. *Koch Shipping Inc.* [1978] 2 All E.R. 254.

[84] See now Arbitration Act 1950, s.4(1).

[85] *Czarnikow* v. *Roth Schmidt & Co.* [1922] 2 K.B. 478. For a different approach in New Zealand, see *CBI NZ Ltd.* v. *Badger Chiyoda* [1989] N.Z.L.R. 669.

[86] Clauses making an arbitrator's decision "final" do not have this effect: see *Ford* v. *Clarkson's Holidays Ltd.* [1971] 1 W.L.R. 1412; *P. & M. Kaye* v. *Hosier & Dickinson Ltd.* [1972] 1 W.L.R. 146.

if he made an award enforcing a wholly illegal agreement. This risk could also arise where the clause did not in terms restrict the right of the parties to ask the court to control the arbitrator's decision, but instead laid down standards which made such control nugatory; and this is a second ground of invalidity at common law. Accordingly, it has been said that "a clause which purported to free arbitrators to decide without regard to law and according, for example, to their own notions of what would be fair would not be a valid arbitration clause."[87] But the parties can validly specify standards which, at least to some extent, guard against this risk: it is, for example, not contrary to public policy to enforce an arbitration award based on "internationally accepted principles of law governing contractual relations."[88] An arbitration clause can also free arbitrators from the need to apply strict legal rules of construction, *e.g.* by enpowering them to interpret a contract "as an honourable engagement rather than in accordance with a literal interpretation of the language."[89] And the courts can to some extent save an arbitration clause which transgresses such limits by striking out such parts of the clause as go "further than the law permits in freeing arbitrators from strict rules of law."[90]

The first of the two common law rules just stated (*i.e.* the rule invalidating an arbitration clause which purported to exclude the right of the parties to ask the court to control an arbitrator's decision on points of law) was open to a practical objection: the resulting total impossibility of excluding judicial control tended in practice to erode the virtues of speed and cheapness that were supposed to be characteristics of arbitration as a method of settling disputes. Two important changes were therefore made by the Arbitration Act 1979.[91] First, the parties can now exclude the powers of the court to control arbitrations by a written "exclusion agreement."[92] The effectiveness of such an agreement is, however, subject to the important limitation that, in the case of a "domestic arbitration agreement,"[93] and in certain other cases,[94] the exclusion agreement must be made after the commencement of the arbitration. Secondly, the Act reduces the scope of judicial control. This control will generally be exercised by way of appeal to the court on a question of law.[95] Such an appeal can only be brought

---

87 *Home and Overseas Insurance Co. Ltd.* v. *Mentor Insurance Co. (U.K.) Ltd.* [1989] 1 Lloyd's Rep. 473, 485; and see *infra*, n. 89.

88 *Deutsche Schachtbau-und Tiefbohrgesellschaft m.b.H.* v. *Ras Al Khaimah National Oil Co.* [1990] 1 A.C. 295, 315 (reversed on other grounds *ibid.* pp. 329 *et seq.*).

89 *Overseas Union Insurance Ltd.* v. *AA Mutual International Insurance Ltd.* [1988] 2 Lloyd's Rep. 63; *Home and Overseas Insurance Co. Ltd.* v. *Mentor Insurance Co. (U.K.) Ltd.*, *supra*, n. 87.

90 *Home Insurance Co.* v. *Administrata Asigurarilor* [1983] 2 Lloyd's Rep. 674, 677.

91 Kerr, 43 M.L.R. 45.

92 Arbitration Act 1979, s.3(1).

93 *Ibid.* s.3(6); "domestic arbitration agreement" is defined in s.3(7) so as to exclude agreements with certain foreign elements.

94 *Ibid.* s.4(1) (Admiralty questions and disputes arising out of contracts of insurance or commodity contracts, unless the award relates to a question governed by foreign law). This restriction on effectiveness of exclusion agreements is intended to be temporary and can be removed by order of the Secretary of State: s.4(3).

95 Arbitration Act 1979, s.1(2). Under s.2 the court also has a power to determine preliminary questions of law.

either with the consent of the parties[96] or with the leave of the court[97]; and leave can only be given where the question of law could substantially affect the rights of one or more of the parties.[98] The House of Lords has held that leave to appeal should not be given *merely* because it is alleged that the arbitrator has gone wrong in law; and it has laid down guidelines to be observed by the courts in considering applications for such leave.[99] The overriding consideration is whether the decision of the court "would add significantly to the clarity and certainty of English commercial law."[1] Thus the court is more likely to grant leave if the issue is as to the true construction of a standard form commercial contract in common use,[2] or if it raises an important general question of law,[3] than if it relates merely to the construction of a "one-off" contract specially drafted for a particular transaction. In the former situation leave will normally[4] be given if there is "a strong prima facie case" that the arbitrator has made an error of law; in the latter, only if his decision is "obviously wrong."[5] A similar distinction has been drawn in relation to *events* bringing contractual provisions into play, or interfering with the performance of a contract. Thus leave is more likely to be given where the event is one that may affect many contracts (such as the hostilities in the Persian Gulf, preventing the movement of shipping there,[6] or an embargo on the export of some commodity from a major exporting country) than where the event is not likely to have this effect (*e.g.* where it is a strike that only affects the export of goods from a particular port).[7]

(iii) *Construction of rules of associations.* A clause in the rules of an association such as a trade union may purport to give to the committee of the association exclusive jurisdiction to construe the rules. But, as the construction of the rules is a question of law, it has been held that any attempt

---

96 s.1(3)(*c*).

97 s.1(3)(*b*); *cf.* s.2(2)(*b*). For further appeals to the Court of Appeal against refusal of leave, see s.1(6A), as inserted by Supreme Court Act 1981, s.148(2); *The Antaios* [1985] A.C. 191; *Aden Refinery Co.* v. *Ugland Management Co.* [1987] Q.B. 650.

98 s.1(4).

99 *The Nema* [1982] A.C. 724. Similar restrictions apply to appeals to the Court of Appeal from decisions of the High Court under s.2 (*supra*, n. 95); *The Oltenia* [1982] 1 W.L.R. 871.

1 *The Nema*, *supra*, at p. 743. For other grounds of public interest that may lead the court to give leave, see *Bulk Oil (Zug) A.G.* v. *Sun International* [1984] 1 W.L.R. 147.

2 *The Rio Sun* [1981] 2 Lloyd's Rep. 489; see also [1982] 1 Lloyd's Rep. 404.

3 *The Alaskan Trader* [1983] 1 Lloyd's Rep. 315.

4 This guideline may be displaced, *e.g.* if there are circumstances indicating that the parties did not intend to accept the arbitrator's decision as final: see *The Emmanuel Colocotronis* [1982] 1 All E.R. 578.

5 *The Nema*, *supra*, at p. 743; *The Nichos A* [1982] 1 Lloyd's Rep. 52; *The Kerman* [1982] 1 Lloyd's Rep. 62; *National Rumour Compania S.A.* v. *Lloyd-Libra Navegacao S.A.* [1982] 1 Lloyd's Rep. 472; *cf. The Kwai* [1981] 2 Lloyd's Rep. 563; *The Yanxilas* [1982] 2 Lloyd's Rep. 444, 457 ("fairly clearly wrong"); *L'Office National du Thé et du Sucre* v. *Philippine Sugar Trading (London) Ltd.* [1983] 1 Lloyd's Rep. 89; *The Antaios* [1985] A.C. 191. *Kansa General Insurance Co. Ltd.* v. *Bishopsgate Insurance plc* [1988] 1 Lloyd's Rep. 503; *cf. The Kelaniya* [1989] 1 Lloyd's Rep. 30. The same tests apply to arbitrators' decisions on the construction of rent review clauses, but such decisions will often fall into the "standard contracts" category because of their likely long-term effects on the rights of the parties: see *Ipswich B.C.* v. *Fisons plc* [1990] Ch. 709 (where leave was given because there was a "strong prima facie case": it was not enough if the court was "in real doubt," as had been held in *Lucas Industries plc* v. *Welsh Development Agency* [1986] Ch. 500, 504).

6 *The Wenjiang* [1982] 1 Lloyd's Rep. 128.

7 As in *The Nema*, *supra*.

to deprive the courts of their jurisdiction over it is invalid.[8] By contrast, the jurisdiction of the Visitor of a University to decide matters governed by the "internal laws" of the University is at common law exclusive, so that his decisions on points of this kind cannot be challenged in the ordinary courts.[9]

(b) SCOPE OF THE RULE. Contracts purporting to exclude the jurisdiction of the courts must be distinguished from promises in honour only.[10] A provision that a promise "shall not be enforced in any court" makes the promise legally unenforceable, but does not purport to oust the jurisdiction of the court to say so. Similar reasoning applies to compromise of a genuine dispute as to legal rights. Such a compromise may vary or supersede the legal rights of the parties; but it does not prevent the courts from determining what those right are. It is therefore not contrary to public policy[11]; and this is true even though the public can be said to have some interest in the dispute, *e.g.* because it relates to the performance of duties under a charitable trust.[12]

(10) Contracts to deceive public authorities

In *Alexander* v. *Rayson*[13] the plaintiff let a service flat to the defendant for £1,200. Two documents were executed: in the first the defendant agreed to pay £450 for the flat and certain services; in the second she agreed to pay £750 for the same services, plus the use of a refrigerator. The plaintiff's object in splitting up the contract in this way was to defraud the rating authorities by showing them the first document only. The contract was therefore held to be illegal. A contract by which an employee gets an expense allowance grossly in excess of the expenses he actually incurs is similarly illegal as a fraud on the Revenue.[14] The same is true where part of the employee's actual pay is fraudulently concealed from the Revenue, with a view to evading tax.[15] But the contract is only illegal if the scheme that it furthers is a fraudulent one. Thus it is perfectly lawful for a contract of employment to provide that the employee is to receive a specified amount "free of tax," so long as the employer accounts to the revenue authorities for the tax due.[16]

---

[8] *Lee* v. *Showmen's Guild of Great Britain* [1952] 2 Q.B. 329; *Baker* v. *Jones* [1954] 1 W.L.R. 1005; *cf. Edwards* v. *Aberayron Insurance Soc. Ltd.* (1876) 1 Q.B.D. 563; *Re Davstone Estate Ltd.'s Leases* [1969] 2 Ch. 378; *Leigh* v. *N.U.R.* [1970] Ch. 326; *Edwards* v. *SOGAT* [1971] Ch. 354. There is no objection to leaving questions of fact to the final determination of a private tribunal: *Brown* v. *Overbury* (1856) 11 Exch. 715; *Cipriani* v. *Burnett* [1933] A.C. 83. *Cf.*, in the law of trusts, *Re Tuck's S.T* [1976] Ch. 99. See also Employment Act 1988, s.2 (right of union members to go to court after six months).

[9] *Thomas* v. *University of Bradford* [1987] A.C. 795 for a statutory exception, see *Pearce* v. *University of Aston* [1991] 2 All E.R. 463.

[10] *Ante*, p. 150.

[11] *Ante*, p. 82. For compromise of a claim known by the claimant to be invalid, see *ante*, p. 83; *post*, p. 426.

[12] *Bradshaw* v. *University College of Wales* [1988] 1 W.L.R. 190.

[13] [1936] 1 K.B. 169; *cf. Palaniappa Chettiar* v. *Arunasalam Chettiar* [1962] A.C. 294; *Mitsubishi Corp.* v. *Aristidis I. Alafouzos* [1988] 1 Lloyd's Rep. 191.

[14] *Miller* v. *Karlinski* (1945) 62 T.L.R. 85; *Napier* v. *National Business Agency Ltd.* [1951] 2 All E.R. 264; *cf. Hyland* v. *J. Barber (North West)* [1985] I.C.R. 861.

[15] *Cf. Corby* v. *Morrison* [1980] I.C.R. 564.

[16] See *Newland* v. *Simmons & Willer (Hairdressers) Ltd.* [1981] I.C.R. 521.

(11) Sale of offices and honours, lobbying, etc.

Certain contracts for the sale of public offices are prohibited by statute[17] while others are illegal at common law.[18] The same rule applies to contracts for the sale of commissions in the armed forces of the Crown.[19] Exceptionally, commissions in the Army could be sold[20] until this practice was prohibited by Royal Warrant in 1871.[21] Contracts of this kind are contrary to public policy because of their tendency to lead to corruption and inefficiency.

Similarly, it was held in *Parkinson* v. *College of Ambulance Ltd.*[22] that a contract to procure a knighthood was illegal as it might lead to corruption and as it was "derogatory to the dignity of the Sovereign."[23] It is now an offence to make such a contract.[24] And a contract by a Member of Parliament to vote in accordance with the direction of some body outside Parliament is invalid.[25]

Similar problems can arise from the practice of "lobbying" for government contracts. While in some cases the practice is "recognised and respectable,"[26] it is in others contrary to public policy. This was, for example held to be the case where the defendant promised large commissions to the plaintiff company for using its influence to secure the renewal of contracts between the defendant and a foreign government. It was essential to the success of the scheme that the government should be kept in ignorance of the plaintiff's financial interest in the matter, while the plaintiffs knew that the original contract provided that no commissions should be paid to third parties. The plaintiff's claim for the commission was therefore rejected on grounds of public policy.[27]

(12) Trading with the enemy

A contract made in time of war is illegal if it involves commercial intercourse with an enemy.[28] An enemy, for this purpose, is a person voluntarily resident or carrying on business in enemy-occupied territory.[29] Such contracts are illegal as they tend to aid the economy of the enemy country. A contract is not illegal if one of the parties to it is an "enemy" but its per-

---

17 Sale of Offices Act 1551, extended by Sale of Offices Act 1809, as amended by Criminal Law Act 1967, s.10 and Sched. 3.

18 *Garforth* v. *Fearon* (1787) 1 H.B.L. 327; *Hannington* v. *Du-Chatel* (1781) 1 Bro.C.C. 124; *Law* v. *Law* (1735) 3 P.Wms. 391; *Parsons* v. *Thompson* (1790) 1 H.B. 322. *Cf.* the rule against assignment of a public officer's salary: *post*, p. 601.

19 *Morris* v. *McCullock* (1763) Amb. 432.

20 *Berrisford* v. *Done* (1682) 1 Vern. 98.

21 An attempt to abolish purchase of Army commissions by statute having failed to get a majority in the House of Lords.

22 [1925] 2 K.B. 1.

23 At p. 14.

24 Honours (Prevention of Abuses) Act 1925.

25 *A.S.R.S.* v. *Osborne* [1910] A.C. 87. The House of Commons has resolved that it is a breach of privilege to make such a contract: Erskine May, *Parliamentary Practice*, (20th ed.), p. 81.

26 *Lemenda Trading Co. Ltd.* v. *African Middle East Petroleum Co.* [1988] Q.B. 448, 458; Collies [1988] C.L.J. 169.

27 *Lemenda* case, *supra*.

28 *Sovfracht (V/O)* v. *Van Udens Scheepvaart en Agentuur Maatschappij (N.V. Gebr.)* [1943] A.C. 203.

29 *Porter* v. *Freudenberg* [1915] 1 K.B. 857.

formance involves no further commercial intercourse with the enemy[30] and it can be enforced if this does not benefit the enemy.[31] It is a statutory offence to trade or to attempt to trade with an enemy.[32]

(13) Contracts which involve doing an illegal act in a friendly foreign country

In the interests of good foreign relations, the courts will not uphold a contract which involves the performance in a friendly foreign country of an act which is illegal by its law. Thus a loan to support an armed attack on such a country is illegal.[33] Similarly, a contract to smuggle whisky into the U.S.A. during the Prohibition period was held illegal.[34] And in *Regazzoni* v. *K. C. Sethia (1944) Ltd.*[35] a contract was made for the export of Indian jute to Italy, with a view to re-export to South Africa. The House of Lords refused to enforce the contract as it contravened an Indian law prohibiting the export of goods produced in India to South Africa, and as it could only be performed by making false declarations in India.

(14) Contracts restricting personal liberty

A contract may be illegal if it so restricts the liberty of an individual as to reduce him to a quasi-servile condition. In *Horwood* v. *Millar's Timber and Trading Co.*[36] a clerk borrowed money from a moneylender and agreed that he would not without the lender's written consent leave his job, borrow money, dispose of his property or move house. The contract was held to be illegal as it unduly restricted the liberty of the borrower.

But a case has to be extreme to fall within this principle. In *Denny* v. *Denny*[37] a father promised to pay his son's debts and to make him an allowance if the son did not become a bankrupt; became and remained a reformed character; gave up some named associates (who were swindlers); did not go within 80 miles of Piccadilly Circus without his father's previous consent; did not borrow money, or bet or directly or indirectly have any business or personal relations with any moneylenders, bookmakers or turf accountants or their servants. This contract was upheld even though, taken literally, it prevented the son from having personal relations with a bookmaker's clerk, who might be perfectly honest. The court was mainly influenced by the fact that the father had imposed the restrictions for the son's benefit, whereas the moneylender in *Horwood's* case had acted from selfish motives.

---

30 *Tingley* v. *Muller* [1917] 2 Ch. 144.

31 *Rodriguez* v. *Speyer Bros.* [1919] A.C. 59.

32 Trading with the Enemy Act 1939.

33 *De Wutz* v. *Hendricks* (1824) 2 Bing. 314.

34 *Foster* v. *Driscoll* [1929] 1 K.B. 470; *cf. Ralli Bros.* v. *Compañia Naviera Sota y Aznar* [1920] 2 K.B. 287; contrast *Libyan Arab Foreign Bank* v. *Bankers Trust Co.* [1989] Q.B. 728, 744–745 (where there was no intention to do or procure an illegal act abroad).

35 [1958] A.C. 301.

36 [1917] 3 K.B. 305; *cf. Hepworth Manufacturing Co.* v. *Ryott* [1920] 1 Ch. 1; *Gaumont-British Picture Corp.* v. *Alexander* [1936] 2 All E.R. 1686. See also *Tailby* v. *Official Receiver* (1888) 13 App.Cas. 533; *King* v. *Michael Faraday & Partners Ltd.* [1939] 2 K.B. 753 (assignment of salary depriving assignor of his sole means of support invalid), and *Syrett* v. *Egerton* [1957] 1 W.L.R. 1130 (whether assignment of *all* a man's property is contrary to public policy).

37 [1919] 1 K.B. 583; *cf. Upton* v. *Henderson* (1912) 28 T.L.R. 398.

3. Contracts in Restraint of Trade[38]

Contracts which prevent or regulate business competition were in early times regarded as invariably void[39]; and persons who made them were even threatened with imprisonment.[40] But it came to be recognised that this inflexible attitude might defeat its own ends. A master might be reluctant to employ and train apprentices if he could not to some extent restrain them from competing with him after the end of their apprenticeship. And a trader might be unable to sell the business he had built up if he could not bind himself not to compete with the purchaser. The courts therefore began to uphold contracts in restraint of trade, and in 1711 the subject was reviewed in *Mitchel* v. *Reynolds*.[41] The effect of that case, as interpreted in later decisions, was that a restraint was prima facie valid if it was supported by adequate consideration and was not general—*i.e.* did not extend over the whole Kingdom.

Since then, the law has changed in three respects. First, restraints are no longer prima facie valid; they are prima facie void, but can be justified if they are reasonable and not contrary to the public interest.[42] Secondly, it is no longer essential that the consideration should be adequate,[43] "though . . . the quantum of consideration may enter into the question of the reasonableness of the agreement."[44] Thirdly, the rule that a restraint must not be general no longer applies. In *Nordenfelt* v. *Maxim Nordenfelt Guns & Ammunition Co.*[45] the owner of an armaments business sold it to a company and covenanted not to carry on such a business for 25 years except on behalf of the company. The covenant was held valid although it prevented competition anywhere in the world.

Although the contrary has been suggested,[46] the general view is that the question whether a restraint is valid must be determined once for all by reference to the circumstances in existence when the contract was made.[47] The view that a restraint which satisfies the tests of validity at that time may become invalid or unenforceable in the light of subsequent events has been generally rejected as it would give rise to an unacceptable degree of uncertainty.

Agreements which have been held to be within the doctrine of restraint of trade can be divided into a number of groups or categories which will be discussed below. It should, however, be stressed at the outset that some

---

38 Heydon, *The Restraint of Trade Doctrine* and 50 A.L.J. 290; Trebilcock, *The Common Law of Restraint of Trade.*

39 *Claygate* v. *Batchelor* (1602) Owen 143.

40 *Dyer's Case* (1414) Y.B. 2 Hen. V, Pasch. pl. 26.

41 (1711) 1 P.Wms. 181.

42 *Post*, pp. 406–412.

43 *Tallis* v. *Tallis* (1853) 1 E. & B. 391.

44 *Nordenfelt* v. *Maxim Nordenfelt Guns and Ammunition Co.* [1894] A.C. 535, 565; *Esso Petroleum Ltd.* v. *Harper's Garage (Stourport) Ltd.* [1968] A.C. 300, 318, 323; *Amoco Australia Pty. Ltd.* v. *Rocca Bros. Motor Engineering Pty. Ltd.* (1973) 47 A.L.J.R. 681 (affirmed without reference to this point [1975] A.C. 561); *Alec Lobb (Garages) Ltd.* v. *Total Oil (Great Britain) Ltd.* [1985] 1 W.L.R. 173, 179.

45 [1894] A.C. 535. For a trace of the older view, see *Home Counties Dairies Ltd.* v. *Skilton* [1970] 1 W.L.R. 526, 530 ("an agreement in restraint of trade may be upheld *if partial*").

46 *Shell U.K. Ltd.* v. *Lostock Garages Ltd.* [1976] W.L.R. 1187, 1198.

47 *Commercial Plastics Ltd.* v. *Vincent* [1965] 1 Q.B. 623, 644 (citing earlier authorities); *Gledhow Autoparts Ltd.* v. *Delaney* [1985] 1 W.L.R. 1366, 1377. *A. Schroeder Music Publishing Co. Ltd.* v. *Macaulay* [1974] 1 W.L.R. 1308, 1309; *Shell U.K. Ltd.* v. *Lostock Garages Ltd.* [1976] 1 W.L.R. 1187, 1203; *Briggs* v. *Oates* [1991] 1 All E.R. 407, 417.

agreements which are, or may be, within the doctrine do not fall readily within any of these categories; and that other agreements which can in a sense be said to restrain trade are not within the doctrine at all, and are therefore not subject to the conditions on which the validity of covenants in restraint of trade depends. We shall return to these questions[48] after discussing the established categories of contracts in restraint of trade.

(1) Sale of a business and employment

In this group of cases, a covenant in restraint of trade is invalid unless three conditions are satisfied: there must be an interest meriting protection; the restraint must be reasonable; and it must not be contrary to the public interest.

(a) THE INTEREST. The interest must arise from the relationship of the parties as buyer and seller or as employer and employee. In the absence of such a relationship, freedom from ordinary trade competition is not, of itself, an interest meriting protection.[49] Thus a bare promise to a shopkeeper not to open (or work for) a competing business would be void; such a promise is known as a covenant in gross. Normally the covenant must be contained in a contract of sale or employment, but this is not absolutely necessary. It is enough if the covenant is closely related to such a contract; for example, if it is contained in a contract made (shortly after the termination of an employment contract) to settle outstanding differences.[50]

(i) *Sale of a business*. Even in the absence of a covenant in restraint of trade, the purchaser of the goodwill of a business can restrain the vendor from canvassing the old customers of the business.[51] This rule would not prevent the vendor from competing in other ways (*e.g.* from dealing with his old customers if they spontaneously came to him); but the purchaser can validly stipulate against such competition by a covenant in restraint of trade. His right to do so is said to depend on his "proprietary interest" in the goodwill of the business which he has bought.[52]

It follows that the purchaser is only entitled to protection in respect of the business which he has bought, and not in respect of some other business which he already carries on or may carry on in the future. If a company which owns shops in all parts of the country buys a village shop it can restrain the seller from competing in or near that village, but not at other places where it happens to carry on business.[53] Similarly, in the *Nordenfelt* case[54] the covenant restrained the seller from engaging not only in the manufacture of armaments but also "in any other business competing or liable to compete with that for the time being carried on by" the buyer. The latter part of the covenant was invalid. Its effect would be to restrain the seller from competing with the company if within 25 years it started to make ploughshares; and he had sold no such business. But a person who buys a business which is about to expand may be able to take a covenant

[48] *Post*, p. 422.
[49] *Cf. Vancouver Malt & Sake Brewing Co.* v. *Vancouver Breweries Ltd.* [1934] A.C. 181.
[50] *Stenhouse Australia Ltd.* v. *Phillips* [1974] A.C. 391.
[51] *Trego* v. *Hunt* [1896] A.C. 7.
[52] There can be such an interest even though the goodwill is inalienable: see *Whitehill* v. *Bradford* [1952] Ch. 236; *Kerr* v. *Morris* [1987] Ch. 90.
[53] *Cf. British Reinforced Concrete Engineering Co. Ltd.* v. *Schelff* [1921] 2 Ch. 563.
[54] [1894] A.C. 535, *ante*, p. 401.

against competition covering the area of the proposed expansion.[55] And the rule that the buyer can only restrain the seller from competing with the business formerly carried on by the seller is subject to a common-sense exception. A person who sells shares in a company which he controls may covenant not to compete in respect of the business carried on by *the company*; and such a covenant may be valid if it was in substance the seller who, through his control of the company, carried on the business.[56] If, however, the *business* carried on by a company, (as opposed to the *shares* in it) is sold, it may be hard to frame a suitable covenant to protect the buyer from competition by associated companies.[57]

(ii) *Employment.* Even in the absence of a covenant in restraint of trade, the law gives an employer some degree of protection against his employee. He can restrain the employee from (i) using or disclosing trade secrets (ii) using or disclosing confidential information[58] falling short of a trade secret[59] and (iii) soliciting the employer's customers. The restriction on the use or disclosure of trade secrets applies at any time[60]; that on the solicitation of customers applies only to solicitation during employment[61]; while that relating to confidential information occupies an intermediate position: it is normally limited to the employee's conduct during employment but in some cases it extends beyond the period of employment. This is the position where, at the end of that period, the employee takes away, copies or memorises lists of the employer's trade connections[62]: he can then be restrained from using such information for his own benefit (or for that of a third party) for so long as such use would give him (or the third party) an unfair competitive advantage over the employer.[63] A similar restriction may apply where the employee *sells* such information, as opposed to using it to earn his living.[64] Certain confidential information acquired by employees in the public service is also subject to a lifelong duty of confi-

---

[55] *Lamson Pneumatic Tube Co.* v. *Phillips* (1904) 91 L.T. 363.

[56] *Connors Bros.* v. *Connors Ltd.* [1940] 4 All E.R. 179; *cf. Kirby* (*Inspector of Taxes*) v. *Thorn E.M.I.* [1988] 1 W.L.R. 445 (covenant on sale by company of shares in its subsidiary).

[57] See *Doyle* v. *Olby* (*Ironmongers*) *Ltd.* [1969] 2 Q.B. 158.

[58] Except where disclosure would be in the public interest, *e.g.* where the employer has been guilty of misconduct which ought to be disclosed: *Initial Services Ltd.* v. *Putterill* [1968] 1 Q.B. 396; North [1968] J.B.L. 32; *cf. Malone* v. *Metropolitan Police Commissioner* [1979] Ch. 344, 361–362; *British Steel Corp.* v. *Granada Television Ltd.* [1981] A.C. 1096, 1168, 1177, 1201; *Lion Laboratories Ltd.* v. *Evans* [1985] Q.B. 526; *Att.-Gen.* v. *Guardian Newspapers Ltd.* (*No.* 2) [1990] A.C. 109, 268; *Re a Company* [1989] 2 All E.R. 248; *W.* v. *Edgell* [1990] Ch. 359. Contrast *Distillers Co. Ltd.* v. *Times Newspapers Ltd.* [1976] Q.B. 613; *Schering Chemicals Ltd.* v. *Falkman Ltd.* [1982] Q.B. 1; *Stephens* v. *Avery* [1988] Ch. 449. For proposals to widen the scope of the "public interest" exception see Law Com. 110 paras. 6.84(i) and 6.134(iii).

[59] See *infra* at n. 73.

[60] *Printers & Finishers Ltd.* v. *Holloway* [1965] 1 W.L.R. 1; *Faccenda Chicken Ltd.* v. *Fowler* [1987] Ch. 117, 136; *Lock International plc* v. *Beswick* [1989] 1 W.L.R. 1268, 1273 (where confidential information or trade secrets were not proved). *Cf. Att.-Gen.* v. *Barker* [1990] 3 All E.R. 257 (express covenant by employee of Royal Household).

[61] *Wessex Dairies Ltd.* v. *Smith* [1935] 2 K.B. 60; if the solicitation occurs during employment it is irrelevant that the actual contract with the customers is made thereafter: *Sanders* v. *Parry* [1967] 1 W.L.R. 753.

[62] *Faccenda Chicken Ltd.* v. *Fowler* [1987] Ch. 117, 139; Miller 102 L.Q.R. 359; *cf. Johnson & Blay* (*Holdings*) *Ltd.* v. *Wolstenholme Rink plc* [1989] F.S.R. 135.

[63] *Roger Bullivant Ltd.* v. *Ellis* [1987] I.C.R. 464.

[64] *Faccenda Chicken Ltd.* v. *Fowler* [1987] Ch. 117, 139.

dentiality.[65] All these rights of the employer are once again said to constitute "proprietary interests" which the employer is entitled to protect by a covenant in restraint of trade; and such a covenant may (as in the cases between vendor and purchaser) afford somewhat greater protection[66] than that provided by law in the absence of a covenant. But the employer cannot justify a covenant in restraint of trade simply on the ground that the covenant would protect the business in which the employee has worked.

Thus the interest meriting protection is more narrowly defined between employer and employee than between buyer and seller,[67] and two reasons have been given for this distinction. First, buyer and seller may bargain on a more equal footing than employer and employee. The courts certainly attach importance to disparity of bargaining power in restraint of trade cases.[68] But this factor would scarcely be significant where the terms of employment were settled between an employer and a powerful trade union, or where the restraint was undertaken by a company director who, though technically an employee, was by no means in a weak bargaining position.[69] In such cases, it is better to fall back on the second justification for the distinction between the two types of contract. The buyer of a business pays for freedom from competition and would lose part of what he paid for if the seller began to compete with him.[70] An employer pays for his employee's services and would not be deprived of what he paid for if the employee competed with him after leaving his service.

Unlike the purchaser of a business, an employer cannot protect himself by a covenant in restraint of trade against his former employee's competition as such. He cannot restrain the employee from using his own skill even though that skill was learnt from the employer.[71] To establish that he has an interest meriting protection, the employer must show *either* that the employee has learnt the employer's trade secrets, *or* that he has acquired influence over the employer's clients or customers. Trade secrets include secret formulae or processes, and certain other similar kinds of highly confidential information[72] (but not information which is merely confidential in the sense that the employee must not disclose it during employment).[73] It used to be thought that "know-how" could not be protected[74] but now that such expertise has become a saleable commodity[75] it is likely that the

[65] *Att.-Gen.* v. *Guardian Newspapers (No.* 2) [1990] A.C. 109, 264, 284; *Lord Advocate* v. *Scotsman Publications Ltd.* [1990] 1 A.C. 812, 821.

[66] See *post*, p. 406.

[67] *Mason* v. *Provident Clothing & Supply Co.* [1913] A.C. 724; *Bridge* v. *Deacons* [1984] A.C. 705, 713.

[68] *A. Schroeder Music Publishing Co. Ltd.* v. *Macaulay* [1974] 1 W.L.R. 1308; *Clifford Davies Management* v. *W.E.A. Records Ltd.* [1975] 1 W.L.R. 61; *post*, pp. 409–410.

[69] "A managing director can look after himself": *M. & S. Drapers* v. *Reynolds* [1957] 1 W.L.R. 9, 19.

[70] *Attwood* v. *Lamont* [1920] 3 K.B. 571; 590; *cf. Leather Cloth Co.* v. *Lorsont* (1869) L.R. 9 Eq. 345, 354; *Herbert Morris Ltd.* v. *Saxelby* [1916] 1 A.C. 688, 701.

[71] *Herbert Morris Ltd.* v. *Saxelby* [1916] 1 A.C. 688; *cf. Eastes* v. *Russ* [1914] 1 Ch. 468 and *Faccenda Chicken Ltd.* v. *Fowler* [1987] Ch. 117, 137. For a proposal to extend this principle to certain persons other than employees, see Law Com. No. 110, para. 6.75.

[72] *Caribonum Co. Ltd.* v. *Le Couch* (1913) 109 L.T. 587; *cf. The Littlewoods Organisation Ltd.* v. *Harris* [1977] 1 W.L.R. 1472. And see *Lansing Linde Ltd.* v. *Kerr* [1991] 1 All E.R. 425, 433, 435.

[73] *Faccenda Chicken Ltd.* v. *Fowler* [1987] Ch. 117, 136.

[74] *Herbert Morris Ltd.* v. *Saxelby*, *supra*; *Sir W. C. Leng & Co.* v. *Andrews* [1909] 1 Ch. 763, 768.

[75] Blanco White, 15 Conv. 89; 26 Conv. 366.

courts will recognise it as an interest meriting protection.[76] In respect of clients or customers, the employer is entitled to protection only if the nature of the employment was such as to enable the employee to acquire influence over them,[77] *e.g.* where the employee was a solicitor's managing clerk,[78] or a hairdresser's assistant[79] but not where he was a factory worker who never came into contact with customers. If the employee comes into contact with some customers, the employer may be able to protect himself also in respect of some others.[80]

The question whether there is any other interest which an employer can protect by a covenant in restraint of trade was raised in *Eastham* v. *Newcastle United Football Club Ltd.*[81] The defendant club employed the plaintiff as a professional footballer subject to the "retain and transfer" system. Under that system, a player who was "retained"[82] by one club could not be employed by another; nor could he be transferred to another club without the consent of both clubs. The defendant club could not claim that this system protected either of the two traditional interests. But Wilberforce J. said that "it would be wrong to pass straight to the conclusion that no . . . interest . . . exists."[83] He considered other possible interests, such as the danger that, but for the "retain and transfer" system, all the best players might go to the richest clubs. He found that such consequences would not in fact follow if the system were abandoned; that there was thus no interest to be protected; and that the system was invalid. But his approach suggests that interests other than the traditional ones might be entitled to protection. A covenant by a film actor not to appear on the stage for three months, made with the object of furthering the success of a new film,[84] might be enforceable even though it did not protect either of the orthodox interests. Such new interests would differ from the traditional ones in that they would be protected *only* if there was a covenant, while the traditional ones are to some extent protected even if there is no covenant. For this reason the new interests may be called "commercial" rather than "proprietary" ones; and we shall see that in some categories of contracts in restraint of trade the law now recognises that such commercial interests may be protected by covenants.[85] It is possible that this recognition will help to modify the strict insistence on the need for a "proprietary" interest in cases between vendor and purchaser, or between employer and employee.

(iii) *Doubtful cases.* The distinction between vendor-purchaser and employer-employee covenants is by no means exhaustive. Thus a covenant

---

[76] In *Commercial Plastics Ltd.* v. *Vincent* [1965] 1 Q.B. 623, 642 Pearson L.J. faintly hints at this possibility.

[77] *Faccenda Chicken Ltd.* v. *Fowler* [1987] Ch. 117, 137.

[78] *Fitch* v. *Dewes* [1921] 2 A.C. 158; *post*, p. 408.

[79] *Marion White Ltd.* v. *Francis* [1972] 1 W.L.R. 1423.

[80] *C. W. Plowman & Son Ltd.* v. *Ash* [1964] 1 W.L.R. 568; and see p. 407, *post*.

[81] [1964] Ch. 413; *cf. Greig* v. *Insole* [1978] 1 W.L.R. 302.

[82] A player could be "retained" by giving him notice and paying him a reasonable wage (determined, in case of dispute, by the Football Association).

[83] *Eastham* v. *Newcastle United Football Club Ltd.*, *supra*, at p. 432.

[84] For this practice, see *Higgs* v. *Olivier* [1951] Ch. 899; *cf. Vaughan-Neil* v. *I.R.C.* [1979] 1 W.L.R. 1283 (covenant by a barrister, on becoming an employee of a company, not to practise at the bar).

[85] *Post*, pp. 413, 419.

by a retiring doctor or solicitor not to compete with his former partners does not fall precisely into either category[86]; but the courts would not subject it to the strict tests of validity that they apply to employer-employee covenants.[87] Again, a person may sell his business to a company of which he then becomes managing director. It seems that a covenant by such a person not to compete should be treated in the same way as a vendor-purchaser covenant, whether it is actually contained in the sale agreement or in the service agreement.[88] On the other hand, a covenant by a writer or composer not to dispose of his work except to a particular publisher may for present purposes be treated in the same way as an employer-employee covenant, even though there was never any contract of employment between the parties.[89]

(b) REASONABLENESS. A restraint is only valid if it goes no further than is reasonably necessary for the protection of the covenantee's interest. Reasonableness is determined by looking at the relationship between that interest and the covenant.[90]

(i) *Area of restraint.* In order for a covenant to be reasonable, it need not be precisely co-terminous with the interest. If there were such a requirement, there would be little point in taking a covenant, since a "proprietary interest" is (by definition) protected even in the absence of a covenant.[91] So long as the employer has trade secrets he can take a covenant which to some extent prevents the employee from using his own skill by restraining him from working in competition with the employer. And an employer who has a "proprietary" interest in his relations with clients or customers can restrain his employee from working in the *area* in which those clients or customers live, even though most of the inhabitants of the area have never dealt with the employer.[92] Such restraints may be necessary for the protection of the employer as the actual infringement of his proprietary interests could be very hard to establish: in particular it would, if the employee were allowed to work for a competitor, be hard to tell whether he was disclosing trade secrets. The covenant may, moreover, be enforced even though the "proprietary interest" infringed is of little value to the employer. Thus a former employee can be restrained from dealing with a client who has decided to deal with the ex-employee, rather than with the employer, since it is precisely this type of competition "against which the covenant is designed to give protection.[93]

On the other hand, such "area covenants" may operate to some extent

---

[86] *Bridge* v. *Deacons* [1984] A.C. 705, 714.

[87] *Whitehill* v. *Bradford* [1952] Ch. 236; *Kerr* v. *Morris* [1986] 3 All E.R. 217. *contra*, *Jenkins* v. *Reid* [1948] 1 All E.R. 471—but the defendant's covenant seems to have been "in gross".

[88] See *Silverman Ltd.* v. *Silverman*, *The Times*, July 7, 1969. *Cf. Blake* v. *Blake* (1967) 111 S.J. 715 (restraints imposed, on dissolution of a company, on its major shareholders: these were treated in the same way as vendor-purchaser covenants); *Allied Dunbar* (*Frank Weisinger*) *Ltd.* v. *Frank Weisinger* [1988] I.R.L.R. 60.

[89] See *A. Schroeder Music Publishing Co. Ltd.* v. *Macaulay* [1974] 1 W.L.R. 1308.

[90] *Allied Dunbar* (*Frank Weisinger*) *Ltd.* v. *Frank Weisinger* [1988] I.R.L.R. 60, 65.

[91] *Ante*, pp. 402, 404.

[92] *Fitch* v. *Dewes* [1921] 2 A.C. 158; *Scorer* v. *Seymour-Johns* [1966] 1 W.L.R. 1419; contrast *Fellowes* v. *Fisher* [1976] Q.B. 122.

[93] *John Michael Design plc* v. *Cooke* [1987] I.C.R. 445, 446.

as pure restraints on competition; and in a number of cases[94] the courts have distinguished them from "solicitation covenants" (against soliciting the employer's old clients or customers). On the facts of those cases the courts have held or said that only solicitation covenants would be regarded as reasonable. The cases do not absolutely rule out the possibility that an "area covenant" may be valid between employer and employee[95]; but such a covenant will be void if it covers a much larger area than is needed for the protection of the covenantee's interest. Thus in *Mason* v. *Provident Clothing & Supply Co. Ltd.*,[96] a canvasser who was employed to sell clothes in Islington covenanted not to enter into similar business within 25 miles of London. The covenant was held void because the area of the restraint was about 1,000 times as large as that in which the canvasser had been employed. It was said that the employer could have protected himself by a covenant restricted to the area in which the canvasser had worked. But if that area is very large and the employee has only dealt with a small number of customers within it, an area covenant will not,[97] though a solicitation covenant might,[98] be upheld.

Between vendor and purchaser (and in analogous cases[99]) area covenants are commonly enforced; and a restraint may be reasonable even though it is *unlimited* as to area. In the *Nordenfelt* case[1] such a restraint was enforced against the vendor of a business since the business in question extended over the whole world. And even between employer and employee a "solicitation covenant" may be valid although it is not expressly limited as to area.[2] A covenant of this kind is more likely to be enforced if it is limited to customers with whom the employee came into contact in the course of his employment[3]; but such a limitation is not essential to the validity of the covenant.[4] A worldwide restraint against disclosing confidential information is unlikely to be upheld if the information in question relates only to business done by the employer in a limited geographical area (*e.g.*, to customers in one country).[5]

(ii) *Duration of the restraint.* The question whether a restraint is invalid for excessive duration depends on the nature of the business to be protected. If it is one to which customers or clients are likely to resort for a long time, a restraint for the lifetime of the covenantor may be valid. Thus

---

94 *S. W. Strange Ltd.* v. *Mann* [1965] 1 W.L.R. 629; *Macfarlane* v. *Kent* [1965] 1 W.L.R 1019, 1024 (doubted on another point in *Peyton* v. *Mindham* [1972] 1 W.L.R. 8); *Gledhow Autoparts Ltd.* v. *Delaney* [1965] 1 W.L.R. 1366; *T. Lucas & Co. Ltd.* v. *Mitchell* [1974] Ch. 129; *Stenhouse Australia Ltd.* v. *Phillips* [1974] A.C. 391; *Spafax* v. *Harrison* [1980] I.R.L.R. 442; *Daily Crest Ltd.* v. *Pigott* [1989] I.C.R. 92; *cf. Bridge* v. *Deacons* [1984] A.C. 705 (non-solicitation covenant in partnership agreement between solicitors upheld).

95 *e.g. Anscombe & Ringland* v. *Butchoff* (1984) 134 N.L.J. 37.

96 [1913] A.C. 724; *cf. Empire Meat Co. Ltd.* v. *Patrick* [1939] 2 All E.R. 85; *Spencer* v. *Marchington* [1988] I.R.L.R. 392; *Office Angels Ltd.* v. *Rainer-Thomas*, *The Times*, March 27, 1991; for conflicting dicta in a borderline case, see *Lyne-Pirkis* v. *Jones* [1969] 1 W.L.R. 1293.

97 *Marley Tile Co. Ltd.* v. *Johnson* [1982] I.R.L.R. 75.

98 *Gledhow Autoparts Ltd.* v. *Delaney* [1965] 1 W.L.R. 1366. Contrast *Office Angels Ltd.* v. *Rainer-Thomas*, *supra*, n. 96.

99 *e.g. Kerr* v. *Morris*, [1987] Ch. 90.

1 [1894] A.C. 535.

2 *G. W. Plowman & Son Ltd.* v. *Ash* [1964] 1 W.L.R. 568.

3 As in *Stenhouse Australia Ltd.* v. *Phillips* [1974] A.C. 391.

4 *Plowman & Son Ltd.* v. *Ash*, *supra*.

5 *Lansing Linde Ltd.* v. *Kerr* [1991] 1 All E.R. 418, 425.

in *Fitch* v. *Dewes*[6] a lifelong restraint on a solicitor's managing clerk not to practise within seven miles of his principal's office was upheld. But this was a somewhat exceptional case; and more usually a lifelong restraint in an "area covenant" would now be regarded as invalid[7] A more lenient view was taken of a "solicitation covenant" for a fixed period in *Bridge* v. *Deacons*[8]: the Privy Council there upheld a covenant by a partner in a firm of solicitors not to act as solicitor in Hong Kong for any client of the firm for five years after ceasing to be a partner. Where the business to be protected is of a more fluctuating nature, long restraints are unlikely to be upheld whether they are contained in "area" or in "solicitation" covenants.[9]

An employee can validly covenant not to disclose confidential information relating to the employer at any time: such a covenant has, for example, been upheld where an employee of the Royal Household undertook not either during or after service to disclose information concerning any member of the Royal Family (and certain other persons) without written authority.[10] Such a limited restraint does not prevent the former employee from working for others, and is therefore not objectionable on grounds of public policy.

(iii) *Scope of restraint.* A restraint must not extend to an activity which is irrelevant to the interest to be protected. Thus a restraint in a tailor's service contract against working as a hatter is unreasonable.[11] Nor can an employer use his proprietary interest in trade secrets and confidential information to support a covenant restraining an employee from disclosing any information whatsoever "relating to the company [*i.e.* the employer] or its customers of which [the employee] becomes possessed while acting as sales director"[12]; for much information of this kind will have nothing to do with the employer's proprietary interest.

(iv) *Drafting problems.* So long as there is an interest meriting protection, some restraint can be validly imposed, but the draftsman may, by drawing the restraint too widely, wholly fail to achieve his purpose.[13] An attempt to evade this difficulty was made in *Davies* v. *Davies,*[14] where the covenant simply restrained competition "so far as the law allows"; but this was held void for uncertainty. The draftsman is therefore forced to use more precise language and this may, if taken literally, impose an excessive restraint even though the parties may not have intended that meaning. For example, in *Lyne-Pirkis* v. *Jones*[15] a covenant in a partnership agreement between doctors in *general practice* provided that a retiring partner should not (within certain limits of time and space) "engage in medical practice." This was held invalid as it prohibited practice even as a *consultant.* On the

---

[6] [1921] 2 A.C. 158.
[7] See *Fellowes* v. *Fisher* [1976] Q.B. 122.
[8] [1984] A.C. 705; the suggestion made *ibid.* at p. 717 that a covenant which is otherwise reasonable will not be struck down "solely because of its duration" is, with respect, not easy to reconcile with *Esso Petroleum Co. Ltd.* v. *Harper's Garage (Stourport) Ltd.* [1968] A.C. 269 (*post*, p. 417), so far as it related to the 21 year tie; and with *Eastes* v. *Russ* [1914] 1 Ch. 468. See further Spowart-Taylor and Hough, 47 M.L.R. 745.
[9] *e.g.*, *M. & S. Drapers* v. *Reynolds* [1957] 1 W.L.R. 9; *cf. Eastes* v. *Russ* [1974] 1 Ch. 468.
[10] *Att.-Gen.* v. *Barker* [1990] 3 All E.R. 257.
[11] *Attwood* v. *Lamont* [1920] 3 K.B. 571.
[12] *Lawrence David* v. *Ashton* [1989] I.C.R. 123.
[13] *Cf. post*, pp. 448–449.
[14] (1887) 36 Ch.D. 359.
[15] [1969] 1 W.L.R. 1293; *cf. Peyton* v. *Mindham* [1972] 1 W.L.R. 8.

other hand the court may sometimes uphold a covenant even though it might, if taken literally, operate in a way that is not reasonably necessary for the protection of the covenantee's interest. In *Home Counties Dairies Ltd.* v. *Skilton*[16] a covenant in a milk roundsman's contract provided that he should not serve or sell "milk or dairy produce." It was argued that this would prevent him from serving cheese as a grocer's assistant, but the court refused to invalidate the covenant as the parties clearly did not intend it to bear this meaning.

(v) *Reasonableness and fairness*. The law of restraint of trade has long recognised two principles: that adequacy of consideration is relevant to the validity of a restraint[17] and that the law has regard to the relative bargaining strengths of the parties.[18] This does not mean that restraint is invalid merely because it was undertaken by the weaker party; for the benefits obtained by that party under the contract may show that the transaction was a perfectly fair one.[19] It is only where the stronger party makes unconscionable use of his superior bargaining power that the resulting bargain may be struck down on account of its unfairness.[20] To this extent, the fairness of the bargain is a *necessary* condition of the validity of the restraint; but it is submitted that it is not a *sufficient* condition. It has indeed been said that a restraint cannot be unreasonable if the parties have freely agreed to it[21] or if it is to their mutual advantage. This is true in the sense that the agreement of the parties may determine how much the covenantee has bought, and hence how much he can protect. But once the interest has been defined, the restraint will only be upheld if it is necessary for the protection of that interest.[22] This will generally depend on the relation between the restraint and the interest.[23] A world-wide restraint in a contract for the sale of a village store would not satisfy this test however much both parties wanted to enter into it and even if the buyer had quite voluntarily paid a greatly enhanced price in view of the restraint. The same point can be made in relation to a partnership agreement. Thus in *Bridge* v. *Deacons* one factor emphasised by the Privy Council was "the mutuality of the contract," by which the five-year restraint "applied equally to all partners."[24] But while this was relevant to the validity of a five year solici-

---

[16] [1970] 1 W.L.R. 526; *cf. G. W. Plowman Ltd.* v. *Ash* [1964] 1 W.L.R. 568; *Marion White Ltd.* v. *Francis* [1972] 1 W.L.R. 1423; *The Littlewoods Organisation Ltd.* v. *Harris* [1977] 1 W.L.R. 1472; (doubting *Commercial Plastics Ltd.* v. *Vincent* [1961] 1 Q.B. 623 on the issue of construction); *Edwards* v. *Worboys* [1984] A.C. 724, note; *Clarke* v. *Newland* [1991] 1 All E.R. 397.

[17] *Ante*, p. 401.

[18] *Ante*, p. 404.

[19] *Alec Lobb (Garages) Ltd.* v. *Total Oil (Great Britain) Ltd.* [1985] 1 W.L.R. 173; this case, and those cited in the next note, were concerned with the type of restraint discussed *post*, pp. 416–420.

[20] *A. Schroeder Music Publishing Co.* v. *Macaulay* [1974] 1 W.L.R. 1308, 1315–1316 (where Lord Diplock did not distinguish between unfairness and unconscionability); *Clifford Davis Management Ltd.* v. *W.E.A. Records Ltd.* [1975] 1 W.L.R. 61. *Quaere* whether it is up to the stronger party to establish the fairness of the restraint (*post*, p. 412) or to the weaker party to establish its unfairness (*ante*, p. 367).

[21] *N.W. Salt Co.* v. *Electrolytic Alkali Co. Ltd.* [1914] A.C. 461, 471; *English Hop Growers Ltd.* v. *Dering* [1928] 2 K.B. 174, 185.

[22] *Cf. A. Schroeder Music Publishing Co. Ltd.* v. *Macaulay*, *supra* at p. 1316 ("reasonably necessary for the protection of the legitimate interests of the promisee.").

[23] *Ante*, p. 406; *Allied Dunbar (Frank Weisinger) Ltd.* v. *Frank Weisinger* [1988] I.R.L.R. 60, 65.

[24] [1984] A.C. 705, 716.

tation covenant it would not, it is submitted, have justified a life-time area covenant covering the whole of Hong Kong since that would have been wholly disproportionate to the interest recognised as meriting protection. The rule that the restraint must not go further than necessary for the protection of the recognised interest of the covenantee is one of public policy and accordingly cannot be excluded merely by the agreement of the parties.

(c) PUBLIC INTEREST. In a broad sense, the requirement of reasonableness can be said to raise issues of public interest. But even if the restraint is "reasonable" in relation to the interest which the covenantee is entitled to protect, it may still be invalid if it is likely to prejudice the public.[25] Many dicta state this rule, but there is little direct authority to support it. In *Wyatt* v. *Kreglinger & Fernau*[26] the employers of a wool broker promised to pay him a pension on his retirement provided that he did not re-enter the wool trade and did nothing to their detriment (fair business competition excepted). Nine years later the Court of Appeal rejected his claim for arrears of pension. Three reasons can be found in the judgments: that the employers' promise to pay the pension was simply a gratuitous promise; that the stipulation against competition was void because it was unreasonable; and that the stipulation against competition was void because it was contrary to the public interest. The view that a restraint imposed on an elderly wool broker at the time of his retirement was likely to injure the public is certainly open to criticism[27]; and it can be said to ignore the countervailing public interest of encouraging young recruits to the profession.[28] Reaction against it at one time went so far that it was said that public interest was not an independent ground of invalidity at all.[29] But *Wyatt's* case was followed in a later similar case[30]; and it is arguable that a restraint on persons whose services are in short supply may be invalid on the ground that it is contrary to the public interest, even though it is reasonable in relation to the interest which the covenantee is entitled to protect. This argument is not, it is submitted, inconsistent with cases holding that it was not contrary to the public interest to restrain a solicitor from acting for a particular client or group of clients *merely* because of the fiduciary relationship between solicitor and client.[31] For the present purpose, the decisive factor is not the nature of the services but the availability of alternative sources of supply: the public interest lies in their general availability and not in their being rendered by a particular individual. Thus a restraint on a former member of a partnership of general medical practitioners would not be invalid merely because patients wished to continue to be treated by that

---

[25] *e.g. Att.-Gen. for Australia* v. *Adelaide SS. Co.* [1913] A.C. 781, 796; *Herbert Morris Ltd.* v. *Saxelby* [1916] A.C. 688, 700; *McEllistrim's Case* [1919] A.C. 548, 562. *Bridge* v. *Deacons* [1984] A.C. 705, 713; *cf. Kerr* v. *Morris* [1987] Ch. 90, where the covenant was admitted to be reasonable in area and duration and public interest was discussed as a separate issue.

[26] [1933] 1 K.B. 793.

[27] 49 L.Q.R. 465.

[28] *Cf. Bridge* v. *Deacons* [1984] A.C. 705, 718.

[29] *Routh* v. *Jones* [1947] 1 All E.R. 179, 182.

[30] *Bull* v. *Pitney-Bowes Ltd.* [1967] 1 W.L.R. 273; Koh, 30 M.L.R. 587.

[31] *Edwards* v. *Worboys* [1984] A.C. 724, n.; *Bridge* v. *Deacons* [1984] A.C. 705, 720; disapproving contrary dicta in *Oswald Hickson Collier & Co.* v. *Carter-Ruck* [1984] A.C. 720, n.

partner,[32] but such restraint might be contrary to the public interest if there was a shortage of doctors in the area in question.

The principle of public interest may, equally, apply to covenants for the sale of a business. In the *Nordenfelt*[33] case some stress was placed on the fact that, as the business sold was a foreign one, a restraint on the vendor would not injure "the public policy of this country"; and more recently the promotion of export sales has been mentioned as a head of public interest.[34] The principle of public interest has, moreover, become increasingly important in relation to other categories of contracts in restraint of trade[35]; and it now seems to be clear that it can be an independent ground of invalidity.

In the common law relating to restraint of trade, the "public interest" refers to legally recognised interests, and in particular to the interest of the public that a person should not be subjected to unreasonable restrictions on his freedom to work or trade. An agreement is unlikely to be invalidated by a common law court because it is alleged to infringe some wider public interest, *e.g.* because it might lead to an improper allocation of economic resources, or prove inflationary. Such allegations often lack precision, and courts of law are not well equipped to evaluate them.[36]

(d) NO ACTUAL COVENANT AGAINST COMPETITION. The restraint of trade doctrine may apply where the terms of the contract provide a party with a financial incentive not to compete, even though he makes no actual promise not to do so: this was the position in *Waytt* v. *Kreglinger & Fernau*[37] where the employee made no promise not to compete, but his right to his pension was conditional on his not doing so. Similarly, in *Stenhouse Australia Ltd.* v. *Phillips*[38] the defendant undertook to pay to his former employers half the gross commission which he might receive in respect of business done with their clients. This was held to be in restraint of trade (though there was no covenant) since it was "in effect . . . likely to cause the employee to refuse business which otherwise he would take . . ."[39] On the other hand in *Alder* v. *Moore*[40] a professional footballer was paid £500 for "permanent total disability." He made a "declaration" not to play professional football again "and in the event of infringing this condition I will be subject to a penalty of £500." He did infringe the "condition" and a majority of the Court of Appeal held that he was liable to repay the £500. The sole question discussed was whether the stipulation to repay was a penalty[41]; and no reference was made to the restraint of trade doctrine.

---

[32] *Kerr* v. *Morris* [1987] Ch. 90, overruling *Hensman* v. *Traill* (1980) 124 S.J. 776.

[33] [1894] A.C. 535, 550; *cf. ibid.* 574.

[34] *Bull* v. *Pitney-Bowes Ltd.* [1967] 1 W.L.R. 273, 276.

[35] *Post*, p. 419.

[36] *Texaco Ltd.* v. *Mulberry Filling Station Ltd.* [1972] 1 W.L.R. 814, 827, a case concerned with the type of restraint discussed at pp. 416–420, *post*; contrast *Bull* v. *Pitney-Bowes Ltd. supra*, n. 34.

[37] [1933] 1 K.B. 793, *per* Scrutton and Slesser L.J.; Greer L.J. interpreted the correspondence to mean that there *was* a covenant not to complete. *Cf. Sadler* v. *Imperial Life Assurance of Canada* [1988] I.R.L.R. 388 (where the stipulation by an agent not to compete after the end of his agency was similarly not a promise but only a condition of his entitlement to future commissions).

[38] [1974] A.C. 391.

[39] *Ibid.* 402–403.

[40] [1961] 2 Q.B. 57.

[41] *Post*, p. 888.

Prima facie, the stipulation appears to fall within that doctrine, though it may have been perfectly reasonable and not contrary to the public interest.

(e) RESTRAINT OPERATING DURING EMPLOYMENT. In the employment cases so far discussed, the issue has been as to the validity of covenants operating *after* the end of the period of service. Restrictions on competition *during* that period are normally valid, and indeed may be implied by law by virtue of the servant's duty of fidelity.[42] In such cases the restriction is generally reasonable, having regard to the interests of the employer, and does not cause any undue hardship to the employee, who will receive a wage or salary for the period in question. But the contract may be a long-term one, and the main purpose of the restraint may be not to secure faithful service, but to protect the employer from competition by sterilising the employee's working capacity. In such a case the restraint may be invalid even though it only operates during the period in which the employee can be required to serve.[43]

(f) ESTABLISHING VALIDITY OF RESTRAINT. The reasonableness of the restraint must be established by the person who seeks to enforce the contract; it is then up to the party resisting enforcement to establish that the restraint is contrary to the public interest. Thus in the ordinary case, in which the covenantee sues to enforce the restraint, he must establish its reasonableness and the covenantor its tendency to injure the public. But where, as in *Wyatt* v. *Kreglinger & Fernau*[44] the action is brought by the covenantor to enforce the promise for which the restraint constitutes the consideration, the roles are reversed: the person under the restraint must show that it is reasonable and the other party that it is contrary to the public interest.

The questions of reasonableness and public interest are questions of law[45] so that it is strictly inaccurate to say that the party claiming enforcement has the *onus of proving* that the covenant is reasonable. What he must do is to prove the circumstances from which the court may conclude that the ratio between the restraint and the interest is reasonable.[46] The same principle applies to the question of public interest.

(2) Restrictive trading and similar agreements

(a) AT COMMON LAW. Agreements betweeen suppliers of goods and services restricting competition between them are subject to the restraint of trade doctrine, so that they are prima facie void, but valid if reasonable and not contrary to the public interest. They also give rise to a number of special problems.

(i) *The interest.* In *McEllistrim's* case Lord Birkenhead said that "in this class of case the covenantee is not entitled to be protected against competition *per se.*"[47] But he accepted the argument that "stability in their lists of

---

[42] *Ante*, p. 189. *Faccenda Chicken Ltd.* v. *Fowler* [1987] Ch. 117, 135–136; *cf. Evening Standard Co. Ltd.* v. *Henderson* [1987] I.C.R. 588; *Provident Financial Group plc.* v. *Hayward* [1989] I.C.R. 160.

[43] *Cf. A. Schroeder Music Publishing Co. Ltd.* v. *Macaulay* [1974] 1 W.L.R. 1308; *Clifford Davis Management Ltd.* v. *W.E.A. Records* [1975] 1 W.L.R. 61; contrast *Greig* v. *Insole* [1978] 1 W.L.R. 302, 326.

[44] [1933] 1 K.B. 793; *ante*, p. 410.

[45] *Dowden & Pook Ltd.* v. *Pook* [1904] 1 K.B. 45.

[46] *Herbert Morris Ltd.* v. *Saxelby* [1916] 1 A.C. 688, 707.

[47] [1919] A.C. 548, 564.

customers"[48] was an interest which producers were entitled to protect. It is not clear how this differs from protection against "competition *per se*," and it seems that in this group of cases, as in those to be discussed below,[49] a "commercial" as opposed to a "proprietary" interest[50] may support a covenant.

(ii) *Conditions of validity*. The broad definition of the interest meriting protection by agreements of the present kind made it relatively easier to establish their validity than that of restraints between vendor and purchaser or between employer and employee. In *English Hop Growers* v. *Dering*,[51] for example, the court upheld an agreement by which hop growers undertook to deliver their crops to a central selling agency in order to avoid cut-throat competition at a time when it was feared that there would be a glut of hops on the market. But the courts were prepared to strike down agreements of this kind if they were plainly unreasonable or contrary to the public interest. They might do this, for instance, where the effect of the agreement was to force one of the parties to close down his business altogether.[52] Similarly, in *McEllistrim's* case[53] an association of farmers in Ireland promised to buy all the milk produced by its members in its area; and the members in turn promised not to sell milk there produced by them to anyone except the association. The agreement was held invalid because it provided that no farmer could withdraw without the consent of the committee of the association, and this consent could be arbitrarily withheld. But for this factor, it seems that the agreement would have been valid.

(iii) *Hardship to a particular group*. An agreement may cause hardship to a particular group of persons, without being contrary to the interests of the public at large. In *Kores Manufacturing Co. Ltd.* v. *Kolok Manufacturing Co. Ltd.*[54] two manufacturers of carbon paper and typewriter ribbons agreed not to employ each other's former employees for five years after they left their original employer. The Court of Appeal held that, although the parties were entitled to protect their trade secrets, the covenant was invalid, as it covered all employees, whether they knew trade secrets or not, and as it was of excessive duration. It was further argued that the parties were entitled to protect their labour supplies, but the court doubted whether "labour supplies" were an interest meriting protection. If they were, employers could, by contracting with each other, achieve what they could not do by contracting directly with the employees themselves. An undertaking by an employee not to work for another employer would be invalid for lack of a proper interest[55] if he knew no trade secrets and had no influence over customers. The same principle should apply where the restraint is contained in a contract between employers and indirectly prejudices their employees' opportunities of finding work.[56] It seems that the

---

48 *Ibid.*
49 *i.e.* at p. 419, *post*.
50 *Ante*, p. 405.
51 [1928] 2 K.B. 174; *cf. N.W. Salt Co.* v. *Electrolytic Alkali Co. Ltd.* [1914] A.C. 461.
52 *Cf. Joseph Evans & Co.* v. *Heathcote* [1918] 1 K.B. 418.
53 [1919] A.C. 548; see also *Collins* v. *Locke* (1879) 4 App.Cas. 674.
54 [1959] Ch. 108; *cf. Mineral Water, etc. Trade Protection Soc.* v. *Booth* (1887) 36 Ch.D. 465; Sales, 104 L.Q.R. 600.
55 *Ante*, p. 404.
56 *Cf. infra*, at n. 61.

court can take hardship to third parties into account and hold that it invalidates a contract of this kind by making it contrary to the public interest.[57]

(iv) *Remedies of third parties.* The above reasoning will only help the third party where one of the parties to the agreement has challenged its validity. In practice, these restrictive agreements were rarely broken, because they were usually beneficial to the contracting parties, however much third parties might suffer from them. The third parties cannot claim damages for conspiracy at common law[58]; and it used to be thought that they had no standing at all to challenge such agreements. But in *Eastham* v. *Newcastle United Football Club Ltd.*[59] a professional footballer sought a declaration that the "retain and transfer" system was invalid. The remedy was granted, not only against his club, but also against the Football Association and the Football League, with whom he had never been in any contractual relationship; and it was said to be available "whether or not the plaintiff has a legal cause of action against the defendants."[60] The weakness of this remedy by way of declaration is that it has no coercive effect: it would not prevent the parties to the invalid agreement from continuing to act in accordance with it. The declaration could only help the third party by giving one of the contracting parties grounds for thinking that he could break the agreement with impunity if it suited him to do so.

Sometimes a third party may, even at common law, have a more effective remedy. There is some support for the view that a person can obtain an injunction against a professional association to restrain it from applying a rule under which he is excluded from membership, and so prevented from exercising the profession,[61] on grounds not relevant to his capacity to do so.[62] This principle appears to be restricted to cases in which the right to work (or perhaps the right to trade) is arbitrarily restricted by a contract between others. It seems unlikely that a buyer of goods or services could at common law get an injunction against a price-ring merely because it operated to his prejudice.

(b) Restrictive trade practices act 1976. A more comprehensive attack[63] on restrictions which may benefit the parties but prejudice third parties is made in legislation going back to 1956 and now consolidated in the Restrictive Trade Practices Act 1976.[64] The legislation, and the relevant case law, are extremely complex and only the barest outline can be given in a book of this nature. The Act specifies certain classes of restric-

---

[57] See *Esso Petroleum Ltd.* v. *Harper's Garage (Stourport) Ltd.* [1968] A.C. 269, 300, 319.

[58] *Mogul SS. Co.* v. *McGregor, Gow & Co.* [1892] A.C. 25, 39, 42, 46, 51, 57, 58.

[59] [1964] Ch. 413; *ante*, p. 405; *cf. Greig* v. *Insole* [1978] 1 W.L.R. 302.

[60] At p. 426.

[61] The rule would not be contrary to public policy unless it had this effect: *Cf. Cheall* v. *APEX* [1983] 2 A.C. 180, 191 (expulsion from a trade union).

[62] See *Nagle* v. *Feilden* [1966] 2 Q.B. 633; A.L.G. (1966) 82 L.Q.R. 319; Rideout, (1966) 29 M.L.R. 424. That case concerned discrimination now unlawful under the Sex Discrimination Act 1975; but the same principle might now apply to (for example) discrimination on religious or political grounds; or if there has been a denial of "natural justice": see *McInnes* v. *Onslow-Fane* [1978] 1 W.L.R. 1520 (where there was no such denial).

[63] For a further statutory provision (enabling the third party prejudiced to rescind the contract), see *post*, p. 422.

[64] Wilberforce, Campbell and Elles, *Restrictive Practices and Monopolies*, (2nd ed.); Lever, *Restrictive Practices and Resale Price Maintenance*; Stevens and Yamey, *The Restrictive Practices Court*.

tive trading agreements[65] or arrangements[66] which must be registered with the Director General of Fair Trading. The most important of these are price-fixing agreements between suppliers of goods, and most services,[67] who carry on business in the United Kingdom. There is also power to require the registration of "information agreements"[68] by which provision is made as to the exchange of information on various matters such as the prices to be charged or quoted for goods. Certain agreements of importance to the national economy, and for holding down prices, may be exempted from the requirement of registration.[69] Once an agreement is registered it is brought by the Director before the Restrictive Practices Court to have its validity determined. In these proceedings an agreement is deemed to be contrary to the public interest unless the parties to it can show that it is beneficial in one of eight ways specified in the Act *and* that such benefit is not outweighed by detriment to the consuming public at large.[70] If the parties fail to justify the agreement it is declared void, and parties may be restrained from acting in accordance with it.[71]

Failure to register a registrable agreement makes the restriction contained in it void[72] and makes it unlawful for the parties to give effect to or to enforce the restrictions or to purport to enforce them.[73] A third party who suffers loss from a contravention of this provision is entitled to damages[74] and the Director can seek an injunction to restrain contravention.[75] An agreement which is justifiable under the Act may theoretically be void at common law: in such a case the parties would be free to act on the agreement, but could not enforce it if one of their number were recalcitrant. Restrictive trade and other anti-competitive practices may also be referred to the Monopolies and Mergers Commission.[76] Effect may be given to reports of the Commission by delegated legislation.[77]

(3) Trade unions and employers' associations

At common law the validity of the rules of a trade union depended nominally on the principles which governed other contracts in restraint of trade. But in practice there was a strong judicial tendency to hold such rules illegal. The courts relied in particular on the fact that the rules of a trade union might require an employee to stop work against his will; and they were no doubt also influenced by the fear that they might be called on to

---

[65] ss.6, 11; certain agreements are excepted by s.28 and Sched. 3, by the Restrictive Trade Practices Act 1977 and by Financial Services Act 1986, s.125; and see *ibid.* s.127.

[66] 1976 Act, s.43(1).

[67] For services not included, see *ibid.* Sched. 1.

[68] *Ibid.* ss.7, 12.

[69] *Ibid.* ss.29, 30.

[70] *Ibid.* ss.10, 19 (as amended by Competition Act 1980, s.28).

[71] According to *Brekkes Ltd.* v. *Cattell* [1972] Ch. 105, the High Court may, in a clear case, restrain the parties from acting on the agreement even before the Restrictive Practices Court has considered it.

[72] 1976 Act, s.35(1)(*a*).

[73] *Ibid.* s.35(1)(*b*).

[74] *Ibid.* s.35(2).

[75] *Ibid.* s.35(3).

[76] Fair Trading Act 1973, Pt. IV; Competition Act 1980, ss.2, 3 and 5; by s.2(2) conduct under an agreement which is registered or registrable under the Restrictive Trade Practices Act 1976 is not, for the purposes of the 1980 Act regarded as an "anti-competitive practice." See also Financial Services Act 1986, s.126.

[77] Fair Trading Act 1973, s.56; Competition Act 1980, s.10.

enforce a strike by injunction. Thus most, though not all, unions were illegal at common law. One serious consequence of this was that union funds were not protected against conversion by fraudulent officers.[78]

So far as trade unions were concerned, this state of the law was, in substance, reversed by statute as long ago as 1871[79]; and the matter is now dealt with by the Trade Union and Labour Relations Act 1974.[80] A detailed analysis of this complicated Act cannot be attempted in this book[81]; but the main point is that under section 2(5) the purposes of a trade union[82] are not, by reason only of the fact that they are in restraint of trade, to be unlawful so as to make void any agreement; nor is any rule of a union (so far as it relates to the regulation of relations between employers and employers' associations and workers) to be unenforceable by reason only of its being in restraint of trade.[83] The Act contains similar provisions with regard to the purposes and rules of employers' associations,[84] which are to the same extent excepted from the scope of the restraint of trade doctrine.[85] But an agreement or rule of a trade union may still be invalid for some other reason. In particular, an employee (or person seeking employment) has in certain circumstances the right not to be unreasonably excluded or expelled from a trade union.[86] If the rules of a union provided for exclusion or expulsion on grounds that were unreasonable, the rules would presumably to that extent be invalid.

(4) Exclusive dealing

The original tendency of the common law was to regard exclusive dealing arrangements as valid. This attitude is illustrated by decisions upholding sole agency and exclusive service agreements,[87] agreements not to buy or sell goods except from or to a particular person,[88] and agreements not to use goods except with others made by the same manufacturer.[89] In other cases, the courts have upheld[90] a covenant on the purchase of land giving the vendor the exclusive right of supplying beer to any public house built on the land; a contract by which the owner of a restaurant agreed to buy all

---

[78] *Hornby* v. *Close* (1867) L.R. 2 Q.B. 153.

[79] Trade Union Act 1871, s.3.

[80] As amended by Trade Union and Labour Relations (Amendment) Act 1976, s.1(*a*).

[81] See Wedderburn, 37 M.L.R. 525.

[82] As defined by s.28(1).

[83] The exact scope of s.2(5) depends on whether or not the union is a "special register body" as defined by s.30(1).

[84] As defined by s.28(2); *semble* that two employers who agree not to "poach" on each other's labour force (as in *Kores Manufacturing Co. Ltd.* v. *Kolok Manufacturing Co. Ltd.* [1959] Ch. 108, *ante*, p. 413) are not, for that reason alone, an "organisation" within s.28.

[85] s.3(5): the exact scope of this subsection depends on whether the association is incorporated.

[86] Employment Act 1980, s.4(1) and (2).

[87] See *Esso Petroleum Co. Ltd.* v. *Harper's Garage (Stourport) Ltd.* [1968] A.C. 269, 294, 307, 336; the last dictum excepts restrictions which are "purely limitative or sterilising" as in *Young* v. *Timmins* (1831) 1 C. & J. 331; *post*, p. 417 and *cf. ante*, p. 412.

[88] *Donnell* v. *Bennett* (1883) 22 Ch.D. 835; *Metropolitan Electric Supply Co.* v. *Ginder* [1901] 2 Ch. 799; *Monkland* v. *Jack Barclay Ltd.* [1951] 2 K.B. 252; *B.M.T.A.* v. *Gilbert* [1951] 2 All E.R. 641.

[89] *United Shoe Machinery Co. of Canada* v. *Brunet* [1909] A.C. 330, criticised in the *Esso* case, *supra*, at p. 297.

[90] *Catt* v. *Tourle* (1869) L.R. 4 Ch.App. 654 (the actual decision is no longer law: Megarry and Wade, *The Law of Real Property* (5th ed.), p. 772).

the burgundy sold there from the plaintiffs[91]; and a contract by a purchaser of garage premises to buy from the vendor all petrol used in the business carried on there.[92] Very occasionally, an exclusive dealing agreement was held invalid: for example, where a brassfounder contracted to execute orders only for a particular firm, which did not bind itself to place any orders with him.[93] Where the agreements were upheld, the rules relating to restraint of trade were in some cases not mentioned at all, while in others the rules were mentioned but the contracts were nevertheless held valid. In these cases, it was not always clear whether the contracts were valid because the restraint of trade doctrine did not apply to them at all or because its requirements were satisfied. The distinction is crucial because if the doctrine did not apply at all it would be unnecessary for the person seeking to enforce the agreement to establish its reasonableness.

The old authorities must now be read subject to a line of cases concerned with the validity of "solus agreements" between oil companies and garage proprietors. These agreements were usually made on an advance of money by the oil company to help with the purchase or development of garage premises; in return, the garage proprietor would usually give three undertakings: a "tying covenant," to buy all petrol (and sometimes certain other products) from the oil company; a "compulsory trading covenant," to keep his garage open at all reasonable times for the sale of petrol; and a "continuity covenant," to extract similar undertakings from any person to whom he might sell the garage during the subsistence of the solus agreement. *Esso Petroleum Co. Ltd.* v. *Harper's Garage* (*Stourport*) *Ltd.*[94] concerned solus agreements made in respect of two garages. One agreement was to last for about four and a half years, and the other for 21 years. The House of Lords held that the solus agreements were within the restraint of trade doctrine; that the four and a half year agreement was valid; but that the 21 year agreement was invalid as it was unreasonable and contrary to the public interest. Undertakings with regard to solus petrol agreements were later given to the Government by oil companies in consequence of a report by the Monopolies Commission[95]; but the decision in the *Esso* case gives rise to a number of general problems which still require discussion.

(a) WHETHER SUCH AGREEMENTS ARE WITHIN THE RESTRAINT OF TRADE DOCTRINE. Before the *Esso* case, many exclusive dealing and service agreements[96] were not considered to be within the restraint of trade doctrine. Others were thought to be within the doctrine but valid because they were reasonable and not contrary to the public interest.

The continued existence of both groups of agreements is recognised in the *Esso* case, where Lord Pearce distinguished between "those contracts which are in restraint of trade and . . . those which merely regulate the

---

[91] *Bouchard Servais* v. *Prince's Hall Restaurant Ltd.* (1904) 20 T.L.R. 574.

[92] *Foley* v. *Classique Coaches* [1934] 2 K.B. 1.

[93] *Young* v. *Timmins* (1831) 1 Cr. & J. 331; the reasoning (based on lack of *adequate* consideration) would no longer be accepted: *Esso Petroleum Co. Ltd.* v. *Harper's Garage* (*Stourport*) *Ltd.* [1968] A.C. 269, 294; and *cf. ibid.* p. 336. The actual decision is also hard to reconcile with the principles stated *post*, pp. 446–447.

[94] [1968] A.C. 269; Heydon, 85 L.Q.R. 229; P.V.B., 83 L.Q.R. 478; Koh [1967] C.L.J. 151; and see Whiteman, 29 M.L.R. 507.

[95] 1965, House of Commons Paper 264; further undertakings were given in 1976: Borrie, L.S.Gaz. Jan. 26, 1977, pp. 71–72.

[96] *Ante*, p. 416.

normal commercial relations between the parties and which are therefore free from the doctrine."[97] He regarded solus agreements as falling within the former class, principally on the ground that the oil company gave no assurance that it would provide a supply of petrol at a reasonable price.[98] Lord Wilberforce said that contracts were not within the doctrine of restraint of trade if they were "such . . . as, under contemporary conditions, may be found to have passed into the accepted and normal currency of contractual or conveyancing relations."[99] The agreement in the *Esso* case was not of a kind which had in this way "passed into acceptance . . . ; the solus system is both too recent and too variable for this to be said."[1] However, Lord Wilberforce reserved the powers of the court to subject even "accepted" contracts to scrutiny in the light of changing social or economic conditions or of special features in individual transactions.[2] Later decisions have, in particular, made it clear that a contract is not taken out of the restraint of trade doctrine merely because it is in standard form and contains only terms which are usual in that type of transaction. This factor may take contracts out of the restraint of trade doctrine if they have been freely negotiated,[3] but the position is different where there is great disparity of bargaining power and the terms are imposed by the stronger on the weaker party. In *A. Schroeder Music Publishing Co.* v. *Macaulay*[4] it was accordingly held that a contract by which an unknown song-writer undertook to give his exclusive services to a publisher who made no promise to publish his work was subject to the doctrine. Lord Reid said: "Normally the doctrine of restraint of trade has no application to such restrictions: they require no justification. But if contractual restrictions appear to be unnecessary or to be reasonably capable of enforcement in an oppressive manner, then they must be justified before they can be enforced."[5]

The tests proposed by Lords Pearce and Wilberforce in the *Esso* case, and by Lord Reid in the *Schroeder* case continue to recognise the possibility that some exclusive dealing and exclusive service agreements may not be subject to the doctrine of restraint of trade. Many of the earlier cases which support this view were cited, and none was overruled, in the *Esso* case. At the same time, the tests are very vague and leave much discretion to the courts in defining the scope of the doctrine in relation to such contracts. It seems probable that in future the doctrine will apply to contracts of this kind if they present any novel or unusual features, or if they contain terms likely to operate harshly on a party of weak bargaining power.

Most exclusive dealing arrangements which only restrain one party are excepted from the scope of the restrictive trade practices legislation.[6]

(b) REQUIREMENTS OF VALIDITY. Where an exclusive dealing or service contract is subject to the doctrine of restraint of trade, the usual requirements must be satisfied before it can be enforced.

---

97 [1968] A.C. 269, 327.
98 *Ibid.* p. 329.
99 *Ibid.* pp. 332–333.
1 *Ibid.* p. 337.
2 *Ibid.* p. 333.
3 *A. Schroeder Music Publishing Co. Ltd.* v. *Macaulay* [1974] 1 W.L.R. 1308, 1314.
4 *Supra*; *cf. O'Sullivan* v. *Management Agency & Music Ltd.* [1985] Q.B. 428.
5 [1974] 1 W.L.R. 1308, 1314.
6 Restrictive Trade Practices Act 1976, Sched. 3, paras. 2 and 7.

(i) *The interest.* We have distinguished elsewhere between "proprietary" and "commercial" interests[7]; and it is clear from the *Esso* case that a "commercial" interest will suffice in the present group of cases. Lord Reid there said that the statement "that a person is not to be protected against mere competition" was "not . . . very helpful in a case like the present"[8] and Lord Pearce, after expressing substantially the same view, seems to have regarded the oil company's "network of outlets"[9] as the interest which they sought to protect. The only difficulty is that Lord Morris described the covenants as "naked covenants or covenants in gross"[10]; but he obviously regarded this, not as a ground of invalidity[11] (for he upheld one of the covenants), but merely as a ground for subjecting the covenants to the doctrine of restraint of trade.

(ii) *Reasonableness.* To satisfy the test of reasonableness, the party seeking to enforce the restrictions must show that they were "no more than what was reasonably required to protect his legitimate interest."[12] Here, as elsewhere,[13] relevant factors include the length of the restraint and the adequacy of the consideration provided for it. We have seen that in the *Esso* case a four and a half-year tie was upheld and a 21-year one struck down.[14] But in a later case a 21-year tie in a solus agreement contained in a lease was upheld since the premises were already, before the lease, subject to a valid three-year tie, since the tenant had the right to break the lease after seven and 14 years, and since the landlord had paid the tenant £35,000 under a previous transaction leading to the execution of the lease.[15]

The fairness of the contract is also a relevant factor, particularly where the restrictions are imposed on the weaker party to a relationship of unequal bargaining power. A solus agreement is not, indeed, open to attack merely because the oil company is by far the more powerful party; for many such agreements are reasonable commercial arrangements, voluntarily entered into for the mutual benefit of both parties and with no element of oppression.[16] By contrast, the restriction imposed on the composer in *A. Schroeder Music Publishing Co. Ltd.* v. *Macaulay*[17] was neither necessary nor fair. It extended over a period of five years, during which he had to submit all his compositions to the publishers, while they were under no obligation to promote his work and had to make no more than minimal payments if they failed to do so. The restriction was accordingly invalid as it went beyond the protection of the publishers' legitimate interests and operated harshly on the other party: "his work will be sterilised and he can earn nothing from his abilities as a composer."[18]

(iii) *Public interest.* Lord Reid in the *Schroeder* case based his decision partly on the ground that "The public interest requires in the interests both

---

[7] *Ante*, p. 405.
[8] [1968] A.C. 269, 301.
[9] *Ibid.* p. 329.
[10] *Ibid.* p. 309.
[11] *Cf. ante*, p. 402.
[12] *A. Schroeder Music Publishing Co. Ltd.* v. *Macaulay* [1974] 1 W.L.R. 1308, 1310.
[13] *Ante*, pp. 406–410.
[14] *Ante*, p. 417.
[15] *Alec Lobb (Garages) Ltd.* v. *Total Oil (Great Britain) Ltd.* [1985] 1 W.L.R. 173.
[16] *Ibid.*
[17] [1974] 1 W.L.R. 1308; *ante*, p. 418.
[18] *Ibid.* p. 1314.

of the public and of the individual that everyone should be free so far as practicable to earn a livelihood and give to the public the fruits of his particular abilities."[19] The *Esso* case, too, is noteworthy for the stress placed on the element of public interest; indeed Lord Hodson bases the invalidity of the 21 year agreement "on the public interest rather than on that of the parties"[20]; Lord Pearce says that the ultimate ground for interference in all cases is public policy so that there is no real separation between "what is reasonable on grounds of public policy and what is reasonable as between the parties."[21] Lord Wilberforce appears to take the same view but adds that it is "important that the vitality of the second limb . . . of the wider aspects of a single public policy rule should continue to be recognised."[22] It is clear from all this that the courts would in these cases reject the once fashionable argument[23] that, if an agreement was shown to be reasonable between the parties, the public interest would also be satisfied.

(5) Covenants affecting the use of land

Such covenants are commonly enforced although they no doubt restrain trade, *e.g.* by imposing restrictions on building, or on the carrying on of some particular business or trade, or by providing that the land shall be used for residential purposes only. In the *Esso* case a majority of the House of Lords explained these cases on the ground that "A person buying or leasing land had no previous right to be there at all, let alone to trade there, and when he takes possession of that land subject to a negative restrictive covenant he gives up no right or freedom which he previously had."[24] It follows that where a person enters into a solus agreement when he acquires land, and the agreement is a term of the conveyance by which the land is transferred, the doctrine of restraint of trade does not apply at all; and since the *Esso* case this conclusion has indeed been drawn by the Court of Appeal.[25] Nevertheless, it is submitted that the reasoning is hard to reconcile with the emphasis placed in the *Esso* case itself on the element of public interest.[26] Restrictions on the use of land may harm the public whether they are undertaken at the time when the land is acquired or later. Of course, generally speaking, the object of a restrictive covenant affecting land is to preserve amenities and not to restrain trade or to prevent competition; and in most cases such a covenant would in any event pass the test of reasonableness because it would only operate in a very small area. But sometimes covenants of this kind do expressly restrain the carrying on of a particular business on the land acquired[27]; and cases of this kind can be imagined in which the covenant would not be reasonable. A person who owned a garage on a 1000-acre estate might sell all the land except for the

---

[19] *Ibid.* p. 1313; Lord Diplock at p. 1315 seems to view this argument with some scepticism.
[20] [1968] A.C. at p. 321; and *cf. ante*, p. 411.
[21] [1968] A.C. 269, 324.
[22] *Ibid.* p. 341.
[23] *Ante*, p. 410.
[24] [1968] A.C. 269, 298; *cf. ibid.* pp. 309, 316–317, 325.
[25] *Cleveland Petroleum Ltd.* v. *Dartstone Ltd.* [1969] 1 W.L.R. 116; Korah, 32 M.L.R. 323; *post*, p. 421. See also *Re Ravenseft Properties Ltd.'s Application* [1978] Q.B. 52 (where exceptions are envisaged at pp. 67–68).
[26] *Ante*, pp. 419–420.
[27] See, for example, *Holloway Bros.* v. *Hill* [1902] 2 Ch. 612; *Newton Abbott Cooperative Society Ltd.* v. *Williamson & Treadgold Ltd.* [1952] Ch. 286; *cf. Rother* v. *Colchester Corporation* [1969] 1 W.L.R. 720.

garage and take a covenant that the purchaser would not carry on a garage business on any part of the land bought. Such a covenant could offend public policy just as much as a covenant not to compete within a given radius of the garage. Moreover, we may vary the example by supposing the original owner sells the garage but keeps the rest of the land, and covenants not to carry on a garage business on it. This covenant would, according to the reasoning of the *Esso* case, be subject to the doctrine of restraint of trade, for the landowner would be giving up a right which he previously had, to carry on a garage business on the land which he kept.[28] It is very hard to see why the doctrine of restraint of trade should not apply to the first as well as to the second of these hypothetical cases. Suppose, further that the owner of a garage sells or leases it to an oil company and then *leases it back* on terms that include a solus agreement. Here it would seem that he did have a "previous right to be there" so that the doctrine of restraint of trade would apply.[29] Attempts have, indeed, been made to evade this result by interposing a company controlled by the garage owner into such an agreement. Thus there is some support for the view that, if the land is leased from a garage owner and leased back to a company controlled by him, then the restraint of trade doctrine should not apply because *the company* had no "previous right to be there."[30] But the distinction between this situation and that in which the two leases are between the same parties can hardly be justified in terms of public policy. Accordingly, it has been held that the restraint of trade doctrine did apply where garage premises were owned by a company controlled by a mother and son, leased by that company to an oil company and then leased back to the mother and son personally.[31] It was said that the court should "pierce the corporate veil" and not give effect to such a "palpable device"[32] for evading the restraint of trade doctrine.

In three further situations the restraint of trade doctrine applies to covenants affecting land. First, it applies where the covenant is given by A to B on the acquisition of land not from B but from a third party C, *e.g.* where (as in the *Esso* case itself)[33] the oil company (B) takes the covenant as one of the terms of a loan to A to enable him to buy a garage from C. Secondly, it applies where the owner of a garage mortgages his existing premises and the mortgage contains a solus agreement.[34] Thirdly, it applies where the

---

28 *Cf. Kerrick* v. *Schoenberg*, 328 S.W. 2d 595, 602 (1959).

29 *e.g. Amoco Australia Pty. Ltd.* v. *Rocca Bros. Motor Engineering Co. Pty. Ltd.* [1975] A.C. 561; Bowman, 38 M.L.R. 571.

30 *Cleveland Petroleum Ltd.* v. *Dartstone Ltd.* [1969] 1 W.L.R. 116, where the claim to enforce the restraint was actually made against an assignee of the company's leasehold interest in the garage.

31 *Alec Lobb (Garages) Ltd.* v. *Total Oil (Great Britain) Ltd.* [1985] 1 W.L.R. 173 (where the restraint was held reasonable).

32 *Ibid.* p. 178.

33 Heydon, 85 L.Q.R. 229, 233 (and *The Restraint of Trade Doctrine*, 58–59) argues that this makes the reasoning in the *Esso* case inconsistent with the decision: as A had "no previous right to be there," the restraint of trade doctrine should not have applied. But it is submitted that the reasoning was only intended to apply where the agreement imposing the restriction is between the same parties as the disposition of the land. *Cf.* also *Petrofina (Great Britain) Ltd.* v. *Martin* [1966] Ch. 146, where a solus agreement with an oil company on the purchase of a garage from a third party was also held invalid for restraint of trade.

34 *Texaco Ltd.* v. *Mulberry Filling Station Ltd.* [1972] 1 W.L.R. 814; *semble* the mortgage in the *Esso* case was similarly executed after the defendant company had acquired the Corner Garage (though it was executed in pursuance of an earlier agreement).

restriction is imposed not in the conveyance itself but in a separate contemporaneous agreement: this was the position in *Foley* v. *Classique Coaches*[35] where it was assumed that the doctrine did apply and this assumption seems to have been accepted in the *Esso* case.[36] But it is once again by no means clear why, if the doctrine of restraint of trade can apply in these cases, it should not apply to a restrictive covenant forming part of a conveyance between the parties to the covenant. Perhaps very similar principles can be applied, if not at common law, then by virtue of section 84 of the Law of Property Act 1925.[37] That section gives the Lands Tribunal a statutory power in certain cases to discharge or modify restrictive covenants affecting land if they have become obsolete by reason of changes in the character of the neighbourhood or because their continued existence "would impede some reasonable user of the land for private or public purposes." This enactment is, in effect, a statutory extension of the doctrine of public policy to these covenants.[38]

(6) Other agreements

In the past the courts were reluctant to apply the doctrine of restraint of trade to new classes of contracts. Thus at common law price-maintenance agreements are valid,[39] though the Resale Prices Act 1976[40] has made many such agreements void. So, too, at common law an agreement between two persons not to bid against each other at an auction is not illegal[41] but if at least one of them is a dealer they may be guilty of a statutory offence under the Auctions (Bidding Agreements) Act 1927.[42] This Act also provides that the contract can be set aside by the owner of the property auctioned; and, although it does not explicitly invalidate the agreement not to bid as between the parties to it, such invalidity probably follows at common law from the criminality of the agreement.[43] In these cases legislative intervention has been necessary to extend the scope of the doctrine of restraint of trade, but there are signs that the courts are now prepared to resume a more creative role in this field. In the *Esso* case Lord Wilberforce said that no exhaustive tests could be stated for defining or identifying contracts in restraint of trade[44]; and that, although such contracts might "be listed, provisionally, in categories . . . the classification must remain fluid and the categories can never be closed."[45]

A new departure occurred in *Pharmaceutical Society of Great Britain* v. *Dickson*,[46] where the House of Lords held that a rule of the Society restricting the trading activities of chemists was invalid. One ground for the

---

35 [1934] 2 K.B. 1.
36 See [1968] A.C. 269, 296, 311, 316, 327, 339.
37 As amended by s.28 of the Law of Property Act 1969.
38 Under the section, the person seeking modification may be ordered to pay compensation. It is arguable that this practice should be extended to some other cases where a person seeks relief from a promise in restraint of trade for which he has received consideration.
39 *Palmolive Co.* (*of England*) v. *Freedman* [1928] Ch. 264.
40 *Post*, p. 569; the Act applies to supply of goods but not to cases like *Re Dott's Lease* [1920] 1 Ch. 281 (covenant to maintain price of tickets at the Garrick Theatre).
41 *Rawlings* v. *General Trading Co. Ltd.* [1921] 1 K.B. 635; *Harrop* v. *Thompson* [1975] 1 W.L.R. 545.
42 As amended by the Auctions (Bidding Agreement) Act 1969.
43 *Ante*, p. 378.
44 [1968] A.C. 269, 332.
45 *Ibid.* p. 337; *cf. Petrofina* (*Great Britain*) *Ltd.* v. *Martin* [1966] Ch. 146, 169.
46 [1970] A.C. 403; Koh, 31 M.L.R. 70.

decision was that the rule was *ultra vires*[47]; but a majority of the House of Lords also held that it was invalid for restraint of trade.[48] The rule was held invalid on this ground even though it was not legally binding, (whether as a contract or otherwise), but was only a part of a professional code of ethics. The decision opens up the possibility that other rules of professional etiquette may be within the doctrine of restraint of trade.

The doctrine of restraint of trade does not apply merely because a contract restricts a party's freedom to deal with its particular subject-matter, for every contract "necessarily limits the freedom to enter into another contract."[49] The essential feature of contracts within the doctrine is that of "fettering a person's freedom in the future to carry on his trade, business or profession."[50] Various further kinds of agreements or arrangements can be imagined which might have this effect: for example, an agreement by A not to manufacture a certain product in competition with B[51]; an agreement on the sale of a ship not to operate it on certain routes; an agreement by a buyer not to export goods to a particular country[52]; or an agreement on the lease of a hall for an exhibition not to hold a similar exhibition there for six months.[53] It is not suggested that all or any of such agreements will be held invalid; but they may require justification under the doctrine of restraint of trade.

(7) European Community Law

Under Article 85 of the Treaty of Rome[54]; "agreements between undertakings,[55] decisions by associations of undertakings and concerted practices which have as their object or effect the prevention, restriction or distortion of competition within the common market" are void unless special exemption is granted by the authorities of the European Economic Community. No attempt can be made in a book of this nature even to summarise this extremely complex topic. It is only necessary to make two points about the territorial scope of these provision. First, an agreement made outside the Community may fall within Article 85 if it restricts competition within the Community, *e.g.* where "undertakings" in non-member states agree to fix prices which they charge to customers in member states.[56] Secondly, Article 85 does not apply to an agreement which affects trade only within a single member state. This means that contracts which

---

47 *Post*, p. 504.

48 Contrast *R.* v. *General Medical Council, ex p. Coleman* [1990] 1 All E.R. 489 (refusal to allow advertising of holistic medical practice not to open to challenge for restraint of trade as the refusal was authorised by statute).

49 *Shearson Lehman Hutton Inc.* v. *Maclaine Watson & Co.* [1989] 2 Lloyd's Rep. 570, 615.

50 *Ibid.*

51 *International Pediatric Products Ltd.* v. *Cuddle-King Products Ltd.* (1964) 46 D.L.R. (2d) 581.

52 As in *National Panasonic (U.K.) Ltd.* v. *Commission of the European Communities* [1981] I.C.R. 51.

53 *Cf. Modern Exhibition Services* v. *Cardiff Corporation* (1965) 63 L.G.R. 316, where restraint of trade was not discussed.

54 Which has the force of law in the United Kingdom: European Communities Act 1972, s.2.

55 For this purpose, an individual can be an "undertaking": *Gottfried Reuter* v. *B.A.S.F.A.G.* [1976] 2 C.M.L.R. D44.

56 *Ahlstrom Osakeyhtio* v. *E.C. Commission*, *The Times*, September 29, 1988.

do not affect trade outside the United Kingdom will remain subject to the domestic rules discussed in this Chapter.[57]

An agreement may be void or exempt under the Treaty and also fall within the Restrictive Trade Practices Act 1976.[58] The Act deals with this possibility so as to give effect to the general policy that Community law should, in case of conflict, prevail.[59]

4. Scope of the Doctrine of Public Policy[60]

Public policy is a variable notion, depending on changing manners, morals and economic conditions. In theory, this flexibility of the doctrine of public policy could provide a judge with an excuse for invalidating any contract which he violently disliked. With this danger in mind judges have sometimes criticised the doctrine of public policy. In 1824 Burroughs J. described it as "a very unruly horse, and when once you get astride it you never know where it will carry you. It may lead you from the sound law."[61] And Lord Halsbury has denied that any court could "invent a new head of public policy."[62]

On the other hand, the law does adapt itself to changes in economic and social conditions, as can be seen particularly from the development of the rules as to contracts in restraint of trade. This point has often been recognised judicially. Thus Lord Haldane has said: "What the law recognises as contrary to public policy turns out to vary greatly from time to time."[63] And Lord Denning has put a similar point of view: "With a good man in the saddle, the unruly horse can be kept in control. It can jump over obstacles."[64]

The present attitude of the courts represents a compromise between the flexibility inherent in the notion of public policy and the need for certainty in commercial affairs.

In the interests of certainty the courts will in general refuse to apply the doctrine of public policy to contracts of a kind to which the doctrine has never been applied before. In *Printing & Numerical Registering Co.* v. *Sampson,*[65] for instance, an inventor assigned a patent to a company and

---

[57] *Esso Petroleum Co. Ltd.* v. *Kingswood Motors Ltd.* [1974] Q.B. 142. *cf. S.A. Fonderies Roubaix-Wattrelos* v. *Soc. Nouvelle des Fonderies A. Roux* [1976] 1 C.M.L.R. 538; Wyatt, 124 N.L.J. 243. The prohibition in Art. 30 against quantitative restrictions on imports may also be relevant in the context of restraint of trade: see *R.* v. *Royal Pharmaceutical Soc. of G.B.* [1989] 2 All E.R. 758 (where Art. 30 was not contravened).

[58] *Ante*, p. 414.

[59] s.10.

[60] Shand [1972] C.L.J. 144.

[61] *Richardson* v. *Mellish* (1824) 2 Bing. 229, 252.

[62] *Janson* v. *Driefontein Consolidated Mines Ltd.* [1902] A.C. 484 491; *cf. Texaco Ltd.* v. *Mulberry Filling Station Ltd.* [1972] 1 W.L.R. 814, 827; *Geismar* v. *Sun Alliance & London Insurance* [1978] Q.B. 383, 389; *Nickerson* v. *Barraclough* [1981] Ch. 426; *Deutsche Schachtbau—und Tiefbohrgesellschaft mbH* v. *Ras Al Khaima National Oil Co.* [1990] 1 A.C. 295, 316 (revsd. on other grounds *ibid.* pp. 329 *et seq.*).

[63] *Rodriguez* v. *Speyer Bros.* [1919] A.C. 59, 79; *cf. Evanturel* v. *Evanturel* (1874) L.R. 6 P.C. 1, 29; *Davies* v. *Davies* (1887) 36 Ch.D. 359, 364; *Nordenfelt* v. *Maxim Nordenfelt Guns & Ammunition Co.* [1894] A.C. 535, 553; *Naylor, Benzon & Co.* v. *Krainische Industrie Gesellschaft* [1918] 1 K.B. 331; *Gray* v. *Barr* [1971] 2 Q.B. 554, 582.

[64] *Enderby Town F.C. Ltd.* v. *The Football Association Ltd.* [1971] Ch. 591, 606.

[65] (1875) L.R. 19 Eq. 462.

also agreed to assign to the company any patent of a like nature thereafter to be acquired by him. He argued that this agreement was contrary to public policy as it tended to discourage inventors. In rejecting the argument, Jessel M.R. said: "You are not to extend arbitrarily those rules which say that a given contract is void as being against public policy."[66] The reason why the courts are less ready to apply the doctrine of public policy to new classes of contracts is that Parliament and its delegates have become more active in this field.[67]

But in some cases (particularly "where the subject-matter is 'lawyers' law' "[68]) judicial intervention may still as a last resort be desirable.[69] The courts may occasionally invalidate a contract even though it is of a kind to which the doctrine of public policy has not been applied before. Such novel applications of the doctrine of public policy are illustrated by decisions to the effect that a moneylending contract is illegal if it imposes quasi-servile obligations on the borrower[70]; that a contract by which a trade journal promises not to comment on the affairs of a company is illegal as it may prevent the journal from exposing frauds perpetrated by the company[71]; that an attempt to contract out of certain statutory provisions governing the liquidation of companies is contrary to public policy[72]; and that the same is true of an attempt to deprive an agricultural tenant of security of tenure where he is entitled to it by statute.[73]

There have been occasional hints that the courts might extend the doctrine of public policy to strike down contracts furthering certain kinds of discrimination[74]; but this suggestion now gives rise to a particularly difficult problem with regard to the relative functions of Parliament and the courts in matters of public policy. Parliament has, in the Sex Discrimination Act 1975[75] and the Race Relations Act 1976,[76] made elaborate provisions against discrimination on grounds of sex, colour, race, nationality or ethnic or national origins in certain carefully defined spheres of activity.

---

66 At p. 465.

67 See *D.* v. *N.S.P.C.C.* [1978] A.C. 171, 235; *Johnson* v. *Moreton* [1980] A.C. 37, 67; *Cheall* v. *APEX* [1983] 2 A.C. 180, 191; *Johnstone* v. *Bloomsbury Health Authority* [1991] I.R.L.R. 118; *cf. Multiservice Bookbinding Ltd.* v. *Marden* [1979] Ch. 84 (Swiss franc uplift clause in mortgage); *Nationwide B.S.* v. *Registry of Friendly Societies* [1983] 1 W.L.R. 1226 (index-linked mortgage). For a similar argument in relation to the limit of the courts' power to create new crimes, see *D.P.P.* v. *Withers* [1975] A.C. 842, 858.

68 *D.* v. *N.S.P.C.C.*, *supra*, at p. 235.

69 *Cf. Monkland* v. *Jack Barclay Ltd.* [1951] 2 K.B. 252, 265.

70 *Horwood* v. *Millar's Timber & Trading Co.* [1917] 1 K.B. 305; *ante*, p. 400.

71 *Neville* v. *Dominion of Canada News Co. Ltd.* [1915] 3 K.B. 556; *cf. Initial Services Ltd.* v. *Putterill* [1968] 1 Q.B. 396, 410 (contract not to disclose contravention of Restrictive Practices Act); *Slater* v. *Raw*, *The Times*, October 15, 1977.

72 *British Eagle International Airlines Ltd.* v. *Cie. Nationale Air France* [1975] 1 W.L.R. 758.

73 *Johnson* v. *Moreton* [1980] A.C. 37. *Featherstone* v. *Staples* [1986] 1 W.L.R. 861; *Gisborne* v. *Burton* [1989] Q.B. 390. The statute in question did not specify the legal effects of attempts to "contract out" of its provisions: contrast the provisions of Rent Act 1977 cited on p. 3, n. 18, *ante*.

74 *Nagle* v. *Feilden* [1966] 2 Q.B. 633, 655 ("the colour of his hair"); *Edwards* v. *SOGAT* [1971] Ch. 354, 382 ("the colour of his skin"). See generally Garner, (1972) 35 M.L.R. 478.

75 Pts. 1, 2, 3 and 4; see also Equal Pay Act 1970, as amended by Employment Protection Act 1975, s.125 and Sched. 16, para. 13; Sex Discrimination Act 1986 (as amended by Employment Act 1989); Courts and Legal Services Act 1990, s.64(1).

76 Race Relations Act 1976, Pts. 1, 2, 3 and 4; Courts and Legal Services Act 1990, s.64(2).

Religious discrimination[77] was deliberately omitted from the scope of the Acts[78]; and the courts might well hesitate to intervene where Parliament had deliberately decided not to do so.[79] On the other hand the courts can take account of these other forms of discrimination in deciding whether a contract satisfies the requirements of validity laid down under an existing head of public policy. In *Nagle* v. *Feilden,*[80] for instance, the Court of Appeal appeared to take the view that, even before the Sex Discrimination Act, a contract in restraint of trade would not be regarded as reasonable, or as consistent with the public interest, if its object was to discriminate against women; and the same might now be true if the object of the contract were to discriminate against some religious group.[81]

There are, finally, cases in which the courts may invalidate contracts or contractual provisions on what are essentially grounds of public policy without, as a general rule, referring to the doctrine of public policy, or to some established "head" of public policy, in so many words. Some of the limitations on contractual capacity could be based on public policy: and indeed the former "incapacity"[82] of a barrister to make a contract with his client[83] and the "incapacity" of a public authority to make a contract not to exercise its statutory powers[84] have been explained on this ground. At one time the invalidity of promises to pay extra wages to seamen who were already bound to serve[85] and of promises not to enforce claims which were known to be invalid[86] was explained on grounds of public policy; though it is now more common to base these rules on lack of consideration.[87] The rule against the assignment of "mere rights of action"[88] was not usually discussed under the heading of public policy, though it might well be considered to belong there.[89] The same is true of the rules which determine the validity of penalty clauses,[90] and of some of the common law rules

[77] Clauses in wills are not void for religious discrimination: *Theobald on Wills*, (14th ed.), § 1566; *Blathwayt* v. *Cawley* [1976] A.C. 397; *Re Tuck's S.T.* [1978] Ch. 49. *cf.* Race Relations Act 1976, s.34(2) and (3), exempting certain charitable instruments and acts done for charitable purposes from the operation of Pts. 2, 3 and 4; and see similar provisions in Sex Discrimination Act 1975, s.43(1) and (2).

[78] Contrast Fair Employment (Northern Ireland) Act 1976, s.16, as substituted by Fair Employment (Northern Ireland) Act 1989, s.49 ("religious belief or political opinions"), and *cf.* s.20 of the 1989 Act.

[79] *Cf.* in another context, *La Pintada* [1985] A.C. 104, 129; *post*, p. 882.

[80] [1966] 2 Q.B. 633.

[81] The statement in *Mandla* v. *Dowell Lee* [1983] Q.B. 1, 8, 12 that discrimination on grounds which are not racial is "perfectly lawful" merely means that it does not amount to a contravention of the Race Relations Act 1976; the actual decision was reversed by the House of Lords [1983] 2 A.C. 548 on the ground that the discrimination did contravene the Act.

[82] *Kennedy* v. *Broun* (1863) 13 C.B.(N.S.) 667, 736.

[83] *Rondel* v. *Worsley* [1969] 1 A.C. 191, 264. See now Courts and Legal Services Act 1990, s.61.

[84] *Cory* v. *City of London Corp.* [1951] 2 K.B. 476. For a similar limit on the scope of estoppel, see *Western Fish Products Ltd.* v. *Penwith D.C.* [1981] 2 All E.R. 204, 217.

[85] *Harris* v. *Watson* (1791) Peake 102; *ante*, p. 88.

[86] *Wade* v. *Simeon* (1846) 2 C.B. 548; 564 ("almost *contra bonos mores*"); *Edwards* v. *Baugh* (1843) 11 M. & W. 641, 646.

[87] *Stilk* v. *Myrick* (1809) as reported in 2 Camp. 317; *Poteliakhoff* v. *Teakle* [1938] 2 K.B. 816; *ante*, pp. 82, 88.

[88] See *post*, p. 598.

[89] *Trendtex Trading Corp.* v. *Crédit Suisse* [1982] A.C. 679, 694.

[90] *Post*, pp. 883–890. In *Robophone Facilities Ltd.* v. *Blank* [1966] 1 W.L.R. 1428, 1446 and *The Angelic Star* [1988] 1 Lloyd's Rep. 122, 127, the rules invalidating penalty clauses are said to be based on public policy.

which limit the operation of exemption clauses.[91] All these rules could be regarded as disguised extensions or applications of the doctrine of public policy.

SECTION 3. EFFECTS OF ILLEGALITY

1. Enforcement

A contract affected by illegality is sometimes unenforceable by one party and sometimes unenforceable by both. Where it is "wholly unenforceable because it is contrary to English law, it may . . . accurately be said to be void as a contract, that is, not to be a contract at all;"[92] or to be "illegal and void."[93] In the restraint of trade cases, the illegality often affects only a single term of the contract, and generally its effect is not to make the contract wholly void: it only makes the stipulation in restraint of trade unenforceable insofar as it has not been performed.[94] A contract in restraint of trade would only be "wholly unenforceable" and "void" (in accordance with the statements quoted above) where the restraint formed the sole or principal subject-matter of the contract.[95]

A court will never "enforce" an illegal contract in the sense of ordering a party actually to do something that is unlawful or contrary to public policy.[96] But if A promises B £10 in return for B's promise to do such an act the court may sometimes award A damages if B fails to do the act, or allow B to claim the £10 if he has actually done it. The law on this question is complex and not very satisfactory.

(1) Position of guilty party

An illegal contract cannot be enforced by a guilty party. Thus a person who hires a hall to deliver blasphemous lectures cannot sue for possession[97]; a landlord who lets premises with guilty intent cannot sue for rent[98]; and the owner of a brougham knowingly let to a prostitute for the purpose of her profession cannot sue for hire.[99] A guilty party cannot evade the rule by enforcing the contract indirectly.[1] Thus the court will set aside an arbi-

---

[91] *e.g. ante*, pp. 223–226.

[92] *Mackender* v. *Feldia* [1967] 2 Q.B. 590, 601; *cf. Arnhold Karberg & Co.* v. *Blythe, Green, Jourdain & Co.* [1915] 2 K.B. 379, 388 ("illegal and void"), affirmed [1916] 1 K.B. 49; *Customs & Excise Commissioners* v. *Oliver* [1980] 1 All E.R. 353, 354, 355 ("void"). *Clarke* v. *Chadburn* [1985] 1 W.L.R. 78, 81 ("void for illegality").

[93] *Phoenix General Insurance Co. of Greece S.A.* v. *Halvanon General Insurance Co.* [1988] Q.B. 216, 249, 267, 268 (as to which see *ante*, p. 382).

[94] *O'Sullivan* v. *Management Agency & Music Ltd.* [1985] Q.B. 428, 469 at least "where, as here, the restriction is during the pendency of the agreement": *ibid.* p. 447.

[95] As in *Amoco Australia Pty.* v. *Rocca Bros. Motor Engineering Pty Ltd.* [1975] A.C. 561, where acts done under the agreement were accordingly annulled with retrospective effect: *post*, p. 451.

[96] *e.g.* to perform a contract if to do so would amount to a criminal offence: *cf. ante.* pp. 379, 382.

[97] *Cowan* v. *Milbourn* (1867) L.R. 2 Ex. 230.

[98] *Cf. Alexander* v. *Rayson* [1936] 1 K.B. 169; *Edler* v. *Auerbach* [1950] 1 K.B. 359.

[99] *Pearce* v. *Brooks* (1866) L.R. 1 Ex. 213; the court stressed that the plaintiff knew of the use to which the brougham was to be put; *cf. post*, pp. 429–430.

[1] *The Angel Bell* [1981] Q.B. 65, 72–73.

tration award based on an illegal contract.[2] Similarly, it will refuse to order an account of money due under an illegal contract,[3] and will not administer the funds of an illegal association.[4]

The traditional justification for the rule is that it exists, "not for the sake of the defendant, but because the courts will not lend their aid to such a plaintiff."[5] Thus it applies even though the defendant shares the plaintiff's guilt and even though its effect may be to allow the defendant to keep a substantial benefit for nothing. For example, where money has been lent under an illegal loan, a guilty lender cannot recover it from the borrower.[6] The rule is capable of producing harsh results, particularly as a party may be "guilty" without being morally to blame.[7] Recent authorities therefore suggest that the defence of illegality should be approached "pragmatically"[8] and that the general principle should be that the courts will not assist the plaintiff where to do so "would be an affront to the public conscience."[9] Such vague criteria are, as has been rightly said, "very difficult to apply"[10]; and it remains to be seen whether the courts will be able to develop them into a body of doctrine capable of distinguishing between those cases in which a guilty party should, and those in which he should not, be allowed to enforce the contract. None of the older authorities applying the rule that the guilty party cannot enforce the contract has been overruled; but the severity of that rule is, in any event, mitigated in two ways.

First, the rule only prevents the guilty party from enforcing *the contract.* Where the defendant's conduct constitutes, not merely a breach of the illegal contract, but also an independent tort, the courts can take account of the fact that the degree of the defendant's guilt exceeds that of the plaintiff.[11] That was the position in *Saunders* v. *Edwards*,[12] where a contract had been made for the sale of a flat and the furniture in it; the purchaser had been induced to enter into the contract by the vendor's fraudulent misrepresentation that the premises included a roof-garden. The contract was

---

[2] *David Taylor & Sons Ltd.* v. *Barnett Trading Co.* [1953] 1 W.L.R. 562. But this principle does not apply to findings of *fact* on which the legality of the contract depend: *Binder* v. *Alachouzos* [1972] 2 Q.B. 151; nor does an arbitrator lack jurisdiction merely because it is alleged that performance of an originally lawful contract subsequently became illegal: *Prodexport* v. *E. D. & F. Man Ltd.* [1973] 1 Q.B. 389.

[3] *Victorian Daylesford Syndicate Ltd.* v. *Dott* [1905] 2 Ch. 624.

[4] *Sykes* v. *Beadon* (1879) 11 Ch.D. 170; disapproved in *Smith* v. *Anderson* (1880) 15 Ch.D. 247, but not on this point; *Shaw* v. *Benson* (1883) 11 Q.B.D. 563. The court can order repayment of such funds to the members or contributors: *Barclay* v. *Pearson* [1893] 2 Ch. 154; *Greenberg* v. *Cooperstein* [1926] Ch. 657.

[5] *Holman* v. *Johnson* (1775) 1 Cowp. 341, 343. It follows that the court can take the point even though illegality is not pleaded: *Snell* v. *Unity Finance Co. Ltd.* [1964] 2 Q.B. 203; but see *Bank of India* v. *Trans Continental Commodity Merchants Ltd.* [1982] 1 Lloyd's Rep. 427 (facts giving rise to illegality must be pleaded where contract not *ex facie* illegal).

[6] *Boissevain* v. *Weil* [1950] A.C. 372; *Spector* v. *Ageda* [1973] Ch. 30.

[7] See *post*, p. 430.

[8] *Euro-Diam Ltd.* v. *Bathurst* [1990] Q.B. 1, 35.

[9] *Ibid. Cf.* (in the context of recovery of property obtained illegally) *Thackwell* v. *Barclays Bank plc* [1986] 1 All E.R. 676, 687. And see *Howard* v. *Shirlstar Container Transport Ltd.* [1990] 1 W.L.R. 1292 (foreign law broken to evade threat to life of plaintiff and of his fiancée).

[10] *Pitts* v. *Hunt* [1990] 3 All E.R. 344, 362.

[11] For similar principle governing claims for the recovery of money paid or property transferred under an illegal contract, see *post*, pp. 437–438.

[12] [1987] 1 W.L.R. 1116.

also illegal[13] in that £5,000 of the agreed price of £45,000 was attributed to the furniture, which was worth no more than £1,000: this was apparently done at the suggestion of the purchasers, with a view to saving them the relatively small sum of £300 in stamp duty. Their claim for damages of over £7,000 for the vendor's deceit was nevertheless upheld. One reason for this result was that the purchasers were "not seeking to enforce the contract"[14] but only to claim damages in tort.[15] Another was that, in deciding whether to allow the tort claim, the court could, and should, have regard to the "relative moral culpability"[16] of the parties: the need to deter tax evasion on a fairly moderate scale was outweighed by the court's desire to strip the defendant of the considerable profit accruing to him as a result of his fraud. Public policy therefore supported the upholding of the plaintiffs' tort claim.[17] It does not follow that a party to an illegal agreement can always succeed merely by formulating his claim in tort. Thus in *Ashton* v. *Turner*[18] one of two persons who had agreed (when drunk) to commit burglary together sued the other for injuries inflicted by the latter when negligently driving the get-away car. The action failed as it would have been obviously contrary to public policy to allow such a claim.

Secondly, there is some latitude in determining who is a "guilty" party where the illegality lies in the method of performance. For the present purposes, a party is not guilty merely because he performs a contract in an unlawful manner. Thus the shipowner in *St. John Shipping Corp.* v. *Joseph Rank Ltd.*[19] succeeded in his claim for freight although he had overloaded his ship; but he could not have enforced the contract if he had at the time of contracting intended to overload his ship.[20] The same rule applies where the offending conduct is not contrary to law, but (for example) immoral. Thus an employee is not precluded from enforcing a contract of employment which was lawful in itself merely because he has, in the course of performing it, procured prostitutes for his employer's clients[21]; but if he had agreed to do this when entering into the contract he could not have enforced it.[22] Where the intention that one party should do an unlawful (or immoral) act exists at the time of contracting, even the other party may be

---

13 On the principle of *Alexander* v. *Rayson* [1936] 1 K.B. 169, *ante*, p. 398.

14 [1987] 1 W.L.R. 1116, 1125.

15 *Cf.* the successful tort claim in *Edler* v. *Auerbach* [1950] 1 K.B. 359 in respect of a bath wrongfully removed by the tenant of premises let under an illegal lease.

16 [1987] 1 W.L.R. at p. 1127.

17 Dicta at p. 1134 might, in their widest sense, support even a contract claim where the balance of public policy considerations comes down on the claimant's side; but such an interpretation would conflict with the (no doubt sometimes Draconian) principle stated at n. 5, *supra*.

18 [1981] Q.B. 137; *semble* there was no *animus contrahendi* and hence no contract. *Cf. Pitts* v. *Hunt* [1990] 3 All E.R. 344.

19 [1957] 1 Q.B. 267; *cf. Shaw* v. *Groom* [1970] 2 Q.B. 504. *S.A. Ancien Maison Marcel Bauche* v. *Woodhouse Drake & Carey (Sugar) Ltd.* [1982] 2 Lloyd's Rep. 516, 529; *Yango Pastoral Co. Pty. Ltd.* v. *First National Chicago Australia Ltd.* (1978) 139 C.L.R. 410, as explained in *Phoenix General Ins. Co. of Greece S.A.* v. *Halvanon General Ins. Co. Ltd.* [1988] Q.B. 216 (as to which see *ante*, p. 382); *Euro-Diam Ltd.* v. *Bathurst* [1990] Q.B. 1.

20 [1957] 1 Q.B. at p. 283; *cf. Fielding & Platt Ltd.* v. *Najjar* [1969] 1 W.L.R. 357. *Quaere* whether in the *St. John Shipping* case the test of intention would have been strictly subjective. If the shipowner had made a single contract for so much cargo that his ship would inevitably be overloaded, would the court have said that he "must have" intended at the time of contracting to break the law?

21 *Coral Leisure Group* v. *Barnett* [1981] I.C.R. 503.

22 *Ibid.* at p. 509.

unable to sue on the contract. In *Ashmore, Benson, Pease & Co. Ltd.* v. *A. V. Dawson Ltd.*[23] a contract to carry two 25-ton loads was performed by using lorries which could not lawfully carry loads of more than 20 tons. This was known both to the carrier and to the owner of the goods, whose claim for damage done to them in the course of transit was rejected as he not only knew of the illegality but "participated" in it. "Participation" here means that he assented to a method of performance which he knew to be illegal, and that he hoped to benefit from it by saving the extra expense of having the goods carried on different vehicles.

(2) Position of innocent party

For the present purpose, a person may be "innocent" because he is mistaken, or ignorant, about either the law or the facts.

(a) IGNORANCE OR MISTAKE OF LAW does not, in general, give a party the right to enforce a contract which is affected by illegality. In *Nash* v. *Stevenson Transport Ltd.*[24] the plaintiff agreed to allow the defendants to use goods vehicle licences taken out by him in his own name. This arrangement was made in good faith, but by statute it involved both parties in criminal liability. It was held that the plaintiff could not sue for the money promised to him under the contract. Similarly a person could not enforce a contract in restraint of trade merely because he thought that such contracts were valid.

In these cases the performance or enforcement of the contract *necessarily* involves a breach of the law, or a result which is contrary to public policy. Where this is not the position, the effect of mistake of law is harder to determine. In *Waugh* v. *Morris*[25] a ship was chartered to carry hay from a French port to London. The cargo was to be taken from the ship "alongside," and the master was orally instructed to deliver it to a wharf in Deptford Creek. This could not lawfully be done because, before the time of contracting, an order had, unknown to the parties, been made prohibiting the landing of hay from French ports in the United Kingdom. The hay was therefore transshipped and exported. It was held that the shipowner could sue on the charterparty as it could have been, and in fact had been, performed lawfully. But in *J. M. Allan (Merchandising) Ltd.* v. *Cloke*[26] a roulette wheel was let on hire for the purpose of enabling the hirer to play roulette royale at a country club. Both parties honestly thought that this game was lawful when it was not. It was held that the owner of the wheel could not sue for payment of the agreed hire. One reason for the decision was that the parties had a "common design to use the subject-matter for an unlawful purpose."[27] But it is equally true that in *Waugh* v. *Morris* the parties had a common design to land the hay in Deptford, and that this was an unlawful purpose. Alternatively, there was in *Cloke's* case an actual contract that the wheel should be used for playing roulette royale[28]: the position was as it would have been in *Waugh* v. *Morris* had the contract there

---

23 [1973] 1 W.L.R. 828; Hamson [1973] C.L.J. 199

24 [1936] 2 K.B. 128; *cf. Corby* v. *Morrison* [1980] I.C.R. 218.

25 (1873) L.R. 8 Q.B. 202; *cf. Hindley & Co. Ltd.* v. *General Fibre Co. Ltd.* [1940] 2 K.B. 217.

26 [1963] 2 Q.B. 340.

27 At p. 348.

28 At p. 351.

been to *land* the hay in London and not deliver it "alongside." It is, of course, possible that the hirer could, without committing a breach of contract, have used the wheel to play some other game; but this would not alter the fact that the owner had contracted to provide facilities for playing roulette royale. Thus if one party cannot perform his obligations without committing or abetting a breach of the law he cannot enforce the contract even though he was "innocent" in the sense that he made a mistake of law.

(b) IGNORANCE OR MISTAKE OF FACT. A party may be innocent in the sense of being unaware of, or mistaken about, the facts which give rise to the illegality. The right of such a party to enforce the contract has been upheld in some cases but denied in others; even where it has been denied, other remedies may be available to the innocent party.

(i) *Cases upholding the innocent party's claim.* One such case has already been considered: a printer can probably recover his charges for printing a document containing statements which, as a result of facts unknown to him, are defamatory.[29] An actual decision in favour of the innocent party is *Bloxsome* v. *Williams*[30] where a person sold a horse on a Sunday and thereby committed an offence under the Sunday Observance Act 1677,[31] as he was a dealer. The buyer did not know that the seller was a dealer and recovered the money he had paid for the horse as damages for breach of warranty. *Bloxsome* v. *Williams* was doubted in the *Bedford Insurance*[32] case, where a company issued insurance policies in violation of a statutory prohibition against "the effecting and carrying out of [certain] contracts of insurance" without government authorisation. The policies were described as "illegal and void *ab initio*"; and it was said that the insured person, though innocent, acquired no rights under the policies "for it would be an offence for the insurer to pay him."[33] In the case of such insurance policies, this result has since been reversed by statute,[34] and, even if the reasoning were sound as a matter of common law, it would not follow that *Bloxsome* v. *Williams* was wrongly decided; for the plaintiff in that case was not claiming delivery of the horse, but the return of his money. In upholding this claim, the court was not ordering the defendant to do an act prohibited by statute. This was also the position in *Archbolds (Freightage) Ltd.* v. *Spanglett Ltd.*,[35] where the defendants contracted to carry the plaintiffs' whisky in a van which was not licensed to carry goods belonging to third parties. In carrying the whisky in this van, the defendants committed a statutory offence. The whisky was stolen and the plaintiffs, who did not know that the van was not properly licensed, recovered the value of the whisky as damages for breach of the contract. And in *Fielding & Platt Ltd.* v. *Najjar*[36] an English seller of machinery agreed to give the foreign buyer an invoice in a form requested by the buyer so that he could use it to

---

29 *Cf. Clay* v. *Yates* (1856) 1 H. & N. 73; *ante*, p. 380.
30 (1824) 3 B. & C. 232; *cf. Newland* v. *Simons & Willer* [1981] I.C.R. 521.
31 The Act does not invalidate contracts between limited companies: *Rolloswin Investments* v. *Chromolit* [1970] 1 W.L.R. 912; 86 L.Q.R. 437; 87 L.Q.R. 156.
32 [1985] Q.B. 966.
33 *Ibid.* p. 982; approved in *Phoenix General Insurance Co. of Greece S.A.* v. *Halvanon Insurance Co. Ltd.* [1988] Q.B. 216; *Re Cavalier Insurance Co. Ltd.* [1989] 2 Lloyd's Rep. 430, see *ante*, p. 382.
34 Financial Services Act 1986, s.132; *ante*, p. 382; *post*, p. 433.
35 [1961] 1 Q.B. 374.
36 [1969] 1 W.L.R. 357.

deceive the authorities in his own country. It was held that the seller could sue on the contract as he did not know of the illegality or actively participate in it.

(ii) *Cases rejecting the innocent party's claim.* The leading case in this group is *Re Mahmoud and Ispahani*,[37] where a contract was made to sell linseed oil at a time when it was (under delegated legislation) an offence to buy or sell such oil without licence. The seller had a licence to sell to other licensed dealers and was induced to enter into the contract by the buyer's fraudulent representation that he also had a licence. The buyer later refused to accept the oil, and it was held that the seller could not claim damages for non-acceptance, even if his lack of *mens rea* would exonerate him from criminal liability. Similarly, it has been held that builders who did work in the bona fide but mistaken belief that the necessary licences had been obtained could not enforce the contracts under which the work was done.[38] And, although the point has not been decided, it seems that mistake of fact would not entitle an innocent person to enforce a contract in restraint of trade or one to trade with the enemy. Thus the buyer of a shop whose customers all lived within one mile of it could not enforce a covenant against competition within 20 miles merely because he believed that the customers lived within the larger area. And a person who made a contract with a resident of an enemy country could not enforce it merely because he did not know that war had just broken out between the United Kingdom and that country.[39]

(iii) *Tests for distinguishing the two groups of cases.* Various tests have been suggested for distinguishing between the cases in which the innocent party can, and those in which he cannot, enforce the contract. One is to say that the contract can be enforced by the innocent party so long as it is not *ex facie* illegal. But if the contract is *ex facie* illegal and one party is innocent his mistake is almost always one of law; and the mere fact that the contract is *ex facie* legal is certainly not enough to enable the innocent party to sue.[40] Another suggestion is that the innocent party can sue where the contract is illegal as performed but not where it is illegal as formed. But in *Bloxsome* v. *Williams* the innocent party could sue even though the contract was illegal as formed. Moreover, in *Archbolds (Freightage) Ltd.* v. *S. Spanglett Ltd.* the Court of Appeal regarded it as irrelevant whether the contract was to carry the whisky in the particular van, and yet this fact would be crucial if enforceability depended on whether the contract was illegal as formed or as performed. A third suggestion is that the innocent party can sue in cases of common law but not of statutory illegality. But this again does not fit the cases: in *Bloxsome* v. *Williams* and *Archbolds (Freightage) Ltd.* v. *S. Spanglett Ltd.* the innocent party succeeded although the illegality was statutory. And if the suggestions made at the end of the last paragraph are sound there are cases in which the innocent party will fail although the illegality is brought about by common law. It is, moreover, hard to see why the innocent party's rights should depend on the distinction between statutory and common law illegality.

The distinction between the two types of illegality can, of course, be

---

[37] [1921] 2 K.B. 716; *cf. Yin* v. *San* [1962] A.C. 304; Williams, 8 C.L.J. 51; Buckley, 38 M.L.R. 535; Treitel, *Essays in Memory of Sir Rupert Cross*, pp. 96–99.

[38] *J. Dennis & Co. Ltd.* v. *Munn* [1949] 2 K.B. 327; and see *post*, p. 434.

[39] For discharge by *supervening* illegality in such cases see *post*, p. 786.

[40] *e.g. Re Mahmoud and Ispahani* [1921] 2 K.B. 716.

decisive where the illegality is statutory and the statute expressly or by implication specifies its effect on contracts. On the one hand, the statute may expressly provide that the validity of the contract is not to be affected. It is, for example, an offence under section 65(1) of the Road Traffic Act 1988 to supply certain vehicles which do not comply with specified safety requirements; and section 65(4) provides that "nothing in subsection (1) . . . shall affect the validity of any contract or any rights arising under or in relation to a contract."[41] On the other hand, the statute may expressly or impliedly provide that even an innocent party is not to be entitled to enforce the contract. This possibility was formerly illustrated by the cases, already mentioned,[42] in which insurance policies were issued in the course of a business carried on without government authorisation, thus making the insurers who had issued them guilty of a statutory offence; the general view was that such policies could not be enforced even by an insured person who was quite innocent of the illegality. This result was thought[43] to follow from the wording of the statute, which was considered to have impliedly invalidated the contract by prohibiting the "carrying out" of the policies. But to deny a remedy to the innocent party certainly did not promote the policy of the statutory requirement,[44] which had been imposed on insurers for the protection of insured persons; and section 132 of the Financial Services Act 1986 now lays down the general principle that the contract is unenforceable only against (and not by) the insured, who has the option of enforcing the contract or of claiming the return of money paid or property transferred by him under it. However, if the insurer is equally innocent the court may (exceptionally) allow him to enforce the contract, or to retain money paid or property transferred under it.[45]

Where the statute does not expressly or by implication specify the effects of the illegality on contracts,[46] those effects are, it is submitted, to be determined by reference to the purpose of the statute. This approach is suggested by Devlin L.J. in *Archbolds (Freightage) Ltd.* v. *S. Spanglett Ltd.*, where he said: "I think that the purpose of this statute is sufficiently served by the penalties prescribed for the offender; the avoidance of the contract would cause grave inconvenience and injury to members of the public *without furthering the object of the statute.*"[47] Although Devlin L.J.

---

[41] *Cf.* Fair Trading Act 1973, s.26; Sex Discrimination Act 1975, ss.66(1), 77; (as amended by Sex Discrimination Act 1986, s.6); Race Relations Act 1976, ss.53(1), 72; Energy Conservation Act 1981, s.18; Financial Services Act 1986. ss.5, 56, 57, 131 and 132; Banking Act, 1979 s.1(8) (now Banking Act 1987, s.3(3)) applied in *SCF Finance Ltd.* v. *Masri.* [1986] 2 Lloyd's Rep. 366.

[42] *Viz.*, the *Bedford* case [1985] 1 Q.B. 966 and the *Phoenix* case, [1988] Q.B. 216, *ante*, p. 382. The statements were strictly obiter since in the *Bedford* case the action was by a *guilty* insurer against an innocent reinsurer while in the *Phoenix* case no offence had been committed. The reasoning of these cases was followed in *Re Cavalier Ins. Co. Ltd.* [1989] 2 Lloyd's Rep. 430.

[43] Though with evident reluctance: see the *Phoenix* case [1988] Q.B. 216. 249. 273; *Re Cavalier Ins. Co. Ltd.* [1989] 2 Lloyd's Rep. 440, 443 ("without enthusiasm").

[44] From this point of view, the result in *Stewart* v. *Oriental Fire & Marine Ins. Co. Ltd.* [1985] 1 Q.B. 988 (giving the innocent party a remedy on the contract against the guilty party) was preferable to the reasoning of the authorities cited in note 42, *supra*. *Cf.* Clarke [1987] L.M.C.L.Q. 201.

[45] Financial Services Act 1986, s.132(3).

[46] There may be a provision which is incomplete: *e.g.* Trade Descriptions Act 1968, s.35, which only deals with contracts for the supply of goods and not with contracts for the supply of services, though both types of contracts may be affected by the Act.

[47] [1961] 1 Q.B. 374, 390.

refers only to statutory illegality, it is submitted that the same approach would be appropriate where the illegality was due to a rule of common law: the court has to consider how it would further the objects of the relevant rule of law to invalidate the contract. Where the rule exists for the protection of a class of persons, its objects will obviously not be promoted by denying a remedy to an innocent member of that class.[48] In other cases, it is more difficult to strike a balance between the interests of the public (which the invalidating rule is meant to protect) and those of the innocent party. Of course specific performance of an act that is unlawful or against public policy will not be ordered. The question is whether the innocent party should get damages if the guilty party fails to perform, or the agreed remuneration if he (the innocent party) has performed his part.[49] In what way does it ever "further the object" of the invalidating rule to deny the innocent party such a remedy?

One possible answer to this question is that the denial of a remedy may induce the innocent party to take greater care not to enter into an illegal transaction. Another is that a remedy should be refused whenever the contract is executory, since the availability of such a remedy might induce the other (guilty) party to perform. But where these arguments are sound, the innocent party should have no remedy at all, or at least no remedy as good as the action on the contract. In fact the innocent party who cannot sue on the contract may have other remedies, and one of these seems to be no worse than an action on the contract.

(iv) *Other remedies of innocent party.* Three such remedies call for discussion. First, the innocent party may be able to recover damages for breach of "collateral warranty." In *Strongman (1945) Ltd.* v. *Sincock*[50] the defendant employed a firm of builders to modernise his house. He promised to get the necessary licences (without which it was illegal to do the work), but he only got licences for part of the work and refused to pay for the rest on the ground that the contract to do it was illegal. The builders could not sue on the contract to do the work although they had acted in good faith. But they recovered damages (amounting to the value of the unlicensed work) for breach of the defendant's collateral undertaking to get the necessary licences. This is a useful device for doing justice to the innocent party, and in *Strongman (1945) Ltd.* v. *Sincock* little harm was done to the public interest. For in that case the defendant was an architect so that the builders were not careless[51] in failing to ask to see the licence. And the work had been completed, so that it would have been futile to deny a remedy on the ground that to grant it might induce the performance of an illegal act. But to allow the innocent party to sue on a "collateral warranty" in a case like *Re Mahmoud and Ispahani*[52] would be quite inconsistent with the rationale of the rule denying him a remedy on the contract. It would be mere sophistry to say: we will protect the public interest by deny-

---

48 See *Nash* v. *Halifax Building Society* [1979] Ch. 584, so far as it relates to the enforcement of the security; *cf. post*, p. 437. The contract cannot of course be enforced *against* a member of the protected class: *Johnson* v. *Moreton* [1980] A.C. 37.

49 It is assumed that the making of the payment is not prohibited.

50 [1955] 2 Q.B. 525.

51 *Ibid.* p. 536.

52 [1921] 2 K.B. 716; *ante*, p. 432.

ing a remedy on the contract, but we will also protect the innocent plaintiff by giving him as good a remedy on a collateral warranty. This remedy should only be granted where it will provide no incentive to do the illegal act and where the innocent party was not careless. But if these conditions are satisfied there seems to be no reason why the innocent party should not be able to sue on the contract itself.

Secondly, the innocent party may be able to recover damages for misrepresentation. In *Shelley* v. *Paddock*[53] the plaintiff was by the fraud of the defendant induced to enter into a contract to buy a house in Spain and to make payments under it which were illegal as they violated exchange control regulations. Since the plaintiff's breach of the law was innocent and resulted from the defendant's fraud, she was entitled to damages for that fraud. Even where the misrepresentation was *not* fraudulent, it is possible that a person who had, as a result of it, innocently entered into an illegal contract could similarly recover damages, either at common law or under the Misrepresentation Act 1967; and he might also be able to rescind the contract. But these remedies could be less advantageous than an action on the contract as they would not give the innocent party damages for loss of his bargain.[54]

Thirdly, innocence may be material in an action for the recovery of money paid or property transferred under an illegal contract. The objects of the invalidating rule are less likely to be defeated by this remedy than by an award of damages for breach of contract since it amounts rather to an undoing[55] than to an enforcement of the contract.[56] The remedy may, however, be less advantageous than any of those so far discussed, for under it the plaintiff can only get back what he gave: he cannot recover in respect of other losses incurred in reliance on the contract, or for loss of his bargain.

(3) De facto enforcement

A contract which is illegal may be enforced de facto in the sense that one party may secure compliance with its terms by using or threatening to use some form of economic pressure. Such measures may be taken in good faith, and the question then arises whether the party who is thus induced to perform a contract that was not binding on him has any remedy in respect of loss suffered in consequence. In *Shell U.K. Ltd.* v. *Lostock Garages Ltd.*[57] a garage proprietor was in effect compelled to observe the terms of a solus agreement by the oil company's threats that, if other suppliers were to sell petrol to him, it would sue them for inducing a breach of the solus

---

53 [1980] Q.B. 348; *cf. Burrows* v. *Rhodes* [1899] 1 Q.B. 816 and *Saunders* v. *Edwards* [1987] 1 W.L.R. 1116 (*ante*, p. 428), where even a "guilty" party recovered damages for a fraud unconnected with the illegality.

54 *Cf. ante*, p. 322, *post*, p. 836. In *Shelley* v. *Paddock*, *supra*, the damages did not include any element of compensation for loss of the plaintiff's bargain: see [1979] Q.B. 120.

55 This was the outcome of *Bloxsome* v. *Williams* (1824) 3 B. & C. 232 (*ante*, p. 431) where the buyer's claim was for "damages" but the amount that he recovered was the price paid by him.

56 This was the nature of the claim unsuccessfully made by the seller in *Re Mahmoud and Ispahani* [1921] 2 K.B. 716 (*ante*, p. 432); if he had actually delivered the oil to the buyer he could no doubt have recovered it back: *post*, p. 438.

57 [1977] 1 W.L.R. 1187.

agreement. Lord Denning M.R. held that the solus agreement was unenforceable and that the garage proprietor was entitled to damages in respect of the loss he had suffered through being nevertheless compelled to observe it.[58] Ormrod L.J. held that no such damages were available,[59] while Bridge L.J. awarded them on a different ground, *viz.* that the oil company was in breach of an implied term of its contract with the garage proprietor.[60] Lord Denning held that no such term could be implied,[61] so that the damages awarded by him cannot have been for breach of contract. His award seems rather to have been based on the novel principle, that the *de facto* enforcement of an illegal contract can, if it causes loss, give rise to a claim for damages. The correctness of this principle, as well as its extent, await further judicial consideration.

2. Recovery of Money or Property

A person who cannot enforce an illegal contract may instead try to recover back money paid or property transferred by him under the contract.

(1) General rule: no recovery

The general rule is that money paid or property transferred under an illegal contract cannot be recovered back.[62] At one time the rule could be justified by saying that the courts should not give any help to a willing party to an illegal transaction; and by the argument that, by leaving one party at the mercy of the other, the rule had a deterrent effect. The first of these arguments is no longer wholly convincing now that a person may in all innocence make a contract that is technically illegal; and the second overlooks the possibility that sometimes illegality may be more effectively discouraged by allowing than by denying recovery. If, for example, a person receives money in the course of conducting an illegal business, the illegality is more likely to be deterred by making him pay the money back, than by allowing him to rely on the rule of non-recovery.[63] It would be better if the law did not adopt a "general rule" but asked in relation to each type of illegality whether it was recovery or non-recovery that was the more likely to promote the purpose of the invalidating rule. In practice the present general rule is subject to so many exceptions that the law, taken as a whole, comes close to achieving this result.

(2) Exceptional cases: recovery possible

(a) CLASS-PROTECTING STATUTES. If a contract is made illegal by a statute passed for the protection of a class of persons, a member of that class can

---

[58] *Ibid.* p. 1200.
[59] *Ibid.* pp. 1200–1201.
[60] *Ibid.* p. 1204.
[61] *Ante*, p. 188, Ormrod L.J. agreed with Lord Denning on this point.
[62] *e.g. Scott* v. *Brown* [1892] 2 Q.B. 724; *Edler* v. *Auerbach* [1950] 1 K.B. 359; *cf. Shaw* v. *Shaw* [1965] 1 W.L.R. 537. See generally Grodecki, 71 L.Q.R. 254; Higgins, 25 M.L.R. 598.
[63] *Cf. Hermann* v. *Charlesworth* [1905] 2 K.B. 123

recover back money paid or property transferred by him under the contract.[64] Some statutes expressly provide that a member of a protected class shall be entitled to recover back money paid or property transferred under an illegal contract. For example, the Rent Act 1977 contains various provisions entitling a tenant to recover back money which he could not lawfully have been required to pay[65]; and in a case decided under an earlier Act it was held that he could recover back an illegal premium even though he was a willing party to a fraudulent scheme to evade the Act.[66] The Financial Services Act 1986 contains a number of similar provisions: for example, where an insurer issues a policy in the course of a business carried on without the requisite government authorisation,[67] the insured can generally recover back money paid or property transferred under the contract[68]; and he can do so even though he also has the option of enforcing the contract.[69]

There was at one time some support for the view that the prevalence of such statutory provisions had made the old class-protecting rules obsolete[70]; but this view no longer prevails. In *Kiriri Cotton Ltd.* v. *Dewani*[71] a landlord had, by accepting an illegal premium from his tenant, committed an offence under a Rent Restriction Ordinance which did not expressly say that such premiums could be recovered back. The Privy Council held that the tenant could recover back the premium under the old rules relating to class-protecting statutes. Similarly, premiums paid under an illegal insurance policy of the kind described above could be recovered back by the innocent policy-holder at common law,[72] even before such a right of recovery was expressly conferred on him by the Financial Services Act 1986.[73]

(b) OPPRESSION. A person can recover back money paid or property transferred under an illegal contract if he was forced by the other party to enter into that contract. "Oppression" is here used in a somewhat broad

---

64 *Browning* v. *Morris* (1778) 2 Cowp. 790; *Barclay* v. *Pearson* [1893] 2 Ch. 154; *Bonnard* v. *Dott* [1906] 1 Ch. 740 (unlicensed moneylender); in *Lodge* v. *National Union Investment Co.* [1907] 1 Ch. 300 it was held that the borrower could not recover his securities unless he repaid the money actually lent to him; but this decision has been distinguished out of existence: *Chapman* v. *Michaelson* [1908] 2 Ch. 612; [1909] 1 Ch. 238; *Cohen* v. *J. Lester Ltd.* [1939] 1 K.B. 504; *Kasumu* v. *Baba-Egbe* [1956] A.C. 539; *cf. Barclay* v. *Prospect Mortgages* [1974] 1 W.L.R. 837. Under Consumer Credit Act 1974, s.40(1), a regulated agreement with an unlicensed moneylender is not illegal but only unenforceable against the debtor unless the Director General of Fair Trading orders otherwise.

65 *e.g.* ss.57, 95, 125. *Cf. Financial Services Act* 1986, ss.5. 6. 56, 57, 131 and 132.

66 *Gray* v. *Southouse* [1949] 2 All E.R. 1019. For enforcement of the remainder of the contract by "unwilling victims" see *Ailon* v. *Spiekermann* [1976] Ch. 158, 165.

67 *Ante*, pp. 382, 431, 433.

68 Financial Services Act, s.132(1); exceptionally, the court may allow the insurer to retain such money or property if it is satisfied that the insurer acted innocently and that it was just and reasonable to allow him to retain the money or property: s.132(3). See also ss.5, 6, 56, 57, and 131.

69 *Ante*, p. 433.

70 *Green* v. *Portsmouth Stadium* [1953] 2 K.B. 190, especially at p. 195.

71 [1960] A.C. 192; *cf. Nash* v. *Halifax B.S.* [1979] Ch. 584, so far as it relates to the money lent; and see *ante*, p. 434.

72 *Re Cavalier Insurance Co. Ltd.* [1989] 2 Lloyd's Rep. 430, 450 (and see *ante*, p. 382). For the position where payments had been made by the insurer under the policy, see *post*, p. 441, n. 4.

73 *Supra* at n. 68.

sense. In *Atkinson* v. *Denby*[74] the plaintiff was insolvent and offered to pay his creditors a dividend of 5s. in the £. All the creditors were willing to accept the dividend in full settlement of their claims, except the defendant, who said he would only accept it if the plaintiff first paid him £50. The plaintiff did so, but was later allowed to recover back the £50 on the ground that he had been forced to agree to defraud the other creditors. To say that the plaintiff was oppressed may not be very convincing; but it was a convenient way of avoiding the general rule of non-recovery where that rule would have led to the undesirable result of enabling one creditor to keep more than his fair share of the assets of the insolvent debtor.

The "oppression" may be due, not to the conduct of the other party, but to extraneous circumstances, and such "oppression" has been recognised as a ground of recovery where the contract is made illegal by a statute passed for the protection of a class. Thus in *Kiriri Cotton Co. Ltd.* v. *Dewani* Lord Denning said that the tenant was not "so much to blame" for evading the Rent Restriction Ordinance as the landlord, who was "using his property rights so as to exploit those in need of a roof over their heads."[75] In an American case oppression not caused by the defendant was recognised as a ground of recovery where a person paid a bribe to escape from the danger of being imprisoned and put to death by the Nazis.[76] Less extreme forms of pressure have in England not been regarded as a ground for recovery. In *Bigos* v. *Bousted*[77] a father made an illegal contract to acquire foreign currency in order to send his daughter to Italy as a cure for her recurrent attacks of pleurisy. This "pressure" did not entitle him to recover back property transferred under the contract.

(c) MISREPRESENTATION. A person can recover back money paid or property transferred under an illegal contract if he entered into the contract as a result of the other party's fraudulent misrepresentation that the contract was lawful. Thus in *Hughes* v. *Liverpool Victoria Legal Friendly Soc.*[78] the plaintiff effected a policy of insurance with the defendants on the life of a person in which he had no insurable interest. The contract was illegal,[79] but the plaintiff was able to recover back the premiums he had paid as he had been induced to make the contract by the fraudulent representation of the defendants' agent that the policy was valid. The decisive factor in these cases is the fraud of the defendant, and not the innocence of the plaintiff. The plaintiff would have failed if the representation that that policy was valid had been innocently made.[80] Similarly, where a tenant was induced by the landlord's misrepresentation to enter into an illegal lease, it was held that he could not recover back a payment of rent without alleging and proving fraud.[81]

The cases on this subject suggest that, where recovery is allowed, the

[74] (1862) 7 H. & N. 934; *cf. Smith* v. *Bromley* (1760) 2 Dougl. 696 n.; *Smith* v. *Cuff* (1817) 6 M. & S. 160; *Davies* v. *London & Provincial Marine Insurance Co.* (1878) 8 Ch.D. 469. In *Osborne* v. *Williams* (1811) 18 Ves. 379 it seems even to have been thought that a father "oppressed" a son by offering him the prospect of financial independence.

[75] [1960] A.C. 190, 205.

[76] *Liebman* v. *Rosenthal* 57 N.Y.S. 2d 875 (1945).

[77] [1951] 1 All E.R. 92.

[78] [1916] 2 K.B. 482; *cf. Reynell* v. *Sprye* (1852) 1 D.M. & G. 660.

[79] Life Assurance Act 1774, s.1

[80] *Harse* v. *Pearl Life Assurance Co.* [1904] 1 K.B. 558. *Semble*, that in such a case the policy of invalidating rule would have been better served by allowing recovery: *cf. ante*, p. 436.

[81] *Edler* v. *Auerbach* [1950] 1 K.B. 359.

basis for it is the invalidity of the contract on the ground of illegality, and not misrepresentation as such. It follows that the right of recovery is not necessarily limited by the bars to rescission for misrepresentation.[82] If no such bar has arisen, it seems that a person who has been induced by even an *innocent* misrepresentation of fact[83] to enter into an illegal contract can rescind it for misrepresentation and so recover back his money or property.[84]

(d) MISTAKE. A party who enters into a contract under a mistake of fact as to its legality can sometimes enforce the contract.[85] In such a situation he should be equally entitled to recover back money paid or property transferred under the contract; for it is inconceivable that this remedy will defeat the purpose of the invalidating rule where enforcement of the contract is allowed because it will not have this effect. Mistake of fact[86] can also be a ground for recovery of money or property even where it does not give the mistaken party the right to enforce the contract.[87] In *Oom* v. *Bruce*[88] the plaintiff, as agent for the Russian owner of goods in Russia, took out a policy of insurance on the goods with the defendant. Neither party knew (or could have known) that Russia had declared war on this country before the contract was made. It was held that the plaintiff could get back his premium as he was not guilty of any fault or blame in entering into the illegal contract. Here again no useful purpose would be served by applying the general rule of non-recovery.

(e) REPUDIATION OF LEGAL PURPOSE.[89] A person may be able to reclaim money paid or property transferred under an illegal contract if he repudiates the illegal purpose in time.[90] By giving a party this right, the law tries to encourage him to give up the illegal purpose. Two conditions must be satisfied to bring the rule into operation.

(i) *Repudiation in time.* A party who repudiates before anything has been done to perform the illegal purpose can recover back his money or property, while one who repudiates after the illegal purpose has been fully carried out cannot recover.[91] The difficult cases are those in which the repudiation takes place after steps have been taken towards the performance of the illegal purpose, but before it has been fully carried out. Two such cases may be contrasted.

In *Taylor* v. *Bowers*[92] the plaintiff was being pressed by his creditors. To prevent certain machinery from falling into their hands, he transferred it to

---

[82] *Ante*, pp. 337–345.

[83] This would not cover a case like *Harse* v. *Pearl Life Assurance Co.*, *supra*, as the misrepresentation there was one of law: *ante*, p. 299.

[84] This was assumed in *Edler* v. *Auerbach* [1950] 1 K.B. 359, but in that case the right to rescind for innocent misrepresentation was barred by execution of the lease. This would no longer be a bar: *ante*, p. 338.

[85] *Ante*, p. 431.

[86] Not mistake of law, as in *Harse* v. *Pearl Life Assurance Co.*, *supra*.

[87] *e.g.* on facts such as those of *Re Mahmoud and Ispahani* [1921] 2 K.B. 716; *ante* p. 435, n. 56.

[88] (1810) 12 East 225; *cf. Edler* v. *Auerbach* [1950] 1 K.B. 359, 374–375, where mistake of the payor alone was said to be insufficient; *sed quaere*.

[89] Beatson, 91 L.Q.R. 313; Merkin, 97 L.Q.R. 420.

[90] *Harry Parker Ltd.* v. *Mason* [1940] 2 K.B. 590, 608.

[91] *Palaniappa Chettiar* v. *Arunasalam Chettiar* [1962] A.C. 294.

[92] (1876) 1 Q.B.D. 291: now a case of "frustration"? *cf. infra*, at n. 99; *Symes* v. *Hughes* (1870) L.R. 9 Eq. 475.

one Alcock. He then called two meetings of creditors in an attempt to reach a settlement with them, but none was reached. The plaintiff successfully claimed the machinery back from the defendant, who was one of the creditors and had obtained the machinery from Alcock with notice of the fraudulent scheme and in the hope of benefiting from it. The decision is based on the fact that the illegal purpose had not been carried out: no creditor had been defrauded.

In *Kearley* v. *Thomson*[93] the plaintiff had a bankrupt friend. He paid the defendants £40 in return for their undertaking not to appear at the bankrupt's public examination and not to oppose his discharge. The defendants duly absented themselves from the public examination, but before any application had been made for the bankrupt's discharge the plaintiff claimed back the £40. His claim failed. Fry L.J. said, first, that the rule permitting recovery on repudiation of the illegal transaction did not exist before *Taylor* v. *Bowers* and he doubted the correctness of that decision. But the principle was at least twice stated in earlier cases[94] and has since been accepted as good law.[95] Secondly, he said that, *Taylor* v. *Bowers* was distinguishable from *Kearley* v. *Thomson*, since in the latter case there had been "a partial carrying into effect of an illegal purpose in a substantial manner."[96] This distinction looks at first sight tenuous, but it must be remembered that the illegal purposes in the two cases were quite different. The illegal purpose in *Taylor* v. *Bowers* was to defraud creditors, and no creditor was defrauded. The illegal purpose in *Kearley* v. *Thomson* was to interfere with the course of public justice,[97] and some such interference took place when the defendants stayed away from the bankrupt's public examination. Thus it seems that the repudiation is in time if it takes place after mere preparation to achieve the illegal purpose, but that it is too late if it takes place after performance of the illegal purpose has actually begun.

There is also a more practical distinction between the two cases. In *Taylor* v. *Bowers* the success of the plaintiff's claim promoted the equal distribution of his property among his creditors; for if the claim had failed, one of the creditors (the defendant) would have benefited at the expense of the others.[98] In *Kearley* v. *Thomson*, on the other hand, the creditors would not have benefited at all if the plaintiff's claim had succeeded; for the £40 would have gone to the plaintiff, and not to the bankrupt's estate.

(ii) *Voluntary repudiation.* Repudiation must be voluntary: it must not be forced on the party claiming recovery by the intervention of the police, or of a third person, or by the other party's breach of contract.[99] This requirement follows from the justification for the present exception to the general rule of non-recovery, which is its tendency to encourage a party to give up the illegal purpose. For this reason it is hard to accept the suggestion[1] that a party to an illegal contract can recover back money paid under it simply because there has been a total failure of consideration[2] brought

---

[93] (1890) 24 Q.B.D. 742.
[94] *Hastelow* v. *Jackson* (1828) 8 B. & C. 221, 226; *Bone* v. *Eckless* (1860) 5 H. & N. 925, 928.
[95] See *Hermann* v. *Charlesworth* [1905] 2 K.B. 123; *Bigos* v. *Bousted* [1951] 1 All E.R. 92.
[96] (1890) 24 Q.B.D. at p. 747.
[97] *Cf. ante*, p. 393.
[98] *Cf. ante*, p. 438.
[99] As in *Bigos* v. *Bousted* [1951] 1 All E.R. 92.
[1] Made in *Shaw* v. *Shaw* [1965] 1 W.L.R. 537, 539.
[2] *Post*, p. 927.

about by the other party's refusal to perform. Where illegality is involved, recovery is often denied (under the general rule of non-recovery) even though there has been a total failure of consideration[3]: and may conversely be allowed (under some of the exceptions to the general rule) even though there is no failure of consideration.[4] In these cases, the need to further the policy of the invalidating rule often excludes the ordinary rules that govern recovery on the ground of failure of consideration under lawful contracts.

(f) NO RELIANCE ON ILLEGAL TRANSACTION. A person may be able to recover money or property which has been transferred under an illegal contract, if he can establish his right or title to it without relying on the contract or on its illegality.

(i) *Recovering back goods transferred under an illegal contract.* Where goods are sold under an illegal contract, the property in them can pass (in accordance with the usual rules as to passing of property) notwithstanding the illegality.[5] The property may pass even though the goods have not been delivered to the buyer.[6] If the property has passed and the goods have been delivered to the buyer, the seller will not be able to get them back—a point of special importance where the sale is on credit and the price has not been paid. Similarly, if property has passed to the buyer and the goods have been delivered to a third party, the seller cannot get them back from the third party, having no longer any title on which he can rely. The extent to which the *buyer* can rely on the passing of property in goods which have not been delivered to him is discussed below.[7]

If something is pledged, hired or lent under an illegal contract, a special property or right to retain possession passes when possession is transferred. So long as that special property endures, the subject-matter cannot be recovered back by the transferor. Thus in *Taylor* v. *Chester*[8] half of a £50 Bank of England note was pledged as security for the expenses of a debauch in a brothel. The effect of the pledge was to transfer a special property in the note to the pledgee, with the result that the pledgor could not recover back the note without tendering the amount due. It seems that the effect of such tender would have been to put an end to the pledgee's special property and to entitle the pledgor to recover back the note on the strength of his title. The same principles would apply where a thing is hired under an illegal contract: the owner cannot recover it back while the hirer's

---

[3] *e.g. Parkinson* v. *College of Ambulance Ltd.* [1925] 2 K.B. 1; *Bigos* v. *Bousted* [1951] 1 All E.R. 92. In *Edler* v. *Auerbach* [1950] 1 K.B. 359, 373–374 recovery was denied on the ground that there was no total failure of consideration; but this aspect of the case is better explained as an application of the general rule of non-recovery.

[4] *e.g., Atkinson* v. *Denby* (1862) 7 H. & N. 934; *Kiriri Cotton Co. Ltd.* v. *Dewani* [1960] A.C. 192. The contrary decision in *Re Cavalier Insurance Co. Ltd.* [1989] 2 Lloyd's Rep. 430, 450 scarcely seems to give effect to the policy of the legislation which had been contravened but may be explicable on the ground that the "guilty" insurer had not intended to violate the law and was in liquidation (so that the effective contest was between policyholders who had been paid and the insurer's creditors). *Cf.* now Financial Services Act 1986, s.132(3); *ante*, p. 437, n. 68.

[5] *Simpson* v. *Nichols* (1838) 3 M. & W. 240, 244; *Scarfe* v. *Morgan* (1838) 4 M. & W. 270, 281; *Elder* v. *Kelly* [1919] 2 K.B. 179; *Singh* v. *Ali* [1960] A.C. 167.

[6] *Belvoir Finance Co. Ltd.* v. *Stapleton* [1971] 1 Q.B. 210; *cf. Kingsley* v. *Sterling Industrial Securities Ltd.* [1967] 2 Q.B. 747, 738; *post*, p. 444.

[7] *Post*, p. 444.

[8] (1869) L.R. 4 Q.B. 309; the same principle would apply to a pledge of goods.

special property lasts, but he can do so after that special property has come to an end, *e.g.* because the period of hire has run out.

In *Bowmakers Ltd.* v. *Barnet Instruments Ltd.*[9] machine tools had been let out under hire-purchase agreements which were illegal as they contravened war-time maximum price and licensing regulations. The hirers failed to pay the instalments due under the agreements, sold some of the goods and kept the rest. The owners successfully claimed damages for the conversion of all the goods. They did not have to "found [their] claim on the illegal contract or . . . plead its illegality in order to support [their] claim,"[10] but relied simply on their title. As the period of hire had not run out, it is at first sight hard to see why the hirers could not resist the owners' claim by relying on their special property under the hire-purchase agreements. The reason why they could not do so seems to be that a hirer's right to possession may come to an end otherwise than by lapse of time. First, it can come to an end as a result of a repudiatory breach on the part of the hirer.[11] Since a hirer is guilty of such a breach if he sells the thing hired, the defendants' special property in the goods which they had *sold* had therefore come to an end.[12] But this does not explain why their special property in the goods which they *simply kept* had come to an end. Failure to pay instalments is a breach of contract, but it is not a repudiatory one. A possible solution of the difficulty is that the special property might come to an end as a result of *any* breach *because the contract expressly so provided*; *i.e.* because it provided that, on failure by the hirer to pay instalments, the agreement should *ipso facto* determine and that the owner should be entitled to take back the thing. If the agreements in *Bowmakers'* case contained some such clause[13] the hirers' right to possess the goods ceased as soon as they defaulted in paying instalments. The case can be reconciled with *Taylor* v. *Chester* by assuming that the agreements did contain such a clause.

The preceding discussion of *Taylor* v. *Chester*[14] and *Bowmakers Ltd.* v. *Barnett Instruments Ltd.*[15] attempts to analyse these cases in the light of the rules governing the transfer of property (general or special) in the subject-matter of illegal contracts. This approach is however open to the objection that it ignores the crucial question: whether to allow the owner to recover his property would tend to promote or to defeat the purpose of the rule of law which makes the contract illegal.[16] In *Taylor* v. *Chester* the policy of that rule was presumably to discourage the keeping of brothels; and the decision can perhaps be explained on the ground that it created a stalemate position: the pledge being of half a bank note, neither pledgor nor pledgee could enforce any rights under the note until its two halves were reunited. On the other hand, it can be argued that, by giving the pledgor an incentive

---

[9] [1945] K.B. 65; Hamson, 10 C.L.J. 249; Coote, 35 M.L.R. 38; Stewart, 1 J.C.L. 134.
[10] At p. 71.
[11] *N. Central Wagon & Finance Co.* v. *Graham* [1950] 2 K.B. 7. Election by the owner to rescind on account of the breach seems to be assumed (*cf. post*, pp. 743–747).
[12] *Cf. Belvoir Finance Co.* v. *Harold G. Cole Co.* [1969] 1 W.L.R. 1877 (where the hirer had sold the entire subject-matter); *Union Transport Finance Ltd.* v. *British Car Auctions Ltd.* [1978] 2 All E.R. 385.
[13] The terms of the agreements are not set out in any of the reports of the case, but such provisions were certainly common.
[14] (1869) L.R. 4 Q.B. 309.
[15] [1945] K.B. 65.
[16] Treitel in *Essays in Memory of Sir Rupert Cross* pp. 99–104.

to redeem his pledge, the decision made it more, rather than less, likely that the brothel-keeper would be paid, and so tended to defeat the purpose of the invalidating rule. In *Bowmakers'* case the purpose of the regulations was presumably to prevent profiteering and to regulate the allocation of scarce resources in time of war; and it is unlikely that these purposes were defeated by upholding the owners' claims, particularly in view of the fact that "their error was involuntary."[17] The position would have been different if the owners had been guilty of a deliberate violation of a regulation made for the purpose of protecting hirers. It is submitted that, if this had been the position, the rule in *Bowmakers'* case should not have been applied; for if it were applied one of the owners' most important remedies for non-payment (that of retaking the goods) would be available irrespective of the legality of the agreement. In the case put, such a result would defeat, rather than promote, the policy of the invalidating rule.

Where goods are let out under a regulated agreement,[18] the owner cannot retake them unless he first serves a default notice; and in certain cases he must in addition obtain a court order.[19] Such steps seem to amount to a reliance on the agreement and thus not to be available if the agreement is illegal.

(ii) *Recovering back money paid under an illegal contract.* A person who pays money under an illegal contract cannot generally recover it back by relying on his title, since the effect of the payment is almost always to transfer the entire property in the notes or coins to the payee. Money can only be recovered back under the present rule in the rare cases in which it is not paid out-and-out, but is paid as a deposit. Thus money deposited with a stakeholder under an illegal wager can be recovered back, so long as the stakeholder has not paid it over, in accordance with his instructions, to the other party to the wager.[20]

(iii) *Illegal leases.* An illegal lease generally vests a term of years in the tenant.[21] Thus if the tenant has gone into possession the landlord cannot rely on his title so as to turn the tenant out during the currency of the lease[22]; but he can do so once the lease has expired. The further question arises whether the landlord could recover possession if the tenant failed to pay rent. If this were possible the rule that a tenant under an illegal lease is not liable for rent[23] would be of small practical importance, for such a tenant, like any other, could be turned out for non-payment of rent. It might be argued that the tenant's right to possession comes to an end if he fails to pay rent, just as the hirers' right to possession in *Bowmakers'* case came to an end when they failed to pay instalments. But the analogy between illegal leases and *Bowmakers'* case is false if the explanation of that case was that

---

17 *Bowmakers'* case [1945] K.B. 65, 68. The owners themselves had not attempted to make "excess" profits out of the transactions, having been brought in only to provide finance after the hirers had decided to acquire the goods from their former owners.

18 *Ante*, p. 163.

19 Consumer Credit Act 1974, ss.87, 90.

20 *Cf. O'Sullivan* v. *Thomas* [1895] 1 Q.B. 698.

21 The general rule does not apply if on the true construction of the relevant legislation no interest is intended to pass to a person who takes a lease in contravention of it, *e.g.* where occupation of the land is meant to be restricted to a particular class: *Amar Singh* v. *Kulubya* [1964] A.C. 142; Hamson [1964] C.L.J. 20; Cornish, 27 M.L.R. 225.

22 *Feret* v. *Hill* (1854) 15 C.B. 207; *semble* that this case would now be differently decided on the ground of fraud; and see *Grace Rymer Investments Ltd.* v. *Waite* [1958] Ch. 831.

23 *Ante*, p. 427.

the hirers' right to possession determined *ipso facto* on the hirers' breach of contract. For a lease cannot determine *ipso facto* on the tenant's breach as the law does not recognise such a thing as a lease for an uncertain period.[24] It is possible to have a lease "for five years, subject to forfeiture if the tenant fails to pay rent," but not "for five years, or for so long as the tenant pays rent, whichever is the shorter period." If the tenant fails to pay rent the landlord's right does not automatically revive. He can only attempt to enforce the forfeiture clause. Such an attempt will fail, as it is an attempt to enforce a term of an illegal contract. Hence a landlord cannot recover possession of premises let under an illegal lease simply because the tenant fails to pay rent. A tenancy may also be terminable by notice, quite irrespective of default. If it is determined in this way, it seems that the landlord can recover possession on the strength of his title when the period of notice has expired.[25]

(iv) *Special cases.* There may be special cases in which a person cannot recover back money or property although his right or title to it can be established without reference to the contract or its illegality. It has been suggested that if the property is such that it is unlawful to deal with it at all (*e.g.* an obscene book) it cannot be recovered back.[26] It has also been suggested that there is no right of recovery if the object of the contract is to enable one party to commit a serious crime,[27] *e.g.* if a dagger is lent to commit murder. On the other hand, a person who undertakes the safe keeping of a burglar's house-breaking tools is apparently bound to give them up to the burglar on demand.[28]

(v) *Recovery of money or property obtained under an illegal contract.* The mere fact that something has been obtained under an illegal contract does not deprive the recipient of the usual remedies for its recovery or protection. Thus if goods are sold and delivered under an illegal contract, and the property in them has passed to the buyer, he can recover them or their value if they are later taken away from him by the seller.[29] Such remedies are also available against third parties, and even (subject to statutory exceptions) against the police.[30] They may, moreover, be available to a buyer who has acquired the property in goods under an illegal sale, even

---

[24] *Lace* v. *Chandler* [1944] K.B. 368; but see Validation of Wartime Leases Act 1944. Contrast *Ashburn Anstalt* v. *Arnold* [1989] Ch. 1, where the terms were sufficiently certain.

[25]1 The contrary assumption seems to have been made in *Amar Singh* v. *Kulubya* [1964] A.C. 142, but was not necessary for the decision.

[26] *Bowmakers Ltd.* v. *Barnet Instruments Ltd.* [1945] K.B. 65, 72. *Aliter* if the book is seditious? See *Elias* v. *Pasmore* [1934] 2 K.B. 164, 174.

[27] Williams, 8 C.L.J. at p. 62, n. 54.

[28] *R.* v. *Lomas* (1913) 110 L.T. 239, as explained in *R.* v. *Bullock* [1955] 1 W.L.R. 1.

[29] *Singh* v. *Ali* [1960] A.C. 167.

[30] *Gordon* v. *Chief Commr. of Metropolitan Police* [1910] 2 K.B. 1080. For police powers in certain cases to seize and retain property for a limited time, see *Malone* v. *Metropolitan Police Commissioner* [1980] Q.B. 49; Police and Criminal Evidence Act 1984, ss.19, 22; for powers to restrain an offender from dealing with the fruits of his crime, see *Chief Constable of Kent* v. *V* [1983] Q.B. 34 and *Chief Constable of Hampshire* v. *A Ltd.* [1985] Q.B. 132 (where the means of identification had failed); contrast *Chief Constable of Leicestershire* v. *M* [1989] 1 W.L.R. 20, 23, and *Chief Constable of Surrey* v. *A*, *The Times*, October 27, 1988 (no common law power to prevent a person, who had been charged with obtaining money by deception, from dealing with *profits* made by use of the money). For statutory powers to order forfeiture or confiscation, see Drug Trafficking Act 1986; Criminal Justice Act 1988, ss.69–70 and Pt. VI Criminal Justice (International Co-operation) Act 1990, ss.25, 26; *cf.* Obscene Publications Act 1959, s.3(3); Video Recordings Act 1984, s.21(1).

though the goods have never been in his possession. In *Belvoir Finance Co. Ltd.* v. *Stapleton*,[31] Belgravia wanted to acquire cars from Francis, finance being provided by Belvoir. In relation to each car, two contracts were made: a sale by Francis to Belvoir and a letting on hire-purchase by Belvoir to Belgravia. All these contracts were illegal. Belvoir never acquired possession of the cars, which were delivered by Francis straight to Belgravia. It was held that Belgravia's assistant manager was liable to Belvoir for conversion of the cars, since the property in them had passed to Belvoir as soon as the contracts of sale between them and Francis were "executed."[32] It should, however, be emphasised that the decision is only concerned with the relative rights of the buyer and a third person. *The seller* had no further interest in the cars and was not in possession of them. The case therefore does not support the proposition that a buyer to whom property in goods has passed under an illegal contract can claim them, or damages for their conversion, *from a seller who has never delivered them at all*. Such a claim would not differ in substance from a claim for the delivery, or for damages for the non-delivery, of the goods under the illegal contract. Its success would thus defeat the policy of the rule against the enforcement of such a contract.

The right to recover money or property obtained under an illegal contract has been extended, sometimes with surprising results, to make an agent employed in an illegal transaction liable to account for its proceeds to his principal. Thus in *Tenant* v. *Elliott*[33] a broker who effected an illegal insurance and later received the policy moneys was held accountable for them to his principal. Similarly, in *Farmer* v. *Russell*[34] a carrier received the price of goods on behalf of his principal, to whom he was held liable to account even though the goods were counterfeit halfpence. The same principle was applied in *Bone* v. *Eckless*,[35] where the captain of a ship was instructed to sell it to the Turkish Government, and told the owner that this could only be done if he paid bribes of £500 to Turkish officials. The owner agreed that the bribes should be paid, and the ship was duly sold for £6,500, of which the captain kept £500 to pay the bribes. He paid away only £300 in bribes, and it was held that the owner could recover the remaining £200 from the captain because he "makes out his title to recover £6,500 by proving the sale of his ship for that sum, and it is the [captain] who is relying on the illegal agreement to justify the non-payment of the money." In all these cases the illegality was in the transaction which the agent was employed to effect. The principle would probably not apply where the agency itself was illegal[36] and recent authority casts some doubt on its validity in suggesting that a plaintiff could not recover damages from a third party for conversion of property obtained by fraud where the property was "the very proceeds of the fraudulent conduct."[37]

---

[31] [1971] 1 Q.B. 210; *cf. Kingsley* v. *Sterling Industrial Securities Ltd.* [1967] 2 Q.B. 747, 783.
[32] [1971] 1 Q.B. 210 at p. 220.
[33] (1791) 1 B. & P. 3.
[34] (1798) 1 B. & P. 296 (approved in *Sykes* v. *Beadon* (1879) 11 Ch.D. 170); *cf. Bousfield* v. *Wilson* (1846) 16 L.J.Ex. 44; *Pye* v. *B.G. Transport Service* [1966] 2 Lloyd's Rep. 300; *contra*, *Griffith* v. *Young* (1810) 12 East 513, 514.
[35] (1860) 5 H. & N. 925.
[36] See *Booth* v. *Hodgson* (1795) 6 T.R 405; *Harry Parker Ltd.* v. *Mason* [1940] 2 K.B. 590.
[37] *Thackwell* v. *Barclays Bank plc* [1986] 1 All E.R. 676, 689.

(3) Scope of the general rule

The general rule that property transferred or money paid under an illegal contract is irrecoverable was not settled without a good deal of hesitation; and in particular equity at one time inclined to the opposite view.[38] Traces of the equitable view can be found in *Hermann* v. *Charlesworth*.[39] The defendant ran a marriage bureau, and the plaintiff promised to pay him £250 if he could find her a husband. She also paid a "special client's fee" of £52, of which £47 was to be repaid if no marriage or engagement took place within nine months. After four months she repudiated the contract and claimed back the £52. One reason for allowing her claim was that equity gave relief against marriage brokage bonds, even after a marriage had taken place,[40] and that, similarly, money actually paid under a marriage brokage contract could be recovered back: in other words, the general rule of non-recovery does not in equity apply to marriage brokage contracts. At one time this equitable principle also applied to other types of contract: thus money paid under a contract to get the plaintiff a commission in the marines could be recovered back.[41] There is no good modern authority for applying the equitable principle except to marriage brokage contracts; but the possibility of its wider application should perhaps not be wholly ruled out. It would enable the courts to allow recovery where this was more likely than the general rule of non-recovery to further the policy of the invalidating rule.[42]

3. Severance[43]

Where a contract is only partly illegal, two problems can arise. The first is the problem of severance of consideration: can a promise be enforced if it is lawful in itself but is in part supported by illegal consideration? The second is the problem of severance of promises: can a promise be enforced if it is lawful in itself but is coupled with an illegal promise?

(1) Severance of consideration

(a) DEPENDS ON WHETHER ILLEGAL PART IS SUBSTANTIAL OR SUBSIDIARY. A promise cannot be enforced if the whole or a substantial part of the consideration for it is illegal. In *Lound* v. *Grimwade*[44] a person who had committed a fraud making him civilly and criminally liable promised to pay the plaintiff £3,000 in return for the plaintiff's promise not to take "any legal proceedings" in respect of the fraud. The plaintiff's claim for the £3,000 failed as a substantial part of the consideration for the promise to pay it was his own illegal promise to stifle a criminal prosecution.[45]

On the other hand, a promise can be enforced if the main consideration for it is lawful, although it is also supported by a subsidiary illegal consider-

[38] *Neville* v. *Wilkinson* (1782) 1 Bro.C.C. 547, 548. The same view was sometimes taken at common law; *e.g. Munt* v. *Stokes* (1792) 4 T.R. 561.
[39] [1905] 2 K.B. 123.
[40] At pp. 134, 137, 138.
[41] *Morris* v. *McCullock* (1763) Amb. 432.
[42] *Cf. ante*, p. 436.
[43] Marsh, 64 L.Q.R. 230, 347.
[44] (1888) 39 Ch.D. 605; *cf. Walrond* v. *Walrond* (1858) Johns. 18.
[45] See *ante*, p. 393.

ation.[46] For example, an employee who enters into too wide a contract in restraint of trade can recover his wages.[47] The main consideration for the employer's promise to pay is the employee's promise to serve, or the performance of it; his promise not to compete is only subsidiary. The position is similar where an employee as a term of his contract of service enters into a pension scheme which contains an invalid stipulation in restraint of trade. That stipulation forms only a subsidiary part of the consideration provided by the employee for the various promises made by the employer under the contract as a whole; and if the stipulation is invalid it can be severed, so that the pension will be payable although the stipulation is not complied with.[48] But if the sole consideration for the promise to pay the pension is an invalid stipulation in restraint of trade the employee cannot recover the pension. This was the position in *Wyatt* v. *Kreglinger & Fernau*[49] where the promise was made on the lawful termination of the contract of service and the employee provided no consideration for the promise except his assent to, or performance of, the invalid stipulation in restraint of trade.

Similar principles apply where the vendor of a business enters into too wide a contract in restraint of trade. If the price is promised mainly for the business premises and stock-in-trade, the illegal promise not to compete is only a subsidiary part of the consideration for the promise to pay, so that the vendor can sue for the price. But if the purpose of the transaction, viewed objectively,[50] was the elimination of a competitor, rather than the purchase of business, it might be held that the vendor's promise not to compete formed a substantial part of the consideration for the purchaser's promise to pay; and that accordingly the vendor could not sue for the price.

The distinction so far drawn may, however, be excluded by the policy of the invalidating rule. In *Ailion* v. *Spiekermann*[51] the vendor of a leasehold interest required the purchasers to pay an illegal premium. He thereby committed a statutory offence, but the purchasers (who were "unwilling victims"[52]) committed none by promising to pay the premium. It was held that they could specifically enforce the vendor's obligations without having to pay the premium. They were able to do this, whether or not their promise to pay the premium constituted a substantial part of the consideration; for such enforcement by them was obviously the most effective way of promoting the legislative policy against illegal premiums.

(b) APPORTIONMENT OF PROMISE TO LEGAL PART. In the cases so far discussed, the plaintiff has either failed or succeeded in full. The plaintiff in *Lound* v. *Grimwade*[53] got nothing, though part of the consideration provided by him was lawful. An employee who enters into too wide a restraint of trade can sue for his entire wages, though the employer loses one of the

---

[46] See *Goodisnon* v. *Goodinson* [1954] 2 Q.B. 118 (the actual decision is obsolete: Matrimonial Causes Act 1973, s.34, *ante*, p. 395; *cf. Kearney* v. *Whitehaven Colliery Co.* [1893] 1 Q.B. 700; *Fielding & Platt Ltd.* v. *Najjar* [1969] 1 W.L.R. 357, 362.

[47] *McFarlane* v. *Daniell* (1938) S.R. (N.S.W.) 337, approved in *Carney* v. *Herbert* [1985] A.C. 301, 311; *cf. Sadler* v. *Imperial Life Assurance Co. of Canada* [1988] I.R.L.R. 388 (similar principle applied to agent's claim for commission).

[48] *Bull* v. *Pitney-Bowes Ltd.* [1967] 1 W.L.R. 273; *semble* the stipulation was not a mere condition but formed part of the consideration for the employer's promise; *cf. ante*, p. 69.

[49] [1933] 1 K.B. 793; *ante*, p. 410.

[50] *Triggs* v. *Staines U.D.C.* [1969] 1 Ch. 10; *ante*, p. 409.

[51] [1979] Ch. 158.

[52] *Ibid.* p. 165.

[53] (1888) 39 Ch.D. 605.

advantages for which he bargained. It might be thought fairer to make the defendant liable in proportion to the legal part of the consideration. The objection to such a rule is that it would often be difficult to apply as the court cannot easily tell what value the parties attributed to the legal and illegal parts of the consideration respectively. But it seems that where the legal and illegal parts can be precisely valued, the plaintiff can recover so much of the promised payment as can be attributed to the lawful part of the consideration. In *Frank W. Clifford Ltd.* v. *Garth*[54] the plaintiff agreed to do building work for the defendant on a "cost plus" basis, so that the total cost of the work could not be known in advance. The bill for the completed work came to £1,911. The defendant refused to pay anything because work costing more than £1,000 was illegal unless licensed, and no licence had been obtained. But he was held liable to pay £1,000: his promise to pay was enforced to the extent to which it was supported by lawful consideration.

(c) SPECIAL CASES. It has been said that the doctrine of severance does not apply where part of the consideration is criminal or immoral,[55] *e.g.* where it is a promise to commit robbery or adultery, or the performance of such a promise. But the fact that part of the consideration is criminal only prevents severance if the party who provides it is guilty of a deliberate violation of the law. Thus in *Frank W. Clifford Ltd.* v. *Garth* the builder recovered £1,000 in spite of the fact that he had committed an offence by doing unlicensed work worth more than £1,000. He would however have recovered nothing if he had agreed to do the work without a licence, knowing from the start that it would cost over £1,000.[56]

(2) Severance of promises

Where the promises of one party to a contract are partly lawful and partly illegal, the court may cut out the illegal promises and enforce the lawful ones alone. The courts will only do this if three conditions are satisfied. It should be stressed that *all* these conditions must be satisfied before the court will sever. It is sometimes suggested that a fourth condition must also be satisfied, but this is probably not law.

(a) THE PROMISE MUST BE OF SUCH A KIND AS CAN BE SEVERED. It has been said that there can be no severance of a criminal or immoral promise.[57] But although this may be generally true, it seems that a criminal promise could be severed if it was made without guilty intent.[58] It has also been said that there can be no severance of a promise to trade with the enemy[59] or of a promise to defraud the Revenue.[60] Promises are in fact most frequently severed in contracts in restraint of trade; and it has been assumed that pro-

[54] [1956] 1 W.L.R. 570; *cf. Ex p. Mather* (1797) 3 Ves. 373; *J. Dennis & Co.* v. *Munn* [1949] 2 K.B. 327; and see *The American Accord* [1983] 1 A.C. 168.
[55] *Bennett* v. *Bennett* [1952] 1 K.B. 249, 254.
[56] *Frank W. Clifford* v. *Garth* [1956] 1 W.L.R. at p. 572; *cf. ante*, p. 429.
[57] *Bennett* v. *Bennett* [1951] 1 K.B. 249, 254.
[58] As in the case of severance of consideration: *supra*, at nn. 55, 56.
[59] *Kuenigl* v. *Donnersmarck* [1955] 1 Q.B. 515.
[60] *Miller* v. *Karlinski* (1945) 62 T.L.R. 85; *Corby* v. *Morrison* [1980] I.C.R. 564; the contrary was assumed in *Napier* v. *National Business Agency* [1951] 2 All E.R. 265 but it was held that the contract was not severable as there was only one promise in substance. In the case of long-term employment, the contract is wholly invalid during the period in respect of which the illegal payments are made, but not in respect of the rest of its duration; *Hyland* v. *J. H. Barber (North-West) Ltd.* [1985] I.C.R. 861.

mises excluding the jurisdiction of the courts can be severed.[61] The question whether other illegal promises can be severed at all is still an open one.

(b) THE "BLUE PENCIL" TEST. The court will only sever an illegal promise if this can be done by cutting words out of the contract. This has been called the "blue pencil" test: it must be possible to sever by simply running a blue pencil through the offending words. The court will not redraft the contract by adding or rearranging words, or by substituting one word for another.[62] Thus in *Mason* v. *Provident Clothing & Supply Co. Ltd.*[63] the House of Lords refused to strike out of the contract the words "within 25 miles of London" and to substitute "in Islington"; to do so would not be to sever but to redraft the contract. The test is of doubtful utility since it can easily be satisfied by skilful draftsmanship, while on the other hand it may entirely prevent enforcement of a restraint drawn up by laymen where some degree of enforcement would be reasonable.[64] Where this is the case, the courts will now apply the test with some latitude. In *T. Lucas & Co. Ltd.* v. *Mitchell*[65] a covenant provided that a sales representative should not within a certain *area* "deal in any goods similar to" those allocated to him for sale; or "*solicit orders* for . . . any *such* goods." It was held that the area covenant was invalid while the solicitation covenant was valid; and that the area covenant could be severed. Strictly speaking, this left no point of reference for the word "such" in the solicitation covenant, but the deleted area covenant could be looked at to give the word meaning.

It used to be thought that promises could be severed merely because the "blue pencil" test was satisfied[66]; but this view no longer prevails. The test may restrict, but it does not determine, the scope of the doctrine of severance. Even if the legal and illegal promises are actually contained in separate documents,[67] the court will refuse to sever if the third requirement is not also satisfied.

(c) SEVERANCE MUST NOT ALTER THE NATURE OF THE COVENANT. The court will not sever if to do so alters the whole nature of the covenant.[68]

In *Goldsoll* v. *Goldman*[69] the seller of an imitation jewellery business in New Bond Street undertook that he would not for two years deal in real or imitation jewellery in the United Kingdom or certain named places abroad. The covenant was too wide in *area* as the seller had not traded abroad, and in respect of *subject-matter* as he had scarcely dealt in real jewellery. But it was held that the references to the foreign places and to real jewellery could be severed, and that the restraint on dealing in imitation jewellery in the United Kingdom could be enforced. The only question discussed by the court was whether the "blue pencil" test was satisfied;

---

[61] *Re Davstone Estate Ltd.'s Leases* [1969] 2 Ch. 378; but severance failed because the "blue pencil" test (below) was not satisfied; *Home Insurance Co.* v. *Administratia Asigurarilor* [1983] 2 Lloyd's Rep. 674, 677.

[62] Contrast the court's statutory power to revise contracts: in the cases described at p. 453 *post*.

[63] [1913] A.C. 724 (*ante*, p. 407).

[64] See *Commercial Plastics Ltd.* v. *Vincent* [1965] 1 Q.B. 623, 647.

[65] [1974] Ch. 129.

[66] *Putsman* v. *Taylor* [1927] 1 K.B. 637, 640; the Court of Appeal held the covenant valid *in toto*, so that severance was not necessary: [1927] 1 K.B. 741.

[67] As in *Kenyon* v. *Darwen Cotton Manufacturing Co. Ltd.* [1936] 2 K.B. 193.

[68] *Putsman* v. *Taylor* [1927] 1 K.B. 637, 646; *cf. Spector* v. *Ageda* [1973] Ch. 30, 45.

[69] [1915] 1 Ch. 292.

but it can be argued that the object of the original covenant was to protect the business which the buyer had bought; that the object of the severed covenant was the same; and that severance had thus not altered the nature of the original covenant.

In the contrasting case of *Attwood* v. *Lamont*[70] the plaintiffs had a general outfitters' business at Kidderminster. It was divided into several departments, each of which was supervised by one of their employees. The head of each department undertook that he would not after leaving the plaintiffs' service "be concerned in any of the following trades or businesses: that is to say, the trade or business of a tailor, dressmaker, general draper, milliner, hatter, haberdasher, gentlemen's, ladies' or children's outfitter" within ten miles of Kidderminster. In an action to enforce this covenant against the head of the tailoring department, the plaintiffs admitted that the covenant was too wide in point of subject-matter, but they argued that everything except the reference to tailoring should be severed, and that part alone enforced. This argument was rejected as severance would have altered the whole nature of the covenant. After severance, the covenant would only protect that part of the business in which the defendant had worked, whereas the original covenant was "part of a scheme by which every head of a department was to be restrained from competition with the plaintiffs, even in the business of departments with which he had no connection."[71] It was "one covenant for the protection of the . . . entire business"[72] and not a series of covenants for the protection of each department.

It was at one time thought that *Goldsoll* v. *Goldman* and *Attwood* v. *Lamont* could be reconciled simply on the ground that the covenant in the first case was between vendor and purchaser while that in the second was between employer and employee.[73] This view was supported by a dictum in *Mason* v. *Provident Clothing & Supply Co. Ltd.* that in employment cases the courts should only sever where the excess was trivial,[74] and by the view expressed in *Attwood* v. *Lamont* that in such cases the courts should be reluctant to sever at all.[75] But if the court is satisfied that there are, as a matter of construction, separate covenants, and that one of them can be removed without altering the nature of the covenant, it can sever a restraint in an employment contract,[76] and it may do so even though the excess was not merely trivial.[77] On the other hand, the court will not sever a covenant between vendor and purchaser merely because the "blue pencil" test is satisfied. Even between vendor and purchaser, severance will

---

70 [1920] 3 K.B. 571.

71 At pp. 579–580.

72 At p. 593.

73 *Ronbar Enterprises Ltd.* v. *Green* [1954] 1 W.L.R. 814, 820.

74 [1913] A.C. at p. 745.

75 [1920] 3 K.B. a pp. 593–596. Contrast the attitude of the court in *Commercial Plastics Ltd.* v. *Vincent* [1965] 1 Q.B. 623, 647 (*ante*, p. 449) and in *The Littlewoods Organisation Ltd.* v. *Harris* [1977] 1 W.L.R. 1472 (where no question of severance arose).

76 *T. Lucas & Co. Ltd.* v. *Mitchell* [1974] Ch. 129; *Stenhouse Australia Ltd.* v. *Phillips* [1975] A.C. 391; *Business Seating (Renovations) Ltd.* v. *Broad* [1989] I.C.R. 729, 734–735; *cf. Commercial Plastics Ltd.* v. *Vincent* [1965] 1 Q.B. 623, 647. *Anscombe & Ringland* v. *Butchoff* (1984) 134 New L.J. 37.

77 *Putsman* v. *Taylor* [1927] 1 K.B. 637; *Scorer* v. *Seymour-Johns* [1966] 1 W.L.R. 1419; and see n. 76 *supra*.

not be allowed where its effect would be to alter the nature of the covenant.[78]

(d) ALLEGED NECESSITY FOR SEPARATE CONSIDERATION. It is sometimes said that a promise can only be severed if it is supported by separate consideration.[79] But this view is inconsistent with the cases just considered. In *Goldsoll* v. *Goldman*, for instance, no separate consideration was provided for the valid and the invalid parts of the covenant. Yet the invalid parts were severed.

(e) WHETHER OTHER PROMISES AFFECTED. In the restraint of trade cases discussed above, the covenant not to compete has formed part of a larger transaction; and the effect of holding that excessive parts of the restraint could not be severed was simply that *that covenant* was wholly void. *Other* promises or obligations of the covenantor under the contract as a whole may nevertheless be enforceable. For example, an employee who has entered into a wholly void covenant in restraint of trade may still be restrained from breaking his duty of fidelity.[80] And a person to whom money has been lent on terms which include an invalid covenant in restraint of trade is nevertheless liable to repay the loan and to pay interest.[81] In such cases, it can be said that the main purpose of the contract is to create the relationship of employer and employee or of lender and borrower; and the fact that the contract seeks to impose an invalid restraint on the employee or borrower does not vitiate the entire relationship.

On the other hand, where the main purpose of the contract is to impose the restraint, the invalidity of that restraint can lead to the nullity of the whole contract. In such cases, the issue is not whether one part of the restraint can be severed from another without altering the nature *of the covenant* in restraint of trade; it is, rather, whether the invalidity of the restraint has left *the contract as a whole* without subject-matter. Two cases which raise the latter question may be contrasted. Both were concerned with solus petrol agreements; in each case the garage proprietor had leased his garage to the oil company which had then leased it back by granting an underlease to the garage proprietor, the solus agreement being contained in the underlease.[82] In the *Amoco*[83] case, the underlease was at a nominal rent for a period just one day shorter than the original lease: in these circumstances it was held that the solus agreement "constituted the heart and soul of the underlease."[84] As the solus agreement was invalid, it followed that neither the underlease nor the original lease (which was part of the same arrangement) could remain in force. On the other hand, in the *Alec Lobb*[85] case the original lease was for a period of 51 years; the oil company had paid a premium of £35,000 (the fair market value) for it; the under-

[78] *British Reinforced Concrete Engineering Co. Ltd.* v. *Schelff* [1921] 2 Ch. 563, a vendor and purchaser case in which *Attwood* v. *Lamont* [1920] 3 K.B. 571 was followed on this point.

[79] *e.g.* in *Putsman* v. *Taylor*, *supra* n. 77, at p. 640; *Kuenigl* v. *Donnersmarck* [1955] 1 Q.B. at p. 538.

[80] *Ante*, p. 189, *Commercial Plastics Ltd.* v. *Vincent* [1965] 1 Q.B. 623.

[81] *Cf. Cleveland Petroleum Co.* v. *Trinity Garage (Bexleyheath)*, *The Times*, September 8, 1965; [1965] C.L.Y. 3881.

[82] *Ante*, p. 421.

[83] *Amoco Australia Pty.* v. *Rocca Bros. Motor Engineering Pty. Ltd.* [1975] A.C. 561.

[84] *Ibid.* p. 578.

[85] *Alec Lobb (Garages) Ltd.* v. *Total Oil (Great Britain) Ltd.* [1985] 1 W.L.R. 173; *cf.* the *Amoco* case, *supra*, at p. 579.

lease was for only 21 years and yielded a rent of £2,250 per annum. The solus agreement was held valid[86]; but it was said that, even if it had been invalid, the lease and underlease would have remained in force since the transaction as a whole would not, merely because of the invalidity of that one term, have "so changed its character as not to be the sort of contract that the parties intended to enter into at all."[87] The contract would have remained one "for letting a petrol station . . . at a rent which was not nominal. It was therefore the sort of contract which the parties intended to enter into."[88]

In cases of the kind just considered, it is sometimes suggested that the agreement as a whole is vitiated if the invalid promise constitutes the whole or main consideration for the valid promise or promises of the other party. This is the test applied in the "severance of consideration" cases[89]; but it is submitted that in the present context the test is unhelpful. In the severance of consideration cases, the test determines whether the person *to whom* the illegal promise is made is liable on his counter-promise. In the *Amoco* and *Alec Lobb* cases the question was whether the person *by whom* the illegal promise was made was liable on *other* promises made by himself. The consideration for all the promises of that party moved from the oil company; no part of that consideration was illegal, nor was any part of it given specifically for the restraint. All this was just as true in the *Amoco* case (where the illegality vitiated the whole agreement) as in the *Alec Lobb* case (where the restraint would, if illegal, not have had this effect). The distinction between the two cases does not lie in the character of the consideration for the promises of the party who has undertaken the restraint[90]: it is to be found by asking whether the invalidity of the promise in restraint of trade destroyed the principal object of the transaction.

The principle just stated is not restricted to cases in which the source of illegality is restraint of trade. In *Carney* v. *Herbert*[91] a contract was made for the sale of shares by instalments; the sellers asked for security for the payment of these instalments, and the form of security agreed on and given was illegal. It was held that the contract as a whole was not vitiated, so that the buyer remained liable for the price since the illegal security "did not go to the heart of the transaction."[92] The sellers had only wanted *some* security and the invalidity of the particular security given did not change the essential character of the contract as one for the sale of the shares.

(3) Statutory severance

Acts of Parliament which make specific terms in certain contracts unlawful sometimes contain provisions which give rise to a kind of statutory sever-

---

[86] *Ante*, p. 419.
[87] [1985] 1 W.L.R. 173, 192, applying the test stated by Buckley L.J. in *Chemidus Wavin Ltd.* v. *Soc. pour la Transformation et l'Exploitation des Resines Industrielles* [1978] 3 C.M.L.R. 514, 520.
[88] [1985] 1 W.L.R. 173, 192.
[89] *Ante*, pp. 446–448.
[90] Failure to perceive this point seems to be responsible for the statement in the *Alec Lobb* case, *supra*, at p. 181 that "The tie provisions . . . were not *either* the sole consideration for the tie *or* the sole object of the transaction" (italics supplied). While the second alternative here stated is (with respect) plainly correct, the first is hard to follow: it seems to suggest that the tie could in part be consideration for itself.
[91] [1985] A.C. 301; *cf. post*, p. 453.
[92] *Ibid.* p. 316.

ance. Under the Sex Discrimination Act 1975[93] and the Race Relations Act 1976,[94] for example, the court may make orders for "modifying or removing" certain discriminatory provisions in contracts. The Resale Prices Act 1976 makes it unlawful for a supplier of goods to include certain resale price maintenance provisions in an agreement relating to the sale of such goods to a dealer[95]; but, although such a provision is void, its inclusion does not affect the validity of the rest of the agreement.[96] Similarly the inclusion of certain terms in a contract may be an offence under the Fair Trading Act 1973[97]; but a contract for the supply of goods or services is not to be void or unenforceable "by reason only" of the commission of the offence.[98]

4. Collateral Transactions

Collateral transactions may be infected with the illegality of a principal contract if they help a person to perform an illegal contract, or if they would, if valid, make possible the indirect enforcement of an illegal contract. Thus a loan of money is illegal if it is made to enable the borrower to make or to perform an illegal contract,[99] or to make an illegal payment,[1] or to pay a debt contracted under an illegal contract.[2] Similarly, a policy of insurance on an illegal venture is illegal[3]; a bond, bill of exchange or pledge given to secure an illegal debt is illegal[4]; and a bank is not liable on a letter of credit[5] to the extent that[6] the underlying contract of sale is prohibited by statute.[7] But if it is the collateral transaction which is illegal, it does not follow that this illegality infects the otherwise lawful principal contract. Thus where an illegal security was in good faith taken to secure the performance of a legal agreement that agreement was not thereby invalidated.[8] Nor is a contract illegal merely because one of the parties to it is also a party to an illegal contract which is remotely connected with the first. Thus a policy of marine insurance on a voyage is not illegal merely because the master has incurred statutory penalties through failing to make the service contracts with his crew in proper form[9]; and a policy of insurance on goods is not

---

93 s.77, as amended by Sex Discrimination Act 1986, s.6.
94 s.72(5).
95 s.9(2)(*a*).
96 s.9(2).
97 *Ante*, p. 245.
98 s.26.
99 *De Begnis* v. *Armistead* (1833) 10 Bing. 107; *M'Kinnell* v. *Robinson* (1838) 3 M. & W. 434.
1 *Cannan* v. *Bryce* (1819) 3 B. & Ald. 179, as explained in *Spector* v. *Ageda* [1973] Ch. 30.
2 *Spector* v. *Ageda, supra.*
3 *Toulmin* v. *Anderson* (1808) 1 Taunt. 227; contrast Financial Services Act 1986, s.132(6) (reinsurance of prohibited insurance).
4 *Fisher* v. *Bridges* (1854) 3 E. & B. 642 (bond); *Clugas* v. *Penaluna* (1791) 4 T.R. 466 (bill of exchange); as to the rights of a holder in due course, see *post*, p. 595, *Taylor* v. *Chester* (1869) L.R. 4 Q.B. 309 (pledge). Contrast *Sharif* v. *Azad* [1967] 1 Q.B. 605 as explained in *Mansouri* v. *Singh* [1986] 1 W.L.R. 1393.
5 *Ante*, p. 138.
6 *Ante*, pp. 447–448.
7 *The American Accord* [1983] 1 A.C. 168 (where the sale was not illegal but only unenforceable under the Bretton Woods Agreement Act 1945). A cheque given in pursuance of such a transaction is likewise unenforceable between the parties to the transaction: *Mansouri* v. *Singh* [1986] 1 W.L.R. 1393.
8 *South Western Mineral Water Co. Ltd.* v. *Ashmore* [1967] 1 W.L.R. 1110; *cf. Carney* v. *Herbert* [1985] A.C. 301; *ante*, p. 452.
9 *Redmond* v. *Smith* (1844) 7 Man. & G. 457.

illegal merely because, in the course of acquiring the goods, the insured had committed a violation of a foreign revenue law.[10] The first contract in these cases will only be illegal if its object was to assist one of the parties in achieving the unlawful purpose under the second contract.[11]

An innocent party to an illegal contract can sometimes recover damages for breach of a "collateral warranty" that the contract was lawful.[12] Such a collateral warranty is not really a separate collateral transaction, but a device invented by law for the protection of an innocent party to an illegal contract.

[10] *Euro-Diam Ltd.* v. *Bathurst* [1990] Q.B. 1; the violation of the foreign law did not benefit the insured but only benefited his supplier; Clarke, [1988] L.M.C. L.Q. 124; Tan, 104 L.Q.R. 523; Tettenborn, [1988] C.L.J. 338.

[11] *See Re Trepca Mines Ltd.* [1963] Ch. 199; A.L.G. 79 L.Q.R. 49; *cf.* [1974] 6 C.L. 266; see now Courts and Legal Services Act 1990, s.58.

[12] *Ante*, p. 434.

CHAPTER TWELVE

STATUTORY INVALIDITY

SECTION 1. IN GENERAL

WHERE a statute prohibits or regulates the making or performance of a contract, breach of the statute may make the contract illegal, void or unenforceable, or leave it perfectly valid. If the breach of the statute amounts to a crime, the effects of its breach depend on the principles discussed in Chapter 11.[1] Apart from these principles, the effect of a breach of a statute depends primarily on its express provisions, which may, for example, make the contract (or the offending term[2]) void[3] or unenforceable.[4] The most difficult cases are those in which the statute gives no clear lead. They may be divided into three groups.

1. "Void" Contracts held to be Illegal

Section 1 of the Life Assurance Act 1774 provides that "no insurance shall be made" by any person on the life of another, or on certain other risks, unless the assured has an interest in the subject-matter of the insurance. Contracts of insurance made in breach of this section are declared to be "void" but have repeatedly been held illegal.[5] The position was the same under section 1 of the Marine Insurance Act 1745, which provided that "no assurance shall be made" on the terms that no further proof of interest than the policy should be required. Policies made in breach of the section were declared to be "void" but held illegal.[6] But when the section was replaced by section 4(1) of the Marine Insurance Act 1906, which simply made such policies void, it was held that they were no longer illegal.[7] The reason for this distinction seems to be that the older Acts first prohibited the contracts (though without penalty) and then declared them void, while the Act of 1906 contains no prohibition but only a declaration of nullity.

---

[1] *Ante*, pp. 378–386.

[2] *e.g.* Sex Discrimination Act 1975, s.77(1) and (2); Race Relations Act 1977, s.72(1) and (2)—"void" but only "unenforceable against" the victim of unlawful discrimination: see *Orphanos* v. *Queen Mary College* [1985] A.C. 761, and *ante*, p. 433.

[3] *e.g.* Resale Prices Act 1976, s.9(1) and (2), making a term or practice "unlawful"—but not criminal; *cf.* Restrictive Trade Practices Act 1976, s.35(1)(*a*), (*b*) ("void," but not criminal: s.35(2)); Matrimonial Causes Act 1973, s.34 (*ante*, p. 395); Insurance Companies Act 1982, s.36 ("void").

[4] Either in so many words (*e.g.* Consumer Credit Act 1974, s.40(1)), Financial Services Act 1986, ss.5, 6, 56, 57, 131, 132) or by saying that "no action shall be brought," or by use of similar expressions: *e.g.* Statute of Frauds 1677, s.4; *ante*, p. 170.

[5] *Harse* v. *Pearl Life Assurance Co.* [1904] 1 K.B. 558; *Hughes* v. *Liverpool Victoria Legal Friendly Society* [1916] 2 K.B. 482; *Re London County Commercial Reinsurance Office* [1922] 2 Ch. 67.

[6] *Lowry* v. *Bourdieu* (1780) 2 Dougl. 468; *Allkins* v. *Jupe* (1877) 2 C.P.D. 375; *Gedge* v. *Royal Exchange Assurance* [1900] 2 Q.B. 214; *contra*, *Tasker* v. *Scott* (1815) 6 Taunt. 234.

[7] *Re London County Commercial Reinsurance Office* [1922] 2 Ch. 67.

2. Consequences of Breach Not Specified

A statute may prohibit the making of a contract without imposing a criminal penalty or specifying all the civil consequences of breach. For example, section 716 of the Companies Act 1985[8] provides that (subject to certain important exceptions)[9] "No company, association, or partnership . . . shall be formed" consisting of more than 20 persons, unless it is registered under the Act. No penalty is imposed for breach of the section but unregistered associations of more than 20 persons have for some purposes been regarded as illegal associations.[10]

3. Formalities Required by Statute

A statute may require some formalities to be observed in making a contract, or require some specific terms to be inserted into the contract, and again fail to specify the consequences of breach.[11] In such cases the question is whether the statutory requirement is to be construed as being "directory only or obligatory."[12] Failure to comply with the statute makes the contract void if the requirement is obligatory, but not if it is only directory. In the case in which the distinction was drawn, statutory requirements as to the execution of a mortgage of a ship were held to be obligatory. Failure to comply with them accordingly invalidated the transaction though this effect of the failure was not specified in the legislation.[13] It seems that in applying the distinction the court will ask whether it is necessary, to promote the object of the statute, to hold that failure to comply with its requirements should invalidate transactions.[14]

SECTION 2. GAMING AND WAGERING CONTRACTS

1. Definitions

(1) Wagering contracts

In *Carlill* v. *Carbolic Smoke Ball Co.*[15] Hawkins J. said: "A wagering contract is one by which two persons, professing to hold opposite views touching the issue of a future uncertain event, mutually agree that, dependent upon the determination of that event, one shall win from the other, and that other shall pay or hand over to him, a sum of money or other stake; neither of the contracting parties having any other interest in that contract than the sum or stake he will so win or lose, there being no other real consideration for the making of such contract by either of the parties." The following points arising out of this definition call for comment.

(a) FUTURE UNCERTAIN EVENT. A wager is generally made on a future event but can equally well be made on a past event which is not, objec-

[8] As amended by Companies Act 1989, s.145 and Sched. 19 para. 15(1) and 2.

[9] *i.e.* partnerships of solicitors, accountants, members of recognised stock exchanges and other partnerships specified by statutory instrument.

[10] *Sykes* v. *Beadon* (1897) 11 Ch.D. 170; disapproved in *Smith* v. *Anderson* (1880) 15 Ch.D. 247, but not on this point: *Shaw* v. *Benson* (1883) 11 Q.B.D. 563; *cf. Greenberg* v. *Cooperstein* [1926] Ch. 657.

[11] See *ante*, pp. 162–164 for cases in which the statute does specify the effects of non-compliance.

[12] *Liverpool Borough Bank* v. *Turner* (1860) 2 D.F. & J. 502, 508.

[13] *Liverpool Borough Bank* v. *Turner* (1860) 2 D.F. & J. 502.

[14] *Cf. St. John Shipping Corp.* v. *Joseph Rank Ltd.* [1957] 1 Q.B. 267; *ante*, p. 377.

[15] [1892] 2 Q.B. 484, 490; affirmed [1893] 1 Q.B. 256.

tively, uncertain at all, *e.g.* which horse won the Derby last year[16]; or on the question whether the earth is flat.[17] The event need only be "uncertain" in the sense that the parties profess to hold opposite views on it. It has been suggested that there cannot be a wager on an event which is wholly within the control of one party.[18] But if A says that he will wear a red tie tomorrow, it is perfectly possible for B to bet him that he will not do so; and it is hard to see why the resulting contract should not be described as a wager.

(b) ONE TO LOSE, OTHER TO WIN. A contract is not a wager if one party cannot win or if one party cannot lose. Thus in *Carlill* v. *Carbolic Smoke Ball Co.*[19] the defendants promised to pay £100 to anyone who, after using a smoke-ball manufactured by them, caught influenza. This was not a wager because the user of the smoke-ball could not lose anything if he failed to catch influenza. Similarly, in *Ellesmere* v. *Wallace*[20] the defendant entered his horse for two races under contracts made with the Jockey Club. If he won the first race, he was entitled to £200 put up by the Club plus the stakes of the other nominators. If he won the second, he was entitled to £200 put up by the Club plus the right to sell his horse by auction for £300. These contracts were not wagers because the Club could lose nothing on the outcome of the races: it paid the £200 to the winner, whoever he was. Similarly, persons who contribute to a totalisator[21] or football pool[22] or who take part in a bingo competition[23] do not wager with the person who runs it, since he merely distributes a predetermined proportion of the total stakes among the winners.[24] And persons who participate in a whist drive at which they can win prizes contributed by third parties do not wager because they cannot lose.[25]

(c) BETWEEN TWO PERSONS. It has been said that there can only be two parties to a wager, or that, if there are more than two, they must be divided into two sides.[26] Thus if A and B bet on the result of an election in which there are two candidates, the contract is a wager. But if A, B and C bet on the result of an election in which there are three candidates, each contributing his stake to a common fund to be paid over to the person whose forecast is correct, the contract is not a wager. The authorities seem to support this distinction, though it is hard to see why the two cases should be treated differently.

---

16 *Cf. Pugh* v. *Jenkins* (1841) 1 Q.B. 631; *Rourke* v. *Short* (1856) 5 E. & B. 904 (*post*, p. 459).
17 *Hampden* v. *Walsh* (1876) 1 Q.B.D. 189.
18 *Ellesmere* v. *Wallace* [1926] 2 Ch. 1, 29.
19 [1893] 1 Q.B. 256. See also *Kloeckner & Co. A.G.* v. *Gatoil Overseas Inc.* [1990] 1 Lloyd's Rep. 177 (agent could not lose as he was remunerated by commission payable in any event); contrast *Richards* v. *Starck* [1911] 1 K.B. 296 (risk of losing interest on money sufficient to make transaction a wager).
20 [1929] 2 Ch. 1.
21 *Cf. Tote Investors Ltd.* v. *Smoker* [1968] 1 Q.B. 509 (but Lord Denning M.R. and Lord Pearson said at pp. 515, 520 that, apart from authority, they would have regarded such transactions as wagers).
22 But where the agreements between the promoters of the pool and the participants contain honour clauses they are not legally binding: *ante*, p. 150.
23 See *Peck* v. *Lateu*, *The Times*, January 18, 1973.
24 *Att.-Gen.* v. *Luncheon & Sports Club Ltd.* [1929] A.C. 400.
25 *Lockwood* v. *Cooper* [1903] 2 K.B. 428.
26 *Ellesmere* v. *Wallace* [1929] 2 Ch. at p. 50; this is another reason why contributors to a totalisator or football pool or participants in a bingo competition do not wager with each other.

(d) NO OTHER INTEREST. A contract is not a wager if the party to whom money is promised on the occurrence of an event has an "interest" in its non-occurrence. Hence contracts of insurance are not wagers if the insured person has some enforceable right or interest (whether contractual or proprietary) in the subject-matter.[27] So long as the insured has an insurable interest, the contract is not a wager merely because the interest is insured for more than its true value.[28] If he has no such interest at all, the contract may be a wager, though this is not necessarily the case since insurer and insured do not necessarily profess to hold opposite views concerning the event insured against. Whether the contract is a wager or not, an insurance without interest is void and may be illegal by statute.[29] Thus a person cannot make a valid contract to insure a third person's property, unless it is pledged to him for a debt: for example, the assets of a company cannot be insured by its principal or even by its sole shareholder.[30] A person cannot in theory insure a mere expectation of benefit, however strong it may be.[31] But "there are many risks which cannot be regarded as legal or equitable in character, but which are not the less real from a business point of view, and which it is therefore important to cover."[32] Policies covering such risks are binding in honour only, but the insurers in practice pay on them in spite of the theoretical lack of interest.

Although a mere expectation of benefit in the commercial sense cannot be insured, it is possible to insure a hope of benefit if it is founded on a legal right. Thus the owner of an orchard can insure "next year's apple crop"[33]; and a person who holds shares in a company can insure against the failure of an enterprise in which the company is engaged.[34]

In cases of life insurance, the interest insured is not strictly proprietary. A man can insure his own life[35] or the life of any relation who is legally bound to support him[36]; and the life of his debtor.[37] Spouses can also insure each other's lives.[38]

A contract may be a wager although it concerns the property of one of the parties. Thus it is a wager for a man to bet on his own horse in a race.[39] The owner has an interest, but it is not the object of the contract to protect that interest. There seems to be no objection in principle to the owner's insuring the prize which his horse may win: this is not necessarily different from insuring a future crop.

(e) NO OTHER REAL CONSIDERATION. Attempts are sometimes made to pass off as valid contracts transactions which are in substance wagers. In

---

[27] *Cf. Wilson* v. *Jones* (1867) L.R. 2 Ex. 139, 150.
[28] *The Maira* (*No.* 2) [1984] 1 Lloyd's Rep. 660, 662, reversed [1986] 2 Lloyd's Rep. 12, but not on this point: see *ibid.* p. 17.
[29] *e.g.* Marine Insurance (Gambling Policies) Act 1909; *cf. ante*, p. 455.
[30] *Macaura* v. *Northern Assurance Co. Ltd.* [1925] A.C. 619.
[31] *Lucena* v. *Craufurd* (1806) 2 B. & P.N.R. 269.
[32] Arnould, *Marine Insurance*, (16th ed.), p. 15; *cf. Strass* v. *Spillers & Bakers Ltd.* [1911] 2 K.B. 759, 768–9.
[33] *Thacker* v. *Hardy* (1878) 4 Q.B.D. 685, 695; *cf. Cook* v. *Field* (1850) 15 Q.B. 460.
[34] *Wilson* v. *Jones* (1867) L.R. 2 Ex. 139.
[35] *Wainwright* v. *Bland* (1835) 1 Moo. & Rob. 481; (1836) 1 M. & W. 32.
[36] Colinvaux, *Laws of Insurance* (5th ed.), p. 339.
[37] *Von Lindenau* v. *Desborough* (1828) 3 C. & P. 353.
[38] *Griffiths* v. *Fleming* [1909] 1 K.B. 805.
[39] *Carlill* v. *Carbolic Smoke Ball Co.* [1892] 2 Q.B. 484, 492.

Brogden v. *Marriott*[40] the defendant sold a horse to the plaintiff on the terms that if the horse trotted at 18 miles per hour within a month the price was to be £200; if not the price was to be 1s. This was a wager: in effect the defendant staked his horse against £200 on the result of a trotting match.[41] Similarly, in *Rourke* v. *Short*[42] the plaintiff agreed to sell rags to the defendant. In the course of fixing the price, the parties began to argue about the price of a previous lot of rags, the plaintiff maintaining that it had been 5s. 9d. per cwt. and the defendant that it had been 6s. This dispute was referred to a third party (who was to receive one gallon of brandy for deciding it) and it was agreed that the price of the present lot was to be 6s. per cwt. if the plaintiff was right, and 3s. per cwt. if the defendant was right. This was held to be a wager on the price of the previous lot. There could be a perfectly genuine bargain for the price of goods to be fixed by reference to that paid for a previous lot. But that was not the bargain here, "for the lower the former price was, the higher the present price is to be."[43]

These cases should be contrasted with the Irish case of *Crofton* v. *Colgan*,[44] where the plaintiff exchanged his horse for the defendant's, who also agreed to pay the plaintiff half the former horse's winnings in its next two races. This was held to be a valid contract, in which the price was made to depend on the horse's profit-earning capacity.

It is, again, possible to contract to pay a reward to a person for making some discovery, or for proving a particular hypothesis. But in *Hampden* v. *Walsh*[45] the plaintiff, who believed that the earth was flat, offered a reward of £500 to any person who could satisfactorily prove the curvature of the earth by actual measurement. This was held to be a wager since the plaintiff's object was not to establish a scientific fact but "to establish his own view in a marked and triumphant manner."[46]

The most important group of contracts which may in substance amount to wagers are contracts for differences.[47] A person may buy shares or commodities on the understanding that they are neither to be transferred nor paid for but that on settlement day one party shall pay to the other the difference between the price on that day and the price on the contract day. Such a contract is a wager.[48] But it is not a wager if a person who has genuinely bought resells to the original seller, and the parties then settle accounts by agreeing that only the difference resulting from the two transactions shall change hands.[49] Many contracts for differences are now bind-

---

40 (1836) 3 Bing.N.C. 88.

41 For an undisguised wager on such a match, see *Batson* v. *Newman* (1876) 1 C.P.D. 573.

42 (1856) 5 E. & B. 904.

43 *Ibid.* p. 912.

44 (1859) 10 Ir.C.L.R. 133.

45 (1876) 1 Q.B.D. 189.

46 *Ibid.* p. 197.

47 Chaikin and Moher, [1986] L.M.C.L.Q. 390.

48 *Universal Stock Exchange Ltd.* v. *Strachan* [1896] A.C. 166; *Re Gieve* [1899] 1 Q.B. 794; *cf. Re The Futures Index* [1985] F.L.R. 147. If the proceeds of the transaction are "winnings from betting" they are not subject to Capital Gains Tax: Capital Gains Tax Act 1979, s.19(4). Under Licensed Dealers (Conduct of Business) Rules (1983 S.I. No. 585), r. 18(2), a licensed dealer (in securities) may not plead the Gaming Act.

49 *Grizewood* v. *Blane* (1851) 11 C.B. 526; *The Filipinas I* [1973] 1 Lloyd's Rep. 349, 357; *Wilson, Smithett & Cope Ltd.* v. *Teruzzi* [1976] Q.B. 683, 710; *Kloeckner A.G.* v. *Gatoil Overseas Inc.* [1990] 1 Lloyd's Rep. 177.

ing by statute, even if they are wagers[50]; but our present concern is with the question whether such a contract is a wager.

In many of the above cases the question whether a contract is a wager or a genuine transaction depended on the intention of the parties. The parties may have different intentions: for example, one may intend to make a contract for differences and the other a real sale. Such a contract is not a wager.[51]

(2) Gaming

(a) Definitions. "Gaming" has been judicially defined to mean the playing of any game for money or money's worth[52]; and for this purpose a "game" includes horse-racing.[53] A gaming contract[54] is simply a contract to take part in such gaming. It is not necessarily a wager since there may be more than two parties to it. If persons other than the participants in a game bet on its outcome, their contract is not a gaming contract, but it may be a wager on a game.[55]

Many kinds of gaming and wagers on games are regulated by various statutes.[56] The Gaming Act 1968 defines "gaming" as "the playing of any game of chance for winnings in money or money's worth, whether any person playing the game is at risk of losing money or money's worth or not."[57] This definition is narrower than the judicial definition in that it is limited to games *of chance*.[58] The judicial definition still applies in relation to enactments which use the word "gaming" without defining it.[59]

(b) Lawful and unlawful gaming. The 1968 Act defines the circumstances in which gaming is *unlawful*. For this purpose it distinguishes gaming on licensed or registered premises (which may be carried on for profit) from gaming elsewhere (which may not be carried on for profit).[60] The Act provides that "no gaming . . . shall take place" under certain conditions:

---

50 Financial Services Act 1986, s.63; *post*, pp. 463, 467; *cf.* the *Kloeckner* case, *supra*, n. 49, at p. 193.

51 *Thacker* v. *Hardy* (1878) 4 Q.B.D. 685; *Weddle, Beck & Co.* v. *Hackett* [1929] 1 K.B. 321.

52 *Ellesmere* v. *Wallace* [1929] 2 Ch. 1, 55 (but see also *ibid.* p. 28); *Ankers* v. *Bartlett* [1936] 1 K.B. 147.

53 *Applegarth* v. *Colley* (1842) 10 M. & W. 723; presumably other kinds of racing could also fall within the definition.

54 There seems to be no difference between a gaming contract and a "contract by way of gaming" within s.18 of the Gaming Act 1845; *post*, p. 462.

55 This depends on whether the elements of the definition discussed at pp. 456–460, *ante*, are satisfied: *e.g.* the contract will not be a wager if there are more than two sides or if one party cannot lose.

56 Particularly by the Betting, Gaming and Lotteries Acts 1963–1971, the Gaming Act 1968 (as amended by Gaming (Amendment) Act 1986, Gaming (Amendment) Act 1987 and Gaming Act 1990) and the Lotteries and Amusements Act 1976.

57 s.52(1); the object of the concluding words ("whether . . . not.") was to reverse the decision in *McCollom* v. *Wrightson* [1968] A.C. 522.

58 Defined by s.52(1) to include "a game of chance and skill combined and a pretended game of chance or of chance and skill combined." The possibility that the element of chance may be eliminated by "superlative skill" is to be disregarded: s.52(6). An "athletic game or sport" is not a game of chance: s.52(1).

59 *e.g.* Gaming Act 1845, s.18 (*post*, p. 462); *cf.* Gaming Act 1710 (*post*, p. 469).

60 See s.1 and Pts. 1 and 2 respectively. For the distinction between licensed and registered premises, see s.11 and Scheds. 3 and 4. Roughly speaking, licensed premises are casinos established principally for commercial gambling while registered premises are clubs established for other purposes which also wish to make a sessional charge for gambling but not to profit from it in other ways.

i.e. if the game involves staking against a bank; or if the chances are not equally favourable to all the players; or if the chances lie between the player or players and some other person and are not as favourable to the player or players as they are to that person; or if a charge other than the stake is made in respect of the gaming; or if a levy is made on the stakes or winnings.[61] But these conditions are subject to a number of qualifications and exceptions; and in particular they may be relaxed in the case of gaming on licensed or registered premises so as to enable the gaming to be carried on at a profit.[62] Gaming in streets or public places is also prohibited.[63] The definition of *unlawful* gaming in the Act is exhaustive; the previous common law and statutory definitions of unlawful gaming no longer apply.[64]

The 1968 Act does not, except in one section,[65] affect the law as to gaming and wagering *contracts*; but it has indirect repercussions on the law of contract in that the effect of a gaming contract or of a wager on a game sometimes depends on the legality of the gaming.

2. Effects of Gaming and Wagering Contracts

(1) Enforcement

(a) AT COMMON LAW wagers were valid and could thus be enforced by the winner.[66] This rule was not much liked by the courts, who refused to enforce wagers on many grounds. Some wagers were illegal: these included wagers on unlawful games[67]; wagers that one of the parties would commit a legal wrong or do an immoral act; wagers which affected the interests and feelings of a third person so as to make a breach of the peace likely; and wagers which were "against sound policy."[68] Thus the following wagers were held void: a wager that peace between England and France would be concluded by September 1797[69]; a wager on the life of Napoleon in time of peace[70]; a wager tending to cause public disorder[71]; a wager with voters in a constituency as to the outcome of an election in that constituency—an obvious cloak for bribery[72]; and a wager on the sex of a living person suspected to be masquerading as a man.[73] The courts also sometimes simply

---

61 See ss.2(1), 3(1), 4, 13(1), 14(1) and 15(1); and regulations made under ss.13–15.

62 See ss.13(2), 14(2) and 15(2). See also s.6 for special exceptions with regard to certain games played in public houses.

63 s.5.

64 This is not expressly provided by any section of the 1968 Act but is the effect of s.32(1) of the Betting, Gaming and Lotteries Act 1963. The repeal of this subsection by s.53(1) of the 1968 Act does not revive the previous statutory and common law rules as to what constituted unlawful gaming: see Interpretation Act 1978, ss.15, 16.

65 s.16 (as amended by Gaming (Amendment) Act 1986) *post*, pp. 471–472, 476–477.

66 *Micklefield* v. *Hipgin* (1760) 1 Anst. 33; *Good* v. *Elliott* (1790) 3 T.R. 693; *Hussey* v. *Crickitt* (1811) 3 Camp. 168.

67 See now *ante*, pp. 460–461. At common law, cock-fighting, card games other than those of mere skill and (probably) all games of chance were unlawful: *Jenks* v. *Turpin* (1884) 13 Q.B.D. 505, 524.

68 *Good* v. *Elliott* (1790) 3 T.R. 693, 695.

69 *Lacaussade* v. *White* (1798) 2 Esp. 629 (as to recovery of money under illegal contract, overruled in *Vandyck* v. *Hewitt* (1800) 1 East 96).

70 *Gilbert* v. *Sykes* (1812) 16 East 150: because this might lead to his assassination (which would be "against sound policy" in time of peace) or to his preservation (which would be "against sound policy" in time of war).

71 *Eltham* v. *Kingsman* (1818) 1 B. & Ald. 683.

72 *Allen* v. *Hearn* (1785) 1 T.R. 56.

73 *Da Costa* v. *Jones* (1778) 2 Cowp. 729.

refused to enforce a wager on the ground that it was an "idle wager" and that it was a waste of the court's time to entertain an action on it.[74] Thus the courts refused to enforce a wager "on the number of ways of nicking 7 on the dice"[75]; a wager, made between persons who had no pecuniary interest in the matter, that the next child of an unmarried woman would be a boy,[76] and a wager on an abstract question of law in which the parties had only an academic interest.[77]

(b) BY STATUTE. Section 18 of the Gaming Act 1845 provides that "All contracts or agreements . . . by way of gaming or wagering shall be null and void; and . . . no suit shall be brought or maintained in any court of law or equity for recovering any sum of money or valuable thing alleged to be won upon any wager. . . . "[78] It follows that the winner cannot enforce the wager by action.[79] It used to be thought that this was the sole effect of the section, and that the loser could be sued if he made a fresh promise, supported by fresh consideration, to pay the amount of the lost bet. In *Hyams* v. *Stuart King*[80] the loser of bets on horse-races made a fresh promise to pay in consideration of the winner's promise not to post him as a defaulter. The Court of Appeal held that the winner could enforce this promise. But this case was overruled by the House of Lords in *Hill* v. *William Hill (Park Lane) Ltd.*[81] It was held, on similar facts, that the winner could not enforce the loser's fresh promise because the second sentence of section 18 prevented the recovery of money alleged to have been won on a wager, whether or not the action was brought on the wagering contract. The fresh promise to pay, though not void by the first limb of the section, was unenforceable by its second limb.

The courts have always resisted attempts indirectly to enforce the wagering contract itself, and have, since *Hill*'s case, resisted attempts to evade the effect of that decision. Thus the winner cannot recover by suing on an account stated[82] or by getting a third party to promise to pay, in return for the winner's promise not to post the loser as a defaulter.[83] The use of such devices came to an abrupt stop after it was held that a solicitor who indorsed a writ based in substance on a wager as a claim on an account stated was guilty of contempt of court, and liable to be imprisoned for having tried to deceive the court.[84] But there may still be three types of cases which are not within section 18.

First, the loser may promise the winner to *sell him something at an undervalue* in return for the winner's promise not to post him as a defaulter. It would be a question of fact whether an action brought to enforce the loser's promise would be one to recover a valuable thing alleged to be won on a wager; and the court "will not be deceived by any

---

74 *Robinson* v. *Mearns* (1825) 6 D. & R.K.B. 26, 27.
75 *Brown* v. *Leeson* (1792) 2 H.Bl. 43.
76 *Ditchburn* v. *Goldsmith* (1815) 4 Camp. 152.
77 *Henkin* v. *Gerss* (1810) 2 Camp. 408.
78 See further *post*, pp. 464, 467, 468.
79 The court can take this point of its own motion, although the loser does not plead the section: *Luckett* v. *Wood* (1908) 24 T.L.R. 617; *Société des Hôtels Réunis (S.A.)* v. *Hawker* (1913) 29 T.L.R. 578. *Semble*, the loser could also obtain a declaration of invalidity.
80 [1908] 2 K.B. 696.
81 [1949] A.C. 530.
82 *Law* v. *Dearnley* [1950] 1 K.B. 400.
83 *Coral* v. *Kleyman* [1951] 1 All E.R. 518.
84 *R.* v. *Weisz* [1951] 2 K.B. 611. See also *L.S.Gaz.* January 1952, p. 17.

specious attempt to conceal the real nature of the promise."[85] If A, having defaulted on a bet of £300 to B and been threatened with exposure, agrees to sell B a car worth £1,000 for £700, and the contract shows a deduction of the £300 lost on the bet, it is clear that B could not enforce the contract. But it does not follow that "there can never be a case where a promise by a defaulting backer given in consideration of a promise by the winner of the bet not to report the defaulter may be enforced."[86]

Secondly, the loser may *bargain for time to pay*, without asking to be released from the debt of honour incurred under the bet. Thus A, having lost a bet of £1,000 to B, may promise to pay B £50 in return for B's promise not to report A as a defaulter for one month. An action to recover this £50 might not be an action "for recovering any sum of money . . . alleged to be won upon any wager."

Thirdly, the first limb of section 18 makes void *all* contracts by way of gaming and wagering but the second limb only precludes the recovery of *money or a valuable thing*. If the loser, in consideration of the winner's promise not to post him as a defaulter, promises to render some *service* to the winner, this promise may not be within section 18.[87]

In the cases in which a new promise can still be enforced, this can only be done subject to the restrictions which, before *Hill*'s case, had been placed on the rule in *Hyams* v. *Stuart King*. The winner must *promise* not to post the loser as a defaulter; it is not enough for him simply to refrain from posting,[88] nor for him to promise not to *sue* the loser, for a promise not to enforce a claim known to be invalid is no consideration.[89] It is also clear that the new promise would not be enforced if it had been obtained by threats amounting to blackmail.[90]

Certain dealings in investments by way of business are excepted from invalidity under section 18 of the Gaming Act 1845 even though they might amount to wagering contracts, *e.g.* because they were contracts for differences.[91]

(2) Recovering back money paid

(a) AT COMMON LAW. At common law a loser could not recover back money paid under a lost bet.[92] Money paid under a valid or unenforceable contract clearly cannot be recovered back, and money paid under an illegal contract is, in general, irrecoverable,[93] although there are exceptions to this rule. But there is no reported case in which the loser was able to rely on any of these exceptions to recover back his losses from the winner.

---

[85] *Hill's Case* [1949] A.C. 530, 559; *cf.* 549, 565; *Re Browne* [1960] 1 W.L.R. 692.

[86] [1949] A.C. at p. 559; *cf. Re Browne* [1904] 2 K.B. 133; discussed in *Hill*'s case at pp. 564–566, 573–574.

[87] The third limb of s.18 (*post*, pp. 467–468) makes it clear that services cannot be a "valuable thing" within s.18; for the "thing" must be of a kind that can be deposited.

[88] *Bob Guiness Ltd.* v. *Salomonsen* [1948] 2 K.B. 42; the case may be reconciled with the rule that actual forbearance to *sue* (without a promise) is good consideration along the lines suggested at pp. 84–85, *ante*.

[89] *Poteliakhoff* v. *Teakle* [1938] 2 K.B. 816. But there might be consideration if the validity of the claim was in doubt, *e.g.* because it was not clear whether the original transaction was a wager.

[90] As defined by Theft Act 1968, s.21

[91] Financial Services Act 1986, s.63 and Sched. 1 paras. 9, 12; *City Index Ltd.* v. *Leslie* [1991] N.L.J.R. 419; for contracts for differences, see *ante*, p. 459.

[92] *Howson* v. *Hancock* (1800) 8 T.R. 575; *Vandyck* v. *Hewitt* (1800) 1 East 96.

[93] *Lowry* v. *Bourdieu* (1780) 2 Dougl. 468.

(b) UNDER THE GAMING ACT 1845. Prima facie money paid under a void contract can be recovered back.[94] Thus in *Re London County Commercial Reinsurance Office*[95] it was held that premiums paid under marine policies which were, or were deemed to be, wagers, and void under section 4 of the Marine Insurance Act 1906, could be recovered back. But it is generally agreed that losses paid under a simple wager are irrecoverable. One possible reason for this rule is that, under the second limb of section 18, a person cannot bring an action to recover "any sum of money . . . alleged to have been won on a wager." But it has been said that the second limb only prevents the winner from recovering, and does not apply to an action by the loser.[96] If this is so, the only reason for the rule is that the loser, by paying, "waives a benefit which the statute has given him and confers a good title to the money on the person to whom he pays it."[97] If the winner cheats, the loser can probably recover back his losses on the ground of fraud.[98]

(c) OVERPAYMENT. It has been held that an overpayment by a bookmaker to his client in respect of a wager cannot be recovered back.[99] But if the client knows when he receives the payment that it is excessive and decides to keep it, he is guilty of theft[1]; and the court by or before which he is convicted can presumably make a compensation order against him.[2]

(3) Recovering back money or property deposited

One party to a wager may deposit a sum of money or other valuable thing with the other before the determination of the wager, as security for the performance of his undertaking.[3]

(a) ILLEGAL WAGERS. Such a deposit is irrecoverable if it was made under an illegal wager,[4] because of the general rule that money paid under an illegal contract cannot be recovered back.[5] But it may be recoverable under one of the exceptions to that rule, *e.g.*, if the depositor repudiates the wager in time.[6] Whether it is actually recoverable then depends on the rules applicable to lawful wagers, discussed below.

(b) LAWFUL WAGERS. Where the wager is lawful,[7] a deposit can, in general, be recovered back by the winner. Thus in *Re Cronmire*[8] Waud

94 *Post*, p. 933.
95 [1922] 2 Ch. 67.
96 *Varney* v. *Hickman* (1847) 5 C.B. 271, 280.
97 *Bridger* v. *Savage* (1884) 15 Q.B.D. 363, 367; *cf. Richards* v. *Stark* [1911] 1 K.B. 296 (losses paid in advance irrecoverable).
98 This was the common law position: *Dufour* v. *Ackland* (1830) 9 L.J.(o.s.) K.B. 3. For a review of conflicting American decisions, see *Berman* v. *Riverside Casino Corp.*, 323F. 2d 977 (1963), where it was alleged that loaded dice had been used in a Nevada casino.
99 *Morgan* v. *Ashcroft* [1938] 1 K.B. 49.
1 *R.* v. *Gilks* [1972] 1 W.L.R. 1341.
2 Powers of Criminal Courts Act 1973, s.35, as amended by Criminal Justice Act 1988, s.104; *ante*, p. 329.
3 For the position where the deposit is made with a third person as stakeholder, see *post*, p. 467.
4 See *ante*, p. 461.
5 *Ante*, p. 436.
6 *Ante*, p. 439; *Tappenden* v. *Randall* (1801) 2 B. & P. 467; *Aubert* v. *Walsh* (1810) 3 Taunt. 277.
7 A wager is lawful unless it falls into one of the categories of illegal wagers described on p. 461, *ante*.
8 [1898] 2 Q.B. 383.

deposited £60 with Cronmire by way of "cover" for gambling transactions on the Stock Exchange, which resulted to Waud's advantage. It was held that he could recover back his £60.

The question whether a deposit can be recovered back by the loser raises more complicated issues, which may be illustrated by reference to the two *Strachan* cases, both of which arose out of the same transactions. Strachan engaged in gambling transactions on the Stock Exchange with a company. He deposited securities and £3,000 in cash by way of "cover," and lost heavily. The House of Lords held that he was entitled to recover back his securities since they were deposited to secure payment of a void debt.[9] But the Court of Appeal held, on another appeal,[10] that the £3,000 deposited in cash was irrecoverable as it had actually been appropriated by the company in discharge of Strachan's "indebtedness." It seems that Strachan could not have recovered the securities if the contract had authorised the company to realise them and if the company had done so and appropriated the proceeds in discharge of Strachan's "indebtedness." It seems also that Strachan could have recovered back the £3,000, had he demanded it back before appropriation of it in discharge of any "indebtedness" under the gambling transactions, *e.g.* if he had made the demand before those transactions had been determined. Thus in *Re the Futures Index*,[11] a bookmaker took sums of money from a client on account of possible future losses. On the bookmaker's going into liquidation, it was held that the sums could be recovered back by the client in so far as they had not yet been appropriated to any wager.

(4) Principal and agent

(a) FAILURE TO OBEY INSTRUCTIONS. An agent who undertakes to make a bet on behalf of his principal is not liable for failing to do so.[12] In *Cohen* v. *Kittell* the reason for this rule was said to be that the principal suffered "no real loss"[13] since he could not have enforced the bet even if it had been made. But the rule applies even though it is clearly proved that the bet would have been paid, had it been made and won. It seems that the better reason for the rule is that "A contract declared by the law to be null and void cannot be either directly or indirectly the basis of a legal claim."[14] An agent is similarly not liable if he makes a bet in a way forbidden by his instructions. In *A. R. Dennis & Co. Ltd.* v. *Campbell*[15] the manager of a licensed betting shop, contrary to his instructions, allowed a customer to place bets on credit to the extent of £1,000. On the customer's failure to pay the bets after he had lost them, it was held that the manager could not be sued by his employers for the £1,000. Even if the employers could prove

---

[9] *Universal Stock Exchange Ltd.* v. *Strachan* [1896] A.C. 166.

[10] *Strachan* v. *Universal Stock Exchange Ltd.* (*No.* 2) [1895] 2 Q.B. 697.

[11] [1985] F.L.R. 147.

[12] *Cohen* v. *Kittell* (1889) 22 Q.B. 680.

[13] *Ibid.* p. 684.

[14] *Cheshire & Co.* v. *Vaughan Bros. & Co.* [1920] 3 K.B. 240, 254. Where gaming or wagering is not involved an agent may well be liable for failing to make an invalid contract if it is unlikely that the third party would have repudiated: see *Fraser* v. *B. N. Furman (Productions) Ltd.* [1967] 1 W.L.R. 898; *Everett* v. *Hogg, Robinson & Gardner Mountain Insurance* [1973] 2 Lloyd's Rep. 216; *Dunbar* v. *A & B Painters Ltd.* [1986] 2 Lloyd's Rep. 38.

[15] [1978] Q.B. 365.

that they had lost this amount,[16] the action was barred by the second limb of section 18 of the Gaming Act 1845.

(b) AGENT'S INDEMNITY. The agent may make the bet, lose it, and pay the winner. It was held in *Read* v. *Anderson*[17] that an agent who paid the winner could recover the sum so paid from his principal on the ground that the latter had impliedly contracted to indemnify his agent[18] against liabilities, whether legally enforceable or not, which arose in the ordinary course of business from the execution of his authority.

This decision provided an easy means of evading the Gaming Act 1845: wagers could be enforced against a loser by simply interposing an agent. It was therefore reversed by section 1 of the Gaming Act 1892, which provides: "Any promise, express or implied, to pay any person any sum of money paid by him under or in respect of any contract or agreement rendered null and void by the Gaming Act 1845, or to pay any sum of money by way of commission, fee, reward, or otherwise in respect of any such contract, or of any services in relation thereto or in connection therewith, shall be null and void, and no action shall be brought or maintained to recover any such sum of money."

In *Levy* v. *Warburton*[19] an agent tried to evade this provision by suing his principal before actually paying the winner. But the court rejected his claim, holding that "paid" included "to be paid." In *Law* v. *Dearnley*[20] it was held that an agent cannot evade the Act by suing on an account stated. Tucker L.J., also said that the principle in *Hill* v. *William Hill* (*Park Lane*) *Ltd.*[21] applied to cases falling within the 1892 Act. That Act, however, only deals with promises *to pay money*.[22] Thus it seems that if the principal promised to deliver some *valuable thing* to the agent in return for the latter's promise not to post him as a defaulter, the agent could[23] enforce the principal's promise.

(c) AGENT'S LIABILITY TO ACCOUNT. An agent who made a bet for his principal which the principal won is liable at common law to account to the principal if he received the money won from the loser. This position is not altered by the 1892 Act: the agent is not sued on an implied promise to pay the principal "any sum of money *paid* by him" (the agent) but on an implied promise to pay over a sum of money *received* by him.[24] It was further held in *Bridger* v. *Savage*[25] that the agent's liability to pay over winnings received by him was not affected by section 18 of the Gaming Act 1845. One reason given was that the section struck only at the wagering contract itself, and not at other transactions. But this argument is untenable after *Hill* v. *William Hill* (*Park Lane*) *Ltd.*[26] and it could plausibly be argued that the principal was suing to recover money "alleged to have been

[16] If the credit had not been allowed, it is more probable that the customer would not have made the bet than that he would have made it for cash.
[17] (1884) 13 Q.B.D. 779.
[18] *Post*, p. 646.
[19] (1901) 70 L.J.K.B. 708.
[20] [1950] 1 K.B. 400.
[21] [1949] A.C. 530.
[22] Contrast "sum of money or valuable thing" in Gaming Act 1845, s.18.
[23] Subject to the exceptions stated *ante*
[24] *De Mattos* v. *Benjamin* (1894) 63 L.J.Q.B. 248.
[25] (1884) 15 Q.B.D. 363.
[26] [1949] A.C. 530; *ante*, p. 462.

won upon any wager." On the other hand, it would certainly not defeat the policy of the Gaming Acts to force the agent to account to his principal for money actually received. The policy of the Acts is not to prevent the winner from getting his winnings but to prevent the loser from being *forced* to pay his losses. *Bridger* v. *Savage* can be justified by saying that, once the loser has paid the bets, "any dispute as to their validity [is] gone."[27]

A person may be called an agent, but in fact bet *with* his "principal" and not *for* him. If so, he is an actual party to the bet and is not accountable under the rule in *Bridger* v. *Savage*.[28]

It seems (although the point has not been decided) that the above principles would apply where several persons agreed to make a bet in the name of one of them and to share any winnings. Thus if the person in whose name the bet was made received any sum won he would have to account to the others, unless he had in fact bet with and not for them.[29]

(d) ADVANCE PAYMENT. An agent who makes a bet for his principal may account to the principal for his winnings before he has himself been paid by the loser. If the loser then defaults, the agent cannot recover back the winnings from the principal: the case falls within section 1 of the Act of 1892.[30]

(e) CERTAIN DEALINGS IN INVESTMENTS. The 1892 Act is subject to a statutory exception which applies where an agent by way of business conducts certain dealings in investments which might at common law amount to wagers, *e.g.* because they were contracts for differences.[31]

(5) Stakeholders

A stakeholder is a person with whom the parties to a wager deposit their stakes on the understanding that he will deliver the stakes to the winner on the determination of the wager.

The third limb of section 18 of the Gaming Act 1845 provides that "no suit shall be brought or maintained in any court of law or equity for recovering any sum of money or valuable thing . . . which shall have been deposited in the hands of any person to abide the event on which any wager shall have been made." In spite of the apparent generality of this provision, it has been held that it only applies "to the non-recovery by the winner of a sum deposited by the other party to abide the event, and not to the right of the depositor to recover back his deposit if demanded before the money was paid over."[32] Thus a loser can recover back his own stake, so long as he demands it back from the stakeholder before the latter has paid it over to the winner.[33] Similarly, the winner can recover back his own stake, but he cannot sue the stakeholder for the entire stakes.[34] These rules

---

[27] (1884) 15 Q.B.D. 363, 365. *Bridger* v. *Savage* was treated as still good law in *The Vasso* [1979] 2 Lloyd's Rep. 412, 419.

[28] *Higginson* v. *Simpson* (1877) 2 C.P.D. 76; *Potter* v. *Codrington* (1892) 9 T.L.R. 54.

[29] *Cf. Higginson* v. *Simpson*, *supra*.

[30] *Cf. Simpson* v. *Bloss* (1816) 7 Taunt. 246 (same rule at common law where wager illegal).

[31] Financial Services Act, 1986 s.63 and Sched. 1 paras. 9, 12. For contracts for differences, see *ante*, p. 459.

[32] *Hampden* v. *Walsh* (1876) 1 Q.B.D. 189, 196; *cf. Re The Futures Index* [1985] F.L.R. 147.

[33] *Varney* v. *Hickman* (1874) 5 C.B. 271; *Hampden* v. *Walsh*, *supra*; *Diggle* v. *Higgs* (1877) 2 Ex.D. 422; *Trimble* v. *Hill* (1879) 5 App.Cas. 342.

[34] *Savage* v. *Madder* (1867) 36 L.J.Ex. 178; a dictum that the winner could not recover even his own stake was unnecessary for the decision, and is not law: *Hampden* v. *Walsh* (1876) 1 Q.B.D. at p. 196.

are not affected by section 1 of the Gaming Act 1892; this section refers to money "paid" out-and-out, and not to money *deposited* with a stakeholder.[35]

A stake deposited in pursuance of an illegal wager is, in general, irrecoverable as money paid under an illegal contract; but it can be recovered back by the payor if demanded back before execution of the illegal purpose. If the wager is illegal because it is a wager on an illegal game, the stake can thus be recovered back if its return is demanded before the game has taken place.[36] According to *Hastelow* v. *Jackson*[37] the stake can be recovered back even though the illegal game has taken place so long as the *contract* has not been executed by payment of the stake to the winner. But it is submitted that the decisive question ought to be whether the *illegal purpose* has been carried into effect[38]; and that the stake should be irrecoverable once the illegal game has taken place. If the wager is illegal because of its intrinsic nature, *e.g.* because it is an illegal lottery, it could be said that the illegal purpose is not "executed" until the stake is paid over to the winner so that the loser could, till then, recover it back.[39]

(6) Prizes for lawful games

Section 18 of the Gaming Act 1845 concludes: "Provided always that this enactment shall not be deemed to apply to any subscription or contribution or agreement to subscribe or contribute, for or towards any plate, prize or sum of money to be awarded to the winner or winners of any lawful game, sport, pastime or exercise."

In *Diggle* v. *Higgs*[40] two persons agreed to enter into a walking match for £200 a side, to be deposited with a stakeholder and paid to the winner. It was held that this was a wager and not saved by the proviso since this only applied where the prize was due under a contract which was not a wager. This view would leave open the possibility that the proviso would apply where the prize was put up by a third party: the contract would not be a wager since the competitors could win, but not lose, money; nor would it be a gaming contract since no money was staked by the competitors. But since such a contract would in any case be valid it seems that the proviso has no effect at all.[41]

(7) Securities

A security given for the payment of money lost under a gaming or wagering contract, or of a debt incurred in connection with such a contract, has, between the parties to the bet, no greater validity than the principal contract. Thus if the loser gives the winner a cheque in payment, the winner cannot sue the loser on the cheque any more than on the original contract.[42] But the position is more complicated when a security which is negotiable[43] later comes into the hands of a third party.

---

[35] *O'Sullivan* v. *Thomas* [1895] 1 Q.B. 698.
[36] *Martin* v. *Hewson* (1855) 10 Exch. 737.
[37] (1828) 8 B. & C. 221.
[38] *Ante*, pp. 439–440.
[39] *Cf. Barclay* v. *Pearson* [1893] 2 Ch. 154 (not a wager, but a lottery).
[40] (1877) 2 Ex.D. 422; *cf. Parson* v. *Alexander* (1855) 5 E. & B. 263; *Batson* v. *Newman* (1876) 1 C.P.D. 573.
[41] *Cf. Ellesmere* v. *Wallace* [1929] Ch. 148, criticising the accepted interpretation.
[42] *Richardson* v. *Moncrieffe* (1926) 43 T.L.R. 32.
[43] *Post*, p. 595.

(a) NON-GAMING WAGERS. Where a negotiable security such as a bill of exchange, cheque or promissory note is given in respect of a wager made void by the Gaming Act 1845, the security is also void between the parties as there is no consideration for it. But it can be enforced by a third party who becomes holder of it, if value has at any time been given for it; and as such a third party will normally be presumed to be a holder in due course, and so to have given value,[44] he can sue on the instrument, unless the defendant proves that value has not been given.[45] It is immaterial that the holder knew that the security was originally given in connection with a wager.[46]

A security may be given in respect of a transaction which is a wager but which is nevertheless valid because it is excepted by statute[47] from invalidity under section 18 of the Gaming Act 1945. In such a case, the fact that the transaction was a wager would have no effect on the validity of the security which could therefore be enforced in the normal way, both between the parties and between one of them and a third party.

(b) GAMING AND WAGERS ON GAMES are governed by special legislation contained in the Gaming Acts of 1710, 1835 and 1968.[47a]

(i) *The Acts of 1710 and 1835*. Section 1 of the Gaming Act 1710 provided that all securities given wholly or in part for any money or valuable thing won by gaming or by playing at any game or by betting on any game,[48] or for repaying any money[49] lent for such gaming or betting or lent at the time and place of play to any person so gaming or betting, shall be "utterly void, frustrate and of none effect." The object of this enactment was to restrict gaming on credit; but it had the unfortunate effect of prejudicing third parties who in good faith gave value for securities within its scope. Section 1 of the Gaming Act 1835 therefore provided that such securities should no longer be void, but that they should be "deemed and taken to have been . . . given . . . for an illegal consideration." Where, as a result of this Act, a bill of exchange is deemed to have been given for an illegal consideration, it still cannot be enforced by a third party who takes it with notice of the circumstances in which it was given, even though he gave value for it.[50] But it can be enforced by a holder in due course,[51] *i.e.* by one who took the bill (provided that it was regular on its face and not overdue) for value, in good faith, and without notice of the illegality[52]; it can also be

---

[44] Bills of Exchange Act 1882, ss.27(2), 29, 30(2); *post*; pp. 595–596.
[45] *Fitch* v. *Jones* (1855) 5 E. & B. 238.
[46] *Lilley* v. *Rankin* (1886) 56 L.J.Q.B. 248.
[47] Financial Services Act 1986, s.63, *ante*, pp. 463, 467.
[47a] As amended by Gaming (Amendment) Act 1986, *post*, p. 472.
[48] Including horse-racing: *Applegarth* v. *Colley* (1842) 10 M. & W. 723, and (*semble*) other forms of racing: *ante*, p. 460, n. 53.
[49] Including gaming chips: *Stuart* v. *Stephen* (1940) 56 T.L.R. 571, *post*, p. 470. The Act seems to contemplate repayment by the borrower; but in *Ladup Ltd.* v. *Shaik* [1983] Q.B. 225 it seems to have been assumed that s.1 also applied to a cheque given by a casino to a loser on cashing in the remainder of his chips.
[50] *Hay* v. *Ayling* (1851) 16 Q.B. 423, 431; *Woolf* v. *Hamilton* [1898] 2 Q.B. 337. Nor will an action lie on a fresh bill made in substitution if, when the holder acquired it, he had notice of the illegal consideration: *Hay* v. *Ayling*, *supra*; *Chapman* v. *Black* (1819) 2 B. & Ald. 588.
[51] Bills of Exchange Act 1882, s.38(2).
[52] *Ibid.* s.29(1) and (2).

enforced by a holder who derives his title from a holder in due course.[53] However, once it is admitted or proved that the bill is affected with illegality, a holder who sues on it cannot rely on the usual presumption that he is a holder in due course. He must show that, subsequent to the illegality, value has in good faith been given for the bill, either by him or by a previous holder through whom he derives title.[54] "In good faith" here means "without notice of the illegality."[55] The same rules would apply where the security was given in respect of an illegal wager which is not a gaming wager: in such a case the consideration would be illegal quite apart from the Acts of 1710 and 1835. This would also be true of a security given in respect of a wager on an illegal game.

The Acts of 1710 and 1835 apply (*inter alia*) to securities given for repaying money "lent for gaming." It has been held that securities given for money lent to enable the borrower to pay bets already lost are not within the Acts, as such money is not "lent for gaming."[56] The loan itself may be void under the Gaming Act 1892,[57] but a security given in respect of it is not "deemed and taken to have been given for an illegal consideration." The Acts of 1710 and 1835 would, however, apply to a security given for money lent if the lender knew that the money would be used to pay a lost bet[58] and either promised to advance the money before the bet was made[59] or stipulated that it should be used to pay the lost bet.[60]

Although the Acts only deal in terms with securities given for *money* lent, it has been held that they also strike at a common gaming practice. In *Stuart* v. *Stephen*[61] the defendant at a gambling party borrowed £150 worth of chips and lost them. He later[62] paid for the chips by cheque. The court held that the Acts of 1710 and 1835 applied even though no *money* was lent at the time of play.

The Acts cannot be evaded by stating a fictitious consideration in the security. Thus in *William Hill (Park Lane) Ltd.* v. *Hofman*[63] a mortgage purported to have been given for money lent, but was really given for money lost at play. The court disregarded the false recital and deemed the mortgage to have been given for an illegal consideration.

There may be a loophole in this legislation. Suppose a person loses bets on horse-races and later promises to pay his losses in consideration of not being posted as a defaulter. This promise cannot be enforced because of section 18 of the Act of 1845.[64] But if the loser now gives a cheque in dis-

---

[53] *Ibid.* s.29(3); this subsection does not apply where the holder who derived title through a holder in due course is himself a party to any illegality.

[54] Bills of Exchange Act 1882, s.30(2).

[55] Bills of Exchange Act 1882, s.90 ("in fact done honestly"); and *cf. Tatam* v. *Haslar* (1889) 23 Q.B.D. 345, 348 (a case of fraud, not of illegality). It is submitted that a person does not act "honestly" if he takes with notice of the illegality.

[56] *Ex p. Pyke* (1878) 8 Ch.D. 754; the actual decision would now go the other way under the Gaming Act 1892.

[57] *Post*, pp. 472–473.

[58] *Humphrey* v. *Wilson* (1929) 141 L.T. 469.

[59] *Parker* v. *Alcock* (1831) You. 361; contrast the position under the 1892 Act, where mere knowledge on the part of the lender is not enough: *post*, pp. 472–473.

[60] *Hill* v. *Fox* (1859) 4 H. & N. 359.

[61] (1940) 56 T.L.R. 571.

[62] For the question whether there is a "loan" if the cheque is given at the time of the delivery of the chips, see *post*, p. 474 n. 96.

[63] [1950] 1 All E.R. 1013.

[64] *Ante*, p. 462.

charge of his liability *under the new promise* the cheque is not tainted with illegality. The reasoning of *Hill* v. *William Hill* (*Park Lane*) *Ltd.*[65] does not apply since section 18 of the Act of 1845, in providing that a promise to pay a lost bet cannot be enforced, does not refer to the consideration for the promise; while securities are only deemed to have been given for an illegal consideration under the Acts of 1710 and 1835 "where the whole or any part of the consideration shall be for money or other valuable thing won by gaming . . . or repaying any money knowingly lent . . . for such gaming."[66] Where the consideration for the loser's cheque is the winner's promise not to post the loser as a defaulter, the cheque may thus not be deemed to have been given for an illegal consideration, since it is arguable that the consideration for the cheque is not "money . . . won by gaming." The cheque cannot be enforced between the original parties since between them it has no greater enforceability than the promise in respect of which it was given; and this promise could not be enforced by reason of the second limb of section 18 of the Gaming Act 1845. But a third person may be able to enforce the cheque, even though he knew of the circumstances in which it was given, unless the defendant proves that the third person did not give value.

(ii) *Section 16 of the Gaming Act 1968*[67] was passed principally to limit credit for gaming on licensed premises[68]; and as part of that policy it restricts the circumstances in which the licensee may accept cheques in exchange for cash or tokens to be used for such gaming. Subsection (2) makes it an offence for him to take post-dated cheques and to take cheques at a discount.[69] Subsection (4) then provides that nothing in the Gaming Acts of 1710, 1835, 1845 and 1892 "shall affect the validity of, or any remedy in respect of, any cheque which is accepted in exchange for cash or tokens to be used by a player in gaming" on licensed or registered[70] premises. The effect of this appears to be that a cheque lawfully accepted for cash or tokens to be used for lawful gaming on licensed or registered premises is enforceable even between the parties.[71] It is true that subsection (4) is not in terms restricted to cheques lawfully accepted or to lawful gaming. But if the acceptance of the cheque, or the gaming, constituted an offence the cheque would be invalid at common law quite apart from the Acts of 1710, 1835, 1845 and 1892.[72] Such common law invalidity is not cured by subsection (4).[73] And the subsection does not affect the validity of any cheque lawfully accepted except in exchange for cash or tokens *to be* used by a player in gaming: it would not, for example, apply to a cheque given on registered premises to pay for a bet already lost.[74] Nor does the subsection

---

65 [1949] A.C. 530.
66 1710 Act, s.1.
67 As amended by Gaming (Amendment) Act 1986, *post*, p. 472.
68 See further *ante*, p. 460, n. 60 and *post*, p. 476.
69 Subs. (2) is clearly restricted to gaming on licensed premises, "the gaming" in the subsection referring back to gaming on licensed premises referred to in subs. (1).
70 Subs. (4) refers to "gaming to which this Part of this Act applies" and this includes gaming on registered premises: see s.9. The offences created by subs. (2), however, are restricted to licensed premises: see last note.
71 See *Lipkin Gorman* v. *Karpnale*, [1989] 1 W.L.R. 1340, 1363–1364.
72 *Ante*, pp. 469–471.
73 *Ladup Ltd.* v. *Shaik* [1983] Q.B. 225; *cf. post*, p. 477.
74 Acceptance of a cheque in such circumstances on *licensed* premises would be unlawful under s.16(1): *post*, p. 476.

apply to cheques accepted in connection with gaming on unlicensed or unregistered premises.

A player who has given a cheque which is enforceable under section 16(4) of the 1968 Act may later redeem that cheque and give the licensee a substitute cheque: *e.g.* where the player has paid for tokens worth £100 and has £40 worth left at the end of the playing session, he may redeem his original cheque in exchange for these tokens and a new cheque for £60. Provided that certain statutory conditions (designed to ensure that the restrictions on giving credit for gaming are not evaded) are satisfied,[75] section 16(4)[76] then allows the licensee to enforce the substitute cheque.

(8) Loans

We shall first discuss the general rules governing the validity of loans connected with gaming and wagering contracts and then consider certain special provisions with regard to credit for gaming on licensed premises.

(a) IN GENERAL. At common law, a loan made to enable a person to play an illegal game is irrecoverable.[77] The same is presumably true of a loan to enable a person to make any other kind of illegal wager, or to pay an illegal bet already lost. Where the wager is not illegal at common law, it may be a valid transaction because it is excepted by statute from invalidity under section 18 of the Gaming Acts of 1845. This is the position with regard to certain dealings in investments which may at common law amount to wagers, *e.g.* because they amount to contracts for differences.[78] In such a case, the fact that the transaction was a wager would have no effect on the validity of a loan made in connection with it. More commonly, lawful wagers would be void and unenforceable under section 18 of the 1845 Act; and loans for such lawful (but invalid) wagers give rise to two problems.

(i) *Loans to pay lost bets.* The loser of a bet may ask another person to pay it for him. If the latter then pays the money straight to the winner, he cannot sue the loser for it, since such a payment is made "in respect of" a wagering contract within section 1 of the Gaming Act 1892.[79] This reasoning was applied in *C. H. T. Ltd.* v. *Ward.*[80] The plaintiffs owned a gaming club and advanced chips on credit[81] to the defendant to enable her to play poker. She lost chips worth nearly £200 and the plaintiffs paid these losses in cash to the winners. It was held that the payments were irrecoverable as they had been made "in respect of" gaming contracts.

But a payment is not necessarily made "in respect of" a wager simply because it enables the person for whose benefit it was made to pay betting debts. In *Re O'Shea*[82] a person guaranteed a gambler's overdraft for £500 which the guarantor ultimately had to pay to the bank. It was held that this payment was not made "in respect of" a wager: it was simply a contribution to the assets of a gambler which he could deal with as he pleased. But

---

[75] Gaming Act 1968, s.16(2A), as inserted by Gaming (Amendment) Act 1986, s.1(2).

[76] As amended by Gaming (Amendment) Act 1986, s.1(6).

[77] *M'Kinnell* v. *Robinson* (1838) 3 M. & W. 434.

[78] Financial Services Act 1986, s.63, *ante*, pp. 463, 467.

[79] *Tatam* v. *Reeve* [1893] 1 Q.B. 44; *cf. Carney* v. *Plimmer* [1897] 1 Q.B. 634 (money paid straight to stakeholder).

[80] [1965] 2 Q.B. 63; following *Woolf* v. *Freeman* [1937] 1 All E.R. 178.

[81] To make such an advance on licensed premises would be an offence under s.16(1) of the Gaming Act 1968; *post*, pp. 476–477.

[82] [1911] 2 K.B. 981.

money may be lent "in respect of" a wager, even though it is paid into the hands of the loser, if the loan is made subject to a stipulation (express or implied) that it is to be used to pay the lost bet. In *MacDonald* v. *Green*[83] the defendant owed gambling debts of £4,200 to a company of which the plaintiff was a director. The plaintiff agreed to lend the defendant money "privately" but only on the terms that the defendant should immediately pay it to the company. The plaintiff accordingly sent the defendant a cheque by a messenger, who waited while the defendant indorsed the cheque, took it away again, and paid it into the company's bank account. It was held that the loan was made "in respect of" the wagers with the company, and was void, since it was never at the free disposal of the borrower.

In *Tatam* v. *Reeve*[84] Wills J. said that a loan paid straight to the winner would be "in respect of" the wager even if the lender did not know that he was paying a betting debt. But this view has been doubted as it might cause grave hardship to the lender[85]; and it can no longer be supported after *MacDonald* v. *Green*. The question whether a loan is made "in respect of" a wager depends, at least to some extent, on the intention of the lender, who cannot have the necessary intention if he is ignorant of the purpose of the loan.

It must be pointed out again that the 1892 Act only invalidates promises to pay money.[86] If the borrower promises to deliver to the lender some valuable thing, or to render him some service in return for the loan, that promise seems to be perfectly valid. On the other hand, it seems clear from the concluding words of the section that the principle in *Hill* v. *William Hill (Park Lane) Ltd.*[87] applies. No action could be brought to enforce a promise supported by fresh consideration to repay a loan originally made "under or in respect of" a wager.

(ii) *Loans for future betting*. A loan to enable the borrower to make bets might be void under the Gaming Act 1892, if it was made subject to a stipulation that it should be used for betting. This seems to follow from *MacDonald* v. *Green*,[88] though the point has not actually been decided.

A loan to enable the borrower to make *gaming* bets may also be affected by the Acts of 1710 and 1835.[89] It is uncertain whether these Acts only invalidate securities, or whether they also invalidate the consideration, *i.e.*, the original loan for which a security was given. Most of the cases decided under the Act of 1710 support the view that only the security is invalidated.[90] But in *Applegarth* v. *Colley*[91] it was said that the Act of 1835 had by implication invalidated the consideration as well: "it is impossible to impute to the legislature an intention so absurd as that the consideration should be good and capable of being enforced, until some security is given . . . and then that by the giving of security the consideration should become bad." The present position depends to some extent on cases in

[83] [1951] 1 K.B. 594.
[84] [1893] 1 Q.B. at p. 48.
[85] *Hyams* v. *Stuart King* [1908] 2 K.B. 696, 714; *cf. MacDonald* v. *Green, supra*, at p. 605.
[86] *Ante*
[87] [1949] A.C. 530; *ante*, p. 462.
[88] [1951] 1 K.B. 594.
[89] *Ante*, pp. 469–471.
[90] *Barjeau* v. *Walmsley* (1746) 2 Stra. 1249; *Robinson* v. *Bland* (1760) 2 Burr. 1077; *Wettenhall* v. *Wood* (1793) 1 Esp. 18; a dictum in *Young* v. *Moore* (1757) 2 Wils.K.B. 67 suggests the contrary, but as to this, see *C.H.T. Ltd.* v. *Ward* [1965] 2 Q.B. at p. 83.
[91] (1842) 10 M. & W. 723, 732.

which loans were made in foreign countries for the purpose of gaming there. Three propositions can be deduced from the cases.

First: the lender cannot sue in England on a cheque drawn on an English bank even though the cheque was given to repay a loan made in a foreign country to enable the borrower to bet on a game that was legal there. In *Moulis* v. *Owen*[92] the plaintiff lent the defendant money in Algiers to enable the defendant to play baccarat there. The defendant gave the plaintiff a cheque drawn on an English bank in payment of the loan. By French law (which then applied in Algiers) baccarat was a legal game, and both the loan and a cheque given in payment of it were valid. But it was held that the plaintiff could not sue on the cheque in England since the cheque was governed by English law and was invalid under the Acts of 1710 and 1835.

Secondly: the lender can sue in England on a loan made in, and governed by the law of, a foreign country to enable the borrower to bet on a game that is legal there. In *Saxby* v. *Fulton*[93] the plaintiff lent money to one Brook in Monte Carlo to enable him to play roulette there. By the law of Monaco, roulette was a legal game, and the loan was valid. It was held that the plaintiff could recover the loan. There were two reasons why the Acts of 1710 and 1835 did not apply: no security had been given upon which those Acts could operate; and the *loan* was wholly governed by the law of Monaco.

Thirdly: the lender can sue in England on a loan made in, and governed by the law of, a foreign country to enable the borrower to bet on a game that is legal there *even though* the borrower gives the lender a cheque drawn on an English bank. In *Baumgart*'s case[94] the plaintiff on such facts originally sued in England on the cheque and on the loan, but later abandoned the claim on the cheque. It was held that he could sue on the loan as this was governed by the law of the foreign country in which it had been made, and was valid by that law. It follows that *Saxby* v. *Fulton* must now be taken to depend solely on the fact that the loan was governed by foreign law.

The effect of these foreign gaming decisions on a case wholly governed by English law was considered in *Carlton Hall Club Ltd.* v. *Laurence.*[95] The plaintiffs advanced chips to the defendant to enable him to play at billiards and poker, and the defendant gave the plaintiffs a cheque for the amount of the chips at the time of the advance. This transaction was treated as a loan of money.[96] The plaintiffs claimed the amount of the loan, but did not rely on the cheque. The claim might have been resisted on the ground that poker was then an illegal game as it is a card game, and not one

---

[92] [1907] 1 K.B. 746; *cf. Browne* v. *Bailey* (1908) 24 T.L.R. 644.

[93] [1909] 2 K.B. 208; *cf. Quarrier* v. *Colston* (1842) 1 Ph. 147.

[94] (1927) 96 L.J.K.B. 789.

[95] [1929] 2 K.B. 153.

[96] In *Cumming* v. *Mackie*, 1973 S.L.T. 242, it was said that there was no "loan" if the cheque was given at the time of the advance but this view was disapproved in *R.* v. *Knightsbridge Crown Court, ex p. Marcrest Properties Ltd.* [1983] 1 W.L.R. 300, where it was held that making an advance against a cheque amounts to a loan, even though the cheque is not post-dated. See also the analysis of a similar transaction as a loan to pay bets already lost in *C.H.T. Ltd.* v. *Ward* [1965] 2 Q.B. 63; *ante*, p. 472. That analysis was not possible in the *Carlton Hall Club* case as there was no evidence that the defendant had lost his chips or that the plaintiffs had made any payments in respect of them to third parties who had won bets with the defendant.

of mere skill.[97] But this is a question of fact and the argument was not open to the defendant as he had not raised it in the court of first instance.[98] The defendant chose, instead, to rely on the Acts of 1710 and 1835, and this defence succeeded. The question raised by the case, bearing in mind that the defendant could no longer allege that the money was lent for illegal gaming, was whether money lent to enable the borrower to play a game which was lawful in England could be recovered. But according to the *Law Reports* that was not the question answered. Shearman J. is reported to have said: "Having regard to the cases as a whole in regard to claims for money lent for the purpose of playing a game which is *unlawful* in this country one finds the law in this curious condition: that where the game is played in a foreign country in which it is lawful . . . the money can be sued for in . . . this country, but where the game is to be played in this country, the weight of opinion is in favour of the view that the money cannot be sued for here because the statute of Anne [*i.e.* of 1710] avoids not only the security but by implication the consideration also."[99] This suggests that the court only held loans for *unlawful* games invalid. But in the *Law Journal Reports* the corresponding passage reads as follows: "The curious position therefore arises that though the decisions on foreign gaming should logically apply to *legal games in this country*, the better authority is that the consideration cannot be sued on because it is avoided under the statute of Anne."[1] This version is preferable[2] to that in the *Law Reports* as it does at least make the court decide the question before it. The *Carlton Hall Club* case is thus authority for the proposition that if money is lent to enable the borrower to play in England a game which is lawful in England and if the borrower gives a cheque for the loan, then the lender cannot sue either on the cheque or on the loan. There are two possible criticisms of this decision.

The first is based on *Baumgart*'s case[3]: if a person who has lent money abroad to enable the borrower to play a game that is legal there can disregard an English cheque which the borrower may have given him, why should not the lender have the same rights if the loan is made and the legal game played in England? But the crucial factor in the foreign gaming cases was not the legality of the game but the validity of the loan under the foreign law. If in *Saxby* v. *Fulton*[4] it had been proved that roulette was a legal game in Monte Carlo but that loans for the purpose of playing roulette were void there, the plaintiff would clearly have failed. The validity of the loan cannot, in a purely English case, be deduced from the legality of the game.

The second objection to the *Carlton Hall Club* case is based on the wording of section 1 of the Act of 1835. To say that a security is "*deemed* and taken to have been . . . given . . . for an illegal consideration" is not to say that the consideration for the security *is* illegal: if it really were illegal, there would be no need to *deem* it so.[5] But the 1835 Act was not drafted

---

97 See *ante*
98 This appears from the report in 45 T.L.R. 195.
99 *Carlton Hall Club Ltd.* v. *Laurence*, [1929] 2 K.B. at p. 164 (italics supplied).
1 L.J.K.B. 305, 307 (italics supplied); *cf.* 140 L.T. 534, 536–537; 45 T.L.R. 195, 196.
2 *C.H.T. Ltd.* v. *Ward* [1965] 2 Q.B. at p. 85.
3 (1927) 96 L.J.K.B. 789, *supra*, at n. 94.
4 [1909] 2 K.B. 208.
5 Diamond, (1938) 54 L.Q.R. 418.

with modern precision. The draftsman probably did not intend to draw any distinction between a consideration which was illegal and one which was deemed to be so. The now repealed section 2 of the Act, in referring back to section 1, uses the words "such illegal consideration."

The decision in the *Carlton Hall Club* case is therefore consistent with the authorities and with the Acts. It could be said to give effect to the policy of the Acts of 1710 and 1835, which was to restrict credit for gaming. But the dispute is not in future likely to be of much practical importance. If the facts of *Carlton Hall Club Ltd.* v. *Laurence* recurred and the premises on which the gaming took place were licensed or registered under the Gaming Act 1968, an action could be brought on the cheque.[6] If the gaming took place elsewhere, an action on the cheque would fail under the Acts of 1710 and 1835; and an action on the loan would probably fail under the Act of 1892 on the ground that there was an implied stipulation to use the loan for gaming.[7] The Acts of 1710 and 1835 would therefore rarely determine the validity of the loan.

Where no security is given for the loan, it seems that the Acts of 1710 and 1835 cannot apply for there is nothing to attract their operation. It has been said that in such a case the loan would be recoverable.[8] But if there is a stipulation that the loan is to be used for gaming or wagering, the loan will again be void under the Act of 1892.

(b) LOANS FOR GAMING ON LICENSED PREMISES. Section 16(1) of the Gaming Act 1968 provides that where gaming takes place on licensed premises the licensee shall not "make any loan or otherwise provide or allow to any person any credit, or release or discharge on another person's behalf, the whole or part of any debt (a) for enabling any person to take part in gaming, or (b) in respect of any losses incurred by any person in the gaming." Thus it is an offence for the licensee to advance money or tokens[9] on credit to enable a person to take part in the gaming, or to pay losses which a player has incurred in the gaming, or to give credit to a loser by paying the winner. But under section 16(2) a licensee who advances cash or tokens in exchange for a cheque will not be guilty of an offence (even though the advance may amount to giving credit) if he gives full value for the cheque and if it is not post-dated.[10] Section 16(2) would not, however, exonerate the licensee where the cheque was a mere sham, *e.g.* where the advance was made against a "house-cheque" drawn on a bank at which the player was known to have no account and not intended to be enforced,[11] and where the licensee took large cheques which he agreed not to bank, and later accepted the smaller sums actually lost in satisfaction of those cheques.[12] An offence will, also be committed if the cheque is accepted in

[6] *Ante*, p. 471; for the possible effect of the 1968 Act on actions on the loan, see *infra*.
[7] *Ante*, pp. 472–473.
[8] *C.H.T. Ltd.* v. *Ward* [1965] 2 Q.B. at p. 86. *R.* v. *Knightsbridge Crown Court, ex p. Marcrest Properties Ltd.* [1983] 1 W.L.R. 300, 309.
[9] The provisions of the subsection are not restricted to loans of money. They would apply to a case like *C.H.T.* v. *Ward* [1965] 2 Q.B. 63 if the gaming took place on licensed premises: *R.* v. *Knightsbridge Crown Court supra*, at pp. 309–310.
[10] *Ante*, p. 471.
[11] *R.* v. *Knightsbridge Crown Court, ex parte Marcrest Properties Ltd.* [1983] 1 W.L.R. 300.
[12] *Ibid.*

payment partly of an advance for future gaming and partly of bets already lost.[13]

Section 16 does not specify the civil consequences of the transactions which it prohibits; but a transaction which amounts to an offence under the section would be an illegal contract at common law.[14] It could clearly not be enforced by the lender; nor, probably, could the borrower claim damages if the lender failed to perform a promise to give credit, *e.g.* if he promised to pay a player's losses and then omitted to do so.[15] The borrower might, however, be able to recover property pledged by him in respect of the contract on the ground that subsection (1) was passed to protect gamblers on licensed premises as a class.[16] Section 16(2) also (at least by implication) permits certain transactions and here section 16(4) does specify one of the civil effects by validating certain cheques accepted in exchange for cash or tokens.[17] Where a cheque is thus validated, the reasoning of *Carlton Hall Club Ltd.* v. *Laurence*[18] would not invalidate the loan: on the contrary, "the implication appears . . . to be quite clear, that the giving of a cheque which does comply with the conditions laid down by section 16(2) results in the lawful grant of credit."[19]

The prohibitions in section 16 only apply where a licensee gives credit or accepts a cheque, for the purposes there specified, in respect of gaming on licensed premises. Other forms of credit for gaming remain subject to the previous law which therefore applies to gaming elsewhere than on licensed premises and may even apply to gaming on licensed premises, *e.g.* if a loan is made there by one player to another. However, a cheque may be validated by section 16(4) even though the gaming takes place on registered and not on licensed premises[20]; and where the cheque is thus validated it would once again seem that the loan could not be invalidated by the reasoning of *Carlton Hall Club Ltd.* v. *Laurence*, though it might be void under the Act of 1892.

(9) Gambling with stolen money

(a) LOSER USING STOLEN MONEY. We have seen that, where a loser pays money lost under a wager, he cannot recover back the amount so paid from the winner.[21] That rule deals with the normal situation in which the payment is made with the loser's own money. But the loser may make such a payment with stolen money, and the victim of the theft may then seek to recover that money from the winner. Because of the negotiable[22] quality of money, the victim cannot recover the money if the winner has received the money in good faith, without notice of the theft and for value; and difficulties may arise in determining whether these conditions have been satisfied.

---

[13] *Ladup* v. *Shaik* [1983] Q.B. 225.
[14] *Ante*, p. 378.
[15] The borrower would be "innocent" only in the sense that he might act under a mistake of law: see *ante*, p. 430.
[16] *Ante*, p. 436.
[17] *Ante*, p. 471. See also Gaming Act 1968, s.16(2A), *ante*, p. 472.
[18] [1929] 2 K.B. 153; *ante*, p. 474.
[19] *R.* v. *Knightsbridge Crown Court, ex p. Marcrest Properties Ltd.* [1983] 1 W.L.R. 300, 310; *Crockfords Club Ltd* v. *Mehta*, *The Times*, March 20, 1991.
[20] *Ante*, p. 471.
[21] *Ante*, p. 464.
[22] See *post*, p. 595.

(b) STOLEN MONEY USED TO BUY GAMING CHIPS. In *Lipkin Gorman* v. *Karpnale Ltd.*[23] a salaried partner in a firm of solicitors stole money from the firm's clients' account. He used the money to buy gaming chips from a club which ran premises licensed[24] for gaming, and eventually he lost those chips in the course of a lawful gaming carried on at the club's premises. The club took the money in good faith and without notice of the circumstances in which it had been acquired; it was held that the club was not liable to refund the money since it had also received the money for value. The club had given value, since the transaction under which it had given chips in exchange for the money was a valid contract made for good consideration. In return for the money, the club had not merely parted with plastic discs of little intrinsic value, but had also made a number of promises: namely, to allow the buyer to exchange the chips for cash on demand, to allow him to use them for the purpose of taking part in the gaming, and to allow him to use them for the purpose of buying refreshments on the premises. The resulting contract was moreover, unaffected by section 18 of the Gaming Act 1845[25] since it was not itself a contract by way of gaming or wagering. Nor was it affected by the Gaming Acts of 1710 and 1835[26] since no security was involved and no credit was given. Nor did the Gaming Act 1892 apply as it was not a term of the contract that the chips were to be used for gaming[27]: a buyer of chips was free not to take part in gaming on any particular occasion; and, if he chose not to take part, he might either not use the chips at all, or use them only to buy refreshments.

The same result was reached in two further sets of circumstances which are also illustrated by *Lipkin Gorman* v. *Karpnale Ltd.* The first arose where cash extracted by the thief from the firm's account was paid by him into his own building society account, from which he later withdrew cash and used it for the purchase of chips in the way already described. The second was that in which the thief apparently paid for chips by cheques drawn on an account of his own, into which he had previously paid cash stolen from the firm.

The second of the above situations fell with section 16 of the Gaming Act 1968, in the sense that the club could have sued on the cheques (its premises being licensed)[28]; and in such circumstances it followed that the club could also keep the proceeds of the cheques when they were paid voluntarily. If the premises had not been licensed for gaming, an action on the cheques would indeed have failed by reason of the Gaming Acts of 1710 and 1835, but it does not seem to follow that the club could not have kept an actual payment, if made voluntarily. Its rights to keep such a payment would seem to depend on the validity of the contract for the purchase of the chips (in pursuance of which the cheque was given) rather than on the validity of the cheque itself. The clubs's right to keep the money would not, in other words, has been affected merely by the fact that it was precluded by the Acts of 1710 and 1835 from bringing an action on the cheques.

On the other hand, the club would have been liable to refund money or the value of a negotiable security obtained (even for value) with notice of

---

[23] [1989] 1 W.L.R. 1340; Jones, [1990] C.L.J. 17.
[24] *Ante*, p. 460.
[25] *Ante*, p. 462; *cf. Ellesmere* v. *Wallace* [1929] 2 Ch 1, 33, 48.
[26] *Ante*, p. 469.
[27] *Ante*, p. 466, and see *ante*, pp. 473–474.
[28] *Ante*, pp. 476–477.

the theft. This point is illustrated by the fact that the club was held liable for the conversion of a banker's draft in favour of the firms which the thief endorsed to the club in payment for chips. The draft had been "improperly accepted . . . by a servant of the club."[29] it seems that "improperly" here refers to the fact that the servant had notice of the fact that the thief was not entitled to deal with the draft as his own.[30]

(c) LOSER GAMBLING WITH STOLEN MONEY ITSELF. In *Lipkin Gorman* v. *Karpnale Ltd.* the club was held to have received the stolen money for value because the money had been paid under a valid contract for the purchase of chips by the thief from the club. This reasoning would not have applied if the thief had not entered into any such contract, but had simply used the stolen money itself for the purpose of gambling at the club. But Parker L.J. said that he would have been "reluctant to hold that the money . . . would have been recoverable if, instead of obtaining chips for cash, [the thief] had actually gambled with the cash under what would clearly have been a gaming and wagering contract made null and void by section 18"[31] of the 1845 Act. He concluded that "What is void is the promise to pay not the payment."[32] That payment, moreover, was not made on a consideration which had failed[33]: "When [the loser] places his bet, *e.g.* on a roulette game, and the casino accepts it, he obtains in exchange the chance of winning and thus being paid, and confers on the casino the like chance of winning and being paid . . . When the bet is paid, whichever way the payment goes the payee takes the money for valuable consideration."[34] On the other hand, Nicholls L.J. took the view that "if money rather than tokens had been used at the table the club would not have given valuable consideration."[35] The money would, in his view, have been paid to the club under a void contract, and in respect of such a payment, the club's position was no better than that of a donee. Nicholls L.J. made his disagreement with Parker L.J. on the present point a crucial part of his reasoning for dissenting in the result. May L.J. expressed no opinion on the point, which therefore remains an open one. Parker L.J.'s reasoning can be supported on the ground that even a defective promise is capable of constituting consideration; and that, even where the promise cannot be so regarded, a party may nevertheless provide consideration by performance of the promise.[36] Thus there is no compelling reason why the club's implied promise to let the thief take part in the gaming, or the club's performance of that promise, should not constitute consideration for the thief's payment, at least where that payment is made before, or at the time of, the gaming. If the payment were not made until after the gaming had taken place, it could be argued that the consideration for the payment was past, unless the gaming and the payment were so close to each other in time as to constitute substantially a single transaction.[37]

Stolen money lost and paid on a wager at the time of the wager was, on

---

[29] [1989] 1 W.L.R. 1340, 1348.
[30] See the report of the decision at first instance: [1987] 1 W.L.R. 987, 995.
[31] [1989] 1 W.L.R. 1340, 1369.
[32] *Ibid.* p. 1370.
[33] *Post*, p. 927.
[34] [1989] 1 W.L.R. 1340, 1370–1371.
[35] *Ibid.* p. 1383; *cf.* p. 1382.
[36] See *ante*, p. 137.
[37] *Ante*, pp. 73–74.

the other hand, held to be recoverable by the victim of the theft from the winner in *Clarke* v. *Shee & Johnson*.[38] The wager in that case was prohibited by an Act of Parliament which made the winnings subject of forfeiture and imposed on the winner a penalty of three times the amount of those winnings. Lord Mansfield said that the victim was entitled to the return of the stolen money as it had come into the hands of the winner "iniquitously and illegally."[39] These words may indicate *either* that the winner was aware of the circumstances in which the money had come into the hands of the thief, *or* merely that the winner had knowingly participated in the violation of the statute. On the former supposition, the case simply illustrates the principle (stated above[40]) that a winner who does not receive the money without notice of the theft must restore it to the victim of the theft. On the latter supposition, the case shows that the winner's right to retain the money (even where he has received it in good faith) can be displaced by special statutory provisions which prohibit particular types of wagers and specify their effects; and in *Lipkin Gorman* v. *Karpnale Ltd.* the case seems to be explained on this ground.[41]

---

[38] (1774) 1 Cowp. 197.
[39] *Ibid.* p. 200.
[40] *Ante*, p. 477 at n. 22.
[41] [1989] 1 W.L.R. 1340, 1370.

Chapter Thirteen

CAPACITY

SECTION 1. MINORS[1]

In the law of contract, persons below the age of majority were formerly called infants; and this expression is used in many of the older cases which deal with their contractual capacity. They are now more generally called minors; and, as this term is used in modern legislation on the subject,[2] it will also be used in this Chapter. When the age of majority was reduced from 21 to 18,[3] the practical importance of the rules which determine the extent to which minors are bound by their contracts was greatly reduced. If the decided cases are any guide, many of the problems in this area have in the past concerned the contracts of persons between 18 and 21, whose contractual capacity is now normal. But the question whether persons under 18 are bound by contracts can still arise today: for example, out of the contracts of young professional entertainers[4] or athletes, or out of hire-purchase agreements or contracts of employment involving minors. Legal problems can also arise where a claim is made by the minor against the other party, either to enforce the contract or to recover back money or property with which the minor has parted under it.

The law on this topic is based on two principles. The first, and more important, is that the law must protect the minor against his inexperience, which may enable an adult to take unfair advantage of him, or to induce him to enter into a contract which, though in itself fair, is simply improvident.[5] This principle is the basis of the general rule that a minor is not bound by his contracts. The second principle is that the law should not cause unnecessary hardship to adults who deal fairly with minors. Under this principle certain contracts with minors are valid; others are voidable in the sense that they bind the minor unless he repudiates; and a minor may be under some liability in tort and in restitution.

1. Valid Contracts

(1) Necessaries

A contract for necessaries is binding "not for the benefit of the tradesman who may trust the infant, but for the benefit of the infant himself."[6] It is assumed, rightly or wrongly,[7] that the tradesman would not give credit to the minor unless the law imposed liability. In this connection it should be

---

[1] For a comparative study, see Hartwig, 15 I.C.L.Q. 780.

[2] Family Law Reform Act 1969 says they "may" be called minors; they are so called in Sale of Goods Act 1979, s.3 and in Minors' Contracts Act 1987.

[3] Family Law Reform Act 1969, s.1; s.9 provides that a person attains 18 "at the commencement of the [18th] anniversary of his birth."

[4] *e.g. Mills* v. *I.R.C.* [1975] A.C. 38, 53.

[5] *e.g.* if the minor for a fair price agrees to buy something that he cannot afford.

[6] *Ryder* v. *Wombwell* (1868) L.R. 4 Ex. 32, 38; *Zouch* v. *Parsons* (1763) 3 Burr. 1794.

[7] *Cf. post*, p. 483.

noted that parents are not liable on their child's contract unless the child acts as their agent[8]; and that in English law a minor's contract cannot be validated by the consent or authorisation of his parent or guardian.

Necessaries include goods supplied and services rendered to a minor. He is only bound by a contract for necessaries if it is on the whole for his benefit: not if it contains harsh and onerous terms.[9] Nor is he bound by an indivisible contract comprising necessaries and non-necessaries.[10]

(a) NECESSARY GOODS. Necessary goods are not confined to necessities: they include "such articles as are fit to maintain the particular person in the state, station and degree . . . in which he is."[11] Thus "a coat of superfine broadcloth may be necessary for the son of a nobleman, although it is impossible not to say that the coarser material of a ploughman's coat would be sufficient to keep a nobleman's body warm."[12] In *Hands* v. *Slaney*[13] a livery for a minor's servant was held to be a necessary; and in *Peters* v. *Fleming*[14] the court refused to disturb a verdict that rings, pins and a watch-chain supplied to the son of a rich man were necessaries. In such cases it can hardly be said that liability is imposed "for the benefit of the infant himself."[15] The wide definition of necessaries was adopted rather for the protection of suppliers who reasonably gave credit to young men from wealthy families.

On the other hand the definition of necessaries was limited so as to exclude "mere luxuries." These were distinguished from "luxurious articles of utility,"[16] which could be necessaries. Since few articles are so luxurious that they cannot be used at all, the real question is whether it is reasonable for the minor, however rich, to be supplied with articles of the kind in question. Thus it was said that if the son of the richest man in the kingdom bought a racehorse, it could not be a necessary[17] but where an apprentice bought a racing bicycle (which was no more expensive than an ordinary one) it was held to be a necessary.[18] It is doubtful whether goods bought by a minor to be given away can normally be necessaries.[19] But an engagement ring bought to be given to the minor's fiancée, whom he later marries, can be a necessary.[20]

Much difficulty was caused in the nineteenth century by the tendency of juries (consisting of 12 shopkeepers) to stretch the definition of necessaries beyond its legitimate limits. In one case "an Oxford jury held that cham-

---

[8] *Blackburn* v. *Mackey* (1823) 1 C. & P. 1; *Law* v. *Wilkin* (1837) 6 A. & E. 718; *Mortimore* v. *Wright* (1840) 6 M. & W. 482.

[9] *Fawcett* v. *Smethurst* (1914) 84 L.J.Ch. 473.

[10] *Stocks* v. *Wilson* [1913] 2 K.B. 235.

[11] *Peters* v. *Fleming* (1840) 6 M. & W. 42, 46.

[12] *Bryant* v. *Richardson* (1866) 14 L.T. 24, 26.

[13] (1800) 8 T.R. 578. But a claim for the price of cockades for soldiers under the minor's command was disallowed.

[14] *Supra*, n. 11.

[15] *Ante*, p. 481.

[16] *Chapple* v. *Cooper* (1844) 13 M. & W. 252, 258.

[17] *Wharton* v. *Mackenzie* (1844) 5 Q.B. 606, 612. Contrast *Barber* v. *Vincent* (1680) Free.K.B. 581 (horse sold to a minor to carry him about his necessary business held a necessary).

[18] *Clyde Cycle Co.* v. *Hargreaves* (1898) 78 L.T. 296.

[19] *Ryder* v. *Wombwell* (1868) L.R. 4 Ex. 32; *Hewlings* v. *Graham* (1901) 84 L.T. 497.

[20] *Jenner* v. *Walker* (1869) 19 L.T. 398.

pagne and wild ducks were necessaries to an infant undergraduate."[21] To counteract this tendency, the courts first distinguished between articles which could, and those which could not, as a matter of law, be necessaries.[22] They held, secondly, that the question whether goods were necessaries was "one of mixed law and fact; in so far as it is a question of fact it must be determined by the jury . . . ; but there is in every case . . . a preliminary question which is one of law, namely whether there is any evidence on which the jury could properly find the question for the party on whom the onus of proof lies."[23] The onus of proving that the goods are necessaries lies on the supplier. Thus in *Ryder* v. *Wombwell*[24] the son of a deceased baronet bought jewelled cuff-links for £12 10s. apiece and an antique goblet to give to a friend. The jury found that these articles were necessaries. But the court set the verdict aside as there was no evidence on which it could properly be based.

The supplier must show not only that the goods are capable of being necessaries, but that they actually are necessaries. Thus in *Nash* v. *Inman*[25] a tailor sued a minor for the price of clothes, including 11 fancy waistcoats. The action failed because the tailor had not adduced any evidence fit to be left to the jury that the clothes were suitable to the condition in life of the minor, *and* that the minor was not already adequately supplied with clothes. The courts have here put on the plaintiff the burden of proving the difficult negative proposition that the minor was not adequately supplied. As a general rule a person is only required to prove a negative if such proof depends on facts peculiarly within his own knowledge; here the proof required of the supplier depends on facts peculiarly within the knowledge of the minor.

The courts have gone even further: the minor is not liable if he already had an adequate supply, even though the supplier did not know this.[26] Such a rule may help to protect minors; but it is difficult to reconcile with the argument that minors are liable for necessaries because, if they were not, traders would not give them credit. For the rule makes it impossible for the tradesman to tell, when the contract is made, whether the minor will indeed be bound by it.

(b) SERVICES RENDERED TO A MINOR. Certain services rendered to a minor may be necessaries. These include education (whether liberal or vocational)[27] and medical and legal advice.[28] The provision of a funeral for her deceased husband has been held a necessary for a minor who was a widow.[29] It seems that any service can be a necessary if it satisfies the tests already stated in relation to necessary goods.

---

21 (1874) *Hansard*, Vol. 219, ser. 3, col. 1225.

22 *Ryder* v. *Wombwell* (1868) L.R. 4 Ex. 32.

23 *Ryder* v. *Wombwell*, *supra*, at p. 38.

24 (1868) L.R. 4 Ex. 32; *cf. Wharton* v. *Mackenzie* (1844) 5 Q.B. 606.

25 [1908] 2 K.B. 1.

26 *Foster* v. *Redgrave* (1867) L.R. 4 Ex. 35n; *Barnes* v. *Toye* (1884) 13 Q.B.D. 410; *Johnstone* v. *Marks* (1887) 19 Q.B.D. 509.

27 *Chapple* v. *Cooper* (1844) 13 M. & W. 252, 258; *Walter* v. *Everard* [1891] 2 Q.B. 369; *Roberts* v. *Gray* [1913] 1 K.B. 520. For contracts to pay school fees, see *Practice Direction* [1980] 1 W.L.R. 1441; Practice Direction [1983] 1 W.L.R. 800; *Sherdley* v. *Sherdley* [1988] A.C. 213, 225.

28 *Huggins* v. *Wiseman* (1690) Carth. 110; *Helps* v. *Clayton* (1864) 17 C.B. (N.S.) 553.

29 *Chapple* v. *Cooper* (1844) 13 M. & W. 252.

(c) Executory contracts.[30] It is disputed whether a minor is bound by an executory contract for necessary goods. Can he only be sued if the goods have actually been delivered, or is he liable if he wrongfully repudiates before delivery? Three main arguments have been used to support the view that the minor is only liable if the goods have been delivered.

First: in *Nash* v. *Inman* Fletcher Moulton L.J. said that the minor was liable, *re*, because he had been supplied, and not *consensu*, because he had contracted. "An infant, like a lunatic,[31] is incapable of making a contract . . . in the strict sense of the word: but if a man satisfies the need of the infant or lunatic by supplying to him necessaries, the law will imply an obligation to repay him for the services so rendered, and will enforce that obligation against the estate of the infant or lunatic."[32] But Buckley L.J. said that a contract for necessaries was "such as the infant, notwithstanding infancy, could make. The defendant, although he was an infant, had a limited capacity to contract."[33] And the analogy of the "lunatic" is, with respect, weak. Where such a person is "incapable of making a contract" the reason is that he cannot consent. When he is supplied with necessaries there is not usually even the shadow of an agreement to accept and pay for the goods. This may also be true when necessaries are supplied to a very young child.[34] But it is not true when a young man of 17 orders a suit and promises to pay for it. He can and does consent[35]: the only question is whether he ought as a matter of legal policy to be held to the agreement.

Secondly: the minor is only liable for a reasonable price, which may not be the same as the contract price. "That does not imply a consensual contract."[36] But the law often interferes with one or more of the terms of a transaction and this does not necessarily deprive it of its essential character as a contract.[37]

Thirdly: section 3 of the Sale of Goods Act 1979 provides:

"(1) Capacity to buy and sell is regulated by the general law concerning capacity to contract, and to transfer and acquire property.

(2) Where necessaries are sold and delivered to a minor . . . he must pay a reasonable price for them.

(3) In subsection (2) above, 'necessaries' means goods suitable to the condition in life of the minor . . . and to his actual requirements at the time of the sale and delivery."

The definition in subsection (3) may seem to suggest that goods cannot be necessaries unless they have actually been delivered. But the definition is of necessaries "In subsection (2) above," and that subsection only deals with necessaries sold and delivered. The definition does not apply to goods sold but not yet delivered.

Thus the arguments in support of the view that the minor is not liable on an executory contract are inconclusive; and the contrary view is supported

---

[30] Miles, (1927) 43 L.Q.R. 389; Winfield, (1942) 58 L.Q.R. 83.
[31] Now called a mental patient: see *post*, pp. 501 *et seq*.
[32] [1908] 2 K.B. 1, 8; *cf. Re J.* [1909] 1 Ch. 574.
[33] [1908] K.B. 1, 12.
[34] See *Sherdley* v. *Sherdley* [1988] A.C. 213, 225.
[35] As is recognised in other branches of the law: *e.g.*, Family Law Reform Act 1969 s.8(1) (consent to medical treatment); *Gillick* v. *West Norfolk Health Authority* [1986] A.C. 112 (consent to contraceptive advice).
[36] *Pontypridd Union* v. *Drew* [1927] 1 K.B. 214, 220.
[37] *Ante*, p. 3.

by *Roberts* v. *Gray*.[38] The plaintiff, a famous billiards player, agreed to take the defendant, who was a minor, on a world billiards tour, and to pay for his board and lodging and travelling expenses. This was a contract for necessaries, mainly because its object was to teach the minor the profession of a billiards player. The defendant repudiated the contract while it was still partly executory. He was held liable in damages. Hamilton L.J. said: "I am unable to appreciate why a contract which is in itself binding . . . can cease to be binding merely because it is still executory."[39] It has been said that the authorities relied on in *Roberts* v. *Gray* concern beneficial contracts of service[40] and that contracts for education are more closely analogous to these contracts than to contracts for the supply of necessary goods.[41] But it is hard to see why any distinction should for this purpose be drawn between necessary goods and education; or between necessaries of either kind and beneficial contracts of service. The reasons for holding a minor liable, and for limiting his liability, are the same in all these cases. It is thought that the minor's overall position might be prejudiced if he could not bind himself, and also that liability should be imposed to protect the legitimate interests of the adult. These considerations have to be balanced against the need to protect the minor. If a balancing of all these factors justifies the view that the minor should be bound by an executory contract for education or of service, it is submitted that it can equally justify the view that he should be bound by an executory contract for the supply of necessary goods.[42]

(d) LOANS FOR NECESSARIES. At common law a person who spends money in buying necessaries for a minor is enitled to recover it from the minor.[43] One who lends money to a minor cannot recover it at law, but can in equity recover such part of the loan as was actually used by the minor to discharge his liability for necessaries supplied to him.[44] A promise in a mortgage deed to repay such a loan is ineffective since the minor is not bound by his deed.[45] The law leaves the lender for necessaries in a somewhat precarious position—perhaps because a loan of money can more easily be misapplied than an actual supply of necessaries.

(2) Service contracts

A minor[46] is bound by a service contract if it is on the whole for his benefit. He may be bound even though some of the terms of the contract are to his disadvantage. Thus in *Clements* v. *L. & N.W. Ry.*[47] a minor who was a railway porter agreed to join an insurance scheme, to which his employers

---

[38] [1913] 1 K.B. 520.
[39] At p. 530.
[40] See *post*, pp. 485–486.
[41] Cheshire, Fifoot and Furmston, *Law of Contract* (11th ed.), p. 415.
[42] The difficulties discussed above would be diminished if parents were liable for necessaries, or at least for necessities, supplied to a child. For an American case in which such liability was imposed, see *Greenspan* v. *Slate*, 12 N.J. 426; 97 A. 2d. 390 (1953).
[43] *Ellis* v. *Ellis* (1689) Comb. 482; *Earle* v. *Peale* (1712) 10 Mod. 67.
[44] *Marlow* v. *Pitfeild* (1719) 1 P.Wms. 558; *Re National Permanent Benefit Building Society* (1869) L.R. 5 Ch.App.309, 313.
[45] *Martin* v. *Gale* (1876) 4 Ch.D. 428.
[46] Contracts of service with children are to some extent regulated by statute: see, for example, Children and Young Persons Acts 1933, s.18; 1963, ss.34, 37; Employment of Children Act 1973.
[47] [1894] 2 Q.B. 482; *Slade* v. *Metrodent* [1953] 2 Q.B. 112; *Mills* v. *I.R.C.* [1975] A.C. 38, 53.

contributed, and to give up any claim for personal injury under the Employers' Liability Act 1880. His rights under the scheme were in some ways more, and in other ways less, beneficial than those under the Act; and it was held that the contract was on the whole beneficial, so that the minor was bound by it. But a term which simply limits or excludes the liability of the employer without giving the minor any rights in return is unlikely to be upheld.[48]

A minor is, on the other hand, not bound by a service contract if it is on the whole harsh and oppressive. In *De Francesco* v. *Barnum*[49] a girl was apprenticed for stage dancing by a deed which provided that she should be entirely at the disposal of the master; that she should get no pay unless he actually employed her, which he was not bound to do; that he could send her abroad; that he could put an end to the contract if, after fair trial, he found her unsuitable; and that she should not accept any professional engagement without his consent. She accepted a professional engagement with the defendant without the master's consent. It was held that the master could not sue the defendant for inducing a breach of the apprenticeship deed as it was unreasonably harsh and thus invalid.

In deciding whether a service contract is on the whole beneficial the court is entitled to look at surrounding circumstances. For example, a service contract with a minor may contain a covenant in restraint of trade. Such a covenant, if otherwise valid,[50] does not invalidate the contract if the minor could not have got similar work on any other terms.[51] But it would invalidate a service contract with a minor if it was of a kind that was not usually found in service contracts in that trade and locality.[52] These principles also apply to contracts connected with service contracts. Thus they determine the validity of contracts to carry minors to work,[53] of compromises of industrial injury claims,[54] and of agreements to dissolve service contracts.[55]

The principles evolved in relation to service contracts also determine the validity of contracts under which a minor makes a living by the exercise of some profession, *e.g.* as an entertainer or author or athlete. In *Doyle* v. *White City Stadium Ltd.*[56] a professional boxer who was a minor made a contract to fight for £3,000, win, draw or lose, subject to the rules of the British Boxing Board of Control, under which a boxer who was disqualified forfeited his "purse." The minor was disqualified for hitting below the

---

[48] *Olsen* v. *Corry and Gravesend Aviation Ltd.* [1936] 3 All E.R. 241. Even if valid at common law, the term may be ineffective, or subject to the requirement of reasonableness, under Unfair Contracts Terms Act 1977, ss. 2 or 3 (*ante*, pp. 231–232).

[49] (1889) 43 Ch.D. 165; (1890) 45 Ch.D. 430.

[50] *Ante*, pp. 402 *et seq.* The fact that the employee was a minor may be relevant to the issue of the reasonableness of the covenant: see *Sir W. C. Leng & Co. Ltd.* v. *Andrews* [1909] 1 Ch. 763, 771–772.

[51] *Bromley* v. *Smith* [1909] 2 K.B. 235; *cf. Leslie* v. *Fitzpatrick* (1877) 3 Q.B.D. 229; *Fellows* v. *Wood* (1888) 59 L.T. 513.

[52] *Sir W. C. Leng & Co. Ltd.* v. *Andrews* [1909] 1 Ch. 763.

[53] *Flower* v. *London and North Western Ry.* [1894] 2 Q.B. 65; in *Buckpitt* v. *Oates* [1968] 1 All E.R. 1145 it seems to have been assumed that any contract to carry the minor (though not connected with his work) would be binding if on the whole for his benefit; *sed quaere.* The actual decision would now go the other way: Road Traffic Act 1988, ss.145, 149.

[54] *Stephens* v. *Dudbridge Ironworks Co.* [1904] 2 K.B. 225.

[55] *Waterman* v. *Fryer* [1922] 1 K.B. 499.

[56] [1935] 1 K.B. 110. *Cf.* also *Lumley* v. *Wagner* (1852) 1 D.M. & G. 604, where a famous soprano was under age, as appears from 5 De G. & Sm. 485.

belt and his claim for the £3,000 was dismissed. Although in the circumstances the rules operated against him, he was bound by them: they were, on the whole, for his benefit as a professional boxer since they encouraged clean fighting. This case was followed in *Chaplin* v. *Leslie Frewin (Publishers) Ltd.*[57] where a minor contracted to give a firm of publishers the exclusive right to publish his memoirs. The Court of Appeal unanimously held that this was the sort of contract which could bind the minor if it was on the whole for his benefit.[58] Applying this test Lord Denning M.R. thought that, having regard to the contents of the memoirs, the contract was not binding, as it was not for the minor's good "that he should exploit his discreditable conduct for money."[59] But Danckwerts and Winn L.JJ. took the more materialistic view that "the mud may cling but the profits will be secured": thus the contract was on the whole beneficial, and bound the minor as it enabled him to "make a start as an author."[60]

The rule that a minor is bound by "beneficial" contracts is restricted to service or analogous contracts. There is no general principle that a minor is bound by a contract merely because it is for his benefit. For example, a minor would not be contractually liable to repay[61] a loan without interest. And it has long been settled that a minor is not bound by a trading contract. Thus he is not liable for goods supplied to him for the purpose of trade, nor for damages if he fails to deliver goods which he has sold as a trader.[62] Nor can he be made bankrupt for trade debts.[63]

It may be asked: why does the law distinguish between a minor who earns his living by the exercise of a profession and one who earns his living by trading? The traditional answer is that "the law will not suffer him to trade, which may be his undoing."[64] A minor who trades thereby necessarily risks his capital. If he exercises some profession or calling he may incur expense, but putting his capital at risk is not of the essence of the matter. Of course there are difficult borderline cases. A minor who is a haulage contractor is a trader,[65] but probably one who was a racing driver would not be so regarded. Similarly, it is probable that a minor who was a house painter would, while one who was a portrait painter would not, be regarded as a trader.[66] There is no precise definition of "trade" for this purpose.

Contracts of apprenticeship were governed by special rules. It was held

---

57 [1966] Ch. 71; the case was later compromised: *The Times*, February 16, 1966.

58 The same rule seems to apply to a contract between an entertainer who is under age and his agent: see *Denmark Productions Ltd.* v. *Boscobel Productions Ltd.* (1967) 111 S.J. 715, reversed on other grounds [1969] 1 Q.B. 699, *post*, pp. 650, 898.

59 [1966] Ch. 71, 88.

60 *Ibid.* p. 95. The majority may have been influenced by the fact that the minor had received considerable payments in advance of royalties. The publishers would have had considerable difficulties—both legal and practical—in getting these back.

61 For liability to make restitution, see *post*, pp. 494–501.

62 *Mercantile Union Guarantee Corp. Ltd.* v. *Ball* [1937] 2 K.B. 498; *Cowern* v. *Nield* [1912] 2 K.B. 491; *post*, p. 500.

63 *Ex p. Jones* (1881) 18 Ch.D. 109; but he can be made bankrupt in respect of tax liability incurred in the course of trade: *Re a Debtor* [1950] Ch. 282. If a minor is made bankrupt as a result of a mistake as to his age, the court has a discretion to set the bankruptcy aside: *Re Davenport* [1963] 1 W.L.R. 817.

64 *Whywall* v. *Campion* (1738) 2 Stra. 1083.

65 *Mercantile Union Guarantee Corp. Ltd.* v. *Ball*, *supra*, n. 62.

66 *Quaere* what the position would be if a minor agreed to sell a picture which he had painted without being commissioned to paint it.

in the seventeenth century that an apprentice who was under age was not liable in damages if he, in breach of contract, departed from service.[67] This rule was originally based on the fact that the master had other remedies such as having the minor ordered by a justice of the peace to return to work. These remedies no longer exist[68] and it seems that contracts of apprenticeship will now be governed by the normal rules. A minor is not bound by an apprenticeship deed as such, but he is bound by it as a simple contract. Thus he is liable to pay any premium which he has agreed to pay.[69] Similarly, a covenant in restraint of trade (if otherwise valid[70]) or an arbitration clause contained in the apprenticeship deed can be enforced against him so long as the deed is on the whole for his benefit.[71]

2. Voidable Contracts

(1) Cases of voidable contracts

In four cases a minor's contract is voidable: that is, it binds both parties but the minor can avoid liability by repudiating before majority or within a reasonable time thereafter. The other party cannot repudiate.[72]

(a) CONTRACTS CONCERNING LAND. A lessee who is under age is liable for rent unless he repudiates.[73] A minor who agrees to purchase freehold land is similarly bound unless he repudiates.[74] It seems that the same principle also applies where a minor lets or agrees to sell land.[75] Actual conveyances to and by minors give rise to special problems which are outside the scope of this book.

According to one case[76] a lessee who is under age is only liable for rent if the subject-matter of the lease is a necessary, but if this were so he could presumably not repudiate. The requirement is not elsewhere stated and is probably not law. On the contrary, it seems that a lessee who is under age is liable unless he repudiates even though the lease is disadvantageous to him.[77]

(b) SHARES IN COMPANIES. A minor who agrees to subscribe for shares in a company, or buys shares which are not fully paid, is liable for calls unless he repudiates. A mere plea that he has not ratified the transaction does not

---

[67] *Gylbert* v. *Fletcher* (1630) Cro.Car. 179.

[68] Family Law Reform Act 1969, s.11.

[69] *Walter* v. *Everard* [1891] 2 Q.B. 369.

[70] See *ante*, p. 486, n. 50.

[71] *Gadd* v. *Thompson* [1911] 1 K.B. 304; *Slade* v. *Metrodent* [1953] 2 Q.B. 112.

[72] *Clayton* v. *Ashdown* (1714) 2 Eq.Ca.Abr. 516.

[73] *Keteley's Case* (1613) 1 Bromnl. 120; *Davies* v. *Benyon-Harris* (1931) 47 T.L.R. 424. A minor can no longer hold a legal estate in land: Law of Property Act 1925, s.1(*b*); but this enactment does not affect the proposition in the text.

[74] *Whittingham* v. *Murdy* (1889) 60 L.T. 956; *Thurstan* v. *Notts P.B.B.S.* [1902] 1 Ch. 1, 9, 13 (affmd. [1903] A.C. 6); *Orakpo* v. *Manson Investments Ltd.*, [1978] A.C. 95, 106, 113.

[75] *Slator* v. *Trimble* (1861) 14 Ir.C.L.R. 342; Williams, *Vendor and Purchaser*, (4th ed.), pp. 847 *et seq.*

[76] *Lowe* v. *Griffith* (1835) 4 L.J.C.P. 94.

[77] *North Western Ry.* v. *M'Michael* (1850) 5 Ex. 114, 128; in *Keteley's Case*, *sub nom. Kirton* v. *Eliot* (1613) 2 Bulst. 69, there is a conflict of opinion on this point. There would be no liability for necessaries in such a case: *ante*, p. 482 at n. 9.

relieve him from liability.[78] If he repudiates he ceases to be liable and can have his name removed from the company's register.[79] If the minor buys shares from a previous owner and fails to repudiate liability for calls on them, *the company* cannot generally avoid the transaction and so make the transferor liable for the calls.[80] But if the company is wound up while the buyer is still a minor, the liquidator can exercise the minor's right of repudiation for him and so make the transferor again liable for calls.[81]

The cases on this subject all concern the relations between the minor and the company or between the company and the person who has transferred shares to a minor. There appears to be no authority on the effect between buyer and seller of a sale of shares by or to a minor. Suppose that a minor buys shares, fails to pay for them on settlement day, and then repudiates after majority. If the contract is voidable this repudiation may be too late,[82] so that the minor will be liable to pay. But he would not be liable if the contract had never been binding on him at all.[83]

(c) PARTNERSHIP. A minor can become a partner and is to some extent bound by the partnership agreement. He cannot be sued during minority by persons who give credit to the firm,[84] or be made liable for its losses.[85] But he is liable if after majority he fails to put an end to the partnership.[86] And he is not entitled to any share in the profits or assets of the partnership until its liabilities have been paid off.[87]

(d) MARRIAGE SETTLEMENTS. It was once thought that a marriage settlement by a minor was binding to the extent to which it benefited him; but was otherwise not binding unless ratified after majority.[88] But the prevailing view is that such a settlement binds the minor unless he repudiates.[89] In certain cases a minor could, by statute, make an absolutely binding settlement with the consent of the court.[90] The statute has been repealed,[91] though not with retrospective effect.

---

78 *North Western Ry.* v. *M'Michael, supra*; *Dublin & Wicklow Ry.* v. *Black* (1852) 8 Ex. 181; *Ebbett's Case* (1870) L.R. 5 Ch.App. 302. The rule was originally thought to be based simply on the provisions of the Act incorporating the company: *Cork & Bandon Ry.* v. *Cazenove* (1847) 10 Q.B. 935; but this reasoning was disapproved in *M'Michael's* case, *supra*, and in *Leeds & Thirsk Ry.* v. *Fearnley* (1849) 4 Ex. 26. Thus the rule applies to shares in all companies, however incorporated.

79 *Dublin & Wicklow Ry.* v. *Black, supra*; *Steinberg* v. *Scala (Leeds) Ltd.* [1923] 2 Ch. 452.

80 *Lumsden's Case* (1868) L.R. 4 Ch.App. 31; *Gooch's Case* (1872) L.R. 8 Ch.App. 266.

81 *Capper's Case* (1868) L.R. 3 Ch.App. 458; *Castello's Case* (1869) L.R. 8 Eq. 504; *Symon's Case* (1870) L.R. 5 Ch.App. 298.

82 *Post*, p. 490.

83 *i.e.* if it fell within the general rule stated at p. 492, *post*.

84 *Goode* v. *Harrison* (1821) 5 B. & Ald. 147, 157; *Lovell & Christmas* v. *Beauchamp* [1894] A.C. 607.

85 *Goode* v. *Harrison, supra*, at p. 159.

86 *Goode* v. *Harrison, supra*.

87 *Lovell & Christmas* v. *Beauchamp* [1894] A.C. 607, 611.

88 See *Simson* v. *Jones* (1831) 2 Russ & My. 365; traces of this view remain in *Kingsman* v. *Kingsman* (1880) 6 Q.B.D. 122 and in *Clements* v. *London and North Western Ry.* [1894] 2 Q.B. 482, 493.

89 *Duncan* v. *Dixon* (1890) 44 Ch.D. 211; *Edwards* v. *Carter* [1893] A.C. 360; [1892] 2 Ch. 278.

90 Infant Settlements Act 1855.

91 Family Law Reform Act 1969, s.11.

(2) Loans for voidable contracts

A minor may borrow money to enable him to make a payment due from him under a voidable contract, and actually use the money borrowed to make the payment. The minor is not for this reason bound by the contract for the loan of the money[92]; but the lender has rights similar to those of a lender for necessaries.[93] In *Nottingham Permanent Benefit Building Society* v. *Thurstan*[94] a minor borrowed money from a building society to buy land. She paid the money to the vendor and executed a mortgage to the society. The mortgage was void,[95] but the society was entitled to stand in the shoes of the vendor and to exercise the lien that he would have had over the property, if he had not been paid.

(3) Rules relating to repudiation

(a) TIME OF REPUDIATION. A voidable contract can be repudiated during minority, but such a repudiation can be withdrawn by the minor before, or within reasonable time of, majority.[96] If the minor repudiates during minority he need take no further steps to avoid liability on reaching full age.[97]

If the minor does not repudiate during minority, he must do so within a reasonable time of reaching full age. This is so even though he did not know of his right to repudiate, and even though his obligation under the contract had not yet matured. Thus a covenant by a minor in a marriage settlement to settle after-acquired property may not become operative for many years after the settlor comes of age. But it binds him unless he repudiates it within a reasonable time of majority. In *Edwards* v. *Carter*[98] it was held that a settlement could not be repudiated nearly five years after the majority of the settlor, although he was for most of that time ignorant of his right to repudiate.

(b) EFFECTS OF REPUDIATION. Two points call for discussion.

(i) *Relief from future liabilities.* Repudiation relieves the minor from liabilities which would, but for the repudiation, have accrued after its date. There are conflicting dicta[99] on the question whether liabilities which have already accrued are extinguished by repudiation. According to an Irish case repudiation has no retrospective effect[1]: thus a lessee who is under age is liable for rent which has become payable before repudiation.

(ii) *No recovery of money.* A minor cannot recover back money paid under a voidable contract unless there has been a total failure of consideration.[2] In *Steinberg* v. *Scala (Leeds) Ltd.*,[3] a minor applied for shares in a

---

[92] It falls within the general rule stated at p. 492, *post*.
[93] *Ante*, p. 485.
[94] [1903] A.C. 6.
[95] See *ante*, p. 485 at n. 45.
[96] *North Western Ry.* v. *M'Michael* (1850) 5 Ex. 114, 127; *Slator* v. *Trimble* (1861) 14 Ir.C.L.R. 342.
[97] *Newry and Enniskillen Ry. v. Combe* (1849) 3 Ex. 565, 575.
[98] [1893] A.C. 360.
[99] *North Western Ry.* v.*M'Michael*, *supra*, n. 96 at p. 125 (retrospective); *Keteley's Case* (1613) 1 Brownl. 120 (not retrospective); dicta in *Steinberg* v. *Scala* (*Leeds*) *Ltd.* [1923] 2 Ch. 452, 463 can be cited on both sides.
[1] *Blake* v. *Concannon* (1870) I.R. 4 C.L. 323.
[2] *Post*, p. 927.
[3] [1923] 2 Ch. 452.

company but repudiated after allotment. She thus avoided liability for future calls, but her claim for the return of money already paid was rejected as there was no total failure of consideration: she had got the very shares she bargained for. It follows that property transferred under a marriage settlement is irrecoverable if the marriage has taken place. On the other hand in *Corpe* v. *Overton*[4] a minor agreed to enter into a partnership and paid a deposit of £100, to be forfeited if he failed to execute the partnership deed. No partnership deed was ever executed because the minor repudiated, and it was held that he could get his deposit back as there had been a total failure of consideration. An adult, too, can recover back money if there has been a total failure of consideration; but a minor (unlike an adult) can do so even though the failure of consideration is due to his own act in repudiating the contract.

(4) Why are these contracts voidable?

In general a minor is not bound by his contracts.[5] He need not repudiate to escape liability. Why must he do so in the four cases discussed above?[6]

The orthodox view is that the minor must repudiate because he has acquired an interest in a subject-matter of a permanent nature to which continuing obligations are attached: it would be unjust to allow him to retain the interest without fulfilling the obligations. But this explanation is not wholly satisfactory. First, it is vague: what is meant by "permanent" here? Is a lease for one year permanent because land is virtually indestructible? Partnerships and shares in companies do not necessarily confer an interest in property which is permanent even in this sense. And marriage settlements can only be brought within the explanation by arguing that the marriage is permanent, whether the settled property is permanent or not. Secondly, the explanation does not cover all cases within the rule. It has been held that a minor's contract to buy freehold land to be paid for in instalments is voidable.[7] Nothing in the judgment suggests that it would have made any difference, had the price been payable in one lump sum. Yet in such a case the contract would not have created any "continuing" obligation between the parties. Thirdly, the explanation proves too much. It is admittedly unjust to allow a tenant who is a minor to retain possession of land without paying rent. But it is equally unjust to allow a minor to keep a car obtained under a hire purchase agreement without paying instalments. Yet the hire purchase agreement does not bind the minor[8]: he need not repudiate.

There seems to be no satisfactory explanation for the existence of this separate class of voidable contracts. It perhaps provides the clearest illustration of the dilemma in which the law sometimes finds itself when it tries at the same time to protect minors and not to cause undue hardship to adults who deal with them. But this dilemma exists in all cases of contracts with minors and scarcely justifies special treatment of the four voidable contracts. Perhaps this is based on social and economic factors which have long since passed away.

---

[4] (1833) 10 Bing. 252; *Everett* v. *Wilkins* (1874) 29 L.T. 846.
[5] *Post*, p. 492.
[6] *Ante*, pp. 488–489.
[7] *Whittingham* v. *Murdy* (1889) 60 L.T. 956.
[8] *e.g. Mercantile Union Guarantee Corp. Ltd.* v. *Ball* [1937] 2 K.B. 498.

3. Other Contracts

(1) Minor not bound

Contracts which are neither valid, nor voidable in the sense just discussed, do not bind the minor but have a number of legal effects.

(2) Other effects

(a) OTHER PARTY BOUND. Contracts in this group bind the other party.[9] However, the remedies available to the minor are somewhat restricted in that he cannot claim *specific* performance of the contract.[10]

(b) RATIFICATION. The minor as a general rule[11] becomes liable on the contract if he ratifies it after reaching full age.[12] Ratification may be express, or implied from conduct: the latter possibility is illustrated by the case in which the former minor continues after majority to act on the contract in such a way as to show that he regards it as binding on himself.[13] Because contracts in this group became binding as a result of ratification, they were sometimes called "voidable." But this is misleading as "voidable" normally means binding unless repudiated, whereas these contracts do not bind the minor unless he ratifies.

(c) EXECUTED CONTRACTS. Once the minor has actually performed the contract he cannot recover back money paid or property transferred by him under it merely on the ground that the contract did not bind him by reason of his minority.[14] He can only recover back such money or property in the same circumstances in which this remedy is available to an adult: for example, he can recover back money paid under the contract if there has been a total failure of consideration.[15] There is, indeed, some doubt as to the scope of the rule that property transferred in pursuance of contracts in this category cannot be recovered back. In *Chaplin* v. *Leslie Frewin (Publishers) Ltd.*[16] a majority of the Court of Appeal accepted the view that the minor would not be able to recover the copyright which he had transferred under the contract even if (contrary to the view of that majority) the contract did not bind him.[17] Lord Denning M.R., on the other hand, said that

---

[9] *Farnham* v. *Atkins* (1670) 1 Sid. 446; *Bruce* v. *Warwick* (1815) 6 Taunt. 118; and see *ante*, p. 481.

[10] *Flight* v. *Boland* (1828) 4 Russ. 298; *Lumley* v. *Ravenscroft* [1895] 1 Q.B. 683; *post*; p. 916.

[11] Exceptionally, a penal bond was regarded as void so that it could not be ratified: *Baylis* v. *Dinely* (1815) 3 M. & S. 477.

[12] See *Williams* v. Moor (1843) 11 M. & W. 256.

[13] This appears from cases which distinguished for the purpose of s.2 of the Infants Relief Act 1874 between a "ratification" (which under that section was not enforceable) and a fresh promise (which was enforceable): *e.g. Brown* v. *Harper* (1893) 68 L.T. 488. Now that s.2 has been repealed by Minors Contracts Act 1987, ss.1(a) and 4(2), a mere ratification is enforceable.

[14] *Wilson* v. *Kearse* (1800) Peake Add. Cas. 196; *Corpe* v. *Overston* (1833) 10 Bing. 252, 259; *Ex p. Taylor* (1856) 8 D.M. & G. 254, 256.

[15] *Post*, p. 927.

[16] [1966] Ch. 71; *ante*, p. 487.

[17] This view was based "on the authorities cited to us" (at p. 94). But these were not strictly in point as the contract in one of them (*Steinberg* v. *Scala* (*Leeds*) Ltd. [1923] 2 Ch. 452) was truly voidable, while in the other two (*Valentini* v. *Canali* (1889) 24 Q.B.D. 166; *Pearce* v. *Brain* [1929] 2 K.B. 310) the contracts were "absolutely void" within s.1 of the Infants Relief Act 1874 (now repealed by Minors' Contracts Act 1987, ss.1(*a*) and 4(2)). The majority's view is more appropriately supported by the authorities cited in n. 14, *supra*.

the rule, by which property could not be recovered back, only applied to transfers by delivery and not to those which require a written document: it would be "absurd to hold that a contract to make a disposition is voidable and that the disposition is not."[18] But it is, with respect, hard to see why this is more absurd when the disposition has to be in writing than when it can, and does, take effect by delivery.[19]

(d) PASSING OF PROPERTY TO MINOR. It was said by Lush J. in *Stocks* v. *Wilson*[20] that, where goods were delivered to a minor under a contract of sale, the property in them passed to him "by the delivery." The view that property can pass to a minor under a contract which does not bind him seems to be supported by section 3(1) of the Minors' Contracts Act 1987: this subsection[21] refers to "property acquired" by the minor under such a contract, and to the power of the court to order him to "transfer" such property.[22] The property, in the case put, seems to pass by delivery with intention to pass property. It may indeed be argued that the seller's intention to pass property is based on the assumption that the contract binds the minor and is nullified if this assumption is untrue, just as the intention of a seller to pass property is nullified if the contract is void for mistake as to the identity of the buyer.[23] But delivery to the wrong person may well differ in effect from delivery for the wrong reason. In the first case there is no intention to pass the property to the person to whom the delivery is made; in the second there is such an intention, though possibly based on a mistaken assumption. Thus it is submitted that property passes to the minor by delivery. The great practical attraction of this view is that it enables the law to protect an innocent third party who later buys the goods from the minor. It is an open question whether property can pass to the minor without delivery,[24] simply by virtue of the contract. The question is of small practical importance since property is unlikely to pass in this way until the price has been paid[25]; and in that case the seller is unlikely to have any interest in claiming that he still has the property in the goods.

(e) PASSING OF PROPERTY FROM MINOR. It is clear from cases such as *Chaplin* v. *Leslie Frewin (Publishers) Ltd.*[26] that property can pass *from* the minor under a contract which does not bind him.[27] The same principle would apply where the minor made a pledge to secure a debt incurred under such a contract. The person taking the pledge would normally be guilty of an offence,[28] but this does not affect the civil consequences of the transaction.[29] Thus it seems that a special property in the thing pledged would pass to the pledgee and that the minor could not get the thing back

18 [1966] Ch. 71, 90; *cf. G (A)* v. *G (T)* [1970] 2 Q.B. 643, 652.
19 No such distinction is drawn where the contract is voidable for misrepresentation *ante*, pp. 331 *et seq*.
20 [1913] 2 K.B. 235, 246; *cf. Watts* v. *Seymour* [1967] 2 Q.B. 647.
21 *Post*, p. 495.
22 See further post, pp. 495–497.
23 *Cundy* v. *Lindsay* (1878) 3 App.Cas. 459; *ante*, p. 262.
24 *e.g.* under Sale of Goods Act 1979, s.18, rule 1.
25 See *R. V. Ward Ltd.* v. *Bignall* [1967] 1 Q.B. 534, 545.
26 [1966] Ch. 71; *ante*, pp. 487, 492.
27 Even Lord Denning accepted this view where the property was alleged to have passed by *delivery*: see *supra* at n. 18.
28 Consumer Credit Act 1974, s.114(2).
29 *Ibid.* s.170(1); *quaere* whether this excludes the rules stated at pp. 436–437 *ante*; *cf.* also pp. 441–448, *ante*.

without paying off the loan. This conclusion may be disadvantageous to the minor, but the argument that property passes by delivery seems to apply as much where the delivery is made *by*, as where it is made *to*, the minor.

4. Liability in Tort

The general rule is that minors are liable in tort in the same way as adults. One possible exception to this rule exists in the case of very young children: this does not concern us here. Another exception exists where a cause of action in tort arises out of, or in connection with, a contract which does not bind the minor.

Conduct amounting to a breach of contract may also be a tort.[30] If a minor engages in such conduct and is sued in tort, he can sometimes set up the invalidity of the contract as a defence to the tort claim. This was the position in *Jennings* v. *Rundall*,[31] where a minor had hired a horse "to be moderately ridden"; and it was held that he was not liable for "wrongfully and injuriously" riding it. To allow such a tort claim would undermine the protection which the law gives the minor by holding his contract invalid. But this rule only applies where the breach consists of wrongfully doing an act authorised by the contract. If the minor does an act forbidden by the contract he is liable in tort. Thus in *Burnard* v. *Haggis*[32] a minor hired a horse for riding: the contract expressly forbade jumping. He was held liable in tort when the horse was killed through being jumped. Similarly, an under-age bailee is liable in tort if he wrongfully disposes of the goods.[33] The distinction between the two lines of cases can be explained as the product of the law's two conflicting desires: to protect minors, but without causing unnecessary hardship to adults who deal with them.

The minor may be immune from liability in tort, not only where he commits a tort in breaking the invalid contract, but also where he commits a tort in procuring it. Thus it was held in *R. Leslie Ltd.* v. *Sheill*[34] that a minor could not be sued in deceit for inducing an adult to lend him money by fraudulent misrepresentations as to his age. Similarly it was held in *Stocks* v. *Wilson*[35] that a minor could not be sued in deceit for inducing an adult by such misrepresentations to sell and deliver goods to him. The practical effect of a judgment in tort in such cases would be to force the minor to repay the money lent or to pay the value of the goods obtained; and this would once again undermine the protection which the law gives the minor by holding the contract invalid.

5. Liability in Restitution

Before the Minors' Contracts Act 1987, a minor could be held liable to restore certain benefits received by him under a contract which did not bind him. Such liability was imposed in equity if the minor was guilty of fraud,[36] and at common law in certain cases in quasi-contract.[37] Section 3(1) of the 1987 Act now gives the court a discretion to order the minor to

---

[30] *Post*, pp. 472–473.
[31] (1799) 8 T.R. 335; *cf. Fawcett* v. *Smethurst* (1914) 84 L.J.K.B. 473.
[32] (1863) 14 C.B. (N.S.) 45.
[33] *Ballett* v. *Mingay* [1943] K.B. 281.
[34] [1914] 3 K.B. 607; *Johnson* v. *Pye* (1665) 1 Sid. 258.
[35] [1913] 2 K.B. 235.
[36] *Post*, pp. 497–499.
[37] *Post*, pp. 500–501.

transfer to the adult party any property acquired by the minor under such a contract, or any property representing it. Section 3(2) goes on to provide that nothing in section 3 "shall be taken to prejudice any other remedy available to the" adult party to the contract: thus in cases which fall outside section 3(1), or in which the court declines to exercise its discretion under that subsection, it remains open to the adult to seek restitution under the old rules of equity or common law. These therefore still require some discussion even though generally claims for restitution are now likely to be made under section 3(1), since the conditions imposed by the subsection are less onerous than those imposed by equity or by the common law rules of quasi-contract.

(1) Minors' Contracts Act 1987, s.3(1)

(a) SCOPE. This subsection deals with the case where a contract has been made with a minor and the contract "is unenforceable against [the minor] (or he repudiates it)[38] because he was a minor when the contract was made." In such a case the court "may, if it is just and equitable to do so, require [the minor] to transfer to the [other party] any property acquired by the [minor] under the contract, or any property representing it."

(i) *Restoration of property acquired.* The subsection would most obviously apply to a case like *Nash* v. *Inman*[39]: the minor could be ordered to return the fancy waistcoats to the seller. Such an order could be made even though the minor was not guilty of fraud, which is essential to liability in equity[40]; and even though there would, in the case put, be no liability in quasi-contract at common law.[41]

(ii) *Proceeds of property acquired.* Section 3(1) goes beyond the simple case just put, in that the court can order the minor to transfer either the "property acquired . . . under the contract" or "any property representing it." Thus if the minor were to exchange the fancy waistcoats for a set of silver candlesticks, he could be ordered to transfer those to the seller of the fancy waistcoats. On the other hand, section 3(1) would not apply where the minor had dissipated the property acquired under the contract or its proceeds: *e.g.* where he had bought champagne and consumed it, or where he had sold property acquired under the contract for cash and had used the money to pay for a holiday. Section 3(1) only empowers the court to order the minor to transfer either the property acquired under the contract or property representing it: the court cannot order him to pay either the price or the reasonable value of what he has obtained out of his other assets. The underlying principle seems to be that the minor should not be enriched by retaining "property" obtained under the contract. But his general assets (other than that "property") are not to be diminished as a result of the exercise of the court's discretion under the section.

The discretion will present few problems where the "property acquired . . . under the contract" is still in the minor's possession; but dif-

---

[38] This phrase refers to the "voidable" contracts discussed *ante*, at pp. 488–491.

[39] [1908] 2 K.B. 1; *ante*, p. 483.

[40] *Post*, pp. 497–498.

[41] English law does not recognise any quasi-contractual claim for the recovery of chattels (as distinct from money): see *Power* v. *Wells* (1778) 2 Cowp. 818. The only possible claim for chattels is in tort for wrongful interference with possession or with an immediate right to possession; and in the case put there would be no such claim as property in the goods would have passed to the minor.

ficulty can obviously arise where the discretion is invoked in respect of "property representing it." The case in which the minor simply exchanges the "property acquired" for something else will be relatively uncommon. More usually, he will sell the "property acquired" and use the money to buy something else; that other thing may have been paid for wholly or in part with the money obtained from the sale of the property acquired. Further problems can arise where that money is paid by the minor into a bank account which is in credit and from which money is then drawn out to pay for the substitute purchase. In such a case it may be very hard to tell whether that substitute is indeed "property representing" the property acquired under the original contract. Even greater difficulties could arise if the substitute had been bought under another contract which was unenforceable against the minor, and if only part of the price due under that contract had been paid by the minor; in such a case claims under section 3 for the transfer of the same thing might be made by two sellers.

(iii) *Meaning of "property."* A final difficulty is to determine what is meant by "property" in the section; and in particular whether "property" includes money.[42] The difficulty arises because the case-law before the Act displayed a somewhat greater reluctance to make a minor liable to "restore" a sum of money than to return goods obtained by him under the contract[43]—apparently because a judgment against him to pay a sum of money was more likely than one for the return of goods to present the appearance of indirectly enforcing the contract. But those cases certainly do not rule out the possibility of making the minor restore money,[44] at least where he was guilty of fraud, and section 3(1) seems to be intended to extend such liability to cases in which there was no fraud.[45] Moreover, it appears from the legislative history of the Act that section 3(1) is intended to produce the result that "the minor can be compelled to hand over the proceeds if he has sold the property[46];" and, in the case of goods at least, the proceeds of a *sale*, by definition, consist of money.[47] This supports the view that the "property representing" the "property acquired" includes money; and if this is so, then it is submitted that the "property acquired" also includes money, since the word "property" must prima facie bear the same meaning in both the places in which it occurs in the subsection. Thus it is submitted that where a minor buys goods under a contract which is unenforceable against him by reason of his minority, and then sells them, he can be ordered to transfer the money to the seller; while if the minor borrows money under such a contract, and uses it to buy goods, he can be ordered to transfer those goods to the lender.

(b) Discretion of the court. Section 3(1) does not entitle the adult party to the transfer of the property as of right: it only provides that the court "may, if it is just and equitable to do so," order the transfer. In exer-

---

[42] The Act contains no definition of property; contrast Theft Act 1968, s.4(1), expressly providing that "property" includes money.

[43] See *R. Leslie Ltd.* v. *Sheill* [1914] 3 K.B. 607 (*post*, p. 498); *Cowern* v. *Neild* [1912] 2 K.B. 419 (*post*, p. 500).

[44] See *Stocks* v. *Wilson* [1913] 2 K.B. 235, *post*, p. 499, and *post*, pp. 500–501.

[45] See Law Com. No. 134 para. 4.21. The Act is based on this Report; for use of such materials as aids to interpretation, see *M/S Aswan Engineering Establishment Co.* v. *Lupdine Ltd.* [1987] 1 W.L.R. 1, 14.

[46] Law Commission Report, *supra*, n. 45, para. 4.21.

[47] Sale of Goods Act 1979 s.2(1) ("for a money consideration").

cising this discretion, the court may take various factors into account. One is the difficulty, where the minor has disposed of the property acquired, of determining whether assets still owned by him are indeed property representing what he originally acquired. The process of "tracing" assets into their product can be complex[48]; and the court may restrict the operation of section 3(1) to cases in which it is relatively clear that the property which the minor is ordered to restore does indeed represent that acquired under the contract. To extend the operation of the subsection beyond this point would obviously increase the danger that an order to transfer property (especially in the form of money) would amount to indirect enforcement of the contract against the minor. The operation of the equitable doctrine of restitution in cases of fraud gave rise to a similar danger, and it was to avert this danger that the courts restricted the scope of that doctrine. The relevant equity cases are discussed below[49] (even though the equitable doctrine has lost much of its former practical importance) because it is thought that they now provide guidance for the exercise of the statutory discretion. A second factor which the court might take into account is the fairness of the original contract: thus if the court regarded the price payable under the contract as too high it might order the minor to return the property unless he paid a reasonable price fixed by the court.[50] In failing to specify the circumstances and manner in which the discretion is to be exercised, the subsection no doubt gives rise to some uncertainty; but it avoids complexity. In the context, the balance that it thus strikes is satisfactory, for the rules which govern a minor's liability in restitution are not of a kind on which either party to the contract relies (or should be encouraged to rely) in conducting his business affairs.

(2) Effects of fraud

(a) COMMON LAW. At common law, a minor cannot be made liable on a contract merely because he has committed a fraud on the other party in inducing him to enter into the contract.[51] The other party can at most rely on the fraud as a defence or as a ground of rescission.[52]

(b) IN EQUITY. The common law rules just stated unduly favoured a class of minors that least deserved protection. Hence equity gave further relief against minors on the ground of fraud. For this purpose, it seems that fraud meant some misrepresentation by the minor as to his age; so that his mere

---

48 *Cf. post*, p. 509.

49 *Post*, pp. 499–500.

50 See the reference in para. 4.21 of the Law Commission's Report (*supra*, n. 45) to para. 6.10 of the Commission's earlier Working Paper No. 81 on Minors' Contracts.

51 *Bartlett* v. *Wells* (1862) 1 B. & S. 836; *De Roo* v. *Foster* (1862) 12 C.B.(N.S.) 272; *Miller* v. *Blankley* (1878) 38 L.T. 527; *Levene* v. *Brougham* (1909) 25 T.L.R. 265; exceptionally a debt incurred by fraud can be proved in an uncontested bankruptcy: *Re King* (1858) 3 D. & J. 63.

52 *e.g. Lemprière* v. *Lange* (1879) 12 Ch.D. 675. No attempt seems to have been made in the cases to argue that the adult could, by rescinding the contract for fraud, avoid the minor's title *at law* (*cf. ante*, p. 331). *Quaere* whether the court could award damages in lieu of rescission against a minor under s.2(2) of the Misrepresentation Act 1967 (*ante*, p. 321). To do this might amount to indirect enforcement of the contract in the sense discussed at p. 499, *post*.

failure to declare that he was under age did not amount to fraud[53]; nor was it fraud for him to keep, without paying, goods obtained by him under a contract which did not bind him.[54] Equitable relief on the ground of fraud took a number of forms.

(i) *Restoration of benefits.* Our principal concern is with the power of equity to order the fraudulent minor to restore benefits obtained under the contract.[55] The remedy, being equitable, was presumably discretionary,[56] and in this respect it resembles the statutory remedy now available under section 3(1) of the Minors' Contracts Act 1987.[57] On the other hand, the statutory remedy is in two respects more favourable to the adult than the old equitable remedy. First, the statutory remedy is available even though the minor was not guilty of fraud. Secondly, there is no doubt that the statutory remedy extends to the proceeds of the thing obtained under the contract,[58] while it was disputed whether the equitable remedy was available in respect of such proceeds.[59] Thus although the equitable remedy is one of those expressly preserved by the 1987 Act,[60] there seems to be no reason why the adult party should wish to resort to it. It follows that questions as to the exact scope and extent of the equitable remedy no longer have any practical importance. The cases concerned with such questions are now useful only as providing illustrations of the factors that the courts may take into account in deciding whether to exercise their statutory discretion to order the minor to transfer property acquired under the contract, or property representing it. Two cases are of particular interest in this context.

The first is *Stocks* v. *Wilson*[61] where a minor had obtained goods under a contract induced by fraud and had disposed of some of those goods. He was held liable to account[62] to the original seller for the proceeds of the goods. The second is *R. Leslie Ltd.* v. *Sheill*[63] where a minor had by fraud obtained a loan of £400 and was held not liable in equity to restore the money. Lord Sumner said: "the money was paid over to be used as the defendant's own and he has so used it, and, I suppose, spent it. There is no question of tracing it, no possibility of restoring the very thing got by fraud, nothing but compulsion through a personal judgment to pay an equivalent sum out of his present or future resources . . ."[64]

The crucial factor in *R. Leslie Ltd.* v. *Sheill* was that there was no question of tracing the money, that is of showing that it, or some asset repre-

---

[53] For the definition of fraud, see *ante*, p. 497. In equity a person could be guilty of fraud even though he had no "actual intention to cheat": *Nocton* v. *Ashburton* [1914] A.C. 932, 954; but in the present context a number of cases state the requirement of a misrepresentation as to age: *Stikeman* v. *Dawson* (1847) 1 De G. & Sm. 90, 103; *Ex p. Jones* (1881) 18 CL.D. 109, 120; *Re Hodson* [1894] 2 Ch. 421, 427.

[54] This must have been assumed in *Nash* v. *Inman* [1908] 2 K.B. 1; for the contrary view, see Atiyah, 22 M.L.R. 273, 275. Because of Minors' Contracts Act 1987, s.3(1), the point no longer has any practical importance: see *infra*, after n. 60.

[55] *e.g. Clarke* v. *Cobley* (1789) 2 Cox 173.

[56] *Cf. ante*, pp. 284, 285, 338; *post*, pp. 907, 919.

[57] *Ante*, p. 496.

[58] See the words "any property representing it" in s.3(1): ante, p. 495.

[59] *Infra*, at nn. 61 to 68.

[60] s.3(2).

[61] [1913] 2 K.B. 235.

[62] *Ibid.* at p. 247—a passage criticised in *R. Leslie Ltd.* v. *Sheill* [1914] 3 K.B. 607.

[63] *Supra.*

[64] [1914] 3 K.B. 607, 619.

senting it, was still in the hands of the minor. If he had still had the £400 he could have been made to restore it in equity[65]; and if he had used the £400 to buy a car he could have been ordered to hand the car over to the lender.[66] An order to "transfer . . . property" could now be made in such circumstances under section 3(1) of the 1987 Act, even in the absence of fraud.[67] Conversely, in a case like *Stocks* v. *Wilson* the minor could be ordered to transfer the proceeds of sale if they could be identified as "property representing" the goods.[68] It is submitted that such an order could be made even if the minor had happened to resell the goods for the exact equivalent of the contract price. It is no objection to a claim for restitution that it leads to the same *measure* of recovery as an action on the contract. To order a minor to pay such an amount (or any amount) only becomes objectionable on account of the *nature* of the judgment: that is, if the judgment is, in Lord Sumner's words, "a personal judgment to pay an equivalent sum out of his present or future resources." The only type of order that can be made against the minor is one to *restore* the property acquired, or its proceeds, in equity, or to *transfer* it under section 3(1). He cannot be made liable to *pay* for the property acquired or to *account* for its proceeds by a personal judgment enforceable against his general assets. This point seems to have been overlooked in *Stocks* v. *Wilson* where the court ordered the minor to *account for* the proceeds of sale without enquiring whether those proceeds were still in the hands of the minor. The purpose of the equitable and statutory remedies is to ensure that the minor is not enriched as a result of the transaction which is not binding on him; but the remedy should not diminish such general resources as he had apart from the transaction. It follows that the remedies are limited by the value of the property in the hands of the minor at the time of judgment. If by then the minor has dissipated part of the property (or its proceeds) the remedy is available only in respect of the remainder.

(ii) *Other forms of relief.* Equity gives relief against fraudulent minors in a number of other cases. A minor who obtains payment of a share in a trust fund by fraudulently pretending to be of age cannot claim a second payment when he reaches full age.[69] A minor remainderman who by fraud enables the tenant for life to mortgage the estate cannot, when the estate vests in him, deny the validity of the charge.[70] These cases do not call for extended discussion here as they are not directly connected with the law of contract. It has, indeed, been suggested that equity recognised a broad principle of relief: *viz.* that if a minor sued without offering to pay he would be guilty of "fraud" which would give the adult an equitable defence,[71] even (apparently) where, under the contract, payment from the minor was not due until after the adult's performance. But the authorities do not support such a broad definition of "fraud": on the contrary, they support the view that, even in equity, relief is only available to the adult

---

[65] There would have been, in Lord Sumner's words (*supra*, at n. 64), a "possibility of restoring the very thing got by fraud."
[66] It is assumed that the money lent could be "traced" into the car, within Lord Sumner's words (*supra*, at n. 64).
[67] *Ante*, p. 495.
[68] *Ibid.*
[69] *Cory* v. *Gertcken* (1816) 2 Madd. 40.
[70] *Watts* v. *Cresswell* (1714) 2 Eq.Ca.Abr. 515.
[71] Atiyah, 22 M.L.R. 273.

where the minor's "fraud" takes the form of a misrepresentation by him as to his age.[72]

(3) Liability in quasi-contract

In certain circumstances a minor who has obtained benefits at the expense of an adult may be liable to the adult at common law in quasi-contract. This remedy is available as of right, and it is expressly preserved by section 3(2) of the Minor's Contracts Act 1987.

The quasi-contractual remedy is illustrated by cases of so-called waiver of tort, in which the victim of a fraud (and of certain other torts) can sue in quasi-contract to recover certain benefits obtained by the tortfeasor. Such an action lies against a minor if he would have been liable to the direct action in tort. Thus in *Bristow* v. *Eastman*[73] a minor who was an apprentice had embezzled[74] his master's property and was held liable in quasi-contract.

But the courts will resist attempts to circumvent a minor's lack of contractual capacity by means of an action in quasi-contract. Thus in *R. Leslie Ltd.* v. *Sheill* the lenders made an alternative claim that the minor was liable to repay the money lent as money had and received to their use. This claim also failed as "the cause of action is in substance *ex contractu* and is so directly connected with the contract of loan that the action would be an indirect way of enforcing that contract."[75] Here again the decisive objection is not that the measure of liability may be the same in a quasi-contractual action as in an action for breach of contract: the crucial point is that, where the money had been spent, the only possible effect of the judgment in either kind of action would be to impose personal liability on the minor, enforceable against his assets generally.[76]

Much difficulty is caused by *Cowern* v. *Nield.*[77] A minor who was a trader sold hay and clover, and was paid in advance. He failed to deliver any hay, and the clover which he delivered was defective, so that the buyer justifiably rejected it. As the contract was a trading contract, the buyer's claim for damages failed; and his claim in quasi-contract for the return of the money that he had paid was also rejected. The court thought that such a claim could succeed if the minor had obtained the money by fraud, and therefore ordered a new trial on the issue of fraud. But this reasoning is, with respect, open to criticism. A minor cannot be made liable in quasi-contract if "the action would be an indirect way of enforcing [the invalid] contract."[78] If (contrary to the submission made above) this means that the judgment must not impose the same *measure* of liability as a judgment in action for breach of contract, then the action for the return of the price should have succeeded in *Cowern* v. *Nield* irrespective of fraud. For the minor's duty under the contract was to deliver the goods, and the damages for their non-delivery might have been quite different from the price. But if (as seems more probable) indirect enforcement refers to the imposition of

---

[72] *Ante*, p. 498.
[73] (1974) 1 Esp. 172. "Even this has been doubted": *per* Lord Sumner in *R. Leslie Ltd.* v. *Sheill* [1914] 3 K.B. 607, 613.
[74] Such conduct would now be theft under Theft Act 1968, s.15.
[75] [1914] 3 K.B. at p. 621; *cf.* p. 613.
[76] *Cf. ante*, p. 499.
[77] [1912] 2 K.B. 419.
[78] *R. Leslie Ltd.* v. *Sheill* [1914] 3 K.B. at p. 621.

personal liability on the minor, the action should not have succeeded merely on proof of fraud. The minor should have been liable only to the extent that the money or its identifiable proceeds were still in his hands. Under section 3(1) of the Minors' Contracts Act 1987 the court could now order the minor to transfer such money, or property representing it, to the buyer, irrespective of fraud; but that remedy is discretionary, so that the buyer might prefer to pursue his remedy in quasi-contract, which is available as of right.

SECTION 2. MENTAL PATIENTS[79]

The law relating to contracts with persons suffering from mental disorder represents a compromise between two principles. The first is that such a person should not be liable on his contracts if he is incapable of intelligent consent. The second is that it might cause hardship to one contracting party to allow the other to "stultify himself."[80]

1. In General[81]

A contract with a mental patient is valid, except in two cases:

(1) Disability known to other party

If the other contracting party knows of the patient's disability, the contract is voidable at the patient's option.[82] The burden is on the patient to show that his disability prevented him from understanding the particular transaction,[83] and that the other party knew this. It seems that the patient becomes absolutely bound if he ratifies the contract after he is cured.[84] There is also some support for the view that the contract is binding so long as it was a fair one, even though the disability of one party was known to the other.[85]

Where the sane party does not know of the other's disability, the contract is valid: it cannot be attacked merely on the ground that it was "unfair" in the sense that its terms were more favourable to the sane party than they were to the party under the disability.[86] The contract can only be attacked on the ground of "unfairness" if the circumstances are such that the party under the disability can rely, like a person of normal capacity, on the equitable rules relating to undue influence or unconscionable bargains.[87]

(2) Property subject to control of the court[88]

If the patient is one whose property is subject to the control of the court[89] an attempt by him to dispose of the property does not bind him, since, if it

---

[79] A convenient, if slightly inaccurate, term to describe a person suffering from mental disorder within the Mental Health Act 1983.
[80] *Beverley's Case* (1603) 4 Co.Rep. 123b.
[81] Hudson [1984] Conv. 32.
[82] *Molton* v. *Camroux* (1849) 4 Ex. 17; *Imperial Loan Co.* v. *Stone* [1892] 1 Q.B. 599.
[83] *Re K* [1988] Ch. 310, *post*, p. 653.
[84] *Birkin* v. *Wing* (1890) 63 L.T. 80; *Manches* v. *Trimborn* (1946) 115 L.J.K.B. 305.
[85] *Dane* v. *Kirkwall* (1838) 8 C. & P. 679.
[86] *Hart* v. *O'Connor* [1985] A.C. 1000.
[87] *Ante*, pp. 366–371.
[88] Jennings, 23 M.L.R. 421; Fridman, 79 L.Q.R. 509–516.
[89] Under Part VII of the Mental Health Act 1983.

did bind him, it would interfere with the court's control over the property.[90] But the contract binds the other party.[91]

The rule that the contract does not bind the patient clearly applies to any contract which purports to dispose of the patient's property. But it is not clear whether the rule applies *only* to such contracts, or whether it extends to *all* contracts with mental patients whose property is subject to the control of the court. On the one hand it can be argued that every contract creates a potential liability to pay money and thus interferes with the court's control over the property. On the other hand there are some negative contracts which can be enforced by injunction against the patient's person which need not interfere with his property. There is no reason, on principle, why such contracts should not be enforced in this way. The question is largely academic as the court only exercises control over the property in cases of serious disorder. The other party will generally know of such disorder and be unable to sue on this ground.

2. Necessaries

Section 3(2) of the Sale of Goods Act 1979 provides that "where necessaries are sold and delivered . . . to a person who by reason of mental incapacity . . . is incompetent to contract, he must pay a reasonable price for them." As a mental patient is by no means always "incompetent to contract" two situations must be considered.

If the patient would be bound by the contract under the rules stated above, his liability for necessaries is not affected by section 3(2). Thus a person who sells and delivers necessaries to the patient without knowing of his disorder can enforce the contract[92]: he is not limited to an action for a reasonable price.

If the patient would not be bound by the contract under the rules stated above, he is liable under section 3(2). Thus a person who sells and delivers necessaries to the patient knowing of his disorder cannot enforce the contract: he can only recover a reasonable price.

Section 3(2) applies "where necessaries are sold and delivered" to the patient. These words are scarcely appropriate where necessaries are simply supplied to a patient whose disorder is so serious that he has no capacity for rational thought; or where a patient in this condition is simply maintained at the expense of another person. In such cases the person who supplies or pays for the necessaries has a remedy at common law under the doctrine of agency of necessity[93] unless he acted gratuitously, without thought of recompense.[94]

We have seen that, in the case of minors, "necessaries" can include services no less than goods[95]; and the same principle can apply in the case of mental patients. For example, medical treatment supplied to such a person can be a necessary. Two questions arise in relation to such services: first, whether the treatment is lawful even though the patient lacks the capacity to consent to it; and secondly, whether the person providing the treatment

[90] *Re Walker* [1905] 1 Ch. 160; *Re Marshall* [1920] 1 Ch. 284.

[91] *Cf. Baldwyn* v. *Smith* [1900] 1 Ch. 588.

[92] *Baxter* v. *Portsmouth* (1826) 5 B. & C. 170.

[93] *Brockwell* v. *Bullock* (1889) 22 Q.B.D. 567; *Pontypridd Union* v. *Drew* [1927] 1 K.B. 214, 220; see also *Re Rhodes* (1889) 44 Ch.D. 94 and *post*, p. 624.

[94] *Re Rhodes, supra.*

[95] *Ante*, p. 483.

is entitled to be paid for it. The first question arose in *Re F.*[96] where it was held that a sterilisation operation could lawfully be carried on on a mental patient if it was necessary to save her life or to secure an improvement in (or to prevent deterioration of) her health. The second question did not arise[97] as the treatment was carried out under the National Health Service; but it seems that, if necessary services are rendered to a mental patient in circumstances in which a charge would normally be made for them, the person rendering them would be entitled to a reasonable remuneration for them.

A person who lends money to a mental patient knowing of his disorder cannot enforce the contract, but can recover so much of the money as has actually been spent on necessaries.[98]

SECTION 3. DRUNKARDS

Extreme drunkenness is a defence to an action on a contract if it prevents the defendant from understanding the transaction, and if the plaintiff knows this.[99] The drunkard is liable if he ratifies the contract when he becomes sober.[1] He is also liable for necessaries[2] in the same way as a mental patient.

A defendant cannot rely at law on drunkenness which merely blurred his business sense: but such drunkenness is a ground on which equity may refuse to decree specific performance.[3]

SECTION 4. CORPORATIONS

1. Common Law Corporations

Corporations are created at common law by Royal Charter. The orthodox view is that a common law corporation has the same contractual capacity as a natural person of full age and capacity. Although this view is only based on dicta,[4] which have been challenged,[5] it is probably good law. Thus a contract with such a corporation is binding although it is forbidden, or not authorised, by its charter. But if the corporation makes such a contract the Attorney-General can take proceedings for the revocation of its charter; and any member of the corporation can restrain it by injunction from

---

[96] [1990] 2 A.C. 1.
[97] *Ibid.* p. 74.
[98] *Re Beavan* [1912] 1 Ch. 196.
[99] *Gore* v. *Gibson* (1843) 13 M. & W. 623.
[1] *Matthews* v. *Baxter* (1873) L.R. 8 Ex. 132.
[2] *Gore* v. *Gibson*, *supra*, at p. 626; Sale of Goods Act 1979, s.3(2).
[3] *Post*, p. 909.
[4] *Case of Sutton's Hospital* (1613) 10 Co.Rep. 1, 30b; *Wenlock* v. *River Dee Co.* (1885) 36 Ch.D. 374, 385; *British S. Africa Co.* v. *De Beers Consolidated Mines* [1910] 1 Ch. 354, 374; *Jenkin* v. *Pharmaceutical Society* [1921] 1 Ch. 392, 398; *Institution of Mechanical Engineers* v. *Cane* [1961] A.C. 696, 724; *Hazell* v. *Hammersmith & Fulham L.B.C.* [1991] 1 All E.R. 545, 563. Furmston, 24 M.L.R. 518. See also *Ayers* v. *South Australia Banking Co.* (1868) L.R. 3 P.C. 548, which appears to assume the correctness of the generally accepted view. For the possibility that the powers of a charter corporation may be restricted by special legislation, see *post*, p. 507.
[5] *e.g.* Holdsworth, *History of English Law*, Vol. 9, pp. 55–66; Street, *Ultra Vires*, pp. 18–22; Carden, 26 L.Q.R. 320.

carrying on a forbidden activity which may lead to the revocation of its charter,[6] or claim a declaration that the activity is *ultra vires*.[7]

2. Statutory Corporations

Statutory corporations can be created in two ways: first, by complying with the formalities required by the Companies Acts; and secondly, by special statute, passed to create the particular corporation in question. Since 1862, most trading companies have been created in the first of these two ways; the principal Act now in force is the Companies Act 1985.

(1) Companies created under the Companies Acts

(a) INTRODUCTION. Where a company is incorporated under the Companies Acts, the objects for which it is formed must be stated in its memorandum of association.[8] The contractual capacity of the company was formerly limited by the *ultra vires* doctrine, under which any act which was not authorised by the memorandum was void in law; and, being a nullity, it could not be ratified even by a unanimous vote of the company's shareholders.[9] It followed that the company was not liable on a contract which was not authorised by its memorandum. The primary purpose of the doctrine was to protect investors in the company by giving them some assurance that the assets of the company would not be used in some wholly unexpected way. On the other hand, a person who made a contract with the company was liable to be prejudiced by the doctrine, since he was unlikely to have read the company's memorandum, or (if he had read it) to have understood it. The doctrine could also prejudice the company itself by preventing it from taking advantage of business opportunities which (perhaps as a result of a defect in drafting) fell technically outside its objects. The company could to some extent avoid this prejudice by altering its objects, but its power to make such alterations could be exercised only for seven specified purposes.[10] It could also draw its objects clause in very wide terms, enabling it to do almost any act which could be done by a company[11]; but such very widely drawn clauses tended to be restrictively interpreted by the courts,[12] since they made the protection which the *ultra vires* doctrine was intended to give to shareholders quite illusory.

(b) THE 1989 REFORMS. The effects of the *ultra vires* doctrine, as described above, were subjected to much criticism[13] and significant reforms were introduced by the Companies Act 1989, which inserted a number of new sections into the Companies Act 1985.

In discussing these reforms, two preliminary points should be noted. First, it is now possible to state the object of a company to be "to carry on

---

6 *Jenkin* v. *Pharmaceutical Society* [1921] 1 Ch. 392.
7 *Phamaceutical Society of Great Britain* v. *Dickson* [1970] A.C. 403.
8 Companies Act 1985, s.2(1)(*c*).
9 *Ashbury Ry. Carriage & Iron Co.* v. *Riche* (1875) L.R. 7 H.L. 653.
10 Companies Act 1985, s.4 (original version), now replaced by the provision referred to at n. 15, *infra*.
11 *Cotman* v. *Brougham* [1918] A.C. 514; *Re Horsley & Weight Ltd.* [1982] Ch. 442; *Brady* v. *Brady* [1989] A.C. 755, 772.
12 *e.g. Rolled Steel (Holdings) Ltd.* v. *B.S.C.* [1986] Ch. 246, drawing the distinction referred to at n. 17, *infra*.
13 See especially Prentice, *Reform of the Ultra Vires Rule*, a consultative paper issued by the Department of Trade and Industry in 1986.

business as a general commercial company." The object of the company will then be "to carry on any trade or business whatsoever" and also to do "all such things as are incidental or conducive to carrying on any trade or business by it."[14] The *ultra vires* doctrine can have very little scope in the case of a company with such an objects clause. Secondly, a company can now alter its objects for any purpose whatsoever, and not only for the seven purposes for which it could formerly do so.[15]

The legal effects of acts done by the company which are not authorised by its memorandum are dealt with by two new sections (35 and 35A) inserted in 1989[16] into the Companies Act 1985. These two sections are based on a distinction which was recognised in the previous English case-law,[17] and was also drawn in an European Economic Community Council Directive,[18] between the *capacity* of the company and the *powers* of the board of directors to bind it. These provisions alleviate the hardship which the *ultra vires* doctrine formerly caused to persons who dealt with the company, while retaining some degree of protection for its shareholders.

(i) *The company's capacity.* So far as the company's capacity is concerned, the new section 35(1) of the 1985 Act provides that the validity of any act done by a company is not (as a general rule[19]) to be called into question on the ground of lack of the company's capacity by reason of anything in (or, presumably, not in) its memorandum. The argument that a contract is void for lack of capacity if it is not authorised by the memorandum is thus no longer available. Section 35(1) will generally operate in favour of persons who enter into contracts with the company, which can no longer rely on its own lack of capacity (by reason of the provisions of the memorandum) against such persons. It is equally true that these persons cannot rely on such lack of capacity against the company.[20]

Members of the company are, in turn, protected by section 35(2), which gives them the right to bring proceedings to restrain the doing of an act which would (but for section 35(1)) be beyond the company's capacity.[21] But no such proceedings lie in respect of an act to be done in the fulfilment of a legal obligation arising from a previous act of the company: in other words, proceedings under subsection (2) cannot be brought to prevent the performance of a contract which cannot be called into question on the ground of lack of capacity by virtue of subsection (1). Members of the company are further protected by section 35(3), by which it remains the duty of directors to observe any limitation on their powers flowing from the company's memorandum. An act which transgresses these limitations can indeed be ratified by the company by special resolution, but a separate

---

14 Companies Act 1985, s.3A, as inserted by Companies Act 1989, s.110(1).

15 Companies Act 1985, s.4, as substituted by Companies Act 1989, s.110(2).

16 By Companies Act 1989, s.108(1).

17 *Rolled Steel (Holdings) Ltd.* v. *B.S.C.* [1986] Ch. 246.

18 68/151/EEC Art. 9. For the construction of legislation based on such directives, see *Litster* v. *Forth Dry Dock & Engineering Co. Ltd.* [1990] 1 A.C. 546, adopting a "purposive" construction "even though, perhaps, it may involve some departure from the strict and literal application of the words which the legislature has elected to use" (at p. 559).

19 For exceptions, see Companies Act 1985, s.35(4), as substituted by Companies Act 1989, s.108(1) (charitable companies and certain transactions with directors).

20 The phrase "shall not be called into question" in s.35(1) applies equally to both parties. Contrast the wording of s.35A(1), set out at n. 24, *infra*.

21 *Cf.* the position in the case of charter corporations, *ante*, p. 504 at n. 6.

special resolution is required to relieve the directors from liability in respect of the act.[22]

(ii) *The powers of the directors.* Where a contract is not within the objects clause of the memorandum, the mere fact that it cannot be called into question on the ground of lack of capacity will not enable a person who deals with the company to enforce it; for the making of such an unauthorised contract is necessarily beyond the powers of the directors. Further protection to such a person is therefore given by the new section 35A(1) of the 1985 Act. This provides that, "In favour of a person dealing with a company in good faith, the power of the board of directors to bind the company, or to authorise others to do so, shall [as a general rule[23]] be deemed to be free of any limitation under the company's constitution."[24] The person who deals with the company is not bound to enquire whether the transaction is permitted by the memorandum or whether the power of the directors to bind the company or to authorise others to do so is limited.[25] He is presumed to have acted in good faith until the contrary is proved[26]; and he is not to be regarded as acting in bad faith "by reason *only* of his knowing that an act is beyond the powers of the directors under the company's constitution."[27] This provision allows for the possibility that it may actually be in the interests of the company to take advantage of a commercial opportunity by entering into a contract which is technically not within its objects. On the other hand, a person would presumably not be dealing with the company in good faith if the transaction in question was not only beyond the powers of the directors but also constituted a breach of their fiduciary duty to it, or was otherwise a collusive attempt on the part of the directors and the person dealing with the company to act in a way that was contrary to the interests of the company. In such a case the fact that a contract was not authorised by the company's memorandum would not, indeed, make it open to challenge on the ground of lack of capacity, but by reason of the element of bad faith the contract would be unenforceable as it was beyond the directors' powers, and it would not be saved by section 35A(1).

Persons who deal with the company are further protected by section 35A(5) which provides that section 35A(1) does not affect any liability incurred by the directors to persons other than members of the company by reason of the directors' exceeding their powers. Where the company is *liable* by virtue of subsection (1), such liability is unlikely to be incurred[28]; though it is possible for a director to undertake additional personal liability under a collateral contract. Where the company is *not* liable because the person dealing with it did so in bad faith, a claim against the directors is unlikely to succeed: it would probably be dismissed on the analogy of the

---

[22] Companies Act 1985, s.35(3) (as substituted by Companies Act 1989, s.108(1)).
[23] *Ibid.* s.35A(6) (excepting charitable companies and certain transactions with directors).
[24] "Limitation under the company's constitution" is broadly defined in s.35A(3) and includes, *inter alia*, a limitation derived from a resolution of the company in general meeting.
[25] Companies Act 1985, s.35B, and see also s.711A (as substituted by Companies Act 1989, ss.108(1) and 142(1)).
[26] *Ibid.* s.35A(2)(*c*).
[27] *Ibid.* s.35A(2)(*b*) (italics supplied).
[28] *e.g.* the remedy for breach of warranty of authority (*post*, p. 509) would not be available if the contract bound the company under s.35A(1): see *post*, p. 642.

rule that a contract to defraud a third party (*i.e.* the company) is illegal and void.[29]

Members of the company are protected, in that they can bring proceedings to restrain the doing of an act which is beyond the powers of the directors.[30] But no such proceedings lie "in respect of an act to be done in fulfilment of a legal obligation arising from a previous act of the company."[31] Presumably it follows that proceedings cannot be brought to restrain a company from performing a contract which a person dealing with the company could enforce against it under section 35A(1). It seems that such a contract will, by virtue of that subsection, be deemed to be an "act of the company" even though the directors actually had no power to enter into it on the company's behalf.

Section 35A(1) only operates "in favour of a person dealing with" the company. It therefore does not confer rights on the company. The company can however acquire such rights by ratifying the transaction.[32]

(2) Corporations incorporated by special statute

These corporations continue to be subject to the *ultra vires* doctrine as developed at common law. The doctrine was originally established in relation to such corporations[33] and is, with respect to them, not affected by the reforms which have been described above.[34] However, before these reforms came into force many of the rules which determine the scope and effects of the doctrine were laid down in cases arising out of the contracts with companies incorporated under the Companies Acts. These cases are obsolete, now that the common law doctrine no longer restricts the capacity of such companies. But the principles stated in them can still (where appropriate) apply to transactions with corporations which are created, or whose capacity is limited, by special statute. For this reason, the following account is to some extent based on such cases.

(a) THE ULTRA VIRES DOCTRINE. The contractual capacity of a corporation created by special statute is restricted by the *ultra vires* doctrine. The objects of such a corporation are set out in the statute by which it was created (or in rules made in pursuance of that statute). Any act done by or on behalf of the corporation which is not authorised by (or under) the incorporating statute is *ultra vires* and ineffective. It follows that an *ultra vires* contract made by such a corporation does not bind the corporation. The corporation can also be restrained from doing *ultra vires* acts.[35] The same rules apply where the corporation has been created in some other way (*e.g.* by Royal Charter) but its capacity is nevertheless defined or limited by statute.[36]

(i) *Whether transaction is ultra vires.* The questions whether a particular transaction falls within the powers of the corporation turns in the first place

---

[29] *Ante*, p. 380.
[30] s.35A(4).
[31] *Ibid.*
[32] *Grant* v. *U.K. Switchback Ry.* (1888) 40 Ch.D. 135.
[33] See *Eastern Counties Ry.* v. *Hawkes* (1855) 5 H.L.C. 331, 347–348 (citing earlier cases).
[34] *Ante*, pp. 504–507.
[35] e.g. L.C.C. v. *Att.-Gen.* [1902] A.C. 165.
[36] *e.g. Hazell* v. *Hammersmith and Fulham Borough Council* [1991] 1 All E.R. 545.

on the construction of the statute[37] by which it is incorporated, or which otherwise defines or limits its capacity. Particular difficulty can arise where the statute, after setting out the specific objects for which the corporation is created, goes on to confer a general power to do other acts which it is necessary or desirable for the company to do in order to achieve these objects. When the *ultra vires* doctrine applied to companies incorporated under the Companies Acts, the courts were faced with similar difficulties arising from analogous, broadly drafted, provisions in memoranda of association.[38] In deciding questions of this kind, they distinguished between the *objects* of a company and its *powers*; they went on to hold that, although powers could only be exercised for the purpose of the objects, their exercise for other purposes was not *ultra vires* but only beyond the powers of the directors; and that their exercise for other purposes could not confer rights on the other party to the transaction if he had notice of the fact that the powers had been so exercised.[39] It is arguable that the same distinction between objects and powers may apply where the officers of a corporation, whose capacity is defined by the incorporating statute, purport to exercise a general power (conferred by the statute) to do acts for the purpose of achieving unauthorised objects: *e.g.* where they give a guarantee and it is alleged that the transaction in respect of which it is given is not an authorised object. In the last resort, however, the question in cases of the present kind turns simply on the construction of the relevant legislation. Thus where the corporation was empowered to do "anything . . . which in its opinion is calculated to facilitate the proper discharge of its functions or is incidental or conducive thereto," it was held that a guarantee given by the corporation could not be challenged on the ground that it was *ultra vires.*[40]

(ii) *Incidental objects*. Even in the absence of widely drafted provisions of the kind just discussed, a corporation can do acts which it is not expressly authorised to do, if they are fairly incidental to the objects for which it was established. For example, in *Foster* v. *London, Dover & Chatham Ry.*[41] it was held that a railway company could validly grant short leases of the spaces of the arches under a viaduct, so long as those leases did not disable it from carrying on its railway business. But this rule does not enable the corporation to carry on activities substantially distinct from those authorised: thus a corporation authorised to run trams could not "incidentally" run buses.[42]

(iii) *Contracts ex facie intra vires*. A contract which is *ex facie* within the capacity of the corporation is not invalid merely because the corporation uses its proceeds for an *ultra vires* purpose: *e.g.* where an *intra vires* loan is

---

[37] *Den Norske Creditbank* v. *The Sarawak Economic Development Corp.* [1988] 2 Lloyd's Rep. 616.

[38] *Ante*, p. 504 n. 11.

[39] *Rolled Steel Products (Holdings) Ltd.* v. *B.S.C.* [1986] Ch. 246; *cf. ante*, p. 505 at n. 17. See also *Introductions Ltd.* v. *National Provincial Bank Ltd.* [1970] Ch. 119; Wedderburn, 32 M.L.R. 563; 46 M.L.R. 204; Gregory, 48 M.L.R. 109.

[40] *Den Norske Creditbank* v. *The Sarawak Economic Development Corp.* [1988] 2 Lloyd's Rep. 616, (where the incorporating legislation was a Malaysian Ordinance).

[41] [1895] 1 Q.B. 711; *cf. Charles Roberts & Co.* v. *British Railways Board* [1965] 1 W.L.R. 396; and, in the case of certain companies incorporated under the Companies Acts, Companies Act 1985, s.3A(b), as substituted by Companies Act 1989, s.110(1).

[42] *L.C.C.* v. *Att.-Gen.* [1902] A.C. 165; *cf. Hazell* v. *Hammersmith & Fulham L.B.C.* [1991] 1 All E.R. 545.

spent on an *ultra vires* purpose.[43] But the corporation would not be bound by the contract if the lender knew that it intended to use the loan for such a purpose, or if he knew facts from which he could reasonably have deduced that the corporation had such an intention.[44]

(b) ALTERNATIVE REMEDIES. Where a transaction with a corporation is *ultra vires*, its invalidity can be a source of hardship to the other party: that party will, for example, have no remedy against the corporation if the corporation defaults on a transaction which has, by reason of market fluctuations, turned out to be disadvantageous to the corporation.[45] In theory, the other party can protect himself against this risk, before entering into the transaction, by reading the statute which defines or limits the corporation's powers. But in practice the other party is unlikely to take this step; and, even if he does take it, he runs the risk that his interpretation of the statute may, in proceedings on the contract, be held by the court to have been erroneous. The law to some extent mitigates this hardship by making a number of alternative remedies available to the other party to the transaction.

(i) *Subrogation.* An *ultra vires* lender can recover so much of his loan as is used by the company to pay debts incurred under *intra vires* contracts.[46]

(ii) *Tracing.* A person who pays money to a corporation under an *ultra vires* contract can trace it into the assets of the company. Thus in *Sinclair* v. *Brougham*[47] the directors of a building society conducted an *ultra vires* banking business. When the society was wound up, it was held that the depositors in the bank were entitled to a share in its assets, representing their *ultra vires* loans. A full discussion of this remedy is outside the scope of this book.[48] But one weakness of it, from the lender's point of view, may be noted. If the money is no longer precisely identifiable, and if the assets of the corporation have shrunk, the lender may not recover his loan in full.

(iii) *Remedy against officers.* A person who is induced to contract with a corporation by the false representation of a director that the contract is *intra vires* may be able to sue the director in tort for deceit or negligence,[49] or in contract for breach of implied warranty of authority.[50] The contractual action lies even though the representation was made innocently and in good faith.[51] But this remedy is not available if the misrepresentation is one of law.[52] In *Rashdall* v. *Ford*[53] the plaintiff wished to lend money to a railway company and at the suggestion of the directors accepted a bond as

---

43 *Re David Payne & Co. Ltd.* [1904] 2 Ch. 608.

44 *Re Jon Beauforte Ltd.* [1953] Ch. 131; *cf. Introductions Ltd.* v. *National Provincial Bank Ltd.* [1970] Ch. 199.

45 *e.g. Hazell* v. *Hammersmith and Fulham Borough Council* [1991] 1 All E.R. 545.

46 *Blackburn B.S.* v. *Cunliffe, Brooks & Co.* (1882) 22 Ch.D. 61; on appeal it was not necessary to decide this point: 9 App.Cas. 857.

47 [1914] A.C. 398.

48 See Snell, *Equity* (28th ed.), pp. 295–303; Hanbury and Maudsley, *Modern Equity* (13th ed.), pp. 619–644; Goff & Jones, *The Law of Restitution* (3rd ed.), pp. 69–77.

49 At common law, but not under s.2(1) of the Misrepresentation Act 1967; see *ante*, p. 313 at n. 55.

50 *Post*, p. 640.

51 *Firbank's Executors* v. *Humphreys* (1886) 18 Q.B.D. 54; *cf. Weeks* v. *Propert* (1873) L.R. 8 C.P. 427; *Cherry* v. *Colonial Bank of Australia* (1869) L.R. 3 P.C. 24.

52 The same is true where damages are claimed in tort: *ante*, p. 298.

53 (1866) L.R. 2 Eq. 750; *cf. Beatttie* v. *Ebury* (1872) L.R. 7 Ch.App. 777; affirmed L.R. 7 H.L. 102.

security. Under its incorporating statute, the company had in the circumstances, which were fully known to the plaintiff, no power to issue bonds. It was held that the directors were not liable for breach of implied warranty of authority. The construction of the company's incorporating statute was a matter of law, so that a director who represented that, on the true construction of the statute, a contract was *intra vires*, had made a representation of law.

An *ultra vires* contractor may, finally, be able to show that the director is personally liable on the contract itself. Intention on the part of an agent to assume personal liability is readily inferred when the principal is non-existent.[54] It is arguable that the inference might also be drawn where the principal exists but lacks capacity.

(c) CAN THE CORPORATION SUE?[55] The *ultra vires* doctrine normally operates so as to prevent a contract from being enforced *against* the corporation. The authorities provide no clear answer to the question whether the *ultra vires* doctrine also precludes enforcement of the contract *by* the corporation.

A similar problem used to arise where a contract with a corporation should have been, but was not, made under its common seal.[56] If such a contract was executory, the company could not sue because its own promise, being invalid, was no consideration for that of the other party.[57] But the company could sue on the contract if it had performed its part and so provided consideration by the actual performance of its void promise.[58] It can be argued that a similar distinction should be applied to *ultra vires* contracts; but it is submitted that the better approach is to ask whether the policy of the statutory limitation on the corporation's capacity would be infringed by allowing it to enforce the contract (rather than to ask whether the corporation had provided consideration).[59] Where the corporation had not yet performed its part, that policy is likely to be infringed, at least where enforcement by the corporation is (as would often be the case)[60] conditional on performance by it: in such cases, the company would be encouraged to satisfy the condition, and so to engage in *ultra vires* activity. It follows that the contract should not be enforceable by the corporation.[61] Where the corporation had performed its part, there is some support for the view that it can enforce the contract,[62] and it is arguable that such enforcement would not encourage furture *ultra vires* activity since (at least

[54] *Kelner* v. *Baxter* (1866) L.R. 2 C.P. 174; *post*, p. 637.
[55] Furmston, 24 M.L.R. 215.
[56] This formal requirement was abolished by Corporate Bodies Contracts Act 1960.
[57] *Kiddermister Corp.* v. *Harwick* (1873) L.R. 9 Ex. 13, *ante*, p. 137.
[58] *Fishmongers' Co.* v. *Robertson* (1843) 5 Man. & G. 131.
[59] This approach would make it inappropriate to apply to *ultra vires* cases the further rule, laid down in *Ecclesiastical Commissioners* v. *Merral* (1869) L.R. 4 Ex. 162, that a corporation could enforce a contract which should have been (but was not) under seal if the *other* party had done such acts of part performance as made the contract enforceable against the corporation.
[60] *Post*, pp. 662–664; exceptions would be cases of independent promises (*post*, p. 665) and of accepted anticipatory breach (*post*, pp. 667–668, 747–748).
[61] See *Pellatt's Case* (1867) L.R. 2 Ch.App. 527; *Triggs* v. *Staines U.D.C.* [1969] Ch. 10; *Bell Houses Ltd.* v. *City Wall Properties Ltd.* [1966] 1 Q.B. 207 (reversed [1966] 2 Q.B. 656 on the ground that the contract was *intra vires*).
[62] *Bell Houses Ltd.* v. *City Wall Properties Ltd.* [1966] 2 Q.B. 656, 694.

in relation to the transaction in question[63]) the *ultra vires* activity had already taken place. But it is submitted that for the purpose of this argument a distinction should be drawn between cases in which the nature of the performance is such that it cannot, and those in which it is such that it can, be restored to the corporation. The first possibility is illustrated by the case in which the corporation has rendered services under an *ultra vires* contract: in such a case, the policy of the rule making the contract *ultra vires* is hardly likely to be defeated by allowing the corporation to sue for the agreed price of the services. The second possibility can be illustrated by supposing that the corporation has purported to sell an article which it was by its incorporating statute prohibited from selling, and that it had actually delivered that article to the buyer. The policy of the statute would, it is submitted, be more effectively promoted by allowing the corporation to sue for the return of the article than by allowing it to sue for the price, or for damages for non-acceptance or for not taking delivery of the subject-matter of the sale.[64]

---

[63] Future *ultra vires* transactions could be restrained: *ante*, p. 505 at n. 21.

[64] *Cf.* the suggestion in the *Bell Houses case*, *supra*, at first instance that the corporation's remedy should be in quasi contract (though this would not be a possible remedy for the recovery of goods in specie).

CHAPTER FOURTEEN

PLURALITY OF PARTIES

A PROMISE may be made by or to more than one person. Such a promise must be distinguished from a multilateral contract.[1] If three persons agree to run a race subject to certain rules, there are three sides to the contract, but each side consists of only one person. If two persons promise to pay a third £10 there may only be two sides to the contract, one consisting of two persons and the other of one person. This Chapter is concerned with promises of this kind.

SECTION 1. PLURALITY OF DEBTORS[2]

1. Definitions

If A and B *each separately* promise to pay C £10 this does not amount to one promise by several to one, but to two independent promises. Thus C is entitled to £10 from A and a further £10 from B. This was, for example, the position where C granted licences to A and B under agreements providing for payment of a weekly sum by each of them.[3] There may be two such separate promises even where both of them are contained in the same written document.[4]

If A and B *together* promise to pay C £10, the promise may be joint, or joint and several. It is joint if A and B only make one promise binding both of them; it is joint and several if they make one promise binding both of them and if in addition each makes a separate promise binding him alone. A joint and several promise is distinguishable from two entirely separate promises in that it does not involve the promisors in cumulative liability. If A and B jointly and severally promise to pay C £10, C is not entitled to more than £10 in all. It is a question of construction whether a promise is joint, or joint and several.[5] A promise by two persons together is deemed to be joint, unless it is qualified in some way.[6] To make a promise joint and several, it is advisable to say expressly "we promise jointly and severally," or "we, and each of us, will pay." But this is not the only way of creating joint and several liability. In *Tippins* v. *Coates*[7] three persons executed a bond by which they bound themselves "jointly and our respective heirs." This was held to be a joint and several promise, since that was evidently the intention of the parties: if it were held to be a joint

---

[1] *Ante*, p. 47.
[2] Williams, *Joint Obligations*.
[3] *Mikeover* v. *Brady* [1989] 3 All E.R. 618.
[4] *Collins* v. *Prosser* (1823) 1 B. & C. 682; *Gibson* v. *Lupton* (1832) 9 Bing. 297; *Lee* v. *Nixon* (1834) 1 A. & E. 201.
[5] *Cf.* Bills of Exchange Act 1882, s.85(1) ("according to its tenour").
[6] *Levy* v. *Sale* (1877) 37 L.T. 709; *White* v. *Tyndall* (1888) 13 App.Cas. 263; *The Argo Hellas* [1984] 1 Lloyd's Rep. 296, 300.
[7] (1853) 18 Beav. 401.

bond, the *respective* heirs of the promisors would not be bound, but only the heir of the survivor.[8]

In some cases the question of whether liability is joint, or joint and several, is expressly dealt with by statute. For example, section 9 of the Partnership Act 1890, provides that "every partner in a firm is liable jointly with the other partners . . . for all debts and obligations of the firm incurred while he is a partner." On the other hand promissory notes made by a number of persons are deemed to be joint and several.[9]

2. Differences Between Joint, and Joint and Several, Promises

(1) Parties to the action

At common law, an action on a *joint* contract had to be brought against all the surviving joint debtors.[10] If this was not done the defendants could plead the non-joinder of their co-debtors in abatement. Although pleas in abatement no longer exist, it is still the general rule that the action must be brought against all the joint debtors.[11] But the court has a discretion to allow the action to proceed against one joint debtor if the other is out of the jurisdiction, or cannot be traced.[12] If one joint debtor is bankrupt, the other or others may be sued without him.[13]

An action on a *joint and several* contract could at common law be brought against one or all the co-debtors but not, it seems, against some (but not all). The creditor could either sue each debtor individually on his several promise or all on their joint promise; but he could not, by suing some, treat the contract as joint without also joining all the others.[14] It seems that in such a case the court now has a discretion to order all the other joint and several debtors to be joined to the action since it may order the names of persons to be joined to an action if their presence is "necessary to ensure that all matters in dispute in the cause or matter may be effectually and completely determined."[15] The court might order such joinder so that the amount of the debt may be conclusively established for the purpose of contribution[16] between all the debtors. It seems that the onus is on the debtor who is sued to bring his co-debtors before the court as third parties, with a view to claiming contribution from them.[17]

(2) Judgment

If one *joint* debtor is sued alone and does not plead non-joinder of the others, judgment may be given against him alone. After the creditor had recovered such a judgment, it was formerly the rule that he could not take

---

8 *Post*, p. 514.
9 Bills of Exchange Act 1882, s.85(2); see also Law of Property Act 1925, s.119 (covenants by a number of mortgagors deemed to be joint and several).
10 *Cabell* v. *Vaughan* (1669) 1 Wms.Saund. 291; *Richards* v. *Heather* (1817) 1 B. & Ald. 29.
11 *Norbury, Natzio & Co. Ltd.* v. *Griffiths* [1918] 2 K.B. 369; it is up to the defendant to take the point; *Wegg-Prosser* v. *Evans* [1895] 1 Q.B. 108. And see R.S.C. Ord. 15, r. 4.
12 *Wilson, Sons & Co. Ltd.* v. *Balcarres Brook SS. Co. Ltd.* [1893] 1 Q.B. 422; *Robinson* v. *Geisel* [1894] 2 Q.B. 685.
13 Insolvency Act 1986 s.345(4).
14 *Cabell* v. *Vaughan* (1669) 1 Wms.Saund. 291, n. 4.
15 R.S.C. Ord. 15, r. 6(2)(*b*).
16 *Post*, p. 518.
17 *Cf. Wilson, Sons & Co. Ltd.* v. *Balcarres Brook SS. Co. Ltd.*, *supra*, n. 12, at p. 428 (where the contract was joint).

further proceedings against any of the other joint debtors, even though the judgment remained unsatisfied, because the original cause of action was merged in the judgment.[18] This rule was, however likely to cause hardship to the creditor; and, after having been mitigated by many exceptions,[19] it was finally abolished by statute[20] with respect to debts becoming due after January 1, 1979. A creditor is therefore no longer precluded from suing one joint debtor merely because he has previously obtained a judgment against another.

Where the contract is *joint and several*, judgment against one debtor was never regarded as a bar to proceedings against another. Each is liable on his separate promise, as well as on the joint promise: hence there are several causes of action only some of which are merged in the first judgment.[21] A claim against joint and several debtors is only barred if one of them satisfies it, whether under a judgment or otherwise.

(3) Survivorship

At common law the liability of a *joint* debtor passed on his death to the surviving joint debtors.[22] The creditor could not sue the estate of the deceased, but only the surviving joint debtors. If they paid, they might be able to recover contribution from the estate of the deceased[23]; but the creditor himself had no direct right against the estate. On the death of the last surviving joint debtor, the creditor could recover the debt from his estate.[24]

On the death of a *joint and several* debtor, on the other hand, his several (though not his joint) liability remained enforceable against his estate.[25]

The rule that joint liability passed to the surviving debtors might be convenient where the debtors were engaged in administering a trust, but it was highly inconvenient in commercial affairs. If only one of a number of joint debtors was solvent, and that one happened to die, the creditor would lose all substantial remedy. This difficulty was particularly acute in partnership cases. Equity therefore treated partnership debts as joint and several to this extent, that they could be enforced against the estate of a deceased partner.[26] This rule is confirmed by section 9 of the Partnership Act 1890.[27]

The equitable right to enforce a joint debt against the estate of a deceased joint contractor was mainly applied in partnership cases, but there is some authority for saying that it was not confined to such cases, nor even to cases involving mercantile transactions.[28] It is therefore arguable

---

[18] *Kendall* v. *Hamilton* (1879) 4 App.Cas. 504.

[19] See R.S.C. Ord. 81, rr. 1, 5 (judgment against partnership in the firm name); Ord. 13 r. 1; Ord. 19 r. 2 (judgment in default of appearance or defence); Ord. 14 r. 8 (summary judgment); *Lechmere* v. *Fletcher* (1863) 1 C. & M. 623 (judgment on a distinct cause of action).

[20] Civil Liability (Contribution) Act 1978, ss.3, 7(1). For a situation not covered by these provisions, see *The Argo Hellas* [1984] 1 Lloyd's Rep. 296, 304.

[21] *Blyth* v. *Fladgate* [1891] 1 Ch. 337.

[22] *Cabell* v. *Vaughan* (1669) 1 Wms.Saund. 291, n. 4(*f*); *Godson* v. *Good* (1816) 6 Taunt. 587, 594.

[23] *Batard* v. *Hawes* (1853) 2 E. & B. 287; *post*, p. 518.

[24] *Calder* v. *Rutherford* (1822) 3 Brod. & B. 302.

[25] *Read* v. *Price* [1909] 1 K.B. 577.

[26] See *Kendall* v. *Hamilton* (1879) 4 App.Cas. 504, 517. Lord Mansfield had anticipated the equitable rule: *Rice* v. *Shute* (1770) 5 Burr. 2611, 2613.

[27] But under this section separate debts of a deceased partner must be paid in priority to the partnership debt.

[28] *Thorpe* v. *Jackson* (1837) 2 Y. & C. Ex. 553.

that, on the question of survivorship, there was, before the Judicature Act 1873, a conflict between common law and equity, so that equity now prevails.[29] It is also arguable that the principle of survivorship has been abolished by section 1(1) of the Law Reform (Miscellaneous Provisions) Act 1934, which provides that all causes of action subsisting against a person at the time of his death shall (with certain exceptions) survive against the estate. The object of this provision was to abolish the common law rule that actions *in tort* could not be brought against the estate of a deceased tortfeasor; but its words seem apt to abolish the rule that the liability of a joint debtor passed on his death to the surviving joint debtors (so that it could no longer be enforced against his estate).

3. Similarities Between Joint, and Joint and Several, Promises

(1) Defence of one

If one of several co-debtors has a defence to the action, the question whether that defence also avails the others depends on its nature. If it goes to the root of the plaintiff's claim, and wholly destroys it, the other debtors can take advantage of it. Thus they can do so if one co-debtor can prove that the debt has been paid, or that the creditor is not entitled to payment because of his own breach of contract, or that a written contract is a forgery, or that the creditor was guilty of fraud.[30] But if the defence is personal to one co-debtor, *e.g.* that he was a minor or that he had been discharged as a result of bankruptcy proceedings, it does not avail the other co-debtors.[31]

Special rules apply to contracts of guarantee, under which the guarantor generally undertakes joint and several liability with the principal debtor.[32] It has been held that the guarantor is not liable if the principal debt is illegal,[33] or if the principal debtor has been discharged as a result of the creditor's breach.[34] A guarantor of a debt that was unenforceable under the Money-lenders Acts could not be sued on the guarantee[35]; and the Consumer Credit Act 1974 (which repeals those Acts) lays down a similar rule in the case of a guarantee given in respect of a regulated agreement.[36] These rules cannot be deduced from the general principles governing joint and several contracts, but appear to be based on considerations of policy.[37] It is obviously undesirable to allow a person who lends for an illegal pur-

---

[29] Judicature Act 1873, s.25(11); now Supreme Court Act 1981, s.49(1).

[30] *Porter* v. *Harris* (1663) 1 Lev. 63; *Gardner* v. *Walsh* (1855) 5 E. & B. 83; *Pirie* v. *Richardson* [1927] 1 K.B. 448.

[31] *Burgess* v. *Merrill* (1812) 4 Taunt. 468; *Gillow* v. *Lillie* (1835) 1 Bing.N.C. 695; *Lovell & Christmas* v. *Beauchamp* [1894] A.C. 607; *King* v. *Hoare* (1844) 3 M. & W. 494, 506; *Pirie* v. *Richardson* [1927] 1 K.B. 448 *cf. Chaplin* v. *Leslie Frewin (Publishers) Ltd.* [1966] Ch. 71.

[32] *e.g. Anderson* v. *Martindale* (1801) 1 East 497; *Re W. E. A., a Debtor* [1901] 2 K.B. 642; *Read* v. *Price* [1909] 1 K.B. 577.

[33] *Swan* v. *Bank of Scotland* (1836) 10 Bli.(N.S.) 627; *Heald* v. *O'Connor* [1971] 1 W.L.R. 497.

[34] *Unity Finance Ltd.* v. *Woodcock* [1963] 1 W.L.R. 455, explained on another ground in *Goulston Discount Co. Ltd.* v. *Clark* [1967] 2 Q.B. 493.

[35] *Eldridge & Morris* v. *Taylor* [1931] 2 K.B. 416; *Temperance Loan Fund Ltd.* v. *Rose* [1932] 2 K.B. 522.

[36] s.113(1) and (2); see *ante*, p. 163 for the meaning of "regulated" agreement.

[37] Mitchell, (1947) 63 L.Q.R. 354.

pose, or a lender who tries to evade the Consumer Credit Act, to recover his loan from any person whatsoever.

On the other hand, a guarantee may be valid where the principal debtor is a corporation acting *ultra vires*. Whether it is actually valid depends on its construction: did the guarantor undertake only what the corporation could lawfully be required to pay, or what it had in fact promised to pay?[38] Where the principal debt is incurred by a company incorporated under the Companies Acts, the validity of that debt can no longer (as a general rule) be called into question on the ground of lack of company's capacity by reason of anything in its memorandum[39]: it follows that the guarantee cannot be called into question on this ground. The position is the same where principal debt arises out of a contract which is made by a person dealing with the company in good faith, but which is, under the company's constitution, beyond the power of the board of directors: in favour of the other contracting party, the power of the board is deemed to be free from any limitation under the company's constitution,[40] so that the contract giving rise to the debt, and consequently also the guarantee, cannot be challenged on the ground that it was beyond the powers of the board. The general rule is that the principal contract will be invalid only if the other party dealt with the company in bad faith; and mere knowledge of the fact that the contract was beyond the powers of the directors is not sufficient to constitute bad faith.[41] It seems that some kind of actual dishonesty is required to constitute bad faith; and if the principal transaction is invalid on this ground, then it is submitted that the guarantee should also be invalid. This submission is based on the analogy of the rule relating to illegal contracts,[42] for the principal contract in our last example would be, or would come close to being, one to defraud the company.[43] The only other situations in which the principal contract is now likely to be invalid on the ground that it is *ultra vires* are those in which the corporation was not incorporated under the Companies Acts, so that the common law doctrine of *ultra vires* still applied to it,[44] and those in which the statutory modifications of the *ultra vires* doctrine, described above, exceptionally do not apply.[45] If in such cases the creditor is induced to enter into the contract in reliance on a guarantee given by one of the corporation's directors or officers, it is submitted that the guarantor should be liable on the guarantee: there seems to be no ground of policy for allowing him to rely on the invalidity of the principal debt.

Similar policy considerations apply where the principal debtor is a minor: it would be wrong to allow the guarantor on this ground to escape from a liability deliberately undertaken since such a result would not be necessary for the protection of minors. It has therefore been provided by statute that the guarantee shall not be unenforceable against the guarantor

---

38 *Yorks. Ry. & Wagon Co.* v. *McLure* (1882) 21 Ch.D. 309; *Garrard* v. *James* [1925] Ch. 616, as explained in *Heald* v. *O'Connor* [1971] 1 W.L.R. 497.

39 Companies Act 1985, s.35(1) (as substituted by Companies Act 1989, s.108(1)); *ante*, p. 505.

40 *Ibid.* s.35A(1).

41 *Ibid.* s.35A(2)(*b*).

42 *Supra*, at n. 33.

43 *Cf. ante*, p. 380.

44 *Ante*, p. 507.

45 Companies Act 1985, ss.35(4) and 35A(6), as substituted by Companies Act 1989, s.108(1) (charitable companies and certain transactions with directors).

merely because the principal obligation was unenforceable against the debtor because he was a minor when he incurred it.[46]

(2) Release of one

If the creditor releases one debtor, the release is available for the benefit of all the co-debtors since it wholly destroys the cause of action.[47] At first sight, the application of this rule to joint and several debtors looks illogical, since there are several causes of action against them; but it may be justified on the ground that it would make the release partly futile to hold that only one of the co-debtors was released. If the others could still be sued, they could claim contribution from the one who had been released, who would thus indirectly be made liable, notwithstanding the release.[48] But in spite of this argument, a covenant not to sue a single co-debtor releases him alone and does not release the other co-debtors.[49]

It used to be thought that a release granted to one co-debtor released the others even though it reserved the creditor's rights against them.[50] But the courts evaded this rule by distinguishing between a release and a covenant not to sue. The former released all the co-debtors: the latter only released the debtor with whom it was made.[51] If a document purports to release one co-debtor but to reserve the creditor's rights against the others the courts tend to construe it as a covenant not to sue and so to give effect to the intention of the parties.[52] But a document which simply released one co-debtor without expressly or impliedly[53] reserving the creditor's rights against the others would still wholly extinguish those rights.[54]

These principles apply only to a release by act of the parties. Where one co-debtor is released by operation of law (*e.g.* by an order of discharge in bankruptcy) the others are not released.[55] If the creditor appoints one co-debtor his executor, both the co-debtor and the others are released when probate is obtained. The reason for this rule is that "the debt is deemed to have been paid by the debtor [*qua* debtor] to himself as executor" and thus discharged.[56] In equity the executor is then deemed to have the amount of the debt in his hands as assets of the testator, and is thus accountable for it to the estate.[57]

---

46 Minors Contracts Act 1987 s.2 (reversing *Coutts & Co.* v. *Browne-Lecky* [1947] K.B. 104); and see s.4, amending Consumer Credit Act 1974 s.113(7).

47 *Nicholson* v. *Revill* (1836) 4 A. & E. 675.

48 *Jenkins* v. *Jenkins* [1928] 2 K.B. at p. 508.

49 See the authorities cited in n. 51, *infra*.

50 *Nicholson* v. *Revill* (1836) 4 A. & E. at p. 683.

51 *Hutton* v. *Eyre* (1815) 6 Taunt. 289; *Kearsley* v. *Cole* (1846) 16 M. & W. 128, 136; *Webb* v. *Hewitt* (1857) 3 K. & J. 438; *Ex p. Good* (1876) 5 Ch.D. 46; *Re Wolmerhausen* (1890) 62 L.T. 541; in *Duck* v. *Mayeu* [1892] 2 Q.B. 511 and *Gardiner* v. *Moore* [1969] 1 Q.B. 55 the same rule was applied in tort; the latter case also shows that reservation of the rights against one of the persons liable may be implied.

52 *Price* v. *Barker* (1855) 4 E. & B. 760; *cf. Appleby Estates Co.* v. *De Bernales* [1947] Ch. 217 (tort).

53 See *Gardiner* v. *Moore*, *supra*.

54 *Cf. Cutler* v. *McPhail* [1962] 2 Q.B. 292.

55 Insolvency Act 1986 s.281(7); *Re Garner's Motors Ltd.* [1937] Ch. 594.

56 *Jenkins* v. *Jenkins* [1928] 2 K.B. 501, 509; Limitation (Amendment) Act 1980, s.10.

57 *Jenkins* v. *Jenkins*, *supra*, at p. 509; *Commissioner of Stamp Duties* v. *Bone* [1977] A.C. 511.

(3) Contribution

If one co-debtor, being liable to pay the entire debt,[58] has paid it in full, he is entitled to recover contribution from the others.[59] Prima facie, he is entitled to recover from each co-debtor the amount of the debt divided by the number of co-debtors. If one of the co-debtors has died, his estate is liable to contribute, even if he was a joint debtor. The general rule may be varied by the terms of the contract or by the bankruptcy of one co-debtor.

(a) TERMS OF THE CONTRACT. The co-debtors can make any provision they like as to contribution. Where the co-debtors are principal debtor and surety, it is implied that the surety, if called on to pay, is entitled to be wholly indemnified by the principal debtor. Conversely, if the principal debtor pays the whole debt, he has no right of contribution against the surety. Several sureties for the same debt are prima facie entitled *inter se* to contribution in proportion to their number; but where one surety (A) only promises to pay if neither the debtor nor another surety (B) does so, and B pays on the debtor's default, then B will not be entitled to contribution from A.[60]

(b) BANKRUPTCY. At common law, the rule that the amount of contribution was the amount of the debt divided by the number of co-debtors prevailed even though some of the co-debtors were insolvent.[61] Equity adopted the fairer rule that the amount of contribution was the amount of the debt divided by the number of sureties who were *solvent* when the right to contribution arose.[62] This equitable rule now prevails.[63]

SECTION 2. PLURALITY OF CREDITORS

1. Definitions

If X promises to pay A and B £10, he may make two promises which are quite separate. If so, A and B are entitled to £10 *each*, *i.e.* X's total liability is to pay £20. No special problems arise out of such promises. But if X makes only one promise to A and B, so that he is only liable to pay £10 in all, it becomes important to determine whether his promise to A and B is made to them jointly, or whether it is made to them severally. At common law, the question whether a contract was made with two persons jointly or with them severally depended on the wording of the contract, and on the interests of the parties in enforcing it.

If the contract was made with a number of persons "jointly" and their interests were joint, it was a joint contract[64]; if it was made with a number of persons severally, *i.e.* "with them and each of them" and their interests

---

[58] For this requirement, see *Legal & General Assurance Society* v. *Drake Insurance Co. Ltd.*, *Financial Times*, January 15, 1991, where a debtor who was liable for only *half* the debt, but had paid it in full, was held not to be entitled to contribution.

[59] For a recent application of this right, see *Davitt* v. *Titcumb* [1989] 3 All E.R. 417, 422; *cf.* *Legal General Assurance Soc. Ltd.* v. *Drake Ins. Co. Ltd.* [1989] 3 All E.R. 923 (contribution between co-insurers).

[60] *Scholefield Goodman & Sons Ltd.* v. *Zyngier* [1986] A.C. 562.

[61] *Lowe* v. *Dixon* (1885) 16 Q.B.D. 455, 458.

[62] *Hitchman* v. *Stewart* (1855) 3 Drew. 271.

[63] *Lowe* v. *Dixon*, *supra*. The rules as to assessment of contribution laid down in Civil Liability (Contribution) Act 1978, s.2 do not alter this position: they apply to *damages* but not to *debts*; for this distinction, *cf. post*, pp. 895–896.

[64] *Cf. Sorsbie* v. *Park* (1843) 12 M. & W. 146, 158.

were several, it was a several contract.[65] If the contract was ambiguous, or did not state whether it was joint and several, then it was joint if the interests of the creditors were joint, and otherwise several.[66] The interests of the creditors were joint if each had the same interest in the performance of the contract, even though they had separate interests in the property affected. Hence a covenant to repair made with a number of lessors jointly was joint, though they did not hold the land jointly, but in common, so that their interests in it were several.[67] On the other hand, where land was sold by tenants in common and the purchaser promised to pay them the price in fixed proportions corresponding with their shares in the land, the promise was regarded as several.[68] The position was less clear where the contract was expressly joint and the interests several, or conversely; but the prevailing view appears to be that the court would give effect to the intention of the parties, as expressed in the agreement.[69] The common law did not originally recognise the possibility that a promise *to* a number of persons could be joint *and* several.[70] The possibility was, however, recognised in the late nineteenth century[71]; and the question is now of little importance as section 81 of the Law of Property Act 1925 provides that a covenant, and a contract made under seal[72] and a bond or obligation under seal made with two or more persons jointly, shall, if made after 1925, "be construed as being also made with each of them"[73] unless a contrary intention is expressed; in relation to instruments made after the coming into force of section 1 of the Law of Property (Miscellaneous Provisions) Act 1989, the instrument need no longer be sealed: it is sufficient if it is executed as a deed in accordance with the requirements of that section.[74] Such covenants, etc., are now prima facie joint and several.[75] Section 81 of the 1925 Act only applies to promises in deeds[76]; its object seems to have been to avoid in relation to such promises the common law rule that on the death of a joint creditor his rights passed by survivorship[77] to the other or others. In this respect, it resembles the rule under which a contract for the repayment

---

[65] *James* v. *Emery* (1818) 5 Price 529.

[66] *e.g. Anderson* v. *Martindale* (1801) 1 East 487; *Palmer* v. *Mallett* (1887) 36 Ch.D. 411.

[67] *Bradburne* v. *Botfield* (1845) 14 M. & W. 559; *Thompson* v. *Hakewill* (1865) 19 C.B. (N.S.) 713. For the position between the tenants in common *inter se*, see *Beer* v. *Beer* (1852) 12 C.B. 60.

[68] *James* v. *Emery* (1818) 5 Price 529.

[69] *Sorsbie* v. *Park* (1843) 12 M. & W. 146, 158; *Keightley* v. *Watson* (1849) 3 Ex. 716; *Beer* v. *Beer* (1852) 12 C.B. 60; for the earlier view that the interest of the parties was always decisive, see *Slingsby's Case* (1588) 5 Co. Rep. 18b; *Withers* v. *Bircham* (1824) 3 B. & C. 254, 256; *Hopkinson* v. *Lee* (1845) 6 Q.B. 964.

[70] *Slingsby's Case*, *supra*; *Anderson* v. *Martindale*, *supra*; *Bradburne* v. *Botfield* (1854) 14 M. & W. 559, 573; *Keightley* v. *Watson*, *supra*, at p. 723 (criticising the rule).

[71] *Thompson* v. *Hakewill* (1865) 19 C.B.N.S., 713, 726; *Palmer* v. *Mallett* (1887) 36 Ch.D. 410, 421.

[72] See now Law of Property (Miscellaneous Provisions) Act 1989, s.1(7).

[73] Re-enacting, with some changes, Conveyancing Act 1881, s.60.

[74] Law of Property (Miscellaneous Provisions) Act 1989, s.1(8) and Sched. 1. And see *ante*, pp. 144–145 for execution of deeds by corporations.

[75] See *Josselson* v. *Borst* [1938] 1 K.B. 723; for a statutory exception, see Law of Property Act 1925, s.119 (covenants with several mortgagees deemed to be joint).

[76] The primary meaning of "covenant" is a promise by deed: see *Rank Xerox Ltd.* v. *Lane (Inspector of Taxes)* [1981] A.C. 629, 639. It seems that in Law of Property Act 1925, s.81, "covenant" refers to a promise which would not be binding unless it were under seal, and "contract . . . under seal" to one which would be binding even if it were not sealed.

[77] *Post*, p. 520.

of money lent by a number of lenders was presumed in equity to create a several right in each lender, even though under the common law rules the contract was joint.[78] The presumption could be rebutted, *e.g.* if the lenders were trustees[79]; here survivorship was administratively convenient, and created no substantive injustice. It seems that promises regarded as several under section 81 and under the equitable presumption will be so regarded not only for the purpose of limiting the doctrine of survivorship,[80] but also for the other purpose to be discussed below.

2. Parties to the Action

Where a promise is made to a number of persons *jointly*, all of them (if living) must be parties to the action.[81] If one joint creditor is unwilling to join, the one wishing to sue must offer him an indemnity as to costs; if he still refuses to join he can then be added as co-defendant.[82]

Where a promise is made to two or more persons *severally* an action can be brought by one or more of them: it is not necessary to join them all.[83]

3. Survivorship

On the death of a *joint* creditor, his rights pass to his surviving co-creditors.[84] On the death of a *several* creditor, his rights do not pass to his co-creditors, but to his personal representatives.[85]

4. Defence Against One

Where a contract is *joint*, a defence available against one creditor can be raised against the others if it goes to the root of the claim. For example, "when two persons are jointly insured and their interests are inseparably connected, so that a loss or gain necessarily affects them both, the misconduct of one is sufficient to contaminate the whole insurance."[86] It seems, although there is no authority precisely in point, that a defence available against one joint creditor does not avail against the other if it is purely personal to the first. Thus, if the debtor can plead *ultra vires* against one joint creditor,[87] he may remain liable to the others.

Where a contract is *several*, a defence available against one creditor cannot be raised against the others. In *Hagedorn* v. *Bazett*[88] an insurance of cargo covered goods some of which belonged to British subjects, some to

---

78 *Steeds* v. *Steeds* (1889) 22 Q.B.D. 537.
79 *Ibid.* p. 542.
80 This seems to have been the sole effect of Conveyancing Act 1881, s.60, but that section did not include the words quoted in the text at n. 73, *supra*.
81 *Jell* v. *Douglas* (1821) 4 B. & Ald. 374; *Sorsbie* v. *Park* (1843) 12 M. & W. 146; *Thompson* v. *Hakewill* (1865) 19 C.B.(N.S.) 713.
82 *Cullen* v. *Knowles* [1898] 2 Q.B. 380; no such indemnity need be offered to one joint creditor who is guilty of a fraud on the other: *Johnson* v. *Stephens & Carter Ltd.* [1923] 2 K.B. 857. If a joint creditor is added as co-defendant without being offered such an indemnity, the only person who can object is that joint creditor, and not the debtor; *Burnside* v. *Harrison Marks Productions Ltd.* [1968] 1 W.L.R. 728.
83 *James* v. *Emery* (1818) 5 Price 529; *Keightley* v. *Watson* (1849) 3 Ex. 716; *Palmer* v. *Mallett* (1887) 36 Ch.D. 411.
84 *Anderson* v. *Martindale* (1801) 1 East 497.
85 *Withers* v. *Bircham* (1824) 3 B. & C. 254.
86 *P. Samuel & Co.* v. *Dumas* [1924] A.C. 432, 445.
87 *Ante*, p. 507.
88 (1813) 2 M. & S. 100.

neutrals and some to an alien enemy. It was held that the policy amounted to a number of separate policies, one with each owner, and was not wholly vitiated by the fact that one of the owners was an alien enemy. "There was no common or joint interest in the whole of the property insured subsisting in the different individuals, nor was there any fraud."[89] The reason why fraud would have vitiated the whole insurance is that the fraud referred to was that of the common agent of all the parties, and thus imputable to them all. It does not follow that the fraud of one several creditor is a defence against others to whom it cannot be imputed. Had the policy been joint, the fact that one of the owners was an alien enemy would have made it wholly illegal since it seems that this kind of illegal promise cannot be severed.[90]

Where a joint bank account is opened in the names of two persons, the amount standing to the credit of the account is owed to them jointly, so that, neither of them can enforce the debt against the bank without joining the other.[91] But a promise by the bank to honour only instructions given by both account holders is made separately to each of them, so that, if the bank allows one of them to draw on the account without the knowledge or authority of the other, the latter can sue alone and recover damages from the bank for breach of this promise.[92]

5. Release by One

A release granted by one *joint* creditor discharges the debt. Unless this were so, the one who granted the release might be able, after the death of his co-creditor, to recover the debt in spite of his own release, under the rule of survivorship.[93] But if the release is given by one creditor in fraud of another, the latter can have it set aside.[94]

A release granted by one of a number of creditors entitled *severally* (whether at law or in equity) only releases the share of the grantor.[95]

6. Payment to One

The general rule is that payment to one of two *joint* creditors discharges the debt.[96] But this rule may be varied by the contract, and such variation may be implied from a course of dealing. Thus where persons have a joint account with a bank, and the usual course of dealing is to make payments only with the authority of them all, a payment made to one without the authority of the others does not discharge the bank.[97] Even where payment to one discharges the debt, it does not discharge any security which may have been given for the debt except to the extent of the payee's beneficial interest in the debt.[98]

Payment to one of a number of *several* creditors clearly does not discharge the whole debt since each is separately entitled to his share.

---

[89] At p. 105.
[90] *Ante*, p. 448.
[91] *Brewer* v. *Westminster Bank Ltd.* [1952] 2 T.L.R. 568 (as to which, see next note).
[92] *Catlin* v. *Cyprus Finance Corporation (London) Ltd.* [1983] Q.B. 759 not following *Brewer's* case, *supra*, on this point; Vroegop, 100 L.Q.R. 25.
[93] *Wallace* v. *Kelsall* (1840) 7 M. & W. 264, 274.
[94] *Jones* v. *Herbert* (1817) 7 Taunt. 421.
[95] *Steeds* v. *Steeds* (1889) 22 Q.B.D. 537.
[96] *Husband* v. *Davies* (1851) 10 C.B. 645; *Powell* v. *Broadhurst* [1901] 2 Ch. 160, 164.
[97] *Husband* v. *Davies* (1851) 10 C.B. 645, 650.
[98] *Powell* v. *Broadhurst* [1901] 2 Ch. 160, 166.

7. Consideration Moving from One[99]

Where a promise is made to A and B *jointly*, it can be enforced by both of them, even though the whole consideration was provided by A.[1] If this were not so, the promise could not be enforced at all; for, if A tried to sue alone, he would be defeated by the rule that all the promisees must be parties to the action.[2] It follows from the doctrine of survivorship[3] that B would be entitled to the entire benefit of the promise after A's death.

None of the above reasoning applies where a promise is made to A and B *severally*. Hence each promisee must provide consideration for the separate promise made to him.

It is, however, uncertain which of the above rules applies to the intermediate case of a promise made to two persons *jointly and severally*.[4] In *McEvoy* v. *Belfast Banking Co.*,[5] a father (A) deposited £10,000 in a bank; the deposit receipt stated that the money had been received from him and his son (B) and that it was payable "to either or the survivor." Lord Atkin said obiter that the contract was not by the bank with A for the benefit of B[6] but "with A and B, and I think with them jointly and severally. A purports to make a contract on behalf of B as well as himself, and the consideration supports such a contract."[7] Of course after A's death (which in *McEvoy's* case had occurred), B would be entitled to sue on any joint promise under the doctrine of survivorship. But it is harder to see how he could sue on any several promise, for this is *ex hypothesi* an independent promise, and on the facts stated no consideration for it moved from B.[8] Indeed, the more probable view of such facts is that the bank makes no promise to B but only has authority to pay him. Hence it is discharged by a payment to B, but is not liable to him.[9] The bank would not, however, be discharged by such payment if it was *not* authorised by its contract with A to pay B. This possibility is illustrated by *Thavorn* v. *Bank of Credit & Commerce S.A.*,[10] where A opened a bank account in the name of her nephew B (who was under age), stipulating that only A should operate the account. It was held that B was a mere nominee and that the bank was not discharged by (or was liable in damages for) paying B at the sole request of B and without any instructions from A. As no promise to (or in favour of) B had been made by the bank, it follows that B could not have sued the bank on its promise to A.

---

[99] Cullity, 85 L.Q.R. 530; Winterton, 47 Can.Bar Rev. 483; Coote, [1978] C.L.J. 301.
[1] This proposition seems to have been accepted in *Coulls* v. *Bagot's Executor and Trustee Co. Ltd.* [1967] A.L.R. 385; although the majority of the court held that no joint promise had in fact been made; *post*, p. 536.
[2] *Ante*, p. 520.
[3] *Ante*, p. 520.
[4] For this type of promise, see *ante*, p. 519.
[5] [1935] A.C. 24.
[6] And so not within the doctrine of privity (*post*, Chap. 15).
[7] At p. 43.
[8] S.J.B., 51 L.Q.R. 419.
[9] See *Coulls* v. *Bagot's Executor and Trustee Co. Ltd.* [1967] A.L.R. 385; *post*.
[10] [1985] 1 Lloyd's Rep. 259.

CHAPTER FIFTEEN

PRIVITY[1]

SECTION 1. STATEMENT

THE doctrine of privity means that a contract cannot, as a general rule, confer rights or impose obligations arising under it on any person except the parties to it. Two questions arise from this statement: who are the parties to the agreement? and has the claimant provided consideration for the promise which he is seeking to enforce?

1. Parties to the Agreement

Normally, the parties to the agreement are the persons from whose communications with each other the agreement has resulted. There may, indeed, be factual difficulties in identifying these persons[2]; but such difficulties do not raise any questions of legal principle. Problems as to the legal analysis of clearly established facts can, however, arise in a number of situations in which there is clearly an agreement, while it is doubtful exactly who the parties to it are, or in which there are several contracts which affect the same subject-matter and involve more than two parties.

(1) Collateral contracts[3]

(a) ILLUSTRATIONS. A contract between two persons may be accompanied by a collateral contract between one of them and a third person relating to the same subject-matter. In *Shanklin Pier* v. *Detel Products Ltd.*,[4] the plaintiffs employed contractors to paint a pier and instructed them for this purpose to buy and use paint made by the defendants. The instruction was given in reliance on a representation made by the defendants to the plaintiffs that the paint would last for seven years. In fact it only lasted for three months. The main contract for the sale of the paint was between the contractors and the defendants, but it was held that there was also a collateral contract between the plaintiffs and the defendants that the paint would last for seven years. The same reasoning can apply where a person buys goods from a dealer and is given a guarantee issued by the manufacturer. The main contract of sale is between the dealer and the customer, but it seems that the guarantee is a collateral contract between the manufacturer and the customer.[5] Again, a contract for the execution of building

---

[1] Finlay, *Contracts for the Benefit of Third Persons*; Dold, *Stipulations for a Third Party*; Wilson, 11 Sydney L.Rev. 300; Flannigan, 108 L.Q.R. 564; Kincaid, [1989] C.L.J. 454; Andrews, 8 Legal Studies 14.

[2] *e.g. The Zinnia* [1984] 2 Lloyd's Rep. 211; *Empresa Lineas Maritimas Argentinas* v. *The Oceanus Mutual Underwriting Association* (*Bermuda*) *Ltd.* [1984] 2 Lloyd's Rep. 517.

[3] Wedderburn [1959] C.L.J. 58.

[4] [1951] 2 K.B. 854; followed in *Wells* (*Merstham*) *Ltd.* v. *Buckland Sand & Silica Co. Ltd.* [1965] 2 Q.B. 170, even though no specific main contract was contemplated when the "collateral" undertaking was given. *Cf.* also *post*, p. 640.

[5] *Cf. ante*, p. 74. For legislative control of exemption clauses in such guarantees, see *ante*, p. 229.

work between A and B may be performed, wholly or in part, through the instrumentality of sub-contractor C, nominated by A but engaged by B. Such an arrangement usually gives rise to a contract between A and B and to one between B and C, but not to one between A and C[6]; but it is possible for a collateral contract to arise between these last two parties,[7] making C contractually liable to A. Yet a further situation in which a single transaction involves several contracts is that in which a supply of goods is paid for by the use of a cheque card or credit card. Such a transaction involves three contracts: one between the supplier and the customer, a second between the customer and the issuer of the card, and a third between the issuer of the card and the supplier of the goods.[8] The supplier can therefore sue the issuer: he is not a mere third-party beneficiary under the contract between the customer and the issuer.

The collateral contract device has also been used to solve a difficulty arising out of hire-purchase agreements. The customer may think of himself as "buying on hire-purchase" from the dealer on whose premises he selects the goods. Actually, the transaction may involve a sale of the goods by the dealer to a finance company which then hires them out to the customer and grants him an option to purchase them. Thus the main contract of hire-purchase is between the customer and the finance company. A representation by the dealer as to the quality of the goods used not to bind the finance company,[9] but it could be enforced against the dealer as a collateral contract.[10] If the transaction is a regulated agreement within the Consumer Credit Act 1974,[11] a dealer who conducts antecedent negotiations is deemed to do so as agent of the finance company as well as in his actual capacity.[12] His representations can therefore make the company liable under the main contract, while he himself may still be liable under a collateral contract.[13]

(b) Consideration for collateral contracts. To be enforceable as a collateral contract, a promise must be supported by consideration,[14] and in the cases so far discussed this requirement was clearly satisfied. In the

[6] *e.g. Simaan General Contracting Co.* v. *Pilkington Glass Ltd.* (*No.* 2) [1988] Q.B. 758.

[7] *Holland Hannen & Cubitts* (*Northern*) v. *Welsh Health Technical Services Ltd.* (1987) 7 Con.L.R. 14; *cf. Welsh Health Technical Service Organisation* v. *Haden Young* (1987) 37 Build.L.R. 130; *Greater Nottingham Co-operative Soc. Ltd.* v. *Cementation Ltd.* [1989] Q.B. 71; for C's possible liability to A in tort, see *post*, p. 539.

[8] *Re Charge Card Services* [1987] Ch. 150, affirmed [1989] Ch. 497; Tiplady, [1989] L.M.C.L.Q. 22; Jones, [1988] J.B.L. 457; *cf. Customs & Excise Commissioners* v. *Diners Club Ltd.* [1989] 1 W.L.R. 1196; *Metropolitan Police Commissioner* v. *Charles* [1977] A.C. 177; *R.* v. *Lambie* [1988] A.C. 449; a different analysis probably applies where the card is issued by *the supplier*, as is the practice of some department stores: *Richardson* v. *Worral* [1985] S.T.C. 693, 720.

[9] *Campbell Discount Co. Ltd* v. *Gall* [1961] 1 Q.B. 431; reversed on other points in *Branwhite* v. *Worcester Works Finance Ltd.* [1969] 1 A.C. 552 and *United Dominions Trust Ltd.* v. *Western* [1976] Q.B. 513.

[10] *Brown* v. *Sheen & Richmond Car Sales* [1950] 1 All E.R. 1102; *Andrews* v. *Hopkinson* [1957] 1 Q.B. 229; Diamond, (1958) 21 M.L.R. 177; *cf. Astley Industrial Trust Ltd.* v. *Grimley* [1963] 1 W.L.R. 584; as to damages, see *Yeoman Credit Ltd.* v. *Odgers* [1962] 1 W.L.R. 215.

[11] See *ante*, p. 163.

[12] s.56(2); *cf.* also s.75, under which the finance company is liable for any breach of contract by the supplier, but entitled to an indemnity from him in respect of such liability.

[13] This follows from s.56(2), *supra*.

[14] *Cf. Brikom Investments Ltd.* v. *Carr* [1979] Q.B. 467, (*ante*, p. 97), where no third party problem arose..

Shanklin Pier case the consideration was the instruction given by the plaintiffs to their contractors[15]; in the guarantee case it is the purchase by the customer of the goods from the dealer; in the sub-contractor case, it is similarly the nomination of the sub-contractor by the client; in the cheque or credit card case it is the supply of goods by the supplier to the customer and the discount allowed by the supplier to the issuer of the card[16]; and in the hire-purchase case it is the entering by the customer into a hire-purchase agreement with the finance company. A case in which the problem of consideration gives rise to rather more difficulty is *Charnock* v. *Liverpool Corporation*.[17] The plaintiff's car was damaged and repaired under a contract between his insurance company and a garage. It was held that there was also a collateral contract by which the garage promised the plaintiff to do the repairs reasonably quickly. Although the plaintiff did not pay or promise to pay the garage anything,[18] he had provided consideration by "leaving his car with the garage for repair."[19] This might not be a detriment to the plaintiff, at least in the factual sense.[20] But it benefited the garage in giving it the opportunity of making a contract for the repair of the car with the insurance company; and this benefit constituted the consideration for the garage's promise to the plaintiff.[21]

(c) CONTRACTUAL INTENTION. In the present context, as in others,[22] a promise will not amount to a collateral contract if it was made without contractual intention. For example, in *Independent Broadcasting Authority* v. *E.M.I. Electronics*[23] E.M.I. had contracted to erect a television mast for the I.B.A., on the terms that the actual work was to be done by a sub-contractor, who was not a party to the main contract. The sub-contractor wrote to the I.B.A., saying: "We are well satisfied that the structure will not oscillate dangerously." The mast having later collapsed, it was held that this letter did not have contractual force as there was no *animus contrahendi*[24] (though the sub-contractor was held liable in negligence).

(2) Agency

A person may negotiate a contract as agent between his principal and a third party. This contract will generally be between the principal and the third party.[25] But it is sometimes doubtful whether a person acted as agent

---

[15] [1951] 2 K.B. 854, 856.
[16] *Customs & Excise Commissioners* v. *Diners Club Ltd.* [1989] 1 W.L.R. 1196.
[17] [1968] 1 W.L.R. 1498.
[18] *Cf. Godfrey Davies Ltd.* v. *Culling and Hecht* [1962] 2 Lloyd's Rep. 349; *Cooter & Green Ltd.* v. *Tyrell* [1962] 2 Lloyd's Rep. 377; *Brown & Davies* v. *Galbraith* [1972] 1 W.L.R. 997.
[19] [1968] 1 W.L.R. at p. 1505.
[20] *Ante*, p. 65.
[21] *Cf. ante*, p. 89. For similar reasoning, see *International Petroleum Refining & Supply Sociedad* v. *Caleb Brett & Son Ltd.* [1980] 1 Lloyd's Rep. 569, 594.
[22] *Ante*, pp. 149, 164, 183–185, 319–320.
[23] (1980) 14 Build.L.R. 1; *cf. Alicia Hosiery Ltd.* v. *Brown Shipley Ltd.* [1970] 1 Q.B. 195; *Lambert* v. *Lewis* [1982] A.C. 225; *ante*, p. 149.
[24] *Cf.* also *Hannam* v. *Bradford C.C.* [1970] 1 W.L.R. 937; *Construction Industry Training Board* v. *Labour Force Ltd.* [1970] 3 All E.R. 220.
[25] *Post*, pp. 630 *et seq*.

or on his own behalf.[26] Thus where a husband booked tickets on a cross-Channel ferry for himself, his wife and children, there was said to be a "contract of carriage between the [wife] and the [carriers],"[27] presumably made by the husband as agent of the wife. Where a husband and wife lunched together at a restaurant, it was again held that there was a contract between the wife and the proprietor, though on the different ground that husband and wife each made a separate contract with the proprietor.[28] But if there were no such separate contracts and the host on such an occasion did not act as agent it has been said that there would be a contract only between him and the restaurant proprietor.[29]

Similar problems arise where an agent employs a sub-agent. In some such cases there is a direct contract between principal and sub-agent; while in others the sub-agent is only in a contractual relationship with the agent who employed him.[30] In these cases it is again clear that there is a contract, but doubtful who the parties to it are.

(3) Multilateral contracts

When a person joins a club or other unincorporated association he may be in direct communication only with the secretary and be quite unaware of the identity of the other members. But his contract of membership is likely to be with them, and not with the secretary.[31] Again, where several persons agree to enter into a competition subject to certain rules it is often doubtful exactly who the parties to the resulting contract are. In *The Satanita*[32] it was held that the competitors in a regatta contracted not only with the committee of the organising club but also with each other. On the other hand in *Ellesmere* v. *Wallace*[33] it was held that persons who entered horses for races organised by the Jockey Club had contracted with the club, and not with each other.

(4) Companies: memorandum and articles[34]

Under the Companies Acts[35] the memorandum and articles of association of a company[36] bind the company and its members as if they had been signed and sealed by each member and contained covenants by each mem-

---

26 *Post*, pp. 609–611; *P. Samuel & Co. Ltd.* v. *Dumas* [1923] 1 K.B. 593; [1924] A.C. 431. Similar problems commonly arise in relation to "forwarding agents": see, *e.g. Jones* v. *European General Express* (1920) 25 Com.Cas. 296; *Elektronska, etc.* v. *Transped, etc.* [1986] 1 Lloyd's Rep. 49.

27 *The Dragon* [1979] 1 Lloyd's Rep. 257, 262; affirmed [1980] 2 Lloyd's Rep. 415.

28 *Lockett* v. *A. M. Charles Ltd.* [1938] 4 All E.R. 170.

29 *Jackson* v. *Horizon Holidays Ltd.* [1975] 1 W.L.R. 1468, 1473 (where *Lockett* v. *A. M. Charles Ltd. supra*, was not cited).

30 *Post*, p. 649, contrast *Robbins* v. *Fennell* (1847) 11 Q.B. 248 with *Collins* v. *Brook* (1860) 5 H. & N. 700; *cf.* also *The Antama* [1982] 2 Lloyd's Rep. 112 (agent failing to specify which of two persons is the principal for the purpose of the transaction).

31 *Hybart* v. *Parker* (1858) 4 C.B.(N.S.) 209; *Gray* v. *Pearson* (1870) L.R. 5 C.P. 568; *Evans* v. *Hooper* (1875) 1 Q.B.D. 45.

32 [1895] P. 248; affirmed *sub nom. Clarke* v. *Dunraven* [1897] A.C. 59, where only Lord Herschell dealt with the point here discussed; *cf. Meggeson* v. *Burns* [1972] 1 Lloyd's Rep. 223; *White* v. *Blackmore* [1972] 2 Q.B. 651 (where there was no contractual intention).

33 [1929] 2 Ch. 1.

34 Gower, *Modern Company Law* (4th ed.), pp. 315–320, Gregory, 44 M.L.R. 526.

35 See now Companies Act 1985, s.14(1); Goldberg, 48 M.L.R. 158. The reference to sealing seems (perhaps inadvertently) to have survived Law of Property (Miscellaneous Provisions) Act 1989, s.1.

36 *Ante*, p. 504.

ber to observe the provisions of the memorandum and articles. The memorandum and articles amount to a contract between each member and the company[37]; and also to one between the members *inter se*.[38] But they only have the latter effect between the members in their capacity as members; a director is not liable or entitled under them in his capacity as director simply because he happens also to be a member.[39]

2. Party to the Consideration

It is disputed whether the rule that consideration must move from the promisee[40] is the same as, or different from, the rule that only a party to the agreement can sue.[41] In the English cases the two rules have always led to the same result, which the judges have sometimes based on the first rule and sometimes on the second.[42] To be entitled to enforce a promise a person must generally show (1) that it was made to him *and* (2) that the consideration for it moved from him. The statement that consideration must move *from the promisee* simply assumes that the first requirement has been satisfied. If the rule were stated to be that consideration must move *from the party seeking to enforce the promise* it would be clearly distinct from the rule that only a party to the agreement can sue. A man might, for example, promise his daughter to pay £1,000 to anyone who married her. A man who married the daughter with knowledge of and in reliance on such a promise might provide consideration for it, but could not sue on it, as it was not addressed to him.

In *Kepong Prospecting Ltd.* v. *Schmidt*[43] a third party made a claim to enforce a contract under the law of Malaysia, by which consideration need not move from the promisee. In rejecting the claim, the Privy Council said: "It is true that section 2(*d*) of the Contracts Ordinance gives a wider definition of 'consideration' than that which applies in England, particularly in that it enables consideration to move from another person than the promisee, but the appellant was unable to show how this affected the law as to enforcement of contracts by third parties."[44] This decision seems therefore to support the view that the doctrine of privity is distinct from the rule that consideration must move from the promisee.

SECTION 2. RATIONALE, DEVELOPMENT AND OPERATION

1. Reasons for the Doctrine

There are two aspects of the doctrine of privity: no one except a party to a contract can acquire rights under it; and no one except a party can be sub-

---

[37] *Hickman* v. *Kent or Romney Marsh Sheepbreeders Association* [1915] 1 Ch. 881; *cf. Cumbrian Newspaper Group* v. *Cumberland and Westmorland Herald Ltd.* [1987] Ch. 1.

[38] *Rayfield* v. *Hands* [1960] Ch. 1; *J. H. Rayner* (*Mincing Lane*) *Ltd.* v. *D.T.I.* [1989] Ch. 72, 190 (approved on this point [1990] 2 A.C. 418, 515); but there is no contract between members on the one hand and third parties on the other: *Eley* v. *Positive, etc., Assurance Co.* (1876) 1 Ex.D. 88.

[39] *Beattie* v. *E. & F. Beattie Ltd.* [1938] Ch. 708; *Rayfield* v. *Hands, supra*, is difficult to reconcile with this principle: L.C.B.G., 21 M.L.R. 401.

[40] *Ante*, p. 77.

[41] Furmston, 23 M.L.R. at pp. 383–384; Jacobs, [1986] J.B.L. 466, 467.

[42] Thus the judgments in *Tweddle* v. *Atkinson* (1861) 1 B. & S. 393 are based on the rule that consideration must move from the promisee; while the judgments of Littledale and Patteson JJ. in *Price* v. *Easton* (1833) 4 B. & Ad. 433 are based on the doctrine of privity.

[43] [1968] A.C. 810.

[44] *Ibid.* p. 826.

jected to liabilities under it. The reason for the second aspect of the doctrine is obvious: a person should not, as a general rule, have contractual obligations imposed on him without his consent. The first aspect of the doctrine is less easy to explain. One possible reason for it is that a contract is a personal affair, affecting only the parties to it; but this is rather a restatement of the doctrine than a reason for its existence. Another possible reason is that it would be unjust to allow a person to sue on a contract on which he could not be sued[45]; but the law enforces unilateral contracts, to which the same argument applies.[46] A third possible reason is that, if third parties could enforce contracts made for their benefit, the rights of contracting parties to rescind or vary such contracts would be unduly hampered: this reasoning has certainly been influential in limiting the development of one of the exceptions to the doctrine.[47] Yet a fourth possible reason is that the third party is often a mere donee. A system of law which does not give a gratuitous promisee a right to enforce the promise is not likely to give this right to a gratuitous beneficiary who is not even a promisee. The doctrines of privity and consideration, though not identical, are closely connected. This connection helps to explain the development of the doctrine of privity.

2. Development

Before the doctrine of consideration was established in its present form,[48] there was a conflict of authority on the question whether a person could enforce a contract to which he was not a party.[49] The most important decision in the third party's favour was *Dutton* v. *Poole*.[50] A father intended to sell a wood to raise portions for his younger children. His eldest son dissuaded him from selling by promising him to pay £1,000 to each of the younger children. One of the daughters successfully sued the eldest son on the promise made to the father. Scroggs C.J. said: "There was such apparent consideration of affection from the father to his children, for whom nature obliges him to provide, that the consideration and promise to the father may well extend to the children."[51] The underlying assumption is that if the promise had been made by the father to the younger children, it would have been binding because natural love and affection was good consideration. The facts that no promise was made to the daughters and that the alleged consideration did not move from them are simply ignored. Lord Mansfield, an opponent of the strict doctrine of consideration, not surprisingly approved of this decision.[52] But when the idea that natural love and affection could constitute consideration was

---

[45] *Tweddle* v. *Atkinson* (1861) 1 B. & S. at p. 398.
[46] *Ante*, pp. 36–40, 138.
[47] *Post*, pp. 563–564.
[48] *Ante*, pp. 75–76.
[49] In *Crow* v. *Rogers* (1724) 1 Str. 592; *Bourne* v. *Mason* (1669) 1 Ventr. 6 and *Price* v. *Easton* (1833) 4 B. & Ad. 433 the third party was not allowed to sue; but he was allowed to sue in *Thomas* v. —— (1655) Sty. 461; *Green* v. *Horn* (1693) Comb. 219 (reversed (1694) 1 Salk. 197 on the ground that the third party must at least be mentioned in the deed) and *Marchington* v. *Vernon* (1786) 1 B. & P. 101. n. (*c*); E.J.P., 70 L.Q.R. 467; Scammel, 8 C.L.P. 134–135; Palmer, 33 Am. Jl. of Legal History 3; Ibbetson in (ed.) Barton, *Towards a General Law of Contract*, 67, 96–99.
[50] (1678) 2 Lev. 210; affirmed by the Exchequer Chambers, T.Raym. 302.
[51] (1678) 2 Lev. at pp. 211–212.
[52] *Martyn* v. *Hind* (1776) 2 Cowp. 437, 443.

rejected in the nineteenth century, the reasoning in *Dutton* v. *Poole* became obsolete.[53] This was made clear in *Tweddle* v. *Atkinson*.[54] The plaintiff was about to marry the defendant's daughter. The defendant promised *the plaintiff's father* to pay the plaintiff a marriage portion. It was held that the plaintiff could not enforce this promise.

Tweddle v. *Atkinson* was generally considered to have established the doctrine of privity in its present form. In 1884 Bowen L.J. said that it was "mere pedantry" to insurrect the old cases so as to cast doubt on the doctrine[55]; and in 1915 the doctrine was approved by the House of Lords in *Dunlop Pneumatic Tyre Co. Ltd.* v. *Selfridge & Co. Ltd.*,[56] where Lord Haldane said: "In the law of England certain principles are fundamental. One is that only a person who is a party to a contract can sue on it. Our law knows nothing of a *jus quaesitum tertio* arising by way of contract."[57] The existence of the doctrine was, indeed, doubted by Denning L.J. in two cases in 1949 and 1954[58]; and for a time his views attracted a certain amount of judicial and academic support.[59] But in 1961 the House of Lords (Lord Denning dissenting) once again affirmed the existence of the doctrine,[60] and this view of the law has been accepted in many later cases.[61]

The leading modern case is *Beswick* v. *Beswick*.[62] A coal merchant transferred his business to his nephew who made various promises in return. One of these was that he would, after the uncle's death, pay £5 per week to the uncle's widow. The uncle died and the widow became his administratrix. She brought an action to enforce the nephew's promise, suing both in her own right and as administratrix. The House of Lords held that the widow could enforce the nephew's promise in her capacity as administratrix of the promisee and that she was entitled to an order of specific performance against the nephew obliging him to make the payments to her for her personal benefit. In the Court of Appeal Lord Denning M.R. had said that the widow could also sue in her own right at

---

[53] *Re Cook's Settlement Trusts* [1965] Ch. 902 provides an interesting modern contrast.

[54] (1861) 1 B. & S. 393.

[55] *Gandy* v. *Gandy* (1884) 30 Ch.D. 57, 69.

[56] [1915] A.C. 847. The actual decision is no longer law; see *post*, p. 569.

[57] [1915] A.C. at p. 853; for a similar, earlier, statement, see *Keighley, Maxsted & Co.* v. *Durant* [1901] A.C. 240, 246.

[58] In *Smith and Snipes Hall Farm Ltd.* v. *River Douglas Catchment Board* [1949] 2 K.B. 500; *Drive Yourself Hire Co. (London) Ltd.* v. *Strutt* [1954] 1 Q.B. 250.

[59] *Pyrene Co. Ltd.* v. *Scindia Steam Navigation Co. Ltd.* [1954] 2 Q.B. 402; *Rayfield* v. *Hands* [1960] Ch. 1; Dowrick, 19 M.L.R. 375; *cf.* Andrews, 8 Legal Studies 14.

[60] *Scruttons Ltd.* v. *Midland Silicones Ltd.* [1962] A.C. 446; *post*, p. 553; see also *Green* v. *Russell* [1959] 2 Q.B. 226.

[61] *Rookes* v. *Barnard* [1964] A.C. 1129 (*post*, p. 742); *Re Cook's Settlement Trust* [1965] Ch. 902, 915; *Hepburn* v. *A. Tomlinson (Hauliers) Ltd.* [1966] A.C. 451; *The Eurymedon* [1975] A.C. 154; *The New York Star* [1981] 1 W.L.R. 138; *Woodar Investments & Development Ltd.* v. *Wimpey Construction U.K. Ltd.* [1980] 1 W.L.R. 277; *Northern Regional Health Authority* v. *Derek Crouch Construction Co. Ltd.* [1984] Q.B. 644, 665; *Balsamo* v. *Medici* [1984] 1 W.L.R. 951, 959–960; *Southern Water Authority* v. *Carey* [1985] 2 All E.R. 1077, 1083; *The Forum Craftsman* [1985] 1 Lloyd's Rep. 291, 295; *Singer (U.K.) Ltd.* v. *Tees & Hartlepool Port Authority* [1988] 2 Lloyd's Rep. 164, 167; *J. H. Rayner (Mincing Lane) Ltd.* v. *D.T.I.* [1990] 2 A.C. 418, 479, 506; *The Captain Gregos* [1990] 1 Lloyd's Rep. 310, 318; the point is perhaps left open in *Esso Petroleum Ltd.* v. *Hall Russell & Co.* [1989] A.C. 643, 662.

[62] [1966] Ch. 538; [1968] A.C. 58; Goodhart, 83 L.Q.R. 465; Fairest [1967] C.L.J. 149; Treitel, 29 M.L.R. 657; 30 M.L.R. 687.

common law,[63] because the doctrine of privity was "at bottom . . . only a rule of procedure"[64] and could be overcome by simply joining the promisee as a party to the action. The House of Lords found it unnecessary to express a concluded view on this point. But the speeches all assume the correctness of the commonly accepted view that a contract can only be enforced by the parties to it[65]; though the House of Lords has on a number of occasions indicated its willingness to reconsider the position.[66] Such reconsideration has indeed been undertaken by a majority of the High Court of Australia, but in a decision in which so many divergent views were expressed, that it provides no firm guidance for the development of the law.[67] The difficulties of reaching satisfactory results in this area through purely judicial reconsideration are formidable: they arise, particularly, in defining exactly what classes of third parties can acquire rights under the contract, and in determining how those rights are to be affected by defences available between the contracting parties themselves.[68] A satisfactory solution of such difficulties is more likely to be achieved by legislative reform than through the accidents of litigations.[69] For the present, the weight of English authority supports the continued existence of the doctrine of privity.

3. Present Operation of the Doctrine

Although a third party cannot generally assert rights under a contract made for his benefit, the contract remains nevertheless binding between promisor and promisee. The fact that the contract was made for the benefit of a third party does, however, give rise to special problems so far as the promisee's remedies against the promisor are concerned. Actual performance of the contract may also lead to disputes between promisee and third party.

(1) Promisee's remedies

(a) SPECIFIC PERFORMANCE. The promisee (or those acting for his estate) may seek specific performance. If, as in *Beswick* v. *Beswick*,[70] this remedy is granted, the third party will in fact receive the benefit contracted for. But the scope of the remedy of specific performance is limited in various ways;

---

[63] For the effect of Law of Property Act 1925, s.56, see *post*, pp. 571–573.
[64] [1966] Ch. at p. 557.
[65] [1968] A.C. at pp. 72, 81, 83, 92–93, 95.
[66] *Ibid.* p. 72; *Woodar Investment Development Ltd.* v. *Wimpey Construction U.K. Ltd.* [1980] 1 W.L.R. 277, 291, 297–298, 300; *Swain* v. *Law Society* [1983] 1 A.C. 598, 611.
[67] *Trident Insurance Co. Ltd.* v. *McNiece Bros. Pty. Ltd.* (1988) 165 C.L.R. 107, where a claim under a liability insurance policy by a person who was not a party to it was upheld by a majority of 5 to 2. But one member of the majority (Deane J.) was only prepared to allow the third party's claim under the well-established trust exception to the doctrine of privity (*post*, p. 562), while another (Gaudron J.) based his decision in favour of the third party, not on contract, but on unjust enrichment (*post*, p. 551), and said that this was "not an abrogation of the doctrine of privity of contract" (at p. 177). Only 3 of the 7 members of the court can be said to have countenanced such an abrogation, and even their view may be restricted to the special insurance context with which the case was concerned. See also Edgell, [1989] L.M.C.L.Q. 139; Kincaid, 2 J.C.L. 160.
[68] See the elaborate discussion of these problems in American law (which in principle recognises the rights of third party beneficiaries) in Corbin on *Contracts*, Chapters 41–44. The effect of rescission or variation by the contracting parties gives rise to particular difficulties: *cf. post*, pp. 563–564, 574–575.
[69] See Treitel, 29 M.L.R. 657, 665; Reynolds, 105 L.Q.R., 1, 3.
[70] [1968] A.C. 58, *ante*, p. 529.

these limitations, and their applicability to cases involving third parties, will be discussed in detail in Chapter 21.[71] It is therefore necessary to consider what other remedies may be available to the promisee if the contract is broken.

(b) RESTITUTION. The promisee may claim restitution of the consideration provided by him. But part performance of the promise in favour of the third party might defeat this remedy,[72] and it might also be unjust to restrict the promisee to such a claim: for example, return of premiums could be a quite inadequate remedy where a policy of life insurance had been taken out for the benefit of a third party and had matured.

(c) AGREED SUM. The promisee may claim payment to himself of the agreed sum. It can be objected that to allow such a claim would force the promisor to do something which he never contracted to do, *viz.* to pay the promisee when he contracted to pay the third party. The objection loses much of its force if the promisor would not in fact be prejudiced by having to pay the promisee rather than the third party.[73] There is little authority on the question, but the most recent pronouncement supports the view that the promisee cannot sue for the agreed sum,[74] save in exceptional circumstances, to be described later in this Chapter.[75]

(d) DAMAGES IN RESPECT OF PROMISEE'S LOSS. The promisee may claim damages where he has suffered loss as a result of the promisor's failure to perform in favour of the third party. But in *Beswick* v. *Beswick* the majority of the House of Lords evidently thought that no such loss had been or would be suffered and that the damages recoverable by the estate for breach of the nephew's promise would be merely nominal.[76] Lord Upjohn explained that this would be the case because the promisee "died *without any assets* save and except the agreement which he hoped would keep him and then his widow for their lives."[77] It seems from this that damages might have been substantial if the promisee had had other assets—either because the widow might have had a claim against those assets if the promise was not performed[78] or because the promisee or his estate would in fact, even if not legally obliged to do so, have made some other, wholly voluntary, provision for the widow. The loss suffered by the promisee would be the cost of making an alternative provision, and there is some authority to support the view that damages for breach of contract may be recovered to compensate for such loss even though the provision is wholly

---

[71] *Post*, pp. 918–919.

[72] As there would be no total failure of consideration; and as "rescission" for breach could probably not be allowed unless the third party was willing to restore any performance received: *post*, pp. 927–928. For the suggestion that *the third party* may have a claim in restitution, see *post*, p. 551.

[73] *Cf. post*

[74] See *Coulls* v. *Bagot's Executor and Trustee Co. Ltd.* [1967] A.L.R. 385, 409–411; *cf. Beswick* v. *Beswick* [1968] A.C. at pp. 88, 101 (dealing with the remedy of damages).

[75] See *Cleaver* v. *Mutual Reserve Fund Life Association* [1892] 1 Q.B. 147, *post*, p. 566.

[76] Lord Pearce, however, thought that damages would be substantial: [1968] A.C. at p. 88.

[77] [1968] A.C. at p. 102 (italics supplied).

[78] *e.g.* under the Inheritance (Family Provision) Act 1938, now Inheritance (Provision for Family and Dependants) Act 1975.

voluntary.[79] *A fortiori* the promisee can recover substantial damages where he is under a legal obligation to make a payment to the third party and where this obligation would have been discharged if the promisor had paid in accordance with the contract.

(e) DAMAGES IN RESPECT OF THIRD PARTY'S LOSS? The view that the damages in *Beswick* v. *Beswick* would only be nominal is based on the general principle that, in an action for damages, a plaintiff cannot recover more than the amount required to compensate him for his loss.[80] That principle is, however, subject to exceptions: for example, substantial damages can be recovered by a trustee even though the loss is suffered by his *cestui que trust*[81]; by an agent even though the loss is suffered by his undisclosed principal[82]; and by the consignor of goods on a ship even though the loss is suffered by a person to whom he has sold them but who has not himself acquired any rights to sue the shipowner for breach of contract.[83] In all these exceptional cases a person recovers substantial damages for breach of contract even though the breach caused loss, not to him, but to a third party. Our present concern is to ask whether the general principle is subject to a further exception, applicable on breach of a contract for the benefit of a third party. Can the promisee recover substantial damages in respect of loss suffered, not by himself, but by the third party?[84]

In *Jackson* v. *Horizon Holidays Ltd.*[85] the defendants contracted with the plaintiff to provide holiday accommodation for the plaintiff, his wife and their two three-year-old children.[86] The accommodation fell far short of the promised standard, and the plaintiff recovered damages, including £500 for "mental distress."[87] James L.J. seems to have regarded this sum as compensation for the plaintiff's own distress.[88] No doubt this was increased by his witnessing the distress suffered by his wife and children, and if the promisee himself suffers loss he should not be prevented from recovering it in full merely because the contract was made partly for the

---

79 *Admiralty Commissioners* v. *SS. Amerika* [1917] A.C. 38, 61 (the actual decision was that payments voluntary made to the victim of an alleged *tort* could not be recovered: on this point see also *Esso Petroleum Co. Ltd.* v. *Hall Russell & Co. Ltd.* [1989] A.C. 643). For the possibility of recovering voluntary payments to third parties in a contractual action, see also the rules as to mitigation and especially *Banco de Portugal* v. *Waterlow & Sons Ltd.* [1932] A.C. 452, where a bank recovered damages in respect of payments which it was not legally liable to make; *post*, p. 868.

80 *Post*, p. 825.

81 See, for example, *post*, p. 562; *cf. Pan Atlantic Ins. Co. Ltd.* v. *Pine Top Ins. Co. Ltd.* [1988] 2 Lloyd's Rep. 505.

82 See, for example, *post*, p. 636.

83 *Dunlop* v. *Lambert* (1839) 2 Cl. & F. 626, 627; *The Sanix Ace* [1987] 1 Lloyd's Rep. 465; *The Chanda* [1989] 2 Lloyd's Rep. 494. The rule was recognised in *The Albazero* [1977] A.C. 774, but held inapplicable as the buyer had acquired his own contractual rights against the shipowner under s.1 of the Bills of Lading Act 1855, *post*, pp. 579, 606–607; Weir [1977] C.L.J. 24.

84 For the ultimate destination of such damages (where, exceptionally, recoverable), see *post*, p. 537.

85 [1975] 1 W.L.R. 1468; Yates, 39 M.L.R. 202.

86 It was assumed that the wife and children were not parties to the contract. Contrast, as to this, *ante*, p. 426 at n. 27.

87 At p. 1472.

88 *Ibid.* at p. 1474.

benefit of third parties,[89] who also suffered loss. Lord Denning M.R., however, said that £500 would have been excessive compensation for the plaintiff's own distress.[90] He nevertheless upheld the award on the ground that the plaintiff had made a contract for the benefit both of himself and of his wife and children[91]; and that he could recover in respect of their loss as well as in respect of his own. But the authorities cited in support of this conclusion seem to contradict rather than to support it.[92] Moreover, in *Beswick* v. *Beswick* the majority of the House of Lords said that the promisee's estate could only have recovered nominal damages as it had suffered no loss.[93] This is scarcely consistent with the view that the promisee under a contract for the benefit of a third party is, as a general rule, entitled to damages in respect of the third party's loss.

The question whether the promisee can recover damages in respect of the third party's loss was again discussed in *Woodar Investment Development Ltd.* v. *Wimpey Construction U.K. Ltd.*[94] In that case a contract for the sale of land provided that, on completion, the purchaser should pay £850,000 to the vendor and also £150,000 to a third party. The vendor claimed damages on the footing that the purchaser had wrongfully repudiated the contract and the actual decision of the House of Lords was that there had been no such repudiation,[95] so that the issue of damages did not arise. But Lord Denning's approach to the question of damages in *Jackson* v. *Horizon Holidays Ltd.*[96] was disapproved; though the actual decision in that case was supported on the ground that the damages were awarded for the plaintiff's own loss,[97] or, alternatively, on the ground that cases such as booking of family holidays or ordering meals in restaurants[98] might "call for special treatment."[99] The question what damages would have been recoverable in the *Woodar* case itself was described as "one of great doubt and difficulty"[1]: presumably it would turn on such factors as whether the vendor was under a legal obligation to ensure that the third party received the payment, or whether, on the purchaser's failure to make the payment, the vendor had himself made it, or procured it to be made, from other resources available to him.

---

89 *Cf. Radford* v. *De Froberville* [1977] 1 W.L.R. 1262 (damages for failure to build a wall not reduced merely because plaintiff had entered into the contract, not only for his own benefit alone, but also for that of his tenants).

90 [1975] 1 W.L.R. at p. 1474.

91 *Ibid.*; *cf. McCall* v. *Abelesz* [1976] Q.B. 585, 594.

92 Lord Denning M.R. relied on a dictum of Lush L.J. in *Lloyd's* v. *Harper* (1880) 16 Ch.D. 290, 331 said to have been quoted by Lord Pearce in *Beswick* v. *Beswick* "with considerable approval": [1975] 1 W.L.R. at p. 1473. In fact Lord Pearce said that the dictum "cannot be accepted without qualification and regardless of the context": [1968] A.C. at p. 88; *cf. ibid.* p. 101; he agreed with the view expressed in *Coulls* v. *Bagots Executor and Trustee Co. Ltd.* [1967] A.L.R. 385, 411 that Lush L.J.'s dictum must be confined to the case in which the contract creates a trust in favour of the third party (*post*, p. 562). This situation falls within the special exception stated at n. 81, *supra*.

93 *Ante*, p. 531.

94 [1980] 1 W.L.R. 227.

95 *Post*, p. 706.

96 *Supra, n. 85.*

97 [1980] 1 W.L.R. 283, 293, 297.

98 *Cf. ante*, p. 526.

99 [1980] 1 W.L.R. 277, 283. *Cf. Calabar Properties Ltd.* v. *Stitcher* [1984] 1 W.L.R. 287, 290 where it was not disputed that a tenant's damages for her landlord's breach of his covenant to repair should include compensation for ill-health suffered by her husband.

1 [1980] 1 W.L.R. at p. 284.

The result of the *Woodar* case thus seems to be that, where a contract for the benefit of a third party has been broken, the promisee cannot generally recover damages in respect of a loss suffered only by the third party. But this position was in that case described as "most unsatisfactory"[2] and said to be in need of reconsideration, either by the legislature or by the House of Lords itself.[3] The general rule was again criticised in *Forster* v. *Silvermere Golf and Equestrian Centre*,[4] where the plaintiff transferred land to the defendant, who undertook to build a house on it and to allow the plaintiff and her children to live there rent free for life. It was held that the plaintiff could recover damages for breach of that undertaking in respect of her own loss, but not in respect of the loss suffered by her children as a result of being deprived of any rights of occupation which they might have enjoyed after her death. Dillon J. described this result as "a blot on our law and most unjust." It is submitted (on the basis of the explanation of *Beswick* v. *Beswick*[5] given above)[6] that, if the plaintiff had incurred expenses in making alternative provision for the accommodation of her children after her death, she could have recovered such expenses as part of her own loss. On the other hand, it is unlikely that the plaintiff could have secured the intended benefit for her children by claiming specific performance, for it does not seem that the defendant's obligation to build was defined with sufficient precision to enable the court to enforce it specifically.[7]

(f) NEGATIVE PROMISE. So far, we have assumed that the promise is positive in nature, *e.g.* to pay money, deliver goods or to do some other act. Where the promise is negative in nature, the promisee's most obvious remedy is an injunction to restrain the promisor's breach. This remedy would, for example, be available where A validly promised B not to compete with C.

One type of negative promise which gives rise to special difficulty is a promise by A to B *not to sue* C, *e.g.* for a debt owed by C to A. If, in breach of such a promise, A nevertheless did sue C, it would not be appropriate for B to start a second action for an injunction to restrain A from proceeding with the first action; for such a step would lead to undesirable multiplicity of legal proceedings.[8] B's remedy is to ask the court to exercise its discretion[9] to stay A's action against C. In *Gore* v. *Van der Lann*[10] the Court of Appeal held that B could only obtain a stay of A's action against C if two conditions were satisfied: there must be a definite promise by A to B not to sue C, and B must have a sufficient interest in the enforcement of A's promise. This last requirement would not be satisfied unless, as a result

---

[2] *Ibid.* p. 291; *cf.* pp. 297–298, 300–301.
[3] *Cf. Beswick* v. *Beswick* [1968] A.C. 58, 72.
[4] (1981) 125 S.J. 397.
[5] [1968] A.C. 58.
[6] *Ante*, p. 531.
[7] *Post*, p. 915.
[8] Supreme Court Act 1981, s.49(2), replacing Supreme Court of Judicature (Consolidation) Act 1925, s.41 which expressly provided that no proceedings in the High Court could be restrained by injunction.
[9] Under Supreme Court Act 1981, s.49(3).
[10] [1967] 2 Q.B. 31; Davies, 1 *Legal Studies* 287; *European Asian Bank A.G.* v. *Punjab and Sind Bank* [1982] 2 Lloyd's Rep. 356; *The Chevalier Roze* [1983] 2 Lloyd's Rep. 438; and see *post*, p. 556.

of A's breach, B were exposed to legal liability to C: for example where B had *contracted with* C to procure his release from a debt or a liability to A, and would be put in breach of that contract by A's action against C.

In *Snelling* v. *John G. Snelling Ltd.*[11] the court went even further in giving effect to a promise of this kind. Three brothers had lent money to a family company of which they were directors. They agreed that if one of them resigned he should "forfeit" any money due to him from the company. One of them did resign and sued the company for the amounts due to him. By way of defence the company relied on the agreement between the brothers, and, if matters had rested there, the defence would have failed as the company was not a party to the agreement.[12] But the other two brothers applied to be joined as defendants to the action, adopted the company's defence and counterclaimed for a declaration that the plaintiff's loan was forfeited. It was held that they were entitled to such a declaration by virtue of the contract between them and the plaintiff.[13] Ormrod J. further held that they could obtain a stay of the action against the company and that the most convenient way of disposing of the action against the company was to dismiss it. So far as the granting of the stay is concerned, the judgment is hard to reconcile with the requirement of a sufficient interest as explained in *Gore* v. *Van der Lann*[14]; but it is submitted that Ormrod J.'s decision is consistent with the spirit of *Beswick* v. *Beswick*.[15] If *the promisee* takes steps specifically to enforce the contract the court should, wherever possible, grant such remedy as is most appropriate for that purpose. Normally this will be an order of specific performance or an injunction. The fact that the latter remedy is not appropriate to enforce a promise not to sue should not deter the court from granting other remedies that serve substantially to enforce the promise. Such a remedy is only available if it is sought *by the promisee*. If the two brothers in the *Snelling* case had not applied to be joined in the action, the company could not have relied on the agreement between them and the plaintiff by way of defence.[16]

(2) Position between promisee and third party

The promisor may be perfectly willing to perform, and may actually perform, in favour of the third party, *e.g.* by paying him the agreed sum. These possibilities give rise to further problems between the third party and the promisee. In discussing these problems we shall at this stage assume that the case does not fall within any of the exceptions to the doctrine of privity which will be considered later in this Chapter.[17]

(a) PROMISOR PAYS OR IS WILLING TO PAY. The first problem arises where the promisor has actually paid the third party or is willing to pay him, and the promisee claims that the third party is not entitled to keep the money

---

[11] [1973] 1 Q.B. 87; Wilkie, 36 M.L.R. 214.
[12] [1973] Q.B. 87, 95.
[13] *Ibid.* p. 96.
[14] [1967] 2 Q.B. 31.
[15] [1968] A.C. 58; *ante*, pp. 529–530.
[16] *Snelling* v. *John G. Snelling Ltd.* [1973] Q.B. 87, 95.
[17] *Post*, pp. 561–573; and see in particular pp. 562–568.

for his own benefit but must hold it on behalf of the promisee. Such a claim is not likely to be made by the promisee himself, as he wants to benefit the third party. But it might be made by the promisee's trustee in bankruptcy, or by his personal representative on death. In *Beswick* v. *Beswick* the House of Lords held that the third party (the widow) was entitled to keep the money which the nephew was ordered to pay her, simply because it appeared from the true construction of the contract that this was the intention of the contracting parties.[18] It seems that the position would be the same where payments were made willingly, *i.e.* without any order of the court.[19] Payments actually received by the third party can only be claimed by the promisee if, on the true construction of the contract, they were made to the third party as nominee for the promisee. Where the money has not yet been paid, the promisor and the promisee can at any time rescind or vary the contract; and if they vary it so as to provide for payment to the promisee, the third party has no claim under the contract. But the question whether the promisee can unilaterally (*i.e.* without the consent of the promisor) demand that payment should be made to himself depends once again on the construction of the contract. If the contract can be construed as one to pay the third party "or as the promisee shall direct," then the promisee is entitled to demand payment to himself.[20] But the contract is not likely to be construed in this way where it is a matter of concern to the promisor that payment should be made to the third party, *e.g.* because the third party is a near relative of the promisor and it matters to the promisor that the third party should be provided for.[21]

The rules just stated only apply if there is indeed a promise to pay the third party. In *Coulls* v. *Bagot's Executor and Trustee Co. Ltd.*[22] an agreement between A and B provided for payment of royalties by B to A and concluded: "I [A] authorise . . . [B] to pay all money connected with this agreement to my wife . . . and myself . . . as joint tenants." The document was signed by A, B and A's wife. A majority of the High Court of Australia held that there was no *promise* by B to A to pay A's wife but only a *mandate* by A authorising B to pay A's wife (so that such payment would discharge B). This mandate was revocable and had been revoked by A's death. Consequently, the money (which B was willing to pay) belonged to A's estate and not to his wife. The third party would, *a fortiori*, not be entitled to the money if he were mentioned in the contract as a mere nominee in such a way as to indicate that no beneficial interest was intended to pass to him, and that payment to him without the request of the promisee should not discharge the promisor.[23]

---

[18] *Beswick* v. *Beswick* [1968] A.C. 58, 71, 96, on this point overruling *Re Engelbach's Estate* [1924] 2 Ch. 348 and doubting *Re Sinclair's Life Policy* [1938] Ch. 799. Earlier cases supporting the view stated in the text include *Ashby* v. *Costin* (1888) 21 Q.B.D. 401; *Harris* v. *United Kingdom, etc., Society* (1889) 87 L.T.J. 272; *Re Davies* [1892] 3 Ch. 63.

[19] This appears from the treatment in *Beswick* v. *Beswick* of *Re Engelbach's Estate* (*supra*), where the money had in fact been paid to the third party: see 93 L.J.Ch. 616, 617.

[20] The same is true where a contract provides for some other performance to be rendered to a third party: *e.g. Mitchell* v. *Ede* (1840) 11 Ad. & El. 888; *The Lycaon* [1983] 2 Lloyd's Rep. 548.

[21] As in *Re Stapleton-Bretherton* [1941] Ch. 482.

[22] [1967] A.L.R. 385; for a similar distinction, see *post*, p. 583.

[23] *Thavorn* v. *Bank of Credit & Commerce S.A.* [1985] 1 Lloyd's Rep. 259.

(b) PROMISEE REFUSES TO SUE. The second problem arises where the promisee fails or refuses to take any action to enforce the promise. Lord Denning has suggested that the third party could in such a case circumvent the doctrine of privity by suing the promisor and joining the promisee as co-defendant.[24] But Diplock and Salmon L.JJ. have said that the action can be brought only by the promisee[25]; and it is submitted that this is the correct view. Lord Denning's view is inconsistent with the continued existence of the doctrine of privity which was recognised in *Beswick* v. *Beswick* and in later cases.[26] It is also inconsistent with the reasoning of the cases on trusts of promises to be discussed below,[27] for if the third party could always sue by joining the promisee to the action, it would be pointless to insist that he must in addition show the existence of a trust.

(c) PROMISEE SUES FOR DAMAGES OR RESTITUTION. The final problem arises where the promisee sues but claims some form of relief other than specific performance in favour of the third party: *i.e.* where he claims recovery of the consideration provided by him, or damages. If such a claim succeeded, it would seem to lead to a judgment for payment to the promisee and not to the third party; and the question would arise whether the promisee could keep the payment for his own benefit or whether he would be bound to hold it for the third party. In tort, a person can sometimes recover damages for a loss suffered not by himself but by another: *e.g.* a husband may get damages for loss of earnings suffered by his wife in giving up her job to nurse him after an accident. There is some authority for the view that such damages are to be held on trust for the other person.[28] Similarly, damages for breach of contract can in certain exceptional situations be recovered in respect of loss suffered by another[29]; such damages must be held for that other person.[30] Where a contract for the benefit of a third party is broken, the promisee normally recovers damages only in respect of his *own* loss,[31] and he cannot be under any obligation to pay over those damages (or any part of them) to the third party.[32] There may, however, be cases "calling for special treatment,"[33] such as the booking of family holidays or ordering meals in restaurants. If, in such cases, the promisee can recover damages in respect of the third party's loss, it may be that those damages, when recovered, would be held by the promisee as money had and received for the use of the third party.[34]

---

[24] *Beswick* v. *Beswick* [1966] Ch. at p. 557; *Gurtner* v. *Circuit* [1968] 2 Q.B. 587, 596.

[25] *Ibid.* pp. 599, 606.

[26] *Ante*, pp. 528–530.

[27] *Post*, pp. 562–568.

[28] *Cunningham* v. *Harrison* [1973] Q.B. 942, 952; *cf. Allen* v. *Waters* [1935] 1 K.B. 200 and *Dennis* v. *L.P.T.B.* [1948] 1 All E.R. 779 as explained in 72 L.Q.R. 187; *Donnelly* v. *Joyce* [1974] Q.B. 545 (where the ultimate destination of the damages was not discussed); *cf. post*, p. 562.

[29] *Ante*, pp. 532–533.

[30] *Ibid, The Albazero* [1977] A.C. 774, 845; *cf. post*, p. 570.

[31] See *ante*, pp. 532–533.

[32] *Cf. Coulls* v. *Bagot's Executor and Trustee Co. Ltd.* [1967] A.L.R. 385, 411.

[33] *Woodar Investment Development Ltd.* v. *Wimpey Construction U.K. Ltd.* [1980] 1 W.L.R. 277, 283; *ante*, p. 533.

[34] This was the view of Lord Denning M.R. in *Jackson* v. *Horizon Holidays Ltd.* [1975] 1 W.L.R. 1468, 1473. The strange result would be that the plaintiff was under quasi-contractual liability to his small children in respect of part of the £500 recovered as damages for distress.

SECTION 3. SCOPE

1. General

The doctrine of privity means that a person cannot acquire rights or be subjected to liabilities *arising under* a contract to which he is not a party.[35] It does not mean that a contract between A and B cannot affect the legal rights of C indirectly. For example, an agreement between A and B under which A accepts from B part payment of a debt owned by C to A in full settlement of that debt can benefit C by precluding A from suing C for the balance of the debt[36]; and *a fortiori* full performance by B of C's obligation to A can discharge that obligation.[37] It is also possible for a contract between A and B to affect C adversely.[38] Of course A and B cannot by a contract between them impose an obligation on C to perform duties arising under the contract. This aspect of the doctrine of privity is so obvious that it scarcely needs to be stated: if A and B agreed that C was to pay £100 to A, no one would suppose that this agreement could oblige C to make the payment. But a contract between A and B may in some other way restrict C's freedom of action: for example it may create rights in or over property, such as a lien[39] or a lease[40] or an equitable interest, or give rise to a constructive trust affecting property[41]; and such rights can often be enforced against third parties.

The following situations, in which contracts can indirectly affect the legal rights of third parties, call for further discussion.

2. Liability in Negligence to Third Parties

(1) Duty of care may be owed to third party

While the primary effect of a contract between A and B is to oblige them to perform their respective promises to each other, the contract may also impose on A a duty of care to C, the breach of which will enable C to sue A in tort for negligence. The contract may have this effect because it gives rise between A and C to the relationship of passenger (or cargo-owner)

---

[35] *Ante*, p. 523.

[36] *Hirachand Punamchand* v. *Temple* [1911] 2 K.B. 330; *ante*, p. 118.

[37] *Post*, p. 656.

[38] *e.g. Northern Regional Health Authority* v. *Derek Crouch Construction Co. Ltd.* [1984] Q.B. 644.

[39] See *Faith* v. *E.I.C.* (1821) 4 B. & Ald. 630; *Tappenden* v. *Artus* [1964] 2 Q.B. 185; contrast *Chellaram & Sons (London) Ltd.* v. *Butler's Warehousing & Distribution Ltd.* [1978] 2 Lloyd's Rep. 412 (third party not bound by agreement purporting to confer on sub-bailee a lien more extensive than that which would, but for such agreement, have arisen at common law).

[40] As in *Ashburn Anstalt* v. *Arnold* [1989] Ch. 1.

[41] See *Ashburn Anstalt* v. *Arnold*, *supra*, where the mere fact that C had notice of an earlier contract between A and B was said at pp. 25–26 to be insufficient to give rise to a constructive trust on C's acquisition of the land affected by that contract; and where Fox L.J. (delivering the judgment of the Court) at p. 17 disapproved dicta in *Errington* v. *Errington* [1952] 1 K.B. 290 (which had been followed in *Re Sharpe* [1980] 1 W.L.R. 219) to the effect that a contractual licence granted by A to B gave rise to an equitable interest binding third parties; Hill, 51 M.L.R. 226; Oakley [1988] C.L.J. 353; *cf.* also *Binions* v. *Evans* [1972] Ch. 359; Smith, [1973] C.L.J. 81; Hornby, 93 L.Q.R. 568; *Pritchard* v. *Briggs* [1980] Ch. 338 (option to purchase); *Lyus* v. *Prowsa Developments Ltd.* [1982] 1 W.L.R. 1044.

and carrier,[42] of occupier of premises and visitor,[43] or of bailor and sub-bailee.[44] In a number of cases professional advisors, such as solicitors,[45] and safety consultants[46] have been held liable in tort to persons other than their immediate clients for negligence in the performance of contracts with those clients. Surveyors, valuers, accountants and auditors can similarly be liable for negligent misrepresentation to third parties: the basis, and limits, of such liability have been discussed in Chapter 9.[47]

The most controversial extension of tort liability to a third party was made in *Junior Books Ltd.* v. *Veitchi Co. Ltd.*[48] where B had undertaken to build a factory for C by a contract which entitled C to nominate sub-contractors. C nominated A as flooring sub-contractor; B in consequence entered into a contract with A by which A undertook to lay the floor; but no contract came into existence between A and C.[49] The floor later cracked and, on the assumption that this was due to A's negligence in doing the work defectively, it was held that A was liable to C for the loss suffered by C in consequence of the fact that the work had to be done again. At first sight, this result represents a considerable encroachment on the doctrine of privity, but later decisions have (as the following discussion will show) taken a highly restrictive view of the scope of the *Junior Books* case.

It is important to emphasise that, in the situations just described, A's liability to C is in tort and not on the contract between A and B as such: both the standard and the basis of liability may differ according to whether A is being sued on the contract by B or in tort by C. Thus in the *Junior Books* case it does not seem that C could have sued A if A had repudiated

---

[42] *Austin* v. *G.W. Ry* (1867) L.R. 2 Q.B. 442; *The Antonis P. Lemnos* [1985] A.C. 771.

[43] Occupiers' Liability Act 1957, s.3; Defective Premises Act 1972, ss.1(1)(*b*), 4.

[44] *Moukataff* v. *B.O.A.C.* [1967] 1 Lloyd's Rep. 396; *Bart* v. *B.W.I.A.* [1967] 1 Lloyd's Rep. 239 (where the claim failed as the sub-bailee's duty was limited to one to keep safely, and did not extend to transmission of the package). Such a sub-bailment may also operate to the disadvantage of C in that he may be bound by an exemption clause in the contract between A and B, as in *Morris* v. *C. W. Martin Ltd.* [1966] 1 Q.B. 716. No "sub-bailment" arises merely because a sub-agent has received the proceeds of sale of the principal's property: *Balsamo* v. *Medici* [1984] 1 W.L.R. 951.

[45] *Ross* v. *Caunters* [1980] Ch. 287; *Al Kandari* v. *J. R. Brown & Co.* [1988] Q.B. 665. For a discussion of these two cases, see *Banque Keyser Ullmann S.A.* v. *Skandia (U.K.) Insurance Co. Ltd.* [1990] Q.B. 665, 794–796 (affirmed on other grounds [1990] 2 All E.R. 947); and see *Van Oppen* v. *Clerk of the Bedford Charity Trustees* [1989] 1 All E.R. 273, 289 (affirmed [1990] 1 W.L.R. 235) where *Ross* v. *Caunters*, *supra*, was said to turn on its "own special facts"; the case is also viewed with some scepticism in *Caparo Industries plc.* v. *Dickman* [1990] 2 A.C. 605, 635, but it was cited with apparent approval in *Murphy* v. *Brentwood D.C.* [1990] 2 All E.R. 908, 934.

[46] *Driver* v. *William Willett (Contractors) Ltd.* [1969] 1 All E.R. 655; *cf. Dove* v. *Banham's Patent Locks Ltd.* [1983] 1 W.L.R. 1436; *Bourne* v. *McEvoy Timber Preservation* (1975) 237 E.G. 496 (timber preservation firm giving estimate of cost of work to vendor of a house held to owe a duty of care to purchaser).

[47] *Ante*, p. 310.

[48] [1983] 1 A.C. 520; Jaffey [1983] C.L.J. 37; Palmer and Murdoch 46 M.L.R. 213. See further Jaffey, 5 Legal Studies 77; Reynolds (1985) 11 N.Z.U.L.R. 215; Stapleton, 104 L.Q.R. 213 and 389; Huxley, 53 M.L.R. 361; Beyleveld and Brownsword, 54 M.L.R. 48.

[49] In *Greater Nottingham Co-operative Society Ltd.* v. *Cementation Piling & Foundations Ltd.* [1989] Q.B. 71 there was a direct contract between A (the subcontractor) and C (the building owner) and it was held that A's duty to C was governed by that contract alone and not by the general law relating to the tort of negligence. But it was recognised that breaches of duty arising out of certain contractual relationships may be actionable in tort as well as in contract: see *post*, pp. 872–873.

his contract with B on an untenable ground and done no work under it at all, with the result that completion of the building was delayed and A suffered loss.[50] Moreover the contract between A and B might have made A strictly liable to B,[51] without proof of negligence, while negligence was an essential element of C's cause of action in tort against A; in contract, B would have a cause of action against A as soon as the defective work was done, but in tort C's cause of action would only accrue when the resulting loss was suffered[52] and in B's action on the contract it is only necessary to show that the contract has been made and broken, while in C's action in tort, C must establish that there was a relationship of "proximity" between himself and A.

(2) Restrictions on scope of the duty

(a) IN GENERAL. A relationship of "proximity," giving rise to a duty of care,[53] is not established merely by showing that C has suffered foreseeable loss as a result of A's defective performance of his contract with B. In the *Junior Books* case, there were many special factors giving rise to the requisite degree of proximity: A were nominated as sub-contractors by C; A were specialists in flooring and knew of C's requirements; C relied on A's special skills in laying floors; and A must have known that defects in the work could necessitate repairs and lead to economic loss.[54] These special factors (and in particular the extent of C's reliance on A's special skills) can be said to have given rise to a "special rėlationship" analogous to that which gives rise to liability in tort for negligent misrepresentation.[55] But such factors are unlikely to arise in the ordinary case where C suffers loss as a result of the defective performance by A of his contract with B. Accordingly later authorities[56] have emphasised tne exceptional nature of the circumstances of the *Junior Books* case. It has been said that those circumstances were "unique"[57]; that the case "cannot now be regarded as a useful pointer to the development of the law"[58] or "as laying down any

---

[50] In *The Zephyr* [1984] 1 Lloyd's Rep. 58, 85, it was said at first instance that even the law of torts can sometimes impose "positive duties . . . recognised . . . only because a party has voluntarily undertaken them." But this suggestion was disapproved on appeal: [1985] 2 Lloyd's Rep. 529. No issue of privity arose in *The Zephyr*; the dispute was as to contractual intention (*ante*, p. 157). For a similar suggestion, see *Punjab National Bank* v. *De Boinville*, *Financial Times*, February 1, 1991.

[51] *Post*, p. 738. Similarly, on facts such as those of *Donoghue* v. *Stevenson* [1932] A.C. 562 liability for breach of contract in respect of defects in the goods sold would be strict, while the tort liability of, or to, a third party would have depended on negligence. This difference between tort and contract liability will be considerably reduced in importance by Consumer Protection Act 1987 Pt. I, introducing strict "product liability" to the ultimate consumer. But such liability is subject to important qualifications and will not extend to many of the situations with which the following discussion is concerned.

[52] *Dove* v. *Banham's Safety Locks Ltd.* [1983] 1 W.L.R. 1463; *cf. Bell* v. *Peter Browne & Co.* [1990] 2 Q.B. 495.

[53] See *ante*, p. 309; the requirements there stated are of general application.

[54] [1983] 1 A.C. 520, 546.

[55] *Murphy* v. *Brentwood D.C.* [1990] 2 All E.R. 908, 919, 930; see *ante*, p. 309.

[56] *Post*, p. 545, nn. 93 and 94.

[57] *D. & F. Estates Ltd.* v. *Church Commissioners for England* [1989] A.C. 177, 202; *cf. Van Oppen* v. *Clerk to the Bedford Charity Trustees* [1989] 1 All E.R. 273, 289, affirmed [1990] 1 W.L.R. 235; *Duncan Stevenson MacMillan* v. *A. W. Knott Becker Scott Ltd.* [1990] 1 Lloyd's Rep. 98.

[58] *Simaan General Contracting Co.* v. *Pilkington Glass Ltd.* (*No.* 2) [1988] Q.B. 758, 784.

principle of general application in the law of tort"[59]; that "it is really of no use as an authority on the general duty of care"[60]; and that the statement of principle in Lord Brandon's dissenting speech is to be preferred to that of the majority.[61] The authority of the case is further undermined by the fact that the reasoning of the majority is to a considerable extent based on earlier decisions[62] which have since been overruled by the House of Lords.[63]

(b) REQUIREMENT OF PHYSICAL HARM. Except in the misrepresentation cases discussed in Chapter 9,[64] a plaintiff can only rely on the breach of a contract to which he was not a party as giving him a cause of action in tort if, as a result of the breach, he has suffered physical harm, in the form either of personal injury or of physical damage to his property.[65] The importance of this factor is illustrated by *Simaan General Contracting Co.* v. *Pilkington Glass Ltd.* (*No.* 2),[66] where the defendants had been nominated as suppliers of glass for incorporation in a building which was being erected by the plaintiffs as main contractors for a client in Abu Dabi. The glass had been sold by the defendants to a subcontractor engaged by the plaintiffs, so that there was no contract between plaintiffs and defendants; the glass was perfectly sound but was not of the colour specified in the contract of sale or in the main building contract. In consequence of this shortcoming, the plaintiffs were not paid by their client and so suffered financial loss; but it was held that the defendants' breach of their contract with the subcontractors did not give the plaintiffs any right of action in tort against the defendants merely because that breach had caused the plaintiffs to suffer financial loss. Similarly, it was held in *Balsamo* v. *Medici*[67] that a sub-agent who had negligently paid over the proceeds of the sale of the principal's property to a fraudulent imposter was not liable in tort to the principal for such negligence in handling the money; nor was he liable to the principal in contract as there was no privity of contract between the sub-agent and the principal. To extend the *Junior Books* case to such a situation would, it was said, "come perilously close to abrogating the doctrine of privity altogether."[68]

(c) DEFECTS IN THE VERY THING SUPPLIED NOT SUFFICIENT. Even where A's negligence in the performance of his contract with B has resulted in damage to "property," the scope of C's tort remedy is further restricted by the fact that "property" in this context normally refers to property belong-

---

59 *D. & F. Estates Ltd.* v. *Church Commissioners for England* [1989] A.C. 177, 202.

60 *Ibid.* at p. 215.

61 *Ibid.* at pp. 202, 215; *Department of the Environment* v. *Thomas Bates & Son Ltd.* [1989] 1 All E.R. 1075, 1084; *Islander Trucking Ltd.* v. *Hogg Robinson & Gardner Mountain* (*Marine*) *Ltd.* [1990] 1 All E.R. 826, 829; *cf. Murphy* v. *Brentwood D.C.* [1990] 2 All E.R. 908, 921.

62 *i.e. Anns* v. *Merton London Borough* [1978] A.C. 728; *Dutton* v. *Bognor Regis Building Co. Ltd.* [1972] 1 Q.B. 373.

63 *Murphy* v. *Brentwood D.C.*, [1990] 2 All E.R. 908.

64 *Ante*, p. 309.

65 *Tate & Lyle Industries Ltd.* v. *G.L.C.* [1983] 2 A.C. 509, 530–531; *cf. London Congregational Union Inc.* v. *Harriss* [1988] 1 All E.R. 15, 25; *Simaan General Contracting Co. Ltd.* v. *Pilkington Glass Ltd.* (*No.* 2) [1988] 1 Q.B. 758, 781; *Greater Nottingham Co-operative Soc. Ltd.* v. *Cementation Piling & Foundation Ltd.* [1989] Q.B. 71, 94.

66 [1988] Q.B. 758.

67 [1984] 1 W.L.R. 951; Whittaker, 48 M.L.R. 86.

68 At pp. 959–960; *cf. Michael Sallis & Co.* v. *E.C.A. Call* (1988) 4 Const. L.J. 125.

ing to C *other* than the very thing supplied by A under that contract. Thus where A sold goods to B who resold them to C, it was held that A would not be liable in tort to C merely because those goods disintegrated on account of a defect in them amounting to a breach of A's contract with B.[69] Nor, where goods are bought from a retailer, is the manufacturer liable to the buyer in tort[70] for negligence if the goods are defective and the defect is discovered before any injury, or harm to other property has resulted. Even if the goods deteriorate by reason of the defect, the buyer's only loss is the financial or economic loss which he suffers because he has to discard or repair the goods, or because the defect has made them less valuable.[71] In the *Junior Books* case, indeed, the present requirement was not satisfied; for the only "property" which could be said to have been damaged was the factory floor (which had cracked), and that damage was no more than a defect in the very thing supplied by A. The fact that A was nevertheless held liable in tort to C is now explicable (if at all) only by reference to the same special, or "unique," factors[72] which gave rise to the relationship of proximity in that case.

(d) PLAINTIFF HAVING NO TITLE TO THING DAMAGED. Even where A's breach of his contract with B does result in physical damage, the mere fact that the loss so occasioned falls on C will not necessarily give C a right of action in tort against A in respect of that loss. In *The Aliakmon*[73] A, a carrier, had contracted with B for the carriage of a quantity of steel coils which B had sold to C. The goods were damaged, as a result of A's negligent breach of the contract of carriage, after the risk in them had passed to C under the contract of sale, but while B remained owner of them. C had no claim under the contract of carriage as he was not a party to it[74]; and the House of Lords held that he also had no cause of action against A in tort in respect of the loss which he had suffered as a result of remaining liable for the full price of the goods in spite of the fact that they had been damaged in transit. This conclusion was based on a long line of authority[75] which had established the "principle of law that, in order to enable a person to claim in negligence for loss caused to him by reason of loss or damage to property, he must have had either the legal ownership of or a possessory title to the property concerned at the time when the loss or damage occurred, and it is not enough for him to have only had contractual rights in relation to

[69] *Aswan Engineering Establishment Co.* v. *Lupine Ltd.* [1987] 1 W.L.R. 1; *cf. D. & F. Estates Ltd.* v. *Church Commissioners for England* [1989] A.C. 177, 202, 216; *Reid* v. *Rush & Tompkins Group plc.* [1990] 1 W.L.R. 212, 224.

[70] For possible liability in contract under a manufacturer's guarantee, see *ante*, p. 523.

[71] *Murphy* v. *Brentwood D.C.* [1990] 2 All E.R. 908, 921, 925.

[72] *Ante*, p. 540, n. 57.

[73] [1986] A.C. 785; Treitel [1986] L.M.C.L.Q. 294; Markesinis, 103 L.Q.R. 354, 384–390; Tettenborn [1987] J.B.L. 12; *cf. Transcontainer Express Ltd.* v. *Custodian Security Ltd.* [1988] 1 Lloyd's Rep. 128; *The Ciudad de Pasto* [1988] 1 W.L.R. 1145. For a possible qualification, see *The Kapetan Georgis* [1988] 1 Lloyd's Rep. 352, where A in breach of his contract with B caused physical harm to B in respect of which C became liable to indemnify B, and C was held to have an arguable case against A.

[74] The benefit of the contract of carriage had not been transferred to C under Bills of Lading Act 1855, s.1 (*post*, pp. 579, 606–607) as the property in the goods had not passed to him.

[75] Stretching from *Cattle* v. *Stockton Waterworks Co.* (1875) L.R. 10 Q.B. 453 through *The Wear Breeze* [1969] 1 Q.B. 219 to *The Mineral Transporter* [1986] A.C. 1.

such property"[76] when the loss or damage occurred. The House of Lords refused to create an exception to this principle where (as in the present case) the contractual right, which C had under his contract of sale with B, was one to have property and possession of the goods transferred to him at the later date. The main reason for this refusal was that the contract of carriage between A and B was expressed to be subject to an international Convention[77] which gave A (as carrier) the benefit of certain immunities from, and limitations of, liability; and to have held A liable in tort to C would have produced the undesirable result of depriving him of the protection of that contract,[78] since C (being a stranger to it) was no more bound by its terms than entitled to assert rights under it.

(3) TORT AND CONTRACT DAMAGES CONTRASTED. Where a third party can recover damages in tort for the negligent performance of a contract between two others, the damages in such a tort action will not normally be assessed in the same way as they would be in a contractual action. In particular, certain kinds of "economic loss" are generally regarded as being recoverable only in a contractual action. This follows from the principle that the object of awarding damages in a contractual action is to put the plaintiff into the position in which he would have been, if the contract had been performed, while in an action in tort that object is to put him back into the position in which he was before the tort was committed.[79] The distinction is well illustrated by *Muirhead* v. *Industrial Tank Specialities Ltd.*[80] where the plaintiff, who owned a lobster farm, had entered into a contract for the installation of pumps which failed because of a defect in their electric motors. There was no contract between the plaintiff and the supplier of the motors but his claim against that supplier succeeded in tort in respect of the physical damage caused by the failure (*i.e.* the value of the lobsters which had died); and in respect of "any financial loss suffered by the plaintiff in consequence of that physical damage."[81] (*i.e.* the loss of profits on the sale of *those* lobsters). But a further claim "in respect of the whole economic loss suffered"[82] by the plaintiff (*i.e.* for loss of the profits that he would have made from the installation, had it not been defective) was rejected: such damages might have been recoverable from the installer of the pumps in contract but they could not be claimed from a third party in tort.

---

[76] [1986] A.C. 785, 809. For the suggestion that the principle may have been qualified by Latent Damage Act 1986 s.3, see Griew (1986) 136 N.L.J. 1201; but there is no suggestion in the legislative history of s.3 that such a qualification was intended. It can, in any event only apply where the damage was still latent when the claimant became owner: this was not the position in *The Aliakmon*.

[77] *i.e.* the Hague Rules set out in the Schedule to the Carriage of Goods by Sea Act 1924, now superseded in England by Carriage of Goods by Sea Act 1971.

[78] *Cf. Simaan General Contracting Co.* v. *Pilkington Glass Ltd.* (*No.* 2) [1988] Q.B. 758, 782–783. For the suggestion that the position may be different where the potential tortfeasor has no such protection, see *Triangle Steel & Supply Co.* v. *Korean United Lines Inc.* (1985) 63 B.C.L.R. 66, 80 (the reasoning of which is in other respects inconsistent with that of *The Aliakmon*).

[79] See *ante*, p. 323; *post*, pp. 830–831.

[80] [1986] Q.B. 507; Whittaker, 49 M.L.R. 369; Oughton [1987] J.B.L. 370.

[81] [1986] Q.B. at p. 533.

[82] *Ibid.*

Considerable difficulty again arises in this connection from the *Junior Books* case.[83] The main question discussed in that case was whether damages for *any* economic or financial loss could be recovered in a tort action in the absence of any allegation that the cracks in the floor were a source of danger to persons or to other property. In the special circumstances of the case, this question was answered in the affirmative and on that basis most of the items of loss, in respect of which damages were said to be recoverable, can be explained in terms of the principles governing the assessment of damages in tort: this is, for example, true of the profits lost and of the wages and overheads wasted while the factory was closed for repairs to the floor. But it was also said that the factory owners were entitled to the *cost of replacing the floor*[84] and such an award would, by putting them into the position in which they would have been if the sub-contractor's promise had been performed, amount to an award of contract damages in spite of the fact that there was no contract between them and the sub-contractors[85]: on the normal basis of assessment in tort, the damages for this item should not have included the cost of replacing the floor with a good one.[86] In the *Junior Books* case, Lord Keith explained this aspect of the case on the ground that, in replacing the floor, the factory owners simply mitigated the loss of profit resulting from the defects in the floor originally provided[87]; and it is well established that expenses reasonably incurred in mitigation are recoverable.[88] But as this reasoning was not adopted by the other members of the House of Lords, an alternative explanation was given in the *Muirhead* case, namely that the same special (or "unique") factors in the *Junior Books* case, which gave rise to the duty of care there,[89] also explain the assessment of damages.[90] This narrow view of the *Junior Books* case is supported by dicta in the *Junior Books* case itself[91]; by the fact that there is no subsequent[92] case in which a third party has recovered damages in tort to put him into the position in which he would have been if the contract between two others *had been performed*

---

[83] [1983] 1 A.C. 520; Grubb [1984] C.L.J. 111; Holyoak, 99 L.Q.R. 591; Smith and Burns, 46 M.L.R. 147.

[84] This was one of the items claimed; the question whether the claim was proved was not before the House of Lords, which only decided that there was a cause of action in respect of it if negligence were established.

[85] The case was governed by Scots law, which recognises a *jus quaesitum tertio*, but the circumstances giving rise to such a right were not satisfied.

[86] *Cf. Murphy* v. *Brentwood D.C.* [1990] 2 All E.R. 908, 918, 921. Lord Roskill in the *Junior Books* case at p. 545 discusses (without reaching a definite conclusion) the question whether the pursuer in *Donoghue* v. *Stevenson* [1932] A.C. 562 could have recovered damages "for the diminished value of the ginger beer"—not for the cost of replacing the contaminated with pure ginger beer. Even the former basis of assessment is hard to reconcile with the authorities cited *ante*, p. 542, n. 69.

[87] [1983] 1 A.C. 520, 536.

[88] *Cf. post*, pp. 867, 869.

[89] *Ante*, p. 540.

[90] [1986] Q.B. 507, 523, 533–535.

[91] [1983] 1 A.C. at p. 533 (*per* Lord Fraser, who took the same narrow view of the *Junior Books* case in *The Mineral Transporter* [1986] A.C. 1, 24–25); and [1983] 1 A.C. at p. 546 (*per* Lord Roskill).

[92] For an earlier case giving rise to similar difficulties, with respect to damages, to those discussed in the text, see *Ross* v. *Caunters* [1980] Ch. 287 (*ante*, p. 539, n. 45); and *cf.* Luntz, 3 O.J.L.S. 284.

(as opposed to that in which he was *before it was broken*); and by the fact that many later decisions[93] have made it highly unlikely that such damages will, in a future tort case, be awarded to a third party. On the contrary, two House of Lords decisions have specifically rejected such claims.[94] In each case, a lessee claimed damages in tort for the cost of remedying defects alleged to be due to the negligence of a building contractor in the performance of a contract to which the lessee was not a party. In each case, the contractor was held not liable in tort, even if he was negligent,[95] since the defects had been discovered before they had caused any personal injury, or damage to other property belonging to the lessees. To make the contractor liable for the purely economic loss suffered by the lessee in remedying the defect would "impose upon [the contractor] for the benefit of those with whom he had no contractual relationship the obligation of one who warranted the quality of"[96] his work. Such a result would have been inconsistent with the doctrine of privity; and the decisions reinforce the view that liability in negligence to third parties has not subverted (though it may have limited the scope of) that doctrine.

3. Interference with Contractual Rights

(1) In general

Although a contract primarily creates rights and duties enforceable by the contracting parties against each other, it also incidentally imposes on third parties the duty not to interfere with the contracting parties in performing the contract. In the leading case of *Lumley* v. *Gye*[96a] the plaintiff engaged Johanna Wagner as an opera singer. The defendant, knowing of this contract, "maliciously"[96b] induced her to refuse to perform it. He was held liable for what has since become known as the tort of wrongful interference with contractual rights.

---

[93] *i.e. Tate & Lyle Industries Ltd.* v. *G.L.C.* [1983] 2 A.C. 509; *Balsamo* v. *Medici* [1984] 1 W.L.R. 951; *The Mineral Transporter* [1986] A.C. 1; *Muirhead* v. *Industrial Tank Specialities Ltd.* [1986] Q.B. 507; *The Aliakmon* [1986] A.C. 785; *Aswan Engineering Establishment Co.* v. *Lupdine Ltd.* [1987] 1 W.L.R. 1. *Cf.* also *Smith* v. *Littlewoods Organisation Ltd.* [1987] A.C. 241, 280; *Yuen Kun-yeu* v. *Att.-Gen. of Hong Kong* [1988] A.C. 175; *Simaan General Contracting Co.* v. *Pilkington Glass Ltd. (No. 2)* [1988] Q.B. 758; *Greater Nottingham Co-operative Soc. Ltd.* v. *Cementation Piling & Foundation Ltd.* [1989] Q.B. 71, 94; *Davies* v. *Radcliffe* [1990] 1 W.L.R. 821; *Parker-Tweedale* v. *Dunbar Bank plc.* [1990] 2 All E.R. 577, 586.

[94] *D. & F. Estates Ltd.* v. *Church Commissioners for England* [1989] A.C. 177; *Department of the Environment* v. *Thomas Bates & Son Ltd.* [1990] 2 All E.R. 943.

[95] In the *D. & F. Estates* case, there was no such negligence as the builders had employed competent sub-contractors.

[96] [1989] A.C. 177, 207; *cf. ibid.* pp. 211–212.

[96a] (1853) 2 E. & B. 216.

[96b] *i.e.* deliberately and with knowledge of the existence of the contract: *British Homophone Ltd.* v. *Kunz* (1935) 152 L.T. 589; *D. C. Thomson & Co Ltd.* v. *Deakin* [1952] Ch. 646, 694; *Jones Bros. (Hunstanton) Ltd.* v. *Stevens* [1955] 1 Q.B. 275, 280. Such knowledge may be inferred from surrounding circumstances: *Merkur Island Shipping Corp.* v. *Laughton* [1983] 2 A.C. 570. But two dicta in *British Industrial Plastics Ltd.* v. *Ferguson* [1940] 1 All E.R. 479, 483 suggesting that liability may be based on constructive knowledge were not necessary for the decision and run counter to the main stream of authority. See further, *post*, p. 548, n. 15.

(2) Contracts affecting property

The principle just stated may help to solve the problem which arises when a person acquires property with notice of a contract concerning it, previously made between two other persons. The problem is: to what extent is the acquirer restricted[96c] by the contract in the use which he is entitled to make of the property? Where the property is land, the law has developed complex rules as a result of which a third party may be bound by (and, indeed, entitled to enforce) the contract, by way of exception to the doctrine of privity.[97] But the law has been reluctant to admit that contracts concerning chattels can bind a third party. If a third party were bound by such contracts at all, he might (as in the land cases) be bound where he had merely constructive notice of them; and it is generally agreed that the doctrine of constructive notice should be kept, so far as possible, out of commercial affairs. On the other hand, too rigid a refusal to allow contracts concerning chattels to affect third parties may itself prove commercially inconvenient.

Such contracts may be divided into four groups.[98] The first consists of contracts restricting the use or disposition of goods. Certain undesirable restrictions of this kind have been expressly invalidated by statute.[99] But others may be perfectly reasonable business arrangements aimed at ensuring consistency of quality or stable markets: for example, contracts that goods shall be sold only in packets sealed by the manufacturer, or that they shall be sold only at certain prices[1] or after a certain time has elapsed.[2] The second group of contracts consists of those requiring the use of *particular* chattels for their performance, without creating any proprietary or possessory interest in those chattels for example, a contract to carry cargo in a particular ship. The third group consists of contracts for the hire of a chattel: and the fourth of options to purchase a chattel. These last two groups are now very common; a hire-purchase agreement is a contract for the hire of a chattel, coupled with an option to purchase it.

(a) PROTECTION AGAINST THIRD PARTIES IN SPECIAL CASES. In a number of special cases, the courts protect the rights arising under such contracts against third parties with notice of them: for example, where restrictions are imposed by a patentee on the use or disposition of patented goods,[3] and where an option to purchase a chattel is specifically enforceable.[4] The same would be true where money was lent on the terms that the loan was to be repaid out of specific property. Since such an undertaking to repay is specifically enforceable, it would create a charge in equity over the property in favour of the lender, and this would prevail against a third party

---

[96c] For the possible effect of a *promise* by the acquirer to perform the contract, see *post*, p. 604.

[97] See Megarry and Wade, *The Law of Real Property* (5th ed.), Chap. 14.

[98] See Chafee, 41 H.L.R. 945; *cf.* Wade, 44 L.Q.R. 51; Gardner, 98 L.Q.R. 278; Tettenborn [1982] C.L.J. 58; Cohen-Grabelsky, 45 M.L.R. 241.

[99] Patents Act 1977, s.44.

[1] *Post*, pp. 568–569.

[2] See *B.M.T.A.* v. *Salvadori* [1949] Ch. 556; *post*, p. 548.

[3] Subject to Patents Act 1977, s.44 (formerly Patents Act 1949, s.57); *Dunlop Rubber Co. Ltd.* v. *Long Life Battery Depot* [1958] 1 W.L.R. 1033. This position is not affected by Copyright, Designs and Patents Act 1988.

[4] *Falcke* v. *Gray* (1859) 4 Drew. 651, as explained in *Erskine Macdonald Ltd.* v. *Eyles* [1921] 1 Ch. 631, 641; *cf. The Stena Nautica* (*No.* 2) [1982] 2 Lloyd's Rep. 336 (where specific enforcement was denied).

who later acquired an interest in it, unless he was a bona fide purchaser for value without notice.[5]

(b) GENERAL PRINCIPLE OF PROTECTION AGAINST THIRD PARTIES REJECTED. An attempt to establish a more general principle was made in *De Mattos* v. *Gibson*,[6] where Knight Bruce L.J. said: "Reason and justice seem to prescribe that, at least as a general rule, where a man, by gift or purchase, acquires property from another, with knowledge of a previous contract, lawfully and for valuable consideration made . . . with a third person, to use and employ the property . . . in a specified manner, the acquirer shall not, to the material damage of the third person, in opposition to the contract and inconsistently with it, use and employ the property in a manner not allowable to the giver or seller." This principle came to be associated with the rule in *Tulk* v. *Moxhay*[7] relating to restrictive covenants concerning land. Originally that rule was thought to apply whenever a defendant bought land with notice, actual or constructive, that it was subject to a restrictive covenant. But it was later confined to cases in which the plaintiff's interest in enforcing the covenant consisted in the ownership of land capable of being benefited by the covenant. This usually meant adjacent land[8]; and since adjacency is hardly a satisfactory criterion of interest in the case of things that can be moved, the tendency of these developments of the rule in *Tulk* v. *Moxhay* was to undermine Knight Bruce L.J.'s principle.[9] Nevertheless, in *Lord Strathcona SS. Co.* v. *Dominion Coal Co.*[10] the Privy Council relied on that principle to hold that the time charterer of a ship had an interest in the ship which he could enforce against a purchaser of the ship with notice of the charterparty; the puchaser was also said to be in the position of a constructive trustee, with obligations which a court of equity would not allow him to violate.[11] The decision provoked adverse criticism,[12] particularly because the land law analogies and the constructive trust reasoning on which it was based might lead to the third party's being made liable where he had only constructive notice of the earlier contract. Where that contract concerned the use or disposition of a chattel, such a conclusion was open to the objection that it might have the undesirable effect of introducing the doctrine of constructive notice into commercial affairs. When a similar problem arose in *Port Line Ltd.* v. *Ben Line Steamers Ltd.*,[13] Diplock J. therefore refused to follow the Privy Council's decision. Alternatively, he was prepared to distinguish it: the

---

5 *Swiss Bank Corp.* v. *Lloyd's Bank Ltd.* [1982] A.C. 584, 598, 613; the actual decision was that the contract of loan did *not* create an obligation to repay out of specific property so that there was no specifically enforceable agreement affecting it.

6 (1858) 4 D. & J. 276, 282.

7 (1848) 2 Ph. 774.

8 *L.C.C.* v. *Allen* [1914] 3 K.B. 642; the actual decision was reversed by statute (see now Housing Act 1985, s.609), but the principle stated in the text remains unimpaired.

9 See *Barker* v. *Stickney* [1919] 1 K.B. 121, 131; for criticism, see *Tito* v. *Waddell* (*No.* 2) [1977] Ch. at p. 300.

10 [1926] A.C. 108.

11 *Ibid.* p. 125.

12 *e.g. Greenhalgh* v. *Mallard* [1943] 2 All E.R. 234.

13 [1958] Q.B. 146. The cases cited in n. 41 at p. 538, *ante*, all apply the constructive trust reasoning to contracts concerning land and do not, it is submitted, undermine the rejection of that reasoning in the *Port Line* case so far as contracts affecting the use of disposition of chattels are concerned.

buyer of the ship in the *Port Line* case knew that she was under charter to the plaintiff, but he did not have actual notice of the precise extent of the plaintiff's rights under the charterparty.[14] Thus the *Port Line* case rejects the principle stated by Knight Bruce L.J.; but it does not decide that a third party can always disregard a contract concerning a chattel. A number of possibilities must be considered.

(c) THIRD PARTY'S LIABILITY IN TORT. A third party who with knowledge[15] of the contract interferes with its performance may be liable in tort.[16] Thus in *B.M.T.A.* v. *Salvadori*[17] A bought a car and covenanted with B that he would not resell it for one year without first offering it to B. During the year, C bought the car from A with notice of the covenant, and was held liable to B for wrongfully interfering with B's contractual rights against A. It has been suggested that the decision of the Privy Council in the *Lord Strathcona* case[18] can be explained on the ground that the purchaser of the ship had committed this tort against the charterer.[19] The tort may be committed even though A was quite willing to break his contract with B. Thus it is immaterial whether A or C began the negotiations leading to the contract between them[20]; indeed, C's tort liability may arise precisely because he has colluded with A in an effort to get rid of a restriction imposed in favour of B by the contract between A and B.[21]

The merit of this approach is that it avoids the danger of importing the doctrine of constructive notice into this branch of the law. On the other hand, it is subject to two limitations. First, the tort is not committed if the defendant's interference was not the cause of the plaintiff's loss. In the *Lord Strathcona* case,[22] the purchasers of the ship (who were the defendants in the Privy Council proceedings) mortgaged her, but were too poor to put her to sea. The mortgage gave the mortgagees the right to sell the ship, and it was held that they were entitled to sell her free from the charterer's rights, though they had notice of those rights. The cause of the failure to perform the charterparty was the shipowners' poverty, and not the mort-

---

[14] See *infra*, n. 15.

[15] The degree of knowledge necessary to make a defendant liable in tort for interference with contractual relations depends on the circumstances. Precise knowledge of the terms of the contract is not *generally* necessary: see *J. T. Stratford & Sons Ltd.* v. *Lindley* [1965] A.C. 269, 332; *Emerald Construction Co. Ltd.* v. *Lowthian* [1966] 1 W.L.R. 691; *Daily Mirror Newspapers Ltd.* v. *Gardner* [1968] 2 Q.B. 762; *Greig* v. *Insole* [1978] 1 W.L.R. 302, 336; and *cf. Distillers Co. (Biochemicals) Ltd.* v. *Times Newspapers* [1975] Q.B. 613; *Merkur Island Shipping Corp.* v. *Laughton* [1983] 2 A.C. 570. But in the *Port Line* case the defendant was not liable in tort as he had assumed that the charterparty with which he was alleged to have interfered was in the same terms as another charterparty which he had made with one of the contracting parties. This assumption was mistaken, but not, in the circumstances, unreasonable.

[16] Wade, 42 L.Q.R. 139.

[17] [1949] Ch. 556; *Rickless* v. *United Artists Corp.* [1987] 1 All E.R. 679, 699.

[18] [1926] A.C. 108.

[19] *Swiss Bank Corp.* v. *Lloyd's Bank Ltd.* [1979] Ch. 548, 574; in the Court of Appeal it was conceded that there was "no substance" in the point in that case: see [1982] A.C. 584, 598 and *post*, p. 549 at n. 32.

[20] *Sefton* v. *Tophams Ltd.* [1965] Ch. 1140, 1161, 1167, reversed without reference to this point [1967] A.C. 50.

[21] *Esso Petroleum Co. Ltd.* v. *Kingswood Motors (Addlestone) Ltd.* [1974] Q.B. 142.

[22] [1926] A.C. 108; *ante*, p. 547.

gagees' sale of the ship.[23] Secondly, liability for interference with contractual rights is based on intentional wrongdoing. It follows that, if a defendant negligently damaged a ship which was subject to a time charterparty, he would not commit this tort against the charterer; nor would he be liable to the charterer in negligence for pecuniary loss, such as hire wasted or profits lost while the ship was, by reason of the damage, out of service.[24]

So far, in discussing the third party's liability for interference with contractual rights, it has been assumed that C either knew, or that he did not know, of the contract between A and B. In the former situation, he could, but in the latter he could not, be liable for the tort.[25] There is also an intermediate situation, in which C at the time of his contract with A had only constructive notice of A's earlier contract with B, but then acquired actual knowledge of that contract before calling for (or receiving) performance of his own contract with A.[26] The question arises whether, on such facts, C is liable to B for the tort of interference with contractual rights. That tort is subject to the defence of "justification,"[27] which is certainly available to C where he had contracted with A *before* B had done so.[28] The defence is a flexible one,[29] and the principle on which it is based appears to be equally applicable where C's contract with A was made *after* B's but in ignorance of it. The exercise by C of rights thus acquired in good faith against A should not, it is submitted, make C liable for the tort to B.[30] Even in such a situation, however, C may be liable to B under the rules stated above[31] if B's contract with A is specifically enforceable. Where the specific enforceability of this contract gives rise to an equitable interest, this can be enforced against C even though he had, when he contracted with A, only constructive notice of A's contract with B. In such a case, the tort claim would be "of no value"[32] if, as has been submitted above, it only arises where C, when he contracted with A, had actual knowledge of B's rights; but it would equally be unnecessary,[33] since B could succeed against C on the different ground that B's contract with A was specifically enforceable and therefore conferred an equitable interest on B.

(d) PROTECTION OF "POSSESSORY RIGHTS." A final possibility relates to contracts under which possession of a chattel is, or is to be, transferred. The contracts in the *Strathcona* and *Port Line* cases were not of this kind: they were time charters, under which a shipowner undertakes to render

---

[23] *The Lord Strathcona* [1925] P. 143; judgment in this case was given four months before judgment in the Privy Council proceedings so that the injunction issued by the Privy Council never took effect. *De Mattos* v. *Gibson* suffered a similar fate: (1858) 4 D. & J. 276. *cf. The Myrto* [1977] 2 Lloyd's Rep. 243; *Lyus* v. *Prowsa Developments Ltd.* [1982] 1 W.L.R. 1044, 1049.

[24] On the principle stated at p. 541, *ante*: *The Mineral Transporter* [1986] A.C. 1.

[25] *Ante*, pp. 545–548.

[26] This was the position in *Swiss Bank Corp.* v. *Lloyds Bank Ltd.* [1982] A.C. 584: see [1979] Ch. 548, 568–569, and see *infra*, n. 30.

[27] See Salmond, *The Law of Torts* (18th ed.), pp. 347–348.

[28] *Smithies* v. *National Association of Operative Plasterers* [1909] 1 K.B. 310, 337; *Edwin Hill & Partners* v. *First National Finance Corp. plc.* [1989] 1 W.L.R. 225, 230.

[29] *Glamorgan Coal Co.* v. *South Wales Miners' Federation* [1903] 2 K.B. 545, 574–575.

[30] This was admitted in *Swiss Bank Corp.* v. *Lloyds Bank Ltd.*, *supra*, n. 26: see [1979] Ch. 548, 569–573.

[31] *Ante*, p. 546.

[32] *Swiss Bank Corp.* v. *Lloyds Bank Ltd.* [1982] A.C. 584, 598, where it was held, on construction, that the contract was *not* specifically enforceable; see *post*, p. 904, n. 7.

[33] [1982] A.C. 584, 598.

services by the use of a particular ship, which remains in his possession.[34] Such charters may be contrasted with demise charters, which are contracts for the hire of a ship under which the shipowner does undertake to transfer possession of the ship to the charterer. The nearest analogy in the land law to a contract for the hire of a chattel is a lease,[35] and not a restrictive covenant. Hence the development of the doctrine of *Tulk* v. *Moxhay*, discussed above, need not affect cases concerning such contracts. One reason given by Diplock J. for his decision in the *Port Line* case was that a time charterer had "no proprietary *or possessory* rights in the ship."[36] It can be inferred that a "possessory right" might have been protected. Where the hirer of a chattel is in actual possession of it he should certainly be protected against a third party who acquires the chattel with notice of the hirer's interest. It is less clear whether, in this context, the words "possessory right" refer only to the right *of* possession, or extend also to a right *to* possession, *i.e.* whether a person who has a contractual right to the *future* possession of a chattel would similarly be protected against the third party. In *The Stena Nautica* (*No.* 2)[37] A had demise-chartered his ship to B under a contract which also gave B an option to purchase her. Later, while A was in possession of the ship, he granted a second demise charter of her to C who had no knowledge of the earlier contract. B exercised his option to purchase and it was held that his only remedy was by way of of damages against A: B could not assert his rights to the ship against C since B's option to purchase was not specifically enforceable.[38] The question whether B could assert his *right to future possession as demise charterer* against C did not, strictly speaking, arise since B was not suing to enforce that right, but rather his right as a person who had exercised an option to purchase. But it seems from the reasoning of the Court of Appeal that B's right to possession as demise charterer would only have been protected if the contract under which the right arose was one in respect of which the court was willing to make an order of specific performance. The argument of commercial convenience which justifies the decision in the *Port Line* case would seem to apply as much where a contract creates a right to the future possession of a chattel as where it creates the right to have some particular use made of the chattel. In each case the right is hard to discover and should not be enforced against a third party *without* actual knowledge of it; and adequate enforcement against a third party *with* such knowledge is provided by the rules relating to the tort of wrongful interference with contractual rights.

4. Intimidation

The tort of intimidation is committed where A induces B to act to the detriment of C by threatening B with some unlawful course of conduct. In *Rookes* v. *Barnard*[39] the House of Lords decided that a threat by A to break his contract with B is for this purpose a threat to do an unlawful act.

---

[34] *The Lancaster* [1980] 2 Lloyd's Rep. 497, 500.
[35] *Cf. ante*, p. 538 at n. 40.
[36] [1958] 2 Q.B. 146, 166 (italics supplied).
[37] [1982] 2 Lloyd's Rep. 336.
[38] *Post*, p. 905.
[39] [1964] A.C. 1129; the actual decision was reversed by statute. See now Trade Union and Labour Relations (Amendment) Act 1976, s.3(2); Employment Act 1980, s.17. But subject to this special exception, the principle stated in the text remains valid.

Such a threat may therefore entitle C to sue A for intimidation. It has been said that this view outflanks the doctrine of privity.[40] No doubt in such a case C bases his cause of action on the threat to break a contract to which he is not a party. But the doctrine of privity only prevents C from enforcing A's promise to B[41]; and in cases of intimidation C is certainly not doing that. If A induces B to dismiss C by threatening to defame B, C may be able to sue A for intimidation, but not for defamation. So, if A induces B to dismiss C by threatening to break A's contract with B, C may be able to sue A for intimidation, but not for breach of contract. In such a case C is not trying to enforce A's promise to B: "his ground of action is quite different."[42] C's complaint is not that A has broken his promise to B but that he has coerced B into acting to C's detriment.[43] The House of Lords has therefore rejected the argument that the doctrine of privity would be outflanked by holding that the tort of intimidation could be committed by threatening to commit a breach of contract.[44]

5. Restitution?

It has been suggested in Australia that the third party may have a claim in restitution where the promisor has received payment (or some other performance) from the promisee and has then failed or refused to perform the promise in favour of the third party; and that the measure of recovery on such a claim is the amount promised.[45] The suggestion was made where premiums under a policy of liability insurance for the benefit of a third party had been paid by the promisee to the promisor (the insurance company) which had then refused to pay the third party. The promisor's liability in restitution was said to be based on his unjust enrichment, and to arise in spite of the fact that there was no correlative impoverishment of the third party. But while it is true that liability in restitution is not based on loss to the claimant, it is (in the case put) based on gain to the defendant and it is hard to see what justification there can be for wholly disregarding this *basis* of restitutionary liability in determining its *measure*. And the argument that, to hold the promisor liable to the third party was "not an abrogation of the doctrine of privity of contract,"[46] merely because the liability was said to arise in restitution, is, it is submitted, inconsistent with the practical result of making the promisor so liable. We have seen that, in England, the promisor is not liable in tort where the practical effect of imposing such liability would be to abrogate the doctrine of privity[47]; and there seems to be no reason why the position should be different merely because the alleged basis of liability is restitution rather than tort. The suggestion that the promisor is liable in restitution to the third party for the

---

40 Wedderburn, 24 M.L.R. 572, 577; in *Rookes* v. *Barnard* the argument was accepted in the Court of Appeal; [1963] 1 Q.B. 623, 695, but rejected by the House of Lords; *infra*, n. 42.

41 *Ante*, p. 523.

42 *Rookes* v. *Barnard* [1964] A.C. at p. 1168; *cf.* p. 1208; if C were trying to enforce the contract, the damages might be quite different.

43 *Rookes* v. *Barnard* [1964] A.C. at p. 1208.

44 *Rookes* v. *Barnard* [1964] A.C. at pp. 1168, 1200, 1208, 1235; Hamson [1961] C.L.J. 189; [1964] C.L.J. 159; Hoffmann, 81 L.Q.R. 116, 124–128.

45 *Trident Insurance Co. Ltd.* v. *McNiece Bros. Pty. Ltd.* (1988) 165 C.L.R. 107, *per* Gaudron J.; this view does not seem to be shared by any other member of the Court; Soh, 105 L.Q.R. 4.

46 165 C.L.R. at p. 177.

47 *Ante*, p. 541.

amount promised, merely because the promisor has received performance from the promisee is, moreover, inconsistent with the reasoning of *Beswick* v. *Beswick*,[48] where it was assumed that the third party had no common law right to sue the promisor in her own name, in spite of the fact that the promisor had received performance in full from the promisee. The view that claims of the kind here discussed fall outside the scope of the doctrine of privity of contract must therefore be regarded with scepticism. The argument based on restitution would in any event be of no avail to the third party where the promisor was willing to pay and the issue was merely whether it should pay the third party or the promisee[49]: in such cases the promisor would not be unjustly enriched so that there would be no basis for restitutionary liability.

SECTION 4. EXEMPTION CLAUSES AND THIRD PARTIES

Where an exemption clause purports to affect a third party, two questions arise. Can the third party take the benefit of the clause? Can he be bound by it? For the purpose of this discussion, it will be assumed that the clause is valid under the rules stated in Chapter 7.[50]

1. The Benefit

Originally, the courts held that a person could only take the benefit of an exemption clause in a contract which he did not make himself if one of the recognised exceptions to the doctrine of privity could be invoked in his favour: for example, if the contract was made through an agent acting either for him or for the other party. Such agency reasoning was often artificial,[51] but it at any rate saved the face of the doctrine of privity.

Whether, in this context, the doctrine must be abandoned altogether depends on the effect of the decision of the House of Lords in *Elder, Dempster & Co.* v. *Paterson, Zochonis & Co.*[52] A company agreed to carry the plaintiff's plam-oil from West Africa to Hull and chartered a ship for this purpose. The contract of carriage, which was between the plaintiffs and the company, exempted "the shipowners, hereinafter called the company,"[53] from liability for bad stowage. The oil was damaged by bad stowage and it was held that the shipowners were protected by the exemption clause, although there was no express contract between them and the plaintiffs. One possible reason for the decision is that, when the plaintiffs entrusted the oil for carriage to the shipowners, a contract between them

[48] [1968] A.C. 58; *ante*, p. 529.

[49] See *ante*, p. 535; *cf.* such cases as *Re Schebsman* [1944] Ch. 83 (*post*, p. 565) and *Re Sinclair's Life Policy* [1938] Ch. 799 (*post*, p. 563).

[50] Many of the cases discussed in this Section concern contracts for the carriage of goods by sea and would not be affected by the Unfair Contract Terms Act 1977: *ante*, pp. 242, 243. Others (*e.g.* those in which the claim was for negligently inflicted personal injuries) would now be differently decided, or decided on other grounds, under the Act: *ante*, p. 228.

[51] *Hall* v. *N.E. Ry.* (1875) L.R. 10 Q.B. 437; *cf. Barrett* v. *Great Northern Ry.* (1904) 20 T.L.R. 175; *The Kirknes* [1957] P. 51; *cf. Texas Instruments Ltd.* v. *Nelson (Europe) Ltd.* [1991] 1 Lloyd's Rep. 146 (where the carrier's wilful misconduct deprived him of the benefit of an exempting provision having the force of law).

[52] [1924] A.C. 522; distinguished in *Gadsden Pty. Ltd.* v. *Australian Coastal Shipping Commission* [1977] 1 N.S.W.L.R. 575, *The Golden Lake* [1982] 2 Lloyd's Rep. 632, in *The Forum Craftsman* [1985] 1 Lloyd's Rep. 291 (especially at p. 295) and in *The Kapetan Markos NL* (*No.* 2) [1987] 2 Lloyd's Rep. 321, 331.

[53] It was admitted that these words were apt to protect the company: [1923] 1 K.B. 422.

could be implied from their conduct, incorporating the terms of the contract of carriage by tacit reference.[54] A second possible reason is that the company acted as the agent of the shipowners for the purpose of making a contract between them and the plaintiffs.[55] Both these lines of reasoning can be reconciled with the doctrine of privity. But a third possible reason for the decision is the so-called principle of vicarious immunity: where a person employs an agent to perform a contract, that agent is entitled, in performing the contract, to any immunity from liability which the contract confers on the principal.[56] Under this principle, the shipowners were protected because they acted as agents of the company in performing its contract with the plaintiffs. This reasoning is inconsistent with the doctrine of privity in the sense that it would enable an agent to rely by way of defence on the terms of a contract to which he was not a party; and it was rejected by the House of Lords in *Scruttons Ltd.* v. *Midland Silicones Ltd.*[57]

In that case a drum of chemicals had been shipped under a contract evidenced by a bill of lading which limited the liability of "the carrier" to $500. After the rights and duties under this contract had passed to the plaintiffs by transfer of the bill of lading,[58] the drum was damaged by the negligence of a firm of stevedores who had been employed by the carrier to unload the ship. The House of Lords[59] held that the stevedores could not rely on the $500 limitation of liability as they were not parties to the contract of carriage; and that the principle of vicarious immunity was not the *ratio decidendi* of the *Elder, Dempster* case. Nor did the other two reasons for that decision help the stevedores here. No implied contract arose since the plaintiffs had not asked the stevedores to perform any service in relation to the drum: the plaintiffs had simply applied to the carrier for its delivery, and that operation was carried out through the instrumentality of the stevedores.[60] Nor did the circumstances support any inference that the carrier had acted as agent for the stevedores to make a contract between the stevedores and the plaintiffs on the terms of the bill of lading; for those terms limited the liability only of *the carrier* and made no reference to the stevedores.

The decision in the *Midland Silicones* case severely limited the effectiveness of exemption clauses. A person who suffered loss or injury as a result of a negligent breach of contract generally had a remedy against someone, if only against the workman who was actually negligent. In practice the employer would often feel morally obliged to pay the damages awarded

---

[54] [1924] A.C. at p. 564; this seems to be what Lord Sumner meant by a "bailment on terms."

[55] *Ibid.* at p. 534 (first sentence).

[56] *Ibid.* at p. 534 (second sentence); *cf. Mersey Shipping & Transport Co.* v. *Rea* (1925) 21 Ll.L.R. 375, 378.

[57] [1962] A.C. 446; *cf. Adler* v. *Dickson* [1955] 1 Q.B. 158; *Cosgrove* v. *Horsfall* (1946) 62 T.L.R. 140; *Genys* v. *Matthews* [1965] 3 All E.R. 24; *Gilchrist Watt & Sanderson Pty. Ltd.* v. *York Products Pty. Ltd.* [1970] 1 W.L.R. 1262; see also *Gore* v. *Van der Lann* [1967] 2 Q.B. 31 (*ante*, pp. 144, 156, 534), where the exemption clause was in any event void by statute.

[58] *Post*, pp. 579, 606–607.

[59] Lord Denning dissenting. See also his judgments in *Adler* v. *Dickson, supra, White* v. *Warwick (John) & Co. Ltd.* [1953] 1 W.L.R. 1285 and *Morris* v. *C. W. Martin & Sons Ltd.* [1966] 1 Q.B. 716.

[60] See [1959] 2 K.B. 171, 188–189, *per* Diplock J.; *cf.* [1962] 1 Q.B. 106, 132, [1962] A.C. 446, 474, 496.

against his employee,[61] and might be legally liable to do so.[62] Hence employers tried to protect their servants or agents by differently worded exemption clauses, and the cases to be discussed below make it clear that they can now do so by using appropriate words. There is no objection to this on policy grounds where the clause is itself valid and constitutes a legitimate device for allocating contractual risks and the burden of insurance. Some statutes which limit the liability of carriers expressly extend these limitations to the carriers' servants or agents.[63] No harm is done by allowing contracts to achieve such a result. The doctrine of privity was never a satisfactory instrument for controlling undesirable exemption clauses,[64] and should no longer be used for this purpose now that the ability of a contracting party to exclude or restrict his liability by means of such clauses is directly controlled under the Unfair Contract Terms Act 1977.[65] Indeed it has been said that some of these statutory controls do not apply to clauses excluding the right to sue a third party,[66] who may thus be protected by a clause which could not exclude or restrict the liability of a contracting party himself. Direct control of exemption clauses between the contracting parties is clearly preferable to indirect evasion by means of a claim against a third party whom the words of the clause seek to protect.

Granted, then, that there are no policy grounds for refusing to allow a third party to take advantage of an exemption clause, the remaining question is how this result may be achieved. The most obvious possibility is by drafting the clause in such a way as to extend its protection to the third party; for one of the reasons for the decision in the *Midland Silicones* case was that the clause there did not refer to the stevedores at all, but only to the carrier. It would not, indeed, suffice simply to say that the third party was to be protected,[67] or that he was to be deemed to be a party to the contract.[68] But a very much more elaborate clause was considered in *The Eurymedon*,[69] where a contract was made between a shipper and a carrier for the carriage of machinery from England to New Zealand. The machinery was damaged by employees of the stevedore while it was being unloaded; and the question was whether the stevedore was protected by the bill of lading issued by the carrier to the shipper as evidence of the con-

[61] In *Adler* v. *Dickson, supra,* n. 57, the employers said that they would satisfy any judgment which might be given against their servants. But, as they would not be obliged to do so, they would not be entitled to have an action by the injured party against the servants stayed: *Gore* v. *Van der Lann* [1967] 2 Q.B. 31.

[62] *i.e.* under an express contract to idemnify the servant or agent.

[63] *e.g.* Carriage by Air Act 1961, Sched. 1, Art. 25A; Carriage of Goods by Sea Act 1971, Sched. Art. 4 bis (stevedores, being independent contractors rather than agents, would not be protected under this provision); Merchant Shipping Act 1979, s.14 and Sched. 3, Part I, Article 11 and s.18(2) and (3).

[64] *Cf. Mason* v. *Uxbridge Boat Centre* [1980] 2 Lloyd's Rep. 593, 598.

[65] *Ante*, pp. 226–241. For example, in cases such as *Cosgrove* v. *Horsfall* (1946) 62 T.L.R. 140, *Adler* v. *Dickson* [1955] 1 Q.B. 158 and *Genys* v. *Matthews* [1965] 3 All E.R. 24 the doctrine was used to allow recovery for personal injury against an employee of the party protected by the exemption clause. Its use for this purpose is no longer necessary now that that party is prevented from relying on the clause by s.2 of the 1977 Act.

[66] ss.2 and 10 of the 1977 Act: *The Chevalier Roze* [1983] 2 Lloyd's Rep. 438, 442 (*post*, p. 556, n. 83). *Semble*, this principle is not restricted to these two sections of the Act.

[67] *Cosgrove* v. *Horsfall* (1946) 62 T.L.R. 140; *Genys* v. *Matthews* [1965] 3 All E.R. 24.

[68] *Cf. Taddy* v. *Sterious* [1904] 1 Ch. 354 (the actual decision is no longer law: *post*, p. 569).

[69] [1975] A.C. 154; Reynolds, 90 L.Q.R. 301; Coote, 37 M.L.R. 453; Palmer [1974] J.B.L. 101, 220; Powles [1979] L.M.C.L.Q. 331; Davies & Palmer [1979] J.B.L. 337. And see *post*, p. 559.

tract the bill provided that no servant or agent (including independent contractor) of the carrier was to be liable for any act or default in the course of his employment; that every limitation applicable to the carrier should be available to such persons; that for the purpose of the clause the carrier should be deemed to be acting as agent or trustee for such persons; and that they should to this extent be or be deemed to be parties to the contract. All the members of the Privy Council agreed that such third persons could be protected by an appropriately drawn clause; and a majority held that the clause in question did protect the stevedore. Lord Wilberforce said that the bill of lading "brought into existence a bargain initially unilateral but capable of becoming mutual, between the shipper and the [stevedore], made through the carrier as agent. This became a full contract when the [stevedore] performed the services by discharging the goods."[70] It may be objected that often stevedores might not be aware of the terms of bills of lading under which goods were carried, so that these could not amount to offers to them which they could accept by performing the services. On the facts of *The Eurymedon* this argument has little substance as the carrier was a subsidiary of the stevedore who probably did know of the terms of the bill of lading.[71] But the more important point is that it is by no means unknown for contracts to come into existence in circumstances which cannot be strictly analysed in terms of offer and acceptance.[72] The decision should therefore be evaluated, not in terms of such analysis, but by asking two questions: (1) was there any objection on grounds of policy to extending the protection of the clause to third parties such as the stevedores? and (2) did that extension give effect to the intention of the parties? It has already been suggested[73] that the first question should be answered in the negative, and this must have been the view even of the dissentients in *The Eurymedon*, for they accepted that a third party could be protected by an appropriately worded clause. The second question is harder to answer but it seems unlikely that the shipper at the time of contracting made any conscious distinction between rights against the carrier and against persons employed by the carrier in the performance of the contract. It is submitted that the majority's interpretation of an admittedly obscure clause did give effect to the intentions and commercial expectations of the parties; and that the decision is therefore to be welcomed.

In other jurisdictions, *The Eurymedon* has been both followed[74] and distinguished.[75] In one case it was held that the stevedore could not rely on the exemption clause as he was in no way previously connected with the

---

[70] At pp. 167–168.

[71] He at least had means of knowledge since one original of the bill of lading had been delivered to him before the goods were unloaded, though only in his capacity as agent of the carrier; see [1975] A.C. 154, 164.

[72] See *The Satanita* [1895] P. 248, affirmed *sub nom. Clarke* v. *Dunraven* [1897] A.C. 59; *ante*, p. 47.

[73] *Ante*, pp. 553–554.

[74] *Ceres Stevedoring Co. Ltd.* v. *Eisen und Metall A.G.* (1976) 72 D.L.R. (3d) 660 (where the third party's defence failed on another ground); *Miles International Corp.* v. *Federal Commerce & Navigation Co.* [1978] 1 Lloyd's Rep. 285. These two cases were decided in Quebec, under a system of law that allows third parties to take the benefit of contracts to which they are strangers.

[75] *Lummus Co. Ltd.* v. *East African Harbours Corp.* [1978] 1 Lloyd's Rep. 317; see also *Herrick* v. *Leonnard and Dingley Ltd.* [1975] 2 N.Z.L.R. 566 (discussed by Palmer and Rose, (1976) 39 M.L.R. 466), where a clause in different terms did not expressly refer to independent contractors.

carrier, who therefore could not be regarded as his agent for the purpose of making a contract between him and the owner of the goods.[76] But in *The New York Star*[77] the Privy Council unanimously followed *The Eurymedon* in holding that stevedores (who were regularly employed and partly owned by the carriers) were protected by a similarly worded clause. Lord Wilberforce said that stevedores would "normally and typically" be protected by such a clause, and that "their Lordships would not encourage a search for fine distinctions which would diminish the general applicability, in the light of established commercial practice, of the principle."[78] Reliance on such distinctions would ignore the commercial realities rightly emphasised by Lord Wilberforce in the two Privy Council cases. For the reasons given in the preceding paragraph, it is submitted that those two cases should be followed in England, and should not be confined to their admittedly special facts.[79] That is, the necessary agency relationship should not be restricted to cases in which carriers and stevedores are associated companies, or in which there is some other previous connection between them.[80] The third party will, of course, only be protected while he is engaged in the performance of the contract in which the exemption clause is contained, and not while he is acting in some other capacity.[81]

The third party could also be protected by a form of words other than that used in *The Eurymedon*. For example, an exemption clause in a contract between A and B may contain an express promise by A to B not to sue C. Under the rules already considered, B can enforce that promise by getting a stay of any action by A against C,[82] particularly if there is a contract between B and C under which B is bound to indemnify C against liability incurred in the performance of his duties under that contract to outsiders.[83] Alternatively, the contract between A and B might provide that A should be liable to pay over to B any sum that A might recover from C.[84]

The preceding discussion is based on the assumptions that C is under a prima facie liability in tort to A and that he seeks to rely on a provision in a contract between A and B in order to exclude or restrict the liability. But it is arguable that the terms of that contract can be relevant at an earlier

---

76 *The Suleyman Stalskiy* [1976] 2 Lloyd's Rep. 609. The same reasoning was applied in *Southern Water Authority* v. *Carey* [1985] 2 All E.R. 1077, 1085 to prevent a building subcontractor from taking the benefit of an exemption clause in the main contract (to which he was not a party); but the sub-contractor succeeded on another ground: *post*, p. 557.

77 [1981] 1 W.L.R. 138; Reynolds, 96 L.Q.R. 506; Coote [1981] C.L.J. 13; Clarke [1981] C.L.J. 17; Rose, 44 M.L.R. 336.

78 [1981] 1 W.L.R. 138, 144.

79 *Cf. The Zinnia* [1984] 2 Lloyd's Rep. 211, 217 (where the third party and one of the contracting parties were again associated companies).

80 See the New South Wales case of *Godina* v. *Patrick Operations Ltd.* [1984] 1 Lloyd's Rep. 333.

81 *Raymond Burke Motors Ltd.* v. *Mersey Docks & Harbour Co.* [1986] 1 Lloyd's Rep. 155.

82 *Snelling* v. *John G. Snelling Ltd.* [1973] 1 Q.B. 87; *ante*, p. 535.

83 See *Gore* v. *Van der Lann* [1967] 2 Q.B. 31; *ante*, p. 534; *The Elbe Maru* [1978] 1 Lloyds's Rep. 206; contrast *The Chevalier Roze* [1983] 2 Lloyd's Rep. 438 (where the contract between A and B had been fully performed before A's cause of action against C arose, and so did not protect C).

84 *Quaere* whether this would be a penalty; see *post*, pp. 883–890. For further possible devices, see the *Midland Silicones* case [1962] A.C. 466, 473 and Hamson [1959] C.L.J. 150.

stage, namely in determining the extent of any duty of care owed to A by C. For example, work under a building contract between A and B may be done by a subcontractor C, who is a party to the sub-contract between himself and B, but not a party to the main contract with A. If C does the work negligently and so causes harm to A (*e.g.* by damaging other property belonging to A[85]) then C may be liable in tort to A, and he cannot rely, as such, on an exemption clause in the main contract between A and B. But in the *Junior Books* case, Lord Roskill suggested that a "relevant exclusion clause in the main contract" might "limit the duty of care"[86] of C and so indirectly provide him with a defence to a claim in tort by A. In *The Aliakmon*, this suggestion was doubted by Lord Brandon on the ground that the exemption clause in the example was contained "in a contract to which the plaintiff [was] a party but the defendant [was] not"[87]: in other words, because there was no privity of contract between them. *The Aliakmon* was, however, concerned with the converse of the situation discussed by Lord Roskill, namely with the case in which the exemption clause was contained in a contract to which the defendant was a party but the plaintiff was not.[88] Both situations raise issues of privity of contract but they are concerned with different aspects of that doctrine: the first with the question whether C can take the *benefit* of an exemption clause in a contract between A and B, and the second with the question whether A can be *bound* by an exemption clause in a contract between B and C. As a matter of policy, there is less objection to giving an affirmative answer to the first question than to the second; for in the first situation A has assented to the clause while in the second no inference of such assent can be drawn merely from the presence of the clause in the contract between B and C.[89] Lord Roskill's suggestion has therefore been followed in a number of later cases in which exemption clauses in the main contract between A and B have been held to negative any duty of care which C might (but for such clauses) have owed to A.[90] In such cases, C is protected, in spite of the absence of privity of contract,[91] because the clause "destroys the duty of [C] if duty there ever was."[92] It follows that the clause may be available not only to C, but also to any other person whose hypothetical duty is in this way affected. It may thus protect C's employees as well as C himself: in one case of this kind it was said that

---

[85] In this respect the facts in the example given in the text differ from those of *Junior Books Ltd.* v. *Veitchi Co. Ltd.* [1983] 1 A.C. 520 and so do not give rise to the difficulties occasioned by that case (see *ante*, p. 540).

[86] [1983] 1 A.C. 520, 546, applied in *Southern Water Authority* v. *Carey* [1985] 2 All E.R. 1077, 1086.

[87] [1986] A.C. 785, 817.

[88] See *post*, p. 558. Lord Brandon's view (*supra*, n. 87) was accordingly questioned in *Pacific Associates Inc.* v. *Baxter* [1990] 1 Q.B. 993, 1022.

[89] For this reason, the suggestion, made in *Muirhead* v. *Industrial Tank Specialties Ltd.* [1986] Q.B. 507, 525, that Lord Roskill intended to refer to an exclusion clause in the *sub*contract, may with respect be doubted. The suggestion is based on a passage in Lord Fraser's speech in the *Junior Books* case at p. 534, which is, however, not concerned with exclusion clauses at all but rather with the type of performance that C has agreed to render under his contract with B: see *post*, pp. 560–561.

[90] *Southern Water Authority* v. *Carey* [1985] 2 All E.R. 1077; *Norwich C.C.* v. *Harvey* [1989] 1 W.L.R. 828; *Pacific Associates Inc.* v. *Baxter* [1990] 1 Q.B. 993; Adams and Brownsword [1990] J.B.L. 23.

[91] *Norwich C.C.* v. *Harvey* [1989] 1 W.L.R. 828, 837.

[92] *Pacific Associates Inc.* v. *Baxter* [1990] 1 Q.B. 993, 1038.

if C owed no duty "then neither can any of their employees have done so."[93] Whether a clause affects the duty of persons other than C depends simply on its construction and not on the doctrine of privity.

Lord Roskill's statement refers only to "a *relevant* exclusion clause": that is, to one which can "limit *the duty of care*." A clause which merely imposed a financial limit on the *amount recoverable* would not be of this kind since such a clause would only come into operation on the assumption that a duty was owed and had been broken.[94]

2. The Burden

The law starts with the principle that a person is not bound by an exemption clause in a contract to which he is not a party, unless one of the recognised exceptions to the doctrine of privity (such as agency) can be invoked against him.[95] In the *Midland Silicones* case[96] the contract between the carrier and the stevedores provided that the stevedores should have "such protection as is afforded by the terms of the bill of lading." The owners of the drum nonetheless recovered full damages from the stevedores. They were not bound by what was, in effect, a limitation clause in the contract between the stevedores and the carrier. Similarly, in *The Aliakmon*[97] the buyers were not bound by exemption provisions in the contract of carriage since the only parties to that contract were the sellers and the shipowners.[98] This position, which may be unsatisfactory in practice, is subject to a number of qualifications.

The first is illustrated by *Pyrene Co. Ltd.* v. *Scindia Navigation Co. Ltd.*,[99] where a fire tender was sold for export. Under the contract of sale, the buyer was to make the shipping arrangements, and he accordingly made a contract with the carrier which limited the latter's liability.[1] In the course of being loaded, the tender was damaged by the carrier while it was still at the seller's risk. It was held that the seller was bound by the limitation clause. The decision was partly based on the doubts expressed by Denning L.J. in earlier cases as to the existence of the doctrine of privity[2]; and it can no longer be supported on this ground. But it can still be justified on the ground that the buyer was the seller's agent in making the contract with the carrier, at least so far as it concerned the seller[3]; or on the ground

---

[93] *Norwich C.C.* v. *Harvey* [1989] 1 W.L.R. 828, 834.

[94] *Cf. post*, pp. 560–561.

[95] *Delaurier* v. *Wyllie* (1889) 17 R. (Ct. of Sess.) 167: *cf. The Kite* [1933] P. 164; *White* v. *Warwick (John) & Co. Ltd.* [1953] 2 W.L.R. 1285, 1294; *Chas. Davis (Metal Brokers) Ltd.* v. *Gilyot & Scott Ltd.* [1975] 2 Lloyd's Rep. 422; *The Eagle* [1977] 2 Lloyd's Rep. 70; *Twins Transport* v. *Patrick Brocklehurst* (1983) 25 Build.L.R. 65 for a statutory exception, see Congenital Disabilities (Civil Liability) Act 1976, s.1(6).

[96] [1962] A.C. 446, *ante*, p. 553.

[97] [1986] A.C. 785, *ante*, p. 542.

[98] Paradoxically, it was the buyers who argued (unsuccessfully) that they *were* bound, their object being to establish that the undesirable consequence of depriving the shipowners of the benefit of those provisions (see *ante*, p. 543) would not follow if the shipowners were held liable to them in tort.

[99] [1954] 2 Q.B. 402.

[1] Under what is now Carriage of Goods by Sea Act 1971, Sched. Art. IV. 5.

[2] At p. 426; and see *ante*, p. 529.

[3] See [1954] 2 Q.B. pp. 423–425.

that an implied contract incorporating the limitation clause arose between seller and carrier when the tender was presented and accepted for loading.[4]

Similar reasoning also explains another aspect of *The Eurymedon*,[5] where the action against the stevedore was brought, not by the shipper, but by the consignee, who was not a party to the original contract of carriage. It was held that the consignee was bound by the exclusion clause. This aspect of the decision was supported on the ground that an implied contract arose[6] between stevedore and consignee, as a result of the consignee's "acceptance of [the bill of lading] and request for delivery of the goods thereunder."[7] This implied contract incorporated the terms of the bill of lading (which protected the stevedore[8]), so that the consignee was bound by the terms of the bill of lading even though it was assumed that he was not a party to the bill of lading contract.[9] In the *Midland Silicones* case, by contrast, there was no implied contract between the plaintiffs and the stevedores incorporating the terms of the contract between the carrier and the stevedores.[10] One reason given for this conclusion was that the stevedores, in delivering the goods were simply performing their contract with the carrier[11]; but this was equally true in *The Eurymedon*.[12] A better distinction between the two cases is that in *The Eurymedon* the consignees had possession of the bill of lading (even though they were assumed not to be parties to it) and so knew its terms or at least had means of knowing them. In the *Midland Silicones* case there was nothing to indicate that the plaintiffs knew anything about the contract with which we are at this stage concerned, *i.e.* the contract between the carrier and the stevedores. The implied contract argument may also fail on other grounds. In *The Aliakmon* the buyers again presented a bill of lading to which they were not parties, and took delivery of the goods; but no implied contract arose since they had there done these acts purely as agents of the sellers.[13]

A second exception to the general rule that a person is not bound by an exemption clause in a contract to which he is not a party arises under the law of bailment. This exception can, for example, apply where a customer sends goods to a cleaner or repairer and allows him to send the work out to

---

4 *Scruttons Ltd.* v. *Midland Silicones Ltd.* [1962] A.C. 446, 471; *The Kapetan Markos N.L.* (*No.* 2) [1987] 2 Lloyd's Rep. 321, 331; *The Captain Gregos (No. 2)* [1990] 2 Lloyd's Rep. 395 (claim by B.P.).

5 [1975] A.C. 154.

6 On the analogy of *Brandt* v. *Liverpool etc. S.N. Co. Ltd.* [1924] 1 K.B. 575. The analogy is not exact. In *Brandt's* case the issue was whether the owner of the goods could enforce an implied promise made *to* him, so that it was necessary to find consideration moving *from him*. In *The Eurymedon*, the issue was whether a promise not to sue made *by* the owner of the goods was binding, and the consideration for this would have to move *from the other parties* to that promise (or at least from the one seeking to rely on it).

7 [1975] A.C. 154, 168.

8 *Ante*, p. 554.

9 It was assumed that the consignee had not become a party to the contract under the Bills of Lading Act 1855, s.1 (*post*, pp. 579, 606–607) since it was not clear that the requirements of the section had been satisfied.

10 [1962] A.C. 446; *ante*, p. 553.

11 [1962] A.C.446, 496; *cf.* [1961] 1 Q.B. 106; for similar reasoning (in a case not concerned with exemption clauses) see *The Aramis* [1989] 1 Lloyd's Rep. 213.

12 See the report of Beattie J.'s decision in [1971] 2 Lloyd's Rep. at p. 403; this decision was eventually affirmed by the Privy Council: [1975] A.C. 154. The reasoning of *The Aramis*, *supra*, is not easy to reconcile with that of *The Eurymedon* on the implied contract point: see Treitel [1989] L.M.C.L.Q. 162, 171.

13 [1986] A.C. 785, 808; this fact was known to the carrier: see [1985] Q.B. 350, 364.

a subcontractor. If the sub-contract contains an exemption clause, the owner may be bound by it on the ground that he has "expressly or impliedly consented to the bailee making a sub-bailment containing those conditions, but not otherwise."[14] It seems that the owner is not bound contractually but on the basis that he voluntarily takes the risk of loss or damage, or perhaps on the ground that he cannot establish a breach of duty against the sub-bailee without relying on all the terms of the sub-bailment, including the exemption clause.[15] This exception is, however, confined to cases in which there is a relationship of bailor and bailee (or sub-bailee) between the plaintiff and the defendant. In *The Aliakmon*, the exception did not apply as no such relationship there existed between the *buyers* and the shipowners: "The only bailment of the goods was one by the sellers to the shipowners."[16] Similarly, in the *Midland Silicones* case the stevedores were not bailees of the drum.[17] They had not been entrusted with the possession of it: they were simply asked to deliver it to the plaintiffs out of a warehouse belonging to the port authority.

It is finally necessary to distinguish here (as elsewhere)[18] between exemption clauses and clauses which define a party's duty. Clauses of the latter kind can adversely affect a plaintiff even though they are contained in a contract to which he is not a party. Breach of that contract may amount also to breach of a duty of care owed to a third party, giving that third party a remedy in tort[19] and the terms of the contract can be relevant to the scope of that duty of care. For example, where work in pursuance of a building contract between A and B is done by C under a roofing subcontract between B and C, the terms of the latter contract would clearly determine the type of work to be done by C.[20] If the subcontract merely required C to tile the roof he would not be liable in tort to A on the ground that the main contract required the roof to be tiled and felted, or even on the ground that tiling and felting was standard practice for the type of building in question. But a clause in the sub-contract limiting C's liability (*e.g.* to the cost of replacing defective tiles) would not be relevant in defin-

---

[14] *Morris* v. *C. W. Martin & Sons Ltd.* [1966] 1 Q.B. 716, 729; *cf. ibid.* 741; *Port Swettenham Authority* v. *T. W. Wu & Co.* [1979] A.C. 580; *The Kapetan Markos NL* (*No.* 2) [1987] 2 Lloyd's Rep. 323, 340; *Singer* (*U.K.*) *Ltd.* v. *Tees & Hartlepool Port Authority* [1988] 2 Lloyd's Rep. 164, 167–168; *The Captain Gregos (No. 2)* [1990] 2 Lloyd's Rep. 395, 405; Palmer [1988] L.M.C.L.Q. 466; Phang, 8 O.J.L.S. 418. Carnegie, 3 Adelaide L.Rev 7. For a similar view, see *Fosbroke-Hobbs* v. *Airwork Ltd.* (1936) 53 T.L.R. 254, 257 (carriage of persons), but contrast *Haseldine* v. *C. A. Daw & Sons Ltd.* [1941] 2 K.B. 343, 379. *Cf.* also Occupiers' Liability Act 1957, s.3; Defective Premises Act 1972, ss.11(*b*) and 4; *White* v. *Blackmore* [1972] 2 Q.B. 651, 676.

[15] For conflicting authorities on the second of the above suggestions, see *Johnson Matthey & Co.* v. *Constantine Terminals Ltd.* [1976] 2 Lloyd's Rep. 215 (where consent to the sub-bailment was present but said at p. 221 to be unnecessary); Coote [1977] C.L.J. 17; *Lee Cooper Ltd.* v. *C. H. Jeakins & Son Ltd.* [1964] 1 Lloyd's Rep. 300 (also reported in [1967] 2 Q.B. 1, but not on this point); *Learoyd Bros. & Co.* v. *Pope & Sons* (*Dock Carriers*) *Ltd.* [1966] 2 Lloyd's Rep. 142.

[16] [1986] A.C. 785. 818; *cf. Swiss Bank Corp.* v. *Brink's-Mat Ltd.* [1986] 2 Lloyd's Rep. 79, 98; *The Captain Gregos (No. 2)* [1990] 2 Lloyd's Rep. 395 (claim by PEAG), but the same case shows that a bailment incorporating the terms of the contract can arise by subsequent attornment of the carrier to the buyer (claim by B.P.).

[17] [1962] A.C. 446, 470.

[18] *Ante*, p. 219.

[19] *Ante*, pp. 538–539.

[20] *Junior Books* case [1983] 1 A.C. 520, 534; *cf. Simaan General Contracting Co.* v. *Pilkington Glass Ltd.* (*No.* 2) [1988] Q.B. 758, 782–783.

ing C's duty to A in tort; for such a clause would not define what C has to do: it would specify the legal consequences of failing to do it.[21] Hence such a clause would as a general rule not bind A contractually, since he was not a party to the contract in which it was contained.

SECTION 5. EXCEPTIONS

The doctrine of privity would, if inflexibly applied, give rise to considerable injustice and inconvenience. Many exceptions to it have therefore been developed, of which the following are the most important.

1. Covenants Concerning Land

Covenants in a lease can benefit or bind persons, other than the original parties to the lease, who later acquire an interest in the property or the reversion; a person may be able to enforce a covenant affecting land made by his predecessor in title, and one who acquires land with notice that it is burdened by a restrictive covenant may be bound by it although he was not a party to the covenant. Detailed discussion of these topics will be found in works on the land law.[22]

2. Agency

Agency is the relationship which arises when one person (the principal) authorises another (the agent) to act on his behalf and the agent agrees to do so. One legal consequence of this relationship is that the principal acquires rights and incurs liabilities under contracts made by the agent on his behalf with third parties. It is sometimes said that this is only an apparent exception to the doctrine of privity, since in such cases the agent is only the instrument of the principal, who is the real contracting party.[23] This may be true where the agent acts within his actual authority. But it is only doubtfully true where the principal is liable under the doctrine of apparent authority although the agent's act is unauthorised, or where the principal ratifies.[24] And the principles of agency constitute a clear exception to the doctrine of privity where the agent acts within his "usual" authority,[25] where the principal is undisclosed,[26] and in certain cases of agency of necessity.[27] These matters are discussed in Chapter 17.

3. Assignment

Assignment is a process whereby a contractual right is transferred to someone other than the original creditor without the consent of the original debtor. It is a clear exception to the doctrine of privity and is discussed in Chapter 16.

---

[21] See *The Aliakmon* where the contract incorporated the Hague Rules which contained an intricate set of provisions some of which defined duties while others provided immunities and limitations; taken together, these could not be "synthesised into a standard of care": [1985] Q.B. 350, 368, approved [1986] A.C. 785, 818; *cf. Twins Transport Ltd.* v. *Patrick Brocklehurst* (1983) 25 Build.L.R. 65.

[22] *e.g.* Megarry and Wade, *The Law of Real Property* (5th ed.), Chap. 14.

[23] *Cf.* Pollock, *Principles of Contract* (13th ed.), p. 163.

[24] *Post*, pp. 615–619, 626–630.

[25] *Watteau* v. *Fenwick* [1893] 1 Q.B. 346; *post*, pp. 619–621.

[26] *Post*, pp. 631–634.

[27] *Post*, pp. 621–625.

4. Trusts of Promises[28]

Equity developed a more general exception to the doctrine of privity by use of the concept of trust. A trust is an equitable obligation to hold property on behalf of another. It may be express or implied; and a person may be trustee not only of a physical thing or of a sum of money,[29] but also of a *chose in action*,[30] such as a debt owed to him. Equity held, further, that a person could be trustee of a promise to pay money, not to himself, but to a third person. Thus in *Tomlinson* v. *Gill*[31] the defendant promised a widow to pay her late husband's debts. Lord Hardwicke held that the widow was trustee of the promise for the husband's creditors, who could thus enforce the promise against the defendant.

This device was applied in a number of nineteenth-century cases[32] and was even recognised by the common law courts, who sometimes allowed the promisee to recover more than he had lost on the ground that he was bound to hold the surplus for a third party.[33] It was finally approved by the House of Lords in *Walford's* case,[34] where a broker (C) negotiated a charterparty by which the shipowner (A) promised the charterer (B) to pay the broker a commission. It was held that B was trustee of this promise for C, who could thus enforce it against A.[35] Many problems arise in determining the scope and effects of this trust device.

(1) Intention to create a trust

A promisee will not be regarded as trustee for a third party unless he has the intention to create a trust.[36]

The intention to create a trust is clear where the word "trust" or "trustee" is used.[37] The only[38] difficulty which may arise in such a case is: in whose favour has the trust been created? In *Gandy* v. *Gandy*[39] a husband entered into a separation agreement by which he promised trustees to

---

[28] Corbin, 46 L.Q.R. 12; *Contracts*, Chap. 46.

[29] If A lends a sum of money to B and stipulates that the money is to be used only for paying a debt which B owes C, then B may hold the money on trust for C: see *Barclays Bank Ltd.* v. *Quistclose Investments Ltd.* [1970] A.C. 567 (where the trust in favour of C failed and it was held that there was a resulting trust for A). In this case, the subject-matter of the trust was *the money* and not a *promise*. A made no promise to B to pay C; nor did B promise A to pay C: B only promised not to use the money for any other purpose.

[30] *Post*, p. 576.

[31] (1756) Amb. 330; *cf. Gregory* v. *Williams* (1817) 3 Mer. 582.

[32] *e.g. Gregory* v. *Williams* (1817) 3 Mer. 582; *Lloyd's* v. *Harper* (1880) 16 Ch.D. 290.

[33] *e.g. Lamb* v. *Vice* (1840) 6 M. & W. 467; *Robertson* v. *Wait* (1853) 8 Ex. 299; *Prudential Staff Union* v. *Hall* [1947] K.B. 685.

[34] *Les Affréteurs Réunis, S.A.* v. *Leopold Walford (London) Ltd.* [1919] A.C. 801; *The Panaghia P* [1983] 2 Lloyd's Rep. 653, 655. Contrast *The Manifest Lipkowy* [1989] 2 Lloyd's Rep. 138, where an agreement for the sale of a ship provided for deduction of commission from the price, but seems to have contained no *promise* by the seller to pay the broker.

[35] Lord Finlay seems to have regarded the broker as a party to the contract.

[36] *Swain* v. *Law Society* [1983] 1 A.C. 598, 620; Feltham, 98 L.Q.R. 17.

[37] *Fletcher* v. *Fletcher* (1844) 4 Hare 67; *Bowskill* v. *Dawson* [1955] 1 Q.B. 13.

[38] For the purpose of the present discussion, it is assumed that formal requirements, such as that imposed by Law of Property Act 1925, s.53(1)(*b*), have been satisfied. As to the effect on the rights of third parties of failure to satisfy such requirements, see Feltham (1987) Conv. 246.

[39] (1884) 30 Ch.D. 57.

pay them an annuity for the benefit of his wife, and to pay them money for the maintenance and education of his daughters. It was held that this agreement created no trust in favour of the daughters, since its sole object was to regulate the relations between husband and wife. Thus the wife could, but the daughters could not, enforce the agreement.[40]

A trust may be created without using any particular form of words, and where the word "trust" or "trustee" is not used, the question of intention to create a trust gives rise to great difficulty. Two cases may be contrasted. In *Re Flavell*[41] a partner retired and the continuing partners promised him that they would, after his death, pay an annuity to his widow. It was held that there was a trust in favour of the widow. But in *Re Schebsman*[42] a company promised one of its employees on his retirement that it would, after his death, pay annuities to his widow for a specified period, or (if she should die within that period) to his daughter. It was held that there was no trust in favour of the widow or daughter.[43]

Similarly, a life insurance policy expressed to be for the benefit of a third party has in some cases been held to create a trust in his favour,[44] but in others to confer no rights on him.[45] And in some cases concerning other types of insurance[46] the courts have held that a third party could take advantage of the policy under the trust device[47] while in others they have held that the third party had no rights because of the doctrine of privity.[48] There is no point in trying to reconcile all these cases. They represent different stages of development and show that the courts became at one stage, reluctant to apply the trust device, because, once a trust was held to have been created, the parties to the contract lost their right to rescind or vary

---

40 Fry L.J. held that the daughters could not sue because the trustees had a discretion as to their upbringing. But when the wife was joined to the action her claim succeeded even though enforcement by her could also be said to interfere with the trustees' discretion.

41 (1883) 25 Ch.D. 89; *cf. Page* v. *Cox* (1852) 10 Hare 163; *Re Gordon* [1940] Ch. 851; *Drimmie* v. *Davies* [1899] 1 I.R. 176.

42 [1944] Ch. 83; see further, *post*, p. 565, n. 65; *cf. Re Stapleton-Bretherton* [1941] Ch. 482. In *Re Miller's Agreement* [1947] Ch. 615 and *Beswick* v. *Beswick* [1968] A.C. 58 it was conceded that there was no trust.

43 Paradoxically, the argument that there was a trust was not advanced on behalf of the third parties but on behalf of the promisee's trustee in bankruptcy. The point of the argument was to have the trust set aside under Bankruptcy Act 1914, s.42 (now superseded by Insolvency Act 1986, s.339): see [1944] Ch. at p. 86. On p. 104 the argument is attributed to "Mr. Denning," who appeared for the third parties. But this must be a mistake; the corresponding passage in [1943] 2 All E.R. 768, 779 correctly attributes it to "counsel for the appellant," *i.e.* for the trustee in bankruptcy. As the company was willing to pay, the outcome of holding that there was *no* trust was that the third parties obtained the intended benefit. In *Re Flavell, supra*, the same result followed from the decision that there *was* a trust.

44 *Re Richardson* (1882) 47 L.T. 514; *Royal Exchange Assurance* v. *Hope* [1928] Ch. 179; *Re Webb* [1941] Ch. 225; *Re Foster's Policy* [1966] 1 W.L.R. 222.

45 *Re Burgess' Policy* (1915) 113 L.T. 443; *Re Clay's Policy of Assurance* [1937] 2 All E.R. 548; *Re Foster* [1938] 3 All E.R. 357; *Re Sinclair's Life Policy* [1938] Ch. 799; *Re Engelbach's Estate* [1924] 2 Ch. 348. For criticism of the last two cases in *Beswick* v. *Beswick* [1968] A.C. 58 (but on another ground), see *ante*, p. 536, n. 18.

46 For statutory exceptions to the doctrine of privity in cases of insurance, see *post*, pp. 569–571.

47 *Williams* v. *Baltic Insurance Co.* [1924] 2 K.B. 282; *cf. Waters* v. *Monarch Assurance Co.* (1856) 5 E. & B. 870, 881. *Cf.* Deane J. in *Trident General Ins. Co. Ltd.* v. *McNiece Bros. Pty. Ltd.* (1988) 165 C.L.R. 107 (*ante*, p. 530).

48 *Vandepitte* v. *Preferred Accident Insurance Corp.* [1933] A.C. 70; *Green* v. *Russell* [1959] 2 Q.B. 226, cited with approval in *McCamley* v. *Cammell Laird Shipbuilders* [1990] 1 W.L.R. 963, 969.

that contract by mutual consent.[49] In this state of the authorities, the most that can be done is to try to extract from them a number of principles which will at any rate serve as guides to the solution of future problems.

(a) THERE MUST BE AN INTENTION TO BENEFIT THE THIRD PARTY. If the promisee intends the promise to be for his own benefit, there will be no trust in favour of the third party. Thus in *West* v. *Houghton*[50] the plaintiff granted a lease of sporting rights to the defendant, who promised him to keep down rabbits "so that no appreciable damage may be done to crops." The land was let to tenants, to whom, under their leases, the plaintiff was not liable for damage done by rabbits. It was held that the plaintiff did not hold the defendant's promise on trust for his tenants: it was not clear that he had taken that promise for their benefit rather than for his own. Conversely, the fact that the promisee had *not* intended to take the promise for his own benefit can be relied on to support the argument that there was a trust in favour of the third party.[51]

The fact that the promise was taken generally for the benefit of third parties will not create a trust in favour of any particular third party unless an intention to benefit that person is clearly proved. In *Vandepitte* v. *Preferred Accident Insurance Corporation*[52] a father took out a motor insurance policy, stated to be "available . . . to any person . . . while . . . legally operating" his car. The question arose whether the father intended to hold the policy on trust for his under-age daughter, who had injured the plaintiff while driving the car with her father's consent. The Privy Council gave two reasons for holding that the father had no such intention. First, the trust device only confers benefits on third parties, "whereas in an insurance . . . serious duties and obligations rest on any person claiming to be insured, which necessarily involve consent and privity of contract."[53] Secondly, the case was governed by the law of British Columbia, under which a father was liable for the torts of his minor children living in his family.[54] Thus if the daughter injured someone, the father might expect that he (and not she) would be sued. It was not clear that he intended to benefit her when taking out the policy, since it was not certain that she would need the benefit. It follows from the second of these reasons that the decision would have gone the other way if the car had been driven by someone for whose torts the assured was not responsible. This assumption is borne out by *Williams* v. *Baltic Insurance Co.*,[55] where the assured was held to be trustee of a similar (though not identical) policy for his sister while she was driving his car with his consent in England.

(b) THE INTENTION TO BENEFIT THE THIRD PARTY MUST BE IRREVOCABLE. It is now[56] settled that a contract will not normally[57] give rise to a trust in favour

---

[49] See *ante*, p. 528; *post*, p. 565.
[50] (1879) 4 C.P.D. 197; criticised in *Re Flavell* (1883) 25 Ch.D. 89, 98 and in *Lloyd's* v. *Harper* (1880) 16 Ch.D. 290, 311.
[51] *Lyus* v. *Prowsa Developments Ltd.* [1982] 1 W.L.R. 1044.
[52] [1933] A.C. 70; R. S. T. C., 49 L.Q.R. 474.
[53] At p. 81.
[54] At p. 80.
[55] [1924] 2 K.B. 282; and see *post*, p. 570.
[56] For the earlier view that a trust may arise although the contracting parties can divert the benefit away from the third party, see *Hill* v. *Gomme* (1839) 5 My. & Cr. 250; *Page* v. *Cox* (1852) 10 Hare 163.
[57] For exceptions, see *infra*, at nn. 59 and 62.

of a third party if, under the terms of the contract, the promisee is entitled to deprive the third party of the intended benefit by diverting it to himself. Thus in *Re Sinclair's Life Policy*[58] a policy of life insurance, taken out by the assured for the benefit of his godson, contained an option enabling the assured to surrender the policy for his own benefit. This fact negatived the intention to create a trust. On the other hand, the existence of such a power to divert the benefit was held not to negative the intention to create the trust where the power was expressed to be exercisable only for a limited period and was not exercised within that period.[59] Nor will the existence of a trust necessarily be negatived where the contract names a group of beneficiaries but reserves to the promisee the power to alter the nature or destination of the benefit as between those beneficiaries. Thus in *Re Webb*[60] insurance policies taken out by a father on the lives of his children, for their benefit and on their behalf, were held to create trusts in favour of the children although the father was entitled to exercise various options under the policies on their behalf which would alter the precise nature of the benefits to be received by them. In *Re Flavell*[61] a promise to pay annuities to the widow *or* children of the promisee as he should appoint, and in default of appointment to the widow, was held, in default of appointment, to create a trust in favour of the widow although the whole benefit could have been diverted away from her to the children. And where a contract *by statute* creates a trust[62] a general provision in the contract entitling the promisee to divert the benefit to whom he pleases will not defeat the trust: on the contrary such power can only be exercised for the benefit of objects of the trust.[63]

The court may conclude that there was no intention irrevocably to benefit the third party even though the contract contains no express provision entitling the promisee to divert the benefit away from the third party. It may do so on the ground that the contract would, if it were held to give rise to a trust, unduly limited the freedom of action of the parties or of one of them, *e.g.* by restricting the promisee's freedom of movement[64] or by depriving the parties of their rights to vary the contract by mutual consent.[65]

(c) THE INTENTION TO BENEFIT IS NOT, WITHOUT MORE, SUFFICIENT. An intention to create a trust must be distinguished from an intention to make a gift.[66] There are many cases in which the courts have refused to apply the trust device although the promisee clearly and without qualification intended to benefit the third party.[67] It seems that an intention to create a

---

58 [1938] Ch. 799; criticised on another ground in *Beswick* v. *Beswick* [1968] A.C. 58, 96; *ante*, p. 536, n. 18.
59 *Re Foster's Policy* [1966] 1 W.L.R. 432.
60 [1941] Ch. 225.
61 (1883) 25 Ch.D. 89.
62 *Post*, p. 569.
63 *Re a Policy of the Equitable Life Assurance of the United States and Mitchell* (1911) 27 T.L.R. 213; *Re Fleetwood's Policy* [1926] Ch. 48.
64 *e.g. Re Burgess' Policy* (1915) 113 L.T. 43 (policy to become void if insured went "beyond the boundaries of Europe" without previously notifying insurers).
65 *e.g. Re Schebsman* [1944] 83, 104 (parties "intended to keep alive their common law right consensually to vary the terms of the obligation").
66 See *Richards* v. *Delbridge* (1874) L.R. 18 Eq. 11.
67 *Re Engelbach's Estate* [1924] 2 Ch. 348 (overruled on another point in *Beswick* v. *Beswick* [1968] A.C. 58; *ante*, p. 536, n. 18); *Re Clay's Policy of Assurance* [1937] 2 All E.R. 548; *Re*

trust will readily be found where the contract for the benefit of the third party is made in performance of a previous contract between promisee and third party, *e.g.* where an employer promises to insure his employee against accident and then does so.[68] An intention to create a trust should, on principle, involve an intention on the part of the promisee to assume fiduciary responsibilities towards the third party.[69] But there is no clear definition of "fiduciary" for this purpose; and the courts did not at one time insist very strictly on proof of the intention to create a trust. The fact that they later came to do so is largely responsible for the present, more restricted, scope of the trust device.

The intention to create a trust may, finally, be negatived on the ground that a trust is not necessary to give rights to the third party because he is entitled to enforce the contract, even in the absence of a trust, under a statutory exception to the doctrine of privity.[70]

(2) Effects of the trust

The effects of a trust in favour of a third party are as follows:

(a) THIRD PARTY CAN SUE. The third party can sue the promisor to enforce the contract. He must join the promisee as a party to the action[71] since otherwise the promisor might be sued a second time by the promisee. As this rule as to joinder of parties exists for the benefit of the promisor, it can be waived by him.[72]

(b) THIRD PARTY ENTITLED TO THE BENEFIT. The third party is (as a general rule[73]) beneficially entitled to any money paid or payable under the contract; the promisee has no right to such money.[74] After *Beswick* v. *Beswick*[75] the third party can generally keep money paid to him even if there is no trust.

(c) FAILURE OF THE TRUST. There are exceptional cases in which the promisee may be entitled to the money even though there was a trust. In *Cleaver* v. *Mutual Reserve Fund Life Association*[76] a husband insured his life for the benefit of his wife by a policy which, by statute, created a trust in her favour.[77] The wife was convicted of murdering the husband and was therefore disqualified from enforcing the trust. It was held that the execu-

---

Foster [1938] 3 All E.R. 357; *Re Stapleton-Bretherton* [1941] Ch. 482; *Green* v. *Russell* [1959] 1 Q.B. 28; *Re Cook's Settlement Trusts* [1965] Ch. 902; *cf. Cleaver* v. *Mutual Reserve Fund Life Association* [1892] 1 Q.B. 147, 152.

68 See *Re Independent Air Travel Ltd., The Times*, May 20, 1961, where counsel, with the approval of the court, conceded this point.

69 See *Harmer* v. *Armstrong* [1934] Ch. 65, where the fact that the promisee was the third party's agent, and so under a fiduciary duty (*post*, p. 647), helped to establish the necessary intention.

70 *Swain* v. *Law Society* [1983] 1 A.C. 598, esp. at p. 621.

71 *Cf. Performing Right Society Ltd.* v. *London Theatre of Varieties* [1924] A.C. 1; *The Panaghia P* [1983] 2 Lloyd's Rep. 653, 655 and *post*, p. 578.

72 As in *Walford's* case [1919] A.C. 801 (*ante*, p. 562); *cf. William Brandt's Sons & Co.* v. *Dunlop Rubber Co.* [1905] A.C. 454.

73 *i.e.* subject to the exception stated at n. 76, *infra*.

74 *Re Flavell* (1883) 25 Ch.D. 89; *Re Gordon* [1940] Ch. 851; *cf. Paul* v. *Constance* [1977] 1 W.L.R. 52.

75 [1968] A.C. 58

76 [1892] 1 Q.B. 147.

77 Married Women's Property Act 1882, s.11; *post*, p. 569.

tors of the husband could sue for the policy moneys. The decision can be criticised on the ground that the promisor should not be held liable to pay the promisee when he promised to pay the third party.[78] But it seems that the destination of the payments was a matter of indifference to the insurance company and that there was nothing to show that the company would (even if there had been no conviction) have been in any way prejudiced by paying the husband's executors rather than the wife.[79] The actual decision may also turn on the interpretation of the statute creating the trust.[80]

(3) Kinds of promises which can be held on trust

The trust device has so far only been applied to promises to pay money or to transfer property.[81] It is sometimes suggested that it might be applied to other kinds of promises, *e.g.* that an employer might hold the benefit of an exemption clause on trust for his employee.[82] But the present judicial tendency is to confine the trust device within narrow limits; and the suggestion has therefore been rejected on the ground that "the conception of a trust attaching to a benefit under an exclusion clause extends far beyond conventional limits."[83] Other techniques for making the benefit of such clauses available to third parties have already been discussed in this Chapter.[84]

(4) Relation between trust device and doctrine of privity

The trust device has here been treated as an exception to the doctrine of privity, of limited if uncertain scope. It has, however, been argued that where a third party was enabled by this device to enforce a contract made for his benefit there was, before the Judicature Act 1873, a conflict between the rules of equity and those of common law; that the rules of equity now prevail[85]; and that therefore the third party generally has a right of action.[86] But this view has not been accepted.[87] Even in equity the third party did not succeed merely because the contract was expressed to have been made for his benefit: he had to show, in addition, that a trust had been created in his favour.[88] And the argument that third parties were entitled to enforce contracts made for their benefit has been rejected in many cases after the Judicature Act 1873. Some of these were admittedly

---

[78] Ames, *Lectures*, 320; *Coulls* v. *Bagot's Executor & Trustee Co. Ltd.* [1967] A.L.R. 385, 410–411, *per* Windeyer J. (dissenting).

[79] *Cf. ante*, p. 536.

[80] See [1892] 1 Q.B. 147, 157.

[81] For a possible extension, see *Swain* v. *Law Society* [1982] 1 A.C. 598, where a promise to provide indemnity insurance was evidently regarded as a possible subject-matter of a trust; though for the reason given at p. 566, *ante*, there was no intention to create a trust.

[82] See the clause in *The Eurymedon* [1975] A.C. 154; *ante*, p. 555.

[83] *Southern Water Authority* v. *Carey* [1985] 2 All E.R. 1077, 1083.

[84] *Ante*, pp. 552–558.

[85] Judicature Act 1873, s.25(11); now Supreme Court Act 1981, s.49(1).

[86] *Drimmie* v. *Davies* [1899] 1 I.R. 176, 182 (the actual decision was that specific performance could be obtained by the executors of the promisee); Corbin, 46 L.Q.R. 12, 36.

[87] *Re Schebsman* [1943] 1 Ch. at p. 370, approved [1944] Ch. at p. 104.

[88] *Colyear* v. *Mulgrave* (1836) 2 Keen 81; the actual decision has been criticised, but the principle remains unimpaired. See *Page* v. *Cox* (1852) 10 Hare 163; *Kekewich* v. *Manning* (1851) 1 D.M. & G. 176.

argued entirely on common law principles,[89] but in others the equitable argument was considered and rejected.[90]

5. Covenants in Marriage Settlements

A covenant to settle after-acquired property contained in a marriage settlement can be enforced by all persons "within the marriage consideration," *i.e.* the spouses and issue of the marriage, but not by anyone else.[91] For example, it cannot be enforced by either spouse's next-of-kin, who are regarded as volunteers.[92] The rule seems to be a relic from the days when it was thought that any stranger who provided consideration could enforce a promise.[93]

6. Statutory Exceptions

A number of exceptions to the doctrine of privity have been created by statute. The most important of these are the following:

(1) Price maintenance agreements

The present law relating to these agreements can only be understood by reference to its history. At common law price maintenance agreements were valid,[94] but a manufacturer who wanted to maintain the retail price of his products at a fixed level was often faced with the difficulty that there was no contract between him and the retailer. He usually sold to a wholesaler who resold to a retailer. Thus a term as to the resale price of the goods could be enforced by manufacturer against wholesaler, or by wholesaler against retailer, but not by manufacturer against retailer. To overcome this difficulty, the manufacturer might claim that the retailer was bound by the agreement between manufacturer and wholesaler; or he might bind the wholesaler to extract from the retailer a promise not to resell below the fixed price and then claim that he could take the benefit of that promise; or he might declare that the wholesaler was his agent for the purpose of selling the goods to the retailer; or he might attach a printed slip to the goods declaring that acceptance of them should be deemed to create a contract between himself and the acceptor. But the courts refused to uphold any of these devices[95]; and manufacturers therefore resorted to self-help. An undercutting retailer could be put on the stop-list of a trade association, or he could be given the option of paying a trade fine instead; such methods of enforcing price maintenance agreements did not amount

---

[89] *e.g. Dunlop Pneumatic Tyre Co. Ltd.* v. *Selfridge & Co. Ltd.* [1915] A.C. 847, as to which see *ante*, p. 529 and *post*, pp. 568–569.

[90] *Re Burgess' Policy* (1915) 113 L.T. 443; *Re Clay's Policy of Assurance* [1937] 2 All E.R. 548; *Re Sinclair's Life Policy* [1938] Ch. 799; *Re Schebsman* [1944] Ch. 83; *Green* v. *Russell* [1959] 1 Q.B. 28.

[91] *Hill* v. *Gomme* (1839) 5 My. & Cr. 250, 254; *Re D'Angibau* (1880) 15 Ch.D. 228, 242; *Green* v. *Patterson* (1886) 32 Ch.D. 95, 107; *Re Plumptre's Marriage Settlement* [1910] 1 Ch. 609, 619.

[92] *Re Cook's Settlement Trusts* [1965] Ch. 902, 915–918; Lee, 85 L.Q.R. 213; Barton, 91 L.Q.R. 326; Meagher and Lehane, 92 L.Q.R. 427.

[93] The statement in *Hill* v. *Gomme, ubi supra*, that the children are "quasi-parties" to the contract is curiously reminiscent of the reasoning of *Dutton* v. *Poole*; *ante*, p. 528.

[94] *Palmolive Co. (of England) Ltd.* v. *Freedman* [1928] Ch. 264; *ante*, p. 422.

[95] *Taddy & Co.* v. *Sterious & Co.* [1904] 1 Ch. 354; *McGruthur* v. *Pitcher* [1904] 2 Ch. 306; *Dunlop Pneumatic Tyre Co. Ltd.* v. *Selfridge & Co. Ltd.* [1915] A.C. 847.

to conspiracy or blackmail.[96] This state of law was open to two criticisms. The first was that, if price-maintenance agreements were to be enforced at all, this should not be done secretly, in private trade courts. Part 1 of the Resale Prices Act 1976[97] therefore makes unlawful agreements for the *collective* enforcement of price-maintenance agreements by stop-lists, trade fines and other similar means. The second criticism was that even the *individual* enforcement of minimum resale price maintenance agreements between the parties to them was generally contrary to the public interest. The Act therefore makes void any provision in a contract purporting to establish the *minimum* price at which goods may be resold,[98] except where the goods have been exempted by the Restrictive Practices Court on one of a number of grounds stated in the Act.[99] Where the goods have been exempted, or where the contract specifies a *maximum* resale price, the resale price maintenance agreement can be enforced not only against a contracting party, but also against a third party who acquires the goods with notice of the agreement.[1] For this purpose "notice" means actual notice. Thus a retailer is not bound by a price maintenance agreement merely because he might by using reasonable diligence have discovered its existence.[2] But a retailer who knows of the existence of a price maintenance agreement is bound by it, although he does not trouble to find out its precise terms.[3]

(2) Insurance

The doctrine of privity applies to contracts of insurance.[4] It was in practice much modified in this field by the trust device and by agency; but the inadequacy of these exceptions has led to the creation of further exceptions to the doctrine by statute.

(a) LIFE INSURANCE. Section 11 of the Married Women's Property Act 1882[5] provides that where a man insures his life for the benefit of his wife or children, or where a woman insures her life for the benefit of her husband or children,[6] the policy "shall create a trust in favour of the objects therein named." This is a good provision so far as it goes, but it is subject to some odd limitations. It only applies where a person insures his or her own life, and not where the policy is on the life of the third party[7]; and it is restricted to policies for the benefit of spouses and children, so that it does

96 *Ware and De Freville* v. *M.T.A.* [1921] 3 K.B. 40; *Thorne* v. *M.T.A.* [1937] A.C. 797, disapproving *R.* v. *Denver* [1926] 2 K.B. 258. The position would probably be the same under s.21 of the Theft Act 1968.

97 The Act consolidates provisions formerly contained in the Restrictive Trade Practices Act 1956 and the Resale Prices Act 1964.

98 Resale Prices Act 1976, s.9.

99 *Ibid.* s.14.

1 *Ibid.* s.26; resale includes letting on hire-purchase (*ibid.* Sched. 1), but not simple letting; *Beechams Foods Ltd.* v. *Northern Suppliers (Edmonton) Ltd.* [1959] 1 W.L.R. 643.

2 *County Laboratories* v. *J. Mindel Ltd.* [1957] Ch. 295.

3 *Goodyear Tyre & Rubber Co. (Great Britain) Ltd.* v. *Lancashire Batteries Ltd.* [1958] 1 W.L.R. 857.

4 See *Boston Fruit Co.* v. *British & Foreign Marine Insurance Co.* [1906] A.C. 336; *Yangtze Insurance Association* v. *Lukmanjee* [1918] A.C. 585. Contrast, in Australia, *Trident General Ins. Co. Ltd.* v. *McNiece Bros. Pty. Ltd.* (1988) 165 C.L.R. 107 (*ante*, p. 530).

5 Replacing Married Women's Property Act 1870, s.10.

6 Illegitimate children are included: Family Law Reform Act 1969, s.19(1).

7 *Re Engelbach's Estate* [1924] 2 Ch. 348, overruled on another point in *Beswick* v. *Beswick* [1968] A.C. 58; *ante*, p. 536, n. 18.

not apply in favour of other dependants, such as informally adopted children.[8] The Law Revision Committee has recommended the removal of these limitations.[9]

(b) MOTOR INSURANCE. In *Williams* v. *Baltic Insurance Co.*[10] it was held that the owner of a car may be trustee of his motor insurance policy for a person driving his car with his consent. By statute such a person can now take the benefit of the owner's insurance policy without having to prove that the owner intended to constitute himself trustee.[11]

(c) FIRE INSURANCE. Where a house which is insured is destroyed by fire, "any person . . . interested" may require the insurance money to be laid out towards reinstating the house[12]; thus a tenant may claim under his landlord's insurance,[13] and a landlord under his tenant's insurance.[14]

(d) INSURANCE BY PERSONS WITH LIMITED INTERESTS. A person may insure property for its full value although he has only a limited interest in it. He may then be able to recover its full value from the insurers but be liable to pay over to the other persons interested any sum exceeding his own loss.[15] A number of real or supposed limitations on this principle have been removed by statute. Thus it has been provided that any person who has an interest in the subject-matter of a policy of marine insurance can insure "on behalf of and for the benefit of other persons interested as well as for his own benefit."[16] On a somewhat similar principle, where property is sold and suffers damage before the sale is completed, any insurance money to which the vendor is entitled in respect of the damage must be held by him for the purchaser, and be paid over to the purchaser on completion.[17]

(e) SOLICITORS' INDEMNITY INSURANCE. Under section 37 of the Solicitors Act 1974, a scheme has been established by the Law Society for the compulsory insurance of solicitors against liability for professional negligence or breach of duty. The scheme takes the form of a contract between the Society and insurers whereby the insurers undertake, on being paid the appropriate premiums, to provide indemnity insurance to solicitors. It has been held that the scheme gives rise to reciprocal rights and duties between the insurers and solicitors.[18] This result follows "by virtue of public law, not the ordinary English private law of contract"[19]; for in operating the

---

[8] *Re Clay's Policy of Assurance* [1937] 2 All E.R. 548.

[9] 6th Interim Report (Cmnd. 5449), Section D.

[10] [1924] 2 K.B. 282; *ante*, p. 564.

[11] Road Traffic Act 1988, s.148(7), replacing Road Traffic Act 1930, s.36(4), discussed in *Tattersal* v. *Drysdale* [1935] 2 K.B. 174; *Austin* v. *Zurich, etc., Insurance Co.* [1944] 2 All E.R. 243, 248.

[12] Fires Prevention (Metropolis) Act 1774, s.83.

[13] *Portavon Cinema Co. Ltd.* v. *Price and Century Insurance Co.* [1939] 4 All E.R. 601; *Mark Rowlands Ltd.* v. *Berni Inns Ltd.* [1986] Q.B. 211.

[14] MacGillivray and Parkington, *Insurance Law* (8th ed.), paras. 1652–1658.

[15] *Waters* v. *Monarch Insurance Co.* (1856) 5 E. & B. 870; *Hepburn* v. *Tomlinson (Hauliers) Ltd.* [1966] A.C. 451; *cf. Petrofina (U.K.) Ltd.* v. *Magnaload Ltd.* [1984] Q.B. 127 (head contractor insuring for the benefit of himself and subcontractors); *Pan Atlantic Ins. Co. Ltd.* v. *Pine Top Ins. Co. Ltd.* [1988] 2 Lloyd's Rep. 505.

[16] Marine Insurance Act 1906, s.14(2).

[17] Law of Property Act 1925, s.47; reversing the rule in *Rayner* v. *Preston* (1881) 18 Ch.D. 1; the section applies to all kinds of "property." *Cf. ibid.* s.108 as to the application of insurance money where property is mortgaged.

[18] *Swain* v. *Law Society* [1983] 1 A.C. 598.

[19] *Ibid.* p. 611.

scheme the Society acts, not in its private capacity as a professional association, but in its public capacity as a body one of whose functions is to protect members of the public against loss which they may suffer from dealings with solicitors.

(f) THIRD PARTIES' RIGHTS AGAINST INSURERS. A contract of insurance may not purport by its terms to confer a benefit on a third party, but may insure the policy-holder against liability to third parties. By statute such a third party may in certain circumstances[20] enforce the rights of the insured under the policy by proceeding directly against the insurance company.[21] In the case of victims of motor accidents, these rights are supplemented by an important agreement originally made between the Motor Insurers' Bureau and the Minister of Transport.[22] This provides that the Bureau wil pay any judgment (to the extent to which it remains unsatisfied) "in respect of any liability which is required to be covered by a policy of insurance" under the statutory scheme of compulsory motor insurance. A person who is injured in a road accident cannot technically enforce the agreement as he is not a party to it. But the agreement may be specifically enforced by the Minister,[23] and, although "the foundations in jurisprudence" of the agreement "are better not questioned,"[24] the Bureau's practice is not to rely on the doctrine of privity as a defence to claims by the injured parties themselves.[25]

(3) Law of Property Act 1925, s.56[26]

At common law a person could not take an immediate interest in property, or the benefit of any covenant, under an indenture purporting to be *inter partes*, unless he was named as a party to the indenture.[27] An indenture was a deed whose top was indented to match with a counterpart, as a pre-

---

[20] *Normid Housing Association* v. *R. John Ralphs* [1989] 1 Lloyd's Rep. 265; *Bradley* v. *Eagle Star Insurance Co. Ltd.* [1989] A.C. 957 (third party unable to sue insurer where insured had gone into liquidation before liability was established); *Duncan Stevenson MacMillan* v. *A. W. Knott Becker Scott Ltd.* [1990] 1 Lloyd's Rep. 98; *Lefevre* v. *White* [1990] 1 Lloyd's Rep. 569, 577; *The Padre Island* [1990] 2 All E.R. 705.

[21] Third Parties (Rights Against Insurers) Act 1930, s.1; Road Traffic Act 1988, ss.151–153; Michel, [1987] L.M.C.L.Q. 228; and see Policyholders Protection Act 1975, s.7 for the rights of such persons if the company is in liquidation.

[22] For the text of the agreement and of a supplementary agreement, see *Hardy* v. *M.I.B.* [1964] 2 Q.B. 745, 770; *White* v. *London Transport* [1971] 2 Q.B. 721, 729. The current agreements are between the Bureau and the Secretary of State for the Environment and are published by H.M.S.O. under the titles *Motor Insurers' Bureau* (*Compensation of Victims of Untraced Drivers*) (1972) and *Motor Insurers' Bureau* (*Compensation of Victims of Uninsurered Drivers*) (1972).

[23] See *Gurtner* v. *Circuit* [1968] 2 Q.B. 587.

[24] *Gardner* v. *Moore* [1984] A.C. 548, 556.

[25] *Persson* v. *London County Buses* [1974] 1 W.L.R. 569; and see *Hardy* v. *M.I.B.*, *supra*, n. 22, at p. 757; *Randall* v. *M.I.B.* [1968] 1 W.L.R. 1900; *Porter* v. *Addo* [1978] R.T.R. 503. As the Bureau is, therefore, interested in the outcome of litigation between the injured party and the driver, it may, at the court's discretion, be added as a party to such litigation: see *Gurtner* v. *Circuit* [1968] 2 Q.B. 587; contrast *White* v. *London Transport* [1971] 2 Q.B. 721.

[26] Elliot, 20 Conv. 43, 114; Andrews, 23 Conv. 179; Wade [1964] C.L.J. 66; Furmston, 23 M.L.R. 380–385; Ellinger, 26 M.L.R. 396; all these comments on s.56(1) must now be read in the light of the decision of the House of Lords, in *Beswick* v. *Beswick* [1968] A.C. 58.

[27] *Scudamore* v. *Vandenstene* (1587) 2 Co.Inst. 673; *Storer* v. *Gordon* (1814) 3 M. & S. 308; *Berkeley* v. *Hardy* (1826) 5 B. & C. 355; *Southampton* v. *Brown* (1827) 6 B. & C. 718; *Gardner* v. *Lachlan* (1836) 8 Sim. 123.

caution against fraud. It was said to be "*inter partes*" if it was expressed to be "between A of the first part, B of the second part . . . " etc. The common law rule did not apply to deeds poll (deeds with a smooth top) or to indentures not *inter partes*.[28] In the case of such deeds the grantee never had to be named *as a party*; and it was eventually settled that he need not be named at all, so long as he was sufficiently designated.[29] Deeds no longer have to be indented for any purposes,[30] but the distinction between deeds *inter partes* and other deeds still exists.

The common law rule with regard to indentures *inter partes* was modified by section 5 of the Real Property Act 1845,[31] which provided that "under an indenture . . . an immediate estate or interest in any tenements or hereditaments and the benefit of a condition or covenant respecting any tenements or hereditaments may be taken although the taker thereof be not named a party to the said indenture." This enactment was limited to estates or interests in, and to conditions or covenants respecting, real property.[32] It was held to be further limited, in the case of covenants, to those which ran with the land.[33]

Section 5 of the 1845 Act was replaced by section 56 of the Law of Property Act 1925, subsection (1) of which provides: "A person may take an immediate or other interest in land or other property, or the benefit of any condition, right of entry, covenant or agreement over or respecting land or other property, although he may not be named as a party to the conveyance or other instrument." The 1925 Act further defines "property" to include "any thing in action."[34] In *Beswick* v. *Beswick* Lord Denning M.R. and Danckwerts L.J. held that a promise in writing by A to B to pay a sum of money to C would, by virtue of this definition of "property," be within section 56(1) and so give C a right to sue A.[35] In their view, section 56(1) was a "clear" provision to this effect, doing away with the doctrine of privity where the contract is written. But the words "although he may not be *named as a party*" are far from clear. They could refer to a number of things: to a party who is not named but only described; to a person who is named but not as a party; and to a person who is neither named nor a party[36] (*e.g.* where A promises B to pay a pension "to any servant of yours who is injured at work"). The House of Lords in *Beswick* v. *Beswick*

---

[28] *Cooker* v. *Child* (1673) 2 Lev. 74; *Chelsea & Waltham Green Building Soc.* v. *Armstrong* [1951] Ch. 853.

[29] *Sunderland Marine Insurance Co.* v. *Kearney* (1851) 16 Q.B. 925; qualifying *Green* v. *Horn* (1694) 1 Salk. 197. The old rule relating to indentures *inter partes* appears still to apply to deeds *inter partes* in cases falling outside s.56(1) of the Law of Property Act 1925; see *Beswick* v. *Beswick* [1968] A.C. 58, 104.

[30] Law of Property Act 1925, s.56(2).

[31] Replacing s.11 of the Land Transfer Act 1844, which was not restricted to real property. For the history of this change, see Davidson's *Concise Precedents in Conveyancing* (2nd ed., 1845), pp. 10 *et seq.*; Treitel, 30 M.L.R. 687, 688–689.

[32] *Beswick* v. *Beswick* [1968] A.C. 58, 87, 104.

[33] *Forster* v. *Elvett Colliery Co. Ltd.* [1908] 1 K.B. 629 (in the House of Lords, Lord Macnaghten reserved the point: *Dyson* v. *Forster* [1909] A.C. 98, 102); *Grant* v. *Edmonton* [1931] 1 Ch. 1.

[34] s.205(1)

[35] [1966] Ch. 538; see also *Smith and Snipes Hall Farm Ltd.* v. *River Douglas Catchment Board Ltd.* [1949] 2 K.B. 500 and *Drive Yourself Hire Co. (London) Ltd.* v. *Strutt* [1954] 1 Q.B. 250; criticised on this point by Wade [1954] C.L.J. 66.

[36] *Cf.* the side-note to s.56: "Persons taking who are not parties."

rejected the view of Lord Denning M.R. and Danckwerts L.J., principally on the ground that the definition of "property" in the Act was stated to apply "unless the context otherwise requires." The context in section 56(1) did otherwise require, since section 56(1) was part of a consolidating Act and was designed to reproduce section 5 of the 1845 Act, which admittedly did not have the wide effect suggested for section 56(1).[37] There was, moreover, nothing in the legislative history of section 56(1) to support the view that the subsection was intended to abolish the doctrine of privity in relation to written contracts.[38]

Section 56(1) therefore does not apply to a bare promise in writing by A to B to pay a sum of money to C; and the correctness of a number of previous decisions to this effect[39] is reaffirmed by *Beswick* v. *Beswick*. But the question, to what other cases the subsection does apply, remains one of great difficulty. There is support in *Beswick* v. *Beswick* for four limitations on its scope: namely, that it applies only (1) to real property[40] (2) to covenants running with the land[41]; (3) to cases where the instrument is not merely for the benefit of the third party but purports to contain a grant to or covenant with him[42]; and (4) to deeds strictly *inter partes*.[43] But there is no clear majority in the speeches in favour of all, some or even one of these limitations, so that the scope of the subsection remains obscure. There appear to be only two cases in which section 56(1) has actually been applied. The first[44] is consistent with all four of the above limitations, while the second[45] is consistent only with the last two. The third limitation was regarded as the operative one in both these cases and also in a number of others in which the courts have refused to apply the subsection.[46] It seems probable that the subsection will be applied only where this limitation is satisfied. There is also much to be said on historical grounds for the fourth limitation, which is consistent with all the cases, though it does not form a ground of decision in any of them. The scope of section 56(1) is further limited by a rule which it was not necessary to consider in *Beswick* v. *Beswick*, namely, that a person cannot take the benefit of a covenant under the subsection unless he, or his predecessor in title, was in existence and identifiable in accordance with the terms of the instrument at the time when it was made.[47]

---

[37] [1968] A.C. 58, 77, 81, 87.

[38] [1968] A.C. 58, 77, 81, 104; *cf.* Treitel, 29 M.L.R. 657, 661.

[39] *Re Sinclair's Life Policy* [1938] Ch. 799 (criticised on another ground in *Beswick* v. *Beswick* [1968] A.C. 58; *ante,* p. 536, n. 18; *Re Foster* [1938] 3 All E.R. 357; *Re Miller's Agreement* [1947] Ch. 615.

[40] See [1968] A.C. pp. 87 and 76; contrast p. 105 See also *Southern Water Authority* v. *Carey* [1985] 2 All E.R. 1077, 1083.

[41] See [1968] A.C. p. 87; contrast pp. 77, 93, 105.

[42] See [1968] A.C. pp. 94, 106; *cf.* pp. 74–75 and 87.

[43] See [1968] A.C. pp. 107 and 94; *cf.* pp. 76–77. See *ante*, p. 572.

[44] *Re Ecclesiastical Commissioners' Conveyance* [1936] Ch. 430; *cf. Re Windle* [1975] 1 W.L.R. 1628, 1631.

[45] *Stromdale and Ball Ltd.* v. *Burden* [1952] Ch. 223.

[46] See the cases cited in n. 39, *supra*; *White* v. *Bijou Mansions* [1937] Ch. 610, affirmed [1938] Ch. 351; *Lyus* v. *Prowsa Developments Ltd.* [1982] 1 W.L.R. 1044, 1049.

[47] *Kelsey* v. *Dodd* (1883) 52 L.J.Ch. 34; *Westhoughton U.D.C.* v. *Wigan Coal Co.* [1919] 1 Ch. 159 (both these cases were decided under s.5 of the Real Property Act 1845, but the position under s.56(1) of the 1925 Act seems to be the same); *White* v. *Bijou Mansions, supra.*

SECTION 6. PROPOSAL FOR REFORM

The rule that no one except a party to a contract can be made liable under it is generally regarded as just and sensible.[48] But the rule that no one except a party to a contract can enforce it may cause inconvenience where it prevents the person most interested in enforcing the contract from doing so.[49] The many exceptions to the doctrine make it tolerable in practice, but they have provoked the question whether it would not be better further to modify the doctrine, or to abolish it altogether.

In 1937 the Law Revision Committee recommended[50] that "Where a contract by its express terms purports to confer a benefit directly on a third party it shall be enforceable by the third party in his own name subject to any defences that would have been valid between the contracting parties." To meet the objection that this might unreasonably restrict the freedom of the contracting parties to vary the contract, the Committee added that "Unless the contract otherwise provides it may be cancelled by the mutual consent of the contracting parties before the third party has adopted it either expressly or by conduct."

In some situations this is clearly a desirable reform. Suppose that A for a consideration provided by B promises B to pay a sum of money to X who agrees with B to accept the money in satisfaction of a debt owed to him by B. In such a case there is probably consideration moving from X[51]; and refusal to allow X to sue A would merely force the parties to resort to a more clumsy procedure to enforce the contract: either B could sue A for specific performance in favour of X; or (if that remedy was not available) X could sue B for the debt and B could then sue A for damages for breach of contract, or for restitution. It would be better to allow X simply to sue A.[52] But where X is a gratuitous beneficiary he has, under the present law, no remedy in his own right, and the problem is whether he should have such a remedy. The doctrine of privity is closely connected with the doctrine of consideration[53]; and it is not at first sight easy to see why a gratuitous third party beneficiary should be better off than a gratuitous promisee. One possible answer to this objection is that such a beneficiary is in a position analogous to that of a gratuitous assignee, who generally does have enforceable rights.[54] But the Law Revision Committee do not treat the third party beneficiary like an assignee[55]: in particular, he can be deprived of his rights by cancellation of the contract before he has "adopted" it. It is not clear just what this means; and it might be more satisfactory to say that

---

[48] *Ante*, p. 528. The rule that the contract cannot, in other respects, bind a third party can, however, be inconvenient in cases involving exemption clauses: *ante*, p. 558.

[49] *e.g. Dunlop Pneumatic Tyre Co. Ltd.* v. *Selfridge & Co. Ltd.* [1915] A.C. 847; *ante*, p. 568.

[50] 6th Interim Report (Cmnd. 5449), Section D; for a partial adoption of these recommendations in the Republic of Ireland, see Dowrick, 21 M.L.R. 98. For a more elaborate legislative reform, see the New Zealand Contract (Privity) Act 1982.

[51] In the shape of an actual forbearance to sue B: *ante*, p. 84. In *Price* v. *Easton* (1833) 4 B. & Ad. 433 Lord Denman C.J. objected that no consideration moved from X to A, but it is now settled that consideration need not move *to the promisor*.

[52] The suggestion that the "creditor beneficiary" should have a right of action is not new: see *Bourne* v. *Mason* (1670) Ventr. 6. For a suggested extension of a similar notion to "network" contracts, see Adams and Brownsword, 10 Legal Studies, 12.

[53] *Ante*, p. 528.

[54] *Post*, pp. 587–592.

[55] An assignment must be communicated to the assignee (*post*, p. 583) but he need not "adopt" the assignment.

the contracting parties' right to cancel the contract should cease when the third party has acted in reliance on the contract so as to prejudice his position in some way.[56] A second possible argument is that, if value has been given by the promisee, the promisor should be made to perform in accordance with his promise; and the best way of ensuring that he does so perform is to allow the third party to sue him. This may be true when no one has any interest in the matter except promisor, promisee and third party; but many of the litigated cases seem to have come to court mainly because of the tensions caused by some outside interest—for example the interest of the creditors or estate of the promisee.[57] A solution which may seem satisfactory between promisor, promisee and third party can be much less satisfactory when such outside interests are brought into the picture. It is by no means obvious that a third party who has not given value should be entitled to the benefit of a promise bought with money which might otherwise have been available to pay the promisee's creditors.[58]

On the other hand the Law Revision Committee's proposal can be criticised on the ground that, in some ways, it does not go far enough. There are at least some cases in which it is arguable that the third party's rights should not be subject to the contracting parties' right of cancellation.[59] And it is unlikely that the recommendation, as it stands, affects the law as to exemption clauses and third parties, which is certainly in need of clarification.[60] The problem of third party beneficiaries is, in short, a very complex one and it is submitted that no simple formula can provide an adequate solution.

---

[56] *Cf.* the Committee's similar recommendation with regard to consideration: *ante*, p. 148.

[57] *e.g. Re Flavell* (1883) 25 Ch.D. 89; *Re Schebsman* [1944] Ch. 83.

[58] Insolvency Act 1986, s.339 only provides a partial answer to this objection: see especially s.341(2).

[59] *e.g.* where an insurance policy is taken out for the benefit of a third party should he at least receive *notice* of cancellation?

[60] *Ante*, pp. 552–561.

Chapter Sixteen

ASSIGNMENT[1]

The benefit of a contract may be transferred to a third party by a process called assignment. This is a transaction between the person entitled to the benefit of the contract (called the creditor or assignor) and the third party (called the assignee) as a result of which the assignee becomes entitled to sue the person liable under the contract (called the debtor). The debtor is not a party to the transaction and his consent is not necessary for its validity.

SECTION 1. AT COMMON LAW

The common law refused to give effect to assignments of "choses in action," that is, of rights which could only be asserted by bringing an action and not by taking possession of a physical thing. The early lawyers found it hard to think of a transfer of something intangible like a contractual right.[2] Later the rule was based on the fear that assignments of choses in action might lead to maintenance,[3] that is, to "intermeddling in litigation in which the intermeddler has no concern."[4] Such conduct was formerly a crime and a tort.[5]

Exceptionally, debts due to and by the Crown[6] and negotiable instruments[7] could be assigned at law. The common law also recognised that assignments were effective in equity: thus a promise by the assignee not to sue the debtor was good consideration for a promise by the debtor to pay the assignee.[8] And although an assignment did not at law entitle the assignee to sue the debtor, it might be binding as a contract between assignor and assignee, for breach of which the assignee could recover damages.[9]

The common law did enforce three kinds of transactions which to some extent did the work of assignment.

---

[1] Marshall, *The Assignments of Choses in Action*; Bailey, 47 L.Q.R. 526; 48 L.Q.R. 248, 547.

[2] Pollock and Maitland, *History of English Law,* Vol. II, p. 226.

[3] *Johnson* v. *Collings* (1880) 1 East 98; *Wilson* v. *Coupland* (1821) 5 B. & Ald. 228, 232; *Liversidge* v. *Broadbent* (1859) 4 H. & N. 603; *Fitzroy* v. *Cave* [1905] 2 K.B. 364, 372.

[4] *Neville* v. *London Express Newspaper Ltd.* [1919] A.C. 368, 385.

[5] Criminal and tortious liability for maintenance were abolished by Criminal Law Act 1967, ss.13(1) and 14(1), but this has (in general) no effect on the validity of contracts: see s.14(2) and p. 379, *ante*. s.14(2). For possible effects on the validity of certain assignments, see *post,* pp. 598 *et seq*.

[6] *Miles* v. *Williams* (1714) 1 P.Wms. 249, 259.

[7] *Ryall* v. *Rowles* (1750) 1 Ves.Sen. 348.

[8] *Forth* v. *Stanton* (1681) 1 Wms.Saund. 210; *cf. Moulsdale* v. *Birchall* (1772) 2 W.Bl. 820; *Master* v. *Miller* (1791) 4 T.R. 320, 341 (for another explanation, see *Israel* v. *Douglas* (1789) 1 H.Bl. 239). For other instances of recognition of assignment at common law, see *Winch* v. *Keely* (1787) 1 T.R. 619; *Legh* v. *Legh* (1799) 1 B. & P. 447; *Carpenter* v. *Marnell* (1802) 3 B. & P. 40; *Crowfoot* v. *Gurney* (1832) 9 Bing. 372.

[9] *Gerrard* v. *Lewis* (1867) L.R. 2 C.P. 305.

1. Novation[10]

Novation is a contract between debtor, creditor and a third party that the debt owed by the debtor shall henceforth be owed to the third party. This is not assignment because the consent of all three parties,[11] including that of the debtor, is necessary, and because the original debt is not, strictly, transferred. The third party's right against the debtor is based on the new contract between him and the debtor.[12] Thus the third party will fail if no consideration moves from him for the debtor's promise to pay him.[13]

2. Acknowledgment[14]

If a creditor asks his debtor to pay a third party, and the debtor agrees to do so, and notifies the third party of his agreement, then the third party may be entitled to sue the debtor.[15] It was for long doubtful whether such a transaction had to be supported by consideration. In the second half of the nineteenth century, the following distinction was established: that consideration was, in general, necessary; but that it was not necessary where the debtor actually had in his hands (*e.g.* as banker) a fund belonging to the creditor.[16] But this distinction, which seems to have little merit, was disregarded in the more recent case of *Shamia* v. *Joory.*[17] The defendant owed some £1,200 to his agent Youssuf, who asked him to pay £500 of this to the plaintiff, Youssuf's brother. The defendant agreed to pay the plaintiff and notified the plaintiff of this. It was held that the plaintiff could sue the defendant for the £500, though no consideration moved from him. If this decision is right,[18] acknowledgment is in one respect more advantageous than assignment, since certain types of assignment have to be supported by consideration.[19] On the other hand, it is less advantageous than assignment in that it requires the consent of the debtor.

3. Power of Attorney

A creditor can give a third party a power of attorney, authorising him to sue for the debt in the creditor's name, without any liability to account to creditor. But this device had many disadvantages from the third party's point of view. The most important of these was that a power of attorney could generally be revoked by the creditor, and was often revoked automatically by his death.[20]

---

[10] Ames, *Lectures,* p. 298.
[11] See *The Aktion* [1987] 1 Lloyd's Rep. 283, 309.
[12] *e.g. Rasbora Ltd.* v. *J.C.L. Marine Ltd.* [1977] 1 Lloyd's Rep. 645.
[13] *Tatlock* v. *Harris* (1789) 3 T.R. 174, 180; *Cuxon* v. *Chadley* (1824) 3 B. & C. 591; *Wharton* v. *Walker* (1825) 4 B. & C. 163.
[14] Davies, 75 L.Q.R. 220; *cf.* Yates, 41 Conv. 49.
[15] *Wilson* v. *Coupland* (1821) 5 B. & Ald. 228; *Hamilton* v. *Spottiswoode* (1842) 4 Ex. 200; *Griffin* v. *Weatherby* (1868) L.R. 3 Q.B. 753.
[16] *Liversidge* v. *Broadbent* (1859) 4 H. & N. 603, 612.
[17] [1958] 1 Q.B. 448.
[18] For criticism, see Goff and Jones, *The Law of Restitution,* (3rd ed.), pp. 518–521.
[19] *Post,* pp. 585 *et seq.*
[20] *Post,* p. 651.

SECTION 2. EQUITABLE ASSIGNMENTS

Equity regarded the common law's fear of maintenance as unrealistic[21] and took the view that choses in action were property[22] which ought, in the interest of commercial convenience, to be transferable, *e.g.* to provide security for a loan. Choses in action were therefore assignable in equity.[23] The precise machinery used for enforcing such assignments varied with the nature of the chose in action, which might be legal or equitable. A legal chose is one which could only be sued for in a common law court, *e.g.* a contract debt. An equitable chose is one which could only be sued for in the Court of Chancery, *e.g.* an interest in a trust fund.

1. Legal Choses

There were four reasons why equity could not simply allow the assignee of a legal chose to sue the debtor in the Court of Chancery. First, equity did not in general enforce purely legal debts. Secondly, the debtor might suffer hardship if he were later sued for a second payment at common law by the original creditor (the assignor): he would have to take separate proceedings in Chancery to make good his defence. Thirdly, the assignor might retain some interest in the debt, *e.g.* he might only assign part of it: in such a case, it was desirable to have him before the court, so that the relative rights of all the parties could be determined in a single action. Fourthly, the assignor might wish to dispute the validity of the assignment: this possibility again made it desirable to have him before the court at some stage.

The machinery devised for solving these difficulties was to allow the assignee to sue the debtor at common law in the name of the assignor. If the assignor refused to cooperate, equity could compel him to do so. In the resulting proceedings in Chancery, the rights of the assignor could be adequately safeguarded. Now that common law and equity are administered in the same courts, the first two reasons[24] for the original method of enforcing equitable assignments are of purely historical interest, but the third and fourth reasons may still apply and sometimes make it important to have all the parties before the court.[25] But the action against the debtor need no longer be brought in the name of the assignor[26]: he is simply joined as co-plaintiff if he is willing to co-operate with the assignee, and as co-defendant if he is not, *i.e.* if he wishes to dispute the validity of the assignment. The machinery of joining the assignor as a party to the action may, however, break down if the assignor has ceased to exist, *e.g.* if the assignor is a company which has been dissolved.[27] Where the assignor is a natural person

---

[21] *Wright* v. *Wright* (1750) 1 Ves.Sen. 409, 411, ("very refined").

[22] *Cf. Alloway* v. *Phillips* (*Inspector of Taxes*) [1980] 1 W.L.R. 888, 893.

[23] *Crouch* v. *Martin* (1707) 2 Vern. 595; *Row* v. *Dawson* (1749) 1 Ves.Sen. 331; *Ryall* v. *Rowles* (1750) 1 Ves.Sen. 348; *Ex p. South* (1818) 3 Swanst. 392.

[24] *i.e.* of those stated in the preceding paragraph.

[25] *The Aiolos* [1983] 2 Lloyd's Rep. 25, 33.

[26] *Weddell* v. *J. A. Pearce & Major* [1988] Ch. 26, 40.

[27] See *M. H. Smith* (*Plant Hire*) *Ltd.* v. *D. L. Mainwaring* (*T/A Onshore*) *Ltd.* [1986] 2 Lloyd's Rep. 244, where subrogation (*post*, p. 599, n. 93) was said at p. 246 in this respect to resemble equitable assignment.

and has died, it would seem to be possible for the assignee to sue, joining the assignor's legal personal representatives.

2. Equitable Choses

The assignee of an equitable chose could in his own name sue the trustee in the Court of Chancery.[28] The chose being equitable, the trustee was not exposed to the danger of a subsequent action in a different (common law) court by the assignor. It was only necessary to make the assignor a party to the proceedings if he retained some interest in the subject-matter. If he wished to dispute the validity of the assignment, he could take separate proceedings for that purpose.[29]

SECTION 3. STATUTORY ASSIGNMENTS

Certain specific contracts, such as life and marine insurance policies and bills of lading, were made assignable by statute during the nineteenth century.[30] A more general provision was made by the Judicature Act 1873, which fused the courts of common law and equity, and so made obsolete some of the reasons for the original machinery for enforcing equitable assignments of legal choses. There was no longer any difficulty in allowing the assignee to sue in any Division of the High Court; and a debtor who was successfully sued by the assignee no longer had to take separate proceedings if he were sued again by the assignor: he could simply rely on his payment to the assignee as a defence in the second action. Thus it was no longer necessary to have the assignor before the court unless he retained an interest in the subject-matter or wished to dispute the validity of the assignment.

Section 136(1) of the Law of Property Act 1925 (re-enacting section 25(6) of the Judicature Act 1873), therefore provides that an absolute assignment by writing under the hand of the assignor (not purporting to be by way of charge only) of any debt or other legal thing in action, of which express notice in writing has been given to the debtor or trustee, is effectual in law to pass the legal right to the debt or thing in action to the assignee. The effect of such an assignment is to enable the assignee to sue the debtor in his own name, and to sue alone, *i.e.*, without joining the assignor as a party to the action. The subsection finally makes provision for enabling the assignor to dispute the validity of the assignment; if he does so, the debtor can drop out of the proceedings and leave the dispute to be fought out between assignor and assignee.

1. Absolute Assignment

The assignee can only sue alone if the assignment is *absolute*; this excludes cases in which the assignor retains an interest in the subject-matter so that

---

[28] *Cator* v. *Croydon Canal Co.* (1841) 4 Y. & C.Ex. 405, 593; *Donaldson* v. *Donaldson* (1854) Kay 711.

[29] *e.g. Bridge* v. *Bridge* (1852) 16 Beav. 315.

[30] *e.g.* Bills of Lading Act 1855, s.1; Policies of Assurance Act 1867 (life insurance); Marine Insurance Act 1868 (see now 1906 Act, s.50(1)).

it is still desirable to have him before the court. Absolute assignments should from this point of view be contrasted with the following:

(1) Assignments by way of charge

In *Durham Bros.* v. *Robertson*[31] a builder to whom £1,080 was due under a building contract borrowed money and assigned the £1,080 to the lender as security for the loan "until the money [lent] . . . be repaid." This was held to be an assignment by way of charge. The builder had not assigned the £1,080 absolutely to the lender, but had only charged that sum with the repayment of the money he had borrowed. But an assignment may be absolute although it is only made by way of mortgage, and does not transfer the subject-matter out-and-out. Thus in *Tancred* v. *Delagoa Bay, etc., Ry.*[32] a debt was assigned as security for a loan of money, with the proviso that if the assignor repaid the loan, the debt should be reassigned to him. This was held to be an absolute assignment.

The distinction between these two cases can best be understood by taking the point of view of the debtor, and assuming that he wants to pay the debt. In *Tancred's* case, he can find out from documents in his own possession whether he ought to pay the assignor or the assignee; for even if the debt is reassigned to the assignor, the debtor can safely pay the assignee until he gets notice of the reassignment.[33] But in *Durham Bros.* v. *Robertson* the debtor does not know whether to pay the assignee until it is settled whether the assignor still owes anything to the assignee. The debtor cannot find this out from documents in his own possession: he would have to investigate the state of accounts between the assignor and assignee. Similarly, if the assignee sued the debtor, the court could not determine whom the debtor should pay without investigating the state of accounts between assignor and assignee; and it cannot satisfactorily do this if the assignor is not before the court. For similar reasons, an assignment of a debt to a bank was held to be by way of charge only where it was expressed to be made as security for a loan and was to become operative only on the assignor's failing to perform his obligations under the original contract which had given rise to the debt or under the loan agreement with the bank.[34]

In *Bank of Liverpool* v. *Holland*[35] a creditor assigned a debt of £285 to a bank "to hold the same absolutely. And it is hereby agreed and declared that the amount recoverable by these presents shall not at any time exceed" £150. This was held to be an absolute assignment of the whole debt, with the proviso that, if the bank recovered more than £150, it was to hold the excess on trust for the assignor. This part of the arrangement did not concern the debtor: he could get a good discharge by paying the bank at any time.

---

[31] [1898] 1 Q.B. 765; *cf. Jones* v. *Humphreys* [1902] 1 K.B. 10; *Mercantile Bank of London Ltd.* v. *Evans* [1899] 2 Q.B. 613.

[32] (1889) 23 Q.B.D. 239; *cf. Hughes* v. *Pump House Hotel Co. Ltd.* [1902] 2 K.B. 190; *The Cebu* [1983] Q.B. 1005, 1016 (where nothing seems to have turned on the distinction between equitable and statutory assignments).

[33] *Post*, p. 585.

[34] *The Halcyon The Great* [1984] 1 Lloyd's Rep. 283.

[35] (1926) 43 T.L.R. 29, *cf. Comfort* v. *Betts* [1891] 1 Q.B. 737; *Fitzroy* v. *Cave* [1905] 2 K.B. 364; *Ramsay* v. *Hartley* [1977] 1 W.L.R. 686.

(2) Assignments of part of a debt

An assignment of part of a debt (*e.g.* of £500 out of the £1,000 which X owes me; or of half of what X owes me) is not absolute.[36] In such a case a debtor who wants to pay may know perfectly well how much to pay to whom. But to hold such an assignment absolute might cause hardship to a debtor who wished to dispute the debt. If the assignment were absolute, the assignee would be able to sue alone. In this action, the debtor might be able to show that there was no debt. But he would have to prove this over again if he were later sued by the assignor for the balance of the alleged debt. And if the assignor split the debt up into a large number of small parts, the debtor might have to defend many actions arising out of the same transaction. Hence it is necessary, for the protection of the debtor, to have all the interested parties before the court. For the same reason, an assign*or* of part of a debt cannot sue for the part he retains without joining the assignee as a party to the action.[37]

The above reasoning does not apply to an assignment of the *balance* of a debt. Suppose A owes B £100 and pays off £25 of the debt. An assignment of the remaining £75 would be absolute as it would be an assignment of B's entire remaining interest in the debt.[38]

(3) Conditional assignments

Section 136(1) of the Law of Property Act 1925, contrasts absolute assignments with assignments by way of charge; but some judgments also distinguish between absolute and conditional assignments.[39] Many assignments by way of charge are, in fact, assignments subject to the condition subsequent that they will determine when the assignor pays off the debt which he owes to the assignee. Assignments which are subject to some other condition (whether precedent or subsequent) should be treated in the same way.[40] Whatever the condition may be, the assignor retains a contingent interest in the debt, and is thus a desirable party to an action to recover it. Suppose that A assigns rent due under a lease "to my daughter until she marries." The assignment should not be absolute since it is desirable that A should be a party to an action brought by his daughter against the tenant for rent. If the daughter could sue without A, she might be able to prove that she was unmarried, and so entitled to the rent. But this would not prevent A, in a subsequent action against the tenant, from proving that the court in the first action had made a mistake in finding that the daughter was unmarried, so that the tenant would have to pay over again. What matters to the tenant is not whether the daughter is married but that the question should be decided, one way or the other, so as to bind both A and the daughter.[41]

---

[36] *Forster* v. *Baker* [1910] 2 K.B. 636; *Re Steel Wing Co.* [1921] 1 Ch. 349; *Williams* v. *Atlantic Assurance Co. Ltd.* [1933] 1 K.B. 81 at p. 100 (the actual decision seems to turn on Marine Insurance Act 1906, s.50(2)).

[37] *Walter & Sullivan Ltd.* v. *J. Murphy & Sons Ltd.* [1955] 2 Q.B. 584.

[38] *e.g. Harding* v. *Harding* (1886) 17 Q.B.D. 442.

[39] *e.g. Durham Bros.* v. *Robertson* [1898] 1 Q.B. 765, 773; *cf. The Balder London* [1980] 2 Lloyd's Rep. 489, 495.

[40] *e.g. The Halcyon The Great* [1984] 1 Lloyd's Rep. 283.

[41] *Cf. The Aiolos* [1983] 2 Lloyd's Rep. 25, 33.

2. Debt or Other Legal Thing in Action

A "debt" in section 136(1) is a sum certain due under contract or otherwise.[42] The phrase "other legal thing in action" has been broadly interpreted: it means any "debt or right which the common law looks on as not assignable by reason of its being a chose in action, but which a court of equity deals with as being assignable."[43] The phrase includes equitable choses in action,[44] though this point is of little practical importance since an assignment of an equitable chose is no more effective under the statute than it is in equity. The phrase also includes a debt not yet due but accruing due,[45] and the benefit of an obligation to do something other than to pay cash,[46] or to forbear from doing something.[47] It does not include choses in action which can only be transferred by complying with some other statute; thus shares in a company cannot be assigned by statutory assignment under section 136, but only in the manner prescribed by the articles of association of the company.[48]

SECTION 4. GENERAL REQUIREMENTS

1. Formalities

A statutory assignment must be "by writing under the hand of the assignor." An assignment which for some reason fails to take effect as a statutory assignment may still be a good equitable assignment. Thus although an oral assignment cannot take effect under the statute, it may be valid in equity.[49] The statute merely provides an alternative method of making assignments; it does not destroy the old method.

Any disposition of an equitable interest "must be in writing signed by the person disposing of the same or by his agent thereunto lawfully authorised."[50] This rule is mandatory: an oral assignment of an equitable chose is therefore void.[51]

As a general rule, writing is not necessary for an equitable assignment of a legal chose in action. But a contract may provide that rights under it shall only be assigned by use of a certain form, such as writing. An attempt to assign such rights without using the stipulated form is probably not effective as an assignment, though it may amount to a contract to assign.[52]

---

[42] *e.g.* under statute: *Dawson* v. *Great Northern & City Ry.* [1905] 1 K.B. 260.

[43] *Torkington* v. *Magee* [1902] 2 K.B. 427, 430 (actual decision reversed on another ground: [1903] 1 K.B. 644); *cf. King* v. *Victoria Insurance Co.* [1896] A.C. 250, 254; *Manchester Brewery* v. *Coombs* [1901] 2 Ch. 608, 619.

[44] *Re Pain* [1919] 1 Ch. 38, 44.

[45] *Brice* v. *Bannister* (1878) 3 Q.B.D. 569, 574; *Walker* v. *Bradford Old Bank* (1884) 12 Q.B.D. 511; *Re Green* [1979] 1 W.L.R. 1211, 1219–1224. Contrast *Law* v. *Coburn* [1972] 1 W.L.R. 1238, where the date on which the debt became due was crucial under the relevant legislation.

[46] *Torkington* v. *Magee, supra.*

[47] *Jacoby* v. *Whitmore* (1883) 49 L.T. 335.

[48] Companies Act 1985, s.182(1).

[49] *Cf. post,* pp. 585, 591.

[50] Law of Property Act 1925, s.53(1)(*c*), formerly Statute of Frauds 1677, s.9. The enactment applies to all "dispositions," whether they are assignments or not. But it does not apply to a transfer of the legal title which is intended to operate as a transfer of the equitable interest, even though before the transfer the legal title and the equitable interest were in different hands; *Vandervell* v. *I.R.C.* [1967] 2 A.C. 291; Strauss, 30 M.L.R. 461; Green, 47 M.L.R. 385. As to joinder of documents, see *ante,* p. 169.

[51] *Oughtred* v. *I.R.C.* [1960] A.C. 206; *cf. Grey* v. *I.R.C.* [1960] A.C. 1.

[52] *Cf. post,* p. 586.

For the protection of the assignor's creditors, provision has been made by various statutes for the registration of certain assignments. Section 344 of the Insolvency Act 1986,[53] for example, requires general assignments of book debts (or any class of them) made by a person engaged in any business to be registered; if they are not registered they are void as against the trustee in bankruptcy to the extent specified in the section.

2. Intention to Assign

Although assignments must sometimes be in writing, no particular formula has to be used to effect an assignment. The document need not on its face purport to be an assignment. As Lord Macnaghten said in *William Brandt's Sons & Co.* v. *Dunlop Rubber Co.*[54] "An equitable assignment does not always take that form. It may be addressed to the debtor. It may be couched in the language of command. It may be a courteous request. It may assume the form of mere permission. The language is immaterial if the meaning is plain. All that is necessary is that the debtor should be given to understand that the debt has been made over by the creditor to some third person."[55]

A creditor does not necessarily assign a debt by asking his debtor to pay a third party. The request may be intended only as a mandate (or instruction) to the debtor to pay the third party.[56] Such a mandate does not give the third party any rights against the debtor, and can be revoked by the creditor. Similarly, a person who draws a cheque on his bank in favour of a third person does not thereby assign part of his bank balance.[57] The bank is not liable to the third party, though if it fails to pay him it may be liable in damages to its own customer.

3. Communication to Assignee

An assignment has no effect unless it is communicated[58] to the assignee by the assignor, or by someone with his authority[59]; or unless it is made in pursuance of a prior agreement between assignor and assignee. The reason for the requirement is not immediately obvious since a person can have property transferred to him without his knowledge, subject to a right to repudiate the transfer when he becomes aware of it.[60] One possible reason for the requirement is that communication to the assignee is evidence of intention to assign[61]; but such an intention could equally well be proved by

---

[53] See also Companies Act 1985, ss.395, 396.

[54] [1905] A.C. 454.

[55] At p. 462. *Cf.* also *Spellman* v. *Spellman* [1961] 1 W.L.R. 921; *Palmer* v. *Carey* [1926] A.C. 703; *The Kelo* [1985] 2 Lloyd's Rep. 85; and see *Swiss Bank Corp.* v. *Lloyd's Bank Ltd.* [1982] A.C. 584, 613 and *Kijowski* v. *New Capital Properties* (1990) 15 Con.L.R. 1 (where there was no assignment).

[56] *Ex p. Hall* (1878) 10 Ch.D. 615; *cf. Re Williams* [1917] 1 Ch. 1; *Timpson's Executors* v. *Yerbury* [1936] 1 K.B. 645; *Dalton* v. *I.R.C.* [1958] T.R. 45. For a similar distinction between a contract for the benefit of a third party and a mandate to pay a third party, see *ante*, p. 536.

[57] Bills of Exchange Act 1882, s.53(1); *Schroeder* v. *Central Bank of London Ltd.* (1876) 34 L.T. 735. Thus if an account is overdrawn the bank is not concerned with the question of priorities between competing payees.

[58] According to *Alexander* v. *Steinhardt, Walker & Co.* [1903] 2 K.B. 208 posting is sufficient communication, but that case was doubted in *Timpson's Executors* v. *Yerbury* [1936] 1 K.B. 645, 657.

[59] *e.g.* by the debtor: *Burn* v. *Carvalho* (1839) 4 My. & Cr. 690.

[60] *Standing* v. *Bowring* (1885) 31 Ch.D. 282.

[61] See *Re Hamilton* (1921) 124 L.T. 737.

other evidence. Alternatively, communication to the assignee may be regarded as the equivalent of the delivery which is necessary to perfect a gift of a chattel made otherwise than by deed.[62] A final possible explanation of the requirement is that it is based on the nature of assignment as a transaction between assignor and assignee.

4. Notice to Debtor

(1) How to give notice

Notice of an equitable assignment may be oral,[63] but if the chose assigned is equitable, oral notice will seldom be effective between successive assignees.[64] Notice of a statutory assignment must be in writing.[65] It need not be given by the assignor, nor at the time of the assignment: it may be given by the assignee and is effective so long as it is given before action brought.[66] No particular form of words is necessary[67]; but the notice must clearly and unconditionally[68] tell the debtor to pay a third party *as assignee*, and not merely as agent for the creditor.[69] A notice which incorrectly states the date of the assignment or, it seems, the amount of the debt, is invalid.[70] But a notice which says nothing at all about these particulars appears to be valid, so long as it describes the debt with sufficient certainty. A notice is valid although it inaccurately states that another notice had been previously given.[71]

A notice sent through the post has been said to take effect when it is received by the debtor.[72] This is clearly right where a dispute arises between assignee and debtor, for it is unreasonable to make the debtor suffer for failing to act on a notice of which he is not yet aware. But where the dispute is between successive assignees, it is at least arguable that the first to post his notice should have priority over any other assignee who has not yet posted his notice (or otherwise communicated with the debtor) when the first notice was posted.[73]

(2) Effects of notice

Notice may affect the relative rights of assignor and assignee, of assignee and debtor, and of a number of successive assignees.

(a) BETWEEN ASSIGNOR AND ASSIGNEE. The rights of these parties may depend on whether the assignment is statutory[74]; and it can only have this character if notice is given.[75] If no notice is given, the assignment may still

[62] *Post*, p. 589.
[63] *Ex. p. Agra Bank* (1868) L.R. 3 Ch.App. 555.
[64] *Post*, p. 585.
[65] Law of Property Act 1925, s.136(1).
[66] *Walker* v. *Bradford Old Bank* (1884) 12 Q.B.D. 511; *Bateman* v. *Hunt* [1904] 2 K.B. 530; *Re Westerton* [1919] 2 Ch. 104; *Holt* v. *Heatherfield Trust Ltd.* [1942] 2 K.B. 1.
[67] *Smith* v. *SS. "Zigurds" Owners* [1934] A.C. 209.
[68] *The Balder London* [1980] 2 Lloyd's Rep. 489, 495.
[69] *James Talcott Ltd.* v. *John Lewis & Co. Ltd.* [1940] 3 All E.R. 592.
[70] *Stanley* v. *English Fibres Industries Ltd.* (1889) 68 L.J.Q.B. 839; *W. F. Harrison & Co. Ltd.* v. *Burke* [1956] 1 W.L.R. 419; criticised by R. E. M., 72 L.Q.R. 321.
[71] *Van Lynn Developments Ltd.* v. *Pelias Construction Ltd.* [1969] 1 Q.B. 607.
[72] *Holt* v. *Heatherfield Trust Ltd.* [1942] 2 K.B. 1, 6.
[73] *Holt* v. *Heatherfield Trust Ltd., supra,* is not inconsistent with this suggestion since the order in which the two claimants communicated with the debtor is not stated in the report.
[74] *Post*, p. 587.
[75] Law of Property Act 1925, s.136(1).

be effective in equity.[76] Notice to the debtor is not necessary to perfect the rights of an equitable assignee against the assignor.[77]

(b) BETWEEN ASSIGNEE AND DEBTOR. Notice is, however, necessary to perfect the title of an equitable assignee against the debtor,[78] since without such notice the debtor is entitled to assume that he remains liable to his original creditor (the assignor) and that he will get a good discharge by paying the assignor.[79] Notice may[80] also turn the assignment into a statutory assignment, in which case the debtor is liable to be sued by the assignee alone: he can no longer insist that the assignor be made a party to the action. Where the assignment is statutory, the debtor ceases, as soon as notice has been given, to be liable to the assignor[81] and becomes liable to the assignee. It is submitted that the same is true where the assignment is equitable; for it has been held that if the debtor in such a case ignores the notice and pays the assignor he is not discharged and will have to make a second payment to the assignee.[82]

(c) BETWEEN SUCCESSIVE ASSIGNEES. A chose in action may be successively assigned by an insolvent assignor to several persons for more than it is worth. It is then necessary to decide in what order the assignees are to be paid. The rule is that successive assignments taken in good faith rank in the order in which notice is given to the debtor. Thus a later assignee may gain priority over an earlier one by giving notice first.[83] Notice of the assignment of an equitable chose should be given in writing, since oral notice of an assignment of such a chose does not give priority over later assignees in good faith and for value.[84]

SECTION 5. CONSIDERATION[85]

The question whether an assignment must be supported by consideration is one of great complexity. Two points must be made to clear the ground for

---

[76] *Holt* v. *Heatherfield Trust Ltd.* [1942] 2 K.B. 1.

[77] *Gorringe* v. *Irwell India Rubber, etc., Works* (1886) 34 Ch.D. 128; *Re Trytel* [1952] 2 T.L.R. 32.

[78] *Warner Bros. Records Inc.* v. *Rollgreen Ltd.* [1976] Q.B. 430; Kloss, 39 Conv.(N.S.) 261.

[79] See *Stocks* v. *Dobson* (1853) 4 D.M. & G. 11.

[80] *i.e.* if the requirements of writing and of "absolute" assignment (*ante*, pp. 579–581), are satisfied.

[81] *Cottage Club Estates Ltd.* v. *Woodside Estates (Amersham) Ltd.* [1928] 2 Q.B. 463, 467; *The Halcyon The Great* [1984] 1 Lloyd's Rep. 283, 289.

[82] *Jones* v. *Farrell* (1857) 1 D. & J. 208; *Brice* v. *Bannister* (1878) 3 Q.B.D. 569 (where the assignment was equitable: see *Durham Bros.* v. *Robertson* [1898] 1 Q.B. 765, 774); *Ex p. Nicholls* (1883) 22 Ch.D. 782, 787. In view of these authorities it is hard to accept the suggestion in *Warner Bros. Records Inc.* v. *Rollgreen Ltd., supra,* at pp. 443, 445 that an equitable assignment (of a legal chose) only gives the assignee rights against the assignor but none against the debtor. The development outlined on p. 578, *ante* seems to have made obsolete any historical support that may once have existed for this view, which seems, with respect, to be based on failure to distinguish between the substantive rights arising in equity out of assignments and the procedure for their enforcement; or between assignments and agreements to assign.

[83] *Dearle* v. *Hall* (1828) 3 Russ. 1; *cf. Stocks* v. *Dobson* (1853) 4 D.M. & G. 11; *Mutual Life Assurance Society* v. *Langley* (1886) 32 Ch.D. 460; *Ellerman Lines Ltd.* v. *Lancaster Maritime Co. Ltd.* [1980] 2 Lloyd's Rep. 497, 503; *The Attika Hope* [1988] 1 Lloyd's Rep. 439, 441; *Pfeiffer Weinkellerei-Weineinkauf GmbH & Co.* v. *Arbuthnot Factors* [1988] 1 W.L.R. 150. See also Goode, 92 L.Q.R. 554–559; Donaldson, 93 L.Q.R. 324; Goode, *ibid.* 487.

[84] Law of Property Act 1925, s.137(3).

[85] Megarry, 59 L.Q.R. 58; Hollond, *ibid.* 129; Hall [1959] C.L.J. 99; Sheridan, 33 Can. Bar Rev. 284.

the discussion. First, the dispute only concerns the relative rights of assignor and assignee. The debtor cannot refuse to pay the assignee on the ground that the assignment was gratuitous[86]; he is liable to pay the debt in any event and his only interest is to see that all possible claimants are before the court, so that he does not run the risk of having to pay twice over. So long as this possibility of prejudice to the debtor is removed by the joinder of all appropriate parties, it is only the assignor who can raise an issue as to the validity of the assignment on the ground that no consideration was given for it; indeed the only purpose of taking the point is to enable the assignor to claim payment of the debt for himself. In practice this most frequently happens if the assignor has died or become bankrupt: his representatives may, for the benefit of his estate or of his creditors, wish to challenge the validity of the assignment. Secondly, the discussion concerns all gratuitous assignments, even those made by deed or for a nominal consideration.[87] The fact that an assignment is so made may make an assignor who disputes it liable in damages for breach of contract,[88] or make an agreement to assign binding contractually. But it does not, of itself, make the assignment effective as a transfer of the debt.

1. Assignments of Future Property

An assignment is the transfer of an existing right. There can be no assignment of rights which do not yet exist or belong to the assignor. Such rights are sometimes called "future property." An attempt to assign future property may operate as an agreement to assign which must be supported by consideration if it is to be binding.[89]

Money payable in the future under an existing contract is not necessarily future property, and a disposition of the right to receive such money may be an assignment and not an agreement to assign. If the contingency on which the money is payable is essentially within the control of the creditor, there is no difficulty in holding that the disposition is an assignment: thus a builder can assign instalments to become due to him under a building contract as the work progresses, for here the contingency on which the money will become due is simply his own performance.[90] If, however, the contingency is not within his control, the disposition is prima facie an agreement to assign: this would be the position where a person purported to assign future dividends in a company which was not under any obligation to him to declare any dividends.[91] But even where the rights of the assignor

[86] *Walker* v. *Bradford Old Bank* (1884) 12 Q.B.D. 511; the question of consideration may also be relevant for revenue purposes, but the question in cases of this kind is always whether the assignor could have denied the validity of the assignment, as against the assignee: *e.g. Re Rose* [1952] Ch. 499; *Letts* v. *I.R.C.* [1957] 1 W.L.R. 201; *Dalton* v. *I.R.C.* [1958] T.R. 45.

[87] *Kekewich* v. *Manning* (1851) 1 D.M. & G. 176 (deed); *Dillon* v. *Coppin* (1839) 4 My. & Cr. 647 (nominal consideration).

[88] *Gerrard* v. *Lewis* (1867) L.R. 2 C.P. 305; *Cannon* v. *Hartley* [1949] Ch. 213.

[89] *Tailby* v. *Official Receiver* (1888) 13 App.Cas. 523; *Glegg* v. *Bromley* [1912] 3 K.B. 474; *Cotton* v. *Heyl* [1930] 1 Ch. 510; *cf. Meek* v. *Kettlewell* (1843) 1 Ph. 342; *The Annangel Glory* [1988] 1 Lloyd's Rep. 45 (actual decision reversed by Companies Act 1985, s.396(2)(*g*), as substituted by Companies Act 1989, s.93); *The Attika Hope* [1988] 1 Lloyd's Rep. 439, 442 (where "*or* future chose" seems to be a misprint for "*of a* future chose"). *Cf. The Cebu (No. 2)* [1990] 2 Lloyd's Rep. 316 (where it was not necessary to distinguish between an assignment and an agreement to assign).

[90] *e.g. Hughes* v. *Pump House Hotel Co. Ltd.* [1902] 2 K.B. 190.

[91] *Norman* v. *Commissioner of Taxation* (1963) 109 C.L.R. 9.

depend on a contingency outside his control, he may purport to assign *either* his present right to future income from a specified source *or* the future income itself. A disposition of the first kind may be regarded as an assignment[92] and a disposition of the second kind as an agreement to assign.[93] The question into which category it falls turns on the construction of the document purporting to effect the disposition.

2. Statutory Assignments

A statutory assignment, whether of a legal or of an equitable chose in action, is effective although it is made without consideration.[94] The reasons for this rule are discussed below.[95]

3. Equitable Assignments

The effects of a "voluntary" equitable assignment (*i.e.* one which is not supported by consideration) must be discussed historically.

(1) Before the Judicature Act 1873

There are two main views as to the position in equity before 1873.

(a) PROCEDURAL VIEW. According to one view, the need for consideration depended on the procedure for enforcing the assignment. In *Re Westerton*[96] Sargant J. gave the following reason for holding that a statutory assignment was effective without consideration: "Apart from the Judicature Act . . . the want of consideration would have been fatal to [the assignee's] claim. Prior to the Judicature Act . . . a legal chose in action such as this debt could not be transferred at law, and the assignee of the debt could only have sued in the name of the assignor, and in the absence of consent . . . or of a binding contract by the assignor . . . the use of the assignor's name could only have been enforced by filing a bill in equity . . . and equity would not have granted that relief unless the assignment had been for valuable consideration."[97] Since a statutory assignee can now sue the debtor without the co-operation of the assignor, "there is no reason for continuing against the assignee those terms which were imposed by equity as a condition of granting relief."[98] In other words, consideration is necessary if the assignee needs the co-operation of the assignor to recover the debt, but is not necessary if the assignee does not need such co-operation. If this were true three things would follow.

First: consideration should not have been necessary in the rare cases in which the assignee could sue alone at law.[99] This assumption is to some extent supported by the rule that the voluntary transferee of a negotiable instrument could sue all the parties liable on it, except the transferor.[1] But

---

92 *Shepherd* v. *Commissioner of Taxation* [1966] A.L.R. 969.
93 *Williams* v. *Commissioner of Inland Revenue* [1965] N.Z.L.R. 395.
94 *Harding* v. *Harding* (1886) 17 Q.B.D. 442; *Re Westerton* [1919] 2 Ch. 104.
95 *Infra* after n. 97 and *post*, p. 589 at n. 11.
96 [1919] 2 Ch. 104.
97 At p. 111.
98 At p. 114.
99 *Ante*, p. 576.
1 *Easton* v. *Pratchett* (1835) 1 Cr.M. & R. 798, 808. Consideration is probably necessary for the transfer of contractual rights evidenced by a bill of lading: *Benjamin's Sale of Goods* (3rd ed.), § 1453.

this rule was based on commercial practice, and not on the fact that the transferee did not need the co-operation of the transferor. It is not clear whether assignments of debts due to and from the Crown had to be supported by consideration.

Secondly: consideration should not have been necessary for absolute assignments of equitable choses, since the assignee could sue without the co-operation of the assignor.[2] This assumption, too, is borne out by many cases in which such assignments were upheld, though they were voluntary. But in most of these cases the fact that the assignee could sue alone is not even mentioned, let alone relied on.[3] The decisions are based on the view that the assignor has made a completed gift.[4] And in some cases voluntary assignments of equitable choses were held invalid as incomplete gifts[5]; these are difficult to explain on the procedural view.

Thirdly: consideration should have been generally[6] necessary for the assignment of a legal chose, since the assignee could not sue the debtor without the co-operation of the assignor. Here the procedural view breaks down. Although some voluntary assignments of legal choses were held invalid, others were upheld.[7] The distinction between valid and invalid assignments was not based on procedural requirements. It depended on the question whether the assignor had made a completed gift.

(b) COMPLETED GIFT VIEW. A person may enter into a contract to dispose of his property, or make a gift of it, or create a trust of the property in favour of another.

Consideration (or a deed) is clearly necessary for the validity of a contract to dispose of property, including a contract to assign a chose in action.

It is equally clear that consideration is not necessary for the validity of a trust of a chose in action.[8] All that is necessary is that the settlor should clearly have expressed his intention to create a trust. As in the case of contracts for the benefit of a third party,[9] a mere intention to benefit is not enough: there must be an intention to create a trust. The settlor must intend to undertake a legally binding obligation to hold the subject-matter for the beneficiary, or to persuade someone else to undertake such an obligation.[10]

---

[2] *Ante*, p. 579.

[3] Exceptionally, the argument is mentioned in *Ward* v. *Audland* (1845) 8 Beav. 201 (the actual decision was doubted in *Kekewich* v. *Manning* (1851) 1 D.M. & G. 176).

[4] *Kekewich* v. *Manning, supra*; *Bentley* v. *Mackay* (1851) 15 Beav. 12; *Voyle* v. *Hughes* (1854) 2 Sm. & G. 18; *Donaldson* v. *Donaldson* (1854) Kay 711; *Nanney* v. *Morgan* (1887) 37 Ch.D. 346; *Re Way's Trust* (1864) 2 D.J. & S. 365.

[5] *e.g. Bridge* v. *Bridge* (1852) 16 Beav. 315; *Beech* v. *Keep* (1854) 18 Beav. 285.

[6] Except where the legal chose was, even before the Judicature Act, assignable by some special statute (*ante*, p. 579) or at common law (*ante*, p. 576).

[7] *Ex. p. Pye* (1811) Ves. 140; *Fortescue* v. *Barnett* (1834) 3 My. & K. 36; *M'Fadden* v. *Jenkyns* (1842) 1 Ph. 153; *Paterson* v. *Murphy* (1853) 11 Hare 88; *Richardson* v. *Richardson* (1867) L.R. 3 Eq. 686; *Re King* (1879) 14 Ch.D. 179 (where the assignment was made before the Judicature Act); *cf. Re Patrick* [1891] 1 Ch. 82 and *Re Griffin* [1899] 1 Ch. 408, in which the provisions of the Judicature Act relating to assignment were not mentioned.

[8] *Ex. p. Pye, supra*; *Bentley* v. *Mackay* (1851) 15 Beav. 12; *Paterson* v. *Murphy, supra*; *Richardson* v. *Richardson, supra*; *Re Richards* (1887) 36 Ch.D. 541; *Paul* v. *Constance* [1977] 1 W.L.R. 527. A declaration of trust is not, strictly, an assignment: see *Grey* v. *I.R.C.* [1958] Ch. 690; affirmed on other grounds: [1960] A.C. 1.

[9] *Ante*, p. 565.

[10] *Bayley* v. *Boulcott* (1828) 4 Russ. 345; *Smith* v. *Warde* (1845) 15 Sim. 56; *Re Caplen's Estate* (1876) 45 L.J.Ch. 280.

Consideration is also unnecessary for the validity of a completed gift. Thus in *Harding* v. *Harding*[11] a voluntary statutory assignment was held binding on the ground that it was a completed gift. In many cases, the law requires a gift to be made in a prescribed way: for example, the gift of a chattel must be made by delivery with intention to pass the property, or by deed of gift.[12] If a purported gift of a chattel is not made in one of these two ways, it is incomplete or imperfect; and equity refuses to complete an imperfect gift by ordering the donor to make it in the proper legal manner.[13]

In the same way, a voluntary assignment of a chose in action did not bind the assignor unless it was made in the manner, if any, required by law. In *Milroy* v. *Lord*[14] the owner of shares in a company voluntarily assigned them by deed poll. This was held to be an imperfect gift since the legal title to the shares could not be transferred except by the execution of a proper instrument of transfer followed by registration of the transfer in the books of the company. Turner L.J. said: "In order to render a voluntary settlement valid and effectual, the settlor must have done everything which, according to the nature of the property comprised in the settlement, was necessary to be done in order to transfer the property and render the settlement binding upon him."[15] The assignment thus failed as a gift but the assignees argued that it could still take effect as a declaration of trust. This argument, too, was rejected, as the donor had no intention to create a trust, but only an intention to make a gift. An imperfect gift cannot be validated by simply construing it as a declaration of trust.

A gift is only incomplete under the rule in *Milroy* v. *Lord* if something more has to be done *by the donor* to transfer the property. If the donor has done all that he needs to do to transfer the property, the gift is complete even though further steps to vest the property in the donee have to be taken by a third party,[16] or even by the donee himself.[17]

The rule in *Milroy* v. *Lord* only applied to gifts which had, by law, to be made in a certain form. The only formal requirement for the assignment of an *equitable* chose was that it must be in writing.[18] Hence in *Kekewich* v. *Manning*[19] a voluntary settlement in writing of an equitable interest in property was held binding on the settlor, since there was nothing more that he could have done to transfer the property. Again, in the absence of special rules, such as those governing the transfer of shares in companies,

---

[11] (1886) 17 Q.B.D. 442.

[12] *Re Breton's Estate* (1881) 17 Ch.D. 416; *Cochrane* v. *Moore* (1890) 25 Q.B.D. 57; *Re Cole* [1964] Ch. 175.

[13] *Ellison* v. *Ellison* (1802) 6 Ves. 656, 662. For a special exception in cases of so-called *donatio mortis causa* see *Sen* v. *Headley* [1991] N.L.J.R. 384.

[14] (1862) 4 D.F. & J. 264; *cf. Antrobus* v. *Smith* (1805) 12 Ves. 39; *Dillon* v. *Coppin* (1839) 4 My. & Cr. 647; *Jones* v. *Lock* (1865) L.R. 1 Ch.App. 25; *Richards* v. *Delbridge* (1874) L.R. 18 Eq. 11; *Heartley* v. *Nicholson* (1875) L.R. 19 Eq. 233; *Re Shield* (1885) 53 L.T. 5; *Macedo* v. *Stroud* [1922] 2 A.C. 330; *Re Wale* [1956] 1 W.L.R. 1346; *McKay*, 40 Conv. 139.

[15] At p. 274.

[16] *Re Rose* [1952] Ch. 499; following *Re Rose* [1949] Ch. 78; *cf. Mascall* v. *Mascall* (1985) P. & C.R. 119 (transfer of a house); contrast *Re Fry* [1946] Ch. 312.

[17] *Cf. Re Paradise Motor Co. Ltd.* [1968] 1 W.L.R. 1125 (defective execution by transferee did not invalidate gift of shares).

[18] *Cf. Chinn* v. *Collins* [1981] A.C. 533, 548.

[19] (1851) 1 D.M. & G. 176; *cf. Re Way's Trusts* (1864) 2 D.J. & S. 365; *Nanney* v. *Morgan* (1887) 37 Ch.D. 346, decided after the Judicature Act, but without reference to its provisions regarding assignments.

equity did not lay down any formal requirements for the transfer of *legal* choses. Thus in *Fortescue* v. *Barnett*[20] a voluntary assignment by deed[21] of a life insurance policy[22] was held binding on the assignor, as there was nothing more that he could do to complete the transfer.

A gift may be imperfect for some reason other than failure to use the proper form. The donor may only have said that he would make a gift in the future, or subject to some condition which can only be satisfied by his doing some further act. Thus a gift "to my daughter when she marries a man of whom I approve" is imperfect until the donor gives his approval.

The "completed gift" view seems to be preferable to the "procedural" view in two respects. It is more consistent with the reasoning of the cases decided before the Judicature Act. And it explains why voluntary assignments of legal choses were sometimes upheld.

(2) After the Judicature Act 1873

An assignment may now fail to be statutory, and so take effect (if at all) in equity, for one of three reasons.

(a) NO WRITTEN NOTICE. An assignment which fails to be statutory merely because written notice has not yet been given to the debtor is effective although it is not supported by consideration.[23] The assignor has done all that need be done *by him* to transfer the property, as notice can be given by the assignee. It would be futile to insist that the assignee must give consideration, since he could evade the requirement by simply writing to the debtor and so making the assignment statutory.

(b) NO WRITING. An oral assignment of an equitable chose is void, quite apart from the question of consideration.[24] It is more doubtful whether a voluntary oral assignment of a legal chose can be valid as a gift.

One possible view is that consideration is not now necessary in cases of this kind because the assignee no longer needs the co-operation of the assignor to sue the debtor: if the assignor refuses to join as co-plaintiff, he can simply be joined as co-defendant. But this argument is based on the "procedural" view of the old rules of equity, which is untenable. The argument would, moreover, fail even if the "procedural" view were sound. It can make no difference whether the assignor is joined as co-plaintiff or as co-defendant. The important point is that he is joined at all. He is not joined out of respect for history, but "to allow him to dispute the assignment."[25] One possible reason for disputing it might be that it was voluntary. If the assignor disputed the assignment on this ground, the debtor would in practice drop out of the action, and leave the assignor and assignee to fight out the dispute. Thus in substance the assignor will be the sole defendant.[26] To argue that he will lose simply because he has been made defendant is to assume the very point in issue.

Another possible view is that an oral voluntary assignment of a legal

---

20 (1834) 3 My. & K. 36; *cf. Edwards* v. *Jones* (1836) 1 My. & Cr. 226; *Re King* (1879) 14 Ch.D. 179; *Re Patrick* [1891] 1 Ch. 82.

21 This would not cure the want of consideration for the present purpose: *ante*, p. 586.

22 See now, *ante*, p. 579: for assignment of life insurance policies.

23 *Holt* v. *Heatherfield Trust Ltd.* [1942] 2 K.B. 1.

24 *Ante*, p. 582.

25 *Durham Bros.* v. *Robertson* [1898] 1 Q.B. 765, 770.

26 *Cf. ante*, p. 579.

chose in action fails as an imperfect gift under the rule in *Milroy* v. *Lord.*[27] On this view, the proper way to transfer a debt is by making a statutory assignment. If the assignor does not put the assignment into writing, he has not done "everything which, according to the nature of the property . . . was necessary to be done [by him] to transfer the property." This view was adopted in the Australian case of *Olsson* v. *Dyson*[28] where a voluntary oral assignment of a debt was accordingly held ineffective.

Under the first of the above views, all oral voluntary assignments of legal choses would be valid; under the second they would all be invalid. Neither of these conclusions can be accepted. The law may recognise two ways of making a gift of a chose in action, just as it recognises two ways of making a gift of a chattel.[29] Before the Judicature Act a gift of a chose in action could be made by equitable assignment and equity laid down no formal requirements for this purpose. The Act provided a second method of making such a gift, without necessarily affecting the first. Thus in *German* v. *Yates*[30] a voluntary oral assignment of a debt was held binding on the personal representatives of the assignor. Lush J. rejected the argument that the gift was imperfect, and said that the Judicature Act had not "destroyed equitable assignments or impaired their validity in any way."[31]

The true position seems to be that oral voluntary assignments of legal choses can be valid so long as they are perfect gifts. They are not imperfect *merely* for want of writing, but they may be imperfect for some other reason. In particular, there may be room for doubt whether an oral statement was a completed gift, rather than a promise to make a gift in the future.

(c) NOT ABSOLUTE. There are three reasons why an assignment may not be absolute.

(i) *Part of a debt.* An assignment of part of a debt may be effective without consideration. This can be deduced from *Re McArdle.*[32] A testator left his estate in equal shares to his five children. The wife of one of them, at her own expense, made improvements to a farm belonging to the estate. Thereafter, the children wrote to the wife: "In consideration of your carrying out certain alterations . . . we . . . hereby agree that the executors shall repay you [£488] from the estate." This promise was clearly based on past consideration[33] and was held to be ineffective because it purported to be a contract and not a gift. It was further said that, even if the letter could be construed as a gift, it was not perfect, because something more had to be done by the donors; the executors could not have paid the wife without referring back to the children to find out whether the work had been done to their satisfaction.[34] On this reasoning, the result would have been different if the letter had on its face been a gift and had involved no reference

---

27 (1862) 4 D.F. & J. 264; *ante*, p. 589.
28 (1969) 120 C.L.R. 365.
29 *Ante*, p. 589.
30 (1915) 32 T.L.R. 52.
31 At p. 53. He also said that the assignor might have been able to revoke the assignment but that his personal representative could not do so; and that there might have been consideration for the agreement because the parties thought there was. No reasons were given for these puzzling statements.
32 [1951] Ch. 669; Stone, 14 M.L.R. 356.
33 *Ante*, p. 74.
34 For criticism of this reasoning, see R. E. M., 67 L.Q.R. 295.

back to the children. A letter simply saying "We hereby agree that the executors shall pay you £488 out of the estate" would have been a valid equitable assignment.

(ii) *By way of charge.* The question whether an assignment by way of charge must be supported by consideration is not likely to arise. Such an assignment is almost always made to secure a debt, so that there will generally be consideration for it in the shape of the assignee's advancing money or promising not to sue or actually forbearing to sue.[35] Moreover, such an assignment is usually intended to operate as a disposition by way of contract, and cannot be construed as a gift merely because, for some technical reason, there is no consideration. Even if the assignment were intended to operate as a gift, the fact that the amount assigned would fluctuate from time to time as the assignor increased or decreased his indebtedness to the assignee would show that the gift was not perfect.

(iii) *Conditional.* The validity of a voluntary conditional assignment depends on the nature of the condition. An assignment "to A until she marries" might well be a perfect gift, and so might an assignment "to A when she marries," unless it is construed as a promise to make a gift in the future. But a gift "to A when she marries a man of whom I approve"[36] would be imperfect as it could not take effect until some further act had been done by the donor.

SECTION 6. SUBJECT TO EQUITIES

An assignee takes "subject to equities,"[37] *i.e.* subject to any defects in the assignor's title and subject to certain claims which the debtor has against the assignor. He takes subject to such defects and claims whether they arise at law or in equity, and whether or not he knew of their existence when he took his assignment.[38] And he cannot recover more than the assignor could have recovered. The object of these rules is to ensure that the debtor is not prejudiced by the assignment.

1. Defects of Title

An assignor cannot confer any title if he had none himself. Thus if a builder assigns money to become due to him under a building contract, and then fails to perform the contract so that no money ever becomes due, the assignee takes nothing.[39] Similarly, the assignee of a contract which is affected by mistake or illegality generally[40] takes no greater rights than the assignor would have had. And the assignee of a contract which is voidable for misrepresentation takes subject to the right of the debtor to set the contract aside.[41] Defences available by the terms of the contract to the debtor against the assignor can similarly be raised against the assignee.[42] On the other hand payment of the debt to the assignor is only a defence against the

---

[35] *Ante,* pp. 82–85.

[36] It is assumed that this is a condition and not consideration (*cf. ante,* p. 69).

[37] *Ord* v. *White* (1840) 3 Beav. 357; *Mangles* v. *Dixon* (1852) 3 H.L.C. 702, 731.

[38] *Athenaeum Soc.* v. *Pooley* (1853) 3 D. & J. 294.

[39] *Tooth* v. *Hallett* (1869) L.R. 4 Ch.App. 242.

[40] An assignee for value may be able to enforce a life insurance policy though the assured could not do so because he died by his own hand: *ante,* p. 385.

[41] *Ante,* pp. 331 *et seq.*

[42] *The League* [1984] 2 Lloyd's Rep. 259 (arbitration clause).

assignee if made before notice of the assignment was given to the debtor[43] and the same is presumably true of rescission of the contract assigned by subsequent agreement between debtor and assignor.

2. Claims by Debtor against Assignor

The debtor may have claims against the assignor which he could set up, if he were sued by the assignor, to diminish or extinguish his liability. Whether he can rely on such claims against the assignee depends on the way in which they arose.

(1) Claims arising out of the contract assigned

If the debtor has claims *arising out of the contract assigned*, on which he could have relied by way of defence or set off against the assignor, he can also rely on those claims against the assignee, and he can do so whether the claims have arisen before or after notice of the assignment is given to him.[44] Thus if a builder assigns money due to him under a building contract, and then commits a breach of that contract, the debtor can set off against the assignee the amount of any damages which he could have recovered from the assignor.[45] If this amount exceeds the sum assigned, the assignee will not be entitled to anything; but he is not liable to the debtor for the excess[46] as he is not himself in breach of contract.

If the debtor has been induced to enter into the contract by a misrepresentation on the part of the assignor, he can rely against the assignee on the right to rescind the contract on that ground; but a difficult problem arises where that right has been lost. In *Stoddart* v. *Union Trust Ltd.*,[47] the defendants were induced by the fraud of one Price to buy a business from him. Price assigned £800, part of the agreed price, to the plaintiffs, who now claimed this sum from the defendants. Two defences were raised. First, the defendants counterclaimed for damages for Price's fraud, but such a claim could not be made against the plaintiffs, as they were not themselves guilty of fraud, nor responsible for the fraud of Price. Secondly, the defendants pleaded that by reason of Price's fraud they had suffered loss exceeding £800, so that no money was due from them. This defence would have succeeded against Price; but it failed against the plaintiffs as the claim for damages did not "arise out of the contract in question at all"[48] but was "something *dehors* the contract."[49] The decision seems to lead to the regrettable result that a contract may be worth more in the hands of the assignee than in the hands of the assignor, and so to defeat the purpose of the rule that an assignee takes "subject to equities." No attempt was made by the defendants to rely simply on their right to rescind the contract. They had disposed of the subject-matter and seem to have assumed that they

---

43 *Ante*, p. 585.

44 *Graham* v. *Johnson* (1869) L.R. 8 Eq. 36; *William Pickersgill & Sons Ltd.* v. *London & Provincial Marine, etc., Insurance Co. Ltd.* [1912] 3 K.B. 614; *The Raven* [1980] 2 Lloyd's Rep. 266; contrast *The Dominique* [1987] 1 Lloyd's Rep. 239, 251, (approved [1989] A.C. 1056, 1109–1101), where the debtor's claim could *not* have been set up against the assignor (*post*, p. 689, n. 88) and was therefore not available against the assignee.

45 *Cf. Govt. of Newfoundland* v. *Newfoundland Ry.* (1888) 13 App.Cas. 199.

46 *Young* v. *Kitchin* (1878) 3 Ex.D. 127.

47 [1912] 1 K.B. 181.

48 At p. 193.

49 At p. 194.

could not rescind as they were unable to make restitution.[50] But the victim of a criminal fraud can rely on it by way of defence without making restitution.[51] This defence would seem to be an "equity" and should have been available against the assignee.

(2) Claims arising out of other transactions

(a) CLAIMS AGAINST ASSIGNOR. The debtor may have a claim against the assignor arising out of some transaction other than the contract assigned: *e.g.* a debtor may owe money under a building contract and in turn have a claim against the builder for the price of goods sold and delivered. Such a claim can only be set up against an assignee of the debt due under the building contract if it arose before notice of the assignment was given to the debtor.[52] If the claim arises later, the debtor is not prejudiced by being unable to raise it against the assignee. He knows that the assignor no longer has any right to dispose of the debt assigned and cannot therefore expect to set it off against any further claims which he may acquire against the assignor.

(b) CLAIMS AGAINST INTERMEDIATE ASSIGNEE. Where a debt which has been assigned to one person is then assigned by him to another, the question may arise whether a claim or defence which the debtor has against the first assignee can be set up against the second assignee. Such a claim or defence should be available against the second assignee, if it arose after the first assignment,[53] but before notice of the second assignment had been given to the debtor. If the debtor *paid* the first assignee before the notice of the second assignment, he would clearly not have to make a second payment to the second assignee. The same rule should apply if the debtor supplied goods to the first assignee on the terms that the price was to be set off against the debt assigned.[54]

(c) PROVISIONS OF THE CONTRACT. The rule that claims arising before notice of the assignment can be set off against the assignee may be excluded by the express provisions of the contract creating the debt. Such provisions are often found in debentures issued by companies to secure loans, since the rule that an assignee takes subject to equities unduly restricts the transferability of such instruments.[55]

3. Assignee Cannot Recover More than Assignor

The assignee cannot recover more from the debtor than the assignor could have done. Thus in *Dawson* v. *G.N. & City Ry.*[56] a landowner had a statu-

---

50. *Ante,* pp. 338 *et seq.*

51 *Ante,* pp. 333–334.

52 *Stephens* v. *Venables* (1862) 30 Beav. 625; *cf. Watson* v. *Mid. Wales Ry.* (1867) L.R. 2 C.P. 593; *Roxburghe* v. *Cox* (1881) 17 Ch.D. 520; *Business Computers Ltd.* v. *Anglo-African Leasing Ltd.* [1977] 1 W.L.R. 578.

53 Not if it arose *before*, since in that case the debtor can have had no expectation of being able to set it up in diminution of the debt assigned: *The Raven* [1980] 2 Lloyd's Rep. 266.

54 According to a dictum in *Re Milan Tramways Co.* (1884) 25 Ch.D. 587, 593 an ultimate assignee takes "free from any equities which only attach on the intermediate assignee"; but this view could cause great injustice, and the actual decision can be explained on the ground that the intermediate assignee's liability to the debtor was not established until *after* the *second* assignment had been made. The actual decision in the *Milan Tramways* case was approved in *Fryer* v. *Ewart* [1902] A.C. 187, 192.

55 Gower, *Modern Company Law,* (4th ed.), pp. 468–470.

56 [1905] 1 K.B. 260.

tory claim against a railway company for injuriously affecting his land. He sold the land to the plaintiff, and also assigned the statutory claim to him. It was held that the railway company's liability to the plaintiff must be measured by the loss which would have been suffered by the assignor and that any extra loss suffered by the plaintiff by reason of a trade carried on by him, but not by the assignor, must be ignored.

SECTION 7. NEGOTIABILITY

Special rules apply to the assignment of certain written contracts, called negotiable instruments. The most important negotiable instruments are bills of exchange, cheques and promissory notes. A bill of exchange is a written order made by one person (the drawer) requiring another (the drawee) to pay a sum of money either to the drawer, or to a named third person, or simply to bearer.[57] The request may be to pay the money on demand, or at some stated future time. If the drawee accepts the request, he becomes liable as acceptor of the bill. A cheque is a bill of exchange drawn on a banker payable on demand.[58] A promissory note is an unconditional promise in writing to pay a person a sum of money.[59] No useful purpose would be served by enumerating in this book all the instruments which have been held to be negotiable. The categories of negotiable instruments are not closed, so that instruments can still become negotiable by mercantile custom, that is, by being regularly so treated by businessmen.[60]

The transfer of a negotiable instrument differs from the assignment of an ordinary chose in action in the following ways.

1. Transfer by Delivery

A negotiable instrument is actually or potentially transferable by mere delivery. A bill of exchange payable to bearer can be transferred by simply handing it to the transferee. If a bill of exchange is payable to A, he can transfer it by indorsing it, *i.e.* by signing his name on it, and then handing it to the transferee. Notice of the transfer need not be given to the person or persons liable on the instrument.

2. Defects of Title

An ordinary assignee takes "subject to equities." But negotiable instruments pass from hand to hand like cash, so that it is particularly important that those who deal with them should be able to rely on their apparent validity. The transferee of a negotiable instrument therefore takes it free from certain defects in the title of prior parties[61] and from defences available among them, if he is a "holder in due course."[62] Such a holder is a person in possession of the instrument who has in good faith given value for it, provided that it is complete and regular on its face, not overdue and that it has not, to his knowledge, been dishonoured. Every holder is presumed to

---

[57] Bills of Exchange Act 1882, s.3.

[58] *Ibid.* s.73.

[59] *Ibid.* s.83(1). A promissory note should be distinguished from an IOU, which is only evidence of a debt.

[60] *Crouch* v. *Crédit Foncier of England Ltd.* (1873) L.R. 8 Q.B. 374.

[61] Bills of Exchange Act 1882, s.38(2).

[62] *Ibid.* s.29. And see Consumer Credit Act 1974, s.125, for special provisions designed to prevent evasions of that Act.

be a holder in due course[63] unless the instrument is affected by fraud, duress or illegality[64]; but even in such a case the holder can still enforce the instrument if he can prove that he in fact gave value for the instrument in good faith. The only cases in which his title is no better than that of the transferor are those in which a party's signature to the instrument is wholly void, *i.e.* for mistake or under statute.[65]

3. Consideration

The holder of a bill of exchange is deemed to be a holder for value if consideration[66] has at any time[67] been given for the bill. Thus he can enforce it against (for example) the acceptor even though he himself gave no consideration for it. This rule should be distinguished from the further rule that consideration is not necessary for the validity of a transfer of a negotiable instrument.[68] Suppose that A draws a bill of exchange on B who accepts it. If A transfers the bill to C, neither A nor B can deny the validity of the transfer on the ground that it was gratuitous. But B can escape liability by showing that his acceptance was gratuitous, and that C gave no consideration for the transfer. Want of consideration may enable the acceptor to resist an action *on the bill.* But it does not entitle the transferor to deny the validity of the *transfer.*

SECTION 8. RIGHTS WHICH ARE NOT ASSIGNABLE

1. Contracts Expressed to be Not Assignable

If a contract provides that the rights arising under it shall not be assigned, a purported assignment of such rights is ineffective, in the sense that it does not give the assignee any rights against the debtor.[69] For example, a hire-purchase agreement may provide that the rights of the hirer shall not be assignable; and if he nevertheless purports to assign them, the assignee cannot enforce them against the owner.[70] But an assignment of the benefit of a contract which is expressed to be not assignable may be binding as a contract between assignor and assignee. Thus it has been held that a settlement of an insurance policy, expressed to be not assignable, could be enforced by the beneficiaries against the settlor.[71]

---

[63] Bills of Exchange Act 1882, s.30(2).

[64] *Ibid.*

[65] *Foster* v. *Mackinnon* (1869) L.R. 4 C.P. 704; for contracts declared to be "void" by statute, see *ante*, p. 455.

[66] An antecedent debt or liability is sufficient by way of exception to the rule that consideration must not be past: Bills of Exchange Act 1882, s.27(1)(*b*).

[67] *Ibid.* s.27(2).

[68] *Easton* v. *Pratchett* (1835) 1 Cr.M. & R. 798, 808. The transferee could not *sue* the transferor, but the transferor could not prevent the transferee from collecting the amount due from the other parties liable.

[69] *Helstan Securities Ltd.* v. *Hertfordshire C.C.* [1978] 3 All E.R. 262; Munday [1979] C.L.J. 50; see generally Alcock [1983] C.L.J. 328.

[70] *United Dominion Trust Ltd.* v. *Parkway Motors* [1955] 1 W.L.R. 719 (disapproved as to the effect of such a provision on measure of damages in *Wickham Holdings Ltd.* v. *Brooke House Motors Ltd.* [1967] 1 W.L.R. 295. Apart from such clauses prohibiting assignment, hire-purchase agreements are assignable: *Whiteley Ltd.* v. *Hilt* [1918] 2 K.B. 808.

[71] *Re Turcan* (1888) 40 Ch.D. 5. *Cf. Spellman* v. *Spellman* [1961] 1 W.L.R. 921.

2. Personal Contracts

The benefit of a contract cannot be assigned if it is clear that the debtor is only willing to perform in favour of one particular creditor, and if it would be unjust to force him to perform in favour of another. In such cases it is sometimes said that the "personal" nature of the contract prevents assignment.

An important application of this principle is that an employer cannot assign the benefit of his employee's promise to serve. It has been said that the right of the employee to choose whom he would serve "constituted the main difference between a servant and a serf."[72] But in the case of an employee of a company, this right of choice will often depend on distinctions which are somewhat technical. Contracts of employment with a company are terminated if the company sells *its business*.[73] But if *the shares* in the company are sold, and its directors are replaced by others in the course of a take-over bid, the employee is, it seems, bound to go on serving the company. In law he still has the same employer[74] but his right of choice is in such cases of more theoretical than real importance.

The same principle applies to all contracts involving personal confidence. Thus a publisher cannot assign the benefit of an author's contract to write a book if the author relied on the publisher's skill and judgment as a publisher.[75] And the holder of a motor insurance policy cannot assign it since the insurer relies on the holder's skill and record as a driver.[76]

The principle may even apply to contracts for the sale of goods. Thus it has been held that the benefit of a contract to supply coal on credit to a retail coal merchant could not be assigned to his successor in the business. In making the contract, the sellers had relied on the original buyer's business experience; and to force them to give credit to his successor (who had no such experience) would subject them to quite a different business risk.[77] Again in *Kemp* v. *Baerselman*[78] a farmer agreed to supply to a baker all the eggs which the latter should need in his business for one year; and the baker agreed not to buy eggs elsewhere during that period. The baker sold his business to a large company, to whom he purported to assign the benefit of his contract with the farmer. It was held that the farmer was justified in refusing to supply eggs to the company. One reason for the decision was that the farmer had contracted to supply the baker's business needs, and the baker no longer had any such needs as he had gone out of business. Another reason was that the baker's promise to deal exclusively with the farmer could not be enforced against the company.[79] Thus if the farmer were compelled to supply eggs to the company he would be subject to all

---

[72] *Nokes* v. *Doncaster Amalgamated Collieries Ltd.* [1940] A.C. 1014, 1026; *cf. Denman* v. *Midland Employer's Mutual Assurance Soc. Ltd.* [1955] 2 Q.B. 437; *Smith* v. *Blandford Gee Cementation Ltd.* [1970] 3 All E.R. 154, 163; *O'Brien* (*Inspector of Taxes*) v. *Benson's Hosiery* (*Holdings*) *Ltd.* [1980] A.C. 562, 572.

[73] *Re Foster Clark Ltd.'s Indenture Trusts* [1966] 1 W.L.R. 125.

[74] *Cf. Re Mack Trucks* (*Britain*) *Ltd.* [1967] 1 W.L.R. 780; *Griffiths* v. *S. of S. for Social Services* [1974] Q.B. 468; *Nicholl* v. *Cutts* 1985 P.C.C. 311; (service contracts not determined by appointment of receiver).

[75] *Stevens* v. *Benning* (1854) 1 K. & J. 168; 6 D.M. & G. 223; *Hole* v. *Bradbury* (1879) 12 Ch.D. 886; *Griffith* v. *Tower Publishing Co.* [1897] 1 Ch. 21.

[76] *Peters* v. *G.A.F.L.A.C.* [1937] 4 All E.R. 628.

[77] *Cooper* v. *Micklefield Coal & Lime Co. Ltd.* (1912) 107 L.T. 457.

[78] [1906] 2 K.B. 604.

[79] For the validity of such exclusive dealing arrangements, see *ante*, pp. 416–420.

the burdens of the original contract, but would lose the privilege of exclusive trading for which he had originally bargained.

But the benefit of a long-term contract for the sale of goods can be assigned if it was expressly or impliedly made with the buyer *or his assigns*. In *Tolhurst* v. *Associated Portland Cement Co.*[80] Tolhurst agreed that he would for 50 years supply to Imperial so much chalk as it should require for the manufacture of cement on certain land which was described in the contract. Imperial sold its business to Associated (a much larger concern), to which it purported to assign the benefit of its contract with Tolhurst. It was held that Tolhurst was not justified in refusing to supply chalk to Associated, since the contract was impliedly made between the parties and their respective assigns. The fact that Associated was a larger concern than Imperial did not increase Tolhurst's burden, since the contract only obliged him to supply so much chalk as was needed on the land originally occupied by Imperial.

It seems that the rule against the assignment of "personal" contracts does not apply where the creditor has an accrued right to a fixed sum of money. A person who is indebted to an indulgent creditor cannot apparently complain if the creditor assigns the debt to the debtor's trade rival (who may make him bankrupt), or to a debt-collecting agency.[81]

In cases of this kind, one party may be able to assign the benefit of the contract while the other cannot do so. Thus an employee can assign his wages,[82] though the employer cannot assign the benefit of the employee's promise to serve.

3. Mere Rights of Action

Equity in general[83] regarded the common law's fear that assignments would lead to maintenance as exaggerated. But where assignments in fact savoured of maintenance[84] or champerty,[85] equity refused to enforce them. The Criminal Law Act 1967 abolishes criminal and tortious liability for maintenance and champerty[86] but goes on to provide that this "shall not affect any rule of law as to the cases in which a contract[87] is to be treated as contrary to public policy or otherwise illegal."[88] The rule against the assignment of certain rights known as "mere rights of action" has therefore survived the 1967 Act.[89] But, partly as a result of the Act, and partly as a result of the current "more liberal attitude"[90] towards maintenance and champerty the courts have considerably restricted the scope of the rule.

---

80 [1903] A.C. 414; *cf. Shayler* v. *Woolf* [1946] Ch. 320.

81 *Cf. Fitzroy* v. *Cave* [1905] 2 K.B. 364. But the "personality" of the creditor may be material to the debtor: see *Gordon* v. *Street* [1899] 2 Q.B. 641.

82 Except to the extent that the assignment is contrary to public policy: *ante*, p. 400, n. 36; *post*, p. 601; or to statute (*post*, p. 601, n. 20).

83 *Ante*, p. 578.

84 *Rees* v. *De Bernardy* [1896] 2 Ch. 437.

85 *Laurent* v. *Sale & Co.* [1963] 1 W.L.R. 829; *Trendtex Trading Co.* v. *Crédit Suisse* [1982] A.C. 679, 694–695. For a champerty, see *ante*, p. 379.

86 ss.13(1) and (2).

87 This seems to include an assignment even though such a transaction may be effective without consideration (*ante*, pp. 585–592) or even agreement: communication *to* the assignee is necessary, but not assent *by* him (*ante*, p. 583).

88 s.14(2).

89 *Trendtex Trading Corp.* v. *Crédit Suisse* [1982] A.C. 679.

90 *Ibid.* p. 702. *Cf.* Courts and Legal Services Act 1990, s.58.

(1) Claims in tort

A right of action in tort cannot generally be assigned.[91] A person who is defamed or assaulted cannot sell his right to sue the tortfeasor. He can, however, sue the tortfeasor and agree to assign any damages he may recover; this is unobjectionable as it does not give the assignee any right to interfere with the conduct of the action.[92] Exceptionally, a right of action can be assigned to an insurance company which has compensated the victim of the tort.[93]

The generality of the rule against assignment of claims in tort is open to criticism. Such claims are often brought to assert rights of property; and it is hard to see why the assignment of a right of action in (for example) conversion is more likely to lead to maintenance than the assignment of a debt. Some tort claims can be enforced by quasi-contractual actions,[94] and it is arguable that the assignment of these, at least, should be allowed.[95]

(2) Liquidated claims

A liquidated sum due under contract (*e.g.* for money lent, or goods supplied, or services rendered) or otherwise[96] can be assigned in spite of the fact that the debtor denies liability. A debtor cannot destroy the assignability of a debt by refusing to pay it.[97] Nor is it relevant that such an assignment is made or taken with an oblique motive. An assignment of a debt is not invalid merely because its object is to enable the assignee to make the debtor bankrupt.[98]

(3) Unliquidated claims

If the benefit of a contract, *e.g.* to deliver goods, is assigned before breach, the assignee can claim damages if the seller subsequently refuses to deliver the goods. But more difficulty arises in determining whether the right to claim unliquidated damages for breach of contract can be assigned after the contract has already been broken.

One view is that such a right is a "mere" right of action and cannot be assigned.[99] But this view causes difficulty where the contract provides for the payment of a fixed sum in the event of its breach. Such a provision may

---

[91] *Defries* v. *Milne* [1913] 1 Ch. 98.

[92] *Glegg* v. *Bromley* [1912] 3 K.B. 474; *Trendtex Trading Corp.* v. *Crédit Suisse* [1982] A.C. 679, 702.

[93] *King* v. *Victoria Insurance Co.* [1896] A.C. 250; *Compania Colombiana de Seguros* v. *Pacific Steam Navigation Co.* [1965] 1 Q.B. 101. Even if there is no assignment, the insurer is, to the extent that he has compensated the victim, entitled to be subrogated to the latter's rights against the tortfeasor: see *Hobbs* v. *Marlowe* [1978] A.C. 16, 37; *cf.* Marine Insurance Act 1906, s.79. The insurer must in such a case sue in the name of the insured: see *The Aiolos* [1983] 2 Lloyd's Rep. 25 (where the claim was in contract); *M. H. Smith (Plant Hire) Ltd.* v. *D. L. Mainwaring (T/A Inshore)* [1986] 2 Lloyd's Rep. 244, where the insured was a company which had been wound up, so that the insurer lost his rights by way of subrogation; *Esso Petroleum Co. Ltd.* v. *Hall Russell & Co. Ltd.* [1989] A.C. 643.

[94] *i.e.* in cases of so-called "waiver" of tort where the tort benefits the defendant, *e.g.* where he converts the plaintiff's property. See Goff & Jones, *The Law of Restitution* (3rd ed.), Chap. 32; Birks, *An Introduction to the Law of Restitution*, Chap. 10.

[95] *Cf. Re Berkeley Securities (Property) Ltd.* [1980] 1 W.L.R. 1589, 1611.

[96] *Dawson* v. *Great Northern and City Ry.* [1905] 1 K.B. 260.

[97] *County Hotel & Wine Co.* v. *London and North Western Ry.* [1918] 2 K.B. 251, 258.

[98] *Fitzroy* v. *Cave* [1905] 2 K.B. 364.

[99] *May* v. *Lane* (1894) 64 L.J.Q.B. 236, 237, 238.

be (i) invalid as a penalty, in which case no more than the actual loss is recoverable; or (ii) valid as an attempt to pre-estimate damages, in which case the fixed sum (no more and no less) is recoverable.[1] According to the present view, the assignment would be valid if the contractual provision were valid (for then the claim would be liquidated), and invalid if the contractual provision were penal. But this distinction has no relevance to the tendency of the assignment to maintenance.

Another view is that a right to claim unliquidated damages for breach of contract can, generally,[2] be assigned. But this view in turn gives rise to difficulty where the claim which has been assigned could be framed in contract or in tort.[3] The assignability of the right to damages can hardly depend on the way in which it is described.

As both the views so far discussed are unsatisfactory, the law has adopted an intermediate view. A right to unliquidated damages for breach of contract may be validly assigned, so long as the assignment does not in fact savour of maintenance or champerty. If, for example, the assignee has a *proprietary* interest in the subject-matter, the assignment is valid since maintenance is committed only where a person interferes in another's litigation without having a genuine or substantial interest[4] in the outcome. Thus a vendor of land can assign to the purchaser the right to claim damages for breaches of covenant committed by the vendor's tenants before the sale.[5] Similarly, a right to rescind a contract for the sale of land on the ground of misrepresentation can be assigned along with the benefit of the contract itself.[6] And a person can assign the benefit of a specifically enforceable contract, though the assignee elects, or is forced, to claim damages.[7]

Even where the assignee has no proprietary interest, the assignment may be valid if he has a "genuine commercial interest"[8] in the subject-matter of the action. Thus in *Trendtex Trading Ltd.* v. *Crédit Suisse*[9] a bank had financed a sale of cement by one of its customers. It was held that the bank could validly have taken an assignment from the customer of his claim for damages for wrongful failure to pay for the cement.[10] But the assignment actually made was held to be champertous and invalid because it was expressed to have been taken for the purpose of enabling the bank to resell the customer's right of action to a third party, so that the profit resulting

---

[1] *Post,* pp. 883–890.

[2] In *County Hotel & Wine Co.* v. *London and North Western Ry., supra,* at p. 259, an exception is made for "personal" contracts.

[3] *e.g. Matthews* v. *Kuwait Bechtel Corp.* [1959] 2 Q.B. 57, 77; and see *post,* p. 873.

[4] *Martell* v. *Consett Iron Co. Ltd.* [1955] Ch. 363.

[5] *Williams* v. *Protheroe* (1829) 5 Bing. 309; *Defries* v. *Milne* [1913] 1 Ch. 98; *Ellis* v. *Torrington* [1920] 1 K.B. 399.

[6] *Dickinson* v. *Burrell* (1866) L.R. 1 Eq. 337, 342.

[7] *Torkington* v. *Magee* [1902] 2 K.B. 427; reversed on another ground: [1903] 1 K.B. 644.

[8] *Trendtex Trading Ltd.* v. *Crédit Suisse* [1982] A.C. 679, 703; *cf. The Aiolos* [1983] 2 Lloyd's Rep. 25; *Brownton Ltd.* v. *Edward Moore Inbucon Ltd.* [1985] 3 All E.R. 499 (where the same result could now be reached without assignment under Civil Liability (Contribution) Act 1978, ss.1(1), 2(1)); *The Kelo* [1985] 2 Lloyd's Rep. 85; *S.E. Regional Health Authority* v. *Lovell* (1985) 33 Build L.R. 127; *Weddell* v. *J. A. Pearce & Major* [1988] Ch. 26, 43.

[9] *Supra*; Thornely [1982] C.L.J. 29.

[10] The claim was not against the buyer for the price but against a bank for damages for failing to honour a letter of credit: *cf. post,* p. 881.

from its enforcement (which was considerable)[11] could be divided between the third party and the bank. The crucial fact was that the assignee contemplated a further sale of the right, as opposed to its enforcement by himself. If he intends to pursue the latter course, the assignment is not champertous merely because he expects to improve his position by taking the assignment: unless this were so, few assignments would be valid.[12]

4. Public Policy

In English law, an assignment of wages or salary is generally valid,[13] so long as it does not deprive the employee of his sole means of support.[14] But a public officer cannot assign his salary.[15] This rule was originally based on two considerations of public policy.[16] First, it was thought that a public officer must not be deprived of the means to maintain the dignity of his office; but this argument now has little force, except, perhaps, in the case of ambassadors. Secondly, it was thought that public officers must have the means to pay damages for wrongs committed by them or by their order; but this is no longer important since the injured party can now sue the Crown.[17] It could perhaps be argued that to allow such assignments might lead to corruption. But this seems to be a remote contingency; and the argument proves too much. Officers who are paid out of local funds can assign their salaries,[18] but are presumably just as corruptible as officers paid out of national funds.

Maintenance and other similar payments to which a wife may become entitled as a result of matrimonial proceedings are inalienable, since to allow the wife to assign them might leave her destitute.[19] There are many other statutory restrictions on assignment, based on various considerations of public policy.[20]

SECTION 9. ASSIGNMENT BY OPERATION OF LAW

1. Death

On the death of a contracting party, his rights generally pass to his personal representatives, who can recover any sums due under the contract or damages for its breach. The representatives may sometimes recover less than the deceased would have done, and sometimes more. Thus, personal

---

[11] The bank paid $800,000 for the claim and sold it for $1,100,000 to the third party who settled it for $8,000,000.

[12] *Brownton Ltd.* v. *Edward Moore Inbucon Ltd.* [1985] 3 All E.R. 499, 506, 509, where the "profit" likely to be made by the assignee was (even proportionately) much more modest than that in the *Trendtex* case.

[13] For a statutory exception, see Merchant Shipping Act 1970, s.11(1)(*b*). See also Wages Act 1986, s.1(5)(*d*) for formal requirements to be satisfied before the amount assigned can be deducted from wages.

[14] *King* v. *Michael Faraday & Partners Ltd.* [1939] 2 K.B. 753.

[15] *Methwold* v. *Walbank* (1750) 2 Ves.Sen. 238; *Barwick* v. *Reade* (1791) 1 H.Bl. 267; *Liverpool Corp.* v. *Wright* (1859) 28 L.J.Ch. 868.

[16] Logan, 61 L.Q.R. 240.

[17] Under the Crown Proceedings Act 1947.

[18] *Re Mirams* [1891] 1 Q.B. 594.

[19] *Watkins* v. *Watkins* [1896] P. 222; Bromley and Lowe, *Family Law* (7th ed.), p. 657.

[20] *e.g.* Superannuation Act 1972, s.5(1); Social Security Act 1975, s.87; Child Benefit Act 1975, s.12; Police Pension Act 1976, s.9.

representatives cannot recover exemplary damages.[21] On the other hand, in *Otter* v. *Church, Adams, Tatham & Co.*[22] solicitors negligently advised a client that he had an absolute interest in property, when in fact he had an entailed interest. Had the mistake been discovered while the client was alive, he could have barred the entail, so that the solicitors would only have been liable for nominal damages. But the mistake was not discovered until after the client's death, with the result that the solicitors had to pay substantial damages as the entailed property was through their negligence lost to the client's estate.

Where at time of death the contract is still partly executory, the personal representatives are generally entitled to complete its performance and to claim the agreed remuneration. But they cannot do so if the contract is "personal" in the sense that one party places confidence in the skill, judgment or integrity of the other. Thus if either party to a contract of employment dies, his right to go on serving, or to be served (as the case may be), does not pass to his representatives: they can only enforce rights which had already accrued.[23] It is possible for one party, but not the other, to rely on such personal considerations. If a painter contracted to paint a house and died when the work was half-done, his representatives might not be entitled to finish the work and claim the contract price; but if the house-owner died, his representatives might well be able to demand further performance from the painter.

2. Bankruptcy

When a person is adjudged bankrupt, things in action forming part of his estate at the commencement of the bankruptcy[24] are "deemed to have been assigned" to his trustee in bankruptcy.[25] Thus the trustee can recover debts due to the bankrupt and claim damages for breach of any contract with the bankrupt. Where the contract is executory, the trustee may be entitled to perform it and claim payment from the other party. Certain "personal" rights do not pass to the trustee. The word "personal" is here used in two senses.

First: rights do not pass to the trustee if they are concerned with the person or personal affairs of the bankrupt. Thus a right to claim damages for injury to reputation does not pass,[26] nor does the benefit of a contract "to carry him [the bankrupt] in safety, [or] to cure his person of a wound or disease. . . . "[27] Such rights do not pass to the trustee, even though they have accrued before bankruptcy. The rule is based on the view that only the bankrupt's property is divisible between his creditors: they are not entitled to benefit from injuries to his person. The "property"[28] of the bankrupt that vests in his trustee[29] includes "things in action"[30] without

---

21 Law Reform (Miscellaneous Provisions) Act 1934, s.1(2)(*a*)(i), as amended by Administration of Justice Act 1982, s.4. Such damages are hardly ever (if at all) recoverable on a breach of contract: *post,* p. 829.

22 [1953] Ch. 280.

23 *Stubbs* v. *Holywell Ry.* (1867) L.R. 2 Ex. 311.

24 For after-acquired property, see Insolvency Act 1986, s.307.

25 Insolvency Act 1986, s.311.

26 *Wilson* v. *United Counties Bank* [1920] A.C. 102.

27 *Beckham* v. *Drake* (1849) 2 H.L.C. 579, 627.

28 Insolvency Act 1986, s.283(1).

29 *Ibid.* s.306.

30 *Ibid.* s.436.

qualification; but this definition does not seem to have been intended to alter the previous rules relating to "personal" rights of the kind just described.

Secondly: the benefit of an *executory* contract does not pass to the trustee if it was "personal" in the sense that the other contracting party relied on the skill and judgment of the bankrupt. It would be unjust in such a case to force the other party to accept performance from the trustee or someone employed by him. Thus where a contract to build a house was "personal" in this sense, the trustee was not entitled to finish the house and then to demand payment.[31] But the trustee may employ the bankrupt to finish the work, and if the other party in this way gets precisely what he bargained for, the trustee can sue him.[32]

Special rules apply to payments in the nature of income to which the bankrupt is from time to time entitled.[33] Such entitlement may not vest in the trustee because the bankrupt's right to the payment may not arise until after the commencement of the bankruptcy.[34] Whether or not the right has so arisen, the trustee may apply to the court for an "income payments order"[35] requiring either the bankrupt or the person from whom the payments are due[36] to pay to the trustee so much of the income as may be specified in the order. In deciding what part (if any) of the income is to be paid over to the trustee, the court takes account of "what appears . . . to be necessary for meeting the reasonable domestic needs of the bankrupt and his family"[37]: an income payments order must not be made if its effect would be to reduce the income of the bankrupt below this level. These provisions will apply to wages or salary earned by the bankrupt. They are not based on the "personal" nature of the contract under which the income is earned (for *ex hypothesi* the bankrupt is himself still rendering the services) but on the need to allow the bankrupt to work to maintain himself and his family.[38]

A trustee in bankruptcy is in a less favourable position than an ordinary assignee in that he cannot gain priority over a previous assignee for value by being the first to give notice to the debtor.[39]

SECTION 10. ASSIGNMENT DISTINGUISHED FROM TRANSFER OF LIABILITIES

Assignment is the transfer of a *right* without the consent of the debtor. The common law does not recognise the converse process of the transfer of a contractual *liability* without the consent of the creditor. A person who lends £100 to X cannot be deprived of his right to sue X merely because X and Y agree that the debt is to be paid by Y and not by X. Although the

---

31 *Knight* v. *Burgess* (1864) 33 L.J.Ch. 727; *cf. Lucas* v. *Moncrieff* (1905) 21 T.L.R. 683.

32 *Oliphant* v. *Wadling* (1875) 1 Q.B.D. 145; *Ex p. Shine* [1892] 1 Q.B. 522. To the extent that the right to the money had not yet vested in the bankrupt at the commencement of the bankruptcy, the trustee could claim it as after-acquired property under Insolvency Act 1986, s.307.

33 Insolvency Act 1986, s.310(7).

34 *Ibid.* s.283(1)(*a*).

35 *Ibid.* s.310(1).

36 *Ibid.* s.310(3).

37 *Ibid.* s.310(2).

38 *Cf. Re Roberts* [1900] 1 Q.B. 122, commenting on the position under earlier legislation.

39 *Re Wallis* [1902] 1 K.B. 719. This rule does not seem to be affected by Insolvency Act 1986, s.311(4).

phrase "assignment of liabilities" is occasionally used, it is highly misleading and should be abandoned.

It is of course possible for Y to perform X's obligation. The question whether the creditor is bound to accept such vicarious performance[40] (so as to discharge X) will be considered in Chapter 18. It is also possible, in the situations to be discussed below, for Y to become liable to perform the obligation originally undertaken by X; but in none of these situations is there a true transfer of liability.

1. Novation[41]

We have seen that it is possible by novation to substitute one creditor for another.[42] Similarly, one debtor may be substituted for another. In *Miller's* case[43] the plaintiff insured his life with the X Co., which was later amalgamated with the Y Co., which agreed to become liable on the policy if the plaintiff paid future premiums to it. The plaintiff did so, and it was held that he could enforce the policy against the Y Co. It has been suggested that a similar analysis may apply where a customer pays by credit card[44] for goods supplied by a retailer: the customer's liability to the retailer is discharged and a new liability to the retailer is undertaken by the company issuing the card.[45] Such arrangements are only binding if they are made with the appropriate contractual intention,[46] and if they are supported by consideration. Usually the creditor provides consideration for the new debtor's promise to pay him by agreeing to release the original debtor or to accept a discount[47]; and the original debtor provides consideration for the creditor's promise to release him by providing a new debtor.[48] The effect of novation is not, in strict theory, to *transfer* a liability, but to extinguish it and put a new one in its place.

2. Benefit and Burden

Generally, a person to whom the benefit of a contract is assigned makes no promise to perform the obligations of the assignor; and in the ordinary case such an assignee does not come under any contractual liability. Suppose, for example, that a builder assigns to a bank moneys due or to become due under a building contract. The bank is under no liability to the builder's client for any breach of contract by the builder; the most that the client can do is to rely on the builder's breach in diminution or extinction of the bank's claim.[49]

There are, however, exceptions, or apparent exceptions, to this general rule. In particular, the discharge of a burden may be a condition of the enjoyment of the benefit, so that the burden can be said to be annexed to

---

40 *Post,* pp. 656–659.
41 Ames, *Lectures,* p. 298.
42 *Ante,* p. 577.
43 (1876) 3 Ch.D. 391.
44 See *post*, p. 655.
45 *Customs & Excise Commissioners* v. *Diners Club Ltd.* [1989] 1 W.L.R. 1196, citing *Re Charge Card Services* [1989] Ch. 497, 513 ("quasi-novation").
46 A requirement not satisfied in *Tito* v. *Waddell* (*No. 2*) [1977] Ch. 106: see p. 287.
47 *Customs & Excise Commissioners* v. *Diners Club Ltd.* [1988] 2 All E.R. 1016, 1023, affd. [1989] 1 W.L.R. 1196.
48 See *ante*, p. 141.
49 See *Young* v. *Kitchin* (1878) 3 Ex.D. 127; *ante*, p. 593.

the benefit, or to the subject-matter of the contract. Where this is the case, a person (other than one of the original contracting parties) to whom the benefit is transferred must perform the burden, or at least forego the benefit if he fails to do so. If, for example, a right to extract minerals is subject to the duty to pay compensation if the surface of the land is let down, such compensation may have to be paid by the assignee of the mining right.[50] This exception, however, does not apply if the burden, though imposed in the same instrument which creates the right, is not a condition of its exercise but an independent obligation undertaken by the original grantee of the right.[51]

But even the burden of such independent obligations may have to be performed by an assignee under a second, and broader, exception to the general rule. This has been called by Megarry V.-C. the "pure principle of benefit and burden"[52]; it was "distinct from the conditional benefit cases, and cases of burdens annexed to property."[53] In *Tito* v. *Waddell* (*No. 2*)[54] a company that was engaged in mining phosphates on a Pacific island had acquired land there under contracts obliging it to return any worked out land to its former owners and to replant it. The rights under these contracts were transferred to commissioners "subject to . . . the covenants . . . therein contained"; and the commissioners undertook to keep the company indemnified against claims by the landowners under the original contracts. Many years after the company had been wound up, it was held that the commissioners were liable to the landowners for failing to perform the covenant to replant. Their liability was based on the "pure principle of benefit and burden."[55]

That principle had been recognised in a number of earlier cases[56]; but it does (as Megarry V.-C. said) give rise to the problem how the principle is to be reconciled with the view "that in general contractual burdens are not assignable, though contractual benefits are."[57] A person is certainly not subject to the burdens of a contract merely because he has taken benefits under it: it has, for example, been held that the equitable assignee of a licence to use a patent was not subject to the burdens imposed by the licence on the original licensee.[58] Such cases may seem to contradict the "pure principle of benefit and burden." But they could be explained either on the ground that the point was not argued, or on the ground that they fell outside the scope of that principle.[59] According to Megarry V.-C. in *Tito* v.

[50] *e.g. Aspden* v. *Seddon* (*No. 2*) (1876) 1 Ex.D. 496 (for earlier proceedings see (1875) L.R. 10 Ch.App. 394); *cf. Chamber Colliery Co. Ltd.* v. *Twyerould* (1893) [1915] 1 Ch. 268n; *Werderman* v. *Société Générale d'Electricité* (1881) 19 Ch.D. 246.

[51] *Radstock Co-operative and Industrial Society* v. *Norton-Radstock U.D.C.* [1967] Ch. 1094; [1968] Ch. 605. For independent obligations, *cf. post,* p. 664.

[52] *Tito* v. *Waddell* (*No. 2*) [1977] Ch. 106, 302.

[53] *Ibid.*

[54] [1977] Ch. 106.

[55] *Ibid.* p. 307; the original contracts between the company and the landowners had not made the benefits conditional on discharge of the burdens.

[56] *Elliston* v. *Reacher* [1908] 2 Ch. 665, 669 (in argument); *Halsall* v. *Brizell* [1957] Ch. 169, 182 (but the point was conceded; see p. 180; and not necessary for the decision); *E. R. Ives Investment Ltd.* v. *High* [1967] 2 Q.B. 379, 394, 399, 400 (where estoppel was another ground of decision).

[57] [1977] Ch. at p. 291; *cf.* p. 299.

[58] *Bagot Pneumatic Tyre Co.* v. *Clipper Pneumatic Tyre Co.* [1902] 1 Ch. 146; *cf. Cox* v. *Bishop* (1857) 8 D.M. & G. 815; *Barker* v. *Stickney* [1919] 1 K.B. 121.

[59] See specially *Bagot's* case *supra,* at p. 156.

Waddell (*No. 2*) the question whether an assignee is subject, under the principle, to a contractual burden "will prima facie depend upon the circumstances in which he comes into the transaction."[60] If only the *benefit* of the contract had been assigned, and the assign*or* had undertaken to continue to discharge the burdens, it would be "remarkable"[61] if the assignee became liable to that burden. But in *Tito* v. *Waddell* (*No. 2*) the commissioners were subject to the burden since they took as "a purported assignee of the whole contract from a company which [was] on the point of going into liquidation, he undertaking to discharge all the burdens and to indemnify the company. . . . "[62] The scope of the "pure principle of benefit and burden" therefore depends on the intention of assignor and assignee as it appears from the terms of the assignment and the surrounding circumstances. An intention to subject an assignee of contractual rights to liabilities under the contract will not generally be inferred[63]; so that the scope of the "pure principle of benefit and burden" is likely to be a narrow one. Even where it applies, it does not strictly transfer a liability; for the assignor remains liable to the other contracting party.

3. Operation of Law

In the following cases, a creditor may by operation of law be entitled to sue someone (other than the original debtor) who has not voluntarily undertaken such liability.

(1) Death

Contractual liabilities pass to the personal representatives of a deceased person in the sense that they must apply his assets in discharging those liabilities. They are not personally liable, so that there is no true transfer of liability.

(2) Bankruptcy

Contractual liabilities of a bankrupt pass to his trustee in bankruptcy in the sense that the latter must distribute the bankrupt's assets among his creditors. Again there is no true transfer of liability as the trustee is not personally liable. He can also disclaim a contract which is wholly or partly executory if it is onerous or unprofitable, *e.g.* a lease at too high a rent.[64] Such disclaimer puts an end to the contract but does not relieve the bankrupt's estate from liability for breach of it.

(3) Statute

Under the Bills of Lading Act 1855, the consignment of goods under a bill of lading or the indorsement of the bill may transfer to a consignee or indorsee

---

60 [1977] Ch. 106, 302.
61 *Ibid.*
62 *Ibid.*
63 *Ibid.* p. 291; *cf.* p. 299.
64 Insolvency Act 1986, s.315; *cf. ibid.* s.178. For exceptions, see Companies Act 1989, s.164

all rights, and also subject the consignee or indorsee to all liabilities, of the original shipper under the bill.[65] But the original shipper normally remains liable as well,[66] so that his liability is not, strictly speaking, transferred. A statute which nationalises or privatises an enterprise may also transfer the liabilities (as well as the assets) of that enterprise to its statutory successor.[67]

---

[65] Bills of Lading Act 1855, s.1. For proposals for reform, see Law Com. No. 196 (1991).

[66] *Ibid.* s.2 (expressly preserving his liability for freight); *Fox* v. *Knott* (1861) 6 H. & N. 630.

[67] See *Re British Concrete Pipe Association* [1983] 1 All E.R. 203, distinguishing *Nokes* v. *Doncaster Amalgamated Collieries Ltd.* [1940] A.C. 1014, on the point made at p. 657, *post*.

CHAPTER SEVENTEEN

AGENCY[1]

SECTION 1. DEFINITION

AGENCY is a relationship which arises when one person, called the principal, authorises another, called the agent, to act on his behalf, and the other agrees to do so. Generally, the relationship arises out of an agreement[2] between principal and agent. Its most important effect, for the purpose of this book, is that it enables the agent to make a contract between his principal and a third party.

1. Agreement

(1) General

The agreement between principal and agent is often a contract. But agency may also arise out of an agreement which does not amount to a contract because one of the parties lacks contractual capacity[3] or because there is no consideration. Thus the committee of a club, though they act gratuitously, may be agents of the members.[4]

(2) Agency without agreement

There may be agency without agreement in the following cases:

(a) OPERATION OF LAW. The law may attribute an agent to a person: for example, when a company is first formed, its original directors are its agents by operation of law.[5] Many statutes have created public corporations, some of which are regarded as agents of the Crown[6]: such agency arises simply by virtue of the incorporating statute. Moreover, by statute, one person, or the court, may have power to appoint an agent to act on behalf of another: thus a mortgagee can in certain circumstances appoint an agent of the mortgagor[7]; an administrative receiver appointed by debenture holders is deemed to be the agent of the company[8]; and a person appointed by the court to manage the affairs of a mental patient has been

---

[1] *Bowstead on Agency* (15th ed.); Powell, *Law of Agency* (2nd ed.); Hanbury, *Principles of Agency* (2nd ed.); Fridman, *Law of Agency* (5th ed.); Stoljar, *Law of Agency*; Markesinis and Munday, *An Outline of the Law of Agency* (2nd ed.).

[2] *Garnac Grain Co. Inc.* v. *Faure & Fairclough Ltd.* [1968] A.C. 1130, 1137; Fridman, 84 L.Q.R. 224; *J. H. Rayner (Mincing Lane) Ltd.* v. *D.T.I.* [1989] Ch. 72, 250 (and see *infra*, n. 5).

[3] *Post*, p. 612.

[4] *Cf. Flemyng* v. *Hector* (1836) 2 M. & W. 172.

[5] *Cf.* Companies Act 1985, s.282. But English law does not regard the company as agent for its shareholders: *J. H. Rayner (Mincing Lane) Ltd.* v. *D.T.I.* [1989] Ch. 72, 188 (approved on this point [1990] 2 A.C. 418, 515).

[6] *e.g. Bank voor Handel en Scheepvaart N.V.* v. *Administrator of Hungarian Property* [1954] A.C. 584.

[7] Law of Property Act 1925, s.101.

[8] Insolvency Act 1986, s.44(1)(*a*).

held to be the patient's agent.[9] At common law, one person may be regarded as the agent of another, even against the latter's will, under the doctrine of agency of necessity.[10]

(b) APPARENT AND USUAL AUTHORITY. Under the doctrines of apparent and usual authority[11] a principal is liable on contracts made by his agent although he has not authorised the agent to make them.

2. Intention to Act on Behalf of Principal

Whether a person intends to act on behalf of another is a question of fact. Thus a person who agrees out of friendship to ferry another's car from one place to another can be regarded as the owner's agent,[12] so that his negligent driving may make the owner liable in tort; but a person who borrows another's car for his own purposes would not be so regarded.[13] Even where the owner is liable for the driver's torts, it does not follow that the driver is his agent for other purposes, such as pledging his credit for repairs. Where a person does intend to act on behalf of another, agency may arise although a contract between the parties declares that there is no such relationship[14]; conversely the mere fact that a person says he is an agent does not make him one if he intends to act on his own behalf and not on behalf of his alleged principal.[15]

The rule that an agent must intend to act on behalf of his principal distinguishes agency from other analogous relationships, and is helpful in cases where it is clear that a person acted as agent, but not clear whose agent he was.

(1) Agency distinguished from other relationships

(a) BUYER AND SELLER. A retailer may describe himself as the "agent" of the manufacturer whose products he sells. This description is legally accurate if the retailer accounts to the manufacturer for the price paid by the customer, and is remunerated by a commission or salary paid by the manufacturer. But generally the retailer does not negotiate a contract between manufacturer and customer.[16] He is a middleman who buys and resells on his own behalf. He is the manufacturer's "agent" only in a commercial, and not in the legal sense. Thus if the goods are defective the customer can only sue the retailer, and not the manufacturer, on the contract of sale. The manufacturer is only liable to the customer in contract if he gives a guarantee[17]; he may also be liable in tort[18] if the customer suffers loss or injury because of a defect in the goods. Again a manufacturer who con-

---

[9] *Plumptom* v. *Burkinshaw* [1908] 2 K.B. 572.
[10] *Post*, pp. 621 *et seq.*
[11] *Post*, pp. 615–621.
[12] *e.g. Ormrod* v. *Crosville Motor Services Ltd.* [1953] 1 W.L.R. 1120; *Vandyke* v. *Fender* [1970] 2 Q.B. 292.
[13] *e.g. Hewitt* v. *Bonvin* [1940] 1 K.B. 188; *Morgans* v. *Launchbury* [1973] A.C. 127.
[14] *McLaughlin* v. *Gentles* (1919) 51 D.L.R. 383.
[15] *Kennedy* v. *De Trafford* [1897] A.C. 180, 188.
[16] Similar problems can arise in determining whether a person who is asked to procure goods for another is his agent or a seller to him: see *Ireland* v. *Livingston* (1871) L.R. 5 H.L. 395; Hill, 31 M.L.R. 623; *Kloekner & Co. A.G.* v. *Gatoil Overseas Inc.* [1990] 1 Lloyd's Rep. 177; *cf. Customs & Excise Commissioners* v. *Paget* [1989] S.T.C. 773.
[17] *Ante*, pp. 74, 523–524.
[18] For negligence at common law and irrespective of negligence under Consumer Protection Act 1987.

tracts to make something for a customer is not the agent of the customer. Although he makes the thing at the customer's request, he acts primarily for his own profit and on his own behalf.[19]

(b) HIRE-PURCHASE. A dealer who negotiates a hire-purchase agreement between a customer and a finance company is considered at common law to act primarily on his own behalf.[20] But he may be the agent of the company for some purposes, *e.g.* to accept offers on the terms of the company's proposal form.[21] And under the Consumer Credit Act 1974 he may be treated as the agent of the company when he makes any representation in the course of negotiations as to the quality of the goods,[22] and when he receives notice from the customer that the agreement has been cancelled or rescinded, or that the customer's offer has been withdrawn.[23]

(c) PROVISION OF SERVICES. Persons who are engaged in the business or profession of supplying services may be described as "agents" in the commercial sense, without being agents in the legal sense: "To carry on the business of an 'agent' is not the same thing as saying that you are contracting as agent."[24] For example, where a "forwarding agent" is engaged to arrange for goods to be transported to a foreign destination, he may act as agent (in the legal sense) in making a contract between the exporter and a carrier; but he may equally well act as principal in undertaking to get the goods to the specified destination.[25] Whether such persons act in the legal sense as agents depends on the responsibilities that they undertake in relation to the particular transaction. The same point may be illustrated by reference to two further examples.

(i) *Client and professional man.* In *Leicestershire C.C.* v. *Michael Faraday & Partners Ltd.*[26] the plaintiffs employed a firm of valuers and later claimed to be entitled to certain documents made by the valuers in the course of the valuation. They based their claim on cases in which it had been held that a principal was entitled to documents created by his agent in the course of his employment. In rejecting the plaintiffs' claim, MacKinnon L.J. said that those cases were "radically different from the present case as being concerned with the relative rights and duties of principal and agent. . . . The present case is emphatically not one of principal and agent. It is the case of the relations between a client and a professional man to whom the client resorts for advice."[27] Some professional advisers, such as solicitors[28] and architects[29] often do act as agents for their clients. Other

---

[19] *Dixon* v. *London Small Arms Co.* (1876) 1 App.Cas. 632.

[20] *Mercantile Credit Co. Ltd.* v. *Hamblin* [1965] 2 Q.B. 242, 269. In *Branwhite* v. *Worcester Works Finance Ltd.* [1969] 1 A.C. 552 Lords Morris, Guest and Upjohn took the view stated in the text, but Lords Reid and Wilberforce thought that the dealer would normally be the finance company's agent.

[21] *Northgran Finance Ltd.* v. *Ashley* [1963] 1 Q.B. 476.

[22] s.56(2); by s.56(3) a provision in a regulated agreement purporting to make the dealer the *customer's* agent is void.

[23] ss.69(6), 102(1), 57(3). See also s.175 for the "agent's" duty to transmit such notices.

[24] *Elektronska etc.* v. *Transped etc.* [1986] 1 Lloyd's Rep. 49, 52.

[25] See *Jones* v. *European General Express* (1920) 25 Com.Cas. 296.

[26] [1941] 2 K.B. 205.

[27] At p. 216.

[28] *e.g. Tudor* v. *Hamid* [1988] 1 E.G.L.R. 251 (vendor's solicitor vendor's agent in receiving deposit); contrast *Hastingwood Property Ltd.* v. *Sanders Bearman Anselm* [1990] 3 All E.R. 107.

[29] *e.g. Gibson* v. *Pease* [1905] 1 K.B. 810.

professional persons are engaged simply to produce specified results: for example, to prepare a report or to paint a picture. Such persons have no power to act on behalf of their clients; and it is to this type of "professional man" that MacKinnon L.J. refers in the *Leicester* case.

(ii) *Estate agents*[30] An estate agent who is instructed to negotiate the sale of a house by private treaty has normally[31] no power to make a contract between his client and a prospective purchaser. He may for certain purposes act on behalf of the client, *e.g.* for the purpose of making representations about the property[32]; and he also owes the client certain duties similar to those owed by an agent to his principal.[33] But "an estate agent, despite the style, is an independent person"[34] who for most purposes does not normally act in the legal sense as the vendor's agent. In particular, he does not so act when he receives a deposit from a person who has agreed, subject to contract, to buy the property.[35] So long as no contract of sale has been concluded, he must not pay the deposit over to his client. He holds the money in trust for the prospective purchaser,[36] and must return it to him on demand[37]; but if he fails to do so the client is not liable for the deposit unless he had expressly authorised the estate agent to receive it on his behalf.[38]

(2) Whose agent?

It may be clear that a person is an agent, but doubtful whose agent he is. Thus it has been held that a London agent employed by a country solicitor is not the agent of the lay client, but that he is the agent of the country solicitor.[39] On the other hand counsel, though briefed by the solicitor, is the client's agent.[40]

In other cases the question is whether a person who is undoubtedly the agent of P may not also for some purposes be the agent of Q. Thus persons employed by an insurance company to solicit proposals for insurance are generally the company's agents,[41] but may become the agents of the proposer when helping him to complete the proposal form.[42] On the other hand insurance brokers are for most purposes agents of the insured persons

---

[30] Murdoch, 91 L.Q.R. 357.

[31] *i.e.* unless specifically so authorised, as seems to have been the case in *Spiro* v. *Lintern* [1973] 1 W.L.R. 1002, 1006. For a statutory definition of "estate agency work," see Estate Agents Act 1979, s.1(1).

[32] *Sorrell* v. *Finch* [1977] A.C. 728, 753.

[33] *e.g. Regier* v. *Campbell-Stuart* [1939] Ch. 766 (agent engaged to *find* a property for the client).

[34] *Sorrell* v. *Finch* [1977] A.C. 728, 753.

[35] *Sorrell* v. *Finch, supra*; *John McCann & Co.* v. *Pow* [1974] 1 W.L.R. 1643, 1647; Reynolds, 92 L.Q.R. 484; Markesinis [1976] C.L.J. 237.

[36] Estate Agents Act 1979, s.13(1)(*a*).

[37] At common law, he is not liable for interest: *Potters* v. *Loppert* [1973] Ch. 399; but regulations made under Estate Agents Act 1979, s.15 may impose such liability.

[38] *Ryan* v. *Pilkington* [1959] 1 W.L.R. 403, as explained in *Sorrell* v. *Finch*, *supra*, at p. 750; *cf. Ojelay* v. *Neosale* [1987] 2 E.G.L.R. 167.

[39] *Robbins* v. *Fennell* (1847) 11 Q.B. 248.

[40] *Grindell* v. *Bass* [1920] 2 Ch. 487.

[41] *Bawden* v. *London Assurance* [1892] 2 Q.B. 534; *Stone* v. *Reliance Mutual Insurance Soc. Ltd.* [1972] 1 Lloyd's Rep. 469; Reynolds, 88 L.Q.R. 462.

[42] *Biggar* v. *Rock Life Assurance Co.* [1902] 1 K.B. 516; *Newsholme* v. *Road Transport Insurance Co.* [1929] 2 K.B. 356; *cf. ante*, p. 303.

and not of the insurers.[43] But they may be agents of the insurers for some purposes, such as the provision of interim insurance cover until the policy is issued.[44] Again, directors of a company are primarily the agents of the company, and not of the shareholders; but they may for some purposes become agents of the shareholders, *e.g.* for the purpose of negotiating a sale of their shares.[45]

SECTION 2. CAPACITY

1. Capacity to Act as Agent

As agency is a consensual but not necessarily a contractual relationship, any person who is capable of consenting can act as agent, although his contractual capacity may be limited. In the days when married women lacked contractual capacity they could nonetheless act as agents.[46] Similarly, a minor can, it seems, be agent to make a contract which he has no capacity to make on his own behalf; and a corporation could probably act as agent in respect of a transaction which was *ultra vires*. But to say that a person of limited contractual capacity can act as agent does not mean that his agreement to do so gives rise to all the legal consequences that usually result from the relationship of principal and agent. It means that he can make a contract between his principal and a third party, but not that he acquires all the rights or is subject to all the liabilities of an agent towards his principal or the third party. The agent could not be made liable if to hold him liable would defeat the protection which the law means to give him by limiting his capacity. Thus he could not be made liable on the contract between principal and third party, even though the circumstances were such that an agent of full capacity would be so liable.[47] On the other hand, there is no reason to suppose that he would be denied the ordinary agent's right of indemnity[48] against his principal.

2. Capacity to Act as Principal

Capacity to act as principal is determined by the rules governing contractual capacity generally. Thus a minor cannot make himself liable for luxuries merely by employing an agent. But he can appoint an agent to make a contract which would have bound him if he had made it personally.[49]

This rule again applies primarily to determine the reciprocal rights and liabilities of principal and third party. It might also protect the principal from liability to the agent. Thus a principal who was under age would not be liable to indemnify an agent employed to buy luxuries. But the rule would not necessarily protect the agent: thus an under-age principal might

---

[43] *Anglo-African Merchants* v. *Bayley* [1970] 1 Q.B. 311, 322; *McNealy* v. *Pennine Ins. Co.* [1978] 2 Lloyd's Rep. 18. For criticism, see *Roberts* v. *Plaisted* [1989] 2 Lloyd's Rep. 341, 345.

[44] *Stockton* v. *Mason* [1978] 2 Lloyd's Rep. 430 (except in cases of marine insurance: *cf. ante*, p. 165).

[45] *Briess* v. *Woolley* [1954] A.C. 333.

[46] *Stevenson* v. *Hardie* (1773) 2 Wm.Bl. 872.

[47] *Post*, pp. 635 *et seq.*

[48] *Post*, p. 646.

[49] See Webb, 18 M.L.R. 861; R.E.M., 69 L.Q.R. 446; a contrary dictum in *Shephard* v. *Cartwright* [1953] Ch. 728, 755 (reversed without reference to this point [1955] A.C. 431) was later corrected in *G. (A.)* v. *G. (T.)* [1970] 2 Q.B. 644, 651–652.

well have a remedy against the agent if the latter accepted a bribe[50] from the third party.

SECTION 3. CREATION OF AGENCY

Agency may arise by express or implied agreement, or without agreement under the doctrines of apparent and usual authority, and where a person has authority of necessity. Finally, agency may arise *ex post facto* by ratification.

1. Agency by Agreement

(1) Express authority

An agent's authority is commonly conferred by express appointment. No formality is required. Oral appointment suffices even where the agent is appointed to make a contract which has to be in writing, or evidenced in writing.[51]

The extent of an agent's express authority depends on the true construction of the words of the appointment. If these are vague or ambiguous, the principal may be bound even if the agent, in good faith, interprets them in a sense not intended by the principal. Thus in *Weigall* v. *Runciman*[52] the principal instructed his agent to "fix" a steamer, intending the agent to *let* a steamer. It was held that the principal was bound when the agent instead *hired* a steamer. But where the terms of the appointment are vague, ambiguous or self-contradictory, the speed of modern communications will often make it reasonable for the agent to seek clarification of his instructions, and if he fails to do so he will not be able to rely on his own erroneous interpretation of his instructions.[53]

(2) Implied authority

(a) EXISTENCE OF AUTHORITY IMPLIED. The very existence of agency may be implied, either from conduct on a particular occasion, or from some other relationship. Thus a husband who lives with his wife impliedly authorises her to pledge his credit for necessary household expenses.[54] This authority is not a legal consequence of marriage, but depends on the inference of fact that the husband has permitted the wife to pledge his credit as manager of the household. The authority therefore does not arise where there is no household because the parties live in an hotel.[55] But where there is a household, the authority can arise even though the parties are not married.[56] As the authority is based on implied consent, it can be negatived if the husband forbids his wife to pledge his credit.[57] The wife's auth-

---

[50] *Post*, p. 648.
[51] *Heard* v. *Pilley* (1869) L.R. 4 Ch. 548.
[52] (1916) 85 L.J.K.B. 1187; *cf. Ireland* v. *Livingston* (1871) L.R. 5 H.L. 395, as explained in *Woodhouse A.C. Israel Cocoa Ltd. S.A.* v. *Nigerian Produce Marketing Co.* [1972] A.C. 741, 757, 771–772.
[53] *European Asian Bank* v. *Punjab & Sind Bank* (*No.* 2) [1983] 1 W.L.R. 642, 656 (where the claim succeeded on another ground).
[54] *Jewsbury* v. *Newbold* (1857) 26 L.J.Ex. 247; *Phillipson* v. *Hayter* (1870) L.R. 6 C.P. 38, 42; *Gage* v. *King* [1961] 1 Q.B. 188 (medical bills).
[55] *Debenham* v. *Mellon* (1880) 6 App.Cas. 24.
[56] *Blades* v. *Free* (1829) 9 B. & C. 167; *post*, p. 651.
[57] *Jolly* v. *Rees* (1864) 15 C.B.(N.S.) 628; *Miss Gray Ltd.* v. *Cathcart* (1922) 38 T.L.R. 562.

ority is also negatived if the husband gives her an adequate housekeeping allowance[58]; if the husband warns the tradesman not to supply goods to the wife on his credit; and if the wife already has an adequate supply of the goods in question.[59] The cases which lay down these rules are unlikely to be of much significance in modern conditions when household supplies are generally paid for either in cash or on credit terms requiring the signature of the debtor personally[60]; but they could still have some practical importance in relation to services supplied to the household. A child has no implied authority to pledge his parents' credit; but such authority may be implied if the parent stands by and acquiesces in a purchase made by the child on his account.[61]

(b) INCIDENTAL AUTHORITY. An agent who is appointed for a particular purpose may have implied authority to do acts incidental to the execution of that authority. For example, a solicitor, or counsel engaged to conduct litigation, may have implied authority to compromise the suit.[62] On the other hand, an agent employed to sell a thing has generally no authority to receive payment for it.[63] The question whether he has authority to warrant its quality is one of fact, depending on the circumstances of each case.[64]

(c) CUSTOMARY AUTHORITY.[65] A principal who employs an agent to act for him in a particular market impliedly authorises the agent to act in accordance with the custom of that market.[66] He is bound by the custom even if he is not aware of it.[67] But the inference that the principal authorised the agent to act in accordance with the custom cannot be drawn if the custom is inconsistent with the instructions given by the principal to the agent, or with the very relationship of principal and agent. The custom is then said to be "unreasonable" and the principal is not bound by it unless he knows of it. Thus in *Perry* v. *Barnett*[68] an agent who had been employed to buy bank shares failed to comply with an Act of Parliament then in force[69] by which such contracts were void unless the numbers of the shares were stated in the contract note. The principal did not know of a custom of the Stock Exchange to disregard the Act, and it was held that he was not bound by the custom. It was inconsistent with the agent's instructions since it resulted in his making a void contract when he was employed to make a valid one. Again, in some markets there is a custom by which an agent

---

58 *Morel Bros.* v. *Westmorland* [1903] 1 K.B. 63; affirmed [1904] A.C. 11.

59 *Miss Gray Ltd.* v. *Cathcart* (1922) 38 T.L.R. 562, 565; *Seaton* v. *Benedict* (1828) 5 Bing. 28.

60 See Consumer Credit Act 1974, s.61(1)(*a*): the requirement of signature "*by* the debtor . . . and *by or on behalf* of the creditor" indicates that signature on behalf of the debtor is insufficient.

61 *Law* v. *Wilkin* (1837) 6 A. & E. 718; some dicta in this case are too sweeping: *Mortimore* v. *Wright* (1840) 6 M. & W. 487.

62 *Waugh* v. *H. B. Clifford & Sons* [1982] Ch. 374.

63 *Mynn* v. *Jolliffe* (1834) 1 M. & Rob. 326; *Butwick* v. *Grant* [1924] 2 K.B. 483. *Cf. ante*, p. 611 as to deposits received by estate agents.

64 Such authority was implied in *Alexander* v. *Gibson* (1811) 2 Camp. 555; *Howard* v. *Sheward* (1866) L.R. 2 C.P. 148; and *Baldry* v. *Bates* (1885) 52 L.T. 620; contrast *Brady* v. *Todd* (1861) 9 C.B.(N.S.) 592.

65 *Cf. ante*, p. 194, for the view that it is artificial to base such authority on actual agreement.

66 *Graves* v. *Legg* (1857) 2 H. & N. 210.

67 *Pollock* v. *Stables* (1848) 12 Q.B. 765; *Cropper* v. *Cook* (1868) L.R. 3 C.P. 194; *Reynolds* v. *Smith* (1893) 9 T.L.R. 494.

68 (1885) 15 Q.B.D. 388; contrast *Seymour* v. *Bridge* (1885) 14 Q.B.D. 460, where the principal knew of the custom.

69 Banking Companies (Shares) Act 1867, repealed by Statute Law Revision Act 1966.

employed by several principals is allowed to buy in bulk to satisfy the needs of all. In *Robinson* v. *Mollett*[70] a custom to this effect in the tallow market was held unreasonable since its effect was to turn an agent into a seller. This was inconsistent with the relationship of principal and agent since an agent must buy for his principal as cheaply as he can, while a seller sells at the highest price he can get. But in *Scott* v. *Godfrey*[71] a custom of the Stock Exchange permitting stockbrokers to buy enough shares for several principals from a single seller was held reasonable because all the parties intended that contracts should be made between the seller and the various buyers.

2. Agency without Agreement

(1) Apparent authority

Where a person represents to a third party that he has authorised an agent to act on his behalf, he may, as against the third party, not be allowed to deny the truth of the representation, and be bound by the agent's act whether he in fact authorised it or not. In *Summers* v. *Solomon*,[72] for instance, the defendant employed a manager to run a jeweller's shop and regularly paid for jewellery ordered by the manager from the plaintiff for resale in the shop. The manager left the defendant's employment, ordered further jewellery in the defendant's name, and absconded with it. The defendant was held liable to pay for this jewellery since he had by his past conduct caused the plaintiff to believe that the manager had authority to pledge his credit, and had not informed the plaintiff that that authority had come to an end.

The following conditions must be satisfied before apparent authority arises:

(a) THERE MUST BE A REPRESENTATION OF AUTHORITY. This may be express but it is more frequently implied: for example, from a course of dealing, as in *Summers* v. *Solomon*; or from placing the agent in such a position that it is reasonable for third parties to assume that he has the principal's authority to make a contract of the kind in question[73]; or from the known relationship of the parties, so that a retiring partner continues to be liable to those who deal with the firm and know that he was a member of it, but not that he has retired.[74] In such cases, the apparent authority is said to be *general* in character since it extends generally to all transactions which a person, in the position in which the principal has placed the agent, is normally regarded as having authority to conclude.[75] Even where the agent

---

[70] (1875) L.R. 7 H.L. 802; *cf. North & South Trust Co.* v. *Berkeley* [1971] 1 W.L.R. 471.

[71] [1901] 2 Q.B. 726.

[72] (1857) 7 E. & B. 879; *cf. Pole* v. *Leask* (1862) 33 L.J.Ch. 155; *The Unique Mariner* [1978] 1 Lloyd's Rep. 438; *The Shamah* [1981] 1 Lloyd's Rep. 40; *Waugh* v. *H. B. Clifford & Sons* [1982] Ch. 374. The following discussion deals only with the extent to which the principal can as a result of the representation be held liable on an unauthorised contract. It is not concerned with any other form of liability for misrepresentation.

[73] *Panorama Developments (Guildford) Ltd.* v. *Fidelis Furnishing Fabrics Ltd.* [1971] 2 Q.B. 711; *The Ocean Frost* [1986] A.C. 717, 777; *United Bank of Kuwait* v. *Hamoud* [1988] 1 W.L.R. 1051; *cf. Strover* v. *Harrington* [1988] Ch. 390, 409–410; contrast *Cleveland Manufacturing Co.* v. *Muslim Commercial Bank Ltd.* [1981] 2 Lloyd's Rep. 646.

[74] Partnership Act 1890, s.14(1); and *cf. Scarf* v. *Jardine* (1882) 7 App.Cas. 345.

[75] *The Ocean Frost* [1986] A.C. 717, 777; contrast *The Suwalki* [1989] 1 Lloyd's Rep. 511 (shipbroker has no such authority).

has no such apparent authority by virtue of his position, he may have *specific* apparent authority to enter into a particular transaction; but since in such cases it must be clear to the third party that the agent does not *normally* have authority to conclude a transaction of that kind, the principal will only be liable on this basis if the third party can show that the principal expressly represented that the agent had authority to enter into the particular contract on his behalf.[76]

(b) THE REPRESENTATION MUST BE OF FACT. A representation of law does not give rise to apparent authority.[77] Thus a third party cannot rely on the doctrine of apparent authority if he has read the terms of the agent's appointment, but has misconstrued them, since the construction of a document is a question of law.

(c) THE REPRESENTATION MUST BE THAT THE "AGENT" IS AUTHORISED TO ACT AS AGENT. Apparent authority does not arise if a person is represented to be the *owner* of a business or other property. In such cases the representor may well be bound under the doctrine of usual authority, or under some analogous doctrine.[78] But these doctrines have only a limited scope, and where they do not apply, the representee can only fall back on the more general doctrine of apparent authority if the representation is one of *agency*.

(d) THE REPRESENTATION MUST BE MADE BY THE PRINCIPAL. Apparent authority can only arise out of a representation made by the principal: it cannot arise out of a representation made by some other person[79] or out of one made by the agent himself.[80] Thus in *Att.-Gen. for Ceylon* v. *Silva*[81] a Crown agent untruly represented that he had authority to sell steel plates which were Crown property. The Privy Council held that the Crown was not bound by the sale since the agent had no actual authority, and since apparent authority could only arise out of a representation made by the principal and not out of one made by the agent. Of course, a principal may represent that the agent has authority to make further representations on his behalf; and such a representation may be made by the principal's conduct, for example, by placing the agent in a position in which he would normally have authority to enter into a transaction of the type in question (even though in the particular case the agent's actual authority to do so had been negatived by the express instructions of the principal).[82] In such a case, the agent may by his own representation enlarge an existing authority,[83] but such a representation cannot create an apparent authority out of nothing.[84]

---

[76] *The Ocean Frost, ubi supra*, where the third party's claim on this basis failed.
[77] *Cf. ante*, p. 298; *post*, p. 641.
[78] *Post*, pp. 619–621.
[79] *The Rhodian River* [1984] 1 Lloyd's Rep. 373.
[80] *Lanyon* v. *Blanchard* (1811) 2 Camp. 597; *British Bank of the Middle East* v. *Sun Life Assurance Co. of Canada (U.K.) Ltd.* [1983] 2 Lloyd's Rep. 9, 17; *The Raffaela* [1985] 2 Lloyd's Rep. 36, 43; *The Ocean Frost* [1986] A.C. 717, 778; *The Suwalki* [1989] 1 Lloyd's Rep. 511.
[81] [1953] A.C. 461; and see *post*, p. 620.
[82] *United Bank of Kuwait* v. *Hamoud* [1988] 1 W.L.R. 1051.
[83] *The Raffaela* [1985] 2 Lloyd's Rep. 36, 43.
[84] *The Ocean Frost* [1986] A.C. 717, 778. *United Bank of Kuwait* v. *Hamoud* [1988] 1 W.L.R. 1051, 1064 ("cannot hold himself out").

(e) THE REPRESENTATION MUST BE MADE TO THE THIRD PARTY. The representation must be made to a third person or group of persons. The old notion of holding a person out as agent "to the world"[85] has long been discredited.[86] Nor does a representation made by principal to agent give rise to apparent authority.

(f) THE THIRD PARTY MUST HAVE RELIED ON THE REPRESENTATION. The third party must have been induced by the representation to deal with the agent in the belief that the principal had authorised the agent to enter into the transaction.[87] Two consequences flow from this requirement. First, the representation must actually be known to the third party; and this requirement cannot have been satisfied if the representation is contained in a document which has not actually come to his attention.[88] Secondly, the third party is not allowed to say that he relied on the representation if he knew that it was untrue, or if he had, but did not take, a reasonable chance of reading the agent's instructions and so of discovering the truth.[89]

These requirements have given rise to particular difficulties in cases in which a third party dealt with a corporation through an agent who had no actual authority to enter into the transaction. In the case of a company incorporated under the Companies Acts, these difficulties arose largly because the authority of such an agent might be set out in, or limited by, the company's memorandum or articles of association; and, before the changes in the law to be discussed below, the rule was that the third party had constructive notice of these documents.[90] This doctrine of constructive notice operated in favour of the company but not against it. Thus if the memorandum or articles *limited* the power of the company's officer, the third party was deemed to know of the limitation and could not rely on an appearance of authority inconsistent with it. But if they *conferred* power, the third party could not base a case of apparent authority on them, for he could not be said to have relied on something of which he was only deemed to know (but did not actually know).[91] This state of the law could cause considerable hardship to third parties, and two important changes in the law were made by the Companies Act 1989.

First, the doctrine of constructive or deemed notice of the company's registered documents has been abolished.[92] A third party may, indeed, still be "affected by notice of any matter by reason of a failure to make such inquiries as he ought reasonably to have made."[93] But the latter provision is of limited importance in the present context because "a party to a trans-

---

[85] *Whitehead* v. *Tuckett* (1812) 15 East 400, 411.

[86] *Dickinson* v. *Valpy* (1829) 10 B. & C. 128, 140.

[87] For cases in which this requirement was not satisfied, see *Kooragang Investments Pty. Ltd.* v. *Richardson & Wrench Ltd.* [1982] A.C. 462; *Bedford Insurance Co. Ltd.* v. *Instituto de Ressaguros do Brasil* [1985] Q.B. 966; *The Ocean Frost* [1986] A.C. 717.

[88] *The Ocean Frost* [1986] A.C. 717, 778.

[89] *Jacobs* v. *Morris* [1902] 1 Ch. 816; *Overbrooke Estates Ltd.* v. *Glencombe Properties Ltd.* [1974] 1 W.L.R. 1335; Coote, [1975] C.L.J. 17; *Rolled Steel* (*Holdings*) *Ltd.* v. *B.S.C.* [1986] Ch. 246, 295–296. The principle seems to have been overlooked in *Mendelssohn* v. *Normand Ltd.* [1970] 1 Q.B. 177.

[90] *Mahony* v. *East Holyford Mining Co. Ltd.* (1875) L.R. 7 H.L. 869.

[91] See *Rama Corp.* v. *Proved Tin & General Investments Ltd.* [1952] 2 Q.B. 147, discussing earlier authorities; for further discussion, see *Freeman & Lockyer* v. *Buckhurst Properties* (*Mangal*) *Ltd.* [1964] 2 Q.B. 480.

[92] Companies Act 1985, s.711A(1) (as inserted by Companies Act 1989, s.142).

[93] *Ibid.* s.711A(2).

action with a company is not bound to enquire as to whether it is permitted by the company's memorandum or as to any limitation on the powers of the board of directors to bind the company *or to authorise others to do so*."[94] The third party is thus not bound to inquire whether the directors actually had the power to authorise the agent, with whom he dealt, to enter into the transaction on behalf of the company.

Secondly, in favour of a person dealing in good faith with the company, the power of the board of directors to bind the company is "deemed to be free of any limitation under the company's constitution."[95] This provision has already been discussed[96]; here it is only necessary to repeat that a person does not act in bad faith merely because he knows that an act is beyond the powers of the directors under the company's constitution.[97] Liability under this provision may therefore arise even though the requirements of the doctrine of apparent authority are *not* satisfied because the third party knows of the limitation on the directors' authority.

The common law principles governing apparent authority can, however, still apply where the third party relies, not on the apparent *existence* of powers, but on their *exercise*. The point may be illustrated by supposing that the board of directors of a company has power under the articles to appoint a managing director, but that the person with whom the third party has dealt as such has not actually been appointed to the post. The third party cannot then rely simply on the fact that the board had power to make the appointment. But the third party's claim will be upheld if he can show that there has been a representation by the persons entitled to make the appointment, to the effect that it has in fact been made. Such a representation need not be express but may be implied from conduct: for example, from the action of the board in allowing the person with whom the third party dealt to act as managing director. The company will then be bound by contracts made by him (even though he has not actually been appointed managing director) so long as those contracts are within the scope of the authority normally conferred on managing directors.[98] A company may also be bound by contracts made by its officers on the ground that they were impliedly authorised to make them; but here the liability is based on actual (implied) and not on apparent authority.[99]

(g) FORGERIES BY AGENT. In two cases company secretaries affixed the common seals of their companies to documents which they had forged. It was held that third parties who were taken in by the forgeries could not, against the companies, rely on them.[1] But in *Uxbridge P.B.S.* v. *Pickard*[2] a solicitor's clerk obtained money by way of mortgage on the strength of forged title deeds alleged to belong to a fictitious client. His principal was held liable. In the former cases, the secretaries had not been held out as having authority to execute the documents (respectively a power of attorney and a share transfer). In the latter case, the clerk had been held

---

[94] *Ibid.* s.35B (as inserted by Companies Act 1989, s.108(1)).
[95] *Ibid.* s.35A(1).
[96] *Ante*, p. 506.
[97] Companies Act 1985, s.35A(2)(*b*) (as inserted by Companies Act 1989, s.108(1)).
[98] *Freeman & Lockyer* v. *Buckhurst Properties (Mangal) Ltd.*, *supra*, n. 91
[99] *Hely-Hutchinson* v. *Brayhead Ltd.* [1968] 1 Q.B. 549, 573; Nock, 30 M.L.R. 705.
[1] *Bank of Ireland* v. *Evan's Trustees* (1855) 5 H.L.C. 389; *Ruben* v. *Great Fingall Consolidated* [1906] A.C. 439.
[2] [1939] 2 K.B. 248.

out as having authority to conclude mortgage transactions. Alternatively, the first two cases can be regarded as cases in which the agent, in effect, forged the principal's signature. When this happens, the third party is not induced to believe that the agent has his principal's authority, but that the signature is the act of the principal himself. Such a belief does not give rise to apparent authority.[3] The person whose signature is forged is only liable if he knew of the forgery and acquiesced in it.[4]

(h) SUBSEQUENT CONDUCT OF "PRINCIPAL." A person may be bound by a contract, even though the requirements of apparent authority are not satisfied, if he is precluded by his subsequent conduct from denying that the contract was made on his behalf. In *Spiro* v. *Lintern*[5] a wife purported to enter into a contract for the sale of her husband's house. She had no actual authority to do so, nor had the husband before the transaction led the purchaser to believe that she was his agent for the purpose. But afterwards the husband met the purchaser, gave him the impression that there was a binding contract and allowed him to incur expenses in connection with the property. It was held that the husband was estopped[6] from denying his wife's authority to make the contract on his behalf.

(2) Usual authority

(a) MEANING. The phrase "usual authority" is used in a number of senses. First, it may mean implied authority, and, in particular, incidental authority.[7] Secondly, it may refer to cases in which an agent has apparent authority because he has been placed by his principal in a situation in which he would have had incidental authority, if this had not been expressly negatived by instructions given to him by the principal (and not communicated to the third party).[8] But the phrase will here be used in a third sense, to refer to cases in which a principal is bound by his agent's contracts although there is no express, implied or apparent authority. This usage is based on *Watteau* v. *Fenwick*,[9] where the owner of a public-house was sued for the price of cigars bought without his authority by his manager for the purposes of the business. The manager had bought the cigars in his own name. Thus the seller could not rely on any appearance of authority since he believed, at the time of the contract, that the manager was contracting on his own behalf. But the defendant was nonetheless held liable. Wills J. said: "The principal is liable for all the acts of the agent which are within the authority usually confided to an agent of that character, notwithstanding limitations, as between the principal and the agent, put upon that authority. It is said that this is only so where there has been a holding out of authority. . . . But I do not think so."[10]

---

[3] *Cf. Kooragang Investments Pty. Ltd.* v. *Richardson & Wrench Ltd.* [1982] A.C. 462.
[4] *Greenwood* v. *Martins Bank Ltd.* [1933] A.C. 51.
[5] [1973] 1 W.L.R. 1002; followed in *Worboys* v. *Carter* [1987] 2 E.G.L.R. 1; *cf. Janred Properties Ltd.* v. *Ente Nazionale Italiano per il Turismo* [1989] 2 All E.R. 444.
[6] Detrimental reliance by the third party is necessary for this type of estoppel (*ante*, p. 361); while for the purposes of apparent authority, "the only detriment that has to be shown . . . is the entering into the contract:" *The Tatra* [1990] 2 Lloyd's Rep. 51, 59.
[7] *Ante*, p. 614.
[8] *The Raffaella* [1985] 2 Lloyd's Rep. 56, 41.
[9] [1893] 1 Q.B. 346.
[10] At pp. 348–349; *cf. The Ocean Frost* [1986] A.C. 717, 734 (affd. *ibid.* 773), where there was no holding out for the different reason stated at pp. 615–616, *ante*.

This decision has been criticised,[11] and has been more often distinguished than followed, but the very fact that later courts have thought it necessary to distinguish the case shows that it is still law.[12] There are, moreover, other cases in which a principal is bound by his agent's acts done outside the scope of his express, implied or apparent authority. Thus if a principal gives his agent documents and authorises him to borrow a fixed sum on the security of them, he may be liable to a third party from whom the agent borrows more, even though the third party did not think that the agent had any authority to borrow.[13] Similarly, at common law a person was bound by an unauthorised sale of his goods by a factor, though the factor sold in his own name.[14] At common law, he was not bound by an unauthorised pledge, but under the Factors Act 1889, he is bound in certain circumstances by any disposition made by such an agent. These rules are, it is submitted, based on the same principle as *Watteau* v. *Fenwick*. That principle seems to be more closely analogous to the doctrine of vicarious liability in tort (under which an employer may be liable even for forbidden acts if done by an employee in the course of employment[15]) than to the doctrine of apparent authority.

Two Privy Council decisions can be said to be inconsistent with the principle of usual authority, in that they simply did not consider it as a possible basis of liability where the requirements of apparent authority were not satisfied. But in the first[16] the question was where a principal could be held *criminally* liable for his agent's unauthorised act in purporting to enter, on the principal's behalf, into a contract which the latter was by statute prohibited from making. The negative answer given to this question can be explained on the ground that the courts are reluctant to impose criminal liability without *mens rea*. And in the second case[17] the contract was a sale of Crown property made without actual or apparent authority. The conclusion that the Crown was not bound was supported on the ground that "The subject derives benefits . . . from property vested in the Crown, and its proper protection is necessary in the interests of the subject, though it may cause hardship to an individual."[18] But this argument proves too much, for the need to give "proper protection" to Crown property would seem to extend to *all* dispositions which were actually unauthorised, *i.e.* even to those within the agent's apparent authority. In fact, the Privy Council's reasoning is an argument only against ordering the Crown to deliver the goods, and such specific relief is not available against the Crown, even where it is bound by a contract.[19] The argument does not explain why the disappointed contractor should not receive damages or compensation; and in deciding whether such a remedy ought to be available it is submitted that

[11] See Montrose, 17 Can.Bar Rev. 693; Hornby [1961] C.L.J. 239; *The Rhodian River* [1984] 1 Lloyd's Rep. 373, 379.
[12] See *Johnston* v. *Reading* (1893) 9 T.L.R. 200; *Lloyds Bank* v. *Swiss Bankverein* (1912) 107 L.T. 309; 108 L.T. 143; *Jerome* v. *Bentley & Co.* [1952] 2 T.L.R. 58.
[13] *Brocklesby* v. *Temperance P.B.S.* [1895] A.C. 173; *Fry* v. *Smellie* [1912] 3 K.B. 282. For criticism of the reasoning of these cases, see *Bowstead on Agency* (15th ed.), pp. 360–362.
[14] *Coles* v. *N.W. Bank* (1875) L.R. 10 C.P. 354. 362.
[15] *Limpus* v. *L.G.O.C.* (1862) 1 H. & C. 526.
[16] *Miles* v. *McIlwraith* (1883) 8 App.Cas. 120.
[17] *Att.-Gen. for Ceylon* v. *Silva* [1953] A.C. 461; *ante*, p. 616.
[18] At p. 481.
[19] Crown Proceedings Act 1947, s.21(1)(*a*).

the principle of usual (no less than that of apparent) authority should be taken into consideration.

(b) SCOPE. The extent of an agent's usual authority depends on the class of agent to which he belongs and on the common understanding of the trade concerning such agents. *Watteau* v. *Fenwick* should from this point of view be contrasted with *Daun* v. *Simmins*,[20] where it was held that the manager of a tied public-house had no usual authority to order spirits from any person he chose. And where the agent does not belong to a well-known class of agents, but is simply appointed for an isolated transaction, the doctrine of usual authority does not apply. Thus in *Jerome* v. *Bentley & Co.*[21] a retired army officer to whom jewellery had been entrusted for sale was held not to have the usual authority which a mercantile agent would have had in the same circumstances.

A principal is only liable under the doctrine of usual authority if there is some dealing between the third party and the agent: the doctrine does not apply if the agent's involvement in the transaction has been concealed so that the third party thinks that he is dealing directly with the principal.[22] The contract must also be made in the course of the principal's business: in *Kinahan* v. *Parry*[23] it was accordingly held that a hotel-owner was not liable for whisky bought without his authority by his manager, since it was not proved that the manager had bought it for use in the hotel rather than for his personal use. Similarly, where the manager of a tied house bought beer from outside suppliers and resold it on the premises on his own account, it was said that his employers could not have been sued for the price of the beer.[24] A person is, *a fortiori*, not liable under the doctrine of usual authority if the business in the course of which the contract was made was not his business at all. Thus in *MacFisheries Ltd.* v. *Harrison*[25] the owner of a public-house sold it as a going concern, but forgot to transfer the licence to the buyer. He was not liable for food supplied to his successor for consumption on the premises, since the latter was carrying on the business entirely on his own behalf.

(3) Authority of necessity[26]

Under this heading, we shall first discuss a number of situations in which one person acts to protect some interest of another without any previous authorisation from that other person. We shall then consider whether any useful purpose is served by attempting to bring all these, somewhat disparate, cases within the scope of a single doctrine.

(a) ACCEPTANCE OF A BILL OF EXCHANGE FOR THE HONOUR OF THE DRAWER. When a bill is not accepted by the person on whom it is drawn, a stranger

---

20 (1879) 41 L.T. 783.
21 [1952] 2 T.L.R. 58.
22 *Kooragang Investments Pty. Ltd.* v. *Richardson & Wrench Ltd.* [1982] A.C. 462.
23 [1911] 1 K.B. 459.
24 *Attorney-General's Reference* (*No. 1 of 1985*) [1986] Q.B. 491, 506.
25 (1924) 93 L.J.K.B. 811.
26 Williston, 22 Can.Bar Rev. 492; Treitel, 3 W.A.A.L. Rev. 1; Wade, 19 Vanderbilt L.Rev. 1183; Birks, 10 C.L.P. 110; Matthews [1981] C.L.J. 340. The old rules under which a deserted wife had authority of necessity were abolished by Matrimonial Proceedings and Property Act 1970, s.41, and are not revived by the repeal of that section by Matrimonial Causes Act 1973: see Interpretation Act 1978, ss.15, 16; for a dispute on the point see 36 M.L.R. 638, 642, 37 M.L.R. 480.

may, with the consent of the holder, accept the bill for the honour of the drawer. If the stranger has to pay on this acceptance, he becomes entitled to the rights of the holder to sue the drawer on the bill.[27]

(b) SHIPMASTERS. Where it is necessary[28] to do so for the further prosecution of the voyage, the master of a ship has authority of necessity to borrow on the shipowner's credit, to hypothecate the ship, cargo and freight, or the cargo alone, to sell part of the cargo,[29] and to enter into a salvage agreement on behalf of the cargo-owner.[30]

(c) SALVAGE. A person who goes to the aid of a ship in distress at sea[31] and saves life or property is entitled to a reward for his efforts. The amount of the reward is, subject to certain limitations, at the discretion of the court.

(d) OTHER CASES. The courts have been reluctant to extend the doctrine of agency of necessity, because it may result in depriving a person of his property, or in subjecting him to an obligation, without his consent.[32] But the doctrine is not confined to the three situations described above. It extends to a number of other situations, in some (but not in all) of which the authority is based on some prior relationship between the parties.[33]

(i) *Powers of sale.* It has been held that land carriers can have authority of necessity to sell.[34] At common law, the courts were reluctant to hold that a bailee with whom goods had been left for storage or repair was entitled to sell them merely because the owner had failed to collect them and could not be traced. By statute, the bailee is now entitled to sell in a number of situations if he has given notice to the bailor of his intention to sell or if he has failed to trace the bailor after having taken reasonable steps to do so.[35] This statutory power extends to cases in which there was, at common law, no authority of necessity to sell.[36] There may be cases in which, though the statutory requirements are not satisfied, a sale can be justified under the common law doctrine of agency of necessity. A buyer of goods may justifiably reject them on the ground that they are not in conformity with the contract of sale. If the seller refuses to accept the return of the goods, the buyer may then have authority of necessity to sell the goods for the account of the seller.[37]

(ii) *Preservation of another's property.* A number of cases raise the question whether a person who preserves another's property has any claim

---

[27] See Bills of Exchange Act 1882, ss.65–68.

[28] *Post*, p. 624.

[29] See *Notara* v. *Henderson* (1872) L.R. 7 Q.B. 225.

[30] *The Winson* [1982] A.C. 939. But where the conditions stated at p. 624, *post* are not satisfied, the master has no *implied* authority to enter into such an agreement: *The Choko Star* [1990] 1 Lloyd's Rep. 516.

[31] For this restriction, see *The Goring* [1988] A.C. 831.

[32] *Falcke* v. *Scottish Imperial Assurance Co.* (1886) 34 Ch.D. 234, 248; *The Winson* [1982] A.C. 939, 962.

[33] *Re F.* [1990] 2 A.C. 1, 75.

[34] *Sims & Co.* v. *Midland Ry.* [1913] 1 K.B. 103, 112; *Springer* v. *Great Western Ry.* [1921] 1 K.B. 257, 265, 267; *cf.* Carriage of Goods by Road Act 1965, Sched., Arts. 14(2), 16(3), for statutory provisions in case of international carriage.

[35] Torts (Interference with Goods) Act 1977, ss.12, 13 and Sched. 1.

[36] *e.g. Sachs* v. *Miklos* [1948] 2 K.B. 23; *Munro* v. *Wilmott* [1949] 1 K.B. 295.

[37] *Graanhandel T. Vink B.W.* v. *European Grain & Shipping Co.* [1989] 2 Lloyd's Rep. 531, 533 (where there was no such agency as the buyer had lost his right to reject); *cf. The Olib, Financial Times*, February 8, 1991.

against the owner. Two eighteenth-century cases decided that such a person has no lien on the property saved[38]; but it does not necessarily follow that he has no claim for reimbursement. In *Tetley* v. *British Trade Corp.*[39] an agent who, contrary to his principal's express instruction, removed goods from Batum to Constantinople (to save them from seizure by an invading army) recovered the expense of the removal from his principal. In *The Winson*[40] a salvor of goods from a stranded ship took them to a place of safety and (to prevent them from deteriorating) had them stored in a warehouse there. It was held that he was entitled to recover the cost of warehousing the goods from their owner. And in *G.N. Ry.* v. *Swaffield*[41] a railway company claimed the cost of feeding and stabling a horse from the owner, who had failed to collect it on arrival at its destination and had not authorised the company to incur these expenses. The claim succeeded on the ground that the company "were bound from ordinary feelings of humanity to keep the horse safely and feed him."[42]

(iii) *Improvement of another's property*. A person who actually improves another's property may do so in the mistaken but honest belief that it is his own. In such a case there is no agency of necessity since the improver's intention is to act on his own behalf, and not on behalf of the owner. If the subject-matter is goods and the owner sues the improver for wrongful interference, the improver is by statute entitled to an allowance in respect of the improvements.[43] A similar rule existed at common law, and presumably applies in relation to property other than goods.[44] It is more doubtful whether the improver has an independent claim for the value or cost of the improvements,[45] *i.e.* one that he can assert even though no action has been brought against him by the true owner.

If the improver knows that he has no title to the property he may again have certain limited rights in respect of the improvements. In *Munro* v. *Wilmott*[46] the plaintiff with the defendant's permission left his car in the defendant's yard. Some years later, the defendant wanted to have the car moved, and, after trying unsuccessfully to contact the plaintiff, spent some £85 on making the car saleable, and sold it. He was held liable for conversion, but the damages were reduced by £85 "not from the point of view of payment for what he has done, but in order to arrive at . . . the true value of the property which the plaintiff had lost."[47] The case would now come within the statutory provisions authorising sales of uncollected goods,[48] so that the defendant would no longer be liable in conversion. Under the statutory provisions the bailee must account for the proceeds of sale to the

---

38 *Binstead* v. *Buck* (1776) 2 Wm.Bl. 1117; *Nicholson* v. *Chapman* (1793) 2 H.Bl. 254.
39 Cited in (1922) 10 Ll.L.R. at p. 678; for a somewhat similar statutory provision, see Carriage of Goods by Road Act 1965, Sched., Art. 14(2).
40 [1982] A.C. 939; Samuel, 98 L.Q.R. 362.
41 (1874) L.R. 9 Ex. 132.
42 At p. 137.
43 Torts (Interference with Goods) Act 1977, ss.6(1), 3(7).
44 *Peruvian Guano Co.* v. *Dreyfus Bros.* [1892] A.C. 166, 176; *Greenwood* v. *Bennett* [1973] Q.B. 915.
45 For a suggestion that there is such a claim, see *Greenwood* v. *Bennett*, *supra* at p. 201 (but see p. 203); Jones, 93 L.Q.R. 273.
46 [1949] 1 K.B. 295.
47 *Ibid.* p. 299.
48 Torts (Interference with Goods) Act 1977, ss.12, 13 and Sched. 1; Palmer [1987] L.M.C.L.Q. 43.

bailor. He is entitled to deduct items such as the costs of sale and sums due to him under the terms of the bailment[49] but nothing is said about the value of improvements.[50] However, the bailee can apply to the court for an order authorising the sale "subject to such terms . . . as may be specified in the order."[51] These could perhaps give him the right to make a deduction in respect of improvements. Even this possibility would not be open to the bailee if he did not sell the goods but simply returned them to the bailor. In such a case he could perhaps invoke the doctrine of agency of necessity.

(iv) *Conditions to be satisfied*. In the sale, preservation and improvement cases just discussed, the common law doctrine of agency of necessity will only apply if certain conditions are satisfied.[52] It must be impossible to communicate with the owner of the goods in time to get his instructions or impossible to obtain such instructions because the owner (though he can be reached) fails to give them[53]; the agent must act reasonably, in good faith and in the interests of the owner; and his acts must have been commercially necessary. It is not "necessary" to sell goods merely because they are causing inconvenience,[54] for there may be a reasonable opportunity of storing them.[55]

(v) *Preservation of life or health*. The doctrine of agency of necessity may apply where one person preserves the life or health of another. Thus it is the basis on which a person can sue for the value of necessaries supplied to a mental patient who has no capacity for rational thought.[56] A doctor who gives medical attention to an unconscious person might recover a fee on the same ground[57]; the case for allowing him to do so would be particularly strong where the doctor's acts are not merely lawful but are done in the performance of a legal duty to render the services in question.[58] A right to payment would of course be negatived if the circumstances were such that the services would not normally be paid for: this would be the position where emergency treatment is given under the National Health Service. Special statutory provisions entitle the doctor to a fee where he gives emergency treatment to the victim of a road accident.[59]

---

[49] *Ibid.* s.12(5).

[50] s.6 of the Act (*supra*, n. 43) would not apply as the defendant knew that he had no title to the car.

[51] s.13(1)(*a*).

[52] See *Springer* v. *G.W. Ry.* [1921] 1 K.B. 257; *Prager* v. *Blatspiel, Stamp & Heacock Ltd.* [1924] 1 K.B. 566. These principles also apply to a shipmaster's authority of necessity: *ante*, p. 622; *cf. The Winson* [1982] A.C. 939.

[53] *The Winson*, *supra* at p. 962; *The Olib*, *Financial Times*, February 8, 1991; the possibility that the owner may fail to give the instructions shows that the difficulty of obtaining them is not invariably "overcome to-day by modern means of communication" (*Re F.* [1990] 2 A.C. 1, 75); *cf. The Choko Star* [1990] 1 Lloyd's Rep. 516, 524); it may also be impracticable for a shipmaster to obtain instructions from *all* the cargo-owners.

[54] *Sachs* v. *Miklos* [1948] 2 K.B. 23, as to which see *ante*, p. 622, n. 36.

[55] As in *Prager* v. *Blatspiel, Stamp & Heacock Ltd.* [1924] 1 K.B. 566. *Semble* the statutory power of sale referred to on p. 622, *ante*, would not extend to the facts of this case.

[56] *Ante*, p. 502.

[57] *Cotnam* v. *Wisdom*, 83 Ark. 601, 104 S.W. 164 (1907); *Re Crisan's Estate*, 102 N.W. 2d 907 (1961). For the right of an accident victim to recover damages in respect of loss suffered by a person who nurses him, *cf. ante*, p. 537.

[58] *Re F.* [1990] 2 A.C. 1, 55, where the issue was whether the treatment was *lawful* (see *ante*, p. 502).

[59] Road Traffic Act 1988, ss.158, 159.

(e) SCOPE OF THE DOCTRINE. It will be seen from the situations discussed above that "agency of necessity" can produce three quite different results. First, it may enable the agent to create a contract between the principal and a third party[60]; secondly it may entitle the agent to dispose of the principal's property[61]; and thirdly it may entitle the agent to recompense or reimbursement in respect of the efforts that he has made, or the expense that he has incurred, to protect the interests of the principal.[62] It has been suggested that the expression "agency of necessity" should no longer be used in its traditional broad sense, to refer to all these consequences, but that it should be used in a narrower sense, to refer only to cases in which the question is whether the agent has, by reason of the necessity, the power to create a contract between his principal and a third party.[63]

The purpose of this suggested departure from the traditional terminology is to emphasise the point that the three consequences described above do not necessarily depend on the same requirements.[64] Thus a person who, to prevent another's goods from deteriorating, arranges for them to be stored in a warehouse, may have a claim against the owner for reimbursement of the charges that he has paid to the warehouseman. It does not follow from this that he also has the power to make a contract between the owner and the warehouseman, so that the warehouseman can sue the owner directly for his charges.[65] On the other hand, the fact that both consequences depend on necessity makes it at least likely that similar factors will often be relevant to each of them. For example, the humanitarian considerations which enabled the railway company in *G.N. Ry.* v. *Swaffield*[66] to claim reimbursement might well have been used in support of the argument that the railway company had power to create a contract between the owner of the horse and a livery stable in which it was housed on his failure to collect it. Similarly, it is relevant for the purpose of both consequences to ask whether the agent acted in the interests of the owner or out of self-interest.[67]

Thus it is submitted that the question whether the label "agency of necessity" should be used in its traditional broad, or in a new narrow, sense is largely one of emphasis, or, as has been said, a "purely terminological"[68] one. It is part of the wider question as to the effects of non-consensual agency, to be discussed later in this Chapter.[69] Such agency scarcely ever produces *all* of the effects of agency based on agreement, but it generally does produce *some* of those effects. This is true of all forms of non-consensual agency; and it is submitted that, so long as the relationships discussed under the present heading produce at least some of the consequences that normally flow from agency by agreement, it is not inappropriate to say that they give rise to "agency of necessity."

---

60 *e.g. ante*, p. 622 at n. 30.
61 *e.g. ante*, p. 622 at n. 34.
62 *e.g. ante*, p. 623 at nn. 39–42.
63 *The Winson* [1982] A.C. 939, 958.
64 *Ibid.*
65 *Ibid.*
66 (1874) L.R. 9 Ex. 132; *ante*, p. 623 at n. 41.
67 *The Winson*, *supra* at p. 962.
68 *Ibid.* at p. 965; *cf. Re F.* [1990] 2 A.C. 1, 75 (using the expression to refer to the intervenor's right to reimbursement).
69 *Post*, p. 649.

3. Ratification

A principal may acquire rights and liabilities as a result of his agent's unauthorised act by ratifying it.

(1) What amounts to ratification

Ratification may be express or implied. It can be implied if the principal by conduct unequivocally affirms the agent's acts even though he purports to repudiate them.[70] Some affirmative act is required, so that mere passive acquiescence does not amount to ratification.[71]

Ratification will not generally be implied from conduct unless the principal has full knowledge of the agent's unauthorised act.[72] But in *Fitzmaurice* v. *Bayley*[73] a principal in effect said to the third party: I do not know what my agent has agreed to, but I must support him in all that he has done for me. It was held that he had ratified. He did not actually know that the agent had exceeded his authority, but deliberately took the risk that this might be the case.

An act will only be regarded as ratification if the principal had a free choice whether to do it or not. Merely taking back one's own property after a third party has, in reliance on unauthorised instructions, done work on it is not ratification.[74]

(2) When ratification possible

Ratification is effective only if the following conditions are satisfied.

(a) THE AGENT MUST PURPORT TO ACT ON BEHALF OF THE PRINCIPAL. A principal can only ratify acts which the agent purported to do on his behalf.[75] The most important consequence of this rule is that if the agent purports to act on his own behalf the principal cannot ratify; or, in other words, that an undisclosed principal[76] cannot ratify. Thus in *Keighley, Maxsted & Co.* v. *Durant*[77] an agent bought corn at a price above that at which he had been instructed to buy. He intended to buy for his principal, but did not disclose this fact to the seller. The undisclosed principal purported to ratify the purchase, but later refused to accept delivery. It was held that the ratification was ineffective and that the principal was not liable. Lord Macnaghten said that "Civil obligations are not to be created by or founded upon undisclosed intentions."[78] It could be objected that this reasoning would destroy the whole law relating to undisclosed principals. But the decision is nonetheless intelligible, having regard to the doctrine of privity of contract. Ratification and the undisclosed principal are two important exceptions to that doctrine. To allow both exceptions to operate on the same set of facts would go far towards overthrowing the doctrine of privity altogether.

---

[70] *Cornwall* v. *Henson* (1750) 1 Ves.Sen. 509.

[71] *Moon* v. *Towers* (1860) 8 C.B.(N.S.) 611; reversed on other grounds: (1860) 9 H.L.C. 78. Contrast the now doubtful case of *Waithman* v. *Wakefield* (1807) 1 Camp. 120.

[72] *Lewis* v. *Read* (1845) 13 M. & W. 834.

[73] (1856) 6 E. & B. 868; *cf. Haseler* v. *Lemoyne* (1858) 5 C.B.(N.S.) 530.

[74] *Foreman & Co. Pty. Ltd.* v. *The Liddesdale* [1900] A.C. 190.

[75] *Wilson* v. *Tumman* (1843) 6 Man. & G. 236.

[76] For the definition of "undisclosed principal," *post*, p. 630.

[77] [1901] A.C. 240; *cf. The Astyanax* [1985] 2 Lloyd's Rep. 109; *Welsh Development Agency* v. *Export Finance Co.* [1990] BCC 393.

[78] At p. 247.

On the other hand, an unnamed principal[79] can ratify. Policies of marine insurance may be taken out "for and on behalf of any person interested"; and such persons can ratify although they are not named in the policy.[80]

The rule that the agent must *purport* to act on behalf of the principal does not mean that he must *intend* to do so. Thus the principal may ratify although the agent intended to defraud him.[81]

In *Brook* v. *Hook*[82] an agent forged his principal's signature to a promissory note. The principal's later ratification was held to be ineffective. This case has given rise to a dispute on the question whether a forgery can ever be ratified. But it does not seem that this question arises in a case of this kind. If an agent forges his principal's signature he does not say "I am signing for my principal" but "this is my principal's signature." The principal cannot ratify because the agent did not purport to act on his behalf.[83] But if the principal stands by knowing that his agent will forge his signature he may be estopped from denying its genuineness.[84]

(b) THE PRINCIPAL'S CAPACITY. At common law, a corporation cannot ratify the unauthorised act of its agent in entering into an *ultra vires* contract.[85] In relation to companies incorporated under the Companies Acts, this rule no longer applies, for two reasons. First, the validity of an act done by such a company can no longer be called into question on the ground of lack of capacity by reason of anything in the company's memorandum.[86] Secondly, it is expressly provided that the act can be ratified.[87] Such ratification would also prevent the company from impugning the transaction on the ground that it was beyond the power of the board of directors.[88] An unauthorised act done on behalf of the company can be ratified even though, when it was done, no officer having authority to do it had been appointed.[89]

A person can become liable on a contract made by him while he was a minor if he "ratifies" it after reaching full age.[90] "Ratification" here seems to refer to confirmation by a person of a contract made by himself; but there seems to be no reason why a person should not be similarly liable on a ratification after full age of a contract made on his behalf, but without his authority, while he was a minor. There are, however, cases in which a per-

---

79 For the definition of "unnamed principal," see *post*, p. 630.

80 *Hagedorn* v. *Oliverson* (1814) 2 M. & S. 485. *Quaere* whether the requirement stated in *Watson* v. *Swann* (1862) 11 C.B.(N.S.) 756, 771, that the person seeking to ratify must be described at the time of the contract in such a way as to be ascertainable at that time is generally accepted: see *Boston Fruit Co.* v. *British & Foreign Marine Insurance Co.* [1906] A.C. 336, 338–339 (a case apparently overlooked in *Southern Water Authority* v. *Carey* [1985] 2 All E.R. 1077, 1085); Arnould, *Marine Insurance* (16th ed.), § 243.

81 *Re Tiedemann & Ledermann Frères* [1899] 2 Q.B. 66.

82 (1871) L.R. 6 Ex. 89.

83 *Imperial Bank of Canada* v. *Begley* [1936] 2 All E.R. 367.

84 *Greenwood* v. *Martins Bank Ltd.* [1933] A.C. 51.

85 *Ashbury Ry. Carriage & Iron Co.* v. *Riche* (1875) L.R. 7 H.L. 653; *Mann* v. *Edinburgh N. Tramways* [1893] A.C. 69; *Rolled Steel Products (Holdings) Ltd.* v. *B.S.C.* [1986] Ch. 246, 304.

86 Companies Act 1985, s.35(1) (as inserted by Companies Act 1985, s.108(1)); *ante*, p. 505.

87 Companies Act 1985 (*supra*), s.35(3).

88 *i.e.* under *ibid.* s.35A(1); it seems to follow that ratification can be effective even if the third party acted in bad faith, at least if the members of the company were aware of this fact when ratifying the contract.

89 *Alexander Ward & Co. Ltd.* v. *Samyang Navigation Co. Ltd.* [1975] 1 W.L.R. 673.

90 *Ante*, p. 492.

son is not liable on a ratification in the sense of a confirmation of a contract made during minority by himself[91]; and it is submitted that he would equally not be liable if, after full age, he ratified a contract of this kind which had during his minority been made on his behalf but without his authority.[92]

(c) THE PRINCIPAL MUST HAVE BEEN IN EXISTENCE WHEN THE ACT WAS DONE. This rule can give rise to inconvenience when promoters contract on behalf of a projected company. It was held in *Kelner* v. *Baxter*[93] that the company could not, after its formation, ratify the promoters' contracts, since it was not in existence when those contracts were made. One possible way of evading this rule is for the promoter to enter into a draft agreement providing that the company, when formed, shall enter into a similar agreement with the third party and that the liability of the promoter shall thereupon cease. But this device is not wholly satisfactory since it creates no binding contract between company and third party: each can with the collusion of the promoter deprive the other of the expected benefit of the contract. The position is somewhat better in equity. The company may be able to enforce the contract against the third party by showing that the promoter acted as trustee for it,[94] and the third party may be able to claim a reasonable remuneration out of any sum which the company has paid, or bound itself to pay, to the promoter for initial expenses.[95] But he has no such right if the company has not made any payment or promise to the promoter[96]; nor has he any claim against the company on a purely executory contract. By statute, a contract which purports to be made by or on behalf of a company before it is formed has effect (subject to contrary agreement) as a contract between the third party and the person purporting to act for the company or as agent for it.[97] But it is still impossible to create a direct contract between the company and the third party by ratification after incorporation. It would be better if the rule in *Kelner* v. *Baxter* were wholly repealed by legislation.[98]

(d) THE PRINCIPAL MUST RATIFY IN TIME. A contract cannot be ratified after the time fixed for its performance has passed[99]; if no such time is fixed, it must be ratified within a reasonable time of the principal's acquiring notice of the unauthorised act.[1] Nor can a contract be ratified at a time when the principal could not validly have made it. Thus a person cannot insure his property after it has been destroyed; and if an agent, without

---

[91] A penal bond could not be ratified as it was considered to be wholly void: *Baylis* v. *Dineley* (1815) 3 M. & S. 477.

[92] On the principle that a nullity cannot be ratified: *post*, p. 629.

[93] (1866) L.R. 2 C.P. 174; *cf. Melhado* v. *Porto Alegre Ry.* (1874) L.R. 9 C.P. 503.

[94] *Ante*, pp. 562 *et seq.*

[95] *Touche* v. *Metropolitan Ry.* (1871) L.R. 6 Ch.App. 671; *cf. Re Hereford, etc., Engineering Co.* (1876) 2 Ch.D. 621 (where the third party lost his rights because of the promoter's fraud); *Re Empress Engineering Co.* (1880) 16 Ch.D. 125. *Spiller* v. *Paris Skating Rink Co.* (1878) 7 Ch.D. 368 states the equitable principle too widely.

[96] *Re Rotherham Alum & Chemical Co.* (1883) 25 Ch.D. 103.

[97] Companies Act 1985, s.36C(1), as inserted by Companies Act 1989, s.130(4); *post*, p. 637.

[98] The Companies Bill 1973 (which was lost at the dissolution of Parliament in February 1974) contained a provision (cl. 6) to this effect. And see Gross, 87 L.Q.R. 367.

[99] *Metropolitan Asylums Board* v. *Kingham* (1890) 6 T.L.R. 217; *Dibbins* v. *Dibbins* [1896] 2 Ch. 348.

[1] *Re Portuguese Consolidated Copper Mines* (1890) 45 Ch.D. 16 *cf. Bedford Insurance Co. Ltd.* v. *Instituto de Ressaguros do Brasil* [1985] Q.B. 966, 987 (and see *ante*, p. 382).

authority, insures his principal's property, the latter cannot ratify the insurance after the destruction of the property.[2] Exceptionally, a policy of marine insurance can be ratified after the destruction of the property insured.[3]

(e) A NULLITY CANNOT BE RATIFIED.[4] Although ratification is not confined to lawful acts, an act which is simply void in law cannot be validated by ratification. Similarly, a principal cannot become liable if the unauthorised contract was prohibited by statute: "life cannot be given by ratification to prohibited transactions."[5] This is an additional reason for saying that a forgery cannot be ratified.[6]

(3) Effect of ratification

The effect of ratification is to put principal, agent and third party into the position in which they would have been if the agent's acts had been authorised from the start: his authority is said to relate back to the time of the unauthorised act. Thus in *Bolton Partners* v. *Lambert*[7] an agent without authority purported to buy a house for his principal from the defendant, who later repudiated the contract. The principal then ratified. It was held that the defendant was bound by the contract. His repudiation was ineffective as the principal's ratification related back to the time of the agent's unauthorised purchase.

The rule that ratification relates back does not apply where the agent contracts "subject to ratification": in such a case the third party can withdraw at any time before ratification.[8] Nor does the rule apply where the agent and the third party have by mutual consent cancelled the unauthorised transaction before the principal ratifies.[9] And the doctrine of relation back will not be allowed to deprive a stranger to the contract of a right of property which had vested in him before ratification[10]; though it may deprive him of a right to sue the agent in tort if the agent's unauthorised act would have been lawful, had it been done with the principal's prior authorisation.[11]

The rule in *Bolton Partners* v. *Lambert* has been criticised on the ground that it puts the third party at the mercy of the principal, who is free to ratify or not as he pleases.[12] But the hardship to the third party should not be exaggerated. If the principal does not ratify, the third party has his remedy against the agent for breach of implied warranty of authority.[13] If the principal does ratify, the third party will be liable to him; but since this is precisely what he expected, he cannot complain. The only hardship is that the

---

[2] *Grover & Grover Ltd.* v. *Matthews* [1910] 2 K.B. 401.

[3] *Williams* v. *N. China Insurance Co.* (1876) 1 C.P.D. 757; Marine Insurance Act 1906, s.86.

[4] For a discussion of this rule, see *Danish Mercantile Co.* v. *Beaumont* [1951] Ch. 680 (where the act was held not to be a nullity).

[5] *Bedford Insurance Co. Ltd.* v. *Instituto de Ressaguros do Brasil* [1985] Q.B. 966, 986. (and see *ante*, p. 382).

[6] *Ante*, p. 627.

[7] (1888) 41 Ch.D. 295; *cf. Maclean* v. *Dunn* (1828) 4 Bing. 722; *Koenigsblatt* v. *Sweet* [1923] 2 Ch. 314.

[8] *Watson* v. *Davies* [1931] 1 Ch. 455; *Warehousing & Forwarding Co. of East Africa Ltd.* v. *Jafferali & Sons Ltd.* [1964] A.C. 1.

[9] *Walter* v. *James* (1871) L.R. 6 Ex. 124.

[10] *Bird* v. *Bird* (1850) 4 Ex. 786.

[11] *Whitehead* v. *Taylor* (1839) 10 A. & E. 210.

[12] Wambaugh, 9 Harv.L.R. 60; and see *Fleming* v. *Bank of New Zealand* [1900] A.C. 577.

[13] *Post*, pp. 640–642.

principal may be able to keep the third party waiting while he decides whether to ratify. But he must ratify within reasonable time; and the extent of such time is considerably abridged if the third party tells the principal that he wishes to withdraw from the contract.[14] Moreover, a principal cannot ratify after he has by words or conduct intimated to the third party that he does not intend to do so.[15] It is probable, therefore, that a principal would not be able to ratify if he remained silent for more than a comparatively short time after notice of the third party's intention to withdraw. Thus the third party need not be kept indefinitely in suspense. He can, in effect, say to the principal: ratify quickly or not at all.

SECTION 4. EFFECTS OF AGENCY

When an agent makes a contract on behalf of his principal with a third party, the transaction gives rise to legal effects between principal and third party, between agent and third party, and between principal and agent. In discussing these effects, we shall first assume that the agency has arisen by consent, and then consider to what extent the same effects result from non-consensual agency.

1. Between Principal and Third Party

(1) Rights of principal against third party

The rights of principal against third party depend in part on the distinction between disclosed and undisclosed principals. A *disclosed principal* is one of whose existence the third party is aware at the time of contracting. He is called a named principal if the third party also knew his name, and an unnamed principal if the third party did not know his name. An *undisclosed principal* is one of whose existence the third party is unaware at the time of contracting. Where a person makes a contract "as agent" or "on behalf of my client" the principal will generally be disclosed. But such words may not make it clear that that person is acting as agent *in the legal sense*[16]; they may merely indicate that he is acting as agent in a commercial sense. If that is the position and the person described as "agent" actually has a principal in the legal sense, that principal may be undisclosed.[17]

(a) DISCLOSED PRINCIPAL. The general rule is that a disclosed principal can sue the third party.[18] The third party is not discharged by settling with the agent unless the principal by his conduct induced the third party to do so, or unless the agent had authority to receive payment.[19] The third party cannot set off against the principal any debt which the agent may owe to

---

[14] *Re Portuguese Consolidated Copper Mines* (1890) 45 Ch.D. 16.
[15] *McEvoy* v. *Belfast Banking Co.* [1935] A.C. 24.
[16] *Ante*, p. 609.
[17] See a difference of opinion on this point in *Teheran-Europe Co. Ltd.* v. *S. T. Belton (Tractors) Ltd.* [1868] 2 Q.B. 545, 552, 556, 561.
[18] *Langton* v. *Waite* (1968) L.R. 6 Eq. 165.
[19] *Yates* v. *Freckleton* (1781) 2 Dougl. 623; *Linck, Moeller & Co.* v. *Jameson & Co.* (1885) 2 T.L.R. 206; *Butwick* v. *Grant* [1924] 2 K.B. 483.

the third party[20]; and a custom enabling the agent to receive payment by such set-off is unreasonable.[21]

There was at one time a usage of trade by which the general rule did not apply where an English agent contracted on behalf of a foreign principal. But modern commercial conditions have made the usage obsolete, and it is now settled that a foreign principal can sue the third party.[22]

(b) UNDISCLOSED PRINCIPAL. An undisclosed principal can also, in general, sue the third party. Attempts have been made to reconcile this rule with the doctrine of privity. One view is that the contract is "in truth" made with the undisclosed principal,[23] but this is scarcely consistent with the rule that the agent is fully entitled and liable under the contract.[24] Other views recognise that the contract is between agent and third party but say that the principal can intervene because his contract with the agent entitles him to do so, or because he is a *cestui que trust* or a quasi-assignee.[25] But the better view seems to be that the undisclosed principal's right to sue is not based on the theory that he has somehow acquired the agent's right. His right is an independent right[26] which constitutes an exception to the doctrine of privity, established in the interests of commercial convenience.

The undisclosed principal's right to sue might prejudice a third party, who thought that he was dealing only with the agent. To avoid such prejudice, the undisclosed principal's right is limited in the following ways.

(i) *Consistency with the terms of the contract.* An undisclosed principal is not allowed to intervene where this would be inconsistent with the terms of the contract. In *Humble* v. *Hunter*[27] a person signed a charterparty as "owner." This was held to mean that he and he alone was owner, so that his undisclosed principal was not allowed to intervene. But in *F. Drughorn Ltd.* v. *Rederiaktiebolaget Transatlantic*[28] the fact that an agent signed a charterparty as "charterer" did not exclude his undisclosed principal's right to enforce the contract. It has been said that after this case, *Humble* v. *Hunter* is no longer law,[29] but the two lines of cases can be distinguished. Persons in general *own* on their own behalf, but often charter on behalf of others. Thus it contradicts the contract to say that someone other than the person named (without qualification) as owner is owner, but not that

---

20 *Pratt* v. *Willey* (1826) 2 C. & P. 350; *Fish* v. *Kempton* (1849) 7 C.B. 687; *Mildred* v. *Maspons* (1883) 8 App.Cas. 874; *Cooke* v. *Eshelby* (1887) 12 App.Cas. 271; unless the agent has authority to receive payment in this way: *Stewart* v. *Aberdein* (1838) 4 M. & W. 211, 228.

21 *Pearson* v. *Scott* (1878) 9 Ch.D. 198.

22 *Teheran-Europe Co. Ltd.* v. *S. T. Belton (Tractors) Ltd.* [1968] 2 Q.B. 545; Reynolds, 85 L.Q.R. 92, 97–103; Hudson, 32 M.L.R. 207. *Semble* the rule also applies to undisclosed principals: *supra*, n. 17.

23 *Keighley Maxsted & Co.* v. *Durant* [1901] A.C. 240, 261.

24 *Post*, p. 636.

25 For discussions of the basis of the doctrine, see Ames, *Essays*, 453; Seavey, 29 Y.L.J. 859; Goodhart and Hamson, 4 C.L.J. 320; Montrose, 16 Can.Bar Rev. 757; Dowrick, 17 M.L.R. 25; Higgins, 28 M.L.R. 167. *cf. The Astyanax* [1985] 2 Lloyd's Rep. 109, 113 (where "*not* a settled part of our law" should probably read "*now* a settled part . . . ," etc.).

26 *Pople* v. *Evans* [1969] 2 Ch. 255; *The Havprins* [1983] 2 Lloyd's Rep. 356, 362.

27 (1842) 12 Q.B. 316; *Formby Bros.* v. *Formby* (1910) 102 L.T. 116; *cf. The Astyanax* [1985] 2 Lloyd's Rep. 109.

28 [1919] A.C. 203; *Danziger* v. *Thompson* [1944] K.B. 654.

29 *Epps* v. *Rothnie* [1945] K.B. 562, 565.

someone other than the person named as charterer is charterer. Alternatively, a person who is described as owner may *contract that* he is owner, while a person who is described as charterer does not make any promise that he alone is the charterer.[30]

(ii) *Personal considerations.* If the third party can show that he wanted to deal with the agent *and with no one else*, the undisclosed principal cannot intervene. Thus in *Collins* v. *Associated Greyhound Racecourses Ltd.*[31] a person agreed to underwrite a new issue of shares to be made by a company, *i.e.* to take up any shares for which the public did not apply. This contract was held to involve such reliance on the business reputation and integrity of the underwriter that his undisclosed principal was not allowed to enforce it. Similarly, in *Greer* v. *Downs Supply Co.*,[32] a person bought timber from a seller who owed him money, on the terms that the debt should be set off against the purchase price: this showed that he intended to deal with the seller and with no one else, so that the seller's undisclosed principal was not allowed to intervene. This conclusion does not seem to have been strictly necessary for the protection of the buyer; for an undisclosed principal can only sue subject to the third party's right to set off any money due to him from the agent.[33]

A third party who has no particular reason for wanting to deal with the agent may nevertheless not want to deal with the principal. If the agent expressly says that he is not acting for the principal, the third party can avoid the contract for fraud.[34] If he makes no such misrepresentation, the law is less clear.

In *Nash* v. *Dix*[35] a committee of Roman Catholics wanted to buy a Congregational chapel from the defendants and to turn it into a place of Roman Catholic worship. The defendants refused to deal with the committee as they disapproved of the proposed user. The committee then told the plaintiff that if he could buy the chapel from the defendants they would buy it from him for £100 more than he had paid for it. The defendants sold the chapel to the plaintiff but repudiated the contract on discovering that the plaintiff intended to resell to the committee. North J. held that the defendants were bound (1) because the plaintiff was not an agent, but simply a person who had bought to resell; and (2) because the plaintiff had not been guilty of any misrepresentation. It appears from the judgment that the plaintiff would have failed if he *had* been the agent of the committee.

In *Said* v. *Butt*[36] the plaintiff wanted to go to the first night of a play, but knew that the proprietors of the theatre would not sell him a ticket as he had in the past strongly criticised their conduct. He therefore sent a friend to the box-office to buy a ticket for him without disclosing his name, but he was later refused admission by the manager of the theatre. In an action

---

[30] *Cf. Cross on Evidence* (7th ed.), p. 699. The position would be different where the word "owner" was qualified in some way. Where a person enters into a charterparty as "disponent owner" or "operating owner" it is a question of construction whether he, or the registered owner, is a party to the contract: see *The Yanxilas* [1982] 2 Lloyd's Rep. 444.

[31] [1930] 1 Ch. 1.

[32] [1927] 2 K.B. 28.

[33] *Post*, p. 633.

[34] *Archer* v. *Stone* (1898) 78 L.T. 34; *cf. Berg* v. *Sadler & Moore* [1937] 2 K.B. 158; *ante*, p. 333.

[35] (1898) 78 L.T. 445.

[36] [1920] 3 K.B. 497.

against the manager for inducing a breach of contract, McCardie J. held that there was no contract between the proprietors and the plaintiff: since the proprietors reserved the right to sell first-night tickets to specially selected persons, the "personality" of the other contracting party was a material element in the contract.

Both these cases were distinguished in *Dyster* v. *Randall & Sons*.[37] The plaintiff wanted to buy land from the defendants, who, to his knowledge, would not deal with him as they distrusted him. He employed an agent to buy the land in the agent's own name, and then claimed that he was entitled to intervene as undisclosed principal. Lawrence J. upheld the claim: he said that it would be futile to deny the plaintiff's right to sue since the agent could have assigned the benefit of the contract to him. But this argument does not satisfactorily distinguish *Said* v. *Butt*: theatre tickets can (unless they expressly provide the contrary)[38] be assigned no less than contracts to buy land. Again it was said that "personal" consideration entered into the two earlier cases but not into *Dyster* v. *Randall & Sons*. While this may distinguish *Said* v. *Butt*, it does not satisfactorily explain why the action in *Nash* v. *Dix* would have failed if the plaintiff had been an agent; for it is hard to see why an objection based on religious grounds is more "personal" than one based on distrust.

It is submitted that an undisclosed principal should not be allowed to intervene if he knows that the third party does not want to deal with him. If the principal directly concealed his identity, the contract would be void for mistake, or voidable for fraud; and the principal should not be able to improve his position by simply employing an agent.

(iii) *Other safeguards*. An undisclosed principal can only sue the third party subject to any defences which the third party has against the agent.[39] This rule is clearly necessary for the protection of the third party, who thinks that he is dealing with the agent alone. Thus if the agent owes money to the third party, the debt can be set off by the third party against the principal, and if the third party pays the agent he can rely on the payment against the principal.[40] This rule is based on the third party's belief that he is deaing with the agent alone: it therefore does not apply where the third party has no such belief. In *Cooke* v. *Eshelby*[41] the third party had no belief one way or the other whether the person with whom he was dealing was principal or agent. He was in fact an agent. The third party was not allowed to set off against the principal a debt which the agent owed to the third party.

The principal may intend the agent to disclose his existence, but the agent may fail to do so because he wants to misappropriate the proceeds of the contract, or to induce the third party to accept the principal's property in discharge of a debt which the agent owes to the third party. In such cases the third party can only rely on his settlement with, or set-off against, the

---

[37] [1926] Ch. 932; *cf. Smith* v. *Wheatcroft* (1878) 9 Ch.D. 223; for a discussion of these cases, see Williams, 23 Can.Bar Rev. 397.

[38] The report of *Said* v. *Butt* does not state whether the ticket contained a condition prohibiting its assignment or transfer.

[39] *Browning* v. *Provincial Insurance Co. of Canada* (1873) L.R. 5 P.C. 263, 272.

[40] *George* v. *Clagett* (1797) 7 T.R. 359; *Rabone* v. *Williams*, *ibid.* p. 360n.; *Mann* v. *Forrester* (1814) 4 Camp. 60; *Montague* v. *Forwood* [1893] 2 Q.B. 350, Derham [1986] C.L.J. 384.

[41] (1887) 12 App.Cas. 271; Reynolds [1983] C.L.P. 119.

agent, in an action brought by the principal, if the latter has so conducted himself as to enable the agent to appear as principal in the transaction.[42]

(2) Liability of principal to third party

The general rule is that a principal, whether disclosed or undisclosed, is liable to the third party. The limitations on the right of an undisclosed principal to intervene exist mainly for the protection of the third party. Hence they do not necessarily apply where the third party sues the principal. But a person who is alleged to have contracted on behalf of another may, on the true construction of the contract, have contracted solely on his own behalf. In that case he alone is liable on the contract[43]: the reason why the other is not liable is not that he is an undisclosed principal whose liability is excluded, but that he is not a principal in the transaction at all.

The principal cannot set off against the third party any money owed to him by the agent.[44] If the principal gives the agent the money with which to pay the third party, but the agent fails to pay it over, the principal remains liable to the third party: he must seek out his creditor and see that he is paid.[45] The principal is only discharged by payment to the agent if such payment is made at the third party's request,[46] or if the third party looked to the agent for payment and so induced the principal to settle with the agent.[47]

In *Heald* v. *Kenworthy*[48] it was assumed that an undisclosed principal is not (any more than one who is disclosed) discharged by settling with his agent. But in *Armstrong* v. *Stokes*[49] the court said that this rule produced "intolerable hardship,"[50] and refused to follow it. Thus it was held that an undisclosed principal who settled with his agent was not liable to make a second payment to the third party if the agent failed to pay over the money. Of course, it is hard for the principal to have to pay twice over; but it is equally hard for the third party not to be paid at all. It could be argued that the law should, in this situation, have no sympathy for the third party since he did not rely on the credit of a principal of whose existence he was unaware at the time of contracting. But this proves too much: whenever an undisclosed principal is sued the third party gets a windfall of this kind. Thus the case for applying a special rule to undisclosed principals in this context is weak. *Armstrong* v. *Stokes* was severely criticised, and doubted by the Court of Appeal in *Irvine* v. *Watson*.[51] It is submitted that an undisclosed principal who settles with his agent should remain liable to the third party.

2. Between Agent and Third Party

Agent and third party may incur reciprocal rights and liabilities under the contract which the agent makes on behalf of his principal, or under a col-

[42] *Drakeford* v. *Piercey* (1866) 14 L.T. 403.
[43] *J.H. Rayner (Mincing Lane) Ltd.* v. *D.T.I.* [1989] Ch. 72, 190–191, approved on this point [1990] 2 A.C. 418, 515.
[44] *Waring* v. *Favenck* (1807) 2 Camp. 85.
[45] *Irvine* v. *Watson* (1880) 5 Q.B.D. 414.
[46] *Smyth* v. *Anderson* (1849) 7 C.B. 21.
[47] See *Wyatt* v. *Hertford* (1802) 3 East 147.
[48] (1855) 10 Ex. 739; Reynolds (1983) C.L.P. 119.
[49] (1872) L.R. 7 Q.B. 598.
[50] At p. 610.
[51] *Supra*, n. 45.

lateral contract. The agent may also be liable for breach of implied warranty of authority.

(1) Under the contract

(a) GENERAL RULE. The general rule is that an agent is neither liable under,[52] nor entitled to enforce,[53] a contract he makes on behalf of his principal.

(b) EXCEPTIONS. An agent may enter into a contract on his own behalf as well as on behalf of the principal and so be liable or entitled under the contract. This possibility is illustrated by the following cases.

(i) *Agent contracting personally.* An agent is liable under the contract if he in fact intended to undertake personal liability. Where the contract is in writing, the question whether he had this intention is one of construction. An agent who is described in a written contract as a party to it and signs it without qualification is liable under it although the third party knew that he was acting as agent.[54] He may be liable even though such a contract also provides that it is signed on behalf of a third person, for such a provision may merely be intended to mean that that person is to be a party to the contract and not that the agent is to be absolved from liability under it.[55] At the other extreme, an agent who is described as agent in the contract and signs as agent is not liable.[56] But an agent may be described as agent in the body of the contract and sign without qualification; or he may be described as a party in the body of the contract but sign as agent.[57] A distinction has been drawn in such cases between words which merely describe the agent's profession, and words of representation, which show that he is acting as agent. The former do not, while the latter do, exonerate him from liability. Thus the words "we, as solicitors, undertake . . . " were held in *Burrell* v. *Jones*[58] to be merely descriptive; and even the words "as agent" when used in their commercial, rather than their legal, sense have been held to be descriptive.[59] The words "on behalf of" or "*per procurationem*" are generally representative. But no particular formula is conclusive; and where the description is equivocal the court will rely on other relevant circumstances in order to determine, on an objective standard, whether an undertaking of personal liability may be inferred. Thus in one case[60] a company director ordered repairs to be done to a boat which the company had hired from him. He gave the order on the company's notepaper and signed it with the addition "Director." He was, nevertheless, held person-

---

52 *Robins* v. *Bridge* (1837) 3 M. & W. 114; *Ferguson* v. *Wilson* (1866) L.R. 2 Ch.App. 77; *N. & J. Vlassopulos* v. *Ney Shipping Ltd.* [1977] 2 Lloyd's Rep. 478.

53 *Lucas* v. *Beale* (1851) 10 C.B. 739; *Fairlie* v. *Fenton* (1870) L.R. 5 Ex. 169.

54 *Basma* v. *Weekes* [1950] A.C. 441; *cf. Davies* v. *Sweet* [1962] 2 Q.B. 300; *Sika Contracts* v. *Gill* (1978) 9 Build.L.R. 11; *Kai Yung* v. *Hong Kong & Shanghai Banking Corp.* [1981] A.C. 787, 795.

55 *The Sun Happiness* [1984] 1 Lloyd's Rep. 381.

56 *Mahony* v. *Kekulé* (1854) 14 C.B. 390.

57 As in *Gadd* v. *Houghton* (1876) 1 Ex.D. 357; *Universal Steam Navigation Co. Ltd.* v. *James McKelvie & Co.* [1923] A.C. 492. (In these cases the agents were held not liable.)

58 (1819) 3 B. & Ald. 47.

59 *Parker* v. *Winlow* (1857) 7 E. & B. 942; *cf. ante*, pp. 609–610.

60 *The Swan* [1968] 1 Lloyd's Rep. 5; Reynolds, 85 L.Q.R. 92; Legh-Jones, 32 M.L.R. 325; *cf. Tudor Marine Ltd.* v. *Tradax Export S.A.* [1976] 2 Lloyd's Rep. 135; *The Primorje* [1980] 2 Lloyd's Rep. 74; contrast *Astilleros Canarios S.A.* v. *Cape Hatteras Shipping Co. S.A.* [1982] 1 Lloyd's Rep. 518.

ally liable as he was the owner of the boat. But for this fact it seems that he would not have been personally liable.

Just as the agent may on the true construction of the contract, be liable, so he may be entitled.[61] The courts will, if possible, hold that "the existence of the liability on the one hand involves the existence of the correlative right on the other."[62] But it is perfectly possible for an agent to be liable without being entitled if that is the true meaning of the contract. So long as the contract is executory, however, he cannot, be entitled without being liable, for unless he is liable there is no consideration moving from him for the third party's promise to him.[63] Where the agent is liable but not entitled the third party is not faced with any similar difficulty. He provides consideration for the agent's promise by undertaking liability towards the principal and it is immaterial that the consideration does not move to the agent: consideration must move from the promisee (the third party) but need not move to the promisor (the agent).[64]

It was at one time thought that the inference that the agent intended to contract personally must be drawn whenever he acted on behalf of a foreign principal,[65] but it is now recognised that this fact is only one of many to be taken into consideration in determining whether the agent had such an intention.[66]

(ii) *Trade usage or custom.* An agent may be personally liable or entitled if that is the usual course of business either between particular parties or in relation to a particular class of agents. For example, "where one attorney does work for another, it is common practice for him to give credit to that other and not to the client."[67] A local or trade custom can have the same effect.[68]

(iii) *Principal undisclosed.* The agent is both entitled and liable where the principal is undisclosed[69]; but this rule does not apply where the agent uses words of representation and the principal is only unnamed.[70] Where an agent does not name his principal, it may be easy to infer that he intended to contract personally; but there is no general rule to that effect.[71]

(iv) *Agent in fact principal.* An agent may purport to act on behalf of a principal when he is in fact acting on his own behalf. If he purports to act for an unnamed principal, he can enforce the contract for his own bene-

---

[61] *Short* v. *Spackman* (1831) 2 B. & Ad. 962; *Clay* v. *Southern* (1852) 7 Ex. 717; *H. O. Brandt & Co.* v. *H. N. Morris & Co. Ltd.* [1917] 2 K.B. 784; *cf. The Yanxilas* [1982] 2 Lloyd's Rep. 444; *Fraser* v. *Thames Television* [1984] Q.B. 44; *Transcontinental Underwriting Agency S.R.L.* v. *Grand Union Ins. Co. Ltd.* [1987] 2 Lloyd's Rep. 409.

[62] *Repetto* v. *Millar's Karri & Jarrah Forests Ltd.* [1901] 2 K.B. 306, 310.

[63] *Evans* v. *Hooper* (1875) 1 Q.B.D. 45.

[64] *Ante*, pp. 77–79.

[65] *Paterson* v. *Gandasequi* (1812) 15 East 62.

[66] *Miller, Gibb & Co.* v. *Smith & Tyrer Ltd.* [1917] 2 K.B. 141; *J. S. Holt & Moseley (London) Ltd.* v. *Sir Charles Cunningham & Partners Ltd.* (1949) 83 Ll.L.R. 141, 145; Hudson, 23 M.L.R. 695; 29 M.L.R. 353; 35 Can.Bar Rev. 336.

[67] *Scrace* v. *Whittington* (1823) 2 B. & C. 11. The above dictum makes the agent *exclusively* liable: *cf. post*, p. 639.

[68] *Fleet* v. *Murton* (1871) L.R. 7 Q.B. 126.

[69] *Sims* v. *Bond* (1833) 5 B. & Ad. 389, 393.

[70] *e.g. Universal Steam Navigation Co.* v. *James McKelvie & Co.* [1923] A.C. 492; *Benton* v. *Campbell, Parker & Co. Ltd.* [1925] 2 K.B. 410.

[71] *N. & J. Vlassopulos* v. *Ney Shipping Ltd.* [1977] 2 Lloyd's Rep. 478.

fit.[72] But if he purports to act for a named principal, he can only enforce the contract after giving due notice to the third party that he acted on his own behalf.[73] Even then the agent will not be allowed to sue if this would prejudice the third party.[74] These safeguards are necessary as the third party may have relied on the principal's solvency or other attributes when he made the contract. It follows that the agent cannot sue if he knew that, for some "personal" reason, the third party was unwilling to contract with him either at all, or on the same terms as those on which he was willing to contract with the principal.[75]. If the plaintiff in *Said* v. *Butt*[76] had gone in person to buy a ticket, pretending that it was not for him but for a friend, he could not later have said that his friend was in fact himself.

The present exception to the general rule, that an agent acquires no rights under the contract, can only apply where two conditions are satisfied: the agent must (i) purport to contract as agent and (ii) in fact contract as principal. The exception therefore did not apply where a father conducted negotiations for the purchase of a house and the resulting contract was drawn up in the name of his son (who was a minor). It was held that the father could not enforce the contract since the contract did not say that he had entered into it on behalf of the son, or indeed mention the father's name at all.[77]

(v) *Principal non-existent.* Where the alleged principal does not exist, it may be easy to infer that the agent intended to assume personal liability. At common law this inference was drawn in *Kelner* v. *Baxter*[78] with the result that promoters were held personally liable on a contract made by them on behalf of a company which had not yet been formed. On the other hand in *Holman* v. *Pullin*[79] it was held that the chairman of the Tunbridge Wells Medical Association could not sue on a contract made by him on behalf of the Association before it existed as a legal person. An agent is therefore not a contracting party merely because he purported to act for a non-existent principal: the question is one of intention in each case.[80] Section 36C(1) of the Companies Act 1985[81] now provides that "a contract which purports to be made . . . on behalf of a company[82] at a time when the company has not been formed has effect, subject to any agreement to

---

72 *Schmaltz* v. *Avery* (1851) 16 Q.B. 655; *Harper & Co.* v. *Vigers Bros.* [1909] 2 K.B. 549. See *Bowstead on Agency* (15th ed.), pp. 477–478 for the suggestion that this rule should only be applied where it was not inconsistent with the terms of the contract to allow the agent to sue.

73 *Bickerton* v. *Burrell* (1816) 5 M. & S. 383; *aliter* if the other party knows that the "agent" is the real principal: *Rayner* v. *Grote* (1846) 15 M. & W. 359.

74 See *Fellowes* v. *Gwydyr* (1829) 1 Russ. & M. 83.

75 *The Remco* [1984] 2 Lloyd's Rep. 205.

76 [1920] 3 K.B. 497; *ante*, p. 632.

77 *Hector* v. *Lyons* (1989) 58 P. & C.R. 156.

78 (1886) L.R. 2 C.P. 174; *ante*, p. 628; *cf. Phonogram Ltd.* v. *Lane* [1982] Q.B. 938; Green, 47 M.L.R. 671.

79 (1884) Cab. & El. 254.

80 *Black* v. *Smallwood* [1966] A.L.R. 744; Baxt, 30 M.L.R. 328; Lücke, 3 Adelaide L.Rev. 102.

81 As substituted by Companies Act 1989, s.130(4) for the former s.36(4) of Companies Act 1985, which had in its turn replaced European Communities Act 1972, s.9(2). The effect of s.36C(1) seems to be the same as that of the earlier provisions, in spite of slight changes in the wording.

82 *i.e.* one incorporated in the United Kingdom: *Rover International Ltd.* v. *Cannon Film Sales Ltd.* (*No. 3*) (1987) 3 B.C.C. 369, revsd. in part on other grounds [1989] 1 W.L.R. 912.

the contrary, as one made with the person purporting to act . . . as agent for" the company. Under this subsection, the agent can no longer escape liability merely on the ground that he entered into the contract "as agent"[83]; it is up to him to establish that there was an "agreement to the contrary" exonerating him from liability. The subsection puzzlingly concludes with the words "and he [*i.e.* the agent, in our examples] is personally liable on the contract accordingly." It seems these words merely spell out *one* consequence of the previous words and do not limit their operation: *i.e.* the agent may be *entitled* as well as liable.

At common law, a distinction was drawn between the cases so far considered where the agent purported to *act on behalf* of the unformed company, and those in which he said that the contract *actually was that* of the company and purported to affix the company's signature. In the latter case it was held that the resulting transaction was a complete nullity,[84] and that the agent could not acquire any rights under it.[85] But the distinction between the two situations has been criticised as highly technical[86] and one which businessmen were unlikely to appreciate. The provisions of section 36C(1) of the Companies Act 1985[87] therefore extend also to "a contract which purports to be made by a company" before it is formed. Such a contract has effect (subject to contrary agreement) "as one made with the person purporting to act for the company"; *e.g.* by the officer purporting to affix the company's signature. The concluding words of the subsection again refer only to the *liability* of such a person, but it seems that he may also be *entitled*. But the subsection does not apply where the contract purports to have been made by a company which had once existed and later been dissolved before the time of the putative contract. That contract is then a nullity and cannot be enforced either by the person purporting to have acted for the company or by a new company formed after the date of contracting to carry on the business of former company. The reason why section 36C(1) does not apply to such a case is that the agent purported to act for the old company rather than on behalf of the new company before it was formed.[88]

(vi) *Deeds.* At common law, an agent who executed a deed was personally liable on it even though the deed said that he had executed it on behalf of his principal.[89] It seems, however, that this rule has been reversed by statute.[90]

(vii) *Statute.* An agent may be personally liable by statute: for example, an administrative receiver appointed by debenture holders, who is deemed

---

[83] *Phonogram Ltd.* v. *Lane* [1982] Q.B. 938, 944; McMullen [1982] C.L.J. 47. And see *supra*, n. 81.

[84] *Cf. Rover International Ltd.* v. *Cannon Film Sales Ltd.* (*No. 3*) [1989] 1 W.L.R. 912—a position described in earlier proceedings in the same case as "a blot on English jurisprudence": [1987] 1 W.L.R. 670, 679.

[85] *Newborne* v. *Sensolid* (*Great Britain*) *Ltd.* [1954] 1 Q.B. 45.

[86] The defendants in Newborne's case escaped from a bad bargain on a technicality: see the comments of Lord Goddard C.J. reported in *The Times*, March 20, 1953. *Cf.* Lord Denning M.R. in *Phonogram Ltd.* v. *Lane* [1982] Q.B. 938, 944.

[87] *Supra*, n. 81.

[88] *Cotronic (UK) Ltd.* v. *Dezonie, The Times*, March 8, 1991.

[89] *Appleton* v. *Binks* (1804) 5 East 148.

[90] Powers of Attorney Act 1971, s.7(1), as amended by Law of Property (Miscellaneous Provisions) Act 1989, ss.1(8) and 4 and Scheds. 1 and 2.

to be the agent of the company,[91] is nevertheless personally liable on a contract into which he enters in carrying out his functions, except in so far as the contract otherwise provides.[92]

(c) ELECTION.[93] Where an agent is liable on the contract, one possible interpretation of the transaction is that he is solely liable, or, in other words, that the contract is simply between him and the third party and not between the third party and the principal at all.[94] Another possibility is that the agent and the principal are both liable under the contract.[95] This is certainly the position where the principal is undisclosed[96] and it may also be true where an agent incurs personal responsibility under a contract made on behalf of a disclosed principal.[97]

Where both principal and agent are liable on the contract, the third party may lose his right to sue one of them on the ground that he has "elected" to hold the other liable. This doctrine is most commonly discussed in relation to cases involving undisclosed principals, though there is some authority for applying it in all cases in which both principal and agent are liable on the contract.[98] The reasons for the doctrine are obscure: it is hard to see why a principal should be released merely because the third party has "elected" to hold the agent liable. It might be more satisfactory to hold that the principal should only be released if he had relied on the third party's conduct in such a way that he would be prejudiced by being subsequently held liable: for example, if the principal had adjusted his accounts with the agent in reliance on the third party's conduct.[99] Election to hold the principal liable may similarly be a ground for releasing the agent if it has led to action in reliance by the agent: for example, to his giving up rights against the principal. Where there has been no action in reliance on the third party's conduct, the courts do not in fact often apply the doctrine of election. What amounts to election is a question of fact; and in the decided cases the courts have been somewhat reluctant to find an election. Merely sending a bill to one of two parties liable has been held not to be an election[1]; and even the commencement of legal proceedings, though strong evidence of election,[2] is not necessarily conclusive. Thus in one case the third party was able to sue the principal although an overzealous clerk had, without the third party's real concurrence, filed a claim in the agent's bankruptcy.[3] In another case a third party was able to sue the agent, even though he had issued a writ against the principal, since he had

---

[91] Insolvency Act 1986, s.44(1)(*a*).
[92] *Ibid.* s.44(1)(*b*); for his right of indemnity, see *post*, p. 646.
[93] Reynolds, 86 L.Q.R. 318.
[94] *e.g. ante*, p. 636 at n. 67, *infra*, n. 94.
[95] See Reynolds, 85 L.Q.R. 92.
[96] *Ante*, pp. 631, 636.
[97] See *The Swan* [1968] 1 Lloyd's Rep. 5, 12; *Teheran-Europe Co.* v. *S. T. Belton (Tractors) Ltd.* [1968] 2 Q.B. 545, 558.
[98] *Debenham* v. *Perkins* (1925) 113 L.T. 252, 254. Other cases which have been cited to support the doctrine of election where the principal was disclosed may turn rather on the point that he was never liable under the contract at all because it was made solely with the agent: *e.g. Addison* v. *Gandasequi* (1812) 4 Taunt. 574; *Thomson* v. *Davenport* (1829) 9 B. & C. 78; *Calder* v. *Dobell* (1871) L.R. 6 C.P. 486.
[99] *Smethurst* v. *Mitchell* (1859) 1 E. & E. 622; *Davison* v. *Donaldson* (1882) 9 Q.B.D. 623.
[1] *Chesterton* v. *Barone* [1987] 1 E.G.L.R. 15.
[2] See *Scarf* v. *Jardine* (1882) 7 App.Cas. 345.
[3] *Curtis* v. *Williamson* (1874) L.R. 10 Q.B. 57.

also threatened to sue the agent, had never withdrawn this threat, and had not prosecuted his action against the principal.[4]

There was formerly a rule that, if the liability of principal and agent was joint, and the third party obtained judgment against one of them, he could not then sue the other, *even though the judgment was not satisfied*.[5] The rule has been abolished with respect to debts becoming due after January 1, 1979.[6] It follows that the mere obtaining of a judgment against principal or agent will not bar proceedings against the other; though it might, presumably, still amount to an "election."

(2) Under a collateral contract

There may be a collateral contract between agent and third party, quite distinct from the main contract between principal and third party. Thus when goods are sold by auction, the auctioneer undertakes certain obligations towards the buyer,[7] but they are not co-extensive with those of the seller. The seller undertakes that he has the right to sell, but the auctioneer only undertakes to give the buyer possession[8] so that he is not liable for the seller's lack of title.[9] The collateral contract may confer rights, as well as impose liabilities, on the agent. Thus an auctioneer can sue the buyer for the price of the things sold.[10]

(3) Implied warranty of authority

(a) NATURE OF LIABILITY. An agent who purports to act for a principal, knowing that he has no authority to do so, is liable to the third party in deceit, even if he believed that the principal would ratify.[11] It was at one time thought that if the agent honestly believed that he had authority when in fact he had none, he was under no liability.[12] But it was settled in *Collen* v. *Wright*[13] that the agent was in such circumstances liable for breach of an implied warranty that he had the authority which he purported to have. Thus in *Yonge* v. *Toynbee*[14] a solicitor was conducting litigation on behalf of a client who went mad. After this had happened but before the solicitor heard of it, he took further steps in the action. It was held that the other party to the litigation could recover from the solicitor the costs incurred by him in consequence of the solicitor's continuing the litigation after his authority to do so had come to an end because of his client's incapacity. It made

---

[4] *Clarkson Booker Ltd.* v. *Andjel* [1964] 2 Q.B. 775; *cf. The Scaplake* [1978] 2 Lloyd's Rep. 380.

[5] *Ante*, p. 513.

[6] Civil Liability (Contribution) Act 1978, s.3.

[7] *Woolfe* v. *Horne* (1877) 2 Q.B.D. 355.

[8] *Wood* v. *Baxter* (1883) 49 L.T. 45.

[9] *Benton* v. *Campbell, Parker & Co.* [1925] 2 K.B. 410.

[10] *Coppin* v. *Walker* (1816) 7 Taunt. 237; *cf. Wilson* v. *Pike* [1949] 1 K.B. 176; *Chelmsford Auctions Ltd.* v. *Poole* [1973] Q.B. 542.

[11] *Polhill* v. *Walter* (1832) 3 B. & Ad. 114.

[12] This was one basis of *Smout* v. *Ilbery* (1842) 10 M. & W. 1; see also *post*, p. 641. The view that fault is essential was still stated (wrongly) in *Salton* v. *New Beeston Cycle Co.* [1900] 1 Ch. 43.

[13] (1857) 8 E. & B. 647; approved by the House of Lords in *Starkey* v. *Bank of England* [1903] A.C. 114 and followed in *V/O Rasnoimport* v. *Guthrie & Co. Ltd.* [1966] 1 Lloyd's Rep. 1; Reynolds, 83 L.Q.R. 189.

[14] [1910] 1 K.B. 215; see *post*, p. 651, for survival of apparent authority in cases of the principal's insanity.

no difference that the solicitor had acted in good faith and with due diligence.

The rule sometimes operates harshly on the agent, and it might be more reasonable to imply a warranty that the agent should not negligently exceed his authority.[15] The agent's position has been alleviated by legislation, so that an agent who acts under a power of attorney incurs no liability if the power of attorney has without his knowledge been revoked.[16]

The agent does not warrant that the contract which he makes between principal and third party will be performed, but only that he has authority to make it. This has an important bearing on damages. If the third party could have obtained full satisfaction from the principal, had the contract been binding on him, the agent is liable to the same extent. But if the principal is insolvent, the third party cannot recover more from the agent than he would have actually got from the principal, had the agent had authority; and this may be very little, or nothing, according to the degree of the principal's insolvency.[17]

(b) RESTRICTIONS ON LIABILITY. An agent is not, or may not be, liable for breach of implied warranty of authority in the following cases:

(i) *Want of authority known to third party.* The agent is not liable where the third party knew, or must be taken to have known, that the agent had no authority.[18] The agent may also not be liable where he and the third party had equal means of knowing that the agent had no authority. In *Smout* v. *Ilbery*[19] a wife ordered goods from the plaintiff as agent for her husband, who, unknown to either party, had died in China before the order was placed. One reason[20] for holding that she was not liable to the plaintiff was that "the continuance of the life of the principal was . . . a fact equally within the knowledge of both contracting parties."[21] But although *Smout* v. *Ilbery* was argued, and discussed by the court, as if it were an action for breach of implied warranty of authority, the claim was in fact for goods sold and delivered, *i.e.* on the main contract of sale. Thus the case may not be authoritative on an agent's liability for breach of implied warranty.[22]

(ii) *Representation of law.* The agent is not liable where the representation of authority is one of law.[23] Since the construction of a document is a matter of law, an agent who misrepresents its meaning is not liable for breach of implied warranty. Thus if the director of a statutory corporation[24] which has, on the true construction of its incorporating statute, no borrowing powers, purports to borrow on its behalf, he is not liable for

---

[15] Negligence may lead to liability in damages at common law or under the Misrepresentation Act 1967; but the measure of such damages could differ from that for breach of implied warranty of authority: *cf. ante*, p. 322.

[16] Powers of Attorney Act 1971, s.5(1).

[17] *Post*, p. 828.

[18] *Jones* v. *Hope* (1880) 3 T.L.R. 247n.; *Lilly, Wilson & Co.* v. *Smales, Eeles & Co.* [1892] 1 Q.B. 456; *Halbot* v. *Lens* [1901] 1 Ch. 344.

[19] (1842) 10 M. & W. 1.

[20] For another reason see *ante*, p. 640, n. 12.

[21] At p. 11.

[22] See *Oliver* v. *Bank of England* [1901] 1 Ch. 652, 660.

[23] *Saffron Walden, etc. B.S.* v. *Rayner* (1880) 14 Ch.D. 406; for representations of law see *ante*

[24] Such corporations remain subject to the *ultra vires* doctrine: *ante*, p. 507.

breach of implied warranty.[25] But if such a corporation has a limited power to borrow up to, say, £10m., and the director purports to borrow on its behalf above that limit, he is liable for breach of implied warranty, for he has misrepresented a fact: namely, that the company has not yet borrowed £10m.[26] If a loan is made to a company incorporated under the Companies Acts by a lender dealing with the company in good faith, the contract of loan will be enforceable against the company even though the directors had, under the company's constitution, no power to enter into the contract.[27] The lender's claim for breach of warranty against the directors will therefore fail on the principle stated in the following paragraph. If the lender had *no* claim against the company because he had acted in bad faith, he would know that the loan was unauthorised. His claim for breach of warranty of authority would fail on the ground already stated, *viz.* that he knew of the agent's want of authority.[28]

(iii) *Principal liable on main contract.* An agent who has no actual authority is probably not liable for breach of implied warranty if the principal is liable to the third party on the ground of apparent or usual authority. In *Rainbow* v. *Howkins*[29] an auctioneer who had authority to sell a horse, subject to a reserve price, sold it without reserve. It was held that he was not liable for breach of implied warranty, as the buyer could have enforced the main contract against the seller on the ground that the auctioneer had apparent authority to sell without reserve.[30] Similarly, an agent would not be liable for breach of implied warranty if he did an unauthorised act which the principal later ratified.

(iv) *Crown agent.* An agent of the Crown is probably not liable for breach of implied warranty of authority. The assumption that such an agent impliedly warrants his authority is "utterly inconsistent with the facts."[31] In view of the enormous value of some government contracts, it would be extremely harsh to impose liability on a civil servant who in good faith and without negligence had misrepresented his authority.

3. Between Principal and Agent

(1) Rights of agent

(a) COMMISSION. Three questions arise in connection with an agent's right to commission.

(i) *Whether payable at all.* Whether an agent is entitled to any commission at all depends on the terms of the agreement between principal and agent. In *Taylor* v. *Brewer*[32] an agent was to receive "such commission . . . as should be deemed right" by the principal. It was held that he had no

---

[25] *Rashdall* v. *Ford* (1866) L.R. 2 Eq. 750.

[26] *Cherry* v. *Colonial Bank of Australasia* (1869) L.R. 3 P.C. 24; *Weeks* v. *Propert* (1873) L.R. 8 C.P. 427.

[27] Companies Act 1985, s.35A(1), as substituted by Companies Act 1989, s.108(1); *ante*, p. 506.

[28] *Supra*, at n. 18.

[29] [1904] 2 K.B. 322; criticised in *McManus* v. *Fortescue* [1907] 2 K.B. 1, 6, but that case can be explained on the ground that the third party knew of the agent's want of authority.

[30] *Cf. Mitsui & Co. Ltd.* v. *Marpo Industrial Ltd.* [1974] 1 Lloyd's Rep. 386, 393. *Quaere* whether this reasoning might have been applied in *Yonge* v. *Toynbee* [1910] 1 K.B. 215 (*ante*, p. 640). *Cf. post*, p. 651, n. 26.

[31] *Dunn* v. *Macdonald* [1897] 1 Q.B. 555, 558.

[32] (1813) 1 M. & S. 290.

legal right to commission. But where the agency is a commercial relationship the courts are reluctant to send the agent away empty-handed.[33] Thus if the agreement merely provides that the *amount* of commission is to be left to the principal's discretion, and he refuses to fix the amount, he may be liable to pay a reasonable sum.[34] On the other hand, the director of a company may agree to work for it "for such remuneration as the other directors may determine" on the understanding that he will receive nothing until the company has "got on its feet." If this never happens, he cannot claim a reasonable remuneration for his work.[35]

(ii) *When earned.* Commission is only payable in respect of a transaction which the agent was employed to bring about. In *Toulmin* v. *Millar*[36] the owner of a house employed an agent to find a tenant. The agent found a tenant, who later bought the house. His claim for commission on the sale failed, since he was only employed to let the house.

The transaction must also be caused by the agent's efforts. In *Tribe* v. *Taylor*[37] a principal employed an agent to raise a loan of money. The lender later entered into partnership with the principal and on this occasion made a further loan. The agent's claim for commission on this second loan failed, since it was not brought about by his efforts. It follows that, unless otherwise agreed,[38] the agent is not entitled to commission in respect of transactions which take place after the termination of the agency.[39] A contract may, however, provide that commission is *earned* when the agent secures the order (so that nothing more need be done by him to perfect his entitlement to it) but that it is only to *become payable* at some later stage, *e.g.* when the order is executed. In such a case the agent is entitled to commission on orders obtained before, though not executed till after, the termination of the agency.[40]

A principal may engage more than one agent: *e.g.* where an owner instructs two estate agents to find a purchaser for his house. Commission will then be due to the agent whose efforts have brought about the sale[41]; and where the efforts of both have contributed to this result, each may[42] be entitled to commission.[43]

The precise point of time at which the right to commission accrues depends on the terms of the contract between principal and agent. This question has given rise to great difficulty in cases concerning estate agents'

---

33 See *Kofi Sunkersette Obu* v. *A. Strauss & Co. Ltd.* [1951] A.C. 243.

34 *Bryant* v. *Flight* (1839) 5 M. & W. 114; *British Bank for Foreign Trade Ltd.* v. *Novinex Ltd.* [1949] 1 K.B. 623; *Powell* v. *Braun* [1954] 1 W.L.R. 401.

35 *Re Richmond Gate Property Co. Ltd.* [1965] 1 W.L.R. 335.

36 (1887) 12 App.Cas. 746. For a fuller report, see 58 L.T. 96.

37 (1876) 1 C.P.D. 505; *cf. Debenham, Tewson & Chinnocks plc* v. *Rimington* [1989] 2 E.G.L.R. 26 (where, however, the agents were awarded a reasonable remuneration for their efforts).

38 *Levy* v. *Goldhill* [1917] 2 Ch. 297; *cf. Brian Cooper & Co.* v. *Fairview Estates (Investments) Ltd.* [1987] 1 E.G.L.R. 18; *Robert Bruce & Partners* v. *Wynyard Developments* [1987] 1 E.G.L.R. 20; *Barnard Marcus & Co.* v. *Ashraf* [1988] 1 E.G.L.R. 7.

39 *Crocker-Horlock* v. *B. Lang & Co. Ltd.* [1949] 1 All E.R. 526; *Bronester Ltd.* v. *Priddle* [1961] 1 W.L.R. 1294.

40 *Sellers* v. *London Counties Newspapers* [1951] 1 K.B. 784.

41 *John D. Wood & Co.* v. *Dantata* (1985) 275 E.G. 1278.

42 Depending on the terms of the contract: see the authorities cited at nn. 45–51 *infra*.

43 *Lordgate Properties* v. *Balcombe* (1985) 274 E.G. 493.

commission.[44] In *Luxor (Eastbourne) Ltd.* v. *Cooper*[45] the contract provided that the landowner should pay the estate agent his commission "on completion of sale." No sale took place because the owner refused to deal with the prospective purchaser introduced by the agent. It was held that the agent was not entitled to commission. Again, a contract for the payment of commission on the agent's "introducing a person ready, willing and able to purchase" does not entitle him to commission if the prospective purchaser makes a conditional offer subject to contract and satisfactory survey; or if he makes an offer and withdraws it before the vendor accepts[46]; or if he signs a contract which cannot be completed because of a defect in the vendor's title[47]; or if, before the prospective purchaser is introduced, the owner has entered into a binding contract to sell the property to a purchaser introduced by another agent.[48] Nor does a promise to pay commission "in the event of your introducing . . . a person prepared to enter into a contract" entitle the agent to commission where the person introduced only agrees to sign a contract which is subject to conditions.[49] Even a contract for the payment of commission "in the event of securing for you an offer" does not entitle the agent to commission unless a firm, unconditional offer is made.[50] But where the contract was to pay commission as soon as "any person introduced by us enters into a legally binding contract to purchase" it was held that the agent was entitled when such a contract was made although the vendor later rescinded it on account of the purchaser's breach.[51]

The law on this topic is far from satisfactory. On the one hand it is hard for the estate agent, who may have gone to much trouble and expense in advertising[52] a house and securing offers, to be deprived of all reward through the caprice of his client. On the other hand it is hard for the client to have to pay commission where it is not his fault that no sale takes place: the common understanding is that the commission should come out of the proceeds of sale. In this conflict of interests, the estate agents usually have the advantage of being able to submit a standard form of contract[53] to the client, who may accept its terms without question. The courts have to some extent redressed the balance in favour of the client. They may, in the first place, refuse to give effect to a stipulation for the payment of commission on the ground that it is too uncertain. This is one reason why the agent's

---

44 Gower, 13 M.L.R. 490; Hardy-Ivamy (1951) C.L.P. 305.

45 [1941] A.C. 108.

46 *Dennis Reed Ltd.* v. *Goody* [1950] 2 K.B. 277; *Graham & Scott (Southgate) Ltd.* v. *Oxlade* [1950] 2 K.B. 257. Contrast *Christie Owen & Davies Ltd.* v. *Rapacioli* [1974] Q.B. 781 (where a vendor who withdrew after a firm offer had been made by the prospective purchaser was held liable for commission).

47 *Dellafiora* v. *Lester* [1962] 1 W.L.R. 1208; *cf. Blake & Co.* v. *Sohn* [1969] 1 W.L.R. 1412.

48 *A. A. Dickinson & Co.* v. *O'Leary* (1979) 254 E.G. 731.

49 *A. L. Wilkinson Ltd.* v. *Brown* [1966] 1 W.L.R. 1914.

50 *Bennett, Walden & Co.* v. *Wood* [1950] 2 All E.R. 134; *cf. Christie, Owen & Davies Ltd.* v. *Stockton* [1953] 1 W.L.R. 1353.

51 *Scheggia* v. *Gradwell* [1963] 1 W.L.R. 1049; *cf. Midgeley Estates Ltd.* v. *Hand* [1952] 2 Q.B. 432; *Drewery & Drewery* v. *Ware-Lane* [1960] 1 W.L.R. 1204; *aliter* if the contract goes off because of the agent's misrepresentation: *Peter Long & Partners* v. *Burns* [1956] 1 W.L.R. 413, 1083.

52 The agent can expressly stipulate for reimbursement of advertising expenses, as in *Bernard Thorpe & Partners* v. *Flannery* (1977) 244 E.G. 129.

53 The Unfair Contract Terms Act 1977 does not affect the validity of the provisions discussed: they confer rights on the agent and do not exclude or restrict his liability.

claim failed in *Jaques* v. *Lloyd D. George & Partners*[54] where the agreement purported to make commission payable "should you [the agent] be instrumental in introducing a person willing to sign a document capable of becoming a binding contract." A second ground for the decision in that case was that the agent had said orally that commission would be payable "if we find a suitable purchaser and the deal goes through": this amounted to a misrepresentation as to the effect of the written agreement and prevented the agent from relying on it. The courts will also construe stipulations for commission very strictly against the agents.[55] But it remains possible for commission to be payable even though there is no sale. It would perhaps be better if the question when an estate agent was entitled to commission ceased to be regarded purely as one of construction. Only legislation could now achieve this result[56]; but the Estate Agents Act 1979 (which regulates the activities of estate agents) does not lay down any rules for this purpose. It merely requires the agent, before a client enters into an agency contract with him, to give the client "particulars of the circumstances in which the client will become liable to pay remuneration to the agent for carrying out estate agency work."[57]

Even where the agent is not entitled to commission, he may have other rights against the client. He may be entitled to damages where the sale goes off as a result of the client's fault.[58] If the sale goes off as a result of the purchaser's default, and the purchaser's deposit is forfeited to the client, it has been suggested that the agent should be entitled to a *quantum meruit* out of the sum so forfeited.[59]

(iii) *Whether principal must give agent a chance to earn commission.* If a principal employs an agent for a fixed period he is not, in general, bound to stay in business merely to enable the agent to earn his commission. In *Rhodes* v. *Forwood*[60] a colliery-owner employed an agent to sell his coal in Liverpool for seven years. It was held that he committed no breach of contract by selling his colliery and going out of business within seven years. But if a principal contracts to stay in business for the agent's benefit he is liable in damages if he fails to do so. This was the effect of the contract in *Turner* v. *Goldsmith*,[61] where the principal employed the agent for five years to obtain orders for shirts "manufactured or sold" by the principal. It was held that he was not justified in putting an end to the agency agreement simply because the factory in which he manufactured shirts was burnt

---

[54] [1968] 1 W.L.R. 625.

[55] *Ante*, p. 644 at nn. 45–51.

[56] Lord Denning's view in *Jaques* v. *Lloyd D. George, supra*, n. 54, at p. 629, that an unreasonable stipulation will not be enforced does not seem to have received any judicial support.

[57] s.18(2)(*a*).

[58] *Dennis Reed Ltd.* v. *Goody* [1950] 2 K.B. 277, 285; for this purpose the default must be wilful, and not merely inability to complete on account of a defect of title: *Blake & Co.* v. *Sohn* [1969] 1 W.L.R. 1412.

[59] *Boots* v. *E. Christopher & Co.* [1952] 1 K.B. 89, 99; *cf. Debenham Tewson & Chinnock plc* v. *Rimington* [1989] 2 E.G.L.R. 26. In the United States, there is authority for holding the prospective *purchaser* liable to the agent for commission where he defaults: *Ellsworth Dobbs Inc.* v. *Johnson* 236 A. 2d. 843 (1967). Contrast *The Manifest Lipkowy* [1989] 2 Lloyd's Rep. 138 (buyer's agent held to have no right to commission against defaulting seller.

[60] (1876) 1 App.Cas. 256; *cf. Lazarus* v. *Cairn Line Ltd.* (1912) 106 L.T. 378; *L. French & Co. Ltd.* v. *Leeston Shipping Co. Ltd.* [1922] 1 A.C. 451; Burrows, 31 M.L.R. 390.

[61] [1891] 1 Q.B. 544; *cf. Re Patent Floor Cloth Co.* (1872) 26 L.T. 467.

down. An agency agreement may, moreover, relate to a specific contract which is actually concluded between principal and third party. In such a case, a term may be implied into the agency agreement that the principal will not break *that contract* so as to deprive the agent of his commission. Thus in *Alpha Trading Ltd.* v. *Dunshaw-Patten*[62] an agent negotiated a contract for the sale of cement by the principal to the third party. The principal defaulted on that contract and settled his claim with the third party. It was held that he was, in addition, liable to the agent in damages for having prevented him from earning his commission. An agency agreement may also contain an express or implied promise not to deprive the agent of the chance of earning commission on future transactions.

A client who employs an estate agent to sell a house is, in general, under no liability if he sells it himself or through a second agent.[63] If the agent is appointed "sole agent" the client cannot sell through another agent, but he can still sell the house himself unless he gives the agent "the sole and exclusive right to sell."[64] A manufacturer's "sole agent" may simply be a buyer and not an agent at all.[65] The manufacturer's undertaking to sell all his output to such a "sole agent" would bind him not to dispose of any of it himself,[66] so long as it was not invalid for restraint of trade.[67]

(b) Indemnity. A principal must indemnify his agent against all liabilities reasonably incurred or discharged by him in the execution of his authority.[68] This right of indemnity exists not only where the agent incurs contractual liability, but also where he incurs tortious liability, *e.g.* as a result of selling a third person's property under the instructions of his principal.[69] The agent is not entitled to any indemnity in respect of an obviously illegal transaction,[70] nor in respect of a liability due to his own breach of duty.[71]

An agent may even be entitled to an indemnity in respect of payments which he was not legally obliged to make. In *Read* v. *Anderson*[72] an agent paid the amount of a bet which he had made on behalf of his principal, and lost. He was able to recover this payment, though, if it had not been made, the winner could not have sued for it. The actual decision has been reversed by the Gaming Act 1892,[73] but the principle would still apply to a case not concerned with a wagering contract.[74] It would, however, only entitle the agent to an indemnity if the payment, though not legally due, was made in the usual course of business, or possibly if it was made under a strong moral obligation.

---

[62] [1981] Q.B. 290; Carter, 45 M.L.R. 220; *cf. ante*, p. 59 and 645 at n. 58; *George Moundreas & Co. S.A.* v. *Navimpex Centrala Navala* [1985] 2 Lloyd's Rep. 515.
[63] *Luxor (Eastbourne) Ltd.* v. *Cooper* [1941] A.C. 108.
[64] *Bentall Horsley & Baldry* v. *Vicary* [1931] 1 K.B. 253; *Hampton & Sons Ltd.* v. *George* [1939] 3 All.E.R. 627.
[65] *Ante*, p. 609.
[66] *W. T. Lamb & Sons* v. *Goring Brick Co. Ltd.* [1932] 1 K.B. 710.
[67] *Ante*, pp. 416–420.
[68] *Thacker* v. *Hardy* (1878) 4 Q.B.D. 685; *Reynolds* v. *Smith* (1893) 9 T.L.R. 494; *cf.* Insolvency Act 1986, s.44(1)(*c*) and (3); contrast *Wilson* v. *Avec Audio Visual Equipment Ltd.* [1974] 1 Lloyd's Rep. 80 (payment made after termination of authority).
[69] *Adamson* v. *Jarvis* (1827) 4 Bing. 66.
[70] *Thacker* v. *Hardy, supra*, at p. 687.
[71] *cf. Lister* v. *Romford Ice & Cold Storage Co. Ltd.* [1957] A.C. 555; *ante*, p. 191.
[72] (1884) 13 Q.B.D. 779.
[73] *Ante*, p. 466.
[74] *Cf. Adams* v. *Morgan* [1924] 1 K.B. 751; 40 L.Q.R. 389.

(c) LIEN. An agent is (unless otherwise agreed)[75] entitled to a lien on all property of the principal which has come into his possession in the course of the agency. Every agent has a *particular* lien: that is, he can hold the property until the principal satisfies all claims of the agent arising out of the agency. An agent may by custom or by special contract also have a *general* lien, entitling him to hold the property until the principal satisfies all claims of the agent, whether they have arisen out of the agency or not.

(2) Duties of agent

(a) TO CARRY OUT HIS INSTRUCTIONS. An agent who is appointed under a contract binding him to carry out his instructions is obviously obliged to carry them out. He may be liable for failing to do so even if the contract which he was instructed to make would not, if made, have been a binding one.[76] An agent who acts gratuitously or under a unilateral contract[77] is not bound to do anything, but may be liable if he starts to perform and then leaves the task unfinished.

(b) TO ACT WITH DUE CARE AND SKILL. The degree of care and skill expected of an agent depends on the circumstances. A person who holds himself out as being skilled in some profession or trade[78] must show greater care and skill than one who merely offers to give what help he can as a friend. There is probably no rigid distinction between paid and gratuitous agents for this purpose. The fact that the agent is paid is taken into consideration, along with other circumstances, in determining the degree of the care and skill to be expected of him; but even a gratuitous agent may be liable in tort for acting negligently.[79]

(c) FIDUCIARY DUTY. An agent is not a trustee[80]; but since the principal places confidence in him he is under a fiduciary duty. The most important consequences of this are the following.

(i) *Conflict of interest and duty*. The agent must not put himself into a position where his interest and duty conflict.[81] He must not, for instance, sell his own goods to the principal when he is employed to buy: his interest as a seller is to get the highest possible price, whereas his duty as agent is to buy at the lowest possible price.[82] Similarly, he must not, if employed to sell, buy the principal's property for himself.[83] Again, he must not subject himself to conflicting duties by acting as agent for both principal and third party,[84] unless he fully discloses the position to each of these persons.[85]

---

75 *Rolls Razor Ltd.* v. *Cox* [1967] 1 Q.B. 552.

76 *Ante*, p. 465, n. 14.

77 *Ante*, pp. 36, 138, 143; *The Zephyr* [1985] 2 Lloyd's Rep. 529, 538.

78 *Ante*, p. 189.

79 *Hedley Byrne & Co. Ltd.* v. *Heller & Partners Ltd.* [1964] A.C. 465, 495, 510, 526–527, 530, 538; approving *Wilkinson* v. *Coverdale* (1793) 1 Esp. 75; *ante*, p. 143.

80 *Lister & Co.* v. *Stubbs* (1890) 45 Ch.D. 1.

81 *Lamb* v. *Evans* [1893] 1 Ch. 218; *cf. Reading* v. *Att.-Gen.* [1951] A.C. 507.

82 *Armstrong* v. *Jackson* [1917] 2 K.B. 822; *Tetley* v. *Shand* (1871) 25 L.T. 658; *Regier* v. *Campbell-Stuart* [1939] Ch. 766; *Guiness plc* v. *Saunders* [1990] 2 A.C 663; *cf.* Companies Act 1985, s.317.

83 *McPherson* v. *Watt* (1877) 3 App.Cas. 254.

84 *Fullwood* v. *Hurley* [1928] 1 K.B. 498, 502; *Anglo-African Merchants* v. *Bayley* [1970] 1 Q.B. 311, 322–323; *North & South Trust Co.* v. *Berkeley* [1971] 1 W.L.R. 470.

85 See *Harrods Ltd.* v. *Lemon* [1931] 2 K.B. 157 (where full disclosure was made). *cf.* Estate Agents Act 1979, s.21 (imposing a statutory duty of disclosure on estate agents: the remedy is disqualification under s.3 of the Act).

A contract made in breach of this fiduciary duty is voidable at the option of the principal. The agent himself cannot avoid a transaction on the ground that it may conflict with his duties to his principal.[86]

(ii) *Bribes and secret profits*. The agent must not make a secret profit or take a bribe.[87] Thus he must not without the principal's consent[88] accept a commission from a third party.[89] Such a secret commission is called a "bribe" if the third party, at the time of paying it, knew that the payee was acting as agent for another. It is immaterial that the third party had no corrupt motive in making the payment.[90] The promise or payment of a bribe has drastic effects. The agent can (even if he has been appointed for a fixed period) be summarily dismissed[91]; he loses his right to commission on the tainted transaction[92]; and he must pay the bribe over to the principal, whether or not the latter has suffered loss.[93] If the bribe has not yet been paid, the agent cannot recover it from the third party, but the principal can do so.[94] The principal can further set the tainted transaction aside and retain the bribe, if it has been paid over to him by the agent[95]; if the bribe has not been paid, the principal can, as an alternative to claiming the bribe,[96] claim damages from the agent and the third party for the loss suffered as a result of the bribery.[97] Agent and third party may also incur criminal liability.[98] Where the secret profit is not a bribe, the third party is under no contractual or tortious liability. The agent is likewise not criminally liable[99] though he will be civilly liable to account for the payment to the principal.

---

86 *Boulting* v. *A.C.C.T.* [1963] 2 Q.B. 606.

87 Needham, 95 L.Q.R. 536.

88 See *Anangel Atlas Compania Naviera S.A.* v. *Ishikawajima-Harima Heavy Industries Co.* [1990] 1 Lloyd's Rep. 167 (where this requirement was not satisfied as the principal knew of the payments).

89 Or from the third party's agent acting within the scope of his authority: *The Ocean Frost* [1986] A.C. 717, 743 (affirmed without reference to this point *ibid*. 773.

90 *Industries & General Mortgage Co.* v. *Lewis* [1949] 2 All E.R. 573.

91 *Boston Deep Sea Fishing & Ice Co.* v. *Ansell* (1888) 39 Ch.D. 339. For the effect of such dismissal on the agent's rights to salary (or recompense for work actually done), see *post*, p. 685.

92 *Solomon* v. *Pender* (1865) 3 H. & C. 639; *Andrews* v. *Ramsey* [1903] 2 K.B. 635 (but commission on other transactions remains payable if they are severable: *Nitedals Taenstickfabrik* v. *Bruster* [1906] 2 Ch. 671); *cf. Boston Deep Sea Fishing & Ice Co.* v. *Ansell*, *supra*, where the fact that the agent had made secret profits on two groups of contracts did not defeat a right to commission on a third group. However, the reason given for this result was not that the transactions were severable but that the right to commission accrued before dismissal; this reasoning is hard to reconcile with such cases as *Andrews* v. *Ramsey*, *supra*.

93 *Reading* v. *Att.-Gen.* [1951] A.C. 507; Sealy [1963] C.L.J. 119, 128–136; *Islamic Republic of Iran Shipping Lines* v. *Denby*, *Financial Times*, October 28, 1986.

94 *Harrington* v. *Victoria Graving Dock Co.* (1878) 3 Q.B.D. 549; *Industries & General Mortgage Co.* v. *Lewis*, *supra*, n. 90

95 *Logicrose* v. *Southend United F.C.* [1988] 1 W.L.R. 1256; Jones, [1989] C.L.J. 22.

96 *T. Mahesan S/O Thambiah* v. *Malaysian Government Officers' Housing Society* [1979] A.C. 374; disapproving dicta in *Salford Corp.* v. *Lever* [1891] 1 Q.B. 168; Tettenborn, 95 L.Q.R. 68.

97 *Salford Corp.* v. *Lever* [1891] 1 Q.B. 168.

98 Prevention of Corruption Acts 1906–1916; corrupt motive is necessary for this purpose.

99 *R.* v. *Cullum* (1873) L.R. 2 C.C.R. 28. This decision has survived the Theft Act 1968; see s.5(3); Criminal Law Revision Committee, 8th Report (1966) Cmnd. 2977, para. 57(iii); *Attorney-General's Reference* (*No.*1 *of* 1985) [1986] Q.B. 491; *R.* v. *Cooke* [1986] A.C. 909, 934.

(d) PERSONAL PERFORMANCE. The general rule is that an agent cannot delegate the performance of his duties, unless the principal expressly or impliedly authorises him to appoint a sub-agent.[1] But an agent does not "delegate" by instructing his own employees to do various necessary acts in connection with the execution of his duty.

An agent may have authority to appoint a sub-agent and to make a contract between the sub-agent and the principal.[2] He may, alternatively, have authority to delegate, in the sense that he commits no breach of duty by performing through another, but have no authority to make a contract between principal and sub-agent.[3] In such a case the agent remains contractually liable to the principal if the sub-agent performs defectively,[4] while the sub-agent is under no contractual duty to the principal. The sub-agent may, however, be liable on other grounds, *e.g.* for breach of fiduciary duty or in tort if he negligently causes damage to the principal's property.[5] But it has been held that the sub-agent is not liable in tort merely for negligence in paying over the proceeds of the principal's property to an impostor[6] (so that the principal suffers financial loss); for such liability would be in practice indistinguishable from contractual liability and so inconsistent with the absence of a contractual relationship between principal and sub-agent.

(e) INDEMNITY. It is an implied term in a contract of employment that the employee will indemnify the employer against any liability to third parties incurred by reason of the employee's negligence in doing what he was employed to do.[7] A contract of agency will generally give rise to a similar liability to indemnify the principal.

4. Effects of Non-consensual Agency

It is a difficult and largely unsolved problem to what extent the effects of agency which have so far been discussed arise where the agency is not created by agreement between principal and agent, *e.g.* in cases of apparent and usual authority, and in cases of agency of necessity.

One effect of apparent or usual authority is to make the principal liable to the third party. But is the third party liable to the principal? When an agent acts within his apparent authority, the principal is liable because he is estopped from denying the agent's authority; but no similar estoppel need arise against the third party. If the principal wants to enforce the contract, he will usually ratify. But there may be some reason why he cannot do so,[8] and, if this is the case, it is far from clear that he could sue the third party simply because the third party can sue him. An agent who does an unauthorised act which binds his principal is clearly not entitled to commission,

---

[1] *e.g. John McCann & Co.* v. *Pow* [1974] 1 W.L.R. 1643.
[2] *De Bussche* v. *Alt* (1878) 8 Ch.D. 286.
[3] *New Zealand & Australian Land Co.* v. *Watson* (1881) 7 Q.B.D. 374; *Calico Printers' Assoc.* v. *Barclays Bank* (1931) 145 L.T. 51; *Royal Products Ltd.* v. *Midland Bank Ltd.* [1981] 2 Lloyd's Rep. 194, 198.
[4] *Powell & Thomas* v. *Evan Jones & Co.* [1905] 1 K.B. 11.
[5] *Meyerstein* v. *Eastern Agency* (1885) 1 T.L.R. 595; *cf. Stewart* v. *Reavell's Garage* [1952] 2 Q.B. 545.
[6] *Balsamo* v. *Medici* [1984] 1 W.L.R. 951
[7] *Lister* v. *Romford Ice & Cold Storage Co. Ltd.* [1957] A.C. 555; contrast *Harvey* v. *R. G. O'Dell Ltd.* [1958] 2 Q.B. 78.
[8] *Ante*, pp. 628 *et seq.*; *e.g.* it may be too late to ratify.

but is probably subject to the usual liabilities if he accepts a bribe or makes a secret profit.[9] An agent of necessity often acquires rights of recompense or reimbursement against his principal, but it is less common for him to be able to create a contract between principal and third party. Thus it is impossible to make any general statement about the effects of non-consensual agency. The problems which may arise must be considered in the light of the considerations of policy which underlie each type of non-consensual agency.

SECTION 5. TERMINATION

Agency as a contract is determined by any event which terminates a contract,[10] and also in certain special ways. After discussing these, we shall discuss the effects of termination and finally consider some cases of irrevocable agency.

1. Modes of Termination

(1) Consensual agency

(a) NOTICE. An agent's authority can be determined by giving him notice: for instance, a wife's implied authority to pledge her husband's credit for necessary household expenses can be terminated in this way.[11] Where the agency is contractual it may be for a fixed term or specify a period of notice. If no term or period of notice is specified, the contract is determinable on reasonable notice.[12] A notice given in breach of contract is, in general,[13] nonetheless *effective*. It determines the agent's actual authority[14] and the relationship of principal and agent. Thus the agent cannot restrain the breach by injunction or obtain a declaration that his dismissal was void or claim his agreed remuneration in respect of periods after the wrongful termination.[15] His normal remedies are by way of damages for wrongful dismissal and a declaration that the dismissal was wrongful.[16] He may also be able to restrain by injunction the breach of a negative stipulation in the agency contract,[17] such as an undertaking by the principal not to appoint another agent to conduct the business in question.[18]

---

[9] *English* v. *Dedham Vale Properties Ltd.* [1978] 1 W.L.R. 93.

[10] *e.g.* by rescission, performance or frustration.

[11] *Ante*, p. 613.

[12] *Martin-Baker Aircraft Co. Ltd.* v. *Canadian Flight Equipment Ltd.* [1955] 2 Q.B. 556; *cf. Re Spenborough U.D.C.'s Agreement* [1968] Ch. 139; *Richardson* v. *Koefod* [1969] 1 W.L.R. 1812, 1814. The "presumption of perpetual duration" in contracts specifying no time limit, stated in *Llanelly Ry. & Dock Co.* v. *L. & N.W. Ry.* (1875) L.R. 7 H.L. 550 (discussed by Carnegie, 85 L.Q.R. 392) does not apply to contracts of agency.

[13] For exceptions, see *post*, p. 911.

[14] *i.e.* the authority based on the wrongfully repudiated contract; as to apparent authority, usual authority and authority of necessity, see *post*, p. 651.

[15] *Denmark Productions Ltd.* v. *Boscobel Productions Ltd.* [1969] 1 Q.B. 699; *Roberts* v. *Elwells Engineering Co. Ltd.* [1972] 2 Q.B. 586; *Gunton* v. *London Borough of Richmond upon Thames* [1981] Ch. 448; *R.* v. *East Berkshire Health Authority, ex p. Walsh* [1985] Q.B. 152, 165; *Delaney* v. *Staples* [1991] 1 All E.R. 609, 616 *post*, p. 898; Freedland, 32 M.L.R. 314; Drake [1969] J.B.L. 113. Remuneration earned before the dismissal but payable thereafter could be claimed on the principle of *Sellers* v. *London County Newspapers* [1951] 1 K.B. 784.

[16] As to damages, see *Denmark Productions Ltd.* v. *Boscobel Productions Ltd., supra;* as to declaration, see *Taylor* v. *N.U.S.* [1967] 1 W.L.R. 532.

[17] *Post*, pp. 919–920.

[18] *Decro-Wall International S.A.* v. *Practitioners in Marketing Ltd.* [1971] 1 W.L.R. 361.

(b) INCONSISTENT CONDUCT. It seems that agency can be determined without notice by conduct inconsistent with its continuance, *e.g.* if the principal sells the subject-matter of the agency.[19] Such conduct may again be a breach of contract but nevertheless puts an end to the agency.

(c) INSANITY. At common law,[20] agency is determined by the supervening insanity of principal or agent if the insanity is inconsistent with the consensual nature of agency. The principal's insanity terminates agency even though the agent has no notice of it.[21]

(d) DEATH. Death of principal or agent terminates agency, whether the survivor has notice of death or not.[22] Dissolution of a company has the same effect, and so has dissolution of a partnership, unless the contract is, on its true construction, with the partners constituting the firm from time to time.[23]

(e) BANKRUPTCY. The principal's bankruptcy terminates the agent's authority.[24] The bankruptcy of the agent terminates his authority if it makes him unfit to perform his duties.[25]

(2) Non-consensual agency

The events listed above terminate an agent's express or implied authority, but do not necessarily terminate apparent or usual authority, or authority of necessity. Notice to the agent obviously does not terminate apparent or usual authority: notice must be given to the third party to have this effect. Again, a principal's insanity terminates his agent's actual authority; but a third party who goes on dealing with the agent without notice of the principal's insanity may be able to sue the principal on the ground that the agent still had apparent authority.[26] In *Blades* v. *Free*[27] the death of the principal was held to terminate the implied authority of his mistress to pledge his credit. Apparent authority was not discussed and it is submitted that the principal's estate could now be held liable on the ground that this type of authority can only be terminated by notice to the third party.

Agency of necessity can sometimes be terminated by notice, *e.g.* a shipmaster's authority would be terminated, just as it could be prevented from arising, in this way. But notice would not terminate such authority where

---

19 *E. P. Nelson & Co.* v. *Rolfe* [1950] 1 K.B. 139.

20 For a statutory exception, see *post*, pp. 652–653.

21 *Yonge* v. *Toynbee* [1910] 1 K.B. 215; *ante*, p. 640.

22 *Campanari* v. *Woodburn* (1854) 15 C.B. 400; *Pool* v. *Pool* (1889) 58 L.J.P. 67.

23 *Salton* v. *New Beeston Cycle Co.* [1900] 1 Ch. 43. And see *Brace* v. *Calder* [1895] 2 Q.B. 253; *Harold Fielding Ltd.* v. *Mansi* [1974] 1 All E.R. 1035; *Tunstall* v. *Condon* [1980] I.C.R. 786; *Briggs* v. *Oates* [1990] I.C.R. 473.

24 *Elliott* v. *Turquand* (1881) 7 App.Cas. 79.

25 *McCall* v. *Australian Meat Co. Ltd.* (1870) 19 W.R. 188.

26 *Drew* v. *Nunn* (1879) 4 Q.B.D. 661; *Yonge* v. *Toynbee* [1910] 1 K.B. 215 is only concerned with the termination of the agent's *actual* authority and his consequent liability for breach of warranty of authority. Normally such liability would not arise if the third party could hold the principal liable on the footing that the agent still had *apparent* authority (*ante*, p. 642). The two cases can, perhaps, be distinguished on the ground that the acts done by the agent in *Yonge* v. *Toynbee* (taking steps in litigation) were acts which the insane principal had no capacity to do at all; while the contract in *Drew* v. *Nunn* was one which could validly be made with an insane principal in accordance with the rules stated at p. 501, *ante*. However that may be, the court did not in *Yonge* v. *Toynbee* consider the possibility that the principal might have been held liable on the footing of apparent authority.

27 (1829) 9 B. & C. 167.

the need to encourage the agent to act was particularly strong. In *G.N. Ry.* v. *Swaffield*,[28] for instance, the railway company's claim was not defeated merely because the owner of the horse had said that he would not be responsible for the cost of feeding and stabling it.

2. Effects of Termination

Termination normally brings to an end the agent's authority to act on behalf of the principal; this is true even if the termination is wrongful and so gives the injured party a claim for damages.[29] Termination also brings to an end the relationship of principal and agent *inter se*, so that after termination no fresh rights between them can arise out of that relationship. On the other hand, rights and liabilities which have accrued before termination are clearly not affected by it. An agent is not, for instance, deprived of an accrued right to commission by the death of his principal, nor is he relieved by that event from liability for breach of duty committed before it occurred.

3. Irrevocable Agency

In the following cases agency is irrevocable in the sense that any attempt to revoke it is not merely a breach of contract but also ineffective. The agent's authority continues in spite of the attempt to revoke it.

(1) Authority coupled with an interest

An authority coupled with an interest is irrevocable. This does not mean that an authority is irrevocable simply because the agent can, by executing it, earn commission. The authority must be given for valuable consideration or by deed to secure some interest of the agent which exists independently of the agency. Thus in *Carmichael's* case[30] one Phillips promoted a company to buy a mine from him. Carmichael agreed to underwrite 1,000 shares in this company—*i.e.* to take up so many of these shares as could not be sold to the public—and authorised Phillips to apply for the shares on his behalf. This authority was held to be irrevocable; it was coupled with an "interest" because, if the shares were not taken up, Phillips would not get the purchase-money for the mine.

This rule only applies if the authority was intended for the protection of the interest.[31] It therefore cannot apply where the interest arises after the creation of the authority. Thus in *Smart* v. *Sandars*[32] an agent to whom goods were entrusted for sale *later* advanced money to the owner. His authority did not thereby become irrevocable.

(2) Irrevocable and enduring powers of attorney

At common law a power of attorney, even though coupled with an interest, was revoked by the death of the donor, *i.e.* of the principal.[33]

This rule might cause hardship both to the agent and to a person who

---

[28] (1874) L.R. 9 Ex. 142; *ante*, p. 623.
[29] *Ante*, p. 650.
[30] [1896] 2 Ch. 643; *cf. Walsh* v. *Whitcomb* (1797) 2 Esp. 565.
[31] *Frith* v. *Frith* [1906] A.C. 254.
[32] (1848) 5 C.B. 895.
[33] *Watson* v. *King* (1815) 4 Camp. 272.

bought from him in ignorance of the principal's death. The Powers of Attorney Act 1971 therefore provides that a power of attorney which is expressed to be irrevocable and is given to secure a proprietary interest of, or the performance of an obligation owed to, the donee shall not be revoked by the donor without the consent of the donee, or by the donor's death, incapacity or bankruptcy, so long as the interest or obligation secured by it remains in being.[34] The Act also protects third parties who deal in good faith with the donee of a power which is expressed to be irrevocable and to be given by way of security. Such persons are entitled to assume (unless they know the contrary) that the power cannot be revoked except by the donor acting with the consent of the donee, and that it has not been revoked in this way.[35]

The Enduring Powers of Attorney Act 1985 makes provision for powers of attorney executed in a prescribed form and expressed to continue in spite of the donor's supervening mental incapacity.[36] To create such an "enduring power" the donor need only have the capacity to understand the act of conferring authority on the donee: it is not necessary for the donor to have the mental capacity of managing his or her own affairs.[37] An enduring power is not revoked by the supervening incapacity of the donor,[38] but when such incapacity occurs the power is, in effect, suspended[39] until it is registered by the court.;.[40] Once an enduring power has been registered, it can no longer be revoked by the donor of the power; it can only be revoked with the consent of the court.[41] The Act further protects the donee of the power and third parties in a number of cases: if they act in good faith in ignorance of the donor's supervening mental incapacity[42]; if they act in good faith in pursuance of an instrument which is registered as an enduring power in spite of not being a valid power of attorney; if an enduring power is invalidly revoked (*i.e.* by the donor without the consent of the court); and if the instrument, though valid as a power of attorney, was not a valid *enduring* power though purporting to be one, and the power has been revoked by the donor's supervening mental incapacity.[43]

---

[34] s.4.
[35] s.5(3); special protection is provided for transferees under stock exchange transactions by s.6.
[36] s.2.
[37] *Re K.* [1988] Ch. 310.
[38] s.1(1)(*a*).
[39] s.1(1)(*b*).
[40] Under s.6.
[41] ss.7(1)(*a*), 8(3).
[42] s.1(1)(*c*).
[43] s.9.

CHAPTER EIGHTEEN

PERFORMANCE

A PARTY who performs a contract in accordance with its terms is thereby discharged from his obligations under it. Such performance also normally entitles him to enforce the other party's undertakings. It is often possible to perform a contract vicariously, *i.e.* by procuring performance by a third party. The legal effects of failure to perform are complex: a discussion of them forms the bulk of this chapter. Special rules govern the effects of failure to perform certain stipulations as to time.

SECTION 1. METHOD OF PERFORMANCE

1. When Performance is Due

The general rule is that performance is due without demand: a debtor must seek his creditor.[1] This rule can be varied by contrary agreement or by mercantile usage. The first possibility is illustrated by a contract which provides for payment to be made "on demand." The effect of these words is that the creditor cannot sue before making the demand,[2] and that the debtor must pay within a reasonable time of receiving the demand.[3] The second possibility is illustrated by the rule that the holder of a bill of exchange is not entitled to payment unless he first presents the bill for payment.[4] A demand or notice of default may also have to be given where the party from whom performance is claimed cannot, without notice, reasonably be expected to know that performance is due. Thus "a landlord is not in breach of his covenant to repair until he has been given notice of the want of repair and a reasonable time has elapsed in which repair could have been carried out."[5] In certain other cases, a demand or notice of default is also necessary to entitle the injured party to rescind,[6] though not to establish breach.

Where a contract provides that money is to be paid on, or by, a specified day, the debtor has the whole of that day to make the payment. The creditor cannot treat him as in default before the end of that day (*i.e.* before midnight) merely because the bank at which payment was, under the contract, to be made had already closed.[7] As a practical matter, the debtor, therefore cannot be treated as in default until the day following that specified in the contract.

---

[1] *Walton* v. *Mascall* (1844) 13 M. & W. 452. *Cf. Carne* v. *Debono* [1988] 1 W.L.R. 1107 (fact that vendor's completion statement contained inaccuracies did not excuse purchaser's failure to pay, since vendor had no duty to send such a statement).

[2] *Esso Petroleum Co. Ltd.* v. *Alstonbridge Properties Ltd.* [1975] 1 W.L.R. 1474 (where a contract under which a debt was payable in instalments provided that the balance was to become due "on demand" if debtor failed to keep up the payments); *Libyan Arab Foreign Bank* v. *Bankers Trust Co.* [1989] Q.B. 728, 748–749.

[3] *Toms* v. *Wilson* (1862) 4 B. & S. 442; *Bank of Baroda* v. *Panessar* [1987] Ch. 335.

[4] Bills of Exchange Act 1882, ss.41(1)(*a*), 40(1).

[5] *Calabar Properties Ltd.* v. *Stitcher* [1984] 1 W.L.R. 287, 298.

[6] *Post*, pp. 681, 728–729.

[7] *The Lutetian* [1982] 2 Lloyd's Rep. 140; *The Afovos* [1983] 1 W.L.R. 195.

2. Tender

A tender of money is ineffective unless the money is actually produced, or unless production is dispensed with by the creditor.[8] It will not do for the debtor to offer to pay and then simply to put his hand in his pocket.[9] Tender of part of a debt is bad.[10] Conversely, tender of too large a sum, *requiring change*, is bad, as this might put an unreasonable burden on the creditor.[11]

Tender of goods due under a contract of sale must be made at a reasonable hour; what is a reasonable hour is a question of fact.[12]

Where a bad tender is rejected and is, within the time fixed for performance, followed by a good tender, the latter must generally be accepted.[13] But if the first tender amounts to a repudiation of the contract, the injured party can treat the contract as discharged,[14] and if he does so he will not be bound to accept the second tender.

3. Payment by Cheque or Credit Card

There is a presumption that payment by cheque or other negotiable security operates only as conditional payment: that is, the payer is not discharged until the cheque or security is honoured. During the currency of the security, the creditor impliedly undertakes not to sue on the original debt.[15] But the presumption of conditional payment can be rebutted by proof of contrary intention *i.e.* by showing that the creditor had accepted the security unconditionally in payment of the debt.[16] The presumption that payment is merely conditional does not apply where a customer pays for goods or services by use of a charge or credit card. Use by the customer of such a card discharges his obligations under the contract with the supplier and makes the customer liable to reimburse the card issuing company in accordance with the contract between these two parties. If the company should fail to pay the supplier (*e.g.* because it has become insolvent) the supplier's sole remedy is against the company.[17] He cannot claim the price

---

[8] *Farquharson* v. *Pearl Insurance Co. Ltd.* [1937] 3 All E.R. 124.

[9] *Finch* v. *Brook* (1834) 1 Bing.N.C. 253.

[10] *Dixon* v. *Clark* (1847) 5 C.B. 365.

[11] *Betterbee* v. *Davis* (1811) 3 Camp. 70; *Robinson* v. *Cook* (1815) 6 Taunt. 336.

[12] Sale of Goods Act 1979, s.29(5).

[13] *Tetley* v. *Shand* (1871) 25 L.T. 658; *cf. Borrowman Phillips & Co.* v. *Free & Hollis* (1878) 4 Q.B.D. 500; *Agricultores Federados Argentinos* v. *Ampro S.A.* [1965] 2 Lloyd's Rep. 157; *Getreide Import Gesellschaft mbH* v. *Itoh & Co. (America) Ltd.* [1979] 1 Lloyd's Rep. 592; *Bremer Handelsgesellschaft mbH* v. *J. H. Rayner & Co.* [1979] 2 Lloyd's Rep. 216, 224–229; *The Playa Larga* [1983] 2 Lloyd's Rep. 171, 186.

[14] *Post*, p. 758.

[15] *Sayer* v. *Wagstaff* (1844) 14 L.J.Ch. 116; *Re Romer & Haslam* [1893] 2 Q.B. 286; *cf. Maran Road Saw Mill* v. *Austin Taylor & Co. Ltd.* [1975] 1 Lloyd's Rep. 156 and *E.D.F. Man* v. *Nigerian Sweets & Confectionery Co.* [1977] 2 Lloyd's Rep. 50 (payment by letter of credit). In *D.P.P.* v. *Turner* [1974] A.C. 357, 367–368, it is suggested that giving a cheque amounts to payment but that the debt revives if the cheque is not met. However, in *Sayer* v. *Wagstaff* (*supra*) "payment" was held to have taken place when the promissory note was *paid*, not when it was *given*.

[16] *Sard* v. *Rhodes* (1836) 1 M. & W. 153.

[17] *Re Charge Card Services Ltd.* [1989] Ch. 497; *cf. Richardson* v. *Worrall* [1985] S.T.C. 693, 717, 720; *Customs & Excise Commissioners* v. *Diners Club Ltd.* [1989] 1 W.L.R. 1196, 1205–1206 where Woolf L.J. rejects the argument that the debt is not extinguished but assigned to the card-issuing company. He leaves open the question whether the same analysis applies "where the contract is not made until the customer hands his card to the retailer in payment."

from the customer; for to allow him to do so would make the customer liable to immediate full payment in cash for the goods or services supplied and so impose on him an obligation substantially more onerous than that to which he agreed when contracting with the supplier on the terms that payment was to be made by means of the card.

4. Alternatives[18]

A contract may provide for performance in two different ways without stating which party is to have the power of choosing between them. In *Reed* v. *Kilburn Co-operative Society*[19] the plaintiff lent £50 to the defendants at six per cent. per annum "for six or nine months." The period of the loan was held to depend on the choice of the borrower. One reason given was that "the alternative was put in for the benefit of the borrower."[20] On this view the result could vary with the state of the market: the alternative might be for the benefit of the borrower if interest rates were thought likely to rise and for that of the lender if they were thought likely to fall. But this is not the law: the choice is always the borrower's, unless the contract expressly provides the contrary. Another reason given was that "the option is in the party who is to do the first act; here the borrower is to do the first act by paying."[21] But this test would not satisfactorily solve all cases. Quain J. during the argument said: "A lease for seven, 14 or 21 years, without saying at whose option, is at the option of the lessee."[22] Yet before one knows whose the option is, it is impossible to tell who is to do the first act, *i.e.* whether landlord or tenant must give notice. No general rule is satisfactory where parties make such obscure contracts. One can only deal with the problem by laying down arbitrary rules in particular cases.[23]

SECTION 2. VICARIOUS PERFORMANCE

A contract may be performed by a third party on behalf of the debtor. The legal effects of such performance depend on whether it is made (or tendered) with or without the creditor's consent.

1. With the Creditor's Consent

If the creditor agrees to accept performance by a third party, the contract is discharged by such performance whether or not it is the same as that stipulated for in the contract. In *Hirachand Punamchand* v. *Temple*[24] a debt was held to be discharged when the creditor accepted a smaller sum from the debtor's father in full settlement.

Payment by a third party can discharge a debt, even though it is made without the knowledge or consent of the debtor,[25] but it will only have this

---

[18] *Cf. post*, p. 778.
[19] (1875) L.R. 10 Q.B. 264; *cf. Price* v. *Nixon* (1813) 5 Taunt. 338.
[20] At p. 265.
[21] At p. 264.
[22] At p. 265.
[23] *Cf. Benjamin's Sale of Goods* (3rd Ed.), §§ 1803, 1827.
[24] [1911] 2 K.B. 330; *ante*, p. 118.
[25] *Cook* v. *Lister* (1863) 13 C.B.(N.S.) 543, 594. If the third party pays under the mistaken belief that he is authorised by the debtor to make the payment, the debt is not discharged: *Barclays Bank Ltd.* v. *W. J. Simms, Sons & Cooke (Southern) Ltd.* [1980] Q.B. 677; unless (presumably) the debtor ratifies.

effect if it is made on behalf of the debtor and with the intention of discharging him. In *Re Rowe*[26] the secretary of a company defrauded a person who had dealt with the company of some £16,500. The company was not liable for this fraud but made an *ex gratia* payment of £6,500 to the defrauded person. The latter was nonetheless entitled to claim the whole of his loss from the secretary, since the company's payment was not made on the secretary's behalf. Similarly, part-payment by one of two persons who are both liable for a debt will not discharge the other, since it will be presumed to have been made on account of his own and not of his co-debtor's liability.[27]

The cases on this subject all concern the payment of debts; but presumably the same principles apply where a creditor agrees to accept vicarious performance of some other obligation, *e.g.* to deliver goods.

2. Without the Creditor's Consent

The question whether a contract can be vicariously performed without the consent of the creditor gives rise to more difficulty. In principle, a creditor cannot object to vicarious performance unless he is prejudiced by the fact that the debtor does not perform personally. Thus a tradesman, to whom money is owed for goods, cannot object if full payment in cash is made on behalf of the debtor by a third party. The same is often true of obligations to do something other than pay cash. Thus in *British Waggon Co.* v. *Lea & Co.*[28] it was held that a contract to let out railway wagons and to keep them in repair for seven years could be vicariously performed: it did not matter to the hirer who kept the wagons in repair so long as the work was efficiently done by someone.

But a creditor may be entitled to object to vicarious performance either on account of the nature of the contract or because of its terms.

(1) Nature of the contract

When a contract is "personal" in the sense that one party relies on the skill and judgment of the other, the latter must perform personally. Thus duties under a contract of service cannot be vicariously performed; an estate agent who has been instructed to find a purchaser for a house cannot perform vicariously, since he "holds a position of discretion and trust"[29]; a person who agrees to store another's goods must perform personally, since the owner of the goods relies on his skill and integrity[30]; and a shipowner must perform a charterparty personally in the sense that he cannot require the charterer to accept performance from a third party to whom the ship has been sold.[31] There are cases in which even a contract for the sale of goods must be personally performed by the seller, *e.g.* if the goods are to be manufactured by the seller and the buyer has relied on the seller's skill

26 [1904] 2 K.B. 483; *Pacific Associates Inc.* v. *Baxter* [1990] 1 Q.B. 993, 1033–1034.
27 *Jones* v. *Broadhurst* (1850) 9 C.B. 173; *Cook* v. *Lister*, *supra*; *Kemp* v. *Balls* (1854) 10 Ex. 607.
28 (1880) 5 Q.B.D. 149; *cf. Phillips* v. *Alhambra Palace Co.* [1901] 1 Q.B. 59.
29 *John McCann & Co.* v. *Pow* [1974] 1 W.L.R. 1643, 1647; *cf. ante*, p. 647.
30 *Edwards* v. *Newland* [1950] 2 K.B. 534.
31 *Fratelli Sorrentino* v. *Buerger* [1915] 3 K.B. 367, 370, but that case shows that the charterer cannot object if, notwithstanding the sale, the shipowner can still perform personally, *i.e.* if he retains the control and management of the ship during the chartered period or voyage; *cf. Humble* v. *Hunter* (1842) 12 Q.B. 310; *ante*, p. 631.

as a manufacturer[32] or if the buyer has in some other way relied on the personal integrity of the seller.[33] Perhaps the most extreme case is *Robson* v. *Drummond*,[34] where it was held that a person who had agreed to keep a carriage in repair for five years and to paint it from time to time was not entitled to delegate performance of the contract to his partner.

(2) Terms of contract

It is obvious that a contract must be personally performed if it expressly so provides. A contract may also contain terms which impliedly rule out vicarious performance. In *Davies* v. *Collins*[35] the defendant accepted a uniform for cleaning under a contract which provided: "Whilst every care is exercised in cleaning . . . garments, all orders are accepted at owners' risk." It was held that the defendant had broken the contract by sending the uniform to be cleaned by a sub-contractor (who had lost it); for the words "whilst every care is exercised in cleaning . . . " were inconsistent with the right to perform the cleaning operation vicariously. If however, the uniform had been properly cleaned, and returned, by the sub-contractor, the owner would not have been prejudiced by the fact of vicarious performance, and it is submitted that he should have been liable to make at any rate some payment.[36] Lord Greene M.R. said that the clause did not preclude every kind of sub-contracting: the cleaner might have employed a sub-contractor to perform some purely ancillary service, such as returning the uniform to the customer. It is arguable that the clause only precluded vicarious performance of the duty to take care of the goods, and that, so long as that duty remained unbroken, the owner was liable to pay the cleaning charges.

3. Vicarious Performance Distinguished from Assignment

The factors which determine whether a contract can be vicariously performed closely resemble those which determine whether the benefit of a contract is assignable.[37] For this reason, vicarious performance is sometimes called *assignment of liabilities*; but this is misleading.[38] Where vicarious performance is permitted no liability is *transferred*; the original debtor remains liable for the due performance of his obligations under the contract[39]; and the sub-contractor does not become liable in contract to the creditor.[40] In *Stewart* v. *Reavell's Garage*[41] the plaintiff took a 1929 Bentley motor-car to the defendants' garage to have the brakes relined. At the

---

[32] *Johnson* v. *Raylton, Dixon & Co.* (1881) 7 Q.B.D. 438.

[33] *Dr. Jaeger's Sanitary Woollen System Co. Ltd.* v. *Walker & Sons* (1897) 77 L.T. 180.

[34] (1831) 2 B. & Ad. 303.

[35] [1945] 1 All E.R. 247; *cf. Kollerich & Cie S.A.* v. *The State Trading Co. of India* [1980] 2 Lloyd's Rep. 32; and see *ante*, p. 210.

[36] *Cf. post*, p. 718.

[37] *Ante*, pp. 597–598.

[38] *Nokes* v. *Doncaster Amalgamated Collieries Ltd.* [1940] A.C. 1014, 1019. *Cf. ante*, p. 603.

[39] For a qualification where performance requires specialist skills which the debtor cannot reasonably be expected to have, see *Investors in Industry Commercial Property Ltd.* v. *Bedfordshire D.C* [1986] 1 All E.R 787, 807 (not reported on this point in [1986] Q.B. 1034).

[40] Unless the main contractor is the other party's agent for the purpose of making a contract between him and the sub-contractor; *ante*, p. 649.

[41] [1952] 2 Q.B. 545; *cf. Basildon D.C.* v. *J. E. Lesser (Properties) Ltd.* [1985] Q.B. 839; *The Superhulls Cover Case* [1990] 2 Lloyd's Rep. 431, 445.

defendants' suggestion, the plaintiff agreed that the work should be done by a sub-contractor, who did it so badly that the brakes failed, and the plaintiff was injured. The defendants were clearly entitled to perform vicariously, as the plaintiff had agreed to their doing so. But they were nonetheless held liable for the sub-contractor's defective workmanship: their liability was not transferred. Nor did the sub-contractor incur any contractual liability to the plaintiff. He might have been liable to the plaintiff in tort for doing the work negligently[42] but he would not have been liable to the plaintiff in contract, had he failed to do the work at all.

Stewart v. *Reavell's Garage* is concerned with the vicarious performance of a defendant's contractual duty, which may be strict, *i.e.* capable of being broken without negligence. A different problem arises where the defendant's alleged duty cannot arise in contract but only in tort. This is the position where A contracts with B to do work and engages a subcontractor to do it. If a third party, C, suffers damage as a result of defects in the subcontractor's work, C cannot sue A in contract as there is no contract between them. C's only cause of action against A will be in tort for negligence; and in such an action it will be a defence for A to show that he had engaged "an apparently competent independent sub-contractor."[43]

SECTION 3. RESCISSION FOR FAILURE TO PERFORM[44]

1. Introduction

(1) Terminology

Failure to perform may (and often will) amount to breach of contract. Where this is the case the injured party can bring actions either for the specific enforcement of the contract, or for damages.[45] In such actions, the injured party seeks to be put (either actually or so far as money can do it) into the position in which he would have been if the contract had been *performed.* But he may also resort to another group of remedies, the object of which is to put him into position in which he would have been, if the contract *had not been made.* These remedies are based on failure in performance rather than on breach[46]: they may therefore be available even though the failure does not amount to a breach because there is some lawful excuse[47] for it. Where there is *no* breach, these remedies are, moreover, the only ones available to the "injured party"; it will be convenient to use this expression to refer to any party who by reason of a failure in per-

---

[42] *Cf. Learoyd Bros.* v. *Pope & Sons* [1966] 2 Lloyd's Rep. 142.

[43] *D. & F. Estates Ltd.* v. *Church Commissioners For England* [1989] A.C. 177, 209, where the claim for a relatively "trivial sum" of £50 in respect of damage to carpets failed on this ground. The larger claim for economic loss failed on other grounds discussed at pp. 541, 545, *ante*.

[44] Devlin [1966] C.L.J. 192; Reynolds, 79 L.Q.R. 534; Shea, 42 M.L.R. 623.

[45] *Post*, Chap. 21, Sections 1 to 3.

[46] *e.g.* in *The Kathleen* (1874) L.R. 4 A. & E. 269, and in *Poussard* v. *Spiers* (1876) 1 Q.B.D. 410; *post*, pp. 676, 678. In *Shell U.K. Ltd.* v. *Lostock Garages Ltd.* [1976] 1 W.L.R. 1187, 1199, Lord Denning M.R. suggests that one party's "unfair conduct," not amounting even to non-performance (let alone to breach) justifies the other's refusal to perform; but acceptance of this view could lead to great uncertainty. *Cf.* Lord Denning's view in *Western Excavating (E.C.C.) Ltd.* v. *Sharp* [1978] Q.B. 761, 770 that for the purpose of constructive dismissal the test of "unreasonable conduct" would be "too indefinite by far."

[47] *Post*, pp. 734–735.

formance (whether excused or not) does not get what he bargained for. One special excuse for non-performance arises where supervening events so fundamentally disrupt performance of the contract as to bring it automatically to an end under the doctrine of frustration. This doctrine is discussed in Chapter 20; our present concern is with cases in which the failure in performance is not such as to frustrate the contract. In cases of this kind, a number of remedies are available to an injured party who wishes to "undo" rather than to "enforce" the contract. One such remedy is a simple refusal by the injured party to perform his own promise, *e.g.* he may refuse to pay for work on the ground that it was defectively done. This remedy is often combined with a refusal to accept further performance from the other party on account of a defect in the performance so far rendered, *e.g.* with a refusal to accept further deliveries under an instalment contract on the ground that one or more of the deliveries so far made are defective. Alternatively, the injured party may wish to undo the transaction by returning the defective performance and claiming back the consideration which he provided for it, *e.g.* he may return defective goods and sue for recovery of the money which he had paid for them.[48]

The first difficulty in discussing this subject is the terminological one of finding a suitable word or phrase to refer to the remedies just described. For this purpose, the courts[49] (and contractual draftsmen[50]) have commonly used words such as "rescission" and "termination"; but this traditional terminology has attracted some criticism. In the *Photo Production* case, Lord Wilberforce said that the use of "rescission" in this sense "may lead to confusion"[51]; and Lord Diplock described the usage as "misleading" unless it was borne in mind that, in cases of breach, such rescission did not deprive the injured party of his right to claim damages for the breach.[52] The Sale of Goods Act 1979 avoids this difficulty by referring to a buyer's "right to reject the goods and treat the contract as repudiated."[53] But even this language is inappropriate where the failure in performance does not amount to a breach; and Devlin J. has described the buyer's right to reject as being "merely a particular form of the right to rescind."[54] The Sale of Goods Act itself, moreover, refers to a contract of sale as being "rescinded" by the seller on account of the buyer's breach; and it meets the point made by Lord Diplock by going on to provide that the rescission is "without prejudice to any claims the seller may have for damages."[55] Since the *Photo Production* case, Lord Roskill has, in *Bunge Corp.* v. *Tradax Export S.A.* once again referred to the right of an injured party to

---

[48] This is more fully discussed in Chap. 21: *post*, pp. 927–933.

[49] Recent examples of this usage can be found in *The Hansa Nord* [1976] Q.B. 44, 66; *Buckland* v. *Farmar & Moody* [1979] 1 W.L.R. 221, 231–232; *Johnson* v. *Agnew* [1980] A.C. 367, 392–393; *cf. Gunton* v. *Richmond-upon-Thames L.B.C.* [1981] Ch. 448, 468 ("determination").

[50] See, for example, the terms of the contracts in *Woodar Investment Development Ltd.* v. *Wimpey Construction U.K. Ltd.* [1980] 1 W.L.R. 227 and *Hyundai Heavy Industries Ltd.* v. *Papadopoulos* [1980] 1 W.L.R. 1129.

[51] *Photo Production Ltd.* v. *Securicor Transport Ltd.* [1980] A.C. 827, 844; *cf.* an earlier criticism in *Heyman* v. *Darwins Ltd.* [1982] A.C. 356, 399.

[52] [1980] A.C. 827, 851; *post*, p. 748.

[53] ss.11(3), 11(4) and 61(1) (definition of "warranty").

[54] *Kwei Tek Chao* v. *British Traders Ltd.* [1954] Q.B. 459, 480.

[55] s.48(4).

"rescind"[56] a contract for breach; Lord Lowry there used the term "rescission" in the same sense[57]; and even Lord Diplock himself has in a number of later cases referred to the injured party's right to "rescind" on account of the other's breach.[58] These expressions are certainly more convenient than the somewhat clumsy circumlocution of "treating a contract as repudiated (or discharged) for breach (or excused non-performance)." In the following discussion we shall therefore continue to use the term "rescission" to refer to the remedies described above, bearing in mind that such rescission does not deprive the injured party of his claim for damages where the failure in performance amounts to a breach. In this respect rescission for breach differs fundamentally from rescission for misrepresentation, discussed in Chapter 9.[59]

(2) Policy Considerations

The law governing the right to rescind for failure in performance is complex and difficult; and in this it reflects the difficulty which the courts have experienced in balancing or reconciling the conflicting interests of the parties in respectively seeking, and resisting, the remedy of rescission.[60]

The interests of the injured party in seeking rescission may be grouped under three heads. First, rescission will be his only remedy where the failure in performance is not a breach. Secondly, rescission may, even where the failure is a breach, lead to a result which is more favourable to the injured party in monetary terms than a claim for damages. This will be true where the contract would have been a bad bargain for the injured party even if it had been duly performed[61]; and also where the loss or injury which he suffers is one for which he might not recover damages in an action for breach of contract: for example, if his loss (or part of it) is irrecoverable because it is too remote.[62] Thirdly, the injured party may, by rescinding, get a quicker and more efficacious remedy. A buyer who has not yet paid for defective goods will often prefer to "rescind" (in the sense of rejecting the goods and refusing to pay) than to perform his side of the bargain and be left to pursue a claim for damages. By rescinding he avoids the delays of litigation, and the risk that the seller's credit may fail. Even if he has already paid, an action for the return of the payment is in many ways more convenient than one for damages. It is an action for a liquidated sum, which avoids many of the difficulties (such as quantification, mitigation and causation) which are liable to arise in an action for damages.[63]

On the other hand, the party who fails to perform in accordance with the

---

[56] [1981] 1 W.L.R. 711, 723, 724; *cf. The T.F.L. Prosperity* [1984] 1 W.L.R. 48, 58.

[57] [1981] 1 W.L.R. at p. 719; *cf.* also *The Cleon* [1983] 1 Lloyd's Rep. 587, 590; *R.H.D. International Ltd.* v. *S.A.S. Animal Air Services Ltd.* [1984] 1 W.L.R. 48, 58; *Peyman* v. *Lanjani* [1985] Ch. 457, 482, 483.

[58] *The Scaptrade* [1983] 2 A.C. 694, 702; *Gill & Duffus S.A.* v. *Berger Co. Inc.* [1984] A.C. 382, 390, 391; *Metro Meat Ltd.* v. *Fares Rural Co. Pty Ltd.* [1985] 2 Lloyd's Rep. 13, 17; for use of the same expression in the present context by other judges, see (for example) *Shine* v. *General Guarantee Corp.* [1988] 1 All E.R. 911, 916; *Nova Petroleum International Establishment* v. *Tricon Trading Ltd.* [1988] 1 Lloyd's Rep. 312, 315.

[59] *Ante*, pp. 329–336, especially at p. 330.

[60] Honnold, 97 U. of Pa.L.Rev. 457.

[61] *e.g.* if he has agreed to pay £100 for something which would, because of a fall in the market, be worth only £50 even if there had been no breach. This is a constantly recurring problem: see *post*, pp. 678–679, 688, 695, 697, 706, n. 29.

[62] *Post*, pp. 854–864.

[63] *Post*, pp. 836–854, 864–871.

contract may have equally strong interests in resisting rescission. He may have incurred expenses in the course of performance, for example by paying a commission on a sale or by transporting the goods to a distant place; and these expenses will be thrown away if the contract is rescinded. He may, in addition, have conferred benefits on the injured party who may be unjustly enriched by being allowed to rescind: rescission of partly performed building contracts is, for example, likely to produce this result. And he may suffer hardship if the injured party is allowed to rescind on a falling market: he may be left with goods whose value has diminished by an amount far in excess of the loss which would have been caused to the injured party by reason of the defect.

In balancing these conflicting interests, the courts have developed a number of rules and distinctions which prima facie determine the availability of rescission as a remedy for failure to perform. Further rules specify that the right to rescind, even where it is prima facie available, may be limited or barred by certain supervening factors.

2. The Order of Performance

The order in which contracting parties must perform their respective obligations depends on the distinction between conditions precedent, concurrent conditions, and independent promises. Somewhat confusingly, English law also uses the expression "condition" in rules which deal with the conformity of one party's performance with that promised (as opposed to the order in which the two performances must be rendered). This usage, and the distinction between these two senses of "condition," are discussed later in this Chapter.[64]

(1) Condition precedent

Performance by one party, A, is a condition precedent to the liability of the other, B, when A has to perform before B's liability accrues. This will most obviously be the case if the contract expressly provides that A's act is to be done before B's.[65] Thus if A agrees to work for B at a weekly wage payable in arrear, B need not pay A until A has done a week's work.[66] Performance by A may be a condition precedent to the liability of B even though the contract does not expressly state the order in which the two acts are to be done. In *Trans Trust S.P.R.L.* v. *Danubian Trading Co.*[67] A bought steel from B to be paid for by "cash against shipping documents from a confirmed credit to be opened by" an American company (to whom A had resold) in favour of B. A undertook that the credit would be opened "forthwith." Performance by A of his undertaking to procure the letter of credit was regarded as a condition precedent to the liability of B although the order in which their acts were to be done was not expressly laid down in the contract. A knew that B could not get supplies of steel unless the credit

---

64 *Post*, pp. 689–704, especially at p. 690.

65 *Société Générale de Paris* v. *Milders* (1883) 49 L.T. 55, 59; *cf. Pioneer Concrete (U.K.) Ltd.* v. *National Employers Mutual, etc.* [1985] 2 All E.R. 395.

66 *Morton* v. *Lamb* (1797) 7 T.R. 125; *Cresswell* v. *Board of Inland Revenue* [1984] I.C.R. 508; *Miles* v. *Wakefield M.D.C.* [1987] A.C. 539, 561, 574; *Wiluszynski* v. *Tower Hamlets L.B.C.* [1989] I.C.R. 493, 498; see further p. 719, *post*.

67 [1952] 2 Q.B. 297. For a similar argument in a different context, see *Films Rover International* v. *Cannon Film Sales Ltd.* [1987] 1 W.L.R. 670, 684; for further proceedings se [1989] 1 W.L.R. 912.

was made available. Hence the nature of the contract made it clear that A should perform before B became liable.

In Chapter 2 we distinguished between contingent and promissory conditions, and noted that "condition" was used to refer either to an event or to a term of a contract.[68] Our present concern is with conditions as events. In this sense, a contingent condition is an event which neither party undertakes to bring about and on which the existence of a contract, or the binding force of its principal obligations, depends. A promissory condition, on the other hand, refers to an event which one party is obliged by the contract to bring about. In the *Trans Trust* case, it was argued that the opening of the credit was a condition of the former kind, so that A was not liable when his sub-buyer failed to open the credit. But the court rejected the argument and held A liable on the ground that the opening of the credit was not a condition precedent to the existence of the contract, but only a condition precedent to the liability of B. In other words, it was not a contingent, but a promissory condition. In its contingent sense, condition precedent is contrasted with condition subsequent. In its promissory sense (with which we are here concerned), condition precedent is contrasted with concurrent condition and independent promise: these concepts are discussed below.

The distinction between a contingent and a promissory condition turns on the question whether the agreement purports to impose on A an obligation to bring about the stipulated event.[69] For example, in one case A undertook to erect buildings on B's land, and B undertook, when A had done so, to grant a lease of the land to A. This was held not to be a (contingently) "conditional contract," but a case in which performance by A was a (promissory) condition precedent to the liability of B.[70] The position is similar where A contracts to buy a house from B and to pay a deposit. As A promised to pay the deposit, that payment is not a contingent condition precedent to the existence of the contract[71] but a promissory condition precedent to the liability of B. If the deposit is not paid, B is, moreover, entitled to rescind the contract,[72] while A can be sued for the unpaid deposit, or for damages for failing to pay it.[73]

(2) Concurrent conditions

The two performances are said to be concurrent conditions when the parties undertake to perform concurrently (or simultaneously). Thus in the case of a contract for the sale of goods delivery and payment are concurrent conditions: this means that the buyer cannot claim delivery unless he is ready and willing to pay, and the seller cannot claim the price unless he is

---

68 *Ante*, p. 58; *cf. post*, p. 690.

69 *Cf. Albion Sugar Co. Ltd.* v. *Williams Tankers Ltd.* [1977] 2 Lloyd's Rep. 457, 464; *The Padre Island* [1990] 2 All E.R. 705, 714.

70 *Eastham* v. *Leigh, London & Provincial Properties Ltd.* [1971] 1 Ch. 871.

71 *Michael Richards Properties Ltd.* v. *St. Saviour's Parish* [1975] 3 All E.R. 416, 420; *Portara Shipping Co.* v. *Gulf Pacifica Navigation Co. Ltd.* [1981] 2 Lloyd's Rep. 180, 184; *Millichamp* v. *Jones* [1982] 1 W.L.R. 1422; *The Blankenstein* [1985] 1 W.L.R. 435. These authorities reject the contrary view stated in *Myton Ltd.* v. *Schwab-Morris* [1974] 1 W.L.R. 326, 330.

72 *Myton Ltd.* v. *Schwab-Morris* [1974] 1 W.L.R. 326, 331, *post*, p. 676. The contract may require B to give notice of termination before he is entitled to rescind, as in *Millichamp* v. *Jones* [1982] 1 W.L.R. 1422 (where this requirement was not satisfied).

73 *Post*, pp. 749, 894–895.

ready and willing to deliver.[74] Of course this rule can be varied by contrary agreement: the seller may agree to give credit or the buyer to pay in advance. Similarly, under a charterparty, delivery of the goods by the shipowner and payment of the freight are (unless otherwise agreed[75]) concurrent conditions.[76]

(3) Independent promises

If promises are "independent" each party can enforce the other's promise although he has not performed his own. The remedy of the party sued is not to withhold performance, but to make a counterclaim to enforce the promise of the party suing. In the old case of *Pordage* v. *Cole*[77] the defendant promised to pay the plaintiff "£775 for all his lands . . . the money to be paid before Midsummer." In an action to recover the £775 it was held that the plaintiff need not aver conveyance or tender of conveyance. A contract for the sale of land would now generally require conveyance and payment to take place concurrently.[78] But a tenant's covenant to pay rent and a landlord's covenant to repair are still regarded as independent, so that the landlord is not entitled to refuse to perform his covenant to repair merely because the tenant is in arrears with his rent.[79] Similarly, in a separation deed the wife's covenant not to molest her husband and the husband's covenant to pay the wife an annuity are independent unless the deed otherwise provides: breach of the wife's covenant is therefore no answer to an action by her for the annuity.[80] And where goods carried on a chartered ship are damaged as a result of the shipowner's breach of the charterparty, before the time fixed for payment of freight, the charterer must nevertheless make the payment when that time comes: his remedy is by way of a cross-action for damages.[81]

(4) Criteria for drawing the distinction

The distinction between conditions precedent, concurrent conditions and independent covenants is easily illustrated by reference to stereotyped situations, such as the employment, sale of goods and tenancy cases referred to in the preceding discussion. In those cases, the distinction is governed by well-settled rules, though these can be excluded by express or implied[82] agreement. But more difficulty arises in drawing the distinction in cases of first impression which fall outside these stereotyped situations. For this

---

74 Sale of Goods Act 1979, s.28; *Morton* v. *Lamb* (1797) 7 T.R. 125.

75 *e.g. The Karin Vatis* [1988] 2 Lloyd's Rep. 330.

76 *Paynter* v. *James* (1867) L.R. 2 C.P. 348, 355; *cf. Stanton* v. *Richardson* (1872) L.R. 7 C.P. 421, 433 (affirmed 45 L.J.Q.B. 78) (shipowner cannot sue for failure to load unless he is ready and willing to receive cargo).

77 (1669) 1 Wms.Saund. 319; *cf. Campbell* v. *Jones* (1796) 6 T.R. 570; *Christie* v. *Borelly* (1860) 29 L.J. Ch. 153.

78 But for this, *Pordage* v. *Cole* would probably have been overruled long ago; it was said to "outrage common sense" as long ago as 1792, in *Goodison* v. *Nunn* (1792) 4 T.R. 761, 764.

79 *Taylor* v. *Webb* [1937] 2 K.B. 283, 290 (reversed, *ibid.*, on another ground which was disapproved in *Regis Property Co. Ltd.* v. *Dudley* [1959] A.C. 370); *cf. Johnstone* v. *Milling* (1886) 16 Q.B.D. 460, 468; *Tito* v. *Waddell* (*No.* 2) [1977] Ch. 106, 290; *The Aegnoussiotis* [1977] 1 Lloyd's Rep. 268, 276; *Yorbrook Investments Ltd.* v. *Batten* (1986) P. & C.R. 51.

80 *Fearon* v. *Aylesford* (1884) 14 Q.B.D. 792.

81 *Post*, pp. 686, 689, n. 88; the rule applies even though the shipowner's breach was repudiatory: see *The Dominique* [1989] A.C. 1056 (not a case of damage but of delay).

82 As in the *Trans Trust* case [1952] 2 Q.B. 297, *ante*, p. 662.

purpose the courts have regard to certain policy considerations, though these can be displaced by evidence of the intention of the parties.

The effect of holding promises to be independent is to expose each party to the risk of having to perform without any security for the performance of the other; the effect of holding performance by one party to be a condition precedent is to expose that party to the same risk. To reduce the first of these risks, the courts have long been reluctant to classify promises as independent[83] unless the intention of the parties to that effect was clear. Both risks would be eliminated if the two performances were held to be concurrent conditions; and for this reason the law should, in doubtful cases, favour such a classification whenever simultaneous performance by both parties is possible.[84]

Where simultaneous performance is not possible (as in the case of contracts to do work over a period of time) performance by one party must necessarily be a condition precedent to the liability of the other. Which party has to perform first depends on their relative bargaining power and on the court's view (right or wrong) as to which of them is more likely to default after the other has performed. These factors no doubt account for the general rule that work must precede pay.[85] The position of the person doing the work is in practice safeguarded by stipulating for interim payments, such as weekly or monthly remuneration under contracts of employment, or progress payments under a building contract.

Even where it is possible for the two performances to be rendered simultaneously, it does not follow that they should invariably be classified as concurrent conditions. There are, in particular, three situations in which it is more appropriate to classify promises as independent.

The first such situation arises where the promise which has not been performed is of only minor importance. This was the position in *Huntoon Co.* v. *Kolynos (Inc.)*,[86] where an agreement was made by which the plaintiffs licensed the defendants to use a patent. By clause 7 the plaintiffs undertook to prosecute all claims for infringement of the patent if requested to do so by the defendants; while by clause 9 the defendants undertook to stamp the number of the patent on all articles incorporating it. These two promises were held to be independent, so that the plaintiffs could enforce clause 9 although they were in breach of clause 7. Lawrence L.J. said: "Where a covenant goes only to part of the consideration on both sides and a breach of such covenant may be paid for in damages, it is an independent covenant . . . ."[87] Clause 7 might apply in relation to quite trivial, or only suspected, infringements: failure to prosecute claims for these would not substantially deprive the defendants of what they had bargained for.

The classification of promises as independent is, secondly, appropriate where the circumstances show that this was the intention of the parties. This was the position in *The Odenfeld*.[88] A charterparty provided that hire was to be assessed by a panel from time to time, but that, if it were assessed at less than some $3.50 per ton, this amount was nevertheless payable. However, the parties also agreed by a "side letter" that, if the amount

---

[83] See *Kingston* v. *Preston* (1773) Lofft. 194; and *Jones* v. *Barkley* (1781) 2 Dougl. 648, 689.
[84] This is the view taken by the Restatement 2d, *Contracts*, § 234(1); *cf. ibid.* § 233(2).
[85] *Ante*, p. 662.
[86] [1930] 1 Ch. 528.
[87] At p. 558.
[88] [1978] 2 Lloyd's Rep. 357.

assessed by the panel fell below the $3.50 per ton, any excess over the amount assessed was to be paid back by the shipowners to the charterers. The freight market having collapsed, the panel assessed the amount payable at $1.50 per ton, but the shipowners failed to perform their promise contained in the "side letter" to repay $2 per ton to the charterers. It was held that the "side letter" constituted an independent promise, so that its breach did not justify the charterers' refusal to perform their obligations under the charterparty. Kerr J. relied mainly on the way in which the transaction had been set up in two documents: this supported the view that the promises were "intended to be independent and not interdependent."[89]

Thirdly, promises may be classified as independent because of their commercial setting. This possibility arises where goods are sold for export on "c.i.f." terms, that is, for an inclusive price covering their cost, insurance and freight. Under such a contract the seller must ship goods that are in conformity with the contract and tender certain shipping documents to the buyer, while the buyer must pay the price on tender of the documents.[90] So long as the documents are in accordance with the contract, the buyer cannot refuse to pay against tender of those documents merely because the goods were not, when shipped, in conformity with the contract.[91] This is true even if the non-conformity of the goods is such that it would justify their rejection when the goods themselves (as opposed to the documents) later reach the buyer. The seller's duty with respect to the conformity of *the goods* can therefore be described as an independent promise in the sense that his failure to perform that duty does not prevent the buyer's duty to pay the price from arising on tender of *documents*. The buyer's remedies, in the case put, are to claim damages for the defects in the goods, or to reject them and reclaim the price if, on their arrival at the agreed destination, it turns out that they suffered, when they were shipped, from defects of a kind that justify their rejection.[92]

(5) Effects of the distinction

It follows from the nature of an independent promise that failure by one party (A) to perform such a promise does not justify rescission by the other party (B). The position where A fails to perform a condition precedent or a concurrent condition is more complex: such a failure justifies B's refusal to perform for so long as the failure continues, but it does not, of itself, justify rescission in the sense of an outright refusal by B to perform, or to accept further performance from A. If A, an employee, fails to perform the condition precedent of doing that agreed work, his employer, B, is prima facie entitled to refuse to pay A so long as that failure continues; and B's refusal to pay may be justified even though he does not dismiss A.[93] But it does not follow that B is entitled to rescind (in the sense of dismissing A) merely on account of A's failure to perform: he would, for example, generally not be so entitled where A's failure was due to a relatively brief temporary ill-

89 *Ibid.* at p. 371. He may also have been influenced by the fact that to hold the promises interdependent would have prejudiced a bank which had taken an assignment of the shipowner's rights under the charterparty without notice of the "side letter."
90 See generally *Benjamin's Sale of Goods* (3rd ed.), §§ 1741–1744.
91 *Gill & Duffus S.A.* v. *Berger & Co. Inc.* [1984] A.C. 382, more fully discussed in *Benjamin's Sale of Goods* (3rd ed.), §§ 1741–1744.
92 *e.g.* from defects amounting to a breach of condition: see *post*, pp. 689–702.
93 *Wiluszynski* v. *Tower Hamlets L.B.C.* [1989] I.C.R. 493.

ness.[94] Similarly, if A, a buyer of goods, fails to perform the concurrent condition of paying or tendering the price, the seller, B, is prima facie justified in withholding delivery; but it again does not follow that B is, merely on account of the failure, entitled to rescind the contract: he may, for example, still be bound to deliver if A tenders the price on the day after that fixed by the contract. In other words, A's failure to comply with a stipulation as to the order of performance which is a condition precedent or a concurrent condition justifies B's refusal to perform only for as long as A's failure continues; but it does not, of itself, justify rescission. It only has the latter effect where A's failure is (in accordance with the principles to be discussed later in this Chapter[95]) *either* sufficiently serious to justify rescission *or* such that it falls within one of the exceptions to the requirement of serious failure.

(6) Wrongful refusal to accept performance

(a) EFFECT OF SUCH REFUSAL ON OTHER PARTY'S DUTY. The general rule, that A's failure to perform a condition precedent or a concurrent condition justifies refusal by B to perform, is subject to an important qualification: this applies where, before any performance from A was due, B had wrongfully refused to accept performance or had indicated that he would do so.

(i) *Repudiation inducing victim's failure to perform.* Suppose that a contract for the sale of goods provides that the goods are to be manufactured by A to B's order. If, before anything has, or should have been, done by A, B wrongfully repudiates the contract A is entitled to rescind; and, if he does so, two things follow: A need no longer manufacture the goods, and he can claim damages from B.[96] It would be pointless to require A to manufacture and tender the goods when the tender was virtually certain to be rejected. His inability to deliver the goods at the agreed time is not allowed to prejudice his rights against B as it was induced by B's wrongful repudiation; another way of putting the point is to say that B is estopped from relying on A's inability to perform.[97] The position is the same where the buyer throughout insists on performance in a manner other than that stipulated by the contract, *e.g.* by demanding that the goods are to be shipped to a non-contractual destination. The seller is clearly not bound to perform in that way, nor is it open to the buyer to argue that the seller could, in any event, not have delivered in accordance with the contract if "it was [the buyer's] insistence on non-contractual destination and not any conduct on the part of [the seller] that prevented [the seller] from delivering" the goods.[98]

(ii) *Victim's inability not induced by the repudiation.* In the situations just described, it has been assumed that A could have performed, and would have done so, if B had not repudiated. But sometimes A can recover damages even though he cannot show that he would, but for B's repudiation, have been able to perform his part. In *British and Beningtons Ltd.* v.

---

[94] See *post*, pp. 677–678, 772–773.
[95] *Post*, pp. 670 to 709.
[96] As to A's remedy in such cases see *The Odenfeld* [1978] 2 Lloyd's Rep. 357, *post*, p. 900.
[97] *The Simona* [1989] A.C. 788, 805–806. *Foran* v. *Wight* (1989) 168 C.L.R. 385 is explicable on this relatively simple ground.
[98] *Bulk Oil (Zug) A.G.* v. *Sun International Ltd.* [1984] 1 Lloyd's Rep. 531, 546.

N. W. Cachar Tea Co. Ltd.[99] A sold tea to B who, before delivery was due, without justification stated that they would refuse to accept it. It was held that A was entitled to damages even though he could not show that he could have delivered the tea at the agreed time and place. B's wrongful refusal to accept was an anticipatory breach,[1] and, once this had been "accepted" by A so as to rescind the contract, later events affecting A's ability to perform did not deprive A of his right of action[2]; for, by rescinding the contract, A had been liberated from his duty of further performance.[3] The position is different if, at the time of B's refusal to accept, A has himself already committed a repudiatory breach,[4] for such a breach would justify B's refusal. It is therefore crucial to determine which party committed the first breach, whether that breach was repudiatory, and whether it was accepted by the other party so as to rescind the contract.

These questions are easy enough to formulate but they can raise difficult issues of fact and law where each party to a commercial dispute in good faith believes that he is acting in accordance with the contract, and that the other is not. The issue is further complicated by two rules. The first is that A is not necessarily in breach merely because he makes a defective tender; for it may be open to him to cure the defect by making a second (and good) tender within the time allowed for performance.[5] The second is that B is not necessarily in breach merely because, at the time of his refusal to accept A's performance, he gives an inadequate reason for the refusal, or none at all; for if he actually had a lawful excuse he can (in general) rely on it later even though he did not state it, or even know of it, at the time of his refusal to accept performance.[6]

---

99 [1923] A.C. 48; *cf. Cort* v. *Ambergate Ry.* (1851) 7 Q.B. 127; *Rightside Properties Ltd.* v. *Gray* [1975] Ch. 72, 87; *Texaxo Ltd.* v. *Eurogolf Shipping Co. Ltd.* [1987] 2 Lloyd's Rep. 541.

1 *Post*, pp. 754–762.

2 *Post*, p. 761; *Braithwaite* v. *Foreign Hardwood Co.* [1905] 2 K.B. 543, as explained in *The Simona* [1989] A.C. 788. The difficulty with this explanation of *Braithwaite's* case is that, when A accepted B's repudiation, A had already shipped non-conforming goods, so that B's repudiation was apparently justified. One possible answer to this objection is that A had not yet tendered those goods: see *Taylor* v. *Oakes Roncoroni & Co.* (1922) 38 T.L.R. 349, 351 (affirmed *ibid.* p. 517); another is that A still had the opportunity to cure his breach and was induced by B's repudiation not to make use of it: *cf. post*, p. 670 at n. 21. If *Braithwaite's* case cannot be explained as one of accepted repudiation, it is wrong: *The Simona, supra*, at p. 805. See further Benjamin's Sale of Goods (3rd ed.), §§ 1745–1748; Lloyd, 37 M.L.R. 351, and *post*, pp. 852–854.

3 *Gill & Duffus S.A.* v. *Berger & Co. Inc.* [1984] A.C. 382, 390; *cf. MSC Mediterranean Shipping Co. S.A.* v. *B.R.E. Metro Ltd.* [1985] 2 Lloyd's Rep. 239, 240; Dawson, 96 L.Q.R. 239 argues that *Universal Cargo Carriers Corp.* v. *Citati* [1957] 2 Q.B. 401 is inconsistent with the explantion of the *British and Beningtons* case given in the text above. But the claim in the *Citati* case was made *against* the party alleged to be unable to perform (the charterer) while in the *British and Beningtons* case it was made *by* that party. Moreover, in the *Citati* case the charterer was already in breach (actual and anticipatory) at the time of the shipowner's refusal to perform while in the *British and Beningtons* case the sellers were not in breach at all at the time of the buyer's refusal. The crucial issue in the *Citati* case was simply whether the charterer's breach was sufficiently serious to justify the shipowner's rescission.

4 *i.e.* one that satisfied the requirement of "substantial failure" (*post*, pp. 670–680) or fell within an exception to that requirement (*post*, pp. 680–709).

5 *Ante*, p. 655.

6 *Post*, p. 735.

(b) QUALIFICATIONS. The rule that A may be entitled to damages for B's repudiation, without having to show that he (A) could have performed his part of the contract, is subject to two important qualifications.

(i) *Pre-rescission non-repudiatory breach by injured party.* Before rescinding the contract on account of B's repudiation, A may himself have committed a breach, but one which did not justify B's repudiation, *e.g.* a breach of an independent promise.[7] Rescission by A does not affect his liability for that pre-rescission breach[8]; so that the damages to which A is entitled on account of B's wrongful repudiation will be reduced by those for which he is liable in respect of his own pre-rescission breach.[9] Those damages will prima facie be the amount by which A's breach reduces the value of his performance.[10]

(ii) *Injured party does not rescind.* The rule that A may be entitled to damages for B's repudiation, without having to show that he could have performed, is based on the argument that, when A accepts B's repudiation, he is liberated from his own duty to perform.[11] That reasoning obviously cannot apply where A does not accept the repudiation. In such a case, A continues to be bound by his own duties under the contract, so that his failure to perform these duties, even after B's repudiation, can (if not induced by B's repudiation[12]) amount to a breach by A. Such a breach will make A liable in damages,[13] and, if it is repudiatory,[14] it will also justify B's refusal to perform and so absolve B from liability in damages to A.[15]

When A does not accept B's repudiation and then commits a breach which does *not* justify B's refusal to perform (*e.g.* because it is a breach of an independent promise[16]), A's breach will nevertheless be relevant to the damages to which A is entitled on account of B's repudiation. At the least, those damages will (as in the case where A has rescinded) be reduced by the damages for which A is liable by reason of his own breach, *e.g.* by the amount by which the value of goods delivered by A is reduced by reason of a defect in them. There are, moreover, circumstances in which, if A has not rescinded, B can rely on A's breach so as to reduce still further the damages for which B is liable by reason of his repudiation. This possibility arises where A's breach, though not originally of such a kind as to justify B's repudiation, later acquires that character. We have seen that where goods are sold on c.i.f. terms, the buyer is not justified in refusing to pay against *documents* merely because the *goods* were not, when shipped, in conformity with the contract; but that such non-conformity may give him the right to reject the goods, a right that he will usually exercise when the goods arrive at the contractual destination and are actually delivered to

---

[7] *Ante*, p. 664.
[8] *Post*, p. 747.
[9] *Gill & Duffus S.A.* v. *Berger & Co. Inc.* [1984] A.C. 382, 390 (where "certification clause" in the contract excluded such liability).
[10] *Post*, p. 841.
[11] *Ante*, p. 668.
[12] *Ante*, p. 667.
[13] *Regent OHG Aisenstadt und Barig* v. *Francesco of Jermyn Street* [1983] 3 All E.R. 327, 335.
[14] In the sense described in n. 4 at p. 668, *ante*.
[15] See *The Simona* [1989] A.C. 788, where A's failure was not a breach but justified cancellation under an express cancelling clause in the contract; Marston [1988] C.L.J. 340; Carter [1989] L.M.C.L.Q. 81.
[16] *Ante*, p. 664.

him.[17] That stage is never reached if the seller rescinds on the buyer's wrongful refusal to pay against documents[18]; but if the seller does *not* rescind, and the defect in the goods is such as to give the buyer the right to reject them on arrival, then the buyer will be able to argue that he would, even if he had duly paid against documents, have rejected the goods on arrival and so have become entitled to the return of the money that he ought to have paid at the earlier stage of tender of documents.[19] The effect of this argument is that the seller's damages will be merely nominal: he will have lost nothing but the worthless right to be paid a sum of money which he would (had it been paid) have later become liable to repay.[20] Such an argument is not, however, available to the buyer where the seller could have cured his breach and his failure to do so was induced by the buyer's wrongful repudiation.[21] If the seller's failure to cure was induced in this way, the buyer cannot rely on it in reduction of damages, any more than he can rely on the seller's original failure to perform (when so induced) on the issue of liability.[22]

(c) EVALUATION. The rule that A is entitled to damages where his own inability to perform is induced by B's repudiation is generally regarded as uncontroversial. But there is dispute about the merit of the rule that A can claim damages for B's repudiation where A could not have performed even if B had not repudiated and where his inability to perform was not in any way induced by B's conduct. This aspect of the rule can be criticised by saying that B is made liable in damages for merely saying that he will not perform, even though he may not thereby cause any prejudice to A.[23] On the other hand, B can avoid this hardship by simply waiting till A's performance is due: if it is not forthcoming at that time it is A, not B, who will be liable in damages; and any remaining hardship that the rule may cause to B is mitigated by the qualifications on its scope that have been stated above.[24] For these reasons, it does not seem that the rule causes undue prejudice to B. It can be justified on the ground that it promotes certainty by discouraging premature repudiation.

3. General Requirement of Substantial Failure

A party may comply with the rules as to the order of performance, just discussed, but his performance or tender may be deficient in quality or quan-

---

[17] *Ante*, p. 666.

[18] As in *Gill & Duffus A.S.* v. *Berger & Co. Inc.* [1984] A.C. 382.

[19] See *Henry Dean & Sons (Sydney) Ltd.* v. *O'Day Pty Ltd.* (1929) 39 C.L.R. 330, 340, so far as it relates to the *seller's* claim; the disapproval of that decision in *Gill & Duffus S.A.* v. *Berger & Co. Inc.*, *supra*, relates to the *buyer's* claim only; and in the *Gill & Duffus* case itself the House of Lords treated the seller's rescission as crucial to the success of his claim.

[20] *Cf. The Mihalis Angelos* [1971] 1 Q.B. 641, *post*, p. 681. An alternative view is that the seller's damages are nominal only if the defect makes the goods worthless: see *Bunge Corp.* v. *Vegetable Vitamin Foods (Private) Ltd.* [1985] 1 Lloyd's Rep. 613, 620; but the buyers case is not that *the goods* are worthless: it is that the seller's *right to have them accepted* is worthless because the buyer's option to reject them would certainly have been exercised.

[21] This is another possible explanation of *Braithwaite* v. *Foreign Hardwood Co.* [1905] 2 K.B. 543, *ante*, p. 668, n. 2: see *Benjamin's Sale of Goods* (3rd ed.), § 1748; for the seller's right to cure, see *ante*, p. 668 at n. 5.

[22] *Cf. ante*, pp. 667–668.

[23] The rule does not seem to apply in the United States: see, for example *Caporale* v. *Rubine*, 105 A. 226 (1918); *Corbin on Contracts*, § 978; *Williston on Contracts*, § 699.

[24] *i.e.* at nn. 7–22, *supra*.

tity or it may be late, *i.e.* after the agreed time. The general principle in such cases is that the defect in performance must attain a certain minimum degree of seriousness to entitle the injured party to rescind. In the following discussion we shall refer to this principle as the requirement of "substantial failure" in performance. Our present concern is with the general principle; it is subject to many important exceptions which will be discussed later in this Chapter.[25]

(1) Historical introduction

In *Boone* v. *Eyre*[26] the plaintiff conveyed to the defendant a plantation in the West Indies, together with the slaves on it, for £500 plus an annuity of £160. He covenanted that he had good title to the plantation and that he was lawfully possessed of the slaves. He later sued for arrears of the annuity and was met by the plea that he was not lawfully possessed of the slaves. Lord Mansfield rejected the plea, saying: "Where mutual covenants go to the whole of the consideration on both sides, they are mutual conditions. But where they only go to a part, where a breach may be paid for in damages, there the defendant has a remedy on his covenant and shall not plead it as a condition precedent. If this plea were allowed any one negro not being the property of the plaintiff would be a bar to the action." In later cases, the contrast between the *whole* and a *part* of the consideration was not, however, taken quite literally. In *Duke of St. Albans* v. *Shore*[27] a contract was made for the sale of land with the timber on it. Before conveyance the vendor cut down a considerable part of the timber, and, on the purchaser's refusal to perform, sued him for the penalty payable under the contract on breach. The action failed for a number of reasons, one of which was that the timber might have been the *chief* inducement to the purchaser to enter into the contract. The fact that the timber formed only *part* of the consideration to be provided by the vendor was not decisive. Later dicta state that the plaintiff in *Boone* v. *Eyre* would have lost if he had had no title *to the land*,[28] or if he had been lawfully possessed only of a single one of the slaves.[29] These discussions of *Boone* v. *Eyre*, rather than the terms of the judgment in that case, may be considered to have established the requirement that a party who has only partly performed his obligations may nevertheless enforce the contract if the failure in performance does not "substantially" deprive the other party of what he bargained for.

(2) When failure is substantial

The question when a failure in performance "substantially" deprives a party of what he bargained for, or (as it is sometimes put) "frustrates" his purpose in making the contract gives rise to very great difficulty. The frequent references in the cases to breaches which "substantially" deprive a party of what he bargained for or "go to the root" of a contract are not particularly helpful in analysing the law or in predicting the course of future decisions. It is submitted that the courts, in applying the general require-

---

25 *Post*, pp. 680–709.
26 (1779) 1 Hy.Bl. 273n.; 2 W.Bl. 1312.
27 (1789) 1 Hy.Bl. 270.
28 *Glazebrook* v. *Woodrow* (1799) 8 T.R. 366, 374.
29 *Ellen* v. *Topp* (1851) 6 Ex. 424, 442.

ment of substantial failure,[30] generally classify a failure in performance with an eye on the consequences. They consider, on the one hand, whether rescission (as opposed to damages) is necessary to protect the injured party and, on the other hand, they take into account the prejudice which rescission will cause to the other party. If, on balancing these factors, they conclude that the injured party should be allowed to rescind, they will classify the failure in performance as "substantial" in order to produce the desired result; and conversely.[31] An attempt will be made in the following pages to illustrate this approach. The decisions are for the most part soundly based on practical considerations; though it must be admitted that these do not always appear very clearly from the judgments.

(a) UNJUST ENRICHMENT. Where the requirement of substantial failure applies,[32] the courts are reluctant to allow a party to refuse to perform if he has received a benefit from the other party's partial or defective performance and cannot, or will not, restore that benefit. The point may be illustrated by a further distinction between *Boone* v. *Eyre* and *Duke of St. Albans* v. *Shore*. In the former case the plantation had actually been conveyed to the defendant,[33] and a judgment in his favour would have enabled him to escape liability for a part of the price which might have exceeded the value of the slaves. In the latter case, however, it was said that "this is not an action of covenant where one party has performed his part, but is brought for a penalty on the other party refusing to execute his contract."[34] In such a case the plaintiff "ought punctually, exactly and literally to perform his part."[35] These words may suggest that an action on an executory contract in a case like *Boone* v. *Eyre* would have failed even if the vendor had lacked title only to a single slave; but if this was indeed ever the law it has been neutralised by the developments about to be discussed.

(b) ADEQUACY OF DAMAGES. Sometimes the main reason for allowing rescission is that damages would not adequately compensate the injured party.

(i) *General principle.* In *Vigers* v. *Cook*[36] an undertaker had contracted to make arrangements for the funeral of the defendant's son, but so negligently constructed the coffin that it could not be taken into the church where the funeral service was held. He was not entitled to recover any part of his charges as it was "an essential part of the funeral that the body should be taken into the church so that the service might be read in its presence."[37] The breach was one for which a money payment could not compensate. But where the loss suffered in consequence of the breach can be valued with relative certainty, an award or allowance of the sum so assessed will be regarded as an adequate remedy, more suitable than

---

30 Different factors govern the exceptions discussed at *post*, pp. 680–709.

31 *Decro-Wall International S.A.* v. *Practitioners in Marketing Ltd.* [1971] 1 W.L.R. 361, 380.

32 In cases falling within an exception to the requirement, rescission often does lead to unjust enrichment, *e.g.* where one party's refusal to pay is justified by the other's failure to perform an "entire" obligation; *post*, pp. 686–687.

33 This is stressed by Ashurst J. in (1779) 2 W.Bl. 1312, 1314n. (*e*).

34 (1789) 1 Hy.Bl. 270, 279; for a similar argument, see *Graves* v. *Legg* (1854) 9 Ex. 709, 717.

35 (1789) 1 Hy.Bl. 270, 279.

36 [1919] 2 K.B. 475; *cf. Sinclair* v. *Bowles* (1829) 9 B. & C. 92.

37 [1919] 2 K.B. at p. 479. Had the defendant claimed damages he would (at least as the law then stood) have recovered nothing for injury to his feelings: *post*, pp. 876–879.

rescission.[38] For example, in one case the fact that a party was persistently late in making payments under a long-term contract was held not to be a ground of rescission, since the other party suffered no prejudice except in having to pay a relatively small amount of interest on the outstanding sums, and this loss could easily have been recovered from the party in breach.[39] In another case a charterer's delay in providing a cargo was held not to justify rescission by the shipowner because the delay did not endanger the common venture and its financial consequences could easily be made good by damages.[40]

(ii) *Specific performance with compensation.* The same principle is illustrated by the equitable jurisdiction to order specific performance of contracts for the sale of land with "compensation"—*i.e.* at a price reduced to take account of a deficiency or defect.[41] In one case[42] compensation was allowed where the area of land sold was stated to be "about 1200 square yards" and was in fact 935 square yards. But the jurisdiction will not be exercised where the defect is "substantial"[43]; and the test for determining whether the defect is of this character appears to be whether adequate compensation can be made for it by a monetary adjustment.[44] The same test applies where the contract itself provides that errors and misdescriptions shall not annul the sale but shall give rise to a claim for compensation. Such a clause can (unlike the equitable jurisdiction) be invoked even after the contract has been performed[45]; but (like the equitable jurisdiction) it is normally inapplicable where the defect is "substantial." In *Flight* v. *Booth*[46] leasehold premises in Covent Garden were sold under particulars of sale which misdescribed the terms of the lease by stating that it prohibited the carrying on of any "offensive trade," when in fact it prohibited the carrying on of a large number of inoffensive trades, including that of selling fruit. The contract went on to provide that errors and misdescriptions should not vitiate the sale but should give rise to a right to compensation. It was held that this provision did not apply to the misdescription which had been made since compensation for it would be much harder to assess than in the case of a simple misdescription as to area. Cases such as *Flight* v. *Booth* seem to apply what later became known as the doctrine of fundamental breach. They would therefore now turn on the construction of the provision in question, rather than on any rule of substantive law making it impossible to exclude the right to rescind.[47] On the other hand, a

---

[38] *Cf.* the rule that specific relief may be refused where the more appropriate remedy is in damages: *post*, pp. 903–907.

[39] *Decro-Wall International S.A.* v. *Practitioners in Marketing Ltd.* [1971] 1 W.L.R. 361. The payments were due under bills of exchange, so that the rule by which interest is not recoverable as general damages for non-payment of money did not apply: see *post*, p. 879; *cf.* also *post*, p. 726.

[40] *The Angelia* [1973] 1 W.L.R. 210.

[41] Harpum [1981] C.L.J. 47.

[42] *Aspinalls to Powell and Scholefield* (1889) 60 L.T. 595.

[43] *Re Fawcett and Holmes' Contract* (1889) 42 Ch.D. 150; *Jacobs* v. *Revell* [1900] 2 Ch. 858; *Watson* v. *Burton* [1957] 1 W.L.R. 19; *Strover* v. *Harrington* [1988] Ch. 390, 411.

[44] *Cato* v. *Thomson* (1882) 9 Q.B.D. 616, 618; *Rudd* v. *Lascelles* [1900] 1 Ch. 815; if the defect is substantial the party prejudiced by it may, instead of rescinding, claim specific performance, but only without compensation: *Durham* v. *Legard* (1865) 34 Beav. 611.

[45] *Bos* v. *Helsham* (1866) L.R. 2 Ex. 72; *Re Turner and Skelton* (1879) 13 Ch.D. 130; *Palmer* v. *Johnson* (1884) 13 Q.B.D. 351.

[46] (1834) 1 Bing.N.C. 370; *cf. Walker* v. *Boyle* [1982] 1 W.L.R. 495 (*ante*, p. 346).

[47] *Ante*, p. 206.

provision of this kind is not subject to the test of reasonableness under sections 2 to 4 of the Unfair Contract Terms Act 1977 since those sections do not apply to any contract so far as it relates to the creation or transfer of an interest in land.[48] This could be an important point where a developer entered into a contract for the sale of a house on written standard terms which would otherwise be subject to the requirement of reasonableness under section 3 of the Act.[49]

A misdescription may not form part of the contract but be a misrepresentation inducing it; or it may originate as such a misrepresentation and be later incorporated in the contract. Under the Misrepresentation Act 1967, there is, in such a case, a right to rescind for misrepresentation,[50] but this is subject to the discretion of the court to declare the contract subsisting and to award damages in lieu of rescission.[51] Where the defect is not "substantial" the court will probably uphold the contract and award "damages"; and it seems likely that these will be assessed in much the same way as that in which "compensation" for misdescription was assessed in equity. The main difference between the old equitable and the new statutory powers is that the latter can be exercised even after conveyance.[52] The further question then arises whether, in cases of the present kind, a contractual provision restricting remedies for misdescription would be ineffective on the ground that it failed to satisfy the test of reasonableness imposed by section 3 of the Misrepresentation Act 1967.[53] Before that Act, it was held that a provision which excluded the right to rescind *and* the right to compensation entitled the vendor to enforce the contract without compensation.[54] Now such a term might well be regarded as unreasonable in so far as it excluded the purchaser's right to compensation, or his right to rescind for a misrepresentation relating to a matter of substantial importance.[55] But if that matter was of only minor importance and the term, while excluding the right to rescind, *provided* for compensation, it is submitted that the requirement of reasonableness would normally be satisfied; for in such a case the term would not prejudice the purchaser. It would only give contractual effect to the right that the vendor would have had, even in the absence of the term, to specific performance with compensation, or to the result that the court would be likely to reach in the exercise of its discretion to declare the contract subsisting and to award damages in lieu of rescission.[56]

These rules as to "compensation" in sales of land should be contrasted with the rule that a quantitative defect in the performance of a contract for the sale of goods justifies rescission,[57] even though it causes little prejudice to the buyer, and even though compensation for it may be quite easy to assess. It is, however, unlikely that this rule applies where a specific parcel

---

[48] Unfair Contract Terms Act 1977, Sched. 1, para. 1(*c*). For attempts to exclude liability for misrepresentation, see *ante*, p. 345; *infra* at n. 53.
[49] *Ante*, p. 231.
[50] s.1(*a*); *ante*, p. 336.
[51] s.2(2); *ante*, p. 321.
[52] s.1(*b*); *ante*, p. 338.
[53] As amended by Unfair Contract Terms Act 1977, s.8; *ante*, p. 345.
[54] *Re Courcier and Harrold's Contract* [1923] 1 Ch. 565.
[55] *Walker* v. *Boyle* [1982] 1 W.L.R. 495; *Cremdean Properties Ltd.* v. *Nash* (1977) 244 E.G. 547; *South Western General Property Co.* v. *Marton* (1982) 263 E.G. 2631.
[56] *Supra*, after n. 51.
[57] *Post*, p. 684.

of goods is sold and is said to contain a different quantity from that which it in fact contains,[58] *e.g.* where the sale is of "a cargo of 1,000 tons" in a named ship which actually contains only 950 tons. Such cases constitute the closest analogy to the land cases, so that the treatment of the two types of contract is not so radically different as might at first sight appear.

(c) Ratio of failure to the performance undertaken. The higher the ratio of the failure is to the performance undertaken, the more likely it is that the court will regard the failure as substantial. Thus where a buyer of oil deliverable in two instalments without justification refused to accept one of them (and added that he would not accept any other delivery) it was held that the seller was entitled to rescind.[59] On the other hand, in *Maple Flock Co. Ltd.* v. *Universal Furniture Products (Wembley) Ltd.*[60] a contract was made for the sale of 100 tons of rag flock to be delivered in instalments of 1½ tons at the rate of three instalments a week. The sixteenth instalment contained an excessive amount of chlorine and the buyers claimed that this breach entitled them to rescind. One reason why the court rejected this claim was that the breach related to a single instalment which bore only a small quantitative ratio to the contract as a whole.[61] Similarly, in *Hongkong Fir Shipping Co. Ltd.* v. *Kawasaki Kisen Kaisha Ltd.*,[62] a ship began service under a 24 month time charterparty. She was later found to be unseaworthy and to need extensive repairs which took altogether 20 weeks to complete. The charterers purported to rescind on a number of grounds,[63] one of which was that the delay caused by the unseaworthiness was such as to "frustrate" their purpose in entering into the contract. One reason why this argument was rejected was that the ship was still available after the completion of repairs for 17 out of the original 24 months of the charterparty.[64]

(d) Uncertainty as to future performance. In the case of continuing contracts, calling for repeated acts of performance over a period of time, the courts are influenced by the need to remove the uncertainty which may result from failure to perform. In *Bradford* v. *Williams*,[65] for example, the plaintiffs chartered the defendant's ship for one year from May to May; but in September they wrongfully refused to provide a cargo. This refusal justified the defendant in putting an end to the contract as "no cross-action for damages would have fully compensated him."[66] In such a cross-action it

---

[58] See *Levi* v. *Berk* (1886) 2 T.L.R. 898, 899; *Benjamin's Sale of Goods* (3rd ed.), § 1953; *Ellis* v. *Hodder & Tolley Ltd.* (1914) 33 N.Z.L.R. 362.

[59] *Warinco A.G.* v. *Samor S.p.A.* [1979] 1 Lloyd's Rep. 450.

[60] [1934] 1 K.B. 148; *cf. Simpson* v. *Crippin* (1872) L.R. 8 Q.B. 14 (failure by buyer to take delivery). For such instalment contracts, Sale of Goods Act 1979, s.31(2) gives virtually no guidance. It merely provides that "it is a question in each case depending on the terms of the contract and the circumstances of the case whether the breach of contract is a repudiation of the whole contract or whether it is a severable breach giving rise to a claim for compensation but not to a right to treat the whole contract as repudiated." Contrast the very rigid rule laid down by s.30(1) with respect to short delivery.

[61] *Cf. Financings Ltd.* v. *Baldock* [1963] 2 Q.B. 104; *Eshun* v. *Moorgate Mercantile Credit Co. Ltd.* [1971] 1 W.L.R. 722.

[62] [1962] 2 Q.B. 26.

[63] See also *post*, pp. 676, 679, 696.

[64] At p. 40, *per* Salmon J. On this issue the Court of Appeal simply approved Salmon J.'s judgment without giving reasons of their own: see [1962] 2 Q.B. at pp. 61, 73.

[65] (1872) L.R. 7 Ex. 259; *The Sankos Iris* [1987] 1 Lloyd's Rep. 487.

[66] (1872) L.R. 7 Ex. 259, 269.

might be alleged that he had failed to mitigate[67] by finding substitute employment for the ship. It would be hard for him to know for how long such employment should be sought, since, if the original charterparty had remained in force, the charterers might later have demanded continuation of performance, and the shipowner would have been bound to have his ship available in response to such a demand. Again, the failure of a house-buyer to pay a deposit in accordance with the contract gives rise to uncertainty in depriving the vendor of an important safeguard against eventual default; and accordingly it justifies rescission by the vendor.[68]

By way of contrast, further reference may be made to the *Hongkong Fir*[69] and *Maple Flock*[70] cases. In the former it was said that, once major repairs were begun, there was no reasonable ground for believing that the ship would not be available for service within a fairly short and predictable time.[71] In the latter case the court stressed that the sellers' business was well conducted, that the source of the defect could easily be tracked down, and that the likelihood of its recurrence was small. Such likelihood has also been stressed where a seller has sought to rescind an instalment contract because of the buyer's refusal to pay in accordance with its terms.[72] Similarly, the insolvency of a buyer who has failed to pay may justify the seller's refusal to perform (at least in the sense that he need no longer deliver *on credit*) if it is unlikely that the buyer or his trustee in bankruptcy will eventually be able to pay in accordance with the contract.[73] On the other hand, mere delay in payment will not of itself justify rescission. In *Decro-Wall International S.A.* v. *Practitioners in Marketing Ltd.*[74] an English company had been appointed "sole concessionaires" for the sale in the United Kingdom of decorative tiles manufactured by a French company. The English company was persistently (though only slightly) late in making payments under the contract. One reason[75] why this did not justify rescission by the French company was that the delays did not give it any reason to doubt that payment would be made as soon as the goods had been disposed of.

The need to remove uncertainty is, again, one factor which helps to explain the distinction between *Poussard* v. *Spiers*[76] and *Bettini* v. *Gye*.[77] In the former case the defendants had engaged Mme. Poussard to play the leading part of Friquette in a new opera which was to open at the Criterion

---

[67] *Post*, p. 866.

[68] *Myton Ltd.* v. *Schwab-Morris* [1974] 1 W.L.R. 331 (for disapproval of this case on another point, see *ante*, p. 663); *Millichamp* v. *Jones* [1982] 1 W.L.R. 1422, 1430 (where the claim to rescind failed on the ground that the vendor should first have given notice of default); *The Blankenstein* [1985] 1 W.L.R. 435, 446.

[69] [1962] 2 Q.B. 26.

[70] [1934] 1 K.B. 148.

[71] *i.e.* by September 1957: [1962] 2 Q.B. at p. 40. *Cf. The Hermosa* [1982] 1 Lloyd's Rep. 570, where it was held that a charterer was not entitled to rescind even though his "demand for reassurance" (p. 580) was not met. The case seems near the line; the American principle of "adequate assurance of performance" (U.C.C. ss.2–609, Restatement 2d, *Contracts* § 251) would be useful in such a situation.

[72] See *Withers* v. *Reynolds* (1831) 2 B. & Ad. 882; *Mersey Steel and Iron Co.* v. *Naylor Benzon and Co.* (1884) 9 App.Cas. 434; *Freeth* v. *Burr* (1874) L.R. 9 C.P. 208; *post*, pp. 704–707.

[73] *Ex p. Chalmers* (1873) L.R. 8 Ch.App. 289; *Bloomer* v. *Bernstein* (1874) L.R. 9 C.P. 588; Insolvency Act 1986, s.345(1) and (2).

[74] [1971] 1 W.L.R. 361.

[75] For another see *ante*, p. 673.

[76] (1876) 1 Q.B.D. 410.

[77] (1876) 1 Q.B.D. 183.

Theatre on November 28, 1874; the engagement was to last for three months "providing the opera shall run for that period."[78] On November 23 Mme. Poussard fell ill and on November 25 the defendants entered into a contract with a Miss Lewis. This provided that Miss Lewis was to be ready to play Friquette on November 28 if Mme. Poussard had not recovered by then; and that, if Miss Lewis did perform on that day, she was to be engaged for four weeks, until December 25. On November 28 Mme. Poussard "continued in bed and ill"[79] so that Miss Lewis performed and acquired the right to go on performing until December 25. On December 4 Mme. Poussard had recovered and offered to take her place, but the defendants refused to take her back. The jury found that the illness was not so "material" as to entitle the defendants to rescind the contract; that the arrangement with Miss Lewis "as made" was reasonable; and that the defendants were liable in damages for their refusal to have Mme. Poussard back at any time. But the court held that the defendants' refusal was justified and that they were not liable in damages. What chiefly influenced the court was that Mme. Poussard's illness "was a serious one of uncertain duration"[80] and that the defendants could not put off the opening night till she had recovered. The court considered the alternative possibility that the defendants might have found a temporary substitute, but rejected it on the ground that "no substitute capable of performing the part adequately could be engaged except on the terms that she should be permanently engaged. . . . "[81] In fact Miss Lewis's engagement expired on December 25 and it would have been perfectly possible for the defendants to take Mme. Poussard back after that date. This was (according to one of the reports)[82] the argument put forward by counsel for the plaintiffs; and it evidently impressed the jury.[83] It is not at all clear from the judgment why it was rejected by the court.

In *Bettini* v. *Gye*[84] the defendant, who was director of the Royal Italian Opera at Covent Garden, engaged the plaintiff "to fill the role of primo tenor assoluto in the theatres, halls and drawing rooms . . . in Great Britain and Ireland" from March 30 to July 13, 1875, that being the period of the Covent Garden season in 1875. The contract provided that the plaintiff should sing "in concerts as well as in operas"; that he should not "sing

---

[78] It in fact ran for more than three months.

[79] (1876) 1 Q.B.D. at p. 413.

[80] (1876) 1 Q.B.D. at p. 415.

[81] *Ibid.*

[82] (1876) 24 W.R. 819.

[83] The damages awarded by the jury amounted to £83 and it is possible to guess how this figure was reached. Mme. Poussard was engaged for three months (or 13 weeks) at £11 per week. Miss Lewis was engaged for four weeks at £15 per week. £83 is the difference between (a) the amount which Mme. Poussard would have earned in the remaining nine weeks (£99), and (b) the extra amount which the defendants had had to pay to Miss Lewis (£4 per week for four weeks, or £16). Of course, this method of assessment cannot be supported in law as it overlooks, on the one hand, the fact that Mme. Poussard was not liable to the defendants for the extra expense of hiring Miss Lewis (see *post*, p. 678); and, on the other, the possibility that Mme. Poussard might have mitigated by accepting another engagement. According to the report of the trial in *The Times* (November 22, 1875, p. 11) Mme. Poussard refused an offer of another engagement in December "thinking that her agreement with the defendants was still in force"; perhaps she was advised by a French lawyer who took the view that the contract could be rescinded only by a court order: see French Civil Code, art. 1184. She finally obtained another engagement in Paris on February 28, 1875—the very day on which her engagement with the defendants expired.

[84] (1876) 1 Q.B.D. 183.

anywhere out of the theatre" (*i.e.* Covent Garden) during 1875 without the written permission of the defendant "except at a distance of more than 50 miles from London *and* out of the season of the theatre"; and that he was "to be in London without fail at least six days before the commencement of his engagement for the purpose of rehearsals." The plaintiff was prevented by temporary illness from being in London until March 28. He gave no advance notice of this delay to the defendant, and when he arrived in London the defendant refused to accept his services. In holding that this refusal was unjustified the court stressed two factors: first, that the plaintiff had been engaged to sing in operas and concerts for a 15-week season and the failure to attend at rehearsals could only affect a small part of this period[85]; secondly, that he had been "deprived of the power of earning anything in London from January 1st to March 30th."[86] The court also said that the defendant "must . . . seek redress by a cross-claim for damages."[87] This carries at any rate a hint that such a cross-claim had some chance of success, though it is hard to reconcile with the statement in *Poussard* v. *Spiers* that the failure to appear in that case "having been occasioned by sickness was not any breach."[88] But there are many other grounds for distinguishing between the two cases. Bettini was not engaged to play any particular part; there is no suggestion that any substitute was engaged to take his place; he was available when the season opened; there is nothing to show that his failure to arrive in London six days before in any way affected the opening night; and once he did arrive, there was no uncertainty about his future availability. *Bettini* v. *Gye* was decided on a demurrer, so that the facts were never established, and it is hard from the facts as pleaded to see any practical justification for the defendant's attitude.

Even where a breach does create uncertainty, the need to remove it may be overcome by the desire to prevent unjust enrichment. Thus in *Cornwall* v. *Henson*[89] it was held that long delay in payment of the *final* instalment due on a sale of land did not justify rescission by the vendor.

(e) ULTERIOR MOTIVES FOR RESCISSION. It sometimes happens that a party's real motive for wishing to rescind is not that there has been some failure in performance, but that the contract was, or has because of market movements become, a bad bargain for him.[90] In such circumstances the courts will often (if the case is one to which the general requirement of substantial failure applies) hold that the failure in performance is not sufficiently serious and so refuse to allow rescission.[91] The underlying policy

---

85 It is this point rather than the fact that the plaintiff's engagement was to sing in *concerts* and operas which should be stressed, for it is clear from the contract read as a whole, that its main purpose was to engage Bettini for the Covent Garden season of 1875. There are many indications of this: for example, the agreement was made in Milan on December 14, 1874, but headed "Royal Italian Opera, Covent Garden, London Year 1875."

86 At p. 188. *Quaere* whether this in fact prejudiced Bettini; he may well have been taking part in an opera season elsewhere during this period.

87 (1876) 1 Q.B.D. at p. 189.

88 (1876) 1 Q.B.D. at p. 414.

89 [1900] 2 Ch. 298.

90 *Cf. ante*, p. 661.

91 In cases falling within exceptions to the requirement, refusal to perform is often allowed even where the object is fairly clearly to escape from a bad bargain, *e.g. Cunliffe* v. *Harrison* (1851) 6 Exch. 901, *post*, p. 688; *Arcos* v. *Ronaasen* [1933] A.C. 470, *post* p. 695.

has been stated by Roskill L.J.: "Contracts are made to be performed and not to be avoided according to the whims of market fluctuation."[92]

The point is illustrated by *Dakin* v. *Oxley*[93] where a shipowner in breach of contract had damaged the cargo, which, on arrival, was worth less than the freight. It was held that the cargo-owner was not justified in abandoning the cargo and refusing to pay freight. One reason given was that "It would be unjust and almost absurd that . . . *the risk of a mercantile adventure should be thrown upon the shipowner* by the mere accident of the value of the cargo [when undamaged] being worth little more than the freight."[94]

Similar considerations may also have influenced the decision in the *Hongkong Fir* case.[95] By the time the ship had been repaired, there had been a "catastrophic fall in the freight market"[96] to 13s. 6d. per ton, as against the 47s. per ton reserved in the charterparty.[97] In a 24 month charterparty the risk of such a fall in the freight market would normally be on the charterer; and the court was probably reluctant to allow him to throw it back on the shipowner by putting an end to the charterparty. It may also be relevant that the shipowner's breaches did not (so far as appears from the report) cause the charterer any loss at all. If, on the other hand, he can show that the owner's breach *is* a source of serious prejudice to him, he will not be prevented from rescinding merely because there has been a steep fall in the freight market. This is particularly true if his conduct shows that his real motive for rescinding was to avoid the prejudice caused by the breach, and not to escape from what has turned out to be a bad bargain.[98]

(f) OTHER FACTORS. The factors influencing decisions as to the availability of rescission by reason of the effects of a failure in performance cannot be exhaustively classified. Even where none of the factors discussed above is present, rescission may nevertheless be justified. In *Aerial Advertising Co.* v. *Batchelor's Peas Ltd.*,[99] for example, the plaintiffs agreed to conduct an advertising campaign for the defendants. On Armistice Day 1937 one of the plaintiffs' aeroplanes set out with a banner bearing the message "Eat Batchelor's Peas." Unfortunately the aeroplane towed the banner over the main square of Salford, Lancashire, at the precise time when a large crowd was gathered there observing the two-minute silence. The effect of this breach of contract was described as "disastrous,"[1] and it was held that the defendants were justified in refusing to accept further performance of the contract. Again, where a contract presupposes the continuation of a relationship involving personal confidence, it is possible for some isolated act of one party to destroy that confidence and so to justify rescission by the other.[2] In some of the cases, rescission was held to be justified because the nature or effects of the breach were regarded as sufficiently "serious" in

---

92 *The Hansa Nord* [1976] Q.B. 44, 71.
93 (1864) 15 C.B.(N.S.) 647.
94 *Ibid.* pp. 667–668; italics supplied.
95 [1962] 2 Q.B. 26; *ante*, p. 675.
96 [1962] 2 Q.B. p. 39.
97 [1961] 2 All E.R. at p. 261.
98 *Cf. Federal Commerce Navigation Co. Ltd.* v. *Molena Alpha Inc.* [1979] A.C. 757.
99 [1938] 2 All E.R. 788.
1 *Ibid.* p. 792.
2 See *Denmark Productions Ltd.* v. *Boscobel Productions Ltd.* [1969] 1 Q.B. 699, where it was held by a majority that rescission was not justified on the facts. *Cf.* also the employers' right to rescind the original service agreement in *Bell* v. *Lever Bros. Ltd.* [1932] A.C. 161 (*ante*, p. 252).

ways that are hard to explain or even to articulate.[3] Such a vague notion has its dangers, but it cannot be altogether eliminated from a discussion of this branch of the law.

4. Exceptions to the Requirement of Substantial Failure

The preceding discussion attempts to identify factors that influence decisions on the issue of substantial failure in performance; but it must be admitted that their practical operation is not easy to predict. In the interests of greater certainty, the law therefore recognises a number of exceptions[4] to the requirement of substantial failure. Inevitably, the resulting certainty is achieved at the expense of justice, so that these exceptions have attracted an increasing weight of criticism.

(1) Express provision for determination

(a) LITERAL ENFORCEMENT IN GENERAL. A contract may expressly provide that one party shall be entitled to rescind in the event of some specified failure by the other to perform. For example, a voyage charterparty may stipulate that the ship is expected to be ready to load at a named port on (or about) a specified date, and that if she fails to arrive there within (say) ten days of that date the charterer shall be entitled to cancel; and a time charterparty may provide either that the owner shall be entitled to withdraw the ship if hire is not punctually paid, or that the charterer shall be entitled to cancel if the ship becomes unavailable for service for more than a specified number of days.[5] The purpose of such clauses is to prevent disputes from arising as to the often difficult question whether the failure in performance is sufficiently serious to justify rescission; and they take effect even though there is no substantial failure.[6] For example, under a clause in a time charterparty entitling the shipowner to withdraw the ship if the charter fails to pay hire by a specified day, the shipowner can exercise his right of withdrawal immediately on such failure[7]; and he can do this even though the charterer tenders payment very soon after it was due, even though the short delay in payment causes him little prejudice, and even though his motive for withdrawal is simply that the freight market has risen. In cases of this kind "certainty is of primary importance"[8]; and the charterer can mitigate the severity of the clause by insisting (if his bargaining position permits) on the inclusion of a so-called "anti-technicality"

---

[3] See *Bright* v. *Ganas*, 189 A. 427 (1936), where a servant forfeited all rights to pay for four-and-a-half years' service by writing a love-letter to his employer's wife.

[4] For a further special exception in the law of agency, see *ante*, p. 648.

[5] *The Span Terza* (No. 2) [1984] 1 W.L.R. 27; such a clause avoids the difficulties that arose in the *Hong Kong Fir* case [1962] 2 Q.B. 26, *ante* pp. 675, 676, 679; *post* pp. 696–697. For similar cancelling clauses in contracts for the sale of ships, see *The Solholt* [1983] 1 Lloyd's Rep. 605; *The Oro Chef* [1983] 2 Lloyd's Rep. 509; *cf.* also *Bettini* v. *Gye* (1876) 1 Q.B.D. 183, 187.

[6] Such clauses are probably not within s.3(2)(*b*)(ii) of the Unfair Contract Terms Act 1977 for the reasons given on p. 232, *ante*, and because rescission under such clauses terminates the primary obligations of *both* parties; *cf. The Super Servant Two* [1990] 1 Lloyd's Rep. 1, 8.

[7] *The Brimnes* [1975] Q.B. 929; *The Laconia* [1977] A.C. 850; Rose, 30 C.L.P. 213; *cf. The Chikuma* [1981] 1 W.L.R. 314; Mann, 97 L.Q.R. 379–382.

[8] *The Laconia* [1977] A.C. 850 at p. 878; *The Lutetian* [1982] 2 Lloyd's Rep. 140, 159; *cf. The Chikuma*, *supra*, at p. 322.

provision allowing days of grace or requiring notice of default before withdrawal.[9]

Although, for the reasons just given, the law normally gives literal effect to express provisions for determination, it does insist on compliance with two requirements. First, the party seeking to terminate must act strictly in accordance with the terms of the clause. For example, a voyage charterparty may provide that the charterer can cancel if the ship is not at the port of loading by September 30. The charterer would not be entitled to cancel on September 29, even though at that time the ship was so far away from the port that she could not possibly get there the next day.[10] Conversely where a time charterparty gives the shipowner the right to withdraw the ship, or to give notice of withdrawal, if hire is not paid on the due day, he is not entitled to exercise that right before the end of that day, even though the bank at which payment was to be made had already closed so that the charterer could not possibly make the payment in accordance with the contract.[11] Secondly, the party relying on the express provision must terminate without undue delay. Thus, in cases of non-payment of hire by a time charterer it has been said that the shipowner must exercise his right to withdraw the ship "within a reasonable time after default."[12]

(b) Relief against forfeiture in certain cases. The willingness of the courts to give effect to express provisions for determination in the cases so far discussed is based on the assumption that the parties have bargained on more or less equal terms.[13] Where this is not the case, the law has developed restrictions on the right of a party to rely on an express provision for determination. This is the position where a lease entitles the landlord to forfeit if the tenant breaks *any* covenant; and where a regulated hire-purchase agreement[14] entitles the owner to terminate it if the hirer defaults in the payment of even a single instalment. In such cases the provision for determination would deprive a party who committed some quite minor breach of the benefit of a contract which he has for a long period performed satisfactorily; and the court may allow him a period of grace within which to make good his default.[15] Sometimes such "relief against forfeiture" is given even though the breach cannot be remedied at all. Thus

---

[9] As in *Libyaville* [1975] 1 Lloyd's Rep. 537; and in *Federal Commerce and Navigation Co. Ltd.* v. *Molena Alpha Inc.* [1979] A.C. 757. *cf. The Laconia*, *supra*, at p. 878; *The Rio Sun* [1981] 2 Lloyd's Rep. 489, [1982] 1 Lloyd's Rep. 404; *The Afovos* [1983] 1 W.L.R. 195.

[10] *The Mihalis Angelos* [1971] 1 Q.B. 164.

[11] *The Afovos* [1983] 1 W.L.R. 195; *cf. ante*, p. 654.

[12] *The Laconia* [1977] A.C. 850, 872; *The Balder London* [1980] 2 Lloyd's Rep. 489, 892–893; *The Scaptrade* [1981] 2 Lloyd's Rep. 425, 430, affirmed without reference to this point [1983] 2 A.C. 699; *The Oro Chef* [1983] 2 Lloyd's Rep. 509; *The Great Marine* [1990] 2 Lloyd's Rep. 245, 249. The rule is based either on waiver or on an implied term that the right to withdraw must be exercised within a reasonable time: see *The Antaios* [1985] A.C. 191. It seems to be restricted to cases of rescission under an express term: see *Nichimen Corp.* v. *Gatoil Inc.* [1987] 2 Lloyd's Rep. 46, 54.

[13] See the judgment of Robert Goff L.J. in *The Scaptrade* [1983] Q.B. 529, 539–540 approved [1983] 2 A.C. 699.

[14] *Ante*, p. 163.

[15] See Consumer Credit Act 1974, ss.88, 89; requiring formal notice of termination and giving the hirer at least seven days to make good his default; and the rules relating to relief against forfeiture of leases: Law of Property Act 1925, s.146. *cf.* also the rules as to damages, discussed on pp. 750–752, *post*. Relief was denied to a hirer, who had been a persistent defaulter, in *Goker* v. *N.W.S. Bank plc*, *The Times*, May 23, 1990.

where a tenant innocently broke a covenant against subletting it was held that the landlord could not enforce a forfeiture clause, as the breach had not prejudiced him in any way.[16]

In some of the time charterparty cases discussed above, it was suggested that relief against forfeiture should be granted to a charterer who failed to pay hire on time, and that the exercise by the shipowner of his right to withdraw the ship under a withdrawal clause should be restricted accordingly.[17] But the House of Lords has rejected these suggestions[18] for two reasons. First, the courts should give effect to commercial agreements concluded (as time charters usually were) between parties who had bargained on equal terms. Secondly, that the principle of relief against forfeiture was restricted to cases where the party in breach would, if the contract were literally enforced, be deprived of "proprietary or possessory rights,"[19] while a time charter conferred only contractual rights, being merely a contract for services to be rendered by the shipowner. In the time charterparty cases both these lines of reasoning supported the conclusion that there should be no relief against forfeiture. But in other situations the two lines of reasoning may tend to support diverging conclusions; and the distinction between terms which deprive the party in breach of "proprietary or possessory rights" and terms which deprive him only of contractual rights can be a fine one. These points can be illustrated by contrasting two cases. In the *Sport International* case[20] it was held that relief against forfeiture was not available where A granted B a licence to use certain trade-marks and the contract provided that the licence was to determine on B's default; but in *B.I.C.C. plc* v. *Burndy Corp.*[21] such relief was held to be available where an agreement by which certain patents were vested in A and B provided that, on B's default, he should assign his rights in the patents to A. No doubt the cases are technically distinguishable on the ground that the actual *assignment* of a patent involves a transfer of "property," while the *termination of a contractual licence* to use a trade-mark does not. But from a commercial point of view a licence to use such forms of "intellectual property" often serves the same purpose as an actual transfer; and the practical effect of the clause in each case was to deprive the party in default of the right to make use of the "property." Moreover the argument that the court should give effect to express provisions for determination in commercial agreements between parties bargaining on equal terms should apply equally to both the situations just described. *B.I.C.C. plc* v. *Burndy Corp.* seems, with respect, to be out of keeping with the requirements of commercial certainty that have been emphasised in a number of recent House of Lords decisions concerned with express provisions for determination.[22]

---

[16] *Scala House & District Property Co. Ltd.* v. *Forbes* [1974] Q.B. 575.

[17] *The Afovos* [1980] 2 Lloyd's Rep. 477, 479, reversed on other grounds [1983] 1 W.L.R. 195; *The Tropwind* [1982] 1 Lloyd's Rep. 232, 234.

[18] In *The Scaptrade* [1983] 2 A.C. 694 and see the authorities cited *ante*, p. 680, n. 8.

[19] *The Scaptrade* [1983] 2 A.C. 694, 702.

[20] *Sport International Bussum BV* v. *Inter-Footwear Ltd.* [1984] 1 W.L.R. 776; Harpum, 100 L.Q.R. 369.

[21] [1985] Ch. 232.

[22] See *The Laconia* [1977] A.C. 850; *The Chikuma* [1981] 1 W.L.R. 314; *The Scaptrade* [1983] 2 A.C. 694.

(c) INVALIDITY ON OTHER GROUNDS. Provisions entitling a party to refuse to make payments under a contract in default of exact performance by the other may be invalid as penalties.[23]

(2) Entire and severable obligations[24]

(a) ENTIRE OBLIGATIONS. A contractual obligation is said to be "entire" when the contract requires it to be *completely* performed by one party (A) before the other (B) is to pay, or to render such other counter-performance as may have been agreed.[25] Complete performance by A is sometimes said to be a "condition precedent" to B's liability; but the cases are not necessarily concerned with disputes as to the *order* of performance.[26] Often the dispute arises because A's purported performance, though rendered in the stipulated order, is in some way incomplete or defective.

Where A fails to complete performance of an entire obligation, B is entitled to refuse to pay even though the deficiency in A's performance causes him little prejudice or none at all. At common law A is not even generally entitled to any other recompense for the partial performance which he has actually rendered. In *Cutter* v. *Powell*[27] a seaman agreed to serve on a ship bound from Jamaica for Liverpool; he was to be paid 30 guineas "ten days after the ship arrives at Liverpool . . . provided he proceeds, continues and does his duty . . . from hence to the port of Liverpool." On August 2 the ship sailed from Jamaica; she arrived at Liverpool on October 9, but the seaman had died on September 20. It was held that his administratrix could not recover for the work he had done before his death; for the contract meant that nothing was to be paid unless and until he had served for the whole voyage. At the ordinary rates of pay then prevailing, he would have earned only £8 for such a voyage. The higher rate of pay seems to have been intended to throw the risk of his completing the voyage on him. Lord Kenyon C.J. said: "It was a kind of insurance."[28] The result was that the administratrix recovered neither the 30 guineas, nor a proportionate part thereof, nor a reasonable sum for the six or seven weeks' service which the deceased had rendered. According to one case, the same rule applies even where a contract of employment is terminated by mutual consent.[29]

Similarly, where a contract for the carriage of goods by sea provides that freight is to become due on arrival of the goods at the agreed destination,

---

23 See *Gilbert-Ash (Northern) Ltd.* v. *Modern Engineeering (Bristol) Ltd.* [1974] A.C. 689; *post*, p. 890.

24 Williams, (1941) 57 L.Q.R. 373, 490. (This article must be read in the light of the Law Reform (Frustrated Contracts) Act 1943.)

25 Such a provision is not affected by Unfair Contract Terms Act 1977, s.3(2)(*b*)(ii) for the reason stated at p. 232, *ante*; and also because B is not claiming to be entitled to render no performance "in respect of his contractual obligation": his case is rather that, before A's performance, he is not under any relevant obligation.

26 *Cf. ante*, p. 662.

27 (1795) 6 T.R. 320; Stoljar, 34 Can.Bar.Rev. 288.

28 At p. 324. *Quaere* whether it was really insurance against the death of members of the crew, or against their desertion. For possible effects of the Apportionment Act 1870 and of the Law Reform (Frustrated Contracts) Act 1943 in a case like *Cutter* v. *Powell*, see *post*, pp. 721, 811.

29 *Lambourn* v. *Cruden* (1841) 2 M. & G. 253.

the shipowner cannot recover either the stipulated freight, or freight *pro rata*, if he is compelled to abandon the voyage by perils of the sea and to discharge the cargo at an intermediate port.[30] The same rule applies where a ship is abandoned at sea and later saved by third parties[31] and it applies even though the shipowner's failure to get to the agreed destination is not due to his breach, but is due to an excepted peril or to the act of a third party for whom he is not responsible.[32] The rule can be excluded by contrary provision in the contract, *e.g.* by one to the effect that freight is to be deemed to have been *earned* on loading.[33] In such a case, the shipowner can recover the freight even though the contract provides that it is to be *paid* on or after unloading: that provision only affects the *time* of payment, not the creation of the obligation to pay.[34]

The same principle is again illustrated by *Sumpter* v. *Hedges*[35] where the plaintiff agreed to build two houses for the defendant on the latter's land for a lump sum of £565. When the houses were still unfinished the plaintiff told the defendant that he had run out of money and could not finish the work; and the defendant later completed the houses himself. It was held that the plaintiff could not recover the agreed sum; nor could he recover a reasonable remuneration for his work as there was no evidence of a "new contract" to pay such a sum.[36]

As a general rule, a contract for the sale of goods is considered to impose an entire obligation with regard to the quantity contracted for.[37] If the seller fails to deliver the correct quantity the buyer is not bound to accept and pay (though if he does accept he must pay at the contract rate).[38] The rule applies where the seller delivers *more* than the quantity contracted for just as much as where he delivers less.[39] The rule is, however, subject to a number of qualifications. First, it can be varied by the provisions of the contract, *e.g.* by one calling for delivery of "about" the stipulated quantity, or for "five per cent. more or less[40] (though such a margin must not be exceeded).[41] Secondly, the rule does not permit rejection for a wholly trivial discrepancy, *e.g.* for an excess of 55 lbs, in a contract calling for

---

[30] *Vlierboom* v. *Chapman* (1844) 13 M. & W. 230; *St. Enoch Shipping Co. Ltd.* v. *Phosphate Mining Co.* [1916] 2 K.B. 624; *cf. The Fort Kip* [1985] 2 Lloyd's Rep. 168.

[31] *The Kathleen* (1874) L.R. 4 A. & E. 269; *The Cito* (1881) 7 P.D. 5; contrast *Bradley* v. *H. Newsom, Sons & Co.* [1919] A.C. 16 (where there was no abandonment).

[32] As in *The Kathleen* (1874) L.R. 4 A. & E. 269.

[33] *The Dominique* [1989] A.C. 1056; Crabtree [1989] L.M.C.L.Q. 289; *The Karin Vatis* [1988] 2 Lloyd's Rep. 330.

[34] See the authorities cited in n. 33; contrast *The Lorna I* [1983] 1 Lloyd's Rep. 373 (where there was no stipulation as to when the freight was *earned*, but only one as to when it was to be *paid*).

[35] [1898] 1 Q.B. 673; *cf. Munro* v. *Butt* (1858) 8 E. & B. 738; *Bolton* v. *Mahadeva* [1972] 1 W.L.R. 1009.

[36] For this requirement, see *post*, pp. 717–718.

[37] See *Oxendale* v. *Wetherell* (1829) 9 B. & C. 386–387; *Reuter* v. *Sala* (1879) 4 C.P.D. 239; *cf. Cobec Brazilian Trading & Warehousing Corp.* v. *Alfred C. Toepfer* [1983] 2 Lloyd's Rep. 386.

[38] Sale of Goods Act 1979, s.30(1). (It is assumed that the goods are not "unsolicited" within Unsolicited Goods and Services Act 1971, s.6). Conversely, the buyer cannot insist on delivery of less than he agreed to accept: *Honck* v. *Muller* (1881) 7 Q.B.D. 92.

[39] Sale of Goods Act 1979, s.30(2).

[40] *e.g. Re Thornett and Fehr and Yuills* [1921] 1 K.B. 219; Sale of Goods Act 1979, s.30(5).

[41] *Tamvaco* v. *Lucas* (1859) 1 E. & E. 581.

delivery of 4,950 tons of wheat.[42] Thirdly, the rule does not apply where the contract provides for delivery by instalments, so that, where short delivery is made of one instalment the buyer is not entitled to refuse to accept either future deliveries, or even the instalment in question.[43]

The rule that a party cannot recover anything for partial performance of an entire obligation also applies where that party was willing to complete performance but was justifiably prevented from completing by the other party, *e.g.* where an employee is dismissed for misconduct.

(b) SEVERABLE OBLIGATIONS. A contract imposes severable obligations if payment under it is due from time to time as performance of specified parts of the contract is rendered. This is the situaton under contracts of employment, which typically provide for payment to be made at weekly or monthly intervals, even though the contract may be expressed to continue for longer periods. Similarly, in building contracts the rule in *Sumpter* v. *Hedges*[44] is often excluded by provision for "progress payments," to be made as specified as stages of the work are completed. The principle can be further illustrated by contrasting *Cutter* v. *Powell*[45] with the case in which a seaman agrees to serve at a fixed rate *per month*; under such a contract, he can recover his pay for each completed month although he fails to complete the voyage for which he was engaged.[46] This would be so even if no money was actually to be *paid over* until the end of the voyage. On the same principle, a piece-rate worker does not forfeit wages already earned simply because it was agreed that nothing should actually be paid out to him till the end of each working week and he left or was lawfully dismissed before the end of the week.[47] Similarly, a contract for the sale of goods may be made severable by providing for delivery and payment in instalments. In all these cases, no more than the specified part of the performance need be rendered before the corresponding payment can be claimed. It is also true that, as a general rule, the specified part must be rendered in full. Thus an employee cannot at common law[48] recover his current pay if he is justifiably dismissed for misconduct during the period at the end of which he is to be paid.[49]

Where a contract imposes severable obligations, a party who has fully performed the specified part can recover the corresponding payment even

---

[42] *Shipton Anderson & Co.* v. *Weil Bros.* [1912] 1 K.B. 574. The Law Commissions recommend an extension of this qualification in non-consumer sales to quantitative discrepancies which are so slight that it would be unreasonable for the buyer to reject: Law Com. No. 160 (1987) para. 6.20. But this proposal is open to the objection that it would cause considerable uncertainty, without significantly promoting the interests of justice.

[43] *Regent O.H.G. Aisenstadt und Barig* v. *Francesco of Jermyn Street* [1981] 3 All E.R. 327: such a case is governed by s.31(2) of the Sale of Goods Act 1979. For the contrast between s.31(2) and s.30(1), see *ante*, p. 675. *Quaere* whether s.30(1) should not apply to the short-delivered instalment itself.

[44] [1898] 1 Q.B. 673; *ante*, p. 684.

[45] (1795) 6 T.R. 320; *ante*, p. 683.

[46] *Taylor* v. *Laird* (1856) 25 L.J.Ex. 329; *Button* v. *Thompson* (1869) L.R. 4 C.P. 330.

[47] *Warburton* v. *Heyworth* (1880) 6 Q.B.D. 1.

[48] For the position under the Apportionment Act 1870, s.2, see *post*, p. 721.

[49] *Ridgway* v. *Hungerford Market Co.* (1835) 3 A. & E. 171; *Boston Deep Sea Fishing & Ice Co.* v. *Ansell* (1888) 39 Ch.D. 339. *Semble* that he can recover remuneration which became due before dismissal though it was earned after a breach of duty justifying dismissal: *Healey* v. *S.A. Française Rubastic* [1917] 1 K.B. 947. As to commission on transactions tainted by bribes, see *ante*, p. 648. For the position where the employee is *not* dismissed see *post*, p. 719.

though his failure to complete the whole of the promised performance is a breach of contract. In *Ritchie* v. *Atkinson*[50] a shipowner agreed to carry a cargo at a stipulated rate *per ton*. He carried only part of the cargo, and was entitled to recover a corresponding proportion of the freight. But he was later held liable in damages for failing to carry the rest of the cargo.[51] There is a similar liability in damages where performance of one of the specified parts is completed but is defective because it in some way falls short of the performance promised. For example, an employee may serve for the full payment period but fail or refuse, in the course of that period, to carry out some task which he was contractually obliged to perform. The employer is then entitled to damages in respect of that failure or refusal even though he may be bound to pay the agreed remuneration.[52] Whether he is so bound, and what other remedies may be available to him, are matters to be discussed later in this chapter.[53]

(c) Distinction between entire and severable obligations. In discussions of the cases so far considered, it is sometimes said that the *contracts* are entire or severable. But this is misleading: what is entire or severable is a particular *obligation*[54] arising under the contract. The point is most easily illustrated by reference to contracts for the carriage of goods by sea. Suppose a shipowner agrees to carry 1,000 tons at a stated rate, due on delivery, for each ton carried to London. If he carries 1,000 tons to Southampton he is not entitled to any freight[55]; if he carries 750 tons to London he is prima facie entitled to three quarters of the freight[56]; and if he carries 1,000 tons to London but the goods arrive damaged, he will be entitled to full freight[57] unless the damage is so serious that the description under which the goods have been shipped ceases to apply to them: for example, where cement solidifies as a result of being damaged by water.[58]

The same point may be illustrated by further reference to *Cutter* v.

---

[50] (1808) 10 East 295.

[51] *Atkinson* v. *Ritchie*, *ibid.* p. 530.

[52] *Sim* v. *Rotherham Metropolitan B.C.* [1987] Ch. 216, where the measure of damages was not in dispute. In *Miles* v. *Wakefield Metropolitan D.C.* [1987] A.C. 539, 560 the measure of damges in case of an employee's refusal to perform the specified contractual duties for part of the agreed working time is said to be the wages for the "lost hours of work." *Cf. ibid.* p. 568. But these dicta were *obiter* (no claim for damages having been made); and strictly speaking the measure of damages should be the loss suffered by the employer, which is not necessarily the same as the wages for the lost hours. *Cf. post*, pp. 825, 932–933.

[53] *Post*, pp. 687, 719.

[54] *Cf. Cobec Brazilian Trading & Warehousing Corp.* v. *Alfred C. Toepfer* [1982] 1 Lloyd's Rep. 528, 531 ("indivisible obligation"); affirmed [1983] 2 Lloyd's Rep. 386.

[55] *Ante*, p. 684; *post*, p. 719.

[56] *Ritchie* v. *Atkinson* (1808) 10 East 295. If the contract provides for a "lump sum" freight, the shipowner will, in such a situation, be entitled to the entire freight: *Merchant Shipping Co.* v. *Armitage* (1873) L.R. 9 Q.B. 99; *Thomas* v. *Harrowing SS. Co.* [1915] A.C. 58. He will also be entitled to the whole freight if the contract provides for freight to be computed by reference to the quantity taken on board though it is only payable after discharge of the cargo: see *The Aries* [1977] 1 W.L.R. 185; *The Metula* [1978] 2 Lloyd's Rep. 5; unless the contract provides for a deduction to be made if the quantity delivered is less that that taken on board, as in *The Olympic Brilliance* [1982] 2 Lloyd's Rep. 205.

[57] *Dakin* v. *Oxley* (1864) 15 C.B.(N.S.) 646; *The Brede* [1974] Q.B. 233 (no freight was allowed in respect of a part of the goods that was *lost:* see [1972] 2 Lloyd's Rep. at pp. 514, 519; but the Court of Appeal was only concerned with the part of the goods that was *damaged*: [1974] Q.B. at p. 245).

[58] *Duthie* v. *Hilton* (1868) L.R. 4 C.P. 138; *cf. The Caspian Sea* [1980] 1 W.L.R. 48; *Dakin* v. *Oxley*, *supra*, at p. 664; *post*, pp. 715–716.

Powell[59]: the obligation to serve for the whole voyage was entire, but it has been said that, if the seaman had completed the voyage and had been guilty during it, of occasional breaches of duty, then the plaintiff could have enforced the contract,[60] subject to a deduction in respect of any loss caused by those breaches.[61] Again, a building contract may provide for payments as the work progresses, subject to a "retention fund" to be paid over on completion. There is then a series of severable obligations to complete each stage as well as an entire obligation to complete the whole.[62] In *Sumpter* v. *Hedges*[63] the builder's obligation was entire with respect to the quantity of work to be done; but his claim would not have been dismissed merely because he had failed in some other way to comply with the contract, *e.g.* by completing a week late[64] or (unless the contract had expressly made his right to payment subject to the work being done strictly in accordance with the contract)[65] by completing the buildings with minor defects. Thus in *Hoenig* v. *Isaacs*[66] the plaintiff contracted to redecorate and furnish the defendant's flat for £750. There were minor defects in the furniture, which could have been made good for £55. The defendant argued that the plaintiff was entitled to no more than a reasonable remuneration for work done in accordance with the contract. But the court held that he was entitled to be paid at the full contract rate (less the cost of making the defects good), as he had substantially completed the work. The obligation of a seller of goods is, again, generally entire as to quantity, but if the correct quantity is delivered he may be able to enforce the contract in spite of the fact that the goods are defective in quality.[67] Of course failure to perform an obligation which is not entire may give the other party a right to rescind on some other ground, *e.g.* that the failure is substantial; but it does not give him this right under the present rule.

In the cases so far discussed the distinction between entire and severable obligations is clearly settled either by the express terms of the contract or by commercial practice recognised by law. But there may be no rule of law on the point and the contract may be silent or self-contradictory, *e.g.* where A employs B to paint A's house for £1,000 but fails to say when it is to be paid; or where the contract provides for payment of "£200 per room payable on completion." In such cases the question whether a particular obligation is entire or severable is one of construction; and where a party agrees to do work under a contract, the courts are reluctant to construe the contract so as to require complete performance before any payment becomes due. "Contracts may be so made; but they require plain words to

---

[59] (1795) 6 T.R. 320.
[60] *Hoenig* v. *Isaacs* [1952] 2 All E.R. 176, 178.
[61] *Cf. Sim* v. *Rotherham Metropolitan B.C.* [1987] Ch. 216; *Miles* v. *Wakefield Metropolitan D.C.* [1987] A.C. 539, 570 (no right to withhold pay for "bad work"). (For statutory restrictions on the right to deduct damages from wages, see Payment of Wages Act 1986, *post*, p. 689, n. 88.
[62] *Ibid.* p. 181.
[63] [1898] 1 Q.B. 673.
[64] *Ibid.*, at p. 676.
[65] *Eshelby* v. *Federated European Bank* [1932] 1 K.B. 423.
[66] [1952] 2 All E.R. 176; approving *Dakin & Co. Ltd.* v. *Lee* [1916] 1 K.B. 566, which had been doubted in *Eshelby* v. *Federated European Bank* [1932] 1 K.B. 423; *Williams* v. *Roffey Bros. & Nicholls (Contractors) Ltd.* [1991] 1 Q.B. 1; *post*, p. 689, n. 82.
[67] *e.g. post*, p. 697.

shew that such a bargain was really intended."[68] In *Roberts* v. *Havelock*[69] a shipwright agreed to repair a ship. The contract did not expressly state when payment was to be made. It was held that the shipwright was not bound to complete the repairs before claiming some payment. If the contract contains contradictory provisions the courts tend to give greater weight to those making the obligation to work a severable one. Thus where a contract provided (1) for payment at a fixed rate per month, but (2) that nothing was to be paid till performance was complete, the first clause prevailed over the second, *i.e.* the contract was construed as imposing severable obligations.[70] In one type of case this hostility towards entire obligations has been reinforced by statute: an agreement by a seaman to abandon his right to wages in case the ship is lost is void.[71]

The courts are reluctant to construe obligations to do work as entire because such a construction will often lead to the unjust enrichment of the party receiving the partial or defective performance.[72] There is no such reluctance in contracts for the sale of goods: we have seen that the buyer is not generally bound to accept a different quantity from that contracted for[73]; nor is he bound, unless the contract so provides,[74] to accept delivery in instalments.[75] This state of the law does not give rise to any danger of unjust enrichment: if a buyer of goods rejects delivery of the wrong quantity, the goods will be returned to the seller. But even in this type of case rejection may cause a different type of hardship to the seller, namely that of throwing back on him the risk of market fluctuations. In *Cunliffe* v. *Harrison*[76] a seller of wine delivered more than the agreed quantity. It was held that the buyer was not bound to accept any part of the wine, "although it may be that the refusal to take the wine was not bona fide but grounded upon the fact that the wine had fallen in price."[77]

(d) SO-CALLED DOCTRINE OF SUBSTANTIAL PERFORMANCE.[78] Cases such as *Hoenig* v. *Isaacs*[79] are sometimes explained on the ground that the plaintiff had "substantially" performed an "entire contract."[80] It is submitted that the explanation is unsatisfactory since it is based on the error that *contracts*, as opposed to particular *obligations*, can be entire.[81] The basis of

---

[68] *Button* v. *Thompson* (1869) L.R. 4 C.P. 330 at p. 342.
[69] (1832) 3 B. & Ad. 404; *cf. Davidson* v. *Jones-Fenleigh* (1980) 124 S.J. 204.
[70] See *The Juliana* (1822) 2 Dods. 504.
[71] Merchant Shipping Act 1970, s.16(1) (reversing the common law rule that freight was the "mother of wages").
[72] *Post*, p. 717.
[73] *Ante*, p. 684.
[74] On this question of construction, contrast *Reuter* v. *Sala* (1879) 4 C.P.D. 239 with *Brandt* v. *Lawrence* (1876) 1 Q.B.D. 344.
[75] Sale of Goods Act 1979, s.31(1).
[76] (1851) 6 Ex. 901.
[77] *Ibid.* p. 907; of course it is possible that the seller was not acting bona fide either but that he was trying to unload an excessive quantity on a falling market.
[78] Beck, 38 M.L.R. 413.
[79] [1952] 2 All E.R. 176; *ante*, p. 687.
[80] *e.g. Dakin* v. *Lee* [1916] 1 K.B. 566, 598; *Sim* v. *Rotherham M.B.C.* [1987] Ch. 216, 253; *Wiluszynski* c. *Tower Hamlets L.B.C.* [1989] I.C.R. 493, 499; *Williams* v. *Roffey Bros. & Nicholls (Contractors) Ltd.* [1991] 1 Q.B. 1, 8–10. *Chitty on Contracts* (26th ed.), Vol. I § 1513; no such doctrine is in terms stated by the court in *Hoenig* v. *Isaacs, supra.*
[81] See *ante*, p. 685.

Hoenig v. *Isaacs* is that the builder, even if he was under an entire obligation as to the quantity of work to be done, was under no such obligation as to its quality.[82] Defects of quality therefore fell to be considered under the general requirement of substantial failure, and on the facts there was no such failure.[83] To say that an obligation is entire *means* that it must be completely performed before payment becomes due. Suppose a contract is made to carry goods from Melbourne to London and the freight is payable on delivery in London. If the goods are carried only to Southampton, the carrier may have "substantially" performed; but he cannot recover the freight.[84] In relation to "entire" obligations, there is no scope for any doctrine of "substantial performance."

(3) Conditions, warranties and intermediate terms

(a) STATEMENT OF THE DISTINCTION. English law has for some considerable time recognised a distinction between two classes of contractual terms: conditions and warranties. "Condition" is here used (in its promissory sense[85]) to refer to a contractual term, the breach of which gives the injured party the right to rescind the contract. Of course he need not rescind but may instead affirm; and he can claim damages whether he affirms[86] or rescinds.[87] A warranty, on the other hand, is a term the breach of which gives the injured party only a right to damages. He can generally set these damages up in diminution or extinction of the price[88]; and if they equal or exceed the price he will not have to pay anything. Subject to this

---

[82] *Williams* v. *Roffey Bros. & Nicholls (Contractors) Ltd.* [1991] 1 Q.B. 1 (where a subcontractor recovered instalments subject to a "small deduction for defective and *incomplete* items" (*ibid.* p. 17) purports to follow *Hoenig* v. *Isaacs*, but that case was concerned only with defective, not incomplete, items.

[83] Contrast *Lawson* v. *Supasink* (1984) Tr.L. 37 (where qualitative defects in kitchen installations were sufficiently serious to justify rescission).

[84] *Ante*, p. 684; *Metcalfe* v. *Britannia Ironworks* (1877) 2 Q.B.D. 423.

[85] *Ante*, p. 58.

[86] *e.g. Aruna Mills Ltd.* v. *Dhanrajmal Gobindram* [1968] 1 Q.B. 655; the test of affirmation seems to be the same here as in the law of misrepresentation so that mere lapse of time will not suffice: *Allen* v. *Robles* [1969] 1 W.L.R. 1193; *cf. ante*, p. 345.

[87] See, *e.g. Millar's Machinery Co. Ltd.* v. *David Way & Son* (1935) 40 Com.Cas. 204; *Lesters Leather & Skin Co. Ltd.* v. *Home & Overseas Brokers Ltd.* (1949) 82 Ll.L.Rep. 203; *Heaven & Kesterton Ltd.* v. *Et. Francois Albiac & Cie* [1956] 2 Lloyd's Rep. 316; *New India Assurance Co. Ltd.* v. *Yeo Beng Chao* [1972] 1 W.L.R. 786; *Microbeads A.G.* v. *Vinshurst Road Markings Ltd.* [1975] 1 W.L.R. 218, 225; *cf. General Billposting Co.* v. *Atkinson* [1909] A.C. 118; *Kwei Tek Chao* v. *British Traders and Shippers Ltd.* [1954] 2 Q.B. 459, 473 (but see *ibid.* p. 477); and *cf. post*, p. 748.

[88] Sale of Goods Act 1979, s.53(1)(*a*); *Gilbert-Ash (Northern) Ltd.* v. *Modern Engineering (Bristol) Ltd.* [1974] A.C. 689. *Sim* v. *Rotherham M.B.C.* [1987] Ch. 216; *U.C.B. Leasing* v. *Holtom* [1987] R.T.R. 362; *cf. Miles* v. *Wakefield M.D.C.* [1987] A.C. 539; for statutory restrictions, see Payment of Wages Act 1986 Pt. I. The process is not available against a claim for freight under a voyage charterparty: *The Brede* [1974] Q.B. 233; *The Aries* [1977] 1 W.L.R. 185. Although this rule was described as "anomalous" in *James & Co. Scheepvaart en Handelmij B.V.* v. *Chinacrest Ltd.* [1979] 1 Lloyd's Rep. 126, 129, and as "arbitrary" in *Dole Dried Fruit and Nut Co.* v. *Trustin Kerwood Ltd.* [1990] 2 Lloyd's Rep. 309, 310 it has been extended in various ways: *The Cleon* [1983] 1 Lloyd's Rep. 587; *R.H. & D. International Ltd.* v. *S.A.S. Animal Air Services Ltd.* [1984] 2 All E.R. 203; *The Elena* [1986] 1 Lloyd's Rep. 425; *The Khian Captain (No. 2)* [1986] 1 Lloyd's Rep. 429; *The Dominique* [1989] A.C. 1059 (applying the rule to a repudiatory breach on account of which the charterer rescinded). For the position under time charterparties, see *Federal Commerce Navigation Co. Ltd.* v. *Molena Alpha Inc.* [1978] Q.B. 927; affirmed without deciding this point [1979] A.C. 997; *The Kostas Melas* [1981] 1 Lloyd's Rep. 18, 25; *The Cebu* [1983] Q.B. 1005, 1011–1012.

possibility the injured party is not entitled to rescind merely[89] on account of a breach of warranty.[90]

(b) NATURE OF THE DISTINCTION. Earlier in this chapter we saw that the phrases "condition precedent" and "concurrent condition" were used to make a point about the *order* of performance.[91] At this stage, the word "condition" is used to make a different point, namely, one about the *conformity*[92] of the performance rendered with that promised. In the first of these two senses, the *performance* by one party may be a "condition precedent" to the liability of the other; in the second it is a *term* of the contract which is described as the "condition." It is perfectly possible for a party to comply with a condition in one of these senses but not in the other: for example, a seller of goods by sample who has agreed to give credit may deliver the goods before being paid and so perform a "condition precedent," but if the goods turn out not to correspond with the sample he will be in breach of "condition."[93] The distinction was formerly obscured by use of the phrase "condition precedent" in cases concerned with conformity, rather than with order of performance[94]: thus "condition precedent" was used to refer both to a term of a contract and to an event, *i.e.* the prior or concurrent performance by one party before that of the other became due. The use of the same phrase in these two senses is, however, confusing since the effects of one party's failure to perform a "condition precedent" or a "concurrent condition" differ in two ways from those of breach of "condition" (as opposed to warranty). First, a failure of the former kind only justifies refusal by the injured party to perform for so long as the failure continues[95]; while breach of condition justifies rescission in the sense of an outright or permanent refusal to perform and to accept further performance from the party in breach. Secondly, the injured party's right to refuse to perform so long as a condition precedent or concurrent condition remains unperformed can be exercised without any previous election by the injured party (whose position is simply that his performance is not yet due[95a]); while such an election is required for the purpose of the more drastic remedy of rescission (in the sense of an outright refusal of the kind just described) for breach of condition.[96] Modern authority accordingly recognises the distinction between the two concepts[96a] and tends[97] to use the phrase "condition" when discussing conformity, and "condition precedent" when discussing the order of performance. That usage is adopted

---

[89] *Post*, p. 703.

[90] See the definition of "warranty" in Sale of Goods Act 1979, s.61(1); *cf. United Scientific Holdings Ltd.* v. *Burnley B.C.* [1978] A.C. 904, 945; and see *post*, p. 698, n. 61.

[91] *Ante*, pp. 662–664.

[92] Conformity includes time of performance: it is perfectly possible for performance to be rendered at the wrong *time* but in the right *order*: *e.g.* where goods are sold for cash on delivery on January 1 and are delivered on January 8.

[93] See *post*, p. 694.

[94] *e.g. Glaholm* v. *Hays* (1841) 2 Man. & G. 257, 267; *Behn* v. *Burness* (1863) 3 B. & S. 751, 755: *Bentsen* v. *Taylor* [1893] 2 Q.B. 274, 281.

[95] See *ante*, pp. 666–667.

[95a] See *The Good Luck*, *The Times*, May 17, 1991.

[96] *Post*, p. 743.

[96a] *e.g. State Trading Corporation of India* v. *M. Golodetz Ltd.* [1989] 2 Lloyd's Rep. 277, 284 treating "condition" and "condition precedent" as distinct concepts; Treitel, 106 L.Q.R. 185.

[97] But not invariably: see, *e.g. The Aktion* [1989] 1 Lloyd's Rep. 283, 285.

in this chapter so that "condition precedent" is contrasted with "concurrent condition" and "independent covenant"; while "condition" (without any qualifying adjective) is contrasted with "warranty" and "intermediate term."

(c) BASES OF THE DISTINCTION. The distinction between conditions and warranties was originally based on two factors. One was the intention of the parties, as expressed in the contract: hence the question into which category a stipulation fell was treated as one of construction.[98] But often the intention of the parties in this respect was not discoverable from the words used; and so the courts relied secondly on the general requirement of substantial failure in performance. If "performance of the stipulation [went] to the very root . . . of the contract,"[99] then the stipulation was treated as a condition. We shall see that a term may also be treated as a condition on other grounds[1]; but the actually or potentially serious effects of breach are still taken into account in deciding, in cases of first impression, whether the term broken is to be classified as a condition.[2] If a contractual term[3] relates to "a substantial ingredient in the identity of the thing sold,"[4] it will be classified as a condition, and its breach will entitle the victim to rescind, on the theory that it would be unjust to hold him liable for refusing to accept and pay for something which differed in an important way from that for which he had contracted. A warranty, on the other hand, concerns some less important or subsidiary element of the contract. Its breach does not entitle the victim to rescind, on the theory that a minor breach can be adequately remedied by the payment of money.

This approach can be seen in a number of cases in which decisions were based on the commercial importance of the term to the injured party: for example, if a buyer said that he would not buy goods at all unless they had a certain quality, then this fact would tend to support the view that an undertaking with respect to that quality was a condition.[5] Where there is no such evidence of intention, the court will base its decision on its own view of the commercial importance of the term. The older authorities on this question must be treated with caution, because in them the word "warranty" was sometimes used to refer to what would now be called a "condition."[6] But the cases do establish that there are certain terms the breach of which prima facie gives rise to a right to rescind and which are therefore

---

[98] *Glaholm* v. *Hays* (1841) 2 Man. & G. 257, 266; Sale of Goods Act 1979, s.11(3); *cf. Tradax Export S.A.* v. *European Grain & Shipping Co.* [1983] 2 Lloyd's Rep. 100.
[99] *Glaholm* v. *Hays*, *supra*, at p. 268; *cf. Bentsen* v. *Taylor* [1893] 2 Q.B. 274, 281.
[1] *Post*, pp. 693–695.
[2] Thus the fact that the breach is *not* likely to cause serious prejudice can support the view that the term is not a condition: see *State Trading Corporation of India* v. *M. Golodetz Ltd.* [1989] 2 Lloyd's Rep. 277, *post*, p. 701.
[3] See *Harlingdon & Leinster Enterprises Ltd.* v. *Christopher Hull Fine Art Ltd.* [1990] 1 All E.R. 737, 739 (where the statement was held *not* to be a contractual term: *ante*, p. 319).
[4] *Couchman* v. *Hill* [1947] K.B. 544, 559.
[5] *Cf. Bannerman* v. *White* (1861) 10 C.B.(N.S.) 844; *ante*, p. 317.
[6] *e.g.* in *Behn* v. *Burness* (1863) 3 B. & S. 751, 755: "a warranty, that is to say a condition . . . ". This usage has survived in insurance law: see, *e.g.* s.33 of the Marine Insurance Act 1906: see *The Good Luck*, *The Times*, May 17, 1991; *cf. Hadenfayre Ltd.* v. *British National Insurance Society* [1984] 2 Lloyd's Rep. 393, 401. See also Food Act 1984, s.102(1)(*a*); *Lambert* v. *Lewis* [1982] A.C. 225, 273, 276, where Lord Diplock refers to the *conditions* implied by s.14 of the Sale of Goods Act 1979 as "warranties"; and see *The Evia* (*No.* 2) [1983] 1 A.C. 736, 765.

"conditions" in the terminology now current. In *Behn* v. *Burness*[7] a ship was described in a charterparty as "now in the port of Amsterdam" when in fact she was elsewhere. It was held that the charterer was entitled to rescind: the statement was a condition because of the commercial importance which charterers usually attach to such descriptive statements. Similarly, a statement that a ship will sail on a certain day has been treated as a condition in a charterparty.[8] The same is true of a statement that a ship is "expected ready to load" under a charterparty on or about a certain day.[9] Such a statement does not amount to a definite undertaking that she will be ready on or about the named day: the shipowner is only in breach if he made the statement dishonestly or without reasonable grounds.[10] This rule weakens the argument that the statement must be a condition because of its commercial importance, for it means that the charterer does not get any firm assurance as to the date of readiness to load. The classification of the statement as a condition can, however, be justified on the ground that a shipowner who has made such a statement dishonestly or without reasonable grounds, is in a poor position to complain of any prejudice which he may suffer as a result of rescission.[11]

The reasoning of the cases discussed above is based on the requirement of serious failure in performance; and emphasis on this requirement gave rise at one time to the view that a term could *only* be a condition if "every breach . . . [of it would] . . . deprive the party not in breach of substantially the whole benefit which it was intended that he should obtain from the contract."[12] But this view was rejected by the House of Lords in *Bunge Corp.* v. *Tradax Export S.A.*, where Lord Roskill said that there were "many cases . . . where terms the breaches of which do not deprive the innocent party of substantially the whole benefit which he was intended to receive from the contract were nonetheless held to be conditions any breach of which entitled the innocent party to rescind."[13] The statement that "conditions . . . have the property that any breach of them is treated as going to the root of the contract"[14] must similarly be viewed with caution. It is accurate only in the sense that a breach of condition, like one going to the root of the contract, gives rise to a right to rescind; but that right arises, in the two cases, for different reasons. Where the breach *actually* "goes to the root of the contract," the right to rescind arises to pro-

---

[7] (1863) 3 B. & S. 751.

[8] *Glaholm* v. *Hays* (1841) 2 Man. & G. 257; *cf. Bentsen* v. *Taylor* [1893] 2 Q.B. 274 (statement that ship "now sailed or about to sail" held to be a condition).

[9] *The Mihalis Angelos* [1971] 1 Q.B. 164; Horton Rogers, 34 M.L.R. 190; Greig, 89 L.Q.R. 93; *cf. The Mavro Vetranic* [1985] 1 Lloyd's Rep. 580, 584 (estimated time of ship's arrival).

[10] *Scrutton on Charterparties and Bills of Lading* (19th ed.), pp. 79–80.

[11] *The Mihalis Angelos*, *supra*, at p. 205. The charterer could also rescind for misrepresentation: *ibid.* p. 194.

[12] *Hongkong Fir Shipping Co. Ltd.* v. *Kawasaki Kisen Kaisha Ltd.* [1962] 2 Q.B. 26, 69, *per* Diplock L.J.; *cf. United Scientific Holdings* v. *Burnley B.C.* [1978] A.C. 904, 928.

[13] [1981] 1 W.L.R. 711, 724; *cf. ibid.* at pp. 715–716, 718. On this point the House of Lords followed the reasoning of Megaw L.J. in the Court of Appeal: see [1980] 1 Lloyd's Rep. 294, 305. Lord Diplock himself took a similar view in *Photo Production Ltd.* v. *Securicor Transport Ltd.* [1980] A.C. 827, 849. His earlier view is, perhaps, reflected in *Gill & Duffus S.A.* v. *Berger & Co. Inc.* [1984] A.C. 382, 391 where he described a c.i.f. buyer's refusal to pay against documents both as a "fundamental breach" and as a "breach of condition." It is submitted that the former is the more accurate description as the refusal showed an intention on the part of the buyer no longer to be bound by the contract: *cf. post*, p. 705.

[14] *Lombard North Central plc* v. *Butterworth* [1987] Q.B. 527, 535.

tect the injured party from serious prejudice; where the breach is one of condition it arises to promote certainty, "without regard to the magnitude of the breach."[15] For this reason, breach of condition is here treated as an exception to, and not as an application of, the requirement of substantial failure in performance.

(d) EXPRESS CLASSIFICATION BY THE PARTIES. One basis for distinguishing conditions from warranties is the intention of the parties[16]; and the courts continue to rely on this factor where that intention can be ascertained.[17] Thus if a contract expressly says that a particular term is a condition,[18] that term will generally be so regarded; and the same is true where the contract expressly states that rescission will be available on breach of the term.[19] But if a term can be broken in a way which will only cause trifling (if any) loss, the court may hold that such a breach will not justify rescission even though the term is called a "condition" in the contract. In *Wickman Ltd.* v. *Schular A.G.*[20] it was a "condition" of a four-year distributorship agreement that the distributor should visit six named customers once a week. The House of Lords held that the contract could not be rescinded *merely* because this term had been broken. The parties could not have intended the agreement to mean that a failure to make only one out of an obligatory total of some 1,400 visits should have such drastic results. More probably they had used "condition" in a nontechnical sense to mean simply a term of the contract (as in the phrase "conditions of sale"). This view was supported by the fact that another clause in the contract conferred an express power of "determination" for any "material" breach.

A term may be classified as a condition either by the express agreement of the parties or by law (*i.e.* by a previous judicial decision[21] or by statute[22]). One possible explanation of the cases in which a term has been classified by law as a condition is that the parties "have agreed . . . by implication of law"[23] that any breach of the term should give rise to the right to rescind. But this does not differ in substance from saying that there is a rule of law giving the injured party the right to rescind for the breach[24]: rescission is allowed, in these cases, even though the parties have not actually agreed that breach of the term should have this effect and even though the breach has not prejudiced the injured party seriously, or at all.

(e) STATUTORY CLASSIFICATION. In some cases the question whether a particular term is a condition or a warranty is determined by statute. The outstanding example of statutory classification is to be found in sections 12 to 15 of the Sale of Goods Act 1979, which lay down in some detail which of the implied terms in a contract for the sale of goods are conditions and

---

15 *Ibid.* (referring, apparently, to terms which are conditions by express classification of the parties).

16 *Ante*, p. 691.

17 *Astley Industrial Trust Ltd.* v. *Grimley* [1963] 1 W.L.R. 584, 590; *Bunge Corp.* v. *Tradax Export S.A.* [1981] 1 W.L.R. 711, 716.

18 *e.g. Dawson's Ltd.* v. *Bonnin* [1922] 2 A.C. 413.

19 *Harling* v. *Eddy* [1951] 2 K.B. 739.

20 [1974] A.C. 235; Baker [1973] C.L.J. 196; Brownsword, 37 M.L.R. 104.

21 *Ante*, p. 691.

22 *Post*, pp. 693–694.

23 *Photo Production Ltd.* v. *Securicor Transport Ltd.* [1980] A.C. 827, 849.

24 *Cf.* the discussion of "terms implied in law" as legal duties at pp. 190–193, *ante*.

which are warranties. A full discussion of these provisions will be found in works on the sale of goods; but it is interesting to note that most of them are implied *conditions* (thus favouring the buyer's right to reject[25]); and a few of them may be mentioned here to illustrate the distinction between conditions and warranties. It is an implied condition that goods sold by description shall correspond with the description,[26] that goods sold by sample shall correspond with the sample,[27] and (in certain cases) that goods shall be merchantable and fit for a particular purpose.[28] There is an implied condition that the seller has the right to sell the goods, but only an implied warranty that they are free from charges or incumbrances in favour of third parties.[29] To allow the seller to enforce the contract, when he had no right to sell, would generally[30] cause hardship to the buyer, as he would have to give the goods up to the true owner. But there is less hardship if the goods are subject to third party charges; these can simply be paid off so that the buyer can adequately and conveniently be compensated by damages.

The distinction between conditions and warranties does not apply to *quantitative* defects in the performance of a contract for the sale of goods. Such defects justify rescission even though they cause little or no prejudice to the buyer.[31]

(f) TECHNICAL APPLICATIONS OF THE DISTINCTION. In some cases, rescission is allowed simply because the term broken has previously been classified as a condition. It is allowed even though there is no indication in the contract that the parties intended the remedy to be available, and even though the breach causes little prejudice, or none at all, to the injured party. Cases of this kind give rise to the question why the injured party should, in such circumstances, be entitled to rescind.

Sometimes, this result is justified by an argument based on hypothetical hardship. Rescission is allowed because the breach *might* have caused serious prejudice, irrespective of the question whether it *actually* did so. In one case,[32] for example, a seller of tinned fruit said to be packed in cases of 30 tins delivered cases of 24 tins. It was held that the buyer could reject. Scrutton L.J. said: "a man who has bought . . . 30 tins to the case may have resold under the same description, and may be placed in considerable difficulty by having goods tendered to him which do not comply with the description under which he bought or under which he has resold."[33]

---

[25] This is also true of the similar terms implied in other contracts for the supply of goods by Supply of Goods (Implied Terms) Act 1973, ss.8–11 (as substituted by Consumer Credit Act 1974, Sched. 4, para. 35) and by Supply of Goods and Services Act 1982, ss.2–5, 7–10. Contrast the Uniform Law on International Sales (ULIS), set out as Sched. 1 to the Uniform Laws on International Sales Act 1967. This law (which only applies if the parties so choose) does not use the distinction between conditions and warranties, but makes the right of "avoidance" generally dependent on a "fundamental breach," thus favouring the seller. But the general principle is subject to many qualifications, and the very complex system of remedies under ULIS is beyond the scope of this book. For the Vienna Convention on international sales (not yet ratified by the U.K.) see *ante*, p. 29, n. 88.

[26] Sale of Goods Act 1979, s.13.

[27] *Ibid.* s.15.

[28] *Ibid.* s.14.

[29] *Ibid.* s.12.

[30] For an exception, see Sale of Goods Act 1979, s.12(3) (agreement to transfer only such title as seller or third party may have).

[31] Sale of Goods Act 1979, s.30(1) and (2).

[32] *Re Moore & Co. Ltd. and Landauer Co.* [1921] 2 K.B. 519.

[33] *Ibid.* p. 525.

In other cases, no attempt is made to justify the result even by reference to such hypothetical hardship. Thus in *Arcos Ltd.* v. *Ronaasen*[34] timber was bought for the purpose of making cement barrels and was described in the contract as half an inch thick. Most of the timber delivered was in fact $\frac{9}{16}$in. thick, but this did not in the least impair its usefulness for making cement barrels. It was held that the buyers were nevertheless entitled to reject and it seems probable that their motive for wishing to do so was not that the timber did not comply with the description but that the market price of the timber had fallen. Similarly, goods may be sold on the terms that they will be (or have been) shipped within a particular month. Such a term is part of the description of the goods and if they are shipped by so much as a day before or after the stipulated period the buyer can reject.[35] He can do this even though the early or late shipment does not in the least affect the value of the goods or prejudice him in any way; and even though his motive for rejection is simply to escape from a bad bargain on a falling market. And it seems that a charterer can rescind for breach of the conditions as to the position of the ship or as to the date when she will sail even though the breach did not cause him any loss and even though his real motive for rescinding was that freight rates had fallen.[36]

Such decisions can perhaps be explained on the ground that they promote certainty. Once a term has been classified as a "condition," the injured party can safely rescind for breach of it, without having to consider the often difficult question whether the breach amounted to a "substantial" failure in performance. On the other hand, in some of the examples given above the exercise of the right to rescind can occasion obvious hardship to the party in breach: it results in his having to bear a loss that was not caused by the breach at all, but by market movements. For this reason, there has been some judicial reaction against the authorities which give a wide scope to the right to rescind.

(g) RESTRICTIONS OF TECHNICAL APPLICATIONS. In *Reardon Smith Line Ltd.* v. *Hansen Tangen*[37] Lord Wilberforce[38] said that some of the authorities just discussed[39] were "excessively technical and due for fresh examination in this House"[40]; and that generally, where goods are sold by description, the court should "ask whether a particular item in a descripand only if it does . . . treat it as a condition."[41] However, he recognised a possible exception in the case of "unascertained future goods (*e.g.* commodities) as to which each detail of the description must be assumed to be

[34] [1933] A.C. 470.
[35] *Bowes* v. *Shand* (1877) 2 App.Cas. 455.
[36] This seems to have been the position in *Glaholm* v. *Hays* (1842) 2 Man. & G. 257.
[37] [1976] 1 W.L.R. 989; *cf. Sanko SS. Co. Ltd.* v. *Kano Trading Co. Ltd.* [1978] 1 Lloyd's Rep.
[38] With whom Lords Simon and Kilbrandon agreed.
[39] *i.e. Re Moore & Co. Ltd. and Landauer Co.* [1921] 2 K.B. 519 and *Behn* v. *Burness* (1863) 3 B. & S. 751 "as interpreted."
[40] [1976] 1 W.L.R. 989, 998. *Cf.* the criticism of the effects of breach of "warranty" in insurance law (*ante*, p. 691, n. 6) in *Forsikringsaktieselskapet Vesta* v. *Butcher* [1989] A.C. 852, 893–894.
[41] [1976] 1 W.L.R. 989, 998.
[42] *Ibid.*

important for each buyer to be able to tell at once whether some defect or misdescription justifies rejection.

One illustration of the judicial reaction against the excessively technical use of the right to rescind is provided by *Reardon Smith Line Ltd.* v. *Hansen Tangen* itself. The case arose out of the subcharter of a tanker then under construction and therefore not yet named. In the contract, she was accordingly described as "Yard No. 354 at Osaka . . . " (the name of the shipbuilder). She was built elsewhere, but by a company under Osaka's control and in accordance with the physical specifications in the subcharter. The tanker market fell and the subcharterers sought to reject, but it was held that they were not entitled to do so. The phrase "Yard No. 354 at Osaka" was not part of the description but a mere substitute for a name. It was only a means of identification, which, in the circumstances, had not failed. The effect of the decision is to reintroduce the requirement of substantial failure into this branch of the law by making it part of the definition of a "description"; and by thus narrowing the scope of an implied term which is undoubtedly a condition, *i.e.* the term requiring the goods to correspond with the contractual description.

(h) INTERMEDIATE OR INNOMINATE TERMS. The courts have also achieved a result similar to that just described by reducing the number of terms which are classified as conditions. They have done so by recognising that the distinction between conditions and warranties is not exhaustive. As Diplock L.J. has said: "There are many . . . contractual undertakings . . . which cannot be categorised as being 'conditions' or 'warranties'. . . . Of such undertakings, all that can be predicated is that some breaches will and others will not give rise to an event which will deprive the party not in default of substantially the whole benefit which it was intended that he should obtain."[43] These "intermediate or innominate terms"[44] differ from conditions, in that breach does not of itself give rise to a right to rescind; and from warranties in that the injured party's remedy is not even prima facie restricted to damages. He can rescind for breach of an intermediate term if, but only if, the requirement of substantial failure is satisfied.[45] Thus it has been held that a shipowner's undertakings in a charterparty to provide a seaworthy ship[46] and to use reasonable despatch[47] are not conditions,[48] so that the *mere* fact thay they are not performed will not entitle the charterer to rescind. The same is true of the charterer's obligation to load within the time stipulated in the charterparty, so that the mere fact of delay will not justify rescission by the shipowner.[49] Similarly, it has been held that a time-charterer's obligation to repair the ship before redelivery is not a condition, so that his failure to repair does not, of itself, justify the shipowner's refusal to accept redelivery.[50] Some terms implied by statute

[43] *Hongkong Fir Shipping Co. Ltd.* v. *Kawasaki Kisen Kaisha Ltd.* [1962] 2 Q.B. 26, 70.

[44] *Bunge Corp.* v. *Tradax Export S.A.* [1981] 1 W.L.R. 711, 714.

[45] *e.g. Freeman* v. *Taylor* (1831) 8 Bing. 124; *cf. The Antaios* [1985] A.C. 191, 200 ("fundamental breach of an innominate term").

[46] *Hongkong Fir* case, *supra*; *cf. The Ymnos* [1982] 2 Lloyd's Rep. 574; *The Torenia* [1983] 2 Lloyd's Rep. 210, 217.

[47] *Clipsham* v. *Vertue* (1843) 5 Q.B. 265; *MacAndrew* v. *Chapple* (1886) L.R. 1 C.P. 643.

[48] See *post* for a justification for this classification.

[49] *Universal Cargo Carriers Corp.* v. *Citati* [1957] 2 Q.B. 401; *The Angelia* [1973] 1 W.L.R. 210.

[50] *Attica Sea Carriers Corp.* v. *Ferrostaal Poseidon Bulk Reederei GmbH* [1976] 1 Lloyd's Rep. 250, 253, 256.

seem also to fall into the category of intermediate terms. This seems to be true of the terms implied by the Supply of Goods and Services Act 1982 into contracts for the supply of services, that the services will be carried out with due care and skill and in a reasonable time; for the Act describes them simply as "terms"[51] (as opposed to the "conditions" and "warranties" implied into contracts for the supply of goods by the same Act).[52]

The availability of rescission for a serious breach of an intermediate term is illustrated by *Federal Commerce & Navigation* v. *Molena Alpha*[53] where a time charter authorised the charterer to sign bills of lading stating that freight had been prepaid. The shipowners wrongfully withdrew that authority and instructed the captain to sign bills of lading only in a form that was commercially useless to the charterer. It was held that, although the term broken was not a condition, the effect of its breach was to deprive the charterer of "substantially the whole benefit of the contract."[54] It followed that the charterer was entitled to rescind.

There was formerly some doubt on the question whether the category of intermediate terms existed in relation to contracts for the sale of goods. One view was that, as the Sale of Goods Act 1979 referred only to two classes of terms (conditions and warranties), the further category of intermediate terms was impliedly excluded. But this view was rejected in *The Hansa Nord.*[55] Citrus pulp pellets were sold for £100,000 under a contract which provided for "shipment to be made in good condition." Part of the goods had not been so shipped; and this fact reduced by some £20,000 the market value of the whole which would, if the goods had been sound, have been £86,000 at the time of their arrival.[56] The buyers rejected the goods which were later resold pursuant to a court order and eventually reacquired by the original buyers for just under £34,000. The buyers then used the goods for the originally intended purpose of making cattle food, though the defective part of the goods yielded slightly lower extraction percentages than sound goods would have done. The Court of Appeal held that rejection was not justified. The provision as to shipment in good condition was neither a condition nor a warranty but an intermediate term; and there was no finding that the effect of its breach was sufficiently serious to justify rejection. The buyers seem to have tried to reject, not because the utility of the goods was impaired, but because they saw an opportunity of acquiring them at well below the originally agreed price. In these circumstances their only remedy was in damages: they were entitled to the difference in value between damaged and sound goods at the agreed destination.[57]

The category of intermediate terms is thus established and is of general application. Its existence does, however, give rise to two further problems:

(i) *Are there three categories of terms?* This is a largely terminological problem.[58] The general view is that there are three classes of contractual

---

[51] Supply of Goods and Services Act 1982, ss.13, 14.
[52] *Ibid.* ss.2–5 and 7–10; *ante*, p. 694, n. 25.
[53] [1979] A.C. 757.
[54] *Ibid.* p. 779. *Cf. The Honam Jade* [1991] 1 Lloyd's Rep. 38.
[55] [1976] Q.B. 44; Reynolds, 92 L.Q.R. 17; Weir [1976] C.L.J. 33; *cf. The Aktion* [1987] 1 Lloyd's Rep. 283.
[56] [1976] Q.B. 44 at pp. 55–56; 68.
[57] *Ibid.* pp. 63–64.
[58] *The Ymnos* [1982] 2 Lloyd's Rep. 574, 583.

terms: conditions, the breach of which invariably gives rise to a right to rescind; warranties, the breach of which gives rise only to a right to damages; and intermediate terms, the breach of which gives rise to a right to rescind if it is sufficiently serious, but otherwise sounds only in damages. There is, however, some support for the alternative view that there are only two categories: conditions and other terms.[59] This view is based on the argument that the injured party may be entitled to rescind even for a breach of warranty, if the effect of the breach is sufficiently serious. There is, as we shall see, considerable force in this argument[60]; and if it is correct a warranty may be said to resemble an intermediate term, in that the availability of rescission as a remedy for its breach depends on the seriousness of the breach. Nevertheless, the weight of authority supports the continued existence of the threefold division of contractual terms.[61] It is respectfully submitted that this is the preferable view since the distinction between warranties and intermediate terms remains for practical purposes an important one. Even if, in extreme cases, rescission is available for breach of warranty, there is at least a prima facie rule that the normal remedy for such a breach is by way of damages. In relation to intermediate terms, there is no such prima facie rule; so that (to put the matter at its lowest) there is a greater likelihood that rescission will be available for breach of an intermediate term than for breach of warranty.

(ii) *Scope of the category of intermediate terms.* Granted that the threefold classification of terms does exist, the question then arises into which category particular terms should be placed. In discussing this question we shall assume that the parties have not provided an express classification of the term in the contract itself; and that the court will generally apply a previous judicial classification of the term.[62] Our main concern will therefore be with previously unclassified terms. Since judicial classification of a term as a warranty is rare,[63] the important issue is whether a previously unclassified term is to be classified as a condition or as an intermediate term. This issue is a difficult one because it gives rise to a conflict between two policies.

The first of these policies is to restrict the right to rescind to cases in which the breach causes serious prejudice to the injured party, and so to

---

59 *e.g.* in *The Hansa Nord* [1976] Q.B. 44, 60 where Lord Denning M.R. says that the court has to ask only two questions: (i) is the term broken a condition; (ii) if not, did the breach go to the root? But he also recognises warranty as a separate category at pp. 59–60 and at p. 61 he expressly distinguishes between the three categories of terms.

60 *Post*, p. 703.

61 *Bunge Corp.* v. *Tradax Export S.A.* [1981] 1 W.L.R. 711, 725 (where Lord Roskill, with whom three of the other members of the House of Lords agreed, referred to a "third class of term"); *Regent O.H.G. Aisenstadt und Barig* v. *Francesco of Jermyn Street* [1981] 3 All E.R. 327, 334; *cf.* Lord Diplock's division of stipulations as to time into three categories in *United Scientific Holdings Ltd.* v. *Burnley B.C.* [1978] A.C. 904, 943; his statement in *Photo Production Ltd.* v. *Securicor Transport Ltd.* [1980] A.C. 827, 849 of a general rule subject to two exceptions similarly amounts to a three-fold classification. For similar statements by Lord Diplock in other cases, see *Bremer Vulkan Schiffbau und Maschinenfabrik* v. *South India Shipping Corp.* [1981] A.C. 909, 980–981; *The Nema* [1982] A.C. 724. 744 *The Afovos* [1983] 1 W.L.R. 195, 203; *The Mavro Vetranic* [1985] 1 Lloyd's Rep. 580, 583.

62 Occasionally the court may wish to reconsider such a classification: *cf.* Lord Wilberforce's suggestion in *Reardon-Smith Line Ltd.* v. *Hansen Tangen* [1976] 1 W.L.R. 989, 998, *ante*, p. 695.

63 For an example of such a classification, see *Palmco Shipping Inc.* v. *Continental Ore Corp.* [1970] 2 Lloyd's Rep. 21.

prevent a party from rescinding for ulterior motives or on grounds that have been criticised as "excessively technical."[64] This policy favours the classification of terms as intermediate. It is illustrated by the *Hongkong Fir*[65] case, the *Hansa Nord*[66] and by a number of later decisions. In *Tradax Internacional S.A* v. *Goldschmidt S.A.*[67] the words "four per cent. foreign matters" in a contract for the sale of barley were held to amount only to an intermediate term, so that the buyer was not allowed to reject merely because the goods were certified to contain 4.1 per cent. foreign matters. Slynn J. said that "in the absence of any clear agreement or prior decision that this was to be a condition, the court should lean in favour of construing this provision as to impurities as an intermediate term, only a serious and substantial breach of which entitled rejection."[68] This policy can, however, be excluded by evidence of contrary intention. In *Tradax Export S.A.* v. *European Grain & Shipping Co.*[69] the words "maximun 7.5 per cent. fibre" in a contract for the sale of solvent extracted toasted soya bean meal were held to be a condition, so that the buyer was entitled to reject when the goods were found to have a fibre content of 9.28 per cent. *Tradax Internacional S.A.* v. *Goldschmidt S.A.* was not cited but the two cases can be distinguished on the ground that in *Tradax Export S.A.* v. *European Grain & Shipping Co.* there was evidence that, in sales of the commodity in question, fibre content was normally a matter for price adjustment. It followed that, by taking the unusual step of specifying a maximum fibre content, the parties had provided evidence of their intention to depart from that normal practice and of giving the buyer the right to reject, should the specified percentage be exceeded.[70] But where there is no such evidence of the intention of the parties, the policy of leaning in favour of classifying stipulations as intermediate terms can be said to promote the interests of justice by preventing the injured party from rescinding on grounds that are technical or unmeritorious.

The second policy, by way of contrast, emphasises the requirement of commercial certainty; and it in turn favours the classification of terms as conditions. Such a classification makes it unnecessary to go into the difficult questions of fact and degree that arise in determining whether a breach is "serious and substantial."[71] And once a term has been classified as a condition, the breach of such a term will, in a future case, enable the injured party to know, as soon as the breach has been committed, that he is entitled to rescind: he will not need to show anything about its effects. These considerations prevailed in *Bunge Corp.* v. *Tradax Export S.A.*[72] A contract for the sale of soya bean meal provided that the goods were to be

---

64 *Reardon-Smith Line Ltd.* v. *Hansen Tangen* [1976] 1 W.L.R. 989, 998; *ante*, p. 695.
65 [1962] 2 Q.B. 26; *ante*, p. 696.
66 [1976] Q.B. 44; *ante*, p. 697.
67 [1977] 2 Lloyd's Rep. 604.
68 *Ibid.* p. 612; *cf. post*, p. 701, n. 86; *Bremer Handelsgesellschaft mbH* v. *Vanden Avenne-Izegem P.V.B.A.* [1978] 2 Lloyd's Rep. 109, 113, and *Federal Commerce & Navigation* v. *Molena Alpha* [1979] A.C. 757 (*ante*, p. 697).
69 [1983] 2 Lloyd's Rep. 100.
70 Another possible distinction between the two cases is that in *Tradax Internacional S.A.* v. *Goldschmidt S.A* it was conceded that "four per cent. foreign matters" was not part of the description and so could not be a condition under Sale of Goods Act 1979 s.13; though that concession would not prevent the words from being a condition on other grounds.
71 *Tradax Internacional S.A.* v. *Goldschmidt S.A.* [1977] 2 Lloyd's Rep. 604, 612.
72 [1981] 1 W.L.R. 711.

delivered during June. Delivery was to begin on a day in that month to be chosen by the buyers and was to be made free on board on a ship provided by the buyers at a U.S. Gulf port to be selected by the sellers. The contract went on to require the buyers to give at least 15 days' notice of the ship's readiness to load the goods. It was held that this provision was a condition, so that the sellers were entitled to rescind on the ground that the notice reached them five days too late. This classification of the term was justified by two arguments. First, the sellers could not, as a practical matter, perform their own obligation of nominating a port until the buyers had given them notice of the ship's readiness to load[73]; but later cases show that a term may be classified as a condition even when there is no such interdependence between the obligations of the parties.[74] The second, and more important, point was that the classification promoted certainty, for it enabled the sellers to tell, immediately on receipt of the notice of the ship's readiness to load, whether they were bound to deliver.

Failure to adhere to similar time-tables laid down by commodity contracts has, in a number of other cases, likewise been held to amount to a breach of condition.[75] One possible explanation for this special treatment of time clauses is that "as to such a clause there is only one kind of breach possible, namely to be late"[76]; while terms that have been classified as intermediate are typically such as might be broken in various ways, some trivial and some serious.[77] It is true that the undertaking as to (for example) seaworthiness can be broken in many different ways; but it is equally true that delay may be trivial or serious; and the law does not always give the injured party the right to rescind for delay which is not serious: we have, for example, seen that a charterer is not in breach of condition merely because he has failed to load within the time stipulated in the charterparty.[78] Stipulations as to the time of performance can, however, be put into a separate category on the ground that breach by delay is uniquely easy to establish: if the injured party has received no performance by the due day, there can be no doubt about the fact of delay; while qualitative breaches (such as unseaworthiness) can give rise to many disputed issues of fact. Delay is also of obvious commercial importance in dealings with commodities, which can fluctuate rapidly in value. It is this combination of a breach which is easy to establish without legal proceedings and which is likely to be important commercially which accounts for the readiness of the courts to treat stipulations as to the time of performance in contracts for

---

73 *Cf. Gill & Duffus S.A.* v. *Société pour l'Exportation des Sucres S.A.* [1986] 1 Lloyd's Rep. 332.

74 *The Mavro Vetranic* [1985] 1 Lloyd's Rep. 580, 583; *Michael J. Warde* v. *Feedex International Inc.* [1985] 2 Lloyd's Rep. 289, 298.

75 *e.g. Krohn & Co.* v. *Mitsui & Co. Europe GmbH* [1978] 2 Lloyd's Rep. 419; *Toepfer* v. *Lenersan-Poortman N.V.* [1980] 1 Lloyd's Rep. 143; *cf. Bremer Handelsgesellschaft mbH* v. *Vanden Avenne-Izegem P.V.B.A.* [1978] 2 Lloyd's Rep. 109 (so far as it relates to the notice under clause 22 of the contract); *Portara Shipping Co.* v. *Gulf Pacific Navigation Co. Ltd.* [1981] 2 Lloyd's Rep. 180; *Nichimen Corp.* v. *Gatoil Overseas Inc.* [1987] 2 Lloyd's Rep. 46; *The Naxos* [1990] 1 W.L.R. 1337; and see the authorities cited in nn. 73 and 74, *supra*.

76 *Bunge Corp.* v. *Tradax Export S.A.* [1981] 1 W.L.R. 711, 715.

77 *Ibid. Cf. The Ymnos* [1982] 2 Lloyd's Rep. 574, 584.

78 *Ante*, p. 696; *cf.* Lord Wilberforce's statement that a charterer's deliberate delay in loading of only one day "can appropriately be sanctioned by damages:" *Suisse Atlantique* case [1967] 1 A.C. 361, 423 (*post*, p. 705).

the sale of commodities as conditions, so that *any* breach of them will justify rescission

It follows from the above reasoning that a stipulation as to the time of performance will not invariably be treated as a condition. It may, for example, not be so treated precisely because the context shows that its due performance is *not* of vital importance[79]; or because to give the injured party the right to rescind for *any* breach of it would make the contract unworkable[80]; or because the stipulation is itself imprecise, so that its classification as a condition would not promote certainty. Thus the House of Lords has held that a stipulation requiring a seller to give notice "without delay" of the occurrence of circumstances entitling him to invoke a prohibition of export clause was an intermediate term only.[81] This case was distinguished in a later decision at first instance, where a contract for the sale of goods required a seller to give the buyer a notice appropriating goods to the contract "as soon as possible after vessel's sailing."[82] It was held that this term was a condition, and the earlier decision of the House of Lords[83] was distinguished on the ground that the decision was concerned with a stipulation governing the machinery of *termination* while the later case was concerned with a stipulation governing the machinery of performance.[84] But the explanation is not entirely convincing since an important question in relation to either kind of term is whether the breach of it entitles the injured party to treat the contract as at an end. The crucial question is whether classification of the term as a condition significantly promotes certainty; and it is submitted that it cannot have this effect when it does not enable the buyer to know in advance precisely when he should have received the notice.[85] Vague expressions such as "without delay," or "as soon as possible" do not enable him to know this, and stipulations containing such expressions should not be classified as conditions in the absence of evidence that the parties clearly intended them to take effect as such.

The foregoing discussion shows that there is considerable support both for the view that the court should "lean in favour"[86] of classifying contractual stipulations as intermediate terms, and for the view that commercial certainty sometimes requires their classification as conditions. It is clear that the first of these views has not been rejected by *Bunge Corp.* v. *Tradax Export S.A.*[87] On the contrary, it was expressly approved by Lord Wilber-

---

[79] *State Trading Corporation of India* v. *M. Golodetz Ltd.* [1989] 2 Lloyd's Rep. 277 (where the stipulation was contained in one contract but related to a different contract between the same parties which was not to be performed for six months and was relatively unimportant in terms of money).

[80] As in *The Honam Jane* [1991] 1 Lloyd's Rep. 39 (where strict compliance with the timetable was impossible in chain contracts).

[81] *Bremer Handelsgellschaft mbH* v. *Vanden Avenne-Izegem P.V.B.A.*, *supra*, n. 75, so far as it relates to the notice under clause 21 of the contract; *cf. Tradax Export S.A.* v. *Italgrani di Francesco Ambrosio* [1986] 1 Lloyd's Rep. 112, 120.

[82] *The Post Chaser* [1981] 2 Lloyd's Rep. 695.

[83] *Supra*, at n. 81.

[84] [1981] 2 Lloyd's Rep. at p. 700.

[85] See *Tradax Export S.A.* v. *Italgrani di Francesco Ambrosio* [1986] 1 Lloyd's Rep. 112, 120.

[86] *Tradax Internacional S.A.* v. *Goldschmidt S.A.* [1977] 2 Lloyd's Rep. 604, 612; *cf. Bremer Handelsgesellschaft mbH* v. *Vanden Avenne-Izegem P.V.B.A.* [1978] 2 Lloyd's Rep. 109, 113; *Federal Commerce & Navigation* v. *Molena Alpha* [1979] A.C. 757; *State Trading Corporation of India* v. *M. Golodetz Ltd.* [1989] 2 Lloyd's Rep. 277, 283; *The Silva Plana* [1989] 2 Lloyd's Rep. 371, 375.

[87] [1981] 1 W.L.R. 711, *ante*, p. 699.

force when he said that "the courts should not be too ready to interpret contractual clauses as conditions"[88]; while Lord Roskill recognised "the modern approach of not being over-ready to construe terms as conditions unless the contract clearly requires the court to do so."[89] The effect of *Bunge Corp.* v. *Tradax Export S.A.* is not to discard, but rather to qualify, that approach by emphasising the importance traditionally attached in certain commercial contracts to exact compliance with stipulations as to the time of performance.[90] If such stipulations are sufficiently precise, they are now likely to be classified as conditions and the same classification may also be adopted in relation to other terms if exact performance of them is regarded as commercially vital[91] or if there is evidence either from the commercial setting or from the course of negotiations that the parties intended them to have the force of conditions.[92] Where a term does not fall within any of these three categories, the judicial attitude continues to be one of not being "too ready" to classify it as a condition. Such other terms are therefore likely to be classified as intermediate, so that rescission will be allowed only where the breach causes serious prejudice to the injured party.

(i) OTHER RESTRICTIONS ON RESCISSION FOR BREACH OF CONDITION. The right to rescind for breach of condition may be limited in one, or possibly two, further ways.

(i) *Exemption clauses.* The right to rescind may be excluded by a clause which validly excludes all liability for breach of condition; or by a "non-rejection" or "non-cancellation" clause which bars the right to rescind without affecting the right to damages. This power to exclude the right to rescind is subject to the rules discussed in Chapter 7, which limit the effectiveness of exemption clauses. In a contract for the supply of goods, a clause purporting to deprive a person who deals as a consumer of the right to reject for breach of the conditions implied by the Sale of Goods Act 1979 will generally have no effect.[93] If the injured party does not deal as consumer, such a clause will commonly be subject to the test of reasonableness.[94] It is submitted that in applying this test to the effectiveness of non-rejection clauses in contracts between businessmen, the courts may be influenced by the likely effects of the breach, and so take into account the same factors which determine whether a failure in performance is sufficiently "substantial" to give rise to a right to rescind. A similar point can be made with regard to the process of strict construction which is applied to

88 [1981] 1 W.L.R. at p. 715.

89 *Ibid.* p. 727; *cf.* also *Toepfer* v. *Lenersan Poortman N.V.* [1980] 1 Lloyd's Rep. 143, 147. *The Ymnos* [1982] 1 Lloyd's Rep. 574, 583.

90 *Cf. Bowes* v. *Shand* (1877) 2 App.Cas. 455; *ante*, p. 695.

91 *The Post Chaser* [1981] 2 Lloyd's Rep. 695 may be explicable on this ground: see p. 700 of the report; or on the ground of concessions made in that case: see *British & Commonwealth Holdings plc* v. *Quadrex Holdings Inc.* [1989] Q.B. 842, 857.

92 This was the position in *Tradax Export S.A.* v. *European Grain & Shipping Co.* [1983] 2 Lloyd's Rep. 100 (*ante*, p. 699) and in *Bergerco U.S.A.* v. *Vegoil Ltd.* [1984] 1 Lloyd's Rep. 440 where a promise to send goods "directly" to Bombay, made after earlier delays in delivery, was held to be a condition; *cf.* also *Michael J. Warde* v. *Feedex International Inc.* [1985] 2 Lloyd's Rep. 284, 288.

93 *Ante*, pp. 229–230.

94 *Ante*, pp. 232–233.

exemption clauses in certain cases of particularly serious breach.[95] If the effect of a breach of condition is wholly to frustrate the injured party's purpose in making the contract, the clause may be held not to apply to the breach at all[96]; and if it is so construed, the injured party will once again be entitled to rescind where the breach gives rise to a substantial failure in performance.

(ii) *Misrepresentation incorporated as condition.* Where a person has been induced to enter into a contract by a false statement of *fact*, his right to rescind for misrepresentation is subject to the discretion of the court under section 2(2) of the Misrepresentation Act 1967,[97] to declare the contract subsisting and to award damages in lieu of rescission. It is arguable that this discretion can be exercised even where the misrepresentation which induced the contract is later incorporated in it as a condition. But the better view seems to be that the subsection only applies to the right to rescind a contract for misrepresentation, and that it has not affected the right to rescind for breach.[98]

(j) RESCISSION FOR BREACH OF WARRANTY? Once a term is classified as a "condition" any breach of it automatically gives right to a right to rescind. It might be thought that, conversely, classification of a term as a "warranty" led to the result that a claim for damages was the only remedy for its breach. But it is submitted that there are two situations in which the injured party may be able to rescind for breach of warranty.

(i) *Misrepresentation incorporated as warranty.* A statement of *fact* made before the contract may give rise to a right to rescind the contract for misrepresentation, and this right will survive the subsequent incorporation of the statement in the contract as a warranty.[99] But if the breach is of relatively small importance, it seems likely that the court will exercise its discretion under section 2(2) of the Misrepresentation Act 1967[1] to declare the contract subsisting and to award damages in lieu of rescission.

(ii) *Substantial failure.* It has been suggested[2] that breach of warranty may justify rescission where it leads (or amounts) to a substantial failure in performance. There is at first sight some difficulty in applying this suggestion to contracts for the sale of goods. The difficulty arises because "warranty" is defined in the Sale of Goods Act 1979 as an agreement "collateral to the main purpose of [the] contract, the breach of which gives rise to a claim for damages but not to a right to reject the goods. . . . "[3] On the other hand, it is arguable that the rule allowing rescission for a "substantial" failure in performance is a rule of common law, preserved by section 62(2) of the Act "except in so far as . . . inconsistent with the express provisions of this Act." In *The Hansa Nord*[4] this subsection was invoked in support of the view that the statutory classification of terms into conditions

---

[95] See *J. Aron & Co. (Inc.)* v. *Comptoir Wegimont* [1921] 3 K.B. 435 for the application of these principles to non-rejection clauses.

[96] See pp. 205 *et seq.*, *ante*.

[97] See p. 320, ante.

[98] *Ante*, p. 336.

[99] Misrepresentation Act 1967, s.1(*a*); *ante*, p. 336.

[1] *Ante*, pp. 320–322.

[2] *Astley Industrial Trust Ltd.* v. *Grimley* [1963] 1 W.L.R. 584, 599. The term broken in this example would now be a condition under Supply of Goods and Services Act 1982, s.9(4) if the party in breach acted in the course of a business.

[3] s.61(1).

[4] [1976] Q.B. 44.

and warranties was not exhaustive. It can similarly be used to support the view that the Act does not exhaustively state the effects of breach of warranty.[5] If in particular circumstances such a breach leads to a substantial failure in performance, rescission should be allowed.

(4) Breach of fundamental term

In the law relating to exemption clauses, a distinction is drawn between conditions and fundamental terms. Breach of a fundamental term and breach of condition both give rise to a right to rescind regardless of the actual effects of the breach.[6] The main differences between them are (1) that it is easier to exclude liability for breach of condition than for breach of a fundamental term[7] and (2) that some of the factors which limit the right to rescind for breach of condition may not similarly limit the right to rescind a fundamental term.[8] Neither of these points is directly relevant to the present discussion, which concerns the question whether any right to rescind ever existed at all.

Usually, the effect of breach of a fundamental term will be serious, so that in most such cases the right to rescind will amount to an *application* of the requirement of substantial failure. But this is not necessarily the case, for in this branch of the law a development has taken place resembling that discussed in relation to breach of condition.[9] Certain terms in particular contracts have been classified by authority as fundamental terms. Once this has happened, any breach of such a term gives rise to a right to rescind, irrespective of its consequences. For example, in contracts for the carriage of goods by sea[10] the term as to the route to be followed has been classified as fundamental.[11] Any unjustified departure from that route by the carrier amounts to deviation and justifies rescission by the injured party. This is so even though the deviation is "for practical purposes irrelevant."[12] The right to rescind here constitutes an exception to the requirement of serious failure in performance; it can be criticised[13] and defended[14] on similar grounds to those which have been discussed in relation to the corresponding exception in case of breach of condition.

(5) Deliberate breach

A breach will not justify rescission *merely* because it is deliberate. For example, a shipowner could not rescind a charterparty simply because the charterer had deliberately and in breach of contract delayed in loading for

---

[5] *Ibid.* at p. 83.
[6] For this reason "fundamental term" is sometimes used in the same sense as condition, *i.e.* to mean any term, the breach of which justifies rescission: see *Millichamp* v. *Jones* [1982] 1 W.L.R. 1422, 1427; *Metro Meat Ltd.* v. *Fares Rural Pty Ltd.* [1985] 2 Lloyd's Rep. 13, 17; and *cf. infra*, n. 11.
[7] *Ante*, pp. 207–213.
[8] *Post*, pp. 715–716.
[9] *Ante*, p. 694.
[10] And probably by land: *ante*, p. 210, n. 2.
[11] *Hain SS. Co. Ltd.* v. *Tate & Lyle Ltd.* (1936) 41 Com.Cas. 350. Lord Diplock in *Photo Production Ltd.* v. *Securicor Transport Ltd.* [1980] A.C. 827, 850, appears to classify deviation as a breach of condition; but, at least in the law relating to exemption clauses, the effect of deviation seems still to differ from that of an ordinary breach of condition: *cf. ante*, p. 222.
[12] *Suisse Atlantique* case [1967] 1 A.C. 361, 423.
[13] See *Farr* v. *Hain SS. Co.* 121 F.2d 940, 944 (1941), *cf. ante*, p. 211.
[14] In that it promotes certainty (*ante*, p. 700, and on grounds stated at p. 210, *ante*).

one day: such a breach "can appropriately be sanctioned by damages."[15] A deliberate breach may, indeed, represent a perfectly honest attempt by the "guilty" party to do his best in the interests of the other party: for example, where a builder who is unable to obtain some minor component called for by the specifications, and who cannot quickly get into touch with the owner, on his own initiative uses a substitute of equal quality. The deliberate nature of the breach is, therefore, not decisive; but it is sometimes relevant to the existence of the right to rescind.

(a) FRAUD. A deliberate breach may amount to fraud and may justify rescission on that ground. This would be the position where a vendor of land knowingly overstated its area and the statement became a term of the contract. In such a case the purchaser can rescind[16] and the vendor cannot compel him to take the land with "compensation,"[17] even though the breach was not "substantial," so that this remedy would have been available, had the misdescription been made innocently.[18]

(b) REPUDIATION. The fact that the breach is deliberate may justify rescission on the ground that it is evidence of "an intention no longer to be bound by the contract,"[19] and so amount to a repudiation, or to an offer to rescind the contract which the other party may accept and so determine the contract.[20] Thus in *Withers* v. *Reynolds*[21] an instalment contract provided for cash *on* delivery. The buyer announced his intention of paying *after* delivery for all future instalments, and it was held that this justified the seller's refusal to make further deliveries. Similarly, the buyer would have been entitled to rescind if the seller had demanded payment *in advance* for all future deliveries.[22] Again, in the *Hongkong Fir* case it was held that unseaworthiness was not of itself a ground for rescission: in general, it could have this effect only if it produced a substantial failure in performance. But it was said that the charterer could have refused to accept the ship if the unseaworthiness had been discovered on or before her delivery and the shipowner had refused to comply with a request to put the matter right within a reasonable time.[23] Such refusal would have been evidence of the shipowner's intention to be no longer bound by the contract. After *The Hansa Nord*[24] a similar rule could, it is submitted, be applied where a seller of goods refused to put right a defect discovered before delivery, even though it did not amount to a breach of condition.[25]

---

[15] *Suisse Atlantique* case [1967] A.C. 361, 435; *cf. Rhymney Ry.* v. *Brecon & Merthyr Tydfil Junction Ry.* (1900) 69 L.J.Ch. 813, 819; *Decro-Wall International S.A.* v. *Practitioners in Marketing Ltd.* [1971] 1 W.L.R. 361, 369.

[16] *Flight* v. *Booth* (1834) 1 Bing.N.C. 370, 376.

[17] *Re Terry & White's Contract* (1886) 32 Ch.D. 14, 29; *Shepherd* v. *Croft* [1911] 1 Ch. 521, 531; *Re Belcham & Gawley's Contract* [1930] 1 Ch. 56.

[18] *Ante*, p. 673.

[19] *Freeth* v. *Burr* (1874) L.R. 9 C.P. 208, 213; *cf. Warinco A.G.* v. *Samor S.p.A.* [1979] 1 Lloyd's Rep. 450; contrast *The Aktion* [1987] 1 Lloyd's Rep. 283.

[20] *Bradley* v. *H. Newsom, Sons & Co.* [1919] A.C. 16, 52.

[21] (1831) 2 B. & Ad. 882.

[22] *Total Oil Great Britain Ltd.* v. *Thompson Garages (Biggin Hill) Ltd.* [1972] 1 Q.B. 318, 322.

[23] [1962] 2 Q.B. 26, 56, 64; *cf. Stanton* v. *Richardson* (1872) L.R. 7 C.P. 421, affirmed (1875) 45 L.J.C.P. 78. It is assumed that the breach is not of a purely trivial kind.

[24] [1976] Q.B. 44; *ante*, p. 697.

[25] *Mantovani* v. *Carapelli S.p.A.* [1978] 2 Lloyd's Rep. 63, 72 ("persisted in and amounted to a refusal"); affirmed [1980] 1 Lloyd's Rep. 375.

On the other hand, the mere fact that a party has deliberately refused what the contract required him to do is not sufficient to show that he intended no longer to be bound by the contract; for he may have acted in good faith, honestly but mistakenly believing that the terms of the contract justified his refusal.[26] In *Woodar Investment Development Ltd.* v. *Wimpey Construction U.K. Ltd.*[27] a contract for the sale of land provided that the purchaser should be entitled to withdraw if proceedings for the compulsory acquisition of the land "shall have commenced." He purported to withdraw on the ground that such proceedings *had already* commenced when the contract was made. In these circumstances, the contract did not, on its true construction, justify his withdrawal; but the House of Lords held that he had not repudiated, for he had acted in the bona fide belief that he was entitled to withdraw and had indicated throughout that he would perform if it should be decided that his interpretation of the contract was wrong. The decision was not unanimous, but it is respectfully submitted that the view of the majority is to be preferred. To regard a refusal to perform as a repudiation in such circumstances would unduly hamper parties in negotiating the settlement of a contractual dispute; for it would expose each of them to the danger that any forthright assertion of his view of their relative rights and duties could, if it turned out to be wrong, justify rescission by the other party. This would be particularly unfortunate if one of the parties had acted on legal advice which was later held by the court to be mistaken. In *Mersey Steel & Iron Co.* v. *Naylor Benzon & Co.*[28] a buyer of steel under an instalment contract refused, on the basis of such advice, to pay for one instalment. It was held that this refusal did not justify rescission by the seller since in these circumstances the buyer's refusal to pay was not evidence of his intention no longer to be bound by the contract.[29]

(c) SUBSTANTIAL BREACH. It does not follow from the cases just discussed that the injured party can *only* rescind when there is evidence of the other party's intention to be no longer bound by the contract. That party "may intend to fulfil [the contract] but may be determined to do so only in a manner substantially inconsistent with his obligations."[30] If so, the injured party can rescind: for example, a buyer can rescind a contract to deliver goods by instalments if over half the goods are seriously defective. He can do so even though the seller's breach is not deliberate or even negligent, and even though the seller protests that he intends to fulfil the contract.[31]

---

[26] *Spettabile Consorzio Veneziano, etc.*, v. *Northern Ireland Shipbuilding Co. Ltd.* (1919) 121 L.T. 628, 635; *James Shaffer Ltd.* v. *Findlay Durham & Brodie* [1953] 1 W.L.R. 106.

[27] [1980] 1 W.L.R. 277; Carter [1980] C.L.J. 256; Nicol and Rawlings, (1980) 43 M.L.R. 696; *cf. The Hazelmoor* [1980] 2 Lloyd's Rep. 351; *The Lutetian* [1982] 2 Lloyd's Rep. 140, 159; *Spencer* v. *Marchington* [1988] I.R.L.R. 392.

[28] (1884) 9 App.Cas. 434; *cf. Payzu Ltd.* v. *Saunders* [1919] 2 K.B. 581; *Peter Dumenil & Co. Ltd.* v. *James Ruddin Ltd.* [1953] 1 W.L.R. 815; *Sweet & Maxwell Ltd.* v. *Universal News Ltd.* [1964] 2 Q.B. 699; *Panchaud Frères S.A.* v. *R. Pagnan & Fratelli* [1974] 1 Lloyd's Rep. 394; *Toepfer* v. *Cremer* [1975] 2 Lloyd's Rep. 118; *Bunge GmbH* v. *C.C.V. Landbouwbeland* [1980] 1 Lloyd's Rep. 458.

[29] Lord Blackburn also refers (9 App.Cas. at p. 443) to the fact that the market price of the steel bought "had risen above the contract price." *cf. ante*, pp. 661, 678–679.

[30] *Smyth & Co.* v. *Bailey Son & Co.* [1940] 3 All E.R. 60, 72; *Peter Lind & Co. Ltd.* v. *Constable Hart & Co. Ltd.* [1979] 2 Lloyd's Rep. 248, 254; *The Splendid Sun* [1981] Q.B. 694, 713; *Bliss* v. *S.E. Thames Regional Health Authority* [1985] I.R.L.R. 308.

[31] *Millar's Karri & Jarrah Co. (1902)* v. *Weddell, Turner & Co.* (1909) 100 L.T. 128; *cf. Robert A. Munro & Co. Ltd.* v. *Meyer* [1930] 2 K.B. 312.

Similarly, where a shipowner wrongfully refused to perform a charterparty except in such a way as made further performance useless to the charterer, the latter was entitled to rescind. It made no difference that the shipowner subjectively intended to perform his part (it being in his interest to do so as freight rates had fallen).[32] Thus if the breach has the effect of substantially depriving the injured party of what he bargained for, it is not necessary to show that the party in breach intended not to fulfil the contract. But proof of such intention may be sufficient to establish the right to rescind where the effect of the breach is less drastic.[33]

There was formerly some support for a special rule in contracts of employment that "wilful disobedience of any lawful order is . . . a good ground of discharge."[34] But a single act of disobedience no longer of itself justifies dismissal. The test is whether the act "shows a determination to disregard any essential term of his contract"[35]: in other words, the courts now apply in employment cases the ordinary rules as to deliberate breaches. Under these rules a teacher's refusal to supervise school meals has been held sufficiently serious to justify dismissal[36]; but a secretary's refusal to stay at a board meeting when her immediate superior walked out did not have this effect.[37] Dismissal may of course, also be justified by a long course of unsatisfactory conduct[38] (as opposed to a single act of deliberate disobedience).

(6) Unilateral contracts and options

So far we have been concerned with the effects of one party's failure to perform a promise, whether or not the failure amounts to a breach. A further possibility is that a party may fail to perform some act which he has not promised to perform, but the performance of which is a contingent condition[39] of the other party's liability. Such a condition must be strictly complied with. The rule may be illustrated by the ordinary case of a unilateral contract.[40] If A promises B £100 if B walks from London to York, B must walk all the way to York before he is entitled to the £100.[41] The requirement of strict performance can be explained on the ground that A has no other remedy than to withhold performance. He cannot recover damages if B fails to complete the walk, since B has made no promise.

The rule that conditions which are not promises must always be strictly complied with gives rise to difficulties where the parties have not made it clear into which category a particular stipulation falls. In *United Dominions Trust (Commercial) Ltd.* v. *Eagle Aircraft Ltd.*[42] the defendants

---

[32] *Federal Commerce and Navigation* v. *Molena Alpha* [1979] A.C. 757; Carter [1979] C.L.J. 270.
[33] *Cf. Bowmakers (Commercial) Ltd.* v. *Smith* [1965] 1 W.L.R. 855, especially at pp. 858–859.
[34] *Turner* v. *Mason* (1845) 14 M. & W. 112, 117.
[35] *Gorse* v. *Durham C.C.* [1971] 1 W.L.R. 775, 781.
[36] *Gorse* v. *Durham C.C.* (*supra*)—but he was not dismissed; *cf. Miles* v. *Wakefield M.D.C.* [1987] A.C. 539, 559–560; *Wiluszynshki* v. *Tower Hamlets L.B.C.* [1989] I.C.R. 493; *post*, p. 719. In none of thses was the employee in fact dismissed.
[37] *Laws* v. *London Chronicle (Indicator Newspapers) Ltd.* [1959] 1 W.L.R. 698.
[38] *Pepper* v. *Webb* [1969] 1 W.L.R. 514; 85 L.Q.R. 325.
[39] *Ante*
[40] *Ante*
[41] It is assumed that A has not attempted to withdraw before B reaches York: see *ante*, p. 37.
[42] [1968] 1 W.L.R. 74.

wanted to dispose of two aircraft to Orion. The transaction was effected by a sale of the aircraft to the plaintiffs, who provided finance for the transaction and let the aircraft out on hire-purchase to Orion. The defendants at the same time undertook that, if the hire-purchase agreements were terminated before the whole amounts payable under them had been paid, they would repurchase the aircraft "when called upon to do so." This undertaking was subject to a "proviso" that the plaintiffs would notify the defendants within seven days of any default by Orion in the payment of hire rentals. Orion defaulted in August 1960 and the hire-purchase agreements were terminated in December 1960. But the plaintiffs did not notify the defendants of Orion's default until October 1960 and only called upon the defendants to repurchase in May 1961. In the Court of Appeal there was a conflict of opinion as to the nature of the "proviso." Two members of the court treated it as a condition and thought that failure to give notice *of Orion's default* discharged the defendants irrespective of its effects; while the third treated it as a promise and thought that the question whether the failure entitled the defendants to rescind, or only gave them a right to damages, depended on its effect, *i.e.* on the extent to which it prejudiced the defendants. But the court unanimously held that there was a further "implied condition" in the contract that the notice *calling on the defendants to repurchase* must be given within a reasonable time. This condition was not a promise, for, as the plaintiffs had not promised to call on the defendants to repurchase at all, they could not have promised to call on them within a reasonable time. As the condition had not been strictly complied with, the defendants were not bound to repurchase the aircraft: they did not have to show that failure to comply with the condition prejudiced them seriously or at all.[43] Yet where a stipulation is classified as a *promise* such prejudice must generally[44] be shown by a party who seeks to rescind. The question whether a stipulation is to be classified as a promise or as a condition may therefore be of crucial importance. It is a question of construction, on which the authorities give little guidance.

The requirement that conditions which are not promises must be strictly complied with also applies to options to purchase. If the grantee fails to comply in any respect with a condition to which the exercise of the option is subject, he cannot enforce the option.[45] It makes no difference that the failure causes only insignificant prejudice, or none at all, to the grantor. Moreover, in the case of an option the rule applies even though the condition is the performance by the grantee of an obligation under another term of the agreement in which the option is contained. Thus in *West Country Cleaners (Falmouth) Ltd.* v. *Saly*[46] a lease gave a tenant an option

---

[43] For criticism, see Atiyah, 31 M.L.R. 332; but the decision was approved in *United Scientific Holdings Ltd.* v. *Burnley B.C.* [1978] A.C. 904, 928, 945, 951. The contract had affinities to suretyship; if it had actually been one of suretyship, the delay in giving notice of Orion's default would probably have discharged the defendants: *cf. Midland Counties Finance Motor Co.* v. *Slade* [1951] 1 K.B. 346.

[44] *i.e.* in cases falling within the general rule discussed at pp. 670–680, *ante*, as opposed to the exceptions discussed at pp. 680–709, *ante*.

[45] *Hare* v. *Nicholl* [1966] 2 Q.B. 160. The rule may be excluded by the terms of the option: see *Millichamp* v. *Jones* [1982] 1 W.L.R. 1422, where the term which the grantee failed to perform was not a condition of the exercise of the option, but a promissory condition of the contract resulting from that exercise: *cf. ante*, p. 663.

[46] [1966] 1 W.L.R. 1485.

to renew "providing all covenants herein contained have been duly observed and performed." The tenant had committed minor breaches of his covenant to paint the interior of his premises; and it was held that he was not entitled to exercise the option, even though it did not appear that the landlord was seriously prejudiced by the breaches. This application of the rule has been explained on the ground that "an option of this character is a privilege—a right which has always been treated by the law as requiring complete compliance with the terms and conditions upon which the option is to be exercised."[47] The severity of the rule is, however, mitigated where the tenant was at one time in breach but has cured that breach by the time of the exercise of the option: *e.g.* if by that time he has paid off rent which had at an earlier stage been overdue. Such "spent" breaches do not prevent him from exercising the option.[48]

5. Limitations on the Right to Rescind

The right to rescind may be lost or limited by waiver (or election), execution of the contract, voluntary acceptance of a benefit or wrongful prevention of performance, and under the Apportionment Act 1870. Where there are several breaches, each giving rise to a right to rescind, the fact that one such right has been lost does not necessarily bar the other or others.[49]

(1) Waiver or election

(a) DIFFERENT SENSES OF "WAIVER." Waiver is used in a number of senses, two of which[50] are relevant to the present discussion.

(i) *Waiver in the sense of election.* A party who is entitled to rescind may indicate that he will nevertheless perform his part of the contract. He is then said to have waived his right to rescind, or to have elected[51] to affirm the contract. For example, in *Bentsen* v. *Taylor*[52] a ship arrived at her port of loading one month after the date stipulated in the charterparty. The charterer could have refused to load on account of this delay, but said that he would nevertheless load, and then refused to do so. It was held that he was liable for failure to load as he had waived his right to rescind.[53] Conversely, in *The Kachenjunga*[54] a charterer in breach of contract nominated a port which was unsafe because of the Gulf war between Iran and Iraq, but the shipowner nevertheless pressed him to load there, and then sailed away. It was held that the shipowner would have been liable in damages, if he had not been protected from such liability by a "war clause" in the charterparty. On the same principle, a shipowner loses his right to put an end to a charterparty under an express term entitling him to withdraw the ship for

---

47 *Ibid.* p. 1486.
48 *Bass Holdings Ltd.* v. *Morton Music Ltd.* [1988] Ch. 493.
49 See *Kwei Tek Chao* v. *British Traders* [1954] 2 Q.B. 459.
50 For other senses, see *ante*, pp. 98–99.
51 *The Kachenjunga* [1990] 1 Lloyd's Rep. 391, 397–398.
52 [1893] 2 Q.B. 274.
53 *Ibid.* at pp. 283, 285.
54 [1990] 1 Lloyd's Rep. 391.

late payment of hire if he accepts such a payment knowing that the time for making it has passed[55]; and a landlord loses the right to forfeit a lease for breach of covenant by the tenant if, knowing of the breach, he makes a demand for rent[56]; and a buyer of goods may lose the right to reject for breach of *one* implied condition if he has agreed with the seller that he will *only* reject for a breach of a *different* implied condition.[57] An important characteristic of waiver in the sense of election is that it only bars the injured party's right to rescind: it does not deprive him of his right to damages for the breach. Thus the shipowner in *The Kachenjunga* would have been entitled to damages if his ship had entered the port and suffered damage there as a result of the charterer's breach.[58]

(ii) *Distinguished from total waiver.* The expression "total waiver" will here be used to refer to the situation in which a contracting party purports wholly to abandon rights under the contract. It differs from waiver in the sense of election in that the injured party indicates that he is giving up, not merely his right to rescind, but also his right to damages[59] or to performance. Section 11(2) of the Sale of Goods Act 1979 recognised both types of waiver in providing that "where a contract of sale is subject to a condition to be fulfilled by the seller, the buyer may *waive* the condition, *or* may *elect* to treat the breach of condition as a breach of warranty and not as a ground for treating the contract as repudiated."[60] Here "waive" is used to refer to total waiver (*i.e.* an abandonment by the buyer of his rights to rescind and to claim damages); while "elect" refers to waiver in the sense of election (*i.e.* to the buyer's abandonment of the right to rescind, while keeping alive his right to damages). It might be better if the courts were to use "waiver" only to refer to total waiver, and to use some other term, such as "election" or "affirmation" to refer to waiver in the sense of election.[61] They have in fact used "waiver" to refer to them both, perhaps because of an important similarity between the two processes; but unfortunately this usage also obscures an equally important difference between them. It will be convenient, in discussing these points, to refer to the two processes respectively as "total waiver" and "waiver in the sense of election."

(b) Requirement of representation. The similarity between the two processes is that the operation of each depends on a "clear and unequivo-

---

[55] *The Brimnes* [1975] Q.B. 929, 954–956; *The Libyaville* [1975] 1 Lloyd's Rep. 537, 554. But there is no waiver if the late payment is made into the owner's bank and rejected by him as soon as he learns of the payment: *The Laconia* [1977] A.C. 850; and acceptance of an underpayment does not amount to waiver if there is still a reasonable possibility that the balance may be paid in time: *The Mihalios Xilas* [1979] 1 W.L.R. 1018.

[56] *David Blackstone Ltd.* v. *Burnetts* [1973] 1 W.L.R. 1487; *Expert Clothing Service & Sales Ltd.* v. *Hillgate House Ltd.* [1986] Ch. 340, 359. For an illustration of waiver by a purchaser of leasehold land see *Aquis Estates Ltd.* v. *Minton* [1975] 1 W.L.R. 1452, 1596.

[57] *S. N. Kurkjan (Commodity) Brokers Ltd.* v. *Marketing Exchange for Africa Ltd.* [1986] 2 Lloyd's Rep. 614.

[58] [1990] 1 Lloyd's Rep. 391, 393, 397, 401.

[59] *Ets. Soules & Cie.* v. *International Trade Development Co. Ltd.* [1980] 1 Lloyd's Rep. 129, 137–138; *cf. Banning* v. *Wright* [1972] 1 W.L.R. 972.

[60] Italics supplied.

[61] *Cf. Kammins Ballroom Ltd.* v. *Zenith Investments (Torquay) Ltd.* [1971] A.C. 850, 882–883; *State Trading Corp. of India* v. *Cie. Française d'Importation et de Distribution* [1983] 2 Lloyd's Rep. 679, 681.

cal" representation.[62] In relation to total waiver, this requirement is discussed in Chapter 3.[63] Our present concern is with waiver in the sense of election: this also requires "an unequivocal act or statement"[64] by which the injured party clearly indicates that he does not intend to rescind, but to affirm, the contract. The reference to an "unequivocal act" shows that the injured party need not make an express statement of his intention to affirm: it is enough if he does some positive act from which that intention can be inferred. If the intention does not clearly appear from his words or conduct, there is no waiver. This is, for example, often the position where the injured party accepts defective performance subject to an express reservation of his rights[65] (though where several grounds of rescission exist and the reservation refers to only some of these, it will not preclude waiver of the others[66]). It has, similarly, been held that the right to rescind was not lost by waiver where a vendor of land, after the purchaser should have performed, said that he would consider a request for an extension of time[67]; where a buyer to whom short delivery had been made called for a "full tender"[68]; where a landlord, after the tenant had committed a breach of covenant, sent him a "negotiating document" designed to resolve the dispute[69]; and where an employee continued, after the employer's breach, to accept wages for such time as was reasonably necessary for him to consider his position.[70] Nor is the right to rescind lost by mere failure to exercise it: such failure is not normally a sufficiently clear indication that the right will not be exercised.[71] But where, as a matter of business, it is reasonable to expect the injured party to act promptly, unreasonable delay in exercising the right to rescind may give rise to the inference that the contract has been affirmed.[72]

(c) NO REQUIREMENT OF ACTION IN RELIANCE. In discussing total waiver, we saw in Chapter 3 that its operation depended on some action in reliance on the statement giving rise to the waiver by the party to whom it was made.[73] There is no similar requirement for the operation of waiver in the

---

62 *Peyman* v. *Lanjani* [1985] Ch. 457, 501; *The Kachenjunga* [1990] 1 Lloyd's Rep. 391, 399; *The Great Marine (No. 1)* [1990] 2 Lloyd's Rep. 245, 249.

63 *Ante*, pp. 102–105.

64 *The Mihalios Xilas* [1979] 1 W.L.R. 1018, 1024; *cf. The Balder London* [1980] 2 Lloyd's Rep. 489; *Bremer Handelsgesellschaft mbH* v. *Finagrain (etc.) S.A.* [1981] 2 Lloyd's Rep. 259, 266; *Cobec Brazilian Trading & Warehousing Corp.* v. *Alfred C. Toepfer* [1983] 2 Lloyd's Rep. 386, 392.

65 *Bremer Handelsgesellschaft mbH* v. *Deutsche Conti Handelsgesellschaft mbH* [1983] 2 Lloyd's Rep. 45; *cf. Nova Petroleum International Establishment* v. *Trican Trading Ltd.* [1989] 1 Lloyd's Rep. 312.

66 *The Wise* [1989] 2 Lloyd's Rep. 451.

67 *Prosper Homes* v. *Hambros Bank Executor & Trustee Co.* (1979) 39 P. & C.R. 395.

68 *Cobec Brazilian Trading & Warehousing Corp.* v. *Alfred C. Toepfer* [1983] 2 Lloyd's Rep. 386.

69 *Expert Clothing Services & Sales Ltd.* v. *Hillgate House Ltd.* [1986] Ch. 340.

70 *Bliss* v. *S.E. Thames Regional Health Authority*, [1987] I.C.R. 700.

71 See *Tyrer & Co.* v. *Hessler & Co.* (1902) 7 Com.Cas. 166; *Allen* v. *Robles* [1969] 1 W.L.R. 1193; *cf. Bremer Handelsgesellschaft mbH* v. *Deutsche Conti Handelsgesellschaft mbH*, *supra*, n. 65; *The Scaptrade* [1981] 2 Lloyd's Rep. 425, 430 (affirmed without reference to this point [1983] 2 A.C. 694).

72 *The Scaptrade* (*supra*, n. 71) [1981] 2 Lloyd's Rep. at p. 430 relying on the analogy of cases of fraudulent misrepresentation (*ante*, p. 345); *The Laconia* [1977] A.C. 850, 872; *The Balder London* [1980] 2 Lloyd's Rep. 489, 491–493; *ante*, p. 681.

73 *Ante*, pp. 105–106.

sense of election. The distinction is recognised in a number of cases[74] and the explanation for it seems to be as follows. In cases of total waiver, the injured party makes a promise wholly to give up his right to some or all of the performance due to him under the contract. Prima facie, this cannot be any benefit to him or any detriment to the party in breach, so that the promise is unsupported by consideration.[75] Action in reliance on the promise is necessary as a substitute for, or alternative to, consideration so as to give at least some legal effect to the promise.[76] In the case of waiver in the sense of election, the injured party has only indicated that he is giving up one particular remedy (*i.e.* rescission). Even if such an indication can be said to amount to a promise not to rescind, the process has never been considered to give rise to any problems of consideration.[77] The injured party is not *necessarily* in a worse position if he elects, instead of rescinding, to keep the contract in being and to claim damages. This *may* be more beneficial to him than rescission; and this possibility is sufficient to satisfy the requirement of consideration.[78]

Thus it is submitted that the difference in the requirements for the two types of waiver is supported by both authority and principle. It is, however, obscured by a number of factors. The first of these is the unfortunate use of "waiver" to describe both processes. This has resulted in the requirement of reliance being sometimes unnecessarily stated where waiver in the sense of election was under discussion, (though inapplicable for want of a sufficiently clear representation)[79]; and occasionally such cases have been argued as if all the requirements of total waiver (including that of reliance) had to be satisfied.[80] The second is that some cases raise issues as to both types of waiver[81]; and in these the issue of reliance tends to be discussed generally, even in relation to the type of waiver to which it is not strictly relevant. The third is that "waiver" is sometimes used interchangeably with "estoppel,"[82] the operation of which does depend on action in reliance. That requirement is therefore assumed to exist where the decision can be based on either of these grounds and the court is not prepared to distinguish between them.[83]

(d) WHETHER KNOWLEDGE REQUIRED. There is some conflict in the authorities on the question whether a party can be said to have "waived" a right

---

[74] *Edm. J. M. Mertens & Co. P.V.B.A.* v. *Veevoeder Import Export Vimex B.V.* [1979] 2 Lloyd's Rep. 372, 384; *The Athos* [1981] 2 Lloyd's Rep. 74, 87–88, affirmed on this point [1983] 1 Lloyd's Rep. 127; *The Scaptrade* [1981] 2 Lloyd's Rep. 425, 430, affirmed on this point [1983] A.C. 694; *Peter Cremer* v. *Granaria B.V.* [1981] 2 Lloyd's Rep. 583, 589; *Peyman* v. *Lanjani* [1985] Ch. 457, 493, 500–501; *The Uhenbels* [1986] 2 Lloyd's Rep. 294, 297; *The Kachenjunga* [1990] 1 Lloyd's Rep. 391, 399.

[75] *Ante*, pp. 94, 96–97.

[76] *Ante*, pp. 98–111.

[77] *The Kachenjunga* [1990] 1 Lloyd's Rep. 391, 398.

[78] *Cf. ante*, pp. 96, 116–118.

[79] *e.g. The Eurometal* [1981] 1 Lloyd's Rep. 337, 341; *cf. Bremer Handelsgesellschaft mbH* v. *Finagrain (etc.) S.A.* [1981] 2 Lloyd's Rep. 259, 265.

[80] See *The Post Chaser* [1981] 2 Lloyd's Rep. 695, esp. at p. 702 where Robert Goff J. points out the difference between the two doctrines; *The Manila* [1988] 3 All E.R. 843, 854, where the point seems not be have been argued; *The Wise* [1989] 2 Lloyd's Rep. 451.

[81] *e.g. Bremer Handelsgesellschaft mbH* v. *C. Mackprang Jr.* [1979] 1 Lloyd's Rep. 221; *Bremer Handelsgesellschaft mbH* v. *Deutsche Conti Handelsesellschaft mbH* [1983] 2 Lloyd's Rep. 45; *Peter Cremer* v. *Granaria B.V.* [1981] 2 Lloyd's Rep. 583.

[82] *Cf. ante*, p. 109.

[83] See *The Wise* [1989] 2 Lloyd's Rep. 451, 460.

to rescind if he does not actually know of the existence of the right. Since the basis of waiver in the sense of election is that the injured party must be "taken to have affirmed"[84] the contract, it should follow that this type of waiver does require knowledge by the injured party of the existence of the right to rescind.[85] This view is supported by *Peyman* v. *Lanjani*[86] where the defendant had obtained a leasehold interest in a restaurant by means of a fraudulent impersonation, and later agreed to sell that interest to the plaintiff. By reason of the fraud, the defendant's title was defective and the plaintiff, with knowledge of the fraud but not of the fact that it gave him the right to rescind, paid £10,000 and went into possession of the restaurant as the defendant's manager. It was held that he had not lost the right to rescind; and one reason[87] for this conclusion was that he could not have elected to affirm the contract until he became aware, not merely of the *facts* giving rise to the right to rescind, but of the *existence of the right* itself.[88] This reasoning does not apply to "total" waiver[89] which, far from being an affirmation of the original contract, generally amounts to an abandonment, or at least to a variation, of it.[90] Statements to the effect that a person can "waive" rights without being aware of their existence are best regarded as referring to such "total" waiver,[91] which is based on action in reliance by the party *to* whom the representation is made rather than on the subjective intention of the party *by* whom it is made. Moreover, it is possible for one party (A) so to conduct himself as to give the other (B) reasonable grounds for thinking that A has affirmed the contract; and B may form this belief even though A does not know of his right to rescind. If B proceeds to act in reliance on A's apparent affirmation, A may (even though he has not actually affirmed) be estopped from denying that he has waived the right to rescind.[92] The *effects* of such an estoppel are the same as those of waiver in the sense of election, and both require an unequivocal representation. Their requirements differ, however, in that this type of waiver requires knowledge by the injured party of the existence of the right to rescind but no reliance on the representation by the party in breach, while an estoppel of the kind described above does not seem to require any such knowledge[93] but does require action in reliance. A party who does not

---

[84] *Kwei Tek Chao* v. *British Traders & Shippers Ltd.* [1954] 2 Q.B. 459, 477.

[85] *Panchaud Frères S.A.* v. *Etablissements General Grain Co. Ltd.* [1970] 1 Lloyd's Rep. 53, 57; The *Mihalios Xilas* [1979] 1 W.L.R. 1018, 1023; *Trustees of Henry Smith's Charity* v. *Willson* [1983] Q.B. 316, 328; *Cobec Brazilian Trading & Warehousing Corp.* v. *Alfred C. Toepfer* [1983] 2 Lloyd's Rep. 386, 392. *Chrisdell Ltd.* v. *Johnson* [1987] 19 H.L.R. 406; *The Manila* [1988] 3 All E.R. 843; *The Kachenjunga* [1990] 1 Lloyd's Rep. 391, 398.

[86] [1985] Ch. 457.

[87] A second was that there had been no unequivocal representation: see *ibid.* pp. 501–502.

[88] Earlier decisions, discussed in *Peyman* v. *Lanjani*, were in conflict on the question whether the injured party could affirm when he was aware only of the facts but not of the right. In *The Kachenjunga* [1990] 1 Lloyd's Rep. 391, 398 it was not necessary to discuss the conflict on this point since the injured party knew of the facts giving rise to the right to rescind *and* of the existence of the right.

[89] A point apparently overlooked in *The Superhulls Cover Case (No. 2)* [1990] 2 Lloyd's Rep. 431, 449.

[90] See *ante*, pp. 98–101.

[91] See *Bremer Handelsgesellschaft mbH* v. *C. Mackprang Jr.* [1979] 1 Lloyd's Rep. 221, 230; contrast *ibid.* p. 229; the case involved *both* types of waiver.

[92] See *Peyman* v. *Lanjani* [1985] Ch. 457, 495, 501.

[93] *i.e.* of the existence of the right: see *Peyman* v. *Lanjani*, *supra*, at pp. 495, 500. According to *National Westminster Bank* v. *Hart* [1983] Q.B. 773, knowledge or notice of *the facts* is

know of the existence of the right to rescind may also lose it on one of the other grounds to be discussed below.[94]

(2) Part performance of the contract

(a) GENERALLY NO BAR. The fact that the contract has been partly performed does not of itself bar the right to rescind. For example, rescission is available where there has been partial performance of an entire obligation, as in *Sumpter* v. *Hedges*.[95] Similarly, express provisions for determination often operate after part performance of the contract.[96]

The above illustrations concern *exceptions* to the requirement of serious failure in performance. In cases to which that requirement *applies*, the courts do sometimes take the fact of part performance into account so as to conclude that the failure is not sufficiently serious to give rise to a right to rescind at all.[97] But once the failure is is found to be of the required degree of seriousness, the injured party will not lose the right to refuse to perform or to accept further performance[98] merely because the contract has been partly performed: for example, in *Aerial Advertising Co.* v. *Batchelor's Peas Ltd.*[99] rescission was allowed after such part performance. Some difficulty is, however, caused in this connection by *Thorpe* v. *Fasey*.[1] Land was sold on the terms that it was to be conveyed in lots as portions of the purchase-money were paid. After some such payments and conveyances had been made, the vendor sought to rescind the contract on account of the purchaser's undue delay in making the remaining payments. The claim was rejected on the ground that the vendor must either rescind *in toto* or not at all. It is not clear from the report exactly what relief the vendor claimed. If he sought the return of the land already conveyed, a valid objection might have been that the purchaser had improved this, so that the vendor would be unjustly enriched by getting it back.[2] If (more probably) he simply sought cancellation of the unperformed balance of the contract, the reasoning is inconsistent with cases[3] in which such relief was granted to a victim of serious breach in spite of partial performance. The refusal to allow rescission in *Thorpe* v. *Fasey* is better explained on the ground that the remedy was never available at all as there was no serious breach or failure in performance.[4]

(b) EFFECT OF ACCEPTANCE ON BREACH OF CONDITION. Although part performance does not usually bar the right to rescind, there is a rule that where this right is based on a breach of condition, it may be lost by reason of the execution of the contract. This rule is most clearly illustrated by section 11(4) of the Sale of Goods Act 1979, which provides that where a

---

necessary; but in *The Kachenjunga* [1990] 1 Lloyd's Rep. 391, 399 there is said to be no need for "particular knowledge."

94 *e.g. infra*, after n. 4.

95 [1898] 1 Q.B. 673; *ante*, p. 684.

96 *e.g. ante*, p. 680.

97 *e.g.* in *Boone* v. *Eyre* (1779) 1 Hy.Bl. 273n., *ante*, p. 671.

98 For the effect of part performance on his right to recover back money paid, see *post*, pp. 927–929.

99 [1938] 2 All E.R. 786; *ante*, p. 679.

1 [1949] Ch. 649.

2 *Cf. Boyd & Forrest* v. *Glasgow & S.W. Ry. Co.* 1915 S.C.(H.L.) 20, *ante*, p. 342.

3 *e.g. supra*, at n. 99.

4 As time was not of the essence of the contract; *post*, p. 726.

buyer has "accepted"[5] goods under a contract which is not severable[6] "the breach of a condition to be fulfilled by the seller can only be treated as a breach of warranty, and not as a ground for rejecting the goods and treating the contract as repudiated." This rule differs from waiver in the sense of election (discussed above) and voluntary acceptance of a benefit (to be discussed below) in that it can apply even though the injured party has no knowledge of the breach.[7] A buyer of defective goods will, for example, be deemed to have accepted them if he retains them for more than a reasonable time without intimating to the seller that he has rejected them; this may, indeed, be so only where he has had a reasonable *opportunity* of examining the goods,[8] but he may lose the right to reject the goods even though he has not actually discovered the defect.[9] The general rule, then, is clear: "acceptance" bars the right to rescind a contract for breach of condition. But the rule is subject to one, and may be subject to two, qualifications.

(i) *Incorporated misrepresentation.* If a misrepresentation made before the contract is incorporated in the contract as a condition, the right to rescind the contract *for misrepresentation* survives and may be exercised in spite of the fact that the contract has been performed.[10] A buyer of goods might be able to exercise this right even though his right to rescind *for breach*[11] was barred by "acceptance." But the right to rescind for misrepresenation is subject to the court's discretion[12] to declare the contract subsisting and to award damages in lieu of rescission. It seems probable that the court will generally follow this course where the right to rescind for breach has been lost by "acceptance," though there may be cases of hardship to a buyer in which the court would not wish to confine him to a remedy in damages.

(ii) *Serious breach.* In Chapter 7 we saw that there was a "strong, though rebuttable, presumption"[13] that exemption clauses were not to be construed to cover certain particularly serious breaches. The distinction between various kinds of breaches there drawn is also relevant in considering the scope of the rule that the right to rescind for breach of condition is barred by acceptance.

One type of serious breach is that which makes "performance totally different from that which the contract contemplates."[14] As a matter of general common law, "execution" of a contract does not bar the right to rescind for a breach of this kind. This appears from *Dakin* v. *Oxley*,[15] where the actual decision was that a charterer could not refuse to pay freight, after the goods had been carried to their destination, merely because the goods had arrived there in a damaged condition; but the court

---

[5] *Ante*, p. 344.

[6] *Ante*, p. 685.

[7] *The Kachenjunga* [1990] 1 Lloyd's Rep. 391, 398.

[8] Sale of Goods Act 1979, ss.34, 35.

[9] *e.g. Bernstein* v. *Pamson Motors* (*Golders Green*) *Ltd.* [1987] 2 All E.R. 220; Reynolds, 104 L.Q.R. 16; *cf. Shine* v. *General Guarantee Corp.* [1988] 1 All E.R. 911 (hire-purchase).

[10] Misrepresentation Act 1967, s.1(*a*); *ante*, p. 336.

[11] For the distinction between this right and the right to rescind for misrepresentation, see *ante*, pp. 330, 336.

[12] Misrepresentation Act 1967, s.2(2); *ante*, pp. 320, 337.

[13] *Suisse Atlantique* case [1967] 1 A.C. 361, 427; *ante*, p. 216.

[14] *Suisse Atlantique* case, *supra*, at p. 393.

[15] (1864) 15 C.B.(N.S.) 646.

added that he would not be liable where "a valuable picture had arrived as a piece of spoilt canvas, cloth in rags, or crockery in broken shreds, iron all or almost rust, rice fermented or hides rotten."[16] The same principle applies where the seller's breach is a breach of condition and its effect is wholly to deprive the buyer of what he bargained for. In *Rowland* v. *Divall*[17] the defendant sold a car to the plaintiff which, unknown to either of them, had been stolen. The defendant was in breach of the implied condition that he had a right to sell the car but the plaintiff did various acts amounting to "acceptance" of the car[18] before it was traced by the police. It was held that the plaintiff could nevertheless rescind the contract (and so recover back the price paid) as "he did not get what he paid for—namely a car to which he would have title."[19] It is submitted that the position would be the same where beans were delivered under a contract to sell peas.[20] In such a case the buyer will not lose his right to rescind *merely* because his conduct amounts to "acceptance,"[21] or would have amounted to "acceptance" if the seller had delivered peas which were not in accordance with the contract. Of course if the buyer knows that beans have been delivered and decides to keep them it may be possible to infer a new contract to buy beans.[22] But "acceptance" can take place without any knowledge of the breach, and "acceptance" without such knowledge should not (it is submitted) deprive the buyer of his right to rescind where the seller has delivered something "totally different" from the thing which he has contracted to sell.

The rule of construction discussed in Chapter 7 can also apply where the breach is serious in the wider sense of causing *substantial* prejudice to the injured party without making the performance rendered *totally* different from that bargained for.[23] In such a case, the right to rescind may be lost by execution of the contract in spite of the fact that the breach is sufficiently serious to prevent the party in breach from relying on an exemption clause. For example, a defect in goods may be sufficiently serious to justify the buyer in rejecting and to deprive the seller (as a matter of construction) of the benefit of an exemption clause. But the breach may nevertheless not be serious enough to allow the buyer to rescind after "acceptance" so as to recover back the money which he has paid.[24]

There are, finally, cases in which a party is prevented from relying on an exemption clause, because he has broken a fundamental term,[25] even though the breach does not deprive the injured party of what he bargained for at all: this would be the position where goods are safely carried to their destination in a ship which has deviated.[26] There is no doubt that in such a case the cargo-owner can rescind the contract. But he may nevertheless have to make some payment under the rules to be discussed below.[27]

---

[16] *Ibid.* p. 667; *cf. The Caspian Sea* [1980] 1 W.L.R. 48.
[17] [1923] 2 K.B. 500; and see further *post*, p. 929.
[18] He had painted it and sold it to a third party.
[19] [1923] 2 K.B. at p. 504.
[20] *Chanter* v. *Hopkins* (1838) 4 M. & W. 399, 404.
[21] For the meaning of "acceptance," see *ante*, p. 344.
[22] *Charterhouse Credit Co. Ltd.* v. *Tolly* [1963] 2 Q.B. 683, 710.
[23] *Ante*, p. 208.
[24] *Cf. Yeoman Credit Ltd.* v. *Apps* [1962] 2 Q.B. 508.
[25] *Ante*, p. 207.
[26] *Ante*, p. 210. *Cf. ante*, p. 704.
[27] *Post*, p. 718.

(3) Voluntary acceptance of benefit

This idea does not strictly limit, but rather attenuates, the right to rescind. Under it, the person who receives partial or defective performance does not lose the right to rescind *the contract*; but if he "voluntarily" accepts the defective performance he must make some payment for it. Thus in *Christy* v. *Row*[28] a contract was made to carry coal to Hamburg. The ship was prevented by restraints of princes from reaching Hamburg, and the master *at the request of the consignees* delivered some of the coal at Gluckstadt. It was held that the shipowner could recover freight in respect of the coal so delivered. In this case the shipowner recovered the full freight, but later cases state the rule that he is only entitled to freight *pro rata itineris*, *i.e.* for freight at the contract rate for the proportion of the voyage originally undertaken which was actually accomplished.[29]

The present principle applies only if the benefit is accepted "voluntarily." A person is not considered to accept a benefit "voluntarily" if he merely takes possession of his own property. Thus a shipowner who discharges cargo at an intermediate port cannot recover freight *pro rata* merely because the cargo-owner has under protest taken possession of his own goods there.[30] In *Sumpter* v. *Hedges*[31] the builder's claim for the reasonable value of his work was dismissed on similar grounds. Such a claim could only succeed if a "new contract" to pay a reasonable sum could be inferred. No such inference could be drawn from the mere fact that the defendant had reoccupied his own land with the partly completed buildings on it; he had no real "option whether he will take the benefit of the work done or not."[32] He did, however, "voluntarily" make use of certain loose materials left by the builder on the site and was held liable for the reasonable value of these materials.

The object of the requirement of a "new contract" is, no doubt, to protect the party receiving the partial or defective performance, who may be prejudiced by having to pay *pro rata* or a reasonable sum. He may have suffered loss in consequence of the failure in performance, and, if the failure does not amount to a breach, rescission may be his only remedy. Even if there has been a breach, the damages legally recoverable for it may fall short of the actual loss suffered. The victim may have stipulated for complete performance before payment precisely in order to protect himself against these risks.

On the other hand the failure in performance may not cause any loss at all,[33] or it may cause a loss worth much less than the value of the partial or defective performance. In such cases the requirement of a "new contract" may lead to the unjust enrichment of the party by whom such performance has been received. Under the rule in *Sumpter* v. *Hedges* a landowner may get nearly completed buildings for nothing. This did not actually happen in

---

28 (1808) 1 Taunt. 300; *cf. Lambourn* v. *Cruden* (1841) 2 M. & G. 253, 256.

29 See *Scrutton on Charterparties* (19th ed.), p. 343. In exceptional circumstances the proper measure of recovery may be a reasonable sum, assessed independently of the contract rate: *Mitchell* v. *Darthez* (1836) 2 Bing.N.C. 555. Obviously, a strict geographical apportionment would be inappropriate where part of the journey was much more expensive than the rest, *e.g.* because it led through the Panama Canal.

30 *Metcalfe* v. *Britannia Ironworks Co.* (1877) 2 Q.B.D. 423; *cf. ante*, p. 684.

31 [1898] 1 Q.B. 673; *ante*, p. 684.

32 [1898] 1 Q.B. 673, 676.

33 *Infra*, at n. 36.

the leading case itself, in which considerable payments had been made to the builder on account of the work.[34] But in *Bolton* v. *Mahadeva*[35] a builder recovered nothing for his defective performance of a contract to install a central heating system for £560, even though no part of this sum had been paid to him, the defects in his work cost only £170 to put right, and the house-owner's other damages were assessed at £15. Again, where a shipowner discharges goods at an intermediate port, the cargo-owner may get the benefit of having them carried a considerable distance for nothing. This possibility is strikingly illustrated by a case in which it was held that the cargo-owner was not bound to pay anything even though the failure to carry the goods to their destination apparently benefited him, the goods having been sold for *more* at the intermediate port than they were worth at the agreed destination.[36] At the same time the requirement of a new contract may bear very harshly on the party conferring the benefit; and therefore the requirement that acceptance of the benefit must be "voluntary" so as to support the inference of a new contract is, or may be, modified in a number of situations.

The clearest modification of the requirement can be seen in cases in which a seller of goods delivers the wrong quantity, *e.g.* a quantity less than that contracted for. In such a case the buyer can generally reject the goods[37] but if he "accepts" them he "must pay for them at the contract rate."[38] This acceptance need not be "voluntary" in the full sense, for the buyer may do acts amounting to "acceptance" before he knows of the defect in delivery.[39]

A second situation in which the requirement of "voluntary" acceptance may be modified arises where a carrier by sea deviates.[40] This undoubtedly gives the cargo-owner the right to rescind; but he may not exercise this right and may accept the goods after the carrier has carried them to their agreed destination. This acceptance of the goods is no more "voluntary" than taking possession of goods which have been discharged without their owner's consent at an intermediate port; but dicta in the House of Lords in *Hain SS. Co. Ltd.* v. *Tate & Lyle Ltd.*[41] support the view that the shipowner may in such a case be entitled to a reasonable freight. This is not necessarily the same as the stipulated freight, so that the risk of any fall in freight rates would be on the carrier; but it seems most unlikely that he would be allowed to rely on the deviation to secure the benefit of any rise in freight rates.

---

[34] The value of the work done is stated to be "about £333" and the builder had received £219 (67 L.J.Q.B. 545) or £119 plus two horses worth £100 (46 W.R. 464). Hence the total enrichment of the defendant appears to have been at the most £114, against which any damages suffered by him should be set off. The actual result may not be unjust; certainly the builder's claim for £230 (78 L.T. 378) or £222 (46 W.R. 464) seems excessive.

[35] [1972] 1 W.L.R. 1009.

[36] *Hopper* v. *Burness* (1876) 1 C.P.D. 137; it was said that there was no hardship to the shipowner as "the proper remedy is by insurance of freight" (p. 141).

[37] *Ante*, p. 684.

[38] Sale of Goods Act 1979, s.30(1). (It is assumed that the goods are not "unsolicited" within Unsolicited Goods and Services Act 1971, s.6).

[39] *Ante*, p. 715.

[40] *Ante*, p. 210.

[41] (1936) 41 Com.Cas 350, 358, 367, doubting contrary dicta in the Court of Appeal 34 Com.-Cas. 259, 285. The dicta in the House of Lords are accepted in *Scrutton on Charterparties*, (19th ed.), p. 262, and in Carver, *Carriage of Goods by Sea* (13th ed.), para. 1197. *cf.* *Bornman* v. *Tooke* (1808) 1 Camp. 376.

A third possible modification of the requirement that acceptance of the benefit must be "voluntary" may exist where breaches of a contract of employment are committed in the course of an industrial dispute. Such a breach may take the form, not only of an outright refusal to work, but also of a refusal merely to carry out certain specified tasks. If (as will often be the case) the refusal amounts to a repudiatory breach,[42] the employer is at common law entitled to dismiss the employee. But he may not exercise that power and instead follow one of the three other courses of action. First, he may voluntarily accept such services as the employee is willing to render. In that case, he can at the very least deduct from the employee's wages, by way of damages, any loss which he has suffered as a result of the breach.[43] Even if he has not suffered any loss, he can deduct from the employee's pay such part of the agreed wages as is attributable to the work which the employee has refused to perform[44]: at least that amount will not have been earned by reason of the employee's failure to perform a condition precedent.[45] Secondly, he may tell the employee that he declines to accept the services (falling short of those due under the contract) which the employee is prepared to render, and actually does render. In that event, the employee is not entitled to any pay, even if the employer does not physically prevent him from rendering the services.[46] Thirdly, the employer may accept the services which the employee is prepared to render, and do so, not voluntarily, but "of necessity"[47]: he may do this either because he has no practical choice (where he cannot in fact prevent the employee from gaining access to his place of work), or because he is required to accept the services offered in order to mitigate his loss.[48] In such a case there has clearly been no "voluntary" acceptance of a benefit; but there is nevertheless some support for the view that the employer must pay a reasonable remuneration for the services actually rendered.[49] This view seems to be based on unjust enrichment rather that on "new contract": the employer is liable because he has received a benefit, not because he has impliedly agreed to pay for it. The difficulty in accepting this view, however, arises precisely because in the case put the employer has *not* rescinded the contract, so that prima facie the rights and duties of the parties continue to be governed by that contract.[50]

It is interesting to compare the various liabilities of a party who receives partial or defective performance under this and the preceding limitations on the right to rescind; of course, where the failure in performance amounts to a breach these liabilities are subject to his right to damages. A

---

[42] *Ante*, p. 705; *post*, p. 742.

[43] *Sim* v. *Rotherham Metropolitan B.C.* [1987] Ch. 216, where the action was not for the agreed wages, but for a declaration that the employer was not entitled to deduct damages: see *Miles* v. *Wakefield Metropolitan D.C.* [1987] A.C. 539, 574–575; Napier, [1987] C.L.J. 44.

[44] *Miles* v. *Wakefield Metropolitan D.C.*, *supra*; McMullen, 51 M.L.R. 234; the contrary assumption made in *Sim* v. *Rotherham Metropolitan B.C.*, *supra*, at p. 255) is no longer maintainable.

[45] *Ante*, p. 662.

[46] *Wiluszynski* v. *Tower Hamlets L.B.C.* [1989] I.C.R. 493; McLean [1990] C.L.J. 28; Mead, 106 L.Q.R. 192; *Macpherson* v. *London Borough of Lambeth* [1988] I.R.L.R. 470.

[47] *Miles* v. *Wakefield Metropolitan D.C.* [1987] A.C. 539, 553.

[48] *Ibid.* pp. 561; *cf. post*, p. 867.

[49] *Ibid.* pp. 553, (*per* Lord Brightman) and 561 (*per* Lord Templeman). The point it left open by Lord Brandon (at p. 552) and Lord Oliver (at p. 576).

[50] *Ibid.* p. 552 (*per* Lord Bridge), and *cf. post*, pp. 934–937.

buyer who "accepts" goods which are defective in a way that amounts to a breach of condition is liable for the contract price. A buyer who accepts short delivery of goods is not liable for the contract price, but for payment at the contract rate. In neither case is it necessary for the "acceptance" to be fully "voluntary," as it may take place before the buyer has any notice of the failure in performance. A cargo-owner who takes delivery at an intermediate port is under no liability at all unless he acts "voluntarily"; and if he does act "voluntarily" he is liable for freight *pro rata itineris*, that is, not for the agreed freight but for a proportion of it at the contract rate. The landowner in a situation similar to that in *Sumpter* v. *Hedges* is again not liable at all unless he "voluntarily" accepts the benefit; but if this requirement is satisfied he is liable for a reasonable sum. A cargo-owner who takes delivery at the agreed destination after the carrier has deviated is again liable (if at all) for a reasonable sum; and it seems that he is liable even though he did not act "voluntarily" but merely took possession of his own goods. An employer who accepts services falling short of those promised may similarly be liable for a reasonable sum, even though his acceptance of the services is not truly voluntary. The reasons for these distinctions have never been satisfactorily explained.

(4) Wrongful prevention of performance

A contract may provide that one party (A) is not to be paid until he completes performance. If, after A has begun to perform, the other party (B) wrongfully refuses to let him complete, A can, no doubt, claim damages for breach of contract. Alternatively, he can claim a *quantum meruit* for the work he has done. In *Planché* v. *Colburn*[51] A agreed to write a book on costume and ancient armour which was to appear in serial form in B's periodical. B stopped publishing the periodical when A had written the greater part of the work, and it was held that A was entitled to a *quantum meruit.* This rule differs from those just discussed[52] in that A's right to a reasonable remuneration does not depend on the receipt of any benefit by B. It only applies where B's refusal was wrongful. Thus an employee who is justifiably dismissed cannot at common law recover a *quantum meruit* or any part of his current salary[53]; and a contractor employed to do building work cannot recover anything for his work if it is done so badly as to justify the customer's refusal to allow him to complete.[54]

(5) Both parties in breach

Where both parties are alleged to have committed breaches, each of which is claimed to be a ground for rescission, the first question to be considered is the order in which the alleged breaches have occurred. If A's breach occurred before B's, the normal position will be that A's breach will give B a right to rescind, and, if B exercises that right, his subsequent failure to perform will not amount to a breach at all (even though it would have done

---

[51] (1831) 8 Bing. 14; *cf. De Bernardy* v. *Harding* (1853) 8 Exch. 822; *Inchbald* v. *Western Neilgherry Coffee Co.* (1864) 17 C.B.(N.S.) 733.

[52] *i.e.* at pp. 717–720, *ante*.

[53] *Ridgway* v. *Hungerford Market Co.* (1835) 3 A. & E. 171; *Boston Deep Sea Fishing & Ice Co.* v. *Ansell* (1888) 39 Ch.D. 339, where it is said at p. 364 that he cannot sue for a reasonable remuneration either. For the possible application of the Apportionment Act 1870, see *post*, pp. 722–723.

[54] *Whitaker* v. *Dunn* (1887) 3 T.L.R. 602.

so, if A had not committed the earlier breach).[55] It is, however, also possible for both parties simultaneously to commit breaches, each of which, standing alone, would justify rescission: for example, because each is a breach of condition. The normal rule in such cases is that each party is entitled to rescind on account of the other's breach[56] There is however some support for a different conclusion where the two breaches are interrelated in the sense that the second consists of failure to perform a duty to avoid the consequences of the first. This was said to be the position in a line of cases concerning agreements to submit claims to arbitration. Where a claimant had committed a breach of such an agreement by undue delay in prosecuting his claim after it had been brought, it was held to be the duty of the respondent to put an end to that delay. It was said to follow that "both claimant and respondent were in breach of their contractual obligations to each other; and neither can rely on the other's breach as giving him a right to treat the primary obligations of each to proceed with the reference as at an end."[57] But this reasoning was, with respect, unsatisfactory; for, granted that both parties were in breach, it is by no means clear why it should follow that *neither* could rescind: it would have been equally possible to conclude that *each* party had the option to do so. The reasoning also had the unfortunate practical consequence that an arbitration might be allowed to continue after so long a delay that a satisfactory trial was no longer possible. The courts were to some extent able to avoid this consequence by relying on the delay as a circumstance giving rise either to a tacit agreement to abandon the arbitration agreement,[58] or to an estoppel[59] precluding a party from insisting on continued observance of that agreement. But these devices had only a limited and uncertain operation. A more satisfactory solution is now provided by legislation which gives arbitrators the power to dismiss a claim for want of prosecution where the delay is such that a satisfactory trial is no longer possible.[60] The reasoning quoted above is therefore obsolete and should no longer be regarded as justifying an exception to the general rule[61] that, where both parties are guilty of breaches justifying rescission, each should have the right to rescind. The justification for that general rule is, it is submitted, that no good purpose is served by holding parties to a contract after each of them has committed a repudiatory breach of it.

(6) Apportionment Act 1870

Section 2 of this Act provides that "All rents, annuities, dividends and other periodical payments in the nature of income . . . shall . . . be considered as accruing from day to day, and shall be apportionable in respect of time accordingly." By section 5 "annuities" includes "salaries and pensions"; and by section 7 the Act does not apply where it is "expressly stipu-

---

[55] *Ante*, p. 668.

[56] *State Trading Corporation of India* v. *M. Golodetz Ltd.* [1989] 2 Lloyd's Rep. 277, 286.

[57] *Bremer Vulkan u. Maschinenfabrik* v. *South India Shipping Co.* [1981] A.C. 909, 987; this reasoning was affirmed, and the decision followed, in *The Hannah Blumenthal* [1983] 1 A.C. 854; *cf. The Matja Gubec* [1981] 1 Lloyd's Rep. 31.

[58] *Ante*, pp. 10, 33.

[59] This was one ground for the decision in *Tracomin* v. *A.C. Nielsen A/S* [1984] 2 Lloyd's Rep. 195.

[60] Arbitration Act 1950, s.13A, as inserted by Courts and Legal Services Act 1990, s.102.

[61] Stated at n. 56, *supra*.

lated that no apportionment shall take place." The Act raises a number of problems, three of which are relevant in the context of this Chapter.

The first is what is meant by a "periodical" payment. It seems that this expression refers to a sum or sums payable under a contract at the end of a stipulated time, or at fixed intervals of time. A single lump sum payable for a specific piece of work would not be a periodical payment; and this is one reason why the Act would not apply to a case like *Cutter v. Powell.*[62] Nor would the payment be periodical merely because the contract stipulated the time within which the piece of work was to be done: thus the Act would not apply to a case like *Sumpter* v. *Hedges*[63] even though the contract in that case contained a completion date.[64]

The second question is whether the Act entitles a person whose salary is payable at the end of a stipulated period to recover a proportionate part of the salary if he only works for part of the period. An Irish case supports the view that the Act does apply in such a case.[65] Similarly, in *Moriarty* v. *Regent's Garage Co.*,[66] the plaintiff was appointed director of the defendant company on the terms that "his fees for so acting shall be £150 per annum." Before the end of the year he ceased (without any breach of contract) to be a director, and the Divisional Court held that he could recover a proportionate part of his salary under the Act.[67] The Court of Appeal reversed this decision on procedural grounds and left open the question whether the Act would apply.[68] The point is of little practical importance because "as a matter of practice the question of apportionment is now usually dealt with by using the words 'at the rate of' in the Articles."[69] Indeed, the Articles often go further and provide expressly that remuneration "shall be deemed to accrue from day to day."[70]

The third question is whether the Act can be invoked by a party in breach of contract, for example by an employee who leaves in breach of contract or who is lawfully dismissed (for breach of duty) during the period at the end of which he is to be paid. In several cases since the Act, claims by such employees for their current pay have failed, but the Act is not mentioned in any of them.[71] In *Clapham* v. *Draper*[72] it was held that a landlord could not recover rent for part of a rent period during which he had wrongfully turned the tenant out. This might be thought to support the view that

---

[62] (1795) 6 T.R. 320; apportionment would also be excluded by the express terms of the contract: see *ante*, p. 683.

[63] [1898] 1 Q.B. 673.

[64] See 67 L.J.Q.B. 545; 78 L.T. 378; 46 W.R. 464.

[65] *Treacy* v. *Corcorran* (1874) I.R. 8 C.L. 40.

[66] [1921] 1 K.B. 423.

[67] In two contrary decisions the Act was not mentioned: *Re Central de Kaap Gold Mines* (1899) 69 L.J.Ch. 18; *McConnell's Claim* [1901] 1 Ch. 728. In two further cases the Act was mentioned but held inapplicable to a claim by a *single* director because the articles provided for payment to *all* the directors of an annual lump sum to be divided between them in such proportion as they thought fit; *Salton* v. *New Beeston Cycle Co.* [1899] 1 Ch. 775; *Inman* v. *Ackroyd & Best* [1901] 1 K.B. 613.

[68] [1921] 2 K.B. 766.

[69] *Ibid.* p. 779. It seems to have been assumed that the Articles had been incorporated in the contract of employment since they would not otherwise form part of the contract between the director and the company; *ante*, p. 526.

[70] See Companies Act 1985, s.8 and S.I. 1985 No. 805, Table A para. 82.

[71] *Boston Deep Sea Fishing and Ice Co.* v. *Ansell* (1888) 39 Ch.D. 339; *Healey* v. *S.A. Française Rubastic* [1917] 1 K.B. 947.

[72] (1885) Cab. & El. 484.

the Act could not be invoked by a party in breach of contract; but another possible explanation of the decision is that "The Act was never intended to deal with *tortious* interferences with the right of any person."[73] In *Moriarty* v. *Regent's Garage Co.* Lush J. said that he would "hesitate to agree"[74] with the view that an employee could base a claim on the Act if he were lawfully dismissed, or left in breach of contract. McCardie J., while expressing "no opinion" on the point, puts the case of an employee whose salary is payable at the end of six months and who is lawfully dismissed in the last fortnight of that period. And he asks: "Is it right that he should be deprived of remuneration for five and a half months' work because during the last fortnight he has done something for which he has been dismissed?"[75] It is submitted that a negative answer should be given to this question, and that there is nothing in the 1870 Act which makes it inapplicable to such a situation.[76]

6. Criticism[77]

The law relating to the effects of failure to perform is hard to state; and parts of it are still harder to justify. It is, in particular, open to criticism on three main grounds. First, it contains (as already noted) a number of distinctions which seem to have no rational or practical basis.[78]

Secondly, many defects in this branch of the law flow from the exceptions to the rule that a failure in performance must be substantial if it is to justify rescission. Some recent decisions[79] have improved the law by restricting the scope of these exceptions; but two major defects remain. The first is that a party may still be entitled to rescind though the breach does not prejudice him seriously or at all, *e.g.* where the breach is of a term previously classified as a "condition," or where a seller fails to deliver the correct quantity.[80] In such cases, the right to rescind can simply provide a party with an excuse for escaping from a bad bargain.[81] It would, it is submitted, be more satisfactory as a general rule to focus attention on the question whether damages were an adequate remedy for the breach; though there are, no doubt, exceptional cases in which the interests of commercial certainty require a clear recognition of the right to rescind for certain breaches, irrespective of their effects.[82] A more limited proposal for reform has been made by the Law Commissions. Under this proposal, where goods are supplied to a person who does not deal as consumer, his right to reject for breach of the conditions implied into the contract by stat-

---

[73] *Murphy* v. *Wood* [1941] 4 D.L.R. 454, 457.

[74] [1921] 1 K.B. 432, 434.

[75] *Ibid.* pp. 448–449; *cf. Sim* v. *Rotherham Metropolitan B.C.* [1987] Ch. 216, 255.

[76] *Cf.* Williams, 57 L.Q.R. 381–383; Goff & Jones, *The Law of Restitution*, (3rd ed.), p. 478; but see Matthews, 2 Legal Studies 302.

[77] Treitel, 30 M.L.R. 139.

[78] See especially the distinction between quantitative and qualitative defects in contracts for the sale of goods (*ante*, p. 694); and the distinctions between the various rights of a party who has failed to perform, under the limitations on the right to rescind (*ante*, pp. 719–720).

[79] Especially *Wickman Ltd.* v. *Schuler A.G.* [1974] A.C. 235; *The Hansa Nord* [1976] Q.B. 44 and *Reardon-Smith Line Ltd.* v. *Hansen-Tangen* [1976] 1 W.L.R. 989.

[80] *Ante*, pp. 684, 689.

[81] *e.g.* in *Cunliffe* v. *Harrison* (1851) 6 Ex. 901; *Acros Ltd.* v. *Ronaasen* [1933] A.C. 47; *ante*, pp. 688, 695.

[82] *e.g. Bunge Corp.* v. *Tradax Export S.A.* [1981] 1 W.L.R. 711 (*ante*, p. 699); *cf.* also *The Laconia* [1977] A.C. 850; *The Chikuma* [1981] 1 W.L.R. 314 (*ante*, pp. 680, 682).

ute[83] would no longer apply if the breach was "so slight that it would be unreasonable"[84] for the acquirer of the goods to reject them. This is, with respect, a regrettable proposal. On the one hand, it does not restrict the right to reject to cases in which the breach is serious, so that it fails adequately to promote the interests of justice. On the other hand it undermines the interests of certainty which exceptions to the requirement of serious breach (such as the right to reject for breach of condition) are intended to promote; for, if the proposal were adopted, the acquirer of the goods could never be sure whether the particular breach of condition which had occurred would indeed justify rejection.[85]

The third main defect in the law is the rule in *Sumpter* v. *Hedges*,[86] under which a party who has partially performed may have no rights at all against the other party to the contract. This rule can plainly lead to the unjust enrichment of the latter party, and seems to go further than necessary for his protection. He should normally be liable to make some payment for that benefit, though he should be entitled to a deduction in respect of any loss that he has suffered as result of the failure in performance.[87]

SECTION 4. STIPULATIONS AS TO TIME

1. In General

Failure to perform a stipulation as to time does not differ intrinsically from any other failure to perform; indeed a number of cases already discussed in this Chapter concern stipulations of this kind.[88] But the subject has a history and terminology of its own; and for this, perhaps not very satisfactory, reason it is usually discussed separately. Certain stipulations as to time are said to be "of the essence" of a contract. Any failure to perform such a stipulation justifies rescission; it makes no difference that the failure is trivial and causes little or no prejudice to the injured party. Where, on the other hand, a stipulation as to time is not of the essence, failure to comply with it only justifies rescission if it amounts to a substantial failure in performance.

The question whether a stipulation as to time is of the essence may be resolved by the terms of the contract itself. Time will obviously be of the essence if the contract expressly so provides.[89] The same is true if the contract provides that, in the event of one party's failure to perform within the stipulated time, the other is to be entitled to rescind[90]; or that the stipulation as to time is to be a condition.[91] In the absence of any contractual pro-

---

[83] *Ante*, p. 693.

[84] Law Com. No. 160 (1987) para. 4.25; although the proposed change in the law is described in para. 4.18 as "slight" (presumably because it would not apply in many cases), its effect would be far-reaching because of the difficulty of identifying in advance the cases in which it would apply.

[85] The proposal to limit the right to reject goods for quantitative defects in a similar fashion (Law Com. No. 160, para. 6.20) is open to the same objection: see *ante*, p. 685, n. 42.

[86] [1898] 1 Q.B. 673; *ante*, p. 684.

[87] See Law Com. 121; not to be implemented: Law Commission, 19th Annual Report, para. 2.11.

[88] *e.g. Glaholm* v. *Hays* (1841) 2 Man. & G. 257; *Bettini* v. *Gye* (1876) 1 Q.B.D. 183; *United Dominions Trust (Commercial) Ltd.* v. *Eagle Aircraft Services Ltd.* [1968] 1 W.L.R. 74.

[89] *Post*, p. 726.

[90] *e.g. ante*, p. 680.

[91] *i.e.* in the sense discussed at pp. 689 *et seq.*, *ante*; *The Scaptrade* [1983] 2 A.C. 694, 703.

visions on the point, the question is often determined by rules of law which have classified certain commonly found stipulations as to time in certain types of contracts as either being, or not being, of the essence. We have, for example, seen that in a charterparty failure by the shipowner to comply with a stipulation as to the time of sailing[92] or as to the ship's expected readiness to load[93] of itself justifies rescission; while the charterer's failure to load within the agreed time only has this effect if the delay is so serious as to frustrate the purpose of the contract.[94] Similarly, in a contract for the sale of goods a stipulation as to the time at which the seller is to deliver the goods is treated as of the essence of the contract[95]; while a stipulation as to the time at which the buyer is to pay for them is not normally so regarded.[96] To the latter rule there are, however, many exceptions: it will, for example, be displaced if the goods are perishable[97]; if the buyer fails to comply with a stipulation as to the time of paying a deposit under a contract with "a very tight time scale"[98]; or if there are other indications of the intention of the parties to treat the stipulation as of the essence.[99] The position is similar with regard to stipulations as to the time of taking delivery: failure by the buyer to comply with such a stipulation will not normally entitle the seller to rescind[1]; but it will have this effect if the goods are perishable,[2] or if the buyer undertakes to provide the ship on which the goods are to be loaded but fails to do so within the agreed time,[3] or if he fails within the time specified by the contract to notify the seller of the ship's readiness to load.[4]

Attempts have been made to formulate some general principle governing the legal classification of stipulations as to time. Thus it has been said, on the one hand, that "In modern English law time is *prima facie* not of the essence of the contract"[5]; and, on the other hand, that "*Broadly speaking* time will be considered of the essence in mercantile contracts."[6] But the italicised words indicate the tentative nature of these generalisations; and a glance at the rules stated in the preceding paragraph shows that they are, with respect, of limited value.[7] The classification of stipulations as to time

---

92 *Glaholm* v. *Hays* (1841) 2 Man. & G. 751; *ante*, p. 692.

93 *The Mihalis Angelos* [1971] 1 Q.B. 164; *ante*, p. 692.

94 *Universal Cargo Carriers Corp.* v. *Citati* [1957] 2 Q.B. 401; *ante*, p. 696; *post*, p. 755.

95 *Hartley* v. *Hymans* [1920] 3 K.B. 475, 484; *cf. Aruna Mills Ltd.* v. *Dhanrajmal Gobindram* [1968] 1 Q.B. 655; *Toepfer* v. *Lenersan Poortman N.V.* [1980] 1 Lloyd's Rep. 143 (time of tender of shipping documents). See also *Bowes* v. *Shand* (1877) 2 App.Cas. 455 (where *early* shipment by the seller justified rejection; *ante*, p. 695).

96 *Martindale* v. *Smith* (1841) 1 Q.B. 389; Sale of Goods Act 1979, s.10(1). For a similar rule as to the effect of delay in payment in a distributorship agreement, see *Decro-Wall International S.A.* v. *Practitioners in Marketing Ltd.* [1971] 1 W.L.R. 361.

97 See *Maclean* v. *Dunn* (1828) 4 Bing. 722, 728; *Ryan* v. *Ridley & Co.* (1902) 8 Com.Cas. 105; *R. V. Ward Ltd.* v. *Bignall* [1967] 1 Q.B. 534, 550; Sale of Goods Act 1979, s.48(3).

98 *The Selene G* [1981] 2 Lloyd's Rep. 180, 185. Contrast *Millichamp* v. *Jones* [1982] 1 W.L.R. 1422, 1431 (deposit paid late by "mere oversight").

99 *e.g.*, where payment was to be by irrevocable letter of credit to be opened within a stipulated time: see *Bunge Corp.* v. *Tradax Export S.A.* [1981] 1 W.L.R. 711, 725.

1 *Woolfe* v. *Horne* (1877) 2 Q.B.D. 355 (rags).

2 *Sharp* v. *Christmas* (1892) 8 T.L.R. 687 (potatoes).

3 *The Osterbek* [1973] 2 Lloyd's Rep. 86.

4 *Bunge Corp.* v. *Tradax Export S.A.* [1981] 1 W.L.R. 711; *ante*, p. 699.

5 *United Scientific Holdings Ltd.* v. *Burnley B.C.* [1978] A.C. 904, 940; *British and Commonwealth Holdings plc* v. *Quadrex Holdings Inc.* [1989] Q.B. 842, 857.

6 *Bunge Corp.* v. *Tradax Export S.A.* [1981] 1 W.L.R. 711, 716.

7 *Cf. ibid.* at p. 729.

seems to be based on considerations of commercial convenience applicable in particular contexts, rather than on any general principle or presumption as to time being, or not being, of the essence.

2. Sale of Land

(1) At common law

At common law, stipulations which specified[8] the time of performance were normally regarded as "of the essence" of contracts for the sale of land.[9] Thus the purchaser could not enforce the contract if he was not ready to pay on the precise day fixed for payment; and the vendor could not enforce the contract if he was not ready to show good title on the precise day on which he had undertaken to do so.

(2) In equity

(a) GENERAL RULE. Equity did not follow the common law rule but took the view that stipulations as to time were not generally "of the essence" of contracts for the sale of land. Thus in *Parkin* v. *Thorold*[10] a vendor contracted to convey on October 25 but could not find his title deeds till January 6 following. He successfully claimed specific performance in spite of this delay. In one case, delay of as much as eight years was not considered fatal to the purchaser's claim for specific performance.[11] The equitable rule, which now prevails,[12] is an application of the general requirement of substantial failure in performance. It is based on the view that delay in completing a contract for the sale of land does not normally deprive the injured party of the substance of his bargain, damages being an adequate remedy.[13] Hence the general rule is that delay will only justify rescission where it does cause serious prejudice to the other party.[14]

(b) EXCEPTIONS. The equitable rule just stated is subject to the following exceptions. For these exceptions to apply, the stipulation must specify a date or time for performance: they cannot apply where a contract merely provides for performance "as soon as practicable."[15]

(i) *Term of the contract.* If the contract expressly provides that time shall be of the essence, it must be performed within the stipulated time.[16] Where there is no such express provision the question whether time is of the essence of the contract is one of construction. A mere provision that the vendor shall produce an abstract of title within seven days has been held

---

[8] *Cf. post*, p. 728.

[9] *Parkin* v. *Thorold* (1852) 16 Beav. 59, 65; unless the contract, on its true construction, provided otherwise: *Rightside Properties Ltd.* v. *Gray* [1975] Ch. 72, 89.

[10] (1852) 16 Beav. 59; *cf. Cole* v. *Rose* [1978] 3 All E.R. 1121.

[11] *Williams* v. *Greatrex* [1957] 1 W.L.R. 31.

[12] *Post*, p. 729.

[13] See *ante*, p. 673; *Chancery Land Development* v. *Wade's Development Stores* (1987) 53 P. & C.R. 306.

[14] *United Scientific Holdings Ltd.* v. *Burnley B.C.* [1978] A.C. 904, 942; *cf. Amherst* v. *James Walker Goldsmith & Silversmith Ltd.* [1983] Ch. 305; *Metrolands Investments Ltd.* v. *J. H. Dewhurst Ltd.* [1986] 3 All E.R. 659. These cases were concerned not with breach but with a landlord's delay in serving notice to increase rent under rent review clauses: they apply the prima facie rule that the stipulated time was not of the essence of the contract.

[15] *British & Commonwealth Holdings plc* v. *Quadrex Holdings Inc* [1989] Q.B. 842.

[16] *e.g. Steedman* v. *Drinkle* [1916] 1 A.C. 275.

not to make time of the essence.[17] But in *Harold Wood Brick Co. Ltd.* v. *Ferris*[18] a contract provided for completion by August 31 and added that "the purchase shall in any event actually be completed not later than September 15." This clause was held to make time of the essence of the contract.

(ii) *Nature of the property.* Time is of the essence in sales of short leaseholds[19] or reversionary interests[20] since the former will depreciate and the latter appreciate rapidly with the passing of time. Generally, time will also be regarded as of the essence where the subject-matter of the contract is of a highly speculative nature.[21]

(iii) *Commercial contracts.* Under the general rules stated above[22] time is often of the essence in commercial transactions. In such cases, equity does not interfere, as it does in contracts for the sale of land. But even contracts for the sale of land are sometimes regarded as "commercial"; and an exception is then made to the general equitable rule that time is not of the essence of such contract. Time has accordingly been held to be of the essence of a contract for the sale of a public-house as a going concern[23]; of a contract for the sale of land which the buyer wanted to develop quickly for business purposes[24]; and, it seems, of a contract for the sale of a brickfield.[25] On the other hand, it has been held that time was not of the essence of a contract to sell 34 plots of land as and when each was built on.[26] This result may be justified on the ground that the completion date was "only a target."[27] But it is hard to accept the further suggestion that a contract under which land is to be developed as a building estate is not a "commercial" contract. Indeed, the notion that some contracts for the sale of land are, while others are not, "commercial" is questionable now that land is an article of commerce, subject to violent fluctuations in value.[28] The crucial question should be whether delay causes substantial prejudice to the injured party, not whether the contract is "commercial."

(iv) *Conditional contracts.* The performance by one party of some stipulated act may be a condition precedent either to the existence of the contract or to the obligation of the other party.[29] Where the very existence of the contract depends on a condition to be performed by one of the parties, that condition must be performed within the time expressly or impliedly fixed by the contract.[30] If no time is expressly fixed, the condition must be

---

[17] *Roberts* v. *Berry* (1858) 3 D.M. & G. 284.
[18] [1935] 2 K.B. 198.
[19] *Hudson* v. *Temple* (1860) 29 Beav. 536.
[20] *Newman* v. *Rogers* (1793) 4 Bro.C.C. 391; unless there is evidence of contrary intention: *Patrick* v. *Milner* (1877) 2 C.P.D. 342.
[21] See *Hare* v. *Nicholl* [1966] 2 Q.B. 130. This would have been the position in *British & Commonwealth Holdings plc* v. *Quadrex Holdings Inc* [1989] Q.B. 842 if the contract had specified a time for performance: see pp. 865–860 of the report.
[22] *Ante*, pp. 724–726.
[23] *Coslake* v. *Till* (1826) 1 Russ. 376; *Lock* v. *Bell* [1931] 1 Ch. 35.
[24] *Bernard* v. *Williams* (1928) 44 T.L.R. 436; *Cf. Hargreaves Transport Ltd.* v. *Lynch* [1969] 1 W.L.R. 215.
[25] See *Harold Wood Brick Co. Ltd.* v. *Ferris* [1935] 2 K.B. 198.
[26] *Williams* v. *Greatrex* [1957] 1 W.L.R. 31.
[27] At p. 35.
[28] *United Scientific Holdings Ltd.* v. *Burnley B.C.* [1978] A.C. 904, 924.
[29] *Ante*, p. 662.
[30] *Cf. Hare* v. *Nicholl* [1966] 2 Q.B. 130.

performed by the date fixed for completion[31]; if no date is fixed for completion, it must be performed within a reasonable time.[32] The equitable principle that time is not of the essence of a contract does not apply in these cases, for until the condition is performed the whole existence of the contract remains in doubt. For the same reason, an option can only be exercised within the time laid down in the agreement by which it was granted.[33]

(c) WAIVER. The general principle that the right to rescind may be lost by waiver[34] applies where time is (under the exceptions just discussed) of the essence of a contract for the sale of land. Accordingly the requirement of punctual performance may be waived by giving the party in breach a further period for performance after the expiry of the period specified in the contract. Such waiver only has the effect of substituting the extended time for the original time; it is "not an utter destruction of the essential character of time."[35]

3. Notice

Where, under the equitable rules, time is not of the essence of a contract for the sale of land, the injured party is not bound to wait indefinitely for performance: he can make time of the essence by giving notice, after the time fixed for performance,[36] calling on the other party to complete. The contract may specify the period of notice required for this purpose; if it fails to do so, the notice must allow a reasonable time for completion. After expiry of the notice, the injured party has a choice: he can either enforce the contract or rescind it. What is a reasonable time is a question of fact. If one party has constantly pressed the other to complete, he can rely on this fact to shorten the amount of time which must be allowed by the notice.[37] If the notice is invalid (or if none is given), the injured party can nevertheless seek specific performance, or rescind the contract, after lapse of a reasonable time.[38] Once notice has been given, it binds *both* parties. Thus if one of them gives notice to complete but is not ready to do so when the notice expires, the other can rescind.[39]

---

[31] *Re Sandwell Park Colliery Co.* [1929] 1 Ch. 277; *Aberfoyle Plantations* v. *Cheng* [1960] A.C. 115; *aliter* where the completion date is only a target date subject to the occurrence of the condition; *Hargreaves Transport Ltd.* v. *Lynch* [1969] 1 W.L.R. 215, 220; and where the condition is subsequent (*ante*, pp. 58–59) and time is expressly stated *not* to be of the essence, as in *29 Equities Ltd.* v. *Bank Leumi* (*U.K.*) *Ltd.* [1986] 1 W.L.R. 1490.

[32] *Re Longlands Farm* [1968] 3 All E.R. 522.

[33] *Hare* v. *Nicholl* [1966] 2 Q.B. 130; *United Dominions Trust* (*Commercial*) *Ltd.* v. *Eagle Aircraft Ltd.* [1968] 1 W.L.R. 74 (*ante*, p. 707); *United Scientific Holdings Ltd.* v. *Burnley B.C.* [1978] A.C. 904, 936.

[34] *i.e.* waiver in the sense of election: *ante*, p. 709.

[35] *Barclay* v. *Messenger* (1874) 43 L.J. Ch. 449; *Nichimen Corp.* v. *Gatoil Overseas Inc.* [1987] 2 Lloyd's Rep. 46.

[36] Notice can be given as soon as the other party is in default: see *Behzadi* v. *Shaftsbury Hotels Ltd.* [1991] 2 All E.R. 477; contrast *British & Commonwealth Holdings plc* v. *Quadrex Holdings Inc.* [1989] Q.B. 842 (where no time was fixed).

[37] *Stickney* v. *Keeble* [1915] A.C. 386.

[38] *Woods* v. *Mackenzie Hill Ltd.* [1975] 1 W.L.R. 613; *cf. Cole* v. *Rose* [1978] 3 All E.R. 1121 (where the delay in performance was *held* not to be unreasonable).

[39] *Finkielkraut* v. *Monohan* [1949] 2 All E.R. 234; *Quadrangle Development and Construction Co. Ltd.* v. *Jenner* [1974] 1 W.L.R. 68; *Oakdown Ltd.* v. *Bernstein & Co.* (1985) 49 P. & C.R. 282.

Notice sometimes has similar effects where the stipulation as to time is not of the essence at common law.[40] For example, an unpaid seller of goods can make time of the essence by giving the buyer notice of his intention to resell the goods.[41] But it does not follow that notice is in all cases sufficient to give rise to a right to rescind. For example, under a charter-party, delay in providing a cargo is only a ground for rescission if it is so prolonged that it "frustrates" the injured party's object in entering into the contract.[42] The contract cannot be rescinded merely because the party in breach has failed to comply with a notice calling on him to perform within a reasonable time. Similarly, a hire-purchaser's failure to pay instalments may not of itself be a ground for rescission; and it has been held that it could not be turned into such a ground by merely giving notice to the hirer that he would be assumed to have repudiated if he did not pay within a stated time.[43]

4. Law of Property Act 1925, s.41

This section, re-enacting section 25(7) of the Judicature Act 1873, provides: "Stipulations in a contract, as to time or otherwise, which according to rules of equity, are not deemed to be or to have become of the essence of the contract, are also construed and have effect at law in accordance with the same rules." It follows from the section that, in contracts for the sale of land, the equitable rules now prevail, so that stipulations as to time in such contracts are no longer of the essence. It has been held that the section is not restricted to cases in which equity would have intervened before the Judicature Acts; it enables the courts also to take into account the subsequent development of equitable principles.[44] The effect of the section is as follows.

First, delay is no longer a ground for rescission merely because it would formerly have been so regarded at common law.[45]

Secondly, a person can now claim damages where formerly he could not do so. For example, a vendor of land may purport to rescind on the ground that the purchaser was not ready with the purchase money on the completion date. At common law the rescission would have been justified as the time of performance was of the essence of the contract. Under section 41, this is no longer the case, so that the purported recission is wrongful and the purchaser is entitled to damages.[46]

Thirdly, delay in performance is a breach giving rise to liability in damages; and this is true even where in equity time is not of the essence. The authorities on this point were formerly in some confusion. It was clear

---

[40] *i.e.* under the rules discussed on pp. 724–726, *ante*.

[41] Sale of Goods Act 1979 s.48(3), as explained in *R. V. Ward Ltd.* v. *Bignall* [1967] 1 Q.B. 534. ULIS (*ante*, p. 28, n. 81) makes extensive use of this technique; see, *e.g.* Arts. 27(2), 31(2), 44(2), 62(2); *cf.* Vienna Convention (*ante*, p. 29, n. 88) Arts. 47, 49 (1)(*b*), 63, 64 (1)(*b*).

[42] *Universal Cargo Carriers Corp.* v. *Citati* [1957] 2 Q.B. 401; *ante*, p. 696.

[43] *Eshun* v. *Moorgate Mercantile Credit Co. Ltd.* [1971] 1 W.L.R. 722.

[44] *United Scientific Holdings Ltd.* v. *Burnley B.C.* [1978] A.C. 904, 925, 957; Baker, 93 L.Q.R. 529.

[45] *Raineri* v. *Miles* [1981] A.C. 1050, 1082–1083.

[46] *Stickney* v. *Keeble* [1915] A.C. 386, 404; *Rightside Properties Ltd.* v. *Gray* [1975] Ch. 72.

that damages for delay were recoverable where the defendant was guilty of negligent or wilful default.[47] But there was some support for the view that the right to damages was restricted to such cases.[48] This view was however, rejected by the House of Lords in *Raineri* v. *Miles*,[49] where is was held that the purchaser of a house was entitled to damages for the vendor's delay in completion, whether or not that delay amounted to wilful default.

[47] *e.g. Jones* v. *Gardiner* [1902] 1 Ch. 191; *Phillips* v. *Lamdin* [1949] 2 K.B. 33.

[48] See *Lock* v. *Bell* [1931] Ch. 35, 44; *e.g. Thorpe* v. *Fasey* [1949] Ch. 649; *Woods* v. *Mackenzie-Hill Ltd.* [1975] 1 W.L.R. 613, 615; *cf. Babacomp Ltd.* v. *Rightside Properties Ltd.* [1973] 3 All E.R. 873, 875.

[49] [1981] A.C. 1050; Samuels, 44 M.L.R. 100.

CHAPTER NINETEEN

BREACH

SECTION 1. WHAT AMOUNTS TO BREACH

A BREACH of contract is committed when a party without lawful excuse fails or refuses to perform what is due from him under the contract, performs defectively or incapacitates himself from performing. Special problems that arise from repudiation *before* performance is due are discussed later in this Chapter.[1]

1. Failure or Refusal to Perform

Failure or refusal to perform a contractual promise when performance has fallen due is prima facie a breach. This point looks obvious enough, but it does raise a number of problems.

The first is whether the stipulation which has not been complied with is indeed a promise, or only a condition. In the standard case of a unilateral contract, where A promises B £100 if he will walk to York,[2] B has not promised to do anything: his walking to York is merely a condition[3] of A's liability. Hence B commits no breach if he does not start the walk, or if, having started, he fails to complete it. But the distinction between the two types of stipulations is sometimes hard to draw.[4] It is, for example, not clearly settled whether an estate agent who is engaged to find a buyer for a house makes any promise to do anything[5]; and it is also possible for a person to commit a breach by failing to complete performance of an act which he was not originally bound to do if, by beginning performance, he impliedly promised to complete it.[6]

The second problem is whether performance has become due. Obviously performance is not due before the stipulated time: a promise to pay £100 tomorrow is not broken by failing to pay today. But greater difficulty arises where the contract, or the liability of one party, is subject to a condition. Where the contract is subject to a *contingent* condition precedent,[7] failure to perform is not a breach if the condition has not occurred; nor does the principal obligation of either party become due if he fails to bring about the condition on which the binding force of that obligation depends. At most, he may be liable for breach of some subsidiary duty: for example, he is often under a duty not actively to prevent the occurrence of the condition; and he may be under a duty to make reasonable efforts to bring its occurrence about.[8] On the other hand, where the liability of A is subject to a *promissory* condition[9] to be performed by B, failure by B to perform that

[1] *Post*, pp. 754 *et seq*.
[2] *Ante*, p. 36.
[3] *i.e.* in the contingent sense (*ante*, p. 58) as B makes no promise.
[4] *Cf. ante*, p. 37; and see *Shires* v. *Brock* (1977) 247 E.G. 127.
[5] *Ante*, p. 39.
[6] *Ante*, p. 37.
[7] *Ante*, p. 58.
[8] *Ante*, pp. 60–61.
[9] *Ante*, p. 662.

promise not only puts B in breach[10] of his principal obligation, but also prevents A's obligation to perform his counter-promise from becoming due.

Thirdly, a contract may contain a promise by one party, but fail to make it clear exactly what has been promised in return by the other. In *Churchward* v. *R.*[11] a contractor agreed with the Admiralty that he would for 11 years carry from Dover to Calais such mail as he should from time to time be asked to carry by the Admiralty or the Postmaster-General. He was not given any mail to carry and claimed damages. One reason why his claim failed was that the agreement did not oblige the Admiralty to employ him: it only obliged him to carry mail if the Admiralty asked him to do so.[12] But a contract often by implication obliges a party to do something which is not expressly stated. "Where there is an engagement to manufacture some article [for a customer] a corresponding engagement on the other party is implied to take it, for otherwise it would be impossible that the party bestowing his services could claim any remuneration."[13]

A similar difficulty arises where the contract clearly obliges a party to do something but fails to specify exactly what it obliges him to do. The question sometimes arises, for example, whether an employer is only bound to pay the agreed wages, or whether he must actually give the employee work. The traditional view is that generally the employer need only pay wages,[14] though this rule does not apply if one of the objects of the contract is to enable the employee to gain, or retain, a skill, or to keep his name before the public. Thus a person who employs a well-known actor must actually give him a part in the play for which he was engaged.[15] More recently, it has been said that the law now recognises a "right to work" so that an employer of (at any rate) a skilled worker must actually give him work.[16] It does not follow that this obligation can be specifically enforced[17]; but an employer who breaks the obligation to provide work may be liable in damages on that account.

Finally, there may be a breach if a party *in substance* refuses to perform, and paradoxically he may do this by insisting with too great literalness on the terms of the contract. "Working to rule" in order to disrupt the employer's business may therefore be a breach of a contract of employment.[18]

---

10 *e.g. Trans Trust S.P.R.L.* v. *Danubian Trading Co.* [1952] 2 Q.B. 297; *ante*, p. 662.

11 (1865) L.R. 1 Q.B. 173; *cf. R.* v. *Demers* [1900] A.C. 109.

12 *Cf. ante*, p. 20.

13 *Churchward* v. *R.*, *supra*, at p. 195. *cf. The Unique Mariner* (*No.* 2) [1979] 1 Lloyd's Rep. 37, 51–52.

14 *Turner* v. *Sawdon* [1901] 2 K.B. 653; *cf. Delaney* v. *Staples* [1991] 1 All E.R. 609, 616 (discussing so called "garden leave").

15 *Herbert Clayton & Jack Waller Ltd.* v. *Oliver* [1930] A.C. 209.

16 *Langston* v. *A.U.E.W.* [1974] 1 W.L.R. 185; *cf. Gunton* v. *Richmond-upon-Thames L.B.C.* [1981] Ch. 448, 472 (exclusion from place of work an "immediate breach" though salary was paid for a further month). Even if the employer is not in breach by failing to provide work, he may be unable to restrain such an employee from working for others in breach of another term of the contract of employment: see *Provident Financial Group plc.* v. *Hayward* [1989] I.C.R. 160, *post*, p. 902. See also Employment Protection (Consolidation) Act 1978, ss.33(1), 45.

17 *Langston* v. *A.U.E.W.* (*No.* 2) [1974] I.C.R. 510; *post*, p. 922.

18 *Secretary of State* v. *A.S.L.E.F.* (*No.* 2) [1972] 2 Q.B. 455; contrast *Power Packing Casemakers Ltd.* v. *Faust* [1983] Q.B. 471 (ban on overtime not a breach).

2. Defective Performance

The phrase "defective performance" arguably contains an element of self-contradiction, in the sense that a person who promises to do one thing does not perform if he does another. Where the defect is of a particularly serious kind, there is indeed no need to distinguish between defective performance and non-performance, as in the case of a seller who promises peas but delivers beans. But where the performance rendered is of the same kind as that promised, differing from it only in point of time, quantity or quality, it is reasonable to refer to it as defective performance. It undoubtedly amounts to a breach; but the effects of such a breach often differ from those of a complete failure or refusal to perform.[19]

3. Incapacitating Oneself

A person may break a contract by incapacitating himself from performing it. Thus a contract to sell a specific thing is broken by selling it to a third party.[20] Similarly, in *Omnium D'Entreprises* v. *Sutherland*[21] a ship which had been chartered was sold by the owner "free from any . . . charter engagement." It was held that he was in breach of the charterparty: the argument that he might be able to perform by getting the ship back was rejected, as it involved "substituting a chance for a certainty."[22] It was further said that the shipowner would have been in breach even if the contract of sale had provided that the buyer must perform the charterparty: such a term could not be directly enforced by the charterer against the buyer because of the doctrine of privity.[23] But the shipowner would not be in breach if the contract of sale entitled him to retain possession of the ship until the charterparty had been performed, or if it gave him the right to perform any charter obligations he had undertaken. Nor does a person who is entitled to make a choice as to the method of performance incapacitate himself merely by declaring that he will perform in a way that is impossible. For example, a seller of generic goods does not put himself in breach merely by telling the buyer that he will make delivery from a source which does not exist.[24] He is normally[25] entitled and bound to deliver from another source, and is only in breach if he fails or refuses to do so.

A person is not incapacitated from performing a contract under which he is obliged to pay money, merely because he is insolvent.[26] If the contract is profitable, his trustee in bankruptcy will probably wish to enforce it and provide funds to discharge his obligations under it. Insolvency only incapacitates a contracting party if no assets are set aside out of his estate for the performance of the contract.[27] Where, after a contract has been made, one party to it is adjudged bankrupt, the other party may apply to the court for

---

[19] *Ante*, pp. 670–709, *post*, pp. 927–933.

[20] *Bowdell* v. *Parsons* (1808) 10 East 359; *Lovelock* v. *Franklyn* (1846) 8 Q.B. 371.

[21] [1919] 1 K.B. 618.

[22] At p. 621.

[23] *Ante*, Chap. 15.

[24] *The Vladimir Ilich* [1975] 1 Lloyd's Rep. 322 at p. 329.

[25] In *The Vladimir Ilich*, *supra*, the seller would not have been entitled to do this under the contract, since this provided that he was to give a "notice of appropriation" and that a valid notice of appropriation, once given, could not be withdrawn. But by treating the notice as *invalid* the buyer had precluded himself from relying on this provision.

[26] *Re Agra Bank* (1867) L.R. 5 Eq. 160.

[27] *Ex p. Chalmers* (1873) L.R. 8 Ch.App. 289; *Bloomer* v. *Bernstein* (1874) L.R. 9 C.P. 588; *cf. Sale Continuation Ltd.* v. *Austin Taylor & Co.* [1968] 2 Q.B. 849.

an order discharging obligations under the contract; and the court may make such an order on such terms as to payment of damages by the bankrupt or by the other party as appear to the court to be equitable.[28]

4. Without Lawful Excuse

There is no breach when non-performance of a contract is justified by some lawful excuse.

(1) Illustrations

In one sense, such an excuse for non-performance exits where one party is entitled to refuse to perform because the other has failed to perform a promissory condition precedent or a concurrent condition. In such cases, performance of the former party's obligation has never become due. This topic has already been discussed[29]; our present concern is with cases in which *after* an obligation has accrued, an extraneous event occurs which interferes with its performance. The event may interfere so seriously with performance that both parties are discharged under the doctrine of frustration (to be discussed in the next Chapter). But even where its effects are less drastic, it may still provide a party with an excuse for non-performance. Thus an employee who does not go to work because he is ill is not in breach,[30] even though the illness is not so serious as to frustrate the contract (so that performance must be resumed when the illness is over). Other extraneous circumstances may similarly justify refusal to perform, or to accept performance, at least in part. In one case it was, for example, held that the owner of a London café, who had engaged the plaintiff to give cabaret performances there, was justified in refusing to allow such performances to take place on the day on which King George V died, and on the following day, but not on the four days after that.[31] Again, if a farmer agrees to sell 500 tons of wheat to be grown on his farm and, through no fault of his, only 200 are produced, he is not liable for failing to produce the other 300 tons, though he will be liable in damages if he fails to deliver the 200 tons.[32]

Excuses for non-performance may be provided by the contract itself, which may contain "exceptions" absolving a party from his duty to perform if he is prevented from doing so by specified circumstances, such as strikes or similar delays. Failure to perform, if brought about by such events, is not a breach at all. The function of the "exception" is not to exclude liability for an assumed breach but rather to define the scope of the contracting party's obligations.[33]

A party relying on an excuse for non-performance must show that the excuse existed at the time of his refusal to perform: it is not enough for him to show that it arose or would (if the other party had not rescinded on

---

[28] Insolvency Act 1986, s.345(1) and (2).

[29] *Ante*, pp. 662–664.

[30] See *ante*, p. 678 at n. 88; *post*, pp. 772–773, but contrast *ante*, p. 678 at n. 87. The excuse may extend to prevention through other causes: see the example given in *Sim* v. *Rotherham Metropolitan B.C.* [1987] Ch. 216, 254 (teacher locked in school lavatory "through no fault of his own").

[31] *Minnevitch* v. *Café de Paris (Londres) Ltd.* [1936] 1 All E.R. 884.

[32] *Howell* v. *Coupland* (1876) 1 Q.B.D. 258; *H. R. and S. Sainsbury Ltd.* v. *Street* [1972] 1 W.L.R. 834; Thornely [1973] C.L.J. 15; Goldberg, 88 L.Q.R. 464; *cf. post*, pp. 774–775.

[33] *The Angelia* [1973] 1 W.L.R. 210; *ante*, pp. 219–220.

account of the refusal) have arisen at some later time.[34] Suppose, for example, that a seller of 100 tons of wheat of a certain description is about to deliver wheat of a different description. If at this stage the buyer declares that he will not accept, and the seller rescinds on that ground, the buyer cannot rely on the non-conformity, for the seller is not actually in breach until he tenders non-conforming goods.[35] Once a defective tender has been made, the buyer is entitled to reject it, but he may not be entitled to rescind the contract; for if, within the time allowed for delivery, the seller can make a further good tender, the buyer is bound to accept it.[36]

(2) Whether excuse must be stated

The general rule is that a refusal to perform by a party who has an excuse for non-performance is not a breach, even though he did not state the excuse, or even know of it, at the time of the refusal. Thus an employer can lawfully dismiss an employee who has committed a breach of duty justifying dismissal, though he did not at the time of the dismissal know of the breach of duty, and though at that time he gave some other, insufficient, reason, or no reason at all.[37] Similarly a buyer can reject goods, if there has been a breach of condition, even though he did not know of the breach; and the rejection will not be wrongful merely because at the time he mistakenly alleged breach of some other condition.[38]

The rule may sometimes be justifiable on the ground that it prevents the party in breach from benefiting from the concealment of his own wrong. But it can also cause surprise and even hardship to the party in breach, and it has therefore been limited in a number of ways. A party cannot rely on an excuse which he did not specify at the time of his refusal to perform "if the point which was not taken is one which if taken could have been put right."[39] This might be the position if a seller lost the opportunity of making a second good tender within the time allowed[40] in consequence of the buyer's failure to state the ground which justified rejection. The case is even stronger if the buyer makes some groundless objection to the seller's tender and the seller incurs trouble or expense in investigating or seeking to cure that objection.[41] In such circumstances, an estoppel can arise, precluding the buyer from alleging the existence of another, sufficient, reason for his refusal to perform. There is moreover, some authority for the view that a buyer who fails to specify a defect in existence at the time of rejec-

---

[34] *British & Beningtons Ltd.* v. *N.W. Cachar Tea Co.* [1923] A.C. 48; *ante*, pp. 667–668; *cf. The Siboen and the Sibotre* [1976] 1 Lloyd's Rep. 293.

[35] *Braithwaite* v. *Foreign Hardwood Co. Ltd.* [1905] 2 K.B. 543, as explained in *Taylor* v. *Oakes Roncoroni & Co.* (1922) 38 T.L.R. 349, 351; for further references see *ante*, p. 668.

[36] *Ante*, p. 655.

[37] *Ridgway* v. *Hungerford Market Co.* (1835) 3 A. & E. 171; *Baillie* v. *Kell* (1838) 4 Bing.N.C. 638; *Spottswood* v. *Barrow* (1850) 5 Ex. 110; *Boston Deep Sea Fishing & Ice Co.* v. *Ansell* (1888) 39 Ch.D. 339; *Cyril Leonard & Co.* v. *Simo Securities Trust Ltd.* [1972] 1 W.L.R. 80. The rule does not apply in cases of *unfair* dismissal (which need not be a breach of contract at all): see *Earl* v. *Slater & Wheeler (Airlyne) Ltd.* [1973] 1 W.L.R. 51; and *cf. Polkey* v. *A.E. Dayton Services Ltd.* [1988] A.C. 344, 355–356.

[38] *e.g. Arcos Ltd.* v. *E. A. Ronaasen & Sons* [1933] A.C. 470.

[39] *Heisler* v. *Anglo-Dal Ltd.* [1954] 1 W.L.R. 1273, 1278; *André & Cie* v. *Cook Industries Inc.* [1987] 2 Lloyd's Rep. 463.

[40] *Ante*, p. 655.

[41] *Cf. The Lena* [1981] 1 Lloyd's Rep. 68, 79; *The Eurometal* [1981] 1 Lloyd's Rep. 337, 341.

tion cannot later rely on it, even though the defect was one which the seller could *not* have cured and even though the seller did not in any way change his position in consequence of the buyer's original failure to specify it. In *Panchaud Frères S.A.* v. *Établissements General Grain Co.*[42] 5,500 tons of maize were sold under a contract which provided that the goods were to be shipped in "June/July." The goods were in fact shipped in August and the buyers could have rejected them on this ground. But they paid against documents which would, if carefully examined, have revealed that the goods were shipped in August; and when the goods arrived the buyers rejected them for defects of quality. This was a bad ground as the goods were sound when shipped and the sellers were not responsible for their subsequent deterioration. The buyers claimed their money back, and, three years after their rejection of the goods, they relied for the first time on the fact of late shipment. Their claim failed, no doubt because the court was impressed by the possibly harsh operation of allowing a party at such a late stage to rely on an originally unstated excuse for non-performance. To allow the buyers to do this would, it was said, be inconsistent with a "requirement of fair conduct."[43] But the vagueness of this requirement makes it virtually impossible to tell which cases will be governed by it and which by the general rule that a party can rely on an originally unstated excuse for non-performance.[44] Hence various other attempts have been made to explain the *Panchaud Frères* case. One suggestion is that the case was one of waiver[45] (in the sense of election)[46]; but this was rejected in the actual judgments in the case on the ground that the buyers did not know of the late shipment when they accepted the documents.[47] Another view is that the buyers' conduct gave rise to an estoppel or equitable estoppel[48]; but it is hard to see in what way the sellers relied on any representation that might be inferred from the buyers' acceptance of the documents.[49] Certainly the sellers lost no chance of curing the defect in their tender, for when that tender was made such a cure was no longer possible. Probably the safest explanation of the case is that the buyers had lost their right to reject by acceptance[50] when they paid against documents which disclosed the fact of late shipment. It follows that the buyers could have relied on the fact of late shipment if they had *rejected* the documents, even though they

[42] [1970] 1 Lloyd's Rep. 53.
[43] *Ibid.* p. 59.
[44] Perhaps for this reason the decision is treated with some reserve in *The Proodos C* [1980] 2 Lloyd's Rep. 390, 392.
[45] *V. Berg & Son Ltd.* v. *Vanden Avenne-Izegem P.V.B.A.* [1977] 1 Lloyd's Rep. 499, 502–503; *Intertradex S.A.* v. *Lesieur-Torteaux* [1978] 2 Lloyd's Rep. 509, 513; *Bremer Handelsgesellschaft mbH* v. *C. Mackprang Jr.* [1979] 1 Lloyd's Rep. 221, 225.
[46] *Ante*, p. 709.
[47] For the requirement of such knowledge, see *ante*, p. 712.
[48] This was the view of Lord Denning M.R. in the *Panchaud Frères* case itself: [1970] 1 Lloyd's Rep. at p. 56; *cf. V. Berg & Son Ltd.* v. *Vanden Avenne-Izegem*, *supra* n. 45, at pp. 502–503; *Intertradex S.A.* v. *Lesieur-Torteaux*, *supra*, at p. 515; *The Manila* [1988] 3 All E.R. 843, 852.
[49] *Cf. Raiffeisen Hauptgenossenschaft* v. *Louis Dreyfuss & Co* [1981] 1 Lloyd's Rep. 345, 352, where the *Panchaud Frères* case was held inapplicable precisely because the requirement of reliance was not satisfied.
[50] *B.P. Exploration Co. (Libya) Ltd.* v. *Hunt* [1979] 1 W.L.R. 783, 810–811; affirmed without reference to this point [1983] 2 A.C. 352.

had, at the time of such rejection, given an inadequate reason, or none at all.[51]

5. Standard of Duty[52]

The question to be discussed under this heading is whether liability for breach of contract is strict, or whether it is based on fault in the sense of want of care, diligence or honesty.

(1) Cases of strict liability

Many contractual duties are strict.[53] The most obvious illustration of this principle is provided by the case of a buyer who cannot pay the price because his bank has failed or because his expectation of raising a loan has not been fulfilled, or because he is prevented by exchange control regulations from remitting money to the place where he has agreed to pay,[54] or because his supply of the currency in which he has agreed to pay has become exhausted and cannot be replenished.[55] In such cases there is no doubt that he is liable[56]: inability to pay money, even if it occurs entirely without the fault of the party who was to make the payment, is not an excuse for failing to make the payment. The same principle of strict liability applies to the duty of a seller of generic goods to make delivery. It is no defence for him to say that he was prevented from making delivery because he was let down by his supplier[57] or because no shipping space was available to get the goods to their agreed destination.[58] A charterparty similarly imposes a strict duty on the charterer to provide a cargo, so that inability to find one is no excuse.[59] In all these cases, the principle of strict liability may be modified by the terms of the contract (for example, by a "*force majeure*" clause),[60] but unless this is done liability is quite independent of fault.

The principle of strict liability also applies to certain cases of defective performance. At common law, a carrier of goods by sea was held to give an "absolute" warranty of seaworthiness[61]: it was not enough for him to show that he had taken reasonable care to make the ship seaworthy. In practice,

---

[51] *Cf. V. Berg & Son Ltd.* v. *Vanden-Avenne Izegem P.V.B.A.* [1977] 1 Lloyd's Rep.
[52] Treitel, in (Ed.) Bos and Brownlie, *Liber Amicorum for Lord Wilberforce*, p. 185.
[53] *Raineri* v. *Miles* [1981] A.C. 1050, 1086.
[54] *Universal Corp.* v. *Five Ways Properties Ltd.* [1979] 1 All E.R. 552.
[55] *Congimex S.A.R.L. (Lisbon)* v. *Continental Grain Export Corp. (New York)* [1979] 2 Lloyd's Rep. 346.
[56] *Cf. Francis* v. *Cowcliffe* (1977) 33 P. & C.R. 368, *Christy* v. *Pilkington* 273 S.W. 2d 533 (1954).
[57] *Barnett* v. *Javeri & Co.* [1916] 2 K.B. 390; *P. J. van der Zijden Wildhandel* v. *Tucker & Cross Ltd.* [1975] 2 Lloyd's Rep. 240; *Intertradex S.A.* v. *Lesieur Torteaux S.A.R.L.* [1978] 2 Lloyd's Rep. 509; *cf. The Al Tawfiq* [1984] 2 Lloyd's Rep. 598 (late delivery).
[58] *Lewis Emanuel & Son Ltd.* v. *Sammut* [1952] 2 Lloyd's Rep. 629.
[59] *The Aello* [1961] A.C. 135 (overruled on another point in *The Johanna Oldendorff* [1974] A.C. 479); *The Zuiho Maru* [1977] 2 Lloyd's Rep. 552; *cf. Hills* v. *Sughrue* (1846) 15 M. & W. 252 (where it was the shipowner who undertook to find the cargo). *Cf. The Athenasia Comninos* [1990] 1 Lloyd's Rep. 277, 282 (shipper's "warranty" that cargo is not dangerous).
[60] There was such a clause in the *Wildhandel* case *supra*, n. 57 but in the circumstances it did not apply so as to protect the seller.
[61] *Steel* v. *State Line SS. Co.* (1877) 3 App.Cas. 72, 86.

sea carriers often contracted out of this strict liability; and in many cases the duty is now reduced by statute to one of due diligence.[62]

Liability is, again, strict where goods delivered under a contract of sale are defective: for example, because they do not comply with the seller's undertakings as to quality.[63] It is no defence for the seller to show that he took all reasonable care to see that there were no defects,[64] or that he could not have discovered the defects because he was a retailer selling goods in packages sealed by the manufacturer.[65] The position appears to be the same where goods are supplied under a control for the supply of goods other than one of sale, *e.g.* under one of hire or hire-purchase.[66]

A contractor who executes repairs or building work is also strictly liable for defects in components fitted by him. He is not exonerated by showing that the components were supplied by a reputable manufacturer and that the defects were latent so that they could not have been discovered by the exercise of reasonable care.[67] Contracts of this kind contain both a supply of goods, and a service, element. Strict liability with regard to the supply element can be justified on the ground that this is closely analogous to sale; and also on the ground that it is the first link in a chain of contractual liability which will stretch back to the manufacturer, on whom the liability should properly rest. The customer has no rights against the manufacturer in contract, as there is no contract between them; and, if contractors were not liable to the customer, the contractor would suffer no loss and so could not recover damages from the manufacturer from whom he had bought the components. The introduction of the maunfacturer's strict "product liability"[68] directly to the customer weakens this argument for the contractor's strict liability in contract to the customer, but does not wholly deprive it of its force since "product liability" is subject to many important qualifications.[69] The "chain of liability" argument is also open to the objection that the chain may be broken by a valid exemption clause.[70] It has therefore been suggested that, if the manufacturer is only willing to sell the components on terms that exclude his liability, and this fact was known both to

---

[62] Carriage of Goods by Sea Act, 1971, s.3.

[63] *e.g.* with those implied under Sale of Goods Act 1979, s.14.

[64] *Frost* v. *Aylesbury Dairy Co. Ltd.* [1905] 1 K.B. 608; *cf. Lockett* v. *A. M. Charles Ltd.* [1938] 4 All E.R. 170; *H. Parsons (Livestock) Ltd.* v. *Uttley Ingham & Co. Ltd.* [1978] Q.B. 791, 799–800.

[65] *Daniels* v. *White & Son* [1938] 4 All E.R. 258.

[66] See Supply of Goods (Implied Terms) Act 1973, s.10 (as substituted by Consumer Credit Act 1974, s.192 and Sched. 4 para. 35); Supply of Goods and Services Act 1983, ss.4 and 9. The wording of these provisions is similar to that of Sale of Goods Act 1979, s.14, under which liability is clearly strict.

[67] *G. H. Myers & Co.* v. *Brent Cross Service Co.* [1934] 1 K.B. 46; *Young & Marten Ltd.* v. *McManus Childs Ltd.* [1969] 1 A.C. 454; *cf. Hancock* v. *Brazier* [1966] 1 W.L.R. 1317; *cf. Wettern Electric Ltd.* v. *Welsh Development Agency* [1983] Q.B. 796 (strict liability for breach of implied undertaking in licence to occupy factory that premises are fit for occupier's purpose). In *The Zinnia* [1984] 2 Lloyd's Rep. 211, 218 the repairer's duty was said to be one to ensure that reasonable care in buying the components was exercised; but as he was found not to have taken such care the further question whether he might be strictly liable did not arise. It is not clear what standard of liability is imposed by Defective Premises Act 1972, s.1(1)(*a*).

[68] Consumer Protection Act 1987, Pt. I.

[69] *e.g.* those arising from the meaning given to "defect" by s.3 of the Act, the defences made available by s.4, and the definition of "damage" in s.5.

[70] As in *Helicopter Sales (Australia) Pty. Ltd.* v. *Rotor Works Pty. Ltd.* (1974) 132 C.L.R. 1.

the contractor and to his customer, then the contractor would not be strictly liable to his customer for defects in those components.[71]

(2) Liability based on fault

Under the Supply of Goods and Services Act 1982, a person who supplies a service in the course of a business impliedly undertakes to "carry out the service with reasonable care and skill."[72] Such liability is clearly based on fault; but the Act also preserves "any rule of law which imposes on the supplier a stricter duty."[73] Hence the question whether the supplier's liability is strict or is based on fault will continue to depend on distinctions drawn at common law.

Where the contract is one for the supply of services and components, liability for defects in the components is (as we have just seen) generally strict[74]; but the contractor's liability with regard to other phases of his operation is often based on fault. For example, a car repairer's duty with regard to the safe-keeping of a customer's car is one of care only.[75] The standard of a building or repairing contractor's duty with regard to the actual carrying out of the work that he is employed to do is less clear. In one of the relevant cases,[76] a sharp distinction was drawn between the "supply of goods" and "service" elements of the contract, and it seems to have been accepted that, in respect of the "service" element, the contractor's duty was one of care only.[77]

Where the contract is one for the supply of services alone, liability is often based on fault. Thus the general rule is that contracts under which services are rendered by professional persons (such as solicitors, architects, accountants or doctors) impose duties of care only.[78] In some at least of such cases, the person rendering the services obviously does not guarantee to produce a result: this is particularly clear in the case of the lawyer engaged to conduct litigation since one party must inevitably lose, and of the doctor since a person who provides medical treatment is not normally

---

[71] In *Young & Marten Ltd.* v. *McManus Childs Ltd.* [1969] 1 A.C. 454, 467; the suggestion is perhaps based on the fact that the building contract specified tiles which could be obtained only from a single manufacturer.

[72] s.13.

[73] s.16(3)(*a*).

[74] *Ante*, p. 738. s.12(3)(*a*) of the Supply of Goods and Services Act 1982 provides that such contracts are contracts for the supply of services for the purposes of the Act; but it does not specify the standard of liability.

[75] See *Hollier* v. *Rambler Motors (A.M.C.) Ltd.* [1972] 2 Q.B. 71; *cf. Alderslade* v. *Hendon Laundry Ltd.* [1945] 1 K.B. 189; *Smith* v. *Eric S. Bush* [1990] 1 A.C. 831, 843 (plumber).

[76] *Young & Marten Ltd.* v. *McManus Childs Ltd.* [1969] 1 A.C. 454.

[77] *Ibid.* at p. 465; *cf. H. Parsons (Livestock) Ltd.* v. *Uttley Ingham & Co. Ltd.* [1978] Q.B. 791, 800; *The Raphael* [1981] 2 Lloyd's Rep. 659, 665. See also *B.P. Exploration (Libya) Ltd.* v. *Hunt* [1979] 1 W.L.R. 783, 796 (affirmed [1983] 2 A.C. 352).

[78] *e.g. Clark* v. *Kirby-Smith* [1964] Ch. 506 (solicitor); *Bagot* v. *Stevens, Scanlan & Co. Ltd.* [1966] 1 Q.B. 197 (architect); *O'Connor* v. *Kirby* [1972] 1 Q.B. 90 (insurance broker); *McNealy* v. *Pennine Insurance Co. Ltd.* [1978] 2 Lloyd's Rep. 18 (insurance broker); *Stafford* v. *Conti Commodity Services* [1981] 1 All E.R. 691 (commodities broker); *Perry* v. *Sidney Phillips & Son* [1982] 1 All E.R. 1005, 1010, varied [1982] 1 W.L.R. 1287 (surveyor); *cf. Investors in Industry Commercial Property Ltd.* v. *South Bedfordshire D.C.* [1986] 1 All E.R. 787, 806 (not reported on this point in [1986] Q.B. 1034); *Luxmoore-May* v. *Messenger May Baverstock* [1990] 1 W.L.R. 1009. See *post*, p. 873, n. 20 as to the first two cases cited in this note.

understood to guarantee its success.[79] All that such persons undertake is to perform the promised services with reasonable care and skill. The same is true of the architect to the extent that he undertakes to supervise the work of others, or the supply of materials by them: in performing this function he cannot be expected to do more than exercise a reasonable degree of professional care and skill.

But the position is different where an architect commits an error, not of supervision, but of design: there is considerable support for the view that, where he designs a structure, he gives an "absolute warranty"[80] that it will be fit for his client's purposes. Similarly, a person who in the course of a profession or business undertakes to *design and supply* an article has been held strictly liable for defects in that article.[81] Some dicta, indeed, suggest that liability is *only* strict where the contract contains a "supply" as well as a "service" element[82]; but this limitation on the incidence of strict liability may, with respect, be doubted. In some of the relevant authorities no defect in the components or raw materials was alleged[83]; and where a defendant is thus held liable for defects in services alone it would be strange if the standard of that liability depended on the existence of another obligation (*i.e.* to supply materials) in respect of which he was not in breach.

(3) Fault and excuses for non-performance

Failure to perform is not a breach where a supervening event either discharges a contract under the doctrine of frustration[84] or provides a party with an excuse for non-performance.[85] An event only has this effect if it occurs without the fault of the party relying on it. In cases of frustration, this requirement is expressed by saying that frustration must not be "self-

---

[79] See *Eyre* v. *Measday* [1986] 1 All E.R. 488 and *Thake* v. *Maurice* [1986] Q.B. 644, where doctors were held not to have guaranteed that sterilisation operations would make patients permanently sterile; though it was recognised that such a guarantee *might* be given. In the latter case, the doctor was held liable in negligence for failing to warn the patient that sterility might not be permanent. Contrast *Gold* v. *Haringey Health Authority* [1988] Q.B. 481, where there seems to have been no contractual relationship, and failure to warn of a very slight risk did not give rise to liability in negligence as it was normal not to give such a warning.

[80] *Greaves & Co.* (*Contractors*) *Ltd.* v. *Baynham Meikle & Partners* [1975] 1 W.L.R. 1095, 1101; *I.B.A.* v. *E.M.I.* (*Electronics*) *Ltd.* (1980) 14 Build.L.R. 1, especially at pp. 47–48 (where the contract contained a supply of goods element but no defect in the goods was alleged).

[81] *Samuels* v. *Davies* [1943] K.B. 526 (dentist supplying false teeth: here the "supply" element predominated and du Parq L.J. regarded the contract as one of sale); *I.B.A.* v. *E.M.I.* (*Electronics*) *Ltd.* (1980) 14 Build.L.R. 1 (contract to design and erect a television mast).

[82] *Basildon D.C.* v. *J. E. Lesser Properties* [1985] 1 All E.R. 20, 26 (not reported on this point in [1985] Q.B. 839); *cf. Cynat Properties Ltd.* v. *Landbuild* (*Investments & Property*) *Ltd.* [1984] 3 All E.R. 513, 523; *Wimpey Construction U.K. Ltd.* v. *D. V. Poole* [1984] 2 Lloyd's Rep. 499, 514 (no undertaking by *designer* as to quality and *execution* of the work); *George Hawkins* v. *Chrysler* (*U.K.*) (1986) 38 Build.L.R. 36 (where the contract contained no supply element).

[83] There was no such allegation in the cases cited in n. 81 *supra*.

[84] *Post*, Chap. 20.

[85] *Ante*, pp. 734–735.

induced."[86] Similarly, a party generally[87] cannot rely as an excuse for non-performance on an event that is due to his fault, *e.g.* a farmer who agreed to sell a quantity of wheat to be grown on his land could not rely on the fact that less was produced if this was due to want of proper cultivation.[88]

Excuses for non-performance may be provided by "exceptions" in the contract itself, and such provisions must be distinguished from exemption clauses. Where performance is prevented by an event specified in an "exception," there is no breach at all, while an exemption clause excludes or restricts liability once a breach has been established. One factor tending to put a provision into the category of "exceptions" is that the specified event was beyond the control of the party relying on the provision, and occurred without fault.[89] Here again fault is relevant in determining whether non-performance is excused or amounts to a breach.

(4) Conditional contracts

Where a contract is subject to a contingent condition,[90] two rules apply which to some extent make fault relevant to the issue of contractual liability. First, a party may be in breach if he deliberately prevents the occurrence of the condition.[91] Secondly, a party may be under some degree of duty to bring about the occurrence of the condition: for example where goods are sold "subject to" export or import licence. In such a case the duty of the party who is to obtain the licence is normally one of diligence only,[92] so that fault is again relevant to the question whether a breach of contract has been committed.

6. Breach Distinguished from Lawful Termination

A contract may give one party the right lawfully to terminate it by notice. If that party says to the other that he no longer intends to perform, it is sometimes hard to tell whether he has broken or terminated the contract. In *Bridge* v. *Campbell Discount Co. Ltd.*[93] a hire-purchase agreement gave the hirer the right to terminate it by notice. He wrote to the owners: "Owing to unforeseen circumstances I am sorry but I will not be able to pay any more payments . . . . Will you please let me know when and where I will have to return the car. I am very sorry regarding this, but I have no alternative." The majority of the House of Lords held that he had not ter-

---

86 *Post*, p. 803.
87 Illness preventing performance of a contract of personal service may be an exception: *cf. post*, p. 804.
88 Lack of fault is mentioned, apparently as an essential ingredient of the excuse, in the cases discussed at p. 734, *ante*.
89 *The Angelia* [1973] 1 W.L.R. 210, 230; *ante*, p. 220. *Cf. The Xantho* (1877) 2 App.Cas. 503: prima facie a party connot rely on an exception if he has negligently brought about the specified event.
90 See *ante*, pp. 58–62.
91 *Ante*, p. 59.
92 *Ante*, p. 60.
93 [1962] A.C. 600; *cf. United Dominions Trust (Commercial) Ltd.* v. *Ennis* [1968] 1 Q.B. 54; *Marriott* v. *Oxford & District Co-operative Society Ltd.* [1970] Q.B. 186.

minated but broken the contract, apparently because that was his intention. "Why should the hirer apologise so humbly, twice, if *he thought* that he was merely exercising an option given to him by the agreement?"[94]

The analogous question has been raised whether a strike or other "industrial action" amounts to a breach of a contract of employment.[95] This depends in the first place on the exact form taken by the conduct in question. While "working to rule" may be a breach,[96] no breach is committed merely because employees who ussually work overtime (without being under any contractual obligation to do so) refuse to continue the practice.[97] In the more common case of a refusal by employees to perform their contractual obligation to work, there is clearly a breach if the contract contains a "no strikes" clause.[98] The same is true if an employee stops work (whether in the course of a strike or not) without giving the notice required by the terms of the contract. If the contract does not contain a "no strikes" clause and if due notice of the strike has been given, one view is that the notice terminates the contract; but this is said[99] to be unrealistic since both parties would expect a return to work under the old contract (suitably modified) after the strike was over. A second view is that a strike notice operates as a lawful suspension of the contract, at least if the notice is no shorter than that required for lawful termination of the contract.[1] This view in turn gives rise to difficulties, particularly as the notion of "suspending" a contract is one with which English law is unfamiliar[2] and to which the courts are generally hostile.[3] The prevailing view, therefore, is[4] that generally a strike is a breach of contract and that it is, moreover, a "repudiatory breach,"[5] *i.e.* one which at common law[6] entitles the employer to dismiss the employee. The employer's other remedies by way of damages and withholding pay have already been discussed.[7]

---

[94] At p. 615 (italics supplied); *cf.* p. 621. Another reason for the decision may be that it was in the hirer's interest to establish that he was in breach: see *post*, p. 889.

[95] Foster, 34 M.L.R. 274.

[96] *Ante*, p. 732.

[97] *Tramp Shipping Corp.* v. *Greenwich Marine Inc.* [1975] 1 W.L.R. 1042; *cf. Power Packing Casemakers* v. *Faust* [1983] Q.B. 471.

[98] As in *Rookes* v. *Barnard* [1964] A.C. 1129.

[99] By Donovan L.J. in *Rookes* v. *Barnard* [1963] 1 Q.B. 623, 682. The statement was approved in the House of Lords by Lord Devlin: [1964] A.C. at 1204, though the decision of the Court of Appeal was reversed. See also Wedderburn, 25 M.L.R. at p. 258; 27 M.L.R. at p. 268.

[1] *Morgan* v. *Fry* [1968] 2 Q.B. 710, 728 *per* Lord Denning M.R.; *cf. ibid.* p. 733, *per* Davies L.J.; O'Higgins [1968] C.L.J. 223.

[2] See *Daily Mirror Newspapers Ltd.* v. *Gardner* [1968] 2 Q.B. 762; *Gorse* v. *Durham C.C.* [1971] 1 W.L.R. 775. A contract can only be "suspended" if it contains a provision to that effect, as in *Bird* v. *British Celanese Ltd.* [1945] K.B. 336.

[3] *Shell U.K. Ltd.* v. *Lostock Garages Ltd.* [1976] 1 W.L.R. 1187.

[4] *Simmons* v. *Hoover Ltd.* [1977] Q.B. 284; Napier [1977] C.L.J. 34; *cf. Rookes* v. *Barnard* [1963] 1 Q.B. 623, 682 (*supra*, n. 99), *per* Donovan L.J. In *Chappell* v. *Times Newspapers Ltd.* [1975] 1 W.L.R. 482, 502 Lord Denning M.R. similarly said that going on strike "wilfully to disrupt the employer's undertaking" was a breach of contract.

[5] *Miles* v. *Wakefield Metropolitan D.C.* [1987] A.C. 539, 562; *Wiluszynki* v. *Tower Hamlets L.B.C.* [1989] I.C.R. 493, 503.

[6] By statute, the dismissal may be *unfair*, even where it is not *wrongful* at common law: see Employment Protection (Consolidation) Act 1978, s.54.

[7] *Ante*, p. 719.

SECTION 2. EFFECTS OF BREACH

A breach of contract may entitle the injured party to claim damages, the agreed sum, specific performance or an injunction, in accordance with the principles discussed in Chapter 21. In appropriate circumstances he may be entitled to more than one of these remedies: *e.g.* to an injunction and damages. Breach may also give the injured party the right to "rescind" the contract in circumstances which have been discussed in Chapter 18.[8] It is with this effect of breach that we are here concerned.

1. The Option to Rescind or Affirm

(1) No automatic termination

A breach which justifies rescission does not automatically determine the contract.[9] It only gives the victim the option either to rescind the contract or to affirm it and to claim further performance. This is generally the case, even if the contract says that it is to become "void" on breach.[10] But normally such a stipulation is construed[11] restrictively so as to prevent one party from relying on his own breach of duty to the other party.[12] The reason for this approach is that the law should not allow the guilty party to rely on his own wrong to obtain a benefit under the contract,[13] to excuse his own failure of further performance, or in some other way to prejudice the injured party's legal position under the contract.[14] Thus the guilty party should not be allowed to take advantage of the breach by arguing that the original contract is discharged, so that he is entitled to a *quantum meruit* for work done by him,[15] or that he need only pay at the market rate (below

---

8 *Ante*, pp. 659 *et seq*.

9 *Michael* v. *Hart & Co.* [1902] 1 K.B. 482, 490; *Heyman* v. *Darwins Ltd.* [1942] A.C. 356, 361; *Decro-Wall International S.A.* v. *Practitioners in Marketing Ltd.* [1971] 1 W.L.R. 361, 368, 375, 381; *Mayfair Photographic Supplies Ltd.* v. *Baxter Hoare & Co. Ltd.* [1972] 1 Lloyd's Rep. 410, 417; *Lakshmijit* v. *Sherani* [1974] A.C. 605; *The Odenfeld* [1978] 2 Lloyd's Rep. 357, 374; *Great Atlantic Insurance Co.* v. *Home Insurance Co.* [1981] 2 Lloyd's Rep. 219, 229; *The T.F.L. Prosperity* [1984] 1 W.L.R. 48, 58; *Lusograin Commercio Internacional de Cereas Ltda.* v. *Bunge A.G.* [1986] 2 Lloyd's Rep. 654, 658; *Evening Standard Ltd.* v. *Henderson* [1987] I.C.R. 588, 593, 595; *The Simona* [1989] A.C. 788, 800; *cf.* the overruling in *Photo Production Ltd.* v. *Securicor Transport Ltd.* [1980] A.C. 827 of *Harbutt's "Plasticine" Ltd.* v. *Wayne Tank & Pump Co. Ltd.* [1970] 1 Q.B. 447. Contrast the use made by ULIS (*ante*, p. 28, n. 81) of a concept of "ipso facto avoidance," which gives rise to many difficulties; and is not used in The Vienna Convention (*ante*, p. 29, n. 88) and see Thompson, 41 M.L.R. 137, suggesting a possible reconsideration of the rule stated in the text.

10 *Cf. Davenport* v. *R.* (1877) 3 App.Cas. 115; *New Zealand Shipping Co.* v. *Société des Ateliers, etc., de France* [1919] A.C. 1; *Cerium Investments Ltd.* v. *Evans*, *The Times*, February 14, 1991. Automatic termination only results if the event on which the contract is expressed to come to an end occurs without breach of duty, as in *Brown* v. *Knowsley B.C.* [1986] I.R.L.R. 102.

11 *e.g. Alghussein Establishment* v. *Eton College* [1988] 1 W.L.R. 587; for the status of the rule as one of construction, capable of being excluded by contrary provision, see *Cheall* v. *Apex* [1983] 2 A.C. 180, 189; *Gyllenhammar & Partners International* v. *Sour Brodogradevna Industrial* [1989] 2 Lloyd's Rep. 403; *Micklefield* v. *S.A.C. Technology Ltd.* [1990] 1 W.L.R. 1002, 1007; *cf. The Bonde* [1991] 1 Lloyd's Rep. 136, 144.

12 For the requirement that the duty must be owed to the other party, see *Thompson* v. *ASDA-MFI Group plc.* [1988] Ch. 241; contrast *Cheall* v. *Apex*, *supra*, (breach of duty to third party).

13 See the *Alghussein* case, *supra*, n. 11.

14 *Ibid*; contrast *Cheall* v. *APEX*, [1983] 1 A.C. 180 (breach of agreement with third party).

15 *Boston Deep Sea Fishing & Ice Co.* v. *Ansell* (1888) 39 Ch.D. 339. 364.

that fixed by the contract) for services rendered to him.[16] Nor should he be allowed to rely on the breach so as to prevent the injured party from enforcing provisions in the contract which are advantageous to him and which may operate after the breach (such as a valid exclusive dealing clause[17]); or so as to deprive the injured party of the chance of claiming specific relief,[18] or of obtaining a lien on the other party's property.[19]

(2) Employment contracts

In some situations, the general rule, that a repudiatory breach does not of itself terminate the contract, clearly applies to employment contracts. For example, in *Rigby* v. *Ferodo Ltd.*[20] an employer had committed such a breach by imposing a wage-cut. The employee nevertheless continued to work and it was held that the contract had not been terminated by the employer's unaccepted repudiation. It followed that employee was entitled to recover the difference between the wages paid and those due under the contract.

But there is some support for the view that the position is different where the employee does *not* continue to work for the employer after the repudiatory breach,[21] either because he has been wrongfully dismissed or because he has left in breach of contract. In such cases, it is sometimes said that wrongful repudiation by one party automatically terminates the contract, without any need for the injured party to exercise the option to rescind. One argument in support of this view is that, where the employee is no longer working for the employer (in consequence of the repudiation), the employment *relationship* has plainly come to an end, even against the wishes of the injured party. But it does not follow from this that the *contract* of employment is similarly terminated[22]: the argument that the repudiating party should not be allowed to rely on his own wrong to deprive the injured party of valuable rights under the contract has much force where the contract is one of employment as it has in relation to other contracts. A further argument for the view that a contract of employment is automatically terminated by repudiatory breach is that, if the contract were not so terminated, a wrongfully dismissed employee would be entitled to sue for his wages until the time of his election to terminate; whereas it is settled

---

[16] Example based on *Timber Shipping Co. S.A.* v. *London & Overseas Freighters Ltd.* [1972] A.C. 1 (where there was no breach).

[17] *e.g. Decro-Wall International* v. *Practitioners in Marketing Ltd.* [1971] 1 W.L.R. 361; *cf. Thomas Marshall (Exports) Ltd.* v. *Guinle* [1979] Ch. 227; *cf. W.P.M. Retail* v. *Laing* [1978] I.C.R. 787 (employee preserving right to bonus after wrongful dismissal); *Lusograin Commercio Internacional de Cereas Ltda.* v. *Bunge A.G.* [1986] 2 Lloyd's Rep. 654 (seller's right to "carrying charges" (*post*, p. 888) after repudiation by buyer). For exclusion of the rule by contrary agreement, see *supra*, n. 11.

[18] See *Decro-Wall International S.A.* v. *Practitioners in Marketing Ltd.* [1971] 1 W.L.R. 361 (where it was held that there was no automatic termination); *Evening Standard Co. Ltd.* v. *Henderson* [1987] I.C.R. 588.

[19] *G. Barker* v. *Eynon* [1974] 1 W.L.R. 462 (where again the view that termination is automatic was implicitly rejected).

[20] [1988] I.C.R. 29.

[21] *Sanders* v. *Ernest A. Neale* [1974] I.C.R. 565; *Kolatsis* v. *Rockware Glass Ltd.* [1974] 3 All E.R. 555, 558; *Gannon* v. *Firth* [1976] I.R.L.R. 415; *cf. Hare* v. *Murphy Bros. Ltd.* [1974] I.C.R. 603 (where the contract seems to have been frustrated on the ground stated at p. 804 *post*); *R.* v. *East Berkshire Health Authority, ex p. Walsh* [1985] Q.B. 152, 161; Thomson, 38 M.L.R. 347; Napier [1975] C.L.J. 36.

[22] *Gunton* v. *Richmond-upon-Thames L.B.C.* [1981] Ch. 448, 474 (doubted on this point in *ex p. Walsh, supra*); *cf. ante*, p. 650. *Micklefield* v. *S.A.C. Technology* [1990] 1 W.L.R. 1002.

that his remedy is in damages and not by action for the agreed wages.[23] But this argument fails to distinguish between the continued existence of the *contract*, and the *remedies* for its breach.[24] This point is by no means restricted to contracts of employment. Suppose, for example, that a buyer wrongfully repudiates an instalment contract for the sale of goods by refusing to accept further instalments. If the seller elects to treat the contract as remaining in existence, it does not follow that he can sue for *the price* of the undelivered instalments. His remedy is normally in damages, though the amount recoverable may depend on whether he elects to terminate.[25] Similarly, where a time charter is wrongfully repudiated by the charterer, the shipowner is not bound to accept the repudiation; but even if he elects to affirm his remedy may be in damages rather than for the agreed hire[26]: "It is . . . the range of remedies which is limited, not the right to elect."[27] The same argument applies to contracts of employment: it does not follow from the continued existence of the *contract* that a wrongfully dismissed employee's *remedy* is by action for the agreed sum. Thus it is submitted that the general rule applies to such contracts, *i.e.*, that a repudiatory breach by either party does not lead to automatic termination, but only gives the injured party an option to rescind the contract.[28]

(3) Restrictions on injured party's choice

Although rescission is at the option of the injured party, that party's option is to some extent curtailed, in particular by the rule that the damages recoverable by the injured party may be reduced if he failed to take reasonable steps to mitigate his loss.[29] This rule will sometimes put pressure on the injured party to rescind, for one common way of mitigating loss is to make a substitute contract; and the effect of doing this will often be to put it out of the injured party's power to perform the old contract. Where this is the case, the making of the substitute contract will involve the rescission of the original one. Thus if a wrongfully dismissed employee mitigates his loss by taking another job he will thereby be "taken to have accepted his wrongful dismissal as a repudiatory breach leading to a determination of the contract of service."[30] The same would be true where a seller, on the buyer's repudiation, disposed elsewhere of the subject-matter. In these cases the injured party is not under any legal obligation to make the substi-

---

23 *Gunton's* case, *supra* [1981] Ch. at p. 474; *Delaney* v. *Staples* [1991] 1 All E.R. 609, 616.

24 *Post*, p. 898, n. 49.

25 *Post*, p. 852.

26 See *post*, p. 900.

27 *The Alaskan Trader* (*No.* 2) [1983] 2 Lloyd's Rep. 645, 651.

28 *Simmons* v. *Hoover Ltd.* [1977] Q.B. 284; *Western Excavating* (*E.E.C.*) *Ltd.* v. *Sharp* [1978] Q.B. 761, 769; *Thomas Marshall* (*Exports*) *Ltd.* v. *Guinle* [1979] Ch. 277; *Gunton* v. *Richmond-upon-Thames L.B.C.* [1981] 1 Ch. 448; *Rasool* v. *Hepworth Pipe Co.* [1980] I.C.R. 494; *London Transport Executive* v. *Clark* [1981] I.C.R. 355; *Burdett-Coutts* v. *Hertfordshire C.C.* [1984] I.R.L.R. 91; *Evening Standard Co. Ltd.* v. *Henderson* [1987] I.C.R. 586, 593, 595; *Dietman* v. *L.B. of Brent* [1987] I.C.R. 737, affd. without reference to this point [1988] I.C.R. 842); *cf.* also *Decro-Wall International S.A.* v. *Practitioners in Marketing Ltd.* [1971] 1 W.L.R. 361, 369–370, 375–376, 380–381; the same assumption seems to underlie *Miles* v. *Wakefield M.D.C.* [1987] A.C. 539, *ante*, p. 719; Thompson, 97 L.Q.R. 8, 235; 98 L.Q.R. 423; 42 M.L.R. 91; McMullen [1982] C.L.J. 110.

29 *Post*, p. 866.

30 *Gunton* v. *Richmond-upon-Thames L.B.C.* [1981] Ch. 448, 468; *Dietman's* case, *supra*, n. 28.

tute contract[31]; so that in this sense he remains free to choose between affirmation and rescission. But his freedom of choice is limited in that, if he acts unreasonably in failing to make such a contract, he will suffer a reduction in the damages to which he is entitled by reason of breach of the original contract.

Conversely, the mitigation rules may require the injured party to accept performance from the party in breach even though it is not in accordance with the contract: *e.g.* they may require a buyer to accept late delivery.[32] In such a case, the mitigation rules again do not, strictly speaking, restrict the injured party's right to rescind, but they do require him, having rescinded, to enter into a new contract for late performance at the original price (subject to damages for delay).[33] The injured party does not commit any breach of duty by failing to enter into such a new contract, but his failure to do so will reduce the damages to which he is entitled for breach of the original contract. Hence his freedom of choice will, as a practical matter, be restricted, this time in the direction of putting him under pressure to accept performance, though subject to relatively minor modifications.

(4) Exercise of the option

It is a question of fact in each case whether the option to rescind has been exercised.[34] Active steps seem to be necessary for this purpose[35]; and notice of the exercise of the option must sometimes be given to the party in breach: for example, where the injured party seeks the return of property with which he has parted under the contract.[36] But it seems that notice of the exercise of the option is not necessary where the injured party puts it out of his power to perform the original contract by making a substitute contract to satisfy the mitigation requirement.[37] The option can also be exercised in the legal proceedings brought on the contract.[38] Obviously the victim affirms the contract by claiming specific performance but there is no inconsistency between claiming damages for a prior breach, or for the breach in question, and exercising the option to rescind.[39] There are, moreover, cases in which the victim merely refuses to perform until the other party either cures his breach or (in the case of contracts calling for continuing performance) resumes performance in conformity with the contract. For example, an employer may refuse to pay wages, or pay them in full, for so long as his employee refuses (in the course of "industrial action") to perform his duties under the contract of employment. Such a

---

31 *Post*, p. 867.

32 *The Solholt* [1981] 2 Lloyd's Rep. 574 (affirmed, [1983] 1 Lloyd's Rep. 605.

33 *The Solholt* [1983] 1 Lloyd's Rep. 605, criticising *Strutt* v. *Whitnell* [1975] 1 W.L.R. 870 for failing to observe the distinction drawn in the text.

34 *Kish* v. *Taylor* [1912] A.C. 604, 617.

35 *State Trading Corp. of India* v. *M. Golodetz Ltd.* [1989] 2 Lloyd's Rep. 277, 286 ("silence and inactivity" insufficient). *Cf. post*, p. 755.

36 *Lackschmijit* v. *Sherani* [1974] A.C. 605.

37 *Gunton* v. *Richmond-upon-Thames L.B.C.* [1981] Ch. 448, 468.

38 It can be exercised even after issue of the writ: *Tilcons Ltd.* v. *Land & Real Estate Investments Ltd.* [1987] 1 W.L.R. 46.

39 *General Billposting Co. Ltd.* v. *Atkinson* [1909] A.C. 118. Contrast *United Dominions Trust (Commercial) Ltd.* v. *Ennis* [1968] 1 Q.B. 54, 65, where it was said that the victim affirms by claiming a sum due under a provision in the contract fixing the amount payable in the event of breach, even though that provision was penal; *sed quaere*.

temporary refusal on the employer's part does not amount to an exercise by him of the option to rescind.[40]

If the victim accepts further performance after breach, he may be held to have affirmed, so that he cannot later rescind the contract.[41] He must, moreover, rescind the contract as a whole: for example, a tenant cannot remain on premises and ignore a particular term of the lease on the ground that the landlord had, in the past, failed to perform his obligations under that term.[42]

2. Effects of Rescission or Affirmation

(1) Rescission

Rescission by the victim is sometimes said to terminate the contract. But this statement is somewhat misleading, and it is best to consider the precise effects of rescission on the obligations of each party.

(a) ON OBLIGATIONS OF THE VICTIM. After rescission, the victim is no longer bound to accept or pay for further performance.[43] He is also entitled to refuse to make payments which had not yet fallen due at the time of rescission, *e.g.* because the other party's performance was incomplete or defective[44]; and he is released from other obligations which, under the contract, were to be performed in the future: for example, a wrongfully dismissed employee is no longer bound by covenants in restraint of trade in his contract of employment.[45]

On the other hand, the victim remains liable to perform obligations which had accrued before rescission. For example, where freight under a charterparty is deemed earned on loading the charterer remains liable to pay it even though he later justifiably rescinds on account of the shipowner's repudiatory breach.[46] The victim may also himself have been in breach at the time of the other party's repudiation, but not in such a way as to justify that repudiation.[47] In such a case, the victim is, in spite of his own breach, entitled to rescind, but he remains liable in damages for his own breach committed before he rescinded the contract.[48]

If, at the time of rescission, the victim has already performed, he may be entitled to recover back that performance. For example, a buyer who justifiably rejects goods for breach of condition is normally entitled to the return of the price.[49] To this extent, rescission has a retrospective effect. It

---

[40] *Wiluszynski* v. *Tower Hamlets L.B.C.* [1989] I.C.R. 493; it is assumed that the breach justified rescission. For the different question whether failure to perform a condition precedent of itself *entitles* the injured party to rescind, see *ante*, p. 666.

[41] *Davenport* v. *R.* (1877) 3 App.Cas. 115; *cf. ante*, pp. 709–715; an *unsatisfied demand* for performance does not have the same effect: *post*, pp. 753–754.

[42] *Total Oil Great Britain Ltd.* v. *Thompson Garages (Biggin Hill) Ltd.* [1972] 1 Q.B. 318.

[43] *Photo Production Ltd.* v. *Securicor Transport Ltd.* [1980] A.C. 827, 849.

[44] *e.g. ante*, p. 683.

[45] *General Billposting Co. Ltd.* v. *Atkinson* [1909] A.C. 118; *Briggs* v. *Oates* [1990] I.C.R. 473.

[46] *The Dominique* [1989] A.C. 1056.

[47] *e.g.* where the victim's own breach is a breach of an independent covenant (*ante*, p. 664); or one which is not sufficiently serious to justify rescission (*ante*, pp. 670–680); or one which occurs simultaneously with the other party's breach, as in *State Trading Corp. of India* v. *M. Golodetz* [1989] 2 Lloyd's Rep. 277, 288.

[48] *Gill & Duffus S.A.* v. *Berger & Co. Inc.*, [1984] A.C. 382, 390.

[49] *Post*, pp. 927–928.

is submitted that, where the victim would thus be entitled, after he has rescinded, to recover back money paid before rescission, he should also be relieved from liability to pay sums which had become due (but had not been paid) before rescission; for it would make no practical sense to hold him liable in one action for a payment which he could then claim back in another.[50]

(b) ON THE OBLIGATIONS OF THE PARTY IN BREACH. For the purpose of stating the effects of rescission on the obligations of the party in breach, it is necessary to distinguish between primary and secondary obligations.[51] The primary obligation is one to render the actual performance promised; the secondary obligation is one to pay damages for failure to perform the primary obligation.

The effect of rescission on the primary obligations of the party in breach is exactly the same as its effect on those of the victim: the party in breach is released from primary obligations which had not yet fallen due at the time of rescission,[52] but he remains liable to perform those which had already fallen due at that time,[53] except where a payment which he should have made before rescission was one which he could, if he had so made it, have recovered back, even on rescission for his own breach.[54]

The important difference between the effects of rescission on the obligations of the two parties is that the party in breach (unlike the victim) as a result of rescission comes under a secondary obligation to pay damages,[55] and that his liability in damages may relate both to breaches committed before rescission and to losses suffered by the victim as a result of the defaulting party's repudiation of future obligations.[56] Suppose, for example, that a hirer under a hire-purchase agreement fails to make the agreed payments in circumstances amounting to a wrongful repudiation and therefore giving the owner the right to terminate. If the owner does terminate, he can sue for instalments which had fallen due *before* the date

---

50 *Cf. McDonald* v. *Denys Lascelles Ltd.* (1933) 48 C.L.R. 457 (*post*, p. 894) where a claim against the party in breach failed on similar reasoning, which should *a fortiori* protect the *victim* of the breach.

51 A distinction drawn by Lord Diplock in a number of cases, *e.g.* in *Lep Air Services* v. *Rolloswin Investments Ltd.* [1973] A.C. 331, 354–355 and *Photo Production Ltd.* v. *Securicor Transport Ltd.* [1980] A.C. 827, 848–849. *Cf.* also *post*, p. 896, n. 34.

52 *Cf. ante*, p. 747.

53 *Hyundai Shipbuilding & Heavy Industries Co.* v. *Pournaras* [1978] 2 Lloyd's Rep. 502; *cf. Fielding & Platt Ltd.* v. *Najjar* [1969] 1 W.L.R. 357, 361; *Lep Air Services* v. *Rolloswin Investments Ltd.* [1973] A.C. 331, 354–355; *Photo Production Ltd.* v. *Securicor Transport Ltd.* [1980] A.C. 827, 844, 849; *Hyundai Heavy Industries Ltd.* v. *Papadopoulos* [1980] 1 W.L.R. 1129; *post*, p. 894. The rule is excluded if the contract validly provides that rescission is to be the *sole* remedy, *e.g. Malcolm-Ellis (Liverpool)* v. *American Electronics Laboratory* (1984) New L.J. 500.

54 *McDonald* v. *Denys Lascelles Ltd.*, *supra*, n. 50.

55 *R. V. Ward Ltd.* v. *Bignall* [1967] 1 Q.B. 534, 548; Thornely [1967] C.L.J. 168; *Lep Air Services Ltd.* v. *Rolloswin Investments Ltd.* [1973] A.C. 331 esp. at p. 350; *Lakshmijit* v. *Sherani* [1974] A.C. 605; *State Trading Corp. of India* v. *M. Golodetz Ltd.* [1989] 2 Lloyd's Rep. 277, 286; Carter, 1 J.C.L. 113 and 249.

56 *R. Leslie Shipping Co.* v. *Westead* [1921] 3 K.B. 420; *Yeoman Credit Ltd.* v. *Waragowski* [1961] 1 W.L.R. 1124; *Overstone Ltd.* v. *Shipway* [1962] 1 W.L.R. 117; *Bridge* v. *Campbell Discount Co. Ltd.* [1962] A.C. 600; *Hyundai Heavy Industries Ltd.* v. *Papadopoulos* [1980] 1 W.L.R. 1129, 1141. *Photo Production Ltd.* v. *Securicor Transport Ltd.* [1980] A.C. 827, 849 ("anticipatory secondary obligation"); *The Rijn* [1981] 2 Lloyd's Rep. 267; *Gill & Duffus S.A.* v. *Berger Co. Inc.* [1984] A.C. 382, 390; *Nova Petroleum International Establishment* v. *Tricon Trading Co.* [1989] 1 Lloyd's Rep. 312.

of termination, the hirer's primary obligation to pay these being unaffected.[57] On the other hand, the hirer is released from his primary obligation to pay *subsequent* instalments, but he is liable in damages for loss suffered by the owner through having, as a result of the premature determination of the agreement, to dispose of the subject-matter elsewhere. For the purpose of these rules, it is important to distinguish between claims for *damages* (which can be brought in respect of future losses) and claims for *agreed sums*[58] (which can be brought only in respect of sums that have become due at the time of rescission). The distinction is sometimes overlooked because there is a tendency to describe any claim for money as one for damages, even when it is actually a claim for the enforcement of a primary obligation to pay an agreed sum. The point can be illustrated by taking the common case of a contract of sale which requires the buyer to pay a deposit and which is rescinded by the seller after, and on account of, the buyer's breach in failing to pay that deposit. In such a case, the seller will be entitled to (i) the deposit as an agreed sum due at the time of rescission; and (ii) damages for the buyer's repudiatory breach,[59] *e.g.* for loss suffered because the seller can only resell the property for an amount which falls short of the contract price by more than the amount of the deposit. In such a case, it is not strictly accurate to say that the seller can "sue for damages *including* the amount of the unpaid deposit."[60] This statement is only accurate where the seller has rescinded on account of some other breach by the buyer *before* the buyer's primary obligation to pay the deposit had accrued. This was the position in *The Blankenstein*,[61] where a contract for the sale of three ships provided for the signing of a formal memorandum and for the payment of a deposit of $236,500 on such signing. The seller rescinded on account of the buyer's wrongful refusal to sign and resold the ships for $60,000 less than the original contract price. As the deposit was only to be paid on signing, the primary obligation to pay it never accrued.[62] But it was held that the seller was entitled to $236,500 as damages for the buyer's repudiation in wrongfully refusing to sign the memorandum. The majority of the Court of Appeal rejected the argument that the seller's damages should be no more than $60,000; and their view seems, with respect, to be correct. At the time of rescission, the seller had been deprived, by the buyer's breach, of his right to receive the full amount of the deposit. He thus became entitled to damages of a precisely ascertainable amount, and later events (*i.e.* the relatively favourable resale of the ships) should not be allowed to deprive him of that accrued right. Such events should only be relevant to the assessment of damages where, at the time of rescission, it is *not* possible to put an exact value on the injured party's loss.

It follows from the authorities discussed in the preceding paragraph that there is no inconsistency between rescinding a contract for breach and at the same time claiming damages for that breach. Accordingly it has been

---

[57] *Brooks* v. *Beirnstein* [1909] 1 K.B. 98; *Chatterton* v. *Maclean* [1951] 1 All E.R. 761; *cf. The Almare Seconda* [1981] 2 Lloyd's Rep. 443; and see *post* p. 894, n. 22.

[58] *Post*, pp. 895–896.

[59] See *ante*, p. 676.

[60] *Millichamp* v. *Jones* [1982] 1 W.L.R. 1422, 1430.

[61] [1985] 1 W.L.R. 435; Carter, 104 L.Q.R. 207.

[62] The doctrine of "fictional fulfilment" of a condition against a party preventing its occurrence would support the argument that the buyer should be liable for the deposit as such, but that doctrine was rejected in *Thompson* v. *ASDA-MFI Group plc* [1988] Ch. 241, *ante*, p. 62.

held that damages can be recovered by a buyer who rejects goods because they are defective,[63] or delivered late[64]; by a wrongfully dismissed employee who has rescinded so as to free himself from a covenant in restraint of trade[65]; by a vendor of land who has rescinded because of the purchaser's failure to comply with a notice to complete[66]; and by a purchaser of land who has rescinded on account of the vendor's breach.[67] Rescission for breach differs in this respect from rescission for misrepresentation, the effect of which is to treat the contract as if it had never existed.[68]

In discussing the effect of rescission on the obligations of the guilty party, we have so far assumed that the right to rescind has arisen under the general rules of law governing that right. It may, however, also arise under an express contractual provision, and such a provision may give the victim the right to rescind for some possibly quite minor breach. So far as the guilty party's *primary* obligations to perform are concerned, the exercise of such a right has exactly the same effects as the exercise of a right to rescind which has arisen under the general law: that is, accrued obligations remain due, while future ones are released.[69] But there is an important difference between the effects of rescission under the general law, and rescission under an express contractual provision, on the guilty party's *secondary* obligation to pay damages. Where the victim rescinds under the general law, he can recover damages in respect of any loss suffered by reason of the premature determination of the contract[70] but he has (unless the contract otherwise provides[71]) no such right where he rescinds for a minor breach under an express contractual provision entitling him to do so.[72] Suppose, for example, that a hire-purchase agreement provides that the owner can terminate for any failure by the hirer to pay an instalment. If the owner terminates for the hirer's failure to pay two out of 24 instalments, he can sue for the two unpaid instalments, but not for any further ones which would

---

[63] *Millar's Machinery Co. Ltd.* v. *David Way & Son* (1935) 40 Com.Cas. 204.

[64] *The Al Tawfiq* [1984] 2 Lloyd's Rep. 598.

[65] *General Billposting Co. Ltd.* v. *Atkinson* [1909] A.C. 118.

[66] *Buckland* v. *Farmar & Moody* [1979] 1 W.L.R. 221; *Johnson* v. *Agnew* [1980] A.C. 367.

[67] The contrary was held in *Horsler* v. *Zorro* [1975] Ch. 302 but that decision was disapproved in *Buckland* v. *Farmar & Moody*, *supra*, and overruled in *Johnson* v. *Agnew*, *supra*. *Horsler* v. *Zorro* had been convincingly criticised by Alberry in, 91 L.Q.R. 337; *cf.* Gummow, 92 L.Q.R. 5 Oakley [1980] C.L.J. 58; but see Dawson, 39 M.L.R. 241; Hetherington, 96 L.Q.R. 401, disputed by Jackson, 97 L.Q.R. 26.

[68] See *ante*, p. 330 and *cf. Johnson* v. *Agnew* [1980] A.C. 367, 395, 398, also disapproving the reasoning of *Barber* v. *Wolfe* [1945] Ch. 187.

[69] *Ante*, p. 651 at nn. 52–53.

[70] *Ante*, p. 651 at n. 56.

[71] As in *The Solholt* [1981] 2 Lloyd's Rep. 574, 579 (affirmed without reference to this point, [1983] 1 Lloyd's Rep. 605).

[72] The crucial question is whether the injured party has a right to determine under the general law (as opposed to one specifically conferred by the contract). If he has such a right, he can recover damages even though, in determining the contract, he relies on an expressly conferred contractual right: *Yeoman Credit Ltd.* v. *Waragowski* [1961] 1 W.L.R. 1124; *Hyundai Heavy Industries Ltd.* v. *Pournaras* [1980] 1 W.L.R. 1129; *The Almare Seconda* [1981] 2 Lloyd's Rep. 433; An apparently contrary dictum in *UCB Leasing Ltd.* v. *Holtom* [1987] R.T.R. 362, 368 is best explained on the ground that repudiation was not established (*ibid.*) so that there was *no* right to terminate except under the express provisions of the contract.

have accrued later if he had not terminated the agreement.[73] Moreover, it was held in *Financings Ltd.* v. *Baldock* that[74] he cannot recover damages in respect of loss suffered by reason of the premature termination of the agreement. The reason for this is that, in the case put, the hirer's *only* breach is his failure to pay the two instalments. He is not, in addition, guilty of a repudiation of the whole contract, for which the additional damages are recoverable where the right to rescind is governed by the general law. This restriction on the right to damages can, it is submitted, be supported on the policy ground that it alleviates the sometimes harsh operation of express provisions which allow a party to rescind even for a minor breach.[75]

The distinction between cases in which the right to rescind arises under general rules of law, and those in which it arises under express provisions may, however, itself give rise to difficulty. The reason for the difficulty lies in the fact that the terms "repudiation" or "repudiatory breach" (which are often used to describe breaches giving rise to the right rescind under general rules of law) can bear at least two meanings. They can refer, first, to breaches which, because of their serious nature, amount to a repudiation and therefore give rise to a right to rescind.[76] But they can also refer, secondly, to all breaches which give rise to a right to rescind; and there are many exceptions to the requirement of serious breach,[77] so that a breach which does not actually amount to a repudiation may nevertheless be described as "repudiatory" in the sense that it gives rise to a right to rescind. This can, for example, be true of a breach of condition[78]: such a breach gives rise to a right to rescind even though it does not cause any serious prejudice to the injured party. Moreover, a term may be a condition on the sole ground that the parties have expressly classified it as such in their contract.[79] Where such a term is broken, it is just as plausible to say that the right to rescind has arisen under a general rule of law (*i.e.* the rule that breach of condition gives rise to a right to rescind) as to say that it has arisen under an express provision of the contract (*i.e.* the express classification by the parties of the term as a condition). A similar point can be made about stipulations as to the time of performance. Breach of such a stipulation justifies rescission if time is "of the essence" of the contract and this will be the position if (a) delay causes, or is likely to cause, serious prejudice to the party in breach,[80] or (b) if the contract expressly provides that time is to be of the essence.[81] In the latter case it is, again, possible to say *either* that the right to rescind for failure to perform at the agreed time has arisen under a general rule of law (*i.e.* the rule giving rise to a right to rescind where time is of the essence) *or* that the right has arisen under an express provision of the contract (*i.e.* the provision making time of the

[73] *Financings Ltd.* v. *Baldock* [1963] 2 Q.B. 104, 110; *Brady* v. *St. Margaret's Trust* [1963] 2 Q.B. 494; *Charterhouse Credit Corp.* v. *Tolly* [1963] Q.B. 683; *U.C.B. Leasing Ltd.* v. *Holtom* [1987] R.T.R. 362.

[74] *Supra*; *Amer-UDC Finance Ltd.* v. *Austin* (1986) 162 C.L.R. 170 (discussing earlier Australian cases); Goode, 104 L.Q.R. 25; Beale, 104 L.Q.R. 355; Opeskin, 106 L.Q.R. 293.

[75] *Ante*, pp. 680–681.

[76] *Ante*, pp. 670–680.

[77] *Ante*, pp. 680–709.

[78] *Ante*, pp. 689–704.

[79] *Ante*, p. 693.

[80] *Ante*, p. 727 at nn. 19–28.

[81] *Ante*, p. 726 at n. 16.

essence). The hire-purchase example given in the preceding paragraph may from this point of view be contrasted with *Lombard North Central plc.* v. *Butterworth*,[82] where a contract of hire provided (1) that the owner could terminate for any failure to pay instalments when due; and (2) that the time of payment was of the essence of the contract. It was held that the second of these provisions made the stipulation as to the time of payment a condition of the contract so that its breach entitled the owners to rescind and also to damages for the premature termination of the agreement. But the decision was reached with evident reluctance[83] since there was no substantial distinction between the facts of this case and those of *Financings Ltd.* v. *Baldock*.[84] In the *Lombard* case the two provisions summarised above were simply two ways of saying the same thing and the policy considerations of alleviating the harsh operation of express provisions for determination are no weaker where the contract contains two such provisions than where it contains only one. For this reason it is submitted that the earlier decision in *Financings Ltd.* v. *Baldock* is to be preferred[85]: *i.e.* that damages for premature determination should not be available merely[86] because the injured party has rescinded under express provisions giving him the right to do so.

(2) Affirmation or failure to rescind

The victim may elect positively to affirm contract, or simply fail to exercise his option to rescind. In either of these cases, the contract remains in force,[87] so that each party is bound to perform his primary obligations when that performance falls due.[88] It must, however, be recalled that, under the rules relating to the order of performance,[89] the effect of the breach may be to prevent performance of the victim's obligations from falling due. For example, an employee may, in breach of contract, refuse to perform his duty to work and so give the employer a right to dismiss him.[90] The mere fact that the employer does not exercise that right does not lead to the result that the employer must continue to pay the agreed wages. On the contrary, he is under no such liability since performance by the employee of his duty to work is a condition precedent of the employer's duty to pay.[91] The position is more complex where the employee's breach takes the form, not of an outright refusal to work, but of a refusal merely to perform specified tasks while continuing to perform the remaining duties of

---

82 [1987] Q.B. 527; Treitel [1987] L.M.C.L.Q. 143; Bojczuk [1987] J.B.L. 353; Nicholson, 1 J.C.L. 64; *cf.* also *The Afovos* [1983] 1 W.L.R. 195, 203.

83 See [1987] Q.B. p. 546 ("with considerable dissatisfaction") and p. 540 ("not a result which I view with much satisfaction").

84 [1963] 2 Q.B. 683, *ante*, p. 751.

85 For the same reason, *Financings Ltd.* v. *Baldock*, *supra*, is (it is submitted) to be preferred to the reasoning of the Supreme Court of Canada in *Keneric Tractor Sales Ltd.* v. *Langille* [1987] S.C.R. 440; Ziegel [1988] L.M.C.L.Q. 277, and 104 L.Q.R. 513.

86 The injured party may be entitled to such damages by virtue of an express term giving him *this* right, even on rescission for a minor breach; but such a term runs the risk of being void as a penalty (*post*, p. 883), as it was in the *Lombard* case, *supra*, n. 83.

87 *Segap Garages Ltd.* v. *Gulf Oil* (*Great Britain*) *Ltd.*, *The Times*, October 24, 1989, a case of *actual* breach. The same rule applies in cases of *anticipatory* breach: *post*, pp. 761–762.

88 For certain effects of victim's inability to perform, see *ante*, pp. 667–670.

89 *Ante*, pp. 662–670.

90 *Ante*, p. 707.

91 *Ante*, p. 662.

his employment. This situation has already been discussed[92]; the only point which needs to be made here is that, if the employer voluntarily accepts such partial performance, he must pay for it at the contract rate,[93] while the employee is liable in damages for loss caused by his breach.[94] It is in this sense that the obligations of both parties "remain in force."

It should be emphasised that the statement just made relates only to the *obligations* of the parties, and not to the *remedies* for their enforcement. To say that a party remains bound under the contract to do or to abstain from doing some act does not mean that these obligations can be enforced by an order of specific performance or by an injunction; and similarly to say that a party remains bound to make certain payments does not mean that an action for the agreed sum can be brought against him.[95] The circumstances in which these remedies are available are discussed in Chapter 21[96]; here it is only necessary to say that, in any of the cases just mentioned, the victim's only remedy may be an action for damages.

(3) Change of course

Once the victim has rescinded, he cannot subsequently affirm and demand performance: this follows from the rule that rescission releases the defaulting party from his primary obligation to perform.[97] On the other hand, where the victim's original reaction to the breach is to continue to press for performance, he plainly does not release the guilty party from any obligation; nor does his demand for performance necessarily give rise to a waiver of the right to rescind, since it is not of itself a "clear and unequivocal" representation[98] that that right will not be exercised. So long as there are no other circumstances from which such a representation can be inferred, the victim can therefore still rescind if the other party does not comply with the demand for performance.[99]

A special application of the rule just stated is to cases in which the injured party has actually obtained an order of specific performance. If the defendant fails to comply with the order, one possible course of action open to the plaintiff is to apply to the court for enforcement of the order. There was formerly some support for the view that this was the only remedy available to him, and that he could not, after having obtained an order of specific performance, then rescind and claim damages.[1] But this view was rejected by the House of Lords in *Johnson* v. *Agnew*.[2] In that case, vendors of land were (as the purchaser knew) relying on the proceeds of the sale to pay off a mortgage on the land. The purchaser failed to com-

---

92 *Ante*, pp. 719.

93 *i.e.* he can make a pro rata deduction in respect of the unperformed services: *Miles* v. *Wakefield Metropolitan D.C.* [1987] A.C. 539.

94 *Sim* v. *Rotherham Metropolitan B.C.* [1987] Ch. 216.

95 *Telephone Rentals* v. *Burgess Salomon*, *The Independent*, April 22, 1987.

96 See especially *post*, pp. 897–902.

97 *Ante*, p. 748; *Johnson* v. *Agnew* [1980] A.C. 367, 393; *cf. Meng Long Developments Pte. Ltd.* v. *Jip Hong Trading Co.* [1985] A.C. 511. The position may be different where the party in breach denies the breach and maintains the continued existence of the contract: see *System Control plc.* v. *Munro Corporate plc.* [1990] BCLC 659, 666.

98 *Ante*, pp. 710–711.

99 *Cf. Tilcon Ltd.* v. *Land and Real Estate Investments Ltd.* [1987] 1 All E.R. 615.

1 See *Capital & Suburban Properties Ltd.* v. *Swycher* [1976] Ch. 319 and the authorities there cited; Dawson (1977) 93 L.Q.R. 232; Oakley [1977] C.L.J. 20.

2 [1980] A.C. 367, disapproving *Capital & Suburban Properties Ltd.* v. *Swycher*, *supra*.

plete, even after specific performance had been ordered against her, with the result that the land was sold by the mortgagee. The vendors were therefore no longer able to enforce the order of specific performance (since they could no longer convey the land) and it was held that they were entitled to damages, not only under the special statutory power to award damages in lieu of specific performance,[3] but also at common law.[4] Such damages may be available even though the party who has obtained the order of specific performance is not, in consequence of the other party's default, disabled from performing his side of the bargain. The reasoning of *Johnson* v. *Agnew* is not restricted to such situations: it is based on the general rules relating to the effects of repudiatory breach. These rules are subject only to the qualification that, where an order of specific performance has been made and not complied with, the party injured by such non-compliance must apply to the court for the dissolution of the order "and ask the court to put an end to the contract."[5]

SECTION 3. REPUDIATION BEFORE PERFORMANCE IS DUE

1. Doctrine of Anticipatory Breach

An "anticipatory breach"[6] is said to occur when, before the time fixed for the performance of a contract, one of the parties *either* renounces the contract *or* disables himself from performing.[7]

Renunciation requires a "clear" and "absolute"[8] refusal to perform; this need not be express but can take the form of conduct indicating that the party is unwilling, even though he may be able, to perform. The conduct must indicate to the other party that the party alleged to have renounced the contract is about to commit a breach of it: an indication given to a third party of an intention to commit a breach at an unspecified time in the future has been held not to amount to a renunciation.[9]

Disablement need not be "deliberate,"[10] in the sense that there may be an anticipatory breach even though it was not the party's intention to disable himself from performing; but the disablement must be due to the party's "own act or default."[11] The latter requirement is most clearly illustrated by cases in which the disablement takes the form of a positive act,

---

[3] *Post*, p. 924; such damages had been awarded in *Biggin* v. *Minton* [1977] 1 W.L.R. 701.

[4] *Semble*, the position would be the same if the order for specific performance were obtained, and then not complied with, by the purchaser. The contrary was decided in *Singh* v. *Nazeer* [1979] Ch. 474; but that case followed *Capital & Suburban Properties* v. *Swycher*, *supra*, which is now disapproved: *supra*, n. 2.

[5] [1980] A.C. 367, 394; *G.K.N. Distributors* v. *Tyne Tees Fabrication* (1985) 50 P. & C.R. 403.

[6] For criticism of this terminology, see *Bradley* v. *H. Newsom, Sons & Co.* [1919] A.C. 16, 53; *The Mihalis Angelos* [1971] 1 Q.B. 164, 196. And see Dawson [1981] C.L.J. 83; Mustill, *Butterworth Lectures*, 1989–1990, 1.

[7] *Universal Cargo Carriers Corp.* v. *Citati* [1957] 2 Q.B. 401, 438; *cf. The Angelia* [1973] 1 W.L.R. 210; Tiplady, 89 L.Q.R. 465.

[8] *The Hermosa* [1982] 1 Lloyd's Rep. 570, 572.

[9] *Laughton and Hawley* v. *B.A.P. Industrial Supplies* [1986] I.C.R. 245.

[10] *Universal Cargo Carriers Corp.* v. *Citati*, *supra*, at p. 438; contrast *The Super Servant Two* [1989] 1 Lloyd's Rep. 149, 155 ("deliberate or at least voluntary").

[11] *Universal Cargo Carriers Corp.* v. *Citati*, *supra*, at p. 441; or (as in that case) from the act or default of another person to whom he had delegated performance of his contractual duty.

such as disposing elsewhere of the specific thing[12] which forms the subject-matter of the contract.

Disablement may, however, also take the form of an omission. For example, a contract may be made for the sale of goods for future delivery, to be manufactured by the seller, or to be acquired by him from a third party, and the seller may fail to take any steps to manufacture the goods or to acquire them from the supplier. The failure will then amount to his "own . . . default" in the sense that he will have failed to do something that he was obliged by the contract to do in order to put himself into the position of being able to perform on the due date. But if, in the second of the above examples, the seller had duly contracted with the third party to acquire the goods, he would not be in anticipatory breach merely because it became highly unlikely that the third party would fail to deliver them under the contract, so that the seller himself would, in turn, be unable to perform. Nor would a buyer be in anticipatory breach merely because, before the time fixed for payment, some external cause (such as exchange control, of the failure of a bank) made it virtually certain that he would be unable to pay on the due date. In neither of the last two examples has there been a disablement by the party's "own . . . default": hence the prospective inability does not amount to an anticipatory breach,[13] even though it would, if it persisted up to the time when performance was due, then amount to an actual breach.[14] Difficulties can obviously arise in deciding whether a prospective inability resulting from an omission is due to the party's "own . . . default." The difficulty is illustrated by the very case in which this requirement is stated, *Universal Cargo Carriers Corp.* v. *Citati*.[15] In that case, a charterer was held to be in anticipatory breach of his obligation to provide a cargo, at the time fixed for loading, because of the prospective failure of a third party, with whom he had contracted for the goods in question, to deliver them within that time. This aspect of the case has been judicially dsecribed as "debatable"[16]; it can perhaps be explained on the ground that the charterer had failed to ensure that his supply contract was effective for the purpose of the performance of his own obligations under the charterparty.

Where one party has committed an anticipatory breach, the other has a choice. He can try to keep the contract alive by continuing to press for performance,[17] in which case the anticipatory breach will have the same effects as an actual breach. Alternatively, he can "accept" the breach, in which case his rights to damages and rescission are governed by certain special rules to be discussed below.

2. Acceptance of the Breach

A breach can be accepted by bringing an action for damages; or by giving notice of intention to accept it to the party in breach, and acting accord-

[12] Disposing of a thing which is *not* specific does not amount to disablement, for the seller may be able to perform, by supplying another thing of the contract description out of stock or from another source: *Texaco Ltd.* v. *Eurogulf Shipping Co. Ltd.* [1987] 2 Lloyd's Rep. 541.

[13] *F.C. Shepherd & Co. Ltd.* v. *Jerrom* [1987] Q.B. 301, 327–328.

[14] This may be so even though the party in breach is in no way at fault, *e.g.* where his source of funds fails: see *ante*, p. 737.

[15] [1957] 2 Q.B. 401 and see *post*, p. 760.

[16] *F.C. Shepherd & Co. Ltd.* v. *Jerrom*, *supra*, at p. 323.

[17] *Michael* v. *Hart & Co.* [1902] 1 K.B. 482; *Harvela Investments Ltd.* v. *Royal Trust of Canada (C.I.) Ltd.* [1986] A.C. 207, 227.

ingly, *e.g.* by buying elsewhere. Such action will normally follow the notice and statements which refer to the need to act on the notice[18] may be explained as descriptive of this normal course of events. Recent authority supports the view that, once the injured party has made it plain that he is treating the contract as at an end, he "does not need to *do* anything more."[19] But mere acquiescence or inactivity does not amount to an "acceptance" for the present purpose.[20]

Acceptance of the breach must be complete and unequivocal.[21] A party cannot accept an anticipatory breach of one term in a contract while treating the contract as still in existence for other purposes. In *Johnstone* v. *Milling*[22] a tenant determined his tenancy by notice and later claimed damages for an anticipatory breach of the landlord's covenant to rebuild. One reason why this claim failed was that the tenant had treated the lease as still in existence when he gave the notice, so that he could not claim damages on the footing that he had previously accepted the landlord's anticipatory breach.

3. Effects of Accepting the Breach

(1) Damages for anticipatory breach

The striking feature of the doctrine of anticipatory breach is that acceptance of the breach entitles the victim to claim damages *at once*, before the time fixed for performance. This rule was established in *Hochster* v. *De la Tour*[23] where the defendant had agreed to employ the plaintiff as courier for three months from June 1, and repudiated the contract on May 11. The plaintiff was able to claim damages at once: he did not have to wait until June 1 before beginning his action. The main reason for the decision was that "if the plaintiff has no remedy for breach of contract unless he treats the contract as in force and acts upon it down to the 1st of June 1852, it follows that, till then, he must enter into no employment."[24] This reasoning has been justly criticised,[25] for the court could have held that the defendant's repudiation gave the plaintiff *the option to rescind* at once but did not *entitle him to damages* until June 1: there is no necessary connection between these two consequences of the repudiation.

Where the interval between repudiation and the time fixed for performance is a long one, there are also practical objections to the rule in *Hochster* v. *De la Tour*, and these are particularly strong where the trial takes place well before the time fixed for performance. One such objection is that the rule may lead to a wrong quantification of damages. If a seller of goods to be delivered in three years' time repudiates and the buyer claims damages at once, the quantification of those damages may depend on the

---

18 *Société Génerale de Paris* v. *Milders* (1883) 49 L.T. 55, 57.
19 *Lefevre* v. *White* [1990] 1 Lloyd's Rep. 569, 574.
20 *Cranleigh Precision Engineering Ltd.* v. *Bryant* [1965] 1 W.L.R. 1293; *Lefevre* v. *White* [1990] 1 Lloyd's Rep. 569, 574, 576–577.
21 *Harrison* v. *Northwest Holt Group Administration* [1985] I.C.R. 668.
22 (1886) 16 Q.B.D. 460.
23 (1853) 2 E. & B. 678.
24 (1853) 2 E. & B. 678, 689.
25 See Williston, *Contracts* (3rd ed.), §§ 1300 *et seq.*; Corbin, *Contracts*, §§ 959 *et seq.*; Vold, 41 Harv.L.Rev. 340 suggests that anticipatory breach might be regarded as a tort; *cf.* Weir [1964] C.L.J. 231; but see Hoffmann, 81 L.Q.R. 116.

market price at the time fixed for delivery[26]; but if the case is tried before that time the court can only guess what that price will be. Another objection to the rule is that it results in an acceleration of the defendant's obligation; he will have to pay damages now, even though under the contract he was not to perform until some future time.[27] Thus if a debtor repudiates liability to repay future instalments of a debt, the creditor can claim damages at once, even though the instalments, or some of them, were not payable until a future day.[28] Of course in assessing those damages the court will allow the debtor "a discount for accelerated payment."[29] Even more strikingly, the defendant will have to pay damages at once although at the time of the action his liability is still contingent and might never mature at all. Thus damages have been recovered for anticipatory breach of a husband's promise to make a will leaving a life interest in property to his wife, although it was uncertain at the time of the action whether the wife would survive the husband.[30]

In spite of these objections, the rule in *Hochster* v. *De la Tour* is well established[31] and at least two points can be made in its favour. First, the rule may help to minimise loss. In a case like *Hochster* v. *De la Tour*, the plaintiff might in fact be more *likely* (whether or not he was *bound*) to keep himself ready to perform if he could not sue at once. The rule giving the plaintiff the right to sue at once provides at any rate some incentive to abandon the contract, and so to avoid this extra loss. Secondly, the rule may sometimes be necessary to protect the injured party: for example, if he has paid in advance for a promise of future performance which is then repudiated. In such a case the injured party could be seriously prejudiced if he had no claim against the other party until the time fixed for performance had arrived; for, having made the advance payment, he might lack the means to procure a substitute contract.

Acceptance of the breach affects not only the plaintiff's entitlement to damages, but also the way in which those damages are assessed. The latter point is discussed in Chapter 21.[32]

---

26 *Post*, p. 849.

27 If the plaintiff affirms the contract and sues for specific performance, the court may give judgment in his favour at once, but the judgment will not order the defendant to perform until the time fixed for performance arrives: see *Hasham* v. *Zenab* [1960] A.C. 316.

28 In the United States, the doctrine of anticipatory breach does not apply in this situation: see Williston, *Contracts* (3rd ed.), § 1326; Restatement 2d, *Contracts*, § 268 Ill. 4. The American rule is convincingly criticised by Corbin, *Contracts*, § 962; and it seems clear that it would not be followed in England: see next note. There is some support for the American rule in Canada and Australia: see *Melanson* v. *Dominion of Canada General Ins. Co.* [1934] 2 D.L.R. 459; *MacKenzie* v. *Rees* (1941) 65 C.L.R. 1, 16–18; *Progressive Mailing House Pty Ltd.* v. *Tabali Pty Ltd.* (1985) A.L.J.R. 373, 385.

29 *Lep Air Services Ltd.* v. *Rolloswin Investments Ltd.* [1973] A.C. 331, 356; *cf.* the position where an insurer wrongfully repudiates liability to make a future payment: MacGillivray & Parkington, *Insurance Law* (8th ed.), para. 800.

30 *Synge* v. *Synge* [1894] 1 Q.B. 466; *cf. Frost* v. *Knight* (1872) L.R. 7 Ex. 111. The actual decision in the latter case has been made obsolete by Law Reform (Miscellaneous Provisions) Act 1970 s.1; but *quaere* whether it could still govern the time at which an order under s.2 could be made: *cf. ante*, p. 387.

31 See *Lep Air Services Ltd.* v. *Rolloswin Investments Ltd.* [1973] A.C. 331, 356, 358; *Woodar Investments Development Ltd.* v. *Wimpey Construction U.K. Ltd.* [1980] 1 W.L.R. 277, 297; *Gunton* v. *Richmond-upon-Thames L.B.C.* [1981] Ch. 448, 467. See, for example, *The Hazelmoor* [1980] 2 Lloyd's Rep. 351.

32 *Post*, pp. 852–854.

(2) Rescission for anticipatory breach

(a) TYPES OF BREACH JUSTIFYING RESCISSION. An anticipatory breach, like an actual breach, can give rise to an immediate right to rescind. Whether it does give rise to such a right depends on the principles discussed in Chapter 18.[33] Generally, therefore, the anticipatory breach will only give rise to a right to rescind if its prospective effects are such as to satisfy the requirement of substantial failure in performance.[34] Thus a charterer's advance announcement of a deliberate delay of one day in loading would not (any more than an actual delay of this kind[35]) justify rescission. In relation to actual breach, however, the requirement of substantial failure is subject to many exceptions[36]; and the question arises whether the right to rescind for anticipatory breach extends to cases falling within those exceptions. There is one type of case in which a negative answer must clearly be given to this question, namely that in which the right to rescind exists only by reason of an express provision in the contract for determination.[37] We have seen that under charterparties charterers cannot exercise their rights to cancel for late arrival of the ship, nor owners withdraw for non-payment of hire, merely because it has become certain that the ship *will not* arrive, or that the hire *will not* be paid in time: they are only entitled to rescind when the specified day has gone by without performance being rendered.[38] In *The Afovos* a shipowner gave notice of intention to rescind on account of the charterer's failure to pay hire in time, but did so while the charterer's breach was merely anticipatory; and Lord Diplock, in holding the purported rescission to be wrongful, said: "it is to fundamental breaches alone that the doctrine of anticipatory breach is applicable."[39] On the facts, the conclusion that the notice of rescission was premature cannot be doubted, for it is clear that the right to rescind for anticipatory breach does not apply to *the particular* exception to the requirement of substantial failure with which *The Afovos* was concerned, *i.e.* the exception under which rescission for actual breach is allowed because of an express provision for determination. But the mere fact that the right to rescind for anticipatory breach does not apply to *one* such exception does not support the conclusion that it does not apply to *any* of them. Indeed, Lord Diplock himself has in a later case recognised that there can be a right to rescind for "an anticipatory breach of a fundamental term."[40] Yet such a breach is not necessarily a "fundamental breach" for it may occur without giving rise to a total or substantial failure in performance.[41] The same is true of a breach of a "condition," *i.e.* of a term *any* actual breach of which justifies rescission[42]; and Lord Diplock's suggestion in *The Afovos*,[43] that there can be no right to rescind for an anticipatory breach of condition may, with respect, be

[33] *Ante*, pp. 659–709.
[34] *Ante*, pp. 670–680.
[35] *Ante*, pp. 704–705.
[36] *Ante*, pp. 680–709.
[37] *Ante*, pp. 680–683.
[38] *Ante*, p. 681.
[39] [1983] 1 W.L.R. 195, 203.
[40] *Harvela Investments Ltd.* v. *Royal Trust of Canada (C.I.) Ltd.* [1986] A.C. 207, 226.
[41] *Ante*, p. 704; in *Metro Meat Ltd.* v. *Fares Rural Co. Pty. Ltd.* [1985] 2 Lloyd's Rep. 13, 15 Lord Diplock seems to use "breach of a fundamental term" to refer simply to a breach evincing an intention not to perform in accordance with the agreed terms.
[42] *Ante*, p. 689.
[43] [1983] 1 W.L.R. 195, 203.

doubted. In part, the question whether there can be such a right is one of terminology. Lord Diplock has elsewhere defined "conditions" as terms the breach of which gives rise to the right to rescind because the parties have so "agreed, whether by express words or by implication of law."[44] Under this definition, express provisions for determination on non-performance *are* "conditions"; but a term is often classified as a "condition" by statute or by judicial decision[45] even though the parties have not expressly agreed that *any* breach of it is to give rise to the right to rescind. This group of conditions is in practice by far the more important group of such terms: and it is submitted that the right to rescind for anticipatory breach does extend to conditions of this kind. Thus in one leading case[46] on anticipatory breach the court asked *first* whether the prospective breaches were breaches of condition and (having reached the conclusion that they were not[47]) proceeded *secondly* to the question whether they were sufficiently serious to justify rescission for anticipatory breach.[48] The first enquiry would have been unnecessary if the doctrine of anticipatory breach could never apply to breaches of condition.

(b) TIME OF JUSTIFICATION FOR RESCISSION. In cases of anticipatory breach, the question arises as to the time when the breach must be such as to justify rescission. Is it sufficient for the injured party at the time of rescission *reasonably to have believed* that the breach would, by the time fixed for performance, have acquired this character? Or must he show that, at the time of rescission, it was *already certain* that the breach was going to be of this kind? This depends on the form taken by the anticipatory breach.

(i) *Renunciation*. The first form of anticipatory breach is by renunciation, *i.e.* by a "clear" and "absolute"[49] refusal to perform. This may be inferred from conduct where the party in breach has "acted in such a way as to lead a reasonable man to conclude that [he] did not intend to fulfil [his] part of the contract."[50] Whether conduct has this effect "is to be considered as at the time when it is treated as terminating the contract, in the light of the then existing circumstances."[51] The court therefore looks to the time of rescission to determine whether the injured party reasonably took the view that the refusal was sufficiently clear and absolute to give him the right to rescind.[52]

(ii) *Prospective inability*. The question whether a failure in performance is sufficiently serious to entitle the injured party to rescind gives rise to special difficulty where a party is alleged to have committed an anticipatory breach by having disabled himself from performing. The failure being wholly prospective, its seriousness is more than usually a matter of speculation; but the injured party may nevertheless seek to rescind before the time fixed for performance. The problem arose in *Universal Cargo Carriers*

---

[44] *Photo Production Ltd.* v. *Securicor Transport Ltd.* [1980] A.C. 827, 849; *cf. ante*, p. 693.
[45] *Ante*, pp. 693–694.
[46] *Universal Cargo Carriers Corp.* v. *Citati* [1957] 2 Q.B. 401.
[47] See *infra*, nn. 54, 55.
[48] See *infra* at n. 57.
[49] *The Hermosa* [1982] 1 Lloyd's Rep. 570, 572.
[50] *Ibid.* p. 580.
[51] *Ibid.* p. 572.
[52] *Ibid.*, p. 573; *Universal Cargo Carriers Corp.* v. *Citati* [1957] 2 Q.B. 401, 439–440; *The Sanko Iris* [1987] 1 Lloyd's Rep. 487; Carter [1988] L.M.C.L.Q. 21.

Corp. v. *Citati*[53] where a charterparty obliged the charterer to provide a cargo of 6,000 tons of scrap iron for carriage to Buenos Aires, to load it at the rate of 1,000 tons a day, and to complete the loading by July 21. He had failed to provide a cargo by July 18 and on that day the shipowners purported to rescind. The charterer's failure to provide a cargo was an actual breach, though not one which of itself justified rescission.[54] It seems that the charterer was also in breach of his obligation to load, for if loading were to be completed at the rate of 1,000 tons a day by July 21 it ought clearly to have begun before July 18. However, perhaps because the obligation to complete loading still lay in the future, the breach was at least in part anticipatory[55]; and the question discussed[56] was whether the charterer's breach, assuming it to be anticipatory, justified rescission by the shipowners on July 18. This depended on the seriousness of the breach: the shipowners had to show "that on July 18 the charterer was unable to load a cargo within such a time as would not have frustrated the venture."[57] It was not sufficient for them to show that on July 18 they had reasonable grounds for believing that such a frustrating delay would occur; they were only justified in rescinding if they could prove that a delay of this kind would actually have occurred.[58]

This rule is likely to prove inconvenient in practice. It does not apply where the contract is alleged to be frustrated.[59] In one such case Scrutton J. said that "Commercial men must not be asked to wait till the end of a long delay to find out from what in fact happens whether they are bound by a contract or not; they must be entitled to act on reasonable commercial probabilities at the time when they are called upon to make up their minds."[60] In the *Citati* case Devlin J. held that this principle did not apply to "questions of breach of contract"[61]; and he added that "An anticipatory breach must be proved in fact and not in supposition."[62] One can to some extent justify the distinction between the two types of cases. Frustration leads only to discharge of the contract, while anticipatory breach can lead both to rescission and to liability in damages. It seems obviously unfair to hold one party (A) liable *in damages*, merely because the other (B) reasonably believed that A would be unable to perform, if it turns out that A is in fact able to perform at the appointed time. But it does not follow that B should not in these circumstances be entitled to rescind. On this point the

---

[53] [1957] 2 Q.B. 401.

[54] [1957] 2 Q.B. 401, 429. He was also in breach of his obligation to nominate a berth. Neither breach was one of condition: *ibid.* and *cf. ante*, p. 696.

[55] Devlin J. at p. 429 discusses whether the breach was actual or anticipatory and concludes that "it must be one or the other." This breach was likewise not one of condition.

[56] See [1957] 2 Q.B. 401, 436.

[57] [1957] 2 Q.B. 401, 450.

[58] *Ibid.* p. 449. The point appears to have been conceded.

[59] *Post*, pp. 789–790.

[60] *Embiricos* v. *Sydney Reid & Co.* [1914] 3 K.B. 45, 54.

[61] [1957] 2 Q.B. 401, 449.

[62] *Ibid.* p. 450; Carter, 47 M.L.R. 422. In *BV Oliehandel Jongkind* v. *Coastal International Ltd.* [1983] 2 Lloyd's Rep. 463 the contract to some extent modified the English rule stated by Devlin J. in the *Citati* case by providing that, if the buyer's financial responsibility were impaired, the seller should be entitled to ask him to pay in advance or give security; but it was nevertheless held that *actual* impairment must be shown before the seller became entitled to exercise these rights. Contrast the American doctrine of "adequate assurance of performance" contained in U.C.C. s.2–609 and somewhat similar rules in civil law systems, *e.g.* German Civil Code § 321.

reasoning of the *Citati* case is open to the same objection as that of *Hochster* v. *De la Tour*[63]: it assumes that in cases of anticipatory breach the right to damages and the right to rescind necessarily arise at the same time. This is, however, no criticism of the actual decision in the *Citati* case, which appears to be consistent with the view here put forward; for the issue in the case was not whether the shipowners were liable for wrongful repudiation, but whether the charterer was liable in damages for an anticipatory breach of his obligation to load.

(iii) *Prospective effects of actual breach.* A reasonable belief that a substantial failure will occur is also sufficient to justify rescission where there has at the time of rescission been an actual breach which gives rise to uncertainty as to future performance. For example, where a ship is unseaworthy, "the charterer may rightly terminate . . . if the delay in remedying any breach is so long in fact, *or likely to be so long in reasonable anticipation*, that the commercial purpose of the contract would be frustrated."[64] In such a case the court need not fear that the shipowner will be held liable in damages merely because it was reasonably anticipated that he could not perform. His liability in damages is already established by reason of the actual breach; all that is in issue is the right of the injured party to rescind. *That right* should, it is submitted, depend on "reasonable anticipation" in cases of anticipatory no less than of actual breach.[65]

(c) CONSEQUENCES OF RESCISSION. Where a plaintiff is entitled to, and does, rescind for anticipatory breach, two results follow. First, he is released from future obligations under the contract: this is so even though between acceptance of the anticipatory breach and the time fixed for performance the party in breach changes his mind and offers after all to perform.[66] Secondly, the injured party is no longer bound to perform in order to establish his right of action on the contract; indeed he need not even show that he could at the time fixed for performance have performed a condition precedent to the other party's liability or a concurrent condition.[67]

4. Effects of Not Accepting the Breach

If the injured party does not accept the breach, he remains liable himself to perform,[68] and he retains the right to enforce the other party's primary obligations.[69] As a practical matter, he also keeps alive the possibility of securing actual performance of the contract without legal action. The fact that the injured party initially calls for performance does not prevent him from later accepting the breach if performance is not rendered,[70] so long as his original demand for performance does not give rise to a waiver of the

---

63 (1853) 2 E. & B. 678, 679; *ante*, p. 756.

64 *Hongkong Fir Shipping Co. Ltd.* v. *Kawasaki Kisen Kaisha Ltd.* [1962] 2 Q.B. 26, 57 (italics supplied); *Snia* v. *Suzuki & Co.* (1929) 29 Com.Cas. 284 (the *Citati* case itself may have been of this kind: see *ante*, p. 760); *cf. The Hermosa* [1982] 1 Lloyd's Rep. 570, 580 (where a mere reasonable *suspicion*, as opposed to a reasonable *conclusion*, of future inability was held insufficient to justify rescission).

65 *Ante*, pp. 675–678.

66 *Danube, etc., Ry.* v. *Xenos* (1863) 13 C.B.(N.S.) 825; *cf. Decro-Wall International S.A.* v. *Practitioners in Marketing Ltd.* [1971] 1 W.L.R. 361, 382.

67 *Ante*, pp. 667–670.

68 *Ante*, pp. 752–753.

69 *Ibid.*

70 *Cf. ante*, p. 753.

right to rescind,[71] or cause some prejudice to the other party (who may have made efforts to perform in response to that demand).

A party who does not accept the breach cannot at common law get damages before the time fixed for performance[72]; and meanwhile he runs the risk of losing his right of action altogether. This could, for example, happen if the contract created a contingent right and events occurred to defeat that right between the time of the anticipatory breach and that fixed for performance[73] The injured party will similarly lose his rights in respect of the anticipatory breach if he does not accept it and if, before performance from the guilty party has become due, that party withdraws his repudiation,[74] or lawfully puts an end to the contract, *e.g.* under an express cancelling clause.[75] The position is the same if, before that time, the contract was discharged by operation of law under the doctrine of frustration.[76] In *Avery* v. *Bowden*,[77] for example, a ship was chartered to carry tallow from Odessa; 45 days were allowed for loading. Within that time the charterer's agent said that he had no cargo, but the captain continued to press for performance. Before the 45 days expired, the charterparty was frustrated by war. If the agent's statement was a breach, the shipowner could have accepted it and claimed damages at once. But he lost his right to do so by choosing to keep the contract alive until it was frustrated, so that both parties were discharged. It would have made no difference if the charterer had been unable to perform, even if war had not supervened.[78]

---

[71] *Ibid.*

[72] For a possible statutory power to award damages in such a case, if the contract was of a kind that is specifically enforceable, see *post*, p. 925.

[73] *e.g.* if in *Synge* v. *Synge* [1894] 1 Q.B. 466, *ante*, p. 757, the wife had died before the husband without accepting the breach.

[74] *Harrison* v. *Northwest Holt Group Administration* [1985] I.C.R. 668.

[75] *The Simona* [1989] A.C. 778; *cf. ante*, p. 680.

[76] *Post*, Chapter 20.

[77] (1855) 5 E. & B. 714; (1856) 6 E. & B. 953; *cf. The Playa Larga* [1983] 2 Lloyd's Rep. 171, 186.

[78] *Continental Grain Export Corp.* v. *S.T.M. Grain Ltd.* [1979] 2 Lloyd's Rep. 460, 470.

Chapter Twenty

FRUSTRATION

Under the doctrine of frustration a contract may be discharged if after its formation events occur making its performance impossible or illegal, and in certain analogous situations.

SECTION 1. DEVELOPMENT

Originally most contractual duties were regarded as absolute, in the sense that supervening events provided no excuse for non-performance. In *Paradine* v. *Jane*[1] a tenant was sued for rent and pleaded that he had for the last three years of his tenancy been dispossessed by act of the King's enemies. This plea was held bad. "When the party by his own contract creates a duty or charge upon himself, he is bound to make it good, if he may,[2] notwithstanding any accident by inevitable necessity, because he might have provided against it by his contract."[3] This doctrine of absolute contracts works well enough (and continues to apply) where it would be reasonable, having regard to the nature of the contract or the circumstances in which it was made, to expect it to provide for the event.[4] But where this is not the case, the doctrine is no longer regarded as a satisfactory way of allocating the loss that is occasioned by supervening events.

The doctrine probably never applied where the contract called for personal performance by a party who died or was permanently incapacitated[5]; and another early exception to it was recognised in cases of supervening illegality.[6] In *Taylor* v. *Caldwell*[7] Blackburn J. relied on the first of these exceptions (and on other analogous cases) as bases for formulating the general rule of discharge which has become known as the doctrine of frustration. The defendants in that case had contracted to allow the plaintiffs to use the Surrey Gardens and Music Hall "for the purpose of giving four grand concerts" on four designated days in the summer of 1861; the defendants were also to provide various side-shows and other entertainments in the gardens. The plaintiffs agreed to pay £100 on the evening of each of the designated days and to provide "all the necessary artistes." Six days before the first concert was to have been given, the hall was destroyed by an accidental fire,[8] so that "it became impossible to give the concerts."[9]

---

[1] (1647) Aleyn 26.

[2] *i.e.* if performance has not become illegal: *post*, p. 786.

[3] At p. 27.

[4] *e.g.* in *Lewis Emmanuel & Son Ltd.* v. *Sammut* [1959] 2 Lloyd's Rep. 629 (where the seller could reasonably have been expected to contract "subject to shipment," but did not do so); *The Zuiho Maru* [1977] 2 Lloyd's Rep. 552.

[5] *Taylor* v. *Caldwell* (1863) 3 B. & S. 826, 836.

[6] *Brewster* v. *Kitchell* (1691) 1 Salk. 198; *Atkinson* v. *Ritchie* (1809) 10 East 530, 534–535.

[7] (1863) 3 B. & S. 826.

[8] Apparently caused by a careless plumber, who had left an unattended flame in the roof: *The Times*, June 12, 1861.

[9] (1863) 3 B. & S. 826, 830.

It was held that the defendants were not liable in damages for the plaintiffs' wasted advertising and other expenses. Blackburn J. said: "Where, from the nature of the contract, it appears that the parties must from the beginning have known that it could not be fulfilled unless . . . some particular specified thing continued to exist, so that, when entering into the contract, they must have contemplated such continuing existence as the foundation of what was to be done; there, in the absence of any express or implied warranty that the thing shall exist, the contract is not to be construed as a positive contract, but as subject to an implied condition that the parties shall be excused in case, before breach, performance becomes impossible from the perishing of the thing without the fault of the contractor."[10]

It should be emphasised that, under this formulation, impossibility is not invariably a ground of discharge. Liability for breach of contract is often strict[11]; and where this is the position a party may be liable for failing to do the impossible. A seller of goods may, for example, be liable for failing to ship goods even though the failure was due to lack of shipping space caused by events entirely beyond his control.[12] By contrast, a shipowner may be excused from liability under a chapterparty if, after the time of contracting, his ship is disabled by an explosion which is not proved to be due to this fault.[13] The distinction between the two situations is not easy to put into words. In neither of them is the party claiming excuse at fault, so that lack of fault is not sufficient (though it is necessary[14]) to discharge the contract. It could be said that lack of shipping space was a risk undertaken by the seller in our first example, while in the second the explosion was not within the contractual risk taken by the shipowner; but this seems to amount to a restatement of the distinction than to an explanation for it. Another way of expressing the distinction is that in the first case the seller *undertook* that shipping space would be available, while in the second the parties merely *assumed* that the particular ship would remain available; and that it is impossibility resulting from the failure of such a common assumption that leads to discharge.

After being established in *Taylor* v. *Caldwell,* the doctrine of frustration entered into a period of growth. It was extended to cases in which performance became impossible otherwise than through the perishing of a specific thing; and finally even to cases where performance did not become impossible at all but the commercial object, or purpose, of the contract was frustrated. In *Krell* v. *Henry*[15] the defendant hired a flat in Pall Mall for the days on which the processions planned for the coronation of Edward VII were to take place. His object was to see the processions, though this was not expressly stated in the contract.[16] The contract was held to be frustrated when the processions were postponed because of the illness of the King. Performance was not physically impossible: the defendant could have used the flat on the days in question. But frustration was not restricted to physical impossibility: it also applied "to cases where the

---

[10] At p. 833.
[11] *Ante*, pp. 737–739.
[12] *Lewis Emanuel & Sons Ltd.* v. *Sammut* [1959] 2 Lloyd's Rep. 629.
[13] *Joseph Constantine SS. Line* v. *Imperial Smelting Corp. Ltd.* [1942] A.C. 154; *post*, p. 807.
[14] *Post*
[15] [1903] 2 K.B. 740. See further p. 784, *post*.
[16] In this respect *Krell* v. *Henry* is unique among the "coronation seat" cases: the contracts in all the other reported cases expressly refer to one or both of the two planned processions.

event which renders the contract incapable of performance is the cessation or non-existence of an express condition or state of things, going to the root of the contract, and essential to its performance."[17]

It can fairly be said that the defendant in *Krell* v. *Henry* would have suffered unacceptable hardship if he had been held to the contract in the altered circumstances. But the courts have refused to extend the doctrine beyond this point; for to do so might enable a party to claim relief merely because circumstances had changed so as to turn the contract, for him, into a very bad bargain. In *British Movietonenews Ltd.* v. *London and District Cinemas*[18] cinema owners argued that a wartime agreement for the supply of newsreels to their cinemas was frustrated because of the following changes of circumstances: the war was over; it was no longer necessary to save film in the national interest; there were no longer patriotic grounds for showing any particular newsreels; and newsreels were no longer uniform as they had been during the war. The Court of Appeal held that this "uncontemplated turn of events"[19] frustrated the contract, but their decision was reversed by the House of Lords. Lord Simon said: "The parties to an executory contract are often faced, in the course of carrying it out, with a turn of events which they did not at all anticipate—a wholly abnormal rise or fall in prices, a sudden depreciation of currency, an unexpected obstacle to the execution, or the like. Yet this does not in itself affect the bargain which they have made."[20] More recently, Lord Roskill has similarly said that the doctrine of frustration was "not lightly to be invoked to relieve contracting parties of the normal consequences of imprudent commercial bargains."[21]

A less strict approach appears at first sight to have been taken by Lord Hailsham in *National Carriers Ltd.* v. *Panalpina* (*Northern*) *Ltd.*, when he described the "proposition that the doctrine was not to be extended" as "untenable."[22] But the point of this observation was that the doctrine applied to contracts generally: thus suggestions that it did not apply to particular contracts, such as time charters, demise charters, and leases of land, have from time to time been rejected by the courts.[23] The actual decision in the *National Carriers* case was that events which temporarily prevented one of the parties from putting the subject-matter to its intended use were not sufficiently serious to frustrate the contract. In this respect, the case, so far from departing from, actually illustrates, the approach adopted in the *British Movietonenews* case.

---

[17] At p. 748.

[18] [1952] A.C. 166.

[19] [1951] 1 K.B. at p. 201, *per* Denning L.J.

[20] [1952] A.C. 166, 185; *cf. Multiservice Bookbinding Ltd.* v. *Marden* [1979] Ch. 84, 112–113; *Watford B.C.* v. *Watford R.D.C.* (1988) 86 L.G.R. 524, 529. Lord Denning has continued to adhere to the views expressed by him (*supra*, n. 19) in the *British Movietonenews* case in spite of their disapproval in the House of Lords: see *Staffs. Area Health Authority* v. *S. Staffs Waterworks* [1978] 1 W.L.R. 1387, 1395 (decided by the majority of the court on other grounds: *post*, p. 782); and *cf. The Nema* [1980] Q.B. 547, 568, 127 (affirmed [1982] A.C. 724).

[21] *The Nema* [1982] A.C. 724, 752; *Atisa S.A.* v. *Aztec A.G.* [1983] 1 Lloyd's Rep. 579, 584; *cf. Tsakiroglou & Co. Ltd.* v. *Noblee Thorl GmbH* [1962] A.C. 93, 115; *The Super Servant Two* [1990] 1 Lloyd's Rep. 1, 8.

[22] [1981] A.C. 675, 689; *cf. ibid.* pp. 694, 712.

[23] *Bank Line Ltd.* v. *Arthur Capel & Co.* [1919] A.C. 435 (time charters); *Blane Steamships Ltd.* v. *Minister of Transport* [1951] 2 K.B. 965 (demise charters); *National Carriers Ltd.* v. *Panalpina* (*Northern*) *Ltd.* [1981] A.C. 675 (leases).

Since that case, there seems to have been some restriction in the scope of the doctrine of frustration. Many factors account for this trend: the reluctance of the courts to allow a party to rely on the doctrine as an excuse for escaping from a bad bargain; the difficulty of drawing the line between cases of frustration and cases where liability for breach of contract is strict; the tendency of businessmen to "draft out" possible causes of frustration by making their own express provisions for obstacles to performance; and the practical difficulties to be discussed in the paragraph that follows. The trend is illustrated by the fact that the Second World War gave rise to few[24] reported cases in which contracts were held to be frustrated otherwise than by supervening illegality.[25] The Suez crisis of 1956 produced only two reported English cases in which frustration was successfully pleaded. Both these cases were later overruled.[26] When the Suez Canal was again closed in 1967, pleas of frustration met with no more success[27]; and the "energy crisis" resulting from further hostilities in the Middle East in 1973 did not lead to any reported cases in England in which frustration was even raised as a defence.[28] All this is not to say that the doctrine will not be applied where performance is actually prevented, as it was in a number of recent charterparty cases in which ships were trapped in port for long periods after the outbreak of hostilities between Iran and Iraq in 1980,[29] so that performance of the agreed services became impossible. In the Suez cases there was (with one exception[30]) no such prevention: performance merely became more onerous for the party alleging frustration. There is now a marked reluctance to apply the doctrine in such circumstances.

From a practical point of view, the doctrine of frustration gives rise to two related difficulties. The first is that it may scarcely be more satisfactory to hold that the contract is totally discharged than to hold that it remains in full force: often some compromise may be a more reasonable solution. Thus in some of the coronation seat cases the contracts provided that, if the procession were cancelled, the ticket-holder should be entitled to use the ticket on the day on which the procession eventually did take place.[31] Similarly, after 1956, contracts for the carriage or sale of goods began to specify which party was to bear any extra expense that might be incurred, should

---

[24] There were some, *e.g. Morgan* v. *Manser* [1948] 1 K.B. 184.

[25] The *Fibrosa* case [1943] A.C. 32, the *Denny, Mott* case [1944] A.C. 265 and the *Cricklewood* case [1945] A.C. 221 were all cases of supervening illegality.

[26] *Carapanayoti & Co. Ltd.* v. *E. T. Green Ltd.* [1959] 1 Q.B. 131; overruled in the *Tsakiroglou* case [1962] A.C. 93; and *The Massalia* [1961] 2 Q.B. 278; overruled in *The Eugenia* [1964] 2 Q.B. 226.

[27] For the Suez cases, see further p. 777, *post.*

[28] *Cf. Sky Petroleum Ltd.* v. *V.I.P. Petroleum Ltd.* [1974] 1 W.L.R. 576, where the only dispute was as to the injured party's remedy; no attempt was made to rely on frustration. In a number of American cases, it was argued (generally without success) that the contracts were discharged by these events on the ground of "impracticability": *e.g.* in *Eastern Airlines Inc.* v. *Gulf Oil* 415 F. Supp. 429 (1975); for an exceptional case giving relief on this ground, see *Aluminum Corp. of America* v. *Essex Group Inc.* 499 F. Supp. 53 (1980), *post*, p. 782.

[29] *The Evia* (*No.* 2) [1983] 1 A.C. 736; *The Agathon* [1982] 2 Lloyd's Rep. 211; *The Wenjiang* (*No.* 2) [1983] 1 Lloyd's Rep. 400; *The Chrysalis* [1983] 1 Lloyd's Rep. 503.

[30] *i.e. The Eugenia* [1964] 2 Q.B. 226; but there the fact that the ship was trapped in the Canal did not lead to frustration as it was due to the charterer's prior breach of the contract: see *post*, p. 803.

[31] For contracts containing such provisions, see *Clark* v. *Lindsay* (1903) 19 T.L.R. 202 and *Victoria Seats Agency* v. *Paget* (1902) 19 T.L.R. 16 (first contract).

the Suez Canal again be closed.[32] In the absence of such express provisions, this kind of solution is not open to the courts: they have no power to *modify* contracts in the light of supervening events. The second difficulty is that the allocation of risks produced at common law by the doctrine of frustration is not always entirely satisfactory. In a case like *Taylor* v. *Caldwell* it may be reasonable that neither party should be liable for loss of the benefit that the other expected to derive from performance, so that the one should not recover his loss of anticipated profits, nor the other the payments promised to him. But it does not follow that loss suffered by one party as a result of acting in reliance on the contract should equally lie where it falls. In *Taylor* v. *Caldwell* the plaintiffs did not in fact make any claim for loss of profits, but only one for expenses thrown away in advertising and preparing for the concerts.[33] No doubt the defendants also incurred expenses on the side-shows and other facilities for entertainment, which the contract obliged them to provide.[34] It might be more satisfactory if such losses could be apportioned. At common law this was only possible where the contract expressly so provided: for example, in one of the coronation cases the contract provided that, if the procession was cancelled, the ticket-holder should get his money back, less a percentage to cover the other party's expenses.[35] A more general, but nevertheless limited, power of adjustment now exists by statute, but it does not cover all cases in which some form of apportionment would seem to be desirable.[36]

SECTION 2. APPLICATIONS

In this section we shall discuss in more detail the circumstances in which the doctrine of frustration operates.

1. Impossibility

(1) Destruction of a particular thing

(a) ILLUSTRATIONS. The most obvious application of the doctrine of frustration is to cases like *Taylor* v. *Caldwell*[37] itself, in which the subject-matter of the contract is destroyed. An agreement for the sale of specific goods is similarly avoided if, without the fault of either party, the goods perish before the risk has passed to the buyer.[38] For the present purpose, destruction need not amount to total annihilation. In *Asfar & Co.* v. *Blun-*

---

[32] *Achille Laura* v. *Total Societa Italiana per Azioni* [1969] 2 Lloyd's Rep. 65; *D. I. Henry Ltd.* v. *Wilhelm G. Clasen* [1973] 1 Lloyd's Rep. 159.

[33] (1863) 3 B. & S. at p. 827.

[34] But these expenses do not seem to have been wholly wasted: it appears from *The Times*, June 12, 1861, that the defendants continued, after the fire, to charge for admission to the Gardens. It also appears from *The Times*, June 13 and December 19, 1861 that the defendants were lessees of the Hall and that it was insured, so that they were to some extent protected against loss.

[35] *Victoria Seats Agency* v. *Paget, supra* n. 31 (second contract); *cf. Elliott* v. *Crutchley* [1903] 2 K.B. 477 (where a contract for the supply of refreshments on a steamer on the day of the naval review provided that the defendants were not to be liable if the review were cancelled "before any expense is incurred by the contractor" *i.e.* the plaintiff). The rule that advance payments could not be recovered back (*post*, p. 809) no doubt produced a sort of rough apportionment, but in a way that was quite unrelated to any expenses actually incurred.

[36] *Post*, pp. 810–814.

[37] (1863) 3 B. & S. 826; *ante*, p. 763.

[38] Sale of Goods Act 1979, s.7; for risk, see p. 768, *post*.

dell[39] a cargo of dates was sunk and so affected by water and sewage as to become "for business purposes something else,"[40] though it was still sold for £2,400. The cargo-owner's liability to pay freight was discharged as the merchantable character of the cargo had been destroyed.

Taylor v. *Caldwell* shows that a contract may be frustrated by destruction of only part of the subject-matter. The contract related to "the Surrey Gardens and Music Hall" and was discharged though only the Hall was destroyed, while the gardens remained in use as a place of entertainment.[41] It is enough if the main purpose of the contract is defeated: we shall see that this idea is also used extensively to determine the scope of the doctrine of frustration in cases not concerned with the destruction of a particular thing.[42] Partial destruction which does not defeat the main purpose of the contract will not frustrate it, though it may provide one party with an excuse for not performing in full[43] or give the other party the option to rescind.[44]

A contract may be frustrated where what is destroyed is not its subject-matter but something essential for its performance. For example, a contract to install machinery in a particular factory can be frustrated by the destruction of the *factory*,[45] even though its subject-matter is the *machinery*. The question whether something is essential for performance depends on the terms of the contract. Thus where an agency agreement related to goods to be "manufacftured *or sold*" by the owner of a factory it was held that destruction of the factory did not frustrate the agreement.[46]

(b) FRUSTRATION AND RISK. Even the destruction of the subject-matter of the contract will not necessarily frustrate it. In certain types of contracts, it will instead be governed by rules which determine when the "risk of loss" passes from one party to the other. Where these rules apply, the contract will not be frustrated by the destruction of the subject-matter; and their effects are radically different from those of frustration. The difference can be summed up by saying that where the destruction leads to frustration it discharges all the contractual obligations of both parties, while where it is governed by the rules as to risk it discharges only some of the obligations of one party. Two types of contracts will serve to illustrate the distinction.

(i) *Sale of goods.* Under a contract for the sale of goods, the general rule is that (unless otherwise agreed) risk passes with property.[47] Property may pass before delivery,[48] so that it is possible for the risk in goods to have passed to the buyer while they are still in the hands of the seller or of a carrier. If the goods are destroyed *after* the risk has passed, the contract is not frustrated: on the contrary, the statement that the risk has passed *means* that the buyer must still pay the price, while the seller is discharged from his duty to deliver. But the seller is not necessarily discharged from *all* his

---

[39] [1896] 1 Q.B. 123.

[40] At p. 128; *cf. The Badagry* [1985] 1 Lloyd's Rep. 395, 399. Contrast *Horn* v. *Minister of Food* [1948] 2 All E.R. 1036.

[41] *Supra* n. 34.

[42] *Post*, pp. 770–771, 777–778, 781, 788–789.

[43] *Ante*, p. 734.

[44] *Post*, p. 772.

[45] *Appleby* v. *Myers* (1867) L.R. 2 C.P. 651.

[46] *Turner* v. *Goldsmith* [1891] 1 Q.B. 544.

[47] Sale of Goods Act 1979, s.20(1).

[48] *e.g.* under Sale of Goods Act 1979, s.18, r. 1.

obligations: he may, for example, have expressly or impliedly undertaken to transfer the benefit of insurance on the goods to the buyer, and this obligation would survive their destruction.[49] If goods are destroyed *before* the risk has passed, the contract is frustrated if the goods are specific,[50] or if they are to be taken from a particular source and all the goods from that source are destroyed.[51] If, on the other hand, the goods are generic the contract is not frustrated merely because the particular goods which the seller intended to supply under the contract were destroyed before the risk had passed. On the contrary, to say that the risk has not passed in this situation means that the seller is bound to deliver other goods of the contract description; and if he does so the buyer must accept and pay.

(ii) *Building contracts.* Under a building contract, the risk of the work is (unless otherwise agreed) on the builder until the agreed work is completed. Thus a contract to build a house or a factory would not be frustrated by destruction[52] of the buildings before completion. On the other hand, where a builder agrees to do work on an existing building, *e.g.* to install new machinery in a factory, a distinction must be drawn.[53] If, before the work is finished, the *factory* is destroyed, the contract is frustrated[54]; but if only the *machinery* is destroyed there is no frustration and the builder will remain bound to complete the installation without extra charge.[55]

(2) Death or incapacity

Certain "personal" contracts, such as contracts of employment, apprenticeship or agency, are discharged by the death of either party.[56] Even a commercial contract may involve reliance by one party on the personal skill of the other[57]; in which case the death of that party (though not that of the other) can discharge the contract. The same rules apply where a party is permanently incapacitated from performing such a contract. Thus a contract to write a book would be frustrated by the supervening insanity of the author[58]; and a contract to render services would be frustrated if continued performance involved a serious risk to the health of the person who had agreed to render them.[59] A contract may likewise be frustrated where it is the capacity of a party to *receive* performance that is affected by the supervening event: *e.g.* where a person who had booked a course of dancing lessons was so seriously injured that he could no longer dance.[60] A contract may also be frustrated by the death or incapacity of a third party: for

---

[49] *e.g. Manbré Saccharine Co. Ltd.* v. *Corn Products Co. Ltd.* [1919] 1 K.B. 198.
[50] Sale of Goods Act 1979, s.7, *ante*, p. 767.
[51] *Post*, p. 773.
[52] It may be frustrated on other grounds: *e.g.* by delay consequent on the destruction, as in *Wong Lai Ying* v. *Chinachem Investment Ltd.* (1979) 13 Build L.R. 81, *post*, p. 794.
[53] Hudson, *Building Contracts* (10th ed.), p. 353; *cf.* in the United States, *Butterfield* v. *Byron* 27 N.E. 667 (1891).
[54] *Appleby* v. *Myers* (1867) L.R. 2 C.P. 651.
[55] *Ibid.* p. 660.
[56] *Cf. Cutter* v. *Powell* (1795) 6 T.R. 320; *Whincup* v. *Hughes* (1871) L.R. 6 C.P. 78; *ante*, pp. 651, 683.
[57] *Cf. ante*, p. 597.
[58] *Jackson* v. *Union Marine Insurance Co. Ltd.* (1874) L.R. 10 C.P. 125, 145.
[59] *Condor* v. *The Barron Knights Ltd.* [1966] 1 W.L.R. 87.
[60] *Parker* v. *Arthur Murray Inc.*, 295 N.E. 2d. 487 (1973).

example, a contract between A and B to paint a portrait of C could be frustrated if C died before work on the portrait had begun.

(3) Unavailability

(a) IN GENERAL. A contract may be frustrated if a thing or person essential for the purpose of its performance, though not ceasing to exist or suffering permanent incapacity, becomes unavailable for that purpose. Thus charterparties have been frustrated where the ship was seized, detained[61] or requisitioned,[62] and where cargo was unavailable because of a strike at the port of loading[63]; a contract for the sale of goods has been frustrated where the goods were requisitioned[64]; a contract to operate and share in the profits of an oilfield has been frustrated where the interests of both parties were expropriated by the government of the country in which the oilfield was situated[65]; and contracts for personal services have been frustrated where one of the parties fell ill[66] or was interned or conscripted.[67]

(b) TEMPORARY UNAVAILABILITY. A person or thing essential for performance may, as a result of the supervening event, be unavailable at the time fixed for performance, but become available later. Such temporary unavailability will most obviously frustrate the contract if it is clear from the terms or nature of the contract that it was to be performed only at, or within, the specified time, and that the time of performance was of the essence[68] of the contract. Thus a contract to play in a concert on a particular day is frustrated by the performer's illness on that day.[69]

Temporary unavailability may frustrate a contract even though no fixed date is expressly specified for performance. For example, in *Jackson* v. *Union Marine Insurance Co.*[70] a charterparty was made in November 1871 for the carriage of rails from Newport to San Francisco; it provided that the ship was to proceed to Newport with all possible despatch. On her way there she went aground in January 1872 and was not repaired until the following August. The contract was held to have been frustrated by the length of the delay, in consequence of which the voyage which the ship was capable of making was substantially different from that envisaged in the contract. It was as if a ship chartered "to go from Newport to St. Michael's . . . in time for the fruit season"[71] did not become available till after the season was over.

The same principle can apply also to time charterparties, under which ships are chartered for a specified period, and not for a particular voyage. In *Bank Line Ltd.* v. *Arthur Capel & Co.*[72] a ship was chartered for 12 months; it was contemplated, though not expressly provided, that the

---

[61] *e.g.* in the Gulf War cases (*ante*, p. 766, *post*, p. 790), and in *The Adelfa* [1988] 2 Lloyd's Rep. 466.
[62] *e.g. Bank Line Ltd.* v. *Arthur Capel & Co.* [1919] A.C. 435.
[63] *The Nema* [1982] A.C. 724.
[64] *e.g. Re Shipton, Anderson & Co.* [1915] 3 K.B. 676.
[65] *B.P. Exploration (Libya) Ltd.* v. *Hunt* [1983] 2 A.C. 352; *post*, p. 812.
[66] *e.g. Hart* v. *A. R. Marshall & Sons (Bulwell) Ltd.* [1977] 1 W.L.R. 1067.
[67] *e.g. Morgan* v. *Manser* [1948] 1 K.B. 184.
[68] *Ante*, p. 724.
[69] *Robinson* v. *Davidson* (1871) L.R. 6 Ex. 269.
[70] (1874) L.R. 10 C.P. 125.
[71] At p. 143.
[72] [1919] A.C. 435; *Hirji Mulji* v. *Cheong Yue SS. Co. Ltd.* [1926] A.C. 497.

period would run from April 1915 to April 1916. She was requisitioned before delivery and the owners did not procure her release till September 1915. In an action by the charterer for damages for non-delivery, the House of Lords held the charterparty frustrated. The contract was, in substance if not in form, an April to April charter; and to hold the parties to a September to September charter would be to impose substantially different obligations from those undertaken. "The requisitioning . . . destroyed the identity of the chartered service and made the charter as a matter of business a totally different thing."[73]

The contract may specify a time for performance but without making time of the essence. Such a contract is not frustrated merely because performance is temporarily impossible at the specified time; but it can be frustrated if performance at a later time would amount to something substantially different from that originally undertaken. In *Acetylene Co. of G.B.* v. *Canada Carbide Co.*[74] shipment of goods under a contract of sale was delayed for three years by war-time requisitioning of all the available shipping space. When performance again became physically possible, it was held that the seller was no longer bound to deliver, as market conditions had radically changed. Similarly, in *Metropolitan Water Board* v. *Dick, Kerr & Co.*[75] war-time restrictions imposed an indefinite delay on the performance of a contract to build a reservoir. It was held that the contract was frustrated since it was likely that there would be a total change in conditions by the time that the restrictions might be lifted.

So far, we have considered cases in which it is claimed that performance should be rendered *in full* when the temporary unavailability ceases. In other cases, involving long-term contracts, the claim is that *the balance* of the contract should then be performed. The outcome in such cases depends on the ratio which the interruption bears, or is likely to bear, to the contract period: the higher that ratio is, the more likely it is that the contract will be frustrated. Thus in *The Nema*[76] a charterparty for six or seven voyages to be made from April to December was frustrated when a long strike at the loading port made it impossible to accomplish more than a further two voyages within the contract period. Similarly, in *Countess of Warwick SS. Co.* v. *Le Nickel S.A.*[77] the war-time requisition of a ship was held to frustrate a one year charter which, at the time of the requisition, still had six months to run, because it was unlikely that the ship would be released in time to render any substantial services under the charter. For the same reason, charterparties were frustrated in a number of cases in which ships became unavailable for service as a result of being trapped for long periods in the course of the Gulf War between Iran and Iraq.[78]

On the other hand, in *Tamplin SS. Co. Ltd.* v. *Anglo-Mexican Petroleum Co.*[79] the war-time requisition of a ship in February 1915 did not frustrate a five year charter which was not due to expire till December 1917:

---

73 At p. 460. Contrast, in a different context, *The Hannah Blumenthal* [1983] 1 A.C. 854, 819 (delay said not to frustrate agreement to submit dispute to arbitration).

74 (1922) 8 Ll.L.Rep. 456.

75 [1918] A.C. 119.

76 [1982] A.C. 724.

77 [1918] 1 K.B. 372.

78 *The Evia* (*No.* 2) [1983] A.C. 736; *The Agathon* [1982] 2 Lloyd's Rep. 211; *The Wenjiang* (*No.* 2) [1983] 1 Lloyd's Rep. 400; *The Chrysalis* [1983] 1 Lloyd's Rep. 503.

79 [1916] 2 A.C. 397; *cf. Port Line* v. *Ben Line Steamers Ltd.* [1958] 2 Q.B. 146.

the majority of the House of Lords took the view that "there may be many months during which the ship will be available before the five years have expired."[80] The effect of such requisition must theoretically be determined at or near the time when it takes place.[81] In practice, the courts no doubt take later events into account, but the *Tamplin* case was decided before the end of the chartered period. Thus the House of Lords had to speculate as to the probable length of the requisition and indirectly as to the probable duration of the war. In the light of later events, the majority may have speculated wrongly. But this is no criticism of the decision, which has also been supported on another ground to be discussed later in this Chapter.[82]

Events such as illness, conscription or internment may interfere temporarily with the performance of long-term contracts involving personal service. Here again one test of frustration is the ratio which the interruption bears, or is likely to bear, to the period specified in the contract. Thus in *Morgan* v. *Manser*[83] a music hall artiste employed a manager for ten years from 1938. He was conscripted in 1940 and demobilised in 1946. The contract was held to be frustrated since in 1940 it was likely that the artiste would remain in the Army for a very long time. On the other hand, in *Nordman* v. *Rayner & Sturgess*[84] a long-term commission agency was not frustrated when the agent (an Alsatian with anti-German sympathies) was interned, since his internment was not likely to last long and in fact only lasted one month.

A contract of employment may be frustrated by the illness of the employee. This is true, not only where the contract is a long-term one, but also where it provides for determination by relatively short periods of notice, since even such a contract is often intended to give rise to an enduring relationship.[85] But temporary illness will not of itself frustrate a contract of employment[86]: it will only have this effect where it is so serious as to put an end to the possibility of performance "in a business sense,"[87] *e.g.* by making resumption within a reasonable time a practical impossibility.[88] An illness which is not serious enough to frustrate the contract does, however, have a number of further legal effects. It gives the employee a *temporary* excuse for non-performance, and it may also give the employer an *option* to rescind.[89] Unless and until this option is exercised, the employee is prima facie entitled to wages during sickness.[90] This prima facie rule can be displaced by an express contrary provision, or by circumstances from which a contrary provision can be implied. To establish such an implied term, it is not necessary to show that the employee would, at the time of

---

80 [1916] 2 A.C. at p. 405.

81 *Post*, p. 789.

82 *Post*, p. 808.

83 [1948] 1 K.B. 184; *cf. Unger* v. *Preston Corporation* [1942] 1 All E.R. 200 (a case very near the line).

84 (1916) 33 T.L.R. 87.

85 *Notcutt* v. *Universal Equipment Co. (London) Ltd.* [1986] 1 W.L.R. 641; Howarth [1987] C.L.J. 47.

86 *Marshall* v. *Harland & Wolff Ltd.* [1972] 1 W.L.R. 899; *cf. Mount* v. *Oldham Corp.* [1973] Q.B. 309.

87 *Jackson* v. *Union Marine Insurance Co. Ltd.* (1874) L.R. 10 C.P. 124, 145.

88 *e.g. Hart* v. *A. R. Marshall & Sons (Bulwell) Ltd.* [1977] 1 W.L.R. 1067; *Notcutt* v. *Universal Equipment Co. (London) Ltd.* [1986] 1 W.L.R. 461.

89 *Ante*, pp. 676–678, 734.

90 *Marrison* v. *Bell* [1939] 2 K.B. 187; *Mears* v. *Safecar Securities Ltd.* [1983] Q.B. 54, 79. *Cf.* Employment Protection (Consolidation) Act 1978, s.19.

contracting, have agreed that he should not be paid during sickness.[91] The rule can be displaced by other circumstances indicating that a term excluding the right to sick pay ought to be implied: for example by the practice of the employers not to make such payments and the failure of the employee to claim them.[92]

(4) Failure of a particular source

A contract may be discharged where the subject-matter was to be obtained from a particular source which without the fault of either party becomes unavailable: *e.g.* where goods were to be taken from a particular crop which fails as a result of drought or disease; or where they are to be imported from a particular country and such import is prevented by war, natural disasters or prohibition of export. Such cases raise two questions: whether the contract is actually frustrated; and what is the position where the source only fails in part.

(a) WHETHER CONTRACT FRUSTRATED. The cases which raise this question can be divided into three groups.

(i) *Express reference to source.* Where the contract expressly provides that the goods are to be taken from the specified source, the contract is frustrated if that source fails. Thus in *Howell* v. *Coupland*[93] a farmer sold 200 tons of potatoes to be grown on land specified in the contract. That crop largely[94] failed, and it was held that the contract was frustrated so that the farmer was not liable in damages for non-delivery. For this purpose it is assumed that the contract specifies an *exclusive* source of supply. Where it refers to several sources, the contract is not frustrated merely because one of them becomes unavailable.[95]

(ii) *Source intended by one party only.* Where the contract contains no reference to the source and only one of the parties intends to use that source, the failure of that source does not lead to frustration. Thus a contract for the sale of "Finland birch timber" was not frustrated merely because the seller expected to get supplies from Finland and could not do so because of the severing of trade routes after the outbreak of war in 1914. For all the buyer knew, delivery might have been made from stocks kept in England.[96] Nor is a contract frustrated merely because the seller is let down by his supplier. This is so even where that supplier is the sole producer of goods of the contract description, so long, at least, as the buyer was unaware of this fact.[97] The same rule applies where a buyer's source of payment fails. Thus a contract is not frustrated merely because the buyer intends (unknown to the seller) to pay with money to be remitted from a foreign country and the remittance is prevented or delayed by changes in

---

91 *Mears* v. *Safecar Securities Ltd.* [1983] Q.B. 54, 74, disapproving *Orman* v. *Saville Sportswear Ltd.* [1960] 1 W.L.R. 1065, and following *O'Grady* v. *Saper* [1940] 2 K.B. 469.

92 *Mears* v. *Safecar Securities Ltd., supra.*

93 (1876) 1 Q.B.D. 258.

94 Not entirely: for a discussion of this aspect of the case, see *post*, pp. 774–775.

95 *e.g. Turner* v. *Goldsmith* [1891] 1 Q.B. 544; *cf. The Super Servant Two* [1990] 1 Lloyd's Rep. 1; and see *post*, p. 778.

96 *Blackburn Bobbin Co. Ltd.* v. *T. W. Allen Ltd.* [1918] 2 K.B. 467.

97 *Intertradex S.A.* v. *Lesieur Torteaux S.A.R.L.* [1978] 2 Lloyd's Rep. 509; *cf. British & Commonwealth Holdings plc* v. *Quadrex Holdings Inc.* [1989] Q.B. 13, 842, 854.

that country's exchange control regulations.[98] *A fortiori*, a contract is not frustrated merely because of the buyer's supply of the currency in which payment was to be made has become exhausted.[99]

(iii) *Source intended by both parties.* The most difficult cases are those in which the contract makes no express reference to the source but *both* parties contemplate that it will be used. Such contracts are sometimes construed as containing an implied reference to the source[1]; but for this purpose it is not enough to show that the parties contemplated the source: they must have intended that that source (and no other), should be used.[2] There is little English authority on the question whether (in the absence of any evidence of such intention) the failure of a source which was merely contemplated by both parties will frustrate a contract. In one case, it was conceded that the partial failure of such a source released the seller in part.[3] The view that the total failure of a mutually contemplated source will frustrate the contract is sometimes said to be supported by *Re Badische Co.*,[4] where a contract for the supply of chemicals was held to be frustrated by illegality on the outbreak of war in 1914 because both parties intended the goods to be obtained from Germany. But this is a very special case: it would clearly be contrary to public policy to allow such a contract to subsist; and this would be so whether the parties had specified the source or merely contemplated that it should be used. The problems raised where the supervening event makes the contract illegal differ significantly from those which arise where it makes performance impossible[5]; and there is no clear English decision on the effect of failure of a mutually contemplated (but unspecified) source of supply. Where that source was contemplated by one party only, the courts have sometimes emphasised this fact in rejecting the plea of frustration[6]; and this may give some support to the view that the plea would succeed where the source was contemplated by both. On the other hand, in some such cases the commercial background may be that it would be usual for the seller to protect himself against the contingency: *e.g.* by a prohibition of export clause. Where this is the position it is less likely that failure of even a mutually contemplated source would frustrate the contract.

(b) PARTIAL FAILURE. A contract for the sale of goods may specify the source from which the goods are to be taken, so that the total failure of that source would undoubtedly lead to frustration. Further difficulties can then arise if the source only fails in part.

(i) *Effects in general.* Such partial failure normally has three consequences. First, the seller is excused to the extent of the deficiency. This was the position in *Howell* v. *Coupland*,[7] where the seller delivered the small

[98] *Universal Corp.* v. *Five Ways Properties Ltd.* [1979] 1 All E.R. 552; *cf. ante*, p. 737.
[99] *Congimex S.A.R.L.* (*Lisbon*) v. *Continental Grain Export Corp.* (*New York*) [1979] 2 Lloyd's Rep. 346, 353; *cf. Janos Paczy* v. *Haendler & Naterman GmbH* [1981] 1 Lloyd's Rep. 302.
[1] *e.g. Ockerby & Co. Ltd.* v. *Murdock* (1916) 19 W.A.R. 1 affirmed (1916) 22 C.L.R. 420.
[2] *Supra*, at n. 95.
[3] *Lipton Ltd.* v. *Ford* [1917] 2 K.B. 647.
[4] [1921] 2 Ch. 331.
[5] *Post*, p. 786.
[6] *Blackburn Bobbin Co. Ltd.* v. *T. W. Allen Ltd.* [1918] 2 K.B. 467.
[7] (1876) 1 Q.B.D. 256; *ante*, p. 773.

quantity actually produced,[8] and the only point actually decided was that he was not liable for the rest of the quantity sold. Secondly, the seller is bound to deliver the quantity actually produced[9]; unless, perhaps, it is so small that it is uneconomical to harvest it.[10] Thirdly, the buyer is not bound to accept the quantity produced if it is less than that contracted for[11]; but as partial crop failures normally lead to a rise in prices this point is of little practical importance.

(ii) *More than one contract.* Additional complications arise where a seller has made a number of contracts to deliver goods from a specified source, and that source fails in part. For example, a farmer who reasonably expects his land to yield 1,000 tons agrees to sell 200 tons to each of five customers, and as a result of partial crop failure only 600 tons are produced; or a seller of goods to be taken from a foreign source similarly agrees to sell 200 tons to each of five customers, and is, as a result of export restrictions, prevented from obtaining more than 600 tons. If total failure of the source would have frustrated the contracts,[12] what difference does it make that the failure was only partial?

One possible view is that it makes no difference, so that all the contracts are frustrated because the seller cannot perform them all in full. But this is unlikely to be accepted because it would enable the seller to keep the available goods and so to make a windfall profit from the rising prices likely to result from the shortage.[13] A second possibility is to say that none of the contracts is frustrated: if the seller delivered 200 tons to each of three buyers, his inability to deliver to the other two would be due to his voluntary act or "election" and would therefore be incapable of frustrating his contracts with these two. This view derives some support from an analogous case[14]; but it will be submitted later in this Chapter that there is no true "election" where the seller's only choice is whether to perform one contract rather than another.[15] The argument that discharge is due to the seller's "election" could also be met by imposing legal restrictions on his choice. This possibility leads to the third view, that some of the contracts are discharged. If this view were interpreted to mean that the seller must deliver to such buyers as were designated by law (*e.g.* by reference to the chronological order in which their contracts were made) it would not be open to the objection that the seller's failure to deliver to the other buyers resulted from his "election." A fourth view adopts the principle of *pro rata*

---

[8] 79½ tons; some of this was produced on land other than that specified in the contract and to this extent the seller did more than he was obliged to do.

[9] *H. R. and S. Sainsbury Ltd.* v. *Street* [1972] 1 W.L.R. 834; *ante*, p. 734.

[10] The contrary seems to have been held in *International Paper Co.* v. *Rockefeller*, 146 N.Y.S. 371 (1914); *sed quaere*: such a case could be regarded as being, in substance, one of total failure of the source.

[11] Sale of Goods Act 1979, s.30(1).

[12] If the seller would have been in breach even in the event of total failure of the source, it clearly makes no difference that the failure was only partial: *Bremer Handelsgesellschaft mbH* v. *Continental Grain Co.* [1983] 1 Lloyd's Rep. 269.

[13] The view that all the contracts are frustrated may at first sight seem to be supported by *Tennants (Lancashire) Ltd.* v. *C. S. Wilson & Co. Ltd.* [1917] A.C. 495; but the only point actually decided was that no single buyer was entitled to delivery *in full.*

[14] *The Super Servant Two* [1990] 1 Lloyd's Rep. 1, *post*, p. 805.

[15] *Post*, p. 806.

division, so that in our example the contracts would not be frustrated, but each buyer would receive 120 tons.[16] The difficulty with this view is that, under it, the contracts would be modified, rather than discharged[17]; and at common law the doctrine of frustration appears to be capable only of leading to a total discharge of the contract.[18] The principle of *pro rata* division does, however, have considerable support in cases in which the seller has relied on the partial failure of the source as discharging him, not under the common law doctrine of frustration, but under an express provision of the contract, such as a *force majeure* or prohibition of export clause. In cases of this kind, there is support for two versions of the *pro rata* principle. One simply states negatively that no buyer is entitled to delivery in full[19]; the other states affirmatively that he is entitled to his *pro rata* share, so that he would be entitled to damages if he received no delivery at all.[20] But there is also support for the view that, if the seller allocates all his supplies to earlier buyers, he is not liable if he delivers nothing to later ones.[21] Probably, the overriding test is whether the seller acted reasonably in allocating the available supplies. In applying this test, the court can also have regard to other circumstances than the order in which the contracts were made, *e.g.* to the fact that the available quantity was "too small to be sensibly apportioned among relevant purchasers."[22] *Pro rata* division is, of course, only possible where the subject-matter is physically divisible. Suppose that a farmer sold to each of five buyers "a calf to be born to my herd," expecting that at least five calves would be so born, and that (for reasons beyond his control) only three calves were born. In such a case, *pro rata* division would not work,[23] and it is submitted that, if the farmer delivered to the first three buyers, his contracts with the other two should be frustrated.[24]

(5) Method of performance impossible

(a) IN GENERAL. A contract may be discharged if it provides for a method of performance which becomes impossible. In *Nicholl & Knight* v. *Ashton*

---

16 *Cf.* in the United States U.C.C. s.2–615(b). The rule there stated, that the seller can take into account "regular customers not . . . under contract," does not seem to represent English law: see *Pancommerce S.A.* v. *Veecheema B.V.* [1983] 2 Lloyd's Rep. 304. Much less are the English courts likely to accept the further rule stated in s.2–615(b) that the seller can take into account "his own requirements for further manufacture": this seems inconsistent with *Maritime National Fish Ltd.* v. *Ocean Trawlers Ltd.* [1935] A.C. 524, *post*, p. 804; see generally Hudson, 31 M.L.R. 535.

17 *The Super Servant Two* [1989] 1 Lloyd's Rep. 148, 158, affirmed [1990] 1 Lloyd's Rep. 1.

18 *Ante*, p. 766; *post*, p. 807.

19 *Bremer Handelsgesellschaft mbH* v. *Vanden Avenne-Izegem P.V.B.A.* [1978] 2 Lloyd's Rep. 109, 115, 128, 131 (where the exact method of division is left open); *cf. Tennants (Lancashire) Ltd.* v. *C. S. Wilson & Co. Ltd.* [1917] A.C. 495, 511–512.

20 *Bremer Handelsgesellschaft mbH* v. *C. Mackprang Jr.* [1979] 1 Lloyd's Rep. 221, 224; the point is left open in *Continental Grain Export Corp.* v. *S. T. M. Grain Ltd.* [1979] 2 Lloyd's Rep. 460, 472.

21 *Intertradex S.A.* v. *Lesieur Torteaux S.A.R.L.* [1978] 2 Lloyd's Rep. 509; *cf. Continental Grain Export Corp.* v. *S.T.M. Grain Ltd.*, *supra*, at p. 473.

22 *Bremer Handelsgesellschaft mbH* v. *Continental Grain Co.* [1983] 1 Lloyd's Rep. 269, 293, citing *Westfalische Genossenschaft GmbH* v. *Seabright Ltd.* (unrep.), *per* Robert Goff J.

23 See I Kings 3: 25.

24 *The Super Servant Two* [1990] 1 Lloyd's Rep. 1 is distinguishable on the ground that the defendant claimed discharge in respect of the *earlier* contract: see *post*, p. 806.

Edridge & Co.[25] a contract was made for the sale of cottonseed "to be shipped per steamship *Orlando* from Alexandria during . . . January." The *Orlando* later went aground in the Baltic so that she could not get to Alexandria in January. It was held that the contract was frustrated since, in the view of the majority of the Court of Appeal, it was to be construed as providing for performance *only* in the stipulated manner. If the stipulated method had not been regarded as exclusive, the seller might have been obliged to perform in a different way, *e.g.* by shipping the goods on a different ship or at a later time.[26] Whether he would actually have been obliged to do this would then have depended on whether the substituted method of performance differed fundamentally from that originally undertaken. This appears from the Suez cases to be discussed below.

(b) THE SUEZ CASES. These cases arose because an agreed or contemplated method of performance became impossible when the Suez Canal was closed as a result of hostilities in the Middle East in 1956 and again in 1967. The first question was whether the parties had actually stipulated for the particular method of performance, or had only expected that it would probably be used. In *Tsakiroglou & Co. Ltd.* v. *Noblee Thorl GmbH*[27] a contract was made for the sale of Sudanese groundnuts at an inclusive price to cover the cost of the goods, insurance and carriage to Hamburg. When the contract was made both parties expected that shipment would be via Suez, but the contract did not either expressly or by implication so provide. It was held that the contract was not frustrated by the closure of the Suez Canal, so that the seller ought to have shipped the goods via the Cape of Good Hope. Although this would have taken two and a half times as long, as shipment via Suez and would have doubled the cost of carriage, the difference between the two methods of performance was not sufficiently fundamental to frustrate the contract.[28] If the difference had been of this kind, it seems that the contract could have been frustrated even though the method of performance was not actually specified in the contract but only contemplated by both parties.[29]

Where, on the other hand, there is no such fundamental difference, the contract may stand even if it does actually provide for performance by the method which becomes impossible. Thus it was suggested in the *Tsakiroglou* case[30] that the contract there would not have been frustrated even if it *had* provided for shipment via Suez. The same view is supported by a number of voyage charterparty cases in which shipowners argued that the contracts were frustrated because of the extra length and expense of the voyage via the Cape of Good Hope. In some of these cases the contracts

25 [1901] 2 K.B. 126; *cf. Maine Spinning Co.* v. *Sutcliffe & Co.* (1918) 87 L.J.K.B. 382, discussed in Benjamin's *Sale of Goods* (3rd ed.), § 1814.

26 *Cf.* in the United States, *Meyer* v. *Sullivan*, 181 P. 847 (1919); U.C.C. s.2–614(1). This rule prevents the seller from making a profit out of frustration on a rising market: *cf. post*, p. 808.

27 [1962] A.C. 93.

28 See further *post* p. 808, at n. 95.

29 *Cf.*, in another context, *Codelfa Construction Pty. Ltd.* v. *State Rail Authority of NSW* (1982) 149 C.L.R. 337.

30 [1962] A.C. at p. 112; *cf. Congimex Companhia General, etc.* v. *Tradax Export S.A.* [1981] 2 Lloyd's Rep. 687, 692 (affirmed [1983] 1 Lloyd's Rep. 250).

expressly referred to Suez[31]; and even where there was no such reference it was no doubt an implied term that the ship should go via the Suez Canal as that was the usual and customary route when the contract was made.[32] Nevertheless the contracts were not frustrated,[33] so that the shipowners were bound to carry the goods at no extra charge by the longer, available, route. The difference between the two routes was not sufficiently fundamental, even though in one case[34] the voyage actually accomplished was twice as long as that originally contracted for and in another added nearly a third to the shipowner's anticipated costs.[35] The same principle can, on the other hand, favour the shipowner where the charterparty provides for a payment calculated by reference to the time taken to accomplish the voyage. In one such case[36] the charterer pleaded frustration but the plea was rejected: once again the court took the view that the voyage via the Cape was not fundamentally different from that via Suez, though exceeding it in length by about a third. To provide an illustration of frustration resulting from the closure of the Canal it is necessary to put a more extreme case, such as that of a contract to carry perishable goods from Port Sudan to Alexandria.

(c) ALTERNATIVE METHODS. Where a contract provides for alternative methods of performance, it is not frustrated if one or more of them become impossible, so long as at least one remains possible. For example, if the contract is to deliver at X or Y, delivery must be made at X if delivery at Y becomes impossible; if the contract is to ship from X or Y, shipment must be made from X if shipment from Y becomes impossible.[37] Such cases have been described as giving a party a "performance option," *i.e.* an option as to various methods of performing what is owed. They must be distinguished from so-called "contract options" which confer a right on a party to choose which of two or more things is to be performed: *i.e.* where the option relates to *what* is to be done under the contract, and not merely to *how* it is to be done. This is, for example, the position where a contract of sale provides for the delivery of X or Y at the seller's option. If X is destroyed, the seller must then deliver Y[38]; but if he had once notified the buyer of his choice to deliver Y and Y were *then* destroyed, the contract would be discharged.[39] It follows that in such a case the seller would not be

---

[31] *e.g. Palmco Shipping Co.* v. *Continental Ore Corp.* [1970] 2 Lloyd's Rep. 21; *The Washington Trader* [1972] 1 Lloyd's Rep. 463; 453 F. 2d. 939.

[32] *Scrutton on Charterparties* (19th ed.), p. 259.

[33] See the authorities cited in n. 31, *supra*, and *Glidden* v. *Hellenic Lines Ltd.*, 275 F. 2d. 253 (1960); *Transatlantic Finance Corp.* v. *U.S.A.*, 363 F. 2d. 312 (1966).

[34] The *Palmco* case, *supra*, n. 31.

[35] *The Washington Trader, supra*, n. 31.

[36] *The Eugenia* [1964] 2 Q.B. 226.

[37] *The Furness Bridge* [1977] 2 Lloyd's Rep. 367; *cf. Warinco A.G.* v. *Fritz Mautner* [1978] 1 Lloyd's Rep. 151 (where there was a "prohibition of export" clause; but the same result would follow under the general common law doctrine of frustration). The rule may be excluded by the terms of the contract, as in *Sociedad Iberica de Molturacion S.A.* v. *Tradax Export S.A.* [1978] 2 Lloyd's Rep. 545.

[38] *Cf. The Super Servant Two* [1989] 1 Lloyd's Rep. 148, 157, affirmed [1990] 1 Lloyd's Rep. 1 (where additional difficulties arose from the "disposal" of Y under another contract: see *post*, pp. 805–806). The position would be different if the contract merely gave the seller a *liberty* to substitute Y for X: [1989] 1 Lloyd's Rep. 148, 157.

[39] See *The Didymi and Leon* [1984] 1 Lloyd's Rep. 583. See further pp. 848–849, *post* for the difference between alternative and contingent obligations.

in breach if he refused to deliver X, and that the buyer would not be in breach if he refused to accept the seller's tender of X.[40]

(6) Statute

The contract (if any) under which a person holds a public office is discharged if the office is abolished by statute.[41]

(7) Impossibility and impracticability

(a) IMPRACTICABILITY DISTINGUISHED FROM IMPOSSIBILITY. The doctrine of frustration originated in cases where performance was said to have become "impossible." That, in itself, is something of a relative term. What is "impossible" depends partly on the current state of technology,[42] and partly on the amount of trouble and expense to which one is prepared to go to achieve it. It has been said that even *Taylor* v. *Caldwell* was not a case of literal impossibility since "by the expenditure of huge sums of money" the music hall could probably have been rebuilt "in time for the scheduled concerts"[43]; but no reasonable businessman would have been expected to incur such expenditure. For this reason the current trend in the United States is to abandon the very words "impossible" and "impossibility" and to use instead the terms "impracticable" and "impracticability."[44] This change seems, moreover, to be intended to widen the scope of the doctrine of discharge by supervening events.[45] "Impracticability" includes "extreme and unreasonable difficulty, expense, injury or loss"[46] to one of the parties. Examples include "A severe shortage of raw materials or of supplies due to war, embargo, local crop failure, unforeseen shutdown of major sources of supply or the like, which . . . causes a marked increase in cost. . . . "[47] The caveat is entered that "Increased cost alone does not excuse performance . . . "[48]—but it is suggested that a price increase "well beyond the normal range"[49] could lead to discharge. In England, dicta to the effect that a contract may be discharged if its performance becomes "impracticable" are occasionally found in the cases.[50] But the weight of English authority rejects this view. Thus it has been said in the House of Lords that "a wholly abnormal rise or fall in prices"[51] would not affect the bargain; and that "The argument that a man can be excused from performance of his contract when it becomes 'commercially' impossible seems to

---

[40] *Cf. The Badagry* [1985] 1 Lloyd's Rep. 395.

[41] *Reilly* v. *R.* [1934] A.C. 176.

[42] See the illustration of "absolute" impossibility given in *Corbin on Contracts* (1962), § 1325: "No-one can go to the moon."

[43] Fuller & Eisenberg, *Basic Contract Law* (3rd ed.), p. 801.

[44] U.C.C. s.2–615; Restatement *Contracts*, 2d, § 261.

[45] *Neal-Cooper Grain Co.* v. *Texas Gulf Sulphur Co.*, 508 F. 2d. 283, 293 (1974) ("less stringent test of impracticability"); *cf. Nora Springs Cooperative Co.* v. *Brandau*, 247 N.W. 2d. 744, 748 (1976).

[46] Restatement, *Contracts*, § 454; Restatement 2d, *Contracts*, § 261 Comment d.

[47] *Ibid.*; U.C.C. s.2–615 Comment 4.

[48] U.C.C. s.2–615 Comment 4.

[49] Restatement 2d, *Contracts*, § 261 Comment d.

[50] *e.g. Horlock* v. *Beal* [1916] A.C. 486, 492; *Nile Co. for the Export of Agricultural Crops* v. *H. & J. M. Bennett (Commodities) Ltd.* [1986] 1 Lloyd's Rep. 555, 581; *cf.*, in another context, *Moss* v. *Smith* (1859) 9 C.B. 94, 103 (a dictum said to be of general application in *Robert H. Dahl* v. *Nelson Donkin* (1881) 6 App.Cas. 38, 52).

[51] *British Movietonenews Ltd.* v. *London and District Cinemas* [1952] A.C. 166, 185.

me a dangerous contention which ought not to be admitted unless the parties have plainly contracted to that effect."[52]

(b) IMPRACTICABILITY GENERALLY NO EXCUSE. A number of cases illustrate the view that "impracticability" is not generally sufficient to frustrate a contract in English law. In *Davis Contractors Ltd.* v. *Fareham U.D.C.*[53] contractors agreed to build 78 houses for a local authority in eight months for £94,000. Because of labour shortages, the work took 22 months and cost the contractors £115,000. They claimed that the contract had been frustrated and that they were therefore entitled to extra remuneration on a *quantum meruit* basis.[54] But the House of Lords rejected the claim as the events which caused the delays were within the ordinary range of commercial probability and had not brought about a fundamental change of circumstances. Lord Radcliffe said: "It is not hardship or inconvenience or material loss itself which calls the principle of frustration into play. There must be as well such a change in the significance of the obligation that the thing undertaken would, if performed, be a different thing from that contracted for."[55] The Suez cases[56] similarly reject the argument that the greater expense caused to the party prejudiced by the closure of the Canal was a ground of frustration. In the words of Lord Simonds, "an increase of expense is not a ground of frustration."[57] Where performance would, in view of changed circumstances, cause not merely extra expense but acute personal hardship to one party, it has been said that "equitable relief may . . . be refused because of an unforeseen change of circumstances not amounting to legal frustration."[58] But in such cases the contract is not discharged: the defendant remains liable in damages even though specific performance is refused on the ground of severe hardship.[59]

(c) POSSIBLE EXCEPTIONS. Four types of cases to be discussed below may at first sight seem to give some support to the view that a contract can be frustrated by "impracticability." But it will be submitted that these cases are all explicable on other grounds and that they do not support the view that impracticability (in the sense of great financial or commercial hardship

---

[52] *Tennants (Lancashire) Ltd.* v. *C. S. Wilson & Co. Ltd.* [1917] A.C. 495, 510 (where the sellers were excused by the express terms of the contract); *cf. Shearson Lehman Hutton Inc.* v. *Maclaine Watson & Co. Ltd.* [1989] 2 Lloyd's Rep. 570, 508 (commodity contract not frustrated by closure of market); and see the cases discussed in the next paragraph.

[53] [1956] A.C. 696.

[54] *Post*, p. 936.

[55] [1956] A.C. at p. 729; *cf. Multiservice Bookbinding Ltd.* v. *Marden* [1979] Ch. 84, 113.

[56] *Ante*, pp. 777–778.

[57] *Tsakiroglou & Co.* v. *Noblee Thorl GmbH* [1962] A.C. 93, 115; *cf. Exportelisa S.A.* v. *Guiseppe Figli Soc. Coll* [1978] 1 Lloyd's Rep. 433; and *Finland Steamship Co. Ltd.* v. *Felixstowe Dock Ry. Co.* [1980] 2 Lloyd's Rep. 287, where no attempt was made to argue that a contract was frustrated by cost increases described at p. 288 as "devastating." Extreme cost increases might, however, be relevant where all that a party was bound to do was to take reasonable steps to produce a specified result. For example, in *Brauer & Co. (Great Britain) Ltd.* v. *James Clark (Brush Materials) Ltd.* [1952] 2 All E.R. 497, 501 it was said that a seller would not be liable for failure to get an export licence if the cost of getting it were 100 times the contract price; the seller's duty in that case would have been limited to one to take reasonable steps (*ante*, p. 61) even if the contract had not been expressly "subject to export licence."

[58] *Patel* v. *Ali* [1984] Ch. 283, 288.

[59] *Post*, p. 908. In *Patel* v. *Ali*, *supra*, the defendant was required to pay £10,000 into court as a condition of the discharge of the order of specific performance against her.

to one of the parties) is of itself sufficient to discharge a contract in English law.

First, there are the cases already discussed[60] in which long delays in performance resulted from war-time restrictions, and it was held that performance need not be resumed in the totally altered conditions which prevailed when those restrictions were removed. It could be said that performance at the later time was "impracticable"; but this was only one factor leading to discharge, the other being that, for a considerable period, the war-time conditions made performance actually impossible.

Secondly, there are cases in which contracts were discharged, not under the general doctrine of frustration, but under express contractual provisions (such as *force majeure* or prohibition of export clauses) which excuse one party, or both, if the specified event prevents performance. Such clauses do not protect a party merely because supervening events make performance more difficult or more expensive for him[61]; nor do they normally protect him where he can perform in alternative ways and only one of them becomes impossible: for example, a seller who cannot obtain the goods that he had undertaken to deliver from the source intended by him (*e.g.* because of being let down by his supplier or because of an export embargo) must obtain them from other sources that remain available.[62] But this rule is subject to an exception which applies where it would be unreasonable to require the seller to perform in this way, because attempts to do so by him, and by other sellers similarly situated, would drive prices up to "unheard of levels."[63] In one case of this kind, it was said that to require the seller to make such an attempt would be "impracticable and commercially unsuitable."[64] But it should be emphasised that these cases are not concerned with discharge under the general doctrine of frustration but with discharge under express contractual provisions for supervening events.[65] Such a provision often operates in circumstances falling short of frustration under the general law.[66] Thus the fact that it may, on its true construction, cover "impracticability" does not support the view that the same circumstances would frustrate a contract which contained no such provision.

The third situation in which it is arguable that impracticability may be a

---

[60] *Metropolitan Water Board* v. *Dick Kerr & Co.* [1918] A.C. 119; *Acetylene Co. of G.B.* v. *Canada Carbide Co.* (1922) 8 Ll.L.Rep. 456; *ante*, pp. 770–771.

[61] See, for example, *Brauer & Co. (Great Britain) Ltd.* v. *James Clark (Brush Materials) Ltd.* [1952] 2 All E.R. 497; *B. & S. Contracts & Designs Ltd.* v. *Victor Green Publications Ltd.* [1984] I.C.R. 419.

[62] *e.g. P. J. van der Zijden Wildhandel N.V.* v. *Tucker & Cross Ltd.* [1975] 2 Lloyd's Rep. 240.

[63] *Tradax Export S.A.* v. *André & Cie* [1976] 1 Lloyd's Rep. 416, 423; *cf. André & Cie S.A.* v. *Tradax Export S.A.* [1983] 1 Lloyd's Rep. 254; *Cook Industries* v. *Tradax Export S.A.* [1983] 1 Lloyd's Rep. 327, 344, affirmed without reference to this point [1985] 2 Lloyd's Rep. 454 and see generally *Benjamin's Sale of Goods* (3rd ed.), § 1721.

[64] *Bremer Handelsgesellschaft mbH* v. *Vanden Avenne-Izegem P.V.B.A.* [1978] 2 Lloyd's Rep. 109, 115. *Cf. The Badagry* [1985] 1 Lloyd's Rep. 385, 399 ("commercially impossible").

[65] The same is true of *Ford & Sons (Oldham) Ltd.* v. *Henry Leetham & Sons Ltd.* (1915) 21 Com.Cas. 55, which is nevertheless cited in support of the general principle of discharge by "impracticability" in U.C.C. s.2–615 Comment 4.

[66] *Post*, pp. 798–799. For the significance of the distinction between discharge by frustration and under an express term, *cf.* also *The Super Servant Two* [1989] 1 Lloyd's Rep. 148, 149, [1990] 1 Lloyd's Rep. 1, 8.

ground of discharge concerns contracts of indefinite duration. In *Staffordshire Area Health Authority* v. *South Staffordshire Waterworks Co.*[67] a hospital had in 1919 contracted to give up to a Waterworks Company its right to take water from a well, and the Company had in return promised "at all times hereafter" to supply water to the hospital at a fixed price specified in the contract. In 1975 the cost to the Company of making the supply had risen to over 18 times the contract price and the Company gave seven months' notice to terminate the agreement. It was held that this notice was effective. Lord Denning M.R. regarded the contract as frustrated by the change of circumstances which had occurred between 1919 and 1975. But this view is, with respect, open to question, as it was based on the very passage of his own judgment in the *British Movietonenews* case which had there been disapproved by the House of Lords.[68] The preferable reason for the decision in the *Staffordshire* case is therefore that of the majority, who held that the agreement was, on its true construction, intended to be indefinite (and not of perpetual) duration[69]: hence the case fell within the general principle that, in commercial agreements of indefinite duration, a term is often implied entitling either party to terminate by reasonable notice.[70] It follows from this reasoning that the decision would have gone the other way if the agreement had been for a fixed term, *e.g.* for ten years. The agreement could then not have been terminated by notice before the end of the ten years, nor would an increase in the suppliers' costs during that period have been a ground of frustration. This view is supported by later authority[71] and seems also to be correct in principle: if parties enter into a fixed term fixed price contract they must be taken thereby to have allocated the risks of market fluctuations. If the parties are not prepared to accept these risks (or to accept them in full) they can adopt the now common practice of providing in the contract itself for flexible pricing.[72]

The three situations so far discussed should be distinguished from a fourth which arose in *The Playa Larga*.[73] Sugar had been sold by a Cuban state trading organisation to a buyer controlled by a state trading organisation in Chile. When the contract was made, Cuba and Chile were both ruled by Marxist governments; but before deliveries under the contract had been completed, the Marxist government in Chile was overthrown; diplo-

---

[67] [1978] 1 W.L.R. 1387; Rose, 96 L.Q.R. 177.

[68] [1952] A.C. 166, 185; *ante*, p. 765.

[69] "At all times hereafter" was (obviously) not to be taken literally, but meant "at all times hereafter during the subsistence of the agreement." The majority view was followed in *Tower Hamlets L.B.C.* v. *British Gas Corp., The Times*, March 23, 1982, affd., *The Times*, December 14, 1983, and approved in *Watford D.C.* v. *Watford R.D.C.* (1988) 86 L.G.R. 524, 529.

[70] *Cf. ante*, p. 650; contrast *Watford D.C.* v. *Watford R.D.C.* (1988) 86 L.G.R. 524, where it was held that no such term could be implied in an agreement to contribute variable amounts towards the maintenance of cemeteries.

[71] *Kirklees M.B.C.* v. *Yorks Woollen District Transport Co.* (1978) L.G.R. 448.

[72] See *Superior Overseas Development Corp.* v. *British Gas Corp.* [1982] 1 Lloyd's Rep. 262; *Wates* v. *G.L.C.* (1983) 25 Build L.R. 1 (*post*, p. 796); *Watford D.C.* v. *Watford R.D.C.* (1988) 86 L.G.R. 524, 548; *Queensland Electricity Generating Board* v. *New Hope Collieries Pty. Ltd.* [1989] 1 Lloyd's Rep. 205. In the American case of *Aluminum Corp. of America Inc.* v. *Essex Group Inc.*, 499 F.Supp. 53 (1980) relief was given even where a fixed term contract contained such a clause, the court substituting its own price-fixing formula for that agreed by the parties; but this seems to be an undue interference with a contract between parties of equal bargaining power.

[73] [1983] 2 Lloyd's Rep. 171.

matic relations between the two countries were severed; and there was a complete breakdown of commercial relations between them. It was held that the contract was frustrated even though its performance had not become impossible in any of the senses discussed in this Chapter. The decision was not, however, based on the argument that performance would cause such extreme hardship to the seller that he ought to be discharged. The basis of discharge simply was that, in the altered conditions, there was no possibility of the implementation of the contract on either side[74]; and that accordingly the contract was, in these conditions, no longer intended to be binding.

(d) INFLATION. In the cases so far discussed, increases in the cost of performing a particular contract have made that contract unprofitable to one party. A similar situation may arise where the general process of inflation reduces in real terms the benefit which that party expected to obtain under the contract. In the *British Movietonenews* case "a sudden depreciation of currency" is listed as one of the uncontemplated turns of events which do *not* frustrate a contract.[75] The passage continues to make the general point that a contract would cease to bind if a "fundamentally different situation" were to emerge. This may refer back to the illustrations of non-frustrating events previously given[76]; but more probably the reference is to *other* (*i.e.* to frustrating) events. Again, in *Wates Ltd.* v. *G.L.C.*[77] a building contract to some extent protected the builder against inflation, by means of a price-escalation clause; and it was said that the fact that "inflation increased not [at] a trot or at a canter but at a gallop . . . was not so radical a difference from the inflation contemplated and provided for as to frustrate the contract."[78] Thus the English authorities do not support the view that inflation is a ground of frustration, though the possibility that extreme (as opposed to merely severe) inflation may be capable of frustrating a contract cannot be wholly ruled out.[79] It is again open to a party who fears that he will be prejudiced by inflation to guard against this risk by an express term, *e.g.* by providing (if his bargaining position permits) for "index-linked" payments.[80]

(e) CURRENCY FLUCTUATIONS. A debtor whose obligations are defined by reference to a foreign currency cannot avoid liability to pay in full merely because the pound sterling has fallen in value in relation to that currency by an unexpectedly large amount.[81]

2. Frustration of Purpose

Frustration of purpose is, in a sense, the converse of impracticability. The two ideas resemble each other in that neither is concerned with cases in which performance has become impossible. Impracticability is said to arise when a *supplier* of goods, services or other facilities alleges that superven-

---

[74] *Ibid.*, p. 188.
[75] [1952] A.C. 166, 185.
[76] *Cf.* Mann, *The Legal Aspects of Money* (4th ed.), p. 111.
[77] (1983) 25 Build.L.R. 1.
[78] *Ibid.* p. 34.
[79] *Cf.* Lord Roskill's reference in *National Carriers Ltd.* v. *Panalpina Northern Ltd.* [1981] A.C. 675, 712, to "inflation" as one of the "circumstances in which the doctrine [of frustration] has been invoked, sometimes with success, *sometimes without*."
[80] See *Nationwide B.S.* v. *Registry of Friendly Societies* [1983] 1 W.L.R. 1226.
[81] *Multiservice Bookbinding Ltd.* v. *Marden* [1979] Ch. 84.

ing events have made performance of his own promise so much more burdensome to him that he should no longer be bound to render it. The argument of frustration of purpose, on the other hand, is put forward by the *recipient* of the goods, services or facilities: it is that supervening events have so greatly reduced the value to him of the other party's performance that he should no longer be bound to accept and to pay the agreed price. Such an argument succeeded in some of the cases which arose out of the postponement of the coronation of King Edward VII. We have seen that in *Krell* v. *Henry*[82] the effect of the postponement was to discharge a contract for the hire of a flat overlooking the route of the proposed processions. The obvious danger of such a rule is that it can all too easily be invoked by a party for whom a contract has simply become a very bad bargain. *Krell* v. *Henry* has therefore attracted much criticism[83]; but the decision can be justified[84] on the ground that the contract was, on its true construction, not merely one for the hire of the flat, but one to provide facilities for viewing the coronation processions. The actual decision may be contrasted with an example given in one of the judgments: a contract to take a cab to Epsom on Derby day "at a suitable enhanced price"[85] would not be frustrated if the Derby were cancelled. Here the contract was evidently regarded as one to get the passenger to Epsom—not as one to get him to the Derby. The contract in *Krell* v. *Henry* was not construed as simply one to hire a flat in Pall Mall because it would then have been an extremely unusual one. Flats in Pall Mall were not commonly hired out by the day[86]; but contracts to take cabs to Epsom were commonly made on days other than Derby day.

Similar reasoning distinguishes *Krell* v. *Henry* from *Herne Bay Steamboat Co.* v. *Hutton*,[87] another of the coronation cases. A pleasure boat was hired "for the purpose of viewing the naval review and for a day's cruise round the fleet." The review, which formed part of the proposed coronation celebrations, was cancelled when the King fell ill, but the contract was not frustrated. It was construed simply as a contract for the hire of a boat, which could still be performed although one of the motives of the hirer[88]—to carry passengers at high prices to see the review—was defeated.

Although the actual decision in *Krell* v. *Henry* appears to be justifiable on the construction of the contract, the case has scarcely ever been followed in England. Normally, a contract is not frustrated merely because supervening events have prevented one party from putting the subject-matter to the use intended by him, even though that use was also contemplated by the other. Thus a contract by which a gas company agreed with a local authority to "provide, maintain and light" street lamps was not frustrated when war-time black-out regulations prohibited the lighting of such

[82] [1903] 2 K.B. 740 (*ante*, p. 764); McElroy and Williams, 4 M.L.R. 241; 5 M.L.R. 1.
[83] *Blackburn Bobbin Co. Ltd.* v. *T. W. Allen & Sons Ltd.* [1918] 1 K.B. 540, 542 (affirmed [1918] 2 K.B. 467); *Larrinaga* v. *Société Franco-Américaine des Phosphates de Medulla* (1923) 92 L.J.K.B. 455, 459; *cf. Maritime National Fish Ltd.* v. *Ocean Trawlers Ltd.* [1935] A.C. 524, 528; *Scanlan's New Neon Ltd.* v. *Toohey's Ltd.* (1943) 67 C.L.R. 169, 191–194; *Corbin on Contracts*, § 1355 at pp. 464–465; Landon, 52 L.Q.R. 168; Gordon, *ibid.* p. 326.
[84] See *Codelfa Construction Pty. Ltd.* v. *State Rail Authority of NSW* (1982) 149 C.L.R. 337, 358.
[85] [1903] 2 K.B. 740, 750.
[86] Especially if the nights are specifically excluded, as they were in *Krell* v. *Henry*.
[87] [1903] 2 K.B. 683.
[88] For the requirement that the purpose of *both* parties must be frustrated, see *The Siboen and the Sibotre* [1976] 1 Lloyd's Rep. 293.

lamps,[89] since performance of the maintenance obligation ("which cannot be regarded as . . . trivial"[90]) remained possible.[91] Similarly, a contract for the sale of goods is not frustrated merely because the buyer's purpose to export the goods from, or to import them into, a particular country is defeated by export or import restrictions.[92] Perhaps the most striking illustration of the reluctance of the courts to apply the principle of frustration of purpose is provided by *Amalgamated Investment & Property Co. Ltd.* v. *John Walker & Son Ltd.*[93] In that case it was held that a contract for the purchase of property for redevelopment was not frustrated when the buildings on the land were listed as being of special architectural or historic interest, so that redevelopment became more difficult or impossible and the property lost most of its value.[94]

The more recent authorities show that "the frustrated expectations and intentions of one party to a contract do not necessarily, or indeed usually, lead to the frustration of that contract."[95] They make it difficult to establish the defence of frustration of purpose; but they do not make it impossible. In *Denny, Mott & Dickinson* v. *James B. Fraser & Co. Ltd.*[96] an agreement for the lease of a timber yard was made for the purpose of enabling the parties to carry out a contract between them for the sale of timber. When performance of the contract of sale was prohibited by wartime regulations, the House of Lords held that the agreement for the lease of the yard was also frustrated. The actual decision may to some extent rest on special policy considerations applicable to cases of supervening illegality; but other situations can be imagined in which the principle of frustration of purpose might also apply. For example, if premises were leased as a warehouse and supervening events made their use as such impossible for the whole period of the lease, it seems that the contract might be frustrated.[97] In such a case, the contract would be discharged, although performance had not become impossible, because the supervening event had destroyed "some basic, though tacit assumption on which the parties had contracted."[98]

---

[89] *Leiston Gas Co.* v. *Leiston-cum-Sizewell U.D.C.* [1916] 2 K.B. 428; on the interpretation of express contractual provisions for such events, *cf. Williams* v. *Mercer* [1940] 3 All E.R. 293 and contrast *Egham & Staines Electricity Co. Ltd.* v. *Egham U.D.C.* [1944] 1 All E.R. 107.

[90] *Leiston* case, [1916] 2 K.B. 428, 433.

[91] For contrasting decisions on the effect of black-out regulations on contracts for the hire of electric advertising signs, see *Scanlan's New Neon Ltd.* v. *Toohey's Ltd.* (1943) 67 C.L.R. 169 (contract not discharged); *20th Century Lites* v. *Goodman*, 149 P. 2d. 88 (1944) (contract discharged).

[92] *e.g. D. McMaster & Co.* v. *Cox McEwen & Co.*, 1921 S.C. (H.L.) 1; *Congimex S.A.R.L. (Lisbon)* v. *Continental Grain Export Corp. (New York)* [1979] 2 Lloyd's Rep. 346; *Congimex Companhia Geral, etc., S.A.R.L.* v. *Tradax Export S.A.* [1983] 1 Lloyd's Rep. 250.

[93] [1977] 1 W.L.R. 164.

[94] The listing was said to have reduced the value of the property to £200,000—against a contract price of £1,710,000.

[95] *Congimex Companhia Geral, etc., S.A.R.L.* v. *Tradax Export S.A.* [1983] 1 Lloyd's Rep. 250, 253.

[96] [1944] A.C. 265.

[97] This seems to be assumed in *National Carriers Ltd.* v. *Panalpina (Northern) Ltd.* [1981] A.C. 675. (*post*, pp. 791–792), where the temporary nature of the interruption was stressed in rejecting the plea of frustration.

[98] *Sir Lindsay Parkinson Ltd.* v. *Commissioners of Works* [1949] 2 K.B. 632, 665.

3. Illegality

A contract may be discharged by a supervening prohibition if the prohibition would have made the contract illegal, had it been in force when the contract was made.[99]

The object of the doctrine of frustration in cases of supervening impossibility or of frustration of purpose is to provide a satisfactory method of allocating or distributing the loss caused by the supervening event. Where, however, a contract is affected by supervening illegality, the court has to take into account, not only the relative interests of the parties, but also the interests of the public in seeing that the law is observed[1]; and this public interest may sometimes outweigh the importance of achieving a fair distribution of loss. For this reason supervening illegality is a separate ground of discharge from supervening impossibility, and is to some extent governed by special rules.

(1) Illustrations

(a) Trading with the enemy. The public interest considerations just mentioned are particularly strong where a contract becomes illegal as a result of the war-time prohibition against trading with the enemy. In the leading *Fibrosa* case[2] a contract for the sale of machinery to be shipped to Gdynia was frustrated when that port was occupied by the enemy during the Second World War. Although it might have been physically possible to get the goods to the destination,[3] the contract was discharged because of the strong public interest in ensuring that no aid should be given to the enemy economy in time of war. The same principle applies where goods are to be imported from an enemy country: the contract is frustrated even though the enemy source is not specified in the contract but only contemplated by the parties.[4] The public interest principle is so strong in these cases that frustration by or as a result of war cannot be excluded even by an express provision in the contract.[5]

(b) Other prohibitions. The cases provide many illustrations of frustration by supervening prohibitions other than that against trading with the enemy. In the *Denny Mott*[6] case, for example, a contract for the sale of timber was frustrated by a war-time prohibition against dealing in goods of the contract description. Contracts can similarly be frustrated by prohibition of export or import, by restrictions on the movement of capital,[7] or by licensing requirements of the kinds to be discussed below. In these cases the public interest in seeing that the prohibition is observed is less strong

---

[99] See *ante*, p. 386 at n. 82.

[1] This book deals only with discharge by supervening illegality which arises under English law. The justification for discharge where the illegality arises under *foreign* law (*e.g.* under a foreign prohibition of export or import) is somewhat different: see *Benjamin's Sale of Goods* (3rd ed.), §§ 1585, 2463.

[2] *Fibrosa Spolka Ackcyjna* v. *Fairbairn, Lawson Combe Barbour Ltd.* [1943] A.C. 32.

[3] The mere outbreak of war does not frustrate a contract: see *The Chrysalis* [1983] 1 W.L.R. 1469, (where the war was one to which the United Kingdom was not a party, so that no question of trading with the enemy could arise).

[4] *Re Badische Co.* [1921] 2 Ch. 331; *ante*, p. 774.

[5] *Ertel Bieber & Co.* v. *Rio Tinto Co. Ltd.* [1918] A.C. 260; *post*, p. 796.

[6] [1944] A.C. 265; *ante*, p. 785.

[7] See *Libyan Arab Foreign Bank* v. *Bankers Trust Co.* [1989] Q.B. 728, 749, though in that case there was no frustration: *ibid.* pp. 771–772.

than in the trading with the enemy cases[8]; and they differ from the trading with the enemy cases in two ways. First, frustration only results if it is an actual term of the contract that the subsequently prohibited act is to be done. Thus a contract for the sale of goods may be frustrated by prohibition of export if it provides that the goods are to be exported,[9] but not merely because the buyer intended to export them, even though the seller knew this.[10] Secondly, frustration can often be excluded by express contractual provisions. Thus provisions suspending performance in the event of prohibition of export are valid[11] since, so far from contravening the policy of the prohibition, they assume that it will be observed. Similar provisions in trading with the enemy cases are contrary to the public interest since they involve continuing relations with an enemy subject, and so may indirectly support the enemy economy.

(2) Supervening and antecedent prohibition

The rules so far stated apply to a supervening prohibition, *i.e.* to one imposed by a law made after the contract. If, at the time of contracting, the prohibition is already in force, the case is one of antecedent prohibition. This may make the contract void *ab initio* for illegality,[12] but it will not bring about frustration. There is, however, an intermediate situation in which at the time of contracting a law is in force under which the contract can only be lawfully performed with the consent of a public authority: *e.g.* if a licence to build, or to export or import goods, is obtained. Such a licence may be sought but refused *after* the contract is made; and it is then possible to regard the refusal as a supervening event which frustrates the contract.[13] But it is submitted that generally there will be no frustration in cases of this kind. The cases fall into three groups.

In the first, the parties intend to perform, or actually perform, without the required licence. In such cases, the contract is not frustrated but illegal *ab initio.*[14]

In the second, the parties intend to perform only if the required licence is obtained. Here the principal obligations under the contract are subject to the condition precedent that the licence will be obtained; and normally one of the parties (*e.g.* a seller of goods for export) will be under a duty to take reasonable steps to obtain the licence.[15] If he takes such steps but the licence is nevertheless refused, he is not liable in damages[16]; but the reason is not that he is prevented from performing but that he *has* performed by doing all that was required of him. Equally, the buyer is not liable, but again the reason is not that his liability is discharged: it is that he never became liable because the seller was unable to deliver and so failed to per-

[8] *Cf. Benjamin's Sale of Goods* (3rd ed.), §§ 1580–1582.
[9] As in *Andrew Miller & Co.* v. *Taylor & Co. Ltd.* [1916] 1 K.B. 402 (see pp. 403, 417); but in that case the plea of frustration failed as the embargo was not permanent: as to this point see *post*, p. 789, n. 31.
[10] *Ante*, p. 785.
[11] *Ante*, pp. 60–61, 781; *post*, pp. 798–799.
[12] *Ante*, pp. 381–382.
[13] This is a possible interpretation of a dictum in *A. V. Pound & Co. Ltd.* v. *M. W. Hardy Inc.* [1956] A.C. 588, 604 that "further performance of the contract was excused"; for another interpretation, see n. 18, *infra*.
[14] *Ante*, p. 429.
[15] *Ante*, pp. 60–61.
[16] *Benjamin's Sale of Goods* (3rd ed.), § 1575.

form a condition precedent to, or a concurrent condition of, the buyer's duty to accept and pay.[17] Thus although neither party is liable the contract is not frustrated.[18] An alternative possibility, in cases of this kind, is that the seller has undertaken absolutely to obtain a licence.[19] If he fails, he is liable in damages; and to avoid conflict with the rules as to illegal contracts it has been said that the seller's liability is based on a collateral contract that he will secure the licence.[20]

In the third group of cases the licensing requirement is in existence at the time of the contract and the parties intend to perform only if a licence is obtained; but afterwards there is a change in government policy with regard to the issue of such licences. If such a change leads to the refusal of licences which previously had been issued as a matter of course,[21] it is possible that the change of policy may be regarded as a supervening event which is capable of frustrating the contract.[22]

(3) Partial and temporary illegality

Partial and temporary illegality gives rise to two problems.

The first is whether it frustrates the contract. This depends (as in cases of partial impossibility[23]) on whether it affects the main purpose of the contract. Thus in the *Denny Mott* case[24] a long-term agreement for the sale of timber provided that "to enable the aforesaid agreement to be carried out" the buyer should let a timber yard to the seller. When dealings in timber under the agreement were prohibited, it was held that the whole contract was frustrated, since its main object, namely trading in timber, had become illegal. Hence the seller could not enforce the part of it that related to the

---

[17] *Ante*, pp. 662–664.

[18] This is an alternative, and preferable, interpretation of the dictum in *A. V. Pound & Co. Ltd.* v. *M. W. Hardy Inc.*, cited *supra*, n. 13; the issue of frustration was specifically left open in that case. *cf. Benjamin's Sale of Goods* (3rd ed.), §§ 1576–1578. The question whether the contract is frustrated, or whether the parties escape liability on other grounds, is of more than academic interest: if there is no frustration the Law Reform (Frustrated Contracts) Act 1943 (*post*, pp. 810–815) does not apply.

[19] *Peter Cassidy Seed Co. Ltd.* v. *Osuustukkukaupa Ltd.* [1957] 1 W.L.R. 273; *Pagnan S.p.a.* v. *Tradax Ocean Transport S.A.* [1987] 3 All E.R. 565; *cf. Congimex Companhia Geral, etc. S.A.R.L.* v. *Tradax Export S.A.* [1983] 1 Lloyd's Rep. 250 (absolute duty to obtain licence undertaken by buyer). "Clear words" are required to impose such an absolute duty, especially where the law prohibiting performance is passed after the time of contracting: *The Playa Larga* [1983] 2 Lloyd's Rep. 171, 191.

[20] *Walton (Grain and Shipping) Ltd.* v. *British Trading Co.* [1959] 1 Lloyd's Rep. 223, 226; *Johnson Matthey Bankers Ltd.* v. *State Trading Co. of India* [1984] 1 Lloyd's Rep. 427, 434.

[21] *Cf.* the example given in *C. Czarnikow Ltd.* v. *Centrala Handlu Zagranicznego "Rolimpex"* [1979] A.C. 351, 372 (dog and television licences); *Johnson Matthey Bankers Ltd.* v. *State Trading Corp. of India* [1984] 1 Lloyd's Rep. 427, 429; contrast *Atisa S.A.* v. *Aztec A.G.* [1983] 2 Lloyd's Rep. 579 (where the foreign government simply broke its contract to supply the seller).

[22] This was assumed in *Maritime National Fish Ltd.* v. *Ocean Trawlers Ltd.* [1935] A.C. 524 (where the plea of frustration failed for reasons discussed at pp. 804–805 *post*); *cf.* also *Walton (Grain and Shipping) Ltd.* v. *British Trading Co.* [1959] 1 Lloyd's Rep. 223, 236 (where the seller was excused by a *force majeure* clause); *Congimex S.A.R.L. (Lisbon)* v. *Continental Grain Export Corp. (New York)* [1979] 2 Lloyd's Rep. 386; *Nile Co. for the Export of Agricultural Produce* v. *H. & J. M. Bennett (Commodities) Ltd.* [1986] 1 Lloyd's Rep. 555, 581–582.

[23] *Ante*, p. 768.

[24] [1944] A.C. 265; *cf. Nile Co. for the Export of Agricultural Crops* v. *H. & J. M. Bennett (Commodities) Ltd.* [1986] 1 Lloyd's Rep. 555, 581 (foreign government imposing change on method of payment).

letting of the yard. But in *Cricklewood Property Investment Trust Ltd.* v. *Leighton's Investment Trust Ltd.*[25] temporary war-time restrictions on building did not frustrate a 99-year building lease; for the illegality did not destroy the main object of the lease as there would probably be ample time for building after the war-time restrictions were removed.

The second question is whether illegality which does not frustrate the contract but only affects some subsidiary obligation excuses non-performance of that obligation. On principle it should have this effect. For example, a charterparty might provide that a ship should call at ten ports. If one of them became an enemy port, the shipowner could hardly be made liable for failing to call there, even if it were physically possible for him to do so.[26] Where temporary illegality does not discharge the contract,[27] it has similarly been held to provide an excuse for non-performance for so long as the prohibition lasted.[28] But in *Eyre* v. *Johnson*[29] a tenant was held liable in damages for breach of his covenant to repair even though war-time regulations made it illegal for him to do the work. The better view, however, is that the tenant ought not to be held liable for refusing to do an act which subsequent legislation has made illegal. Though the lease as a whole is not frustrated, the illegality should provide the tenant with an excuse for non-performance of the part that has become illegal.[30]

4. Prospective Frustration

A claim that a contract has been discharged may be made before there actually *has* been any (or any sufficiently serious) interference with performance, on the ground that supervening events have made it highly probable that there *will* be such interference. As a general rule, the effect of those events must then be determined by reference to the time when they occur. The point is well illustrated by *Embiricos* v. *Sydney Reid & Co.*[31] where a Greek ship had been chartered for a voyage involving passage of the Dardanelles. On the outbreak of war between Greece and Turkey, it was held that the charterer was justified in treating the contract as frustrated, even though later the Turkish authorities unexpectedly announced that Greek ships were to be allowed through the straits during an "escape period" which would have made performance of the contract voyage possible. Similarly, where requisition interferes with performance of a charterparty, the question whether it frustrates the contract is to be determined by reference to the time of requisition.[32] The reason for the rule is so that rights should not be left indefinitely in suspense.[33]

---

[25] [1945] A.C. 221.
[26] *Cf. Hindley & Co. Ltd.* v. *General Fibre Co. Ltd.* [1940] 2 K.B. 517.
[27] As in the *Cricklewood* case, *supra*, n. 25.
[28] *Libyan Arab Foreign Bank* v. *Bankers Trust Co.* [1989] Q.B. 728, 772 ("suspended but not discharged").
[29] [1946] K.B. 481.
[30] *Cricklewood* case, *supra* n. 25, at pp. 233, 244; *Sturcke* v. *S. W. Edwards Ltd.* (1971) 23 P. & C.R. 185, 190; *cf. Brewster* v. *Kitchell* (1691) 1 Salk. 198 ("the statute repeals the covenant"); *Grimsdick* v. *Sweetman* [1909] 2 K.B. 740.
[31] [1914] 3 K.B. 45; so far as *contra, Andrew Miller* v. *Taylor & Co. Ltd.* [1916] 1 K.B. 402 is criticised in *Watts, Watts & Co. Ltd.* v. *Mitsui & Co. Ltd.* [1917] 2 A.C. 227, 245.
[32] *Bank Line Ltd.* v. *Arthur Capel & Co.* [1919] A.C. 435; *cf.* also *National Carriers Ltd.* v. *Panalpina (Northern) Ltd.* [1981] A.C. 675, 706; *Wong Lai Ying* v. *Chinachem Investment Co.* (1979) 13 Build. L.R. 81.
[33] *Bank Line* case, *supra*, at p. 454; *cf. Embiricos* v. *Sydney Reid & Co.* [1914] 3 K.B. 45, 54, quoted *ante*, p. 760.

The rule is based on the assumption that the event is of such a kind that a reasonable view of its probable effect on the contract can be taken as soon as it occurs. Where this cannot be done, because the event is one which may equally well cause slight or serious interference with performance, the rule is necessarily subject to some qualification. This is, for example, the position where a strike of dockworkers interferes with performance of a charterparty.[34] The contract is not frustrated at once, as soon as the strike begins. It is "necessary to wait upon events—"[35] not, indeed, until the strike is over,[36] but until it has gone on for so long that a reasonable person would conclude that it was likely to interfere fundamentally with performance. This test determines not only the question whether the contract is frustrated, but also the date of frustration. The point arose in a number of cases in which ships which had been time-chartered were detained in the Shatt al Arab in the course of the Gulf War between Iran and Iraq.[37] That war is generally regarded as having begun on September 22, 1980; but at that time commercial opinion was that the war would soon be brought to an end and that foreign vessels would be speedily released.[38] These optimistic forecasts were falsified by later events and there was no doubt that the length of the detention which occurred was sufficient to frustrate the charterparties. But it was held that the contracts could be frustrated before the detention had *actually* gone on for this length of time, and that they were frustrated as soon as "a sensible commercial prognosis"[39] could be made, that the delay *would* continue for such time as to prevent the resumption of substantial services under the charterparties.[40] Similarly, where an employee suffered from a heart attack, his contract of employment was not discharged at once, but only when the effects of his heart attack could be assessed and "both sides accepted that . . . [he] was not going to work again."[41]

5. Events Affecting only one Party's Performance

In *Taylor* v. *Caldwell*[42] the court was directly concerned only with the liability of the defendants, performance of whose obligation to supply the Music Hall was made impossible by the fire. Yet the court clearly regarded the plaintiffs as also having been discharged,[43] even though their principal obligation (to pay the agreed hire) had in no way become impossible. This is a very common situation: in a typical bilateral contract one party undertakes to perform some act or abstention, while the other undertakes to pay

---

34 As in *The Nema* [1982] A.C. 724.

35 [1982] A.C. at p. 753.

36 *The Nema*, *supra*, at p. 753 ("businessmen must not be required to await events too long"); *cf. Chakki* v. *United Yeast Ltd.* [1982] I.C.R. 140.

37 *The Evia* (*No.* 2) [1983] 1 A.C. 736; *The Wenjiang* (*No.* 2) [1983] 1 Lloyd's Rep. 400; *The Chrysalis* [1983] 1 W.L.R. 1469.

38 See *The Wenjiang* (*No.* 2), *supra*, at p. 403; *The Chrysalis, supra*, at p. 1472.

39 *The Wenjiang* (*No.* 2), *supra*, at p. 408; *cf. The Adelfa* [1988] 2 Lloyd's Rep. 466 (delay in unloading due to arrest of ship).

40 Commercial arbitrators had fixed the date of frustration as October 4, 1980 in *The Evia* (*No.* 2) *supra*, and as November 24, 1980 in *The Wenjiang* (*No.* 2), *supra*, and in *The Chrysalis, supra*. The courts expressed no opinion of their own as to the dates of frustration, merely holding that the arbitrators had applied the correct principle of law in fixing those dates.

41 *Notcutt* v. *Universal Equipment Co.* (*London*) *Ltd.* [1986] 1 W.L.R. 641, 644.

42 (1863) 3 B. & S. 826; *ante*, p. 763.

43 3 B. & S. at p. 840 ("both parties are excused").

for it. Supervening impossibility normally affects only the former undertaking (though illegality may equally affect both[44]). This fact was at one time thought to support the view that a time charter could not be frustrated by the unavailability of the ship: "if the shipowner's object is to receive the chartered hire . . . he does not care how much the charterer's adventures are frustrated, so long as he is able to pay."[45] But the argument was rejected on the ground that the "common object"[46] of the parties was frustrated; for even the owner's object "is not only to get hire but to afford services."[47] Many other examples can be given of cases in which the parties have the same object in view but expect to benefit from it in different ways. This reasoning applies not only to cases of impossibility but also to cases of frustration of purpose. In *Krell* v. *Henry*[48] the object of the contract was to provide facilities for seeing the coronation processions: this was what one party had to sell and the other wanted to buy. It made no difference that the one expected to benefit by receiving a sum of money and the other by seeing the processions.

Hence when it is said that "performance becomes impossible," or that the purpose of the contract is frustrated, the reference is to the common object of the parties as described above. It follows that both will be discharged even though the supervening event only affects the performance of one.

6. Special Factors Affecting Land

(1) Leases

It was formerly thought that a lease of land could not be frustrated[49] because, in giving the tenant the right to exclusive possession for the specified time, it created a legal estate in the land. This estate was the subject-matter of the contract and survived even if subsequent events prevented the tenant from making any use of the premises. But the commercial reality is that, generally, the tenant bargains for use and occupation and not simply for a legal estate; and in *National Carriers Ltd.* v. *Panalpina (Northern) Ltd.*[50] the House of Lords has held that the doctrine of frustration could apply to leases of land.

At the same time it was emphasised that the frustration of a lease will be a very rare event.[51] One reason for this is that a lease for a long period of years is in the nature of a long-term speculation. Such a transaction is hard to frustrate since the parties must contemplate that circumstances may change radically during its currency, and so to a large extent take the risk of supervening events.[52] Nor would interruption of enjoyment which was likely to last for only a few years frustrate a lease for a long term, such as 99

---

[44] *Cf. Libyan Arab Foreign Bank* v. *Bankers Trust Co.* [1989] Q.B. 728, 749, recognising that "an obligation to pay money can be frustrated" by illegality.

[45] *Budgett* v. *Binnington & Co.* [1891] 1 Q.B. 35, 41.

[46] *Hirji Mulji* v. *Cheong Yue SS. Co. Ltd.* [1926] A.C. 497, 507; contrast *Scanlan's New Neon* v. *Tooheys Ltd.* (1943) 67 C.L.R. 169, 196–197.

[47] *Bank Line Ltd.* v. *Arthur Capel & Co. Ltd.* [1919] A.C. 435, 453.

[48] [1903] 2 K.B. 740; *ante*, pp. 764, 784.

[49] See the authorities cited in nn. 57–62, *infra*.

[50] [1981] A.C. 675.

[51] *Ibid.* pp. 692, 697.

[52] *Cf. post*, p. 799.

years, since the ratio of the interruption to the whole would be too small.[53] Even the physical destruction of the premises would not usually frustrate since it would normally be covered by express provisions[54] in the lease, such as covenants to repair and to keep the premises insured. A further reason why frustration of leases is uncommon is that to hold a long-term lease frustrated by the destruction of the buildings on the land could, paradoxically, operate to the prejudice of *tenants*, especially in a period of rising land values. Frustration operates automatically,[55] so that its effect in the case put would be to deprive the tenant of a valuable site long before the end of the agreed term.

For these reasons, the House of Lords in the *National Carriers*[56] case did not disapprove any of the earlier decisions to the extent that they held that the leases in question *were not* frustrated.[57] In those cases it had been held that leases were not discharged by the destruction of the premises by enemy action[58]; by the requisitioning of the premises[59]; by war-time legislation which prevented the tenant from residing on the premises[60] or from developing the land[61]; or by the death of the tenant of furnished rooms.[62] In the *National Carriers* case itself a tenant claimed that a ten-year lease of a warehouse had been frustrated when, four and a half years before the end of the term, the only access road to the premises had been closed by the local authority and had remained closed for 20 months. The claim was rejected on the ground that the interruption was not sufficiently serious to bring about frustration.[63]

The doctrine of frustration is most likely to apply where the lease is a short-term one for a particular purpose: *e.g.* where a holiday cottage which has been rented for a month is burnt down without the fault of either party. Similarly, the contracts in cases like *Taylor* v. *Caldwell*[64] and *Krell* v. *Henry*[65] could be frustrated, even if the transactions were expressed as leases and not (as they actually were) as licences. In Scotland the lease of a salmon fishery was held to be frustrated when construction of a nearby bombing range prevented the tenant from using the fishery[66]; and this case might now be followed in England. A lease could also be frustrated if "some vast convulsion of nature swallowed up the property altogether, or buried it in the depths of the sea"; or if, in the case of a building lease,

---

[53] *Cf. ante*, pp. 771–772.
[54] *Cf. post*, p. 796.
[55] *Post*, p. 807.
[56] [1981] A.C. 675.
[57] Though at p. 715 *Matthey* v. *Curling* [1922] 2 A.C. 180 was described as "a singularly harsh decision from the tenant's point of view."
[58] *Redmond* v. *Dainton* [1920] 2 K.B. 256; *Denman* v. *Brise* [1949] 1 K.B. 22; *Cusak-Smith* v. *London Corp.* [1956] 1 W.L.R. 1368.
[59] *Whitehall Court Ltd.* v. *Ettlinger* [1920] 1 K.B. 680; *Matthey* v. *Curling* [1922] 2 A.C. 180; *Swift* v. *Macbean* [1942] 1 K.B. 375.
[60] *London & Northern Estates Ltd.* v. *Schlesinger* [1916] 1 K.B. 20.
[61] *Cricklewood Property and Investment Trust Ltd.* v. *Leighton's Investment Trust Ltd.* [1945] A.C. 221.
[62] *Youngmin* v. *Heath* [1974] 1 W.L.R. 135.
[63] *Cf. ante*, p. 000. See also, in the United States, *Lloyd* v. *Murphy*, 153 P. 2d. 47 (1944).
[64] (1863) 3 B. & S. 826; *ante*, p. 763.
[65] [1903] 2 K.B. 740; *ante* pp. 764, 784.
[66] *Tay Salmon Fisheries Co.* v. *Speedie*, 1929 S.C. 593.

"legislation were subsequently passed which permanently prohibited private building in the area or dedicated it as an open space for ever."[67]

The doctrine of frustration can apply to an agreement for a lease, no less than to an executed lease.[68]

Even where the lease is not frustrated, supervening events can nevertheless provide a party with an excuse for not performing a particular obligation imposed by the lease. In *Baily* v. *De Crespigny*[69] a landlord covenanted that neither he nor his assigns would permit building on a paddock adjoining the land let. The paddock was compulsorily acquired by a railway company, which built a station on it. It was held that the landlord was not liable in damages for breach of his covenant, first because on the true construction of the covenant "assigns" did not include assigns by compulsion of law, and secondly because it was impossible for him to secure performance of the covenant.[70] Similarly, a tenant who covenanted to build would not be liable in damages if war-time conditions or legislation made building impossible or illegal.[71]

(2) Sale of land

The doctrine of frustration applies to contracts for the sale of land,[72] but its operation in relation to such contracts is somewhat restricted.

Land is commonly bought for the sake of the house or other buildings on it; but the contract is not frustrated if those buildings are destroyed or seriously damaged between contract and completion. The premises are, moreover, at the buyer's risk, so that he must pay the full price even though the premises are damaged or destroyed between those dates.[73] The rule promoted certainty by making it unnecessary to ask whether partial damage was sufficiently serious to bring about frustration[74]; and the hardship which the rule could cause was mitigated by the fact that the purchaser had the benefit of the vendor's insurance.[75] But as he could not be sure of the adequacy of this insurance he would normally take out his own insurance as soon as contracts were exchanged. This position provided a windfall for insurers, who for the period between contract and completion received two premiums while being liable for no more than the amount for

---

67 *Cricklewood* case [1945] A.C. 221, 229; *cf.* p. 240.

68 *Denny, Mott & Dickinson* v. *James B. Fraser & Co. Ltd.* [1944] A.C. 265 (a decision not confined to Scots Law: see the *National Carriers* case [1981] A.C. 675, 704); *Rom Securities Ltd.* v. *Rogers (Holdings) Ltd.* (1968) 205 E.G. 427; *cf. Property Discount Corp. Ltd.* v. *Lyon Group Ltd.* [1980] 1 W.L.R. 300, 305.

69 (1869) L.R. 4 Q.B. 180.

70 The actual decision seems to be very unjust. The landlord presumably got compensation from the railway company and was able to keep this for himself though the tenant's interests were prejudiced by the erection of the station.

71 *Cricklewood* case [1945] at p. 233; *Eyre* v. *Johnson* [1946] K.B. 481, *contra*, is doubted at p. 789, *ante*.

72 This is assumed in *Amalgamated Investment and Property Co. Ltd.* v. *John Walker & Co. Ltd.* [1977] 1 W.L.R. 164, where the plea of frustration failed for reasons stated at p. 785, *ante*.

73 *Paine* v. *Meller* (1801) 6 Ves. 349. The rule is criticised by the Law Commission (see Law Com. No. 191 para. 4.2), but legislative reform is not recommended in view of the developments described at n. 76, *infra*.

74 This is the test adopted in some of the United States: see *Skelly Oil Co.* v. *Ashmore*, 365 S.W. 2d. 582 (1963); Uniform Vendor and Purchaser Risk Act; Uniform Land Transactions Act, s.2–406. It may seem to be more just, but it is also less convenient, than the English rule.

75 Law of Property Act 1925, s.47 (*ante*, p. 570).

which the property was insured. The rule is therefore commonly varied by contract: for example, by provisions leaving the risk with the seller till completion, and giving a right to rescind the contract *either* to the purchaser if the property has become unusable for its purpose at the date of contract, *or* to the vendor if the property has been destroyed and he cannot get planning permission to rebuild it.[76]

The rule stated above applies where the land is sold with buildings already on it. Where a developer sells land with a house *to be built* on it, the destruction of the partly completed building likewise does not of itself frustrate the contract, so that the vendor must (unless the contract otherwise provides) do the work again at no extra cost.[77] But the contract may be frustrated on other grounds. Thus where a landslip not only destroyed a partly completed block of flats, but also delayed the construction for two and a half years, it was held that a contract for the sale of one of the flats was frustrated *by the delay*; for in the interval market conditions had changed to such an extent as to make performance at the end of the delay radically different from that originally undertaken.[78]

It has been held that a purchaser of land can be compelled to perform even though, after contract, a compulsory purchase order is made in respect of the land.[79] He will of course get the compensation paid by the acquiring authority. But where land is sold with vacant possession and requisitioned before completion, the vendor cannot enforce the contract[80] as he cannot perform his obligation to give possession; and in such a case the purchaser can get back his deposit.[81]

7. Fact or Law

The question whether frustration is a matter of fact or law used to be important in determining the respective functions of judge and jury. Trial by jury is now rare in civil cases; but the question whether frustration is a matter of fact or law is still important in determining whether a court can control an arbitrator's finding. Such a finding is generally conclusive on matters of fact,[82] but does not bind the court when determining appeals from arbitrators on points of law.

The point is illustrated by the Suez cases where such questions as the greater length and cost of a voyage round the Cape of Good Hope and its physical effect on the ship or the goods were clearly questions of fact. In the *Tsakiroglou* case[83] the arbitrator found, in general terms, that performance of the contract by shipping via the Cape was "not commercially or fundamentally different from" performance by shipping via Suez. The House of Lords agreed with this finding, but added that it did not bind the

---

76 Law Society's Standard Conditions of Sale (1990) Conditions 5.1.1 to 5.1.4.
77 *Ante*, p. 769.
78 *Wong Lai Ying* v. *Chinachem Investment Co.* (1979) 13 Build. L.R. 81.
79 *Hillingdon Estates Co.* v. *Stonefield Estate Co.* [1952] Ch. 627. The mere making of such an order does not affect ownership of the land.
80 *Cook* v. *Taylor* [1942] Ch. 349.
81 *James Macara Ltd.* v. *Barclays Bank Ltd.* [1945] K.B. 148.
82 See, *e.g. Universal Petroleum Co. Ltd.* v. *Handels und Transport Gesellschaft mbH* [1987] 1 Lloyd's Rep. 517.
83 [1962] A.C. 93.

court as the question whether the difference was fundamental was one of law[84] or one of mixed law and fact.[85]

In *Jackson* v. *Union Marine Insurance Co. Ltd.*[86] the jury found that the delay caused by the stranding of the ship was "so long as to put an end in a commercial sense to the commercial speculation"; and Bramwell B. described this finding as "all-important."[87] One possible distinction between this attitude and that of the House of Lords in the *Tsakiroglou* case is that the jury's finding related to the effect of a specific factor (delay) on the contract, whereas the arbitrator's findings were in general terms.[88] But it does not seem that the court's control over an arbitrator's finding on the issue of frustration will be excluded merely because he makes a number of findings as to the effects of specific factors, instead of one finding in general terms. A better distinction is that the relations between judge and jury differ from those between court and arbitrator. The question of frustration depends on the inference to be drawn from known or primary facts. The drawing of such inferences was often left to juries, and for some purposes these inferences are called facts, or secondary facts.[89] But inferences of this sort are not treated as "facts" for the purpose of limiting the appellate or supervisory function of the court over lower tribunals. Thus an issue of negligence could be left to a jury; but appeals lie from findings of negligence made by courts whose decisions are subject to appeals only on points of law.[90] The same is true of issues of frustration.

It does not follow from the description of the issue of frustration as one of law that the court will substitute its own view for that taken by an arbitrator merely because it disagrees with his conclusion. It will only do so if the arbitrator has applied the wrong legal test or, while purporting to apply the correct test, has reached a conclusion which no reasonable person would have reached on the primary facts as found.[91]

SECTION 3. LIMITATIONS

Even if an event occurs which would normally frustrate a contract under the rules so far considered, the doctrine of frustration may be excluded if the contract provides for the event; if the event was foreseen or foreseeable; or if it was due to the "fault" of one of the parties.

1. Contractual Provision for the Event

(1) In general

The object of the doctrine of frustration is to find a satisfactory way of allocating the risk of supervening events. There is, however, nothing to pre-

---

[84] *Cf. Palmco Shipping Inc.* v. *Continental Ore Co.* [1970] 2 Lloyd's Rep. 21; *cf. Peter Lind & Co. Ltd* v. *Constable Hart & Co. Ltd.* [1979] 2 Lloyd's Rep. 248, 253; *The Wenjiang* [1982] 2 All E.R. 437; *The Wenjiang* (*No.* 2) [1983] 1 Lloyd's Rep. 400, 402.

[85] [1962] A.C. at pp. 116, 123. *The Chrysalis* [1983] 1 W.L.R. 1469, 1475.

[86] (1874) L.R. 10 C.P. 125, *ante*, 770.

[87] At p. 141.

[88] *Tsakiroglou* case *supra*, n. 85, at p. 130.

[89] See *Benmax* v. *Austin Motor Co. Ltd.* [1955] A.C. 370; *National Carriers Ltd.* v. *Panalpina (Northern) Ltd.* [1981] A.C. 675, 688; *The Adelfa* [1988] 2 Lloyd's Rep. 466, 471.

[90] Goodhart, 74 L.Q.R. 402.

[91] *The Nema* [1982] A.C. 724 (disapproving on this point *The Angelia* [1973] 1 W.L.R. 210); *The Wenjiang* (*No.* 2) [1983] 1 Lloyd's Rep. 400; *The Chrysalis* [1983] 1 W.L.R. 1469, 1475.

vent the parties from making their own provisions for this purpose. Thus they can expressly provide that the risk of supervening events shall be borne by one of them and not by the other[92] or they can apportion it or deal with it in various other ways.[93] Such provisions exclude frustration: as Lord Simon has said: "There can be no discharge by supervening impossibility if the express terms of the contract bind the parties to performance, notwithstanding that the supervening event may occur."[94]

A provision that excludes frustration may also be implied: for example, where the nature of the contract makes it clear that the parties intended the risk of supervening events to lie where it falls. In *Larrinaga & Co.* v. *Société Franco-Américaine des Phosphates de Médulla*[95] a contract was made in 1913 for the carriage of six cargoes of phosphates between March 1918 and November 1920. After the end of the First World War, the carriers argued that the contract was frustrated because of the altered shipping conditions then prevailing. The argument was rejected by the House of Lords. A contract of this kind, not to be performed for many years, was essentially speculative,[96] since each party had consciously taken the risk that conditions might alter. An implied agreement to exclude frustration may also be based on other characteristics of a transaction. In *The Maira* (*No.* 2) agents had undertaken to manage a ship which was subsequently lost. It was held that this did not frustrate the management contract since the parties could hardly have intended "that the managers should be entitled to wash their hands of all duties concerning the vessel as soon as [the ship] was lost[97]: they would be expected to attend to such matters as the repatriation of the crew and the settlement of claims arising out of the loss.

The general rule that frustration can be excluded by provision for the supervening event is not seriously disputed[98]; but the rule is subject to a number of qualifications.

(2) Qualifications

(a) TRADING WITH THE ENEMY. A contract may be frustrated by supervening illegality on the ground that it involves trading with the enemy; and such frustration is not excluded by a contrary provision in the contract. In *Ertel Bieber & Co.* v. *Rio Tinto Co. Ltd.*[99] an English company contracted to deliver copper ore to a German company from 1911 to 1919. It was held that the contract was wholly frustrated on the outbreak of war in 1914 even though it provided that, in the event of war, certain obligations should only be suspended; for to give effect to this provision would, for reasons stated

---

[92] *Budgett* v. *Binnington & Co.* [1891] 1 Q.B. 35, 41; *Thiis* v. *Byers* (1876) 1 Q.B.D. 244. For an extreme case of this kind, see *Claude Neon Ltd.* v. *Hardie* [1970] Qd.Rep. 93.

[93] *e.g.* by provisions of the type mentioned at p. 766, *ante*, or by provisions for flexible pricing (*ante* p. 782), as in *Wates Ltd.* v. *G.L.C.* (1983) 25 Build. L.R. 1.

[94] *Joseph Constantine SS. Line Ltd.* v. *Imperial Smelting Corp. Ltd.* [1942] A.C. 154, 163.

[95] (1923) 92 L.J.K.B. 455.

[96] *Cf. ante*, p. 2.

[97] [1985] 1 Lloyd's Rep. 300, 311, affirmed on other grounds [1986] 2 Lloyd's Rep. 46.

[98] A dictum in *W. J. Tatem Ltd.* v. *Gamboa* [1939] 1 K.B. 132, 138 suggests the contrary, but is immediately contradicted on the same page and on p. 139; *post*, pp. 801, 821.

[99] [1918] A.C. 260; such clauses may also be narrowly construed, so as not to refer to war between the countries to which the contracting parties belong: *Re Badische Co. Ltd.* [1921] 2 Ch. 331, 379; *cf. Pacific Phosphate Co. Ltd.* v. *Empire Trading Co. Ltd.* (1920) 36 T.L.R. 750; *Fibrosa* case [1943] A.C. 32.

earlier in this Chapter, be contrary to public policy.[1] The rule is based on the particular strength of the policy against giving aid to the economy of an enemy in time of war. It does not apply to express provisions that deal with other kinds of supervening illegality, such as prohibition of export. If, for example, a contract provides for a payment to be made in the event of such a prohibition,[2] or for suspension of the contract, followed by its termination if the prohibition is not lifted by the end of a specified period,[3] frustration is effectively excluded. Clauses of this kind are not contrary to public policy[4] since they assume that the prohibition is going to be observed, and since the continuation of the contractual relationship in cases of this kind does not have any tendency to subvert the purpose of the prohibition.

(b) PROVISION NARROWLY CONSTRUED. A clause may be literally wide enough to cover the event, but be held on its true construction not to have this effect. In *Metropolitan Water Board* v. *Dick, Kerr & Co.*[5] contractors agreed in July 1914 to construct a reservoir in six years; in the event of delays "however occasioned," they were to be given an extension of time. In February 1916, the contractors were required by a Government Order to stop work, and to sell their plant. It was held that the contract was frustrated although the events which had happened were literally within the delay clause. That clause was meant to apply to temporary difficulties, such as labour shortages, bad weather, or failure of supplies. It did not "cover the case in which the interruption is of such a character and duration that it vitally and fundamentally changes the conditions of the contract, and could not possibly have been in the contemplation of the parties to the contract when it was made."[6] *A fortiori,* an express provision in a contract for *some* events which might otherwise frustrate it does not exclude the possibility of frustration by *other* events.[7] Thus a charterparty which expressly provides for the effects of delays in the availability of the *ship* may nevertheless be frustrated by delays in the availability of the *cargo*.[8]

(c) PROVISION INCOMPLETE. A clause may make some provision for the event which happens, but fail to make complete provision for it. In *Bank Line Ltd.* v. *Arthur Capel & Co.*[9] a shipowner was sued for damages for failing to deliver a ship due under a charterparty. He pleaded that the contract was frustrated by the requisition of the ship. The charterer argued that frustration was excluded by two clauses giving him, but not the owner, the option to cancel if the ship was commandeered by the Government or if

---

[1] [1918] A.C. at p. 286; *ante*, p. 786.

[2] *e.g. Johnson Matthey Bankers Ltd.* v. *State Trading Corp. of India* [1984] 1 Lloyd's Rep. 427.

[3] *e.g.* in the *Tsakiroglou* case [1962] A.C. 93, 95.

[4] *Johnson Matthey* case, *supra*, at p. 434.

[5] [1918] A.C. 119; *The Penelope* [1928] P. 180 (approved, though with some reservations, in *The Nema* [1982] A.C. 724, 754); *cf. C. Czarnikow Ltd.* v. *Centrala Handlu Zagranicznego Rolimpex* [1979] A.C. 351; *Wong Lai Ying* v. *Chinachem Investment Co.* (1979) 13 Build. L.R. 81; *The Playa Larga* [1983] 2 Lloyd's Rep. 171, 189; *Notcutt* v. *Universal Equipment Co. (London) Ltd.* [1986] 1 W.L.R. 641, 647; *F. C. Shepherd & Co. Ltd.* v. *Jerrom* [1987] Q.B. 301.

[6] At p. 126.

[7] *Intertradex S.A.* v. *Lesieur-Torteaux S.A.R.L.* [1978] 2 Lloyd's Rep. 509, 515.

[8] *The Nema* [1982] A.C. 724.

[9] [1919] A.C. 435; *cf. B.P. Exploration (Libya) Ltd.* v. *Hunt* [1979] 1 W.L.R. 783, 830 (affirmed [1983] 2 A.C. 352); *The Evia* [1982] 1 Lloyd's Rep. 334 (affirmed [1983] 1 A.C. 736, 767).

she was not delivered by April 30, 1915. But the House of Lords held that the charterparty was frustrated. Lord Sumner said that a contract could not be frustrated by a contingency for which it made "full and complete"[10] provision; but he added: "A contingency may be provided for, but not in such terms as to show that the provision is meant to be all the provision for it. A contingency may be provided for, but in such a way as shows that it is provided for only for the purpose of dealing with one of its effects and not with all."[11] Requisition or delay might frustrate the charterparty, but would not necessarily have this effect, *e.g.* if performance were only delayed by one week. The cancelling clauses entitled the charterer to cancel even if the contract was *not* frustrated. He could *escape* liability in that event. It did not follow that the shipowner should *remain* liable if requisition or delay did amount to frustration.

This principle is further illustrated by *Jackson* v. *Union Marine Insurance Co.*[12] where a charterparty provided that the ship should proceed with all possible dispatch (dangers and accidents of navigation excepted) to Newport. On the way there she was so badly damaged that she was not ready for service for eight months. The charterparty was held to be frustrated in spite of the provision excepting dangers and accidents of navigation. One possible explanation is that these words were not intended to cover so long a delay as had actually occurred.[13] But the reason given by the court was that the words of the exception "excuse the shipowner, but give him no right."[14] A delay caused by dangers and accidents of navigation might (but for the exception) have amounted either to a breach or to a frustrating event. The effect of the exception was to prevent the delay from constituting a breach. It did not deal with the effect of such delay as a possible frustrating event, and thus did not rule out frustration. To say that the shipowner is not liable for delay does not lead necessarily to the conclusion that he can enforce the contract in spite of delay.

(3) Provision for non-frustrating events

Under the doctrine of frustration, it is often hard to tell whether the change brought about by a supervening event is indeed sufficiently serious to discharge the contract. To avoid this difficulty, the contract may provide for discharge on the occurrence of specified events (for example by prohibition of export, or by other events beyond the control of the parties or of one of them)[15] and such a provision may take effect whether or not the effect of the event is such as to frustrate the contract under the general law. Such a clause may either give one of the parties the option to cancel the contract,[16] or provide for its automatic determination.[17] A clause of the latter

---

[10] At p. 455.
[11] At p. 456.
[12] (1874) L.R. 10 C.P. 125.
[13] *Sir Lindsay Parkinson & Co. Ltd.* v. *Commissioners of Works* [1949] 2 K.B. 632, 665.
[14] At p. 144. *Cf. Blane Steamships Ltd.* v. *Minister of Transport* [1951] 2 K.B. 965, where the words of the charterparty excused the charterer but were held to give him no rights.
[15] A party can only rely on such a clause as excusing performance if he had taken all reasonable steps to avoid the operation of the event or to mitigate its results: see *Channel Island Ferries Ltd.* v. *Sealink UK Ltd.* [1988] 1 Lloyd's Rep. 323.
[16] *e.g. Bank Line Ltd.* v. *Arthur Capel & Co.* [1918] A.C. 119.
[17] *e.g.* in the *Tsakiroglou* case: [1962] A.C. at p. 95.

kind has been described as a "contractual frustration clause."[18] The point of this description is, however, simply that the *effect* of the clause resembles that of frustration, in giving rise to automatic discharge.[19] The question *when* the clause operates depends simply on its construction and not on the tests of frustration developed by the general law; and, if the clause does come into operation, the contract is discharged under one of its express terms and not under the general doctrine of frustration.[20]

2. Foreseen and Foreseeable Events[21]

(1) In general

Where the parties can foresee the risk that a supervening event may interfere with performance, the normal inference is that they have contracted with reference to that risk. If, for example, the event would make performance more expensive for one party, he is likely to increase his charges; if, on the other hand, it would frustrate the other's purpose, he is likely to reduce the price that he is willing to pay. Having thus allocated the risk, the parties should not be discharged if the event indeed occurs[22]; the loss caused by the event should lie where it falls. As Vaughan Williams L.J. has said, "The test [of frustration] seems to be whether the event which causes the impossibility was or might have been anticipated . . . "[23] Many other dicta similarly support the view that a contract cannot be frustrated by foreseen or foreseeable events[24]; and in other jurisdictions pleas of frustration have been rejected on this ground.[25] There is no English authority which squarely supports the same view; but it has been held that a party cannot rely, as a ground of frustration, on an event which was, or should have been, foreseen by him but not by the other party. In *Walton Harvey Ltd.* v. *Walker & Homfrays Ltd.*[26] the defendants granted the plaintiffs the right to display an advertising sign on the defendants' hotel for seven years. Within this period the hotel was compulsorily acquired, and demolished, by a local authority acting under statutory powers. The defendants were held liable in damages. The contract was not frustrated because the defendants knew, and the plaintiffs did not, of the risk of compulsory acquisition. "They could have provided against that risk, but they did not."[27]

There is thus considerable support both in principle and in the authorities for the view that foresight or foreseeability of the supervening event

---

[18] *Bremer Handelsgesellschaft mbH* v. *Vanden Avenne-Izegem P.V.B.A.* [1978] 2 Lloyd's Rep. 109, 112.

[19] *Post*, p. 807.

[20] So that the Law Reform (Frustrated Contracts) Act 1943 (*post*, pp. 810–815) will not apply.

[21] Hall, 4 *Legal Studies*, 300.

[22] See *Comptoir Commercial Anversois* v. *Power, Son & Co.* [1920] 1 K.B. 868.

[23] *Krell* v. *Henry* [1903] 2 K.B. 740, 752.

[24] *Baily* v. *De Crespigny* (1869) L.R. 4 Q.B. 180, 185; *Tamplin* case [1916] 2 A.C. 397, 426; *Bank Line* case [1919] A.C. 435, 455, 462; *Re Badische Co. Ltd.* [1921] 2 Ch. 331, 379; *Cricklewood* case [1945] A.C. 221, 228; *Fareham* case [1956] A.C. 696, 731; *Denmark Productions Ltd.* v. *Boscobel Productions Ltd.* [1969] 1 Q.B. 699, 725; *Lloyd* v. *Murphy*, 153 P. 2d. 47, 50 (1944); *The Hannah Blumenthal* [1983] 1 A.C. 854, 909.

[25] *Baetjer* v. *New England Alcohol Co.*, 66 N.E. 2d. 748 (1946); *Glidden* v. *Hellenic Lines*, 275 F. 2d. 253, 256 (1960).

[26] [1931] 1 Ch. 274.

[27] At p. 282.

excludes frustration. Nevertheless, that proposition is subject to a number of important qualifications.

(2) Qualifications

(a) Trading with the enemy. A contract may be frustrated by supervening illegality resulting from the war-time prohibition against trading with the enemy, in spite of the fact that the war was a foreseeable event. Even an express provision against frustration does not save the contract in such a case[28]; and the policy considerations which justify this rule apply just as strongly where the event was or should have been foreseen. Thus contracts made in the summer of 1939 could be frustrated as a result of the outbreak of war with Germany although this event was foreseeable.[29]

(b) Degree and extent of foreseeability. The inference that the parties contracted with reference to the event (and so took the risk of its occurrence) can only be drawn if the event was either actually foreseen or if the degree of foreseeability was a very high one. It is not sufficient if the low degree of foreseeability which constitutes the test of remoteness in tort[30] is satisfied. In this sense, it was no doubt "foreseeable" that King Edward VII (who was 60 years old at the time) might fall ill on the day fixed for his coronation.[31] To support the inference of risk-assumption, the event must be one which any person of ordinary intelligence would regard as likely to occur. Moreover, the event or its consequences must be foreseeable in some detail. It is not sufficient that *a* delay or *some* interference with performance can be foreseen if *the* delay or interference which occurs is wholly different in extent. We have seen that this distinction restricts the scope of express provisions for a supervening event[32]; and there is no reason why it should not equally apply in relation to events alleged to have been foreseeable or foreseen. It is submitted that the points made above as to the degree and extent of foreseeability provide the best explanation for cases, in which it was said that a contract could be frustrated by foreseen or foreseeable events.

The first such case is *W. J. Tatem Ltd.* v. *Gamboa.*[33] During the Spanish civil war, the defendant, as agent for the Republicans, chartered the plaintiffs' ship "for the evacuation of civil population from North Spain" for 30 days from July 1. Hire was to be paid at the rate of £250 per day "until her redelivery to the owners," but was to cease if the ship was "missing." On July 14 the ship was seized by the Nationalists, who kept her until September 7, so that she was not redelivered to the owners till September 11. The charterers had paid hire in advance up to July 31, but the owners claimed further hire from August 1 to September 11. Goddard J. rejected the claim on the ground that the charterparty was frustrated. The actual decision can be explained on the ground that it was *not* foreseeable that the

---

[28] *Ante*, pp. 796–797.
[29] But see Taylor, *The Origins of the Second World War*.
[30] *Post*, p. 856.
[31] *Cf.* the express provisions made in some of the contracts for this possibility. According to D.N.B., 2d Supp. p. 591, "A few days before the date appointed for the great ceremony rumours of the King's ill-health gained currency and were denied."
[32] *Ante*, p. 797.
[33] [1939] 1 K.B. 132.

ship would be detained "not only for the period of her charter but for a long period thereafter."[34] But Goddard J. added that the contract would have been frustrated even if that risk had been foreseen. "If the true foundation of the doctrine [of frustration] is that once the subject-matter of the contract is destroyed or the existence of a certain state of facts has come to an end, the contract is at an end, that result follows whether or not the event causing it was contemplated by the parties."[35] Frustration could only be prevented by an express provision that one of the parties should bear the loss. But it is submitted that a contract is not necessarily at an end if the existence of a certain state of facts has come to an end; for the parties may have been engaged in a deliberate speculation on this point.[36] A similar objection applies to the more recent suggestion[37] that an event can frustrate a contract, even though it "was or ought to have been foreseen," if it was "outside the scope of the contract on its true construction." It is submitted that it would be wrong first to construe the contract and *then* to have regard to the fact that the event was foreseen; for that fact must be of crucial importance in determining "the scope of the contract," *i.e.* whether the parties took the risk of the occurrence of the event. Where they actually foresaw the event, the more natural inference is that each of them took that risk unless the contract expressly protected him. In *W. J. Tatem Ltd.* v. *Gamboa* the contract did not expressly protect the defendant from liability if the ship were seized and detained. The inference that he accepted the risk of these events (to the extent to which they were foreseen) is strengthened by the fact that the contract did expressly protect him against another foreseen risk, namely, that the ship might be lost; in that event his liability to pay hire was to cease.[38]

In *The Eugenia*[39] the defendants wished, in September 1956, to charter the plaintiffs' ship to carry iron goods from Russian Black Sea ports to India. At that time "mercantile men realised that there was a risk that the Suez Canal might be closed"[40] because of the Suez crisis. The agents of the parties appreciated this risk and each made a suggestion for dealing with it.[41] But when the charterparty was concluded on September 19, nothing was expressly said about the risk of closure. The reason may be that before November 16 "mercantile men would not have formed any conclusion as to whether the obstructions in the Canal were other than temporary."[42] The actual decision was that the contract was not frustrated by the closure of the Canal on October 31, resulting in the detention of the ship: the charterers could not rely on the detention as it was due to their prior breach of contract and thus "self-induced"[43]; nor on the extra length of the voyage as

---

[34] At p. 135.
[35] At p. 138; *cf. Palmco Shipping Inc.* v. *Continental Ore Corp.* [1970] 2 Lloyd's Rep. 21, 31.
[36] *Cf. ante*, pp. 2, 799.
[37] *Nile Co. for the Export of Agriculture Crops* v. *H. & J. M. Bennett (Commodities) Ltd.* [1986] 1 Lloyd's Rep. 555, 582.
[38] The shipowners may have found it easier to insure against loss than against detention and have distinguished for this reason between the effect of the two events.
[39] [1964] 2 Q.B. 226.
[40] [1963] 2 Lloyd's Rep. at p. 159. The facts are more fully stated in this report.
[41] *Ibid.*
[42] *Ibid.* p. 162.
[43] *Post*, p. 803.

the difference between a voyage via the Canal and one via the Cape was not sufficiently fundamental.[44] But Lord Denning M.R. also seemed to reject the further argument that frustration might have been excluded on the ground that at the time of contracting the closure of the Canal was foreseeable. He said: "It has often been said that the doctrine of frustration only applies where the new situation is 'unforeseen' or 'unexpected' or 'uncontemplated' as if that were an essential feature. But it is not so. The only thing that is essential is that [the parties] should have made no provision for it in the contract."[45] But these remarks are *obiter* and it is respectfully submitted that this aspect of the decision can be explained on other grounds. At the time of contracting, the risk of the Canal's being closed for a *very considerable time* was not foreseen; nor was it foreseeable on the high standard of foreseeability[46] required to exclude frustration. To the extent that the parties did foresee the risk, they seem to have allocated it by the terms of the charterparty. This provided that the voyage was to be paid for by the time it took,[47] so indicating an intention to throw the risk of delay on the charterers. There seems to be no reason why the court should, by applying the doctrine of frustration to foreseen events, reverse such an allocation of risks deliberately made by the contracting parties.

(c) CONTRARY INDICATIONS. The inference that the parties have assumed the risk of foreseen (or readily foreseeable) events is only a prima facie one and can be excluded by evidence of contrary intention. The parties may foresee an event and intend, if it occurs, "to leave the lawyers to sort it out"[48]; or they may actually provide that if the event occurs they will then determine how it is to affect the contract.[49] If the lawyers cannot "sort it out" or if the parties cannot reach agreement, the contract may then be frustrated even though the event was foreseen.

Similar reasoning explains *Bank Line Ltd.* v. *Arthur Capel Ltd.*[50] where a charterparty was frustrated although the parties foresaw that the ship might be requisitioned and actually made some provision for this event. But it is by no means clear that the parties foresaw a requisition of such long duration as would frustrate the contract. Even if they foresaw this, the very fact that they had made *some* provision for the event complicated the issue. The contract entitled the charterer to cancel on requisition, so that the risk of the event was clearly not meant to be on him. The effect of requisition on the owner's liability was not mentioned. One could infer from this silence that the parties had decided to throw the risk of requisition on him, or that they had not thought about its effect on his liability at all. If the latter inference is correct, the contract could be frustrated although requisition was foreseen, and the House of Lords so held. The

---

[44] *Ante*, p. 777.

[45] [1964] 2 Q.B. at p. 239; *cf. Transatlantic Finance Corp.* v. *U.S.* 363 F. 2d. 312, 318 (1966); *Opera Co. of Boston* v. *Wolf Trap Foundation for the Performing Arts* 817 F. 2d. 1094, 1101–1102 (1986).

[46] *Ante*, p. 800.

[47] Making use of the "time charter trip" which has become common: see *The Cebu* [1983] 1 Lloyd's Rep. 302, 305.

[48] *The Eugenia* [1964] 2 Q.B. at p. 234.

[49] *Autry* v. *Republic Productions* 180 P. 2d. 888 (1947).

[50] [1919] A.C. 435; *ante*, p. 797.

normal inference that parties take the risk of foreseen events was displaced by the special terms of the contract.[51]

3. Self-induced Frustration

A party cannot rely on "self-induced frustration, that is, on frustration due to his own conduct or to the conduct of those for whom he is responsible."[52]

(1) Events brought about by one party's conduct

The doctrine of frustration obviously does not protect a party whose own breach of contract actually is, or brings about, the frustrating event. Nor does it protect him if the breach is only one of the factors leading to frustration. Thus a charterer who in breach of contract orders a ship into a war-zone, so that she is detained, cannot rely on the detention as a ground of frustration.[53] Similarly, unseaworthiness amounting to a breach of contract may cause delays in the prosecution of the voyage; and if war intervenes, so that the voyage cannot be completed, the carrier will be liable in damages.[54] Frustration is likewise excluded where the circumstances alleged to have brought it about result partly from the breach of one party and partly from that of the other, *e.g.* where both breaches contribute to an allegedly frustrating delay.[55]

Where the allegedly frustrating event results from one party's deliberate act, that party cannot rely on it as a ground of frustration, even though the act is not in itself a breach of the contract[56]; but the other party may be able to rely on it for this purpose. Thus where an employee has been prevented from performing the agreed work because he has been imprisoned for a criminal offence, the employer can rely on this circumstance as a ground of frustration, so as to defeat a claim by the employee for unfair dismissal; and he can do this even though the offence had no connection with the employment, so that its mere commission did not amount to a

---

[51] *Cf. Autry* v. *Republic Productions* 180 P. 2d. 888 (1947).

[52] *Bank Line* case, *supra* n. 50, at p. 452; *Sudbrook Trading Estate Ltd.* v. *Eggleton* [1983] 1 A.C. 444, 497; Swanton, 2 J.C.L. 699. Frustration is not self-induced where the cause of the delay is the act of a third party for whom the defendant is *not responsible*: see *The Adelfa* [1988] 2 Lloyd's Rep. 466, 471; nor merely because one of the parties is an enterprise controlled by a State which has by some legislative or executive act prevented performance of the contract or made it illegal: *C. Czarnikow Ltd.* v. *Centrala Handlu Zagrancicznego "Rolimpex"* [1979] A.C. 351, 372; *The Playa Larga* [1983] 2 Lloyd's Rep. 171, 192.

[53] *The Eugenia* [1964] 2 Q.B. 226; *The Lucille* [1984] 1 Lloyd's Rep. 244; *cf. Mertens* v. *Home Freeholds Co.* [1921] 2 K.B. 526.

[54] See *Monarch SS. Co.* v. *A/B Karlshamns Oljefabriker* [1949] A.C. 196. The position is different where the breach has no causal connection with the frustrating event: *The Silver Sky* [1981] 2 Lloyd's Rep. 95, 98.

[55] *The Hannah Blumenthal* [1983] 1 A.C. 854, rejecting suggestions in *The Splendid Sun* [1981] Q.B. 694, 703, *The Argonaut* [1982] 2 Lloyd's Rep. 214, 221, and *The Kehera* [1983] 1 Lloyd's Rep. 29 that there could be frustration "by mutual default." In *The Hannah Blumenthal* the plea of frustration failed on the further ground that the delay did not produce a radically different state of affairs; *cf.*, on this point, *Stockport M.B.C.* v. *O'Reilly* [1983] 2 Lloyd's Rep. 70. And see *ante*, p. 10 for a statutory solution of the problem which arose in *The Hannah Blumenthal* [1987] Q.B. 301.

[56] *Denmark Production Ltd.* v. *Boscobel Productions Ltd.* [1969] 1 Q.B. 699; *Black Clauson International Ltd.* v. *Papierwerke Waldhof-Aschaffenburg A.G.* [1981] 2 Lloyd's Rep. 446, 457.

breach of the contract.[57] But an attempt by the employee to set up the imprisonment as a ground of frustration, in an action against him by the employer on the contract, would fail[58] on the ground that the employee could not rely on self-induced frustration.

(2) Negligence

Lord Simon has put the case of a prima donna who lost her voice through carelessly catching cold. He seemed to incline to the view that she could plead frustration so long as the incapacity "was not deliberately induced in order to get out of the engagement."[59] This particular result can perhaps be justified by the difficulty of foreseeing the effect of conduct on one's health.[60] But it is submitted that generally negligence should exclude frustration: for example, the plea should have failed in *Taylor* v. *Caldwell*[61] if the fire had been due to the negligence of the defendants, for in such a case it would be unjust to make the other party bear the loss. Similarly, a shipowner cannot rely on the loss of his ship as a ground of frustration of a contract to carry goods in her if the loss is due to his negligence.[62] It will be seen from these examples that "negligence" in this context is not restricted to "breach of an actionable legal duty": it includes "an event which the party relying on it had means and opportunity to prevent but nevertheless caused or permitted to come about."[63] A negligent omission can suffice to exclude frustration.[64]

(3) Choosing between several contracts

Where a party has entered into a number of contracts, supervening events may deprive him of the power of performing them all, without depriving him of the power of performing some of them. He may then claim that one or more of the contracts are frustrated because the supervening event was one for which he was not responsible; but in two cases such claims have failed.

The first is *Maritime National Fish Ltd.* v. *Ocean Trawlers Ltd.*,[65] where the defendants operated a fleet of five trawlers for fishing with otter trawls. Three of the trawlers were owned by the defendants through their subsidiaries,[66] while two were chartered from other owners. Of these two, one was the *St. Cuthbert,* owned by the plaintiffs. The use of otter trawls with-

---

[57] *Harrington* v. *Kent CC* [1980] I.R.L.R. 353; *F. C. Shepherd & Co. Ltd.* v. *Jerrom* [1987] Q.B. 301; *Hare* v. *Murphy Bros.* [1974] I.C.R. 603, 607; *contra Norris* v. *Southampton CC* [1982] I.C.R. 177. Whether the imprisonment actually frustrates the contract depends on such circumstances as the length of the sentence and the nature of the employment: see *Chakki* v. *United Yeast Ltd.* [1982] I.C.R. 140 and *F. C. Shepherd & Co. Ltd.* v. *Jerrom, supra.*

[58] *Cf. Sumnall* v. *Statt* (1984) 49 P. & C.R. 367 (imprisonment of tenant no excuse for failing to perform covenant to "reside constantly" at farmhouse).

[59] *Joseph Constantine SS. Co.* v. *Imperial Smelting Corp. Ltd.* [1942] A.C. 154, 166–167.

[60] Restatement 2d, *Contracts*, § 262 Comment (a).

[61] (1863) 3 B. & S. 826. Lack of "fault" is mentioned in the passage on p. 833 quoted at p. 764, *ante.*

[62] *The Super Servant Two* [1990] 1 Lloyd's Rep. 1.

[63] *Ibid.* p. 10.

[64] *Cf. Amalgamated Investment & Property Co. Ltd.* v. *John Walker & Sons Ltd.* [1977] 1 W.L.R. 164 (failure to take any steps to obtain planning permission).

[65] [1935] A.C. 524.

[66] See [1934] 1 D.L.R. 621, 623; [1934] 4 D.L.R. 288, 299.

out licence was illegal, and because of a change in government policy[67] the defendants only secured three out of the five licences for which they had applied. Having allocated two of these to two of their own trawlers and one to the other chartered trawler,[68] they argued that the charter of the *St. Cuthbert* had been frustrated. The argument was rejected by the Canadian courts on the ground that the defendants had taken the risk of not getting licences for all five trawlers, the licensing requirement being known to both parties at the time of contracting. The Privy Council, though not dissenting from this view, preferred to base its decision on the ground that frustration was self-induced: "it was the act and election of [the defendants] which prevented the *St. Cuthbert* from being licensed for fishing with an otter trawl."[69] On the facts, there clearly was such an election, for the defendants could have allocated one of the three licences to the *St. Cuthbert* rather than to one of their own trawlers. But suppose that the defendants had operated only the two chartered trawlers, had obtained only one licence, and that the licensing requirement had been introduced after both charterparties were concluded. The question would then have arisen whether their choice to allocate their only licence to one of the trawlers would have been an "election," so as to exclude the doctrine of frustration in relation to the charter of the other.

An affirmative answer to a similar question was given in *The Super Servant Two*,[70] where a contract was made to carry the plaintiff's drilling rig in one of two ships, the *Super Servant One* or the *Super Servant Two*, at the carrier's option. The *Super Servant Two* was lost and the carried claimed that the contract was frustrated by this event because the *Super Servant One* was the subject of another fixture and hence not available for the purposes of performing the carrier's contract with the plaintiffs. The argument was rejected on the ground that the carrier's decision to use the *Super Servant One* for the purpose of performing the other contract amounted to an "election" by him, thus precluding his reliance on the loss of the *Super Servant Two* as a ground of frustration, even if that loss was in no way due to his fault. Three grounds for the decision appear from the judgments but it is submitted with great respect that none of them is wholly convincing. First, it was said that the *Maritime National Fish* case had established that a party could not rely on frustration where his failure or inability was due to his "election"; and that the Court in *The Super Servant Two* should follow that decision.[71] It is, however, submitted that the two cases are readily distinguishable: in the *Maritime National Fish* case it was possible for the charterer to perform *all* the contracts which he had made with the owners of the other trawlers, even though only three licences had been allocated to him; while in *The Super Servant Two* it was no longer possible, after the loss of the ship, for the carrier to perform all the contracts which he had made to carry drilling rigs during the period in question. Secondly, it was said that, if the carrier were given the choice which of the contracts he would

---

[67] See *ante*, p. 788.

[68] See the references in n. 66, *supra*.

[69] [1935] A.C. at p. 529.

[70] [1990] 1 Lloyd's Rep. 1, affirming [1989] 1 Lloyd's Rep. 148; McKendrick [1990] L.M.C.L.Q. 153.

[71] [1990] 1 Lloyd's Rep. 1, 10, 13 (rejecting the contrary submission made earlier editions of this book).

perform, frustration of the other or others could only come about as a result of the exercise of that choice, and such a position would be inconsistent with the rule that frustration occurs automatically, *without* any election by either party.[72] Again, it is submitted that this line of reasoning is not conclusive since the rule that frustration operates automatically is subject to qualification precisely in cases of allegedly self-induced frustration[73]: we have seen, for example, that the imprisonment of an employee is a circumstance on which the employer, but not the employee, can rely as a ground of discharge,[74] so that discharge cannot in such cases be described as automatic. Even where the rule that frustration operates automatically does apply, we shall see that this rule forms one of the least attractive aspects of the doctrine of frustration,[75] and one which should not be extended. Moreover, the element of "election" could be eliminated if the question which of the contracts was to be discharged were left to be determined, not by the free choice of the promisor, but by a rule of law: *e.g.* by a rule to the effect that the various contracts should for this purpose rank in the order in which they were made.[76] It may, from this point of view, be relevant that, in *The Super Servant Two*, some of the contracts which the carrier chose to perform (by the use of his other ship during the relevant period) had not been made "at any rate finally"[77] until *after* the contract with the plaintiffs, and that, even after the loss of the *Super Servant Two*, the carrier had continued to negotiate for extra fees to be paid under one of those contracts, "before finally allocating the *Super Servant One* to the performance of these contracts."[78] The third argument in support of the decision is that "It is within the promisor's own control how many contracts he enters into and the risk should be his."[79] But this argument seems to undermine the whole basis of the doctrine of frustration: it has just as much force where the promisor enters into a single contract as where he enters into two or more, with different contracting parties. This, indeed, is the fundamental objection to the reasoning of *The Super Servant Two*, and it is submitted that the rationale of the doctrine should lead to discharge of some of the contracts where the supervening event which makes it impossible to perform them all occurs without the fault of the party claiming discharge.[80] Consistency with the reasoning of the *Maritime National Fish* could be preserved by holding that *which* contracts were to be discharged should depend, not on the election of the party who can no longer perform, but on a rule of law. On this view, the actual decision in *The Super Servant Two* could be justified by reference to the order in which the various contracts with the carrier were made.

---

72 [1990] 1 Lloyd's Rep. 1, 9, 14.
73 See *post*, p. 808.
74 *Shepherd & Co. Ltd.* v. *Jerrom* [1987] Q.B. 301, discussed at pp. 803–804, *ante*.
75 *Post*, p. 808.
76 *Cf. ante*, p. 775.
77 [1990] 1 Lloyd's Rep. 1, 9.
78 *Ibid.* p. 13.
79 [1989] 1 Lloyd's Rep. 148, 158 (at first instance); the reasoning of this judgment was approved on appeal in [1990] 1 Lloyd's Rep. 1.
80 *Cf. Bremer Handelsgesellschaft mbH* v. *Continental Grain Co.* [1983] 1 Lloyd's Rep. 269, 292–293; the treatment of the 92 tonnes in *Bremer Handelsgesellschaft mbH* v. *Vanden Avenne-Izegem P.V.B.A.* [1978] 2 Lloyd's Rep. 109, 115; and see *ante*, p. 775.

(4) Burden of proof

The onus of proving that frustration is self-induced is on the party who alleges that this is the case. In *Joseph Constantine SS. Line* v. *Imperial Smelting Corp. Ltd.*[81] a ship was disabled by an explosion from performing her obligations under a charterparty. The owners were sued for damages and pleaded that the explosion frustrated the charterparty. The charterers argued that the owners must prove that the explosion was not due to their fault, but the House of Lords rejected this argument and upheld the defence of frustration although the cause of the explosion was never explained. A possible objection to the rule is that the charterer is much less likely than the owner to be able to show how the explosion occurred. This reasoning does, indeed, prevail in one group of cases: a person to whom goods have been bailed, and who seeks to rely on their destruction as a ground of frustration of the contract of bailment, must show that the destruction was not due to any breach of his duty as a bailee.[82] But, this special situation excepted, the rule as to burden of proof laid down in the *Joseph Constantine* case, can be defended on the ground that generally catastrophic events which prevent performance do occur without the fault of either party. To impose the burden of disproving fault on the party relying on frustration is therefore less likely than the converse rule to lead to the right result in the majority of cases.

SECTION 4. EFFECTS OF FRUSTRATION[83]

1. General

Frustration determines a contract automatically at the time of the frustrating event.[84] The court may therefore hold that the contract was frustrated even though the parties for some time after the event went on behaving as if the contract still existed.[85] "Whatever the consequences of the frustration may be upon the conduct of the parties, its legal effect does not depend on their opinions, or even knowledge, as to the event."[86] Accordingly, "what the parties may say or do" has been described as "only evidence, and not necessarily weighty evidence, of the view to be taken of the event by informed and experienced minds."[87] This does not mean that the courts disregard the views of the parties as to the effect of the event: thus in one case Lord Sumner said: "Both [parties] thought its result was to terminate their contractual relations . . . and as they must have known more about it than I do there is no reason why I should not think so too."[88] The

---

[81] [1942] A.C. 154; Stone, 60 L.Q.R. 262. A contrary dictum in *F. C. Shepherd & Co. Ltd.* v. *Jerrom* [1987] Q.B. 301, 319 seems to have been made *per incuriam*.

[82] *The Torenia* [1983] 2 Lloyd's Rep. 210, 216.

[83] Williams, *The Law Reform (Frustrated Contracts) Act 1943*.

[84] *Hirji Mulji* v. *Cheong Yue SS. Co. Ltd.* [1926] A.C. 497, 505; *B.P. Exploration (Libya) Ltd.* v. *Hunt* [1979] 1 W.L.R. 783, 809 (affirmed [1983] 2 A.C. 352); *The Super Servant Two* [1990] 1 Lloyd's Rep. 1, 8, 9, 14.

[85] *Cf. The Agathon* [1982] 2 Lloyd's Rep. 211, 213.

[86] *Hirji Mulji* case, *supra*, at p. 509.

[87] *Ibid.*

[88] *Bank Line Ltd.* v. *Arthur Capel & Co.* [1919] A.C. 435, 460. See also *Black Clauson International Ltd.* v. *Papierwerke Waldhof-Aschaffenburg A.G.* [1981] 2 Lloyd's Rep. 446, 457 where the fact that a party had "affirmed the contract" was said to exclude frustration.

true position is that "the parties' beliefs are not determinative, but nor are they irrelevent."[89]

As frustration operates automatically, it is generally thought to determine the contract without any election by either party: in this respect it differs from breach, which enables the victim to choose whether to treat the contract as discharged.[90] It follows that frustration can be invoked by either party, and not only by the party likely to suffer from the frustrating event. Thus where a ship under charter is requisitioned, frustration is sometimes, paradoxically, claimed by the shipowner, even though the charterer is perfectly willing to pay the agreed hire[91]; for if the compensation paid by the Government for the requisition exceeds that hire, the shipowner will actually profit from frustration. The courts are understandably reluctant to allow the doctrine of frustration to be used in this way. Thus the rejection of the plea of frustration in the *Tamplin*[92] case has been explained precisely on the ground that the House of Lords saw no good reason why the shipowner should be allowed to make a profit of the kind just described.[93] It seems that the seller in the *Tsakiroglou*[94] case would have made a similar profit if his plea of frustration had been upheld, for the market price of the goods had risen by more than the extra cost of carriage via the Cape of Good Hope[95]; and this fact may have had some influence on the decision that the contract remained in force. But in other cases the rule of automatic termination has, no doubt, enabled a party to profit from frustration.[96] It is doubtful whether such a result is necessary, and it might be better if frustration only gave an option to determine to any party who would be prejudiced by the frustrating event. There is, indeed, some support for this view in the cases relating to self-induced frustration. Where an allegedly frustrating event is brought about by the deliberate act of one party (not amounting in itself to a breach), that party cannot rely on it as frustrating the contract; but the other party may be able to rely on it. This is, for example, the position where an employee is imprisoned for a criminal offence and so unable to perform his part of a contract of employment. The employer can plead frustration in such circumstances[97]; but the employee cannot do so since a party cannot rely on self-induced frustration.[98]

Two results follow from the rule that frustration determines the contract at the time of the frustrating event. Rights accrued before frustration remain enforceable; rights not yet accrued at the time of frustration remain

[89] *The Wenjiang* (*No.* 2) [1983] 2 Lloyd's Rep. 400, 408.

[90] *F. C. Shepherd Ltd.* v. *Jerrom* [1987] Q.B. 301, 327.

[91] *e.g. Bank Line Ltd.* v. *Arthur Capel & Co.* [1919] A.C. 435.

[92] [1916] 2 A.C. 397; *ante*, pp. 771–772.

[93] *Metropolitan Water Board* v. *Dick Kerr & Co.* [1918] A.C. 119, 129; *cf.* also *Port Line Ltd.* v. *Ben Line Steamers Ltd.* [1958] 2 Q.B. 146.

[94] [1962] A.C. 93; *ante*, p. 777.

[95] Shortly after the end of the shipment period, the market price of the goods had risen by £18 15s. per ton above the contract price, while the cost of shipment via the Cape was only £7 10s. per ton more than the cost of shipment via Suez.

[96] A striking illustration is *The Isle of Mull*, 278 F. 131 (1921); *cf.* also *Nickoll & Knight* v. *Ashton Edridge & Co.* [1901] 2 K.B. 126 (*ante*, pp. 776–777) where the market price of the goods rose above the contract price so that the seller seems to have made a profit out of frustration.

[97] *F. C. Shepherd & Co.* v. *Jerrom* [1987] Q.B. 301; *ante*, pp. 803–804.

[98] *Ibid.*

unenforceable. As the following discussion shows, these rules sometimes caused hardship which has now been mitigated by statute.

2. Rights Accrued Before Frustration

(1) Common law

The rule that rights which had accrued before frustration remain enforceable can be illustrated by supposing that in *Taylor* v. *Caldwell*[99] the fire had occurred after the first, but before the second, of the four specified days. The rest of the contract would then have been discharged, while each party would have remained liable for any failure to perform obligations which had fallen due on the first day. But the application of this principle could lead to injustice where one party's performance under the contract became due before the frustrating event while that of the other was only to be rendered thereafter; for in such a case the former party would have still to perform, without getting anything in return. For example, in *Chandler* v. *Webster*[1] a contract for the hire of a room overlooking the proposed route of Edward VII's coronation processions provided for payment of £141 15s. in advance: this was due, and £100 of it had been paid, before the day on which the processions were cancelled. The hirer was held liable to pay the remaining £41 15s. as the payment had fallen due before the contract was frustrated.

To some extent the common law remedied this injustice. The obligation to pay in theory remained but it could sometimes be neutralised[2] by allowing the payor to recover back his money on the ground of "total failure of consideration."[3] In *Chandler* v. *Webster*, indeed, the hirer's claim to recover back the £100 already paid had failed: it was thought that there was no total failure of consideration as frustration only released the parties from further performance, and did not make the contract void *ab initio*. But this aspect of *Chandler* v. *Webster* was overruled in *Fibrosa Spolka Akcyjna* v. *Fairbairn, Lawson, Combe, Barbour Ltd.*[4] An English company had agreed to sell machinery to a Polish company for £4,800, of which £1,600 was to be paid in advance. When £1,000 had been paid, the contract was frustrated by the German occupation of Gdynia after the outbreak of war in 1939. The House of Lords held that the Polish company could recover back the £1,000 as the consideration for the payment had wholly failed: no part of the machinery had been delivered.

But this solution was defective in two ways. First, the payment could only be recovered back where the consideration had *wholly* failed.[5] In *Whincup* v. *Hughes*[6] the plaintiff apprenticed his son to a watchmaker for six years at a premium of £25. After one year the watchmaker died. The plaintiff could not recover back any part of the premium as the failure of consideration was only partial. Secondly, to allow the payor to recover

---

[99] (1863) 3 B. & S. 826, *ante*, p. 763.
[1] [1904] 1 K.B. 493; *cf. Blakeley* v. *Muller* (1902) 88 L.T. 90 and *Civil Service Cooperative Society* v. *General Steam Navigation Co.* [1903] 2 K.B. 756. For criticism, see Buckland, 46 Harv.L.Rev. 1281.
[2] *Cf. Fibrosa* case [1943] A.C. 32, 53.
[3] *Post*, p. 927.
[4] [1943] A.C. 32; *ante*, p. 786.
[5] *Cf. post*, p. 927.
[6] (1871) L.R. 6 C.P. 78.

back the whole of his advance payment might in turn cause injustice to the payee, who might (and in the *Fibrosa* case did) use the advance payment to finance the initial stages of the contract. If, in consequence of frustration, that expenditure was wasted, the resulting loss would fall entirely on the payee.

(2) Statute

To remedy the defects just described, section 1(2) of the Law Reform (Frustrated Contracts) Act 1943 lays down three rules:

(a) SUMS PAYABLE. All sums payable under the contract before the time of discharge cease to be payable on frustration: thus in *Chandler* v. *Webster* the claim for the unpaid £41 15s. would now fail.

(b) SUMS ACTUALLY PAID. All sums actually paid in pursuance of the contract before the time of discharge are recoverable from the payee "as money received by him to the use of the" payor. As the subsection does not refer to total failure of consideration, this statutory right to recover back money arises even where the failure is only partial, for example, in such cases as *Whincup* v. *Hughes*.

(c) EXPENSES. If the party to whom sums were paid or payable in pursuance of the contract has before the time of discharge incurred expenses in or for the purpose of the performance of the contract, the court may allow him to retain or recover the whole or any part of the sums so paid or payable; but the court cannot allow him to retain or recover more than the actual amount of his expenses. The court can only make an award in respect of expenses under section 1(2) if the contract contains a stipulation for prepayment; a party who incurs expenses without asking for a prepayment, or who incurs greater expenses than the amount of the prepayment, does so at his own risk.[7]

The court is not bound to award anything in respect of expenses and has a discretion as to the amount awarded. The court's discretion is subject to two upper limits: it cannot award more than the amount of the expenses actually incurred, or more than the amount of the stipulated prepayment. No doubt in exercising its discretion the court is influenced by the degree to which the expenses have been made useless by the frustrating event. If machinery made for one customer can easily be sold to another, very little will be awarded; if it cannot be disposed of except as scrap, the court is likely to make a substantial award. Even in such a case, however, the court will not necessarily award the maximum amount available under the Act. Suppose that in the *Fibrosa* case the seller had received a prepayment of £1,600 and had incurred expenses of exactly that amount. Under the common law rule he would have had to pay back the whole £1,600, and this was unjust because it left him to bear the entire loss of the wasted expenditure. Under the Act, the court could allow him to retain the whole £1,600, but this would be equally unjust as it would leave the buyer to bear the whole of that loss. In the exercise of its discretion under section 1(2) the court

---

[7] An award in respect of expenses can only be made under s.1(2) where a *sum of money* was paid or payable to the party who has incurred expenses. Where that party has received *property* a similar result may, however, be reached under s.1(3)(*a*): *post*, p. 811.

could split the loss (instead of merely shifting it from one party to the other) in such proportions as it thought just.[8]

3. Rights Not Yet Accrued

(1) Common law

At common law, rights not yet accrued at the time of frustration are unenforceable.[9] If a builder agrees to build a house for £100,000 payable on completion he cannot recover the £100,000 if the contract is frustrated before completion. This rule is perfectly reasonable: it would be unjust to make the building-owner pay the full price for an unfinished house. But, further, at common law the builder could not recover anything at all for partial performances before frustration. He could not recover a *quantum meruit* as no agreement to pay a proportionate sum for doing part of the work could be implied in the teeth of an express agreement for payment on completion. Thus in *Cutter* v. *Powell*[10] a seaman whose wages were to become due on completion of a voyage died during it: his executrix recovered nothing for the services he had rendered. And in *Appleby* v. *Myers*[11] the plaintiffs agreed "to make and erect the whole of the machinery" in the defendant's factory "and to keep the whole in order for two years from the date of completion." After part of the machinery had been erected, an accidental fire destroyed the factory with such of the machinery as was already in it, and frustrated the contract. It was held that the plaintiffs could recover nothing for the machinery which they had erected. The general view is that this result is unsatisfactory and that the builder should get something for his work.

(2) Statute

The common law rule stated above was modified by section 1(3) of the Law Reform (Frustrated Contracts) Act 1943, which provides that "Where any party to the contract has, by reason of anything done by any other party thereto in, or for the purpose of, the performance of the contract, obtained a valuable benefit (other than a payment of money to which [section 1(2)] applies) before the time of discharge, there shall be recoverable from him by the said other party such sum (if any), not exceeding the value of the said benefit to the party obtaining it, as the court considers just, having regard to all the circumstances of the case" and in particular to (a) the amount of any expenses incurred by the benefited party before the time of discharge, and (b) "the effect, in relation to the said benefit, of the circumstances giving rise to the frustration of the contract." Thus if A agrees to decorate B's house for £2,500 payable on completion but dies after decorating half the house, A's personal representatives can recover under this subsection. Similarly, the executrix in *Cutter* v. *Powell* could now rely on

---

8 s.1(2) refers to "the whole *or any part* of the sums so paid or payable." Legislation in other jurisdictions provides for *equal* division of the loss: British Columbia Frustrated Contracts Act 1974 s.5(3); New South Wales Frustrated Contracts Act 1978, s.11(2)(*b*)(ii) and *cf.* s.13; South Australian Frustrated Contracts Act 1988, ss.3(3), 7(2)(c); but equal division is not necessarily appropriate in all circumstances: New South Wales Act, *supra*, s.15; South Australian Act, *supra*, s. 7(4).

9 *The M. Vatan* [1987] 2 Lloyd's Rep. 416, 426.

10 (1795) 6 T.R. 320.

11 (1867) L.R. 2 C.P. 651.

the subsection as the defendant would have had the benefit of the deceased seaman's services during part of the voyage.[12]

Section 1(3) was applied in *B.P. (Exploration) Libya Ltd.* v. *Hunt.*[13] The case arose out of an elaborate agreement between B.P. and Mr. Hunt for the exploitation of an oil concession in Libya belonging to Mr. Hunt. B.P. were to do all the work of exploration and to provide the necessary finance; they were also to make certain "farm-in" payments in cash and oil. In return, they were to get a half share in the concession; and, as soon as the field began to produce oil, they were to receive "reimbursement oil" (to be taken at the rate of three-eighths of Mr. Hunt's share) until they had recouped 125 per cent. of their initial expenditure. A large oil field was discovered and oil began to flow from it in 1967; but in 1971 the contract between B.P. and Mr. Hunt was frustrated when their respective interests in the concession were expropriated by Libyan decrees. At this time, B.P. had received only about one third of the "reimbursement oil" to which they were entitled in respect of their initial expenditure; and they brought a claim under section 1(3) of the 1943 Act. The claim was allowed by Robert Goff J., whose decision was (subject to relatively minor modifications[14]) upheld by the Court of Appeal and the House of Lords. The learned judge held that, in considering a claim under section 1(3), the court must proceed in two stages: it must first identify and value the benefit obtained, and then assess the just sum (not exceeding the value of the benefit) which it was proper to award. At the first stage, he held that "benefit," on the true construction of section 1(3), referred not to the cost of performance incurred by the claimant, but to the end product received by the other party.[15] In the case before him, that end product was the enhancement of the value of Mr. Hunt's share in the concession resulting from B.P.'s work; but because section 1(3)(*b*) required the court to have regard to "the effect, in relation to the said benefit, of the circumstances giving rise to frustration," the value of that benefit had to be reduced to take account of the expropriation. In view of this fact, the total benefit obtained by Mr. Hunt was the net amount of oil he had received from the concession, plus the compensation paid to him by the Libyan government. Of this total, half was attributed to B.P.'s efforts and half to Mr. Hunt's original ownership of the concession. The value of this benefit was quantified at some $85m. In assessing the "just sum" to be awarded, however, Robert Goff J. adopted a criterion which he had rejected in valuing the benefit, *viz.* the cost to B.P. of the work to the extent that it was done for Mr. Hunt. To this was added the value of the "farm in" oil[16] and the resulting total was then reduced by the

[12] Unless the contract was literally one of insurance: see *ante*, p. 683, and *post*, p. 816. In any case the *quantum meruit* should not be based on the exceptionally high rate of pay contracted for, but on current market rates (*cf. ante*, p. 683).

[13] [1979] 1 W.L.R. 783; affirmed [1981] 1 W.L.R. 236, [1983] 2 A.C. 352; Baker [1979] C.L.J. 266.

[14] Recovery of a "farm-in" payment of $2m in *cash* had been allowed under s.1(3) when it plainly should have been allowed under s.1(2): see [1981] 1 W.L.R. 236, 240; [1983] 2 A.C. 352, 370; and see *infra*, n. 17.

[15] For this reason a claim for the "time value of money"—*i.e.* for the use that Mr. Hunt could have made of the proceeds of the sale of the oil—was rejected for it was not shown that he did make such use. But interest on the award from the time of frustration was allowed under Law Reform (Miscellaneous Provisions) Act 1934, s.3 (see now Administration of Justice Act 1982, s.15); *post*, p. 875.

[16] This value seems also to be relevant to the identification of the benefit.

amount of the reimbursement oil already received by B.P. On this basis, the just sum was some $34.67m.[17] and, as the valuable benefit exceeded this amount, B.P. recovered the just sum in full.

The machinery of the Act worked satisfactorily in *B.P. (Exploration) Libya Ltd.* v. *Hunt* because the valuable benefit, even when reduced in the light of the frustrating event, exceeded the just sum. But the position would have been different if the expropriation had occurred immediately before oil had begun to flow and if no compensation for expropriation had been paid. On the reasoning of the judgment, there would then have been no valuable benefit (beyond the "farm-in" oil); for that reasoning has regard to "the circumstances giving rise to the frustration" within section 1(3)(*b*) in *valuing the benefit* rather than in *assessing the just sum.* The same reasoning is adopted in an example which closely resembles *Appleby* v. *Myers*[18]: "Suppose that a contract for work on a building is frustrated by a fire which destroys the building and which therefore destroys a substantial amount of the work already done by the plaintiff. Although *it might be thought just* to award the plaintiff a sum assessed on a *quantum meruit* basis, the effect of s.1(3)(*b*) will be to reduce the award to nil. . . . "[19] If this is right, *Appleby* v. *Myers* would not be affected by the Act; but in view of the evident reluctance with which the learned judge reached this conclusion it is submitted that an alternative interpretation of section 1(3) is to be preferred. This would make the destruction of the benefit relevant, not to the identification of the benefit, but to the assessment of the just sum. Two points seem to support such an interpretation. First, section 1(3) applies where a valuable benefit has been obtained *before* the time of discharge: thus to identify the benefit in a case like *Appleby* v. *Myers* the court must look at the facts as they were before, and not after, the fire. The partly completed installation would at least prima facie be a benefit, in that completion of the installation would be likely to cost less after part of the work had been done. Secondly, there is the structure of the subsection. This begins by setting out the circumstances in which the court has power to make an award (*i.e.* when a valuable benefit has been obtained) and then provides guidelines for the exercise of that power. The guideline contained in section 1(3)(*b*) is introduced by the words "such sum as the court thinks just having regard to . . . (b) . . . "; and these words seem to link the guideline to the *exercise* rather than to the *existence* of the court's discretion. This interpretation cannot cause any injustice, for if the court thinks that very little or nothing should be awarded it can exercise its discretion to that effect; and for this purpose the court can certainly take the destruction of the benefit into account so as to split the loss in such proportions as the court thinks just.[20] But if such destruction necessarily led to the

---

[17] [1981] 1 W.L.R. 236, 241; this contrasts with the figure of some $35.40m. in [1979] 1 W.L.R. 783, 827. The difference is not explained and may be due to the adoption of different currency conversion factors at first instance and in the Court of Appeal.

[18] (1867) L.R. 2 C.P. 651.

[19] [1979] 1 W.L.R. 783, 801 (italics supplied); *cf. Parsons Bros. Ltd.* v. *Shea* (1966) 53 D.L.R. 2d 36, decided under a Newfoundland Act in similar (but not identical) terms to those of the English Act.

[20] Under the British Columbia, New South Wales and South Australian Acts referred to on p. 811, n. 8 *supra*, the loss would be split equally; but s.1(3) of the English Act gives a more flexible discretion.

conclusion that no valuable benefit had been obtained before frustration, the court would have no discretion to award anything at all. It would be a pity if this useful discretion were restricted in a way that is neither clearly required by the words of the subsection nor necessary to promote justice.

The discretion is in any case restricted to cases in which the defendant has received something of value. It is not enough for the plaintiff to incur trouble and expense.[21] Thus a person who orders goods from a manufacturer does not receive a valuable benefit merely because the manufacturer has bought the raw materials and started to make the goods. The manufacturer can only recover in respect of these expenses if he has stipulated for an advance payment, so that he can invoke section 1(2).

The power to make an award in respect of a valuable benefit under section 1(3) is, in theory, additional to the power to make an award in respect of expenses under section 1(2). Thus if a party who has incurred expenses has also both conferred a valuable benefit and received (or stipulated for) a prepayment he can claim under both subsections. But any amount awarded in respect of expenses will be taken into account in deciding how much should be awarded in respect of valuable benefit, and vice versa.[22] If the party who has incurred expenses has *received* a valuable benefit other than money (for example, a "prepayment" in kind) he cannot make any claim in respect of expenses under section 1(2) as that subsection only applies where a *sum of money* is paid or payable. But the court can reach much the same result under section 1(3), for it can take the expenses into account in deciding how much the recipient of the valuable benefit should pay for it.[23]

4. Casus Omissus?

Under section 1(2), sums of money payable before frustration cease to be payable on frustration. The subsection is restricted to payments of money. Section 1(3), by contrast, applies to other benefits, *e.g.* where A renders services or transfers property to B before frustration. But nothing in section 1(3) in terms releases A where before frustration he ought to have performed an obligation to do something other than to pay cash and has failed to do so. Thus if A has promised to make an advance payment *in cash* and has failed before frustration to do so, he is released by section 1(2); but if the stipulated payment had been *in kind* he would not be released by section 1(3). Nor can he, in the latter case, neutralise his liability by making a claim under section 1(3), for B has not "by reason of anything done [by A] obtained a valuable benefit . . . *before* the time of discharge." On the contrary, B has failed to obtain an expected benefit by reason of something not done by A. B may *after* the time of discharge obtain a benefit by suing A, but this does not bring the case within section 1(3) as the benefit is obtained too late. Nor would it help A to argue that before the time of discharge B had a valuable benefit, namely, his right to sue A, for this benefit would not have been obtained "by reason of anything done [by A] in or for the purpose of the performance of the contract." It is hard to believe that these consequences were intended. The failure of the Act to provide for the

---

[21] This was precisely the position in *Taylor* v. *Caldwell* (1863) 3 B. & S. 826: see *ante*, p. 767.
[22] See s.1(3)(*a*).
[23] *Ibid.*

release obligations other than those to pay money seems to be a *casus omissus*.

5. Special Cases

(1) Severability

A contract may provide for payments to be made from time to time in response to various acts of performance. The common law rule was that, if the contract was frustrated, such payments as were due at the time of frustration could be recovered. In *Stubbs* v. *Holywell Ry.*[24] a consulting engineer was appointed for 15 months for £500 payable in five equal quarterly instalments. After two quarters he died. His administrator successfully claimed the £200 due to him at the date of his death. But he could have recovered nothing more had the deceased worked for another two months in the next quarter. Under the 1943 Act he can do so. Section 2(4) provides that if parts of a contract which have been wholly performed can properly be severed from the remainder, they are to be treated as separate contracts; and that the provisions of section 1 (discussed above) shall apply to the remainder of the contract.

Section 2(4) also affects the rights of a person to recover back money paid under such a contract. At common law money could be recovered back if paid for some severable part of the consideration which had wholly failed, even though the consideration for the whole payment had not failed.[25] If in *Stubbs* v. *Holywell Ry.* the whole £500 had been paid in advance, £200 could have been recovered back as no work at all was done by the deceased in the last two quarters; but nothing could have been recovered back in respect of the third quarter, if the deceased had done so much as a week's work in it. Now money paid in respect of the third quarter could be recovered back, but the personal representative could claim under section 1(3) in respect of the work done by the deceased in that week.

(2) Contrary agreement

The common law rule that money is recoverable on the ground of total failure of consideration can be excluded by contrary agreement: the money may be paid out-and-out, with the intention that the payee shall keep it in any event.[26] The provisions of the Act can similarly be excluded by contrary agreement[27]; whether a term has this effect depends on its construction. In *B.P. Exploration (Libya) Ltd.* v. *Hunt*[28] the contract provided that the defendant was not to be personally liable to repay any advances and that the plaintiffs' rights were to be exercisable only against the defendant's share of the oil. This provision did not exclude the Act as, on its true construction, it was not intended to deal with the risk of expropriation but with the different risk that no oil might be found.

---

24 (1867) L.R. 2 Ex. 311.

25 See *Tyrie* v. *Fletcher* (1777) 2 Cowp. 666, 668; Marine Insurance Act 1906, s.84(2) (divisible insurance policies); *post*, p. 927.

26 *Fibrosa* case [1943] A.C. 32, 43, 77.

27 s.2(3).

28 [1983] 2 A.C. 352.

(3) Contracts excluded from the operation of the Act

The Act does not apply to:

(a) VOYAGE CHARTERPARTIES AND OTHER CONTRACTS FOR THE CARRIAGE OF GOODS BY SEA.[29] The object of this exception is to preserve two rules which are well established and known to businessmen: first, that freight which has become due or been paid before frustration remains due and (if paid) cannot be recovered back, even though the cargo is lost[30]; and, secondly, that a person who contracts to carry goods by sea to a specified port cannot recover freight *pro rata*, even if he is forced by events outside his control to discharge them at an intermediate port.[31]

(b) CONTRACTS OF INSURANCE.[32] The object of this exception is to preserve the rule that there can, in general, be no apportionment of premiums under an insurance policy once the risk has begun to run. The whole essence of a contract of insurance is that "the contract is for the whole entire risk, and no part of the consideration shall be returned."[33] Thus if a ship is insured but lost in some way not covered by the policy after part of the period of insurance has run, no part of the premium can be recovered back. This is obviously in accordance with the intention of the parties, for such a contract is essentially speculative. Had the ship been lost by one of the perils insured against on the first day, the insurer would have had to bear the whole loss. Conversely, he can keep the whole premium if the ship is lost by a peril that is not covered by the policy at any time during the period of insurance.

(c) CERTAIN CONTRACTS FOR THE SALE OF GOODS. Section 2(5)(*c*)[34] provides that the Act shall not apply to—

(i) *Any contract to which section 7 of the Sale of Goods Act 1979 applies.* Under section 7 of that Act, an agreement to sell specific goods is avoided if the goods perish without any fault on the part of the seller or buyer before the risk[35] has passed to the buyer. That is, the buyer is not liable for the price and neither party is liable in damages. The same result would normally follow from the common law rules of frustration, as the destruction of specific goods would frustrate the contract. The cases in which the 1943 Act would (if it were not excluded by s.2(5)(*c*)) make a difference are those in which there has been an advance payment or part-delivery.

If the buyer pays in advance but does not get any of the goods, he can recover back his payment on the ground of total failure of consideration.[36]

---

[29] s.2(5)(*a*); provides that the Act shall not apply "to any charterparty, except a time charterparty or a charterparty by way of demise, or to any contract (other than a charterparty) for the carriage of goods by sea." These words make it clear that the Act does not apply to voyage charterparties, but leave open the question whether it applies to a charterparty of the kind used in *The Eugenia* [1964] 2 Q.B. 665 (*ante*, p. 778).

[30] *Byrne* v. *Schiller* (1871) L.R. 6 Ex. 319; unless the contract provides the contrary, as in *The Oliva* [1972] 1 Lloyd's Rep. 458; contrast *The Lorna I* [1983] 1 Lloyd's Rep. 373 where, on the true construction of the contract, freight was not to become due till after frustration. Freight may be *earned* before it is *payable*: *ante*, p. 684.

[31] *St. Enoch Shipping Co. Ltd.* v. *Phosphate Mining Co.* [1916] 2 K.B. 625; *ante*, p. 684.

[32] s.2(5)(*b*).

[33] *Tyrie* v. *Fletcher* (1777) 2 Cowp. 666, 668. For a contractual provision displacing the normal rule, see *The M. Vatan* [1987] 2 Lloyd's Rep. 416.

[34] As amended by Sale of Goods Act 1979, s.63 and Sched. 2, para. 2.

[35] See *ante*, pp. 768–769.

[36] *Logan* v. *Le Mesurier* (1846) 6 Moo.P.C. 116.

The exclusion of the Act does not affect this right, but it does prevent the seller from setting off any expenses which he may have incurred, *e.g.* in putting the goods into a deliverable state.

Part-delivery followed by frustration raises two problems. First, a buyer of a specific parcel of goods may have paid the whole price in advance and received only part-delivery. He probably cannot recover back any part of the payment at common law as the failure of consideration is not total.[37] Nor can he rely on the 1943 Act, as that is excluded. But it has been suggested that he may be able to recover back a proportionate part of the advance payment simply on the ground that the undelivered goods are still at the seller's risk.[38] Secondly, a seller may have delivered part of the goods and been paid nothing. He cannot rely on the 1943 Act to recover anything in respect of the valuable benefit obtained by the buyer. He may be able to recover something at common law if a new contract can be implied from the buyer's keeping the goods after frustration. But it would be hard to imply such a contract if the buyer no longer had the goods, *e.g.* because he had used or resold them before frustration.

(ii) *Any other contract for the sale, or the sale and delivery, of specific goods, where the contract is frustrated by reason of the fact that the goods have perished.* These words seem to refer to a case which would not fall within section 7 of the Sale of Goods Act 1979, because the risk *has* passed to the buyer. It is difficult to imagine how such a contract could be frustrated by the perishing of the goods. Perhaps the point of excepting such a case from the 1943 Act is to make it clear that the buyer is liable for the whole price and that there is no power to order restitution or to apportion expenses.

Section 2(5)(*c*) can produce some entirely capricious distinctions.

The 1943 Act is only excluded where the goods are specific. Suppose that a farmer agrees to sell 200 tons out of a crop to be grown on his land, and the crop is destroyed by events for which he is not responsible.[39] As the goods are not specific,[40] the 1943 Act is not excluded and the farmer can set off his expenses of cultivating the crop[41] against any advance payment made by the buyer. But if the agreement were made after the crop had been lifted, the goods would be specific so that the 1943 Act would be excluded. Hence if the agreement in such a case had provided that the farmer was to put the goods into sacks, and if the goods had been destroyed before this operation had been completed, the farmer would have to return the whole of any advance payment made by the buyer,[42] without any right to deduct any part of the expenses of packaging.

The 1943 Act is only excluded where the cause of frustration is the per-

---

37 It is assumed that the case is not within *Ebrahim Dawood Ltd.* v. *Heath* (*Est.* 1927) *Ltd.* [1961] 2 Lloyd's Rep. 512; *post*, p. 927.

38 Atiyah, *Sale of Goods* (8th ed.), p. 336.

39 See *Howell* v. *Coupland* (1876) 1 Q.B.D. 258; *ante*, p. 773.

40 Mellish L.J. in *Howell* v. *Coupland* at p. 262 called the potatoes "specific things," but they were clearly not "specific goods" within the definition given in s.61(1) of the Sale of Goods Act 1979 ("identified and agreed upon at the time a contract of sale is made"): see *Re Wait* [1927] 1 Ch. 606, 631; and *cf. ante*, p. 774: the agreement was for the sale of an unidentified *part* of a future crop.

41 At least if incurred *after* the contract. In *Howell* v. *Coupland* 25 of the 68 acres of the defendant's land at Whaplode had been sown *before* the contract; *quaere* whether such expenditure would be recoverable under the Act.

42 Under the rule in the *Fibrosa* case [1943] A.C. 32; *ante*, p. 809.

ishing of the goods. Thus the Act applies where the contract is frustrated by illegality or requisition.

The reason for these distinctions is far from clear; and one might ask why contracts for the sale of goods were singled out for separate treatment at all. As a matter of abstract justice, there seems to be no reason why the powers of restitution and apportionment provided by the Act should apply to a contract to build a house but not a contract to supply a specific piece of machinery. The main reason for not applying the Act to contracts for the sale of goods is that in such contracts certainty is more important than justice; and the certainty which the rules as to the passing of risk are meant to provide would be disrupted if their effects could be modified by the exercise of the discretionary powers conferred on the courts by the 1943 Act. But on this view contracts for the sale of goods should have been wholly excluded from the operation of the 1943 Act. Their partial exclusion does not satisfy the requirements of either certainty or justice.

SECTION 5. JURISTIC BASIS[43]

1. Theories of Frustration

Much discussion is to be found in the cases as to the so-called theoretical or juristic basis of the doctrine of frustration. The first puzzle is why judges have devoted so much attention to this question. Perhaps the reason is that they still feel the need to justify in some way their departure from the doctrine of absolute contracts. The second puzzle is to know exactly what the discussion is about. Two questions have become, perhaps inevitably, intertwined: *why* are contracts frustrated, and *when*?[44] Discussions of the juristic basis of the doctrine of frustration attempt sometimes to justify the doctrine, and sometimes to evolve some general formula for describing the conditions in which it operates. The main theories of frustration which have been put forward are as follows.

(1) Implied term

The first theory is that the contract is discharged because it impliedly provides that in the events which have happened it shall cease to bind. This theory is put forward by Lord Loreburn in the *Tamplin* case. "No court has absolving power"[45] but the court will not regard an obligation as absolute if the parties themselves did not intend it to be absolute. If they "must have made their bargain on the footing that a particular thing or state of things would continue to exist . . . a term to that effect will be implied."[46]

In a purely subjective sense this theory is clearly untenable. The parties often have no common view at all as to the effects of frustrating event. If one party is in a stronger bargaining position than the other, he would probably not agree to discharge, while the other would want it. Even if the parties could reach some agreement on the point, they would probably not

---

[43] McNair, 56 L.Q.R. 173; *Legal Effects of War*, pp. 143 *et seq.*

[44] Thus in *Davis Contractors Ltd.* v. *Fareham U.D.C.* [1956] A.C. 696, 729 Lord Radcliffe said that "Frustration occurs *whenever*" the changed circumstances make performance "radically different from that which was undertaken." This seems to deal with the second of the questions put in the text; but it has also been regarded as providing an answer to the first: *e.g.* in *National Carriers Ltd.* v. *Panalpina (Northern) Ltd.* [1981] A.C. 675, 688, 717.

[45] *Tamplin* case [1916] 2 A.C. 397, 404.

[46] *Ibid.* at p. 403.

agree to total, unconditional discharge. As Lord Wright has said, "they would almost certainly on the one side or the other have sought to introduce reservations or qualifications or compensations."[47]

In fact Lord Loreburn did not put forward a purely subjective version of the implied term theory. He said: "From the nature of the contract it cannot be supposed that the parties *as reasonable men* intended it to be binding on them under such altered conditions. Were the altered conditions such that, had they thought of them, they would have taken their chance of them, or such that, *as sensible men*, they would have said, 'if that happens, of course, it is all over between us?' What, in fact, was the true meaning of the contract?"[48] But in this form, the implied term theory loses its chief attraction, which is that frustration merely gives effect to the intention of the parties themselves. There is an element of contradiction between saying that the court has no absolving power and saying that the court will absolve the parties if they would have agreed to this course, had they been sensible or reasonable men. The role of the parties in bringing about frustration really disappears. As Lord Radcliffe said in the *Fareham* case: "By this time it might seem that the parties themselves have become so far disembodied spirits that their actual persons should be allowed to rest in peace. In their place there rises the figure of the fair and reasonable man. And the spokesman of the fair and reasonable man, who represents after all no more than the anthropomorphic conception of justice, is and must be the court itself."[49]

(2) Just solution

Lord Sumner once described the doctrine of frustration as "a device by which the rules as to absolute contracts are reconciled with a special exception which justice demands."[50] Lord Wright in the *Denny, Mott* case, found "the theory of the basis of the rule"[51] in this statement; he added that the doctrine of frustration did not depend on the possibility of implying a term, but was "a substantive and particular rule which the common law has evolved."[52] And in the *Constantine* case he said: "The court is exercising powers, when it decides that a contract is frustrated, in order to achieve a result which is just and reasonable."[53] This "just solution" theory does not purport to explain why the courts sometimes abandon the doctrine of absolute contracts: it simply says that they do so. The theory should not, moreover, be interpreted to mean that the courts can do what they think just whenever a change of circumstances causes hardship to one

---

47 *Denny, Mott* case [1944] A.C. 265, 275; *cf. Shell U.K. Ltd.* v. *Lostock Garages Ltd.* [1976] 1 W.L.R. 1187, 1196: *Atisa S.A.* v. *Aztec A.G.* [1983] 2 Lloyd's Rep. 579, 586 (describing the implied term theory as "now rejected."); *F. C. Shepherd & Co. Ltd.* v. *Jerrom* [1987] Q.B. 301, 322; *The Super Servant Two* [1989] 1 Lloyd's Rep. 145, 154, affd. [1990] 1 Lloyd's Rep. 1; *cf.* Trakman, 46 M.L.R. 39. For a possible power of the court to introduce "reservations" etc. by means of an implied term while holding the contract *not* frustrated, see *The Maira* (*No.* 2) [1985] 1 Lloyd's Rep. 300, 311 (affirmed on other grounds [1986] 2 Lloyd's Rep. 12).

48 [1916] 2 A.C. 397, 404.

49 [1956] A.C. 696, 728.

50 *Hirji Mulji* v. *Cheong Yue SS. Co. Ltd.* [1926] A.C. 497, 510. In the *Bank Line* case [1919] A.C. 435, 455 he had supported the implied term theory.

51 [1944] A.C. 265, 275.

52 *Ibid.* at p. 274.

53 [1942] A.C. 154, 186; *cf. National Carriers Ltd.* v. *Panalpina* (*Northern*) *Ltd.* [1981] A.C. 675, 696; *The Super Servant Two* [1990] 1 Lloyd's Rep. 1, 8.

party: it does not supersede the strict rules which determine the scope of the doctrine of frustration.[54] Nor does it determine the type of relief which can be given. When a contract is frustrated, both parties are at common law discharged, though the "just solution" might be an apportionment of loss.

(3) Foundation of the contract

This theory was stated by Lord Haldane in the *Tamplin* case. "When people enter into a contract which is dependent for the possibility of performance on the continued availability of a specific thing, and that availability comes to an end by reason of circumstances beyond the control of the parties, the contract is prima facie regarded as dissolved. . . . Although the words of the stipulation may be such that the mere letter would describe what has occurred, the occurrence itself may yet be of a character and extent so sweeping that the foundation of what the parties are deemed to have had in contemplation has disappeared, and the contract itself has vanished with that foundation."[55] In *W. J. Tatem Ltd.* v. *Gamboa*[56] Goddard J. regarded this as "the surest ground on which to rest the doctrine of frustration."

At first sight this theory has the merit of simplicity as it does not involve speculation as to the intention of the parties. It is particularly appropriate where performance depends on the continued availability of a specific thing. But in other cases the metaphor "foundation" is unhelpful. How can one tell whether passage through the Suez Canal is the "foundation" of a charterparty? What is the "foundation" of a contract in which the parties take a deliberate risk as to the continued availability or existence of a specific thing or of some state of affairs? Such doubts as to what is the "foundation" of the contract can, in the last resort, only be resolved by construing the contract. If this is so, there is no real difference between the "foundation" theory and the "implied term" theory in its objective sense. Indeed, exponents of one sometimes use the language of the other. Thus in the *Tamplin* case Lord Loreburn, after stating the implied term theory, said that the court "can infer from the nature of the contract and the surrounding circumstances that a condition which is not expressed was a foundation on which the parties contracted."[57]

(4) Construction

All the theories so far stated depend in the last resort on the construction of the contract: to this extent, they "shade into one another."[58] After stating the implied term theory, Lord Loreburn proposed, as the ultimate test: "what, in fact, is the true meaning of the contract?"[59] Similarly, in *Taylor* v. *Caldwell,* Blackburn J. said "the contract is not to be *construed* as a positive contract, but subject to an *implied condition* that the parties shall be excused in case, before breach, performance becomes impossible. . . ."[60]

---

[54] *British Movietonenews* v. *London & District Cinemas* [1952] A.C. 166; *ante*, p. 000.
[55] [1916] 2 A.C. 397, 406. Lord Haldane's was a dissenting speech.
[56] [1939] 1 K.B. 132, 137.
[57] [1916] 2 A.C. 397, 404.
[58] *National Carriers Ltd.* v. *Panalpina (Northern) Ltd.* [1981] A.C. 675, 693.
[59] [1916] A.C. 397, 404.
[60] (1863) 3 B. & S. 826, 833.

Construing the contract and implying a term are in these cases only alternative ways of describing the same process. Similarly, the "foundation" theory raises a question of construction whenever it is at all doubtful what the "foundation" of the contract is. And Lord Wright, in the course of stating the "just solution" theory, said: "What happens is that the contract is held on its true construction not to apply at all from the time when the frustrating circumstances supervene."[61] It seems that this is the most satisfactory explanation of the doctrine of frustration.

(5) Failure of consideration

This theory is sometimes used to explain why *both* parties are discharged in the situation (discussed earlier in this Chapter[62]) in which the supervening event makes the performance of only *one* party impossible. Thus destruction of a specific thing may make performance of the *supplier's* obligation impossible; but it has no such effect on the *recipient's* obligation to pay, and it can be said that the latter is discharged by failure of consideration,[63] *i.e.* because he does not receive the performance for which he bargained. In England, however, these cases are explained on the ground that the "common object" of the parties is frustrated.[64] Moreover, insofar as the present theory suggests that the failure of consideration must be total[65] it is plainly wrong since frustration can occur in cases of partial destruction or after part performance; and the theory has for this reason been rejected in the House of Lords.[66]

2. Practical Importance

It is sometimes asked whether this theoretical discussion has any practical importance. It seems to have none.[67] A number of possibilities must be discussed.

(1) In *W. J. Tatem Ltd.* v. *Gamboa* Goddard J. said that the contract would be frustrated although the parties foresaw that the ship would be seized and detained. He even said: "If the foundation of the contract goes, it goes whether or not the parties have made a provision for it."[68] These statements could only be made by an adherent of the "foundation" theory. But the first has been doubted earlier in this Chapter,[69] while the second was qualified later in the judgment: "*Unless the contrary intention is made plain,* the law imposes this doctrine of frustration."[70]

(2) In the *Davis Contractors* case, Lord Reid said that no review was

---

[61] *Denny, Mott* case [1944] A.C. 265, 274; *cf. The Eugenia* [1964] 2 Q.B. 226, 239; *The Sibeon and the Sibotre* [1976] 1 Lloyd's Rep. 293, 235.

[62] *Ante*, pp. 790–791.

[63] This explanation is commonly given in the United States: *e.g. Earn Line SS. Co.* v. *Sutherland SS. Co. Ltd.*, 254 F. 126, 131 (1918); Corbin, *Contracts*, §§ 1320, 1322; Restatement 2d, *Contracts*, Introductory Note to Chap. 11, p. 310.

[64] *Hirji Mulji* v. *Cheong Yue SS. Co. Ltd.* [1926] A.C. 497, 510; *ante*, p. 791.

[65] For total failure of consideration, see *ante*, pp. 809–810; *post*, p. 927.

[66] *National Carriers Ltd.* v. *Panalpina (Northern) Ltd.* [1981] A.C. 675, 687, 702.

[67] This seems to be the view of Lords Wilberforce and Roskill in *National Carriers Ltd.* v. *Panalpina (Northern) Ltd.* [1981] A.C. 675, 693, 717. Lord Hailsham (*ibid.*, at p. 687) regards "the theoretical basis of the doctrine as clearly relevant to the point under discussion"; but he does not specify in what respect it is relevant.

[68] [1939] 1 K.B. 132, 138.

[69] *Ante*, pp. 796, n. 98, 801.

[70] [1939] 1 K.B. 132, 139.

possible of the arbitrator's decision on the "foundation" theory, as the question whether the "foundation" had disappeared was one of fact; while such review was possible on the "implied term" or "construction" theories as implication and construction were questions of law.[71] But a question of law would be involved even on the "foundation" theory if the question: what is the "foundation"? is itself one of construction. And after the *Tsakiroglou* case[72] it is difficult to argue that the right to review an arbitrator's decision is restricted by any particular theory.

(3) In the *Davis Contractors* case, Lord Reid also said that there might be a practical difference between the "implied term" and "construction" theories. On the latter theory "there is no need to consider what the parties thought or how they or reasonable men in their shoes would have dealt with the new situation if they had foreseen it. The question is whether the contract which they did make is, on its true construction, wide enough to apply to the new situation: if not, then it is at an end."[73] But in construing the contract the court does not wholly disregard the intention of the parties. The court may not have to ask: what would the parties have said, had they thought of the frustrating event? But it does have to ask: in what circumstances did the parties intend the contract to operate? It is only after this question has been answered that the intention of the parties becomes irrelevant: that is, it is not necessary to go on and ask whether they would have agreed to discharge or to some compromise. But this question does not arise under the implied term theory either, as frustration at common law always results in total discharge of the contract.

3. Frustration and Mistake

A comparison is sometimes made between frustration and mistake which nullifies consent[74] because the supposed subject-matter of the contract does not exist or is fundamentally different from the subject-matter as it was believed to be. Thus in *Krell* v. *Henry*[75] a contract for the hire of a room overlooking the route of the coronation processions was frustrated when the processions were *later* cancelled; in *Griffith* v. *Brymer*[76] a similar contract was held void for mistake when the processions had *already* been cancelled when the contract was made.

This analogy is interesting and sometimes helpful; but it should not be pressed too far. Mistake and frustration are "different juristic concepts,"[77] the one relating to the formation and the other to the discharge of contracts. Events which frustrate a contract would not necessarily avoid it if,

---

71 *Davis Contractors Ltd.* v. *Fareham U.D.C.* [1956] A.C. 696, 720.

72 [1962] A.C. 93; see generally *ante*, pp. 794–795.

73 [1956] A.C. 696, 721.

74 *Ante*, pp. 249–261. *Associated Japanese Bank* (*International*) *Ltd.* v. *Crédit du Nord S.A* [1989] 1 W.L.R. 255, 264 ("related areas").

75 [1903] 2 K.B. 740.

76 (1903) 19 T.L.R. 434; comparison of these two cases shows that effects of frustration and mistake are not the same. In *Griffith* v. *Brymer* the hirer recovered his advance payment, while in *Chandler* v. *Webster* (*ante*, p. 809) he did not. If similar circumstances were to recur, the powers of apportionment provided by the Law Reform (Frustrated Contracts) Act 1943 would not apply to cases of mistake, though it is arguable that the equitable jurisdiction to rescind on terms (*ante*, pp. 281–284) could produce similar results if the contracts were only voidable in equity.

77 *Constantine* case [1942] A.C. 154, 186; *cf. Bell* v. *Lever Bros. Ltd.* [1932] A.C. 161, 237; *Fibrosa* case [1943] A.C. 32, 77.

unknown to the parties, they had already happened at the time of formation. A contract of carriage may be frustrated by the blocking of the route,[78] but would probably not be void for mistake on this ground. Similarly, parties may validly agree on a contractual term "requiring one of them to do the impossible,"[79] *e.g.* on a term requiring a seller of goods to deliver them from a named ship at a specified port which the ship could not enter. The seller would then be liable for failing to deliver in accordance with that term; but he could be discharged if after the time of contracting an event happened which made it impossible for the ship to get into the port, *e.g.* "if a sudden storm had silted up the harbour"[80] there. The law seems to be less ready to hold a contract void for mistake than discharged by frustration, perhaps because it is, in general, easier to be sure of present facts than to foresee the future.

[78] As in the example given, *ante*, p. 778.
[79] *The Epaphus* [1987] 2 Lloyd's Rep. 215, 218.
[80] *Ibid.* p. 220.

CHAPTER TWENTY-ONE

REMEDIES[1]

A BREACH of contract is a civil wrong. To break a contract can also occasionally be a criminal offence[2]; and some statutes penalise dangerous or deceptive conduct which amounts,[3] or may amount,[4] to a breach of contract. Conviction in such cases makes the offender liable not only to punishment, but also to an order requiring him to pay compensation for any personal injury, loss or damage resulting from the offence.[5] In most cases, however, a breach of contract will involve only civil liability; and our sole concern in this Chapter will be with remedies available in civil proceedings. In such proceedings, the injured party may claim either specific relief, or damages or restitution.

A claim for specific relief is one for the actual performance of the defaulting party's undertaking. Where that undertaking is one to do, or to forbear from doing, some act, a claim for specific relief is made by the equitable remedies of specific performance or injunction; where the undertaking is one to pay a sum of money, a claim for specific relief is made by the common law action for an agreed sum. A claim for damages is one for compensation in money for the fact that the claimant has not received the performance for which he bargained. This is the remedy most frequently discussed in the reported cases, and the bulk of this Chapter is therefore devoted to it. A person who has performed his part of the contract but has not received the agreed counter-performance may, finally, claim back his performance or its reasonable value. These restitutionary remedies are not confined to cases of breach of contract; but as they are often available in such cases they can conveniently be considered in this Chapter.

SECTION 1. DAMAGES

The action for damages is always available, as of right, when a contract has been broken. It should, from this point of view, be contrasted with claims

---

[1] Beale, *Remedies for Breach of Contract*; Treitel, *Remedies for Breach of Contract: a Comparative Account*; Harris, *Remedies in Contract and Tort*; Burrows, *Remedies for Torts and Breach of Contract*.

[2] For example, cutting off a tenant's gas supply may be an offence: *McCall* v. *Abelesz* [1976] Q.B. 585 (as to which see *post* p. 876, n. 49); the offence may be committed even though the tenant is not a contractual tenant, so that there is no breach of contract: Protection from Eviction Act 1977, s.1(1); *R.* v. *Yuthiwattana* (1985) Cr.App.R. 55; *R.* v. *Burke* [1991] 1 A.C. 135. See further, Treitel in *Essays in Memory of Sir Rupert Cross*, pp. 82–92.

[3] Conspiracy and Protection of Property Act 1875, s.5, as amended by Criminal Law Act 1977, s.6 and Sched. 13.

[4] *e.g.* Trade Descriptions Act 1968, s.1; Consumer Protection Act 1987, Pt. II: under these provisions, offences may be committed even though no contract is ever made or broken. Sometimes, the law also provides administrative remedies in respect of conduct that may amount to a breach of contract: *e.g.* under Fair Trading Act 1973, Pt. 3; Sex Discrimination Act 1975, s.67(1)(*a*).

[5] Powers of Criminal Courts Act 1973, s.35, as amended by Criminal Justice Act 1988, s.104; *cf.* also Consumer Protection Act 1987, s.41.

for specific relief and for restitution, which are either subject to the discretion of the court or only available if certain conditions (to be discussed later in this Chapter) are satisfied. An action for damages can succeed even though the victim has not suffered any loss: in that event, it will result in an award of nominal damages. In such a case, the purpose of the action may simply be to establish what the rights and liabilities of the parties under a contract are, though for this purpose the action for a declaration now provides a more convenient remedy. Generally the victim will claim damages for a substantial loss; and our concern is with the law governing the award of such damages. We shall consider, first, the general principles which govern awards of damages; secondly, the way in which damages are assessed or quantified; thirdly, certain rules limiting the damages which can be recovered; and finally, contractual provisions purporting to establish in advance the amount that can be recovered (or retained) by the victim.

1. General Principles

(1) Damages are compensatory

Damages are awarded to compensate the plaintiff.[6] Three aspects of this principle require discussion at this point.

(a) LOSS TO PLAINTIFF[7] THE CRITERION. In general, damages are based on loss to the plaintiff and not on gain to the defendant.[8] In a Scottish case,[9] a financier broke a contract to invest £15,000 in the business of a timber merchant and instead invested the same sum in a distillery. It was held that the timber merchant's damages were based on the loss to his business and not on the much larger profits which the financier had derived from the distillery. Similarly, where a shipowner in breach of contract withdraws his ship from a charterparty, damages are based on the charterer's loss, and not on any profit that the shipowner may make from other employment of the ship.[10] Likewise, an employee who left in breach of contract to take up a better paid job would not be liable to account to his employer for the extra pay, but only to compensate him for any loss that he may have suffered. The same principle again applies where a person who has agreed to sell goods for future delivery for £x fails to deliver because he has disposed elsewhere of the goods for £x + 100. If the buyer can in fact get goods of the same description for £x or less at the time fixed for delivery, he will have suffered no loss and will get no (substantial) damages: it is irrelevant that the seller has, in a sense, made a profit of £100 out of the breach.[11]

---

[6] *Tai Hing Cotton Mill Ltd.* v. *Kamsing Knitting Factory* [1979] A.C. 95, 104.

[7] For exceptional cases in which the plaintiff can recover damages in respect of a third party's loss see *ante*, p. 533.

[8] *Tito* v. *Waddell* (*No.* 2) [1977] Ch. 106, 332; *The Solholt* [1983] 1 Lloyd's Rep. 605, 608; *cf. The Ypatianna* [1987] 2 Lloyd's Rep. 286, 297. According to *Samson & Samson* v. *Proctor* [1975] N.Z.L.R. 665, a builder may be liable to his client for expenses saved through failure to comply with the agreed specifications, even though no loss to the client results; but no reason is given for this departure from the generally accepted principle stated in the text. See also Jones, 99 L.Q.R. 443, Friedmann, 80 Col.L.Rev. 504, Farnsworth, 94 Yale L.J. 1339; Birks, [1987] L.M.C.L.Q. 421; Friedmann, 104 L.Q.R. 383; *cf.* Stoljar, 2 J.C.L.1.

[9] *Teacher* v. *Calder* (1889) 1 F.(H.L.) 39.

[10] *The Siboen and the Sibotre* [1976] 1 Lloyd's Rep. 293, 337.

[11] *Acmé Mills* v. *Johnson* 133 S.W. 784 (1911); *cf. The Solholt* [1983] 1 Lloyd's Rep. 605, where the buyer's damages were nominal as he had failed to mitigate (*post*, p. 867) and it was irrelevant that the seller (who was in breach) had made a profit on resale.

There are, however, a number of exceptions to the general rule that a contract-breaker is not bound to hand over any profits that he has made out of the breach. If, for example, the subject-matter of a sale is land, the vendor is, after the conclusion of the contract, considered to hold the land as trustee for the purchaser; and if the vendor wrongfully resells the land to a third party, the purchaser is entitled to the proceeds of that sale, even though they may exceed his loss.[12] Again, an account of profits may be ordered against a person who wrongfully uses another's trade secret or confidential information[13]; and this remedy is, no doubt, available where the wrongful use amounts to a breach of a contract of (for example) employment.[14] Similarly, an agent who commits a breach of his fiduciary duty by selling his own property to a principal, when he has been employed to buy for him, is liable to account for any profit made in this way.[15]

A defendant may, in breach of contract, use, or interfere with, another's property without, at first sight, inflicting on the latter any loss. In one case[16] the buyer of a floating dock failed, in breach of contract, to remove it from its berth. He argued that no substantial damages should be awarded because the sellers would not have made any use of the berth. The argument was rejected, Lord Denning saying that "the test of the measure of damages is not what the plaintiffs have lost, but what benefit the defendant obtained by having the use of the berth." But the actual award was based on the fair rental value of the berth, and could be explained on the basis that the plaintiffs lost *the chance* of reletting it. It seems that if the defendant had made a *greater* profit, he would not have been liable for it.[17]

Similar reasoning explains a case where a developer built houses in breach of a restrictive covenant.[18] The breach did not diminish the value of the estate for the benefit of which the covenant had been made, but the owners of the estate nevertheless recovered damages based on the amount which they might have charged the developer for granting him permission to build. This chance to charge was valued at only 5 per cent. of the developer's anticipated profit, thus indicating that it was not the profit as such which formed the basis on which damages were awarded.

(b) WHAT CONSTITUTES LOSS. For the present purpose, loss includes any harm to the person or property of the plaintiff, and any other injury to his economic position. The question to what extent harm to the person includes injury to feelings is discussed later in this Chapter.[19] Harm to

[12] See *Lake* v. *Bayliss* [1974] 1 W.L.R. 1073. *Cf.* also Housing Act 1988, ss.27 and 28(1) (damages in tort for wrongful eviction).

[13] *Peter Pan Mfg. Corp.* v. *Corsets Silhouette Ltd.* [1964] 1 W.L.R. 96; *Att.-Gen.* v. *Guardian Newspapers (No. 2)* [1990] A.C. 109, 262, 288. *Cf.* Law Com. 110, paras. 4.86 and 6.114(2)(*b*).

[14] *Cf. Printers & Finishers Ltd.* v. *Holloway* [1965] 1 W.L.R. 1.

[15] *Regier* v. *Campbell-Stuart* [1939] Ch. 766; *cf.* now Estate Agents Act 1979, s.21 (*ante*, p. 647).

[16] *Penarth Dock Engineering Co. Ltd.* v. *Pound* [1963] 1 Lloyd's Rep. 359; *cf.* in tort, *Swordheath Properties Ltd.* v. *Tabet* [1979] 1 W.L.R. 285.

[17] *Cf. Strand Electric and Engineering Co. Ltd.* v. *Brisford Entertainments Ltd.* [1952] 2 Q.B. 246, 252, 256.

[18] *Wrotham Park Estate Co.* v. *Parkside Homes Ltd.* [1974] 1 W.L.R. 798, approved in *Stoke-on-Trent City Council* v. *W. & J. Wass Ltd.* [1988] 1 W.L.R. 1406. *Cf. Bracewell* v. *Appleby* [1975] Ch. 408 (tort); *General Tire & Rubber Co.* v. *Firestone Tyre & Rubber Co.* [1975] 1 W.L.R. 819 (patent infringement—a claim for an account of profits, available under Patents Act 1949, s.60, was not pursued); Sharpe and Waddams, 1 O.J.L.S. 290.

[19] *Post*, pp. 876–877.

property covers damage to or destruction of particular things, while injury to the plaintiff's economic position includes any amount by which he is worse off than he would have been if the contract had been performed. For example, if a seller in breach of contract fails to deliver goods, or to deliver them on time, the buyer prima facie suffers loss in not having the goods, or in not having them at the agreed time.

(i) *Overall position taken into account.* In determining whether the victim has suffered loss, his overall position is taken into account.[20] If, for example, a buyer has not yet paid and is released from his obligation to do so by the seller's wrongful failure to deliver, his loss will prima facie be the value of the goods less the price; and if he has agreed to pay no more than the goods are worth he may have suffered no loss at all.

The court will similarly take the plaintiff's overall position into account in determining the basis on which damages are to be assessed: it will not generally order the defendant to pay an amount which will actually make the plaintiff's position better than it would have been, if the contract had been performed. The principle is illustrated by *Phillips* v. *Ward*[21] where a surveyor in breach of contract failed to draw his client's attention to the fact that the roof timbers of a house, which the latter was about to buy, were rotten. It was held that the client was not entitled to damages based on the cost of making the defects good. Such an award would put him into a better position than that in which he would have been if the contract had not been broken; for it would enable him to have a new roof with new timbers, which would be less expensive to maintain than an old roof with sound timbers. Hence the plaintiff was only entitled to recover the difference between the price that he paid and the value of the house when he bought it[22]; or the difference between the price actually paid and that which would have been paid if the surveyor had made his report with due care.[23] But the cost of making the defect good can be recovered if it was reasonably incurred by the plaintiff to mitigate his loss.[24] Where costs are incurred for this purpose, the principle that the plaintiff should not actually be enriched by an award of damages is, moreover, not an inflexible one. In *Harbutt's "Plasticine" Ltd.* v. *Wayne Tank & Pump Co. Ltd.*[25] the plaintiff's factory was burnt down as a result of the defendant's breach of contract. It was held that the plaintiff could recover the cost of rebuilding the factory without making any allowance for the fact that he would then have

---

[20] *e.g. The Baleares* [1990] 2 Lloyd's Rep. 130 (and see [1991] 2 All E.R. 110). *Cf. post*, p. 869.

[21] [1956] 1 W.L.R. 471.

[22] See *Perry* v. *Sidney Phillips & Son* [1982] 1 W.L.R. 1297, 1305, 1306; Burrows, 47 M.L.R. 357; *Treml* v. *Ernest W. Gibson & Partners* (1984) 272 E.G. 68 *Westlake* v. *Bracknell D.C.* (1987) 19 H.L.R. 375 (where it is not clear whether the damages were awarded in contract or in tort); *Cross* v. *David Martin & Mortimer* [1989] 1 E.G.L.R. 154; *Stewart* v. *Rapley* [1989] 1 E.G.L.R. 159. Where the client pays *more* than the valuation, such excess may be irrecoverable: see *Lucas* v. *Ogden* [1988] 2 E.G.L.R. 176.

[23] *Perry* v. *Sidney Phillips & Son* [1982] 1 W.L.R. 1297, 1302; on the facts of this case the two formulae stated in the text would have yielded the same result, for the actual value of the property was assumed to be the amount that the buyer would have paid, if the surveyor's report had been accurate.

[24] *Cross* v. *David Martin & Mortimer* [1989] 1 E.G.L.R. 154; *Hipkins* v. *Jack Cotton Partnership* [1989] 2 E.G.L.R. 157.

[25] [1970] 1 Q.B. 447, followed on this point in *Bacon* v. *Cooper Metals Ltd.* [1982] 1 All E.R. 397, and *Dominion Mosaics & Tile Co. Ltd.* v. *Trafalgar Trucking Co. Ltd.* [1990] 2 All E.R. 246, though overruled on another point in *Photo Production Ltd.* v. *Securicor Transport Ltd.* [1980] A.C. 827.

a new (and therefore more valuable) factory. The case can be explained on the ground that the plaintiff had no reasonable alternative but to rebuild, or that he did so in order to mitigate his loss.[26]

(ii) *Intended use of subject-matter.* It is sometimes argued that a plaintiff has suffered no loss because, even if the contract had been performed, he would not have used the subject-matter profitably, or at all. In one case,[27] contractors were sued for agreed damages[28] for delay in delivering warships to the Spanish government. It was held to be no defence that warships are not put to profitable use, or that the ships, if delivered on time, would probably have been sunk in a naval battle in which the fleet which they were to have joined suffered defeat. Prima facie, the mere fact that the plaintiff did not receive the performance for which he bargained is itself considered to amount to a loss to him. However, his intended use of the subject-matter may affect the amount of his loss: this is, for example, the case where a buyer of goods has made a subsale of the very goods comprised in the original sale.[29] Similarly, by statute a landlord cannot recover damages for breach of his tenant's obligation to repair if the tenant can prove that the landlord was going to demolish the premises.[30]

(c) BREACH HAVING NO ADVERSE EFFECT. A further consequence of the compensatory principle is that the plaintiff cannot recover substantial damages if the breach has not adversely affected his position. This principle is most readily illustrated by the case in which a seller of goods wrongfully fails to deliver on a falling market. If the buyer has not paid and if, at the time fixed for delivery, he can buy substitute goods more cheaply elsewhere, the breach will prima facie have had no adverse effect on him, so that he will not be entitled to substantial damages. Similarly, a shipowner cannot get substantial damages for breach of the charterer's obligation to load if he finds alternative and more profitable employment for the ship.[31] Nor can a buyer recover substantial damages merely because the seller delivers goods which are not of the contract description if they are in fact no less valuable than goods which are of the contract description.[32]

The same principle was applied in *Ford* v. *White*[33] where the plaintiffs bought a house and adjoining plot for £6,350 after being advised by their solicitors that they could build on the plot. The solicitors had negligently and in breach of contract overlooked a covenant against building on the plot. The property subject to the covenant was in fact worth £6,350 but it would have been worth an extra £1,250 if there had been no covenant. It was held that the solicitors were not liable for this sum.[34] The plaintiffs would not have bought at all, had they been told of the covenant (so that

---

[26] *Post*, p. 867.
[27] *Clydebank Engineering Co.* v. *Don Jose Ramos Isquierdo y Castaneda* [1905] A.C. 6.
[28] *Post*, p. 885.
[29] *Re R. & H. Hall Ltd. and W. H. Pim Jr. & Co.'s Arbitration* (1928) 139 L.T. 50; *post*, p. 840.
[30] Landlord and Tenant Act 1927, s.18(1).
[31] *Staniforth* v. *Lyall* (1830) 7 Bing. 169.
[32] *Taylor* v. *Bank of Athens* (1922) 27 Com.Cas. 142.
[33] [1964] 1 W.L.R. 885.
[34] It seems that, if the property had been resold, the solicitors would have been liable for expenses incurred in connection with, and loss suffered on, resale: *cf. County Personnel (Employment Agency) Ltd.* v. *Pulver* [1987] 1 W.L.R. 916; *Hayes* v. *James and Charles Dodd* [1990] 2 All E.R. 815.

they did not lose the chance of a good bargain); nor had they paid more for the property than it was actually worth.

So far it has been assumed that the plaintiff has suffered no loss at all. The position is the same where he does suffer a loss but would have suffered the same loss if there had been no breach.[35] This would have been the position in *Ford* v. *White* if the property had, because of the covenant, been worth less than £6,350, but it had been shown that the plaintiffs would nevertheless have paid that sum for it, even with knowledge of the covenant.[36] Again, an agent who without authority purports to contract on behalf of his principal is liable for breach of implied warranty of authority.[37] The normal result of this breach is that the agent must pay the same amount that the principal would have had to pay, had he been bound by the contract and not performed it. But if the principal is utterly insolvent the agent need only pay nominal damages. The third party has not lost anything through the breach of warranty, for, had the agent had authority, the third party would only have acquired an empty right against the principal.[38]

(d) NO PUNITIVE DAMAGES. Punitive (or exemplary) damages can be awarded in certain tort cases.[39] The purpose of such damages is not to compensate the plaintiff, nor even to strip the defendant of his profit,[40] but to express the court's disapproval of the defendant's conduct, *e.g.* where he has deliberately committed a wrong (such as defamation[41]) with a view to profit.

As a general rule punitive damages cannot be awarded in a purely contractual action,[42] since the object of such an action is not to punish the defendant but to compensate the plaintiff.[43] Punitive damages are not available even though the breach was committed deliberately and with a view to profit. If the court is particularly outraged by the defendant's conduct, it can sometimes achieve much the same result by awarding damages for injury to the plaintiff's feelings.[44] In theory such damages are meant to compensate the plaintiff for mental suffering, rather than to punish the defendant. But in practice the distinction is often hard to draw and—from

---

[35] *e.g. Stratton Ltd.* v. *Weston*, *Financial Times*, April 11, 1990; *cf. Banque Keyser Ullmann S.A.* v. *Skandia (U.K.) Ins. Co. Ltd.*, [1990] 2 All E.R. 947.

[36] *Cf. Sykes* v. *Midland Bank Executor & Trustee Co. Ltd.* [1971] 1 Q.B. 113; A.L.G., 87 L.Q.R. 10. *Semble*, it would not be enough to show that the plaintiffs *might* have bought for the same price even if they had been told the truth: *cf. Brikom Investments Ltd.* v. *Carr* [1979] Q.B. 467, 483.

[37] *Ante*, p. 640.

[38] *Richardson* v. *Williamson* (1871) L.R. 6 Q.B. 276, 279; *Weeks* v. *Propert* (1873) L.R. 8 C.P. 427, 439; *Re National Coffee Palace Co.* (1883) 24 Ch.D. 367, 372.

[39] See Lord Devlin's speech in *Rookes* v. *Barnard* [1964] A.C. 1129.

[40] In *Stoke-on-Trent City Council* v. *W & J Wass Ltd.* [1988] 1 W.L.R. 1406, 1414 the damages awarded in the *Wrotham Park* case [1974] 1 W.L.R. 798 (*ante*, p. 826), which were based on the defendant's profit, were described as "something akin to . . . exemplary damages for breach of contract." The purpose of true exemplary damages, however, is punitive rather than restitutionary.

[41] *Cassell & Co. Ltd.* v. *Broome* [1972] A.C. 1027.

[42] *Perera* v. *Vandiyar* [1953] 1 W.L.R. 672; *Paris Oldham & Gustra* v. *Staffordshire B.G.* [1988] 2 E.G.L.R. 39; *Reed* v. *Madon* [1989] Ch. 408; and see *infra*, n. 44.

[43] *Calabar Properties Ltd.* v. *Stitcher* [1984] 1 W.L.R. 287, 297.

[44] *Post*, pp. 876–877. *Cf.* the suggestion in *McCall* v. *Abelesz* [1976] Q.B. 585, 594 that damages for injury to feelings could now be awarded in a case like *Perera* v. *Vandiyar*, *supra*.

the defendant's point of view—to perceive.[45] However where the plaintiff has a cause of action both in tort and for breach of contract, he may be able to recover punitive damages by framing the claim in tort. For example, a landlord who unlawfully evicts his tenant is guilty both of a breach of contract and of a trespass; and punitive damages have been awarded in such a case.[46] Another type of case in which a defendant seeks to profit from a deliberate wrong which is both a breach of contract and a tort is that in which he gives a fraudulent warranty as to the subject-matter of a contract of sale. In the United States, punitive damages have been awarded in such a case[47]; but in England conflicting views have been expressed on the question whether such damages can be awarded in an action based on fraud even if the action is brought in tort.[48] It can be argued, on the one hand that the tort of deceit is generally one from which the defendant seeks to profit, so that it falls into the category of wrongs for which punitive damages are available; and, on the other, that deceit generally involves the wrongdoer in criminal liability and that he should not suffer double punishment by being in addition ordered to pay punitive damages.[49]

Punitive damages should be distinguished from multiple damages which may sometimes be awarded to coerce the defendant rather than to express disapproval of his conduct. This seems to be the purpose of the statutory provision by which a tenant who wrongfully holds over after having been given notice to quit can be held liable for *twice* the annual value of the land for the period of his wrongful occupation.[50]

(2) Compensation for what?

The principle that damages are compensatory naturally gives rise to the question: for what is it that the victim of a breach of contract is entitled to be compensated? This question calls for an analysis of the various types of losses for which the victim of a breach of contract can recover damages[51]; and it also gives rise to certain related problems.

(a) Loss of bargain. The basic object of damages for breach of contract is to put the plaintiff "so far as money can do it . . . in the same situation . . . as if the contract had been performed."[52] In other words, the plaintiff is entitled to be compensated for the loss of his bargain, so that his

---

[45] See, for example, *Chelini* v. *Nieri* 196 P. 2d 915 (1948) where damages of $10,000 were awarded for breach of contract against a Californian embalmer.

[46] *Drane* v. *Evangelou* [1978] 1 W.L.R. 455; *cf. Guppys* (*Bridport*) v. *Brookling* (1984) 269 E.G. 846 (nuisance and landlord's breach of covenant to repair); *McMillan* v. *Singh* (1984) 17 H.L.R. 120 (where the claim seems to have been in contract only, but the plaintiff was said at p. 125 also to have had a claim in tort); *Millington* v. *Duffy* (1984) 17 H.L.R. 232.

[47] *Grandi* v. *Le Sage* 399 P. 2d 285 (1965).

[48] *Mafo* v. *Adams* [1970] 1 Q.B. 548; *Cassell & Co. Ltd.* v. *Broome*, *supra*, n. 41, at pp. 1076, 1131; *Metall und Rohstoff A.G.* v. *A.C.L.I. Metals* (*London*) *Ltd.* [1984] 1 Lloyd's Rep. 598, 612; *Smith Kline & French Laboratories Ltd.* v. *Long* [1989] 1 W.L.R. 1.

[49] *Archer* v. *Brown* [1985] Q.B. 401, 418–423.

[50] Landlord and Tenant Act 1730, s.1.

[51] Fuller and Perdue, 46 Yale L.J. 52, 373; *cf.* Burrows, 99 L.Q.R. 217; Owen 4 O.J.L.S. 393. For judicial recognition of the distinctions drawn in the following discussion, see *The Alecos M* [1990] 1 Lloyd's Rep. 82, 84 (reversed, without reference to this point, [1991] 1 Lloyd's Rep. 120).

[52] *Robinson* v. *Harman* (1848) 1 Ex. 850, 855. Atiyah's emphasis in 94 L.Q.R. 193 on reliance loss and restitution (discussed below), fails adequately to account for the principle stated in this dictum; or indeed for the availability of the action for the agreed sum (*post*, pp. 895–902) or other specific relief (*post*, pp. 902–924).

expectations arising out of or created by the contract are protected. This protection of the plaintiff's expectations must be contrasted with the principle on which damages are awarded in tort: the purpose of such damages is simply to put the plaintiff into the position in which he would have been, if the tort had not been committed.[53] Of course, in many tort actions the plaintiff can recover damages for loss of expectations: *e.g.* for loss of expected earnings suffered as a result of personal injury, or for loss of expected profits suffered as a result of damage to a profit-earning thing. But these expectations exist quite independently of the tortious conduct which impairs them: it is the nature of most torts to destroy or impair expectations of this kind, rather than to create new ones. The tort of misrepresentation does, indeed, create new expectations, but the purpose of damages even for that tort is to put the plaintiff into the position in which he would have been, if the misrepresentation had not been made, and not to protect his expectations by putting him into the position in which he would have been, if the representation had been true.[54] In a contractual action, on the other hand, damages are recoverable as a matter of course for loss of the expectations created by the very contract for breach of which the action is brought.[55] That is why damages of this kind are the distinctive feature of a contractual action.

A contract may give rise to two quite separate expectations: that of receiving the promised performance and that of being able to put it to some particular use. For example, a buyer of goods (such as machinery or raw materials) may expect not only to receive the goods but also to use them for manufacturing purposes. If the seller fails to deliver, the buyer is entitled to damages based on the value of the goods that he should have received and also[56] to damages for loss of profits[57] suffered as a result of not receiving the promised delivery.

(b) RELIANCE LOSS. An alternative principle is to put the plaintiff into the position in which he would have been if the contract had never been made, by compensating him for expenses incurred (or other loss suffered) in reliance on the contract. Sometimes the expenses are of a kind which the plaintiff *must* incur if he is to perform his part of the contract. For example, a contract for the sale of goods may provide that the seller is to deliver the goods at the buyer's premises; and if the buyer wrongfully refuses to accept them when they are tendered there, the seller can recover the expenses of delivery as an element of reliance loss. Wasted expenses may, moreover, be recoverable as reliance loss even though the plaintiff was *not*, under the contract, actually obliged to incur them. In *McRae* v. *Commonwealth Disposals Commission*,[58] for example, the defendants were held liable for breach of a contract that there was a wrecked tanker lying in a specified

[53] For an exception (now severely restricted in scope) see the disucssion at pp. 539–545, *ante* of *Junior Books Ltd.* v. *The Veitchi Co. Ltd.* [1983] 1 A.C. 520.

[54] See *ante*, pp. 322–325.

[55] In *The Unique Mariner* [1979] 1 Lloyd's Rep. 37, 54 it is said that damages in contract are assessed "on the usual principle of *restitutio in integrum*." This might suggest that the plaintiff is to be restored to his pre-contract position; but the method of assessment actually adopted in that case was such as to put the plaintiff into the position in which he would have been if the contract had been *performed*.

[56] See *The "Ile aux Moines"* [1974] 1 Lloyd's Rep. 262 (where in fact loss of profits was not proved).

[57] Provided that these are not too remote: *post*, pp. 854 *et seq*.

[58] (1951) 84 C.L.R. 377, esp. at p. 411.

position[59]; and the plaintiffs recovered, *inter alia*, the £3,000 which it had cost them to send out a salvage expedition to look for the tanker.

So far it has been assumed that the reliance loss is incurred after the contract; but even expenditure incurred before the contract may be recoverable on this basis. In *Anglia Television Ltd.* v. *Reed*[60] the defendant broke his contract to take a leading part in the plaintiffs' television play: and he was held liable for expenses of £2,750 incurred by the plaintiffs on the production before they had entered into the contract with him. Although the plaintiffs had not incurred the expenditure in reliance on their contract with the defendant, it could be said that they had relied on that contract in allowing the expenditure to be wasted: in other words, in forbearing to look for another leading actor to take the part until it was too late. The pre-contract expenditure in such cases is recoverable because it leads to a loss which, after breach, can no longer be avoided.[61]

Pre-contract expenditure may also be recoverable if it was incurred in reliance on an *agreement* before that agreement had become a legally binding *contract*. In *Lloyd* v. *Stanbury*[62] a person who had contracted to sell land was accordingly held liable for certain expenses incurred by the purchaser in reliance on the agreement while it was still subject to contract.[63]

(c) RESTITUTION.[64] A claim for restitution may not, strictly speaking, be one for "damages"; its purpose is not to compensate the plaintiff for a loss, but to deprive the defendant of a benefit. The simplest case of restitution arises where a seller has been paid in advance and then fails to deliver. He is bound to restore the price and the effect of this is to put *both parties* into the position in which they would have been if the contract had *not been made*. The restitution claim obviously differs from a loss of bargain claim, which is meant to put the plaintiff into the position in which he would have been if the contract had been performed. It also differs from a claim for reliance loss, which is meant to put the plaintiff into the position in which he would have been if the contract had not been made, and which will often leave the defendant in a worse position. In practice there is considerable overlap between reliance and restitution. Performance by the plaintiff is a form of reliance which often benefits the defendant; and the requirement in restitution claims that the defendant must have "benefited" from that performance is a somewhat elastic one.[65]

(d) RELATIONSHIP BETWEEN LOSS OF BARGAIN, RELIANCE LOSS AND RESTITUTION. The relationship between the three types of claim so far discussed is a complex one, but it seems to be governed by the following principles.

(i) *Plaintiff's choice.* Where more than one type of claim is available the choice between them (if it has to be made) is the plaintiff's: the defendant cannot force the plaintiff to make one of the available claims rather than another. Suppose that a seller has been paid in advance and then fails to deliver. The buyer can choose between claiming the return of his money

---

59 *Ante*, p. 259.
60 [1972] 1 Q.B. 60; A.L.G., 88 L.Q.R. 168; Ogus, 35 M.L.R. 423; Clarke [1972] C.L.J. 22.
61 *C.C.C. Films (London) Ltd.* v. *Impact Quadrant Films Ltd.* [1985] Q.B. 16; Owen [1985] C.L.J. 24; Burrows, 100 L.Q.R. 27.
62 [1971] 1 W.L.R. 535.
63 *Ante*, p. 52.
64 See further, *post*, pp. 926–937.
65 See especially *ante*, p. 720; *post*, p. 935.

(restitution) and the value of the goods at the time fixed for delivery (loss of bargain). Obviously he will take the former course if he has made a bad bargain and the latter if he has made a good bargain. If the seller could force him to choose restitution, the buyer could easily be deprived of the benefit of a good bargain.

(ii) *Limitations on plaintiff's choice.* It does not follow from the mere fact of breach that the three types of claim are always available to the plaintiff, or that they are available in full.

The claim for loss of bargain damages is, in principle, always available. But on such a claim the plaintiff must prove the value of his expectations. If he cannot do so with reasonable certainty, he may be limited to his reliance and restitution claims. The point may be illustrated by further reference to *McRae* v. *Commonwealth Disposals Commission*[66] where the plaintiffs claimed damages for loss of their bargain, alleging that the value of the supposed tanker and its contents (for which they had paid £285) would have been £300,000. This basis for quantifying damages was dismissed as "manifestly absurd"[67]; and the plaintiffs recovered their payment of £285 (restitution) plus the £3,000 spent on their fruitless salvage expedition (reliance loss).

At the other extreme, the plaintiff's right to claim restitution is severely limited, in particular by the rule that he can (in general) only recover back money paid under the contract if there has been a *total* failure of consideration. This rule will be discussed later in this Chapter[68]; but a point to be emphasised here is that, if a restitution is available, it is no objection to such a claim that it will leave the plaintiff better off than he would have been, if the contract had been performed. Indeed, this will be the result of a successful restitution claim whenever the plaintiff has made a bad bargain, *e.g.* by paying more for goods than they are worth.

Claims for reliance loss occupy an intermediate position. The Court of Appeal has held that such claims are normally available when a reliance loss has been suffered; and that the plaintiff is entitled to choose between such a claim and one for loss of bargain damages.[69] One type of case in which he will claim reliance loss is where he cannot prove the value of his expectations. This is no doubt why the plaintiffs claimed reliance loss in *Anglia Television Ltd.* v. *Reed*[70]: they could not prove what profit (if any) they would have made out of the play. Similarly, in *McRae's* case the plaintiffs could not prove the value of the supposed tanker, and nevertheless recovered £3,000 by way of reliance loss. But the plaintiffs should not have been awarded the *whole* of this reliance loss if the defendants could have proved that the tanker, if it had existed, would have been worth only £2,000. In such a case the plaintiffs would have lost £1,000, even if there had been no breach; and where the plaintiff has in this way made a bad bargain, the court will not shift that loss to the defendant by allowing the

---

[66] (1951) 84 C.L.R. 377.

[67] *Ibid.* at p. 411.

[68] *Post*, pp. 927–932.

[69] *Cullinane* v. *British "Rema" Mfg. Co.* [1954] 1 Q.B. 292, 303; *Anglia Television Ltd.* v. *Reed* [1972] 1 Q.B. 60, 63–64; *C.C.C. Films (London) Ltd.* v. *Impact Quadrant Films Ltd.* [1985] Q.B. 16, 32; *cf. Lloyd* v. *Stanbury* [1971] 1 W.L.R. 535, 547.

[70] [1972] 1 Q.B. 60.

plaintiff to recover the whole of his wasted expenditure.[71] Similarly, in a case like *Anglia Television Ltd.* v. *Reed* the plaintiffs could not have recovered the whole of their reliance loss if the defendant could have shown that the plaintiffs' expenses would have exceeded the amount that they could have earned from the play. It has been held that the burden of proof on this issue is on the defendant: in other words, it is not up to the plaintiff to show that his venture would have been profitable but up to the defendant to show that it would have been unprofitable.[72] As much of the relevant information on this issue will usually be more readily available to the plaintiff than to the defendant, it is likely that the defendant will find this burden a hard one to discharge.

By contrast, a plaintiff who claims restitution can shift a loss flowing from the fact that he has made a bad bargain (and not from the breach) to the defendant. The reason for this rule is that the defendant would otherwise be enriched; and there is no such enrichment merely because a plaintiff's reliance loss exceeds the value of his bargain.

(iii) *Whether claims can be combined.* There is sometimes said to be an inconsistency between combining the various types of claim so far discussed. An award which seeks to put the plaintiff into the position in which he would have been if the contract had been *performed* cannot, on this view, be combined with one which seeks to put him (or both parties) into the position which would have existed, if the contract *had not been made.* But the courts have not accepted this kind of reasoning and have, in appropriate cases, allowed the claims to be combined. In one case[73] machinery was bought, paid for and installed. The buyer rejected the machinery because it was not in accordance with the contract; and he recovered the price (restitution), installation expenses (reliance loss) and his net loss of profits resulting from the breach (loss of bargain).

The true principle is not that there is any logical objection to combining the various types of claim, but that the plaintiff cannot combine them so as to recover more than once for the same loss. Suppose that a buyer has paid in advance for goods which are not delivered. He obviously cannot recover both his payment (restitution) and the full value of the goods at the time fixed for delivery (loss of bargain). The point has been well put by Corbin: "*full* damages and *complete* restitution . . . will not both be given for the same breach of contract."[74]

The principle against double recovery also applies where a plaintiff seeks to combine a claim for reliance loss with one for the loss of his bargain. If the plaintiff in *McRae's*[75] case had been able to establish the value of the hypothetical tanker, he should clearly not have been entitled to that amount *and* to the £3,285, for he would have had to spend the latter amount to acquire the former. Similarly, in *Cullinane* v. *British "Rema" Manufacturing Co. Ltd.*[76] the defendants sold a clay pulverising machine to

---

71 See *C. & P. Haulage* v. *Middleton* [1983] 1 W.L.R. 1461; *Bowlay Logging* v. *Domtar* [1978] 4 W.W.R. 105; *cf. C.C.C. Films (London) Ltd.* v. *Impact Quadrant Films* [1985] Q.B. 16, 38.

72 *C.C.C. (London) Films Ltd.* v. *Imperial Quadrant Films* [1985] Q.B. 16.

73 *Millar's Machinery Co. Ltd.* v. *David Way & Son* (1935) 40 Com.Cas. 204; *cf. Naughton* v. *O'Callaghan* [1990] 3 All E.R. 191, 198; and see *ante*, pp. 749–750.

74 Corbin on *Contracts*, § 1221. *Cf. The Unique Mariner* [1979] 1 Lloyd's Rep. 37, 53.

75 (1951) 84 C.L.R. 377.

76 [1954] 1 Q.B. 292; Macleod [1970] J.B.L. 19; Stoljar, 91 L.Q.R. 68.

the plaintiff, warranting that it could process clay at six tons per hour. The plaintiff claimed damages for breach of this warranty under two heads: first, the capital cost of the machine and its installation and, secondly, loss of profits. It was held that the plaintiff could not recover under both of these heads as "a claim for loss of profits could only be founded upon the footing that the capital expenditure had been incurred."[77] To allow the plaintiff to recover the capital expenditure and also his *full* profit would give him damages twice over for the same loss. It was however not established that the profits which would have been derived from the machine over the whole of its useful "life" would have *exceeded* its capital cost. If this had been proved the plaintiff could, according to a decision of the High Court of Australia, have recovered (a) the capital cost of the machinery less its actual value; plus (b) the excess of the estimated profits over the sum calculated under (a).[78] This alone would put the plaintiff into as good a financial position as if the contract had been performed.

A problem of double recovery again arose in *George Mitchell (Chesterhall)* Ltd. v. *Finney Lock Seeds Ltd.*,[79] where a seed merchant sold defective seed to a farmer so that the latter's crop failed. It was said that the damages included "all the costs incurred by the [farmer] in the cultivation of the worthless crop as well as the profit [he] would have expected to make from a successful crop if proper seeds had been supplied."[80] Here "profit" must mean the proceeds of a successful crop less the cost of cultivating *such* a crop. That cost might well have been lower than the cost of attempting to cultivate an unsuccessful crop; for such an attempt might have involved the farmer in trouble and expense beyond the normal, until the hopeless nature of the situation became apparent. But the expense of cultivating a successful crop would have been incurred by the farmer even if the seed had not been defective, so that the farmer would be over-compensated if that expense were not taken into account in computing the profit.

(e) INCIDENTAL AND CONSEQUENTIAL LOSS. The victim of a breach of contract can often recover loss which does not fit easily into the categories so far discussed.

First, he may incur expenses after a breach has come to his attention, such as the administrative costs of buying a substitute[81] or of sending back defective goods. Such expenses are hardly incurred in reliance *on the contract*; and they will in this Chapter be called "incidental" loss.[82]

Secondly, the injured party may suffer "consequential" loss. This expression is used in the law of contract in a number of senses. It may mean simply loss of profits (as opposed to the mere failure to obtain the thing contracted for): in this sense it is merely an element of expectation loss. Alternatively, it may refer to reliance loss: *e.g.* to the expense wasted by a seller in delivering goods which the buyer wrongfully refuses to accept. But the expression is also used (and will be used here) to refer to further harm, such as personal injury or damage to property, suffered as a result of breach: for example, where a cow is sold under a warranty of soundness

---

[77] At p. 302.
[78] *T.C. Industrial Plant Pty. Ltd.* v. *Robert's (Queensland) Ltd.* [1964] A.L.R. 1083.
[79] [1983] A.C. 803.
[80] *Ibid.* p. 812.
[81] See, *e.g.*, *Robert Stewart & Sons Ltd.* v. *Carapanayoti* [1962] 1 W.L.R. 34.
[82] *Cf.* U.C.C. s.2–715(1).

but is diseased and infects other cattle of the buyer, which die. The seller is prima facie liable for the loss of the other animals,[83] even though, when the buyer put the cow with them, the possibility of disease, or the risk of its spreading, was not present to his mind at all. In this situation he cannot have relied on the cow's not being diseased, since reliance presupposes an affirmative belief. Nor can it be said that he *expected not* to lose the other animals; he simply *did not expect* to lose them, which is a wholly different state of mind.

2. Quantification

Damages always consist of a sum of money, so that the plaintiff's loss has to be quantified in terms of money. This process of "quantifying" or "measuring" or "assessing" damages gives rise to a number of problems.

(1) The bases of assessment

(a) RELIANCE AND RESTITUTION. Relatively little difficulty arises where the plaintiff claims reliance loss or restitution. In the first case, the basis of assessment is the cost to him of his action in reliance on the contract; and in the second it is generally[84] the benefit obtained by the defendant under the contract. These assessments are particularly straightforward where the plaintiff has expended or the defendant received a sum of money. Where the reliance loss or the benefit to be "restored" consists of goods or services, a reasonable value must be placed on them. This may give rise to practical difficulties, but there is no doubt about the principle on which such assessment proceeds.

(b) LOSS OF BARGAIN. Where the plaintiff claims to be put into "the same situation . . . as if the contract had been performed,"[85] there are two distinct bases of assessment:

(i) "*Difference in value*" *and* "*cost of cure.*" The distinction between these two cases is strikingly illustrated by an American case[86] in which a coal company took a mining lease of farmland, covenanting to restore the land to its original state at the end of the lease. The cost of doing the work would have been $29,000, but the result of not doing it was to reduce the value of the land by only $300. Damages for the company's failure to do the work were assessed at the latter sum. In English law damages for breach of a tenant's covenant to repair are by statute assessed on a "difference in value" basis.[87] Apart from such statutory provisions, the law starts with certain prima facie assumptions for choosing between the two bases; but these assumptions can be displaced. The point can be illustrated by

---

[83] *Smith* v. *Green* (1875) 1 C.P.D. 92; *cf. The Batis* [1990] 1 Lloyd's Rep. 345 (expenses incurred in complying with directions wrongfully given by party in breach).

[84] Not always: see, *e.g.*, *Planché* v. *Colburn* (1831) 8 Bing. 14 (*ante*, p. 720), where there is no evidence that the defendant benefited at all; and see *post*, p. 935.

[85] *Robinson* v. *Harman* (1848) 1 Ex. 850, 855.

[86] *Peevyhouse* v. *Garland Coal Co.* 382 P. 2d 109 (1962); *cf. Attica Sea Carriers Corp.* v. *Ferrostaal Poseidon Bulk Reederei GmbH* [1976] 1 Lloyd's Rep. 250.

[87] Landlord and Tenant Act 1927, s.18; *Culworth Estates Ltd.* v *Society of Licensed Victuallers*, *The Times*, February 28, 1991. But in the absence of evidence as to difference in value, cost of repairs is a "starting point": *Drummond* v. *S.U. Stores* (1980) 258 E.G. 1293, 1294; *cf. infra*, n. 90.

reference to contracts for the supply of goods and for the execution of building work.

Where a seller delivers goods which are not of the contract quality, the damages are prima facie assessed on a difference in value basis, so that the buyer can recover "the difference between the value of the goods . . . and the value they would have had"[88] if they had been in accordance with the contract. But this is only a prima facie rule, and if the defect in the goods can be cured at a reasonable cost there is little doubt that the cost of such cure can be awarded. This rule has certainly been stated in analogous hire-purchase cases[89] and there seems to be no reason for not applying it to sales.[90] Even the cost of an attempted cure which fails—such as veterinary fees spent on a sick animal which nevertheless dies—can be recovered.[91]

A defendant who is in breach of an obligation to do building work is prima facie liable on a "cost of cure" basis: *i.e.* he must pay for the cost of putting the defects right or of completing the work.[92] It must be emphasised, however, that this is only a prima facie rule, which can be displaced where the cost of putting the defect right would be out of all proportion to the advantage which cure would confer on the injured party. This would, for example, be the position where components not in accordance with the contractual specifications had been built into a structure which would have to be substantially demolished to effect a cure[93]; where the cost of cure was greater than the value of the whole building[94]; or where execution of the promised building work would confer no economic benefit at all on the plaintiff.[95] In such cases, difference in value (if any[96]) would form the normal[97] basis of assessment.[98] This basis of assessment is, in turn, liable to be displaced by further circumstances. There is some support in the authorities for the view that the plaintiff can recover damages on the higher cost of cure basis if he can show *either* that he has in fact incurred that cost *or*

---

88 Sale of Goods Act 1979, s.53(3).

89 *e.g. Charterhouse Credit Co. Ltd.* v. *Tolly* [1963] 2 Q.B. 683, 711–712.

90 *Jacovides* v. *Constantinous*, *The Times*, October 27, 1986 (a sale of land case where damages were awarded for misrepresentation apparently having contractual effect). In *Keeley* v. *Guy McDonald* (1984) 134 New L.J. 522 the *cost of repairing* an unmerchantable car was awarded *as the difference in value* between the car as it was and as it would have been if it had been merchantable.

91 *Harling* v. *Eddy* [1951] 2 Q.B. 739.

92 *Mertens* v. *Home Freeholds* [1921] 2 K.B. 526; *Hoenig* v. *Isaacs* [1952] 1 T.L.R. 1360; *William Cory & Sons* v. *Wingate Investments Ltd.* (1978) 248 E.G. 687; *cf. Radford* v. *de Froberville* [1977] 1 W.L.R. 1262 (breach of covenant to build a boundary wall); *Calabar Properties Ltd.* v. *Stitcher* [1984] 1 W.L.R. 287; and see, in insurance law, *Pleasurama* v. *Sun Alliance* [1979] 1 Lloyd's Rep. 389.

93 *e.g. Jacob & Youngs* v. *Kent* 129 N.E. 889 (1921).

94 *Cf. Morris* v. *Redland Bricks Ltd.* [1970] A.C. 652.

95 *James* v. *Hutton* [1950] 1 K.B. 9 (where peformance of the defendant's promise to restore a shop front to its pre-contract appearance would not have affected its value).

96 There being no such difference in *James* v. *Hutton*, *supra*, the damages were held to be nominal.

97 For a possible exception in cases of "deliberate" breach, see *Glaer* v. *Schwartz*, 176 N.E. 616 (1913).

98 See *Jacob & Youngs* v. *Kent*, *supra*; McGregor on *Damages* (15th ed.), § 1092; Hudson, *Building Contracts* (10th ed.), p. 589; Keating, *Building Contracts* (4th ed.), p. 263; analogous tort cases support the same view: *e.g. Jones* v. *Gooday* (1841) 8 M. & W. 146; *Darbishire* v. *Warran* [1963] 1 W.L.R. 1067; *R. C. Taylor (Wholesale) Ltd.* v. *Hepworth Ltd.* [1977] 1 W.L.R. 659.

that he will incur it by getting the work done.[99] He is, however, required to mitigate his loss,[1] and it is submitted that he would have failed to do so if he had insisted on cure even though its cost was wholly disproportionate to the resulting benefit to him. Where this is the position, he should recover only on a difference in value basis.[2] For this purpose, the disporportion would have to be a clear one, since the mitigation rules only require the injured party to act reasonably. Cost of cure which is actually incurred or going to be incurred may therefore be recoverable where the effect of cure on the value of property is speculative[3]; and where the cost of cure, though not resulting in any improvement to the property, is not excessive in relation to the initial value of that property.[4]

(ii) *Cases where cure is not undertaken.* Even where the plaintiff is prima facie entitled to cost of curing a defect in the defendant's performance, damages will not be assessed on this basis if he does not undertake, or propose to undertake, cure but disposes of the defective subject-matter.[5] Difference in value would, in such circumstances, be the appropriate measure.[6]

(iii) *Both bases may lead to same result.* The two bases of assessment will not invariably lead to diverging results. For example, in *Dean* v. *Ainley*[7] a vendor of land broke her contractual undertaking to seal a patio so as to prevent water from leaking into a cellar. The purchaser recovered the cost of doing the promised work, and this sum was variously described as the "cost of the works,"[8] or as the extent to which the property was "clearly less valuable"[9] as a result of the vendor's failure to perform her undertaking. Where the only reliable evidence of difference in value is cost of cure,[10] the two methods of assessment will lead to the same practical result.

Sometimes the process of assessment can with equal plausibility be des-

---

[99] *Tito* v. *Waddell* (*No.* 2) [1977] Ch. 106, 332, 335; *Radford* v. *De Froberville* [1977] 1 W.L.R. 1262; *Dean* v. *Ainley* [1987] 1 W.L.R. 1729 (cost of cure); *cf. County Personnel* (*Employment Agency*) *Ltd.* v. *Alan R. Pulver & Co.* [1987] 1 W.L.R. 916 (cost to client of extricating himself from a transaction in which he had been negligently advised by his solicitor). For the position in tort, see *Heath* v. *Keys*, *The Times*, May 28, 1984; *Ward* v. *Cannock Chase D.C.* [1986] Ch. 546; *cf. Minscombe Properties* v. *Sir Alfred McAlpine & Son* (1986) 279 E.G. 759 (where the development potential of the damaged property was taken into account). Contrast *Wigsell* v. *School for Indigent Blind* (1882) 8 Q.B.D. 357 (difference in value); and, see Harris, Ogus and Phillips, 95 L.Q.R. 581.

[1] *Post*, pp. 866–869.

[2] *Cf.*, for example *Darbishire* v. *Warran*, *supra* n. 98.

[3] *Sunshine Exploration Ltd.* v. *Dolly Varden Mines Ltd.* (1969) 8 D.L.R. (3d) 441.

[4] Corbin on *Contracts*, § 1091. The position may be the same even where the work would actually *reduce* the value of the property: *ibid.* § 1089.

[5] In such circumstances it was admitted in *Perry* v. *Sidney Phillips & Son* [1982] 1 W.L.R. 1297 that cost of cure was not the appropriate basis for assessing damages against a negligent surveyor; for the proper basis of assessment in such a case, see *ante*, p. 827 at nn. 22–23. See also *Hole & Son* (*Sayers Common*) *Ltd.* v. *Harrisons Ltd.* [1973] 1 Lloyd's Rep. 345; *Yeoman Credit Ltd.* v. *Apps* [1962] 2 Q.B. 508, so far as *contra*, was disapproved in *Charterhouse Credit Ltd.* v. *Tolly* [1963] 2 Q.B. 683.

[6] *Calabar Properties Ltd.* v. *Stitcher* [1984] 1 W.L.R. 297, 299; *cf.* also, in insurance law, *Leppard* v. *Excess Insurance Co. Ltd.* [1979] 1 W.L.R. 512, where it was clear that reinstatement was not going to be effected. For the basis of assessment in *Perry* v. *Sidney Phillips & Son supra*, see *supra*, at n. 5.

[7] [1987] 1 W.L.R. 1729.

[8] *Ibid.* p. 1736.

[9] *Ibid.* p. 1738.

[10] *e.g. Stewart* v. *Rapley* [1989] 1 E.G.L.R. 159.

cribed as being based on difference in value or cost of cure. This is the position where a buyer is entitled to the difference between the contract and the market price of goods which the seller has failed to deliver.[11] It makes no difference whether such damages are described as the cost of curing the seller's breach or as the difference in value between what the buyer has received (*i.e.* nothing) and what he should have received (*i.e.*, the goods). The buyer is, moreover, entitled to such damages whether or not he has actually made the substitute purchase.[12]

(2) Actual and market values

Where damages are based on difference in value (or on the cost of a substitute) they may be assessed by reference either to actual or to market values. There is said to be a "market" for goods if they can be freely bought or sold at a price fixed by supply and demand.[13]

(a) WHERE THERE IS A MARKET, the loss is prima facie quantified by reference to it; but other factors may also have to be taken into account.

(i) *Non-delivery.* If a seller of goods fails to deliver, the buyer can go into the market and buy substitute goods at the prevailing price. Thus his damages will prima facie be based on the amount (if any) by which the market price exceeds the contract price.[14] Similarly if a carrier completely fails to deliver goods which he has contracted to carry, the injured party's damages are based on the market value of the goods at the place and time fixed for delivery.[15]

The principle of assessment by reference to the market price normally applies even though the injured party has resold an equivalent quantity of goods at a different price, in the expectation of receiving those due under the contract. Such a subsale neither reduces the damages if made below the market price nor increases them if made above the market price. In *Williams Bros.* v. *E. T. Agius Ltd.*[16] coal was sold at 16s. 3d. per ton. The buyers resold an equivalent amount at 19s. per ton. When the sellers failed to deliver, the market price was 23s. 6d. per ton. The sellers argued that the buyers had lost no more than the difference between 16s. 3d. and 19s. per ton. But the House of Lords held that the buyer was "entitled to recover the expense of putting himself into the position of having those goods, and this he can do by going into the market and purchasing them at the market price."[17] Thus the sellers were liable for the difference between

---

[11] Sale of Goods Act 1979, s.51(3), *infra*, at n. 14.

[12] *Cf. Shearson Lehman Hutton Inc.* v. *Maclaine Watson & Co.* (*No.* 2) [1990] 1 Lloyd's Rep. 441, 443 (seller's damages); and (in tort) *Dominion Mosaics & Tile Co. Ltd.* v. *Trafalgar Trucking Co. Ltd.* [1990] 2 All E.R. 246.

[13] *Dunkirk Colliery Co.* v. *Lever* (1878) 9 Ch.D. 20; *W. L. Thompson Ltd.* v. *Robinson* (*Gunmakers*) *Ltd.* [1955] Ch. 177; *Charter* v. *Sullivan* [1957] 2 Q.B. 117. A "black" market may be taken into account: *Mouatt* v. *Betts Motors Ltd.* [1959] A.C. 71. See further *Building and Civil Engineering Holiday Scheme Management* v. *Post Office* [1966] 2 Q.B. 247 for a different interpretation of "market value" in Crown Proceedings Act 1947, s.9(2)(*b*) (now Post Office Act 1969, s.30, as amended by British Telecommunications Act 1981, s.70).

[14] Sale of Goods Act 1979, s.51(3); *cf. The Elena D'Amico* [1980] 1 Lloyd's Rep. 75 (failure to provide a ship under charterparty); *Murray* v. *Lloyd* [1989] 1 W.L.R. 1060 (market cost of substitute accommodation awarded against negligent solicitor).

[15] *Watts, Watts & Co. Ltd.* v. *Mitsui & Co. Ltd.* [1917] A.C. 227. For damages for delayed delivery, see *post*, pp. 840–841.

[16] [1914] A.C. 510; *cf. Rodocanachi, Sons & Co.* v. *Milburn Bros.* (1886) 18 Q.B.D. 67; *Brading* v. *F. McNeill & Co. Ltd.* [1946] Ch. 145.

[17] At p. 531.

16s. 3d. and 23s. 6d. per ton. As the subsale was not of the identical coal bought under the main contract, the buyer might have been able to supply his sub-buyer from some other source before the market rose. He could then have resold the coal bought from the defendant to a third party and made a further profit.

Conversely in *Williams* v. *Reynolds*[18] cotton was sold at $16\frac{3}{4}$d. per lb.; the buyer resold an equivalent amount at $19\frac{3}{4}$d. per lb.; when the seller failed to deliver, the market price was $18\frac{1}{4}$d. The buyer's damages were assessed at only $1\frac{1}{2}$d. per lb. as he could have bought in the market at $18\frac{1}{4}$d., on the day of breach, to supply his sub-buyer. The seller's knowledge that the buyer intended to resell would not alter this result.[19] The buyer's extra loss is either not caused by the seller's breach, but by the buyer's failure to go into the market; or it is irrecoverable as the buyer ought to have mitigated by going into the market to buy a substitute to satisfy his sub-buyer.[20] Once again, however, the position would have been different if the subsale had been "of the self-same thing"[21]; for in that case the buyer would not have been able to satisfy his sub-buyer with substitute goods. Consequently, he would have lost his profit on the subsale and could have recovered that loss, so long as it was not too remote.[22]

(ii) *Late delivery.* Where delay in delivery is a ground of rejection, and the right to reject is exercised, damages are assessed in the same way as for non-delivery.[23] But where late delivery is accepted, damages are assessed on a different basis, the contract price being irrelevant. The buyer's complaint in such a case is not that he has to go into the market to buy a substitute for more than he had originally agreed to pay. It is that he gets the goods at a time that is less advantageous to him than the delivery date fixed by the contract. If he intended, on receipt of the goods, to resell them in the market, he will accordingly have lost the amount by which their market value when they were delivered to him was less than their market value when they should have been delivered; and this amount will be recoverable provided that the chance of resale is not too remote a contingency.[24] It is, however, disputed whether a buyer's damages will be reduced if he has actually resold the goods *above* the market price at the time of delivery. In *Wertheim* v. *Chicoutimi Pulp Co.*[25] wood pulp was sold for delivery in September/November but not delivered till the following June. The market price per ton was 70s. at the time fixed for delivery and 42s. 6d. at the time of actual delivery. Prima facie the buyers' loss was therefore 27s. 6d. per ton. But they had resold the pulp at 65s. per ton and were able to pass it on

---

[18] (1865) 6 B. & S. 495.

[19] *Kwei Tek Chao* v. *British Traders Ltd.* [1954] 2 Q.B. 459, 489.

[20] *Cf. post*, p. 866.

[21] *Williams Bros.* v. *E. T. Agius Ltd.* [1914] A.C. 510, 523; *cf. Seven Seas Properties Ltd.* v. *Al-Essa* [1988] 1 W.L.R. 1272.

[22] *Post*, pp. 854 *et seq.*; *Re R. & H. Hall Ltd. and W. H. Pim Jr.* (1928) 139 L.T. 50, where the contract itself expressly provided for resale, and it was not suggested that the resale prices were "out of the ordinary course of business": *ibid.* p. 54; *The Honam Jade* [1991] 1 Lloyd's Rep. 38.

[23] *e.g. The Almare Seconda* [1981] 2 Lloyd's Rep. 433; *cf. ante*, p. 724.

[24] *Post*, pp. 856–857, 863–864. In tort it has been held that this amount is not recoverable as damages for detention where the plaintiff's purpose was not to resell the goods but to use them for manufacturing purposes: *Brandeis Goldschmidt & Co. Ltd.* v. *Western Transport Ltd.* [1981] Q.B. 864.

[25] [1911] A.C. 301.

to their sub-buyers at that price. The Privy Council held that the sellers could rely on the subsale to reduce the damages to 5s. per ton. To allow the buyers to recover 27s. 6d. would, it was said, enable them to make a profit out of the breach. But this is hard to fit in with the principles normally governing the assessment of damages.[26] Two possibilities exist in cases of this kind. First, the buyer has resold the very goods comprised in the main contract.[27] If so he has admittedly not lost 27s. 6d. per ton but it is difficult to see that he has lost anything at all; he would not have been free to sell the pulp in the market at 70s. per ton as he was bound to deliver it to his sub-buyer. Secondly, the buyer has resold an equivalent quantity. If so the subsale should be disregarded. Had the pulp been delivered in September/November it could have *then* been sold to a third party, and the sub-buyer could still have been satisfied with an equivalent quantity bought in June at 42s. 6d. per ton. It is improbable that the buyer would have kept the pulp throughout this period on a falling market. On the other hand, if (in view of the delay) the buyer "had bought other goods and used them for the sub-contract he would have been left with the goods delivered at the time when the market price was 42s. 6d. instead of when it was 70s."[28] Nor is it right to say that the buyer would make a profit *out of the breach* of contract if he were awarded 27s. 6d. a ton. He would make a *profit out of the advantageous subsale*.

(iii) *Defective delivery*. Where defective goods are delivered, and are not (or cannot be) rejected, the buyer's loss is prima facie the difference between the actual value of the goods that he has received and the value that they would have had if they had been in accordance with the contract.[29] As in cases of late delivery, the difference between the contract and the market price is not relevant[30]: the buyer's complaint is not that he will have to buy an equivalent elsewhere, but that he has got something of lower value than that which he should have received. A subsale is again ignored[31]; unless it is of the very goods comprised in the original contract.[32]

Where the market value of the goods has fallen between the making of the contract and its breach, the buyer will normally wish to reject; for in this way he will be able to avoid the loss resulting, not from the breach, but from the fall in the market. If, however, he has lost the right to reject, he will only be entitled to damages, and those damages are prima facie recoverable only in respect of the defect, and not in respect of the fall in the market. In one case,[33] a contract for the sale of beans stipulated for shipment by the end of August but the seller delivered a September shipment. By the time of breach the market value of the beans had fallen some £2,000 below the contract price, so that the buyer would certainly have rejected if he had known of the defect in time. But he had "accepted"[34] the goods and it was held that he could recover only nominal damages as there

---

[26] *Slater* v. *Hoyle & Smith* [1920] 2 K.B. 11, 23.
[27] *Cf. Williams Bros*. v. *E. T. Agius Ltd*. [1914] A.C. 510, 530.
[28] *Slater* v. *Hoyle & Smith* [1920] 2 K.B. 11, 23–24.
[29] Sale of Goods Act 1979, s.53(3).
[30] *Cf. Commercial Fibres (Ireland) Ltd*. v. *Zabiada* [1975] 1 Lloyd's Rep. 27.
[31] *Slater* v. *Hoyle & Smith* [1920] 2 K.B. 11.
[32] As in *Champanhac Ltd*. v. *Waller Ltd*. [1948] 2 All E.R. 724.
[33] *Taylor* v. *Bank of Athens* (1922) 27 Com.Cas. 142.
[34] *Ante*, pp. 344, 714–715.

was no difference between the market value of an August and a September shipment. There may, however, in cases of this kind, be a defect, not only in the goods, but also in the documents which the seller is obliged by the contract to tender[35] and the buyer may have accepted the documents without knowing of the defects in them,[36] paid the price, and so have been deprived (whether as a matter of law or of business[37]) of the chance to reject the goods. In such a case the buyer can claim damages on the footing that the defect in the documents has deprived him of the chance to reject the goods on a falling market; and he can do so even though the fact that the goods are not of the contract description has in no way affected their value.[38] For this reason it has been rightly said that there is "little merit"[39] in such a claim; and it is available only where there is a defect both in the documents and in the goods, each giving rise to an independent right to reject.[40]

(iv) *Refusal to accept and pay.* If a buyer refuses to accept and pay for goods sold to him, the seller can go into the market and sell them at the prevailing price. Thus he will prima facie lose the amount (if any) by which the contract price exceeds the market price[41]; and it is normally[42] irrelevant that the seller has actually resold for a different price.[43] If the market price exceeds the contract price, the seller generally suffers no loss. But this is not always true. The contract may provide for an advance payment without which the seller himself cannot get the goods. If the buyer fails to make this payment, the seller suffers loss even though the market price has risen above the contract price: he loses a good bargain because he is not in a position to take advantage of a rising market. Subject to the rules of remoteness,[44] the buyer will be liable for such a loss.[45]

(b) WHERE THERE IS NO MARKET, the loss must be quantified in some other, and sometimes more speculative, way.[46]

(i) *Failure to deliver.* If a seller or carrier fails to deliver goods which cannot be replaced by buying in the market, the court must assess the loss as best it can: relevant factors include the cost of the goods and of their car-

---

[35] Especially under c.i.f. contracts, as to which see *ante*, pp. 666, 669–670.

[36] For the significance of this point, see *Vargas Pena* v. *Peter Cremee GmbH* [1987] 1 Lloyd's Rep. 392, *infra*, n. 38.

[37] This was the position in *Kwei Tek Chao* v. *British Traders* [1954] 2 Q.B. 459.

[38] *James Finlay & Co. Ltd.* v. *N.V. Kwik Hoo Tong H.M.* [1929] 1 K.B. 400; *Kwei Tek Chao* v. *British Traders Ltd.* [1954] 2 Q.B. 459; *Kleinjan & Holst N.V. Rotterdam* v. *Bremer Handelsgesellschaft mbH* [1972] 2 Lloyd's Rep. 11; *The Kastellon* [1978] 2 Lloyd's Rep. 203. Contrast *Vargas Pena* v. *Peter Cremer GmbH* [1987] 1 Lloyd's Rep. 394 where such damages were held not to be available to a buyer who knew of the defect *in the documents* when he accepted them, for in that situation the loss was not caused by the breach but by the buyer's decision to accept the documents.

[39] *The Kastellon*, *supra*, at p. 207 (where the seller was not to blame for the defect in the documents).

[40] *Benjamin's Sale of Goods* (3rd ed.), §§ 1762–1770; *Procter & Gamble Philippine Manufacturing Corp.* v. *Kurt A. Becher* [1988] 2 Lloyd's Rep. 21; Treitel [1988] L.M.C.L.Q. 457.

[41] Sale of Goods Act 1979, s.50(3). For administrative expenses, see *ante*, p. 835.

[42] *i.e.* subject to the qualifications stated (in the converse case of breach by the seller) on p. 840 at nn. 21–22.

[43] *Campbell Mostyn Provisions Ltd.* v. *Barnett Trading Co.* [1954] 1 Lloyd's Rep. 65; *Texaco Ltd.* v. *Eurogulf Shipping Co. Ltd.* [1987] 2 Lloyd's Rep. 541, 546; *cf. Jamal* v. *Moola Dawood Son & Co.* [1916] 1 A.C. 175 (shares).

[44] *Post*, pp. 854–866.

[45] *Cf. Trans Trust S.P.R.L.* v. *Danubian Trading Co. Ltd.* [1952] 2 Q.B. 297.

[46] *Cf. Luxmoore-May* v. *Messenger May Baverstock* [1990] 1 All E.R. 1067, 1081.

riage, and a reasonable profit.[47] Where the goods have actually been resold, the resale price is evidence of their value, but not conclusive evidence. In *France* v. *Gaudet*[48] champagne was sold at 24s. per dozen and shortly afterwards converted by the defendant. The sale price was successfully relied upon as evidence of the value of the champagne at the time of conversion. But in *The Arpad*[49] a carrier committed a breach of contract (and a tort) in failing to deliver a quantity of wheat which, five months earlier, had been subsold at 36s. a quarter. This figure was not treated as good evidence of the value of the wheat at the time of the breach, for, in the long interval between the subsale and the breach, the price of other wheat had fallen by between a third and a half. Although there was no market for wheat of the actual kind in question, the court took into account the market price of other similar goods. Where goods are bought for use, the cost of acquiring a substitute is in principle the correct measure. In one case[50] this was assessed as the scrap value of the goods, and this assessment, though described in the Court of Appeal as "surprising"[51] was held not to be incorrect in principle. As the scrap value seems to be the likely proceeds of the goods, rather than the cost of acquiring them, this method of assessment may, with respect, be doubted where the goods have (with the seller's knowledge) been bought for use rather than for resale.

(ii) *Failure to accept and pay.* If there is no market, the seller's damages for non-acceptance would prima facie be quantified by reference to the actual proceeds of a substitute sale,[52] so long as that transaction was in all the circumstances a reasonable one. As in the case of failure to deliver, the substitute transaction would only be evidence of the value of the goods at the time of breach if it was concluded at, or close to, that time. If the seller did not resell, the value of the goods left on his hands would have to be assessed according to the general criteria stated in the preceding paragraph; and his damages would prima facie be the amount (if any) by which the contract price exceeded that value.

(c) OTHER LOSS. The market and related rules just stated do not form the limit of recovery. They deal only with the problem of valuing one element of the plaintiff's loss, namely his expectation of getting either the goods or the price. In addition, the plaintiff may be able to recover damages for loss of profits. Suppose that a seller has wrongfully failed to deliver goods which the buyer has subsold at a profit. Even if the resale price is *not* evidence of value,[53] it may nevertheless be taken into consideration in assessing the buyer's damages for loss of profits.[54] Under the rules of remoteness, however, the seller is only[55] liable for loss of resale profit if he

---

[47] *O'Hanlan* v. *G.W. Ry.* (1865) 6 B. & S. 484; *Schulze* v. *G.E. Ry.* (1887) 19 Q.B.D. 30; *cf. The Pegase* [1981] 1 Lloyd's Rep. 175, 183 (late delivery); *Shearson Lehman Hutton Inc.* v. *Maclaine Watson & Co.* (*No.* 2) [1990] 1 Lloyd's Rep. 441, 443.

[48] (1871) L.R. 6 Q.B. 199; *cf. Stroud* v. *Austin & Co.* (1883) Cab. & El. 119.

[49] [1934] P. 189.

[50] *The Alecos M* [1991] 1 Lloyd's Rep. 120.

[51] *Ibid.* p. 125.

[52] *Janred Properties Ltd.* v. *Ente Nazionale per il Turismu* [1989] 2 All E.R. 444; *cf. The Noel Bay* [1989] 1 Lloyd's Rep. 361 (damages for charterer's repudiation based on substitute voyage).

[53] As in *The Arpad, supra.*

[54] *Cf.* also *Re R. & H. Hall Ltd. and W. H. Pim Jr. & Co.'s Arbitration* (1928) 139 L.T. 50 (seller liable to buyer for damages paid by buyer to sub-buyer).

[55] *Schulze* v. *G.E. Ry.* (1887) 19 Q.B.D. 30.

knew or could have contemplated[56] that the goods were required for resale,[57] and even then he is not liable for loss of an extraordinary profit unless he is notified of the possibility that such a profit may accrue.[58] If, on the other hand, there is no market and the resale price *is* evidence of the value of the goods the defendant is liable up to the amount of it, quite irrespective of his state of knowledge.[59]

The possibility of claiming additional damages for loss of profits also exists where a buyer wrongfully refuses to accept and pay for goods. Here the seller may expect both to get the price and to make a profit; and he may lose the profit even though he manages to resell the goods for exactly the same (or even a higher) price to another buyer. The point may be illustrated by cases in which car-dealers have claimed damages for loss of profits from customers who had agreed to buy cars and then in breach of contract refused to accept them. Three situations can be distinguished. First, the sale is of a new car and the supply of cars of the contract description at the dealer's disposal exceeds the demand. Here the dealer's claim will succeed[60]; for he would, if the original customer had not defaulted, have been able to make a sale both to him and to the second customer: hence he would have made two profits,[61] one of which has been lost. Secondly, the sale is of a new car and the demand for cars of the contract description exceeds the supply available to the dealer. Here his claim will fail[62]; for the number of sales that he can make depends on the number of cars that he can get and not on the number of customers that he can find. Hence the default of the original customer does not reduce the number of profits that he can earn. Thirdly, the sale of a second-hand car. In *Lazenby Garages Ltd.* v. *Wright*,[63] it was held that a second-hand B.M.W. car was a "unique" object; and as the car was resold for more than the original price to a second customer, the original customer (who had refused to take it) was not liable for loss of profit. No such loss had been suffered in respect of the car in question; and the possibility that the dealer might have sold a different car to the second customer was dismissed as too remote.[64] Whether it is too remote perhaps depends on the type of car concerned. If the car had been of a kind more commonly sold after use as a "fleet" car, the dealer's chance of selling another (virtually identical) car to a second customer might have been regarded as sufficiently great to satisfy the test of remoteness. Even where the original customer is not liable for loss of

---

[56] See *post*, pp. 854–866.

[57] *Borries* v. *Hutchinson* (1865) 18 C.B. (N.S.) 445; *Grébert-Borgnis* v. *Nugent* (1885) 15 Q.B.D. 85; *Patrick* v. *Russo-British Grain Export Co. Ltd.* [1927] 2 K.B. 535; *Household Machines* v. *Cosmos Exporters Ltd.* [1947] 1 K.B. 217; *J. Leavey & Co. Ltd.* v. *G. H. Hirst & Co. Ltd.* [1944] K.B. 24.

[58] *Post*, pp. 860–861.

[59] *Post*, pp. 863–864.

[60] *W. L. Thompson Ltd.* v. *Robinson* (*Gunmakers*) *Ltd.* [1955] Ch. 177; *cf. Re Vic Mill* [1913] 1 Ch. 465. For the application of similar principles to breach by a hirer of a contract to hire a chattel, where supply exceeds demand, see *Inter-Office Telephones Ltd.* v. *Robert Freeman & Co. Ltd.* [1958] 1 Q.B. 190; *Robophone Facilities Ltd.* v. *Blank* [1966] 1 W.L.R. 1428.

[61] *Cf. Jebsen* v. *E. & W. India Dock Co.* (1875) L.R. 10 C.P. 300.

[62] *Charter* v. *Sullivan* [1957] 2 Q.B. 117.

[63] [1976] 1 W.L.R. 459.

[64] *Post*, pp. 854 *et seq*.

profits, any expense of negotiating the second sale can presumably be recovered from him as "incidental" loss.[65]

(3) Speculative damages

A contracting party may, as a result of a breach, lose the chance of gaining some benefit. So long as the contingencies on which that chance depends are not wholly within the control of the party in breach,[66] the injured party can recover damages for loss of such a chance; he need not show that it was certain that he would have got the benefit if the contract had been performed. Thus damages can be recovered for loss of the chance of taking part in a beauty contest,[67] or for loss of the chance of earning tips.[68] Similarly damages can be recovered for loss of profits expected to arise from transactions not yet concluded at the time of breach. A carrier of samples who delays in delivering them may thus be liable for loss of profits on contracts which the owner might have made, had he got the samples in time.[69] And a person who breaks a contract to deliver a profit-earning thing may be liable for the profits which the other party might have made by using the thing.[70]

The quantification of damages in such cases is necessarily speculative. It depends on the value of the expected benefit and the likelihood of the plaintiff's actually getting it. The chance of winning a beauty contest is obviously worth less than the full prize. In deciding how much the chance is worth the court will consider (1) the number of contingencies on which it depends: "the more contingencies, the lower the value of the chance"[71]; and (2) the likelihood of their being satisfied in the plaintiff's favour: the greater this likelihood, the higher the value of the chance.[72]

In *Sapwell* v. *Bass*[73] the defendant broke a contract that his stallion would serve the plaintiff's mare. It was held that the plaintiff could not recover damages for loss of the foals that might have been born if the contract had not been broken. Jelf J. thought that such damages were too speculative; but the better explanation of the case is that the plaintiff failed to prove that the foals would be worth more than the stud fee.[74]

The court will award speculative damages where no other course is, in the nature of things, open to it. It will not do so where the plaintiff could have provided evidence as to the value of the bargain that he has lost, and has simply failed to do so.[75] But in such a case the plaintiff may be entitled to recover his proved reliance loss and to restitution.[76]

---

65 *Ante*, p. 835.

66 See *Laverack* v. *Woods of Colchester Ltd.* [1967] 1 Q.B. 278. *Quaere*, whether *Blackpool & Fylde Aero Club Ltd.* v. *Blackpool B.C.* [1990] 1 W.L.R. 1195 (*ante*, p. 15) was not a case of this kind.

67 *Chaplin* v. *Hicks* [1911] 2 K.B. 786; *cf. Watson* v. *Ambergate, etc., Ry.* (1851) 15 Jur. 448.

68 *Manubens* v. *Leon* [1919] 1 K.B. 208.

69 *e.g. Simpson* v. *L. & N.W. Ry.* (1876) 1 Q.B.D. 274; *post*, p. 860.

70 *e.g. Victoria Laundry (Windsor) Ltd.* v. *Newman Industries Ltd.* [1949] 2 K.B. 528; *post*, p. 855.

71 *Hall* v. *Meyrick* [1957] 2 Q.B. 455, 471 (actual decision reversed on another ground, *ibid.* p. 474).

72 *e.g. Dickinson* v. *Jones Alexander & Co.* (1990) 20 Fam.L. 137.

73 [1910] 2 K.B. 486.

74 *Chaplin* v. *Hicks* [1911] 2 K.B. 786, 796.

75 *Clark* v. *Kirby-Smith* [1964] Ch. 506, 512.

76 *Ante*, pp. 831–832.

(4) Taxation

The value of the plaintiff's loss may be affected by the incidence of taxation. In *B.T.C.* v. *Gourley*[77] the plaintiff was injured by the negligence of the defendant's servants, and claimed damages for loss of earnings. It was estimated that, but for the accident, the plaintiff would have earned £37,000. Had he actually earned this sum, it would have been taxed and £6,000 would have been left to him. But had he been awarded damages of £37,000 he could have kept the whole amount, since damages for loss of earnings resulting from personal injury are not taxable. The House of Lords held that the proper measure of damages was £6,000, that being the amount of the plaintiff's actual loss. *Gourley's* case was an action in tort, but the same principle can apply where the liability is contractual, *e.g.* in assessing damages for wrongful dismissal.[78]

The reason for the rule is that the plaintiff ought not to make a profit out of the tort or breach of contract by getting tax-free damages to compensate for loss of a benefit which would have been taxable. Thus the rule only applies if two conditions are satisfied. First, the damages must be compensation for loss of a taxable income or gain, and not simply for loss of a capital asset. Thus the rule would probably not apply if a buyer of goods claimed the amount by which their market value exceeded the contract price. These damages are meant to compensate him for failure to obtain a capital asset (out of which he might make a profit or a loss.)[79] Secondly, the damages themselves must not be taxable. In *Diamond* v. *Campbell-Jones*[80] a dealer in real estate lost profits of £8,500 through the defendant's breach of a contract to sell him a house. The argument that damages should be reduced because of tax liability was rejected because the actual damages were taxable in the dealer's hands. Tax liability would similarly be irrelevant in assessing damages claimed by a buyer of goods for loss of profits if those profits would have been taxable as income or capital gains, for in such a case the damages would be taxable in the buyer's hands. For the same reason tax liability might be disregarded in assessing a seller's damages for the buyer's refusal to accept and pay for the goods. Damages for wrongful dismissal are now taxable to the extent that they exceed £30,000.[81] Hence such damages must be reduced by reference to the plain-

[77] [1956] A.C. 185; Jolowicz [1959] C.L.J. 85; Tucker, *ibid.* 185; Hall, 73 L.Q.R. 212; Smith, 1956 S.L.T. 13; Baxter, 19 M.L.R. 373; Bishop and Kay, 103 L.Q.R. 211. *Cf. Otter* v. *Church, Adams, Tatham & Co.* [1953] Ch. 280 (death duties). *Cooper* v. *Firth Brown Ltd.* [1963] 1 W.L.R. 418 (national insurance contributions); *Dews* v. *N.C.B.* [1988] A.C. 1 (compulsory pension contribution).

[78] *Beach* v. *Reed Corrugated Cases Ltd.* [1956] 1 W.L.R. 807; *Re Houghton Main Colliery* [1956] 1 W.L.R. 1219; *Phipps* v. *Orthodox Unit Trusts Ltd.* [1958] 1 Q.B. 314. Contrast the position in cases of breach of trust: *Bartlett* v. *Barclays Bank Trust Co.* [1980] Ch. 515; *Re Bell's Indenture* [1980] 1 W.L.R. 1217; *cf. John* v. *James* [1986] S.T.C. 352 (liability to account for breach of fiduciary duty under contract).

[79] *Cf. Spencer* v. *MacMillan's Trustees*, 1958 S.C. 300; *Lim Foo Yong Ltd.* v. *Collector of Land Revenue* [1963] 1 W.L.R. 295.

[80] [1961] Ch. 22; *P.C. Producers* v. *Dalton* [1957] R.P.C. 199; *Herring* v. *B.T.C.* [1958] T.R. 401; *Rajah's Commercial College* v. *Gian Singh & Co. Ltd.* [1977] A.C. 312; *Dickinson* v. *Jones Alexander & Co.* [1989] N.L.J.R. 1525.

[81] Income and Corporation Taxes Act 1988, ss.148 188(4), as amended by Finance Act 1988, s.74. Payments in lieu of damages for dismissal must be distinguished from payments made as part of an agreed variation of a contract which continues after the variation: such payments are taxable even if they are less than £30,000: see *McGregor* v. *Randall* [1984] 1 All E.R. 1092.

tiff's income-tax liability where his loss of income is less than £30,000[82]; where it is more, the court will assess his net loss and then award such sum as, after tax on the sum so assessed, would be equal to that loss.[83]

The rule in *Gourley's* case has been much criticised. It is said to involve a paradox: for revenue purposes damages for loss of earnings are treated as compensation for loss of a capital asset, since otherwise they would be taxable; while in assessing damages they are treated as compensation for loss of income, since otherwise the plaintiff's tax liability would be irrelevant.[84] A possible solution of this paradox is to say that the damages compensate the plaintiff for loss of *earning capacity*, which is a capital asset whose value depends on (amongst other things) the incidence of taxation.[85] Other criticisms are concerned with the practical effects of the rule. It is said that the rule enables the defendant to take advantage of wholly extraneous circumstances, *e.g.* that the plaintiff has a large private income; that it makes the assessment of damages highly speculative; and that the rule may make it cheaper to break a contract than to perform it. But similar criticisms could be made of other rules relating to damages, which have so far remained immune from them. Thus a seller can sometimes take advantage of an extraneous event, such as a subsale made by the buyer, in reducing damages for non-delivery[86]; speculative damages are by no means uncommon[87]; and it may often be cheaper to break a contract than to perform it: for example, where damages are assessed on a difference in value basis amounting only to a small fraction of the cost of performance.[88]

In 1958 the rule in *Gourley's* case was referred to the Law Reform Committee.[89] Three views were put forward. First, the plaintiff should recover his gross loss and not have to pay tax on the damages. But, setting aside the attractiveness of tax-free benefits, it is hard to see why the injured party should in this way make a profit out of the wrong. Secondly, the plaintiff should recover his gross loss but should have to pay tax on the damages. The objection to this view is that the assessment of the tax payable necessarily involves speculation.[90] It is one thing to accept the need for speculative damages; speculative tax should be strongly resisted. Thirdly (and this was the majority view), the rule in *Gourley's* case is the most satisfactory solution of the problem, as it gives effect to the principle that damages are only meant to compensate the plaintiff for his actual loss. This seems to be the best view.

A breach of contract may actually *reduce* the victim's tax liability. The amount of the reduction is then deducted from the damages for the breach, on the principle that the benefit of having to pay less tax in fact mitigates the victim's loss.[91]

---

[82] *Parsons* v. *B.N.M. Laboratories Ltd.* [1964] 1 Q.B. 95.

[83] *Bold* v. *Brough, Nicholson & Hall Ltd.* [1964] 1 W.L.R. 201; *Shove* v. *Downs Surgical plc* [1984] I.C.R. 582; Lee, 47 M.L.R. 471; *Stewart* v. *Glentaggart* 1963 S.C. (Ct. of Sess.) 300.

[84] Jolowicz, *supra*, n. 77.

[85] Tucker, *supra*, n. 77.

[86] *Ante*, p. 840.

[87] *Ante*, p. 845.

[88] *Ante*, p. 825.

[89] 7th Report (1958) Cmnd. 501.

[90] *e.g.* as to the allowances which the plaintiff could, over the years, have claimed, and as to rates of tax.

[91] *Levison* v. *Farin* [1978] 2 All E.R. 1149; *post*, pp. 869–871.

(5) Alternatives

Where a contract entitles the party in breach to perform in alternative ways, damages are, as a general rule, assessed on the assumption that he would have performed in the way that is least burdensome to himself and least beneficial to the plaintiff.[92] Thus if a voyage charterparty gives the charterer the power to choose between a number of different ports of discharge, damages for his failure to load will be assessed on the assumption that he would have chosen the most distant port and so have reduced the shipowner's profit.[93] Similarly, where a seller of goods has an option as to the exact quantity to be delivered, damages for non-delivery will be based on the assumption that he would have delivered the smallest quantity.[94] In the examples so far given, it is assumed that the contract clearly specifies the options available to the party in breach; but where it fails to do so the court will have to determine, as a matter of construction, just what those options are. In one case,[95] a sole distributorship agreement required the distributor to buy 16,000 dresses a year from his supplier. Having broken that agreement, the distributor argued that damages were to be assessed on the basis that he would order only the very cheapest dresses. But it was held that the contract, on its true construction, required the distributor to make a reasonable selection and that damages were to be assessed "in terms of that reasonable selection which would yield the lowest price."[96]

The general rule is, moreover, subject to a number of qualifications. A contract of sale may, for example, give the seller an option as to the time of delivery by providing that he can deliver at any time chosen by him in a stated month. In such a case, damages for non-delivery will prima facie be assessed by reference to the market price at the end of the period. They will not be assessed by reference to the time during it when the market was lowest[97]; for such a rule would give rise to too much uncertainty. Moreover, the party who has the option may declare before breach that he will exercise it in a particular way. Damages will then be assessed on that basis[98] if the effect of the declaration is to bind him contractually to perform in the specified way.[99]

The above rules only apply where the obligation of the defendant is truly alternative. In *Deverill* v. *Burnell*[1] the defendant undertook to transmit the proceeds of certain drafts to the plaintiff if they were paid: "and if the drafts should not be paid, the defendant should either return the same to

---

[92] *Abrahams* v. *Herbert Reiach Ltd.* [1922] 1 K.B. 477; *Withers* v. *General Theatre Corp.* [1933] 2 K.B. 536; *The Rijn* [1981] 2 Lloyd's Rep. 267; the rule may be excluded by express contrary stipulation: *Yeoman Credit Ltd.* v. *Waragowski* [1961] 1 W.L.R. 1124; *Bremer Handelsgesellschaft mbH* v. *Bunge Corp.* [1982] 1 Lloyd's Rep. 108, affirmed without reference to this point [1983] 1 Lloyd's Rep. 476.

[93] *Kaye S.N. Co. Ltd.* v. *W. & R. Barnett Ltd.* (1932) 48 T.L.R. 400; *The Rijn* [1981] 2 Lloyd's Rep. 267, 270; *cf. Phoebus D. Kyprianou Co.* v. *Wm. H. Pim Jr.* [1977] 2 Lloyd's Rep. 570.

[94] *Re Thornett & Fehr and Yuills Ltd.* [1921] 1 K.B. 219.

[95] *Paula Lee Ltd.* v. *Robert Zehil Ltd.* [1983] 2 All E.R. 390.

[96] *Ibid.* p. 397.

[97] *Cf. Harlow & Jones Ltd.* v. *Panex (International) Ltd.* [1967] 2 Lloyd's Rep. 509; *Phoebus D. Kyprianou Co.* v. *William H. Pim Jr.*, *supra* (buyer's breach); *Benjamin's Sale of Goods* (3rd ed.), §§ 1893, 1908.

[98] See *The Delian Spirit* [1972] 1 Q.B. 103, 111–112; *Shipping Co. of India Ltd.* v. *Naviera Letasa S.A.* [1976] 1 Lloyd's Rep. 132; *Toprak Mahsulleri Ofisi* v. *Finagrain Cie. Commerciale* [1979] 2 Lloyd's Rep. 98.

[99] Contrast *The Rijn*, *supra*, n. 93, at p. 270 (where the declaration was not of this kind).

[1] (1873) L.R. 8 C.P. 475.

the plaintiff *or* pay him the amount." The drafts were not paid but the defendant neither returned them nor paid the amount. In an action for the amount of the drafts the defendant argued that the obligation was alternative; that he could perform by returning the drafts; and that, as these were worthless, he was only liable for nominal damages. But he was held liable for the full amount. His undertaking was "not in the strictest sense an alternative promise, but a promise that the defendant would return the bills, and if he did not return them he would pay the amount of them."[2] It was a contingent, rather than an alternative, obligation.

(6) Time for assessment

In times of fluctuating costs and values, it is important to know by reference to what point of time damages will be assessed.

(a) TIME OF BREACH. The starting principle is, or is generally assumed to be, that damages are assessed by reference to the time of breach. For example, where a buyer of goods fails to accept and pay for them [or a seller fails to deliver] the damages are prima facie the difference between the contract price and the market price "at the time or times when the goods ought to have been accepted [or delivered], or (if no time was fixed for acceptance [or delivery]) at the time of the refusal to accept [or deliver]."[3] The same principle of assessment by reference to the time of breach has been applied where a vendor of land wrongfully refused to convey.[4] The theory behind the rule is that any loss suffered by reason of market movements after the time of breach is not caused by the breach, but rather by the injured party's failure to mitigate[5] by making a substitute contract. Since under the mitigation rules the plaintiff need only act reasonably, it follows that even the principle of assessment by reference to the time of breach is applied with some latitude. In *C. Sharpe & Co. Ltd.* v. *Nosawa*[6] peas were sold by sample. They should have been, but were not, delivered on "about July 21." Goods of the precise contract quality were not available in the market. It was held that the buyers had "a reasonable time to consider their position"[7]; and accordingly the damages were assessed by reference to the market price of similar goods at the end of July.[8]

The principle of assessment by reference to the time of breach is based on two assumptions: that the injured party knows of the breach as soon as

---

2 At p. 477.

3 Sale of Goods Act 1979, ss.50(3), 51(3); *cf. Jamal* v. *Moola Dawood Sons & Co.* [1916] 1 A.C. 175; *The "Ile aux Moines"* [1974] 1 Lloyd's Rep. 262; *Phillips* v. *Ward* [1956] 1 W.L.R. 471, 474, 475, 478.

4 *Diamond* v. *Campbell-Jones* [1961] Ch. 22, 36; *Janred Properties Ltd.* v. *Ente Nazionale Italiano per il Turismu* [1989] 2 All E.R. 444, 457 (purchaser refusing to complete).

5 *Post*, p. 866.

6 [1917] 2 K.B. 814; *cf. The Good Friend* [1984] 2 Lloyd's Rep. 586, 596; *Shearson Lehman Hutton Inc.* v. *Maclaine Watson & Co.* (*No.* 2) [1990] 2 Lloyd's Rep. 441, 447.

7 At p. 821; *cf. Techno Land Improvements Ltd.* v. *British Leyland* (*U.K.*) *Ltd.* (1979) 252 E.G. 805, 809; *The Playa Larga* [1983] 2 Lloyd's Rep. 171, 181.

8 For similar reasons of convenience, the contract itself may provide for assessment by reference to a date other than that of breach: see, for example *Bremer Handelsgesellschaft mbH* v. *Vanden Avenne-Izegem P.V.B.A.* [1978] 2 Lloyd's Rep. 109, 117; *Lusograin Comercio Internacional de Cereas Ltda* v. *Bunge A.G.* [1986] 2 Lloyd's Rep. 654, 658.

it is committed, and that he can at that time take steps to mitigate the loss which is likely to flow from it. Where the facts negative these assumptions, the courts will depart from the principle, and assess the damages by reference to "such other date as may be appropriate in the circumstances."[9] In particular they will have regard to the time when the breach was, or could have been discovered; and to the question whether it was possible or reasonable for the injured party to make a substitute contract immediately on such discovery.

(b) Time of discovery of breach. The injured party may not have known of the breach when it was committed and may have been unable, acting with reasonable diligence, to discover it at that time. The damages will then prima facie[10] be assessed by reference (at the earliest[11]) to the time when that party, so acting, could have made the discovery. For example, a seller may first "appropriate" goods to the contract by indicating which particular goods he intends to deliver under a contract for the sale of generic goods, and then deliver them. If those goods turn out to be defective, the seller will be in breach at the time of appropriation, but the damages are prima facie assessed by reference to the later time of *delivery*.[12] Where the goods are sent to the buyer in sealed packages, the damages may be assessed by reference to an even later point of time, namely that at which it is reasonable to expect the packages to be opened and their contents examined.[13] Similarly, where a builder does defective work and damages are based on cost of cure, they will normally be assessed by reference to the time when the customer, acting with reasonable diligence, could have discovered the defect.[14] Delay in discovering the defect may affect not only the time but also the whole basis of assessment; for if at the time of discovery the cost of cure is disproportionately high in relation to the value of a sound building, or if cure has become as a practical matter impossible, the court will award damages on a difference in value basis.[15]

(c) Possibility of acting on knowledge of breach. Even if the injured party knows of the breach, it may be impossible for him to act on that knowledge by making a substitute contract so as to reduce the loss. For example, a buyer might wrongfully refuse to pay for goods after they had

---

[9] *Johnson* v. *Agnew* [1980] A.C. 367, 401; *County Personnel (Employment Agency) Ltd.* v. *Pulver* [1987] 1 W.L.R. 916.

[10] The rule is only a prima facie one and will not apply to the extent that delay in discovering the breach had no adverse effect on the plaintiff's position: *cf. ante*, p. 828 and see *Re Bell's Indenture* [1980] 1 W.L.R. 1217 (a case of breach of trust).

[11] For assessment by reference to later times, see the following paragraphs (c) to (f) of the text.

[12] Sale of Goods Act 1979, s.53(3).

[13] *Van den Hurk* v. *R. Martens & Co. Ltd.* [1920] 1 K.B. 850; *cf. The Hansa Nord* [1976] Q.B. 44 (damages assessed by reference to time of *arrival*, though breach occurred on *shipment*); *Naughton* v. *O'Callaghan* [1990] 3 All E.R. 191(damages in tort for misrepresentation).

[14] *East Ham B.C.* v. *Bernard Sunley Ltd.* [1966] A.C. 406; subsequent increases in cost may be taken into account if it is reasonable to delay the work: see (in tort) *Dodd Properties (Kent) Ltd.* v. *Canterbury C.C.* [1980] 1 W.L.R. 433; *London Congregatioal Union Inc.* v. *Harris* [1985] 1 All E.R. 334, varied on other grounds [1987] 1 All E.R. 15; and see Feldman and Libling, 75 L.Q.R. 271; Duncan Wallace, 96 L.Q.R. 101; Waddams, 97 L.Q.R. 445; Duncan Wallace, 98 L.Q.R. 406; Waddams, 1 O.J.L.S. 134.

[15] *Applegate* v. *Moss* [1971] 1 Q.B. 406; *King* v. *Victor Parsons Ltd.* [1972] 1 W.L.R. 801.

been despatched to him, and it might be impossible for the seller to resell them until they had reached their destination. In such a case the damages would be assessed by reference to the time at which the seller could reasonably resell, and not to the time of the buyer's refusal to pay.[16]

Impossibility of acting on knowledge of the breach may also affect the time for assessment where a buyer lacks the means to buy a substitute on a rising market. In *Wroth* v. *Tyler*[17] the defendant had contracted to sell his house to the plaintiffs for £6,000. The sale was to be completed in October 1971, when the value of the house had risen to £7,500; but in July 1971 the defendant had wrongfully repudiated the contract. The plaintiffs started proceedings for specific performance and damages; judgment was given in January 1973, when the house was worth £11,500. It was held that specific performance should not be ordered[18]; that damages should be awarded in lieu[19]; and that these should be assessed by reference to the value of the house at the time, not of breach, but of judgment,[20] *i.e.* not at £1,500 but at £5,500. Since the plaintiffs had (as the defendant knew)[21] no financial resources beyond the £6,000 they had raised to buy the house, they could not act on their knowledge of the breach by making a substitute purchase on a rapidly rising market.

(d) Reasonableness of acting on knowledge of breach. Even where it is possible for the plaintiff to make a substitute contract on discovering the breach, it may not be reasonable to expect him to do so because at that time there is still a reasonable probability that the defendant will make good his default. In such cases damages are prima facie assessed by reference to the time when that probability ceased to exist.[22] Thus if a seller of goods, after the delivery date has gone by, assures the buyer that he will deliver, but then declares his final inability to perform, the damages will be assessed by reference to the market at the date of that declaration.[23] Again, the injured party may continue to press for performance after the agreed time, but finally elect to terminate on account of the breach: in such a case damages are assessed by reference to the date of termination.[24] A similar principle applies where the injured party brings an action for specific performance: thus a further explanation of the decision in *Wroth* v. *Tyler*[25] is that the plaintiffs could not be expected to make a substitute contract so long as their claim for specific performance was being main-

---

16 See *Benjamin's Sale of Goods* (3rd ed.), § 1907; *cf. Shearson Lehman Hutton Inc.* v. *Maclaine Watson & Co. Ltd.* [1989] 2 Lloyd's Rep. 570, 647 (dealings suspended at time of alleged breach).

17 [1974] Ch. 30; for further discussion see *infra* at n. 25 and *post*, pp. 862–863, 925–926.

18 *Post*, p. 908.

19 *Post*, p. 925.

20 For the possibility of assessment by reference to an even later time, see *Grant* v. *Dawkins* [1973] 1 W.L.R. 1406.

21 *Wroth* v. *Tyler* [1974] Ch. 30, 57; but for this fact, the loss might (at least in part) have been too remote: *post*, pp. 862–864.

22 *Radford* v. *De Froberville* [1977] 1 W.L.R. 1262; *Johnson Matthey Bankers Ltd.* v. *State Trading Corp. of India* [1984] 1 Lloyd's Rep. 427, 437–438.

23 *Barnett* v. *Javeri & Co.* [1916] 2 K.B. 390.

24 *Toprak Mahsulleri Ofisi* v. *Finagrain Cie. Commerciale* [1979] 2 Lloyd's Rep. 98; *The Aktion* [1987] 1 Lloyd's Rep. 283.

25 [1974] Ch. 30.

tained.[26] The same is true where an order of specific performance has actually been made but is not complied with, so that the plaintiff is eventually driven to abandon his attempt to enforce performance and to seek his remedy in damages: these are then assessed "as at the date when . . . the contract is lost."[27]

(e) LATE PERFORMANCE. If the party in default performs late and the other party suffers loss by reason of the delay, the damages for that loss will be assessed by reference to the date when performance actually was (and not by reference to the date when it should have been) rendered.[28]

(f) DAMAGES FOR ANTICIPATORY BREACH. The victim of an anticipatory breach can either continue to press for performance, or "accept" the breach.[29]

(i) *Breach not accepted.* If the injured party does not accept the breach, the principles (discussed above) as to the time for assessment apply. Assuming that subsequent events have not deprived the injured party of his right to damages,[30] the general rule is that those damages will be assessed by reference to the time when the contract ought to have been performed[31] and not by reference to the time of repudiation. The injured party is under no obligation to "accept" the breach. It follows that if the market moves so as to increase his loss between the time of repudiation and the time fixed for performance, he is entitled to damages assessed by reference to the latter time.[32]

(ii) *Breach accepted.* Where the injured party does accept the breach, he can start his action before the time fixed for performance; but the principle of assessment by reference to that time applies even in this type of case.[33] If the action comes to trial before the time fixed for performance, the damages will therefore necessarily be speculative, as they will be based on forecasts or guesses as to future market movements.[34] But where the injured party accepts the breach, the principle of assessment by reference to the time fixed for performance is subject to an important qualification: his damages will be reduced if, after accepting the breach, he fails to take reasonable steps to mitigate his loss.[35] Under this rule, the injured party may, and if there is a market generally will, be required to make a substitute contract; and his damages will be assessed by reference to the time

---

[26] *Wroth* v. *Tyler*, *supra*, as explained in *Radford* v. *De Froberville* [1977] 1 W.L.R. 1262, 1285–1286; *Meng Long Development Pty. Ltd.* v. *Jip Hong Trading Co. Pte. Ltd.* [1985] A.C. 511; *Domb* v. *Isoz* [1980] Ch. 548, 559, where the plaintiff had bought another house *before* abandoning his claim for specific performance. This was said (at p. 559) to be irrelevant—presumably because, so long as the plaintiff was pursuing his claim for specific performance, it could not be said that the second house had been bought as a *substitute* for the first.

[27] *Johnson* v. *Agnew* [1980] A.C. 367, 401; *cf. Suleman* v. *Shasavari* [1988] 1 W.L.R. 1181.

[28] *Ozalid Group (Export) Ltd.* v. *African Continental Bank Ltd.* [1979] 2 Lloyd's Rep. 231.

[29] *Ante*, pp. 755–762. *Garnac Grain Co. Inc.* v. *Faure & Fairclough Ltd.* [1968] A.C. 1130, 1140.

[30] See *ante*, pp. 761–762 and *infra* after n. 38.

[31] *Tai Hing Cotton Mill Ltd.* v. *Kamsing Knitting Factory* [1979] A.C. 91.

[32] *Tredegar Iron & Coal Co. Ltd.* v. *Hawthorn Bros. & Co.* (1902) 18 T.L.R. 716; under U.C.C. s.2–610(*a*) the injured party may only await performance "for a commercially reasonable time."

[33] *Roper* v. *Johnson* (1873) L.R. 8 C.P. 167; *Melachrino* v. *Nicholl & Knight* [1920] 1 K.B. 693, 699.

[34] As in *Roper* v. *Johnson*, *supra*.

[35] *Post*, p. 866.

when that contract should have been made. This will usually be the time of acceptance of the breach[36] (or such reasonable time thereafter as may be allowed under the rules stated above[37]). If it is disputed whether a substitute contract could indeed have been made, the burden of proving that the injured party could have made such a contract lies on the party in breach. If that burden is not discharged, the damages will prima facie be assessed by reference to the time fixed for performance.[38]

Under the rules just stated, market movements after acceptance of an anticipatory breach may be relevant to the assessment of damages; but it is further possible for the very existence of the right to damages to depend on other events that occur, or will probably occur, between acceptance of the breach and the time fixed for performance. This possibility is illustrated by a number of cases in which charterparties gave charterers a right to cancel if the ship were not ready to load at a named port by a specified date, and the charterers then committed anticipatory breaches by purporting to cancel before that date. In *The Simona*[39] it was held that, if the shipowner affirmed the contract in such circumstances, he was not entitled to damages if the charterer then lawfully cancelled again, after the cancelling date. From the emphasis placed in that case on the fact of affirmation,[40] it appears that the shipowner's claim could have succeeded if, instead of affirming, he had accepted the original wrongful cancellation as an anticipatory breach. But in *The Mihalis Angelos*[41] it was said that the shipowner's damages for such a wrongful[42] cancellation would (even if he had so accepted it) have been merely nominal, since in that case it was already clear at the time of that cancellation that the ship could not possibly have reached the port of loading by the specified date. Hence the charterer could have relied on the point that he would have been entitled to cancel on the ship's late arrival; and as it was found that he would certainly have exercised that right, the contract was of no value to the shipowner.[43] In *The Simona* it was, indeed, also accepted that the ship was not ready to load by the time of the second cancellation,[44] but it does not appear that this prospective inability was already clearly established at the time of the original (wrongful) cancellation. Hence if that cancellation had been accepted as an anticipatory breach at that time, it would not *then* have been clear that the shipowner's rights under the contract were worthless; and the charterer could not have relied on the fact that they subsequently became worthless, since this state of affairs could have been induced by his wrongful repudiation, which could have led the shipowner to abandon any efforts which he might (but for the repudiation) have made to get the ship ready for loading by the cancelling date.

An important feature of the cases just discussed is that a cancelling clause confers an "independent option" on the charterer to cancel if the

---

36 *Roth & Co.* v. *Taysen Townsend & Co.* (1895) 1 Com.Cas. 240; (1896) 12 T.L.R. 211.
37 See *C. Sharpe & Co. Ltd.* v. *Nosawa* [1917] 2 K.B. 814; *ante* p. 849.
38 *Roper* v. *Johnson* (1873) L.R. 8 C.P. 167.
39 [1989] A.C. 788.
40 *Ibid.* pp. 800–801; *cf. ante*, p. 762.
41 [1971] 1 Q.B. 164; George [1971] J.B.L. 109.
42 The actual decision was that the cancellation was justified by the shipowner's breach of condition: *ante*, p. 692.
43 [1971] 1 Q.B. 164, 209–210; *cf. ibid.* pp. 196, 202–203; *cf. The Noel Bay* [1989] 1 Lloyd's Rep. 361, 365.
44 [1989] A.C. 788, 800.

ship is not ready to load by the specified date: it does "not impose any contractual obligation on the owners to commence loading by the cancelling date."[45] In other words, the right to cancel under such a clause is exercisable on the occurrence or non-occurrence of an *event*, and does not depend on any *breach* by the shipowner. The reasoning of *The Mihalis Angelos* would not apply (so as to reduce damages to a nominal amount) where a defendant's case was that he would have been entitled to rescind on account of the plaintiff's future breach; for once the plaintiff had accepted the defendant's repudiation and so rescinded the contract for that anticipatory breach, the plaintiff would be relieved of any further obligation to perform, so that his failure to perform on the due day could no longer be a breach.[46] This would for example be the position where a buyer of goods repudiated by wrongfully refusing to pay: if the seller accepted the repudiation as an anticipatory breach, he would no longer be under any obligation to deliver, and so his prospective inability to do so could not be relied on by the buyer to reduce the damages to a nominal amount. The buyer could only rely on the seller's prospective inability to deliver where the seller had not rescinded before delivery became due and had so kept alive his own obligation to deliver.[47] Even in such a case, however, the seller could recover substantial damages if his continuing inability to deliver was induced by the buyer's repudiation: *e.g.* if the seller had abandoned attempts to deliver on time because the buyer had wrongfully declared that he would not under any circumstances accept and pay for the goods.[48]

3. Methods of Limiting Damages

To compensate a plaintiff fully for all loss that can, in some sense, be said to flow from a breach of contract would often lead to undesirable results. The point can be illustrated by reference to a case, said to have been decided early in the 17th century, "where a man going to be married to an heiress, his horse having cast a shoe on the journey, employed a blacksmith to replace it, who did the work so unskilfully that the horse was lamed, and, the rider not arriving in time, the lady married another; and the blacksmith was held liable for the loss of the marriage."[49] This result has rightly been called absurd.[50] Such complete protection of the injured party's interests would either deter the other party from entering into the contract at all, or lead to an undue raising of charges. The law has therefore developed a number of rules for the purpose of limiting damages for breach of contract.

(1) Remoteness

A defendant is not liable for loss which is "too remote." The test of remoteness is whether the loss was within the reasonable contemplation of the parties; the application of this test gives rise to many problems.

---

[45] *Ibid.* p. 795.

[46] *Gill & Duffus S.A.* v. *Berger & Co. Inc.* [1984] A.C. 382, 291, *ante*, p. 666. After this case, apparently contrary dicta in *Regent O.H.G. Aisenstadt und Barig* v. *Francecso of Jermyn Street* [1981] 3 All E.R. 327 and *Bremer Handelsgesellschaft mbH* v. *J. H. Rayner & Co.* [1979] 2 Lloyd's Rep. 216, 224, 229 can no longer be supported.

[47] See *ante*, p. 668.

[48] *Ante*, p. 667.

[49] Referred to in *British Columbia Saw-Mill Co. Ltd.* v. *Nettleship* (1868) L.R. 3 C.P. 499, 508.

[50] *Ibid.*

(a) THE "REASONABLE CONTEMPLATION" TEST IN GENERAL. The general rules on this topic were formulated in *Hadley* v. *Baxendale*.[51] A shaft in the plaintiffs' mill broke and had to be sent to the makers at Greenwich to serve as a pattern for the production of a new one. The defendants agreed to carry the shaft to Greenwich but, as a result of their breach of the contract, its delivery was delayed so that there was a stoppage of several days at the mill. The plaintiffs claimed damages of £300 in respect of their loss of profits during this period. At the trial the case was left generally to the jury, who returned a verdict of £50 for the plaintiffs. The defendants successfully applied for a new trial on the ground of misdirection. Alderson B. stated the principles in accordance with which the jury should have been directed: "The damages . . . should be such as may fairly and reasonably be considered *either* arising naturally, *i.e.* according to the usual course of things, from such breach of contract itself, *or* such as may reasonably be supposed to have been in the contemplation of both parties at the time they made the contract as the probable result of the breach."[52] Here the stoppage was not the "natural" consequence of the delay: it could not have been contemplated by a carrier that delay in delivering the shaft would keep the mill idle. "In the great multitude of cases of millers sending off broken shafts to third persons by a carrier under ordinary circumstances, such consequences would not, in all probability, have occurred."[53] The plaintiffs might have had a spare shaft[54] or been able to get one.[55] Nor could the stoppage, though it was no doubt anticipated by the *plaintiffs*, have been contemplated by *both* parties at the time of contracting as the probable result of breach. "The only circumstances here communicated by the plaintiffs to the defendants at the time the contract was made were that the article to be carried was the broken shaft of a mill, and that the plaintiffs were the millers of that mill."[56] The defendants were not told that any delay by them would keep the mill idle. If they had been told this, they might have attempted to limit their liability "and of this advantage it would be very unjust to deprive them."[57]

These principles were reformulated in *Victoria Laundry (Windsor) Ltd.* v. *Newman Industries Ltd.*[58] The defendants sold a boiler to the plaintiffs, knowing that the plaintiffs wanted it for immediate use in their laundry business. The boiler was delivered some five months after the agreed date, so that the plaintiffs suffered loss of profits. Asquith L.J. said that the test of remoteness was whether the loss was "reasonably foreseeable as liable

---

[51] (1854) 9 Exch. 341; Simpson, 91 L.Q.R. 272–277; Danzig, 4 *Journal of Legal Studies* 249; Pugsley 126 N.L.J. 420; Barton, 7 O.J.L.S. 40.

[52] At p. 354.

[53] At p. 356.

[54] *Ibid.*

[55] 23 L.J.Ex. at p. 180.

[56] (1854) 9 Exch. at p. 355. This statement is hard to reconcile with the account of the facts given at p. 344: "The plaintiffs' servant told the [defendants'] clerk that the mill was stopped and that the shaft must be sent immediately." In the *Victoria Laundry* case [1949] 2 K.B. 528, 537 Asquith L.J. said that the court "rejected this evidence"; but it is hard to see how the court could do this on an application for a new trial on the ground of misdirection. The more likely explanation of the apparent discrepancy is that the defendants were not told the crucial fact that the mill would *remain* idle if the shaft was delayed. According to 18 Jur. 358, "Although there was evidence that the defendant knew that the mill was standing still, *he did not know that this was for want of the shaft*."

[57] (1854) 9 Ex. 341, 355.

[58] [1949] 2 K.B. 528.

to result from the breach."[59] This depends on the state of the defendant's knowledge. Every defendant has imputed to him knowledge of what happens in the ordinary course of things. He may also have actual knowledge of special circumstances, which would enable a reasonable man to foresee extraordinary loss. Here the defendants knew that the plaintiffs wanted the boiler for immediate use in their business: they were thus liable for loss of profits that would ordinarily result from such use. But they were not liable for loss of exceptionally lucrative contracts with the Ministry of Supply, which the plaintiffs would have been able to make if they had received the boiler in time: they knew nothing of these contracts and could not reasonably have foreseen such loss.

The judgment in this case, and in particular the phrase "reasonably foreseeable as liable to result" gave rise to the view that the same test of "reasonable foreseeability" that governs remoteness in tort applies also in contract. But this interpretation of the *Victoria Laundry* case can no longer be accepted after the decision of the House of Lords in *The Heron II*.[60] In that case a ship was chartered to carry sugar from Constanza to Basrah. At the time of contracting, the charterer intended to sell the sugar as soon as it reached Basrah. The shipowner did not actually know this; but he did know that there was a market for sugar at Basrah, and "if he had thought about the matter he must have realised that at least it was not unlikely that the sugar would be sold in the market at market price on arrival."[61] The shipowner in breach of contract deviated and reached Basrah nine days late. During these nine days the market price of sugar at Basrah fell; and it was held that the charterer was entitled to damages for the loss suffered by reason of the fall in the market.[62] On the one hand, the House of Lords rejected the argument that in contracts for the carriage of goods by sea damages for delay were governed by a special rule, under which losses were too remote unless they were "reasonably certain" to result.[63] On the other hand, the House also rejected the view that the test of remoteness in contract was "reasonable foreseeability," at least if this phrase referred to the very low degree of probability required to satisfy the test of remoteness in tort.[64] Lord Reid said that if this test was laid down for contract in the *Victoria Laundry* case it was wrong.[65] But when Asquith L.J. referred to "loss reasonably foreseeable *as liable to result*" he may have had a higher degree of probability in mind; and in this sense his judgment was (subject to one qualification[66]) approved by the other members of the House of Lords. Various expressions are used in *The Heron II* to describe the degree of probability required to satisfy the test of remoteness in contract. There

---

59 *Ibid.* p. 539.

60 *Sub nom. Koufos* v. *C. Czarnikow Ltd.* [1969] 1 A.C. 350; Pickering, 31 M.L.R. 203.

61 [1969] 1 A.C. 350, 382.

62 That loss amounted to some £4,000, which was *less* than the freight charge of about £9,000. In *Hadley* v. *Baxendale* and the *Victoria Laundry* case this relationship was reversed: the losses considerably exceeded the amounts paid under the contracts to the defendants.

63 *The Parana* (1877) 2 P.D. 118, 123, overruled in *The Heron II*.

64 [1969] 1 A.C. 350, 385, 411, 425; *cf.* 413; *The Rio Claro* [1987] 2 Lloyd's Rep. 173, 175.

65 [1969] 1 A.C. at p. 389.

66 At one point in the *Victoria Laundry* case ([1949] 2 K.B. 528 at p. 540) Asquith L.J. suggested that the test was whether the occurrence of the loss was "on the cards." This test was rejected in *The Heron II* [1969] 1 A.C. 350, 390, 399, 415, 425.

must be a "serious possibility"[67] or a "real danger"[68] or a "very substantial"[69] probability of loss; it must be "not unlikely"[70] or "easily foreseeable"[71] that loss will occur. The result of the decision is that a higher degree of probability is required to satisfy the test of remoteness in contract than in tort. When used in contract cases, the word "foreseeability" refers to this higher degree of probability.

The distinction established in *The Heron II* between the tests of remoteness in contract and tort was further considered in *H. Parsons (Livestock) Ltd.* v. *Uttley Ingham & Co. Ltd.*[72] The defendants in that case supplied to the plaintiffs a hopper for storing pig food; they failed, in breach of contract, to provide for proper ventilation, so that the food became mouldy and many of the pigs died from a rare intestinal disease. Swanwick J., gave judgment for the plaintiffs for damages to be assessed for the value of the pigs which had died, for the plaintiffs' expenses in dealing with the infection, and for "loss of sales and turnover." This judgment was affirmed on appeal, but for divergent reasons which give rise to three main difficulties. The first is to determine exactly what test of remoteness was applied. Lord Denning M.R. said that the higher degree of foreseeability stated in *The Heron II* applied only where the plaintiff's claim was for purely financial loss; where his claim was for physical damage the test of remoteness was the same in contract as in tort. He accordingly found for the plaintiffs on the ground that the tort test was satisfied, even though that laid down in *The Heron II* was not: it was enough that the defendants could have foreseen a "slight possibility"[73] that eating mouldy food might make the pigs ill. Orr and Scarman L.JJ., on the other hand, took the view that there neither was nor should be any distinction between financial loss and physical damage for the purpose of remoteness. Their decision in favour of the plaintiffs was based on the view that the test of remoteness laid down in *The Heron II* was satisfied as the defendants could have contemplated a "serious possibility"[74] that the pigs might become ill as a result of the defect in the hopper. The second difficulty is to account for the fact that, although two different tests of remotness were applied, all the members of the Court of Appeal upheld Swanwick J.'s award of damages for "loss of sales and turnover."[75] In what appears to be a reference to this point, Lord Denning M.R. said that the plaintiffs were not entitled to damages "for loss of profit on future sales or future opportunities of gain"[76]; while Orr and Scarman L.JJ. agreed with Lord Denning in the result, but "by a different route."[77] It is not easy to reconcile these positions with each other or with the different ways (discussed above) in which the members of the Court formulated and applied the test of remoteness. Lord Denning's

---

[67] *Ibid.* pp. 414–415.
[68] *Ibid.* p. 425.
[69] *Ibid.* p. 388.
[70] *Ibid.* p. 383.
[71] *Ibid.*
[72] [1978] Q.B. 791.
[73] *Ibid.* at p. 804.
[74] *Ibid.* p. 812; Orr L.J. expressed his agreement with the reasoning of Scarman L.J.
[75] *Ibid.* at p. 793; the Court of Appeal, while affirming Swanwick J's decision, disagreed with his reasoning that the test of remoteness did not have to be satisfied as liability was strict (*ante*, p. 738).
[76] [1978] Q.B. 791, 804.
[77] *Ibid.* p. 806.

views on these points might seem to lead to the conclusion that there should be *no* recovery for "loss of sales and turnover,"[78] while the reasoning of Orr and Scarman L.JJ. makes it hard to understand why they agreed with Lord Denning's conclusion that there should be no recovery "for loss of profit on future sales."[79] The most plausible reconciliation of the apparent conflict is that the plaintiffs recovered damages for loss of the profits that they would have made from the pigs which had died, but not for loss of further profits which they would have been able to make (if the hopper had not been defective) by rearing and selling additional animals. The third difficulty is to determine whether, in the view of Orr and Scarman L.JJ., the test of remoteness in contract differs from that in tort. At one point, Scarman L.J. said that it was "absurd that the test of remoteness of damage should, in principle, differ according to the legal classification of the cause of action"; and that the law did not "differentiate between contract and tort save in situations where the agreement, or the factual relationship, of the parties with each other requires it in the interests of justice."[80] But he also accepted that "the formulation of the remoteness test is not the same in tort and contract because the relationship of the parties in a contract situation differs from that in tort."[81] It differs because, as Lord Reid said in *The Heron II*, a contracting party "who wishes to protect himself against a risk which to the other party would appear to be unusual, . . . can direct the other party's attention to it before the contract is made. In tort, however, there is no opportunity for the injured party to protect himself in that way . . . ."[82] Perhaps one may conclude that, where the same facts give rise to liability in both contract and tort, the plaintiff will be entitled to damages in respect of loss falling within the (to him more favourable) tort test[83]; and that the same may be true even where the cause of action arises in contract alone but the plaintiff does not in fact have the opportunity of protecting himself to which Lord Reid refers in *The Heron II*. Subject to these qualifications, the distinction drawn in that case between the contract and tort tests of remoteness continues to apply.[84]

(b) LOSS OCCURRING IN THE ORDINARY COURSE OF THINGS. A defendant is (even without knowledge of special circumstances) liable if the loss occurs "in the ordinary course of things," that is, if the probability of its occurrence comes up to the standard described in *The Heron II*. On this ground it has been held that a person who agrees to supply or repair an obviously profit-earning thing is liable for loss of profits resulting from delay[85]; that a seller of poisonous cattle-food is liable for loss of the cattle to which it is fed[86]; that a merchant who sells defective seed to a farmer is liable for loss

---

[78] Since this loss was financial and the test in *The Heron II* was (in Lord Denning's view) not satisfied.
[79] Since (in their view) the *Heron II* test was satisfied.
[80] *Ibid.* p. 806.
[81] *Ibid.* p. 806.
[82] [1969] 1 A.C. 350, 385–386, cited in the *Parsons* case [1978] Q.B. 791, 806.
[83] *Cf. Archer* v. *Brown* [1985] Q.B. 401, 418 (where both tests seem to have been satisfied).
[84] *The Pegase* [1981] 1 Lloyd's Rep. 175, 181, where *H. Parsons (Livestock) Ltd.* v. *Uttley Ingham & Co. Ltd.* [1978] Q.B. 791 does not seem to have been cited.
[85] *Fletcher* v. *Tayleur* (1855) 17 C.B. 21; *Wilson* v. *General Iron Screw Colliery Co. Ltd.* (1887) 47 L.J.Q.B. 239; *cf. Mira* v. *Aylmer Square Investments Ltd.* [1990] 1 E.G.L.R. 45.
[86] *Pinnock Bros.* v. *Lewis & Peat Ltd.* [1923] 1 K.B. 690; *cf. Cointat* v. *Myham & Son* [1913] 2 K.B. 220; *ante*, p. 382; *Ashington Piggeries Ltd.* v. *Christopher Hill Ltd.* [1972] A.C. 441.

of the expected crop[87]; that a supplier of defective components to a manufacturer is liable for loss of business suffered by the latter when customers, dissatisfied with the end-product, do not place repeat orders[88]; that a shipowner, whose ship arrives too late to perform the agreed services under a charterparty, so that the charterer cancels, is liable for the extra cost of transporting the goods in another ship[89]; and that a person who sells goods to which he has no title, and which are later taken away from the buyer, is liable for money spent on repairing the goods.[90] On the other hand, it has been held that money spent on *improvements* to a house could not be recovered from a vendor who refused to convey[91] or from a builder owing to whose breach of contract the house collapsed.[92] The line between repairs and improvements can obviously be a fine one; and where property is bought for restoration or development expenses incurred for this purpose would not be too remote.[93] In the last resort, the question whether the test of remoteness has been *satisfied* is one of fact[94]; though the question whether the correct test has been *applied* is one of law.[95]

A defendant is not normally liable for a loss which might occur in the ordinary course of things if it is not suffered[96]; nor for a loss which is suffered if it is too remote. But these rules are qualified where the plaintiff actually suffers a loss which is too remote while the defendant could have anticipated that he would have suffered another, smaller, loss. In *Cory* v. *Thames Ironworks Co.*[97] the defendants agreed to supply to the plaintiffs the hull of a floating boom derrick, but delivered it six months late. The defendants expected the plaintiffs to use the hull as a coal store, and, if it had been so used, the plaintiffs would, as a result of the delay, have lost £420. But, unknown to the defendants, the plaintiffs intended to use the hull for a revolutionary method of transferring coal from colliers to barges, and lost profits of £4,000. The plaintiffs admitted that they could not recover £4,000 and claimed £420. The defendants were held liable for the latter sum: the court rejected their argument that, as the £420 represented a loss not actually suffered, they were not liable even to this extent. There could be "no hardship or injustice"[98] in making the seller liable for the smaller sum when the buyer had lost a larger amount.[99] It is more doubtful whether damages can be recovered if the loss actually suffered is quite different in kind from that which would have occurred in the ordinary course of things. Suppose A sells B poisonous cattle-food. B eats it himself in the course of an unforeseeable nutritional experiment, and dies. Can his executor sue A for the loss of a cow?

---

[87] *George Mitchell (Chesterhall) Ltd.* v. *Finney Lock Seeds Ltd.* [1983] 2 A.C. 803; and see *ante*, p. 835.

[88] *G.K.N. Centrax Gears Ltd.* v. *Matbro Ltd.* [1976] 2 Lloyd's Rep. 555.

[89] *The Almare Seconda* [1981] 2 Lloyd's Rep. 433.

[90] *Mason* v. *Burningham* [1949] 2 K.B. 545; *cf. Bunny* v. *Hopkinson* (1859) 27 Beav. 565.

[91] *Lloyd* v. *Stanbury* [1971] 1 W.L.R. 535.

[92] *King* v. *Victor Parsons Ltd.* [1972] 1 W.L.R. 801.

[93] *Cf. post*, p. 861 as to loss of profit.

[94] *Bulk Oil (Zug) A.G.* v. *Sun International Ltd.* [1984] 1 Lloyd's Rep. 531, 544.

[95] *The Yanxilas (No. 2)* [1984] 1 Lloyd's Rep. 676, 682.

[96] *Sunley (B.) & Co. Ltd.* v. *Cunard White Star Ltd.* [1940] 1 K.B. 740.

[97] (1868) L.R. 3 Q.B. 181.

[98] At p. 190.

[99] *Building & Civil Engineering Holidays Scheme Management Ltd.* v. *Post Office* [1966] 1 Q.B. 247, 261; the *Victoria Laundry* case (*ante*, pp. 855–856) illustrates the same principle.

(c) KNOWLEDGE OF SPECIAL CIRCUMSTANCES. In *Hadley* v. *Baxendale* it was suggested that the defendants might have been liable for the plaintiffs' loss of profits if they had known, at the time of contracting, that their delay would keep the mill idle. But mere knowledge of special circumstances is no longer regarded as sufficient.[1] Something more must be shown; and attempts have been made in a number of later cases to define that additional requirement.

In *Horne* v. *Midland Ry.*[2] the defendants contracted with the plaintiff to carry a consignment of shoes to London by February 3, but delivered it a day late. As a result of this delay, the plaintiff lost the opportunity of selling the shoes at an exceptionally high price. The defendants were not liable for this loss: they knew that the plaintiff would have to take the shoes back if they were not delivered by February 3, but not that he would lose an exceptional profit.[3] Blackburn J. said that "in order that the notice [of special circumstances] may have any effect, it must be given under such circumstances as that an *actual contract* arises on the part of the defendant to bear the exceptional loss."[4] But the decision can be explained on the ground that the defendants' knowledge of the special circumstances was incomplete; and it is clear that there need be no *express* contract to bear the exceptional loss.[5] Liability for loss caused by known special circumstances can perhaps be based on an "implied undertaking . . . to bear it,"[6] but the reference seems to be to an undertaking implied in law (and not in fact), and so to mean that the defendant is liable for the exceptional loss, irrespective of any actual agreement to bear it.[7]

Simpson v. *L. & N.W. Ry.*[8] illustrates the circumstances in which such liability can arise. The defendants had contracted to carry the plaintiff's samples of cattle-food from an agricultural show at Bedford to another at Newcastle. They had an agent on the showground at Bedford specifically to attract such custom, and the goods were marked "must be at Newcastle by Monday certain" but no express reference was made in the contract of carriage to the Newcastle show. The samples failed to arrive "by Monday" and did not reach Newcastle until after the show there was over. It was held that the defendants were liable for loss of the profits which the plaintiff would have made, had the samples reached Newcastle in time. This should be contrasted with an example given in an earlier case: a barrister going to Calcutta, where he has briefs awaiting him, cannot sue the carriers for getting him there late, even if they know why he is going to Calcutta.[9] The distinction between the cases lies in the nature of the two contracts. In

[1] *e.g. Kemp* v. *Intasun Holidays Ltd.* (1988) 6 Tr.L. 161 (package tour operator not liable for discomfort suffered by holiday-maker because of asthmatic condition of which his wife told travel agent in casual conversation while booking holiday).

[2] (1873) L.R. 8 C.P. 131.

[3] *Cf. Coastal International Trading Ltd.* v. *Maroil Ltd.* [1988] 1 Lloyd's Rep. 92, 97.

[4] At p. 141.

[5] *Robophone Facilities Ltd.* v. *Blank* [1966] 1 W.L.R. 1428, 1448; *cf. Hydraulic Engineeering Co. Ltd.* v. *McHaffie, Goslett & Co.* (1878) 4 Q.B.D. 670, 674; *The Heron II* [1969] 1 A.C. 350, 422; *The Pegase* [1981] 1 Lloyd's Rep. 175, 182; *Panalpina International Transport Ltd.* v. *Densil Underwear Ltd.* [1981] 1 Lloyd's Rep. 187.

[6] *Robophone Facilities Ltd.* v. *Blank*, *supra* n. 5.

[7] *Cf. ante*, p. 190.

[8] (1876) 1 Q.B.D. 274; *Jameson* v. *Midland Ry.* (1884) 50 L.T. 426.

[9] *B.C. Saw-Mill Co. Ltd.* v. *Nettleship* (1868) L.R. 3 C.P. 499, 510; *cf. The Panalpina* case, *supra*, n. 5, where a carrier knew that goods were wanted for the Christmas trade but delivered them too late.

the first, the contract was in substance one to carry samples to the Newcastle show—not simply to Newcastle. In the second the contract was one to carry the barrister to Calcutta—not to the Calcutta law sittings. Liability depends on "some knowledge *and acceptance* by one party of the *purpose and intention* of the other in entering the contract."[10]

The party in breach may only know some of the circumstances which lead to extra loss. He may then be liable for so much of that loss as he could have anticipated on the basis of the facts known to him. Thus a seller of goods who fails to deliver them may be liable to the buyer for loss of profit on a subsale, of the likelihood of which he knew; but he will not be liable for loss resulting from further subsales by the sub-buyer (for which the buyer was liable) unless these, too, were contemplated by the seller.[11] Similarly, a carrier may be able to contemplate that *some* delay will result from his breach, and so be liable for loss which flows from such delay; but he will not be liable for further loss flowing from further delay which results from circumstances which were outside the contemplation of the parties.[12] The defendant's liability increases with his degree of knowledge. Thus one reason why some loss of profits was recovered in the *Victoria Laundry* case, but none in *Hadley* v. *Baxendale*, was that in the former the defendants knew that the boiler was wanted for immediate use, while in the latter case they did not know that want of the shaft would keep the mill idle. Again, in *The Heron II* the defendants' knowledge that there was a sugar market at Basrah made them liable for loss due to market movements there. But in *The Rio Claro*[13] the late arrival of a ship caused loss to a charterer who had contracted to *buy* oil at the destination at the official government selling price, and this price was raised between the time when the ship should have arrived and the time when she actually arrived. The resulting loss was too remote because the shipowner only knew that the charterer was an oil trader and did not know of the details of the contractual arrangements which the charterer had made with his suppliers. The point is further illustrated by two cases in which vendors wrongfully refused to convey land which the purchasers intended to redevelop. In the first,[14] the vendor was held liable for loss of development profits as he knew that the purchaser intended himself to carry out the development; in his second,[15] the vendor was not liable for such loss as he knew only that the purchaser was a dealer in real estate and not that he intended to develop the land.

What the defendant should have deduced from the facts known to him is generally judged by the standard of the reasonable person. Thus in *Hadley* v. *Baxendale* the defendants could not reasonably be expected to deduce

---

10 *Weld-Blundell* v. *Stephens* [1920] A.C. 956, 980; contrast *G.K.N Centrax Gears Ltd.* v. *Matbro Ltd.* [1976] 2 Lloyd's Rep. 555, 580.

11 *Borries* v. *Hutchinson* (1865) 18 C.B. (N.S.) 445; *cf. International Minerals & Chemicals Corp.* v. *Karl O. Helm A.G.* [1986] 1 Lloyd's Rep. 81, 102 (exchange loss recoverable as damages for late payment in a currency known not to be "the currency of [the seller]"; *Danecroft Jersey Mills* v. *Crigee*, *The Times*, April 14, 1987.

12 *The Forum Craftsman* [1991] 1 Lloyd's Rep. 81, 85–86.

13 [1987] 2 Lloyd's Rep. 173; *cf. The Baleares* [1990] 2 Lloyd's Rep. 130 (and see [1991] 2 All E.R. 110).

14 *Cottrill* v. *Steyning & Littlehampton Building Society* [1966] 1 W.L.R. 753; *cf. G. & K. Ladenbau (U.K.) Ltd.* v. *Crawley & de Reya* [1978] 1 W.L.R. 266; *Seven Seas Properties Ltd.* v. *Al-Essa* [1988] 1 W.L.R. 1272.

15 *Diamond* v. *Campbell-Jones* [1961] Ch. 22.

from the facts known to them[16] that their delay would keep the mill idle, as the plaintiffs might have had a spare shaft.[17] In the *Victoria Laundry* case the supposition that the plaintiffs kept a spare boiler would have been fantastic.

In deciding what the defendant should reasonably have deduced from the facts known to him, the court can also take into account the capacity in which he contracted. Thus in *Hadley* v. *Baxendale* the defendants were carriers and less well able to foresee the effects of delay than the defendants in the *Victoria Laundry* case, who were qualified engineers and knew more than the uninstructed layman of the purposes for which such boilers were likely to be used.[18] But even a carrier can be made liable for loss of the chance of making profits on resale[19] and for loss of profits suffered by a manufacturer through non-delivery of raw materials known to be wanted for manufacturing purposes.[20]

A plaintiff may suffer extra loss because his financial position is such that he cannot avoid the adverse consequences of the breach. Damages can be recovered for such loss if the defendant knew of the plaintiff's lack of means and if the extra loss resulting from it "was such as might reasonably be expected to be in the contemplation of the parties as likely to flow from a breach of the obligation undertaken."[21]

(d) WHAT MUST BE "CONTEMPLATED." In tort cases, it is often said that the defendant is liable if he could have foreseen the type or kind of loss suffered, even though he could not have foreseen its extent or quantum.[22] Similar reasoning was used in *Wroth* v. *Tyler*.[23] The defendant argued that he should not be liable for the full difference between the contract price and the market price because, though he could have contemplated some rise in house prices, he could not have contemplated the exceptionally large rise which occurred between 1971 and 1973. In rejecting this argument Megarry J. said that a defendant might escape liability for a "type or kind of loss"[24] which he could not have contemplated; and that "No authority was put before me which appeared to provide any support for the alleged requirement that the quantum should have been in contem-

---

16 *Ante*, p. 855.

17 *Cf. Gee* v. *Lancs. & Yorks. Ry.* (1860) H. & N. 211 (carrier ignorant that manufacturer had no stocks of raw material); *The Pegase* [1981] 1 Lloyd's Rep. 175.

18 [1949] 2 K.B. 528, 540.

19 *e.g. The Heron II* [1969] 1 A.C. 350; *Panalpina International Transport Ltd.* v. *Densil Underwear Ltd.* [1981] 1 Lloyd's Rep. 187.

20 *Monte Video Gas Co.* v. *Clan Line Steamers Ltd.* (1921) 37 T.L.R. 866; *The Pegase* [1981] 1 Lloyd's Rep. 175; *cf. The Ocean Dynamic* [1982] 2 Lloyd's Rep. 88.

21 *Muhammed Issa el Sheik Ahmed* v. *Ali* [1947] A.C. 414, as explained in *Monarch SS. Co.* v. *Karlshamns Oljefabriker (A/B)* [1949] A.C. 196, 224; *cf. Trans Trust S.P.R.L.* v. *Danubian Trading Co. Ltd.* [1952] 2 Q.B. 297; *Wroth* v. *Tyler* [1974] Ch. 30 (as explained at p. 851, *ante*). *Robbins of Putney Ltd.* v. *Meek* [1971] R.T.R. 345; *Perry* v. *Sidney Phillips & Son* [1982] 1 W.L.R. 1297; contrast *Pilkington* v. *Wood* [1953] Ch. 770 (where defendant did not know of plaintiff's overdraft), and *Ramwade Ltd.* v. *W. J. Emson & Co.*, *The Times*, July 11, 1986 (which may be explicable on the same ground).

22 *e.g. Smith* v. *Leech Brain & Co. Ltd.* [1962] 2 Q.B. 405, 415; *cf. Muirhead* v. *Industrial Tank Specialities Ltd.* [1986] Q.B. 507, 532.

23 [1974] Ch. 30; *ante*, p. 851.

24 *Ibid.* p. 61; *cf. G.K.N. Centrax Gears Ltd.* v. *Matbro Ltd.* [1976] 2 Lloyd's Rep. 555, 568 ("loss of a certain kind").

plation."[25] The distinction between "type" and "quantum" is, however, an elusive one; and the *Victoria Laundry*[26] case is hard to reconcile with the view that contemplation of the "quantum" is necessarily irrelevant. The most obvious description of the "type" of loss within the defendants' contemplation in that case is "loss of business profits"; and for some such loss the defendants were held liable. The reason why they were not held liable for all the lost profits appears to be that those on the government contracts exceeded normal profits in amount. *Wroth* v. *Tyler* is, it is submitted, best explained on the ground that the problem posed by the increase in house prices was not one of remoteness at all but one of quantification.[27]

The view that a defendant is liable if he could contemplate the type of loss, as opposed to its degree, was again put forward in *H. Parsons (Livestock) Ltd.* v. *Uttley Ingham & Co. Ltd.*[28] The defendants were held liable for the loss of the pigs because they could have contemplated that, as a result of their breach, the pigs would become ill[29]: it was not necessary for them to have contemplated that the pigs would be affected by the particular disease which affected them, and which turned out to be fatal. One explanation for this aspect of the decision is that, where physical harm is caused, there is no need to show that its degree should have been anticipated.[30] But Scarman L.J. added that the same principles applied in cases of financial loss, though in such cases "the factual analysis will be very different."[31] Again, no reference is made at this point to the *Victoria Laundry*[32] case, which gives rise here to difficulties similar to those discussed above in relation to *Wroth* v. *Tyler*.[33] An alternative explanation of the *Parsons* case is that the only thing which the defendants failed to foresee was the *manner* in which the injury to the pigs might be caused.[34] On this view, no issue arose as to the distinction between *type* and *degree* of loss.

(e) SCOPE OF THE "REASONABLE CONTEMPLATION" TEST. "Reasonable contemplation" is a test of remoteness and not one of quantification.[35] It determines whether a plaintiff is entitled to compensation for a particular item of loss, but not how that loss is to be translated into money terms. If a seller of goods fails to deliver them, there is no doubt that he is liable for the loss that the buyer has suffered in simply not having the goods. Where there is a market, the buyer's loss will prima facie be valued by reference to

---

25 [1974] Ch. at p. 61; *cf. The Rio Claro* [1987] 2 Lloyd's Rep. 173, 175 (where, however, the loss suffered was said at p. 176 to have been of a "different category" from that which could have been contemplated.

26 [1949] 2 K.B. 528; *ante*, p. 855. *Cf.* also *The Forum Craftsman* [1991] 1 Lloyd's Rep. 81, 85–86

27 See *post*, pp. 863–864 for discussion of the scope of the reasonable contemplation test.

28 [1978] Q.B. 791; *ante*, p. 857; P.V.B., 94 L.Q.R. 171.

29 [1978] Q.B. 791, 812.

30 *McGregor on Damages* (13th ed.), para. 188, approved [1978] Q.B. 791, 813.

31 *Ibid.* at p. 813.

32 [1949] 2 K.B. 528.

33 [1974] Ch. 30.

34 See [1978] Q.B. 791, 813.

35 For this distinction, see *Re National Coffee Palace Co.* (1883) 24 Ch.D. 367, 372: *J. D. D'Almeida Araujo Lda.* v. *Sir Frederick Becker & Co. Ltd.* [1953] 2 Q.B. 329. The distinction is said to be between "remoteness" and "measure" of damages, but in view of the ambiguity of the latter term, this usage has given rise to difficulties: see *N. V. Handel etc.* v. *English Exporters Ltd.* [1955] 2 Lloyd's Rep. 69, 72 (affmd. *ibid.* 317).

that market[36]; and this process of valuation does not raise any issue as to what was within the reasonable contemplation of the parties. In such cases, it is sometimes said that market fluctuations are *always* foreseeable; but this is either a fiction[37] or just another way of saying that foreseeability is, for purposes of quantification, irrelevant. It follows that the damages are not affected by the fact that the market has risen or fallen in an unusually sharp way, or because of circumstances which were not within the contemplation of the parties.[38] The same reasoning applies where the loss is quantified by reference, not to a market, but to other factors mentioned earlier in this Chapter.[39] It applies also to *Wroth* v. *Tyler* where the plaintiff was undoubtedly entitled to compensation for his loss in not getting the house, and the question how much the house was worth at the relevant date was simply one of quantification. A question of remoteness might have been raised in that case if the plaintiff had, in addition, lost a profit that he could have made by reselling the house or by redeveloping the site; but no attempt was made to show that any such loss had been suffered.

All this is not to say that loss due to market movements can never be subject to the "reasonable contemplation" test. It was so subject in *The Heron II*[40] where the charterer had lost, not *the goods*, but *the chance of going into the market to sell them* on a particular day. The question was whether *that chance* was something that the shipowner could have contemplated; and, once this issue had been settled in the charterer's favour, no serious attempt seems to have been made to show that market fluctuations in general, or the particular fluctuations which occurred, were unpredictable, so as to make the loss too remote.[41] In two of the speeches, it is said that the fall in the market was not due to "any unusual or unpredictable factor"[42]; and it may be possible to infer that, had it been due to some such factor, this might have affected the result. But it is submitted that a similar argument should not prevail where the market rule is used simply as a test of quantification.

(2) Causation

The statement that a plaintiff cannot recover damages because the breach "caused him no loss" is sometimes found in the cases (already mentioned) in which a state of affairs was clearly brought about by the breach, but was not disadvantageous to the plaintiff.[43] Our present concern, however, is with cases in which there is a breach, followed by a state of affairs clearly disadvantageous to the plaintiff, but the defendant argues that the breach did not bring about that state of affairs. For example, a shipowner may be technically in breach of contract because his ship was not equipped with a

---

36 *Ante*, p. 839.
37 *i.e.* if it relates to *particular* fluctuations.
38 *e.g. Kwei Tek Chao* v. *British Traders Ltd.* [1954] 2 Q.B. 459.
39 *Ante*, pp. 842–843.
40 [1969] 1 A.C. 350; *cf. The Ulyanovsk* [1990] 1 Lloyd's Rep. 425, 433.
41 Contrast dicta in *Smeed* v. *Foord* (1859) 1 E. & E. 602, 616 and (in argument) 608. It is submitted that these dicta would not now be followed. The actual decision can be explained on the ground that, at the time of contracting, the defendant could not have contemplated that his delay in delivering the threshing machine would deprive the plaintiff of the chance of going into the market to sell his crop; for the plaintiff might have been expected to hire a substitute.
42 [1969] 1 A.C. 350, 394, 417.
43 *Ante*, p. 828.

proper medicine chest; but if the ship later foundered in a storm, the owners of goods on board could not claim that the breach was the cause of their loss.[44] On the other hand, a plaintiff can often recover damages although the breach is not the *sole* cause of the loss.

(a) CONCURRENT CAUSES GENERALLY. "If a breach of contract is one of two causes, both co-operating and both of equal efficacy, . . . it is sufficient to carry a judgment for damages."[45] One such case has already been mentioned: the victim of a breach of contract can recover damages for a loss caused partly by the breach and partly by his own lack of means (so long as the loss is not too remote).[46] Again, unseaworthiness is hardly ever the sole cause of a maritime loss: the shipowner is liable though ordinary sea perils have co-operated with unseaworthiness to produce the loss.[47] But he would not be liable if, as a result of delay, the ship ran into a typhoon as such a catastrophe may occur anywhere[48] and as the delay would not be causally "of equal efficacy" with the typhoon. The special case where the concurrent cause is the plaintiff's own conduct is discussed below.[49]

(b) INTERVENING ACTS OF THIRD PARTY. Where loss results partly from the breach and partly from the act of a third party,[50] the party in breach is nevertheless liable for the loss if (but only if)[51] the third party's act was "foreseeable" on the standard of probability which governs remoteness in contract.[52] Thus a shipowner who in time of impending war commits breach of a charterparty is liable for the resulting loss though it was aggravated by government action[53]; a person who in breach of contract recommends a dishonest stockbroker is liable for loss caused by the broker's dishonesty[54]; and a painter who in breach of contract leaves his client's house unlocked is liable for the value of goods taken from it by thieves.[55] These cases illustrate the proposition that, although remoteness and causation are "quite different concepts" nevertheless "some of the relevant considerations are the same."[56]

In *Weld-Blundell* v. *Stephens*[57] the plaintiff employed an accountant to investigate the affairs of a company and wrote him a letter defaming two of

---

44 See *Monarch SS. Co.* v. *Karlshamns Oljefabriker (A/B)* [1949] A.C. 196, 226.

45 *Heskell* v. *Continental Express Ltd.* [1950] 1 All E.R. 1033, 1048; disapproved on another point in *Hedley Byrne & Co. Ltd.* v. *Heller & Partners Ltd.* [1964] A.C. 465, 532.

46 *Ante*, p. 862. In tort the loss resulting from the plaintiff's lack of means has been said to arise from a "separate and concurrent cause": *Liesbosch Dredger* v. *S.S. Edison* [1933] A.C. 449, 460. But this position is viewed with some scepticism in *Perry* v. *Sidney Phillips & Son* [1982] 1 W.L.R. 1297, 1302, 1305, 1307 and is now much qualified even in tort cases: see *Dodd Properties (Kent) Ltd.* v. *Canterbury C.C.* [1980] A.C. 433; *Archer* v. *Brown* [1985] Q.B. 401, 417; more recently, *The Liesbosch* has been applied in contract: *Ramwade Ltd.* v. *Emson & Co.*, *The Times*, July 11, 1986, as to which see *ante*, p. 862, n. 21.

47 *Smith, Hogg & Co. Ltd.* v. *Black Sea Insurance Co. Ltd.* [1940] A.C. 997.

48 *Monarch Steamship* case [1949] A.C. 196, 215.

49 *Post*, pp. 866, 868, 871–875.

50 Where the act is that of the injured party, problems of mitigation and contributory negligence arise: *post*, pp. 866–869, 871–875.

51 *The Silver Sky* [1981] 2 Lloyd's Rep. 95.

52 *Ante*, pp. 855–858.

53 *Monarch Steamship* case [1949] A.C. 196.

54 *De la Bere* v. *Pearson Ltd.* [1908] 1 K.B. 280.

55 *Stansbie* v. *Troman* [1948] 2 K.B. 48.

56 *The Yanxilas (No. 2)* [1984] 1 Lloyd's Rep. 676, 682.

57 [1920] A.C. 956.

the company's directors. The accountant's partner negligently dropped the letter in the company's office, where it was picked up by the manager and shown to the two directors. They recovered heavy damages from the plaintiff in an action for libel. The plaintiff claimed this amount from the accountant as damages for breach of contract. The House of Lords gave two reasons for dismissing the claim. First, the plaintiff's liability for defamation *existed* quite apart from the breach of contract, which simply brought that liability to the director's attention.[58] Secondly, the loss was not caused by the breach, but by the act of the manager in showing the letter to the directors, and this act was not one which the defendant could have foreseen. The view that the manager's act was not foreseeable may be regarded with some scepticism, particularly as the jury found that it was the defendant's duty to keep the letter secret. But it forms one basis of *Weld-Blundell* v. *Stephens*. The case does not support the proposition that a party who breaks a contract can escape liability for loss caused by a foreseeable intervening act.

(3) Mitigation

Two ideas are usually discussed under this heading. The first is that the plaintiff cannot recover for a loss that he ought to have avoided. He is said to be under a "duty to mitigate." This expression will be used here even though it is open to the objection that breach of the "duty" gives rise to no legal liability[59] but only reduces the amount that the plaintiff can recover. The second idea is that the plaintiff has to give credit for certain benefits accruing to him in consequence of the breach. Here it can be said that his loss is in fact mitigated.

(a) THE DUTY TO MITIGATE has two aspects: in the first place, the plaintiff must take reasonable steps to minimise his loss; and secondly he must forbear from taking unreasonable steps that increase his loss.[60]

(i) *Minimising loss.*[61] If the plaintiff fails to take reasonable steps to minimise his loss, he cannot recover anything in respect of extra loss due to that failure. Commonly, he is required to make a substitute contract. For example, where a seller of goods fails to deliver, the buyer must go into the market[62] at the relevant time[63] to buy substitute goods. If he fails to do so he cannot recover any further loss that he may suffer because the market continues to rise or because he is deprived of the opportunity of making a profit out of the use or resale of the goods.[64] Conversely, a seller of shares who kept them after the buyer's breach could not recover any extra loss that he might suffer as a result of a later fall in the market.[65] On the same

---

[58] *Cf. Clark* v. *Kirby-Smith* [1964] Ch. 506.

[59] *The Solholt* [1983] 1 Lloyd's Rep. 605, 608; Lomnicka, 99 L.Q.R. 495; *The Good Friend* [1984] 2 Lloyd's Rep. 586, 597; *The Alecos M* [1991] 1 Lloyd's Rep. 120, 124.

[60] For the burden of proof on this issue, see *post*, p. 901 at n. 71.

[61] Bridge, 105 L.Q.R. 398.

[62] If there are several markets, a transaction in any market that it was reasonable for the injured party to use can form the basis of assessment: *Gebruder Metelmann GmbH & Co. K.G.* v. *N.B.R. (London) Ltd.* [1984] 1 Lloyd's Rep. 614, a case of buyer's breach.

[63] *Ante*, pp. 849–854.

[64] *Hussey* v. *Eels* [1990] 1 All E.R. 449, 453 ("deemed mitigation"); *cf. The Elena D'Amico* [1980] 1 Lloyd's Rep. 75, 79 (charterparty); and see *ante*, p. 839.

[65] *Jamal* v. *Moolla Dawood Sons & Co.* [1916] 1 A.C. 175, 179.

principle, a wrongfully dismissed employee must make reasonable efforts to find a comparable job.

The injured party need only take such steps as are reasonable; and it has been held that he need not take steps which would involve him in complicated litigation[66] or which would ruin his commercial reputation.[67] Similar reasoning was applied where a building society had lent money to a house purchaser on the basis of a negligent surveyor's report (which failed to disclose defects making the house worthless). In an action against the surveyor, it was held that the society was not bound to mitigate by trying to extract money from its borrower under the covenant in the mortgage which rendered him personally liable to repay the loan where the security was inadequate.[68] And where the plaintiffs were induced to buy a house by the vendor's negligent misrepresentation that the house had not suffered from subsidence, it was held that they were not bound to mitigate by moving out of the house, and reselling it.[69]

Sometimes the injured party will be required to mitigate by accepting from the party in breach a performance which differs in some way from that originally bargained for. Thus where a charterer fails to load the agreed cargo, the shipowner may be bound to mitigate by accepting the charterer's reasonable offer of alternative cargo, even at a lower rate[70]; where a seller agrees to give credit and then refuses to deliver except for cash, the buyer may be bound to mitigate by accepting such delivery instead of buying against the seller on a rising market[71]; and where a seller cannot deliver at the agreed time the buyer may be required to mitigate by accepting late delivery.[72] In these cases, any loss suffered by the injured party by reason of the difference between the performance rendered and that originally bargained for can easily and adequately be allowed for in damages. He is not required to mitigate by accepting an offer of modified performance which purports to extinguish his right to such damages.[73] Nor is the injured party bound to mitigate by accepting an offer of modified performance if the modification causes him substantial prejudice: for example, a buyer of goods need not mitigate by accepting the seller's tender of goods of a lower quality than contracted for, even with an allowance for the inferiority.[74] On a somewhat similar principle, an employee who has been wrongfully dismissed need not accept an offer of re-employment involving a reduction in status,[75] or a lower grade of work[76]; nor need he accept the former employer's offer to take him back, even on the original

---

[66] *Pilkington* v. *Wood* [1953] Ch. 770.

[67] *James Finlay & Co. Ltd.* v. *N.V. Kwik Hoo Tong H.M.* [1929] 1 K.B. 400.

[68] *London & South of England Building Society* v. *Stone* [1983] 1 W.L.R. 1242.

[69] *Hussey* v. *Eels* [1990] 2 Q.B. 227.

[70] *Harries* v. *Edmonds* (1845) 1 Car. & K. 686.

[71] *Payzu Ltd.* v. *Saunders* [1919] 2 K.B. 581; contrast *Harlow & Jones Ltd.* v. *Panex International Ltd.* [1967] 2 Lloyd's Rep. 509, 530 (plaintiff "not bound to nurse the interests of the contract breaker").

[72] *The Solholt* [1983] 1 Lloyd's Rep. 605.

[73] *Shindler* v. *Northern Raincoat Co. Ltd.* [1960] 1 W.L.R. 1038; *cf. Strutt* v. *Whitnell* [1975] 1 W.L.R. 870 (said in *The Solholt* [1983] 1 Lloyd's Rep. 605, 609 to turn "on its own special facts").

[74] *Heaven & Kesterton Ltd.* v. *Et. François Albiac & Cie* [1956] 2 Lloyd's Rep. 316, 321.

[75] *Yetton* v. *Eastwood Froy Ltd.* [1967] 1 W.L.R. 104.

[76] *Cf. Edwards* v. *SOGAT* [1971] 1 Ch. 354.

terms, if the wrongful dismissal occurred in circumstances of personal humiliation, *e.g.* on a charge of misconduct made before others.[77]

(ii) *Not augmenting loss.* If the plaintiff acts unreasonably in attempting to mitigate, he cannot recover extra loss which he suffers as a result.[78] Thus in general he should not, for example, spend more on curing a defect in performance than the subject-matter without the defect would be worth[79]; nor should he continue to incur expense for the purpose of tendering performance after the other party has clearly indicated that he will refuse to accept it. But these are only general rules: the crucial question in each case is whether the plaintiff has acted reasonably. The point is strikingly illustrated by *Banco de Portugal* v. *Waterlow & Sons Ltd.*[80] The defendants had contracted to print banknotes for the plaintiff bank, and in breach of contract delivered a large number of these to a criminal, who put them into circulation in Portugal. On discovering this, the bank withdrew the issue and undertook to exchange all the notes in question for others. The defendants argued that they were liable only for the cost of printing the notes: any further loss was due to the bank's own act.[81] But the House of Lords, by a majority, held the defendants liable for the full face value of the notes as the conduct of the bank was reasonable, having regard to its commercial obligations towards the public.[82]

On the same principle, the plaintiff may be able to recover amounts paid in reasonable settlement of a liability to a third party incurred in consequence of the breach.[83] Conversely, if the plaintiff decides to resist a claim brought against him by a third party as a result[84] of the breach, he may be able to recover legal expenses incurred in the proceedings between him and the third party. Thus a buyer can recover from the seller costs reasonably incurred in defending an action brought against him by a sub-buyer on account of a defect for which the seller is liable.[85] Similarly a person who sues an agent for breach of implied warranty of authority can recover costs thrown away in a previous action brought against the principal on the assumption that the agent had the authority he claimed to have.[86] But the

---

77 *Payzu Ltd.* v. *Saunders* [1919] 2 K.B. 581, 589; in the absence of such circumstances it was held in *Brace* v. *Calder* [1895] 2 K.B. 253 that an offer of re-employment should have been accepted.

78 *The Borag* [1981] 1 W.L.R. 274; *Seven Seas Properties Ltd.* v. *Al-Essa* [1988] 1 W.L.R. 1272, 1276 (the reasoning of the case is obsolete on its facts in view of Law of Property (Miscellaneous Provisions) Act 1989, s.3).

79 *Cf. Darbishire* v. *Warran* [1963] 1 W.L.R. 1067—a tort case; *Grant* v. *Dawkins* [1973] 1 W.L.R. 1406; for an exception see *O'Grady* v. *Westminster Scaffolding Ltd.* [1962] 2 Lloyd's Rep. 238—another tort case.

80 [1932] A.C. 452.

81 Portuguese currency was not convertible into gold; the bank had a monopoly of issuing notes as legal tender; and, although the amount of notes it could issue was limited by law, the limit had not been reached.

82 *Cf. ante*, p. 865; and see *Buildings and Civil Engineering Holidays Scheme Management Ltd.* v. *Post Office* [1966] 1 Q.B. 247 (where the claim was not in contract).

83 *Bulk Oil (Zug) A.G.* v. *Sun International Ltd.* [1984] 1 Lloyd's Rep. 531, 544, where the contract limited liability but the amount of the settlement was less than the contractual limit.

84 See *The Antaios* [1981] 2 Lloyd's Rep. 284, 299.

85 *Hammond & Co.* v. *Bussey* (1887) 20 Q.B.D. 79; *Agius* v. *Great Western Ry.* [1899] 1 Q.B. 413; *Lloyd's & Scottish Finance Ltd.* v. *Modern Cars & Caravans (Kingston) Ltd.* [1966] 1 Q.B. 764; *Bowmaker (Commercial) Ltd.* v. *Day* [1965] 1 W.L.R. 1396.

86 *Hughes* v. *Graeme* (1864) 33 L.J.Q.B. 335; *Godwin* v. *Francis* (1870) L.R. 5 C.P. 295; *Farley Health Products* v. *Babylon Trading Co.*, *The Times*, July 29, 1987.

costs must be reasonably incurred: the plaintiff cannot recover them if he persists in litigating when it is clear that he has no chance of success.[87]

Finally, it is possible for steps taken in performance of the duty to mitigate to be reasonable, but actually to increase the loss. For example, a buyer who accepts a seller's anticipatory breach is bound to mitigate by buying a substitute in the market at the time of acceptance. If, when he makes the substitute purchase, the market price exceeds the contract price, he can recover the excess. This is so even though by the time fixed for delivery the market price has fallen below the contract price so that the buyer, if he had not performed the duty to mitigate, would have suffered no loss at all.[88]

(b) MITIGATION IN FACT. Loss is sometimes said to be mitigated where some benefit in fact accrues to the plaintiff as a result of the breach. For example, the breach may release him from his own obligation to perform, and this fact is taken into account in deciding whether there has been an overall loss.[89] Or he may benefit from performing his duty to mitigate, *e.g.* by finding a job comparable to that from which he was wrongfully dismissed.[90] Here again his earnings in the other job will be taken into account in assessing his damages for wrongful dismissal.[91]

There is a further group of cases in which the plaintiff benefits from something that he was *not required* to do in performance of his duty to mitigate: for example, a wrongfully dismissed employee may take a job involving a reduction in status. His actual earnings in that job are taken into account in assessing damages, even though it was a job that he was not required to take in performance of his duty to mitigate.[92] But not all benefits of this kind are taken into account; and the distinction between the two kinds of benefit is illustrated by *Lavarack* v. *Woods of Colchester Ltd.*[93] The plaintiff was wrongfully dismissed from his employment with the defendants and so freed from a provision in his contract with them that he should not, without their written consent, be engaged or interested in any other concern (except as a holder of investments quoted on a stock exchange). After his dismissal, the plaintiff (1) took employment with the X Co. at a lower salary than he had earned with the defendants; (2) acquired half the shares in the X Co.; and (3) invested money in shares in the Y Co. The shares in both companies having appreciated, it was held that the increase in the value of the X Co. shares, but not that of the Y Co. shares, must be taken into account in reducing the plaintiff's damages. The former was regarded as a disguised remuneration, while the latter was "not a direct result of his dismissal" but a "collateral benefit."[94]

---

87 *Pow* v. *Davies* (1861) 1 B. & S. 220; *Baxendale* v. *London, Chatham & Dover Ry.* (1874) L.R. 10 Ex. 38.

88 *Melachrino* v. *Nicholl & Knight* [1920] 1 K.B. 693, 697.

89 *Ante*, p. 827. See also *Levison* v. *Farin* [1978] 2 All E.R. 1149; *C. & P. Haulage* v. *Middleton* [1983] 1 W.L.R. 1461.

90 *Cf. Evans Marshall & Co.* v. *Bertola* [1976] 2 Lloyd's Rep. 17.

91 For the position in cases of unfair dismissal (which generally does not involve any breach of contract) see Employment Protection (Consolidation) Act 1978, s.74(4).

92 *Ante*, pp. 867–868; see *Edwards* v. *SOGAT* [1971] Ch. 354; *S. of S. for Employment* v. *Wilson* [1978] 1 W.L.R. 568; *cf. Techno Land Improvements Ltd.* v. *British Leyland (U.K.) Ltd.* (1979) 252 E.G. 805, 809; *The Concordia C* [1985] 2 Lloyd's Rep. 55.

93 [1967] 1 Q.B. 278.

94 *Ibid.* p. 290; *cf. Aruna Mills Ltd.* v. *Dhanrajmal Gobindram* [1968] 1 Q.B. 655, 669.

The question whether a benefit is "collateral" or a "direct result" of the breach can give rise to difficult problems of causation. In *British Westinghouse Co.* v. *Underground Electric Rys. Co. of London*,[95] A agreed to supply B with turbines of a stated efficiency but supplied less efficient ones, which used more coal. B accepted and used them, reserving his right to claim damages. After some years, and before A's turbines were worn out, B replaced them with others. These were so much more efficient than A's would have been, even had they been in accordance with the contract, that, over the whole period during which A's turbines might be expected to last, B actually used less coal than he would have done by using turbines of the efficiency stated in the contract. The House of Lords held that B was under no duty to mitigate by buying new turbines.[96] But as he had bought the new turbines in consequence of A's breach, the financial advantage he gained by using them had to be set off against the cost of buying them. As B's savings in coal exceeded that cost, he recovered nothing in respect of it. This was so even though it could be argued that the benefit thus obtained by B was only in part the result of the breach; for the turbines originally contracted for had become obsolete so that a reasonable businessman would have replaced them even if they had been in accordance with the contract.[97] On the other hand, B had also, *before* replacing the turbines, suffered loss because the cost of operating them was greater than it would have been if they had been in accordance with the contract. This loss was not diminished as a result of the purchase of the new turbines and was accordingly recoverable.[98]

In the *British Westinghouse* case, it was said that a benefit is only taken into account if it is "one arising from the consequences of the breach."[99] It follows from this requirement that damages will not be reduced by reason of any insurance taken out by the injured party against the consequences of the breach[1] (unless the contract provides that the injured party's sole rem-

---

[95] [1912] A.C. 673; *cf. Erie County Natural Gas Co.* v. *Carroll* [1911] A.C. 105; *Levison* v. *Farin* [1978] 2 All E.R. 1149; *Merrett* v. *Capitol Indemnity Corp.* [1991] 1 Lloyd's Rep. 169.

[96] In this respect the case differs from *Bellingham* v. *Dhillon* [1973] Q.B. 304 (a tort case purporting to follow the *British Westinghouse* case).

[97] [1912] A.C. at p. 691.

[98] [1912] A.C. 675, 688.

[99] *Ibid.* at p. 690.

[1] *Cf. Bradburn* v. *Great Western Ry.* (1874) L.R. 10 Ex. 1; *The Yasin* [1979] 2 Lloyd's Rep. 45; *Foxley* v. *Olton* [1965] 2 Q.B. 306 (national assistance); *Hewson* v. *Downs* [1970] 1 Q.B. 73 (state retirement pension); *Basnet* v. *J. & A. Jackson* [1976] I.C.R. 63 (redundancy payment); *McCamley* v. *Cammell Laird Shipbuilders Ltd.* [1990] 1 W.L.R. 963 (voluntary payment from employer for injury at work); *Smoker* v. *London Fire and Civil Defence Authority* [1991] 2 All E.R. 449 (employee's contributory disability pension); contrast *Parsons* v. *B.N.M. Laboratories* [1964] 1 Q.B. 95; and *Nabi* v. *British Leyland (U.K.) Ltd.* [1980] 1 W.L.R. 529 (unemployment benefit); *Gaskill* v. *Preston* [1981] 3 All E.R. 427 (family income supplement); *Plummer* v. *P. W. Wilkins* [1981] 1 W.L.R. 831 and *Lincoln* v. *Hayman* [1982] 1 W.L.R. 488 (supplementary benefit); *Westwood* v. *S. of S. for Employment* [1985] A.C. 20 (unemployment and earnings related benefit); *Hussain* v. *New Taplow Paper Mills* [1988] A.C. 514 (sickness benefit under insurance paid for by employer); *Colledge* v. *Bass Mitchells & Butler Ltd.* [1988] I.C.R. 125 (voluntary payment which would not have been made but for the accident); Administration of Justice Act 1982, s.5; Social Security Act 1989, s.22 (socialy security benefits to be deducted from victim's damages, but to be paid by wrongdoer to Secretary of State); *Beriello* v. *Felixstowe Dock & Ry. Co.* [1989] 1 W.L.R. 695 (payments from foreign State benefit fund which were recoverable by the fund out of the damages). See generally *Parry* v. *Cleaver* [1970] A.C. 1.

edy is to be against the insurer[2]). Nor will damages be reduced merely because the injured party has resold the defective subject-matter for more than the contract price. In *Hussey* v. *Eels*[3] the plaintiffs had been induced to buy a house as their home by a misrepresentation[4] that there had been no subsidence. More than two years later, they decided to demolish the house and resold the site for one and a half times the price which they had paid, having obtained planning permission for two dwellings on the site. On the assumption that this resale yielded a profit[5] to the plaintiffs, it was held that this was not to be taken into account: the wrong which had caused their loss had not also caused the gain as the resale was "not . . . part of a continuous transaction of which the purchase . . . was the inception."[6] Similarly, where a buyer is entitled to damages based on the market price, those damages will not normally be reduced on the ground that he has made a good bargain by buying a substitute below the market price. But if a buyer who has rightfully rejected goods then buys *those very same goods* from the seller below the market (and the contract) price, this fact will be taken into account to reduce or extinguish the seller's liability.[7]

(4) Contributory negligence[8]

Where a plaintiff fails to perform the "duty" to mitigate, his damages are reduced because it can be said that he is at fault in failing to avoid loss. He may also be at fault in the sense of actually helping to bring about the loss or the event causing it. In the law of tort, such conduct is called "contributory negligence." At common law, it in some cases totally barred the plaintiff's tort claim, while in others it was completely ignored, so that he recovered in full. The Law Reform (Contributory Negligence) Act 1945 now provides that, where a person suffers damage as a result partly of his own "fault" and partly of the "fault" of another person, his claim is not to be defeated, but his damages are to be reduced in proportion to his degree of responsibility. Two questions arise for discussion here.

The first is whether *the common law doctrine of contributory negligence* applied in contract at all. Usually it did not,[9] for a contracting party is not bound to guard against breach. He may, indeed, be required to take steps to avoid the consequences of a known breach; but this follows from the rules as to mitigation, or the maxim *volenti non fit injuria*, rather than from the doctrine of contributory negligence. Where, however, a breach of con-

---

2 *Mark Rowlands Ltd.* v. *Berni Inns Ltd.* [1986] Q.B. 211, where the party in breach was a tenant who had paid for the insurance by way of an "insurance rent": hence the normal justification for disregarding insurance moneys (*viz*. that the *injured party* had paid for the insurance) did not apply.

3 [1990] 2 Q.B. 227.

4 Not incorporated in the contract, so that the cause of action was in tort; but the judgment is based on earlier decisions in contract cases.

5 This depended on the cost of comparable accommodation at the time of the resale, as "The plaintiffs were not property speculators but residents:" [1990] 2 Q.B. 227, 233; *cf.* (in tort) *Dominion Mosaics & Tile Co. Ltd.* v. *Trafalgar Trucking Co. Ltd.* [1990] 2 All E.R. 246, 252.

6 [1990] 2 Q.B. 227, 241.

7 *R. Pagnan Fratelli* v. *Corbisa Industrial Agropacaria Ltd.* [1970] 1 W.L.R. 1306; this case differs from the *British Westinghouse* case (which it purports to follow) in that the opportunity to buy the goods more cheaply would never have arisen but for the seller's breach.

8 Williams, *Joint Torts and Contributory Negligence*, § 59, Swanton, 55 A.L.J. 278.

9 *The Shinjitsu Maru* (*No.* 5) [1985] 1 W.L.R. 1270, 1287 (where this was conceded); *cf. The Nogar Marin* [1988] 1 Lloyd's Rep. 412 (where the point was not argued).

tract was also a tort, the doctrine of contributory negligence was not excluded merely because there was a contractual relationship between the parties. Thus a carrier, when sued for negligently injuring a passenger, could no doubt rely on the passenger's contributory negligence.

The second question is whether *the Act of 1945* applies in cases of breach of contract. This depends on the interpretation of the definition of "fault" in the Act as "negligence, breach of statutory duty, or other act or omission which gives rise to liability in tort or would, apart from this Act, give rise to the defence of contributory negligence."[10] It has been argued that this includes *all* negligence, whether contractual[11] or tortious, and all *other* acts giving rise to liability in tort.[12] But the word "other" seems to suggest that negligence is here used in its tortious sense, and this view is supported by the most recent decision on the point.[13]

It does not, however, follow from this interpretation of "fault" that the Act can never apply to cases of breach of contract. Two further distinctions must be drawn. The first is between breaches of contract that are, and those that are not, negligent. Here the phrase "negligent breach of contract" refers to situations in which liability arises for breach of a contractual duty of care[14]—not to cases in which liability for breach of contract is strict,[15] but the breach happens to have been committed negligently.[16] The second distinction is between breaches of contract which also amount to torts and those which do not. The mere fact that a contract has been carelessly broken, and that loss has resulted from the breach, does not, of itself, give rise to liability in tort. For example, where a building sub-contractor had entered into a direct contract with the building owner (and not merely into one with the main contractor[17]) it was held that the relations between the sub-contractor and the owner were governed by the contract alone. It followed that the sub-contractor was liable to the owner only under the contract, and not also under the general law relating to the tort of negligence.[18] But in a number of other situations it has been held that the same careless conduct can give rise to liability under both heads. For example, a careless statement inducing a contract may give rise to liability in tort for misrepresentation and in contract for breach of collateral warranty.[19] The liability of many professional persons for breach of the duties of care that they owe to their clients similarly arises both in contract and

---

[10] s.4. For an extension to include "product liability" see Consumer Protection Act 1987 s.6.
[11] *Infra*, at nn. 14 and 20–21.
[12] Williams, *ubi supra* (n. 8).
[13] *Forsikringsaktieselskapet Vesta* v. *Butcher* [1989] A.C. 852 (CA), affirmed, without reference to this point, *ibid* pp. 880 *et seq.*; Newman, 53 M.L.R. 201.
[14] *Quinn* v. *Burch Bros. (Builders) Ltd.* [1966] 2 Q.B. 370, 378–379 (affd. on other grounds *ibid.* p. 381).
[15] *Cf. ante*, pp. 737–739.
[16] *Quinn* v. *Burch Bros. (Builders) Ltd.*, *supra*, at pp. 378–379.
[17] *Cf. ante*, p. 539.
[18] *Greater Nottingham Co-operative Society Ltd.* v. *Cementation Piling & Foundation Ltd.* [1989] Q.B. 71; *cf. Tai Hing Cotton Mill Ltd.* v. *Liu Chong Hing Bank* [1986] A.C. 80, 107; *Welsh Technical Services* v. *Haden Young* (1987) 37 Build.L.R. 130; *Sonat Offshore S.A.* v. *Amerada Hess Development Co.* [1988] 1 Lloyd's Rep. 145, 159; *Parker-Tweedale* v. *Dunbar Bank plc* [1990] 2 All E.R. 577, 587; *Johnstone* v. *Bloomsbury Health Authority* [1991] I.R.L.R. 118.
[19] *Esso Petroleum Co. Ltd.* v. *Mardon* [1976] Q.B. 801, approved on the point that liability could, on such facts, arise in contract and tort in *The Maira (No. 3)* [1990] 1 A.C. 637, 650 (revsd. on other grounds *ibid.* pp. 672, *et seq.*).

tort.[20] The same is true of duties arising out of a number of other contractual relationships, such as those between carrier and passenger, employer and employee, bailor and bailee, or occupier of premises and visitor.[21] It follows from these distinctions that three categories of cases must be considered in discussing the application of the 1945 Act to cases involving breach of contract.[22]

(i) The defendant without negligence commits a breach of a strict contractual duty; his conduct does not also amount to a tort; and the plaintiff is careless. For example, A contracts with B to repair B's car. In doing the work, A without negligence[23] fits components which are defective. B is injured as a result partly of the defect and partly of his own negligent driving. The Act does not apply: A's conduct, being neither negligent nor an act or omission giving rise to liability in tort, must fall outside the definition of "fault."[24] Hence at common law the result will, in a contract case,[25] depend on which party's conduct caused the loss. Thus in *Lambert* v. *Lewis*[26] a dealer supplied a defective trailer coupling to a customer who

---

20 *Esso Petroleum Co. Ltd.* v. *Mardon* [1976] Q.B. 801, 819 (disapproving on this point *Bagot* v. *Stevens, Scanlan & Co.* [1966] 1 Q.B. 197); *Arenson* v. *Arenson* [1977] A.C. 405, 420–421; *Batty* v. *Metropolitan Realisations Ltd.* [1978] Q.B. 554 (disapproved as to damages in D & F. *Estates Ltd.* v. *Church Commissioners for England* [1989] A.C. 177). *The Zephyr* [1985] 2 Lloyd's Rep. 529, 537; *Dunbar* v. *A. & B. Painters* [1985] 2 Lloyd's Rep. 616, 620 (affirmed [1986] 2 Lloyd's Rep. 38); *Forsikringsaktieselskapet Vesta* v. *Butcher* [1989] A.C. 852, 860 (affirmed on other grounds *ibid.* pp. 880 *et seq.*); *Duncan Stevenson Macmillian* v. *A. W. Knott Becker Scott Ltd.* [1990] 1 Lloyd's Rep. 98, 101; *Islander Trucking Ltd.* v. *Hogg Robinson & Gardner Mountain (Marine) Ltd.* [1990] 1 All E.R. 826; *Murphy* v. *Brentwood D.C.* [1990] 2 All E.R. 908, 918; *The Superhulls Cover Case (No. 2)* [1990] 2 Lloyd's Rep. 431; *Punjab National Bank* v. *De Boinville*, *Financial Times*, February 1, 1991; Jolowicz [1979] C.L.J. 54. There are conflicting authorities on the question whether a solicitor's liability for negligence to his client arises only in contract or also in tort: see *Groom* v. *Crocker* [1939] 1 K.B. 194; *Clark* v. *Kirby-Smith* [1964] Ch. 506, disapproved on this point in *Esso Petroleum Co. Ltd.* v. *Mardon* [1976] Q.B. 801, 819; *Midland Bank Trust Co. Ltd.* v. *Hett, Stubbs & Kemp* [1979] Ch. 384; *D. W. Moore & Co. Ltd.* v. *Ferrier* [1988] 1 W.L.R. 276; *Lee* v. *Thompson* [1989] 2 E.G.L.R. 151; *Bell* v. *Peter Browne & Co.* [1990] 2 Q.B. 495; *Rowe* v. *Turner Hopkins & Co.* [1980] N.Z.L.R. 550; Kaye 100 L.Q.R. 680.

21 *Bagot* v. *Stevens, Scanlan & Co. Ltd.*, *supra*, at pp. 204–205; *cf. Matthews* v. *Kuwait Bechtel Corpn.* [1959] 2 Q.B. 57; *Sayers* v. *Harlow U.D.C* [1958] 1 W.L.R. 623. But where the same facts are alleged to give rise to a claim on contract and in tort, the plaintiff cannot, after failing in contract, succeed by simply reclassifying his claim as one in tort: *Tai Hing Cotton Mill Ltd.* v. *Liu Chong Hing Bank* [1986] A.C. 80, 107; *The Maira (No. 3)* [1990] 1 A.C. 637, 650 (reversed on other grounds *ibid.* pp. 672 *et seq.*); *Reid* v. *Rush and Tompkin Group plc* [1990] 1 W.L.R. 212; *The Good Luck* [1990] 1 Q.B. 818, 900 (revsd. on other grounds, *The Times*, May 17, 1991); *cf. McNerney Lambeth L.B.C.* [1989] N.L.J.R. 114 (no claim in tort at common law where claim for breach of implied covenant under Landlord and Tenant Act 1985, s.11 failed).

22 *Forsikringsaktieselshapet Vesta* v. *Butcher* [1986] 2 All E.R. 488, 508 (affd. without reference to this point [1989] A.C. 852. The Law Commission has provisionally recommended that powers to apportion loss should be available in all these cases: Working Paper 114).

23 This is no defence to an action for breach of contract.

24 *Basildon D.C.* v. *J. E. Lesser Properties* [1985] Q.B. 839 (as explained in *Forsikringsaktieselskapet Vesta* v. *Butcher* [1989] A.C. 852, 865, affirmed *ibid.* pp. 880 *et seq.*, without reference to this point); *The Good Luck* [1990] 1 Q.B. 818, 904; (where the actual decision was that the defendant was not liable under either in contract or in tort, so that the issue of contributory negligence did not arise); *Tenant Radiant Heat Ltd.* v. *Warrington Development Corp.* [1988] E.G.L.R. 41, 43.

25 In tort cases the result depended at common law on the question who had the "last opportunity" of avoiding the accident: see Williams, *op. cit.*, Chap. 9.

26 [1982] A.C. 225.

went on using it after it was obviously broken. Eventually there was an accident when the coupling gave way. It was held that the dealer was not liable to the customer: the accident had been caused by the customer's continued use of the coupling with knowledge of its condition, and not by the fact that it was defective when sold.

(ii) The defendant commits a breach of a contractual duty of care; his conduct does not also amount to a tort, because the relations of the parties are intended to be governed by the contract alone[27]; and the plaintiff is also careless. In *De Meza* v. *Apple*[28] an auditor carelessly made a mistake in completing certain certificates, with the result that the client suffered loss through being underinsured. The client was also careless and his damages were reduced under the Act. The case seems to have been regarded as falling into the present category[29]; but it is equally plausible to say that the auditor's liability for professional negligence arose in both contract and tort.[30] On that view, the case would belong to our third category: this was said to be the position in a more recent case involving a careless insurance broker, and it was further said that the Act would not apply to cases in the second category, where the defendant was liable only in contract but not in tort.[31]

(iii) The defendant commits a breach of a contractual duty of care; his conduct also amounts to a tort; and the plaintiff is also careless. The Act can apply to such a situation: for example, where the plaintiff is injured partly through his own carelessness and partly through circumstances amounting both a breach of contract by the defendant and to a breach of his duties as an occupier of dangerous premises[32]; or where loss is caused partly by the professional negligence of the defendant, amounting both to a breach of contract and to a tort against his client, and partly by that client's own carelessness.[33] There was formerly some support for the view that, even in cases in this category, the Act only applied where the plaintiff framed his claim in tort.[34] But the most recent judicial discussion[35] rightly rejects this view, which is not supported by the definition of "fault" in the

---

27 See n. 18, *supra*.

28 [1974] 1 Lloyd's Rep. 508 (affirmed [1975] 1 Lloyd's Rep. 498 where the applicability of the Act was left open); *Quinn* v. *Burch Bros. (Builders) Ltd.* [1966] 2 Q.B. 370, 380–383.

29 *Forsikringsaktieselskapet Vesta* v. *Butcher* [1986] 2 All E.R. 488, 508, as to which see *infra*, n. 31.

30 *Supra*, n. 20.

31 *Forsikringsaktieselskapet Vesta* v. *Butcher* [1989] A.C. 852, 866 (affirmed without reference to this point *ibid.* pp. 880 *et seq.*) where *De Meza* v. *Apple*, *supra*, n. 28 was cited at p. 861 without disapproval; *Rowe* v. *Turner Hopkins & Co.* [1980] N.Z.L.R. 550.

32 *Sayers* v. *Harlow U.D.C.*, *supra*, n. 21.

33 *Forsikrigsaktieselskapet Vesta* v. *Butcher* [1989] A.C. 852, affirmed without reference to this point *ibid.* pp. 880 *et seq.*; *The Superhulls Cover Case* (*No.* 2) [1990] 2 Lloyd's Rep. 431.

34 *Sole* v. *W. J. Hallt* [1973] Q.B. 574; *The Shinjitsu Maru* (*No.* 5) [1985] 1 W.L.R. 1270; *cf.* *Basildon D.C.* v. *J. E. Lesser* (*Properties*) *Ltd.* [1985] Q.B. 839 849, 30 (as to which see *ante*, p. 873, n. 24); Andrews [1986] C.L.J. 8; Burrows, 101 L.Q.R. 161; Spowart-Taylor, 49 M.L.R. 102.

35 *Forsikringsaktieselskapet Vesta* v. *Butcher*, *supra*; [1989] A.C. 852 (where at p. 875 in the Court of Appeal, Neill L.J. acknowledged the error of his former contrary view in *The Shinjitsu Maru* (*No.* 5), *supra*); *Lipkin Gorman* v. *Karpnale Ltd.* [1989] 1 W.L.R. 1340, 1360 *cf.* *Wheeler* v. *Copas* [1981] 3 All E.R. 405 (where no express reference to the Act is made in the report).

Act, and which would, moreover, be unsatisfactory[36] in enabling a plaintiff to evade the Act by simply suing in contract where he also had a claim in tort. On the other hand the Act would not apply where, though both parties were careless, the court took the view that the loss was entirely caused by the carelessness of one. In *O'Connor* v. *B. D. Kirby & Co.*[37] an insurance broker made a careless misstatement in completing a proposal form on behalf of a client who was also careless in failing to check the form when it was handed to him for signature. The insurance company successfully relied on the misstatement as a defence to a claim on the policy. It was held that the broker was not liable for the loss suffered by the client through being uninsured, since that loss had been entirely "caused" by the client's own carelessness in failing to detect the misstatement.[38]

In the three situations so far discussed, the loss is caused partly by the defendant's breach of contract and partly by the plaintiff's own careless conduct; but that conduct does not amount to a legal wrong against the defendant. Where the loss to each party results in part from a breach of contract committed by one of them and in part from an independent legal wrong committed by the other, the losses may be apportioned (quite apart from the Act) on the ground that they resulted from two independent actionable wrongs. Each party can then recover in respect of his own loss to the extent that it was caused by the other's wrongful act. This was, for example, held to be the case where goods belonging to the tenant of part of a warehouse, and the warehouse itself, were damaged as a result partly of the tenant's breach of covenant to repair and partly of omissions of the landlord giving rise to liability in tort. Each party was held liable for the other's loss to the extent that it had been caused by his own wrong.[39] The position would have been the same if the wrongs of both parties had been breaches of contract[40] *e.g.* if the tenant had undertaken to do internal and the landlord external repairs and the damage had been due to the failure of both to perform their respective undertakings.

It should finally be noted that, in all the situations so far discussed, the defendant's breach of contract is at least *a* cause of the loss. These situations must be distinguished from those in which the defendant's contractual undertaking is to compensate the plaintiff for a loss not brought about by any act or omission on the part of the defendant at all: for example, where a bank issues travellers' cheques to a customer and promised to compensate him for their face value in the event of his losing them. If the loss is due to the customer's failure to guard against loss, the bank may, if the contract so provides,[41] escape liability for the loss; but such cases raise no issues of contributory negligence as the loss is due entirely to the lack of care of the customer.

---

36 This was admitted in *The Shinjitsu Maru* (*No.* 5), *supra*, at p. 1288.

37 [1972] 1 Q.B. 90; *cf. Quinn* v. *Burch Bros.* (*Builders*) *Ltd.* [1966] 2 Q.B. 370; *Mint Security Ltd.* v. *Blair* [1982] 1 Lloyd's Rep. 188, 201.

38 The trial court's view that the client should recover *two thirds* of the loss was described at p. 99 as "somewhat novel."

39 *Tenant Radiant Heat Ltd.* v. *Warrington Development Corp.* [1988] 1 E.G.L.R. 41; distinguished from contributory negligence cases in *The Good Luck* [1990] 1 Q.B. 818, 904 (revsd. on other grounds *The Times*, May 17, 1991).

40 Where each party commits a tort, the outcome was governed at common law by the "last opportunity" rule (*supra* n. 25) and is now governed by the 1945 Act.

41 *Braithwaite* v. *Thomas Cook Travellers Cheques Ltd.* [1989] Q.B. 553; contrast *El Awadi* v. *Bank of Credit and Commerce International S.A.* [1990] 1 Q.B. 606.

(5) Other restrictions

(a) INJURED FEELINGS AND REPUTATION.[42] A plaintiff can sometimes[43] recover damages in tort for injury to his feelings, far exceeding any financial loss suffered by him. In *Hurst* v. *Picture Theatres Ltd.*[44] the plaintiff was forcibly ejected from a cinema seat for which he had paid 6d. He recovered £150 in an action for assault and false imprisonment. In substance this was compensation for the indignity he had suffered.

In a contractual action, the right to recover such damages is restricted by the decision of the House of Lords in *Addis* v. *Gramophone Co. Ltd.*,[45] where a company wrongfully dismissed its manager in a way that was "harsh and humiliating."[46] He recovered damages for loss of salary and commission, but not for the injury to his feelings caused by the manner of his dismissal. One possible justification for the rule is that such injury is not within the contemplation of the parties and is thus too remote; but an employer considering the effects of *such* a dismissal could surely contemplate injury to the employee's feelings. More probably the rule results from a failure to distinguish between punitive damages (which are not generally available in a contractual action) and damages for injured feelings (which are meant to compensate the plaintiff for a loss, though it is not a pecuniary one).[47] In spite of these objections to the rule, it continues to restrict the damages recoverable in an action for wrongful dismissal,[48] at least until it is reconsidered by the House of Lords.

Addis v. *Gramophone Co. Ltd.* is, strictly speaking, an authority only on damages for wrongful dismissal; but it was formerly also considered to support the wider proposition that damages for injured feelings could not be recovered in any contractual action.[49] Such a general proposition has, however, been viewed with increasing scepticism; and it is now subject to many qualifications. First, it is clear that, where a breach of contract causes personal injury, damages can be recovered for pain and suffering.[50] Such an award takes account of the plaintiff's mental anguish and to this extent

---

[42] Jackson, 26 I.C.L.Q. 502.

[43] For a list of such cases, see McGregor, *Damages* (15th ed.), §§ 411–423; Street, *Damages*, p. 31; Ogus, *Damages*, pp. 230–246. They include assault, false imprisonment, malicious prosecution, defamation, deceit (*Archer* v. *Brown* [1985] Q.B. 401), and trespass to land where it is deliberately committed with the intention to molest or annoy: *cf. Wilkes* v. *Wood* (1763) Lofft 1. Such damages are also available for unlawful discrimination under Sex Discrimination Act 1975, s.66(4) and Race Relations Act 1976, s.57(4). *Quaere* whether negligent or innocent torts or torts of strict liability (other than defamation if that can be so classified) give rise to a claim for injury to feelings. By s.1A of the Fatal Accidents Act 1976, as amended by Administration of Justice Act 1982, s.3, damages of up to £7,500 (S.I. 1990 No. 2575) for "bereavement" are available in certain cases in respect of the death of the claimant's spouse or unmarried minor child.

[44] [1915] 1 K.B. 1.

[45] [1909] A.C. 488.

[46] At p. 493.

[47] See *ante*, p. 829; *McCarey* v. *Associated Newspapers Ltd.* [1965] 2 Q.B. 86.

[48] *Shove* v. *Downs Surgical plc* [1984] I.C.R. 532; *Bliss* v. *S.E. Thames Regional Health Authority* [1987] I.C.R. 700, overruling *Cox* v. *Phillips Industries Ltd.* [1976] 1 W.L.R. 638; Carty, 49 M.L.R. 240.

[49] *Cf. Kenny* v. *Preen* [1963] 1 Q.B. 499; *Semble* the conduct of the landlord in this case would now be an offence under Protection from Eviction Act 1977, s.1 (replacing Rent Act 1965, s.30), but breach of that section gave rise at common law to no separate civil claim: *McCall* v. *Abelesz* [1976] Q.B. 585. See now Housing Act 1988, s.27.

[50] *e.g. Godley* v. *Perry* [1960] 1 W.L.R. 9.

includes damages for injured feelings.[51] Moreover, it seems that personal injury can include physical or mental illness resulting from injury to feelings and that damages for such illness can be recovered,[52] so long as they are not too remote. Secondly, damages can be recovered for physical inconvenience. Thus in *Bailey* v. *Bullock*[53] a solicitor who negligently failed to take proceedings for the recovering of his client's house was held liable for the inconvenience (but not the indignity) that the client suffered in having to live for nearly two years with his wife's parents. Obviously no very sharp distinction can be drawn between these two kinds of injury.[54] This is also true of a third (and expanding) group of cases in which damages for distress or vexation have been awarded because one important object of the contract was to provide enjoyment, security, comfort or sentimental benefits, and it was therefore reasonable to award such damages for a breach which defeated that object. Such awards have, for example, been made aginst a travel agent who broke his contract to provide a couple with accommodation for their honeymoon[55]; against a package-tour operator who provided accommodation falling short of the standard promised and so spoilt his client's holiday[56]; against a carrier for breach of a contract to convey guests to a wedding[57]; against a photographer for breach of a contract to take wedding photographs[58]; against a cemetery for breach of a contract to grant exclusive burial rights[59]; against a landlord for breach of his covenant to repair, which left a flat so damp as to make it uninhabitable,[60] and for breach of a covenant for quiet enjoyment where he so abused and terrified the tenants that they left the premises[61]; against a surveyor who negligently failed to draw his client's attention to defects in a house which the client later bought as his home[62]; and against the seller of a new car which broke down and would not restart, so that the buyer suffered "a totally spoilt day comprising nothing but vexation."[63]

In *Addis* v. *Gramophone Co. Ltd.*[64] it was further held that the plaintiff could not recover damages for the loss that he might suffer because the dismissal made it more difficult for him to get another job. But the alleged rule that damages cannot be recovered for loss of employment prospects,

---

51 See *H. West & Sons Ltd.* v. *Shephard* [1964] A.C. 326.

52 *e.g. Chelini* v. *Nieri* 196 P. 2d 915 (1948); and see *post*, p. 879 at n. 77.

53 (1950) 66 T.L.R. (Pt. 2) 791; *Hobbs* v. *London & South Western Ry.* (1875) L.R. 10 Q.B. 111; *Mafo* v. *Adams* [1970] 1 Q.B. 548.

54 *Cf. McCall* v. *Abelesz* [1976] Q.B. 585 (ante, p. 876, n. 49), at p. 594, where "mental upset and distress" and "inconvenience" seem to be used interchangeably.

55 *Cook* v. *Spanish Holiday Tours Ltd.*, *The Times*, Februay 6, 1960.

56 *Jarvis* v. *Swan Tours Ltd.* [1973] Q.B. 233; *cf. Jackson* v. *Horizon Holidays Ltd.* [1975] 1 W.L.R. 1468; *Wings Ltd.* v. *Ellis* [1985] A.C. 272, 287; *Spencer* v. *Cosmos Air Holidays Ltd.*, *The Times*, December 6, 1989; and (in tort) *Ichard* v. *Frangoulis* [1977] 1 W.L.R. 556.

57 *Chandle* v. *East African Airways Corp.* [1964] E.A. 78.

58 *Diesen* v. *Sampson* 1971 S.L.T. (Sh.Ct.) 49.

59 *Reed* v. *Madon* [1989] Ch.408.

60 *Calabar Properties Ltd.* v. *Sticher* [1984] 1 W.L.R. 287; *cf. Inglis* v. *Cant* [1987] C.L.Y. 1132 (delay and defects in renovation of house); *Chiodi* v. *De Marney* [1988] 2 E.G.L.R. 64 (breach of statutory repairing covenant).

61 *Sampson* v. *Floyd* [1989] 2 E.G.L.R. 49.

62 *Perry* v. *Sidney Phillips & Son* [1982] 1 W.L.R. 1287.

63 *Bernstein* v. *Pamson Motors (Golders Green) Ltd.* [1987] 2 All E.R. 220, 231; the case was later compromised when *the manufacturers* agreed to compensate the buyer in full: see (1987) N.L.J. 1194.

64 [1909] A.C. 488.

or for injury to reputation, is again hard to justify. There are now many situations in which such damages can be awarded. First, a trader can recover damages for injury to his business reputation, *e.g.* if his reputation suffers because his bank wrongfully refuses to honour his cheques[65] or because his wholesaler supplies him with defective goods[66]; on the same principle a travel agent can recover damages for loss of "goodwill" from a shipowner who breaks his contract to supply accommodation for passengers on a pleasure cruise.[67] Secondly, an actor or author can recover damages for "loss of publicity," that is, for loss of the chance to enhance his reputation,[68] though not for injury to his existing reputation.[69] Thirdly, an apprentice who is wrongfully dismissed before the end of his period of training can recover damages for diminution of his future prospects, since "the very object of an apprenticeship agreement is to enable the apprentice to fit himself to get better employment."[70] Fourthly, a person who is wrongfully expelled from a trade union can recover damages for the resulting loss of employment opportunities.[71] Finally, it has been suggested that the alleged rule that damages are not available for injury to reputation should not apply where the contract "had as its purpose, or one of its purposes, the protection of the claimant against the sort of damage suffered."[72] Thus damages of this kind were said to be recoverable for breach of a contract not to broadcast a programme concerning the activities of the plaintiffs until after the publication of a report concerning those activities.[73]

There is a separate rule that damages cannot be recovered for the "anxiety" which a breach of contract may cause to the injured party.[74] The rule is a perfectly sensible one, for anxiety is an almost inevitable concomitant of expectations based on promises, so that a contracting party must be deemed to take the risk of it. Damages for anxiety or mental stress cannot, in particular, be recovered for breach of a contract made in the course of, or in connection with, a business and resulting in the failure of that business.[75] Such damages can, however, be recovered if the very purpose of the contract is to secure relief from an existing state of anxiety, *e.g.* where a

---

[65] *Rolin* v. *Steward* (1854) 14 C.B. 595. A person who is *not* a trader cannot in such a case recover *general* damages for loss of reputation, but only *special* damages for loss proved to have resulted from the bank's breach: see *Gibbons* v. *Westminster Bank Ltd.* [1939] 2 K.B. 882; *Rae* v. *Yorkshire Bank*, [1988] F.L.R. 1.

[66] *Cointat* v. *Myham & Son* [1913] 2 K.B. 220.

[67] *Anglo-Continental Holidays Ltd.* v. *Typaldos Lines* (*London*) *Ltd.* [1967] 2 Lloyd's Rep. 61.

[68] *Herbert Clayton & Jack Waller Ltd.* v. *Oliver* [1930] A.C. 209; *Joseph* v. *National Magazine Co. Ltd.* [1959] Ch. 14; *Malcolm* v. *Chancellor, Masters and Scholars of the University of Oxford*, *The Times*, December 19, 1990.

[69] *Withers* v. *General Theatre Corp. Ltd.* [1933] 2 K.B. 536.

[70] *Dunk* v. *George Waller & Sons Ltd.* [1970] 2 Q.B. 163.

[71] *Edwards* v. *SOGAT* [1971] Ch. 354, 378–379.

[72] *Cambridge Nutrition Ltd.* v. *B.B.C.* [1990] 3 All E.R. 523, 540.

[73] *Cambridge Nutrition* case, *supra*.

[74] *Cook* v. *Swinfen* [1967] 1 W.L.R. 457; *Hutchinson* v. *Harris* (1978) 10 Build L.R. 19; *Reed* v. *Madon* [1989] Ch. 408, 426. In *Kemp* v. *Sober* (1851) 1 Sim. (N.S.) 517 (where the running of a girls' school in breach of covenant was restrained) Lord Cranworth said at p. 520: "The feeling of anxiety is damage." But the better explanation is that an injunction to restrain breach of a negative stipulation can be granted *without* proof of damage: *Tipping* v. *Eckersley* (1855) 2 K. & J. 254; *Doherty* v. *Allman* (1878) 3 App.Cas. 709, 729; *post*, p. 919.

[75] *Hayes* v. *James & Charles Dodd* [1990] 2 All E.R. 815; Soh, 105 L.Q.R. 43.

solicitor in breach of contract fails to take necessary steps in non-molestation proceedings, so that the molestation of his client continues.[76] Moreover, if actual mental illness results from anxiety, damages can be recovered in respect of it, so long as it is not too remote.[77]

(b) NON-PAYMENT OF MONEY. The general rule of common law was that interest could not be recovered as damages for failure to pay a debt when due. This rule applied both where the debtor wholly failed to pay and was sued for the debt, and where he paid voluntarily but after the due day.[78] At common law,[79] interest could be awarded only if the debt arose out of a mercantile security or, there was an agreement to pay interest[80] in the events which had happened.[81] Since 1833 the courts have by statute had a discretionary power to award interest when giving judgment for a debt or damages[82]; and more recently they have been empowered to award interest where proceedings are brought for recovery of a debt and the defendant pays the debt before judgment.[83] The court in exercising this discretion will look at the overall position of the injured party in consequence of the breach. Thus if he retains the inome of property sold till payment, the court will not award him interest on the price, for this would amount to allowing double recovery.[84]

The statutory discretion to award interest is subject to a number of limitations. If the contract has been rescinded by the injured party before payment under it from the party in breach has become due, no action for *debt* will be available to the injured party[85]; and in such a case the statutory power to award interest will be exercisable only in relation to the *damages* to which that party is entitled.[86] This is a significant restriction: the damages suffered on a purchaser's default in completing a contract for the sale of a house are prima facie the difference between the contract price and the proceeds of resale,[87] a much smaller sum than the contract price. The statutory power to award interest does not moreover, extend to the case where an overdue debt is paid *before* any proceedings for recovery of the debt have begun. Nor do the relevant statutory provisions enable the courts to award *more* than interest; and at common law the general rule

---

[76] *Heywoodv. Wellers* [1976] Q.B. 446; *Dickinson* v. *James Alexander & Co.* (1990) 20 Fam.L. 137.

[77] *Cook* v. *Swinfen*, *supra*; *Esso Petroleum Co. Ltd.* v. *Mardon* [1976] Q.B. 801, 822; *Attia* v. *British Gas plc* [1988] Q.B. 304 (where it is not clear whether the claim was in contract or in tort).

[78] *London, Chatham & Dover Ry.* v. *South Eastern Ry.* [1893] A.C. 429; *La Pintada* [1985] A.C. 104; *Alex Lawrie Factors Ltd.* v. *Modern Injection Moulds Ltd.* [1981] 3 All E.R. 658, 683; *The Lips* [1988] A.C. 395, 423; *Janred Properties Ltd.* v. *Ente Nazionale Italiano per il Turismo* [1989] 2 All E.R. 444, 456.

[79] Interest could be awarded by way of ancillary relief in equity, and on damages and on salvage in Admiralty: see *La Pintada* [1985] A.C. 104, 115.

[80] *Higgins* v. *Sargent* (1823) 2 B. & C. 348.

[81] See *Janred Properties Ltd.* v. *Ente Nazionale Italiano per il Turismo* [1989] 2 All E.R. 444 (where the event on which interest was to be paid was held not to have occurred).

[82] See now s.35A(1) of the Supreme Court Act 1981, as amended by Administration of Justice Act 1982, s.12 and Sched. I, Part I. Parts II and IV of the Schedule confer the same powers on county courts and arbitrators; see Practice Direction [1983] 1 All E.R. 934.

[83] Supreme Court Act 1981, *supra*, s. 35A(3); for power to award interest *on damages* under s. 35A, see *Edmunds* v. *Lloyds Italico, etc.* [1986] 1 W.L.R. 492.

[84] *Janred Properties Ltd.* v. *Ente Nazionale Italiano per il Turismo* [1989] 2 All E.R. 444, 456.

[85] *Ante*, p. 748.

[86] *Janred Properties* case, *supra*, n. 84.

[87] *Ante*, p. 843.

was formerly thought to be that a debtor who defaulted was not liable for any further loss (beyond the interest available under the rules just stated) even though he knew that the creditor would be ruined by his default.[88] Over 100 years ago this rule was described by Jessell M.R. as "not quite consistent with reason"[89]; and its scope is now considerably restricted by reference to two distinctions. The first is that between claims for interest and claims for other types of loss; the second is that between "general" and "special" damages. The later distinction is, in turn, used (in the present context) in two senses.[90] In the first sense, "general" damages are those recoverable under the first rule in *Hadley* v. *Baxendale*,[91] while "special" damages are those recoverable under the second rule in that case; in the second sense, "general" damages are those which can be recovered without proof of loss, while "special" damages are those which can be recovered only as compensation for loss actually shown by the plaintiff to have been suffered.[92]

Claims for interest are prima facie claims for "general" damages in both these senses: loss of interest clearly arises (in the words of the first rule in *Hadley* v. *Baxendale*) "according to the usual course of things from such breach of contract itself"[93]; and, under the statutory provisions described above an award of interest can be made without proof that any loss of interest has been suffered. In *The Lips*[94] the House of Lords had limited the general common law rule (that interest was not normally recoverable as damages for delay in payment) to claims for interest by way of "general" damages in the two senses just described. It follows that damages for loss of interest can be recovered if the plaintiff can show (i) that such loss has actually been suffered, and (ii) that this loss was at the time of contracting within the reasonable contemplation of the defendant, so as to satisfy the second rule in *Hadley* v. *Baxendale*.[95] For example, in *Wadsworth* v. *Lydall*[96] the defendant was late in making a payment of £10,000 due to the plaintiff and needed by him (as the defendant knew) for completing the purchase of a farm as his home. As a result, the plaintiff incurred interest (and other) charges; and it was held that these were recoverable as damages for late payment. It should be noted that the interest recovered in this way was interest *incurred* by the plaintiff: not interest *forgone* by him. It is the later type of loss which is irrecoverable at common law even though it occurred (as it normally does) "according to the usual order of things" within the fist rule in *Hadley* v. *Baxendale*.

According to *The Lips*, the common law rule precluding recovery of

---

88 *Fletcher* v. *Tayleur* (1855) 17 C.B. 21, 29; *Williams* v. *Reynolds* (1865) 6 B. & S. 495, 506; *British Columbia Saw-Mill Co. Ltd.* v. *Nettleship* (1868) L.R. 3 C.P. 499, 506.
89 *Wallis* v. *Smith* (1882) 21 Ch.D. 243, 257; Mann, 101 L.Q.R. 30; *Jobson* v. *Johnson* [1989] 1 W.L.R. 1026, 1041.
90 *International Minerals & Chemical Corp.* v. *Karl O. Helm A.G.* [1986] 1 Lloyd's Rep. 81, 103.
91 *Ante*, p. 858.
92 *International Mineral & Chemical Corp.* v. *Karl O. Helm A.G.* [1986] 1 Lloyd's Rep. 81, 103.
93 *Hadley* v. *Baxendale* (1854) 9 Exch. 341, 354.
94 [1988] A.C. 395, 423, 429.
95 *Ante*, p. 860; *International Minerals & Chemical Corp.* v. *Karl O. Helm A.G.* [1981] 1 Lloyd's Rep. 81, 103–105; *Knibb* v. *N.C.B.* [1987] Q.B. 906, 913; *Dods* v. *Coopers Creek Vinyards* [1987] N.Z.L.R. 530.
96 [1981] 1 W.L.R. 598; approved in *La Pintada*.

interest applies *only* to claims *for interest* as damages for late payment of money.[97] Claims for other losses suffered as a result of late payment are therefore not affected by the rule; and such claims are claims "special" damages in the sense that they can succeed only if the plaintiff proves his loss. On the other hand, such losses "are subject to the same rules as apply to claims for damages for breach of contract generally,"[98] so that damages in respect of such losses can be recovered if *either* rule in *Hadley* v. *Baxendale* is satisfied: they do not have to be "special" in the first of the two senses distinguished above, *i.e.* in the sense of falling within the *second* rule of remoteness laid down in that case. For example, late payment of money due in a foreign currency may cause loss to the plaintiff because of exchange rate fluctations. Such loss is recoverable even if only the first (and not the second) rule in *Hadley* v. *Baxendale* is satisfied.[99]

Where the plaintiff can show that he has suffered loss (other than interest) as a result of the defendant's failure to pay money when due, he will have suffered "special" damage in our second sense (*i.e.* of loss actually proved). Many cases in which the courts have awarded damages can now be explained by saying that the damages were "special" in this sense, and that, being claims for damages other than interest, they were subject only to the ordinary rules of remoteness. Such damages can be recovered from a banker who wrongfully repudiates liability, or delays in making payments due, under a letter of credit,[1] or who wrongfully fails to honour a customer's cheque[2] from a buyer of goods who fails to provide a confirmed credit in accordance with the terms of the contract of a sale[3] from a person who breaks a contract to subscribe for debentures in a company or who fails to pay calls on shares[4] from a hire-purchaser or instalment buyer whose wrongful failure to pay instalments amounts to a repudiation of the contract[5] and perhaps from any person who breaks a contract to lend or advance money.[6]

The decision in *Wadsworth* v. *Lydall*,[7] and the restriction in *The Lips* of the original common law rule to claims for interest by way of general damages, are welcome developments: they both recognise and mitigate the unsatisfactory nature of that rule as it was formerly understood.[8] But even after the statutory and common law developments so far described, we are left with the rule that interest cannot generally be recovered as "general" damages from a debtor who pays late, but before proceedings for recovery of the debt have been begun. This rule was criticised in the very case in

---

97 [1988] A.C. 395, 424.
98 *Ibid.*
99 *Ibid.*; *International Minerals & Chemical Corp.* v. *Karl O. Helm A.G.* [1986] 1 Lloyd's Rep. 81.
1 *Prehn* v. *Royal Bank of Liverpool* (1870) L.R. 5 Ex. 92; *Larios* v. *Bonany y Gurety* (1873) L.R. 5 P.C. 346; *Urquhart Lindsay & Co.* v. *Eastern Bank Ltd.* [1922] 1 K.B. 318; *Ozalid Group (Export) Ltd.* v. *African Continental Bank Ltd.* [1979] 2 Lloyd's Rep. 231.
2 *Rolin* v. *Steward* (1854) 14 C.B. 595.
3 *Trans Trust S.P.R.L.* v. *Danubian Trading Co. Ltd.* [1952] 2 Q.B. 297; *ante*, p. 662.
4 *Wallis Chlorine Syndicate Ltd.* v. *American Alkali Co. Ltd.* (1901) 17 T.L.R. 565.
5 *Yeoman Credit Ltd.* v. *Waragowski* [1961] 1 W.L.R. 1124, 1128; *Overstone Ltd.* v. *Shipway* [1962] 1 W.L.R. 117; *Urquhart Lindsay & Co.* v. *Eastern Bank Ltd.* [1922] 1 K.B. 318, 323; *cf.* pp. 748–749, *ante*.
6 See Sedgwick, *Damages* (9th ed.), s.622; Corbin, *Contracts*, § 1065.
7 [1981] 1 W.L.R. 598.
8 See *ante*, p. 880 at nn. 88 and 89.

which the House of Lords first recognised its existence[9]; and that criticism was repeated when the House of Lords in 1984 reluctantly recognised the continued existence of the rule.[10] In times of high inflation or high interest rates, the rule can cause real hardship to a creditor; and it cannot be justified by reference to any of the general principles governing damages for breach of contract. No doubt the creditor can protect himself by expressly stipulating for interest. But although such stipulations will generally be made in contracts for the loan of money, they are less likely to be found in contracts for the supply of goods or services on credit. In one case where such a contract contained no such express stipulation the court nevertheless construed the contract as containing a promise to pay interest.[11] The decision is a further (and welcome) indication of the courts' dislike of the rule. Its abolition was recommended by the Law Commission[12]; but in view of Parliament's failure to implement this recommendation when it last had the matter under consideration,[13] the House of Lords has decided that it could not reverse the rule by judicial decision.[14]

The discussion so far has been concerned with damages for late payment of a *debt*. This must be contrasted with the problem which arises where a defendant incurs liability in damages and unjustifiably delays in paying those damages. In such cases there is a statutory power to award interest on damages,[15] but there is "no such thing as a cause of action in damages for late payment of damages."[16] This may be true even if the damages are a fixed sum payable under a valid liquidated damages clause.[17] Such a clause does not necessarily fix the *time* when the payment is to be made; and where no such time is fixed, late payment is not a breach of contract. Where the clause fixes both the amount payable and the time of payment, it seems that special damages for late payment can be recovered, subject to the usual tests of remoteness.[18]

(c) FAILURE TO MAKE TITLE TO LAND. A special rule formerly governed the damages recoverable by a purchaser of land if the contract went off through a defect in the vendor's title. In *Bain* v. *Fothergill*,[19] the House of Lords held that the purchaser could only get damages in respect of his expenses in investigating the title. He could not get damages for loss of his bargain or for expenses incurred otherwise than in investigating the title.

---

9 *London, Chatham & Dover Ry.* v. *South Eastern Ry.* [1893] A.C. 429, 437 (*per* Lord Herschell L.C.); Mann, 101 L.Q.R. 30.

10 *La Pintada* [1985] A.C. 104; Bowles and Whelan, 48 M.L.R. 235. As the principal debt was paid after arbitration proceedings had commenced, interest could now be awarded on the facts of the case under the provisions of Administration of Justice Act 1982, s.15 and Sched. I Pt. I; but at the relevant time those provisions were not yet in force.

11 *F. G. Minter* v. *Welsh Health Technical Services Organization* (1980) 13 Build. L.R. 1. Contrast *Alsabah Maritime Services* v. *Philippine International Shipping Corp.* [1984] 1 Lloyd's Rep. 291 where a provisions in an agency agreement that "no other *charges* will be made . . . " was held to exclude *interest*.

12 *Report on Interest* (Law Com. 88) paras. 35–44.

13 *Other* parts of the Law Commission's Report (*supra*) were implemented by Administration of Justice Act 1982, s.15 and Sched. I Pt. I, *ante*, p. 879, n. 82.

14 *La Pintada* [1985] A.C. 104.

15 See *ante*, p. 879, nn. 82 and 83.

16 *The Lips* [1988] A.C. 395, 425; *Ramwade Ltd.* v. *W. J. Emson & Co. Ltd.*, [1987] R.T.R. 72; *The Arras and Hoegh Rover* [1989] 1 Lloyd's Rep. 131.

17 This was the position in *The Lips, supra.*

18 *The Lips* [1988] A.C. 395, 427.

19 (1874) L.R. 7 H.L. 158.

The rule was subjected to much criticism[20] and its scope was limited by a number of significant exceptions. These no longer call for discussion now that the rule has been abolished by section 3 of the Law of Property (Miscellaneous Provisions) Act 1989 in relation to contracts made after September 27, 1990. It remains possible for the vendor by the terms of the contract to limit his liability for breach by reason of a defect in his title. Such a term would not be affected by the Unfair Contract Terms Act 1977 (a) in the case of a private sale, because the vendor's liability would not be "business liability"[21]; and (b) in the case of a sale in the course of a business (*e.g.* by a property developer) because the relevant provisions[22] of the Act do not apply to "any contract so far as it relates to the creation or transfer of an interest in land."[23] A term excluding or restricting the vendor's liability for making a misrepresentation as to his title could, however, be ineffective if it did not satisfy the requrement of reasonableness imposed by section 3 of the Misrepresentation Act 1967.[24]

4. Damages Fixed by Contract

A contract may provide for the payment of a fixed sum on breach. Such a provision may serve the perfectly proper purpose of enabling a party to know in advance what his liability will be; and of avoiding difficult questions of quantification and remoteness. On the other hand the courts are reluctant to allow a party, under such a provision, to recover a sum which is obviously and considerably greater than his loss. They have therefore divided such provisions into two categories: penalty clauses, which are invalid, and liquidated damages clauses, which will generally be upheld.

(1) Distinction between penalty and liquidated damages

A clause is penal if it provides for "a payment of money stipulated as *in terrorem* of the offending party"[25] to force him to perform the contract. If, on the other hand, the clause is a genuine attempt by the parties to estimate in advance the loss which will result from the breach, it is a liquidated damages clause. This is so even though the stipulated sum is not precisely equivalent to the injured party's loss. It seems that, if the stipulated sum is a genuine pre-estimate of the *actual* loss, the clause is valid even though part of that loss is *irrecoverable* because it is too remote.[26]

The question whether a clause is penal or a pre-estimate of damages depends on its construction and on the surrounding circumstances at the time of contracting (not at the time of breach).[27] The fact that the payment is described in the contract as a "penalty" or as "liquidated damages" is relevant, but not decisive.[28] Clauses in identical terms may be held penal

---

20 As long ago as *Day* v. *Singleton* [1899] 2 Ch. 320, 329 ("anomalous"); see generally Law Com. No. 166.

21 Unfair Contract Terms Act 1977, s.1(3); *ante*, p. 226.

22 *i.e.* those of s.3, *ante*, p. 231.

23 *Ibid.* s.1(2) and Sched. 1 para. 1(b); *ante*, p. 241.

24 As amended by Unfair Contract Terms Act 1977, s.8; *ante*, p. 345.

25 *Dunlop Pneumatic Tyre Co. Ltd.* v. *New Garage & Motor Co. Ltd.* [1915] A.C. 79, 86.

26 *Robophone Facilities Ltd.* v. *Blank* [1966] 1 W.L.R. 1428, 1448.

27 *Dunlop Pneumatic Tyre Co. Ltd.* v. *New Garage & Motor Co. Ltd.* [1915] A.C. 79, 87.

28 *Kemble* v. *Farren* (1829) 6 Bing. 141 ("liquidated damages" held penalty); *Elphinstone* v. *Monkland Iron & Coal Co. Ltd.* (1886) 11 App.Cas. 332 ("penalty" held liquidated damages); *cf. Pagnan & Fratelli* v. *Coprosol S.A.* [1981] 1 Lloyd's Rep. 283.

or not, according to the subject-matter of the contracts and to the circumstances in which the contracts were made.[29]

In *Dunlop Pneumatic Tyre Co. Ltd.* v. *New Garage & Motor Co. Ltd.*[30] Lord Dunedin formulated four rules of construction:

(a) "It will be held to be a penalty if the sum stipulated for is extravagant and unconscionable in amount in comparison with the greatest loss that could conceivably be proved to have followed from the breach": to quote a rather far-fetched example, a clause in a contract to do building work worth £50 would be penal if it provided that the builder should pay £1 million if he failed to do the work.[31]

(b) "It will be held to be a penalty if the breach consists only[32] in not paying a sum of money, and the sum stipulated is a sum greater than the sum which ought to have been paid." A clause making a debtor liable to pay £1,000 if he failed to pay £50 on the due day would thus be penal. One explanation formerly given for this rule was that the only amount recoverable, as damages for failure to pay money when due, was interest, when available by statute or by special agreement[33]; but this reasoning is no longer convincing now that it is clear that *special* damages can be recovered for loss caused by such a breach.[34] Alternatively, it was suggested that the rule was based on an equitable jurisdiction to reform unconscionable bargains[35]; but this explanation, too, is suspect, for the rule applies even though the contract is fair. Thus in *Betts* v. *Burch*[36] a contract for the sale of the furniture and stock-in-trade of a public-house at a valuation provided that if either party defaulted he should pay the other £50. The court regarded this as a perfectly fair bargain but felt bound to hold the clause penal because the buyer would have to pay £50 even if he defaulted in payment of only £1.

Where the bargain is a fair one, the courts are reluctant to apply the present rule. One way of escape is by narrow construction of the clause alleged to be penal. In *Wallis* v. *Smith*[37] £5,000 was payable "on any substantial breach" of a contract to develop land as a building estate; one of the terms of the contract was that the defendant should pay £500 on signing the agreement. When the defendant wholly repudiated the contract, the plaintiff successfully claimed the £5,000. The court was able to escape from the present rule by holding that failure to pay the £500 was not a "substantial" breach.

The rule does not apply merely because a contract under which a sum of money is payable in instalments provides that, on default of any payment,

---

[29] Contrast *Phonographic Equipment* (1958) *Ltd.* v. *Muslu* [1961] 1 W.L.R. 1379 with *Lombank Ltd.* v. *Excell* [1964] 1 Q.B. 415.

[30] [1915] A.C. 79, 87–88.

[31] Example given in *Clydebank Engineering Co.* v. *Don Jose Ramos Isquierdo y Castaneda* [1905] A.C. 6, 10, *per* Lord Halsbury L.C.

[32] See *Thos. P. Gonzales Corp.* v. *F. R. Waring (International) Pty. Ltd.* [1980] 2 Lloyd's Rep. 160, 163 (rule inapplicable where breach consists of buyer's failure to *accept and* pay).

[33] [1915] A.C. at p. 87.

[34] *Ante*, pp. 880–881.

[35] [1915] A.C. at p. 87.

[36] (1859) 4 H. & N. 506. This case was decided in a common law court before the Judicature Acts 1873–75; but the same rule was recognised, if reluctantly, in the Chancery Division after 1875: *Wallis* v. *Smith* (1882) 21 Ch.D. 243.

[37] (1882) 21 Ch.D. 243.

the whole balance is to become immediately due.[38] Such a clause is said to accelerate, and not to increase, the liability of the debtor. But early payment in fact is generally more expensive to the debtor; and a provision for an extra payment equal in value to this expense would be undeniably penal.[39] In strict logic, such acceleration clauses should therefore fall within Lord Dunedin's second rule; the fact that they have been held not to do so is a further indication of the courts' reluctance to apply that rule. The parties can also circumvent this rule by providing that a high sum is to be paid as the contract price, subject to a discount if payment is made by a specified date; or for providing for the payment to be made by a third party under a performance bond.[40] These provisions for acceleration, for discounts, and for payments by third parties may be perfectly fair; and the relative ease with which Lord Dunedin's second rule can, by use of them, be evaded suggests that it serves no useful purpose and should be abandoned. Cases of real extortion could still be dealt with under Lord Dunedin's first rule; and it seems that under this rule an acceleration clause may be penal.[41]

(c) There is a presumption (but no more than a presumption) that a clause is penal when "a single lump sum is made payable . . . on the occurrence of one or more or all of several events, some of which may occasion serious and others but trifling damage." Under this rule, a sum is not presumed to be penal if it is expressly proportioned to the seriousness of the breach, *e.g.* if a lease provides for payment of £100 *per acre*[42] for land not restored to its former condition, or if a contractor agrees to pay £500 *per week* for delay.[43] Such stipulations are only penal if extravagant.

On the other hand, a sum payable on one of several events will be treated as penal if one of those events is the non-payment of a smaller sum,[44] or if one event is *bound* to cause greater loss than another.[45] A sum may, therefore, be regarded as penal if it *might* have become due on a trifling breach, even though the breach which *actually* occurred was quite a serious one, and one for which the sum could be regarded as a genuine pre-estimate.[46] In this way, the rule can invalidate perfectly fair bargains. The courts will do their best to avoid such results by construing the contract so as to make the sum payable only on major breaches, for which it is a valid

---

38 *Protector Loan Co.* v. *Grice* (1880) 5 Q.B.D. 529; *Wallingford* v. *Mutual Society* (1880) 5 App.Cas. 685; *cf. Sport International Bussum B.V.* v. *Inter-Footwear Ltd.* [1984] 1 W.L.R. 776, 793, and *White & Carter (Councils) Ltd.* v. *McGregor* [1962] A.C. 413, where it was conceded that the acceleration clause was valid; *The Angelic Star* [1988] 1 Lloyd's Rep. 122; contrast *O'Dea* v. *Allstates Leasing Systems (W.A.) Pty. Ltd.* (1983) 57 A.L.J.R. 172; Muir, 10 Sydney L.R. 503.

39 A stipulation for accelerated payment of a loan *plus interest* for the whole contractual period was said to be penal in *The Angelic Star* [1988] 1 Lloyd's Rep. 122, 125.

40 *Post*, p. 888.

41 This seems to be the best explanation for *Wadham Stringer Finance Ltd.* v. *Meany* [1981] 1 W.L.R. 39, 48, where such a clause was said to be subject to the rules as to penalties, though not penal in effect.

42 *Elphinstone* v. *Monkland Iron & Coal Co.* (1886) 11 App.Cas. 332.

43 *Clydebank Engineering* case [1905] A.C. 6. Such a provision will not operate where the contract is totally abandoned (since otherwise the payments would have to go on for ever): *British Glanzstoff Mfg. Co.* v. *General Accident, etc. Co.* [1913] A.C. 143.

44 As in *Kemble* v. *Farren* (1829) 6 Bing. 141.

45 *Wilson* v. *Love* [1896] 1 Q.B. 626 (on such facts, see now Agricultural Holdings Act 1986, s.24); *cf. post*, p. 890.

46 *Ariston S.R.L.* v. *Charly Records Ltd.*, *Financial Times*, March 21, 1990.

pre-estimate.[47] Even where this construction is not possible, it is submitted that the validity of the clause should depend on what is likely to be its normal operation. It should not be struck down merely because, in extraordinary circumstances (which have not in fact occurred), the stipulated sum might greatly exceed the plaintiff's loss.[48]

(d) "It is no obstacle to the sum stipulated being a genuine pre-estimate of damage that the consequences of breach are such as to make precise pre-estimation an impossibility. On the contrary, that is just the situation when pre-estimated damage was the true bargain between the parties." Thus in *Dunlop Pneumatic Tyre Co. Ltd.* v. *New Garage & Motor Co. Ltd.* itself the defendants bought tyres from the plaintiffs and agreed that they would not (i) tamper with the manufacturer's marks; (ii) sell to the public below list price; (iii) sell to any person "suspended" by the plaintiffs; (iv) exhibit or export the tyres without the plaintiff's written consent. They further agreed to pay £5 to the plaintiffs for every tyre sold or offered in breach of the agreement. The defendants sold to the public below list price. It was held that the provision for payment of £5 per tyre was not penal. The presumption that a sum payable on several events was penal was "rebutted by the very fact that the damage caused by each and every one of those events, however varying in importance, [was] of such an uncertain nature that it cannot be accurately ascertained."[49] But even in such circumstances the sum will be penal if it is extravagant.[50]

(2) Effects of the distinction

Often the stipulated sum will exceed the plaintiff's loss. In such a case, the plaintiff can nevertheless recover that sum if the stipulation is a liquidated damages clause, while if it is a penalty he cannot recover the stipulated sum but only the amount to which he would have been entitled if the contract had not contained the penalty clause.[51] This follows from the nature of the distinction between the two kinds of provision. Two further possibilities, however, require discussion.

First, a clause may be intended to provide for payment of a sum below the estimated loss. Such a clause is not invalid as a penalty as its object is not to act *in terrorem*. In *Cellulose Acetate Silk Co. Ltd.* v. *Widnes Foundry (1925) Ltd.*[52] a contract for the construction of an acetone recovery plant provided that if completion was delayed the contractors were to pay "by way of penalty £20 per working week." The plant was completed 30 weeks late, during which period the owners suffered losses of £5,850. It was held that they could recover £600 only. Both parties must have known that the actual loss would exceed £20 per week, so that one object of the clause was to limit the contractors' liability. But it was not a pure limitation clause, for the contractors would still have had to pay £20 per week even if the owners

---

47 *Webster* v. *Bosanquet* [1912] A.C. 394; *cf. ante*, p. 884 at n. 37.
48 See *International Leasing Corp. (Vic.) Ltd.* v. *Aiken* (1966) 85 W.N. (Pt. 1) N.S.W. 766.
49 [1915] A.C. 79, 96; *cf. Robophone Facilities Ltd.* v. *Blank* [1966] 1 W.L.R. 1428. For the now discarded view that a sum payable on several different events was necessarily penal, see *Astley* v. *Weldon* (1801) 2 B. & P. 346.
50 *Ford Motor Co. (England) Ltd.* v. *Armstrong* (1915) 31 T.L.R. 267.
51 *Jobson* v. *Johnson* [1989] 1 W.L.R. 1026, 1038.
52 [1933] A.C. 20.

had lost less.[53] For this reason, liquidated damages clauses are probably not subject to the Unfair Contract Terms Act 1977.[54]

Secondly, the clause may be a penalty even though the stipulated sum falls short of the plaintiff's loss.[55] This apparently paradoxical situation can arise *either* because changing conditions have made an originally extravagant sum inadequate, *or* because a perfectly reasonable sum is nevertheless penal on technical grounds (*i.e.* under the second or third rules of construction stated above).[56] The question then arises whether the clause is nevertheless effective to limit the defendant's liability to the amount of the penalty. According to one view, the clause is effective for this purpose; for penalty clauses are struck down to prevent oppression and the party in breach cannot be oppressed by the clause when it actually works in his favour.[57] But this view can cut across the general principle that the validity of contractual provisions should be determined once for all by reference to the time of contracting[58]; for under it a clause which was originally invalid as a penalty could become valid as a limitation simply by reason of a change of circumstances. Hence in *Wall* v. *Rederiaktiebolaget Lugudde*[59] it was held that a shipowner could disregard a penalty clause in a charterparty and sue for his actual loss, which exceeded the amount of the penalty. In the *Widnes Foundry* case the question whether a penalty clause could always be disregarded in this way was left open as it is possible for a clause on its true construction to be both a penalty and a limitation clause. But this is an implausible construction of a clause which provides for payment of a fixed sum irrespective of proof of loss; and it seems that generally such a clause would be disregarded under the rule in *Wall's* case.

(3) Analogous provisions

The penalty clauses with which the foregoing discussion is concerned are all stipulations for the payment of *money*. It is equally possible for a clause which requires some other performance from the party in breach to be a penalty. This could, for example, be the position where the clause required that party to make a "payment in kind," or to transfer shares at an undervalue.[60]

A number of other commonly found contractual provisions resemble penalties in their commercial purpose of putting pressure on a party to perform, but are nevertheless valid. This is, for example, true of acceleration clauses, of discounts for punctual payment[61] and of express provisions for termination on breach[62]; it is also sometimes true of provisions as to the

---

[53] *Ante*, p. 219.
[54] *Ante*, p. 227.
[55] Hudson, 90 L.Q.R. 30; Gordon, *ibid.* 296; Hudson, 91 L.Q.R. 20; Barton, 92 L.Q.R. 20.
[56] *Ante*, pp. 884–885.
[57] *Elsley* v. *J. G. Collins Insurance Agencies* (1978) 3 D.L.R. (3d) 1; Hudson, 101 L.Q.R. 480.
[58] *Ante*, pp. 236, 401, 883.
[59] [1915] 3 K.B. 66 (not cited in the *Elsley* case, *supra*); *cf. Dingwall* v. *Burnett* 1912 S.C. 1097; *W. & J. Investments Ltd.* v. *Bunting* [1984] 1 N.S.W.R. 331.
[60] *Jobson* v. *Johnson* [1989] 1 W.L.R. 1026, where it was conceded that such a clause was penal.
[61] *Ante*, p. 885.
[62] *Ante*, p. 680.

forfeiture of deposits and part payments to be discussed below.[63] Two further types of clauses, however, give rise to considerable dispute.

(a) SUMS PAYABLE OTHERWISE THAN ON BREACH. The distinction between penalties and liquidated damages normally applies to sums payable *on breach* of the contract in which the stipulation for payment is contained. A clause under which a sum is payable *only* on some other event is therefore not a penalty. In *Alder* v. *Moore*[64] a professional footballer received £500 from an insurance company in respect of an injury which was thought to have disabled him permanently; and he undertook to repay the money in the event of his again playing professional football. This was not a penalty[65] since he committed no breach when he did play again, as he had made no promise not to do so. Again, a contract for the sale of goods may give the buyer the option of postponing the date on which he is to take delivery, on payment of a "carrying charge." Such a provision is not a penalty since the permitted delay is not a breach and the extra charge is simply the price which the buyer pays for exercising the option conferred on him by the contract.[66] A stipulation is, similarly, not penal if it provides for the payment of a sum of money on breach of another contract with a third party. In one case A had contracted to build a refinery for B; C had undertaken responsibilities as guarantor for the financing of the project; and A had promised C that, in the event of a breach of A's contract with B, A would pay to C sums equivalent to those which C would have to pay under the guarantee. It was held that the latter stipulation was not a penalty as it "provided for payment of money on a specified event other than a breach of a contractual duty owed by the contemplated payor to the contemplated payee."[67] Similar reasoning seems to apply to performance bonds by which C promises to pay a sum of money to A if B fails to perform his contract with A. Such a promise is independent of the contract between A and B[68] and can be enforced by A against C even if A cannot show that B's breach has caused him any loss, or if the loss which A suffered is less than the amount payable by C.[69]

It is less clear whether a clause in a contract can be penal if it provides for a payment on several events one of which is a breach of that contract while another is not. The problem has arisen under so-called minimum payment clauses in hire-purchase agreements. Such a clause commonly provides

---

[63] *Post*, pp. 892–894.
[64] [1961] 2 Q.B. 57; 77 L.Q.R. 300; Goff, 24 M.L.R. 637.
[65] [1961] 2 Q.B. 57, 76.
[66] *Thos. P. Gonzales Corp.* v. *F. R. Waring (International) Pty. Ltd.* [1980] 2 Lloyd's Rep. 160; *Toepfer* v. *Sosimage S.p.A.* [1980] 2 Lloyd's Rep. 397, 402; *Fratelli Moretti S.p.A.* v. *Nidera Handelscompagnie B.V.* [1981] 2 Lloyd's Rep. 47; *Lusograin Comiercio Internacional de Cereas Ltda.* v. *Bunge A.G.* [1986] 2 Lloyd's Rep. 654; *The Bonde* [1991] 1 Lloyd's Rep. 136, 145. But demurrage clauses in charterparties (*ante*, p. 219) assume that the detention of the ship is a breach and provide for the payment of liquidated damages: *The Lips* [1988] A.C. 395 In *Interfoto Picture Library Ltd.* v. *Stiletto Visual Programmes Ltd.* [1988] Q.B. 433 (discussed *ante*, p. 246) the question whether the "holding fee" was a "disguised penalty clause" was left open at pp. 445–446.
[67] *Export Credit Guarantee Department* v. *Universal Oil Products Co.* [1983] 1 W.L.R. 399, 402.
[68] *Edward Owen Engineering Ltd.* v. *Barclays Bank International* [1978] Q.B. 159.
[69] If A recovers more from C than he has lost, B may seek to recover the excess from A; the availability of such a claim was left open in *Comdel Commodities Ltd.* v. *Siporex Trade SA (No. 2)* [1989] 2 Lloyd's Rep. 13 (affd. on other grounds [1991] 1 A.C. 148).

that on premature determination of the agreement the hirer shall bring his payments under it up to a specified proportion of the hire purchase price (or the whole of it) "by way of agreed compensation for depreciation." It then specifies the events on which the agreement may be determined. The owner is usually given the right to determine if the hirer commits a breach of the agreement, and in certain other events.[70] The hirer also often has a right to return the goods on bringing his payments up to the specified amount.

The question whether the law as to penalties applies to such clauses has given rise to much dispute. It is said, on the one hand, that only a sum payable on breach can be a penalty; and, on the other, that the whole law as to penalties could be evaded, if it did not apply to these clauses, by simply including, among the events on which the sum was payable, one event which was not a breach. The common law does not fully adopt either of these views. If the agreement is in fact determined on the ground of the hirer's breach, the law as to penalties applies.[71] If the agreement is determined on some ground other than the hirer's breach, *e.g.* because the hirer exercises his right to return the goods, the law as to penalties does not apply.[72] This compromise is unsatisfactory; for under it a hirer who wishes to return the goods may be better off if he simply defaults than he would be if he exercised his lawful right to determine the agreement.[73]

In the case of a regulated agreement within the Consumer Credit Act 1974,[74] the hirer has a statutory right to determine on payment of one-half of the hire-purchase price. But if the court is satisfied that a smaller sum will adequately compensate the owner for his loss, it may make an order for the payment of such smaller sum.[75] Under these provisions, a hirer who terminates lawfully will no longer be worse off than one who commits a breach. But where the Act does not apply (*e.g.* because the amount of credit exceeds £15,000 or because the hirer is not an "individual") the unsatisfactory rules of common law still prevail.

Where the law as to penalties applies, the question whether a minimum payment clause is penal is determined in accordance with the principles already discussed. In *Lamdon Trust Ltd.* v. *Hurrell*[76] a minimum payment clause providing for payment of about three-quarters of the hire-purchase price on determination was held to be penal, *inter alia*, because this sum was payable whether the hirer defaulted in payment of the first or of the last instalment: the loss caused by these two breaches would clearly be very different. As this factor is present in many cases of this kind, it seems that

---

70 *e.g.* the hirer's bankruptcy. Provisions for termination on the hirer's death used to be common but are ineffective if the agreement is a regulated agreement (*ante*, p. 163) within the Consumer Credit Act 1974, ss.86, 87.

71 *Cooden Engineering Co. Ltd.* v. *Stanford* [1953] 1 Q.B. 86; *Lamdon Trust Ltd.* v. *Hurrell* [1955] 1 W.L.R. 391.

72 *Associated Distributors Ltd.* v. *Hall* [1938] 2 K.B. 83; *Re Apex Supply Co. Ltd.* [1942] Ch. 108; *Campbell Discount Co. Ltd.* v. *Bridge* [1961] 1 Q.B. 445; reversed, on other grounds [1962] A.C. 600, where the House of Lords was equally divided on the point discussed in the text.

73 *Cf.* Law Commission Working Paper No. 61, para. 22.

74 *Ante*, p. 163.

75 s.100(1) and (3).

76 [1955] 1 W.L.R. 391; *cf. Anglo-Auto Finance Co. Ltd.* v. *James* [1963] 1 W.L.R. 1042; *United Dominions Trust* (*Commercial*) *Ltd.* v. *Ennis* [1968] 1 Q.B. 54.

mimimum payment clauses will often be penal, unless the minimum payment is very small.[77]

We have seen that a clause is not presumed to be penal if the sum payable is proportioned to the seriousness of the breach.[78] An attempt to use this principle to support a minimum payment clause was rejected in *Bridge* v. *Campbell Discount Co. Ltd.*[79] The sum payable under the clause was said to be compensation for depreciation. Yet it *decreased* with each payment made by the hirer, while the depreciation obviously increased the longer the hirer kept the goods. "It is a sliding scale of compensation, but a scale that slides in the wrong direction."[80] Hence the clause was held to be penal. If the scale slides in the right direction, the clause may be upheld[81]; but it will still be invalid if it may result in excessive payment for any particular breach.[82]

(b) WITHHOLDING PAYMENTS. Normally, a penalty clause requires the defaulting party to *make* a payment to the victim; but it has been suggested that a provision entitling the victim to *withhold* a payment can also be penal. In *Gilbert-Ash (Northern) Ltd.* v. *Modern Engineering (Bristol) Ltd.*[83] a building subcontract entitled the subcontractor to the agreed payments on the issue of architect's certificates; and it then gave the main contractor the "right to suspend or withhold payment" if the subcontractor failed "to comply with any of the provisions" of the contract. This was said to be invalid as a penalty.[84] But it seems that the contract could have achieved in substance the desired result by providing that nothing was to become due until performance precisely in accordance with its terms had been completed. Effect is commonly given to such provisions[85] without any reference to the law as to penalties.

5. Deposit and Part-Payment[86]

(1) In general

A contract may provide that one party shall make an advance payment, without specifying what is to happen to the payment if the contract is not performed. Clearly, the money must be paid back if the *payee*, in breach of contract, refuses to perform. But the more difficult question (with which the following discussion is concerned) is whether the money must also be paid back where it is the *payor* who, in breach of contract, refuses to perform. This depends on the intention with which the money was paid: it may have been paid as a deposit or as a part-payment. A deposit is a sum of

---

[77] See *Lombank Ltd.* v. *Kennedy* [1961] N.I. 192.
[78] *Ante*, p. 885.
[79] [1962] A.C. 600.
[80] *Ibid.* p. 623.
[81] *Phonographic Equipment (1958) Ltd.* v. *Muslu* [1961] 1 W.L.R. 1379; *cf. Essenda Finance Corp. Ltd.* v. *Plessnig* (1989) 63 A.L.J.R. 238; Wilkin [1990] L.M.C.L.Q. 16; Carter, 2 J.C.L. 78.
[82] *Lombank Ltd.* v. *Excell* [1964] 1 Q.B. 415; the Court of Appeal felt unable to overrule *Muslu's* case on the ground of inconsistency with *Bridge's* case. See Ziegel [1964] C.L.J. 108.
[83] [1974] A.C. 689.
[84] *Ibid.* pp. 698, 703, 711, 723; *cf. The Vainqueur José* [1979] 1 Lloyd's Rep. 557.
[85] *e.g. Eshelby* v. *Federated European Bank* [1932] 1 K.B. 423; *ante*, p. 687.
[86] Beatson, 97 L.Q.R. 389; Milner, 42 M.L.R. 508; Harpum [1984] C.L.J. 134.

money paid as "a guarantee that the contract shall be performed."[87] At common law,[88] it is generally[89] irrecoverable[90] unless the contract otherwise provides.[91] A part-payment is simply a payment of part of the contract price: it is generally[92] recoverable[93] unless the contract validly provides the contrary.

(2) Deposits and penalties

A deposit is distinguishable from a penalty on the ground that it is payable before, and not after breach.[94] But the function of the two devices is similar: the only difference between "a guarantee that the contract shall be performed"[95] and "a payment of money stipulated as *in terrorem* of the offending party"[96] lies in the emotive force of the words used. The law as to penalties should, therefore, apply to deposits; and the view that it does so apply is supported by *Public Works Commissioners* v. *Hills*.[97] A contract for the construction of a railway provided that a security deposit of £50,000 paid by the contractor should be forfeited if the work was not punctually completed. It was held that the contractor, who had failed to complete punctually, was entitled to the return of the deposit as the forfeiture provision was penal. On the other hand, where the deposit is reasonable in relation to the loss likely to be suffered, it can be forfeited, particularly if the loss is such that it cannot be accurately assessed in advance.[98]

(3) Law of Property Act 1925, s.49(2)

This subsection gives the court power "if it thinks fit" to order the return of a deposit paid under a contract for the sale of land. Originally, the courts took the narrow view that the subsection only applied in the exceptional situation in which, though the purchaser was in breach, the vendor could not, for some reason, have obtained specific performance.[99] This restriction on the scope of the subsection may have had some support in the legis-

---

87 *Howe* v. *Smith* (1884) 27 Ch.D. 89, 95; *cf. Public Works Commissioners* v. *Hills* [1906] A.C. 368 (so far as it relates to the retention fund); *The Selene G* [1981] 2 Lloyd's Rep. 180, 185.

88 For the position under Law of Property Act 1925, s.49(2) see *infra* after n. 98.

89 For an exception, see the discussion of deposits and penalties, nn. 94–98, *infra*.

90 *Howe* v. *Smith, supra*; *Ex p. Barell* (1875) L.R. 10 Ch.App. 512; *Harrison* v. *Holland* [1921] 3 K.B. 297; [1922] 1 K.B. 211.

91 *Palmer* v. *Temple* (1839) 9 A. & E. 508.

92 For a possible exception, see *post*, p. 895 at n. 32.

93 *Mayson* v. *Clouet* [1924] A.C. 980; *Dies* v. *British International Mining Corp.* [1939] 1 K.B. 725.

94 *Cf. Corpe* v. *Overton* (1833) 10 Bing. 252, 257.

95 *Supra*, at n. 87.

96 *Ante*, at p. 883.

97 [1906] A.C. 368; *cf. Starside Properties Ltd.* v. *Mustapha* [1974] 1 W.L.R. 816, 819; *Jobson* v. *Johnson* [1989] 1 W.L.R. 1026, 1036, 1041.

98 *Pye* v. *British Automobile Commercial Syndicate Ltd.* [1906] 1 K.B. 425; *cf. Starside Properties Ltd.* v. *Mustapha* [1974] 1 W.L.R. 816, 819.

99 See *James Macara* v. *Barclays Bank Ltd.* [1944] 2 All E.R. 31, 32, affirmed [1945] K.B. 148. See also *Michael Richards Properties Ltd.* v. *St. Saviour's Parish* [1975] 3 All E.R. 416 (where a contractual provision excluding the statutory power was relevant, though obviously not decisive); *Cole* v. *Rose* [1978] 3 All E.R. 1121; and *Windsor Securities Ltd.* v. *Loreldal Ltd., The Times*, September 10, 1975 (where no attempt seems to have been made to invoke the power); *Zieme* v. *Gregory* [1963] V.R. 214.

lative history.[1] But the restriction derives no support from the actual words of the subsection; nor does it have any other merit. It was, moreover, open to the objection that, on a rising market, the purchaser's breach might cause the vendor no loss at all; and to allow him nevertheless to keep the deposit could be said to enrich him unjustly, while causing considerable hardship to the purchaser. A number of more recent cases therefore take the broader view that the subsection is "designed simply to do justice between vendor and purchaser"[2] and that the discretion conferred by it is to be exercised "where justice requires it."[3] This rejection of the original, and unsatisfactory, restriction on the scope of the subsection is certainly to be welcomed; but it is unfortunate that the recent cases give no clear indication of the circumstances in which the courts will exercise their discretion under the subsection. It is submitted that the courts might adapt to this situation the distinction between penalties and liquidated damages and order the return of a deposit where its retention would be penal in effect.

(4) Forfeiture of instalments

A contract of sale may provide for payment of the price in instalments and add that, on default in payment of any one instalment, those already paid shall be forfeited. In such cases equity can sometimes relieve the purchaser against forfeiture if he is able and willing to perform after the agreed time[4] that is, it can extend the time for payment,[5] or order repayment of the forfeited instalments if the purchaser was able and willing to perform, but the vendor was for some reason justified in refusing to accept late performance.[6]

It is more doubtful whether equity could order the repayment of forfeited instalments to a purchaser who was *not* able and willing to perform. In *Mussen* v. *Van Diemen's Land Co.*[7] land was sold for £321,000 payable in instalments and the contract provided that the vendor was to have the right to rescind, and to forfeit any money paid, in the event of the purchaser's default. Such default occurred after the purchaser had paid £40,200.[8] His claim for the return of the money was rejected as it was not

---

[1] It was thought that the subsection was intended to do no more than to reverse *Re Scott & Alvarez' Contract* [1895] 2 Ch. 603 (so far as it related to irrecoverability of the deposit).

[2] *Universal Corp.* v. *Five Ways Properties Ltd.* [1979] 1 All E.R. 552, 555; Oakley [1980] C.L.J. 24.

[3] *Schindler* v. *Pigault* (1975) 30 P. & C.R. 328, 336; for other examples of the exercise of the discretion, see *Maktoum* v. *South Lodge Flats Ltd.*, *The Times*, April 21, 1980; *Wilson* v. *Kingsgate Mining Industries Ltd.* [1973] 2 N.S.W.L.R. 713; *Yammouni* v. *Condidorio* [1975] V.R. 479. contrast *Carne* v. *Debono* [1988] 1 W.L.R. 1107, where no attempt was made to invoke the subsection.

[4] See *Jobson* v. *Johnson* [1989] 1 W.L.R. 1026, where the defendant failed to comply with this requirement; and *Goker* v. *NWS Bank plc*, *The Times*, May 23, 1990, where relief was denied to a persistent defaulter.

[5] *Re Dagenham (Thames) Dock Co.* (1873) L.R. 8 Ch.App. 1022; *Kilmer* v. *B.C. Orchard Lands Ltd.* [1913] A.C. 319; *Starside Properties Ltd.* v. *Mustapha* [1974] 1 W.L.R. 816; *cf. Millichamp* v. *Jones* [1982] 1 W.L.R. 1422 (time for payment of deposit extended); Lang, 100 L.Q.R. 427. For other applications of the principle of relief against forfeiture, see *ante*, pp. 681–682.

[6] *Steedman* v. *Drinkle* [1916] 1 A.C. 275, as explained in *Mussen* v. *Van Diemen's Land Co.*, [1938] Ch. 253; but see *Stockloser* v. *Johnson* [1954] 1 Q.B. 476.

[7] *Supra.*

[8] Land equal in value to other payments had been conveyed to him.

"unconscionable on the part of the vendor, who has contracted to part with his land on agreed terms, to enforce the contract . . . ."[9]

This case left open the possibility of ordering repayment when it *was* unconscionable for the vendor to keep the money. In *Stockloser* v. *Johnson*[10] quarrying machinery was sold under a contract which provided for payment in instalments, and for forfeiture of instalments paid in the event of the buyer's default. The buyer failed to keep up the agreed payments and his claim for the return of the forfeited instalments was rejected as, in the circumstances, it was not unconscionable for the seller to keep them: the buyer had speculated on the success of the quarry, and lost. Somervell and Denning L.JJ. thought that repayment could have been ordered if the mere act of keeping the money had been unconscionable.[11] Romer L.J. disagreed: repayment could only be ordered if the vendor was guilty of fraud, sharp practice or other unconscionable conduct; and there was "nothing inequitable *per se* in a vendor, whose conduct is not open to criticism in other respects, insisting on his contractual right to retain instalments of purchase-money already paid."[12]

Later dicta, as well as a decision at first instance,[13] support Romer L.J.'s view, which is based on the principle that the law should not interfere with contracts freely made. But this principle is discarded in the law as to penalties. Since forfeiture provisions often resemble penalties in their purpose and effect,[14] it is submitted that their validity should depend on the same tests that differentiate penalties from liquidated damages clauses. The court should accordingly have power to grant relief where, on these tests, the forteiture provision is penal in nature.[15]; That relief, in the cases discussed above, would take the form of ordering repayment of the forfeited instalments; but *Jobson* v. *Johnson*[16] illustrates the possible availability of other forms of relief. In that case a contract for the sale of shares to be paid for by instalments provided that, if the buyer defaulted, he should retransfer the shares for £40,000. It was admitted that this clause was penal in effect[17]; and, on the buyer's default, it was held that the seller was entitled to an order for *either* the sale of the shares and the payment out of the proceeds of sale of the unpaid instalments, *or* the transfer of the shares so long as their value did not exceed the unpaid instalments by more than £40,000. This amounted to putting the seller into the same position as that in which he would have been if the penal element of the clause had been

---

9 At p. 262.

10 [1954] 1 Q.B. 476; Diamond, 19 M.L.R. 498; Price, 20 M.L.R. 620 *cf.* Hodkinson, 3 O.J.L.S. 393, discussing *Legione* v. *Hateley* (1983) 152 C.L.R. 406.

11 [1954] Q.B. 476, 483, 485, 489–490. According to *Hyundai Shipbuilding and Heavy Industries Co. Ltd.* v. *Pournaras* [1978] 2 Lloyd's Rep. 502, 508 Somervell L.J.'s views are limited to cases of "default" (*sc.* by the buyer), while Denning L.J. went "somewhat further"; but exactly how much further is not made clear, nor is it apparent from the report in *Stockloser's* case.

12 [1954] 1 Q.B. 476, 501.

13 *Galbraith* v. *Mitchenall Estates Ltd.* [1965] 2 Q.B. 473, citing dicta from *Campbell Discount Co. Ltd.* v. *Bridge* [1961] 1 Q.B. 445 (reversed on other grounds [1962] A.C. 600).

14 *Jobson* v. *Johnson* [1989] 1 W.L.R. 1026, 1041.

15 *Cf. Stockloser* v. *Johnson* [1954] 1 Q.B. 476, 491; Law Commission Working Paper No. 61, paras. 65, 66. For a special statutory provision giving the court a discretion to order repayment, see Consumer Credit Act 1974, s.132(1); this would now apply on the facts of *Galbraith's* case, *supra*, n. 13.

16 [1989] 1 W.L.R. 1026; Harpum [1989] C.L.J. 370.

17 *Ante*, p. 887.

struck out: in this respect it resembled the legal consequence of a penalty clause in the normal sense of that expression.[18]

The foregoing discussion is concerned with contracts of sale, in which, as a result of the buyer's default, the contract is rescinded and the subject-matter remains the property of, or is restored to, the seller. The position is different where the contract is one for services to be rendered over a period of time in return for payments to be made at stated intervals. If the recipient of the services fails to keep up the payments and the contract is rescinded on that ground, he will not be able to recover payments made before rescission, at least if they "represent the agreed rate of hire [for the services] and not a penny more."[19] In such a case the reasoning even of the majority in *Stockloser* v. *Johnson* cannot apply as the payor will have received pro rata what he bargained for in exchange for his payments. The position might be different if those payments contained a heavy element of "front loading."

(5) Failure to pay

The preceding discussion of deposits and part-payments deals with the situation in which a payment has been made and the contract is *then* broken by the payor. The main issue in such cases is whether the payor can get back the payment that he has made. But the breach may also consist in failing to make the payment; and if the injured party rescinds the contract on account of this breach,[20] the question arises whether the payment can be sued for by the prospective payee. The view that it can be sued for is supported by the principle that rescission does not retrospectively release the party in breach from accrued obligations[21]; and, after some conflict of judicial opinion, this view has prevailed where the money was to have been paid as a *deposit*[22] which, if it had been duly paid, could not have been claimed back by the payor.[23] But acceptance of the same view in the case of a *part-payment* might lead to the absurdity that the prospective payee could sue for the money because it was due before breach, while the payor could then sue for its return because a part-payment can be recovered back by the payor.[24] Hence in cases involving contracts for the sale of land the position is that a part-payment which was due but remained unpaid at the time of rescission cannot be sued for by the prospective payee.[25] It is submitted that the same reasoning should apply even to a claim for an unpaid deposit where the case is one of those exceptional ones in which the deposit would, if paid, have been recoverable by the payor, either at common

---

[18] *Ante*, p. 886.
[19] *The Scaptrade* [1983] 2 A.C. 694, 703; *cf. ante*, p. 885.
[20] *Ante*, pp. 663, 676.
[21] *Ante*, p. 748.
[22] *Hinton* v. *Sparkes* (1868) L.R. 3 C.P. 161; *Dewar* v. *Mintoft* [1912] 2 K.B. 373; *Millichamp* v. *Jones* [1982] 1 W.L.R. 1422, 1428, 1430; Carter 99 L.Q.R. 503; *The Blankenstein* [1985] 1 W.L.R. 435, 451, disapproving *Lowe* v. *Hope* [1970] 1 Ch. 94, where the court may have been reluctant to enforce what it regarded as in substance a penalty. For a possible way of giving effect to that reluctance, see *infra*, n. 28.
[23] *Ante*, pp. 890–891.
[24] *Ante*, p. 891, at n. 90.
[25] *McDonald* v. *Denys Lascelles Ltd.* (1933) 48 C.L.R. 457, cited with approval in *Johnson* v. *Agnew* [1980] A.C. 367, 396 and in *Hyundai Heavy Industries Ltd.* v. *Papadopoulos* [1980] 1 W.L.R. 1129, 1141.

law[26] or under section 49(2) of the Law of Property Act 1925[27]; and that a claim by the prospective payee for the payment of such a deposit should therefore be rejected.[28]

In the cases just considered, the outcome can be justified on the ground that the seller will, as a result of rescission, keep or get back the land, which constituted the entire consideration for the promised part payment. Hence if liability to make the payments is discharged, each party will be left in, or restored to, his pre-contract position (though the buyer will be liable in damages). This is also true where a part payment is to be made *in advance*, for work to be done in the future, *i.e.* after the part payment had become due. In *Rover International Ltd.* v. *Cannon Films Ltd.* (*No.* 3)[29] it was accordingly held that a payment in respect of services to be rendered in the future under an agreement for the distribution of films on television could not be recovered by the prospective payee, even though the payment had fallen due before rescission. But the position was different where part payments under shipbuilding contracts became due from time to time (as the work progressed) and the builder rescinded for the other party's failure to make one of the payments when due.[30] It was held that the builder was entitled to sue for that part-payment since the consideration, for which the part-payment was to be made, was not merely the delivery of the finished product, but also the builder's work. So far as the work is concerned, he could be restored to his pre-contract position: hence it was proper to allow him to recover a part-payment due before recsission. For the same reason, instalments due under a hire-purchase agreement before rescission can be sued for after rescission[31]: their legal character is that of payment for the hire of the subject-matter, and the benefit of possession during each period for which such a payment was due is one that cannot be restored by the hirer to the owner. It is submitted that the same reasoning should also apply where the part-payment has actually been made before rescission, and that, accordingly, the prima facie rule by which part-payments can be recovered back by the payor[32] should be restricted to cases in which, as a result of rescission, each party can be restored to his pre-contract position.

SECTION 2. ACTION FOR AN AGREED SUM

1. Distinguished from Damages

A contract commonly provides for the payment by one party of an agreed sum in exchange for some performance by the other. Goods are sold for a fixed price; work is done for an agreed remuneration, and so forth. An action for this price or other agreed remuneration is, in its nature, quite

---

26 *Ante*, p. 891.
27 *Ante*, p. 891.
28 In a case like *Lowe* v. *Hope*, *supra*, n. 22, a court could justify its refusal to allow the prospective payee's claim on the ground that it would have ordered the return of the deposit (if paid) under s.49(2) of the 1925 Act.
29 [1989] 1 W.L.R. 912; Beatson, 105 L.Q.R. 179; Andrews [1990] C.L.J. 15.
30 *Hyundai Shipbuilding and Heavy Industries Co. Ltd.* v. *Pournaras* [1978] 2 Lloyd's Rep. 502; *Hyundai Heavy Industries Ltd.* v. *Papadopoulos* [1980] 1 W.L.R. 1129 (Lords Russell and Keith *dubitante* on this point). In both these cases, as in *McDonald* v. *Denys Lascelles Ltd.* (1933) 48 C.L.R. 457, the action was against a guarantor, but the judgments fully discuss the principal debtor's liability.
31 *Ante*, pp. 748–749.
32 *Ante*, p. 891 at n. 93.

different from an action for damages.[33] It is a claim for the *specific* enforcement of the defendant's primary obligation to perform what he has promised[34]; though, as it is simply an action for money, it is not subject to those restrictions which equity imposes on the remedies of specific performance and injunction,[35] on the ground that it would be undesirable actually to force the defendant to perform certain acts (*e.g.* to render personal service) or that it would be difficult to secure compliance with the court's order. Obviously, these factors have no weight where the plaintiff simply claims a sum of money. Of the reasons given for refusing specific performance, only one calls for discussion in relation to an action for the agreed sum: this is the possibility that damages may be an "adequate" remedy.[36]

The action for the agreed sum differs from a claim for damages not only in its nature, but also in its practical effects. The plaintiff in an action for the agreed sum recovers that sum—neither more nor less; no questions of quantification or remoteness can arise. It is quite irrelevant in an action for the price of goods to ask how much they are worth or how much they cost the seller. The argument that the plaintiff should have mitigated can, however, arise in an action for the agreed sum.[37] If successful, it will lead to the conclusion that the action is not available at all—not to recovery of a reduced price.

Where the agreed sum is not paid and the plaintiff also suffers additional loss, he may be able to bring *both* the action for the agreed sum *and* an action for damages.[38]

2. Availability of the Action

The availability of the action for an agreed sum depends on three factors.

(1) Duty to pay the price

Obviously an action for the agreed sum cannot be brought if the duty to pay it has not arisen. Whether it has arisen depends primarily on the terms of the contract. Suppose that a contract of employment provides that the

---

33 The distinction is sometimes obscured by the fact that damages may be *equal to* the agreed sum, as in *The Blankenstein* [1985] 1 W.L.R. 435, *ante*, p. 749. But sometimes the claim is said to be for "damages equal to" the agreed sum, when the action appears to be one for the agreed sum, not for damages of an equivalent amount, *e.g.* in *UCB Leasing Ltd.* v. *Holtom* [1987] R.T.R. 362, 366.

34 See *ante*, p. 748. Where A (an insurer) promises B (the insured) to pay to B any damages for which B may become liable to C, B's claim against A for the amount of such damages has been described as being itself a claim for damages: see *Chandris* v. *Argo Insurance Co. Ltd.* [1963] 2 Lloyd's Rep. 65. In *Phoenix General Insurance Co. of Greece S.A.* v. *Halvanon Insurance Co. Ltd.* [1988] Q.B. 216, 233 (reversed on other grounds *ibid.* p. 248 *et seq.*) it was said to follow from this view that the action against the insurer was not one to enforce his primary obligation. But in the case put A's only promise is to repay B the damages for which B is liable to C; hence A's primary obligation is to make that payment; and an action to recover it is, it is submitted, one for the specific enforcement of A's promise. It is an action for an agreed sum, in the sense of a sum determined by reference to the agreement, rather than one calculated by reference to the consequences of breach.

35 *Post*, pp. 907–918, 920–924.

36 *Post*, pp. 903–907; *Attica Sea Carriers Corp.* v. *Ferrostaal Poseidon Bulk Reederei GmbH* [1976] Lloyd's Rep. 250.

37 *Post*, pp. 900–901.

38 *Overstone Ltd.* v. *Shipway* [1962] 1 W.L.R. 117; *cf. The Halcyon Skies* [1977] Q.B. 857; *Lawlor* v. *Gray* [1984] 3 All E.R. 345; and see *ante*, pp. 879–882.

employee is to be paid wages after working for a month and that he is wrongfully dismissed after a week. He cannot sue for his wages but only for damages for wrongful dismissal.[39] On the other hand, in *Mount* v. *Oldham Corp.*[40] a local authority wrongfully withdrew boys from a school without giving the customary one term's notice. It was held that the headmaster was entitled to bring an action for the term's fees as it was an implied term of the contract that these should be paid in advance. Similarly, where a contract for the sale of goods provides that the price is to be paid "on a day certain irrespective of delivery" the seller can sue for the price at any time after that day.[41]

So far, we have assumed that the only breach is by the party who was to make the payment. There may also be a breach by the other party, *e.g.* where the employee commits a breach of duty or the seller appropriates defective goods to the contract. Such breaches may prevent the duty to pay from arising or discharge it: this topic is discussed in Chapter 18.[42]

(2) Rules of law

The *action* for the price is not available merely because the *duty* to pay the price has arisen. The contract specifies the *duties* of the parties, but the law determines their *remedies*. This is generally recognised when specific performance is sought, and it is also true of the action for the agreed sum.

The distinction appears clearly in the Sale of Goods Act 1979. The *duty* to pay the price arises when the seller is ready and willing to deliver the goods (unless, of course, the sale is on credit or stipulates for an advance payment[43]). But section 49 of the Act provides that the *action* for the price is available to the seller if either the property in the goods has passed to the buyer or the price is payable "on a day certain irrespective of delivery." In *Stein Forbes & Co Ltd.* v. *County Tailoring Co. Ltd.*[44] a contract for the sale of sheepskins provided for payment in cash "against documents on arrival of steamer." This provision did not name a "day certain"; and the buyer's wrongful refusal to pay on tender of documents prevented the property in the goods from passing to him. It was held that the seller could not claim the price, but only damages. The effect (and probable purpose) of this restriction on the seller's action for the price is to encourage him to dispose of the goods elsewhere and so to mitigate his loss.

The *Stein Forbes* case should be contrasted with *Workman Clark & Co.* v. *Lloyd Brasileno*[45] where a contract for the construction and sale of a boat provided for payments in instalments, the first of which was to become due when the keel was laid; and property was not to pass until this payment had been made. After the keel had been laid, the builder successfully sued for the first instalment. The case is hard to reconcile with the wording of section 49; but it nevertheless accurately reflects the underlying policy. At the stage which the work had reached it must have been hard for

---

[39] *Ante*, pp. 650, 774–775.
[40] [1973] Q.B. 309; *cf. Denman* v. *Winstanley* (1887) 4 T.L.R. 127.
[41] Sale of Goods Act 1979, s.49(2).
[42] *Ante*, pp. 659 *et seq*.
[43] Sale of Goods Act 1979, ss.27, 28.
[44] (1916) 115 L.T. 215; *cf. Tradax Internacional S.A.* v. *Goldschmidt S.A.* [1977] 2 Lloyd's Rep. 604; *Regent O.H.G. Aisenstadt und Barig* v. *Francesco of Jermyn Street* [1981] 3 All E.R. 327.
[45] [1908] 1 K.B. 968; this report differs in some significant respects from those in 77 L.J.K.B. 953; 99 L.T. 481; and 11 Asp.M.L.C. 126.

the builder to mitigate his loss by finding another customer for a boat built to the defendant's order—much harder, probably, than it was for the seller in the *Stein Forbes* case to resell the sheepskins.

(3) Conduct of the injured party

On wrongful repudiation of a contract, the injured party has a choice: he can either "terminate" the contract or keep it alive.

(a) ELECTS TO TERMINATE. If the injured party elects to terminate, he cannot sue for any sum which, under the contract, was to accrue to him only after the date of termination.[46] He can claim damages for wrongful repudiation, and in assessing these the court may take into account any sums which he should have received under the broken contract. For example, if a hire-purchase agreement is wrongfully repudiated by the hirer and terminated by the owner, the owner cannot sue for instalments which were to accrue after the date of termination. But his damages may be based on the difference between the amount which the repudiating hirer was to have paid and the benefits obtained by the owner as a result of termination, *e.g.* in regaining possession of the goods.[47]

(b) ELECTS TO KEEP THE CONTRACT ALIVE. Where the injured party elects to keep the contract alive, he can bring the action for the agreed sum if, at the time of repudiation, he has already done all that is required to make the action available: for example, if he is a seller of goods and has already transferred the property in them to the buyer.[48]

If the injured party has not yet done all that is required to make the action available, there are some cases in which he cannot bring the action for the agreed sum. This is the position where it is impossible for him to do the required acts without the co-operation of the guilty party, who refuses to give it. For example, if a singer wrongfully repudiates his contract with his agent, the latter cannot continue performance without the co-operation of the former; and the agent's only claim is for damages.[49] The position is similar where work is to be done by A on the land or goods of B, who wrongfully refuses to allow A to have access to or possession of the property. In such a case, A cannot do the work without some co-operation from B and so his only remedy is an action for damages.[50] A could only do the work without B's co-operation if he already had possession of the goods or if he could get them without B's co-operation (*e.g.* from a warehouseman who had been effectively directed to deliver them to A).[51]

It is disputed whether the action for the agreed sum is available to the injured party where, at the time of repudiation, that party has not yet done all that was required of him to make the action available, but where he can, and does, continue performance without the co-operation of the other

---

[46] *Ante*, p. 748.

[47] See *ante*, pp. 748–750.

[48] Sale of Goods Act 1979, s.49(1); in *Mackay* v. *Dick* (1881) 6 App.Cas. 251 (where there was no discussion as to the remedy) property had apparently passed to the buyer, so that the action for the price would now be available under s.49(1).

[49] *Denmark Productions Ltd.* v. *Boscobel Productions Ltd.* [1969] 1 Q.B. 699; *cf. Roberts* v. *Ellwells Engineering Ltd.* [1972] Q.B. 586; *ante*, p. 650.

[50] *Hounslow (London Borough)* v. *Twickenham Garden & Builders Ltd.* [1971] Ch. 233, 252–254; *cf. Finelli* v. *Dee* (1968) 67 D.L.R. (2d) 393; *Attica Sea Carriers Corp.* v. *Ferrostaal Poseidon Bulk Reederei GmbH* [1976] 1 Lloyd's Rep. 250, 256.

[51] *e.g. George Barker Transport Ltd.* v. *Eynon* [1974] 1 W.L.R. 462, 468.

party. In *White & Carter (Councils) Ltd.* v. *McGregor*[52] the appellants agreed to advertise the respondents' garage business for three years on plates attached to litterbins. Payment was to be at the rate of 2s. per week per plate, plus 5s. per annum towards the cost of each plate. The respondents repudiated the contract on the very day on which it was made but the appellants nevertheless prepared the plates, displayed them, and claimed the full amount due on the contract: £187 4s. for the space and £9 in respect of the plates. A majority of the House of Lords upheld the claim. The main reason given was that repudiation did not, of itself, bring a contract to an end. It only gave the injured party an option to determine the contract; and if he chose instead to affirm, the contract remained "in full effect."[53] But this reasoning does not, of itself, lead to any conclusion as to the *particular remedy* available to the injured party. This appears from the cases in which the injured party *cannot* perform without the co-operation of the other party. Even here, repudiation does not of itself bring the contract to an end[54]; but the injured party's only remedy is an action for damages.[55]

None the less, the principle of *White and Carter (Councils) Ltd.* v. *McGregor* may sometimes be justifiable. The problem in cases of this kind is whether an award of the agreed sum is, on the one hand, necessary to protect the injured party, and, on the other, likely to cause undue hardship to the party in breach. In some cases it may make no difference to the injured party whether (1) he incurs the expense of performance and recovers the agreed sum, or (2) saves that expense by not performing and recovers the difference between it and the agreed sum by way of damages. If this is the position, damages are a perfectly adequate remedy. But there are other situations in which the injured party would be prejudiced by discontinuing performance and claiming damages: *e.g.* where this leads to injury to his reputation, for which damages (if recoverable at all)[56] could not be accurately assessed; where the injured party has entered into commitments with third parties which he must honour as a matter of business[57]; or where part of the loss which the injured party would actually suffer is legally irrecoverable because it is too remote.[58] It is only in cases of this kind that the rule in *McGregor's* case will be applied, for Lord Reid there said that, if the injured party has "no substantial or legitimate interest"[59] in completing performance, he can only claim damages. If the injured party does have such an interest, it is hard to see why he should not

---

52 [1962] A.C. 413; Goodhart, 78 L.Q.R. 263; Nienaber [1962] C.L.J. 213.

53 [1962] A.C. 413, 427.

54 *Ante*, p. 743.

55 See the authorities cited in n. 49, *supra*; *cf. The Alaskan Trader* [1983] 2 Lloyd's Rep. 645, 651 (quoted *ante*, p. 745).

56 *Ante*, pp. 877–878, *cf. The Odenfeld* [1978] 2 Lloyd's Rep. 357 (damages very hard to assess).

57 See *Anglo-African Shipping Co. of New York Inc.* v. *Mortner* [1962] 1 Lloyd's Rep. 81, 94; affirmed on other grounds, *ibid.* 610; *The Odenfeld* [1978] 2 Lloyd's Rep. 357; *post*, pp. 900–901.

58 *Ante*, pp. 854–866.

59 [1962] A.C. 413 at p. 431; *The Alaskan Trader*, [1983] 2 Lloyd's Rep. at p. 651; this qualification brings the English rule close to the American rule, with which it is said to conflict: under Restatement, *Contracts* s.338, Comment *c*: the innocent party must not "unreasonably" continue performance after breach; *cf.* Restatement 2d, *Contracts* § 350 Comment *b*. The legitimate "interest" may be in acquiring a security in the subject-matter: *George Barker Transport Ltd.* v. *Eynon* [1974] 1 W.L.R. 462.

be entitled to complete performance and claim the agreed sum; but three contrary arguments must be considered.

(i) *Mitigation.* The first, and most important, argument is that the injured party should mitigate his loss. It has been said, in reply, that mitigation is relevant only to a claim for damages and not to a claim for an agreed sum[60]; and in many cases this is no doubt true. A seller of goods who claims damages for non-acceptance may be under a duty to mitigate by reselling the goods; but once he has acquired the right to sue for the price[61] there seems, in English law,[62] to be no suggestion that he must mitigate even though he can easily resell and even though he is in a much better position than the buyer to do so. But even if this rule always[63] applies in cases involving sale of goods, it does not follow that it must necessarily apply to cases involving other kinds of contracts. In particular, it is submitted that the policy of the mitigation rules (which is to prevent needless waste) should make those rules applicable, even in an action for the agreed sum, where at the time of repudiation the claimant has not yet done all that is required of him to make the action for the price available. This submission is supported by the *Attica Sea Carriers*[64] case, which arose out of a demise charterparty imposing continuing obligations on both parties. The charterer undertook to execute certain repairs before redelivery of the ship and to pay the agreed hire till then; and for the present purpose it was assumed[65] that the contract did not require the owner to accept redelivery until the repairs had been done. On the charterer's refusal to do the repairs, it was nevertheless held that the owner's remedy was not an action for the agreed hire. As the cost of the repairs far exceeded the value of the ship when repaired,[66] the owner had no "legitimate interest" in insisting on continued performance. Hence the mitigation rules required him to accept redelivery of the unrepaired ship and to seek his remedy in damages.

It does not follow that the mitigation rules will always require the injured party to take such a course, since they only require him to act reasonably.[67] In *The Odenfeld*[68] a time charterer wrongfully repudiated the charterparty by refusing to pay the agreed hire. It was held that the shipowners were not bound at once to accept the repudiation and seek their remedy in damages, but that they could sue for the agreed hire until they finally did accept the

---

[60] Scott [1962] C.L.J. 12.

[61] *Ante*, pp. 897–898.

[62] Contrast U.C.C. s.2–709(1)(*b*), by which the seller can only sue for the price of goods identified to the contract if he is "unable after reasonable effort to resell them at a reasonable price," or the circumstances indicate that such an effort would be unavailing. *Cf.* also ULIS (*ante*, p. 28, n. 81, Art. 61(2)).

[63] If the seller is "bound to do something to [specific] goods for the purpose of putting them into a deliverable state, the property does not pass until the thing is done and the buyer has notice that it has been done": Sale of Goods Act 1979, s.18, r. 2. Thus before the seller does the required act the action for the price is not generally available: s.49(1). It is sometimes assumed that, if the buyer repudiates at this stage, the seller can nevertheless do the act and sue for the price, but there is no actual decision to this effect.

[64] [1976] 1 Lloyd's Rep. 250; Kerr, 41 M.L.R. 1, 20–21; *cf. The Alaskan Trader* [1983] 2 Lloyd's Rep. 645 where a shipowner had no legitimate interest in spending more money than the ship was worth on repairing her so as to keep her available for service; Carter and Marston [1985] C.L.J. 18.

[65] The assumption was in fact regarded as ill-founded: *ante*, p. 696.

[66] *Cf. ante*, pp. 836, 868.

[67] *Ante*, p. 868.

[68] [1978] 2 Lloyd's Rep. 357.

repudiation. They had acted reasonably in requiring continued performance since the ship remained available for service,[69] and since they had entered into an obligation to third parties (to whom they had assigned hire due under the charterparty) to keep the contract in existence.

The argument that the appellants should have mitigated by discontinuing performance was no doubt open to the respondents in *McGregor's* case; but it is submitted that the result in that case was consistent with the mitigation rules. There are, as will be recollected,[70] two such rules. The first is that the appellants should have minimised loss by reletting the advertising space. But the burden of proving that they could indeed have done this was on the respondents[71] and does not seem to have been discharged.[72] The argument required proof that the demand for space exceeded the appellants' available supply[73] and no evidence seems to have been directed to this issue. The second rule is that the appellants should not have augmented loss by spending money on the preparation of the plates. This has to be considered on the assumption that the space could not have been relet, or that it was doubtful whether it could be relet. As a matter of strict law, the appellants could (on this assumption) have abandoned the contract and recovered the difference between the agreed rental and any expenses thus saved by way of damages.[74] Hence it could be said that the expense of preparing the plates should not have been incurred as it did not benefit anyone. But the mitigation rules do not require the injured party to act in accordance with the strict law. They only require him to act reasonably[75]; and if there was no possibility of reletting the space, or only a doubtful one, it seems that the appellants did act reasonably in incurring the expense necessary to substantiate their claim for the agreed sum.

(ii) *Indirect specific performance*. The second argument against *McGregor's* case is that the award of the agreed sum amounted to indirect specific performance[76] of a contract which was not specifically enforceable; but, even if this argument is doctrinally sound, it does not seem that any of the reasons for refusing direct specific performance of such a contract applied in the circumstances of the case. Possible reasons for such refusal are that enforcement of the decree would require "constant supervision"; that there was no "mutuality"; and that the contract involved "personal" service.[77] But the first two reasons do not apply where the contract has been fully performed by one party and the only outstanding liability of the other

[69] *Ibid.* at p. 374; the owners could perform without the charterer's co-operation by simply (in the absence of orders) laying up the ship; contrast, on this point, *The Alaskan Trader* [1983] 2 Lloyd's Rep. 645, 652.

[70] *Ante*, pp. 866–869.

[71] *Roper* v. *Johnson* (1873) L.R. 8 C.P. 187; *Regent O.H.G. Aisenstadt und Barig* v. *Francesco of Jermyn Street* [1981] 3 All E.R. 327, 332 (in these cases, the claims were for damages, but there is no reason to suppose that a different rule as to burden of proof would apply in an action for the agreed sum).

[72] Lord Morton [1962] A.C. 413 at p. 432, states that the appellants "made no effort" to relet the space. But there is nothing to show whether efforts to relet would have succeeded; *cf.* Roger, 93 L.Q.R. 168.

[73] Unless this were so, the appellants would be under no duty to relet the space originally let to the respondents: they would be entitled to let *other* space to other customers, *cf. ante*, p. 844.

[74] *Cf. British and Beningtons Ltd.* v. *N.W. Cachar Tea Co. Ltd.* [1923] A.C. 48; *ante*, p. 844.

[75] *Ante*

[76] [1962] A.C. 413, 433.

[77] *Post*, pp. 910–914, 916–918.

is to pay cash.[78] Nor does the third reason seem to apply (even if one makes the doubtful assumption that the services were "personal") where one party has been able to perform *without any co-operation from the other.*[79]

(iii) *Hardship.* A third argument against *McGregor's* case is that it is hard on the party in breach to have to pay for a performance which he does not want. But the injured party will not be entitled to the agreed sum if he has no "substantial or legitimate interest"[80] in completing performance; and even if he has such an interest, his action for the agreed sum may still fail if he ought to have mitigated by discontinuing performance. When these qualifications are borne in mind, it is submitted that the rule in *McGregor's* case represents a reasonable compromise between the interests of the two contracting parties.

SECTION 3. EQUITABLE REMEDIES[81]

1. Specific Performance[82]

The common law did not specifically enforce contractual obligations except those to pay money. Specific enforcement of other contractual obligations was available only in equity. It was (and is) subject to many restrictions. These are based partly on the drastic character of the remedy, which leads (more readily than an award of damages or of the agreed sum) to attachment of the defendant's person.[83] But this is an important factor only where the contract calls for "personal" performance, *i.e.* for acts to be done by the defendant himself.[84] Where the contract is not of this kind, it can be specifically enforced without personal constraint: for example, by sequestration,[85] by the execution of a formal document by an officer of the court,[86] or by a writ of delivery. Other reasons for restricting specific enforcement are that this form of relief may be unnecessary, undesirable or impracticable on various grounds to be considered in the discussion that follows. But many of these reasons, too, are no longer regarded as wholly convincing.[87] The more recent authorities, therefore, support some expansion in the scope of the remedy.[88]

---

78 *Post*, pp. 913, 917–918. The contract in *McGregor's* case was to display the advertisements for three years from November 1957 and the action was commenced in October 1958, the claim being brought under an acceleration clause (*ante*, p. 885). In view of this clause nothing turned on the fact that performance had not been completed when the action was brought: see [1962] A.C. 413, 426–427.

79 [1962] A.C. 413, 429.

80 *Ibid.* at p. 431.

81 Spry, *Equitable Remedies* (4th ed.); Sharpe, *Injunctions and Specific Performance.*

82 Fry, *Specific Performance* (6th ed.); Jones and Goodhart, *Specific Performance.*

83 *Cf. Enfield L.B.C.* v. *Mahoney* [1983] 1 W.L.R. 749, where even imprisonment failed to induce compliance with an order for specific restitution. Imprisonment for debt has been abolished (subject to exceptions not here relevant) by Debtors Act 1869, ss.4, 5, and Administration of Justice Act 1970, s. 11.

84 Corbin, *Contracts*, s.1138.

85 *Miliangos* v. *George Frank (Textiles) Ltd.* [1976] A.C. 443, 494, 497.

86 *The Messianiki Tolmi* [1983] 2 A.C. 787.

87 *e.g. post*, pp. 907, 910–914.

88 A trend forecast by Lord Justice Fry in his work on *Specific Performance*: see (6th ed.), p. 21; *cf.* Burrows, 4 Legal Studies 102.

(1) Granted where damages not "adequate"

The traditional view is that specific performance will not be ordered where damages are an "adequate" remedy. After illustrating this requirement, we shall see that it now requires some reformulation.

(a) AVAILABILITY OF SATISFACTORY EQUIVALENT. Damages are most obviously an adequate remedy where the plaintiff can get a satisfactory equivalent of what he contracted for from some other source. For this reason specific performance is not generally ordered of contracts for the sale of commodities, or of shares, which are readily available in the market.[89] In such cases the plaintiff can buy in the market and is adequately compensated by recovering the difference between the contract and the market price by way of damages. Indeed, he is required to make the substitute purchase in performance of the duty to mitigate his loss.[90] If he fails to do so, he cannot recover damages for extra loss suffered because the market has risen after the date when the substitute contract should have been made. To award him specific performance in such a case would, in substance, conflict with the principles of mitigation[91] as well as being oppressive to the defendant.[92] Similar reasoning seems to underlie the rule that a contract to lend money cannot be specifically enforced by either party[93]: it is assumed that damages can easily be assessed by reference to current rates of interest.

Damages will, on the other hand, not be regarded as an adequate remedy where the plaintiff cannot obtain a satisfactory substitute. The law takes the view that a buyer of land or of a house[94] (however ordinary) is not adequately compensated by damages, and that he can therefore get an order of specific performance.[95] Even a contractual licence to occupy land, though creating no interest in the land,[96] may be specifically enforced.[97] A vendor of land, too, can get specific performance, though his only claim is

---

89 *Cud* v. *Rutter* (1719) 1 P.Wms. 570; *Re Schwabacher* (1908) 98 L.T. 127, 128; *cf. Fothergill* v. *Rowland* (1873) L.R. 17 Eq. 137; *Garden Cottage Foods Ltd.* v. *Milk Marketing Board* [1984] A.C. 130; *aliter* if the shares are not readily available: *Duncuft* v. *Albrecht* (1841) 12 Sim. 189; *Langen & Wind Ltd.* v. *Bell* [1972] Ch. 685; *Jobson* v. *Johnson* [1989] 1 W.L.R. 1026; or if the contract is for the sale of shares giving a controlling interest in the company: *Harvela Investments Ltd.* v. *Royal Trust Co. of Canada (C.I.) Ltd.* [1986] A.C. 207.

90 *Ante*, p. 866.

91 See *Buxton* v. *Lister* (1746) 3 Atk. 383, 384.

92 See *Re Schwabacher* (1908) 98 L.T. 127, where shares rose in value after breach. In such a case the defendant could be given the option of transferring the shares or paying the difference between contract and market price on the day fixed for performance, as in *Colt* v. *Nettervill* (1725) 2 P.Wms. 301). See also *Whiteley Ltd.* v. *Hilt* [1918] 2 K.B. 808; *M.E.P.C.* v. *Christian Edwards* [1978] Ch. 281, 293 (affirmed on other grounds [1981] A.C. 205); *Chinn* v. *Hochstrasser* [1979] Ch. 447 (reversed on other grounds [1981] A.C. 533).

93 *Rogers* v. *Challis* (1859) 27 Beav. 175 (suit by lender); *Sichel* v. *Mosenthal* (1862) 30 Beav. 371 (suit by borrower: decision based on lack of mutuality (*post*, p. 916) rather than adequacy of damages); *cf. Larios* v. *Bonnany y Gurety* (1873) L.R. 5 C.P. 346. By statute the court can specifically enforce a contract to take debentures in a company, that is, to make a secured loan to the company: Companies Act 1985, s.195 reversing *South African Territories Ltd.* v. *Wallington* [1898] A.C. 109. A contract to subscribe for shares in a company is also specifically enforceable: *Odessa Tramways Co.* v. *Mendel* (1878) 8 Ch.D. 235; *Sri Lanka Omnibus Co.* v. *Perera* [1952] A.C. 76.

94 Fry, *Specific Performance* (6th ed.), § 62.

95 Unless he elects to claim damages, as in *Meng Long Developments Pte. Ltd.* v. *Jip Hong Trading Co. Pte. Ltd.* [1985] A.C. 511.

96 See *Ashburn Anstalt* v. *Arnold* [1989] Ch. 1.

97 *Verrall* v. *Great Yarmouth B.C.* [1981] Q.B. 202.

for money.[98] One reason for this is that it is just to allow the remedy *to* him as it is available *against* him. Another is that damages will not adequately compensate him for not getting the whole price, as he may not easily be able to find another purchaser.[99] And he may be anxious to rid himself of burdens attached to the land.[1] But the rule seems to apply though the land is readily saleable to a third party; and it has even been applied where after contract but before completion a compulsory purchase order was made in respect of the land.[2] Yet in such a case damages (consisting of the amount by which the contract price exceeded the compensation payable on compulsory acquisition) would normally be an adequate remedy.

(b) DAMAGES HARD TO QUANTIFY. A second factor which is relevant (though not decisive[3]) in considering the adequacy of damages is the difficulty of assessing and recovering them. This is one reason why specific performance has been ordered of contracts to sell (or to pay) annuities,[4] and of a sale of debts proved in bankruptcy,[5] the value of such rights being uncertain. Similarly, a contract to execute a mortgage in consideration of money lent at, or before, the time of the contract can be specifically enforced[6] for the value of obtaining security for a debt cannot be precisely quantified. The same is true of the right to have a loan repaid out of specific property; and a term in a contract of loan conferring such a right is therefore specifically enforceable.[7] Even where there is no such difficulty in *quantifying* the loss, damages may be an inadequate remedy because the plaintiff's loss is difficult to prove,[8] or because certain items of loss (such as injury to prospects of employment or to reputation)[9] may not be legally recoverable,[10] or quite simply because the defendant may not be "good for the money."[11]

---

[98] *e.g. Walker* v. *Eastern Counties Ry.* (1848) 6 Hare 594; *Miliangos* v. *George Frank (Textiles) Ltd.* [1976] A.C. 443, 496. Where the purchaser has been allowed to go into possession and has then failed to complete, and the vendor has not elected between rescission and specific performance, the court may (unless the contract otherwise provides) order the purchaser either to perform or to vacate the premises: see *Greenwood* v. *Turner* [1891] 2 Ch. 144; *Maskell* v. *Ivory* [1970] Ch. 502; *Attfield* v. *D. J. Plant Hire & General Contractors* [1987] Ch. 141.

[99] *Lewis* v. *Lord Lechmere* (1722) 10 Mod. 503.

[1] Fry, *Specific Performance* (6th ed.), § 72.

[2] *Hillingdon Estate Co.* v. *Stonefield Estates Ltd.* [1952] Ch. 627

[3] *Soc. des Industries Metallurgiques S.A.* v. *Bronx Engineering Co. Ltd.* [1975] 1 Lloyd's Rep. 465.

[4] *Ball* v. *Coggs* (1710) 1 Bro. P.C. 140; *Kenney* v. *Wexham* (1822) 6 Madd. 355; *Adderley* v. *Dixon* (1824) 1 C. & S. 607, 611; *Clifford* v. *Turrell* (1841) 1 Y. & C.C.C. 138; *Beswick* v. *Beswick* [1968] A.C. 58; see however Fry, *Specific Performance* (6th ed.), pp. 30, 111, 112; *Crampton* v. *Varna Ry.* (1872) L.R. 7 Ch.App. 562.

[5] *Adderley* v. *Dixon* (1824) 1 C. & S. 607.

[6] *Ashton* v. *Corrigan* (1871) L.R. 13 Eq. 76; *Swiss Bank Corp.* v. *Lloyd's Bank Ltd.* [1982] A.C. 584, 595, affirmed *ibid.* p. 610.

[7] *Swiss Bank Corp.* v. *Lloyd's Bank Ltd.* [1979] Ch. 548, reversed [1982] A.C. 584, but on the ground that the contract did not on its true construction contain any such term.

[8] *Decro-Wall International S.A.* v. *Practitioners in Marketing Ltd.* [1971] 1 W.L.R. 361.

[9] *Hill* v. *C. A. Parsons Ltd.* [1972] 1 Ch. 305; *Evans Marshall & Co. Ltd.* v. *Bertola S.A.* [1973] 1 W.L.R. 349.

[10] *Ante*, pp. 877–878.

[11] *Evans Marshall & Co. Ltd.* v. *Bertola S.A.*, *supra*, at p. 380; *cf. The Oakworth* [1975] 1 Lloyd's Rep. 531, 583; *The Oro Chef* [1983] 2 Lloyd's Rep. 509, 521.

(c) DAMAGES NOMINAL. In *Beswick* v. *Beswick*[12] specific performance was ordered of a contract to pay an annuity to a third party. A majority[13] of the House of Lords took the view that damages were an inadequate remedy because they would be purely nominal, the promisee or his estate having suffered no loss. The point here seems to be, not that the promisee would be inadequately compensated, but that the defendant would be unjustly enriched (if damages were the sole remedy) by being allowed to retain the entire benefit of the promisee's performance while performing only a small part of his own promise.

(d) SALE OF GOODS. Section 52 of the Sale of Goods Act 1979 gives the court a discretion to order specific performance in an action for breach of a contract to deliver "specific or ascertained" goods.[14] Although the section only deals with cases in which this remedy is sought by the buyer, the court also has power to order specific performance at the suit of the seller.[15]

Section 52 is based on an earlier enactment, which had been passed to broaden the scope of the remedy.[16] This seemed to have been restricted to cases in which the buyer could not get a satisfactory substitute because the goods were "unique." Heirlooms and great works of art are regarded as "unique" for this purpose[17]; and it seems that the courts go some way towards recognising a concept of "commercial uniqueness." Thus they may order specific performance of a contract to supply a ship, or machinery or other industrial plant which cannot readily be obtained elsewhere.[18]

Under section 52, the discretion to order specific performance is no longer limited to cases in which the goods are "unique"; but the courts nevertheless at one time took the view that the discretion should be sparingly exercised.[19] One reason for this view is that the specific enforceability of a contract for the sale of goods might give the buyer an equitable interest in the goods; and if the seller were insolvent the buyer could in this way

---

12 [1968] A.C. 58; *ante*, pp. 529–530, *post*, p. 918.

13 For Lord Pearce's view, see *post*, p. 918, n. 53.

14 "Specific" means "identified and agreed on at the time a contract of sale is made": s.61(1); "ascertained" is not defined in the Act but seems to mean "identified in accordance with the agreement after the time a contract of sale is made": *Re Wait* [1927] 1 Ch. 606, 630; or identified in any other way: *Thames Sack & Bag Co. Ltd.* v. *Knowles* (1918) 88 L.J.K.B. 585, 588.

15 *The Messiniaki Tolmi* [1982] Q.B. 1248, affirmed without reference to this point [1983] 2 A.C. 787 (sale of ship). For earlier authorities on the availability of the remedy to the seller, contrast *Shell-Mex Ltd.* v. *Elton Copy Dyeing Co.* (1928) 34 Com Cas. 39, 47 with *Elliott* v. *Pierson* [1948] 1 All E.R. 939, 943. The practical effect of ordering specific performance at the suit of the seller is to enable him to get an order for the payment of the price in a case falling outside Sale of Goods Act 1979, s.49 (*ante*, p. 897).

16 s. 2 of the Mercantile Law Amendment Act 1856; Treitel [1966] J.B.L. 211.

17 *Pusey* v. *Pusey* (1684) 1 Vern. 273; *Somerset* v. *Cookson* (1735) 3 P.Wms. 390; *Lowther* v. *Lowther* (1806) 3 Ves. 95; *Falcke* v. *Gray* (1859) 4 Drew. 651, 658.

18 See *Nutbrown* v. *Thornton* (1804) 10 Ves. 159; *North* v. *G.N. Ry.* (1860) 2 Giff. 64; *Behnke* v. *Bede Shipping Co.* [1927] 1 K.B. 649; *The Oro Chef* [1983] 1 Lloyd's Rep. 509, 520–521; *The Star Gazer* [1985] 1 Lloyd's Rep. 370; *Batthyany* v. *Bouch* (1881) 50 L.J.Q.B. 421; *cf. Lingen* v. *Simpson* (1824) 1 S. & S. 600 (pattern books). Contrast *Soc. des Industries Metallurgiques S.A.* v. *Bronx Engineering Co. Ltd.* [1975] 1 Lloyd's Rep. 465 (machinery available from another source); *The Stena Nautica (No. 2)* [1982] 2 Lloyd's Rep. 336; *Gyllenhammer Partners International* v. *Sour Brodogradevna* [1989] 2 Lloyd's Rep. 403, 422.

19 A little-noticed exception is *Rawlings* v. *General Trading Co.* [1921] 1 K.B. 635, where specific performance was granted without argument as to the remedy.

gain an undeserved priority over other creditors.[20] But a restrictive view of the scope of specific performance has been taken even where this factor of insolvency was not present. For example, in *Cohen* v. *Roche*[21] the court refused specific performance to a buyer of a set of Hepplewhite chairs, saying they were "ordinary articles of commerce and of no special value or interest."[22] It is hard to see what legitimate interest of the seller was protected by the court's refusal to grant specific performance in this case; nor is the notion that damages are necessarily an adequate remedy for breach of a contract to sell goods unless they are "unique" an easy one to defend. The buyer may not in fact be able to get a substitute; his loss may be hard to assess; and part of it may be irrecoverable (*e.g.* because it is too remote).

Section 52 refers only to goods which are "specific or ascertained."[23] The section therefore does not apply where the goods are purely generic (*e.g.* where the sale is of "1,000 tons of wheat") or where they form an undifferentiated part of an identified bulk (*e.g.* 500 tons out of the 1,000 tons of wheat on a named ship[24]). It is, however, an open question whether the court may not in appropriate circumstances have a discretion to order specific performance of such contracts even though they fall outside section 52. The section does not in terms say that specific performance can be ordered *only* where the goods are "specific or ascertained"; and it is arguable that the remedy should be available, even where the goods are not of this kind, if to grant it would give effect to the general principle governing its scope. This might, for example, be the position where a contract was made to supply a manufacturer with goods urgently needed by him for the purpose of his business. Damages might be an inadequate remedy in such a case, for they "would be a poor consolation if the failure of supplies forces a trader to lay off staff and disappoint his customers (whose affections may be transferred to others) and ultimately forces him towards insolvency . . . ."[25] The view that specific performance could be ordered on such grounds[26] seemed at one time to have been abandoned[27]; but the more recent cases give it fresh support. During a steel strike in 1980 a manufacturer sought an order for the specific delivery of a quantity of steel belonging to him against the British Railways Board who (in fear of strike action) refused to allow it to be moved. The court made the order because, during

---

[20] It was no doubt to secure such priority that specific performance was (unsuccessfully) sought in *Re Wait* [1927] 1 Ch. 606. But the specific enforceability of the contract does not *necessarily* give rise to an equitable interest in the subject-matter: see *Tailby* v. *Official Receiver* (1888) 13 App.Cas. 533, 548; *Re London Wine Co.* (*Shippers*) [1986] P.C.C. 121, 149. *Cf.* also *The Aliakmon* [1986] A.C. 785, 812–813 (denying that equitable title passed on "appropriation" of goods to a contract for the sale of unascertained goods); but in that case damages would clearly have been an adequate remedy (*ante*, p. 903 at n. 89), so that it does not conclude the question whether an equitable interest *may* pass under a specifically enforceable contract for the sale of goods.

[21] [1927] 1 K.B. 169.

[22] At p. 181. Contrast *Phillips* v. *Lamdin* [1949] 2 K.B. 33 (Adam-style door).

[23] See n. 14, *supra*.

[24] As in *Re Wait* [1927] 1 Ch. 606.

[25] *Howard E. Perry & Co.* v. *British Railways Board* [1980] 1 W.L.R. 1375, 1383.

[26] *Taylor* v. *Neville* (unrep.), cited with approval in *Buxton* v. *Lister* (1746) 3 Atk. 383 and in *Adderley* v. *Dixon* (1824) 1 S. & S. 607.

[27] See *Fothergill* v. *Rowland* (1873) L.R. 17 Eq. 137; *Pollard* v. *Clayton* (1885) 1 K. & J. 462; *Dominion Coal Co.* v. *Dominion Iron & Steel Co.* [1909] A.C. 293. *Donnell* v. *Bennett* (1883) 23 Ch.D. 835 takes a more liberal view.

the strike, "steel [was] available only with great difficulty."[28] It is submitted that, in such circumstances, specific performance should similarly be available to a buyer. This view is supported by a case[29] in which, during the petrol shortage in 1973, an interim injunction was granted to stop an oil company from cutting off supplies of petrol to a garage, since alternative supplies were not available. As the goods were purely generic, the case gives some support to the view that an obligation to deliver goods may be specifically enforced in a case falling outside section 52 of the Sale of Goods Act because the goods are not "specific or ascertained."[30]

(e) APPROPRIATENESS OF THE REMEDY. The more satisfactory approach found in the cases just discussed is also expressed in dicta to the effect that the availability of specific performance depends on the *appropriateness* of that remedy in the circumstances of each case.[31] The question is not simply whether damages are an "adequate" remedy, but whether specific performance will "do more perfect and complete justice than an award of damages."[32] The point was well put in a case concerned with the analogous question whether an injunction should be granted: "The standard question . . . , are damages an adequate remedy? might perhaps, in the light of the authorities in recent years, be rewritten: is it just in all circumstances that the plaintiff should be confined to his remedy in damages . . . ?"[33]

A similar approach has been adopted to the analogous question whether specific performance can be ordered where the action for the agreed sum is also available. At one time a negative answer was given to this question, apparently because the common law remedy was an "adequate" one.[34] The current view, however, is that specific performance can be ordered in such a case if it is, in the circumstances, the most appropriate remedy.[35]

(2) Discretionary

Specific performance is a discretionary remedy: the court is not bound to grant it merely because the contract is valid at law and cannot be impeached on some specific equitable ground such as misrepresentation or undue influence. "Equity will only grant specific performance if, under all the circumstances, it is just and equitable to do so."[36] The discretion is, however, "not an arbitrary . . . discretion, but one to be governed as far as possible by fixed rules and principles."[37] The court will, in particular, have regard to the following factors:

---

28 *Howard E. Perry & Co.* v. *British Railways Board, supra*, at p. 1383.

29 *Sky Petroleum Ltd.* v. *V.I.P. Petroleum Ltd.* [1974] 1 W.L.R. 576; *cf. Total Oil (Great Britain) Ltd.* v. *Thompson Garage (Biggin Hill) Ltd.* [1972] 1 Q.B. 318, 324; *Redler Grain Silos Ltd.* v. *B.I.C.C. Ltd.* [1982] 1 Lloyd's Rep. 435.

30 This possibility was doubted in *Re London Wine Co. (Shippers)* [1986] P.C.C. 121, 149 but it was not necessary in that case to reach a final conclusion on the specific enforceability of the contract: see *ante*, p. 906, n. 20.

31 *Beswick* v. *Beswick* [1968] A.C. 58, 88, 90–91, 102; *cf. Coulls* v. *Bagot's Executor & Trustee Co. Ltd.* [1967] A.L.R. 385, 412.

32 *Tito* v. *Waddell (No. 2)* [1977] Ch. 106, 322.

33 *Evans Marshall & Co. Ltd.* v. *Bertola S.A.* [1973] 1 W.L.R. 349, 379.

34 *e.g. Crampton* v. *Varna Ry.* (1872) L.R. 7 Ch.App. 562, 567 ("a money contract not enforceable in this court").

35 *e.g. Beswick* v. *Beswick* [1968] A.C. 58. The burden is on the plaintiff to show that damages are not an adequate remedy: *The Stena Nautica (No. 2)* [1982] 2 Lloyd's Rep. 336, 348.

36 *Stickney* v. *Keeble* [1915] A.C. 386, 419.

37 *Lamare* v. *Dixon* (1873) L.R. 6 H.L. 414, 423.

(a) SEVERE HARDSHIP. Specific performance can be refused on the ground of severe hardship to the defendant. Thus in *Denne* v. *Light*[38] the court refused to order specific performance against the buyer of farming land wholly surrounded by land which belonged to others and over which there was no right of way. Specific performance may similarly be refused where the cost of performance to the defendant is wholly out of proportion to the benefit which performance will confer on the plaintiff.[39] The court is also "slow" to order specific performance against a person who can only put himself into a position to perform by taking legal proceedings against a third party, especially where the outcome of such proceedings is in doubt.[40] Severe hardship may be a ground for refusing specific performance even though it results from circumstances which arise after the conclusion of the contract, which affect the person of the defendant rather than the subject-matter of the contract, and for which the plaintiff is in no way responsible. For example, in *Patel* v. *Ali*[41] specific performance of a contract for the sale of a house was refused after a four-year delay (for which neither party was responsible), the vendor's circumstances having during this time changed disastrously as a result of her husband's bankruptcy and of an illness which had left her disabled. On the other hand, "mere pecuniary difficulties" would "afford no excuse."[42] Thus the purchaser of a house will not be denied specific performance merely because the vendor, on a rising market, finds it difficult to acquire alternative accommodation with the proceeds of the sale.[43] Nor will specific performance be refused merely because compliance with the order exposes the defendant to the risk of a strike by his employees.[44]

(b) UNFAIRNESS. The court may refuse specific performance of a contract which has been obtained by means that are unfair, even though they do not amount to grounds on which the contract can be invalidated.[45] Thus in *Walters* v. *Morgan*[46] the defendant agreed to grant the plaintiff a mining lease over land which he had only just bought. Specific performance was refused because the defendant was "surprised and was induced to sign the agreement in ignorance of the value of his property."[47] But specific performance will not be refused merely because the plaintiff fails to disclose circumstances which affect the value of the property or the defendant's willingness to contract with him.[48] The plaintiff must have taken unfair advantage of his superior knowledge: in *Walters* v. *Morgan* the court relied on the fact that the plaintiff had produced a draft lease during the negotiations, and had hurried the defendant into signing it before he could dis-

---

[38] (1857) 8 D.M. & G. 774; *cf. Wedgwood* v. *Adams* (1843) 6 Beav. 600; *Sullivan* v. *Henderson* [1973] 1 W.L.R. 333.

[39] *Tito* v. *Waddell* (*No.* 2) [1977] Ch. 106, 326; *cf. Morris* v. *Redland Bricks Ltd.* [1970] A.C. 652.

[40] *Wroth* v. *Tyler* [1974] Ch. 30, where an additional ground for refusing specific performance was that the proceedings would have to be between the defendant and his wife thus tending to split up the family. *Cf. Watts* v. *Spence* [1976] Ch. 165, 173.

[41] [1984] Ch. 283.

[42] *Ibid.* p. 288; *cf. Francis* v. *Cowcliffe* (1977) 33 P. & C.R. 368.

[43] *Mountford* v. *Scott* [1975] Ch. 258; *cf. Easton* v. *Brown* [1981] 3 All E.R. 278.

[44] See *Howard E. Perry* v. *British Railways Board* [1980] 1 W.L.R. 1375.

[45] *Cf. ante*, p. 503.

[46] (1861) 3 D.F. & J. 718.

[47] 3 D.F. & J. at p. 723. For the validity of the contract at law, see *ante*, p. 349.

[48] *Cf. ante*, pp. 349, 632–633.

cover the true value of the property. On the same principle specific performance may be refused if the plaintiff has taken advantage of the defendant's drunkenness, though it was not so extreme as to invalidate the contract at law.[49]

(c) INADEQUACY OF CONSIDERATION. The authorities on inadequacy of consideration as a ground for refusing specific performance are not easy to reconcile. On the one hand it is settled that *mere* inadequacy of consideration is not a ground for refusing specific performance.[50] On the other hand the statement that inadequacy of consideration is not a ground for refusing specific performance unless it is "such as shocks the conscience and amounts in itself to conclusive and decisive evidence of fraud"[51] is probably too narrow, even when allowance is made for the possibility that fraud may have had a wider meaning in equity than at law. The best view seems to be that specific performance may be refused where inadequacy of consideration is coupled with some other factor, not necessarily amounting to fraud or other invalidating cause at law—for example, mistake that is operative only in equity,[52] surprise[53] or unfair advantage taken by the plaintiff of his superior knowledge or bargaining position.[54] Specific performance may be refused on the ground of inadequacy of consideration even though the circumstances do not justify rescission of the contract.[55]

(d) CONDUCT OF PLAINTIFF. "The conduct of the party applying for relief is always an important element for consideration."[56] Thus specific performance can be refused if the plaintiff fails to perform a promise which induced the defendant to enter into the contract, but which is neither binding contractually, nor (because it relates to the future) operative as a misrepresentation.[57] For this purpose it may suffice that the plaintiff has acted unfairly in performing the contract, though he has not broken any promise. Specific enforcement of a solus agreement[58] has accordingly been denied to a petrol company on the ground that it had given discounts to other garages, making it impossible for the defendant garage to trade on the terms of the agreement except at a loss.[59]

An action could formerly be brought on a contract for the sale of land against a party who had provided written evidence of it by one who had not.[60] It had, however, been held that specific performance would not be granted to a purchaser of land if he refused to perform a stipulation to which he had agreed, but which could not be enforced against him for want

---

49 *Malins* v. *Freeman* (1837) 2 Keen 25, 34; *ante*, p. 503.
50 *Collier* v. *Brown* (1788) 1 Cox C.C. 428; *Western* v. *Russell* (1814) 3 V. & B. 187; *Haywood* v. *Cope* (1858) 25 Beav. 140.
51 *Coles* v. *Trecothick* (1804) 9 Ves. 234, 246.
52 *Webster* v. *Cecil* (1861) 30 Beav. 62.
53 *Supra* at n. 47; *cf. Mortlock* v. *Buller* (1804) 10 Ves. 292.
54 *Falcke* v. *Gray* (1859) 4 Drew. 651.
55 See *Mortlock* v. *Buller*, *supra*.
56 *Lamare* v. *Dixon* (1873) L.R. 6 H.L. 414, 423; *cf. Chappell* v. *The Times Newspapers Ltd.* [1975] 1 W.L.R. 482; *Wilton Group* v. *Abrams* [1990] BCC 310, 317 ("commercially disreputable" agreement).
57 *Lamare* v. *Dixon*, *supra*; *ante*, p. 296.
58 *Ante*, p. 417.
59 *Shell U.K. Ltd.* v. *Lostock Garages Ltd.* [1976] 1 W.L.R. 1187.
60 Law of Property Act 1925, s.40, replacing part of Statute of Frauds 1677, s.4, and now repealed by Law of Property (Miscellaneous Provisions) Act 1989, ss.1(8) and 4 and Sched. 2; and see *ante*, p. 168.

of written evidence.[61] A contract for the sale of land must now be made (and not merely evidenced) in a writing signed by all the parties and incorporating all the terms on which they have expressly agreed.[62] Hence if the stipulation in question was such a term, but was not contained in the documents, specific performance would now be refused on the different ground that no contract had come into existence. An alternative possibility is that the stipulation might have been intended to take effect as a collateral contract.[63] In that event, the main contract would be valid but the reasoning of the cases referred to above might still lead the court to refuse specific performance to the purchaser if it considered that the vendor would not be adequately protected, after being ordered to perform, by his claim for damages for breach of the collateral contract.[64]

(e) IMPOSSIBILITY. Specific performance will not be ordered against a person who has agreed to sell land which he does not own and cannot compel the owner to convey to him,[65] "because the court does not compel a person to do what is impossible."[66] The position is the same where a person has agreed to assign a lease and the landlord withholds his consent, without which the assignment cannot lawfully be effected.[67] Impossibility of enforcing an order of specific performance (*e.g.* because the defendant is not, and has no assets, within the jurisdiction) may also be a reason for refusing to make such an order.[68]

(f) OTHER FACTORS. The factors so far discussed operate negatively, as grounds for refusing specific performance. Others may operate positively, as grounds for awarding the remedy. Thus specific performance has been ordered of a contract to grant a licence to use a hall for a political meeting, and one reason for making the order was that it would promote freedom of speech and assembly.[69]

(3) Contracts not specifically enforceable

(a) CONTRACTS INVOLVING PERSONAL SERVICE. It has long been settled that equity will not, as a general rule, enforce a contract of personal service.[70] Specific enforcement against the employee was thought to interfere unduly with his personal liberty. Legislative force has now been given to this principle by the Trade Union and Labour Relations Act 1974, section 16 of which provides that no court shall compel an employee to do any work by ordering specific performance of a contract of employment or by restrain-

---

[61] See *Martin* v. *Pycroft* (1852) 2 D.M. & G. 785, 795; *Scott* v. *Bradley* [1971] Ch. 850.

[62] Law of Property (Miscellaneous Provisions) Act 1989, s.2(1); *ante*, p. 163.

[63] *Ante*, p. 164.

[64] *i.e.* on the principle of "mutuality" as now understood: *post*, pp. 916–918.

[65] See *Castle* v. *Wilkinson* (1870) L.R. 5 Ch.App. 534; *Watts* v. *Spence* [1976] Ch. 165; *cf. Elliot & Elliot (Builders) Ltd.* v. *Pierson* [1948] Ch. 453 (where the vendor sold land owned by a company that he controlled).

[66] *Forrer* v. *Nash* (1865) 35 Beav. 167, 171.

[67] *Wilmott* v. *Barber* (1880) 15 Ch.D. 96; *Warmington* v. *Miller* [1973] Q.B. 877; *cf. Sullivan* v. *Henderson* [1973] 1 W.L.R. 333.

[68] *The Sea Hawk* [1986] 1 W.L.R. 657, 665.

[69] *Verrall* v. *Great Yarmouth B.C.* [1981] Q.B. 202.

[70] *Johnson* v. *Shrewsbury and Birmingham Ry.* (1853) 3 D.M. & G. 358; *Brett* v. *East India and London Shipping Co. Ltd.* (1864) 2 H. & M. 404; *Britain* v. *Rossiter* (1883) 11 Q.B.D. 123, 127; *Rigby* v. *Connol* (1880) 14 Ch.D. 482, 487. *Cf. Taylor* v. *N.U.S.* [1967] 1 W.L.R. 532. *Chappell* v. *Times Newspapers Ltd.* [1975] 1 W.L.R. 482 (injunction); *The Scaptrade* [1983] 2 A.C. 694, 700–701 (*post*, pp. 912–913).

ing the breach of such a contract by injunction. Conversely, an employer could not be forced to employ: it was thought to be difficult or undesirable to enforce the continuance of a "personal" relationship between unwilling parties. This principle is reflected in the provisions of the Employment Protection (Consolidation) Act 1978, as to the remedies for "unfair" dismissal (which is not normally a breach of contract at all). Under the Act, a tribunal may order the reinstatement or re-engagement of the employee. Such an order is intended to be the employee's primary remedy; but if it is not complied with, the employer can, in the last resort, only be made to pay compensation.[71] Where an employee is dismissed in breach of contract, his normal remedy is a claim for damages or a declaration that the dismissal was *wrongful*: not specific enforcement,[72] or a declaration that the dismissal was *invalid*.[73]

The arguments usually advanced in support of the equitable principle are no longer wholly convincing[74]; and the principle is subject to a growing list of exceptions. A person who is dismissed from a public office in breach of the terms of his appointment may be entitled to reinstatement[75]; and the visitor of a University has power to order the reinstatement of a wrongfully dismissed lecturer, even when such a remedy would not be available in the ordinary courts.[76] The continuance or creation of a "personal" relationship may also be enforced where an injunction is granted against expulsion from a social club,[77] or against the refusal of a professional association to admit a person to membership.[78]

More generally, the modern relationship of employer and employee is often much less personal than the old relationship of master and servant

---

[71] ss.69–71 (as amended by Employment Act 1980, Sched. 1); and Employment Act 1982, s.5). Under ss.77(9) and 78 orders may be made for the continuation of the contract, but these do not give rise to the remedy of specific enforcement. *Cf.* Sex Discrimination Act 1975, ss.65(1)(*c*), 65(3)(*a*); Race Relations Act 1976, ss.56(1)(*c*), 56(4); Reserve Forces (Safeguard of Employment) Act 1985, ss.10, 17 and 18; Employment Act 1990 s.3(5), Sched. 1 para. 5.

[72] *Ante*, p. 650, n. 16; *post*, p. 920, n. 65.

[73] *Francis* v. *Kuala Lumpur Councillors* [1962] 1 W.L.R. 1411; *Vidyodaya University Council* v. *Silva* [1965] 1 W.L.R. 77; *Gunton* v. *Richmond-upon-Thames L.B.C.* [1981] Ch. 448 (declaration that dismissal was "ineffective *lawfully* to determine the contract"). A declaration may also be made that a decision of a disciplinary committee leading to a dismissal is void: *Stevenson* v. *United Road Transport Union* [1977] I.C.R. 893; but this does not amount to a declaration that the *contract* remains in operation: *ibid.* p. 906.

[74] See Clark, 32 M.L.R. 532.

[75] *Ridge* v. *Baldwin* [1964] A.C. 40; Ganz, 30 M.L.R. 288; *Malloch* v. *Aberdeen Corp.* [1971] 1 W.L.R. 1578; *Chief Constable of the North Wales Police* v. *Evans* [1982] 1 W.L.R. 1155; *Jones* v. *Lee* (1979) 78 L.G.R. 213. The line between ordinary and public employment is by no means clear-cut: see criticisms of the *Vidyodaya University* case, *supra*, in *Malloch* v. *Aberdeen Corp.*, *supra*, at p. 1595. But the distinction is one factor which determines the availability of judicial review as a remedy for alleged wrongful dismissal of public employees: see *R.* v. *East Berkshire Health Authority, ex p. Walsh* [1985] Q.B. 152 (judicial review not available to senior nursing office); *R.* v. *Civil Service Appeal Tribunal ex p. Bruce* [1989] I.C.R. 171 (judicial review available to Inland Revenue executive officer but refused as other, preferable remedies available); *R.* v. *Secretary of State for the Home Department, ex p. Broom* [1986] Q.B. 198); *R.* v. *Derbyshire C.C., ex p. Noble* [1990] I.C.R. 808 (judicial review available to police surgeon); *cf. McLaren* v. *Home Office* [1990] I.C.R. 824 (claim by prison officer raised no issue of public law).

[76] *Thomas* v. *University of Bradford* [1987] A.C. 795, 824.

[77] *Young* v. *Ladies Imperial Club Ltd.* [1920] 2 K.B. 522.

[78] *cf. Nagle* v. *Feilden* [1966] 2 Q.B. 633. See also Sex Discrimination Act 1975, s.71(1) and Race Relations Act 1976, s.62 (injunction against "persistent" discrimination).

was believed to be; and there are signs that the courts are prepared to re-examine or qualify the old equitable principles in the light of this development.[79] Industrial conditions may in fact force an employer to retain an employee whom he would prefer to dismiss or to dismiss one whom he is perfectly willing to retain. For example, in *Hill* v. *C. A. Parsons Ltd.*[80] employers were forced by union pressure to dismiss an employee. The dismissal amounted to a breach of contract and the court issued an injunction to restrain the breach, thus in effect reinstating the employee. As the employers and the employee were perfectly willing to maintain their relationship, the decision does not seem to violate the spirit of the general equitable principle against the specific enforcement of employment contracts.

The equitable principle applies to all contracts involving personal service even though they are not strictly contracts of service. Thus an agreement to allow an auctioneer to sell a collection of works of art cannot be specifically enforced[81] by either party, though specific enforcement would hardly be an undue interference with personal liberty, even in a suit against the auctioneer. Again, an agreement to enter into a partnership will not be specifically enforced as "it is impossible to make persons who will not concur carry on a business jointly, for their common advantage."[82] The court can, however, order the execution of a formal partnership agreement, and leave the parties to their remedies on the agreement.[83] Similarly, the court can order the execution of a service contract even though that contract, when made, may not be specifically enforceable.[84]

The equitable principle of refusing specific performance is limited to contracts for services of a personal nature. There is no general rule against the specific enforcement of a contract merely because one party undertakes to provide services[85] under it. Thus specific performance can be ordered of a contract to publish a piece of music[86] and sometimes of contracts to build.[87] It has, indeed, been suggested that a time charterparty cannot be specifically enforced against the shipowner because it is a contract for services[88]; but the services that the shipowner undertakes under such a contract will often be no more personal than those to be rendered by a builder

---

79 See *C. H. Giles & Co. Ltd.* v. *Morris* [1972] 1 W.L.R. 307.

80 [1972] Ch. 305; Hepple [1972] C.L.J. 47; *cf. Irani* v. *Southampton, etc. Health Authority* [1985] I.C.R. 590 (where the employers retained confidence in an employee but had dismissed him because of differences between him and another employee); *Powell* v. *Brent L.B.C.* [1988] I.C.R. 176; *Hughes* v. *Southwark L.C.B.* [1988] I.R.L.R. 55.

81 *Chinnock* v. *Sainsbury* (1861) 30 L.J.Ch. 409; *cf. Mortimer* v. *Beckett* [1920] 1 Ch. 571.

82 *England* v. *Curling* (1844) 8 Beav. 129, 137.

83 As in *England* v. *Curling* (*supra*), where the object of obtaining such a decree was to ascertain the exact terms that had been agreed, and then to prevent one of the contracting parties from competing in business with the other.

84 *C. H. Giles & Co. Ltd.* v. *Morris* [1972] 1 W.L.R. 307; *cf. Posner* v. *Scott-Lewis* [1987] Ch. 25.

85 *e.g. Regent International Hotels* v. *Pageguide*, *The Times*, May 13, 1985 (injunction against preventing plaintiff company from managing a hotel); *Posner* v. *Scott-Lewis* [1987] Ch. 25 (*post*, p. 913, at n. 4).

86 *Barrow* v. *Chappell & Co.* (1951), now reported in [1976] R.P.C. 355, and cited in *Joseph* v. *National Magazine Co. Ltd.* [1959] Ch. 14; contrast *Malcolm* v. *Chancellor Masters and Scholars of the University of Oxford*, *The Times*, December 19, 1990, where specific performance of a contract to publish a book was refused on the ground that continued co-operation between author and publishers would have been required.

87 *Post*, p. 915.

88 *The Scaptrade* [1983] 2 A.C. 694, 700–701.

under a building contract. Denial of specific performance in the case of time charters is best explained on other grounds.[89]

(b) CONTRACTS REQUIRING CONSTANT SUPERVISION. Specific performance will not be ordered of continuous contractual duties, the proper performance of which might require constant supervision by the court.[90] In *Ryan* v. *Mutual Tontine Association*[91] the lease of a service flat gave the tenant the right to the services of a porter who was to be "constantly in attendance." Specific enforcement of this right was refused as it would (it was said) have required "that constant superintendence by the court, which the court in such cases has always declined to give."[92] For the same reason the courts have refused specifically to enforce an undertaking to cultivate a farm in a particular manner[93]; a contract to keep a shop open[94]; a contract to keep an airfield in operation[95]; a contract to deliver goods in instalments[96]; and obligations to operate railway signals[97] and to provide engine power.[98] And it has been held that a voyage charterparty cannot be specifically enforced against the shipowner.[99]

This "difficulty" of supervision is much exaggerated. In most cases the mere existence of the court's order will suffice to deter a deliberate breach. No practical difficulty seems to have arisen in the cases in which the courts have specifically enforced building contracts.[1] If the defendant were recalcitrant, the court could appoint an expert as its officer to supervise performance. This is no more "difficult" than appointing a person to run the business of a bankrupt or to manage the property of a mental patient. The court has appointed a receiver to run a mine in a rescission action[2] the same thing could be done in an action for specific performance. Alternatively, the plaintiff could be empowered to appoint a person to act as agent of the defendant to supervise the enforcement of the order: this would not be radically different from the statutory power of a mortgagee to appoint a receiver to act as agent of the mortgagor.[3] Where the acts to be done under the contract are not to be done by the defendant personally, the court can order him simply to enter into a contract to procure those acts to be done. From this point of view, *Ryan* v. *Mutual Tontine Association* may be contrasted with the later case of *Posner* v. *Scott-Lewis*[4] where the lessor of a

---

[89] See *infra* at n. 99.

[90] The principle does not apply to continuous obligations to pay money: thus an agreement to pay an annuity can be specifically enforced (*ante*, p. 904).

[91] [1893] 1 Ch. 116.

[92] At p. 123.

[93] *Rayner* v. *Stone* (1762) 2 Eden 128; *Phipps* v. *Jackson* (1887) 56 L.J.Ch. 350.

[94] *Braddon Towers Ltd.* v. *International Stores Ltd.* [1987] 1 E.G.L.R. 209 (decided in 1959).

[95] *Dowty Boulton Paul Ltd.* v. *Wolverhampton Corp.* [1971] 1 W.L.R. 204; for later proceedings see [1973] Ch. 94.

[96] *Dominion Coal Co.* v. *Dominion Iron & Steel Co.* [1900] A.C. 293; but see *ante*, p. 906.

[97] *Powell Duffryn Steam Coal Co.* v. *Taff Vale Ry.* (1874) L.R. 9 Ch. 331.

[98] *Blackett* v. *Bates* (1865) L.R. 1 Ch. 177.

[99] *De Mattos* v. *Gibson* (1858) 4 D. & J. 276 (voyage charter). The view expressed in *The Scaptrade* [1983] 2 A.C. 694, 700–701, that a time charter is not specifically enforceable, is best explained on the ground that such enforcement would require too much supervision.

[1] *Post*, p. 915; *cf. Storer* v. *G.W. Ry.* (1842) 2 Y. & C.C.C. 48 (specific performance ordered of an agreement "for ever . . . to maintain one neat archway"); *Kennard* v. *Cory Bros. & Co.* [1922] 2 Ch. 1 (mandatory injunction ordering defendant to keep a drain open).

[2] *Gibbs* v. *David* (1870) L.R. 20 Eq. 373.

[3] Law of Property Act 1925, s.101; *cf.* Insolvency Act 1986, s.44.

[4] [1987] Ch. 25.

block of luxury flats covenanted, so far as lay in his power, to employ a resident porter to perform a number of specified tasks. It was held that the covenant was specifically enforceable in the sense that the lessor could be ordered to appoint a resident porter for the performance of the specified services. In the light of all these possible methods of enforcement, it is submitted that "difficulty" of supervision is not of itself a bar to specific performance but only one of many factors to be taken into account in determining whether this form of relief is to be granted.[5] If the court attaches sufficient importance to the interest which the plaintiff wishes to protect, it will not be deterred from granting specific relief by the argument that such relief will require constant supervision.[6]

(c) CONTRACTS WHICH ARE TOO VAGUE. An agreement may be so vague that it cannot be enforced at all, even by an action for damages.[7] But although an agreement is definite enough to be enforced in some form of legal proceeding, it may still be too vague to be enforced specifically.[8] Thus specific performance has been refused of a contract to publish an article as to the wording of which the parties disagreed.[9] In such a case the court would find it difficult or impossible to state in its order exactly what the defendant was to do; and precision is essential[10] since failure to comply with the court's order may lead to attachment for contempt. An agreement is not, however, too vague to be specifically enforced merely because it is expressed to be subject to such amendments as may reasonably be required by one (or by either) party.[11]

The difficulty of precisely formulating the court's order was at one time thought to prevent the specific enforcement of contracts for the sale of goodwill alone (without business premises): it was considered impossible for the court in its decree to state precisely what the vendor was to do.[12] But in *Beswick* v. *Beswick* it was said that such a contract could be specifically enforced.[13] The older, contrary, authorities were not cited; and it seems that they have been made obsolete by the growing legal and commercial precision of the concept of goodwill.[14]

---

[5] *Tito* v. *Waddell* (*No.* 2) [1977] Ch. 106, 321–322; *cf. Shiloh Spinners Ltd.* v. *Harding* [1973] A.C. 691, 724, where difficulty of supervision is said to be no longer a bar to relief against forfeiture (as it had been in *Hill* v. *Barclay* (1870) 16 Ves.Jun. 402); but the possibility is recognised that such difficulty sometimes "explains why specific performance cannot be granted . . . ."

[6] *Luganda* v. *Service Hotels* [1969] 2 Ch. 209 (mandatory injunction ordering defendants to allow a protected tenant, who had been wrongfully locked out of a room in a residental hotel, to resume his residence in the hotel); *cf. Films Rover International Ltd.* v. *Cannon Films Sales Ltd.* [1987] 1 W.L.R. 670, 682 (for further proceedings, see [1989] 1 W.L.R. 912); *Sutton Housing Trust* v. *Lawrence* (1987) 19 H.L.R. 520.

[7] *Ante*, p. 48; *Waring & Gillow* v. *Thompson* (1912) 29 T.L.R. 154.

[8] *Tito* v. *Waddell* (*No.* 2) [1977] Ch. 106, 322–323.

[9] *Joseph* v. *National Magazine Co. Ltd.* [1959] Ch. 14; *cf. Slater* v. *Raw*, *The Times*, October 15, 1977.

[10] *Cf. Lock International plc.* v. *Beswick* [1989] 1 W.L.R. 1268; *Lawrence David Ltd.* v. *Ashton* [1989] I.C.R. 123, 132.

[11] *Sweet & Maxwell Ltd.* v. *Universal News Services Ltd.* [1964] 2 Q.B. 699; *Alpenstow Ltd.* v. *Regalian Properties plc* [1985] 1 W.L.R. 721.

[12] *Bozon* v. *Farlow* (1816) 1 Mer. 459, 472; *cf. Baxter* v. *Connolly* (1820) 1 J. & W. 576; *Coslake* v. *Till* (1826) 1 Russ. 376; *Thornbury* v. *Bevill* (1842) 1 Y. & C.C.C. 554, 565; *Darbey* v. *Whitaker* (1857) 4 Drew. 134, 139.

[13] [1968] A.C. 58, 89, 97.

[14] *Trego* v. *Hunt* [1896] A.C. 7.

(d) BUILDING CONTRACTS. The general rule is that a contract to erect a building cannot be specifically enforced.[15] There seem to be three reasons for this rule. First, damages may be an adequate remedy if the building owner can engage another builder to do the work. Secondly, the contract may be too vague if it fails to describe the building with sufficient certainty. Thirdly, specific enforcement of the contract may require more supervision than the court is willing to give.

But where the first two reasons do not apply, the third will not be allowed to prevail. Specific performance of a contract to build can therefore be ordered if (i) the work is precisely defined with sufficient certainty; (ii) damages will not adequately compensate the plaintiff, and (iii) the defendant is in possession of the land on which the building is to be done.[16] Thus in *Wolverhampton Corporation* v. *Emmons*[17] the plaintiff corporation acquired land for an improvement scheme and sold part of it to the defendant, who covenanted to demolish the houses on it and to build new ones. The demolition was carried out and plans for the new houses were approved. The court ordered specific performance of the covenant to build. The defendant's obligations were precisely defined by the plans; damages would not adequately compensate the corporation if a site in the middle of the town were left vacant instead of being occupied by houses yielding rates; and, as the defendant had possession of the site, the corporation could not get the work done by employing another builder.

(e) CONTRACTS SPECIFICALLY ENFORCEABLE IN PART ONLY. In *Ryan* v. *Mutual Tontine Association*[18] the court refused specifically to enforce a landlord's undertaking to have a porter "constantly in attendance"; and it seems unlikely that the court would, even now, order the landlord to enter into a contract with a porter *on such terms* (though it could make an order of a similar nature where the lease *specified the tasks* to be done by the porter[19]). A further claim that the landlord should be ordered simply to appoint a porter was also rejected on the ground that "when the court cannot grant specific performance of the contract as a whole, it will not interfere to compel specific performance of part of a contract."[20] But where parts of the contract are severable specific performance of each part can be separately ordered.[21] And where a monetary adjustment can be made in respect of the unperformable part the court may order specific performance with compensation.[22]

---

15 *Flint* v. *Brandon* (1808) 3 Ves. 159; and see *Wolverhampton Corporation* v. *Emmons* [1901] 1 Q.B. 515; *cf. Gyllenhammar Partners International* v. *Sour Brodogradevna Industria* [1989] 2 Lloyd's Rep. 403, 422 (contract to build a ship).

16 *Wolverhampton Corporation* v. *Emmons* [1901] 1 Q.B. 515, p. 525, as modified by *Carpenters Estates Ltd.* v. *Davies* [1940] Ch. 160.

17 *Supra*; *cf. Jeune* v. *Queens Cross Properties Ltd.* [1974] Ch. 97; *Calabar Properties Ltd.* v. *Stitcher* [1984] 1 W.L.R. 287; *Price* v. *Strange* [1978] Ch. 337, 357; Landlord and Tenant Act 1985 s.17; *Gordon* v. *Selico* (1986) 278 E.G. 53; *Barrett* v. *Lounova* [1990] 1 Q.B. 348. For the converse question, whether a builder can, in effect, compel the owner to allow him to complete the work, contrast *Hounslow* (*London Borough*) v. *Twickenham Garden & Builders Ltd.* [1971] Ch. 233 with *Mayfield Holdings* v. *Moana Reef* [1973] 1 N.Z.L.R. 309; and *cf. Finelli* v. *Dee* (1968) 76 D.L.R. (2d.) 393.

18 [1893] 1 Ch. 116, *ante*, p. 913.

19 As in *Posner* v. *Scott-Lewis* [1988] Ch. 25 (*ante*, pp. 913–914).

20 [1893] Ch. at p. 123.

21 *Odessa Tramways Co.* v. *Mendel* (1878) 8 Ch.D. 235.

22 *Ante*, p. 673.

(f) TERMINABLE CONTRACTS. If the party against whom specific performance is sought is entitled to terminate the contract, the order will be refused as the defendant could render it nugatory by exercising his power to terminate. This principle applies whether the contract is terminable under its express terms[23] or on account of the conduct of the party seeking specific performance.[24]

(g) PROMISES WITHOUT CONSIDERATION. On the principle that equity will not aid a volunteer,[25] specific performance will not be ordered of a gratuitous promise even though it is binding at law because it is made by deed or supported by nominal consideration[26]; so that damages or the agreed sum can be recovered by the promisee. Where such a promise is made to a trustee for the benefit of a third party, it has been held that the trustee ought not to enforce the promise at law against the promisor,[27] unless the promise can be regarded as constituting a trust which is "already perfect."[28]

The principle that equity will not aid a volunteer does not apply where an option to buy land is granted by deed but without consideration, or for only a nominal consideration. Such an option is for the present purpose regarded as an offer coupled with a legally binding promise not to revoke; and it may therefore be exercised in spite of an attempt to revoke it. The resulting contract of sale can then be specifically enforced[29]—always assuming that it is supported by substantial consideration.

(4) Mutuality of remedy

The court will sometimes refuse to order specific performance at the suit of one party unless it can order it at the suit of the other. Thus a party who undertakes to render personal services or to perform continuous duties cannot get specific performance as the remedy is not available against him[30]; and for the same reason a minor cannot claim specific performance.[31] Such cases were explained on the ground that the remedy of specific performance must be mutual; and it was said that this requirement had to be satisfied at the time when the contract was made.[32]

There are, however, many cases in which specific performance can be

---

[23] *e.g. Sheffield Gas Co.* v. *Harrison* (1853) 17 Beav. 294; but *cf. Allhusen* v. *Borries* (1867) 15 W.R. 739.

[24] *Gregory* v. *Wilson* (1851) 9 Hare 683.

[25] *Ante*, p. 73.

[26] See *Re Parkin* [1892] 3 Ch. 510; *Cannon* v. *Hartley* [1949] Ch. 213. Contrast *Gurtner* v. *Circuit* [1968] 2 Q.B. 587, 596 where an agreement by deed between the Minister and the Motor Insurer's Bureau was said to be specifically enforceable by the Minister. The fact that no consideration moved from him was not mentioned by the court. *Cf. ante*, p. 571.

[27] *Re Pryce* [1917] 1 Ch. 234; *Re Kay* [1939] Ch. 239; Elliot, 76 L.Q.R. 100; Hornby, 78 L.Q.R. 288; Matheson, 29 M.L.R. 397; Lee, 85 L.Q.R. 213; Barton, 91 L.Q.R. 236; Meagher and Lehane, 92 L.Q.R. 427; Macnair, 8 Legal Studies 172. The rule does not apply where a promise for the benefit of a third party volunteer is made to a promisee who has provided consideration: *Beswick* v. *Beswick* [1968] A.C. 58.

[28] *Fletcher* v. *Fletcher* (1844) 4 Hare 67, 74.

[29] *Mountford* v. *Scott* [1975] Ch. 258.

[30] *Ogden* v. *Fossick* (1862) D. F. & J. 426; *Blackett* v. *Bates* (1865) L.R. 1 Ch.App. 117; *cf. Page One Records Ltd.* v. *Britton* [1968] 1 W.L.R. 157 (injunction). A dictum in *Warren* v. *Mendy* [1989] 1 W.L.R. 853, 866 rejects the requirement of mutuality even in this situation (but specific enforcement was refused for reasons discussed on p. 921, *post*).

[31] *Flight* v. *Bolland* (1828) 4 Russ. 298; *Lumley* v. *Ravenscroft* [1895] 1 Q.B. 683.

[32] Fry, *Specific Performance* (6th ed.), pp. 219, 386.

obtained by a party even though it could not at the time of contracting have been ordered against him.[33] Thus, if A agrees to grant a lease of land to B, who agrees to build on it, B cannot normally be forced to build; but if he actually does build he can get specific performance of A's promise to grant the lease.[34] Specific performance cannot be ordered against a person who sells land which he does not own[35] but if he becomes owner before the purchaser repudiates[36] he can get specific performance.[37] Conversely a vendor with defective title may be ordered to convey for a reduced price although he could not himself have obtained specific performance.[38] It seems that a person of full age can get specific performance of a voidable contract made during minority even though he could have elected to repudiate the contract.[39] And a victim of fraud or innocent misrepresentation can get specific performance although he may be entitled to rescind the contract so that it could not be enforced against him.[40]

Such cases show that the requirement of mutuality does not have to be satisfied at the time of contracting; the crucial time is that of the hearing. The rule was reformulated by Buckley L.J. in *Price* v. *Strange*: the court "will not compel a defendant to perform his obligations specifically if it cannot at the same time ensure that any unperformed obligations of the plaintiff will be specifically performed, unless perhaps damages would be an adequate remedy for any default on the plaintiff's part."[41] The defendant in that case had promised to grant an underlease to the plaintiff who had in return undertaken to execute certain internal and external repairs. It was admitted that the plaintiff's undertakings were not specifically enforceable; and it seems clear that he could not have obtained specific performance of the promise to grant the underlease before any of the repairs had been done. For in that case the only remedy available to the defendant for default on the plaintiff's part might have been in damages, and this might have been inadequate,[42] especially if the plaintiff was of doubtful solvency. But in fact the plaintiff had done the internal repairs and was wrongfully prevented from doing the external ones by the defendant, who later had these done at her own expense. As by the time of the hearing all the repairs had been completed, specific enforcement of the

---

[33] This possibility was formerly illustrated by the rule that specific performance of a contract for the sale of land could be enforced against a party who had signed a memorandum of the contract by one who had not: see *Seton* v. *Slade* (1802) 7 Ves. 265; *Martin* v. *Pycroft* (1852) 2 D.M. & G. 785, 795. Now neither party could sue since no contract would come into existence unless the writing was signed by both: Law of Property (Miscellaneous Provisions) Act 1989, s.2(1), *ante*, p. 164.

[34] *Wilkinson* v. *Clements* (1872) L.R. 8 Ch.App. 96.

[35] *Ante*, p. 910.

[36] *Halkett* v. *Dudley* [1907] 1 Ch. 590, 596; *Salisbury* v. *Hatcher* (1842) 2 Y. & C.C.C. 54; *Cleadon Trust* v. *Davies* [1940] 1 Ch. 940.

[37] *Hoggart* v. *Scott* (1830) 1 Russ. & My. 293; *Wylson* v. *Dunn* (1887) 34 Ch.D. 569.

[38] *Mortlock* v. *Buller* (1804) 10 Ves. 292, 315; *Wilson* v. *Wilson* (1857) 3 Jur.(N.S.) 810.

[39] *Clayton* v. *Ashdown* (1714) 9 Vin.Abr. 393 (G.4) 1.

[40] *Ante*, Chap. 9, Section 4.

[41] [1978] Ch. 337, 367–368; adopting Ames, 3 Col.L.Rev. 1. *cf. Lyus* v. *Prowsa Developments Ltd.* [1982] 1 W.L.R. 1044, 1053, and *Sutton* v. *Sutton* [1984] Ch. 184 where the argument of lack of mutuality was rejected because one of the claimant's promises had been performed, even though another was not binding. Specific performance was refused on grounds of public policy, *ante*, p. 395.

[42] If he can be ordered to give additional, satisfactory security, the plaintiff can obtain an order of specific performance even though he has not yet performed and is not ordered immediately to do so: *Langen & Wind Ltd.* v. *Bell* [1972] Ch. 685.

defendant's promise to grant the underlease would not expose her to the risk of having no remedy except damages in the event of the plaintiff's default; and specific performance was ordered on the terms that the plaintiff make an allowance in respect of the repairs done by the defendant. The principle that mutuality is judged by reference to the time of the hearing similarly accounts for the rule that a person who has been induced to enter into a contract by misrepresentation can specifically enforce it against the other; for by seeking this remedy he affirms the contract[43] and so gives the court power to hold him to it.[44] The court has no such power when specific performance is claimed on behalf of a minor: "the act of filing the bill by his next friend cannot bind him."[45]

(5) Specific performance and third parties

In *Beswick* v. *Beswick*[46] A promised B to pay an annuity to C in consideration of B's transferring the goodwill of his business to A. It was held that, although the promise did not give C any right of action, it could be specifically enforced by B's personal representative[47] against A; with the result that A was ordered to make the promised payments to C. In reaching this conclusion, the House of Lords stressed three points: that B's remedy at law was inadequate as the damages which he could recover would be purely nominal[48]; that A had received the entire consideration for his promise as the business had been transferred to him[49]; and that the contract could have been specifically enforced by A, if B had failed to perform his promise to transfer the business.[50] It is also worth pointing out that A's promise, being one to pay an annuity, was of a kind which would have been specifically enforceable if it had been made to B for his own benefit[51]; and that, if the promise had been in these terms, none of the grounds for refusing specific performance which have been discussed in this Chapter would have applied.

It does not, however, follow from *Beswick* v. *Beswick* that specific performance in favour of a third party will be granted *only* if the circumstances are such that the remedy would have been available in a two-party case. Thus it seems that specific performance could be ordered of a promise to pay a single lump sum to a third party,[52] though in a two-party case such an obligation would be enforceable by a common law action for the agreed sum. Again, it seems that specific performance in favour of a third party would not be excluded merely because substantial damages, constituting an "adequate" remedy, were available to the promisee. As Lord Pearce[53]

---

[43] *Ante*, p. 343.
[44] This reasoning still holds good in the situation described in the text above. It was formerly used to explain the now obsolete rule stated in n. 33, *supra*: see *Martin* v. *Mitchell* (1820) 2 J. & W. 413, 427; *Flight* v. *Bolland* (1828) 4 Russ. 298, 301.
[45] *Flight* v. *Bolland*, *supra*, at p. 301.
[46] [1968] A.C. 58; *ante*, p. 529.
[47] Who happened to be C.
[48] [1968] A.C. 58, 73, 81, 83, 102. Nor did A have any other more satisfactory remedy at law, *e.g.* he could not have sued for the amount to be paid to C, or for the return of the goodwill (*ante*, p. 531).
[49] *Ibid.* pp. 83, 89, 97, 102; *cf. ante*, p. 905.
[50] [1968] A.C. 58, 89, 97.
[51] *Ante*, p. 904.
[52] As in *Gurtner* v. *Circuit* [1968] 2 Q.B. 587 (as to which see *ante*, p. 916, n. 26).
[53] Who thought that the damages in *Beswick* v. *Beswick* would be substantial: [1968] A.C. 58, 88.

said in *Beswick* v. *Beswick*, such damages "would be a less appropriate remedy since the parties to the agreement were intending an annuity . . . ; and a lump sum of damages does not accord with this."[54] On the other hand specific performance will obviously not be ordered where A contracts with B to render personal services to C, for the policy of the rule against the specific enforcement of service contracts applies no less where the services are to be rendered to a third party than where they are to be rendered to the promisee. Again, A may contract with B to pay C £10,000 immediately in return for B's promise to serve A for one year. If A repudiates before B has performed the service, specific performance in favour of C should probably be refused on the ground that it would offend the mutuality requirement[55]: A would have no security for the performance of B's promise to serve except a common law action for damages.

The above examples show that specific performance should not be granted merely because the contract provides for performance in favour of a third party, nor refused merely because it would not have been ordered had there been no third party in the case. As a general principle, it is submitted that specific performance in favour of a third party should prima facie be available when it is the *most appropriate* remedy for the enforcement of the contract. But it should be open to the defendant to resist specific enforcement by showing that this remedy would lead to one of the undesirable results against which the established limitations on the scope of the remedy are meant to provide protection.

2. Injunction

(1) General

Where a contract is negative in nature, or contains a negative stipulation, breach of it may be restrained by injunction. In such cases, an injunction is normally granted as a matter of course, even though it is an equitable (and thus in principle a discretionary) remedy. In particular, a defendant cannot resist an injunction simply on the ground that observance of the contract is burdensome to him[56] and that the breach would cause little or no prejudice to the plaintiff[57] the court in such cases is not concerned with "the balance of convenience or inconvenience."[58] This rule, however, only applies to a *prohibitory* injunction restraining a defendant from *future* breaches. Where the breach lies entirely in the past (*e.g.* where the defendant has fenced land that he had covenanted to leave open), the plaintiff may seek a *mandatory* injunction, ordering the breach to be undone. Such an order *is* subject to a "balance of convenience" test and may therefore be refused if the prejudice suffered by the defendant in having to restore the original position heavily outweighs the advantage that will be derived from such

---

[54] [1968] A.C. 58, 88; *cf. ibid.* p. 102 and the citation at pp. 90–91 with approval of a dictum of Windeyer J. in *Coulls* v. *Bagot's Executor & Trustee Co. Ltd.* [1967] A.L.R. 385, 412.

[55] *Ante*, pp. 916–918.

[56] *Cf. ante*, p. 908.

[57] *Kemp* v. *Sober* (1851) 1 Sim. (N.S.) 517; *Tipping* v. *Eckersley* (1855) 2 K. & J. 264; *Marco Productions Ltd.* v. *Pagola* [1945] K.B. 111.

[58] *Doherty* v. *Allman* (1878) 3 App.Cas. 709, 720; *cf. Warner Bros. Pictures Inc.* v. *Nelson* [1937] 1 K.B. 209, 217 and (in tort) *Kennaway* v. *Thompson* [1981] Q.B. 88.

restoration by the plaintiff.[59] In applying the "balance of convenience" test, the court will, however, also take the nature of the breach into account. Thus where the defendant in breach of a restrictive covenant erected a building so as to block the plaintiff's sea view, a mandatory injunction was granted as the breach had been committed deliberately, with full knowledge of the plaintiff's rights, and as damages would not be an adequate remedy.[60]

The "balance of convenience" test also applies to interlocutory injunctions,[61] except where there is "a plain and uncontested breach of a clear covenant not to do a particular thing."[62]

(2) No indirect specific performance

An injunction will not be granted if its effect is directly or indirectly to compel the defendant to do acts which he could not have been ordered to do by a decree of specific performance. Thus an employee cannot be restrained from committing a breach of his positive obligation to work, for that would amount to specific enforcement of a contract of service.[63] Nor can an employer generally[64] be restrained from dismissing his employee in breach of contract.[65]

(a) Express negative promises. A contract of employment may contain negative promises which can be enforced by injunction without indirectly compelling the employee to work, or the employer to employ.[66] Covenants in restraint of trade contained in such contracts are commonly enforced by injunction: this does not compel the employee to work for the employer, as such covenants generally begin to operate after the period of service is over. But some negative stipulations are expressed to operate during that period. These may be enforceable by injunction if the injunction merely provides an inducement to perform the positive obligation, but not if it in effect compels the employee to do the agreed work.

---

[59] *Sharp* v. *Harrison* [1922] 1 Ch. 502; *Shepherd Homes Ltd.* v. *Sandham* [1971] Ch. 340; for subsequent proceedings, see [1971] 1 W.L.R. 1062; *Sutton Housing Trust* v. *Lawrence* (1988) 55 P. & C.R. 320 (mandatory and prohibitory injunction); *Reed* v. *Madon* [1989] Ch. 408.

[60] *Wakeham* v. *Wood* (1982) 43 P. & C.R. 40; *Chelsea* v. *Muscut* [1990] 2 E.G.L.R. 48.

[61] *Texaco Ltd.* v. *Mulberry Filling Station Ltd.* [1972] 1 W.L.R. 814; *Evans Marshall & Co.* v. *Bertola* [1973] 1 W.L.R. 439; *Clifford Davis Management Ltd.* v. *W.E.A. Records Ltd.* [1975] 1 W.L.R. 61; *Mike Trading & Transport Ltd.* v. *R. Pagnan & Fratelli* [1980] 2 Lloyd's Rep. 546; *The Sea Hawk* [1986] 1 W.L.R. 657; *Kerr* v. *Morris* [1987] Ch. 90, 112; *Films Rover International* v. *Cannon Film Sales Ltd.* [1987] 1 W.L.R. 670 (for further proceedings, see [1989] 1 W.L.R. 912); *Evening Standard Co. Ltd.* v. *Henderson* [1987] I.C.R. 588; *Provident Financial Group plc* v. *Hayward* [1989] I.C.R. 160; *Lock International plc* v. *Beswick* [1989] 1 W.L.R. 1268; *Cambridge Nutrition Ltd.* v. *B.B.C.* [1990] 3 All E.R. 523; *Lansing Linde Ltd.* v. *Kerr* [1991] 1 All E.R. 418. For the general principles governing such injunctions, see *American Cyanamid Co.* v. *Ethicon* [1975] A.C. 396; *Fellowes* v. *Fisher* [1976] Q.B. 122; *Lawrence David Ltd.* v. *Ashton* [1989] I.C.R. 123.

[62] *Hampstead and Suburban Properties Ltd.* v. *Diomedous* [1969] 1 Ch. 248, 259; *cf. A.G.* v. *Barker* [1990] 3 All E.R. 257.

[63] *Whitwood Chemical Co.* v. *Hardman* [1891] 2 Ch. 416; *cf.* Trade Union and Labour Relations Act 1974, s.16(*b*).

[64] For an exception to the general rule, see *Hill* v. *C. A. Parsons & Co. Ltd.* [1972] 1 Ch. 305; *ante*, p. 912.

[65] *Chappell* v. *Times Newspapers Ltd.* [1975] 1 W.L.R. 482; Hepple [1975] C.L.J. 212; *cf. City & Hackney Health Authority* v. *NUPE* [1985] I.R.L.R. 252; *Alexander* v. *Standard Telephone and Cables Ltd.* [1990] I.C.R. 291.

[66] *Cf. Evans Marshall & Co. Ltd.* v. *Bertola S.A.* [1973] 1 W.L.R. 349.

Thus in *Lumley* v. *Wagner*[67] Mlle. Wagner undertook that for three months she would sing at Mr. Lumley's theatre in Drury Lane on two nights a week and that during those three months she would not use her talents at any other theatre without Mr. Lumley's written consent. She then agreed, for a larger payment, to sing for Mr. Gye at Covent Garden, and to abandon her agreement with Mr. Lumley. Lord St. Leonards granted Mr. Lumley an injunction to restrain her from singing for Mr. Gye. Similarly, a manufacturer can be restrained from breach of a "sole distributorship" agreement, in the sense that he can be prevented from engaging a different distributor, even though the court might not order him specifically to perform the positive part of the contract to keep up the original distributor's supplies.[68] But a promise by an employee not to work in *any capacity* except for the employer[69] cannot be enforced by injunction since the effect of the injunction would be "to drive the defendant either to starvation or to specific peformance of the positive covenants"[70] to work.

Lumley v. *Wagner* has been much criticised,[71] particularly in relation to contracts of employment. An injunction may put so much economic pressure on the employee as in effect to force him to perform the positive part of the contract. In *Warner Bros. Pictures Inc.* v. *Nelson*[72] a film actress agreed to act for the plaintiffs for a period of time during which she undertook not to act for anyone else without the plaintiffs' written consent. She was restrained by injunction from breaking this undertaking; and it was said that this would not force her to act for the plaintiffs as she could earn a living by doing other work. But it might be quite unreasonable to expect her to do this; and more recent cases support the view that an injunction should not be granted except where it leaves the employee with some other *reasonable* means of earning a living. They have arisen where professional entertainers or athletes have entered into long-term exclusive contracts with managers, in whom they then lost confidence. It has been held that the managers could not obtain injunctions either against their clients,[73] or against third parties with whom those clients had entered into substitute management contracts,[74] if the effect of the injunction would "as a practical matter"[75] force the clients to make use of the services of the original manager; and this would commonly be the case since such persons cannot successfully work without a manager.

The question whether an injunction would put undue pressure on an employee to perform his positive obligation to work can give rise to diffi-

---

67 (1852) 1 D.M. & G. 604.

68 *Decro-Wall International S.A.* v. *Practitioners in Marketing Ltd.* [1971] 1 W.L.R. 361; *Evans Marshall & Co. Ltd.* v. *Bertola S.A.* [1973] 1 W.L.R. 349 (for subsequent proceedings, see [1976] 2 Lloyd's Rep. 17); *cf.* Mr. Lumley's undertaking in *Lumley* v. *Wagner*, *supra*, that certain parts were to "belong exclusively" to Mlle. Wagner.

69 *Ehrman* v. *Bartholomew* [1898] 1 Ch. 671.

70 *Warner Bros. Pictures Inc.* v. *Nelson* [1937] 1 K.B. 209, 216.

71 Stevens, 6 Cornell L.Q. 235; Ashley, 6 Col.L.Rev. 82; Clark, 17 Col.L.Rev. 687.

72 [1937] 1 K.B. 209.

73 *Page One Records Ltd.* v. *Britton* [1968] 1 W.L.R. 157.

74 *Warren* v. *Mendy* [1989] 1 W.L.R. 853, citing criticism of *Warner Bros. Inc.* v. *Nelson* (*supra*, n. 72) in *Nichols Advance Vehicle Systems Inc.* v. *De Angelis* (1979, unrep.); McLean [1990] C.L.J. 15.

75 *Page One Records Ltd.* v. *Britton* [1968] 1 W.L.R. at p. 166. *Lumley* v. *Wagner* was distinguished at p. 165 on the ground that Mr. Lumley had no obligation except to pay money; but in fact he also made certain promises which were negative in substance: *supra*, n. 68.

cult questions of fact and degree. In one case[76] a newspaper reporter undertook during the term of his contract not to work for others; the contract provided for termination by twelve months' notice. The reporter gave only two months' notice of termination, and it was held that he could be restrained by injunction from breach of the negative stipulation. This was said not to subject him to undue pressure since the employers had undertaken to go on paying him, to allow him to go on working for them for the rest of the contract period, and not to claim damages if he should choose simply to draw his pay without doing such work. But the position might have been different if the employers had merely undertaken to go on paying him, without allowing him to work. In such cases, the court can balance the employee's interest in continuing to work (so as to maintain his skill and reputation) against any prejudice likely to be suffered by the employer if the employee works for a third party; and, where the remedy is discretionary,[77] the court may refuse to grant the injunction if it is satisfied that breach of the negative stipulation will not seriously prejudice the employer.[78]

(b) RESTRAINT OF TRADE. A further danger of the rule in *Lumley* v. *Wagner*[79] is that the injunction may help to stifle competition. It is arguable that this was the purpose of the negative stipulation, and the effect of the injunction, in the leading case itself, for it might have been physically possible for Mlle. Wagner to sing at Drury Lane for two nights a week and to sing elsewhere on other nights. Yet the question whether the contract was invalid for restraint of trade was not discussed at all. It used to be thought that this question only arose where the relevant contractual provisions came into effect *after* the period of employment. A possible reason for this view is that, where the period of employment is fairly short (as in *Lumley* v. *Wagner*), the negative stipulation is reasonable (and therefore valid[80]) because of its limited duration.[81] But this reasoning loses much of its force where the employer has options to extend the term of service, sometimes for very long periods.[82] The present position is that stipulations which operate *during* employment are less likely to be invalid for restraint of trade than those which operate thereafter; but that even a stipulation of the former kind may have its *validity* (and not merely the *remedy* for its enforcement) called into question.[83] If this were not so, the law as to restraint of trade could, to a considerable extent, be evaded by simply giv-

---

[76] *Evening Standard Co. Ltd.* v. *Henderson* [1987] I.C.R. 588.
[77] *Ante*, p. 920 at n. 59.
[78] *Provident Financial Group plc* v. *Hayward* [1989] I.C.R. 160.
[79] (1852) 1 D.M. & G. 604.
[80] *Ante*, pp. 407, 412.
[81] Though in *Lumley* v. *Wagner* it was unlimited as to area; *cf. Evening Standard* v. *Henderson* [1987] I.C.R. 588.
[82] As in *Warner Bros. Pictures Inc.* v. *Nelson* [1937] 1 K.B. 209; *cf.* the contract in *Riley* v. *Coglan* [1967] 1 W.L.R. 1300, where a rugby league player agreed to serve his club "for the remainder of his football career . . . if the club should so long require." Contrast *Eastham* v. *Newcastle United Football Club Ltd.* [1964] Ch. 413, where the argument that the contract gave the employers a series of options was rejected.
[83] *Esso Petroleum Ltd.* v. *Harper's Garage (Stourport) Ltd.* [1968] A.C. 269, 294, 328–329, discussing *Young* v. *Timmins* (1831) 1 Cr. & J. 331; *A. Schroeder Music Publishing Co. Ltd.* v. *Macaulay* [1974] 1 W.L.R. 1308; *cf.* Restatement, *Contracts*, s.380(2), where illustration 1 reproduces *Lumley* v. *Wagner* while the next illustration reproduces the *Nordenfelt* case (*ante*, p. 401).

ing the employer options to extend the period of service.[84] A converse suggestion may also be made. Even where a covenant in restraint of trade takes effect after the period of service and is valid, it should not be enforced *by injunction* (but only by action for damages) if the injunction would leave the employee with no other reasonable means of making a living.

(c) IMPLIED NEGATIVE PROMISES. An injunction to restrain the breach by an employee of a stipulation in a contract of employment will only be issued if the contract contains an *express* negative promise.[85] The remedy has been restricted in this way because an injunction may put so much economic pressure on the employee as in effect to force him to perform his positive obligation to work; and this is traditionally regarded as undesirable.[86] But where the defendant's obligation is not one to render personal services, there is less objection to an injunction which puts pressure on him to perform his positive undertaking, even though that undertaking may not be specifically enforceable; and in cases of this kind the courts have *implied* negative stipulations and restrained their breach by injunction. Thus an injunction can be issued to restrain a shipowner from using a ship under charter inconsistently with the charterparty[87]; to restrain breach of a promise to give a "first refusal" to purchase land[88]; and to restrain breaches of various exclusive dealing agreements.[89] Similarly, a seller of uncut timber has been restrained from interfering with the right of the buyer to enter the land to cut down the timber and take it away: this was "not specific performance in the sense of compelling the vendor to do anything. It merely prevents him from breaking his contract."[90]

In the above cases, a negative stipulation, though not express, can readily be implied. The position would be different where the vagueness of the positive part of the contract made it impossible to say precisely what the defendant had undertaken *not* to do[91]; and also where the only negative stipulation which could be implied was one that would embrace the whole positive obligation. For example, if a contract were made for the sale of unascertained generic goods (such as "100 tons of coal") an injunction "not to break the contract" or "not to withhold delivery" would be

---

[84] It is no answer to an attack on the validity of the clause say that the employee may get paid since (a) he will not be entitled to any payment if he refuses to work for the employer, unless the contract expressly so provides; and (b) the mere fact that he gets paid does not oust the principles of restraint of trade: *cf. Wyatt* v. *Kreglinger and Fernau* [1933] 1 K.B. 793. If the covenant is valid, the fact that the employee actually gets paid is relevant to the employer's *remedy*: *ante*, p. 922 at nn. 76–78.

[85] *Mortimer* v. *Beckett* [1920] 1 Ch. 571; but breaches of negative obligations *imposed by law* can be restrained by injunction even though there is no express negative stipulation: *e.g. Hivac* v. *Park Royal Scientific Instruments* [1946] Ch. 169.

[86] *Cf.* Trade Union and Labour Relations Act 1974, s.16.

[87] *Sevin* v. *Deslandes* (1860) 30 L.J. (Ch.) 457; *The Oakworth* [1975] 1 Lloyd's Rep. 581.

[88] *Manchester Ship Canal* v. *Manchester Racecourse Co.* [1901] 2 Ch. 37.

[89] *Donnell* v. *Bennett* (1883) 22 Ch.D. 835; *Metropolitan Electric Supply Co.* v. *Ginder* [1901] 2 Ch. 799; *Decro-Wall International S.A.* v. *Practitioners in Marketing Ltd.* [1971] 1 W.L.R. 361; *Evans Marshall & Co.* v. *Bertola S.A.* [1973] 1 W.L.R. 349. *Fothergill* v. *Rowland* (1873) L.R. 17 Eq. 132, *contra*, is surprising in view of the reluctance with which Jessel M.R. decided for the defendants. As to the validity of exclusive dealing agreements, see *ante*, pp. 416–420.

[90] *Jones & Sons Ltd.* v. *Tankerville* [1909] 2 Ch. 400, 443; *cf. Hounslow (London Borough)* v. *Twickenham Garden and Builders Ltd.* [1971] Ch. 233; *ante*, p. 915, n. 17.

[91] *Bower* v. *Bantam Investments Ltd.* [1972] 1 W.L.R. 1120.

indistinguishable from an order of specific performance,[92] and would not normally[93] be granted. And the implication of a narrower negative stipulation (*e.g.* not to sell to anyone else) would not fairly arise from the contract.

(d) SEVERANCE. A negative stipulation which is too widely expressed may be severed and enforced in part. Severance is not here governed by the rules which govern severance of promises in illegal contracts[94]: the question is not (as it is in the restraint of trade cases) whether severance alters the nature of the contract, but simply whether an injunction to enforce such part of the negative stipulation as the pleader specifies amounts to indirect specific performance. Thus in *Warner Bros. Pictures Inc.* v. *Nelson*[95] the actress undertook, not only that she would not *act* for third parties, but also that she would not "*engage in any other occupation*" without the plaintiffs' written consent. She could clearly not be restrained from breach of the latter undertaking as this would force her to choose between idleness and performance of her obligation to work. But as the plaintiffs only sought an injunction to restrain her from acting for third parties the objection that the whole of her undertaking could not be enforced by injunction was "removed by the restricted form in which the injunction is sought."[96] Of course if the negative stipulation, though operating during employment, is as a whole invalid for restraint of trade, the question of severance will be determined by the principles governing severance of illegal promises in illegal contracts.

3. Damages and Specific Performance or Injunction[97]

Power to award damages in addition to or "in substitution for . . . specific performance" was conferred on the Court of Chancery by section 2 of the Chancery Amendment Act 1858 (also known as Lord Cairns' Act). That power is now vested in the High Court by section 50 of the Supreme Court Act 1981. It applies where the court has "jurisdiction to entertain an application for an injunction or specific performance." So long as the court has such jurisdiction,[98] it can award damages in lieu even though, in its discretion, it refuses to order specific relief.[99] Under section 49 of the Act, common law damages can also be awarded where specific performance or an injunction is claimed, even though the case is not one in which specific relief could have been ordered.[1]

---

[92] *Cf.* Fry, *Specific Performance* (6th ed.), s.857; *Whitwood Chemical Co.* v. *Hardman* [1891] 2 Ch. 416, 426. *The Scaptrade* [1983] A.C. 694, 701.
[93] For exceptions, see *ante*, pp. 906–907, 912.
[94] *Ante*, pp. 448–452.
[95] [1937] 1 K.B. 209.
[96] *Ibid.* at p. 219; see *ante*, pp. 921–922 for the question whether an injunction in even these limited terms should be granted. *Cf. William Robinson & Co. Ltd.* v. *Heuer* [1898] 2 Ch. 451; *Provident Financial Group plc* v. *Hayward* [1989] I.C.R. 150, 160. Where the contrast is illegal, *e.g.* for restraint of trade, the objection that an unseverable restraint is too wide cannot be met by claiming part-enforcement: contrast *Warner Bros. Pictures Inc.* v. *Nelson* with *Gledhow Autoparts Ltd.* v. *Delaney* [1965] 1 W.L.R. 1366.
[97] Jolowicz [1975] C.L.J. 224; Pettit [1977] C.L.J. 369; [1978] C.L.J. 51.
[98] *Hipgrave* v. *Case* (1885) 28 Ch.D. 356; *Lavery* v. *Pursell* (1888) 39 Ch.D. 508; *Price* v. *Strange* [1978] Ch. 337, 359.
[99] *e.g. Wroth* v. *Tyler* [1974] Ch. 30; *ante*, p. 908, n. 40.
[1] As in *Dominion Coal Co. Ltd.* v. *Dominion Iron & Steel Co.* [1909] A.C. 293; *cf. Proctor* v. *Bayley* (1889) 42 Ch.D. 390.

Since claims for damages can now be combined with claims for specific performance or injunction,[2] it is normally unnecessary to resort to the special power to award damages in lieu of these remedies. But it may sometimes be to the plaintiff's advantage to invoke that power where he has no completed cause of action at law, and its exercise has also given rise to certain special problems with regard to the assessment of damages.

(1) No completed cause of action at law

Damages may be awarded in lieu of specific performance or injunction even though there is no completed cause of action at law. For example a court can issue a *quia timet* injunction in respect of a threatened tort which has not yet been committed; and damages can be awarded in lieu of such an injunction.[3] A similar possibility exists where an anticipatory breach of contract has been committed and *not* been accepted. In such a case, specific performance may be ordered at once[4]; and damages can be awarded in lieu under the Act even though there was (when the proceedings were commenced) no right to damages at common law.[5] Again, an injunction is sometimes available against a refusal to contract; and it may be that damages can be awarded in lieu even though the refusal gives rise to no cause of action at common law.[6]

(2) Assessment of damages

There was formerly some support for the view that the assessment of damages might be more favourable to the plaintiff under the Act than at common law, particularly where the value of the subject-matter had risen between the time of breach and the time of judgment. It was assumed that, at common law, damages were necessarily based on the difference between the contract price and the value of the subject-matter *at the time of breach*. In *Wroth* v. *Tyler*[7] one reason given for nevertheless assessing the damages by reference to the *time of judgment* was that they were awarded, not at common law, but under the Act, "in substitution for . . . specific performance." Such damages must, it was said, "constitute a true substitute for specific performance,"[8] and "be a substitute, giving as nearly as may be what specific performance would have given."[9] But even at common law the aim of damages is to put the plaintiff "in the same position . . . *as if* the contract had been *performed*"[10]; and it is hard to see any difference in principle between the two phrases "as if . . . performed" and "in substitution for . . . specific performance." Both state the same general objective; neither is followed through to its logical conclusion. The judgment in

---

2 This follows from Supreme Court Act 1981, s.49.

3 *Leeds Industrial Co-operative Society Ltd.* v. *Slack* [1924] A.C. 851.

4 *Hasham* v. *Zenab* [1960] A.C. 316 (but the order will be for performance on the due day).

5 *Cf. Oakacre Ltd.* v. *Claire Cleaners (Holdings) Ltd.* [1982] Ch. 197. For another former illustration of the exercise of the power (now made obsolete by Law of Property (Miscellaneous Provisions) Act 1989, s.2, *ante*, p. 164) see *Price* v. *Strange* [1978] Ch. 337, 358.

6 *Ante*, p. 4; where the refusal is wrongful by statute, the right to damages will often be regulated by that statute, *e.g.* Sex Discrimination Act 1975, ss.65, 66; Race Relations Act 1976, ss.56, 57; Resale Prices Act 1976, s.25(3).

7 [1974] Ch. 30; *ante*, p. 851, and see *Grant* v. *Dawkins* [1973] 1 W.L.R. 1406; Pettit, 90 L.Q.R. 297.

8 [1974] Ch. 30, 58.

9 *Ibid.* p. 59.

10 *Robinson* v. *Harman* (1848) 1 Ex. 850, 855; *ante*, p. 830.

Wroth v. *Tyler* itself seems to recognise the possibility that part of the plaintiff's loss would have been irrecoverable if it had been too remote[11]; and the mitigation rules can also reduce the amount recoverable as damages in lieu of specific performance.[12] In *Johnson* v. *Agnew*[13] the House of Lords accordingly expressed the view that the assessment of damages was governed by the same principles whether the damages were awarded at common law or in lieu of specific performance. Even at common law, damages are not invariably assessed by reference to the date of breach. This method of assessment is adopted where it would have been reasonable for the plaintiff, at that date, to have mitigated his loss, *e.g.* by making a substitute contract; but if, for some reason, this is not the case, the damages will be assessed by reference to some other date.[14] In *Wroth* v. *Tyler* the plaintiffs were not at the time of breach in a position to make a substitute contract; and, so far as the assessment of damages is concerned, the decision must now be explained on that ground.[15]

(3) Damages and specific performance

Damages may be awarded in addition to specific performance. For example, where a vendor is in breach because his title is subject to an encumbrance, the purchaser can get specific performance ordering the vendor to convey what title he has, plus damages based on the cost of discharging the encumbrance.[16] The court may also award damages for delay in completion in addition to specific performance.[17]

SECTION 4. RESTITUTION[18]

A party who has wholly or in part performed his side of the contract and not received the agreed counter-performance in full may sometimes be entitled to restitution in respect of his own performance. Where this consists of a payment of money, the payor will simply seek to get it back; where it consists of some other benefit he will claim recompense (or a *quantum meruit*) in respect of it.

1. Recovery of Money Paid

An action lies, in the cases to be discussed below, to recover back money paid under a contract or purported contract. The action is also available in a number of other cases which have nothing to do with the law of contract, being only connected with it historically in that the form of action used in them was also used to enforce claims arising out of contracts. Our sole concern in this book is with the use of the action in its contractual context.

---

[11] *Ante*, p. 862.
[12] See *Radford* v. *De Froberville* [1977] 1 W.L.R. 1262, 1286; *Malhotra* v. *Choudhury* [1980] Ch. 52; the point was, in effect, conceded in *Grant* v. *Dawkins*, *supra*; *cf. ante*, p. 868, n. 79.
[13] [1980] A.C. 367, 400.
[14] *Ibid.* p. 401; *ante*, pp. 850–852.
[15] *Ante*, p. 851.
[16] *Grant* v. *Dawkins* [1973] 1 W.L.R. 1406.
[17] *Ford-Hunt* v. *Ragbhir Singh* [1973] 1 W.L.R. 738; *cf. Oakacre Ltd.* v. *Claire Cleaners (Holdings) Ltd.* [1982] Ch. 197 (damages for delay in substitution for specific performance). For damages for delay see *ante*, pp. 729–730.
[18] Beatson, 2 J.C.L. 65.

(1) Total failure of consideration[19]

(a) DEFINITION. A contracting party can recover back money paid under a contract if there is a "total failure of consideration," *i.e.* if he has not got any part of what he bargained for. In the *Fibrosa*[20] case, for example, a buyer of goods recovered back an advance payment when frustration had prevented the delivery of any part of the goods. Lord Simon explained the meaning of "consideration" in this context: "In the law relating to the formation of contract, the promise to do a thing may often be the consideration, but when one is considering the law of failure of consideration and of the quasi-contractual right to recover money on that ground it is, generally speaking, not the promise which is referred to but the performance of the promise."[21] This is only "generally speaking" the case because a party may bargain for the promise itself. Thus a person who insures against the destruction of a thing by fire bargains for the insurer's promise. If the thing is then destroyed by water the insured person cannot recover back his premium: there is no total failure of consideration as he had the benefit of the insurer's promise for some time.[22] He could only recover back his premium if the insurer was never at risk, *e.g.* if the thing had been destroyed the day before the policy had begun to run.[23]

(b) PARTIAL FAILURE. In the above cases, there is either a total failure of consideration or no failure at all. There is also an intermediate situation in which there has been a *partial* failure; and in such cases the general rule is that there is no right to recover back money paid.[24] If A employs B for a lump sum, paid in advance, to paint A's house, and B abandons the job before it is finished, A cannot recover back any part of the payment: his sole remedy is in damages. The reason for the rule appears to be that the law cannot easily apportion the contract price to the amount of work actually done by B. Where apportionment is in fact easy, the law will allow partial recovery: for example, a buyer who had paid in advance for 100 tons could get back half his money if only 50 tons were delivered.[25] By statute, money paid in advance under a contract which is later frustrated can be recovered even though the failure of consideration is only partial.[26] The difficulty of making an apportionment is here outweighed by the fact that restitution is the payor's only possible remedy, since frustration provides the payee with a defence to any claim for damages.

(c) RETURNABLE AND NON-RETURNABLE BENEFITS. A party who has received only partial or defective performance may, on that ground, be entitled to rescind the contract.[27] If he does rescind, and restores what he has received under the contract, he brings about a total failure of consider-

---

[19] Stoljar, 75 L.Q.R. 53.
[20] [1943] A.C. 32; *ante*, p. 809.
[21] At p. 48; *cf. Rover International Ltd.* v. *Cannon Films Ltd.* (*No.* 3) [1989] 1 W.L.R. 912, 923.
[22] *Cf. Tyrie* v. *Fletcher* (1777) 2 Cowp. 666.
[23] *Cf. Stevenson* v. *Snow* (1761) 3 Burr. 1237; and see Marine Insurance Act 1906, s.84.
[24] *Whincup* v. *Hughes* (1871) L.R. 6 C.P. 78; the actual decision is no longer law: *ante*, p. 810. Proposals for reform, in Law Commission Working Paper 65, Part III were later abandoned: Law Com. 121 para. 3.11.
[25] *Whincup* v. *Hughes*, *supra*, at p. 81; *cf. Ebrahim Dawood Ltd.* v. *Heath Ltd.* [1961] 2 Lloyd's Rep. 512; *Clough Mill Ltd.* v. *Martin* [1985] 1 W.L.R. 111, 117–118.
[26] *Ante*, p. 810.
[27] See Chap. 18, section 3.

ation and can therefore recover any money that he has paid. For example, a buyer who has paid in advance for goods may find, on delivery, that they suffer from a defect amounting to a breach of condition, or that they are not of the agreed quantity. In that case, he can reject the goods and get his money back.[28] Of course, the requirement that he must restore the subject-matter does not apply where his inability to do so is due to the very defect on which the right to reject was based: *e.g.* if the goods were so defective that they disintegrated; or if they were taken away from the buyer because the seller had no title to them.[29] The position seems to be the same where restoration of the subject-matter is made impossible by some external cause for which neither party was responsible.[30]

Where, on the other hand, the partial or defective performance is of such a nature that it cannot be returned, the mere fact that it has been rendered prevents the failure of consideration from being total: for example, where work to be done under a building contract has been paid for in advance, but is left unfinished or is done defectively. In such cases, the client could not get back the payment, but only damages. There would only be a total failure of consideration if the builder's breach were so serious that the work was wholly useless to the client.[31] Similarly, an employee may commit breaches of duty justifying his dismissal; but if he is not dismissed and is paid his salary or wages, the employer will not, on subsequently discovering the breaches of duty, be able to recover back the payments[32]: his remedy is in damages.

Even if the subject-matter of the contract is returned (or if its return is not required under the rules stated above) the injured party may have derived some benefit from it: *e.g.* by using or occupying it. Use for the sole purpose of testing is disregarded and so does not impair the right of the injured party to get his money back.[33] But any further use or occupation may prevent the failure of consideration from being total. In *Hunt* v. *Silk*[34] an agreement for a lease provided that possession was to be given immediately; that certain repairs were to be done by the landlord; that the lease was to be executed within 10 days; and that, on execution of the lease, the tenant was to pay £10. The tenant went into possession and paid the £10 before the execution of the lease, but the landlord failed to do the repairs, or to execute the lease within 10 days. After a few more days, the tenant vacated the premises and claimed the return of his £10. The claim was rejected,[35] and (although other explanations are possible[36]) the case has generally been taken to lay down the strict rule that, if a party has received

---

[28] *e.g. Bragg* v. *Villanova* (1923) 40 T.L.R. 154; *Baldry* v. *Marshall* [1925] 1 Q.B. 260. Contrast *Linz* v. *Electric Wire Co. of Palestine* [1948] A.C. 371 (where a buyer of shares forming part of an invalid issue had sold, and was therefore unable to restore, them).

[29] *e.g. Rowland* v. *Divall* [1923] 2 K.B. 500.

[30] *e.g. Head* v. *Tattersall* (1871) L.R. 7 Ex. 7.

[31] *Heywood* v. *Wellers* [1976] Q.B. 446, 458; *cf. The Mikhail Lermontov* [1990] 1 Lloyd's Rep. 579, 615 (holiday cruise ending in shipwreck).

[32] *Horcal* v. *Gatland* [1984] I.R.L.R. 288. For the employer's right to withhold pay, see *ante*, pp. 662, 719.

[33] *e.g. Baldry* v. *Marshall*, *supra*.

[34] (1804) 5 East 449.

[35] Contrast *Wright* v. *Colls* (1848) 8 C.B. 149, where the premium was paid specifically for execution of the lease and was held recoverable when the landlord failed to execute it.

[36] *e.g.* Goff and Jones, *The Law of Restitution* (3rd ed.), 461.

any part of the benefit that he contracted for,[37] there is no total failure of consideration. The rule is open to the objection that it may bar a claim for the recovery of money even though the benefit received is only slight or technical. On the other hand, the actual decision in *Hunt* v. *Silk* does not seem to be unreasonable; for there is nothing in the reported facts to suggest that the tenant did not have a perfectly adequate remedy in damages.

(d) BENEFITS OTHER THAN THOSE BARGAINED FOR. It does not follow from *Hunt* v. *Silk* that the receipt of *any* benefit by the injured party will bar his right to get his money back. If the benefit received was *different in kind* from that bargained for, there may be a total failure of consideration[38] even though the benefit cannot be returned in specie. This idea has made it possible to temper the rigidity of the rule in *Hunt* v. *Silk*, but it has led to rules and distinctions which have in turn attracted criticism.

In *Rowland* v. *Divall*[39] the plaintiff, who was a car dealer, bought a car from the defendant for £334, repainted it and resold it to a customer for £400. Subsequently the car was seized by the police as it had (unknown to any of the above parties) been stolen. The plaintiff thereupon repaid his customer the £400[40] and sued the defendant for the return of the £334. Meanwhile the original owner of the car had been compensated by his insurance company, who "took over the car themselves and then sold it to the plaintiff for £260."[41] The defendant took the position that his liability was limited to this sum and paid it into court.[42] But the Court of Appeal held that there had been a total failure of consideration, so that the plaintiff could recover back his payment of £334. He had not "received any portion of what he agreed to buy. . . . He did not get what he paid for—namely a car to which he would have title."[43] As the plaintiff was a dealer, this seems (with respect) to be a reasonable view: he did not want to use, but to resell, the car. For this purpose he needed a marketable title and not mere possession, which was wrongful against the owner. Moreover, the fact that he did not get title caused him serious prejudice beyond having to buy the car a second time; for it resulted in his losing a presumably profitable resale.[44]

The same rule has, however, also been applied in the absence of such cir-

---

[37] The same principle was applied in *Thorpe* v. *Fasey* [1949] Ch. 649 to the converse situation where a vendor claimed rescission. But it is hard to see why he should be deprived of this remedy merely because the *purchaser* had had some benefit from the subject matter. Perhaps the case can be explained on other grounds: *cf. ante*, p. 714.

[38] For this distinction, contrast *Wilkinson* v. *Lloyd* (1845) 7 Q.B. 27 with *Stray* v. *Russell* (1859) 1 E. & E. 889, 916; and *Knowles* v. *Bovill* (1870) 22 L.T. 70 with *Taylor* v. *Hare* (1805) 1 B. & P.N.R. 260 and *Lawes* v. *Purser* (1856) 6 E. & E. 930; *cf.* also *Rover International Ltd.* v. *Cannon Films Ltd.* (*No*. 3). [1989] 1 W.L.R. 912, 924, where the contract under which the payment was made was void. (*post*, p. 933). The definition of "total failure of consideration" gives rise to some difficulty in such a situation since no performance can be *due* under a void contract, though it is arguable that one may nevertheless have been *bargained for*.

[39] [1923] 2 K.B. 500.

[40] He could now reduce his liability to the customer for failure of consideration by any increase in value attributable to the repainting: Torts (Interference with Goods) Act 1977, s.6(3).

[41] This fact is stated in the report of the case in 129 L.T. 757.

[42] *Ibid.*

[43] [1923] 2 K.B. 500, 504.

[44] The eventual fate of the car is not known; *cf. ante*, pp. 843–844.

cumstances. In *Butterworth* v. *Kingsway Motors Ltd.*[45] a car owned by a finance company was let out on hire-purchase to a hirer who wrongfully sold it before she had paid all the instalments. It passed through a number of hands until it was sold for £1,275 by the defendant to the plaintiff, both of whom acted in good faith. Nearly a year later, the finance company notified the plaintiff that the car was theirs and asked for its return. Alternatively, they offered to allow the plaintiff to acquire title for £175,[46] this being all that remained due under the hire-purchase agreement as the hirer had kept up her payments under it. Meanwhile, however, second-hand car prices had fallen, so that the car was worth only £800. Two days after hearing from the finance company, the plaintiff claimed the return of the £1,275. After another eight days, the original hirer paid off the £175 and acquired a good title which could at that stage have been passed to the plaintiff. In these circumstances, the court rightly described the plaintiff's claim as "somewhat lacking in merits"[47]—but nevertheless allowed it in full. The decision represents a regrettable extension of *Rowland* v. *Divall*. It is hardly realistic to say that the plaintiff did not get any part of what he bargained for: he bought the car for use and did use it for nearly a year. Moreover, any prejudice to the plaintiff from the defendant's lack of title was removed when the amount outstanding under the hire-purchase agreement was paid off.

A similar criticism may be levelled at a line of hire-purchase cases. According to these, there is a total failure of consideration if the person letting a car out has no title, so that he cannot give the hirer a valid option to purchase.[48] But once a valid option has been conferred, there is no total failure because the hirer is for some reason prevented from exercising it[49]; or because the car suffers from defects of such a serious nature that it cannot, for practical purposes, be used at all.[50] It seems unrealistic to say that a hirer who actually uses the car for a substantial period is wholly deprived of what he bargained for merely because there was no valid option, while one who cannot use the car at all because of a physical defect is not so deprived.

The view that the buyer in *Rowland* v. *Divall* itself did not get *the* benefit for which he bargained is (as has been suggested above) a perfectly reasonable one. But the decision has nevertheless been criticised on the ground that the buyer recovered the *whole* of the price even though he and his sub-buyer had had the use of the car for some months. One way of meeting this criticism would be to reduce the buyer's claim for the return of the price by giving the seller the right to an allowance in respect of the benefit obtained

---

45 [1954] 1 W.L.R. 1286.

46 This was all that the finance company could recover as damages from the plaintiff: see *Wickham Holdings Ltd.* v. *Brook House Motors Ltd.* [1967] 1 W.L.R. 295. If the value of the car had been *less* than the amount outstanding under the agreement, the company could not have recovered more than that value: *Chubb Cash Ltd.* v. *John Grilley & Son* [1983] 1 W.L.R. 599.

47 At p. 1291.

48 See *Karflex Ltd.* v. *Poole* [1933] 2 K.B. 251; *Warman* v. *Southern Counties Car Finance Corp. Ltd.* [1959] 2 K.B. 576 (where the point arose on a counter-claim against the hirer).

49 *Kelly* v. *Lombard Banking Co.* [1959] 1 W.L.R. 41; *cf. C.C.C. Films (London) Ltd.* v. *Impact Quadrant Films* [1985] Q.B. 16, 28.

50 *Yeoman Credit Ltd.* v. *Apps* [1962] 2 Q.B. 508.

by the buyer from his use of the subject-matter.[51] But this suggestion in turn gives rise to the problem of valuing that benefit. It would clearly be unfair to the buyer to assess it at a "reasonable rental value" since a person who is buying or hire-purchasing a car would not want to incur the cost of hiring one. An alternative possibility is that the buyer's benefit should generally[52] be valued at the amount by which the cost of replacing the goods when the buyer was deprived of them was less than the contract price.[53]

A further problem arises because the true owner may have a claim in tort against either the buyer[54] or the seller[55] or both; he may be entitled not only to the return of the property or its value, but also its reasonable rental value.[56] If the owner has already claimed the rental value from the buyer, it seems clear that the seller should restore the *whole* price[57]; for if the buyer also had to give credit to the seller for the use of the goods, he would be required to pay twice over for the same benefit. Similar considerations apply where the true owner has not yet made his claim: if the buyer had to give credit to the seller he could later be sued for a similar sum by the owner. He might be able to claim that second payment back from the seller as damages; but the seller may have disappeared or the right to sue him may be barred by lapse of time. As a practical matter the buyer should certainly not be exposed to the risk of having to pay twice for the use of the subject-matter. Of course the true owner may choose not to assert his claim for rental value; and in that case the buyer would no doubt be enriched by having had the use of the subject-matter and nevertheless being allowed to get back the whole price from the seller. But the enrichment could be said to be at the expense of the *owner* and not at the expense of the seller, who accordingly should not have a claim in respect of it.[58] In view of the buyer's possible liability to the true owner, the buyer should only have to make an allowance to the seller for the benefit of the use of the goods if the claim of the true owner has first been satisfied.[59]

A final criticism of the rule in *Rowland* v. *Divall* is based on the following example[60]: B in good faith buys whisky from a thief and sells it to A, who drinks it. Can A recover back the whole price? It seems clear that he cannot,[61] because he is unable to restore the whisky, and this is entirely

[51] Law Commission Working Paper 65, paras. 56–57; for an earlier proposal for reform, see Law Reform Committee (1966) Cmnd. 2958, para. 56, discussed by Treitel, 30 M.L.R. 139, 147–149; Law Commission Working Paper 85, paras. 6.11 to 6.13 lists various possible reforms without deciding between them. The Law Commissions (Law Com. No. 160, Scot. Law Com. No. 104, para. 6.5) have concluded that the subject is too complex for legislative reform.

[52] For a suggested exception where the buyer has made a bad bargain, see Law Commission Working Paper 65, paras. 74–75; *quaere*, whether a special provision for this situation is desirable where (ex hypothesi) buyer and seller have both acted in good faith.

[53] *Ibid*. para. 73.

[54] *Hilberry* v. *Hatton* (1864) 2 H. & C. 822.

[55] *Martindale* v. *Smith* (1841) 1 Q.B. 389.

[56] *Strand Electric & Engineering Co. Ltd.* v. *Brisford Entertainments Ltd.* [1952] 2 K.B. 246; *Hillsden Securities Ltd.* v. *Ryjack Ltd.* [1983] 1 W.L.R. 959.

[57] As in *Newsome* v. *Graham* (1829) 10 B. & C. 234 (where the subject-matter was an interest in land). *Cf. Hizzett* v. *Hargreaves* [1987] C.L.Y 1164.

[58] See *Warman* v. *Southern Counties Car Finance Corp. Ltd.* [1959] 2 K.B. 576, 582–583; *Argens* v. *Whitcomb* 147 P. 2d 501, 504 (1944).

[59] Law Commission Working Paper No. 65, paras. 68–70.

[60] Atiyah, *Sale of Goods* (8th ed.), pp. 88–89.

[61] This seems to be admitted by Atiyah, *ubi supra*.

due to his voluntary act in drinking it.[62] But then it is said to be unjust to A that he *cannot* recover back his money: the true owner may sue him in conversion so that he will (in effect) have to pay for the whisky twice over. But B has also converted the whisky and is also liable in respect of that damage. Hence A can recover contribution from him (which may amount to a complete indemnity[63]) under the Civil Liability (Contribution) Act 1978.[64] The result is perfectly fair. A has paid for the whisky; the true owner has its value. B has admittedly lost the amount he paid the thief for the whisky, but that is a risk to which everyone who deals, even innocently, with a thief is exposed.

(e) RELATION TO DAMAGES. In a number of cases it has been held or said that a plaintiff may be able to get back money paid under a contract *as damages* for the defendant's breach. For example, in one case a cow had been sold warranted healthy but in fact she suffered from a disease from which she died; and the buyer recovered the price as one item of damages for breach of warranty.[65] Payments made under hire purchase agreements by hirers have likewise been recovered by them as damages where the goods were so defective that they were completely useless or rightfully rejected by the hirers.[66] Similar relief has been given to buyers and hire purchasers of stolen goods who elected to claim damages[67]; and to tenants who left premises which had been leased to them in consequence of abusive conduct on the part of their landlord, amounting to breach of his covenant for quiet enjoyment.[68] Strictly speaking, the injured party's damages in such cases should be the *value of the subject-matter* at the relevant date,[69] and not *the price* as such. The cases can perhaps be explained on the ground that in them the price was the best, and indeed the only, evidence of value. It is also possible for the price paid under one contract to be recoverable as reliance loss by way of damages for breach of a second contract between the same parties.[70]

In an action for damages the plaintiff can often recover more than the money he has paid to the defendant. For example, if in consequence of a breach he is deprived of goods, he may be able to recover, not only what he has paid for them,[71] but also money spent on them[72] or loss of profits (subject to the normal limitations on damages, such as remoteness and mitigation). Again, where tenants were evicted by their landlord's abusive conduct, they recovered not only the amount which they had paid for the

---

62 *Cf. ante*, pp. 927–928.
63 Civil Liability (Contribution) Act 1978, s.2(2).
64 *Ibid.* s.1.
65 *Harling* v. *Eddy* [1951] 2 K.B. 739.
66 *Charterhouse Credit Co. Ltd.* v. *Tolly* [1963] 2 Q.B. 683; *Farnsworth Finance Facilities Ltd.* v. *Attryde* [1970] 1 W.L.R. 1053; *Doobay* v. *Mohabeer* [1967] 2 A.C. 278.
67 *Mason* v. *Burningham* [1949] 2 K.B. 545; *Warman* v. *Southern Counties Car Finance Corp. Ltd.* [1949] 2 K.B. 576.
68 *Sampson* v. *Floyd* [1989] 2 E.G.L.R. 49.
69 *Ante*, pp. 830, 839 *et seq.*; *Greenwood* v. *Bennett* [1973] Q.B. 195, 201 ("the value of the car as he sold it to them"); *The Rio Sun* [1985] 1 Lloyd's Rep. 351, 368 ("the value of the oil . . . on the date when [the buyers] received it."; *cf.*, in case of failure to render services *Miles* v. *Wakefield M.D.C.* [1987] A.C. 539, 568, *ante*, p. 686, n. 52).
70 *C.C.C. Films (London) Ltd.* v. *Impact Quadrant Films Ltd.* [1985] Q.B. 16.
71 *Supra*, at nn. 65 and 66.
72 See the authorities cited in nn. 65 and 66 *supra*.

lease but also their conveyancing costs and damages for distress.[73] On the other hand, when a plaintiff claims damages, benefits obtained by him under the contract are, in principle, taken into account; and he will also recover less than the price if he has paid more for the subject-matter than it was worth, or than it would cost to replace. A claim for damages is also subject to practical difficulties, such as quantification and remoteness, which do not arise on a claim for the recovery of money. The question which action should be brought, where both are available, requires a careful weighing of the above factors. It should certainly not be assumed that the action for the recovery of money is necessarily the better remedy.

(2) Money paid under a void contract

The law starts with the assumption made by the law is that money paid under a void contract can be recovered back.[74] Thus in *Bell* v. *Lever Bros. Ltd.*[75] it was clearly assumed that the money paid by the plaintiffs under the compensation agreements could have been recovered back, had those agreements been void for mistake. Where a hire-purchase agreement was wholly void for mistake it was accordingly held that the hirer could recover back his deposit[76]; and it does not seem that he was under any liability to pay for the use of the subject-matter of the agreement, which had been in his possession for over three months.[77] Where a contract was void because one of the parties was a company not yet in existence when the contract was made,[78] it was similarly held that instalments paid under it could be recovered back by the payor.[79]

The rule that money paid under a void contract is recoverable is not an invariable one; the precise result depends on the ground of invalidity in each case. The rules governing the recovery of money paid under contracts which are void for illegality, or by statute have already been discussed.[80]

2. Quantum Meruit

Here we are concerned with cases in which a party claims a reasonable recompense for some benefit (other than a payment of money) conferred, or for work done, by him under contract or purported contract. Many such cases have already been discussed and need only be mentioned here for the sake of completeness.

(1) Where there is no express provision for remuneration[81]

Two situations must be distinguished here.

(a) CONTRACTS NOT PROVIDING FOR REMUNERATION. A party can claim a *quantum meruit* for work done or goods delivered under a contract which

---

[73] *Sampson* v. *Floyd* [1989] 2 E.G.L.R. 49.
[74] *e.g. Re London County Commercial Reinsurance Office* [1922] 2 Ch. 67. And see Arrowsmith, 9 Legal Studies 121 and 307.
[75] [1932] A.C. (*ante*, p. 252); Landon, 51 L.Q.R. 650; Tylor, 52 L.Q.R. 27; Landon, *ibid.* 478; Hamson, 53 L.Q.R. 118.
[76] *Branwhite* v. *Worcester Works Finance Ltd.* [1969] 1 A.C. 552.
[77] No claim of this kind was made by the finance company in *Branwhite's* case.
[78] *Ante*, p. 638.
[79] *Rover International Ltd.* v. *Cannon Films Ltd.* (*No. 3*) [1989] 1 W.L.R. 912; Birks, 2 J.C.L. 227.
[80] *Ante*, pp. 436–446, 463–464, 490–491, 492–493, 494–497.
[81] Birks, (1974) C.L.P. 13; Jones, (1977) 93 L.Q.R. 273.

does not expressly provide how much he is to be paid. This will be the case where the whole agreement is implied from conduct,[82] or where it is simply silent as to the rate of payment. Sometimes it may be clear from the terms of the agreement, or from the circumstances in which it was made, that the plaintiff was not intended to have any legal right to be paid at all.[83] But if he was intended to have such a right the court will award a reasonable sum. Thus if a contract for the sale of goods does not fix the price, the buyer must pay a reasonable price[84]; and if a contract for services does not fix the remuneration, a reasonable sum must be paid.[85]

A similar situation arises where the contract makes some, but not a full, provision for payment. In *Sir Lindsay Parkinson & Co. Ltd.* v. *Commissioners of Works*[86] contractors agreed to erect works for a payment consisting of the cost of the works plus £300,000. It was thought that the works would cost about £5 million, but the Commissioners exercised their right under the contract to ask for additional works worth £1½ million. It was held that the express provision as to payment only applied to works worth about £5 million and that the contractors were entitled to a *quantum meruit* in respect of the additional works.

(b) NO CONCLUDED CONTRACT. Work may be done where the parties believe that there is a contract but this is not the case because there was never a clear acceptance of an offer. In one such case a *quantum meruit* was awarded to the party who had done the work.[87] Such an award may also be made where one party does work at the request of the other during negotiations which are expected to lead to a contract between them but are broken off before its conclusion.[88]

(2) Where there is an express provision for remuneration

The general rule is that where a contract expressly provides for a fixed remuneration on specified events, the court cannot award any other remuneration on those events, nor can it award any remuneration if they do not occur.[89] To allow *quantum meruit* claims in such cases would contradict the agreement reached by the parties, and the courts will only do this if there are special circumstances justifying such interference. Such circumstances exist in the following cases.

(a) INCAPACITY. Where necessaries are sold and delivered to a minor, he need only pay a reasonable price for them, although he may have agreed to

[82] *Ante*, pp. 9, 17; *Paynter* v. *Williams* (1833) 1 C. & M. 810; *cf. The Batis* [1990] 1 Lloyd's Rep. 345.

[83] *Ante*, pp. 153–154, 642–643.

[84] Sale of Goods Act 1979, s.8(2).

[85] Supply of Goods and Services Act 1982, s.15(1); *cf.* at common law *Way* v. *Latilla* [1937] 3 All E.R. 759; and see *ante*, pp. 642–643.

[86] [1949] 2 K.B. 632; *cf. Steven* v. *Bromley & Son* [1919] 2 K.B. 722; *The Gregos* [1985] 2 Lloyd's Rep. 347; *The Saronikos* [1986] 2 Lloyd's Rep. 277.

[87] *Peter Lind & Co. Ltd.* v. *Mersey Docks & Harbour Board* [1972] 2 Lloyd's Rep. 234; *ante*, p. 16; Arrowsmith, *supra*, n. 74.

[88] *William Lacey (Hounslow) Ltd.* v. *Davis* [1954] 1 Q.B. 428; *B.S.C.* v. *Cleveland Bridge & Engineering Co. Ltd.* [1984] 1 All E.R. 504; Ball, 99 L.Q.R. 572; *Marston Construction Co.* v. *Kigas* (1990) 15 Con.L.R. 116.

[89] *Britain* v. *Rossiter* (1879) 11 Q.B.D. 123; *Gilbert & Partners* v. *Knight* (1968) 112 S.J. 155; *Wiluszynski* v. *Tower Hamlets L.B.C.* [1989] I.C.R. 493.

pay more.[90] There are obvious reasons of policy for interfering with the agreement in such a case. There would be no such reasons where the minor had agreed to pay less than a reasonable price.

(b) WRONGFUL PREVENTION OF PERFORMANCE. If one party starts to perform a contract but is prevented from completing it by the other party's breach, he can claim a *quantum meruit* at the contract rate[91] for work done, even though the unperformed obligation is entire.[92] The party in breach here cannot complain of having to pay in circumstances other than those provided for by the contract.

(c) OTHER PARTIAL PERFORMANCE. In Chapter 18 we saw that, in general, a person who failed to complete performance of an entire obligation could not recover anything[93]; but that this rule was subject to a number of exceptions.[94] Under some of these, there is a right to payment of the contract price or at the contract rate. Under others, there is a right to a *quantum meruit* (or reasonable remuneration): for example, where a benefit conferred by partial performance of services is "voluntarily" accepted by the other party. This rule can be explained on the ground that the parties have agreed to abandon the original contract, and that a new one is made when the benefit is accepted.

In a number of further exceptional cases, a reasonable sum is, or may be, payable for services rendered by the party in breach even though the services differ from, or fall short of, those bargained for, even though there has been no "voluntary" acceptance of them by the injured party, and even though the contract remains in force. For example, it has been said that a carrier by sea who deviates but carries the goods to the agreed destination can recover a reasonable freight[95]; and conflicting views have been expressed on the question whether an employer who "of necessity" accepts services falling short of those bargained for is liable to his employee for a *quantum meruit*.[96] Such exceptional cases are controversial precisely because they reveal a conflict between two principles. One is that the court should not unjustifiably contradict a subsisting contract by awarding a reasonable sum for services falling short of those promised; the other is that the court should not allow the injured party to have the benefit of those services for nothing, since this would lead to his being unjustly enriched. The exact scope and rationale of the present group of exceptional cases must therefore remain very much in doubt.

---

[90] *Ante*, p. 848; the same is also sometimes true where necessaries are sold and delivered to a mental patient or drunkard: *ante*, pp. 502–503.

[91] *Lodder* v. *Slowey* (1901) 20 N.Z.L.R. 321, 356, affirmed [1904] A.C. 442; *Kehoe* v. *Borough of Rutherford*, 27 A 912 (1893). According to *Boomer* v. *Muir*, 24 P. 2d. 570 (1933) he can recover a reasonable sum even though it greatly exceeds the contract price; but it is submitted that this would not be followed in England, for it seems absurd that the injured party should recover more for partial, than he could recover for full, performance. Where one party, after the other's breach, does *extra* work, the reasonable sum recoverable for the work may exceed the damages recoverable for the breach: *The Batis* [1990] 1 Lloyd's Rep. 345.

[92] *Ante*, p. 720.

[93] *Ante*, pp. 683–685.

[94] *Ante*, pp. 717–720.

[95] *Hain S.S. Co. Td.* v. *Tate & Lyle Ltd.* (1936) 41 Com. Cas. 350, 358, 367; *ante*, p. 718, n. 41.

[96] *Miles* v. *Wakefield Metropolitan D.C.* [1987] A.C. 539, 552–553 (*per* Lord Brightman) and 561 (*per* Lord Templeman); *contra*, *ibid*. p. 552 (*per* Lord Bridge); *ante* p. 719.

(d) CONTRACT VOID. In *Craven-Ellis* v. *Canons Ltd.*[97] the plaintiff worked for the defendant company as managing director. His service agreement with the company was void as neither he nor those who appointed him held the necessary qualification shares. Thus he could not recover his agreed pay.[98] But the Court of Appeal held that he was entitled to a *quantum meruit*. The position is the same where a contract with a company is void because the company was not yet in existence or had been dissolved[99] when the contract was made.[1] A similar principle may apply where goods have been supplied under a contract of sale which is void for a mistake as to the identity of the buyer.[2]

Where the express contract is a nullity, the argument that the court must not interfere with the bargain between the parties loses much of its force. It does not seem that liability in these cases is based on an agreement which can be implied from voluntary acceptance by the defendant of the plaintiff's services,[3] for the parties usually think that they are acting under an existing valid contract. In *Craven-Ellis* v. *Canons Ltd.* Greer L.J. said that the liability to pay a *quantum meruit* "is an inference which a rule of law imposes on the parties where work has been done or goods have been delivered under what purports to be a binding contract but is not so in fact."[4]

The principle just stated may, however, be displaced by countervailing policy considerations. In *Guinness plc* v. *Saunders*[5] a company director did work for the company in the course of negotiations for a take-over bid which was being made by the company. The agreement under which the work was done was void because those who purported to make it on behalf of the company had no authority to do so. It was held that the director was not entitled to *quantum meruit* since the terms of the agreement (by which his remuneration increased with the amount paid by the company) gave rise to a conflict between his own financial interest and his fiduciary duty to the company as one of its directors.

(e) CONTRACT FRUSTRATED. Work done under a contract *before* it is frustrated does not give rise to any *quantum meruit* claim at common law, though a claim in respect of a valuable benefit conferred by such work can be made under the Law Reform (Frustrated Contracts) Act 1943.[6] But if work is done under the contract *after* frustration, it may be possible to claim a *quantum meruit* on the principle of *Craven-Ellis* v. *Canons Ltd.* The argument that the court must not interfere with the express contract is here met by the fact that the contract has no longer any legal force. A con-

---

97 [1936] 2 K.B. 403; Denning, (1939) 55 L.Q.R. 54.

98 *Cf. Re Bodega Co.* [1904] 1 Ch. 276; if he is paid his contractual remuneration he must pay it back.

99 *Ante*, pp. 637–638.

1 *Rover International Ltd.* v. *Cannon Films Ltd.* (*No. 3*) [1989] 1 W.L.R. 912; *Contronic (UK) Ltd.* v. *Dezonie*, *The Times*, March 8, 1991.

2 *e.g.* on the facts of *Boulton* v. *Jones* (1857) 27 L.J. Ex. 117, for the exact nature of the appropriate remedy in such a situation, see *ante*, p. 269.

3 *Contra*, Denning, *supra*, n. 89.

4 At p. 410. *cf. Lawford* v. *Billericay R.D.C.* [1903] 1 K.B. 772 (the actual decision has been made obsolete by the Corporate Bodies Contracts Act 1960; *ante*, p. 510, n. 56).

5 [1990] 2 A.C. 663; Beatson and Prentice, 106 L.Q.R. 365.

6 *Ante*, p. 811.

tract for the carriage of goods may be frustrated because the method of performance becomes impossible. The carrier may nonetheless get the goods to their destination in some other way. So long as he acts reasonably in doing so, he can claim a *quantum meruit*. It is irrelevant that a new contract cannot be implied from the mere fact that the cargo-owner accepts the cargo at its destination.[7]

[7] *The Massalia* [1961] 2 Q.B. 278; overruled in *The Eugenia* [1964] 2 Q.B. 226, but not on this point.

INDEX